Magill's
Cinema
Annual
1 9 9 9

Magill's Cinema Annual 1 9 9 9

18th Edition
A Survey of the Films of 1998

Michelle Banks, Editor

Carol Schwartz, Contributing Editor

Christine Tomassini, Associate Editor

A VideoHound® Reference

The Gale Group

DETROIT • SAN FRANCISCO • LONDON • BOSTON • WOODBRIDGE, CT

Michelle Banks, Editor
Devra M. Sladics, Brad Morgan, and Carol Schwartz,
Contributing Editors
Christine Tomassini, Associate Editor
Mary Beth Trimper, Production Director
Cindy Range, Production Assistant
Rita Wimberley, Senior Buyer
Cynthia Baldwin, Product Design Manager
Michelle S. DiMercurio, Senior Art Director
Sherrell Hobbs, Macintosh Artist
Randy Bassett, Image Database Supervisor
Robert Duncan and Mikal Angari, Imaging Specialists
Pamela A. Hayes, Photography Coordinator
Jeffrey Muhr and Wayne Fong, Editorial Technical Services Specialists

∞ ™ The paper used in this publication meets the minimum requirements of American National Standard for Information Sciences—Permanence Paper for Printed Library Materials, ANSI Z39.48-1984.

♻ This book is printed on recycled paper that meets Environmental Protection Agency standards.

Copyright © 1999 by
The Gale Group
27500 Drake Road
Farmington Hills, MI 48331-3535
A Cunning Canine® Production

ISBN 0-7876-2902-2
ISSN 0739-2141

Printed in the United States of America

Table of Contents

Preface

Magill's Cinema Annual 1998 continues the fine film reference tradition that defines the VideoHound series of entertainment industry products published by The Gale Group. The eighteenth annual volume in a series that developed from the 21-volume core set, *Magill's Survey of Cinema*, the *Annual* was formerly published by Salem Press. Gale's fifth volume, as with the previous Salem volumes, contains essay-reviews of significant domestic and foreign films released in the United States during the preceding year.

The *Magill's* editorial staff at Gale, comprising the VideoHound team and a host of *Magill's* contributors, continues to provide the enhancements that were added to the *Annual* when Gale acquired the line. These features include:

- More essay-length reviews of significant films released during the year

- Photographs which accompany the reviews and illustrate the obituaries and Life Achievement Award sections

- Trivia and "fun facts" about the reviewed movies, their stars, the crew and production

- Quotes and dialogue "soundbites" from reviewed movies, or from stars and crew about the film

- More complete awards and nominations listings, including the American Academy Awards, Golden Globe, New York Critics Awards, Los Angeles Film Critics Awards, and others (see the User's Guide for more information on awards coverage)

- Box office grosses, including year-end and other significant totals

- Critics' and publicity taglines featured in film reviews and advertisements

In addition to these elements, the *Magill's Cinema Annual 1999* also features:

- An interview with actor Nick Nolte

- An essay reviewing the career and accomplishments of the recipient of the American Film Institute's Life Achievement Award presented each year to Holly-

wood luminaries. Actor Dustin Hoffman is the 1998 award recipient profiled in this volume.

- An obituaries section profiling major contributors to the film industry who died in 1998

- An annotated list of selected film books published in 1998

- Nine indexes: Director, Screenwriter, Cinematographer, Editor, Art Director, Music, Performer, Subject, and Title (now cumulative)

Compilation Methods

The *Magill's* editorial staff reviews a variety of entertainment industry publications, including trade magazines and newspapers, as well as online sources, on a daily and weekly basis to select significant films for review in *Magill's Cinema Annual*. *Magill's* staff and other contributing reviewers, including film scholars and university faculty, write the reviews included in the *Annual*.

Magill's Cinema Annual: A VideoHound Reference

The *Magill's Survey of Cinema* series, now supplemented by the *Annual*, was honored with the Reference Book of the Year Award in Fine Arts by the American Library Association.

The Gale Group, an waward-winning publisher of reference products, is proud to offer *Magill's Cinema Annual* as part of its popular VideoHound® product line, which includes *VideoHound's Golden Movie Retriever, The Video Source Book, VideoHound's Independent Film Guide, VideoHound's Vampires on Video, VideoHound's Epics, VideoHound's Complete Guide to Cult Flicks and Trash Pics, VideoHound's Horror Show, VideoHound's World Cinema*, and many more. Other Gale film-related products include *The St. James Film Directors Encyclopedia, The St. James Women Filmmakers Encyclopedia*, and the *Contemporary Theatre, Film, and Television* series.

Acknowledgments

Thank you to Judy Hartman, GGS Information Services, for her typesetting expertise, and Jeff Muhr and

Wayne Fong for their technical assistance. The Video-Hound staff is thanked for its contributions to this project, especially Christine Tomassini, Brad Morgan, Devra Sladics, and Carol Schwartz for their hard work, generosity, and goodwill, as well as Marty Connors, Christa Brelin, and Julia Furtaw for their guidance and direction.

We most appreciate Bob Cosenza, the Kobal Collection, for his assistance in obtaining photographs.

Introduction

Unlike 1997, no one film or movie event came to prominence in 1998. But that's not to say that 1998 wasn't a memorable or exciting year. Trends and audiences' moods spoke loud and clear in Hollywood, and the collective efforts from studios—still green with envy at *Titanic*'s continued success early in the year—encouraged moviegoers to rack up a record $7 billion in ticket sales and help make 1998 a triumphant year at the movies. Clearly while *Titanic* was destined for the history books, Hollywood, once again, proved that it could make 'em the way it use to—even if it meant repeating itself.

Déjà vu was prevalent throughout 1998 as studios competed against each other for box office dollars with similarly themed movies. The results, surprisingly, were favorable, with some of these films grossing over $100 million. Asteroids destroying the earth was a powerful enough premise to propel two films: first, DreamWorks' melancholy *Deep Impact*, then Touchstone's action-packed, special-effects marvel *Armageddon*, to top spots on weekly box office tallies during the summer of '98, with *Armageddon* becoming the clear winner with a box office take of over $200 million. The insect world, or more specifically, the world according to ants, became two premiere showcases in the newly developed art form of computer animation with the arrival of DreamWorks' *Antz*, followed a month later by Disney's *A Bug's Life*. Geared toward a more adult audience, *Antz* scored with its neurotic main character ant named Z, voiced appropriately by Woody Allen, whereas *A Bug's Life* delighted children with its cuteness and with the wit of naïve ant Flik, voiced by Dave Foley. Of course, with the fast-food tie-ins and the mass marketing of Flik's other adorable six-legged pals, *A Bug's Life* was victorious with a handsome slice of the Christmas box office take.

The mass moviegoing public became reacquainted with the horrors American soldiers faced in combat with two World War II films. DreamWorks' *Saving Private Ryan*, directed by Steven Spielberg, was an unexpected summer hit, while 20th Century Fox's Christmas release of *The Thin Red Line* welcomed the return of director Terrence Malick from a twenty-year absence from behind the camera. Unlike asteroids or cute little insects, there was only room for one brutal combat movie, and *Saving Private Ryan* won the battle hands down. Malick's all-star cinematic turn, considered a visually stunning piece on war's destruction to nature, was overshadowed by the behemoth *Saving Private Ryan*.

After stumbling with the slave drama *Amistad* and losing some credibility for the dinosaur sequel to *Jurassic Park*, Spielberg regained the prestige he'd enjoyed with *Schindler's List* as critics and the public declared *Saving Private Ryan* the best WWII movie ever made. High praise indeed when a month before *Ryan*'s release, the American Film Institute publicized their Top 100 Films of All Time, featuring timeless World War II dramas such as *Bridge on the River Kwai*, *From Here to Eternity*, *Patton*, and *The Best Years of Our Lives*. What placed *Saving Private Ryan* in such good company was Spielberg's gifted filmmaking ability to deglamorize war's violence with an unflinching camera—much as he had shown the brutal conditions of the Nazi concentration camps in *Schindler's List*, which incidentally was number nine on the AFI list. His meticulous and bloody re-creation of the soldiers' storming the beaches of Normandy created arguably the most memorable twenty minutes in film history. Veterans who fought in the war were brought to tears while those too young to have witnessed the war's devastation were immediately moved to find ways to thank those brave soldiers who gave up so much for what we take for granted. *Saving Private Ryan* was also a pinnacle for its star, Tom Hanks, who had not lost his appeal with audiences or critics. After his first Oscar win for *Philadelphia* in 1993, Hanks has been on one of the hottest streaks in Hollywood. His impeccable and emotional performance as Capt. John Miller, the man leading a group of cynical men to find Private Ryan through war-torn France, is evidence that Hanks's career has reached the height of legendary actor James Stewart as the Everyman audiences are willing to follow anywhere. *Saving Private Ryan* surely looked to be the movie to beat come Oscar time.

As a breath of fresh air from the crude re-creations of combat came the sprawling and romantic tale of how a young, lovelorn William Shakespeare fell in love with a wealthy countess and turned his first draft of a play entitled "Romeo and Ethel the Pirate's Daughter" into one of his most famous plays of forbidden love. The clever *Shakespeare in Love* quietly charmed audiences and critics with its robust and comical musing about a passionate love that changed Shakespeare from a poor, inarticulate writer to a prosperous and prolific playwright. Aside from the film's enchanting take on what might have happened in Shakespeare's life, *Shakespeare in Love* also benefitted from the sultry chemistry between its young leads, Joseph Fiennes as Shakespeare and Gwyneth Paltrow as Viola De Lesseps. As *Shakespeare* picked up momentum, *Saving Private Ryan*'s road to Oscar gold wasn't so smoothly paved. To make the ride even bumpier for Spielberg was an unsuspecting Italian comic who would take Hollywood by storm with his own personal story set during World War II.

Life Is Beautiful, the title of Roberto Benigni's successful serio-comic tale, also became his motto for 1998. Overwhelming audiences as it played in various film festivals, *Life Is Beautiful* was a sparkling showcase for Benigni's physical comedy and a powerful examination of a father's love for his family during their imprisonment in a Nazi concentration camp. Benigni was criticized for combining comedy with the tragedy of the Holocaust, but any negativity was brushed aside by the film's poetic and powerful message and by the film's director, writer, and star—Benigni himself, who was a bubbly, energetic, and humble recipient of the praise. When Oscar finally did speak, history was made by awarding Spielberg a Best Director Oscar; *Shakespeare in Love* a Best Picture Oscar; Paltrow the Best Actress award; and Benigni the honors for both Best Actor and Best Foreign Film, the first person to receive awards in those categories for the same movie.

Spielberg may not have walked away with as many Oscars as he would have liked, but with the financial successes of *Saving Private Ryan, Antz,* and *Deep Impact* in 1998, his DreamWorks (created along with Jeffery Katzenberg and David Geffen) was now considered a full-fledged studio with quality and content that could surpass that of other well-established studios.

With healthy doses of love and war, audiences craved comedy. *There's Something about Mary* was a hilarious farce with gross-out comedic scenes that have now become the signature mark for the directors, the Farrelly brothers. It reset the standards of comedy by lowering them, and with a steady flow of positive word of mouth, *Mary* became a sleeper hit for the summer of '98 and shot its star, Cameron Diaz, into the stratosphere of Julia Roberts–type superstardom. Comedy was good for Adam Sandler, too, who also scored with the breezy romance *The Wedding Singer* and KO'd the box office with his low-brow *The Waterboy.* These back-to-back hits placed Sandler in the exclusive $20 million club alongside Mel Gibson, Tom Hanks, and Harrison Ford and turned this once puerile comic into a major Hollywood player.

The man who paved the way for the likes of Adam Sandler ironically made a successful leap from comedy to drama in one of 1998's most original films. Jim Carrey startled audiences and critics with his subdued role as Truman Burbank in Peter Weir's cultural satire *The Truman Show* and set aside any doubt that he was a man with real talent, not just a blunt, adolescent sense of humor and a natural ability for facial contortions.

One earmark of 1998 was its proliferation of animation. No longer was Disney the sole provider of family entertainment and high-quality animation. Other studios such as DreamWorks (with *Antz* and *Prince of Egypt*) and Paramount (with *The Rugrats Movie*) bludgeoned the market with their brand of animation—and received impressive grosses for their efforts.

Even though twenty of the highest-grossing films of 1998 were big-budget Hollywood studio releases, independent films had substantial and impressive representation throughout 1998, which provided career highlights to a few established actors. Veteran British actor Ian McKellen garnered many kudos for his penetrating performance as horror film director James Whale in *Gods and Monsters*; the pairing of salty men James Coburn and Nick Nolte as a father and son duo provided a potent combination in Paul Schrader's dark drama *Affliction*, with both receiving acting nominations plus a Best Supporting Actor Oscar for Coburn; actresses Christina Ricci and Lisa Kudrow matured and redefined their careers in Don Roos's comedy *The Opposite of Sex*; Edward Norton donned a radical look for a risky and bravado performance in the controversial *American History X*; Bill Murray gained respect with his supporting role in the quirky comedy *Rushmore*; and the solid performances by the ensemble cast in Todd Solondz's black comedy of extremely dysfunctional sisters in *Happiness* proved that Solondz's breakthrough feature, *Welcome to the Dollhouse,* was no fluke.

Nine films grossed over $100 million and two grossed over $200 million. Studios shared in both the successes and failures, with some of the most expensive, high-profile box-office flops to come around since *Ishtar*. Oprah Winfrey's labor of love, *Beloved,* was a complicated post-slavery drama that could not find an audience who could both understand the film and appreciate its eerie subject matter. Warren Beatty, always a filmmaker with a message, misfired heavily with his sharp, hip-hop music–enhanced political satire *Bulworth*. Universal Studios' *Babe: Pig in the City* succumbed to an overpopulated children's market and went quietly out of theaters in a matter of weeks. Another nail to the coffin of Universal's production chief was the glossy but boring Brad Pitt vehicle *Meet Joe Black*. Budgeted at $90 million, *Black* put Universal in the red and prompted its studio chief to resign.

In 1998, the entertainment world witnessed the passing of some of its biggest and brightest stars: the Chairman of the Board himself and cultural icon Frank Sinatra, who was not only a giant in music, but in films, too; singing cowboys Gene Autry and Roy Rogers; old-style Hollywood leading lady Alice Faye; prolific and influential Japanese director Akira Kurosawa; comedian and actor Phil Hartman; and veteran character actor J. T. Walsh. See the Obituaries section in the back of this book for profiles of these and other major performers in the film industry who passed away in 1998.

On a separate note, this editor would like to recognize the passing of a man who had a lasting impression on her and anyone else who loved the movies as much as he did. Goodbye, Gene Siskel (1946–1999). You are truly missed.

With no single standout film, 1998 can best be remembered as the year following the most profitable film in history (*Titanic*) and preceding perhaps the most anticipated film in history—*Star Wars Episode 1—The Phantom Menace.*

As the silver screen fades out upon another year of moviemaking, the *Magill's* staff looks forward to preparing the 2000 *Annual*, for which additional changes and enhancements are planned. We invite your comments. Please direct all questions and suggestions to:

Michelle Banks
Editor, *Magill's Cinema Annual*
The Gale Group
27500 Drake Rd.
Farmington Hills, MI 48331-3535
Phone: (248) 699-4253
Toll-free: 800-347-GALE
Fax: (248) 699-8067

Contributing Reviewers

Michael Adams
Graduate School, City University of New York

Vivek Adarkar
Long Island University

Michael Betzold
Freelance Reviewer

David L. Boxerbaum
Freelance Reviewer

Beverley Bare Buehrer
Freelance Reviewer

John Carlos Cantu
Freelance Reviewer

Reni Celeste
University of Rochester

Peter N. Chumo II
Freelance Reviewer

J. M. Clark
Gwinnett Daily Post (Atlanta) Film Editor

Paul B. Cohen
L.A. Weekly Theatre Critic

Jarred Cooper
Freelance Reviewer

Roberta Cruger
Freelance Reviewer

Bill Delaney
Freelance Reviewer

Beth Fhaner
Freelance Reviewer

David Flanagin
Howard Payne University

G. E. Georges
Freelance Reviewer

Robert F. Green
Virginia Polytechnic Institute and State University

Jill Hamilton
Freelance Reviewer

Diane Hatch-Avis
Freelance Reviewer

Mary Hess
Freelance Reviewer

Glenn Hopp
Howard Payne University

Patricia Kowal
Freelance Reviewer/Script Consultant

Leon Lewis
Appalachian State University

Robert Mitchell
University of Arizona

Lisa Paddock
Freelance Reviewer

Carl Rollyson
Baruch College, City University of New York

Jacqui Sadashige
University of Pennsylvania

Rich Silverman
Freelance Reviewer

Kirby Tepper
Freelance Reviewer

Hilary Weber
Freelance Reviewer

James M. Welsh
Salisbury State University

Jerry White
University of Alberta

User's Guide

Alphabetization

Film titles and reviews are arranged on a word-by-word basis, including articles and prepositions. English leading articles (A, An, The) are ignored, as are foreign leading articles (El, Il, La, Las, Le, Les, Los). Other considerations:

- Acronyms appear alphabetically as if regular words.

- Common abbreviations in titles file as if they are spelled out, so *Mr. Nice Guy* will be found as if it was spelled "Mister Nice Guy."

- Proper names in titles are alphabetized beginning with the individual's first name, for instance, *Jack Frost* will be found under "J."

- Titles with numbers, for instance, *54*, are alphabetized as if the number were spelled out, in this case, "Fifty-Four." When numeric titles gather in close proximity to each other, the titles will be arranged in a low-to-high numeric sequence.

Special Sections

List of Awards. An annual list of awards bestowed upon the year's films by ten international associations: Academy of Motion Picture Arts and Sciences, Directors Guild of America Award, Golden Globe Awards, Golden Palm Awards (Cannes International Film Festival), Los Angeles Film Critics Awards, National Board of Review Awards, National Society of Film Critics Awards, New York Film Critics Awards, and the Writer's Guild Awards.

Life Achievement Award. An essay reviewing the career and accomplishments of the recipient of the American Film Institute's Life Achievement Award presented each year to Hollywood luminaries. Actor Dustin Hoffman is the 1998 award recipient profiled in this volume.

Obituaries. Profiles major contributors to the film industry who died in 1998.

Selected Film Books of 1998. An annotated list of selected film books published in 1998.

Indexes

Film titles and artists are arranged into nine indexes, allowing the reader to effectively approach a film from any one of several directions, including not only its credits but its subject matter.

Director, Screenwriter, Cinematographer, Editor, Music, Art Director, and *Performer Indexes* are arranged according to artists appearing in this volume, followed by a list of the films on which they worked.

Subject Index. Films may be categorized under several of the subject terms arranged alphabetically in this section.

Title Index. The title index is a cumulative alphabetical list of nearly 4,870 films covered in the eighteen volumes of the *Magill's Cinema Annual,* including over 300 films covered in this volume. Films reviewed in past volumes are cited with the year in which the film was originally released; films reviewed in this volume are cited with the film title in bold with a bolded Arabic numeral indicating the page number on which the review begins. Original and alternate titles are cross-referenced to the American release title in the Title Index. Titles of retrospective films are followed by the year, in brackets, of their original release.

Sample Review

Each *Magill's* review contains up to sixteen items of information. A fictionalized composite sample review containing all the elements of information that may be included in a full-length review follows the outline below. The circled number preceding each element in the sample review on page XVII designates an item of information that is explained in the outline on the next page.

1 Title: Film title as it was released in the United States.

2 Foreign or alternate title(s): The film's original title or titles as released outside the United States, or alternate film title or titles. Foreign and alternate titles also appear in the Title Index to facilitate user access.

3 Taglines: Up to ten publicity or critical taglines for the film from advertisements or reviews.

4 Box office information: Year-end or other box office domestic revenues for the film.

5 Film review or abstract: A one-paragraph abstract or 750 to 1500–word signed review of the film, including brief plot summary, and for full-length reviews, an analytic overview of the film and its critical reception.

6 Principal characters: Up to 25 listings of the film's principal characters and the names of the actors who play them in the film. The names of actors who play themselves are cited twice (as character and actor).

7 Country of origin: The film's country or countries of origin if other than the United States.

8 Release date: The year of the film's first general release.

9 Production information: This section typically includes the name(s) of the film's producer(s), production company, and distributor; director(s); screenwriter(s); author(s) or creator(s) and the novel, play, short story, television show, motion picture, or other work, or character(s), that the film was based upon; cinematographer(s) (if the film is animated, this will be replaced with Animation or Animation Direction); editor(s); art director(s), production designer(s), set decorator(s) or set designer(s); music composer(s); and other credits such as visual effects, sound, casting, costume design, and song(s) and songwriter(s).

10 MPAA rating: The film's rating by the Motion Picture Association of America. If there is no rating given, the line will read, "no listing."

11 Running time: The film's running time in minutes.

12 Reviewer byline: The name of the reviewer who wrote the full-length review. A complete list of this volume's contributors appears in the "Contributing Reviewers" section which follows the Introduction.

13 Reviews: A list of up to 25 brief citations of major newspaper and journal reviews of the film, including publication title, date of review, and page number.

14 Awards information: Awards won by the film, followed by category and name of winning cast or crew member. Listings of the film's nominations follow the wins on a separate line for each award. Awards are arranged alphabetically. Information is listed for films that won or were nominated for the following awards: American Academy Awards, Australian Film Institute, British Academy of Film and Television Arts, Canadian Genie, Cannes Film Festival, Directors Guild of America, French Cesar, Golden Globe, Independent Spirit, Los Angeles Film Critics Association Awards, Montreal Film Festival, MTV Movie Awards, National Board of Review Awards, National Society of Film Critics Awards, New York Critics Awards, Sundance Film Festival, Toronto-City Awards, Writers Guild of America, and others.

15 Film quotes: Memorable dialogue directly from the film, attributed to the character who spoke it, or comment from cast or crew members or reviewers about the film.

16 Film trivia: Interesting tidbits about the film, its cast, or production crew.

(2)

(1) The Gump Diaries (Los Diarios del Gump)

(3) "Love means never having to say you're stupid."
—Movie tagline

"This was a really good movie. I liked it." —Joe Critic, *Daily News*

(4) **Box Office Gross:** $10 million
(December 15, 1994)

CREDITS

(6) **Jim Carroll:** Leonardo DiCaprio
Swifty: Bruno Kirby
Jim's Mother: Lorraine Bracco
Mickey: Mark Wahlberg

(7) **Origin:** United Kingdom
(8) **Released:** 1993
Production: Liz Heller, John Bard Manulis for New Line Cinema; released by Island Pictures
(9) **Direction:** Scott Kalvert
Author: Bryan Goluboff; based on the novel by Jim Carroll
Cinematographer: David Phillips
Editing: Dana Congdon
Production design: Christopher Nowak
Set decoration: Harriet Zucker
Sound: William Sarokin
Costume design: David C. Robinson
Music: Graeme Revell
(10) **MPAA rating:** R
(11) **Running time:** 102 minutes

(5) In writer/director Robert Zemeckis' *Back to the Future* trilogy (1985, 1989, 1990), Marty McFly (Michael J. Fox) and his scientist sidekick Doc Brown (Christopher Lloyd) journey backward and forward in time, attempting to smooth over some rough spots in their personal histories in order to remain true to their individual destinies. Throughout their time-travel adventures, Doc Brown insists that neither he nor Marty influence any major historical events, believing that to do so would result in catastrophic changes in humankind's ultimate destiny. By the end of the trilogy, however, Doc Brown has revised his thinking and tells Marty that, "Your future hasn't been written yet. No one's has. Your future is whatever you make it. So make it a good one."

In *Forrest Gump*, Zemeckis once again explores the theme of personal destiny and how an individual's life affects and is affected by his historical time period. This time, however, Zemeckis and screenwriter Eric Roth chronicle the life of a character who does nothing but meddle in the historical events of his time without even trying to do so. By the film's conclusion, however, it has become apparent that Zemeckis's main concern is something more than merely having fun with four decades of American history. In the process of re-creating significant moments in time, he has captured on celluloid something eternal and timeless—the soul of humanity personified by a nondescript simpleton from the deep South.

(15)
"The state of existence may be likened unto a receptacle containing cocoa-based confections, in that one may never predict that which one may receive." —Forrest Gump, from *The Gump Diaries*

The film begins following the flight of a seemingly insignificant feather as it floats down from the sky and brushes against various objects and people before finally coming to rest at the feet of Forrest Gump (Tom Hanks). Forrest, who is sitting on a bus-stop bench, reaches down and picks up the feather, smooths it out, then opens his traveling case and carefully places the feather between the pages of his favorite book, *Curious George*.

In this simple but hauntingly beautiful opening scene, the filmmakers illustrate the film's principal concern: Is life a series of random events over which a person has no control, or is there an underlying order to things that leads to the fulfillment of an individual's destiny? The rest of the film is a humorous and moving attempt to prove that, underlying the random, chaotic events that make up a person's life, there exists a benign and simple order.

Forrest sits on the bench throughout most of the film, talking about various events of his life to others who happen to sit down next to him. It does not take long, however, for the audience to realize that Forrest's seemingly random

The action shifts to the mid-1950's with Forrest as a young boy (Michael Humphreys) being fitted with leg braces to correct a curvature in his spine. The action shifts to the mid-1950's to a in his spine. When the first U.S. Ping-Pong team to This movie magic has not accomplished by special effects or computer-altered images, by something much more impressive and harder to achieve.

AWARDS AND NOMINATIONS

(14) **Academy Awards 1994:** Best Film, Best Actor (Hanks), Best Special Effects, Best Cinematography
Nominations: Best Actress (Fields), Best Screenplay, Best Director (Zameckis)
Golden Globe Awards 1994: Best Film,
Nominations: Best Actor (Hanks), Best Supporting Actress (Wright), Best Music, Best Special Effects

(16)
Hanks was the first actor since Spencer Tracy to win back-to-back Oscars for Best Actor. Hanks received the award in 1993 for his performance in *Philadelphia*. Tracy won Oscars in 1937 for *Captains Courageous* and in 1938 for *Boys Town*.

chatter to a parade of strangers has a perfect chronological order to it. He tells his first story after looking down at the feet of his first bench partner and observing, "Mama always said that you can tell a lot about a person by the shoes they wear." Then, in a voice-over narration, Forrest begins the story of his life, first by telling about the first pair of shoes he can remember wearing.

The action shifts to the mid-1950's with Forrest as a young boy (Michael Humphreys) being fitted with leg braces to correct a curvature in his spine. Despite this traumatic handicap, Forrest remains unaffected, thanks to his mother (Sally Field) who reminds him on more than one occasion that he is no different from anyone else. Although this and most of Mrs. Gump's other words of advice are in the form of hackneyed cliches, Forrest whose intelligence quotient is below normal, sincerely believes every one of them, namely because he instinctively knows they are sincere expressions of his mother's love and fierce devotion.

(12) —*John Byline*

REVIEWS

(13) *Entertainment Weekly.* July 15, 1994, p. 42.
The Hollywood Reporter. June 29, 1994, p. 7.
Los Angeles Times. July 6, 1994, p. F1.

Interview with Nick Nolte

Born in Omaha, Nebraska, in 1940, Nick Nolte never considered acting as a career while growing up. Nolte was impetuous, regularly got into trouble, his scholarly achievements were less than stellar, but he didn't really seem to care. A gifted athlete, he was considered one of the premier high school football players in the state and was counting on an athletic scholarship to take him to the next level. The scholarships came just like he'd hoped—four of them, in fact. But every time Nolte took to the field at school, he'd ignore his academics and the scholarships would be rescinded. With a lifetime of bad grades behind him, he abandoned the idea of a career as a jock and hit the road, beginning a 15-year stretch, appearing in regional stage productions and forgettable TV films. His big break came in 1976 when he landed one of the title roles in the landmark TV mini-series *Rich Man, Poor Man.*

As Tom Jordache, Nolte established a screen persona that would rule his career for the next decade: wild, irascible, quick-tempered; a basic garden variety hot-head. Considering his personal life at the time, these performances weren't much of a stretch for Nolte, who was in a constant state of upheaval. In addition to going through a slew of failed relationships, he was married and divorced three times and was later slapped with a $4.5 million palimony suit by actress Karen Louise, his companion of eight years. He regularly made the gossip columns with tales of abhorrent behavior attributed to his longtime love affair with the bottle.

Despite his personal tribulations, Nolte became one of the top leading men of the era. First came *The Deep,* followed by the highly regarded football comedy *North Dallas Forty* and finally, in 1982, *48 HRS.,* one of the most successful mismatched-buddy films of all time. Although he didn't know it then, Nolte had reached his commercial zenith. With the exception of 1986's *Down & Out in Beverly Hills,* Nolte churned out a decade's worth of artistically barren box office bombs. In 1991, Nolte took the romantic lead in the Barbra Streisand film *The Prince of Tides,* which earned him his first Oscar nomination. *Tides* led to Scorsese's remake *Cape Fear* and the drama *Lorenzo's Oil,* both highly acclaimed efforts that did only marginally well at the box office. It looked as if he was on his way to a comeback until the release of five straight commercial duds: *I'll Do Anything, Jefferson in Paris, Blue Chips, I Love Trouble,* and (the much underrated) *Mulholland Falls.* These films varied in subject matter and, in the case of *I'll Do Anything* and *I Love Trouble,* cast Nolte against his rugged persona. At age fifty-five and without a substantial hit in fifteen years, Nolte had come to a personal and professional crossroads, which led to his decision to rearrange his priorities and re-direct his career.

December 1998 saw the release of two new Nolte films, *Affliction* and the highly anticipated World War II epic, *The Thin Red Line,* writer/director Terrence Malick's reverie into the horrors of war. A recluse on a par with Salinger or Garbo, Malick has only made two other movies (*Badlands* [1974], *Days of Heaven* [1978]), both considered modern marvels of storytelling and technical prowess. *The Thin Red Line* will almost certainly become required study for film students. The story is based on a novel by James Jones chronicling the attack on Guadalcanal in the South Pacific and also acts as a sequel of sorts to his *From Here to Eternity* (1953).

During a series of interviews in Los Angeles to promote his two new films, Nolte sat down with *Magill's* contributor J. M. Clark and looked back on those lost years with reflective wisdom.

What are the most unattractive aspects of fame and success?

The problem with finding success in films is what it does to your perspective. You do a movie or two that makes a bunch of money and suddenly you're under pressure to repeat the magic, which rarely ever happens. You begin questioning your decisions and your talent and you forget why you got into the business in the first place. It took me ten years to figure that out.

Was there a point where you finally said to yourself, "I've had enough of Hollywood?"

About four years ago, with *Mother Night,* I made the decision that I would only consider doing projects that I liked. Not because of the actors involved or the money or whether it was commercial or not. The studios will ask you to repeat the same exact formula but as an actor, you want to try something new. I had done the same thing for twenty years and frankly, I was miserable. I made the change with the knowledge that I might go broke, but there comes a point in your life where your soul becomes your main concern and I was long overdue. I had ignored my artistic passion for too long.

Tell us more about your *Thin Red Line* character, Col. Tall.

Lt. Col. Gordon Tall is a soldier without a war. He was too young for World War I and during the period between 1920 and 1940, the armed forces had scaled down; practically demilitarized. The majority of the troops enlisting at the time were men who couldn't get work elsewhere; drunks and homeless types who basically were looking for a warm bed and a hot meal. They trained with fake guns. The funds from the government had been reduced to a trickle; it was a stark contrast to how the military currently operates. By the time World War II rolled around, Tall was getting a little long in the tooth and saw the Guadalcanal invasion as his last real opportunity for glory. He was a military career man, a West Point graduate who feared his career would be over before he ever had a chance to prove himself in the field and that scared the hell out of him. It made him take chances with lives a more rational commander would never have considered.

What was it like working with [writer/director] Terrence Malick?

People think Terry's an eccentric but he's really not. He's an incredibly smart man with a wide-open mind. He can talk with authority on more subjects than anyone I've ever met. One of the scenes he gave me contained a poem by Homer. It was a piece that romanticized war and gave it a sort of wistful timelessness. He wanted to show that man, despite all of his advancements in other arenas, can never fully relinquish this barbaric need to fight and conquer. I think that's where the story distinguishes itself from other war pictures; it looks at it from other perspectives—philosophically, emotionally, spiritually—and shows us things we haven't seen before.

Many of the actors who've previously worked with Malick in the past labeled him an "obsessive/compulsive." How did you feel about working with him?

At various points during the filming, Terry would have five or six scenes going at a time and quite often would leave them incomplete. It was a style I hadn't seen before and it had quite a strong impact on some of the younger actors; they weren't sure that they could get back to the same point, emotionally, but I could see what Terry was doing. Most directors will stick with a scene until they feel that they've got it perfect, which isn't always a good idea. You do forty or fifty takes of the same scene and it begins to get stale. Repeating it over and over isn't always the solution. Giving the actors time to absorb the material, to mature with the scenes and rethink their performances is a great way of keeping it new. Days or even weeks later, he'd come back to the scenes when everyone would be fresh and have a completely different perspective; it was a very innovative method of filmmaking.

How close was the movie to the book?

Every character in the film is based on a piece of author James Jones's personality. He was there, he participated in the battle, got wounded and was sent home. He felt that war was a horrific experience that no one should ever be asked to go through. What really drew me to the project was the tension between Tall and Staros [Tall's second-in-command, played by Elias Koteas]. Tall has his own personal agenda to fulfill and butts heads with the more compassionate Staros, who sees that Tall is losing his grip. The problem is, and this is where I think Jones really nailed it, is presenting the question, is it possible to attain victory in war and still be compassionate? I think that Terry's adaptation works so well because it leaves the answer open ended. [Ironically, the film role Nolte was to play after completion of *The Thin Red Line* was that of Jones himself in the recent Merchant/Ivory film *A Soldier's Daughter Never Cries*. Because of production over-runs, Kris Kristofferson wound up with the role.]

Talk about the events that led up to your taking the lead in *Affliction*.

It took me a long time to prepare for it. [Screenwriter/director] Paul Schrader approached me to do it years ago but the timing wasn't right. Looking back, I'm glad it didn't work out then because I couldn't have pulled it off at the time. *The Thin Red Line* experience taught me how to summon up the emotions I needed for *Affliction* and how to direct the rage. The two movies have a lot in common; they both examine the co-existence of violence and compassion within all of us. We always think that it's the other person who is violent; we conveniently find excuses for it—drugs, gangs, movies, ideology, what have you, but it's present within all of us and ignoring it only makes it worse, which is unfortunate. It's in our genes and it's not going to go away any time soon.

How do you feel about taking on back-to-back roles that required such extreme anger?

You have to build up to it. Doing this type of material delivers an adrenaline rush that feeds off of raw emotion. The secret is to make it look unrehearsed and spontaneous. Both films gave me the chance to reflect on violence, what it is and where it comes from. There's been more wars and confrontation in this century than at any other time in man's history. We've seen more unnecessary bloodshed than ever before. Violence is at our core. Our ability to call on this rage is always there. It was fine when man had to survive among the elements—it was needed then, but we're beyond that need now. Why can't we shake this desire for confrontation? It amazes me sometimes.

Has giving up acting in commercial films in favor of more meaningful, lesser publicized, lower-paying projects had any kind of negative affect on your lifestyle?

I know an actor who would consider it a failure if one of his movies failed to make $100 million at the box office. Compounding that rather twisted perspective, what makes it worse, are the suits whose only concern is the bottom line. For the most part, studio films are trying to reach a core audience between the ages of fourteen and twenty-six. In those movies, you're required to pick up a gun and shoot everybody. Those films do nothing to help us understand violence or our core emotions; they glorify violence. Make it sexy. That's something that's hard for me to believe in. It's not even that interesting. I want to do movies that speak to an audience about the truths of life. I know it's not commercial and I know what I've done recently isn't really considered 'entertainment,' but that's the path I've chosen and I never been happier or more at peace with myself.

Affliction

"One of the year's top ten. Paul Schrader has made his best movie yet."—*Entertainment Weekly*

"One of the year's strongest dramas! A great performance by Nolte. Rarely have a novelist and filmmaker been better matched."—Jack Mathews, *Los Angeles Times*

"One of the Top Ten Films of 1998."—Dave Kehr, *New York Daily News*

"The Best Film of the Year."—Thelma Adams, *New York Post*

"Volcanic! Nick Nolte gives the performance of his career in Paul Schrader's quietly stunning new film. A shockingly savage performance [by] James Coburn."—Janet Maslin, *New York Times*

"Nolte is nothing short of perfection."—Leah Rozen, *People*

"Terrific!"—Peter Travers, *Rolling Stone*

"Two thumbs up!"—*Siskel & Ebert*

"Already an American classic."—Amy Taubin, *Village Voice*

"Brilliant! Nolte should finally win his Oscar"—John Powers, *Vogue*

"This is a great performance by a great actor at the top of his form. If it doesn't win him an Oscar there's no justice under the sun or among the stars."—Joe Morgenstern, *Wall Street Journal*

Small town sheriff Wade Whitehouse (Nick Nolte) is haunted by bad memories of his childhood while investigating a hunter's death in *Affliction*.

 Box Office: $900,506

Adapted from Russell Banks's novel, Paul Schrader's *Affliction* is an intense character study of a man's gradual descent into madness and violence. Nick Nolte stars as Wade Whitehouse, a divorced, middle-aged man perpetually out of sync with his community and even with himself. In *The St. James Film Directors Encyclopedia*, G.C. Macnab and Rob Edelman assert that "the image of the condemned man/woman attempting to escape his/her fate is a leitmotif in Schrader's work." For Wade, this unshakable "fate" is the legacy of his ultra-macho father's alcoholism and violence, a cycle of abuse and despair depicted in flashback throughout the film.

Schrader's adaptation is faithful to the complex novel, but, because so much of the novel's action takes place internally, the movie is often slow-moving, and ultimately each plot strand becomes yet another reflection of Wade's turbulent consciousness and wrong-headed attempts to make things right. Nonetheless, because Nolte gives a performance of such depth and nuance, *Affliction* contains moments of incredible power.

Wade lives an ordinary life in the small, dreary town of Lawford, New Hampshire. He works for Gordon LaRiviere (Holmes Osborne) doing odd jobs like digging wells and plowing snow off the roads. Wade is also the town's police officer, which amounts to being a crossing guard for the school. When we first meet him, he is taking his daugh-

> Wade (Nick Nolte): "I got a feelin' like a whipped dog. Someday I'm gonna bite back."

ter, Jill (Brigid Tierney), to the Halloween party at the town hall, a sad little gathering that Jill, now living in another city with her mother, Lillian (Mary Beth Hurt), and rich stepfather, seems to have outgrown. Jill does not even want to be with her father and calls her mother to pick her up that night. Wade means well but cannot connect with his daughter, who is uneasy just being around him. He wants to be a good father, though, and one of his preoccupations throughout the film is a custody suit. However, prospect of victory seems bleak.

Jack Hewitt (Jim True), one of Wade's co-workers, is assigned to go deer hunting with a union official named Evan Twombley (Sean McCann), a novice hunter who is killed with his own rifle. Jack tells the authorities that it was an accident, but Wade suspects there may be something more to it. Twombley was supposed to testify about organized crime and the union, and Wade gradually concocts a theory about a Mafia hit involving Jack. As Wade discusses his theories with his younger brother, Rolfe (Willem Dafoe), it seems the film could be a detective thriller with Wade slowly putting all the pieces together and becoming the hero he desperately wants to be. *Affliction*, however, is not a thriller; there was no murder, we finally learn, and the mystery plot exists only in Wade's mind—a fixation to take his mind off of his other problems.

Indeed, Wade has difficulty focusing on the right things at the right time. When he is directing traffic the morning of the hunting accident, he is thinking about his daughter's rejection of him and standing in the middle of the road with arms outstretched for a long time, as if he were frozen. The cars are backed up, the drivers become irritated, and one BMW goes racing by him. Wade develops a silly grudge and later goes to the home of the driver, Mel Gordon (Steve Adams), Twombley's son-in-law, to give him a ticket, even though the family is in grief. When Wade serves the ticket, Mel refuses it and even threatens to get him fired.

Wade's best hope for the future seems to be Margie Fogg (Sissy Spacek), a waitress at the local diner who truly cares about him. In the film's sweetest, most hopeful scene, he looks in her face and says that he can see what she looked like as a kid and later cautiously proposes thinking about marriage, an idea she seems hesitant about. They go to visit

CREDITS

Wade Whitehouse: Nick Nolte
Margie Fogg: Sissy Spacek
Glen Whitehouse: James Coburn
Rolfe Whitehouse: Willem Defoe
Lillian: Mary Beth Hurt
Jack Hewitt: Jim True
Alma Pittman: Marian Seldes
Gordon LaRiviere: Holmes Osborne
Jill: Brigid Tierney
Evan Twombley: Sean McCann
Nick Wickham: Wayne Robson

Origin: USA
Released: 1998
Production: Linda Reisman for Kingsgate/Largo Entertainment production; released by Lion Gates Films
Direction: Paul Schrader
Screenplay: Paul Schrader; based on the novel by Russell Banks
Cinematography: Paul Sarossy
Editing: Jay Rabinowitz
Music: Michael Brook
Production design: Anne Pritchard
Art direction: Michel Beaudet
Costumes: Francois Laplante
Sound: Patrick Rousseau
MPAA rating: R
Running Time: 113 minutes

AWARDS AND NOMINATIONS

Academy Awards 1998: Supporting Actor (James Coburn)
New York Film Critics 1998: Actor (Nick Nolte)
Academy Awards 1998 Nominations: Actor (Nick Nolte)

Wade's parents and find his father, Glen (James Coburn), disoriented and drunk as usual. He says his wife is asleep upstairs, but, when Wade finally goes to find his mom, she is dead. She froze to death because Glen never got around to fixing the broken furnace. His complicity in her death—his neglect—may be the most monstrous thing about him. On the whole, Coburn delivers a largely one-note performance—an angry man drinking heavily, growling at the world, and lumbering around his house. He does what the part requires, but he never transcends the type he is playing—the scary patriarch—the way Nolte breathes life into the frustrated, bruised son.

Director Paul Schrader was raised in Michigan by a strict Calvinist father.

The funeral of their mother brings the Whitehouse siblings together. Rolfe, who was able to flee the town and make a decent life, comes, as does the sister, a born-again Christian. When her husband leads everyone in prayer, Glen interrupts them—mocking his sons as "candy asses" and his daughter and son-in-law as "Jesus freaks." Wade soon lashes out at Glen in an outburst that suggests he is very much like his father. After the funeral, Wade decides to move in with Glen because the old man cannot take care of himself.

As time passes, Wade gets carried away with his murder theory and soon ordinary events begin to look more suspicious to Wade. He sees LaRiviere and Mel Gordon having a private meeting together. Then LaRiviere starts showing Wade appreciation—offering to get his car's transmission fixed and charging it to the town. At the same time, LaRiviere encourages Wade to forget about his grudge with Mel Gordon, who is doing business with LaRiviere, and expresses an interest in buying the Whitehouse place.

Wade progressively loses touch with reality. One night he chases Jack, who ends up shooting the tires and window of Wade's truck, which is on loan from LaRiviere. When Wade goes to the town clerk to expound his theories on Twombley's death, she reveals the truth about the dealings in town. Mel Gordon and Gordon LaRiviere are getting rich buying up everyone's land and converting the area into a resort; that is why LaRiviere was interested in buying Wade's place. Wade, however, is not deterred from thinking something more is going on. He explodes at LaRiviere and gets fired. Later the same day, he finds out he has been fired as town cop.

Some elements that worked in the novel, like Wade not recognizing himself in a mirror and a troublesome toothache constantly gnawing away at him (he finally pulls the tooth himself in a harrowing scene), feel too literary and symbolic on film and make the film an overly cerebral exercise. Wade's self-alienation is obvious—we do not need so many reminders that he is also alienated from his body.

Wade experiences more misfortunes. Another visit with Jill goes badly, he learns that Jack has his old policeman's job, and he goes home to find Margie leaving him. She is fearful of the hints of violence she has seen in Wade, the legacy he has inherited from his father. When he tries to stop her, Jill intervenes, and he ends up knocking her down.

A sense of inevitable tragedy weighs Wade down. All of Wade's plans and ideas lead to dead ends, and, because every possible avenue of redemption—as crackerjack detective, good father, loyal son, future husband—leaves him stymied, the film feels a bit like a dead end too. If a lesser actor were playing the part, we might stop caring altogether, but Nolte rivets our attention with his subtle portrayal of a man tightly wound up and slowly coming undone. He plays a wide range of emotions, from tenderness to despair to anger, and explodes in sudden outbursts of long-suppressed rage.

When his father wants to use the truck to go to town to buy booze and Wade ignores him—he hates his father for thinking they are alike—Glen hits Wade with a bottle, and Wade swings at Glen with a rifle, accidentally killing him. In a tender yet chilling moment, Wade bends down next to his father, gently strokes his forehead, then strokes his own—as if acknowledging the bond between them. Wade then sets his father's body on fire, and soon the whole barn is engulfed in flames. In one of the most disturbing images of the year, Wade, who seems to have accepted the violence within him, in essence his fate, goes into the house and pours himself a drink while the inferno rages in the background. Next, he kills Jack, and then disappears from the community. Rolfe, who narrates both the novel and the film, delivers an awkward concluding voice-over, cobbled together clumsily from various passages in the novel—an overarching lesson about the tradition of violence being passed from fathers to sons.

While *Affliction* lacks the poetry, beauty, and formal complexity of Atom Egoyan's 1997 adaptation of *The Sweet Hereafter,* another Banks novel, Schrader's film succeeds, due in large part to Nolte's richly textured performance, as a study of troubled manhood and the disturbed psychology of one particular individual.

—*Peter N. Chumo*

REVIEWS

Boxoffice. February, 1998, p. 51.
Chicago Tribune. February 5, 1999, p. 5
Entertainment Weekly. January 15, 1999, p. 40.
Los Angeles Times. December 30, 1998, p. F2.
San Francisco Chronicle. February 12, 1999, p. C1.
San Francisco Examiner. February 12, 1999, p. C1.
Variety. September 1, 1997, p. 76.

Air Bud: Golden Receiver

The Timber Wolves are about to unleash their secret weapon.—*Movie tagline*

"The best family film of the summer!"—*Kansas City Sun*

 Box Office: $10,031,536

Animals doing amazing tricks have been a staple of family movies since Walt Disney was in knee pants. The surprise 1997 hit *Air Bud* featured a golden retriever named Buddy who could play basketball—a nice feat for a pooch, though hardly more astounding than anything Lassie would do in a typical TV episode. The unexpected success of *Air Bud* inevitably spawned a sequel. In *Air Bud: Golden Receiver*, the canine wonder takes up football. There's one basic problem: while not many dogs can manage a jump shot, any fairly agile mutt can catch a football in its mouth.

So the second *Air Bud* is a movie centered around a supposedly astounding animal who does pretty mundane things. Jumping up and snaring a long pass in its teeth, Buddy looks like most dogs catching frisbees in the local park. Some pedestrian camera tricks exaggerate the height of Buddy's jumps. And he does look bizarrely cute in shoulder pads and a helmet. He doesn't seem to run very well with the gear on, though, and that makes it all the more incredible that every time he grabs the ball he eludes everyone on the field.

This sequel is woefully short on concept and would never have been made on its own merit. It's distressing to watch a fading film franchise, especially one that had little originality to begin with. The first *Air Bud* succeeded on its own terms mostly because it brought some energy to tired plots and overworked characters. Almost everything about the follow-up seems forced and stale.

The film is once again set in the mythical town of Fernfield, in Washington state, a picturesque seaside town "where everything is possible," according to the welcome sign. Among the plausible things that have happened since the first *Air Bud* are that Buddy's owner and pal, Josh (Kevin Zegers) has grown from a shy and unconfident 12-year-old into a handsome and well-liked but still insecure 14-year-old. He still has an impossibly cute little toddler sister, Andrea, who fortunately has few lines.

Among the less plausible changes are that he has a new actress playing his mother, Jackie (Cynthia Stevenson, replacing Wendy Makkena). His father is still dead, a heroic test pilot killed in a car crash, and the garage is still a sort of shrine to him.

The film's writers remain the same—Paul Tamasy and Aaron Mendelsohn, but there is a new man in charge. The original *Air Bud* was overseen by Charles Martin Smith, the actor best known for playing Terry the Toad in the original *American Graffiti*. Smith, who also appeared in the first film, has been replaced as director by Richard Martin, who gives his father, the comic Dick Martin of the old Rowan and Martin comedy team, a cameo role. Martin portrays an addled "color commentator" who announces the big game with straight man Tim Conway. Even their occasionally funny schtick is rendered implausible. The duo provide running commentary over a public address system at the stadium. Who ever heard of public address announcers doing color? By all rights they should be on a radio broadcast.

This sort of studied indifference to plausibility is a hallmark of *Golden Receiver*. It's as if logic doesn't matter because the primary audience for the film is children. For instance, Josh is now in high school—or is it junior high? His friend Tom notes that one of the nice things about entering high school is that "the girls have grown into women."

CREDITS

Josh Framm: Kevin Zegers
Jackie Framm: Cynthia Stevenson
Dr. Patrick Sullivan: Gregory Harrison
Natalya: Nora Dunn
Popov: Perry Anzilotti
Coach Fanelli: Robert Costanzo
Fred Davis: Tim Conway
Phil Phil: Dick Martin
Referee: Jay Brazeau

Origin: USA
Released: 1998
Production: Robert Vince for Keystone Pictures; released by Dimension Films
Direction: Richard Martin
Screenplay: Paul Tamasy and Aaron Mendelsohn; based on the character created by Kevin DiCicco
Cinematography: Mike Southon
Editing: Bruce Lange, Melinda Seabrook
Music: Brahm Wenger
Production design: Rex Raglan
Art direction: Eric Norlin
Costumes: Patricia Hargreaves
Sound: Kevin Sands
MPAA rating: G
Running Time: 90 minutes

They go into a building that is labeled a high school, yet they play for a junior high football team. One must conclude that eighth grade is part of junior high and that junior high is in the high school building, but there are never any older kids around.

The sequel labors long and hard to get the pooch into his football gear, as if trying to eat up time. Josh is still getting over his dad's death, and when his mom starts dating again, it's too much for him to take, especially when she starts getting serious with the new veterinarian in town. As Jackie, Stephenson is a ditz who goes all gooey at the sight of a man and is constantly half-closing her eyes and smiling dreamily at the adventures of her son. Stephenson lampooned this same sort of self-absorbed, clueless suburban mom in the black comedy *Happiness* (reviewed in this edition); here she plays the very character she so deftly satirizes in the latter film. It's unnerving. Jackie meets the hunky Dr. Patrick Sullivan (Gregory Harrison) by skateboarding off a pier and landing on top of him in his boat.

What follows is a totally implausible sequence in which Josh and Tom take Buddy to the vet and pretend there is something wrong with his tail. Obligingly, Dr. Sullivan offers to take an X-ray. In doing so, he conveniently leaves the boys alone in an examining room, and also leaves his wallet behind, so that Josh can rummage through and find photos of the doctor with other women! Thus the boys confirm their suspicions that the sailor vet is a cad with a woman in every port. How the boys figured out in advance that they would have the chance to rifle his wallet is another thing the filmmakers don't care about.

As Josh frets about his mom's beau, two heavily caricatured Russian villains (Nora Dunn and Perry Anzilotti) are scheming about how to get their hands on Buddy. They need the dog to complete a menagerie of amazing animals which they are hiding in a marina warehouse and preparing to abscond with to Russia. This over-the-top pair make Boris and Natasha in the old *Rocky and Bullwinkle* TV cartoon series look like authentic Russians. They camp and vamp, act impossibly clumsy and stupid, and pursue their prey in an ice-cream truck. They pop in and out of the movie, making a few lame attempts at snaring Buddy. The tone of their performances is so out of sync with the syrupy seriousness of the rest of the film that it's jarring.

Dr. Sullivan gives Josh a football for a present, and Tom is eager to get Josh to join him in trying out for the team. What finally convinces Josh to go out for football is his desire to get away from the house after school. Dr. Sullivan, who apparently works banker's hours as the town's only vet, comes over every afternoon to help Jackie build a gazebo in the backyard.

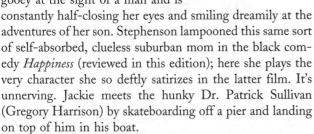

The original Buddy died shortly after the first movie; six dogs were used in the sequel.

Of course, Josh effortlessly can throw 50-yard passes at his first practice. But his path is blocked by a star quarterback, whom the grizzled, kindly veteran coach (Robert Costanzo) says is "the hottest in the league" even though the season hasn't started yet.

When Josh trudges home late that night wearing a football uniform, Jackie looks up from playing with Andrea and casually asks "You joined the football team?" This is the kind of mother whose son disappears for hours with no explanation and when he comes home, she's not even upset.

Finally, Josh discovers, long after the audience has, that Buddy can play football. Before the first game, Josh happens to be in the right place at the right time to overhear the school principal telling the coach that he's going to be fired if the team doesn't have a winning season. Then, the star quarterback is injured, suffering a separated shoulder and neatly getting that potential plot conflict out of the way. *Air Bud* avoids any issues that are more complicated than a paint-by-numbers drawing.

Buddy shows up just in time to rescue Josh from his confidence problems. Josh must convince the coach to let Buddy be part of the team, but the coach is a pushover. So are all the opponents and referees, who never raise a single question about the dog's eligibility—isn't there a minimum grade-point-average for athletes in this state, or at least a requirement that team members be human?

It would be unfair to raise such questions if *Air Bud* played lightheartedly or fanciful. But instead it's morose and earnest. The last half of the film is unabashedly formulaic. Josh runs away upon learning Doc Sullivan has offered to marry his mom. He is talked out of leaving town by the coach, who uses a sports analogy to awaken Josh to the idea that he doesn't have to stop loving his dad to accept a stepdad. "You still love basketball but you can love football too," observes the coach.

As Josh prepares to go to the big state championship game, he finds Buddy has finally been dog-napped by the Ruskies. Buddy's absence sends the team into a tailspin of despair and allows the coach to indulge in a corny halftime speech about believing in yourself.

The fact that the film has no confidence in its own central plot is betrayed when the ending cross-cuts between the big game and much longer sequences that involve Buddy and the other animals in the villains' menagerie. In the warehouse Buddy doesn't just help the animals escape; they launch nefarious schemes to physically punish their abductors. The action includes the Russians drowning in a vat of fish guts—such vats being common in marina warehouses. It's like a cartoon has gotten stuck in the middle of a soap opera.

Of course, Patrick steps in to save the day. But even after the big game, there is no reconciliation scene. That's so

Patrick can sail off on his boat as Josh and Buddy run onto the pier and holler and bark until he turns around. It's that kind of a movie—squeaky-clean, straight-arrow, completely predictable, and absolutely unremarkable.

It would be horrible to imagine what might happen if the sequel machine keeps spinning and Buddy decides to take up baseball.

—*Michael Betzold*

REVIEWS

Los Angeles Times. August 14, 1998, p. F10.
New York Times. August 14, 1998, p. E14.
Variety. August 10, 1998, p. 43.

An Alan Smithee Film: Burn Hollywood Burn

"One of the funniest movies to turn up in ages."—Martin Grove, *Hollywood Reporter*
"Hilarious! Unrelenting in its viciousness."— Charles Fleming, *LA Weekly*
"It's fun . . . peppered with uproarious touches."—Stephen Farber, *Movieline*

There is a tradition in Hollywood that is meant to protect a director from the meddling of others in the making of his film. Should he or she decide that his studio and/or his producers have made a mess of his work of art—usually by recutting it—then he or she has the right to remove his or her name from the film. But since a movie can't be released without a director listed in the credits, the Directors Guild has a generic pseudonym to put on these orphans...Alan Smithee (also sometimes Allen Smithee).

Since its first use in 1967 when Don Siegel replaced Robert Totten 25 days into shooting on Richard Widmark's *Death of a Gunfighter* and neither director wanted his name on the film, "Alan Smithee" has had some 30 credits to his name. Perhaps one of the more interesting stories has Alan Smithee's name as director on the 1981 high school killer comedy *Student Bodies* (instead of Michael Ritchie) complete with an extensive press kit bio. (But hey, *The New York Times* and *Variety* gave Smithee rave reviews for *Death of a Gunfighter!*) Smithee's name has even been employed to hide the original director of several TV shows (a *MacGyver* and a *Twilight Zone* episode). But in reality, besides becoming an interesting piece of movie trivia, the name Alan Smithee has become a signal to knowing movie viewers that what they're watching is basically a bungled production.

Alan (Eric Idle) about his destroyed film: "I ended its suffering. I ended the suffering of those who would have had to watch it!"

But what happens when the director who wants his name removed from a film is actually named Alan Smithee? If he takes his name off, the Directors Guild will slap the name Alan Smithee on it! That's the basic premise of this film.

Alan Smithee (Eric Idle) has made quite a name for himself as the editor of choice for big-budget action films. Consequently it becomes an obvious career move for some studio to offer him his own film to direct. The property he is given is a $200 million film called *Trio* starring Sylvester Stallone, Whoopi Goldberg and Jackie Chan (who do cameos).

Eventually, however, Smithee's producer James Edmunds (Ryan O'Neal) and studio head Jerry Glover (Richard Jeni) commandeer the film and recut it into something Smithee hates. It's his first film, he can't take his name off it because the Directors Guild will put it back on, and it looks as if his career is over. So, seeing no other option, five days before the movie is to open in 7,000 theaters, Alan steals the master print.

Panic stricken, Edmunds and Glover hire private investigator Sam Rizzo (Harvey Weinstein— one of the brothers who cofounded Miramax Films) to find Alan and bring them the master print. Eventually, Smithee is befriended by two filmmaking African-American brothers, Dion (Coolio) and Leon (Chuck D) Brothers, the Brothers brothers. "Is it really that bad?" they ask? "It's fucking horrible," Smithee replies, "It's worse than *Showgirls!*"

With the Brothers brothers sharing Smithee's love of film as an art, they act as negotiators for the victimized director and meet Edmunds and Glover at the studio. They manage to pry final cut rights from Edmunds and it looks as if Smithee has a victory, but the brothers are followed from the studio. A police raid just misses catching Smithee as he slips out a bedroom window.

But Smithee is not willing to inflict the botched production he now holds hostage on unsuspecting audiences. "If we believe in film, and we do, then don't we have a responsibility to protect the world from bad ones?" Alan asks. And in final protest, feeling he has no other recourse, Alan burns the film at the La Brea Tar Pits. When caught, Smithee is not sent to prison, but is sent for therapy at the Keith Moon Psychiatric Facility in Kent England.

But there's one last bit of drollery left in the film. With all the publicity surrounding Smithee's theft, his story is now a hot property and Edmunds finds himself offering $5 million for the film rights to Smithee's biography.

An Alan Smithee Film: Burn Hollywood Burn, sounds as if it could be a savvy and witty insider's satire on all that's wrong with the American filmmaking system. Something like Robert Altman's 1992 film *The Player.* Unfortunately, it's nothing like *The Player.* Its first problem is that it is filmed as a documentary. It's filled with cameos of both real and fictional people who are interviewed for their take on the main events of the film. Stallone, Goldberg and Chan amongst the big cameos, Larry King, Dominic Dunne, Billy

Bob Thornton in smaller walk-ons. Every time one of these people is introduced he or she appears with his or her name along with a list of credits and not-so-subtle character traits. (i.e. "liar," "celibate," "slept in the White House," "wants to sleep at the White House," "hyena," and "scum," for example.) However, because these interviews mean we're being told the story instead of being shown it, the film seems to just plod along and the boredom factor increases.

So, who was the director of this misfired satire? Well, in a final irony, the director of *An Alan Smithee Film . . .* is Alan Smithee. This may be the funniest thing about this whole movie. The director, Arthur Hiller, was so disgusted by the final cut of this film that he requested that the Directors Guild take his name off it. And when they did, guess whose name went on it. For this reason alone *An Alan Smithee Film* probably will garner a special niche in film history, because it certainly won't get one as film art.

Oddly enough, Hiller does appear in the film. During the final credits there are some outtakes from the film. And there he is, talking to the person who truly had creative control of the film and saying, "The last thing any director needs is you, of all people, to stick up for us." And to whom is he speaking? Joe Eszterhas.

For those not in the know, Joe Eszterhas is probably Hollywood's highest paid screenwriter. Tinseltown has made him rich turning his scripts (*Jagged Edge, Basic Instinct*) into film. But his last film, the infamous *Showgirls,* was so soundly trounced by everyone that it seems that Eszterhas has decided to bite the hand that feeds him. As a result *An Alan Smithee Film* is nothing more than a hamhanded, self-indulgent attack against all the negative Hollywood stereotypes he could come up with, especially the fact that moviemaking can be a sleazy business more than a statement of art. But knowing Eszterhas' body of work, one can't help but feel that he has probably done more than his share of contributing to this problem. There is something disingenuous about his tirade here.

There's little art to the movie. There's no wit to the writing, no style to the visuals, no rhythm to the editing, no dramatic arc to the story, and no interest in the movie. Even the actors—either as themselves or as fictional characters—

CREDITS

James Edmunds: Ryan O'Neal
Dion Brothers: Coolio
Leon Brothers: Chuck D
Alan Smithee: Eric Idle
Jerry Glover: Richard Jeni
Michelle Rafferty: Leslie Stefanson
Ann Glover: Sandra Bernhard
Myrna Smithee: Cheri Lunghi
Sam Rizzo: Harvey Weinstein
Gary Samuels: Gavin Palone
Sister II Lumumba: Mc Lite
Stagger Lee: Marcello Thedford

Origin: USA
Released: 1998
Production: Ben Myron for Cinergi; released by Hollywood Pictures
Direction: Alan Smithee
Screenplay: Joe Eszterhas
Cinematography: Reynaldo Villalobos
Editing: Jim Langlois
Production design: David L. Snyder
Art direction: Melanie J. Baker
Set decoration: Claudette Didul
Costumes: Laura Cunningham-Bauer
Sound: Felipe Borrero
MPAA rating: R
Running Time: 86 minutes

REVIEWS

Boxoffice. March, 1998, p. 53.
Chicago Sun Times. February 27, 1998.
Chicago Tribune. February 27, 1998.
Entertainment Weekly. March 13, 1998, p. 51.
Los Angeles Times. February 27, 1998, p. F1.
New York Times. February 27, 1998, p. E10.
People. March 9, 1998, p. 21.
Rolling Stone. March 19, 1998, p. 72.
USA Today. February 27, 1998, p. 9D.
Variety. October 6, 1997, p. 54.
Village Voice. March 10, 1998, p. 118.

look more like victims of *Hard Copy* hit-and-run type interviews than insiders who want to tell their view of the facts.

An Alan Smithee Film was billed as "the movie Hollywood doesn't want you to see," as if this is THE film about Hollywood's dirt and there's some kind of conspiracy between Hollywood's powers that is trying to keep it from au-

diences. But the truth is, the film garnered such bad reviews and such bad boxoffice numbers that it was pulled from distribution only two weeks after its release. It's not that Hollywood doesn't want you to see it, it's that audiences didn't want to see it.

—*Beverley Bare Buehrer*

The Alarmist

Don't be alarmed. . . . they're professionals.—
Movie tagline

"An amusing drama!"—Anne Marie O'Connor,
Mademoiselle

"David Arquette and Stanley Tucci are a kick! Dizzyingly precise. They're in such sync they seem telepathic."—Matt Zoller Seitz, *New York Press*

"A dark, funny comedy. An ensemble piece that showcases everybody's talent."—Stephen Holden,
New York Times

"A black comedy with heart. *The Alarmist* is sharp, suspenseful and often hysterically funny. . . David Arquette and Kate Capshaw are outstanding."—Karen Butler, *United Press International*

"Stanley Tucci is superb in this darkly comedic role."—Paul Wunder, *WBAI*

"Fresh, funny, nasty!"—Dr. Joy Brown, *WOR*

The *Alarmist*, directed by Evan Dunsky and adapted from Keith Reddin's play *Life During Wartime*, is a comedy about paranoia, desperation and loneliness. Despite some valiant performances by Stanley Tucci and Kate Capshaw, this film falters and stumbles where it should trip along swiftly, hampered by weak direction and limp pacing.

Tommy Hudler (David Arquette) is a new hire at Grigoris Security, run by Heinrich Grigoris (Stanley Tucci). Heinrich is outrageous, bold, and determined to get new jobs at any cost. He is aided by Sally Brown (Mary McCormack), a drab dresser who is nevertheless as sharp as Heinrich about people and business. Tommy stumbles through his first few job calls, and finally scores (literally and figuratively) with Gale Ancona (Kate Capshaw), an attractive widow who buys an alarm system from him. Despite their age difference (she has a high school son,

Howard [Ryan Reynolds]), they embark on a hot and heavy affair.

Out drinking one night with Heinrich, Tommy is shocked to discover that Heinrich uses fear to ensure his customers' loyalty; Heinrich thinks nothing of breaking into a client's home to rattle their cage, and make them thank their lucky stars they use Grigoris Security. "We're not selling security — we're selling fear." Heinrich solemnly tells Tommy. Disgusted, Tommy takes Gale to Barstow to visit his family. Although Gale initially resists (it is obvious that she doesn't take their relationship as serious as Tommy does) she agrees to spend the weekend away from her home. The scenes that follow at the white

CREDITS

Tommy Hudler: David Arquette
Heinrich Grigoris: Stanley Tucci
Gale Ancona: Kate Capshaw
Sally Brown: Mary McCormack
Howard Ancona: Ryan Reynolds

Origin: USA
Released: 1997
Production: Dan Stone and Lisa Zimble for Key Entertainment and Bandeira Entertainment; released by Lion's Gate Films
Direction: Evan Dunsky
Screenplay: Evan Dunsky; based on the play *Life During Wartime* by Keith Reddin
Cinematography: Alex Nepomnaschy
Editing: Norman Buckley
Costumes: Denise Wingate
Production design: Amy B. Ancona
Music: Christophe Beck
MPAA rating: R
Running Time: 92 minutes

trash Hudler home are actually the best-acted and directed scenes in the film. Gale becomes drunk, has a "what am I doing here?" epiphany, and takes off back to Los Angeles in Tommy's car. As she sits with her son watching late night television and crying on his shoulder about her weird, young boyfriend, they both hear a noise from an intruder.

Heinrich (Stanley Tucci) to a potential customer: "You want to live your life with all this terror?"

When Tommy returns to Los Angeles, he is heartbroken to learn that Gale and her son have both been murdered in their home. Wracked with grief, Tommy begins to suspect Heinrich and all of his thoughts turn to making his boss pay for Gale's death.

Dunsky's faults lie with the languid, aimless pacing of the story. Individual scenes seem to drag on forever and lack a strong impact. Even wry comedic bits like Grigoris' smarmy television commercial isn't as funny as it probably was when it was fleetingly referred to on the stage. Ar-

quette is usually an appealing character actor but here he shifts and twitches so much that when he decides to take the law into his own hands near the climax, it is simply too unbelievable to see him act in a decisive manner. Tucci is wonderful, as always, and Capshaw is radiant in her small part. Playwright Reddin's works are well-known around Los Angeles, but this is not a fair representation of his work.

—*G.E. Georges*

REVIEWS

New York Times. October 16, 1998, p. E12.
San Francisco Chronicle. November 6, 1998, p. C5.
Village Voice. October 20, 1998, p. 60.

Almost Heroes

Almost History . . . Almost Legends . . . *Almost Heroes* . . . Mostly Ridiculous . . . —Movie tagline

Box Office: $6,175,688

A t one point in the movie *Almost Heroes,* the story of two Lewis and Clark wannabes, Leslie Edwards (Matthew Perry), the foppish, glory-seeking leader of the 1804 expedition, asks his second in command, the boorish Bartholomew Hunt (Chris Farley), "must you and the others reduce everything to its crudest terms?" The question might also be asked of the film's scriptwriters. Filled with sophomoric humor, broad slapstick, rubberfaced overreactions, and more scatological jokes than an *Ace Ventura* film, *Almost Heroes* marks a very sad end note to the career of *Saturday Night Live* comedian Chris Farley who died last December at the age of 33. (It is also eerily similar to *Wagons East,* the last film of fellow comedian John Candy.) And sadly, someone must not have felt the film was

Hunt (Chris Farley): "The worst will never be over as long as this dandy is in charge."

even good enough for an "in memorium" screen credit to mark it as Farley's last film.

The basic story on which all these bad jokes hang involves Hunt and Edwards in a race to find the overland route to the Pacific ahead of Lewis and Clark who have a two-week head start. Edwards is the effete organizer of the expedition. He travels with all the amenities a civilized man would need, even in the backwoods: a slave, Jonah (Bokeem Woodbine), a bathtub, a four-poster bed and a paisley robe for lounging around the evening's campfire. Hunt, on the other hand, is inclined towards coarse, blustering antics which include being able to drink a group of conquistadors under the table. However, Hunt's knowledge of the backwoods may be more than appears on the surface and Edwards desperately needs his help.

They are accompanied on their trip by the usual assortment of ne'er-do-wells. There's Guy Fontenot (Eugene Levy), a French-Canadian who is supposed to speak all the native American languages from the Mississippi to the Pacific, but seems to know none of the dialects they run in to. He is accompanied by Shaquinna (Lisa Barbuscia), a beautiful Indian maiden he recently purchased and jealously guards. There's Jackson (Patrick Cranshaw), an old man who desperately wants to see the Pacific before he dies and wheedles his way into the crew by playing on Edwards' sense of pity. And there's Bidwell (David Packer), who is perpetually perky and upbeat despite losing several body parts on the trip.

On the journey the group encounters crazy Indians and geriatric Indians, bears and eagles, waterfalls and prostitutes made from straw. Their main nemesis, however, turns out to be a silly Spanish conquistador named Hidalgo (Kevin Dunn) who is searching for who-knows-what and takes an obsessive pride in his hair. Insult him and you end up running a gauntlet consisting of soldiers delivering blows, hot coals underfoot, and a trail of corn. . .yes, corn.

Silliness is the operative word here. *Almost Heroes* wants

> Wilderness locations in northern California and the Big Bear region were used for the film.

to be a funny road film with Farley and Perry the latest Hope and Crosby, or more likely, the newest Abbott and Costello.

The skinny guy and the fat guy bouncing jokes off each other. But what Perry and Farley are given to do isn't funny. It's old. It's all been done before. There's barely a joke whose punch line isn't known to any adult long in advance. Barely a gag that doesn't telegraph its coming. Barely a piece of scenery that hasn't been chewed by one lead actor or another. The film's pace lends itself to a lot of clockwatching and the ending is pure disappointment.

This is thin material that even talented actors couldn't salvage, and neither, it seems, could a talented and funny director like Christopher Guest (*The Big Picture, Waiting for Guffman*). Perhaps best known as the character Nigel Tufnel in the hilarious mockumentary *This is Spinal Tap*, Guest is unable to inject any spark of originality or real humor into this endeavor. (Even though he has enlisted the help of fellow Spinal Tapsters Harry Shearer as the narrator and Michael McKean as a "project consultant"—whatever that means.)

It would seem that even *Almost Heroes*' distributor wasn't too inspired to push the film. Originally produced by the short-lived Turner Pictures studio, the film's release was delayed for quite some time until Turner merged with Time-Warner. When it finally was released, the film was not made available for advanced press previews and consequently received few reviews. As Hunt says when he's describing the animal terrors awaiting the crew, "[it] gives a man courage to know what he's up against." Evidently Warner Bros. hoped most theatergoers wouldn't find any reviews to reveal what's awaiting them inside. "Sir, I've been to hell and back," says Bidwell after losing yet another body part. It might also describe how an intelligent audience member feels exiting the theater after seeing *Almost Heroes*.

—*Beverley Bare Buehrer*

CREDITS

Bartholomew Hunt: Chris Farley
Leslie Edwards: Matthew Perry
Hidalgo: Kevin Dunn
Jonah: Bokeem Woodbine
Jackson: Patrick Cranshaw
Guy Fontenot: Eugene Levy
Shaquinna: Lisa Barbuscia
Father Girard: Christian Clemenson
Higgins: Steven M. Porter
Bidwell: David Packer
Pratt: Hamilton Camp
Narrator: Harry Shearer

Origin: USA
Released: 1998
Production: Denise Di Novi for Di Novi Pictures and Turner Pictures; released by Warner Bros.
Direction: Christopher Guest
Screenplay: Mark Nutter, Tom Wolfe and Boyd Hale
Cinematography: Adam Kimmer, Kenneth MacMillan
Editing: Ronald Roose
Production design: Joseph Garrity
Costumes: Durinda Wood
Art direction: Pat Tagliaferro
Sound: Mark Weingarten
Music: Jeffery CJ Vanston
MPAA rating: PG-13
Running Time: 90 minutes

REVIEWS

Detroit Free Press. May 30, 1998, p. 2A.
Entertainment Weekly. June 12, 1998, p. 48.
Los Angeles Times. June 1, 1998, p. F4.
New York Times. May 30, 1998.
People. June 15, 1998, p. 37.
Variety. June 1, 1998, p. 34.

American History X

Some legacies must end.—Movie tagline

"*American History X* jumps off the screen with a power and impact matched by few films."—Jay Carr, *Boston Globe*

"A forceful, mesmerizing performance by Edward Norton."—Kenneth Turan, *Los Angeles Times*

"*American History X* makes its impact felt. Its willingness to take on political realities gives it a substantial raison d'etre . . . it knows which raw nerves to hit."—Janet Maslin, *New York Times*

"Explosive! Edward Norton gives a blistering, brilliant performance."—Peter Travers, *Rolling Stone*

"Two thumbs up!"—*Siskel and Ebert*

 Box Office: $6,045,176

Written by David McKenna and directed by the temperamental novice Tony Kaye, *American History X* is an urban story about two working-class brothers in Venice Beach, California, Derek Vinyard (Edward Norton) and his younger brother Danny (Edward Furlong), who have become involved with a skinhead gang of neo-Nazis controlled by an older hatemonger, Cameron Alexander (Stacy Keach). Derek is a born leader, angry at the world after the death of his father, Dennis (William Russ),

Derek (Edward Norton): "All that anger, all that hate. I don't want it anymore."

a firefighter murdered in the line of duty, while trying to put out a fire at a crack house. Derek and his skinheads have antagonized a black gang that later attempts to steal Derek's car. Danny notices them outside the house and warns his brother, who charges outside with a loaded weapon and kills two of them, stomping one of them to death. As a result, Derek is sent to prison for a three-year term.

Danny idolizes his brother and himself becomes involved with Derek's white-power group of skinheads while his brother serves time. Both brothers are unusually bright, but Danny is quite young, and Derek has not been able to control his rage. Serving time in prison teaches him control and tolerance. On the day Derek is released from prison, Danny turns in a high-school history paper on *Mein Kampf,* and as a result is brought before the African-American high-school principal, Bob Sweeney (Avery Brooks), who had also been Derek's teacher. Sweeney therefore knows the family history and gives Danny a new assignment, a paper to be

written for him entitled "American History X," in which Danny will be expected to write about his brother and the events leading to Derek's incarceration.

The film's narrative therefore shifts between past and present. Past events are filmed in black and white, present events in color. The past events leading up to Derek's arrest come from Danny's memories, but these are also augmented by Derek's memories of his time served in prison, first under the protection of prison skinheads, later under the protection of fellow inmate Lamont (Guy Torry), with whom Derek works in the prison laundry. Lamont takes a liking to Derek and is able to influence the brothers in prison not to murder Derek after Derek comes to his senses and breaks with his skinhead protectors, who turn against him, then victimize him with homosexual rape in the prison showers and ultimately disown him. Everyone in prison knows what Derek is serving time for, but by the time he is released, he is rehabilitated and a new man, no longer a skinhead, and at ease with the African-American who has befriended him.

Sweeney, whom Derek has also always respected, despite his race, visits Derek in prison and asks him a question that makes him think: "Has anything you've done made your life better?" Derek knows the answer to this question and decides not to let Danny fall into the same trap. Sweeney believes that the Vinyard boys are merely misguided and confused, and he offers clarity to the madness that consumes their lives. Released from prison, Derek is determined to break with the neo-Nazi ringleader Cameron Alexander, which he does, dramatically, at a rally held in his honor. Cameron plans to exploit Derek's charisma, celebrity, and leadership, but Derek refuses, emphatically, and the two come to blows, whereupon Cameron tells him "You're a dead man." Danny cannot understand his brother's defection, but Derek is determined to remove Danny from this vicious world of violence and racial hatred. He succeeds in winning his brother over, but the very day Danny takes his completed paper to school, he is shot in the men's room by a young black student he had earlier antagonized.

AWARDS AND NOMINATIONS

Academy Awards 1998 Nominations: Actor (Edward Norton)

The film is notable for its graphic violence and therefore difficult to watch. Particularly repulsive scenes involve Derek's gang wrecking a Korean market and sexually humiliating the cashier, Derek's "curbing" of one of the black youths that attempted to break into his car, Derek's homosexual rape in prison, and also Derek's hateful anti-Semitic tirade against his mother's Jewish suitor (Elliott Gould), who has been invited over to dinner. What is especially impressive about this picture is Edward Norton's ability to convey broad mood swings effectively, a talent he had also shown brilliantly in *Primal Fear* (1996), the actor's debut film appearance. The film is also graced with a very talented supporting cast, especially Edward Furlong, Avery Brooks, and Guy Torry, all of whom make the screenplay seem plausible.

Edward Norton also served as co-editor after director Tony Kaye disowned the film.

The black and white cinematography serves a thematic purpose since the monochrome flashbacks relate to an earlier time when Derek was blinded by his hatred, while scenes set in the cinematic present tense, after Derek has seen the error of his ways, are in color. One monochrome flashback attempts to trace Derek's racism to its source, a nasty break-fast conversation between Derek and his father involving affirmative action. Derek speaks well at this point of Sweeney, his teacher, and his respect for this African American is apparently maintained even after his father's death, a detail that does not quite seem to fit with the whole picture, though it does suggest that even while enraged and immersed in white-supremacy hatred, the possibility of open-mindedness still exists within him. "The point I tried to make in the script," David McKenna noted in the New Line press kit, "is that a person is not born a racist. It is learned through environment and the people that surround you. My premise was that hate starts in the family," and this would seem to explain the flashback. The controversial script was in development for over three years.

Presumably Derek is driven by his rage into the company of neo-Nazis who are far below his intellectual level. McKenna claimed he wanted to make the characters "as real as possible" and avoid turning them into "shallow, stereotypical backwoods idiots," but that goal is not easily achieved. Derek and Danny seem to seek out the company of cretins, male and female, who are not worthy of their attention. Derek's only reason might be that he gets a rush from controlling these animals. Stereotypes abound, including one character identified in the cast simply as a "Huge Aryan," the screenwriter to the contrary.

The film gets credit for daring to be controversial at a time when most films intend merely to entertain and avoid controversial issues. Writing for *The New York Times*, Diane Cardwell objected to the "pornographic violence" of the film and was especially horrified by Vinyard's "curbing" of a young black man, "a particularly vicious practice in which a victim's open mouth is placed on a curb and the head is stomped, breaking at least the jaw, if not the neck." In her *Family Filmgoer* column for the *Washington Post,* Jane Horwitz wrote "this terrifically acted tragedy is visually stunning and emotionally draining," but warned "it contains moments of sickeningly realistic violence, " as well as "vicious ethnic and racial slurs." In other words, this film was not for the fainthearted.

Another controversy surrounding this picture concerned the director's anger over not being permitted to shape the film as he wanted to. This was Tony Kaye's debut picture, yet he demanded final-cut privileges, claiming himself, absurdly, to be "the greatest English filmmaker since Alfred Hitchcock," according to *Entertainment Weekly.* Producer John Morrissey told *Entertainment Weekly* that Kaye treated the picture like Hype Art: "like all of Tony's work, HE was its subject." Known mainly for his daring and experimental European commercial work, Kay claimed that "If [Stanley] Kubrick gets the time he needs" to edit his work, "I deserve

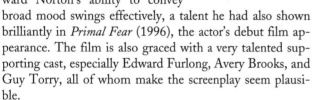

CREDITS

Derek Vinyard: Edward Norton
Danny Vinyard: Edward Furlong
Stacey: Fairuza Balk
Doris Vinyard: Beverly D'Angelo
Bob Sweeney: Avery Brooks
Cameron Alexander: Stacy Keach
Davina Vinyard: Jennifer Lien
Murray: Elliott Gould

Origin: USA
Released: 1998
Production: John Morrissey for a Truman-Morrissey production; released by New Line Cinema
Direction: Tony Kaye
Screenplay: David McKenna
Cinematography: Tony Kaye
Editing: Jerry Greenberg, Alan Heim
Music: Anne Dudley
Production design: Jon Gary Steele
Art direction: Dan Olexiewicz, James Kyler Black
Set decoration: Tessa Posnansky
Costumes: Doug Hall
Sound: Steve Nelson
Casting: Valerie McCaffrey
MPAA rating: R
Running Time: 118 minutes

the same." Kaye wanted his name removed from the picture and went to the Director's Guild demanding the Alan Smithee pseudonym, but he was denied since he had already protested, publicly and noisily, what he called his artistic abuse and had taken out ads in *Variety* claiming that Edward Norton and New Line had ruined his film. "In two or three years, these people are going to be humbled into oblivion by me," he ranted to *Entertainment Weekly*. "All of them will crawl and beg to work with me again. But my door is closed to them. I will crush them," he vowed, pointlessly.

Such displays of temperament and egotism could have resulted in many negative reviews, but in general, reviews, though mixed, treated the film respectfully, especially for Norton's performance. It was favorably reviewed by *Variety* and *Entertainment Weekly*. Stephen Hunter of the *Washington Post* criticized the film, however, for its "melodramatic formula hidden under pretentious TV-commercial-slick photography, postmodernist narrative stylings and violations of various laws of probability," but he objected most of all to its "rank, repellent hypocrisy," as it exploits the racist violence it "pretends to disapprove of." The film is as flam-

boyant as its director, energetic, excessive, repulsive, but fascinating, and certainly visual. It carries a punch, and it leaves an impact that will not soon be forgotten.

—*James M. Welsh*

REVIEWS

Detroit Free Press. November 13, 1998, p. 2E.
Entertainment Weekly. October 23, 1998, p. 28.
Entertainment Weekly. November 6, 1998, p. 51.
Los Angeles Times. August 7, 1998, p. F1.
New York Times Magazine. October 11, 1998, p. 26.
Philadelphia Inquirer Weekend. October 30, 1998, p. 7.
Rolling Stone. November 12, 1998, p. 121.
Time. November 2, 1998, p. 100.
USA Today. October 30, 1998, p. E2.
Variety. October 12, 1998, p. 41.
Village Voice. November 3, 1998, p. 140.
Washington Post. October 30, 1998, p. D1.
Washington Post Weekend. October 30, 1998, p. 64.
Washington Times Metropolitan Times. October 30, 1998, p. C12.

Antz

"Fresh, exhilarating, funny. *Antz* is king of the hill."—Jay Carr, *Boston Globe*

"A sophisticated and funny animated epic."—Lisa Schwarzbaum, *Entertainment Weekly*

"Very smart and very, very funny."—Joel Siegel, *Good Morning America*

"Funny. As amusing for adults as for children."—Janet Maslin, *New York Times*

"Adults will really get a kick out of this one."—Leah Rozen, *People*

"Refreshingly naughty and nice. A lively ride."—Peter Travers, *Rolling Stone*

"Two big thumbs up!"—*Siskel & Ebert*

 Box Office: $88,668,349

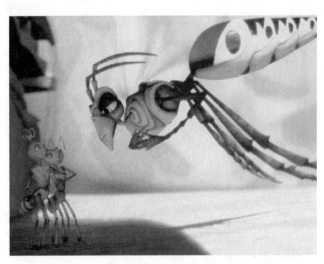
Neurotic worker ant Z-4195 (voice of Woody Allen) gets in a tight spot along with Princess Bala (voice of Sharon Stone) in DreamWorks' *Antz*.

*A*ntz is the first animated film to be released by DreamWorks, the recently-formed studio headed by Steven Spielberg, Jeffrey Katzenberg, and David Geffen. This computer-generated insect tale was completed ahead of schedule and rushed into theaters to beat the arrival of the similarly-themed movie *A Bug's Life* (reviewed in this edi-

tion), produced by rival studio Disney and Pixar Animation Studios, the partners responsible for the 1995 blockbuster *Toy Story*. With two animated films about insects (and both involving ants as main characters) headed to the theaters in close proximity, the commercial advantage could conceivably go to the one that arrived first—assuming, of course, that the two were similar in quality. The quality and financial success of Disney's best animated films has long gone unsurpassed by rival studios, but the release of *Antz* suggested that DreamWorks could pose a real (if small) challenge to the dominance of Disney's animation division. Performing above expectations at the boxoffice, *Antz* quickly became the highest-grossing animated film without Disney's hallowed name attached.

The continuing evolution of computer-generated animation has enabled filmmakers to create increasingly realistic and elaborately-designed characters, movement, and scenery, and this is certainly one of the appeals of *Antz*. The film is a visual marvel, showcasing a fascinatingly intricate environment for its insect characters and serving up a feast of clever sight gags. The ant colony, for example, is a wonderfully complex little world with so much activity that repeated viewings are necessary to appreciate all the details. Scenes like one in which two ants get stuck to a piece of chewing gum on the bottom of a shoe are fun, inventive, and surprisingly realistic. The wizardry of the animation in *Antz* creates a rich fantasy world that easily draws the viewer into the convincing magic of its landscape. Yet it is not the artistry and ingenuity of the animation alone that makes *Antz* a successful film. The most enjoyable aspect of *Antz* lies in its story and the interesting characters that populate its world.

The main character in this story is a dissatisfied ant named Z (technically Z-4195, but "Z" for short), voiced by Woody Allen. From the opening of the film, which shows Z discussing his feelings of "insignificance" with a therapist, one promptly realizes that this story is not standard "children's" fare but is a tale with sophisticated, adult overtones. In a society with strict class divisions between worker ants and soldier ants, in a world where one's fate in life is determined at birth and where uniformity and conformity are expected and go unquestioned, Z finds himself in the middle of a sort of identity crisis. His life seems unfulfilled, as a member of society he feels unimportant (in the ant colony, it is the colony that matters, not the individual), and even though he has a few friends such as fellow worker Azteca (voice of Jennifer Lopez) and soldier Weaver (voice of Sylvester Stallone), he experiences a sense of loneliness. However, his life gets a dose of excitement one evening when he meets a beautiful female at the neighborhood night spot. She asks him to dance and immediately catches his eye.

The female happens to be Princess Bala (voice of Sharon Stone)—daughter of the colony's Queen (voice of Anne Bancroft)—who has been longing to see what life is like outside of the strict, dull, aristocratic confines of her highborn environment and who is not looking forward to an impending marriage with General Mandible (voice of Gene Hackman), the colony's military leader. She sneaks out with a couple of her friends to see what kind of fun the worker and soldier ants (the commoners) are used to having, and when she meets Z, she really has no interest in him except as a dance partner with whom she can enjoy herself. Z, however, is immediately taken with her, undoubtedly attracted not only to Bala physically but also to her daring, unconventional personality.

Z (Woody Allen): "It's just your average boy meets girl, boy likes girl, boy changes underlying social order story."

Hoping to see Bala again, Z works up a scheme with his friend Weaver in which the two of them trade places; Weaver takes Z's place among the workers, and Z assumes Weaver's position in the army. Unfortunately, the scheme is ill-timed. General Mandible, a power-hungry elitist who believes worker ants are inferior and who has devised a plot to destroy all workers and rebuild a stronger colony, has chosen this occasion to send an army of ants loyal to the queen into battle against a neighboring termite colony, knowing that the termites will overwhelm and massacre the soldiers. Soon Z finds himself marching into battle, and as a result of an accident in which he becomes trapped under a dead termite, the little worker ant emerges as the only survivor. Upon his return to the colony, Z is hailed by the ants as a hero and for awhile becomes a symbol of independence and self-determination for the workers when they hear that it was Z—one of their own—who survived the battle.

However, when Z is presented to the queen to be honored, he makes the mistake of trying to flirt with Princess Bala, who recognizes him and exposes him as a worker. The truth comes as a pleasant surprise to General Mandible, who orders his men to arrest Z, but Z takes Bala hostage and escapes from the colony. As they soon find themselves lost, Z begins to see that, despite her excursion into the world of the commoners several nights before, Bala retains a certain class prejudice, believing herself better than he. He refuses to take her back to the colony but tells her she is free to find her own way back. Having lit-

To make *Antz,* DreamWorks partnered with pioneering animation studio PDI who was responsible for the "morphing" sequence in Michael Jackson's video "Black and White."

tle desire to return to his unimportant life in the ant colony, Z sets out to find the fabled "Insectopia," a paradise where there is food aplenty and where one is free to do whatever he or she chooses. Bala, who dreads the idea of having to take her mother's role one day, decides to take a chance that Z might be right about Insectopia and agrees to go with him.

After surviving a dangerous misadventure in which they mistake a picnic site for Insectopia, Z and Bala finally do come across the legendary paradise—an overflowing trash receptacle. It seems their dreams have come true. They and the many other insects in the area have more than enough food and can spend their time in fun and games instead of performing jobs that others have dictated for them; Z and Bala also begin to fall for each other. Unfortunately, the fun does not last long. General Mandible sends his right-hand ant, Colonel Cutter (voice of Christopher Walken), to find Bala and bring her back. Cutter soon locates the princess and spirits her away back toward the ant colony. Z has no choice but to return to the colony to rescue her.

Z reaches the colony and manages to rescue Bala just as Mandible is hatching his plot to destroy the workers and the queen by flooding part of the colony. With a little inspired ingenuity from Z and a lot of dedicated teamwork from the worker ants, they all escape from the watery doom Mandible had planned for them. Witnessing the noble strength, courage, loyalty, and determination of the workers, Colonel Cutter turns against Mandible and aids the colony. This time Z has become a true hero. The story concludes with a voice-over by the little ant explaining that life has improved and he has finally found fulfillment in a revitalized colony that now treasures the importance of the self-determined individual.

As with most animated adventures of this kind, *Antz* is filled with humor, but what makes the film so enjoyable is that much of the humor (though not all of it) is relatively sophisticated and presumes intelligence on the part of the

audience. More often than not this humor is verbal and arises from the dry wit of the somewhat neurotic Z himself. In talking with his therapist during the opening scene, for instance, Z says, "I think everything must go back to the fact that I had a very anxious childhood. You know, my mother never had time for me. You know, when you're the middle child in a family of five million, you don't get any attention." Sometimes the wit is surprisingly of a more adult tone, as when Z sarcastically tells Bala that, by refusing to go with him and rejecting him, she will not get to participate in his wild sexual fantasies. Instances like this make the film seem even less targeted toward younger audiences.

The thematic issues addressed by *Antz* are timeless and useful for children and adults alike. On one level, the story deals heavily with the evils of prejudice—in this case, the prejudice involves class distinctions and stereotypes, dramatized by the attitudes of the royalty toward all the commoners and the soldiers toward the workers (perhaps these three divisions of ant society are akin to the upper, middle, and lower class). The royalty (as represented by the Queen and for awhile by Bala) and the soldiers believe that each ant is born to belong in a specific class, limited to a particular role in life and in society, and that the workers are inferior and less important than the stronger soldiers and the wiser royalty. Although in this story the specific problem depicted is class prejudice, the principles can of course be broadened to apply to any social groupings, whether they are based on gender, ethnicity, religious affiliation, or any other identity.

On another level *Antz* is about non-conformity and individualism. Z lives in a world of blind conformity, where each ant in his or her social class is expected to play the same basic role as everyone else, all supposedly for "the good of the colony." Everyone even dances the exact same dance—except, of course, for Z and Bala, who dare to be different (and get in trouble for it). The soldiers blindly follow orders and the workers do the same, never even realizing that they do not have to conform until they hear about Z's defiance of the system by making his own choices. Therein lies what may be the most important message that *Antz* conveys, a message that any human society may find instructive: the source of heroism lies in the courage to follow one's own heart.

—*David Flanagin*

CREDITS

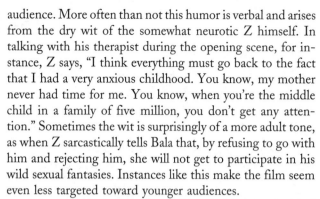

Z: Woody Allen (voice)
Princess Bala: Sharon Stone (voice)
Mandible: Gene Hackman (voice)
Weaver: Sylvester Stallone (voice)
Cutter: Christopher Walken (voice)
Queen: Anne Bancroft (voice)
Azteca: Jennifer Lopez (voice)
Chip: Dan Aykroyd (voice)
Muffy: Jane Curtin (voice)
Barbatus: Danny Glover (voice)
Drunk Scout: John Mahoney (voice)
Psychologist: Paul Mazursky (voice)

Origin: USA
Released: 1998
Production: Brad Lewis, Aron Warner, and Patty Wooton; released by DreamWorks Pictures
Direction: Eric Darnell, Tim Johnson
Screenplay: Todd Alcott, Chris Weitz, and Paul Weitz
Editing: Stan Webb
Music: Harry Gregson-Williams, John Powell
Production design: John Bell
Art direction: Kendal Cronkhite
Sound: Steve Maslow, Gregg Landaker
MPAA rating: PG
Running Time: 83 minutes

REVIEWS

Chicago Tribune. October 2, 1998, p. 5.
Entertainment Weekly. October 9, 1998, p. 54.
Los Angeles Times. October 2, 1998, p. F1.
New York Times. October 2, 1998, p. E12.
People. October 12, 1998, p. 37.
Sight and Sound. December, 1998, p. 41.
Variety. September 21, 1998, p. 104.
Washington Post Weekend. October 2, 1998, p. 47.

Apt Pupil

"A blood-chilling, heart-stopping thriller!"—
Dennis Cunningham, *CBS-TV*

"One of the boldest films of the year! Scarily brilliant."—John Polly, *Genre Magazine*

"An astonishing movie! It is an extraordinary film and an extraordinary story."—Rod Lurie, *KABC-Radio*

"Spine-tingling direction by Bryan Singer. Powerful and riveting. Original, well-crafted and hair-raising."—Rex Reed, *New York Observer*

"An ambitious investigation into the nature of evil."—David Ansen, *Newsweek*

 Box Office: $8,841,516

As any movie fan will tell you, from the most casual viewer to the most ardent critic, the success or failure of any film is predominantly dependent on the successful performance of the villain. If the bad guy isn't bad enough (and that's meant in a good way), the film, no matter how good its intentions will be bad. If you find this introduction oddly poetic, confusing or annoying, it is because *Apt Pupil,* the most recent film from sophomore director Bryan Singer, is also at various points oddly poetic, confusing, and annoying. On paper, it is a movie that shows limitless potential, but, as is the case with many projects, it fell victim to a plethora of peripheral detours in the pre-, post- and actual production phases, which ultimately took their toll on the final print.

Adapted from a Stephen King novella of the same name, *Apt Pupil* had been in the Hollywood pipeline long before it got around to being made. Several screenwriters had attempted an adaptation before Brandon Boyce, a friend of Singer's who had never had one of his screenplays go to production, gave it a go. Perhaps the most read, if not the most prolific writer of the 20th century, virtually all of King's works have been, at one time or another, chosen for screen adaptation. Anyone who ever considers adapting King has two strikes against them from the start. A man of many words, King crafts his stories slowly and methodically; they take a great deal of time to unfold. In trimming what movie people call the 'superfluous' filler, the minute details that are left by the wayside, are the very dollops of information that often binds the stories together. When the text is compromised to such a large de-

 Todd (Brad Renfro) to Kurt (Ian McKellen) about the Holocaust: "I want to hear about it. The stories. Everything. Everything they're afraid to tell us in school."

gree, it is nearly impossible to get the point across with any measurable success. This is the reason the majority of all the King adaptations have failed. Secondly, the bulk of King's audience, fervent and ardent to the core, in large part resent most, if not all, of the films due to what they feel are the glaring, indiscriminate omissions and butchering of the text. It's also a safe assumption that despite his mammoth base of readers, only a fraction of them even go to the movies. Add these factors to the image that comes to mind when most people hear the name 'Stephen King' - horror - not a genre mainstream audiences tend to embrace, and you've got an uphill battle. Of all the films made from King's works, only Stanley Kubrick's *The Shining,* Rob Reiner's *Stand By Me* and *Misery,* and Frank Darabont's *The Shawshank Redemption* have enjoyed any type of critical acclaim or longevity beyond their brief lives at the boxoffice.

King himself has written a combination of 11 adaptations and original works for both the large and small screens which has resulted in only a fraction of the success he has enjoyed writing prose. All eight of the feature film pieces fall well below the mediocre level. Even *Maximum Overdrive,* King's sole effort as both writer and director fell limp. The only three that made any sense at all were the teleplays *It, The Stand,* and the remake of *The Shining.* It's no coincidence that these productions were all presented in a miniseries format. When given extended amounts of film stock, his works can make an impact beyond the printed page. So it would figure that this theory would hold true for King's short stories, which some refer to as novellas. If the source material is shorter in length, the probability of a successful transfer to feature film length goes up. Ironically, the source that has provided the film industry with its most successful King projects is also one that is the least known outside of King's fan base. *Different Seasons,* a collection of four short stories, included "Apt Pupil, Rita Hayworth & The Shawshank Redemption, The Body" and (the as of yet unmade) "The Breathing Method."

Bryan Singer took the motion picture industry by storm in 1995 with *The Usual Suspects.* Written by his friend Christopher McQuarrie (who won an Oscar for his efforts), it broke many conventions and became the sleeper hit of the year. It has garnered a fervent cult following and is one of the few mystery/thrillers that can be watched repeatedly and still manage to reveal something new to the viewer. Suddenly, the young twenty-something wunderkind Singer was the hottest thing in town. Why he didn't choose to enlist McQuarrie for his follow-up is anybody's guess. Perhaps a rift had developed between them or maybe McQuarrie didn't have anything in the hopper. Or perhaps Singer saw the successful transfer of "The Body" (*Stand By Me*) and "Shawshank" and must have figured he had a sure thing in his hands, but as they say 'the best laid plans of mice and men . . .'

The first obstacle Singer faced was several last-minute changes to the script, which wasn't a big deal considering he was also waiting for Sir Ian McKellen to finish *Gods and Monsters*. The classically-trained McKellen, easily the finest living stage performer in the world, finally got the widespread acclaim he deserves. Starting as an apprentice player at Sir Laurence Olivier's National Theatre Company at London's Old Vic, McKellen's roster of roles contains virtually every work by William Shakespeare. Only in the last decade has he transferred his considerable skills to the screen. One of those efforts, *Richard III* surely must have been the film that caught Singer's eye. Very few of Shakespeare's works have ever been reset in a time period different than that of the original play. As Baz Lehrman did recently with *Romeo + Juliet* and Kenneth Branagh with *Hamlet*, McKellen chose to update Shakespeare by setting *Richard* in the 20th Century and made his king out to be a fascist. Dressed in Nazi-like garb, McKellen's portrayal of the diabolically underhanded Richard laid the groundwork for his role here of Kurt Dussander, a former Nazi who, at war's end, started his life over in the cookie-cutter suburbs of California in hopes of living out the remainder of his years in quiet obscurity. Changing his name to Arthur Denker and keeping to himself was working fine until he was recognized by one of his neighbors, a 16-year-old named Todd Bowden (Brad Renfro).

An inquisitive, straight A-student, Todd has just finished a phase of his history class that concentrated on the Holocaust, which left him with more than just a passing interest in the Nazi movement. For reasons that are never explained, Todd's interest turns to obsession and after spotting Kurt, he assembles a thick archive of incriminating evidence and decides to confront the old man. Much in the same manner as Clarice Starling in *The Silence of the Lambs*, Todd wants to get into the head of his chosen subject to find out how he ticks. Kurt wants nothing to do with the boy but has his hand forced when Kurt threatens to expose him to the authorities. Todd will remain silent only if he is told every last gruesome detail of Kurt's past. After hearing one horrific tale after another for months on end, Todd begins having nightmares which, in turn, causes his 4.0 average to backslide.

Renfro, like McKellen, is one of the most gifted actors of his generation. Still in his teens, he has rapidly become one of the most sought after adolescent performers in Hollywood. Starting at age 10, he has appeared in *The Client*, *The Cure*, *Tom & Huck*, *Telling Lies in America* and, in what is largely considered his best work to date, playing the streetwise victim of child abuse in *Sleepers*. Erudite and composed beyond his years, Renfro's potential for superstardom is limitless.

While the fine, unlikely pairing of McKellen and Renfro shows a seasoned veteran and a talented upstart mixing it up nicely, Singer never explains why Todd wants or needs to spend countless hours with an aging, sinister, alcoholic ex-Nazi. A Rock star yes, an athlete maybe, but a Nazi?! For what? To satisfy his own morbid curiosity? A 16-year-old California boy has better things to do with his time. After nearly a year of time spent in close proximity with Kurt, not only do his grades spiral, but he also begins to have hallucinations. One in particular, a scene where he imagines the shower in a school gym morphing into a gas chamber, became the source of Singers' biggest headache. Failing to get parental consent forms in advance for the dozen or so underage actors who stripped down to their birthday suits, Singer and Columbia Pictures faced not only an onslaught of negative publicity but a half-dozen lawsuits, mostly citing questionable child labor practices. Many of these suits have yet to be settled.

At this point, Singer gets back on track by having Kurt turn the tables on his young blackmailer. We first see the tide turning when Todd orders Kurt to don an outfit he

CREDITS

Kurt Dussander: Ian McKellen
Todd Bowden: Brad Renfro
Richard Bowden: Bruce Davison
Monica Bowden: Ann Dowd
Archie: Elias Koteas
Dan Richler: Joe Morton
Isaac Weiskopf: Jan Triska
Joey: Joshua Jackson
Becky: Heather McComb
Edward French: David Schwimmer

Origin: USA
Released: 1998
Production: Jane Hamsher, Don Murphy and Bryan Singer for Phoenix Pictures and Bad Hat Harry; released by TriStar Pictures
Direction: Bryan Singer
Screenplay: Brandon Boyce; based on the novella by Stephen King
Cinematography: Newton Thomas Sigel
Editing: John Ottman
Music: John Ottman
Production design: Richard Hoover
Art direction: Kathleen M. McKernin
Costumes: Louise Mingenbach
Sound: Geoffrey Lucius Patterson
MPAA rating: R
Running Time: 111 minutes

picked up at a costume store—a Nazi SS uniform. The crisp wool suit itches its wearer, which is made even worse by the in-place goose-stepping demanded by the tormentor. However, the next time we see Kurt in his wartime regalia, he seems oddly pleased with the transformation; so much so that he sports a knowing smirk. The unearthing of his past has rekindled a fire in his long-dormant soul. In another episode that gets under his skin, Todd arrives at the family dinner table and discovers that Kurt has been invited by his parents who want to know more of the man who spends so much time with their son. While dining, Kurt gather a few slivers of information about Todd's family that he will use a few days later. By posing as his grandfather, Kurt takes a meeting with Todd's guidance counselor Ed French (David Schwimmer), who expresses grave concern over the star pupil's grades. In a previous scene, Singer plants doubts in our minds as to whether French is gay and whether his concern carries with it a hidden agenda.

The final act of the story introduces a half-dozen new characters that unnecessarily convolute an already iffy plot. It's as if Singer knew his story was weak and in desperation, wanted to divert the audience's attention away from the loose ends. To Singer's credit (or perhaps McKellen's), we actually end up feeling sorry for a ruthless Nazi and hold deep contempt for the child whose biggest sin (at least at the onset) was trying to find out more about what makes people tick. Again, paralleling McKellen to Anthony Hopkins'

Hannibal Lecter in *The Silence of the Lambs*, we have a dark character whose past is riddled with abhorrent acts, but with whom we form a mild kinship and almost find ourselves rooting for. If Singer hadn't latched onto an actor of McKellen's considerable caliber, this would not have happened.

There is no denying the collective talent involved with this picture. It's hard to fathom that Singer's success with *The Usual Suspects* was a fluke and given the history of Stephen King on the screen, it will be easy to label *Apt Pupil* as the sophomore slump of a budding genius. With three of *Different Season*'s four stories in the can, it raises the question and a line in the imaginary creative sand: is there a visionary out there with the nerve to tackle "The Breathing Method?"

—*J. M. Clark*

REVIEWS

Chicago Tribune. October 23, 1998, p. 5.
Cinefantastique. October, 1998, p. 117.
Entertainment Weekly. October 23, 1998, p. 48.
Los Angeles Times. October 23, 1998, p. F8.
New York Times. October 23, 1998, p. E14.
People. October 26, 1998, p. 36.
Variety. September 14, 1998, p. 35.
Washington Post Weekend. October 23, 1998, p. 55.

Armageddon

The end is near.—Movie tagline

Heads up.—Movie tagline

"It rocks the planet. Don't miss it!"—Paul Chambers, *CNN Radio*

"Hands down, the movie event of the summer!"—Scott Patrick, *Encore*

"It'll suck the air right out of your lungs! Check your pulse at the door!"—Diane Kaminsky, *KHOU-TV*

"The summer's most sensational movie!"—Bobbie Wygant, *KXAS-TV*

"The summer popcorn movie of all time!"
—Jimmy Carter, *Nashville Network*

"This is it! The real blockbuster of the year we've been waiting for!"—Bill Zwecker, *WMAQ-TV*

 Box Office: $201,578,182

Armageddon, the big and baffling boom and doom movie of the summer season, excels in computer-generated images, technology, and special effects that assault the eye while a deafening soundtrack offends the ear. There is little to delight the mind, however, apart from a few comic one-liners generated by a platoon of writers to punctuate the action. In 1997 James Cameron's *Titanic* gamble upped the ante for blockbuster epic filmmaking to unprecedented budget levels and won the jackpot with boxoffice revenues and Academy Award recognition. By contrast *Armageddon*, Disney's most expensive project to date, is not likely to pick up many Academy Award nominations, but it follows

Bruce Willis and Ben Affleck are two unlikely heroes preventing an asteroid from destroying Earth in the summer blockbuster *Armageddon*.

Cameron's lead in excessiveness in its attempt to sweep the summer market.

The film begins with a huge cosmic flashback 65 million years ago (so the narrator claims) to frame the disaster concept. At that time a piece of rock six miles wide entered the Earth's atmosphere and exploded with the force of 10,000 nuclear bombs, creating a nuclear winter that killed off the dinosaurs. "It happened before; it will happen again," the narrator warns portentously. Then, cutting to the present, the film shows an astronomer at work as he discovers that an asteroid "the size of Texas" is headed towards the Earth. The government is quickly alerted, but citizens are not, until later. Meanwhile, a meteor shower precedes the asteroid and wreaks havoc on New York City after demolishing the space shuttle Atlantis, providing an initial spectacle of destruction that frightens New Yorkers and kills a few of the more obnoxious ones, including a vendor of Godzilla toys. The snide screenplay makes fun of a Japanese couple in a taxicab: "I just want to go shopping," the lady tells the cabbie as buildings are demolished around her. This spectacle is merely a distracting prelude.

NASA chief Dan Truman (Billy Bob Thornton) advises the military of the magnitude of the impending disaster. "It's what we call a global killer," he says. "Nothing would survive, not even bacteria." The problem has to be solved in 18 days. A nuclear hit on the asteroid would barely scratch the surface and not solve the problem. The only hope for salvation, according to this loony screenplay, is to send a crew into space to intercept the asteroid, land on it, and drill 800 feet down to plant a nuclear device that would break the rock into two chunks, each of which would be deflected

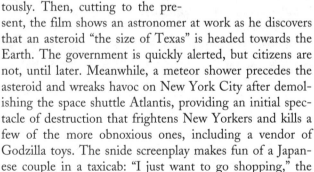

Grace (Liv Tyler): "Listen, Harry, A.J. is my choice—my choice—and not yours." Harry (Bruce Willis): "He's the only one in your age bracket, Grace. It's not a choice, it's a lack of options."

past the Earth. This solution might seem reasonable for an asteroid six or seven miles wide—the size of the comet in *Deep Impact* (reviewed in this edition), for example, but is it likely that one bomb could break up a rock the size of Texas, or Delaware, or Rhode Island, even? Since this is a Jerry Bruckheimer summer blockbuster, the asteroid has to be as big as possible. The Bruckheimer approach makes no concessions for logic or probability.

After establishing the impending threat, the film cuts to an oil rig on the South China Sea to introduce roughneck tycoon Harry S. Stamper (Bruce Willis), who amuses himself by hitting golf balls towards an annoying Greenpeace ship until he discovers his daughter, Grace (Liv Tyler) in bed with one of his crew, A. J. Frost (Ben Affleck), whom he goes after with a shotgun, screaming "Make your peace with God, A. J." When A. J. explains "I love her," Harry responds "Way wrong answer!" He intends to shoot A. J.'s foot off. This bizarre comic interlude is interrupted when a military helicopter arrives and duty calls.

Harry Stamper, who happens to be the world's best deep-core driller, designed the drill that is supposed to get the job done. After he is flown to NASA headquarters in Houston, Harry agrees to do the job only if he can take his own crew of roughnecks with him, a quirky bunch with cute names like Rockhound (Steve Buscemi), Bear (Michael Clark Duncan), and Chick (Will Patton). This group of louts has to be trained for a space mission in less than two weeks' time, another absurdity. When the NASA flight crew sees them, one of them jokes, "Talk about the wrong stuff!" Truman explains the problem: "It's coming at 22,000 miles per hour. No one on Earth can escape from it." Harry tells his roughneck friends, "The United States government just asked us to save the world. Anybody want to say no?" Of course, they all want to be heroes; otherwise they would not belong in this movie.

The team is divided between two space shuttles, Freedom and Independence. Both crafts have to dock with a Russian space station in order to refuel. The station is manned by mad Russian Lev Andropov (Peter Stormare), who is stir crazy after having been in space for 18 months. When the space station is threatened by a meteor shower (since the action plot calls for a crisis every half hour), An-

AWARDS AND NOMINATIONS

Academy Awards 1998 Nominations: Sound; Sound Effects Editing; Song ("I Don't Want to Miss a Thing"); Visual Effects

dropov leaves with the Independence crew. The next crisis comes when the two space shuttles approach the asteroid and have to avoid the debris in its wake. Independence is struck, managed, and disabled and crashes to the surface, but A. J., Bear, and the Russian survive, liberate the land vehicle (called the "Armadillo"), and go in search of Freedom.

NASA allowed the production to film at the Johnson Space Center, Cape Canaveral, and Cape Kennedy.

The Freedom crew has its own problems, naturally, and their "Armadillo" is accidentally launched into space, but A. J. arrives just in time to help. It's a race against time to get the hole dug and the bomb placed. Back on Earth, the President is advised to detonate the device before the hole is completed, but events conspire to buy time. The detonation is stopped three seconds short of exploding, and when the hole is ready, someone has to volunteer to stay behind and detonate the bomb. The survivors draw straws, and A. J. gets the honor, but at the last minute, Harry tricks him and takes the detonator himself so that A. J. can be reunited with Grace, who spends half the picture hanging around NASA and wringing her hands. So the world is saved; the survivors of the space flight return to earth; and Harry is honored for biting the big bullet. The film ends with shots of A. J. and Grace's wedding.

The picture's faults are all too obvious. Though an army of writers, headed up by executive producer Jonathan Hensleigh and J. J. Abrams, labored to develop the screenplay, the results are incoherent and illogical, if not chaotic. Writers hired to tune up the script included Robert Towne, Tony Gilroy, Scott Rosenberg, and Ann Biderman; but the story is star-driven rather than character-driven. The characters are merely defined by their flaws and their appetites. The Willis character, inspired by troubleshooting oilman Red Adair, is a maverick but also a tyrannical father; the Will Patton character is a bad father who has abandoned his wife and young son; the Buscemi character is a lecher; the rest are gamblers and daredevils. Michael Bay's direction propels the story from one crisis and disaster to the next. The lulls between disasters are filled with comedy (inept physical and psychological training, followed by a few hours of wild R&R before the dirty dozen roughnecks are launched into space) and a few tender romantic moments between Ben Affleck and Liv Tyler. In general bad writing and lame jokes coupled with faux patriotism and special effects dominate the picture, which Bay described to *Premiere* magazine as "an Astronaut recruiting poster." The producers obviously kept the fourth of July opening weekend clearly focused. It's a sort of fireworks movie with flags rampant and in your face.

The style of director Michael Bay is hardly subtle. After studying film with Jeanine Basinger at Wesleyan College, he directed his debut Hollywood feature, *Bad Boys*

(1995), which was a hit. This was followed by a bigger hit, *The Rock* (1997), which earned $332 million and made Bay extremely bankable. David Ansen of *Newsweek* thought Bay was an excellent choice to direct *Armageddon* because of the director's ability to recycle "Hollywood clichés with such velocity and slickness they almost seem newly minted."

The problem was that even the script idea seemed recycled by the time *Armageddon* was released. Disney Studios gambled over $150 million on this oversized action-adventure spectacle which had to make a larger impact at the boxoffice than Mimi Leder's *Deep Impact*, the season's first asteroid disaster movie and one that even follows a similar scenario. The Jerry Bruckheimer-produced

CREDITS

Harry S. Stamper: Bruce Willis
A.J. Frost: Ben Affleck
Dan Truman: Billy Bob Thornton
Grace Stamper: Liv Tyler
Charles (Chick) Chapple: Will Patton
Lev Andropov: Peter Stormare
Rockhound: Steve Buscemi
Oscar Choi: Owen Wilson
Bear: Michael Clarke Duncan
Gen. Kinsey: Keith David
Col. William Sharp: William Fichtner
Jennifer Watts: Jessica Steen
Gruber: Grayson McCouch
Narrator: Charlton Heston

Origin: USA
Released: 1998
Production: Jerry Bruckheimer, Gale Anne Hurd and Michael Bay; released by Touchstone Pictures
Direction: Michael Bay
Screenplay: Jonathan Hensleigh, J. J. Abrams
Cinematography: John Schwartzmann
Editing: Mark Goldblatt, Chris Lebenzon, Glen Scantlebury
Music: Trevor Rabin
Production design: Michael White
Art direction: Geoff Hubbard, Lawrence A. Hubbs, Bruton Jones
Costumes: Michael Kaplan, Magali Guidasci
Sound: Keith A. Wester
Visual effects supervision: Pat McClung, Richard Hoover
MPAA rating: PG-13
Running Time: 150 minutes

Armageddon put Bruce Willis rather than Robert Duvall in charge of the crew sent to board the asteroid so as to divert it. Of course, typically Bruckheimer took the bigger is better approach using a bigger budget to create a bigger spectacle, a bigger cast led by Bruce Willis (or at least a more expensive one), and a bigger asteroid, the size of Texas this time around. In *Deep Impact* the meteor was only "as big as Mt. Everest."

Understandably *Time* critic Richard Schickel sniffed "Been there, done that, just a month ago." The only significant difference Schickel noticed was that the second asteroid epic seemed to be about class conflict, which generated some amusing business as the NASA nerds attempted to train Willis and his oil-riggers for their space mission. *Newsweek*, on the other hand, preferred Bay's "slap-happy adventurism" to the more somber approach of *Deep Impact*, which took "the possibility of the planet's demise seriously." Stephen Hunter of *The Washington Post* found the movie "as dumb as it is loud, and it's way too loud." Plucking a cliché himself, Hunter claimed "It leaves no stone unturned in its search for the perfect cliché, for the lowest common denominator."

Nonetheless, *Armageddon* proved to be (momentarily) disappointing for the most expensive film ever made by the Walt Disney Company. Though it grossed just over $52 million during its gateway fourth of July weekend opening, it fell short of *Men In Black*, which grossed $79 million in 1997, and *Independence Day*, which grossed $85 million in 1996, according to industry reporter Bernard Weinraub. The week after its opening, *Armageddon* was quickly challenged by *Lethal Weapon 4* and then *The Mask of Zorro* slashed into its profits. Meanwhile, by that time *Deep Impact* had already made $137 million. As the unnamed head of a rival studio told Bernard Weinraub, the "lesson" of *Armageddon* was "Don't be second." It could also be, however, that *Deep Impact* succeeded because of the lighter, woman's touch of Mimi Leder, whose characters are more humanly appealing than the heavy-handed louts who dominate Bruckheimer's space epic. (It should be noted though that *Armageddon* eventually surpassed *Deep Impact* in boxoffice and has made more than $200 million worldwide.)

—*James M. Welsh*

REVIEWS

Baltimore Sun. July 1, 1998, p. E1.
Christian Science Monitor. July 3, 1998, p. B3.
Entertainment Weekly. July 10, 1998, p. 46.
New York Times. July 1, 1998, p. B1.
New York Times. July 10, 1998, p. B18.
New Yorker. July 13, 1998, p. 78.
Newsweek. July 6, 1998, p. 64.
Philadelphia Inquirer. July 1, 1998, p. C1.
Premiere. July, 1998, p. 76.
Time. July 6, 1998, p. 88.
USA Today. July 1, 1998, p. D1.
Variety. June 29, 1998, p. 37.
Washington Post. July 1, 1998, p. D1.
Washington Post Weekend. July 3, 1998, p. 46.

Artemisia

The story of an extraordinary woman.—Movie tagline

"A triumph of committed workmanship! Richly textured and strongly felt!"—Jay Carr, *Boston Globe*

"Ravishing to watch!"—Stephen Farber, *Movieline*

"A lushly appointed epic!"—Manobla Dargis, *New Times*

Based on a true story about painter Artemesia Gentileschi (Valentina Cervi) in 17th century Rome, this historical film portrays the awakening of her artistry and her sexuality. This independent Italian Baroque artist embraced her creative urges as deeply as romance gripped her. The emotional turmoil during this pivotal part of her youth can be seen in such fierce paintings as "Judith Beheading Holofernes."

Artemisia snatches candles from church to illuminate her body. Attempting to satisfy her voracious appetite for learning anatomy, she studies and sketches her own limbs in the reflection of a mirror. When her drawings are discovered by nuns, they summon her father ready to shame and expel the teenager. However, Orazio Gentileschi (Michel Serrault) recognizes "she's the daughter of a painter," and surprises the sisters by bringing Artemisia home.

Under his tutelage, she blossoms into a master painter, with the ability to "paint like a man." Artemisia can finish her father's commissioned portraits, making sophisticated aesthetic choices and receives tough lessons in the commerce aspects of her trade— there is more at stake than talent, her father advises. Elaborate tableaus, complete with models hanging angelic-like with feathered wings fill his studio as Orazio works. Stuck behind a curtain, Artemisia is forbidden to view the nude males—it is against the law for women to paint men's bodies naked—a restriction that fuels her defiant curiosity.

In a touching moment on the beach, fascinated with a couple making love, she lays in their sand impression as if to absorb the sensation. Whether it's sexual or artistic interest that is aroused—or both—Artemisia lures a flirtatious young boy into a hidden cave and persuades him to undress—as her model, allowing her an opportunity afforded to men painters. She examines his body, amazed at his different muscles while enthusiastically drawing his physique from every angle.

During one of these excursions, they encounter the outdoor encampment of artist Agostino Tassi (Miki Monojlovic). With admiration and intrigue, she comments on his techniques and his unusual choice of landscapes for his canvases. Tassi has a powerful command with the church, and while visiting from Florence is assigned to share a cathedral fresco commission with Artemisia's renowned and respected father.

She arranges to meet Tassi to show him her painting but he thinks the work is her father's art. Asking to be his

Director Agnes Merlet: "The only records left of the trial are the preliminary cross-examinations,... So, I relied on my imagination."

Agnes Merlet originally produced a 35-minute experimental film investigating Artemisia Gentileschi's painting "Judith Beheading Holofernes."

pupil, she says "my father taught me all he can." But Tassi refuses. But when her father, who is furious that the Academy won't accept girls as students, requests he take her on, the girl's education broadens.

Artemisia is a spirited young woman of 18 with artistic skills beyond her age. Although she understands perspective, Tassi desires that she see things differently— to paint the vast world outdoors and he sets out to teach her advanced techniques. She asks him to pose for her in bed, and in the midst of the session, he seduces her, perhaps assuming she's also more experienced in the physical realm. The passionate couple fall in love as her work further develops.

When rumor of the affair reaches her disbelieving father, Gentileschi verifies Tassi's liaison with his daughter, confronting his colleague and having him arrested for rape to clear Artemisia's disgraced name. In court, the artist admits to his love for the girl and she tries to protect him by denying they had sexual relations. But his sister arrives to announce Tassi has a wife in Florence and Artemisia is proven wrong in an examination.

Artemisia is then put on trial. Her drawings of the naked boy are exposed to reveal her scandalous and illegal behavior. Sitting before the judge, and with Tassi watching, she is tortured as leather strips tighten around her hands so her delicate fingers bleed. He "confesses" to the charge and is imprisoned. At her studio she can hear the voice of her former lover and muse describe the lovely view from his cell.

Nominated for a Golden Globe for best foreign film, *Artemisia* is a beautifully composed, exquisitely acted and sensitively drawn story that ironically may be more relevant today than it would appear. Caught in a ratings controversy for nudity and sex scenes, life seemed to imitate art until an appeal changed the NC-17 to an R. As with her dilemma, talent won out. Although her work is often attributed to her father and the scandalous rape trial was how history remembered her, Artemisia was the first woman commissioned by the Academy of Florence and her work can be admired in the Metropolitan Museum of Art.

CREDITS

Artemisia Gentileschi: Valentina Cervi
Orazio Gentileschi: Michel Serrault
Agostino Tassi: Miki Manojlovic
Cosimo Quorli: Luca Zingaretti
Tuzia: Brigitte Catillon
Roberto: Frederic Pierrot
The Judge: Maurice Garrel

Origin: France, Italy, Germany
Released: 1997
Production: Patrice Haddad for Premiere Heure, France 3 Cinema, Schlemmer Film, and 3 Emme Cinematografica; released by Miramax Zoe
Direction: Agnes Merlet
Screenplay: Agnes Merlet, Christine Miller, and Patrick Amos
Cinematography: Benoit Delhomme
Editing: Guy Lecorne
Music: Krishna Levy
Production design: Antonello Geleng
Costumes: Dominique Borg
Sound: Francois Waledisch, Jean-Pierre Laforce
MPAA rating: R
Running Time: 95 minutes

REVIEWS

Hollywood Reporter. February 17, 1998, p. 69.
Los Angeles Times. May 8, 1998, p. F10.
Movieline. May, 1998, p. 46.
New York Times. May 8, 1998, p. E12.
People. May 18, 1998, p. 38.
Variety. September 29, 1997, p. 64.

Agnes Merlet's second feature, which she also co-wrote, *Artemisia* is a visually dramatic, intimate depiction of a young woman's determined vision, her love of art and life. The only problem with the subtitles is tearing away from the com-

pelling imagery on the screen. "It's as much about art as about sex," said Roger Ebert in the *Chicago Sun-Times*.

—*Roberta Cruger*

August 32nd on Earth; Un 32 Aout sur Terre

"The acting sparkles . . ."—*The Globe and Mail*
"Thoughtful and polished, funny and frightening . . ."—*Telluride Daily Planet*
"A pic where virtually every scene is shot with style and panache . . ."—*Variety*

Moving gradually from Montréal to the white desert of Utah and back again, *August 32nd on Earth* is a kind of road movie of the soul. Its young director Denis Villeneuve, like many of his colleagues in the new Québec cinema, is an artist who is able to bring countless areas of influence to bear: experimental art, MTV, and earlier generations of French and French-Canadian filmmaking all figure somehow in this film. *August* is a visual marvel, and the cinematography deserves special mention—the director of photography is André Turpin, whose own 1995 feature debut *Zigrail* never found the audience it deserved. This is not to discount the magnificent acting in the film. The two thespians in question, Pascale Brussières (*Twilight of the Ice Nymphs, Elo-rado, When Night Is Falling*) and Alexis Martin (*No, Cosmos*) have been in so much recent Québec cinema that they are becoming stars in that small cinematic universe: their performances in this film show why. *August* is a forceful combination of the dramatic, narrative, and the purely cinematic: it is part of a *jeune cinema* that is slowly changing the face of North American film.

August 32nd on Earth begins on a road somewhere outside Montréal, where a young fashion model named Simone (Brussières) has a nearly fatal car crash. The existential crisis that this prompts leads her to convince her best friend Phillipe (Martin) to conceive a child with her—on a purely platonic level, since Alexis is already involved with someone. Of course he's secretly in love with Simone, but agrees to the conception plan, as long as they do the deed in the desert. They jump the next plane to Utah (the closest desert Simone could find), and of course all does not go exactly as

 Philippe (Alexis Martin) to Simone (Pascale Bussieres) at one of their highway adventures: "How do you say 'burned-up corpse' in English?"

planned. After a symbolically laden journey through the white desert, they manage to get back to the airport, hoping to head home. This second bit in the airport, which moves the viewer seamlessly from the dusty, barren brush to a surreal, spacepod-like hotel "room" where they have to spend the night (and end up getting blasted on Muscatel), itself constitutes some of the most visually dynamic filmmaking of the year. On the way home, Phillipe writes a letter to Simone telling her how he feels but that he doesn't think they should be together. When they return to Montréal, Phillipe becomes the victim of an act of random violence, Simone reads the letter and decides she wants to be with him, and is left waiting for him to wake up at the side of his hospital bed.

This is a dense, almost collage-like film, full of allusions to other historically important films. The French New Wave and Québec's cinema of the 1960s are obvious points of contact (there are moments of lyricism and hysteria that recall the early films of Jean-Luc Godard or Jean-Pierre Lefebvre), but the desert images look just a little bit like Michelangelo Antonioni's *Zabriskie Point*. What's impressive, though, is that despite this range of influences, *August 32nd* never feels derivative. Instead, Villeneuve is trying to invest these styles and themes with some new meaning, bringing them out of the 1960s into an age that is just as confusing and unstable but which fails to offer the clear moral solutions that marked the rhetoric of an earlier age. There is a real faith in love, the value of friendship and the desire for children that is often absent in the hipper, more airy art films of twenty years ago. Villeneuve also centralizes a sense of real, physical danger—here embodied by the attack at the film's climax—that is also missing in the earlier films, which generally depicted an alienated but at least safely bourgeois world.

These little updates show Villeneuve to be a filmmaker of both great originality and engagement with the masters of the medium. Unlike so many young filmmak-

CREDITS

Simone: Pascale Bussieres
Philippe: Alexis Martin
The Driver: Serge Theriault
The Taxi Driver: Richard S. Hamilton
The Doctor: Paule Baillargeon

Origin: Canada
Released: 1998
Production: Roger Frappier for Max Films Production Inc.; released by Alliance Atlantis
Direction: Denis Villeneuve
Screenplay: Denis Villeneuve
Cinematography: Andre Turpin
Editing: Sophie Leblond
Music: Nathalie Boileau, Robert Charlebois, Pierre Desrochers, Jean Leloup
Art direction: Jean Babin
MPAA rating: Unrated
Running Time: 88 minutes

ers, he's not simply making an ironic imitation of earlier movies. He's genuinely trying to learn something from them, something that will be able to enrich his own very different picture. The way that he works with his collaborators—both actors Brussières and Martin and cinematographer Turpin—seems a model of interaction, given the film's common excellence in matters both visual and theatrical. *August* is a fully rounded film, so much so that it's quite a surprise that it was made by someone so early in his career.

—*Jerry White*

REVIEWS

eye weekly. December 17, 1998.

The Avengers

Saving the world in style.—Movie tagline

Two amazing secret agents. One diabolical madman. Conditions are dark. The forecast is deadly. Tea, anyone?—Movie tagline

"Connery is absolutely delightful."—Chuck O'Leary, *Pittsburgh/Greensburg, PA Tribune*

"Fiennes and Thurman are a match made in hip-couture heaven."—David Elliott, *San Diego Union Tribune*

 Box Office: $23,523,710

A film version of the stylish, witty 1960s British television series *The Avengers* sounds like a good idea, but whenever such suggestions come up, the first question should be "Why do it?" What can be improved over the original series? The casting? The style? The scale? Too often, the answer is the latter with the big-screen version of the small-screen program simply being bigger and louder than the original, as with Brian De Palma's *The Untouchables* (1987) and *Mission: Impossible* (1996), actually two of the better entries in this genre. The big-screen version of *The Avengers*

is bigger and louder than the original but has little else to offer.

Many television series are beloved because they were important in the lives of viewers when they were young, as with *Leave It to Beaver, Star Trek,* and *The Brady Bunch,* not necessarily because they were well written, directed, or cast. *The Avengers* is beloved, especially by those who were in their teens and twenties in the 1960s, because it is good, unlike most of the preachy, poorly paced, indifferently acted programs of its era. From a relatively prosaic beginning on Britain's commercial ITV network in 1961, with Ian Hendry and Patrick Macnee, the spy series gradually developed more style after Honor Blackman replaced Hendry and especially after Diana Rigg replaced Blackman. When the Rigg-Macnee episodes began on American television in 1966, the series, which never received huge ratings, was an instant cult success. The program effectively blends humor and adventure and could be enjoyed as a spoof of both James Bond and John le Carre. With the aid of a seemingly endless supply of wonderful character actors, *The Avengers* celebrates the nastiness lurking just beneath the calm surface of English eccentricity while the stars toss double entendres all over the place. The series is also a joy because of the sexual chemistry between Macnee and Rigg as John Steed and Mrs. Peel, who clearly would like to go to bed together but seem to

When a diabolical madman takes control of the weather, John Steed (Ralph Fiennes) and Emma Peel (Uma Thurman), better known as *The Avengers*, are called to foil his plans.

Reviewers aimed considerable criticism at Fiennes and Thurman, but they did not write this pathetic script. Fiennes is a wonderfully offbeat actor compelling in both good films, *The English Patient* (1996), and lesser ones, *Oscar and Lucinda* (1997), but he does not seem to have the sense of humor necessary for Steed. Macnee seemed to realize that Steed is a tad arch and ridiculous, while Fiennes' Steed comes across like someone at a party who does not get the others' humor but nevertheless tries to weigh in with a lame joke of his own. Thurman is a limited performer who can be effective if used properly, as in *Pulp Fiction* (1994), but she appears strangely ill at ease in several scenes, seemingly distracted, almost amateurish. Her sex appeal, her main virtue in the past, is inferior to those of Keeley Hawes and Carmen Ejogo, who appear in small roles. Even Connery, whose Bond was tweaked by the original series, is undone by the material. Connery has always maintained a degree of presence and style even in bad films—and he has made many—but as de Wynter, he just rants and raves, like a ham actor in a television sketch.

Connery also cannot be faulted much for trying to inject some juice in Don Macpherson's innervated screenplay. Macpherson co-wrote *Absolute Beginners* (1986), another noisy but empty film-that-would-be-hip. He creates no interesting situations and writes dialogue that aims at wit but rarely even gets off a shot. In an interview in *Premiere*, director Jeremiah Chechik compared the film's dialogue to that of Noel Coward. The sophisticated playwright would hardly have de Wynter say, "John Steed. What a horse's arse of a name," or have Steed react to a sudden snowstorm in the middle of summer by exclaiming, "I say. This is a bit much."

Chechik's films include the sentimentally whimsical *Benny and Joon* (1993) and the stillborn Sharon Stone remake *Diabolique* (1996). Nothing in his previous work gives the slightest indication that he could pull off *The Avengers*, even with a good script. The director told *TV Guide*, "I tried very hard to make what the TV show would have been if it had had the money, the time, the palette and the wideness of the screen." Budget and size do not, however, necessarily translate into content or style. This material, if done properly, demands the kind of light, sophisticated touch and directorial confidence missing here.

Chechik is a former fashion photographer, and the film at least looks good, mostly because of the work of the director's talented collaborators. Cinematographer Roger Pratt shot *Brazil* (1985), *Mona Lisa* (1986), and *Batman*

enjoy hinting at the possibility even more. It was a cliché at the time for critics and journalists to refer to Rigg's Mrs. Peel as both the sexiest and the smartest woman character ever to appear on television, and many commentators in 1998, inspired by the film version, claimed that she is still the television epitome of feminine charms and wiles. *The Avengers* was the first prime-time series on American television that took for granted that its viewers had minds and libidos.

The main problem with the big-screen *The Avengers* is the ineptness of the screenplay and direction. The film is not sexy or charming or exciting or witty. The sad thing is that it is not truly bad in the sense (dumb, tasteless, cruel) that big-budget action films usually are. It is just lifeless, evaporating from memory moments after its end credits close.

What passes for a plot involves British agents John Steed (Ralph Fiennes) and Emma Peel (Uma Thurman) being thrown together to stop Sir August de Wynter (Sean Connery) from extorting some huge sum from the world's governments through controlling weather with a climate machine he has invented. Peel and Steed confront de Wynter. De Wynter shouts a lot. De Wynter causes it to rain or snow. De Wynter's thugs (and once giant mechanical flying insects) chase Peel and Steed, who escape narrowly. Peel and Steed confront de Wynter again, and so on. If someone simply suggested sending a commando unit to de Wynter's estate, there would be no film.

Sir August de Wynter (Sean Connery) to his victims: "Now is the winter of your discontent."

John Wood, who appears in *The Avengers* as John Steed's tailor, is also in an episode of the original series entitled "The Bird Who Knew Too Much" as an expert in exotic birds.

(1989), and the film has a crisp look, although given Pratt's previous efforts, it might be expected to be a bit darker and moodier. Production designer Stuart Craig is a veteran of such stylish productions as *Dangerous Liaisons* (1988), *The Secret Garden* (1993), and *The English Patient* (1996), and the sets, especially de Wynter's estate, are impressive. Costume designer Anthony Powell contributed to *Sorcerer* (1977), *Tess* (1979), and *Indiana Jones and the Last Crusade* (1989). His outfits for Steed and Peel recall those of the originals without exactly duplicating them. Powell's main contribution to *The Avengers* comes when de Wynter meets with his board of directors and to keep the identity of each a secret, all are dressed as teddy bears, each a different color. These witty costumes, with each bear seemingly able to express pleasure and displeasure, are one of the few things about *The Avengers* reminiscent of the television series, which often employs the nursery artifacts of the privileged English past.

Warner Bros., which had counted on *The Avengers* as its big summer film, invited the extremely hostile response in both the United States and the United Kingdom by not allowing reviewers to see it before its first day of release. This meant, in the United States, that reviews that would have appeared in newspapers on the Friday the film opened did not appear until Saturday or Monday. Although distributors justify this common practice by saying they want the film in question to be available to the public for at least part of the opening weekend without the tarnish of negative reviews, they are tarnishing the film more severely themselves. What reviewer is going to praise a film even its distributor thinks is a stinker? Not only are reviewers not to blame because Warner Bros. spent over $60 million making a film that took in around $23 million in its first four weeks of release in the United States, but Chechik and MacPherson may not really be to blame either.

Producer Jerry Weintraub, who has produced such notable films as *Nashville* (1975) and *Diner* (1982), as well as less distinguished efforts like *The Specialist* (1994) and the four entries in *The Karate Kid* series, bought the rights to *The Avengers* in 1985, seemingly enough time to come up with a workable script. Weintraub explained to *The Guardian* his sensitivity about the British response to the film, the possibility that he, as an American producer, would be the scapegoat: "From a marketing standpoint, nobody can write before it opens that I ruined the picture. Maybe some of them will do that after the film opens, but the hell with them." Supposedly efforts were made to rescue the film by reediting it after disappointing test screenings, but perhaps too much was taken out. Patrick Macnee told *The Los Angeles Times* that Fiennes' best scenes, which appeared in the original screenplay he read, are not in the final product.

The television *The Avengers* was droll, camp, self-mocking, ahead of its time, which is why it holds up so well three decades later. The film, on the other hand, is all about the corporate mentality of its time. Ironically, Macnee is in the film as the voice of an invisible inventor. An invisible Macnee is a fitting metaphor for the film's insufficient charms.

—*Michael Adams*

CREDITS

John Steed: Ralph Fiennes
Emma Peel: Uma Thurman
Sir August de Wynter: Sean Connery
Mother: Jim Broadbent
Father: Fiona Shaw
Alice: Eileen Atkins
Bailey: Eddie Izzard
Trubshaw: John Wood
Tamara: Keeley Hawes
Brenda: Carmen Ejogo
Invisible Jones: Patrick Macnee

Origin: USA
Released: 1998
Production: Jerry Weintraub; released by Warner Bros.
Direction: Jeremiah Chechik
Screenplay: Don McPherson; based on the television series created by Sydney Newman
Cinematography: Roger Pratt
Editing: Mick Audsley
Production design: Stuart Craig
Art direction: Neil Lamont
Costumes: Anthony Powell
Sound: Clive Winter
Music: Joe McNeely
Special effects: Joss Williams, Nick Davis
MPAA rating: PG-13
Running Time: 91 minutes

REVIEWS

Atlanta Constitution. August 17, 1998, p. B1.
Boston Globe. August 15, 1998, p. C3.
Chicago Tribune. August 17, 1998, p. 1.
Cinefantastique. February, 1998, p. 7.
Entertainment Weekly. September 4, 1998, p. 54.
Los Angeles Times. August 17, 1998, p. F5.
New York Times. August 15, 1998, p. A13.
Newsweek. August 24, 1998, p. 59.
People. August 31, 1998, p. 33.
San Francisco Chronicle. August 15, 1998, p. E1.
Sight and Sound. October, 1998, p. 38.
Time. August 24, 1998, p. 74.
USA Today. August 17, 1998, p. D3.
Variety. August 17, 1998, p. 35.
Washington Post. August 15, 1998, p. B1.

Ayn Rand: A Sense of Life

"Intellectually stimulating."—Jeff Craig, *Sixty Second Preview*

Ayn Rand: A Sense of Life is an epic overview of the life, loves, and career of one of the most interesting, controversial, and influential people of the 20th century. Born Alice Rosenbaum in St. Petersburg, Russia, on February 2, 1905, writer/philosopher Ayn (rhymes with 'vine') Rand become the embodiment of the great American Dream.

Having witnessed firsthand the 1917 Bolshevik revolution, she soon grew fearful of the new totalitarian rule and became diametrically opposed to the mysticism and collectivism of Russian culture. Amidst the increasingly dismal atmosphere enveloping her homeland and fascinated with the images of America she saw in the movies, she fled the Soviet Union in 1926 and landed in Hollywood where she began working as an extra for Cecil B. DeMille. It was during this time she met actor Frank O'Connor, whom she remained married to for 50 years until his death in 1979. After her stint with DeMille, she began reading then penning screenplays for Universal (which included *Red Pawn* and *Night of January 16th*) but soon graduated to prose. Her first novel, the largely biographical *We the Living* (1933) suffered countless rejections until it was optioned by MacMillan in 1936.

Before *Living* even saw the light of day, she had already started on her next novel, *The Fountainhead,* the story of a rebellious architect who refused to conform, which was also met with indifference by publishers until 1943. It languished in obscurity for two years until receiving widespread attention in 1945 when it became a landmark best-seller. Returning to Hollywood that same year, this time to write the screenplay version of *Fountainhead,* yet another of Rand's works remained unproduced (in this case, war-time restrictions were the cause). Finally, in 1948, the film starring Gary Cooper and directed by King Vidor was released to almost unanimous praise.

These many, often confounding delays of Rand's work went far in pinpointing the narrow mind-set of the world at the time. An iconoclast in every sense of the word, Rand's views, which many consider patently humorless and little more than recycled Nietzsche, were light years beyond what was being espoused at the time. The often vehement reactions to her work further cemented, in her own mind at least, the need for pure, unadulterated individualism, which she herself bafflingly labeled as "objectivism."

Rand's final tenure in Hollywood lasted a full eight years where she worked as a screenwriter and producer for Hal Willis. During this period, she began writing *Atlas Shrugged,* the novel for which she is most remembered. Also, her last work of fiction, *Atlas* was a highbrow mystery that integrated elements of ethics, metaphysics, economics, politics, and sex. It grabbed the attention of the literary world in the post World War II era and still hasn't let go. Its labyrinthine design and multi-faceted perspective made it (many feel by design) unadaptable for film (ironically, Rand was working on a mini-series teleplay for *Atlas* at the time of her death in 1982. The project was never finished). The timelessness of the book and its staying power is perpetually re-enforced; it still sells hundreds of thousands of copies each year.

In 1958, perhaps sensing she had reached her zenith (fiction-wise) with *Atlas,* Rand directed her energies into lengthy, esoteric, complexly literate essays and became a staple on the lecture circuit. Exclusively socio-political in nature, her output during this time was staggering and always controversial. While the pieces often championed capitalism and the individual, she distanced herself from the conservatives (and they from her). Her artsy/bohemian idealism made her a natural as a liberal poster child but she regularly blasted the democratic platform. The basis of all of her work at this time came from a deep-seated, venomous disdain for Communism and the overwhelming need for the nonconformist in our society.

Rand is obviously a figure ripe for meticulous examination and writer/director Michael Paxton's Oscar-nominated documentary on her, which clocks in at a taxing 145 minutes, leaves nary an aspect of her life untouched. However, after watching it, the viewer can walk away feeling that Paxton's overwhelmingly favorable bias towards his subject sacrificed, in a very measurable degree, his objectivity, the ultimate no-no for a documentarian. Sadly, his story about the founder of objectivism is anything but objective. After spending an inordinate amount of time glorifying her anti-Communist stance,

CREDITS

Narrator: Sharon Gless

Origin: USA
Released: 1998
Production: Michael Paxton for AG Media Corporation Ltd. and Copasetic Inc.; released by Strand Releasing
Direction: Michael Paxton
Screenplay: Michael Paxton
Cinematography: Alik Sakharov
Editing: Lauren Schaffer, Christopher Earl
Music: Jeff Britting
Sound: Michael M. Moore
MPAA rating: Unrated
Running Time: 145 minutes

Paxton unexplainably glosses over Rand's about-face actions when she appeared as a witness for the prosecution before the House Un-American Activities Committee. The plethora of interviews featured are with those who knew and loved her and these clips come off (understandably) as *de facto* testimonials. He completely avoids the opinions of noteworthy critics, commentators, and detractors of her work and as a result, the film takes on the questionable air of an infomercial.

One such example of this rose-colored perspective arises when Paxton describes, in what can only be regarded as Rand's personal mid-life crisis, a period where she carried on a brief affair with a man almost half her age, which was done with her husband's blessing no less. While giving further proof of her "individualism," Paxton points out just how malleable Rand's husband was, how she rarely considered the feelings of others and how she surrounded herself with sycophants. Whether aware of it or not, Paxton (through a number of clips taken from talk-shows done in her later years) shows just how touchy Rand was when it came to others criticizing her.

In the end, while sprawling and fascinating to watch, Paxton's fact-filled documentary (warmly narrated by actress Sharon Gless) must be noted with a huge, nagging caveat. It preaches the gospel of Rand to a throng of entrenched believers rather than as a treatise to the uninitiated. It is less of the definite biography it pretends to be and more of a smitten homage, a self-indulgent soliloquy, a long-winded love letter from a die-hard admirer.

—*J. M. Clark*

REVIEWS

Entertainment Weekly. March 6, 1998, p. 58.
Los Angeles Times. February 13, 1998, p. F14.
New York Times. February 13, 1998, p. E16.
Variety. February 16, 1998, p. 57.

Babe: Pig in the City

In the heart of the city, a pig with heart.—Movie tagline

"Magical! More magical than the original . . . delightful and funny. Filled with wonders large and small."—Roger Ebert, *Chicago Sun-Times*

"Amazing! Beautifully staged, fast-paced, highly imaginative."—Dave Kehr, *New York Daily News*

"Irresistible! Hog heaven . . . irresistible charm. *Babe* is engaging as ever. Good work pig."—Bob Campbell, *Newark Star-Ledger*

"Terrific! Amazing. A solid hit. A real squeal of a sequel, building on the magical qualities of the first film while telling a completely new story in a new and inventive landscape."—Jack Mathews, *Newsday*

"Two very enthusiastic thumbs way up! One of the year's best films—even better than the first one!"—*Siskel & Ebert*

 Box Office: $17,300,000

The original *Babe* (1995), based on the children's book by Dick King-Smith, was a surprise hit among audiences and critics alike, a magical, unique picture about a talking pig that appealed to both children and adults and became the first film of its kind to be nominated for a Best Picture Oscar. *Babe: Pig in the City,* co-written and directed by *Mad Max* creator George Miller, is a sequel that promised to be another success and that Universal hoped would lead to more film adventures for the little pig. Upon its release, a number of critics heralded *Babe: Pig in the City* with glowing reviews and placed the film on their Top Ten lists of 1998. Audiences didn't seem to agree. Apparently either something unique was missing from this second picture or audiences had lost interest in the heroic little animal, because the movie rapidly faded from view and Universal had an unexpected boxoffice failure on its hands. Budgeted at over $90 million and shortly after the film's final boxoffice take was tabulated, the president of Universal was fired.

The most common complaint from the relatively small number of people who went to the theater to see the film seemed to be that it was a much darker picture than the original *Babe.* While it is true that *Pig in the City* occasionally explores the cruelty and heartlessness found in the world, the much-loved *Babe* did so as well, delving into such subjects as the butchering of animals and such issues as hatred, revenge, and prejudice. One might even argue that *Babe* had even darker elements than its sequel. The gap between the lackluster public response to *Pig in the City* and the critical praise lavished on the film might be better explained by the sharp contrasts between the sequel and its predecessor. At a time when the worst thing about most sequels is that they

Babe the pig looks out into a strange new world as he travels to the big city to save the family farm in *Babe: Pig in the City*.

finally Esme locates a strange little hotel run by an eccentric landlady (Mary Stein) who has covertly set up her establishment as a refuge for disenfranchised animals. The hotel is full of various animals—a room full of singing cats, a number of dogs (including one whose lower body is paralyzed), a family of chimpanzees, and an intelligent orangutan named Thelonius (voice of James Cosmo)—and the only other human occupant seems to be the landlady's strange, seemingly mute uncle Fugly Floom (Mickey Rooney), a clown who uses Thelonius and the chimpanzees in his act. While Mrs. Hoggett is away trying to call her husband, the primates kidnap Babe and Fugly forces the pig to perform in his animal show—which Babe ruins by unintentionally starting a fire.

Later, while out trying to steal food, the chimps trick Babe into going into a yard with savage dogs, and the poor fellow finds himself being chased through town by a mean pit bull (voice of Stanley Ralph Ross). Because of his own carelessness the pit bull winds up hanging from a bridge with his head submerged in the water. Spectator animals who have been watching the chase stand by and do nothing, watching the dog drown, but Babe, the gallant pig, dives into the water to save the savage canine. Not surprisingly, the dog is grateful to Babe for saving his life and instantly becomes the pig's loyal companion. After witnessing Babe's kindness, the stray animals in the neighborhood (many of whom have been mistreated by humans), ask the pig for

often do nothing more than try to duplicate the originals, Babe's second adventure ironically fails to match the success and magic of his first because the sequel actually departs too much from the innovation of the original. *Babe: Pig in the City* is a magical and unique movie in its own right, but in many ways it almost seems to be *too* disconnected from its predecessor.

When Babe (voice of Elizabeth Daily) returns home with Farmer Hoggett (James Cromwell) after becoming a prize-winning "sheep-pig," it is not long before trouble strikes. The innocent and careless pig accidentally causes Hoggett to fall into a well. With the farmer injured and laid up in bed, Mrs. Hoggett (Magda Szubanski) attempts to do all the farm work herself, but it is too much for one person to handle. Soon the farm is threatened with foreclosure. With hopes of making enough money to save their home, Mrs. Hoggett decides to take Babe to a fair in the city. Babe's paranoid duck friend Ferdinand warns the pig that "You'll be in the company of a serial killer" (referring to the fact that Esme Hoggett routinely cooks animals such as himself), but the ever-loyal Babe tells the duck, "The boss can't lose the farm." Thus, off he goes with Mrs. Hoggett to save the homestead.

At the airport, the duo runs into trouble when a canine sniffer leads security to mistakenly arrest Esme for drug possession. Mrs. Hoggett is later released but finds herself stranded with Babe in the city. Unfortunately, most hotels in the city do not allow animals, but

Pitbull (voice of Stanley Ralph Ross) to his animal friends: "What the pig says, goes!"

help, and he suggests they all move into the hotel and band together to help each other. The pit bull names Babe the "chief" of their community, and the animals look to the kindhearted pig as their leader.

Disaster and yet more conflict arrives in the form of the animal regulation authorities, who—having been alerted to the animal hotel by a nosy neighbor—invade the refuge like a military unit and begin rounding up the dogs, cats, and monkeys. Luckily, a few of them escape capture, including Babe. The pig and his fortunate companions decide to go after their friends and find a way to free them. Meanwhile, after

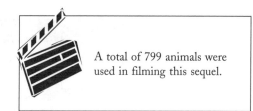

A total of 799 animals were used in filming this sequel.

a long series of misfortunes, Mrs. Hoggett returns to the hotel and sees the place is empty. She finds out what happened to Babe and the other animals and sets out to rescue her beloved and valuable pig. In the end, Babe frees his friends and Mrs. Hoggett saves Babe. The story concludes when Mrs. Hoggett, Babe, the landlady, and all the city animals return to the Hoggett farm. Hence, as the narrator tells us, their "two worlds come together," and as Babe rejoins his "boss" the "pig and farmer were content again."

As with *Babe,* this sequel contains humor aplenty, the best of which comes from the animal characters and their interactions with each other. The animals perform so well and the lip-synched dialogue is so harmonious with their actions that it is easy to suspend disbelief and accept them as real talking animals. Many of these interesting characters quickly become endearing, including the very intelligent but shady chimpanzees and Thelonius. The most fascinating and the most clever parts of the film involve the relationships between these believable characters. However, the less effective elements of humor in *Pig in the City* involve comedy of the more slapstick variety, particularly with regard to Mrs. Hoggett, who seems to be played for laughs more than anything else. The climactic scene in which Babe and Esme disrupt a charity event benefiting a medical institute has its humor but is a far cry from the clever, suspenseful ending of *Babe,* which featured the pig winning a sheep-dog contest.

CREDITS

Esme Hoggett: Magda Szubanski
Arthur Hoggett: James Cromwell
Landlady: Mary Stein
Fugly Floom: Mickey Rooney
Neighbor: Julie Godfrey
Babe: E. G. Daily (voice)
Ferdinand: Danny Mann (voice)
Zootie: Glenn Headly (voice)
Bob: Steven Wright (voice)
Thelonius: James Cosmo (voice)
Pitbull/Doberman: Stanley Ralph Ross (voice)
Narrator: Roscoe Lee Browne

Origin: USA
Released: 1998
Production: George Miller, Doug Mitchell, and Bill Miller for Kennedy Miller; released by Universal Pictures
Direction: George Miller
Screenplay: George Miller, Judy Morris, and Mark Lamprell; based on the characters created by Dick King-Smith
Cinematography: Andrew Lesnie
Editing: Jay Friedkin, Margaret Sixel
Production design: Roger Ford
Art direction: Colin Gibson
Set design: Tony Raes
Costumes: Norma Moriceau
Sound: Ben Osmo
Special effects supervisor: Tad Pride
Music: Nigel Westlake
MPAA rating: G
Running Time: 97 minutes

AWARDS AND NOMINATIONS

Academy Awards 1998 Nominations: Song ("That'll Do")

The set design and visual effects of *Babe: Pig in the City* are impressive and imaginative. The streets around the animal hotel look like something lifted from a theme park, with a quaint little building sitting at the corner of narrow streets running alongside a narrow, winding river. Views of the cityscape reveal an intriguing but surreal set of images: the Golden Gate Bridge, the Statue of Liberty, and Hollywood are all there. This is not one specific city, evidently, but *every* major city. The symbolism in suggesting that this city actually represents many real cities works nicely in accordance with some of the film's themes (such as the prevalence of heartlessness and corruption in city life), but at the same time the juxtaposition of various locales creates an unexpectedly fantastical setting that might detract from the magical "believability" that characterized the first movie. In *Babe,* the setting could have been almost anywhere, but it at least appeared to be a *real* place. In *Pig in the City,* the sudden revelation that Babe's world is not our own, but instead some kind of dreamlike amalgam representing the world we know, might be seen as a weakening of the story's appeal, if for no other reason than its violations of the audience's expectations.

One of the most charming elements of *Babe* was the developing relationship between the pig and his owner, Farmer Hoggett. Though Hoggett actually said very little, he was truly a major character, and the bond he developed with Babe was a special one that provided the movie with a thematic focus: it was Arthur Hoggett who believed in the little pig and saw his potential. In *Babe: Pig in the City,* Farmer Hoggett makes only two appearances—at the beginning and at the end—and his presence is sorely missed throughout the film. Mrs. Hoggett does not have a close connection to Babe and mainly seems to care about him be-

REVIEWS

Boxoffice. January, 1999, p. 52.
Chicago Tribune. November 11, 1998, p. 1.
Detroit Free Press. November 25, 1998, p. 3D.
Detroit News. November 25, 1998, p. 6D.
Entertainment Weekly. December 4, 1998, p. 61.
Los Angeles Times. November 25, 1998, p. F1.
New York Times. November 25, 1998, p. E1.
People. December 7, 1998, p. 31.
Sight and Sound. February, 1999, p. 38.
Variety. November 30, 1998, p. 64.
Washington Post. November 27, 1998, p. 56.

cause of his value; also, as mentioned before, her character is used more for humor than for the dramatic element of the film. Perhaps the film would have been more successful story-wise if Hoggett had been a major character again and the further development of his relationship with Babe had been a central focus.

The original *Babe* shared a useful, instructive message about prejudice and racial and class divisions. The farm world to which Babe belonged represented the human world, with its biases, stereotypes, and complacency. Once again, Babe's world in *Pig in the City* speaks to the audience about the necessity of rising above differences and working together to make a happier, kinder world. Near the beginning of the film, the narrator states the theme of the story: "A kind and steady heart can heal a sorry world." The message is a useful one, but it might have come across more resoundingly if the tone of *Babe: Pig in the City* had modeled itself a little more closely after its predecessor.

—*David Flanagin*

Barney's Great Adventure

Share the magic of the movie . . . you know your children will love!—Movie tagline

Box Office: $12,218,638

News reports have been made stating that young children have been harming themselves whenever they see the sight of Barney on the television. While watching the popular PBS television show *Barney and Friends,* they are compelled to hug their t.v. sets, which in some cases, would cause the television to fall on top of them, thus resulting in injury. With this evidence, along with Barney merchandise netting millions of dollars, it became inevitable for this purple phenomenon to carry his reign over to the big screen. The end result is the banal *Barney's Great Adventure.*

From a physical aspect, the challenge to bring Barney to the big screen was not too daunting a task. Everything about the film is elemental. Three young kids are being driven to their grandparents' farm to spend the summer. Siblings Cody (Trevor Morgan), and Abby (Diana Rice) are accompanied on this trip by Abby's best friend Marcella (Kyla Pratt). Since Cody puts on the front that he's too cool to spend his summer at a boring farm, Abby and Marcella add to their excitement with a stuffed Barney doll. Cody is immediately insulted when Abby and Marcella try to convince Cody that playing with Barney is fun if you use your imagination. Further saddened by the prospect of no cable or Gameboy at the farm, Cody dismisses their theory, and continues to sulk during his stay on the farm. Ironically, through a prank engineered by Cody, the stuffed Barney doll comes to life, turning Cody into a true believer of the power of the imagination.

Barney: "The dreams you see most clearly are the ones most likely to come true."

Soon Barney and the kids unite by singing a few preschool lullabies and hop around the chicken barn. Even with Barney as company, Cody still wishes for some excitement to shake up the monotony of milking cows and stacking hay. After Barney serenades Cody with "Twinkle Twinkle Little Star," a mysterious egg falls from the night sky. Cody discovers the unusually large and multicolored egg and alerts the others of its existence. The grandparents suggest taking the foreign egg to a women down the road who specializes in birds and maybe she'll be able to determine what kind of egg it is. The group reaches the eccentric bird lady's quarters and begin shifting through a myriad of books to ascertain what type of egg they have in their possession. Mysteriously, a book appears informing the gang that the egg is a magical one that has the power to grant wishes. The five colorful rings that surround the egg will glow in succession and once that happens, it has to be taken to the place it was found in order for it to hatch. Upon reading the instructions, Barney and crew suddenly lose the egg and spend the remainder of the film chasing the egg through several colorful musical sequences, such as a parade down Main Street, a posh French restaurant, a circus, and a hot air balloon race.

Children who have watched the show religiously would be excited to see Barney prancing outside of the two-dimensional studio where his program is taped. Even though the locale has changed, the wholesomeness and lessons to be learned that have made the *Barney and Friends* show one of the most popular preschool shows are fully intact in the film. Barney's words of wisdom resound with positivity, if you can ignore his trademark silly laugh, when projected on high, without being too overbearing. The children learn how to work as a team and when it seemed that they had lost the egg for good, to not give up trying to reach their goal. The movie even makes room for Barney's other dinosaur friends such as the green Baby Bop and bright yellow B.J. Even though her presence in the film is unnecessary, Baby Bop encourages audience participation when she asks the young audience if they have seen her "blankey." Younger kids will be most anxious to help her.

The young actors, Morgan, Rice, and Pratt, are a bit older than Barney's real target audience, which gives *Barney's Great Adventure* an air of superficiality. Although it would be nice to think that eight or nine-year-olds could be interested in prancing around with an innocent, goofy purple dinosaur than getting finger blisters from playing Nintendo or calling up to request their favorite rap video on MTV, it's not realistic. The acting of the three youngsters isn't too far removed from an elementary school play, but the good news is, these kids aren't as eager to overact and become annoying as the younger actors on the series soon become. Cody, Abby, and Marcella are a likable group of kids that helps make *Barney's Great Adventure* bearable.

Film opened initially with a four day run at New York's Radio City Music Hall before opening in general release.

But *Barney's Great Adventure* lacks pizazz and flair. Unlike the Muppets, who made a successful leap from the small screen with the help of the late, great Jim Henson, Barney has no such talent behind him. The look and feel of *Barney's Great Adventure* is flat. Not much imagination or money went into bringing the big purple guy to the big screen, which means it's a downhill slide for adults once the movie begins. The majority of the film's songs are public domain titles such as "Old MacDonald" and "Twinkle Twinkle . . ." and the original ones, like the tune the actors sing at the bird lady's sanctuary, seem to be the result of hearing instrumental music on the stage and having the cast improvise words that rhyme to create a song.

You would think that director Steve Gomer would compensate for such a shortcoming with elaborate special effects, but you would be quite wrong. Even Barney's entrance into the film is less than magical, you could even say it was just economical. The stuffed doll is placed in a tub and the faucet is turned on, growing Barney into his full size. Uninterestingly enough, he just steps his big old self out the tub and asks for a towel. No psychedelic colors, no computer generated effects to somehow birth an animal that has been dead millions of years through some porthole from another dimension. It seems Gomer's vision of Barney's big screen debut harkens back to the grass roots days of filmmaking when newfangled movie effects were the talk of mad men. Because of the narrow reaches the film's narrative takes the audience, both young and old, the huge dinosaur with a message seems very limited. On the big screen, he's just an even bigger guy hidden behind a big purple dinosaur suit.

It's unfortunate that such a popular and educational character for toddlers was stuck with such a lackluster film. But then again, for those t.v. hugging youngsters, I'm quite sure they wouldn't mind a sequel.

— *Michelle Banks*

CREDITS

Grandpa: George Hearn
Grandma: Shirley Douglas
Cody: Trevor Morgan
Marcella: Kyla Pratt
Abby: Diana Rice
Barney (Body): David Joyner
Barney (Voice): Bob West
Baby Bop (Body): Jeff Ayres
Baby Bop (Voice): Julie Johnson

Origin: USA
Released: 1998
Production: Sheryl Leach and Dennis DeShazer for a Polygram Filmed Entertainment and Lyrick Studios production; released by Polygram Films
Direction: Steve Gomer
Screenplay: Stephen White
Cinematography: Sandi Sissel
Editing: Richard Halsey
Production design: Vincent Jefferds
Art direction: Collin Niemi
Set decoration: Diane Lamothe
Special visual effects: Cinemotion Pictures
Choreography: Debra Brown
Sound: Don Cohen
Casting: Ronna Kress
MPAA rating: G
Running Time: 75 minutes

REVIEWS

Boxoffice. April, 1998.
Entertainment Weekly. April 17, 1998, p. 98.
Los Angeles Times. April 3, 1998, p. F20.
New York Times. March 27, 1998, p. E28.
San Francisco Chronicle. April 3, 1998, p. C3.
Variety. March 30, 1998, p. 41.
Washington Post. April 3, 1998, p. 53.

BASEketball

From the director of *Naked Gun* starring the creators of *South Park*—Movie tagline

"*South Park*'s Parker and Stone are the comedy duo for the 90's!"—Steve Tilley, *Edmonton Sun*

"Funny and gleefully offensive."—Stephen Holden, *New York Times*

"*BASEketball* scores! A comedy that is as smart as it is funny!"—Scott Siegel, *Siegel Entertainment Syndicate*

 Box Office: $7,042,541

Writer/director/producer David Zucker (*Airplane!* [1980] and *The Naked Gun* [1988]) scored a coup when he signed Trey Parker and Matt Stone to act in his film *BASEketball*. Zucker had chosen them after seeing Parker in Parker's $125,000 student film *Cannibal! The Musical* (1996). By the time *BASEketball* arrived in theaters in August of 1998, Stone and Parker were better known as the creators of the goofy *South Park*, Comedy Central's ratings bonanza. The deal worked out on both sides. Zucker got about the hottest comedy guys in the business and Stone and Parker got to work with one of their heroes.

 Coop (Trey Parker) to Remer (Matt Stone) or Remer to Coop: "Dude!"

Unfortunately, the deal didn't work out as well for the audience. *BASEketball* never approaches the inspired, rapid-fire joke pace of Zucker's *Airplane!* or *The Naked Gun* and it never reaches the loopy genius of a good episode of *South Park*.

Parker and Stone play Coop and Remer, two slackers who don't do much more than play Nintendo. Coop's boyhood dream of one day becoming a famous sports figure like his hero Reggie Jackson has been pushed to the wayside until he and Remer figure out a new game in their driveway. It's BASEketball, a game that involves making free throws while being distracted by the other team's

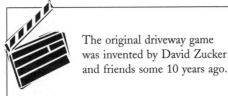 The original driveway game was invented by David Zucker and friends some 10 years ago.

"psych outs." A psych-out can range from pedestrian fare like insulting the thrower's mother or chewing on aluminum foil to more advanced moves like pretending to squirt milk out of one's nipples. ("Got milk?" says Remer, when he employs the move.)

Helped by generous millionaire Ted Densmore (Ernest Borgnine), the guys form a national BASEketball league shaped by Coop's idealistic visions. Everyone is paid the same, players can't switch from one team to another and there is no merchandising allowed. Naturally, this can't last since an evil rival owner (Robert Vaughn) wants to exploit the game for all it's worth. When Densmore dies, he leaves the team to Coop, with the provision that Coop's team, The Milwaukee Beers, must win the game or the team will revert to his widow, Yvette (Jenny McCarthy). So, as sports movies inevitably must, it all comes down to the big game.

The movie gives the Zucker treatment to the world of organized sports. The cheerleaders sport absurdly risque costumes, ranging from flimsy Victoria's Secret-like nighties to full S & M gear. The team names are things like the Miami Dealers or the L.A. Riots. When there is a newscast about a team's big victory, a newscaster comments on the town's "huge celebration" adding "Final tally: 14 injured, 3 dead."

Bob Costas and Al Michaels make an appearance as BASEketball sportscasters who have to endure the absurdly long length of the BASEketball season.

There are plenty of other cameos in the film too. The best use of a cameo is TV veteran Robert Stack, who spews out a stream of vulgarities in his usual dignified style on an "Unsolved Mysteries" show. Kareem Abdul-Jabar also makes an appearance, as do Reggie Jackson and even Kato Kaelin.

The surprising bonus in *BASEketball* is how good Stone and Parker are at acting. With his blond hair and innocent, big blue eyes, Parker has the right look to play Coop, the goody-goody Mr. Perfect. Stone, with his mad scientist brown hair and nerdy glasses, is the more obnoxious, goofy one. The pairing makes for a good comedy team. The two guys, friends in real life, make a charismatic duo, the kind of funny, confident guys who seem like they'd be easy to hang out with.

The rest of the cast are just there to toil in Stone and Parker's shadows. Yasmine Bleeth plays their object of desire, a sweet do-gooder who takes care of a group of lovable, terminally ill kids (or, as she insists "health challenged and survival-impaired" kids.) Part of the joke is supposed to be that this famous pin-up is playing the nice girl-next-door role. Dian Bachar plays Squeak, the guys' object of wrath. As their mas-

CREDITS

Joe Cooper: Trey Parker
Doug Remer: Matt Stone
Squeak Scolari: Dian Bachar
Jenna Reed: Yasmine Bleeth
Yvette Denslow: Jenny McCarthy
Baxter Cain: Robert Vaughn
Ted Denslow: Ernest Borgnine
Joey: Trevor Einhorn
Dirk Jansen: Mark Goodson

Origin: USA
Released: 1998
Production: David Zucker, Robert LoCash, and Gil Netter; released by Universal Pictures
Direction: David Zucker
Screenplay: David Zucker, Robert LoCash, Lewis Friedman, and Jeff Wright
Cinematography: Steve Mason
Editing: Jeffrey Reiner
Music: James Ira Newborn
Production design: Steven Jordan
Art direction: Bill Hiney
Costumes: Catherine Adair
Sound: Hank Garfield
MPAA rating: R
Running Time: 103 minutes

cot, Squeak suffers repeated and generally unfunny abuse at their hands like being called "bitch." Jenny McCarthy, who demonstrated on her MTV show that she's actually a fine comedic actress, is wasted in a role as a bombshell gold-digger type.

While not the glorious meeting of the comedic minds that this film could have been, it's an enjoyable, fast-paced flick. And it proved that Parker and Stone have the charisma to handle big film roles. If nothing else, *BASEketball* whets the appetite for things to come.

—*Jill Hamilton*

REVIEWS

Entertainment Weekly. August 7, 1998, p. 47.
Los Angeles Times. July 31, 1998, p. F10.
New York Times. August 31, 1998, p. E10.
People. August 17, 1998, p. 30.
Variety. August 3, 1998, p. 35.

Beloved

"Deeply moving and emotionally explosive."—Bill Diehl, *ABC Radio*

"One of the best films of the decade. A magnificent film. Ms. Winfrey is shattering perfection."—Dennis Cunningham, *CBS-TV*

"A movie of rare power with knockout performances."—Leah Rozen, *People*

"*Beloved* is triumphant. Winfrey's pitch-perfect performance resonates with beauty, terror and the kind of truth that invades dreams."—Peter Travers, *Rolling Stone*

"Jonathan Demme has made a movie that enriches the cinematic vocabulary. Oprah Winfrey tosses out the glamour and replaces it with heart, soul and grit."—*Time*

"Extraordinarily powerful and provocative."—Paul Wunder, *WBAI Radio*

"Haunting and powerful. One of the best movies of the year."–Pat Collins, *WWOR-TV*

   Box Office: $22,747,234

Beloved is the much anticipated adaptation of the novel by Nobel Prize winner Toni Morrison. The advance publicity and press have suggested how much is at stake in the release of a three-hour epic dealing with America's fraught history of slavery and black/white relationships. Will white audiences flock to the film? Will black audiences not only see it but see it again? For successful films nowadays require repeat attendance, the fans who will return to see a film again and again. In an era that relies on polling and audience research, it is already anticipated that the major audience for *Beloved* will be urban and predominantly composed of African-American middle-aged women. The data suggest that a younger audience—white and black—won't sit for a three hour history lesson, even if it comes packaged with all-star talents such as Oprah Winfrey and Danny Glover.

The first week's grosses evidently confirmed the conventional wisdom. The film played well in cities and did poorly in suburbs. It made less than nine million dollars—certainly a disappointment when hit films make several times that in their first week. Still *Beloved* did place fifth in the week's list of popular films, and Disney executives pronounced themselves satisfied, if not thrilled, with the public response.

Why should there be such a discussion of boxoffice in a film review? Surely *Beloved* should be evaluated on its own terms as a work of art. Yes, although Hollywood films have always married art and commerce, and it is a fact that *Beloved* would not have received epic treatment if its star and producer, Oprah Winfrey, had not put her own power and prestige behind it. Hollywood film has always been about the personalities of actors, of what they are presumed to stand for onscreen and off. Films are previewed and sometimes edited to account for audience reactions. Filmmakers can never imagine—as writers sometimes do—that they are creating for themselves.

So what kind of art, what kind of commercial product, is *Beloved*? In one respect, it is uncompromising. The brutality of slavery and racism are presented in sudden, shocking, and brief scenes—flashbacks to an evil time that is not sentimentalized in the slightest. Ex-slaves populate this film as victims suffering from a kind of post-traumatic stress syndrome. There are no good masters. There is only the legacy of injustice and horror. Whites have absolute power, and absolute power not only corrupts, it makes the whites act perversely—degrading slaves for the sheer sadistic pleasure of it. Thus Sethe (Oprah Winfrey) is deprived of her mother's milk by white men who assault her and literally suck her dry. Sethe later compulsively repeats the line "they took my milk" to another ex-slave, Paul D. (Danny Glover). The flashback to the white men on top of Sethe and the scene with Paul D. are crucial because they explain Sethe's passionate feeling that slavery deprived her of a chance to sustain and perpetuate life for her children. She will *never* allow herself or her loved ones to submit to that anti-human world again.

When her white master shows up to claim Sethe and her children (she has run away), Sethe goes berserk, murdering her youngest daughter (slashing her throat with a saw) rather than allow the white man his "property." It is a confusing moment. Is the Civil War over? Why does the

white man leave, tears in his eyes, looking at Sethe as if she is the monster, not him? The film has already made clear that the master is inhuman. Why wouldn't he simply call Sethe crazy and take her other children away? What is the source of his incredulity and disgust?

The curious problem with *Beloved* is that it seems as unconscious of its own presumptions and prejudices as did an earlier generation of Hollywood movies like *Gone With the Wind* (1939), which treated blacks as background music or comic relief, showing the humanity of African-Americans only briefly in scenes where the give-and-take of dialogue establishes their humanity. *Beloved* is as manipulative as any Hollywood potboiler epic, even though its values are reversed, and whites are shown as subhuman and marginalized. The problem with marginalization—no matter who is practicing it—is that it tends to stereotype the marginalized. Of course, *Beloved* is not suggesting that all whites are evil. There are cameos in the film that cut against its otherwise simplified moral agenda. Yet the film develops no persuasive story line, no complex reading of characters—black or white—that makes it a compelling work of art. Instead, *Beloved* is, sadly, just another piece of commercial filmmaking. And the irony is that its commercial qualities will probably not gain it a broad enough audience for Hollywood to consider it a resounding success.

The soundtrack is an obvious example of how the film fails as art. It functions like the soundtrack of Barbra Streisand's *Yentl* (1983), which overlays music that is supposed to inspire awe; nothing in the scenes themselves is awe-inspiring, any more than similar scenes in *Beloved*, although the music insists on making the audience think it has somehow been elevated. This forcing of the issue through music replaces any real character or plot development.

As a reviewer in *Salon* observes, Sethe's killing of her child is reminiscent of *Sophie's Choice* (1982), in which the concentration camp mother has to choose which of her children will be sacrificed. Like Styron's novel and the film on which it is based, Morrison's novel, and the film on which it is based, tries to make of a horrendous history a domestic story. And in both cases, there is something demeaning about the authors' arrogance—their efforts to make a fictional plot out of the Holocaust and out of slavery. Not that history and its horror cannot be fictionalized; rather, with-

> Paul D (Danny Glover) on viewing Sethe's literally haunted house: "What kind of evil you got in there?" Sethe (Oprah Winfrey) replies: "It ain't evil, just sad."

AWARDS AND NOMINATIONS

Academy Awards 1998 Nominations: Costume

out an extraordinary sense of tact, a sense that history has to be used sparingly, novels and films feel factitious, superficial, and unauthentic.

Some viewers may not be able to get beyond Sethe's murder of her own child. Granted that she did not want to return to a condition of servitude, does her act make sense? The film certainly suggests Sethe's action is hard to accept. She is ostracized by both the white and black communities. Paul D., who becomes her lover, advises her that perhaps it is best to love many things a little than to focus love so exclusively that it isolates one from the rest of humanity and leaves one bereft. Sethe is reminiscent of Nancy Mannigoe in William Faulkner's *Requiem for a Nun,* one of his most problematic novels. Nancy murders a child to prevent her mistress, Temple Drake, from leaving home and breaking up her marriage. Nancy has much of the same moral fervor—the nun or saint-like quality—that distinguishes Sethe. And Nancy is also ostracized and thought of as unnatural by her community. Like Faulkner, Morrison seems to believe—and the

Oprah Winfrey bought the film rights to Toni Morrison's book shortly after its publication in 1987.

film follows her conviction—that her murderer/saint poses extreme questions about love and morality, about life and death, that the community would otherwise not confront. Neither author excuses murder, yet both focus on the murder of a child in such a way as to deprive the murderer of any real sympathy—no matter how great the evil their extreme act is supposed to prevent. Nancy's murder does indeed incite Temple Drake to reflect on her corrupt past, but what exactly is the function of Sethe's murder?

Winfrey and Glover perform their roles with considerable dignity and sophistication, but the story (or lack thereof) lets them down again and again. After the first scene the horror of slavery is a given. But then what? That's what Paul D. wants to know, and he asks the question like a character who wishes he had another story in which to function. Beah Richards (Baby Suggs) has wonderful character written into her face and she performs her role as grandmother and preacher with conviction, yet the scenes in which she urges children to laugh and men to dance are embarrassing. She is supposed to be a holy woman and a life force, but her story (whatever her story might be) is not integrated into the film. *Beloved* is static, a series of set pieces, of scenes meant to illustrate an allegory of right and wrong.

The real disaster of *Beloved,* however, is Thandie Newton, who plays Beloved, the child Sethe murdered but who comes back to life—a drooling, demanding, ghost-made-flesh who is just irritating to watch. She craves her mother's love, but she is all consuming and vanishes when the black community comes to exorcise her from Sethe's house. (Why the community comes around to Sethe is puzzling. It is another one of those poorly motivated scenes in the film.)

Director Jonathan Demme has to be held responsible for not disciplining Newton's performance and for giving in to moralism—the same kind of good intentioned bad art that marred his film on AIDS, *Philadelphia* (1993). Too many of the characters in his recent films, including *The Silence of the Lambs* (1991), are too good or too evil to be true. Not much has changed in Hollywood film. Even the earnest, well-meaning productions just have to jerk tears and project a cloying vision of the moral high ground.

—*Carl Rollyson*

CREDITS

Sethe: Oprah Winfrey
Paul D: Danny Glover
Beloved: Thandie Newton
Denver: Kimberley Elise
Baby Suggs: Beah Richards
Younger Sethe: Lisa Gay Hamilton
Stamp Paid: Albert Hall
Ella: Irma P. Hall
Mr. Bodwin: Jason Robards

Origin: USA
Released: 1998
Production: Edward Saxon, Jonathan Demme, Gary Goetzman, Oprah Winfrey, and Kate Forte for Harpo Films and Clinica Estetico; released by Touchstone Pictures
Direction: Jonathan Demme
Screenplay: Akosua Busia, Richard LaGravenese, and Adam Brooks; based on the novel by Toni Morrison
Cinematography: Tak Fujimoto
Editing: Carol Littleton, Andy Keir
Music: Rachel Portman
Production design: Kristi Zea
Art direction: Tim Galvin
Costumes: Colleen Atwood
Sound: Willie D. Burton
MPAA rating: R
Running Time: 172 minutes

REVIEWS

Entertainment Weekly. October 23, 1998, p. 45.
New York Times. October 16, 1998, p. E1.
People. October 19, 1998, p. 39.
Variety. October 5, 1998, p. 67.
Village Voice. October 20, 1998, p. 155.

The Best Man; Il Testimone dello Sposo

On her wedding day she was very much in love. Unfortunately, not with the groom.—Movie tagline

A tale of uncontrollable passion and undeniable love.—Movie tagline

"Wonderful!"—Gayle Lee, *CBS Radio*

"A lovely portrait. Ines Sastre is extraordinarily stunning."—Elizabeth Weitzman, *Time Out New York*

B eautiful Francesca Babini (Ines Sastre) is a very good daughter. She must be because, although her intended revolts her, she is going to go through with an arranged marriage because if she doesn't it will mean the financial ruin and humiliation of her middle-class family. Set in 1899, in the provincial northern Italian town of Sasso, Pupi takes a look at bourgeois society and its strictures with his film *The Best Man*.

Francesca's fiancé is homely Edgardo Osti (Dario Cantarelli), an older, wealthy, and pompous businessman

Francesca (Ines Sastre) to Angelo (Diego Abantantuono): "You came to save me!"

who has a reputation as a womanizer. But the unexpected happens to Francesca as she heads for the altar—she gets a gander at the bridegroom's best man, Angelo Beliossi (Diego Abantantuono). Angelo has just returned to his hometown from a long stay in the U.S., where he apparently made a substantial fortune. Instantly smitten by the handsome millionaire, a dazzled Francesca secretly says her vows with Angelo in mind—as she tells the bewildered man during the wedding reception when she madly throws herself at him. Angelo may not be similarly love struck but, as the reception gets underway, he can't help but be flattered (and eventually does fall for the girl).

There's a string of amusing moments as old rituals clash headlong with would-be modern sensibilities (it is literally the end of the century since the wedding is taking place on New Year's Eve). Everyone at the reception gets involved with the gift-giving and the preparing of the bridal chamber, while being scandalized by the new bride's less-than-uxorious behavior. Angelo makes a wedding toast to the effect that it's nice to see that his old hometown has prospered only to learn that it's mostly cosmetic and that the rich have only gotten richer at the expense of the poor. Angelo also finally admits to the love struck Francesca that his own fortune was not self-made, indeed he failed in America, but is the result of a legacy from his brother. Meanwhile, the groom is deciding just how to handle his awkward situation (Francesca has no intention of consummating their union).

Pupi's is a lightweight romance with an attractive leading actress whose character wavers between petulance, wilfulness, and hysteria and two capable, if unexciting, leading men. The film provides a number of visual treats and a sweeping orchestral score to highlight its old-fashioned escapism. 🎞

—*Christine Tomassini*

CREDITS

Francesca Babini: Ines Sastre
Angelo Beliossi: Diego Abantantuono
Edgardo Osti: Dario Cantarelli
Olimpia Babini: Valeria D'Obici
Sisto Babini: Mario Erpichini

Origin: Italy
Released: 1997
Production: Aurelio De Laurentiis and Antonio Avati for Filmauro-Duea Film; released by October Films
Direction: Pupi Avati
Screenplay: Pupi Avati
Cinematography: Pasquale Rachini
Editing: Amedeo Salfa
Music: Riz Ortolani
Production design: Alberto Cottignoli, Steno Tonelli
Costumes: Vittoria Guaita
MPAA rating: PG
Running Time: 100 minutes

REVIEWS

Austin Chronicle. September 14, 1998.
Los Angeles Times. August 21, 1998, p. F6.
New York Times. August 14, 1998, p. E12.
San Francisco Chronicle. August 21, 1998, p. C5.
Variety. February 9, 1998, p. 71.

Beyond Silence

A German nominee for Best Foreign Language Film at the 1998 Academy Awards, Caroline Link's *Beyond Silence* is the sensitive, touching story of a girl born to deaf-mute parents and her struggle to realize her musical talents in a household that cannot appreciate her gift. The film is a fine treatment of the complex ways parents and children relate to each other, and, if it loses its focus near the end and turns increasingly melodramatic, it is nonetheless a beautifully told story.

At the center of the film is Lara (played as a child by Tatjana Trieb and as an 18-year-old by Sylvie Testud), the daughter of Martin (Howard Seago) and Kai (Emmanuelle Laborit). Lara herself is not hearing-impaired; she communicates with her parents through sign language and often serves as a translator for them to the hearing world. The film is in German and German sign language, and all forms of communication are subtitled so that the film is accessible to everyone.

Young Lara seems to have a fairly happy childhood and is quite mature and strong-willed for her years, although her parents' dependence on her seems to be holding her back in school. At Christmas, Martin's sister, Clarissa (Sibylle Canonica), plays the clarinet, and Lara's luminous smile shows she is drawn to the music. Clarissa gives Lara the clarinet she had as a child, and Lara immediately shows great interest and aptitude for the instrument. Lara is attracted not just to the music but to her pretty, sophisticated aunt, who represents a life beyond Lara's mundane world. Clarissa even introduces Lara to make-up and cuts her hair to look like hers as a child. In some sense, Clarissa is the stereotypical childless aunt who lures the niece away from her parents, and yet Clarissa is more than that—she is opening up a new world to the little girl. Lara rides bicycles with her aunt and Uncle Gregor (Matthias Habich), and, when she comes home, asks her mother why she cannot ride a bicycle; Kai's deafness makes it hard for her to keep her balance, but Lara does get her mother to give it a try.

Clarissa's gift actually re-opens old family rivalries between her and Martin, who felt shut out of his sister's world and now fears losing his daughter to the world of music. The screenplay is very insightful about the ways family conflicts can simmer over the years and resurface in a new context. According to Clarissa, her brother was the favorite in the family and could do no wrong. In a flashback to their childhood, we learn of Martin's jealousy of his sister's talent and see him laugh during her first concert; she never played in front

Martin (Howard Seago) in sign language: "Lightning is loud." Daughter Lara (Tatjana Trieb) replies: "Lightning is silent, like the moon."

of him again. Kai is more sensitive than her husband and urges him to be more accepting of Lara so that mistakes of the last generation will not be perpetuated in the next.

Despite her father's disapproval, Lara continues to play. She becomes part of the school orchestra, where the music teacher takes her under his wing. She has a clarinet solo at a school production, but sadly her parents are conspicuously missing from the audience. During this scene, the film makes a transition to a performance years later when Lara is 18. Both her teacher and Clarissa want Lara to fulfill her potential, but of course the inevitable conflict with her parents will have to be faced. The matter comes to a head at a family dinner where it is revealed that Lara is planning to leave home to live with Clarissa in Berlin. There she will be able to practice for an entrance audition into a prestigious conservatory. Martin is outraged at the news and even throws his wine at his sister. No matter how badly Martin behaves, however, Seago never plays him as an unsympathetic brute trying to stifle his daughter. (The father-daughter dynamic in *Beyond Silence* is a tender version of the father-son conflict in 1996's *Shine*—both films feature young protagonists trying to break free of their families to study music, but Martin's treatment of Lara never comes close to the abuse depicted in *Shine*.) Martin has lived so long with Lara helping him that he fears losing her and her help. In a poignant yet disturbing moment, he even confesses that sometimes he wishes she were deaf so she would be totally in his world. However, Martin's lack of understanding is balanced by Kai's empathy when she buys two tickets to a clarinet concert she and Lara can attend together.

While *Beyond Silence* eloquently explores large issues of parent-child relationships, it distinguishes itself in the small moments, the everyday ways deaf parents and their children relate. There are, for example, humorous scenes of little Lara as a translator for her parents. When Martin and Kai are having financial problems and Lara is the intermediary at the bank, she does not translate everything her father signs because she does not want to beg, and, later, at a parent-teacher conference, she selectively edits the conversation to make herself look good. Even as Lara dutifully helps her parents, Trieb shows us the independent spirit inside this little girl. There are also touching scenes like Lara sitting in front of a television and translating the romantic movie her mom is watching and a teenage Lara explaining to her father the sound of snow and finally settling on the notion that it makes the world quieter.

When Lara goes to Berlin, the world opens up for her. Clarissa takes her to a nightclub, where Clarissa plays the clarinet and even asks her niece to join her onstage. We see Lara take great joy in her music and begin to prepare for her entrance exams, but her aunt does not like the melancholy pieces of music she has chosen—a bone of contention that could have been explored more fully.

While the first part of the film focuses on Lara's love of music and the conflict this rekindles in a family already fractured in the past, once Lara is on her way to realizing her dream, the film devolves into a series of clichéd plot turns that detract from Lara's music. Lara meets a teacher of the deaf, Tom (Hansa Czypionka), and they eventually go on a date. While their scenes show Lara opening up to new people beyond her family and are quite sweet, the love interest feels like obligatory plot filler designed to give Lara something to do in the big city. Then Lara learns of her mother's death in a bicycle accident—a heavily foreshadowed event since Kai first rode a bike very unsteadily. Since Lara herself had encouraged her mother to take up bicycle riding, predictably enough her father ends up blaming Lara for the accident. Between the romance and the mother's death, the plot flounders, as if the filmmakers did not know what to do with Lara in Berlin (daily clarinet practice would be too boring). Indeed, the mother's death becomes a plot device to bring Lara back home to renew her conflict with her father.

 Howard Seago speaks American Sign while Emmanuelle Laborit speaks French Sign; both learned German Sign Language for the film.

Lara goes to the clarinet recital she was supposed to have attended with her mother (in a heavy-handed shot, a chair remains conspicuously empty next to her). Tom comes to visit her and spends the night, and the next morning Martin discovers them asleep together. Later, in an argument in which Martin confronts Lara with her transgression and she articulates her resentment for her father's deafness and the way it has trapped her, he ends up kicking her out of the house.

Lara then returns to Clarissa, and, in an underwritten confrontation, accuses her aunt of wanting her to do well but not better than she has done and of not encouraging her. The problem is that Lara's anger bursts out of nowhere. While it is true that Clarissa tried to influence Lara's choice of music, without her aunt, Lara probably would have never begun a musical career in the first place. It feels as if, after Lara's falling-out with her father, the filmmakers want to balance it with a falling-out with the aunt so we can see Lara's burgeoning independence from everyone. At the very least, the conflict with Clarissa should have been more fully developed.

To prepare for her entrance exam, Lara moves in with her uncle, who has separated from Clarissa, and Lara's nine-year-old sister comes to visit. Since she is 300 miles from home, Clarissa must drive her back, which culminates in a rather moving scene in which Clarissa tries to get Martin to come back with her to see Lara. Sitting in her car, Clarissa uses sign language to communicate with him standing in his house but is unable to break down his barriers. Nonetheless, they seem to acknowledge the stubbornness they share, and the scene plants the seeds for the film's reconciliation.

In the film's concluding scene, Lara goes to her entrance exam. She has chosen a piece of klezmer music, which she has grown fond of. Just as she is about to start playing, though, her father appears in the back of the auditorium. At first she is flustered by his appearance but sees he has taken a big step in coming to see her perform, and soon she regains her footing and plays her piece well. Communicating through sign language, they reach a kind of understanding as Lara assures her father, "You'll never lose me."

CREDITS

Lara: Sylvie Testud
Lara as a child: Tatjana Trieb
Martin: Howard Seago
Kai: Emmanuelle Laborit
Clarissa: Sibylle Canonica
Tom: Hansa Czypionka
Gregor: Matthias Habich

Origin: Germany
Released: 1997
Production: Thomas Wobke, Jacob Claussen, and Luggi Waldleitner; released by Miramax Films
Direction: Caroline Link
Screenplay: Caroline Link and Beth Serlin
Cinematography: Gernot Roll
Editing: Patricia Rommel
Music: Niki Reiser
Production design: Susann Bieling
MPAA rating: PG-13
Running Time: 97 minutes

REVIEWS

Detroit Free Press. June 26, 1998, p. 9D.
Detroit News. June 26, 1998, p. 9C.
Entertainment Weekly. June 19, 1998, p. 52.
Los Angeles Times. June 5, 1998, p. F18.
New York Times. June 5, 1998, p. E12.
New York Times. June 11, 1998, p. E11.
Village Voice. June 9, 1998, p. 148.
Washington Post. June 12, 1998, p. B5.
Washington Post Weekend. June 12, 1998, p. 44.

The film does not offer easy solutions but suggests at the end that Martin may be on his way to making peace with his daughter's choice. The performances are universally fine, and Tatjana Trieb is especially charming as the young Lara. Even when the film veers toward melodrama, the actors keep the emotions realistic, and the film does not turn Martin (or anyone else) into a stock villain. *Beyond Silence* finally is quite illuminating about the challenges for the child of deaf parents but also insightful about the grudges that poison family relationships, the barriers between parents and children in general, and the pain of separation when a child strikes out on a path a parent cannot share.

—Peter N. Chumo II

The Big Hit

Nothing's more dangerous than some nice guys ...with a little time to kill.—Movie tagline

"An outrageous action comedy!"—Sarah Edwards, *ABC-TV*

"*The Big Hit* is the last word in good-time mayhem."—Jay Carr, *Boston Globe*

"A direct hit to the funny bone. Wahlberg delivers a pitch-perfect, comically straight performance."—Michael Rechtstaffen, *Hollywood Reporter*

"*The Big Hit* is fun, big time!"—Susan Wloszcyna, *USA Today*

"*Hit* is hot, hip and hilarious."—Bill Bregoli, *Westwood One*

 Box Office: $27,066,941

Hitman Melvin Smiley (Mark Wahlberg) finds himself in some hot water with his crime boss after a kidnapping scheme goes haywire in the action/comedy *The Big Hit*.

In the wild and hilarious action satire *The Big Hit*, Mark Wahlberg continues his career of portraying innocents at the center of mayhem and sleaze. In *Traveller* (1997), the baby-faced Wahlberg was a novice con man who can't stomach the ruthless ways of an Irish-American clan. In *Boogie Nights* (1997), he was a babe in the woods of the porno industry, a lame-brained innocent oblivious to the human wreckage surrounding him. In *The Big Hit*, Wahlberg portrays a hit man with a heart of gold who so much wants to be loved that he is thoroughly exploited by his girlfriends and partners in crime.

Wahlberg eats up these kind of roles. In *The Big Hit*, he gets to exaggerate both his cartoonish machismo and his soft-voiced cuddliness. Mostly, he wears a hangdog expression. The wisecracking conceit of *The Big Hit* is that Walhberg's character, called Melvin and nicknamed Skipper, is just another working stiff who gets taken advantage of at home and at the office. He's like Dagwood on speed.

Once again, Wahlberg's performance is mesmerizing. Even in the thinnest situations, his characters have tremendous appeal. It's hard not to like the guy, even when he's blowing people away. Wahlberg and the filmmakers take full advantage of his puppy-dog appeal, exploiting the discrepancy between his powerful physical artillery and his emotional helplessness. *The Big Hit* is so savvy it makes Walhberg's own style a key element of its take-no-prisoners satire.

The Big Hit is veteran Hong Kong director Che-Kirk Wong's first American release. With the aid of executive producer John Woo and producer Wesley Snipes, it is a snappy debut. Writer Ben Ramsey's screenplay has the cartoonish swagger and broad visual and verbal gags that fit the Hong Kong action-comedy genre. To American audiences, the combination of over-the-top action sequences played straight and outrageous slapstick spoof is a mixture that seems fresh.

It takes half a reel into the film to understand what Wong is aiming for. Melvin and his buddies stage an elaborate and completely unexplained hit job on a businessman and his cronies in a hotel. They prepare by dressing as construction workers but wear infrared helmets. One crew member cuts the electricity, the place goes dark, and Melvin and the team enter spraying bullets, hurling explosives, executing jump-kicks, swinging from ropes, and generally acting like action superheroes. Melvin does most of the work while his buddies stop for a coffee break or to ogle the women held hostage by the bad guys. The sequence climaxes in spectacular fashion as Melvin bungees out an upper floor of the high rise and is snapped back toward the inferno just as his explosive device detonates. He's fine, of course: just another day at the office.

After the hit, Cisco, an over-the-top trash-talking killer played with gusto by Lou Diamond Phillips, steals the credit for taking out the prime target and claims the $25,000 reward from big boss Paris (Avery Brooks). Even though Melvin shot the man, he lets his co-worker take the money. Melvin is a professional killer, but he can't stand up to anybody.

Melvin's whipped by not one, but two, gold-mining girlfriends: a Jewish American princess fiancee, Pam (Christina Applegate), and an African-American party girl, Chantel (Lela Rochon). Pam is always hitting him up for money to loan her parents, while Chantel wants a constant flow of cash to keep her in expensive cars and jewels. Melvin's so eager to please that he keeps taking on hit jobs to earn more money just to keep his women satisfied. The dual relationships are treated as if Melvin is the henpecked husband in both. No wonder he's constantly gulping down Maalox.

Film debut of China Chow.

Melvin also can't stand to lose his one-sided friendship with Cisco. As played with ridiculous swagger by Phillips, Cisco is an obviously out-for-himself hood who delights just as much in shafting Melvin as he does in offing his targets. Melvin is also bedeviled by a neighbor upset because Melvin keeps driving into his driveway in their cookie-cutter subdivision. And tense scenes are often interrupted by calls from

a screaming nerd of a video store manager (Danny Smith) who wants Melvin to return an overdue copy of *King Kong Lives!*

These and other peripheral characters are absurdly drawn. One gang member named Crunch (Bokeem Woodbine) has just discovered masturbation and no longer is interested in bedding down females, as he'd done since he was 10. There's another knit-cap-wearing gang member who is such a dolt that he can't complete a simple sentence. Paris is a Black Godfather stereotype. Pam's very stereotyped Jewish parents are played by little-used veterans Lainie Kazan and Elliott Gould. Kazan's Jeanne is an aging multiple-plastic-surgery victim, all big hair, jewels and outrageous outfits. Gould's Morton is a burping, beer-bellied, long-suffering alcoholic prone to fits of devastating honesty when drunk.

When Melvin desperately agrees to a freelance job headed by Cisco, the movie shifts into high gear as kung-fu screwball comedy. The gang's target is Keiko Nishi (China Chow), the daughter of a Japanese industrialist. Unfortunately, the gang isn't aware that Keiko's father has gone bankrupt bankrolling a flop biopic titled "Taste the Golden Spray." They also don't know that he's a bosom buddy of Paris. And their victim is uncooperative in the extreme. Keiko is a preppy schoolgirl with a smart mouth. In one of the funniest send-ups in the film, Keiko tries to read an ungrammatical ransom note into a tape recorder. "I have been abduct," she deadpans. "These men mean businesses."

Chow is a real find who helps the last half of the movie sizzle. She's sharp as a tack and disarmingly sensual. Before her Keiko ensnares Wahlberg's Melvin, he must keep her hidden in his garage as Pam's parents pay a visit. She keeps escaping, hopping through the house bound and gagged, narrowly missing encounters with the folks.

Wong has great fun with the clash between Melvin's suburban, middle-class ambitions and his unusual avocation. Melvin keeps his huge arsenal of weapons in a concealed case behind a tool cabinet in the garage. He drags bags of dismembered victims out to the garbage, trying to avoid the neighbor's dogs. He forgets that he has left his kidnap victim in the trunk of his sports utility vehicle as Pam and her parents drive it away to go to the synagogue.

As her parents try to convince Pam to dump Melvin because he's not Jewish, Melvin plans to win them back by cooking a kosher dinner. Keiko offers to help, and they find romance while stuffing a chicken. It's a wonderfully sensual scene, but even this is played as satire. Just as Melvin and

Keiko (China Chow) to her kidnappers: "What's up with you guys? You supposed to be the Spice Boys or something?"

Keiko are about to go at it, she bops him over the head with a rolling pin.

All this is prelude to a wild ending which features a shootout in front of Pam's parents, car chases and crashes, narrow escapes, and Melvin on foot trying to outrun Cisco's predatory automobile. Melvin wants to return the videotape and run away with Keiko, but he never considers renounc-

CREDITS

Melvin Smiley: Mark Wahlberg
Cisco: Lou Diamond Phillips
Keiko Nishi: China Chow
Pam Shulman: Christina Applegate
Vince: Antonio Sabato Jr.
Crunch: Bokeem Woodbine
Paris: Avery Brooks
Jeanne Shulman: Lainie Kazan
Morton Shulman: Elliott Gould
Chantel: Lela Rochon

Origin: USA
Released: 1998
Production: Warren Zide and Wesley Snipes for Amen Ra Films, Zide-Perry, and Lion Rock; released by TriStar Pictures
Direction: Che-Kirk Wong
Screenplay: Ben Ramsey
Cinematography: Danny Nowak
Editing: Robin Russell, Pietro Scalia
Music: Graeme Revell
Production design: Taavo Soodor
Art direction: Andrew Stern, Craig Lathrop
Costumes: Margaret Mohr
Sound: Douglas Ganton
MPAA rating: R
Running Time: 91 minutes

ing his profession as part of his romantic vows. For her part, Keiko says she'd like the "constant adrenaline rush" provided by his hit man pursuits. The final confrontation takes place in the video store, underlining the point that *The Big Hit* is intended as escapist entertainment.

The Big Hit has the makings of a cult favorite. It's relentlessly bizarre and funny with a refreshing, unabashed directness. This is broad, raucous, slick, and wondrous fun. Writer Ramsey and director Wong have a fine ear for the stock phrases that litter the films they satire. Wahlberg makes another step in building a career as a versatile, charming and solid actor. And Chow is a real discovery. Her Keiko combines sass, smarts, and sex appeal. Phillips is hilarious, and Gould even manages a showstopping scene, berating his wife and daughter in a drunken stupor as the hit men draw guns on each other beneath the dinner table.

As a cartoonish piece of live action, *The Big Hit* never pauses for breath. Both the action and the comedy come nonstop. Wong doesn't worry about loose ends; his is a slapstick style that manages to make the Hong Kong action-comedy genre more accessible to American audiences. Wong takes aim at all manner of movie conventions, and scores much more often than he misses. *The Big Hit* is daring, ribald, wacky, and a whole lot of fun if you're in the mood for offbeat entertainment.

—*Michael Betzold*

REVIEWS

Boxoffice. June, 1998, p. 76.
Detroit Free Press. April 24, 1998, p. 4D.
Detroit News. April 24, 1998, p. 3C.
Entertainment Weekly. May 8, 1998, p. 51.
Los Angeles Times. April 24, 1998, p. F6.
USA Today. April 24, 1998, p. 6E.
Variety. April 27, 1998, p. 59.
Village Voice. May 5, 1998, p. 124.

The Big Lebowski

"A wildly entertaining comedy!"—Dan DiNicola, *CBS-TV*

"Hilarious, highly entertaining! It put a smile on my face that never left."—Michael Wilmington, *Chicago Tribune*

"Excellent! The funniest spin on the detective film in years!"—Marshall Fine, *Gannett Newspapers*

"A big winner! Jeff Bridges is hilarious!"—Anne Marie O'Connor, *Mademoiselle*

"Mr. Bridges finds a role so right for him that he seems never to have been anywhere else." —Janet Maslin, *New York Times*

"A blazingly original comedy!"—Bruce Williamson, *Playboy*

"Hilarious and wicked fun!"—Peter Travers, *Rolling Stone*

 Box Office: $17,498,804

In one scene in *The Big Lebowski*, the latest film by the Coen Brothers, a pornographer named Jackie Treehorn (Ben Gazarra) complains about the falling standards in adult entertainment: "We're competing with those amateurs who can't afford to invest in those little extras like story, production value, feelings." His pose as the serious artist in a world of profit-minded hacks may be a joke by the Coens at the expense of critics who have faulted many of their films for a lack of structure and purpose. A phone call interrupts Jackie's artistic lament, and the Dude (Jeff Bridges), who has been brought to Treehorn to explain the whereabouts of a missing briefcase with a million dollars, watches Jackie jot some notes, tear off the page, and hurry away. Thinking he can now finally learn something about these bizarre events, the Dude colors in on the scratch pad the impression left by Jackie's writing and discovers that Jackie had drawn an obscene picture while talking on the phone. The hint of some longed-for meaning has led only to another dead end. Welcome to the world of Joel and Ethan Coen.

The film's quirky appeal combines the flavors of Cheech and Chong, Busby Berkeley, and Raymond Chandler or to phrase the analogy in the world of the Coen Brothers, the film noir of *Blood Simple,* the comedy of *Raising Arizona,*

The Stranger (Sam Elliott): "This is how the whole durned human comedy perpetuates itself."

and the moral starkness of *Fargo*. The Dude's real name is Jeff Lebowski. He is a drugged-out derelict of the sixties. In the opening scene he wears his bathrobe to the grocery store, samples the milk at the dairy case, and writes a check for sixty-seven cents at the register. When he gets home, two thugs await in his darkened house. They grab the Dude, drag him to the bathroom, and repeatedly submerge his head in the toilet while they shout, "Where's the money, Lebowski?" The Dude's unflappable nature can be heard in his cool reply after the third dunking: "It's down there somewhere; let me take another look." They oblige him. "Our lead characters always seem to be dopes and schmoes," said Ethan Coen, "and this one is no exception."

It soon develops that there are two Jeff Lebowskis. The other one (David Huddleston) is a wealthy mogul whose young wife Bunny (Tara Reid) is deeply in debt to Jackie Treehorn, the porn tycoon. The Dude and his bowling buddy Walter (John Goodman), a Vietnam vet who finds endless analogies to the war in everyday life, reason out the mistake behind the thugs' attack while they practice for their upcoming tournament. (Bowling, the Coens explained, was chosen since it is "the only sport you can do when you're drinking and smoking.") The Dude pays a visit to the wealthy Lebowski and asks him to replace the Oriental rug Treehorn's thugs ruined. When Bunny Lebowski later disappears and a ransom note arrives, the rich Lebowski remembers the Dude and enlists him as the perfect bag man to make the drop. Wanting only to get a new rug and perhaps a percentage of Bunny's recovery fee, the Dude agrees. Walter, however, wants the whole million. He stuffs his dirty underwear ("whites only," he explains to the Dude) into a satchel to substitute for the briefcase with the million, which they put in the trunk of the Dude's car (without opening the briefcase, a deficiency in the plotting that the Coens' do not hide very well). When they later return to the parking lot after bowling a few frames, the car with the briefcase is gone. The remainder of the film becomes a wild pursuit of the briefcase by a growing number of interested parties, among them three vicious German nihilists (Peter Stormare, Flea, Torsten Voges) and the rich Lebowski's avant-guard artist-daughter Maude (Julianne Moore).

The strength of this and of the Coens' other six films is in their not "on-the-nose" quality. In screenwriting parlance it is ineffective to be too on-the-nose (too pat, too predictable). The Coens specialize in avoiding this deficiency. Nearly every scene in *The Big Lebowski* eventually springs for at least a moment to unpredictable life, and a handful of scenes maintain their surprises. Can you have too much of a good thing? Those who fault the Coens probably do so for the same reasons, arguing that they have taken their love of originality and fear of the predictable and pushed them too far, resulting too often in eccentricity for its own sake.

There is evidence for both claims. The first meeting between the Dude and Lebowski, for example, ends with the rich man refusing to pay for the Dude's rug and ejecting him with a series of shouts about freeloaders. In the hall, however, the Dude calmly tells Lebowski's attendant that the meeting went fine, that Lebowski told him to take any rug in the house, which he does. He also meets Bunny outside painting her toenails purple and inviting him to blow on them. Later, when the Dude meets again with Lebowski after the botched payment

Steve Buscemi and Peter Stormare appeared as the criminal partners in the Coen film *Fargo.*

of ransom money, he unwraps the gauze around a severed toe with a purple toenail that Lebowski had received in the mail, both a sign that the kidnappers are serious about harming their victim and a plot point that injects fresh energy into the film. In another example, when the German nihilists crash into the Dude's house to threaten him, they do so by dropping a hungry ferret into his bubble bath. (Or is it a marmot, as the Dude calls it? The Coens told interviewers that a marmot was actually too big but that they liked the Dude's confidence in thinking he could identify the ferret on the leash.)

However, for each of these not on-the-nose moments that bring the film to life, there is another that seems merely bizarre. Julianne Moore's mannered speaking voice, for example, recalls the inflections of the young Katharine Hepburn, which also describes the way Jennifer Jason Leigh delivered her lines in the Coens' *The Hudsucker Proxy.* One film's not on-the-nose touch can become the next film's cliche. One of the best expressions of these two views of the Coens' work is Owen Gleiberman's review of the film in *Entertainment Weekly* (March 6, 1998, pp. 52-53).

The many reviewers who documented the off-kilter nature of *The Big Lebowski* and concluded simply that audiences will either love or hate the film based on their overall response to the movies of the Coen Brothers may have misperceived the film's sometime fumbling, uncertain pace. Many scenes begin with extraneous material—characters being led into rooms through doors and down hallways against the conversational backdrop of the Dude's ongoing ramblings—and other scenes continue past a point of maximum dramatic interest. For example, in the Dude's second scene with Maude Lebowski, he strolls into her studio and meets another eccentric, Knox Harrington (David Thewlis), who is described as a video artist. The Dude tries unsuccessfully to determine who this John Waters look-alike is while he makes himself a drink. Knox giggles through most of the conversation between the Dude and Maude. Like other such moments, the anticipation and build-up fail to find a satisfactory resolution.

In another example, Walter later smashes the new car that he believes has been bought by a boy who stole the million-dollar briefcase. The punchline to this scene (that the car really belongs to the boy's neighbor) is telegraphed by the many cutaways to lights being turned on up and down the street while Walter bangs away with his crow bar. It is as if the Coens cannot resist savoring their own comic ingenuity by adding these needless shots. On the whole, the Coens are better at designing than at executing their jokes. Some trimming for pace would make the film more accessible to a larger audience since many viewers will lose pa-

CREDITS

The Dude: Jeff Bridges
Walter Sobchak: John Goodman
Maude Lebowski: Julianne Moore
The Big Lebowski: David Huddleston
Donny: Steve Buscemi
Jesus Quintana: John Turturro
Brandt: Philip Seymour Hoffman
Jackie Treehorn: Ben Gazzara
Knox Harrington: David Thewlis
Bunny Lebowski: Tara Reid
The Stranger: Sam Elliott
Nihilist: Peter Stormare
Nihilist: Flea
Nihilist: Torsten Voges

Origin: USA
Released: 1998
Production: Ethan Coen for Working Title; released by Polygram Filmed Entertainment
Direction: Joel Coen
Screenplay: Joel Coen and Ethan Coen
Cinematography: Roger Deakins
Editing: Roderick Jaynes, Tricia Cooke
Music: Carter Burwell
Production design: Rick Heinrichs
Art direction: John Dexter
Set decoration: Chris Spellman
Costumes: Mary Zophres
Sound: Allan Byer
Visual effects supervisor: Janek Sirrs
MPAA rating: R
Running Time: 127 minutes

tience with scenes that take so long to become coherent. The publicity for the film reported that the Coen Brothers not only write, produce, and direct but also edit their films (sometimes under pseudonyms). This hands-on approach may be effective for realizing their artistic vision, but it may also insulate them from the viewpoints of others that might prune and thereby improve their work.

In spite of its many clever and offbeat touches, *The Big Lebowski* was still something of a disappointment for the Coens after the critical and popular success of *Fargo*. The earlier film not only won two 1996 Oscars but also earned $24.4 million against a cost of only $6.5 million. The newer film received no nominations and barely earned back its cost of $15 million. The biggest part of the disappointment, however, may be in what was perceived as an artistic backward step for the Coens after the dark intelligence and cinematic discipline of *Fargo,* the most recent film named to the American Film Institute's list of the one hundred best American movies. Amid the higher expectations resulting from that success, the Coens chose merely to return to the self-indul-

gence and in-jokes of making movies seemingly for themselves and their most devoted fans. With more discipline *The Big Lebowski* could have accomplished much more.

—*Glenn Hopp*

REVIEWS

Entertainment Weekly. March 6, 1998, p. 52.
Hollywood Reporter. January 20, 1998, p. 20.
Los Angeles Times. March 6, 1998, p. F1.
New York Times. March 6, 1998, p. E31.
New Yorker. March 23, 1998, p. 98.
People. March 16, 1998, p. 19.
Rolling Stone. March 19, 1998, p. 71.
Time. March 2, 1998.
USA Today. March 6, 1998, p. 4D.
Variety. January 26, 1998, p. 68.
Village Voice. March 10, 1998, p. 61.
Washington Post Weekend. March 6, 1998, p. 50.

The Big One

The creator of *Roger & Me* and *TV Nation* is now protecting the Earth from the scum of corporate America.—Movie tagline

"Sensational! Witty and savagely intelligent!"
—*Entertainment Weekly*

"A lively and entertaining film!"—*New York Times*

"Wickedly funny!"—*Newsweek*

Michael Moore's anti-corporate message was well received in his book *Downsize This!*, which topped the *New York Times* bestseller list at one point. But his film *The Big One*, which documents the publicity tour for the book, suffers from a surprising lack of nerve, wit and wisdom and by Moore's fascination with his own persona.

Moore became a well-known gadfly of the rich and powerful with his 1989 film *Roger and Me*. In that film, he stalked former General Motors chairman Roger Smith with a camera and documented the automaker's abandonment of Moore's hometown, Flint, Michigan. His celebrity continued with a hit-and-miss television series, *TV Nation* and a dead-on-arrival John Candy fictional satirical film, *Canadian Bacon* (1996).

The latter film is much funnier and better realized than the overrated *Roger and Me*. And it is far superior to *The*

Big One, which is something of a belated sequel to *Roger and Me*. The trouble with Moore is that he has become enamored of his celebrity as a self-proclaimed champion of the working class. Few authors, even those who have achieved much more than Moore, would have the temerity to consider their own book tour a sufficient subject for a feature movie.

Moore attempts to use the book tour to paint a somewhat subversive picture of the United States at the close of the 20th century. In his view, the official story about a robust economy is a thin cover-up for the massive downsizing that has threatened the existence of an American middle class. And by far the best sequences in *The Big One* are the ones in which real people speak plainly about their difficult lives.

In one restaurant interview, an unnamed woman talks about how her struggle to make ends meet by working two jobs leaves her little time for her children. It's a direct and powerful if depressingly familiar statement about what's happened to the average American worker. Even more gripping is the woman standing in line to have Moore sign her book who reveals through teary eyes that she's been laid off that very day. "I don't know how they expect people to support their parents without health insurance," she says.

Moore's response is to give her a hug, tell her "you are not alone" and to "hang in there" and write in her book "downsized but not out." She tells him she feels better just by coming to see him. The trouble is not only that Moore's response to her is inadequate, even though it's probably his most genuine statement in the film. It's that Moore seems to revel in his own status as a self-made cult figure for the disenfranchised.

There are far too many scenes in this film of audiences cheering in lecture halls, of Moore doing rambling monologues that are rarely as funny or precious as he seems to think they are, and of empty sequences that go nowhere, such as Moore riffing with a member of the rock band Cheap Trick. Moore singing his own half-remembered version of Bob Dylan's classic "The Times They Are A Changin'" is downright embarrassing. A worse piece of celebrity self-stroking could not be found in a Barbra Streisand film.

Michael Moore: "If it's just about profit, why doesn't GM sell crack?"

Moore's direct statements are more forceful, particularly an excerpt from his appearance on Studs Terkel's radio show, in which he talks about corporate downsizing as a form of economic terrorism. But most of the movie is like too many other celebrity tour documentaries. Moore fills time by making fun of Random House book tour escorts, at one point even staging a ruse to get rid of one. It's pointless.

Worse yet, there's something disturbingly inauthentic about Moore's modus operandi. "Me, I've been out of work," he narrates at the film's beginning, attempting to place himself among the common people he champions. But in truth, Moore has been gainfully employed on a low tier of the American entertainment industry, attempting to use his wits to make a living espousing a populist point of view. There's nothing wrong with that, except Moore's insistence that he's been unemployed.

Going from town to town, Moore seems to stumble across displaced workers at opportune moments. Employees who make Pay Day candy bars for Leaf Corporation in Centralia, Illinois, have been laid off the very day Moore is in town. And the company has been sold to Hershey's the day he shows up at its Chicago headquarters. When he comes to Milwaukee, Johnson Controls is shutting down operations and moving to Mexico.

Whether or not these are real coincidences, *The Big One* has a sort of studied serendipity that seems forced if not downright faked. And Moore's main shtick, showing up at various corporate headquarters to try to meet with company executives, quickly grows tiresome. His gimmicks this time are to bring giant paychecks to company bosses and to present "Downsizer" awards.

These on-the-fly confrontations produce only what one might expect: various sorts of encounters with low-level flunkies, flacks, and security personnel. When the corporation tries to produce spokespeople to spar with Moore, he makes them look lame or silly. When staffers get heavy-handed, they look bad too. Moore uses the encounters to get in some jabs at corporate policies, but in the main he succeeds in making some working people look ridiculous. The lobby personnel he skewers are just as likely to be downsized as anyone else, but he never makes that connection.

Moore is never prepared to do anything really audacious or threatening to the corporations he visits. His antics never rise anywhere near the potent level of guerilla theater; he is not willing to risk that much. His is a sort of excuse-me presence that trades on his notoriety. Whenever authorities challenge him, he is apt to say "I'm Michael Moore," and fall back on his celebrity status as a talking point.

Since Moore has made a career out of stalking CEOs, one might think that an invitation to him from Nike chairman Philip Knight would produce a confrontation of great proportions. But although the surprise stop in Portland serves as the climax to the movie, it reveals Moore to have more bark than bite. Knight comes off looking a little ridiculous and quite pained; you can see the veins bulging out of his forehead as Moore gently questions his conscience over the issue of Indonesian sweatshops. But whenever Knight tries to enjoin a debate, there is an edit and a jump to another topic. Moore either has no good answer or doesn't want to "slow down" his book tour movie with real discussion.

Instead, we get characteristically meaningless Michael Moore theatre. Knight says the reason he doesn't make shoes in the United States is that Americans don't want jobs making shoes. So Moore flies back to Flint and asks workers who want to make Nikes to show up for a video. Some come in their Nikes, a point of delicious irony which is glossed over. Moore returns to Nike's Portland headquarters, shows Knight the video, and Knight backs out of what seemed to be an agreement to open a Flint factory. Moore finally extracts a pledge from Knight to donate $10,000 to Flint schools but only as a match for Moore's own donation. For doing that, Moore shakes his hand.

What's disturbing about this confrontation between gadfly and corporate boss is how deferential Moore seems to be and how willing to accept token offers of help from Knight and Nike. If corporations are really engaging in economic terrorism, Moore must be either incredibly naive or disingenuous to believe he can negotiate with a terrorist leader by simply being a friendly celebrity. And it speaks volumes that Moore can wave a free plane ticket to Asia, pledge $10,000 in cash, and crisscross the land by jet to make a point. Quite a cash reserve for a guy who says he's been out of work.

Moore occupies a unique position. He's one of the few filmmakers with his beliefs who can command at least the limited resources and clout to make a feature documentary that has a chance to be seen by more than a handful of political dissidents. If he did his homework, his movies could be powerful. But he tells viewers little beyond what everyone already knows, and he offers no real solution. For the most part he settles for playing the buffoon. And his buf-

foonery is not engaging. That's too bad. Moore's kind of populist challenge strikes a chord because it captures some disturbing truths about the American economy. But he flubs the opportunity to make a difference due to his endless enchantment with his own celebrity status. Moore has taken the same short road heavily traveled by many a rock star: from adolescent challenges to authority to comfort at being a show biz personality.

—*Michael Betzold*

CREDITS

Narrator: Michael Moore

Origin: USA
Released: 1998
Production: Kathleen Glynn for Dog Eat Dog Films and BBC Television; released by Miramax Films
Direction: Michael Moore
Cinematography: Brian Dantz, Chris Smith
Editing: Meg Reticker
Music: World Famous Blue Jays
Sound: Sarah Price
MPAA rating: PG-13
Running Time: 89 minutes

REVIEWS

Boxoffice. April, 1998, p. 200.
Detroit News. April 24, 1998, p. 3C.
Los Angeles Times. April 10, 1998, p. F12.
New York Times. April 10, 1998, p. E1.
People. May 4, 1998, p. 32.
Variety. September 15, 1997, p. 75.
Village Voice. April 7, 1998, p. 63.
Washington Post. April 10, 1998, p. B7.
Washington Post. April 19, 1998, p. G6.

Billy's Hollywood Screen Kiss

". . . crosses Pedro Almodovar with Woody Allen and adds gay camp!"—Cliff Rothman, *Los Angeles Times*

"Hilarious! . . . just try not laughing!"—Marc S. Malkin, *Out Magazine*

 Box Office: $2,100,430

Ever since Arthur Hiller's landmark *Making Love* (1982), gay-themed films have been slowly but steadily finding their way into the cultural mainstream. *In & Out* (1997) and *Jeffrey* (1995) have been two of the biggest films to deal directly with gay protagonists in a wide-release film. Most gay and lesbian-themed films, however, are small independent films which still play exclusively to gay audiences in few cities. *Billy's Hollywood*

Billy's (Sean P. Hayes) opening monologue: "My name is Billy, and I am a homosexual."

Screen Kiss is an independent film that deserves to be seen by more than just a gay audience.

An audience favorite at the 1998 Sundance Film Festival, this film requires nothing of its audience except a willingness to laugh and to get a little teary at the idea of romance. It is the story of Billy (Sean P. Hayes), a cute gay man who is having trouble meeting a man to love. He has trouble, that is, until he meets the ultra-handsome Gabriel (Brad Rowe) at a coffee house. Billy sets his cap for Gabriel immediately, and figures out a way to spend time with him: he convinces Gabriel to model for him (Billy's a photographer) for a series of photographs about the ultimate romantic screen kiss. Gabriel presumably will play a matinee idol in each of the photos, although Billy's artistic vision of the photo shoot is unclear.

After a series of misunderstandings and mishaps, Billy and Gabriel finally discover the true nature of their relationship, and the enigmatic Gabriel (is he or isn't he gay?) makes his intentions clear. Until then, the film, written and directed by Tommy O'Haver, is a breezy, charming romantic comedy, intended to be a gay/'90s version of the Doris Day films of the late '50 and early '60s, such as *Pillow Talk* (1959), with a few drag musical numbers thrown in for good measure. O'Haver has a way of making ordinary moments fun, such as when Billy begins to tell the sad story of his camera under a spotlight and soft music in the middle of his living room. When he tells the story later in the film, only with a different twist, we get the sense that O'Haver doesn't take anything too seriously, and it's delightful.

Writer/director O'Haver credits his debut feature *A Tommy O'Haver Trifle*

The film is romantic as well. Whether an audience member is gay or straight, they will surely identify with the wonderfully directed and performed scene in which Billy and Gabriel share a bed, each man having uncertainties about what he is doing there. It is tender and funny and thoroughly human, and that sense of humanity makes the film an effervescent charmer.

Now the bad news: there is a silly subplot involving Paul Bartel (director of *Eating Raoul*, 1982), which is excruciatingly overacted by Bartel and by Matthew Ashford, formerly of television's *General Hospital*. Production standards are very low-budget as well, and oftentimes the lighting and the two-person setups in front of obvious stage sets are awkward. Finally, some gay audiences have felt that this film's emphasis on a heterosexual-style romance is a betrayal to the realities of day-to-day living for gays and lesbians in the U.S. Be that as it may, none of these aforementioned problems are enough to bring down the film.

The biggest reason to see this film is Sean P. Hayes as Billy. When the film was a hit at the Sundance Film Festival, Hayes was tapped immediately to co-star in a major new series for NBC's fall 1998 schedule called *Will & Grace*. And for good reason: Hayes is a winning screen presence who has the ability to travel between sarcastic, self-deprecating humor and genuine pathos without missing a beat. His first sequence (a funny title sequence in which he tells the audience a bit about himself) is a fine contrast to the film's climax, where his sadness about his unrequited love is palpable. Hayes plays the true romantic without commenting on it, just as did Doris Day in those old movies. He's a winner.

Brad Rowe has also found success since the film was released, and though he doesn't seem to be quite the actor that Hayes is, it might be said that his pretty-boy role doesn't allow for as much, either. But Rowe is excellent as a young enigmatic man who must deal with the new world filled with gay people. Rowe as Gabriel learns something along the way, and it's a testament to him that he finds this aspect of the material.

O'Haver has done an excellent job with this film. One wonders what he'll be able to do with a big budget and a subject matter that general audiences won't shy away from.

— *Kirby Tepper*

CREDITS

Billy: Sean P. Hayes
Gabriel: Brad Rowe
Georgiana: Meredith Scott Lynn
Rex Webster: Paul Bartel
Perry: Richard Ganoung
Fernando: Armando Valdes-Kennedy
Gundy: Carmine Giovinazzo

Origin: USA
Released: 1998
Production: David Moseley for Revolutionary Eye; released by Trimark Pictures
Direction: Tommy O'Haver
Screenplay: Tommy O'Haver
Cinematography: Mark Mervis
Editing: Jeff Betancourt
Music: Alan Ari Lazar
Production design: Franco-Giacomo Carbone
Costumes: Julia Bartholomew
Sound: Jeff Bennett
MPAA rating: R
Running Time: 92 minutes

REVIEWS

Boxoffice. April, 1998, p. 181.
Entertainment Weekly. July 31, 1998, p. 50.
Los Angeles Times. July 24, 1998, p. F6.
New York Times. July 24, 1998, p. E14.
People. August 17, 1998, p. 28.
San Francisco Chronicle. July 24, 1998, p. C3.
San Francisco Examiner. July 24, 1998, p. C11.
Variety. February 2, 1998, p. 32.

Black Dog

The only way to stay safe is to stay moving.
—Movie tagline

"Great action movie."—Adam Weissler, *KCBS*

"If you like action you'll love *Black Dog*."—Lisa Sanders, *KCOP*

"Spectacular."—Gene Wyatt, *The Tennessean*

Box Office: $12,951,088

Black Dog is a chase film in the tradition of *Smokey and the Bandit* (1977), with elements of *The Road Warrior* (1982) and *Runaway Train* (1985) thrown in. Perhaps the prototype is *Wages of Fear* (*Le Salaire de la Peur* [1955]), or even John Ford's classic *Stagecoach* (1939). *Black Dog* delivers what it promises: a hair-raising series of battles between big rigs sideswiping each other, shootouts with assault rifles and Uzis, hand-to-hand fights aboard careening trucks, and plenty of voluptuous explosions. The viewer who is not swept away by the plot can at least appreciate the painstaking attention that went into choreographing the action. Evidently these sequences are shot while the vehicles are crawling at a snail's pace and the film is subsequently speeded up to create the illusion of impossible derring-do at breakneck speed. Director Kevin Hooks, cinematographer Buzz Feitshans IV, editors Debra Neil-Fisher and Sabrina Plisco-Morris, and their many assistants do a thoroughly professional job throughout.

Jack Crews (Patrick Swayze) used to be a knight of the road, but his career took a nosedive when he fell asleep behind the wheel of a truck and caused a fatal accident. This was the time he saw "the black dog," a legendary creature that appears to truck drivers who have been pressing themselves too hard and are about to pay the penalty. Crews spent two years in prison for vehicular manslaughter and lost his driver's license for life. He now works as a grease monkey for a big trucking firm and earns only a fraction of what he used to make in his glory days as a long-haul trucker.

His imprisonment and subsequent drop in income have created severe financial problems. His wife Melanie (Brenda Strong) tells him they are in foreclosure for a past-due amount of $9000. They are like a lot of couples these days: plagued by debt, squeezed by shrinking income, and bewildered by the invisible economic forces that are destroying their Amer-

ican dream. Crews decides to take a gamble for the sake of his wife and daughter Tracy (Erin Broderick). He has been offered $10,000 to make an "off the books" delivery of a suspect cargo from Georgia to New Jersey, a 15-hour trip if all goes well. Young Tracy adores her father and is adored by him. The viewer (who knows that all is certainly *not* going to go well on this little outing) will recognize Tracy as one of Hollywood's standard hostages-in-waiting. She is pretty, sweet, innocent, vulnerable, and just old enough so that when she is kidnapped by the bad guys, her father has to worry about her being sexually assaulted as well as murdered.

One has to wonder about the management of a firm that would pay an ex-con with no driver's license $10,000 to deliver a load of toilets, but the plot is not one of the movie's strong points. The shipper has no intention of letting Crews complete the delivery anyway. He plans to hijack his own load. To further complicate matters, both the F.B.I. and the Bureau of Alcohol, Tobacco and Firearms (ATF) have Crews' truck under close surveillance, hoping to track the concealed cargo to a kingpin dealing in AK-47s and other contraband weapons. The feds have planted an electronic tracking device in the trailer and have a helicopter discreetly following the big rig from the air. Aboard Crews' truck and in the sports car following him for protection are undercover agents working for the feds and for Bible-toting "Red" (Meat Loaf), a man who is so twisted that he hires people to high-jack his own merchandise. No one knows who anybody else really is. They all have portable telephones and place cryptic long-distance phone calls at every stopping point. Typically of 1990s movies, the paranoia and plot complications are piled precariously high on a routine story.

The producers undoubtedly expected their main profits to come via home video (what *Variety* likes to call "ancillary venues") over the longer haul. To keep their product from becoming dated-looking, they have employed the increasing popular practice of what might be called "pre-antiquing" it. When Crews is offered a brand-new rig for his run to New Jersey,

Eddie Rabbit's country classic "Drivin' My Life Away" is performed by Rhett Akins on the soundtrack.

he turns it down as being too conspicuous. This provides a palatable excuse for using a venerable Peterbilt 18-wheeler instead. The cars and trucks that escort and chase him, as well as the few vehicles they pass on the road, are all older models too. The producers avoid showing late-model police cars by having the interactions with highway patrol officers occur at weigh-in stations. The truckers all wear the kind of blue-collar work clothes that haven't changed in 50 years and will not change in another 50.

The winding roads are as sparsely traveled as roads in television commercials for luxury passenger cars. There are no farm houses or gas stations or billboards or fast-food joints in sight—nothing but hills and trees. There are not even any cows because they might get in the way of the vehicles when the drivers decide—as they frequently do—to leave the paved surface and plow through the open fields. The film is supposed to showcase Crews' exceptional driving ability, but he is no more or less talented than the other maniacs who are pursuing him. The bad guys never think of shooting out their quarry's tires; that would bring the story to a halt and spoil the fun. Instead they spray the sides of the Peterbilt with bullets and shoot out the windows in the cab.

Patrick Swayze has never been a great actor but has recorded some successes in his career, most notably in *Dirty Dancing* (1987) and the smash-hit *Ghost* (1990). *Black Dog* does not make the most of Swayze's limited acting talents. He has little to do but look worried all the time. Critic Bob Heisler of the *Los Angeles Times* wrote: "There's a camera in front of your windshield, Patrick. Do something for it." Heisler noted that Randy Travis, who plays Crews' partner, Earl, "acts rings around Swayze." Earl is an aspiring country music singer and composer. He provides an excuse for the relaxed country music soundtrack, which sometimes seems appropriate to the peaceful scenery and sometimes seems contrapuntal to all the vehicular pandemonium.

Crews manages to shake off one set of bad guys but still has to cope with the other set who work for his employer Cutler (Graham Beckel). In order to assure his loyalty, Cutler has quite predictably taken Melanie and Tracy as hostages. He tells Crews over the phone, "You've got a very pretty daughter," conveying manifold threats in standard bad-guy innuendo. Melanie and Tracy have nothing to do throughout this macho story except to hug each other and look scared. If this is anything like the typical way of getting illegal weapons distributed in this country, the operations obviously need a great deal of fine-tuning.

Three people are killed, and another wounded before the chase ends. By this time, Crews has wisely decided to throw in his hand with the law, even though he is risking jail time and the lives of his family. He arranges a rendezvous with Cutler and his men in one of those deserted dockyard settings so popular in action films where he says he will exchange the contraband goods for his wife and daughter. The feds show up and all hell breaks loose.

Black Dog could have used a little of the comic relief that was provided by Jackie Gleason in *Smokey and the Bandit*. It has that unremitting grimness and point A-to-point B relentlessness of *Runaway Train*. Scriptwriters William Mickelberry and Dan Vining have not given their story witty dialogue or funny sight gags but have provided one extra twist that makes it a little different from its bumper-car predecessors. The French might call the variation a *faux denouement*. Less cultured Hollywood types might call it a "fake wrap-

up." All of Crews' problems appear to be resolved after the big shootout. His wife and daughter are rescued unharmed. They enjoy the obligatory clinch. The F.B.I. and A.T.F. agents quickly assure Crews that (1) he will not be prosecuted for his participation in the smuggling operation, (2) his mortgage will be paid off as a reward for his cooperation, and (3) he will get his driver's license reinstated and will be able to go back to being a long-haul knight of the road.

At the request of the feds, Crews, along with Melanie and Tracy, is driving the tractor (the front part of the rig that consists of the cab and the diesel engine) to the impound yard. There is no traffic and the sun is shining on the peaceful landscape. The audience is expecting the superimposed credits to start crawling up from the bottom of the screen. Then, from out of nowhere, Red, the maddened villain, appears in another tractor. He is intent on killing Crews for foiling his beautiful operation. He will kill Melanie and Tracy for good measure.

Red is one of those villains who only exist in Hollywood movies. Like the criminal mastermind played by John Lithgow in *Cliffhanger* (1993), Red has been exposed and ruined. He is facing really hard time in a federal pen. He

CREDITS

Jack Crews: Patrick Swayze
Red: Meat Loaf
Earl: Randy Travis
Sonny: Gabriel Casseus
Wes: Brian Vincent
Melanie: Brenda Strong
Cutler: Graham Beckel
Agent McClaren: Stephen Tobolowsky
Agent Ford: Charles Dutton
Tracy: Erin Broderick

Origin: USA
Released: 1998
Production: Raffaella De Laurentiis, Peter Saphier, and Mark W. Koch for Prelude Pictures; released by Universal Pictures
Direction: Kevin Hooks
Screenplay: William Mickelberry and Dan Vining
Cinematography: Buzz Feitshans IV
Editing: Debra Neil-Fisher, Sabrina Plisco-Morris
Music: George S. Clinton
Production design: Victoria Paul
Art direction: Ken Hardy, Randall Richards
Costumes: Peggy Stamper
Sound: Mary Ellis
MPAA rating: PG-13
Running Time: 88 minutes

would be well advised to head for Mexico or South America without a moment's delay. Instead of that, he defies the U.S. government and single-handedly takes on the one man who has proven he can out-hustle and out-muscle any other lunatic on the road. This second ending (which leads to a predictable crash and explosion) provides a more appropriate conclusion to a wild action feature, while still including the happy reunited family.

—Bill Delaney

REVIEWS

Boxoffice. June, 1998, p. 75.
Detroit Free Press. May 2, 1998, p. 2A.
Entertainment Weekly. May 15, 1998, p. 74.
Los Angeles Times. May 4, 1998, p. F7.
New York Times. May 2, 1998, p. A20.
People. May 18, 1998, p. 37.
Variety. May 4, 1998, p. 84.

Blade

The power of an immortal. The soul of a human. The heart of a hero.—Movie tagline

"Ultra cool."—John Schofer, *Arizona Republic*

"Dazzling."—Tom Maurstad, *Dallas Morning News*

"Heart-stopping."—Jeanne Wolf, *Jeanne Wolf's Hollywood*

"*Blade* is a rock'em escapist romp."—Rod Dreher, *New York Post*

"Mesmerizing." William Arnold, *Seattle Post Intelligencer*

"Two thumbs up!"—*Siskel & Ebert*

Box Office: $70,095,974

Vampires do walk among us and it's up to half human/half vampire *Blade* (Wesley Snipes) to save us from their evil frenzy.

Marvel Comics' 1973 black superhero comes to the big screen in *Blade,* a high-octane gore-fest that grips you in its jaws (kinda like a pit bull) and refuses to let go. A brief prologue, set in 1967, shows a bloody, pregnant black woman being wheeled into hospital emergency. She's been bitten by a vampire and has gone into labor. The baby survives but, thanks to infected blood from the umbilical cord, has been genetically changed—he's half-mortal/half-vampire, with a vampire's strength but able to withstand sunlight. He's the "Day Walker" and he goes by the name of "Blade" (Wesley Snipes).

Cut to the "now," only it's a "now" that may be hard to recognize. A trampy young woman (Traci Lords) takes a clueless young man to a techno-throbbing dance club (located within a meat-packing plant) and then abandons him to a decidedly surly crowd. Soon blood is pouring out of the overhead sprinklers and our would-be Lothario realizes he's the only human in a club full of vampires looking for a snack. That's when Blade shows up—dressed in black leather and body armor and impressively accessorized with a variety of nasty weapons (including his samurai sword) and some very serious martial arts skills. Blade proceeds to destroy any bloodsucker that gets in his way, using a combination of garlic and silver that causes the vamps to shatter in lots of tiny pieces. But when he catches up with the trash-talking Quinn (Donal Logue), Blade decides to go with old-fashioned fire. But before Blade can make sure the job is finished, the cops show up and he has to make a quick exit.

Quinn's crispy critter body is taken to the morgue, where Curtis (Tim Guinee) tries to convince his hematol-

> Blade (Wesley Snipes) to Deacon Frost (Stephen Dorff): "It's open season on all night-stalkers."

ogist ex-girlfriend Karen Jenson (N'Bushe Wright) that something is odd with the blood sample he's taken from the latest arrival. When they both start to examine the body, they get a nasty surprise when the not-quite-dead Quinn takes a bite out of each of them. (And I do mean bite—these vampires like to rip throats out—no dainty fang-piercing for them.) Again Blade shows up but so do the cops and he still can't finish Quinn off. When he sees the bleeding Karen, rather than leave her behind Blade takes her to his sanctuary, where his grizzled mentor Abraham Whistler (Kris Kristofferson) castigates him for "bringin' home strays." Nevertheless, Quinn tries a garlic concoction on Karen, hoping it's not too late to keep her from turning into a vampire. Naturally, Karen is not too hip to what's going on when she regains consciousness and Blade has to explain to her that vampires are everywhere and into every aspect of society.

Marv Wolfman created *Blade* in 1973 as a supporting character in Marvel Comics *Tomb of Dracula* horror series.

Meanwhile, a group of respectable "pure" vampires, i.e. those who were born vampires, are having an unfriendly discussion with hot-tempered punk-with-an-attitude Deacon Frost (Stephen Dorff). Frost is the head of a motley collection of "turned" vampires and the owner of the nightclub that Blade destroyed. The old-world vampires, led by Dragonetti (Udo Kier), have survived because of their ability to blend in and be discreet. Two traits Frost has complete contempt for—he regards all humans merely as an easy food supply. The ruthlessly ambitious Frost has his own ideas about how vampires should rule and he's investigating some ancient texts in the vampire archives to aid him in his master plan.

Blade's told Karen it's best if she gets out town and she's gone back to her apartment, where an overly friendly cop suddenly shows up—and yes, so does Blade (are you sensing a pattern here?). The cop is a vampire "familiar" or vampire wannabe. He's been snacked upon by a certain vampire and is considered property—even having a certain glyph or tattoo inscribed on the back of the neck with the owner's name. The cop happens to belong to Deacon Frost, whom Blade is anxious to find. The cop does lead Karen and Blade to where the vampire archives are kept and they torture a 1,000 pound Asian vampire named Pearl (Eric Edwards), who looks like a cross between Jabba the Hutt and a very large sumo wrestler, to find out what Frost is after. It seems he's researching the Books of Arabis, the vampire bible, for information on a blood god called "La Magra," who's activated by a ritual involving the "Spirits of the 12."

Frost sends Quinn and his vampire minions to get Blade—alive—but thanks to constant radio contact, Whistler comes in, guns-a-blazin', and the trio manage to get out of a tight situation, leaving a lot of carnage behind them. It's also occurred to Karen that Blade just might not

be human: "You're one of them, aren't you?" But Blade explains he's a genetic mix of both vampire and human, although he ages like a human, rather than very slowly as a vampire does. Whistler warns Karen that Blade has inherited a vampire's thirst for human blood, but has managed to keep the cravings at bay, thanks to a serum that suppresses the worst of the urges. However, the serum is losing its effectiveness and Karen tries using her specialist skills to help find a cure. Using some experimental gene therapy, she does manage to prevent herself from becoming a vampire (after Whistler's garlic concoction fails) and also adds to Blade's arsenal of vampire-killing weapons when she discovers that anti-coagulant drugs cause a vampire's blood cells to literally (and graphically) explode. This becomes very useful later.

Frost has put his plan in motion by kidnapping Dragonetti, killing him by exposing him to a sunrise, and taking over the vampire circle. He also has a little chat with Blade, telling him that he can't deny what he is, and reiterating his ideas that humans are merely cattle and vampires will soon rule as a new and improved race. Blade summarily rejects Frost's offer to join him. Frost and his goons find Whistler's hideout and leave him just alive enough to tell Blade what's happened and that Frost wants to trigger a vampire apocalypse. Whistler knows he'll turn into a vampire unless he's killed and Blade gives him his gun so Whistler can commit suicide. Frost has also taken Karen, though he doesn't actually need her as part of his plan, he just wants to get rid of her in a particularly unpleasant way, Frost being a consummate sadist.

As it turns out, Blade is the key is Frost's big plans. It's his half-breed blood that is needed to trigger a release of power so that the blood god can be resurrected. Blade is captured by Frost after he discovers his mother Vanessa (Sanaa Lathan) is actually alive. She survived her bite and was turned into a vampire. And the vamp who did the honors? Why none other than Deacon Frost himself. (Hmmm, does this mean Frost is Blade's vampire daddy?) Blade and the rest of the old-world vampires are taken to the forgotten "Temple of Eternal Night." The other vampires are the sacrificial 12, while Blade is encased in a special box that cuts his wrists and allows his blood to drip down a complicated series of channels cut into the temple's walls.

A power vortex is established, with Deacon Frost in the middle of all the action. But Karen's managed to escape her deadly fate and gets Blade out of his trap. However, without his serum the thirst has come upon him and he's begun to change. Since he's also weakened by blood loss, Karen nobly offers herself as Blade's liquid nourishment. Blade regains his strength and takes care of the rest of Frost's cohorts before battling the would-be blood god himself. But all that power has given Frost the ability to instantly regenerate any injury or loss of limb that Blade manages to inflict. It's then that Blade spots Karen's discarded vials of anti-coagulant, which Frost had dismissed as Blade's serum. Blade manages to throw all the vials onto Frost and he explodes in a most satisfyingly disgusting fashion.

CREDITS

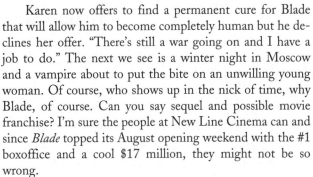

Blade: Wesley Snipes
Deacon Frost: Stephen Dorff
Abraham Whistler: Kris Kristofferson
Karen Jenson: N'Bushe Wright
Quinn: Donal Logue
Dragonetti: Udo Kier
Vanessa: Samaa Lathan
Mercury: Arly Jover
Racquel: Traci Lords
Curtis Webb: Tim Guinee
Pearl: Eric Edwards

Origin: USA
Released: 1998
Production: Peter Frankfurt, Wesley Snipes, and Robert Engleman for Amen Ra Films and Imaginary Forces; released by New Line Cinema
Direction: Stephen Norrington
Screenplay: David S. Goyer; based on the characters created by Marv Wolfman and Gene Colan
Cinematography: Theo Van De Sande
Editing: Paul Rubell
Music: Mark Isham
Production design: Kirk M. Petruccelli
Art direction: Barry Chusid
Set design: Tomhas C. Reta, Chad S. Frey, A. Todd Holland
Costumes: Sanja Mikovic Hays
Sound: Lee Orloff
Makeup effects: Greg Cannom
Stunt coordinators: Jeff Ward, Henry Kingi Jr.
MPAA rating: R
Running Time: 121 minutes

Karen now offers to find a permanent cure for Blade that will allow him to become completely human but he declines her offer. "There's still a war going on and I have a job to do." The next we see is a winter night in Moscow and a vampire about to put the bite on an unwilling young woman. Of course, who shows up in the nick of time, why Blade, of course. Can you say sequel and possible movie franchise? I'm sure the people at New Line Cinema can and since *Blade* topped its August opening weekend with the #1 boxoffice and a cool $17 million, they might not be so wrong.

Blade has a distinctive high-tech, souped-up look, feel, and sound, thanks to its pulsating, hypnotic techno soundtrack. Since vampires apparently process visual information faster than humans, their world has a speeded-up quality, while normal human life is in slow-motion. During Blade and Frost's sunlight tête-a-tête, humans move slowly around them, seemingly not aware of the vampires presence (except, of course, for the young human girl that Frost is holding hostage). The fight scenes are also done with hyperkinetic Hong Kong cinematic flair, since vampires are more agile, stronger, and faster than humans. While the amount of movie blood that flows throughout, and the grotesque, constant comic book violence hardly make for family entertainment, *Blade* does offers a "wow, cool" escapist experience.

—*Christine Tomassini*

REVIEWS

Chicago Tribune. August 21, 1998, p.4.
Cinefantastique. November, 1997, p. 7.
Cinefantastique. February, 1998, p. 16.
Detroit News. August 21, 1998.
Los Angeles Times. August 21, 1998, p. F4.
New York Times. August 21, 1998, p. E27.
People. August 31, 1998, p. 32.
San Francisco Chronicle. August 21, 1998.
San Francisco Examiner. August 21, 1998.
USA Today. August 21, 1998.
Variety. August 24, 1998, p. 27.
Village Voice. September 1, 1998, p. 114.
Washington Post Weekend. August 11, 1998, p. 39.

Blues Brothers 2000

The Blues are back.—Movie tagline

"A blast. A Rock 'n' Roll Hall of Fame induction party."—Joanna Connors, *Cleveland Plain Dealer*

"Great music. I love the music and I love the car crashes too."—Joel Siegel, *Good Morning America*

"That's entertainment."—Lawrence Van Gelder, *New York Times*

 Box Office: $14,089,198

One would have to be awfully coldhearted to not like *Blues Brothers 2000*. Yes, sequels are almost always weaker than the original. Yes, the plot is lame. Yes, it misses John Belushi. But, darn it, it's awfully good natured. . .and then there's the music!

When the first Blues Brother's film was released in 1980, it became an instant boxoffice success that spawned a new pop culture phenomenon, an easy Halloween costume, and dreams of a sequel. When John Belushi died in 1982, however, he took half the Blues Brother's team with him and hopes for a sequel faded. But time heals wounds and soon it seemed possible to cash in on a past success. And so it is that 18 years later, the other half of the duo, Dan Aykroyd, has reteamed with the original film's director, John Landis, added a few new "brothers," and set out on the celluloid highway to reintroduce the blues to yet another generation of filmgoers.

This latest version of the Blues Brothers mythology is heavy on music and light on intelligence. In fact, the plot trudges along with a very heavy-handed use of "deus ex machina" (the gods intervening to move the story along because the writers can't think of a creative way to do it themselves). This explains why Elwood (Aykroyd) is constantly exclaiming, "God works in mysterious ways."

And is anything more mysterious than the fact that at the opening of the film, Elwood is released from prison and never knows that Jake (Belushi) has died? (Weren't they in the same prison at the end of the first film?) Luckily the band's old drummer, Willie Hall (himself), now owns a strip club and has sent one of his dancers to pick Elwood up when he is liberated.

Elwood (Dan Aykroyd): "No pharmaceutical product could ever beat the rush when the band hits the groove and the people are dancing."

When Elwood visits Mother Mary Stigmata (Kathleen Freeman) who ran the orphanage where Jake and Elwood were raised, he's in for another shock. Curtis (Cab Calloway), the janitor who was like a father to the boys, has also passed on. Elwood is now totally disconnected from the world, with no family whatsoever to give his life meaning. That's when Mother Mary lets it slip that Curtis had an illegitimate son, Cabel Chamberlain (Joe Morton), who is now a commander with the Illinois State Police. Well, that's enough of a connection for Elwood, and he's off in search of his new "brother," not only to make his acquaintance, but also in the hopes of borrowing $500 from him in order to buy a new Bluesmobile—a retired canine patrol police car.

Tagging along is Buster (J. Evan Bonifant), a ten-year-old orphan in Mother Mary's charge who is now placed in Elwood's care for two hours so he can mentor him. Unfortunately, Elwood hasn't a clue what mentoring means, and he also has little concept of time. Buster, however, is an accomplished pickpocket, and when Cabel rejects all Elwood's advances (both monetary and familial), Buster swipes the commander's wallet in which the gods have placed exactly $500. What are the odds?

While working at Willie's club, Elwood soon discovers that his old drummer buddy is being shaken down for protection money by the Russian mafia. After a hilarious lecture on Marxist economics, and with the help of the club's bartender, Mighty Mack McTeer (John Goodman), Elwood takes on the Russian rogues. But when the Ruskies retaliate by burning down the club, Elwood decides it's a good time to get the band back together and go on the road.

So with Buster still in tow, and Mack having proved that he can sing blues with the best of them, Elwood sets off to lure his old compatriots away from their current jobs (funeral director, talk radio duo, and Mercedes Benz salesmen) in order to put the band together again.

The Blues Brother's easily identifiable costumes (black suits and hat) are derived from an old 1950 John Lee Hooker album cover. Aykroyd and Belushi added the Ray Ban sunglasses.

The first gig their agent Maury Sline (Steve Lawrence) can get for them is at a county fair in Kentucky where Maury has billed them as the Bluegrass Brothers (unbeknownst to the band). Their ultimate goal, however, is to take part in a battle of the blues bands at the Louisiana mansion of a 130-year-old voodoo queen named Moussette (Erykah Badu).

Along the road south, the boys have their usual share of misunderstandings, money trouble, menacing villains, and motor vehicle chases. This time around, the band is being pursued by three different groups. First the Russians are still after Elwood, but now added to the hunt is Cable and his deputy (Nia Peeples) as well as several other police departments who are after him for allegedly kidnapping Buster, and, as the story progresses, they attract the enmity of a militia group for good measure.

Well, one can't have a Blues Brother's movie without car crashes, and this one is supposed to have the largest one ever filmed. Appearing on screen for less than 2 minutes, it took four months to plan, three days to shoot, and involved 60 cars, a tar spreader, a dump truck, and a trailer. The Bluesmobile, by the way, was a 1990 Crown Victoria Ford.

CREDITS

Elwood Blues: Dan Aykroyd
Mighty Mack McTeer: John Goodman
Cabel Chamberlain: Joe Morton
Buster: J. Evan Bonifant
Warden: Frank Oz
Malvern Gasperon: B.B. King
Mother Mary Stigmata: Kathleen Freeman
Lt. Elizondo: Nia Peeples
Queen Moussette: Erykah Badu
Marco: Paul Shaffer
Mrs. Murphy: Aretha Franklin
Reverend Cleophus James: James Brown
Reverend Morris: Sam Moore
Maury Sline: Steve Lawrence
Ed's Love Exchange Janitor: Johnny Lang
Bob: Jeff Morris
Robertson: Darrell Hammond

Origin: USA
Released: 1998
Production: John Landis, Dan Aykroyd, Leslie Belzberg; released by Universal Pictures
Direction: John Landis
Screenplay: Dan Aykroyd and John Landis; based on *The Blues Brothers* by Dan Aykroyd and John Landis
Cinematography: David Herrington
Editing: Dale Beldin
Production design: Bill Brodie
Art direction: Dan Yarhi
Set decoration: Steve Shewchuk, Clive Thomasson
Costumes: Deborah Nadoolman
Choreographer: Barry Lather
Stunt coordinator: Rick Avery
Music: Paul Shaffer
Sound: Glen Gauthier
MPAA rating: PG-13
Running Time: 121 minutes

A former police car fitted with a 400 hp NASCAR stock engine and a "nitro" button which allowed it to reach speeds of 700 mph. But the Bluesmobile was not one of the vehicles sacrificed to the gods who move this story along.

Finally the band reaches Queen Moussette's where her majordomo, Marco (Paul Shaffer), prepares them to audition to see if they're good enough to take part in the definitive battle of the bands. It is a contest that is the film's high point. In it, the Blues Brothers take on a group called the Louisiana Gator Boys. Headed by B.B. King, it's a sprawling ensemble composed of the likes of Steve Winwood and Billy Preston on keyboards, Clarence Clemons on horn, Lou Rawls, Koko Taylor, Isaac Hayes and Dr. John on vocals, and Bo Diddley, Travis Tritt, and Eric Clapton on guitars.

And it's music like this that makes *Blues Brothers 2000* come alive. It's worth sitting through the preposterous plot when we're also allowed to hear Aretha Franklin belt out a new rendition of "R.E.S.P.E.C.T." and Junior Welles and Lonnie Brooks backing up the Blues Brothers in "Cheaper to Keep Her." (As a sad note, this film was Junior Welles' final performance, he died in January of this year.)

But there's more. There's Eddie Floyd and Wilson Pickett sharing vocals on "634-5789" (which has now become the number of a phone sex business) with the help of a young Johnny Lang, and John Popper and Blues Traveler singing "Maybe I'm Wrong." But it's a rousing tent-revival version of "John the Revelator" sung by Reverend Morris (Sam Moore of Sam and Dave fame), Reverend Cleophus James (James Brown), and Joe Morton, who proves he's not only a great actor but can also hold his own with the masters, that really brings the house down.

And even when the credits roll at the end of the film, the music's still rockin' and audiences are dancin' in the aisles as they are shown the identification of all the great musical talent packed into the movie. And along with the delightful discovery of matching names to faces, one will also be treated to James Brown doing a new rendition of "Please, Please, Please" with Aykroyd and Goodman singing backup.

Now I ask you, how bad can a film be that offers all that?

—Beverley Bare Buehrer

REVIEWS

Chicago Sun Times. February 6, 1998.
Chicago Tribune. February 6, 1998.
Entertainment Weekly. February 20, 1998, p. 88.
Los Angeles Times. February 6, 1998, p. F2.
New York Times. February 6, 1998, p. E14.
People. February 23, 1998, p. 21.
USA Today. February 6, 1998.
Variety. February 9, 1998, p. 70.
Village Voice. February 17, 1998, p. 120.
Washington Post. February 6, 1998, p. 41.

Bongwater

Bongwater concerns a group of pot-smoking twenty-somethings in Portland, Oregon who find their lives changed by the appearance of Serena (Alicia Witt), a headstrong, determined woman who inexplicably lands among them, bringing chaos with her. She attaches herself to pot dealer David (Luke Wilson), but despite their obvious attraction, the relationship stays platonic. As David's friends watch, Serena tries to mold the lazy and unmotivated David into the next hot Artist, introducing him to "patrons" who could help him, and tries to put a "poseur" look on David, who is otherwise just too dumb and naïve to know what is going on.

Director Richard Sears has brought together a fine group of actors (Luke Wilson of *Bottle Rocket,* Alicia Witt of TV's *Cybill* and the independent film *Fun,* and poster boy for anti-establishment stand-up and star of TV's *News Radio,* Andy Dick), but the weak, non-linear storyline gives them no room for growth or expression. The screenplay by Nora Maccoby and Eric Weiss (based on Michael Hornburg's book) leads one to theorize that this story is loosely based on the relationship between the fiercely ambitious Courtney Love and her sweet, disenfranchised husband Kurt Cobain, but even that thought cannot lift this film out of its uneven funk.

CREDITS

David: Luke Wilson
Serena: Alicia Witt
Jennifer: Amy Locane
Mary: Brittany Murphy
Devlin: Jack Black
Tony: Andy Dick
Robert: Jeremy Sisto

Origin: USA
Released: 1998
Production: Alessandro Uzielli and Laura Bickford; released by Alliance Independent Films
Direction: Richard Sears
Screenplay: Nora Maccoby and Eric Weiss; based on the novel by Michael Hornberg
Cinematography: Richard Crudo
Editing: Lauren Zuckerman
Costumes: Nancy Steiner
Production design: Gideon Ponte
Music: Mark Mothersbaugh, Josh Mancell
Sound: John Brasher
MPAA rating: Unrated
Running Time: 98 minutes

The film starts out promisingly; a man and woman argue inside a house, the man stomps out and ends up drinking at a bar, the woman leaves soon after, whereupon a bong tips over and sets the house ablaze. The young man returns to his home to reconcile with his girlfriend and instead finds firemen hosing down the smoldering remains of his house. David's friends try to pull him back into their bacchanalian ways of life (cross-dressing, pot smoking, intense cartoon watching) but he mourns the loss of Serena, without really knowing himself what their relationship was.

Unfortunately, the film then detours into watching David hang out with his friends in Portland and cutting to Serena in New York City diving headfirst into a series of abusive relationships. Although Serena's particular brand of '90s brashness is meant to be quirky and endearing, she comes off as merely obnoxious, abrasive, and completely unsympathetic; she never reveals one thing about where she's come from, where she's going, or what she wants. David, the most sympathetic character in the group, eventually wears on one's nerves with his aimless, passive attitude.

Without a clear-cut goal or plot, the film meanders into small, intermittently funny vignettes highlighting the various characters in both David and Serena's lives. There's Tommy (Jamie Kennedy of *Scream*), the paranoid who can't remember who Serena is and chases her out of his apartment with a gun; Mary (Brittany Murphy), the wealthy stoner girl with a crush on David—but who just can't stop giggling for one minute; and Tony (Andy Dick) and Robert (Jeremy Sisto), boyfriends who seem to get the best one-liners in the film. Sears even includes an unbearably long scene where revelers drop acid and trip happily (and hilariously—to them) throughout the woods.

By the time Serena leaves New York (she has been brutally raped at a party and, in true enigma fashion, doesn't even tell her girlfriend) and returns to Portland to find David, the dramatic pace of the film has slowed to a crawl. If Serena is meant to be the dramatic centerpiece of the story, she needs more exposition (even *Breakfast at Tiffany's* muse Holly Golightly broke down and revealed her family issues). Otherwise, when David and Serena finally do hook up, the audience is left as cold and unfeeling as she appears to be.

—G. E. Georges

REVIEWS

Variety. May 11, 1998, p. 82.

The Borrowers

Their space is in your place!—Movie tagline
"The rare children's comedy that gets laughs from viewers large and small."—*Premiere*
"An absolutely delightful treat."—Jeffrey Lyons, *WNBC-TV*

 Box Office: $22,619,589

F ew movies are as much unpretentious, imaginative fun as *The Borrowers*. This magically lunatic story about a family of "little people" who live under the floorboards of a British family's home is that rarest of family films, a treat for all ages. The movie can make little tykes squeal and adults chuckle. It's a film that exploits the wonders of moviemaking without grandstanding. The special effects are enjoyable, but they don't overwhelm the storytelling.

The Borrowers is based on Mary Norton's 1950s stories about sneaky household gremlins who live off their unwitting human hosts. In its story about how a boy comes to care for a group of tiny creatures, *The Borrowers* is evocative of *The Indian in the Cupboard* (1995), another recent film based on a British novel. In its climactic battle scenes between hordes of miniature people and a huge, ugly giant, it is reminiscent of *Gulliver's Travels*.

The elfin creatures call themselves "borrowers" as a way of excusing their thievery. They appropriate small objects to fashion a homestead, and they take human food to survive. The concept is an amusing take on post-war materialism. The host family has many doodads that often seem to get misplaced. In fact, an underground proletariat is living off the remnants of their wealth. Never has "trickle down" economics been more vividly realized.

The borrowers in this story are the Clock family. Their human hosts—whom the Clocks call "beans"—are named the Lenders, appropriately. The borrowers have lived for years without being noticed. That's because the parents, Pod (Jim Broadbent) and Homily (Celia Imrie), are very cautious. But their daring teenage daughter, Arrietty (Flora Newbigin), is getting too reckless in her explorations around the house, putting the family at risk of exposure and getting her kid brother Peagreen (Tom Felton) into constant trouble.

An extended opening sequence details how resourceful the borrowers are and how they live in constant danger of discovery. With Peagreen's help, Arrietty opens a freezer and climbs inside, the better to enjoy what to her is a pool-

Greedy and conniving landowner Ocious P. Potter (John Goodman) thinks up a scandalous plot to rid his property of the little people known as *The Borrowers*.

sized carton of ice cream. But she gets locked inside, and her father must exercise some Himalayan feats to save her, just as the dour human masters of the household, Joe (Aden Gillett) and Victoria (Doon Mackichan) return home. Right away the perilousness of the Clock family's life is palpable.

Attention to details also gives this film its unique charm. As the borrowers move through their miniature world, viewers will have fun identifying bits of household flotsam and jetsam which the borrowers have adapted for their use. For example, a retractable tape measure serves as a quick getaway ladder. The Clock family's dwelling is well-stocked and cozy, though always tenuous. Sitting at their dining table, they are suddenly rocked by what seems to be an earthquake and windstorm, and tiny Peagreen is sucked up to the floorboards. The family has been caught unprepared because Victoria Lender is absentmindedly vacuuming at an unusual time.

The Clocks are costumed to look like Nordic gypsies. Their hair is reddish and frizzy, and the females' long tresses are knotted in huge ponytails. Everything about their dress and demeanor evokes the old Celtic traditions of the "little people." They are metaphors for the poor and homeless who are shuffled aside and dying out. Indeed, Arrietty, who has never seen another borrower, worries that they are the last of their kind.

Some reviewers familiar with the novel thought the film short shrifted the borrowers' character development and grossly speeded up and Americanized the story. But screenwriters Gavin Scott and John Kamps need not apologize for

 The Borrower credo: "Borrowers are alert, ingenious, brave, prudent, faithful and good at climbing."

making this into an action story. Director Peter Hewitt was wise not to linger over the everyday lives of the little creatures. The plot, though a bit contrived, keeps them in constant peril, and that prevents the story from being saccharine. There's an intriguing mixture of horrible threats and sweet escapes, an appreciation of the menace in children's fantasy lives that is much like the tone of Roald Dahl stories (as in *Matilda* or *James and the Giant Peach*). The frightful situations that befall the borrowers and their pluck in meeting them make this film a heady adventure saga.

The Borrowers has previously been filmed as a 1973 *Hallmark Hall of Fame* movie and as a 12-episode BBC series in 1992/93.

When the Lenders' son Peter (Bradley Pierce) discovers Arrietty in his room, he tells her the family is about to move and the house to be demolished. Hiding the Clocks from his parents, he tries to transport them (in a plastic detergent container) inside the moving van, but bumps on the road cause the Clock children to spill out. Peagreen lands in a dog turd. This is one of two crude bits in the film, the other involving a farting dog. By modern standards, that's remarkably little grossness.

As soon as the Lenders leave, the villain arrives. He is Ocious C. Porter (John Goodman), a leering, greedy attorney who is trying to steal the Lenders' rightful inheritance, their home. Trying to find a will, he smashes walls with a hammer. The Clock children, separated from their parents, are in mortal jeopardy. With the erratic help of a rather sentimental exterminator named Jeff (Mark Williams), Porter flushes out Arrietty and Peagreen, and a war of wits ensues. Of course, Porter gets the worst of it.

Goodman displays a comic genius that never before had this much opportunity to burst forth. His is a marvelous villain, completely heartless and vile. Goodman's punch-me face makes him the perfect foil. Goodman obviously had fun with this role and he plays it at a perfect fever pitch.

While Goodman's character is large and goony, he gets more subtle comic help from Williams, the inept exterminator with a heart. A smaller, wry role is that of Officer Steady (Hugh Laurie), a very polite and gracious policeman. Laurie's hilarious character is a triumph of incongruity and could fit easily into a Monty Python skit.

Pete, the "bean" boy, and the Clock parents have rushed to the rescue when Porter's pursuit of the young borrowers leads to a milk factory. In this marvelous sequence, the daredevil stunts, aided by special effects imagery, come to the fore. Peagreen is trapped in a milk bottle and about to drown. Fortunately, along the way Arrietty has met up with Spud, a resourceful outdoor-dwelling borrower. Riding to the rescue on a candle-powered roller-skate rocket which zooms through a water pipe, Spud is the Luke Skywalker of this mini-epic.

There are some jarring notes. Production designer Gemma Jackson has concocted a London set which seems to be intended to look artificial. There is also much playing with confusion of eras. Anachronisms abound. Cars and clothes evoke the 1950s. Yet there is a remote control (switching channels on a black-and-white set); an icemaker in the refrigerator, and a cellular phone. The effect is puzzling. What the filmmakers intended isn't clear at all.

Apart from that, *The Borrowers* is nearly perfect, considering it has no grand ambitions; it's a simple story, told on a small scale. Yet it contains many pleasures for the child in all of us: fantasies of a parallel world; the wondrous imagination of adapting household things for other purposes, something all children do; the excitement of battle against a pompous villain; and the alliance of a boy with creatures of another dimension. It's done without a bit of pretension. It's pure moviemaking fun.

This film also has dignity. Disney would have made a big romantic deal out of the attraction between Arrietty and Spud; Hewitt does better with a faint suggestion of their shared interest in adolescent joy riding . Arrietty is the familiar spunky adolescent heroine without all the Disney bag-

CREDITS

Ocious P. Potter: John Goodman
Pod Clock: Jim Broadbent
Exterminator Jeff: Mark Williams
Officer Steady: Hugh Laurie
Peter Lender: Bradley Pierce
Arrietty Clock: Flowa Newbigin
Peagreen Clock: Tom Felton
Homily Clock: Celia Imrie
Spiller: Raymond Pickard
Joe Lender: Aden Gillett
Victoria: Doon Mackichan

Origin: Great Britain
Released: 1997
Production: Tim Bevan, Eric Fellner, and Rachel Taladay for Working Title; released by Polygram Films
Direction: Peter Hewitt
Screenplay: Gavin Scott and John Camps; based on the novels by Mary Norton
Cinematography: John Fenner, Trevor Brooker
Editing: Annie Kocur
Music: Harry Gregson-Williams
Production design: Gemma Jackson
Costumes: Marie France
Sound: David Stephenson
Visual effects supervisor: Peter Chiang
MPAA rating: PG
Running Time: 83 minutes

gage. *The Borrowers,* like its namesakes, travels light. It is a straightforward, imaginative tale, executed with loving attention, right down to the smallest detail.

The proletarian subtext of the film sneaks through near the end, when Goodman is defeated by a rescue squad that eventually numbers in the hundreds. Here is the "under-class" personified, a bit romantically, as a group of dignified, inconspicuous folk who claim their share of Earth's bounty, even if they have to take it from the dominant class. In the closing credits, the "little folk" of filmmaking are honored, as legions of carpenters, painters, and other ordinary workers are mentioned. Clearly, this film is a product made by people who take pride in their work. For attentive adults, there is a message here, but it goes down smoothly. For children, there is nothing but delight.

—*Michael Betzold*

REVIEWS

Boston Globe. February 13, 1998.
Boxoffice. March, 1998, p. 53.
Cinefantastique. February, 1998, p. 8.
Cinefantastique. March, 1998, p. 56.
Entertainment Weekly. February 13, 1998, p. 44.
Los Angeles Times. February 13, 1998, p. F8.
New York Times. February 13, 1998, p. E28.
People. February 23, 1998, p. 22.
San Francisco Chronicle. February 13, 1998.
Sight and Sound. December, 1997, p. 39.
USA Today. January 13, 1998, p. 3D.
Variety. December 8, 1997, p. 112.
Village Voice. February 17, 1998, p. 116.
Washington Post. February 13, 1998, p. D1.

Bride of Chucky

Chucky gets lucky.—Movie tagline
The honeymoon's gonna be a killer.—Movie tagline

 Box Office: $32,305,400

How many people have childhood memories of peering apprehensively around a darkened bedroom at familiar, harmless objects which seemed to turn eerily sinister and malevolent in the shadows? Perhaps it was a doll whose toothy grin suddenly seemed a little bit menacing and a little too toothy. *Poltergeist* (1982), for example, exploited this common fear to great effect, as have many other films of lesser quality. One of these was *Child's Play* (1988), which bears responsibility for introducing the notoriously-treacherous toy named Chucky, a doll possessed by the soul of a murderous fiend whose life came to a violent end amongst the shelves of a toy store. In that film, directed by Tom Holland (1985's *Fright Night*), a six-year-old boy receives Chucky as a seemingly-harmless gift from his parents, only to be terrorized by the doll, which spews nasty cracks and wreaks bloody havoc during his quest to inhabit the youngster's body. Chucky behaved no better in *Child's Play 2* (1990) and *Child's Play 3* (1991), by which time the Chucky franchise had lost touch with the creepy chord it had struck

Tiffany (Jennifer Tilly) concocts a voodoo ritual that she hopes will bring back her killer boyfriend who now embodies the doll known as Chucky in the thriller *Bride of Chucky*.

to at least some effect in the first film. In the latter film, the boy is suddenly sixteen (apparently you grow up fast when you have been through what he has been through) and no longer a wide-eyed child, and Chucky's perpetually tart tongue and gory violence had lost much of its initial shock value. The latest installment, *Bride of Chucky*, continues the downward trend.

Having been ripped apart at the end of *Child's Play 3*, Chucky's remains are lying on a shelf in the police department's evidence room. They are retrieved by an unscrupulous policeman at the request of Tiffany (Jennifer Tilly), Chucky's psychotic girlfriend back when he was in human form. After thanking the officer by slashing his throat, Tiffany proves she is as handy with a needle as she is with a knife by sewing her former paramour back together. Using a copy of *Voodoo for Dummies*, she brings the doll back to life. Tiffany is soon disillusioned, however, when Chucky (voiced once again by Brad Dourif) reveals that he would rather play the field than limit himself by being

Bride of Chucky marks the American directorial debut of Hong Kong director Ronny Yu.

Chucky (voice of Brad Dourif): "Do I have a rubber? Look at me. I am rubber."

a one bimbo guy. Enraged, she locks him up in her trailer, but the maniacal midget retaliates by electrocuting her in the bathtub with a television playing *The Bride of Frankenstein* (1935). A few voodoo chants later, Chucky successfully transfers Tiffany's soul into the bride doll she had spitefully given him during his confinement. Now both in the same predicament, the two set out to retrieve an amulet that Chucky was buried with in New Jersey which will enable them to enter into any two human bodies of their choosing. They set their sights on Jesse (Nick Stabile) and Jade (Katherine Heigl), who accept Tiffany's offer of big bucks over the phone to pick up the dolls in the trailer and transport them to Hackensack. (When Tiffany dolls herself up for the adventure, she looks unsettlingly like Pamela Anderson Lee). The two teenaged, star-crossed lovers are soon on the run from the authorities, who blame them for Chucky and Tiffany's lengthening trail of carnage. At this point, *Bride of Chucky* goes through the motions of offering up the various obligatory scenes of bloodshed, as well as a rather repellent sex scene between the two dolls. When the teens finally realize the true nature of their cargo, Jesse and Jade are horrified to be at the toys' mercy. Reaching the cemetery, the young couple fight for their lives. They narrowly escape becoming vessels for Chucky's and Tiffany's souls when the latter, apparently touched by the obvious feeling between the young lovers, bashes Chucky with a shovel. After much commotion, Chucky ends up shot and lying in his grave, and Tiffany lies charred and battered nearby. Jade flees the cemetery with Jesse (who, while having been stabbed in the back by Chucky, seems not much worse for the wear), and a policeman has the misfortune of witnessing the utterly revolting birth of Chucky's child as it squirms out from Tiffany's repulsive remains.

Bride of Chucky, like the other *Child's Play* films, was written by Don Mancini, who describes his latest effort as "a really cool blend of the genuinely creepy and the really funny." While the film is decidedly insipid and obnoxious, it is neither enjoyably scary nor even passably humorous. With the recent proliferation of teen horror films begun by *Scream* (1996) and *I Know What You Did Last Summer* (1997), the creators of *Bride of Chucky* apparently decided that putting their character together with two attractive young people would also make a killing at the boxoffice. After viewing *Bride of Chucky*, one harks back to the words of Janet Maslin when she reviewed *Child's Play 2* in the *New*

CREDITS

Tiffany/Tiffany Doll: Jennifer Tilly
Jade: Katherine Heigl
Jessie: Nick Stabile
Chief Warren Kincaid: John Ritter
Damien Baylock: Alexis Arquette
David: Gordon Michael Woolvett
Chucky: Brad Dourif (voice)

Origin: USA
Released: 1998
Production: David Kirschner and David Gilroy; released by Universal Pictures
Direction: Ronny Yu
Screenplay: Don Mancini; based on his original characters
Cinematography: Peter Pau
Editing: David Wu, Randolph K. Bricker
Music: Graeme Revell
Production design: Alicia Keywan
Art direction: James McAteer
Puppet effects: Kevin Yagher
Costumes: Lynne MacKay
Sound: Owen Langevin
MPAA rating: R
Running Time: 89 minutes

York Times eight years ago: "This proves," she wrote, "that movie ideas truly never die, not even when they ought to." Judging by the ending of *Bride of Chucky* and the continued interest in the series at the boxoffice, we are in for *Son of Chucky* or *Spawn of Chucky*, a thought which truly makes this reviewer want to up-Chucky.

—*David L. Boxerbaum*

REVIEWS

Boston Globe. October 17, 1998, p. A18.
Detroit Free Press. October 17, 1998, p. 2A.
Entertainment Weekly. October 30, 1998, p. 84.
Los Angeles Times. October 19, 1998, p. F4.
New York Times. October 17, 1998, p. B16.
People. November 2, 1998, p. 33.
San Francisco Chronicle. October 17, 1998, p. E1.
Variety. October 19, 1998, p. 77.

Broadway Damage

Greetings from Greenwich Village.—Movie tagline

Victor Mignatti's feature debut, *Broadway Damage,* is a boy-knows-boy-but-boy-doesn't-realize-that-his-best-friend-is-also-Mr.-Right comedy set among aspiring actors, writers, and musicians in

Mara Hobel portrayed the young Christina Crawford in 1981's *Mommie Dearest.*

a seedy New York City milieu. Unfortunately, neither the banal script nor the bewildered performances of the would-be actors are worth a viewer's time.

Handsome and shallow Marc (Michael Shawn Lucas) is only interested in a romance with the "perfect 10," which leaves out his best friend Robert (Aaron Williams), who has an unrequited interest in his buddy. Of course, since Marc has the brains of a gnat, he falls for handsome-but-manipulative singer David (Hugh Panaro) and proceeds to get what he deserves.

Encouraging sad-sack Robert is Marc's fag-hag Greenwich Village roomie, neurotic rich girl, Cynthia (Mara Hobel—the only performer with some verve). Not much more happens—there's some predictable crises (both work and romance related), a modicum of self-evaluation, and things end on a clichéd happy note. You want to watch a good gay romance? Try another film.

—*Michelle Banks*

CREDITS

Cynthia: Mara Hobel
Marc: Michael Shawn Lucas
David: Hugh Panaro
Robert: Aaron Williams

Origin: USA
Released: 1998
Production: David Topple for Village Art Pictures; released by Jour de Fetê Films
Direction: Victor Mignatti
Screenplay: Victor Mignatti
Cinematography: Michael Mayers
Editing: Victor Mignatti
Music: Elliot Sokolov
Costumes: Jill Kilber
Production design: Dina Goldman
MPAA rating: Unrated
Running Time: 110 minutes

REVIEWS

Boxoffice. July, 1998, p. 134.
Los Angeles Times. June 12, 1998, p. F8.
New York Times. May 29, 1998, p. E18.
San Francisco Chronicle. August 28, 1998, p. C7.
San Francisco Examiner. August 28, 1998, p. C6.

Broken Vessels

B*roken Vessels* is an audacious, gutsy first feature from director Scott Ziehl that offers up an unflinching examination of Los Angeles paramedics on the edge. Photographed in a raw-in-your-face manner, populated with characters that you would barely trust to park your car—much less save your life—this film exposes the seamy underside of big city life in a way that has rarely been so well documented onscreen.

Tom Meyer (Jason London) arrives in Los Angeles from Pennsylvania and lands a job as a paramedic with a small ambulance company. Though Tom has no medical experience and even seems to have a somewhat shady background (shadowy flashbacks indicate a car accident of some sort) the owner of the ambulance company, Mr. Chen (James Hong), seems to take a liking to earnest Tom (when Tom tells him he is from Altoona, PA, Chen hereafter refers to him as "Tuna-fish") and hires him on the spot. Tom is introduced to his partner, Jimmy Warzniak (Todd Field) and heads out to face the mean streets of Los Angeles, completely unaware of the turn his life is about to take.

Jimmy seems a bit of a hard-ass at first, but very dedicated to his job; the only indication of his problematic character is that he seems to go through a lot of partners. But when Tom goofs on his very first job, inadvertently tagging a live victim for dead, Jimmy covers up for him and doesn't chew his ass off. Tom admires how Jimmy can charge into a difficult situation, assess what's going on, and rectify matters. But it soon becomes evident that Jimmy is out for Jimmy—and only Jimmy—and everyone else just better stay out of the way. When a drug addict and his girlfriend get out of control in the back of the van, Jimmy doesn't hesitate to put them in their place—with a zap from his electric paddles. The shock from this quickly dissipates; considering some of the awful characters they are called upon to help, any form of self-defense seems understandable. Tom is surprised when Jimmy diverts from their regular duties to stop off to buy street drugs. Jimmy merely smiles and explains that he needs to smooth out the rough edges that the job brings up.

Director Ziehl has fashioned a powerful story that once again beckons the chicken-egg quandary: Does an outrageously stressful job like this screw up people, or are already screwed up, on-the-edge people attracted to the kind of thrills that this job provides? The ironic side to all of this is that these medics have virtually no medical training beyond the most rudimentary basic emergency training. They have literally fallen into this work; Jimmy confesses that he once

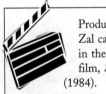

Producer and actress Roxana Zal came to fame as a teenager in the ground-breaking TV film, *Something About Amelia* (1984).

dreamt of being a policeman while Tom seems to just need a job rather than consider this a life long career.

Although Tom seems the more stable, easy going of the two, in no time at all he finds himself pulled into Jimmy's decadent lifestyle. Tom is certainly not hampered by anything so meaningful as a backbone or character. When Tom is kicked out of his apartment by a persnickety roommate, he moves in with Jimmy and the drugs, drink, and revelry begin full time.

In the course of their shift, Tom and Jimmy encounter drug and alcohol addicts, gang members, crazy and indigent people and just plain ordinary folk. In what seems like no time at all, the boys fall into nights of easy sex (prostitutes and young girls are brought into the van and the boys take turns with them), dangerous drug deals, and just barely responding to their calls. In one powerful scene, Jimmy even steals from a middle-class elderly couple who has called because of a possible heart attack. Tom is horrified to be offered lemonade and cookies while Jimmy is rifling through the couple's drawers. When the police look into this misdeed, Jimmy emerges smiling from his grilling with the police captain; apparently Jimmy's got more than drugs in his pocket.

Jimmy's neighbor Susy (Susan Traylor) provides both amusement and drugs for the two men. Stealing every scene she is in, Traylor plays Susy with horrifying twitching energy, flopping around the room like a caught fish. Susy is planning on doing everything from singing in a band in Japan to fixing up her house herself (she wields saws and drills at dangerous angles). Tom keeps Susy at a distance until Elizabeth Capalino (Roxana Zal, also the film's co-producer) appears as a temporary roommate. Elizabeth is sweet and sexy in a small town way; they begin to see each other and talk about their grand futures in the big city, and even make love. But the next night, as Elizabeth waits for Tom to meet her, he is drawn into a better time with Jimmy, and leaves her in the lurch.

Ziehl and screenwriters David Baer and John McMahon have created characters that are alive and realistic as any ever seen before, and actors Field and London are fully up to the task of illuminating them. Despite the outrageous happenings, the actors never overplay and bring a sense of reality to the downward spiral. Both appear to be wounded in ways that become slowly evident. Tom's flashbacks seem to indicate that he was the perpetrator of a fatal drunk driving accident. Jimmy's background is more mysterious; his one link to a "normal" family life is his drug-addicted grandfather, Gramps (Patrick Cranshaw), who lives in a local nursing home. (Gramps and his tendency to play "Possum" provide many amusing exchanges). Jimmy plays the good grandson and keeps his doddering grandfather flush with illegal drugs.

Predictably, things progress from bad to worse. Gramps overdoses and sends Jimmy into a tailspin. In a neurotic fit, Susy blows herself and a drug dealer friend up while trying to mix a huge batch of amphetamines. Gramps' death sends Jimmy into a depression so deep that he starts to mainline heroin (previously he had only been snorting it). Seeing what a state his life is in, Tom makes a last-ditch effort to reach out to someone who could help him—former lover and nurse, Elizabeth. But when she astutely picks up on what is making him profusely perspire and tremble, he cannot face her and runs away.

When Jimmy tries to screw over his usual drug dealers one last time, a chase ensues and they volley off a round of shots that fatally wound Jimmy, and nearly kill Tom. Tom stumbles out of the hospital, starting once again at ground zero in Los Angeles, but with the knowledge that his addictions cannot be ignored.

In the tradition of wretched excess shown in *The Lost Weekend* (1945), *Days of Wine and Roses* (1962), and *Rush* (1991), Ziehl solidly illuminates the lives of characters that are determinedly and doggedly engaged in self-destructive behavior. The ride may be uncomfortable, but once we are on board, we are committed to the end. All of the production credits are first-rate, overcoming the obvious low-budget restraints. Cinematographer Antonio Calvache brings vibrancy to the action that never lets up; the skewed, disturbing vision perfectly expresses the damaged lifestyles of the characters. This film packs an emotional, visceral wallop rarely seen in bigger budget films, much less in a smaller film. The story, coupled with the assured acting and direction, provides an unforgettable portrait of two troubled characters.

—*G. E. Georges*

CREDITS

Jimmy Warzniak: Todd Field
Tom Meyer: Jason London
Elizabeth Capalino: Roxana Zal
Susy: Susan Traylor
Mr. Chen: James Hong
Gramps: Patrick Cranshaw

Origin: USA
Released: 1998
Production: Roxana Zal and Scott Ziehl
Direction: Scott Ziehl
Screenplay: David Baer, John McMahon, and Scott Ziehl
Cinematography: Antonio Calvache
Editing: David Moritz, Chris Figler
Costumes: Roseanne Fiedler
Production design: Rodrigo Castillo
Sound: Clive Taylor
MPAA rating: Unrated
Running Time: 90 minutes

REVIEWS

Variety. April 27, 1998, p. 60.

Brother; Brat

"A terrifically stylish gangster film!"—Stephen Holden, *New York Times*

"Tough, mordantly comic! A two-fisted travelogue through the vast thieves' market of the former Soviet Union. Highly entertaining!"—J. Hoberman, *Village Voice*

The Police sang: "When the world is running down/You make the best of what's still around," which is exactly what twentysomething Danila Bragov (Sergei Bodrov, Jr.) is trying to do in Alexei Balabanov's Russian thriller *Brother*. Danila is demobilized after two years military service (where he was a office clerk) and, with no particular prospects, decides to head for St. Petersburg and look up his older brother, Viktor (Viktor Sukhoroukov). Even before finding his brother, Danila gets into a scuffle with security guards when he walks through a park and accidentally disrupts a video shoot for a pop group that happens to be Danila's favorite band, Nautilus. Danila, who is constantly listening to his CD player and whose headphones seem welded to his skull, will spend his downtime as casu-

Danila (Sergei Bodrov, Jr.) on St. Petersburg: "The city is a force and everyone here is weak."

Director Balabanov is said to be planning a sequel, which he wants to partially film in Chicago.

ally as any other young man by checking out the record stores looking for the band's latest CD, and attending one of their concerts.

As Danila explores the city, he sees that St. Petersburg runs on the premise of survival of the fittest. And for all his baby-faced looks, Danila is supremely capable of casual violence. When he notices a thug with a gun shaking down a street vendor, he punches out the extortionist and takes his pistol, which he then uses to threaten a deadbeat who won't pay his trolley fare. This wins him the attention of trolley driver Sveta (Svetlana Pismichenko), who shows her appreciation in bed.

When Danila finally hooks up with Viktor, he is undismayed to discover his bro is a killer-for-hire—running a business where his customers are rival Russian mafia who are feuding over turf. Viktor hires Danila and he finds himself on stakeouts in drab apartments, wandering around the city's outdoor markets and clubs where the crooks seem to congregate, and getting casually involved with a number of people, including druggie disco-loving Kat (Maria Joukova), and a street vendor (Yuri Kouznetzov) who takes a fatherly interest in Danila.

Finally, Viktor gives Danila the task of killing a Chechin mobster. He completes his assignment but is wounded in the process and now has the gangster's men after him. This, however, doesn't worry Danila, who turns out to be smarter than first impressions imply and is certainly lethal, with his own strange sort of morality. He also enjoys the power both the weaponry and the money he's paid gives him. Casual betrayals also don't seem to bother him and, after Danila makes his mark in St. Petersburg's underworld, he becomes confident enough to decide to travel to Moscow and more lucrative opportunities.

Director Balabanov's somewhat slow-moving gangster film is shot as a series of vignettes, with the majority of its

CREDITS

Danila Bragov: Sergei Bodrov Jr.
Viktor Bragov: Viktor Sukhoroukov
Sveta: Svetlana Pismitchenko
Kat: Maria Joukova
The German: Yuri Kouznetzov
Boutoussov: Viatcheslav Boutoussov

Origin: Russia
Released: 1997
Production: Alexei Balabanov for STW Film Co. and Roskomkino; released by Kino International Films
Direction: Alexei Balabanov
Screenplay: Alexei Balabanov
Cinematography: Sergei Astakhov
Editing: Marina Lipartiya
Music: Viatcheslav Boutoussov
Production design: Vladmir Kartakov
MPAA rating: Unrated
Running Time: 96 minutes

REVIEWS

Boston Phoenix. July 27, 1998.
Boxoffice. September, 1997, p. 110.
Los Angeles Times. September 4, 1998, p. F6.
New York Times. July 8, 1998, p. E5.
San Francisco Chronicle. November 20, 1968, p. C6.
Variety. May 26, 1997, p. 69.
Village Voice. July 14, 1998, p. 141.

violence discreetly offscreen. He's been blessed by a low-key and naturally charismatic performance by his star, Sergei Bodrov Jr., who first came to U.S. attention playing another once innocent soldier in his father's 1996 film *Prisoner of the*

Mountains. Balabanov winds up giving a tough look at the chaotic, impoverished, crisis-ridden world that is post-Soviet Russia. 🎞️

—*Michelle Banks*

Buffalo 66

"A triumph!"—Dale Peck, *Artforum*

"Glamorously gritty!"—Dave Kehr, *Daily News*

"Beautiful . . . intriguing!"—Gavin Smith, *Film Comment*

"Hilarious, audacious, memorable, original!" —Janet Maslin, *New York Times*

"Gorgeously photographed . . . stunningly surreal!"—J. Hoberman, *Village Voice*

 Box Office: $2,380,606

The scope of narrative and formal freedom open to the actor-as-filmmaker under the low-cost economics of the new independent cinema becomes strikingly evident in Vincent Gallo's flawed but lively first feature, *Buffalo 66.* Moreover, the confidence and flamboyance that mark his directorial debut force us to consider a largely submerged facet of audience identification, also noticeable in the contemporaneous *Hav Plenty* (reviewed in this volume).

Gallo's narrative would ordinarily have required us to identify with Billy Brown, his brash young protagonist, who is released from prison at the start of the film. The fact that the role is played by Gallo himself compounds the issue. For one, Gallo's filmic style is as bold as Billy's demeanor. We thus enjoy Gallo's portrayal of Billy as both that of a fictional protagonist, as well as of the overriding intelligence behind the film made flesh, as it were.

After Billy walks out the prison gates, he huddles against the cold on a bench, while waiting for a bus that will take him into town. The screen then splits into smaller screens, each showing some aspect of the life he has left behind, but which continues to haunt him, from immaculately clean trash bins to taking a semi-private shower. Within the snowscape of his newfound freedom, what now becomes all-important for Billy is, of all things, finding a men's room where he can

urinate. His need for a toilet facility in the first place is, we soon come to know, just the first of the many internal contradictions racking his life, most of them bordering on incredulity.

As it happens, one circumstance after another prevents Billy access to what he seems to need most. Even when he gets to the nearby town, he rushes across vacant lots, clutching his groin. By this time, the gag has worn thin, mainly because Billy looks the kind of macho man who could pee in the middle of Times Square with the Giants backfield around him. When Billy does at last reach an urinal, the man next to him gives him a case of bladder shyness, a debility that persists even when Billy has the rest room to himself.

It soon becomes clear that Billy's unnatural naturalistic urge to relieve himself is a mere narrative ploy intended to have his path cross that of Layla (Christina Ricci), a baby-faced, voluptuous dance student, who functions as a straight-woman for Billy's sarcastic rage. What we find most difficult to believe about Billy seems to endear him most to Layla, whom he abducts outside the washroom. He then forces her to act as his wife, for the sake of his eccentric parents, who have been ignorant of his incarceration.

Before having generated an ounce of drama, the film launches into its next sequence, which comprises role playing before Billy's mother, Janet (Anjelica Huston), a maniacally obsessed fan of the Buffalo Bills and Jimmy (Ben Gazzara), an embittered one-time lounge crooner who, like his son, is given to fits of sudden rage. The internal contradictions that rack Billy from within become extended to the characters of his parents, so that the film begins to take on the guise of a chamber piece of eccentricities, which in turn proves amusing and original, but nothing more.

The film, at this stage, is further crippled when Gallo, as director, brings on a double whammy by resorting to visual tricks that distance us from the action. When Billy, his parents and Layla (introduced to them as Wendy) are seated around the family dining table, Gallo dispenses with conventional tightly-framed point-of-view

 Billy (Vincent Gallo) to the kidnapped Layla (Christina Ricci): "Just look like you like me."

shots in favor of foreground space no doubt intended to jolt our conditioning to realism. When Japanese filmmakers use space in such a presentational manner, it appears culturally in-built, in keeping with narrative codes which eschew audience identification in favor of presenting a bird's-eye view of the situation. Gallo clearly wants us to involve ourselves with Billy, and so his experimentation in framing comes across as mere directorial self-consciousness.

Once the couple take leave of the parents, Billy and Layla wander into a bowling alley, then into a diner, where Billy encounters 'the real Wendy' (Rosanna Arquette) at, of all places, the next table. It is however only in the motel room sequence that Billy and Layla become intimate.

CREDITS

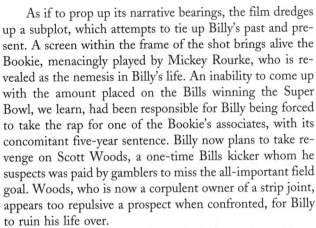

Billy Brown: Vincent Gallo
Layla: Christina Ricci
Janet Brown: Anjelica Huston
Jimmy Brown: Ben Gazzara
Goon: Kevin Corrigan
Bookie: Mickey Rourke
Wendy: Rosanna Arquette
Sonny: Jan-Michael Vincent

Origin: USA
Released: 1998
Production: Chris Hanley for Muse production; released by Lions Gate Films
Direction: Vincent Gallo
Screenplay: Vincent Gallo and Alison Bagnall
Cinematography: Lance Accord
Editing: Curtiss Clayton
Music: Vincent Gallo
Production design: Gideon Ponte
Sound: Brian Miksis
MPAA rating: Unrated
Running Time: 112 minutes

As if to prop up its narrative bearings, the film dredges up a subplot, which attempts to tie up Billy's past and present. A screen within the frame of the shot brings alive the Bookie, menacingly played by Mickey Rourke, who is revealed as the nemesis in Billy's life. An inability to come up with the amount placed on the Bills winning the Super Bowl, we learn, had been responsible for Billy being forced to take the rap for one of the Bookie's associates, with its concomitant five-year sentence. Billy now plans to take revenge on Scott Woods, a one-time Bills kicker whom he suspects was paid by gamblers to miss the all-important field goal. Woods, who is now a corpulent owner of a strip joint, appears too repulsive a prospect when confronted, for Billy to ruin his life over.

The film ends with Billy, who hitherto has found "all women evil," discovering a new meaning in life with the compliantly beautiful Layla, about whom Billy, and we, know virtually nothing.

Critics have been hard put to forgive the film its narrative lapses, noting its lack of "psychological realism" (David Denby in *New York* magazine) and its "drawn out scenes" which "look more like acting school exercises" (Geoffrey Macnab in *Sight and Sound*). Even so, Richard Schickel in *Time* notes the "demonic charm" of Gallo as Billy combining with Gallo's "directorial boldness" to create "a sort of casual but strangely haunting weirdness."

—Vivek Adarkar

REVIEWS

Boxoffice. April, 1998, p. 177.
Entertainment Weekly. July 10, 1998, p. 50.
Los Angeles Times. July 10, 1998, p. F12.
New York. July 20, 1998.
People. July 6, 1998, p. 38.
Sight and Sound. October, 1998, p. 39.
Time. July 13, 1998.
Variety. February 2, 1998, p. 32.
Washington Post Weekend. July 10, 1998, p. 42.

A Bug's Life

An epic of miniature proportions.—Movie tagline

"This bug's for you! *A Bug's Life* is all-embracing—funny . . . full of fun scares and endless sight gags. It's such great fun—the giddiest, most inventive family movie of the year."—David Ansen, *Newsweek*

"*A Bug's Life* should delight everyone—young, old or six-legged."—Tom Gliatto, *People*

"Two thumbs up!"—*Siskel & Ebert*

"Hilarious! A must-see."—Susan Granger, *SSG Syndicate*

"One of the most inventive movies in years. Stick around for the end credits or be sorry."—Mike Clark, *USA Today*

 Box Office: 127,589,564

Inventor ant Flix (voice of Dave Foley) is chosen to free his colony from the menacing grasshopper gang in Disney's computer animated *A Bug's Life*.

The second full-length animated film to be produced by partners Disney and Pixar Animation Studios, *A Bug's Life* was put into active development in the summer of 1996, following the enormous success of the two studios' first joint venture, 1995's *Toy Story*. However, while *A Bug's Life* took more than two years to complete, it was beat into the theaters by the animated DreamWorks picture *Antz* (reviewed in this edition), a project begun much later. When DreamWorks and Disney realized both studios were concurrently developing similarly-themed movies about ants, DreamWorks rushed *Antz* through production to get it into theaters ahead of schedule—and, most importantly, ahead of *A Bug's Life*. As it so happened, once both films opened, the earlier opening of *Antz* may have benefited both studios and at the same time may have cut into the potential profits of Disney's ant story. *Antz* met with more success than expected, becoming one of the highest-grossing non-Disney animated films to date, but *Bug's* opened to even more business, quickly passing the $100 million mark. Still, following so closely in the wake of *Antz,* the Disney film may not see the ultimate boxoffice results of *Toy Story* because it may have shared some of its potential profits with DreamWorks' own insect epic. Seeing *A Bug's Life* become an undisputed hit, Walt Disney Pictures must be delighted with its arrangement with Pixar. The two companies split production costs and profits evenly after Disney recovered its marketing costs and was paid a distribution fee. In March of 1998, Pixar's CEO Lawrence Levy

said that about 50 toy-licensing agreements had already been lined up for *Bug's,* compared to about eight to ten that had been arranged at the same point in *Toy Story*'s development. Fortunately for moviegoers, though, the film is not simply another money-making machine for Disney. While it may be that, it is also an inventive and delightful film that can be enjoyed by audiences of all ages.

The story of *A Bug's Life* opens with the introduction of a friendly colony of ants carrying seeds and other food to an altar-like setting atop a stone located near the anthill. Mr. Soil (voice of Roddy McDowall), supervising the process alongside the overseeing eyes of the royal family, encourages the ants to hurry. Time is running out. The grasshoppers are coming soon, and the ants must leave them an acceptable offering of food in exchange for peace. The little princess Dot (voice of Hayden Panettiere) questions her mother the Queen (voice of Phyllis Diller) about the offering to the grasshoppers, but the Queen replies, "That's our lot in life. It's not a lot, but it's our life." The ambitious ant Flik (voice of Dave Foley) appears on the scene with his newest invention, a one-man-band grain-transport system to revolutionize the harvesting process. The ant colony, unimpressed, continues to harvest the offering. Flik is discouraged and humbly walks away, but he stops to encourage Dot (his only admirer), who is upset that her wings are not fully grown and that she cannot fly. He tells her that, like a seed which is small but one day grows into a beautiful tree, she will in time become a princess.

 Hopper (voice of Kevin Spacey): "It's a bug-eat-bug world out there. Someone could get hurt."

Suddenly the colony hears the great rumble of the approaching grasshoppers, and the ants retreat to safety in their anthill. However, in his fumbling attempt to make it to the hill with his harvesting contraption, Flick inadvertently topples the food offering into a puddle. When the grasshoppers, led by the intimidating Hopper (voice of Kevin Spacey), arrive to find no food waiting for them, they angrily invade the anthill. Hopper tells Princess Atta (voice of Julia Louis-Dreyfus) and the Queen that he will give the ants one more opportunity to gather food, but that this time they must double the offering. Warning that they will return at the end of summer "when the last leaf falls," Hopper and his band leave.

The leaders of the colony are at a loss as to what to do about Flik and hold a trial to decide how to punish him. Flik, however, comes up with a plan to rid the colony of the grasshoppers by leaving the ant island to find help in the form of stronger bugs who can come back and fight Hopper's gang. The leaders are thrilled at the prospect of getting Flik out of their hair so they may get on with their work, so they readily agree that he should embark on his quest. Flik, in his leaf hat and with his bedroll, heads out to the cheering of the crowd and the escort of the small children, led by Dot. He climbs a dandelion, plucks a seed, and takes off with the wind, shouting to the children below, "For the colony and for oppressed ants everywhere!" At that moment he smacks into a rock, one of the many humorous sight gags that help give the movie its charm.

The scene shifts to a "flea circus" performing for a rough crowd. The circus performers, led by owner P.T. Flea (voice of John Ratzenberger), have come up with a new act called "Flaming Death." However, the clumsy performers botch the act, and they wind up abandoning the circus. They go to a local bar to nurse their wounds, but there they are confronted by a group of seedy flies that didn't care for their performance in the circus, and they resort to theatrics. Meanwhile, Flik arrives in the "city"—a trash heap outside a trailer house—and makes his way to the bar, where he enters just in time to hear one of the circus performers, a ladybug by the name of Francis (voice of Denis Leary), declaring to the angry crowd that they are "mighty warriors." Having stepped in too late, Flik misunderstands and believes the performers really are warriors. He tells them, "I've been looking for bugs with your talents." The performers believe him to be a talent scout and accompany him back to the ant island under the false assumption that Flik wants them to put on a show for the ant colony and their guests the grasshoppers.

Back at the anthill, the performers are greeted with cheers by the ants, who are amazed that Flik has actually returned with help. Invigorated by the applause, Francis announces that "When those grasshoppers get here, we're gonna knock them dead!" The crowd roars in excitement, taking his words literally. However, as the celebration continues, the circus bugs finally realize with horror what they were brought here to do, and they flee. Realizing that the bugs are not warriors leaves Flik in a horrible dilemma. Facing the colony with his blunder would mean total humiliation. He tries desperately to convince the troupe (ironically thought of as a "troop" by the ants) to stay, but they refuse. Suddenly a bird attacks the group, and the troupe works together to prevail. Discovering that they are indeed brave and resourceful, and finding themselves once again applauded by the ants, they decide to stay and work with the ants to overcome the grasshoppers. Flik recalls Hopper's fear of birds and suggests that the colony build an artificial bird with which to scare away Hopper and his band of thieves forever. The circus bugs and ants work happily side by side to accomplish this goal.

With disastrous timing, P.T. Flea suddenly arrives at the ant colony looking for his missing troupe. Infuriated by the deception and feeling betrayed by Flik and the circus bugs, Princess Atta tells the troupe and Flik to leave and never return. Convinced that he is a failure, Flik sadly departs with the other bugs, who are also saddened at leaving the colony, where they had gained many friends. However, shortly after the troupe leaves, Hopper and his gang return. Hopper, of course, is enraged to discover there is no food waiting for him, and he secretly plans to squash the Queen in order to prove his superiority to the ants. Fortunately, however, Dot and her friends manage to escape, and Dot goes in search of Flik. She finds him and the circus bugs and convinces Flik to return. Finding inspiration once again, Flik and the young ants man the artificial flying bird while the circus performers create a diversion. The plan works perfectly until P.T. Flea returns and catches the bird on fire, causing it to crash. Realizing he has been duped, Hopper regains the upper hand and beats up Flik, but the ant rises from the ground and stands up to the grasshopper, declaring that "ants are not meant to serve grasshoppers" and that ants are not an inferior species. In fact, since the grasshoppers rely on the ants for their food, Flik tells Hopper that, "It's you who need us." The other ants begin to realize the

Last film for Roddy McDowall (the voice of Mr. Soil).

AWARDS AND NOMINATIONS

Academy Awards 1998 Nominations: Original Musical or Comedy Score

truth in Flik's words, and they also realize that they have the greater strength because they outnumber the grasshoppers—something Hopper has known all along. The grasshopper makes a last-ditch effort to take revenge on Flik, but the day is saved when a real bird appears and grabs up Hopper, taking him to her nest to feed her young.

On a visual level, *A Bug's Life* offers enough activity and detail to repeatedly fascinate the viewer. The realistic, three-dimensional, textured computer animation combines with the cartoonish features of the delightful characters to create an arresting surrealism that in some ways offers a richer landscape than conventional animation. This was also true to an extent with *Toy Story*, but the animation process has been even more refined in *A Bug's Life*. The colors, the move-

ments, the depth, and the elaborate details are almost enough in themselves to make this film worth watching at least once.

Visual magic is not enough to constitute a good film, of course, and fortunately *Bug's* also features an engaging storyline, endearing and often hilarious characters, and various forms of humor, which the film has aplenty. Some of the humor is simple slapstick or physical comedy, as when Flik flies into a rock or when chubby caterpillar Heimlich (voice of Joe Ranft) gets stuck in a crack in the ground. Several characters, such as the goofy, clueless grasshopper Molt (voice of Richard Kind), seem to exist almost solely for their comic appeal, but they remain consistently appealing and never become tiresome. Dialogue is often witty and cleverly written, a trait that adults should appreciate even more so than children. The film also manages to include a few comic allusions. Hopper, for instance, talks about Nature's order and how the ants are meant to serve the grasshoppers, referring to it as "the circle of life," an obvious reference to Disney's 1994 blockbuster *The Lion King*. When Manny the preying mantis, voiced by Jonathan Harris, moans "The pain, the pain," fans of the 1960s series *Lost In Space* will recognize the line as one made famous by Harris' portrayal of Dr. Smith. Finally, the filmmakers cleverly inserted humor into the end credits, with a series of "outtakes" and "bloopers" featuring bugs running into cameras, forgetting their lines, and bursting out into laughter during takes.

The moral of this story, that one individual, with the interests of society in mind, can change the world order of things for the good of all, is a lesson that children of all ages can take to heart. In a world full of drones marching to the beat of another drum, few dare to initiate the very change that may take life as we know it to a higher level of existence. Without innovators we would still be living in the dark ages.

—*David Flanagin, Gina Blevins,* and *Becci Scarborough*

CREDITS

Flik: Dave Foley (voice)
Hopper: Kevin Spacey (voice)
Princess Atta: Julia Louis-Dreyfus (voice)
Dot: Hayden Panettiere (voice)
Queen: Phyllis Diller (voice)
Molt: Richard Kind (voice)
Slim: David Hyde Pierce (voice)
Heimlich: Joe Ranft (voice)
Francis: Denis Leary (voice)
Manny: Jonathan Harris (voice)
Gypsy: Madeline Kahn (voice)
Rosie: Bonnie Hunt (voice)
P.T. Flea: John Ratzenberger (voice)
Mr. Soil: Roddy McDowall (voice)

Origin: USA
Released: 1998
Production: Darla K. Anderson and Kevin Reher for Pixar Animation Studios; released by Walt Disney Pictures
Direction: John Lasseter
Screenplay: Andrew Stanton, Bob Shaw, and Donald McEnery
Cinematography: Sharon Calahan
Editing: Lee Unkrich
Music: Randy Newman
Production design: William Cone
Art direction: Tia W. Kratter, Bob Pauley
Sound: Gary Rydstrom
MPAA rating: G
Running Time: 96 minutes

REVIEWS

Chicago Tribune. November 25, 1998, p. 1.
Entertainment Weekly. November 27, 1998, p. 53.
Los Angeles Times. November 20, 1998, p. F1.
New York Times. November 25, 1998, p. E1.
People. November 30, 1998, p. 36.
Sight and Sound. February, 1999, p. 39.
Variety. November 16, 1998, p. 33.
Village Voice. December 1, 1998, p. 122.
Washington Post Weekend. November 27, 1998, p. 56.

Bulworth

"Brilliant! *Bulworth* is savagely funny."—Bill Diehl, *ABC Radio Network*

"*Bulworth* is more outrageous than *Being There,* more slashing than *Network.*"—Bob Thomas, *Associated Press*

"Outrageous, outlandish, beyond brilliant. The most intelligently funny film of the decade." —David Sheehan, *CBS-TV*

"*Bulworth* shocks, surprises and always entertains. It may be the most keenly astute and honest film about politics ever."—Sam Rubin, *KTLA Morning News*

"This movie is a scandal and irresistibly entertaining."—David Denby, *New York Magazine*

"*Bulworth* is the best political comedy of its generation, and one of the best ever made by Hollywood."—Peter Kaplan, *New York Observer*

"Wonderful. *Bulworth* is a singular summer movie."—David Ansen, *Newsweek*

"Warren Beatty has made a movie that is fast, funny, furiously original!"—Leah Rozen, *People*

"Warren Beatty is playing with fire here. If you're stirred by the sight of a high-wire artist working without a net, catch Beatty's act."—Peter Travers, *Rolling Stone*

Senator Jay Billington Bulworth (Warren Beatty) suffers a nervous breakdown while running for re-election in the controversial political satire *Bulworth.*

 Box Office: $26,528,684

During his four decades in film, Warren Beatty has been one of Hollywood's most outspoken social commentators, both on and off the screen. Despite his carefully calculated persona of the aloof, reckless lothario, Beatty uses his star status to make statements, although he'll be the first to tell you he eschews 'message' movies. In a recent interview he quoted Samuel Goldwyn saying, "If you have a message, don't make a movie, call Western Union."

Beatty has only made 18 films since his debut in 1961 but has spent much of his downtime as a champion for assorted causes, most with a decidedly liberal agenda. After an unimpressive start in mostly lightweight, throwaway romantic fare, Beatty took the title male lead in a film many consider to have been the harbinger of the last cinematic

 Bulworth (Warren Beatty) to a group of Hollywood filmmakers: "Most of your films are not very good. You must be doing it for the money. You turn everything to crap."

revolution in 1967 with *Bonnie & Clyde* (this period [1967–1982] is examined in fine detail in Peter Biskind's enthralling 1997 best-seller *Easy Riders, Raging Bulls*). Since then, the bulk of his roles have leaned towards the anti-hero. Subsequent projects such as *McCabe & Mrs. Miller* [1971], *The Parallax View* [1974] and *Bugsy* [1991] have found Beatty to be the rebel *with* a cause. He has taken villains and infused them with admirable traits along with heavy doses of redeeming social value. Conversely, when he plays the more conventional leading man (*Shampoo* [1975], *Heaven Can Wait* [1978], *Reds* [1981], etc.), he manages to taint them with splashes of unsavory behavior and questionable moral fiber. He likes to keep the audience guessing and begs you to consider several different points of view. In short, he wants you to think for yourself.

With *Bulworth,* Beatty has released one of the great films of 1998 and arguably the most socially aware project taking place in this decade. In *Reds,* he examined the birth of communism. Considering when it came out (just a few years shy of the death of communism), it was a bold and iffy choice, but was rewarded with 11 Academy Award nominations and three Oscars (including one for Beatty for Best Director). It was a movie of epic proportions (read: long and serious) and one of the greatest political statements in movie history. *Bulworth* is *Reds'* funnier, ugly stepsister. Think *Liar Liar* [1997] meeting *Network* [1976] for the political crowd. Already deeply awash in controversy, this brash, in-your-face satire examines the growing chasm between race and class in America.

California senator Jay Billington Bulworth has reached a professional, personal, and spiritual nadir. Days before the '96 election, he has a nervous breakdown. The double-dealing and perpetual state of moral selling-out have taken their toll on him. He sits in his Washington office, watching his most recent campaign ad, chock-full of recycled sound bites, for literally days on end. He is four points behind in the race to retain his seat and Murphy (Oliver Platt), his wickedly efficient campaign manager, has arranged a virtual nonstop homestretch campaign to help boost his sagging numbers. This includes a strategic photo-op with Bulworth's wife Connie (Christine Baranski), who we can surmise has grown weary of playing the devoted wife/political ornament and remains married to her husband solely for the incidental perks the position offers.

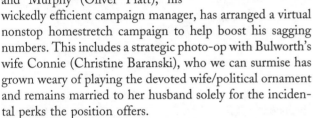

The *Bulworth* soundtrack includes such rap stars as Dr. Dre; LL Cool J; Mack 10; Ice Cube; and Public Enemy.

Before heading out on the final campaign tour, Bulworth hires an assassin with himself as the target. Going days without food or sleep has left him a little loopy, but he is quite clear headed when it comes to arranging his own murder. He's also secured a life insurance policy with a representative (Paul Sorvino) of a nameless company, which is also, ironically, one of the largest contributors to his election campaign. Bulworth's daughter (also unnamed and never seen) is to be the sole recipient of the inflated $10 million policy.

With absolutely nothing to lose and assured that his child will be well taken care of, Bulworth heads back to Los Angeles to begin his mini whistle-stop tour. First up is a visit to Grace Church in South Central. Everything starts off as expected; the same pat speech as heard in the TV commercial, beginning with "we stand at the doorstep of a new millennium," et. al. Suddenly realizing he no longer needs to placate any of his constituents, Bulworth abandons the speech altogether and begins a frank, stream-of-consciousness purging of his soul. Accusing the parishioners of eating too many chicken wings, drinking too much malt liquor and getting behind "a running back who stabs his wife," he reminds them that they are the only ones who can institute change. Of course, they don't hear it that way and, quite understandably, become outraged. Handler Murphy cuts the proceedings short by setting off a fire alarm, but it's too late. The C-SPAN crew covering the event has captured every last word and the crew's producer (Laurie Metcalf) suddenly realizes she sitting on top of a powder keg.

The free-form insults continue to flow at the next stop, a Beverly Hills cocktail party, loaded down with entertainment executives who are predominantly Jewish. While the audience is the polar opposite of the South Central group in every way, Bulworth is no less candid with his opinions. Spouting more ethnic slurs and slamming the movie industry as a whole, Bulworth exits the room with even more jaws agape. For a control freak like Murphy, this type of improvisation is completely unwelcomed and lays waste to his carefully orchestrated plans. Not understanding the reasons why, Murphy is stunned the next day when the expected fallout from the verbal tirades turns out to be a popularity windfall with polls indicating the voters actually prefer an honest politician. Many voters have indicated that they cast their ballots for Bulworth as a write-in candidate for president.

Having freed his mind, Bulworth's body soon follows as he picks up his second wind and heads for an after-hours club in Compton. There he has his first contact with members of the hip-hop crowd and cuts loose for the first time in who knows how long. He also begins to second-guess his decision to off himself. With his awareness of the urban culture and increasing paranoia regarding his own impending assassination, Bulworth becomes one of the faceless members of society he had ignored for so long. Beatty has caught a lot of flak for *Bulworth*'s preoccupation with profanity and what many perceive to be a mocking of urban culture. Obviously, these detractors are unaware that successful, biting satire has to cut a little close to the bone. Bulworth also starts in earnest a mid-life crisis, *Jungle Fever*-flavored fling with Nina (Halle Berry in arguably the best performance of her career), a girl-in-the-'hood who mysteriously shows up at each of Bulworth's stops.

Despite his own personal liberal platform, Beatty made Bulworth a democrat who has soured on the '60s idealism with which he began and, out of necessity, adopted the republican-initiated "family values" mantra. It's as if he made a conscience decision to show how the lines separating the two parties has blurred. *Bulworth* finds Beatty, for really the first time in his career, writing and executing true comedy. Not just the whimsy of *Heaven Can Wait* or failed song-and-dance of *Ishtar*, but actual double-over, bellyaching hilarity. In his typical style he has spread the dialogue around. Knowing a film can only be as good as its weakest links, he is sure to feed even the smallest bit player beefy lines. In addition to Berry, there is Isaiah Washington as Nina's

AWARDS AND NOMINATIONS

Los Angeles Film Critics 1998: Screenplay
Academy Awards 1998 Nominations: Original Screenplay

layabout brother; Sorvino, longtime Beatty associate Jack Warden; Don Cheadle as a drug lord with a conscience; and the scene-stealing Platt.

Followers of Beatty's career are sure to draw comparisons between Jay Bulworth and Beatty himself. Both men, as it turns out, are mavericks who understand that, while it is nearly impossible to change the system, it's easy to subvert it; to get in and agitate it from the center out. When *Bonnie & Clyde* made him a household name, Beatty knew he'd never have to return to the mainstream romance/comedy/drama assembly line. He'd paid his dues and now had the clout to pick and choose his projects carefully. Bulworth speaks the truth and while it shakes people up initially, they grow to accept and actually embrace him. Beatty, much like his contemporary Clint Eastwood, has never lost sight of the commercial demands of his industry and as a result, the mainstream audiences, as well as studio honchos, recognize his commercial viability.

This is just the third time in his career where Beatty has taken on the mammoth task of serving as actor, director, producer, and writer on the same project. With *Heaven Can Wait* and *Reds*, he achieved a major feat by receiving Oscar nominations in all four of those categories. It is not beyond the realm of possibility for him to receive Oscar nominations in those four categories again in 1998. Unlike the relatively polite and genteel *Wag the Dog* [1997] and (practically comatose) *Primary Colors* [reviewed in this issue], Beatty has crafted a political film with bark, bite, *and* a heart. He made an intelligent, socially relevant film that was devoid of pretense and overflowed with humanity. Anyone concerned with the future of this country needs to watch it. Soon.

—*J. M. Clark*

CREDITS

Jay Bulworth: Warren Beatty
Nina: Halle Berry
L.D.: Don Cheadle
Dennis Murphy: Oliver Platt
Graham Crockett: Paul Sorvino
Eddie Davers: Jack Warden
Darnell: Isaiah Washington
Constance Bulworth: Christine Baranski
Mimi: Laurie Metcalf

Origin: USA
Released: 1998
Production: Warren Beatty and Pieter Jan Brugge; released by 20th Century Fox
Direction: Warren Beatty
Screenplay: Warren Beatty and Jeremy Pikser
Cinematography: Vittorio Storaro
Editing: Robert C. Jones, Billy Weber
Music: Ennio Morricone
Production design: Dean Tavoularis
Art direction: William F. O'Brien
Costumes: Milena Canonero
Sound: Thomas Causey
MPAA rating: R
Running Time: 107 minutes

REVIEWS

Chicago Tribune. May 22, 1998, p. 4.
Entertainment Weekly. May 22, 1998, p. 42.
Los Angeles Times. May 15, 1998, p. F1.
New York Times. May 15, 1998, p. E19.
New Yorker. May 11, 1998, p. 62.
People. May 18, 1998, p. 35.
Sight and Sound. February, 1999, p. 40.
Time. May 11, 1998.
USA Today. May 15, 1998, p. 9E.
Variety. May 11, 1998, p. 57.
Washington Post Weekend. May 22, 1998, p. 20.

The Butcher Boy

"Vital & original. A keenly felt, startlingly dark comedy."—Jay Carr, *Boston Globe*

"Neil Jordan's funniest film. He mixes humor with sadness. An excellent performance by Stephen Rea."—Richard Raynor, *Harper's Bazaar*

"Remarkable. Simultaneously comic and horrific, it is the rare film for which there are few descriptions still pure enough. Newcomer Eamonn Owens leaves us speechless."—Elizabeth Weitzman, *Interview*

"Unique and unforgettable. Distinctive, memorable, haunting and hypnotic."—Peter Travers, *Rolling Stone*

"Neil Jordan's best movie yet. Destined to be one of the best movies of 1998!"—John Powers, *Vogue*

 Box Office: $2,063,722

Neil Jordan has, over the last ten years or so, become the most internationally famous filmmaker from Ireland. He serves as a kind of microcosm of that country's recent cinematic re-birth, starting off making low-budget, often television-supported films, spending some time in Britain and Hollywood (where he made *Mona Lisa, High Spirits, We're No Angels,* and *Interview with the Vampire*) and eventually moving to multinational hits about Ireland, such as *The Crying Game* (1992) or *Michael Collins* (1996). He has made a career out of trying to mix the global and the local, Hollywood/City of Dreams with Ireland/The Emerald Isle. His newest film, *The Butcher Boy* is arguably the pinnacle of this mixture, rigorously local and yet moving very much like a multinational arthouse film. Therein lies its downfall.

The film follows the travails of a wisecracking 12-year-old kid named Francie (Eamonn Owens), who is fond of pop culture and prone to outbursts of intense violence. His dad (Stephen Rea) is an alcoholic and his mom (Aisling O'Sullivan) is slowly deteriorating, so Francie spends most of his time running around his small town, Monaghan, getting into trouble with the neighbors and local authorities. If this sounds like a spare plot summary, it's because the narrative itself is quite minimal: most of the film is spent following Francie around,

watching as he tortures neighbors and playmates, and seeing in some pretty grim detail his insanely dysfunctional home life.

The Butcher Boy is in some ways even more local in its orientation than *Michael Collins,* Jordan's epic of the Irish War of Independence. *Michael Collins,* while ostensibly set in colonial era Ireland, was about how war is hell and Julia Roberts is beautiful in a much more central way than it was about Irish history as such, despite all the argument that it generated in the British and Irish press. *The Butcher Boy* is, in a similar way, about a psychopathic little kid, Francie, who struggles, in vain, to rise above all of the factors, cultural and interpersonal, that might destroy him. An obsession with British and American pop culture figures centrally in his attempts to make some sense of his world, and of course this ends up causing as many problems as it promises to solve.

However, the film is also set in the 1960s, a period that, in Ireland, was marked by an extremely repressive, isolationist culture that was totally dominated by a harsh Catholic ethic. Not to mention that Monaghan has got to be one of the least scenic parts of the island of Ireland, a place lacking in any kind of distinct landscape, flat and dull and kind of ugly. This sense of time and place is central in *The Butcher Boy,* for it doesn't take long to understand that out little anti-hero's psychotic lapses into violence are very much a reaction to the repression that surrounds him, a way of letting everyone know that he's nowhere near as beaten or spiritual dead as they are. The violence with which he responds, in this context, serves more to emphasize just what an uphill battle he's waging.

The flip side of this cultural baggage, of course, is that Francie's hallucinogenic lapses are not so much a reaction against as a product of the Catholic ethic that has defined Irish life. Patrick MacCabe, who wrote the novel that the film is based on, told the *New York Times* that "There's nothing more tedious than Irish novelists banging on about the oppression of Catholicism ... I found Catholicism quite imaginative and a rich kind of inheritance, particularly in that period. I always found it a kind of vast and exotic mine to chip away at and use in terms of imagery." This kind of approach to the faith's impact on the nation is also present in *The Butcher Boy,* especially in the way that Francie's hallucinations often draw upon intensely religious imagery, such as a vision of the Virgin Mary, played by a not very virginal looking Sinéad O'Connor. Catholicism provides a rich bank of of-

 Francie (Eamonn Owens): "She had some voice, that Blessed Virgin Mary. You could listen to it all night. It was like the softest woman in the world mixed up in a huge baking bowl, and there you have Our Lady at the end of it."

ten surreal and otherworldly images, and Jordan has certainly made the most of this legacy, showing Francie's inner life in a kind of intense, iconic detail that wouldn't be out of place in religious paintings of the 13th or 14th century.

Some viewers, no doubt, will be extremely put off by the film's protagonist, who *Variety* reviewer Emmanuel Levy has called a combination of Huckleberry Finn and Hannibal Lecter. What makes this kid the most disturbing, however, is not his raw violent impulse, which is troublesome enough, but

Author Patrick McCabe has a cameo as the drunken Jimmy-the-Skite.

the smarmy, smart-ass way that he acts throughout the entire film, whether he's beating on the irritating mother of one of his friends or trying to impress his little buddies with his quick wit. He's completely even throughout the film: an arrogant, terminally ironic little scamp. He is in many ways the portrait of '90s hipdom, always having a remarkably fast, funny, and unfeeling answer to whatever it is that Monaghan has thrown in his way. Jordan seems to be trying to create a character that counters the sterility and austerity of the culture around him with a kind of excess and smartness, and showing the kinds of crises that can occur when this kind of reactionary strategy goes awry.

CREDITS

Francie Brady: Eamonn Owens
Joe: Alan Boyle
Benny Brady: Stephen Rea
Mrs. Nugent: Fiona Shaw
Philip: Andrew Fullerton
Mrs. Brady: Aisling O'Sullivan
Uncle Alo: Ian Hart
Our Lady: Sinead O'Connor

Origin: USA
Released: 1997
Production: Redmond Morris for Geffen Films; released by Warner Bros.
Direction: Neil Jordan
Screenplay: Neil Jordan and Patrick McCabe; based on the novel by McCabe
Cinematography: Adrian Biddle
Editing: Tony Lawson
Production design: Tony Pratt
Art direction: Anna Packard
Costumes: Sandy Powell
Sound: Kieran Horgan
Special effects supervisor: Joss Williams
MPAA rating: R
Running Time: 105 minutes

In that way, *The Butcher Boy*, and especially the very melancholy end of this very hyperactive film, feels altogether coherent and sensible, essentially reminding us that excess of one kind—the oppression of Monaghan—can only be repaid with more excess, the violence of Francie, with Jordan finding a way out only in the mental hospital where Francie winds up a tottering old man. This old man is played by Stephen Rea, who also plays Francie's alcoholic, abusive father, so Jordan is making it pretty obvious just how cyclical this kind of violence is, and how hard it can be to find a way out of it. This peculiar casting decision is especially notable, since it is a very clear example of how Jordan renders the clearly fantastic or surreal— a boy literally growing up to become his father—with a kind of clear, cool detachment. It's a strategy that defines the film overall, and it's a strategy that compromises the film's effectiveness.

Indeed, the way that *The Butcher Boy* is put together really has a way of undercutting the power of some of its most jarring, violent moments. Jordan's early films, such as *Angel* (also released as *Danny Boy*), about a washed-up sax player turned avenger, or even *Mona Lisa*, which was set in London's underworld, had a genuine, uncomfortable sleaziness to them. Shot in grainy stock with highly subdued performances, these films immersed their viewers in the squalor and violence that they sought to narrate. Jordan seems unwilling in *The Butcher Boy* to transplant this kind of cinematic strategy to the world of Monaghan. Instead of a dreary, repressed setting, then, we have a kind of highly artificial and indeed hyper-real rendering of a dreary, repressed setting.

The link with religious painting is especially important here: Jordan's earlier works were sketchy and rough; this film seeks to make the unimaginable so intense and clear that the viewer becomes quite disoriented. Jordan obviously means for this cinematic strategy to correspond to Francie's worldview, a worldview which is embodied by his artificially acid wit. Overall, though, this unwillingness on Jordan's part to simply evoke a sense of place, rather than build a setting from the ground up and then show in great detail why it's so awful, feels forced and insincere. The emotional power of his previous films came from a kind of willingness to be plain, which, admittedly, was probably more the product of a small budget and modest reputation than any kind of commitment to a simple, minimalist style. Nevertheless, these early films get much of their power from their minimalism.

Jordan is in a very different stage of his career now, but *The Butcher Boy* is in large part an attempt to return to the kinds of films that he made when he was just getting his start in Ireland and Britain. What he doesn't seem to understand, though, is that form was central in those early films, and form is exactly what has changed here, with Jordan's visual sense now firmly ensconced in the United States. He has tried to make, then, a very Irish film— set in Monaghan, which is an ugly but deceptively complex place and obsessed with Catholic-influenced themes of repression and innocence—but he has tried to make it in a very Hollywood way—putting a smart, smarmy, but ultimately empty kid at the center of a smartly, expressively evoked setting that is, like the kid, ultimately empty. The results of this unholy marriage are less than satisfying.

—*Jerry White*

REVIEWS

Boxoffice. September, 1997, p. 108.
Chicago Tribune. April 17, 1998, p. 5.
Detroit News. April 17, 1998, p. 3C.
Entertainment Weekly. April 17, 1998, p. 44.
Los Angeles Times. March 29, 1998, p. 7.
Los Angeles Times. April 3, 1998, p. F1.
New York Times. March 29, 1998, p. A17.
People. April 13, 1998, p. 23.
Rolling Stone. July 16, 1998, p. 88.
Sight and Sound. March, 1998, p. 44.
Time. April 6, 1998.
Variety. July 21, 1997, p. 37.
Village Voice. April 7, 1998, p. 68.

Can't Hardly Wait

Yesterday's history. Tomorrow's the future. Tonight's the party.—Movie tagline

"A kind of *American Graffiti* for the millennium. *Can't Hardly Wait* scores points simply for being what it seems like, the first teenage comedy of the 90s."—John Urbancich, *Cleveland Sun Newspapers*

"A refreshingly fast-paced bit of nostalgic fun. A true ensemble piece."—Stephen Thompson, *The Onion*

"Totally enjoyable."—Paul Wunder, *WBAI Radio*

Box Office: $25,605,015

Worthwhile teen flick, if only to catch momentary glimpses of one of a plethora of today's hot young television faces: *Sabrina* star Melissa Joan Hart, *Buffy the Vampire Slayer*'s Seth Green, *Sliders*' Jerry O'Connell and *Dharma & Greg* lead Jenna Elfman. Jennifer Love Hewitt (who plays Amanda Beckett), of course, is one of the *Party of Five*ers. All this small-screen star power adds up to a flicker on the big screen in a loosely put together ensemble romantic comedy effort that has passable humor but fails to produce an engaging main focus.

Preston Meyers (Ethan Embry) is one of the graduating class at Huntington Hills High and the movie's protag-

onist. At the big graduation party on the eve of his departure to study writing with Kurt Vonnegut, the sensitive and overly earnest Preston decides it's finally time to confess his four-year crush on HHH's prom queen, Amanda, after he hears that she and her popular, long time boyfriend Mike (Peter Facinelli) have broken up. The wide-eyed writer-to-be's unending professions of love and tortured inner monologues about Amanda are sometimes delivered to his cute and saucy best friend Denise (Lauren Ambrose) and at other times, delivered directly to the camera, a'la Ferris Bueller, but without the latter's impact. Intending to pour out his heart in a love letter, Preston will deliver the missive to her in person at the party that night. The Preston/Amanda premise is to be the main thread of the picture that incorporates a number of overlapping stories that take place during the evening's festivities.

The usual number of stereotypical characters of this genre (nerd, jock, prom queen) are certainly present and accounted for, but balanced by the originality of some fresh faces portraying them. Standouts include the ever-amusing Seth Green as the slick rapper/hipster Kenny, who sports hugely oversized pants, ski goggles, and two equally clueless sidekicks. Tom Cruise look-alike Facinelli also injects his dumb jock with a dose of depth in a later scene where he gives a drunken apology to the class nerd William (Charlie Korsmo) and actually comes off as

Mike (Peter Facinelli): "I'm a loser. I broke up with the hottest girl in school, my friends all sold me out . . . and somebody in there just called me a fag!"

sincere, dimensional, and most difficult of all, believably drunk. Additionally, Ambrose's fresh-faced sincerity gives loads of appeal to a rebellious, misunderstood character that could've easily been broadly mishandled. Hart lights up the screen as a crazed yearbook signature collector ("These are memories frozen in time, people!")

Although not exclusively a Jennifer Love Hewitt vehicle, it's clear that hers is the star power driving this film. Amanda has little to do here, however, but sneer and listen to the loud praise lavished on her by just about everyone at the party, including her friends ("You're so Gwyneth, but with bigger boobs!"), acquaintances, and just about every stranger she comes into contact with ("You're such a hottie!"). She doesn't seem to even like any of her closest friends, brushing off their concern for her post breakup emotional state in the first few minutes of the party and never talking to them again. She is also forced to haughtily rebuff the advances of more than a few amorous suitors and, finally, dismisses her four-year relationship with Mike, even wondering why she stayed with him at all. Why she is at the party at all is a mystery, other than to wait around for her unknown true love to finally make himself known. Once he

does, there is nothing to stop them from getting together as Amanda brushes off everyone in sight, anyway.

The party itself really doesn't get going until over halfway into the movie. The scene where the nerdy William dips into a keg for the first time is flatter than the beer itself and when the nervous party's hostess thinks she smells feces presumably tracked in by a wayward guest, one is tempted to think it may instead be coming from the script. In all fairness, however, the action does pick up as Denise and Kenny get locked in the bathroom and begin to lose their affectations and inhibitions, making a unlikely love connection. Korsmo's character also takes an interesting turn as he manages, in one high-energy lip-synced moment, to become the life of the party and instant chick-magnet.

Still lacking a clear message up to this point, one is finally hand-delivered to the film in the form of a stripping Angel, played by Elfman. The frustrated Preston, still unable to get Amanda alone to deliver his love letter, leaves the party and pulls over to make a frantic call to request Barry Manilow's "Mandy" to remind him of his beloved Amanda. He is suddenly confronted by the aggressive Angel, who later sits him down to discuss the meaning of fate and responsibility. It's just the thing he needs to hear and roars back to the party to woo his reluctant love.

Continually pumping out the jams, the fast-paced soundtrack, with classics from the past three decades aids in keeping the movie watchable, even during the raw, early moments. Co-writers/directors Harry Elfont and Deborah Kaplan (*A Very Brady Sequel* [1996]) have their fingers on the pulse of today's youth culture and put together a film with some keen observations. While it's still no *Clueless* [1995], there are moments that bring the film to life and separate it from some of the lesser efforts of this genre.

—*Hilary Weber*

CREDITS

Amanda: Jennifer Love Hewitt
Preston: Ethan Embry
William: Charlie Korsmo
Denise: Lauren Ambrose
Mike: Peter Facinelli
Kenny: Seth Green
Girl Whose Party It Is: Michelle Brookhurst

Origin: USA
Released: 1998
Production: Jenno Topping and Betty Thomas for Tall Tress; released by Columbia Pictures
Direction: Harry Elfont, Deborah Kaplan
Screenplay: Deborah Kaplan and Harry Elfont
Cinematography: Lloyd Ahern
Editing: Michael Jablow
Music: David Kitay, Matthew Sweet
Production design: Marcia Hinds-Johnson
Art direction: Bo Johnson
Costumes: Mark Bridges
Sound: David Kirschner
MPAA rating: PG-13
Running Time: 98 minutes

REVIEWS

Chicago Tribune. June 12, 1998, p. 5.
Entertainment Weekly. June 19, 1998, p. 50.
Los Angeles Times. June 12, 1998, p. F6.
New York Times. June 12, 1998, p. E14.
People. June 29, 1998, p. 35.
USA Today. June 12, 1998, p. 13E.
Variety. June 8, 1998, p. 67.
Washington Post Weekend. June 12, 1998, p. 45.

Caught Up

This game has only two rules. Do or die.—Movie tagline

 Box Office: $6,754,958

Caught Up was released in theaters in February of 1998 and by June, it was already languishing on the shelves at video stores. During that time, it barely made a ripple on the public consciousness. That is, if it made any ripple at all. But it's not a big cinematic injustice that the movie didn't catch on because it shouldn't have—the movie really isn't that great. Although *Caught Up* is not hideously bad, it does lack anything that would make it stand out in its genre.

Caught Up focuses on Darryl Allen (Bokeem Woodbine), a hapless ex-con trying to make an honest living. He has spent most of his life in prison (once for a crime he did commit and once for a crime he didn't) and wants to make a clean start. For Darryl, living the straight life proves to be pretty impossible since almost immediately strangers start leaping out of dark corners and trying to shoot him. He hooks up with beautiful fortune teller. Vanessa (Cynda Williams), who, in the first of several improbable plot elements, happens to be a lookalike of his ex-girlfriend Trish. Darryl inadvertently gets caught up in a confusing mess of angry Rastafarians, an unscrupulous cop, and a limo service owner who traffics in dead bodies.

Caught Up has a few interesting touches that make it obvious that writer/director Darin Scott was really trying to make a good film. The story is told in amusing voiceovers by Darryl. In one scene, where Darryl is dancing eagerly at a club, while other dancers look at him quizzically, he says dryly in a voiceover, "I figured out that the dances had changed since I went to prison." The voiceovers also lend the movie, a kind of fairy tale, I'm-going-to-tell-you-a-story feel. And there's some stylish camera work. In a scene where Darryl is being questioned by a police officer, the set is completely dark except for a dramatic spotlight on the two. If nothing else, Scott was wise in choosing his cinematographer Tom Callaway.

Unfortunately, Scott didn't have the same skill in choosing actors. Lead Bokeem Woodbine (who was also in *Jason's Lyric* [1994]) is handsome enough to be a leading man and seems to have some good comedic chops, but some of his acting is really off. It's hard to say whether it was the director choosing bad takes, or that Woodbine really couldn't get a grasp on certain scenes. Sometimes he just yells out a line with a sudden fury that is not merited at all in the scene. It's often hard to tell what his character's mood is in a scene because Woodbine's expressions and line readings will jump

around so much. But Woodbine's acting almost is there—a good acting coach could do wonders for him.

Unfortunately, a team of acting coaches working day and night wouldn't be able to help Cynda Williams. Her blank-faced stares and unexplainably twitchy expressions look lifted directly from the Tori Spelling School of Acting With Facial Tics. Her character is supposed to be a mysterious psychic who can read men's thoughts, but her idea of looking inscrutable is to squint disingenuously at Darryl. She is a looker, however, so one part of her role is done well.

Of course it doesn't help that some of the dialogue is awkward, to say the least. It would be difficult for anyone to make a line like "You are a strong black man who's been through hell and been able to keep your pride and character in tact. You can do anything you want to do," sound natural. Also subpar is the sound quality. In some scenes, characters lines are mumbled or so quiet that they're nearly impossible to hear without changing the volume. In some cases, these scenes are followed by a really loud scene causing more quick dashes to the volume control.

Still, there are several witty or at least unusual touches throughout the film. When Darryl describes prison as being like hell, for example, there is a cut to roaring flames. There are also attempts at tough guy one-liners, a'la *The*

CREDITS

Daryl Allen: Bokeem Woodbine
Vanessa/Trish: Cynda Williams
Billy Grimm: Joseph Lindsey
Herbert/Frank: Clifton Powell
Ahmad: Basil Wallace
Jake: Tony Todd
Roger: LL Cool J
Kool Kitty Kat: Snoop Doggy Dog

Origin: USA
Released: 1998
Production: Peter Heller for Live Film, Mediaworks, and Heller Highwater; released by Live Entertainment
Direction: Darin Scott
Screenplay: Darin Scott
Cinematography: Tom Callaway
Editing: Charles Bornstein
Music: Marc Bonilla
Production design: Terrence Foster
Costumes: Tracey White
Sound: Ben Patrick
MPAA rating: R
Running Time: 97 minutes

Terminator. When Darryl comes across one bad guy playing a shoot 'em up video game, Darryl takes out his own gun and says, "Let me play." After shooting the screen out of the game, Darryl says, "Well, I guess I won that round." As dumb as the line is, maybe it could have worked if Rambo or someone was saying it, but Woodbine's typically awkward reading makes the line fall flat.

But at least *Caught Up* tries to be creative, and compared to many action films, that's something in itself.

—*Jill Hamilton*

REVIEWS

Entertainment Weekly. March 13, 1998, p. 52.
Los Angeles Times. February 27, 1998, p. F6.
Variety. March 2, 1998, p. 84.
Washington Post Weekend. February 27, 1998, p. 43.

Celebrity

A new comedy about people who will do anything to get famous . . . or stay famous.—Movie tagline

"Leonardo DiCaprio juices *Celebrity* with a power surge!"—*Entertainment Weekly*

"A rich, dazzling comedy! A triumphant masterpiece! Leonardo DiCaprio is riotous. Kenneth Branagh's bravura performance is positively amazing!"—Rex Reed *New York Observer*

"The show-stopping Leonardo DiCaprio is shrewdly perfect!"–*New York Times*

"A circus of fun! Leonardo DiCaprio is a live wire. Winona Ryder has never been more bewitching. Charlize Theron is a knockout."–Peter Travers, *Rolling Stone*

"4 stars! Uproarious! Winona Ryder is showstopping"—Mike Clark, *USA Today*

 Box Office: $5,009,081

After the holes punched in his reputation following the scandal over his breakup with Mia Farrow and affair with and subsequent marriage to Soon-Yi Previn, Farrow's adopted daughter, Woody Allen would seem to have something insightful or, at least, amusing to say about nature of celebrity in contemporary America. Considered in the context of the attention his private life has received in recent years, Allen's treatment of

 Robin (Judy Davis) to ex-husband Lee (Kenneth Branagh): "I'm everything I ever hated and I've never been happier."

the incestuous relationship between the media and those they help make famous in *Celebrity*, his twenty-seventh full-length film, is surprisingly superficial.

The film follows the misadventures of New York journalist Lee Simon (Kenneth Branagh) and the wife he has recently divorced after sixteen years of marriage, Robin (Judy Davis), as they encounter celebrities from the worlds of film, television, fashion, and publishing. Lee has a flirtatious encounter with Nola (Winona Ryder), an aspiring actress, and goes with Nicole Oliver (Melanie Griffith), a star he is interviewing, on a visit to her childhood home. After covering a fashion show, he has an impromptu date with a supermodel (Charlize Theron) that ends disastrously. A trip to Atlantic City with Brandon Darrow (Leonardo DiCaprio), a temperamental young actor, and his entourage is even more unpredictable.

Robin, an English teacher, is convinced by friends to visit a famous plastic surgeon, Dr. Lupus (Michael Lerner), and meets Tony Gardella (Joe Mantegna), the producer of a television news unit shooting a segment about the doctor. Tony is instantly smitten with Robin, but she is too damaged by Lee's rejection of her to trust her emotions, as is demonstrated at the showing of a film when she and Tony encounter Lee and his new girlfriend, Bonnie (Famke Janssen), an editor at a publishing house. Lee and Robin disrupt the screening by engaging in a shouting match.

Robin goes to work for Tony and eventually becomes the host of a television talk show.

Celebrity is a portrait of the journalist as parasite. Lee turns to celebrity journalism after his first two novels are poorly received. He tries to exploit his position as interviewer by trying to interest any stars he encounters in the armored-car-heist screenplay he is writing. With Bonnie's encouragement, he abandons that project to write another novel. When he dumps her for Nola, she destroys the manuscript.

Allen's previous film, *Deconstructing Harry* (1997) ends with its despicable protagonist abandoned by everyone but the fictional characters he has created. *Celebrity* takes this motif even further with Lee attending a screening alone and meeting the now happily married Robin and Tony. The film ends with a lingering shot of the pathetically lonely Lee whom Nola has dropped after quickly becoming bored with him. The writer is being punished for failing to be true to his talent, for being selfish and superficial, for mistreating all the women in his life. Because of similar themes in Allen's recent films, especially *Deconstructing Harry*, this period can easily be interpreted as one of self-flagellation.

Allen's last completely satisfying film is the delightful *Manhattan Murder Mystery* (1993). *Bullets over Broadway* (1994), *Mighty Aphrodite* (1995), *Everyone Says I Love You* (1996), and *Deconstructing Harry*, the four films preceding *Celebrity*, all have virtues and flaws, but each offers at least a few moments reminiscent of Allen in his prime. *Celebrity* has not a single memorable scene and only a handful of mildly amusing moments. Some scenes, especially the two involving Tony's large family, are deadly.

Allen's straining for effect can be seen in the arbitrary traffic accident that ends Lee's date with the supermodel and Bonnie's tossing the only copy of his novel from a Hudson River ferry. Do many professional writers Lee's age, especially nationally known journalists, not use word processors and save their manuscripts to disks and hard drives? (Allen told *Newsweek* that he writes his screenplays on the Olympia typewriter he has had since he was sixteen.) Robin asks a prostitute (Bebe Neuwirth) for lessons in oral sex, and the expert gets choked on a banana. This is funny?

There has been a streak of misanthropy and perhaps even misogyny in Allen's films beginning with *Stardust Memories* (1980). This tendency has never been more apparent than in *Celebrity* which seems to sneer at stupid people who think they are bright or creative, superficial young people, smugly superior critics, neurotic and vain women, Italian-Americans, and Catholics. *Stardust Memories*, the Allen film *Celebrity* most closely resembles, looks at the demands fans make on the famous while *Celebrity* implies that fame corrupts and taints everyone who comes into contact with the famous. Darrow strikes Vicky (Gretchen Mol), his girlfriend, and everyone, including Vicky, thinks it is all right for him to get away with such behavior. Lee is concerned less with her welfare than with getting the young star interested in his screenplay.

Reviewers of *Celebrity* commented most often on Branagh's apparent imitation of Allen's patented acting style: stammering, pausing, slowing down at the end of a line. Branagh has said in interviews that he is simply delivering the lines as written and is not consciously imitating Allen. Many other performers in Allen's recent films, notably Edward Norton in *Everyone Says I Love You*, have given readings reminiscent of Allen, but Branagh stands out a bit more perhaps because his voice has a similar pitch to that of Allen. Branagh, a likable actor, is perhaps too likable for this part. Lee is too weak, leaving a gaping hole at the center of the film. The character might have been more effective as a more clearly cynical, self-destructive opportunist, like Tony Cur-

Allen's movie opened the prestigious New York Film Festival in 1998, making it the first film in Woody Allen's career to open a film festival.

CREDITS

Lee Simon: Kenneth Branagh
Robin Simon: Judy Davis
Tony Gardella: Joe Mantegna
Bonnie: Famke Janssen
Nola: Winona Ryder
Supermodel: Charlize Theron
Nicole Oliver: Melanie Griffith
Brandon Darrow: Leonardo DiCaprio
Prostitute: Bebe Neuwirth
Dr. Lupus: Michael Lerner
Philip Datloff: Larry Pine
David: Hank Azaria
Psychic: Aida Turturro
Film director: Greg Mottola
Vicky: Gretchen Mol
Cheryl: Kate Burton
Iris: Patti D'Arbanville
Frankie: Frank Pellegrino
Bruce Bishop: Isaac Mizrahi
Off-Off Broadway director: Jeffrey Wright
Bill Gaines: Douglas McGrath

Origin: USA
Released: 1998
Production: Jean Doumanian for Sweetland Films; released by Miramax Films
Direction: Woody Allen
Screenplay: Woody Allen
Cinematography: Sven Nykvist
Editing: Susan E. Morse
Production design: Santo Loquasto
Set decoration: Susan Kaufman
Costumes: Suzy Benzinger
Sound: Les Lazarowitz
MPAA rating: R
Running Time: 113 minutes

tis' immortal Sidney Falco in *The Sweet Smell of Success* (1957), still the best film about fame.

Davis, a wonderful actress, gives only a slight variation on the insecure, hysterical women she has portrayed in several Allen films, most recently in *Deconstructing Harry*, and Mantegna, an underrated actor, plays almost the same nice guy as in Allen's *Alice* (1990). The most notable performances in Celebrity are those of DiCaprio and Theron, both of whom display considerable presence and energy.

Along with *Manhattan* (1979) and *Stardust Memories*, *Celebrity* is another in the surprisingly long line of black-and-white Allen films. The director has said that he simply likes working in black and white, especially because he loves the way New York City, the setting of most of his films, looks without color. The images remind him of the way the city looked, when he was growing up, in photographs in tabloid newspapers, a fitting similarity given the tabloid nature of *Celebrity*. The film is the fourth collaboration between Allen and Sven Nykvist, the great cinematographer most closely associated with the director's idol, Ingmar Bergman, but the first in black and white. Nykvist captures the grit and glamour of Manhattan. He has always highlighted the physical features of the actresses whom he has shot, and Nykvist's lighting is flattering to all the women in *Celebrity*, particularly Janssen, Theron, Griffith, and Ryder. Branagh is made to look appropriately harried, almost seedy, in his desperation.

What finally does *Celebrity* have to say about its subject? There is a lot of it around these days. The presence of such real celebrities as writer Erica Jong, basketball star Anthony Mason, and business mogul Donald Trump (who has one of the few funny lines) does little to enhance Allen's satire. *Wild Man Blues* (1998), Barbara Kopple's enormously entertaining documentary about Allen's jazz tour of Europe, (also reviewed in this edition) has more to say in any one scene about the demands of fame and how the famous exploit their celebrity than anything Allen does here. Allen is admirable for turning out, without fail, a film every year that reflects his artistic vision. The problem is that his vision is becoming a tad cloudy.

—*Michael Adams*

REVIEWS

Boston Globe. November 20, 1998, p. C5.
Entertainment Weekly. November 20, 1998, p. 92.
Interview. November, 1998, p. 63.
Los Angeles Times. November 20, 1998, p. F10.
Nation. October 26, 1998, p. 36.
New York Times. September 25, 1998, p. B1.
New Yorker. November 23, 1998, p. 113.
Newsweek. November 23, 1998, p. 88.
People. November 30, 1998, p. 34.
Rolling Stone. November 26, 1998, p. 131.
Time. November 16, 1998, p. 104.
USA Today. November 20, 1998, p. E10.
Variety. August 31, 1998, p. 49.
Washington Post. November 20, 1998, p. F5.

Central Station; Central do Brasil

He was looking for a father he never knew. She was looking for a second chance.—Movie tagline

"Like De Sica and Renoir, a richly tender and moving experience!"—Owen Gleiberman, *Entertainment Weekly*

"A personal triumph and a rich cinematic experience!"—Kevin Thomas, *Los Angeles Times*

"A bravura performance!"—Janet Maslin, *New York Times*

"Montenegro has a particular skill shared by great actresses as disparate as Bette Davis, Jeanne Moreau and Giulietta Masina."—David Denby, *New Yorker*

 Box Office: $3, 468,000

A search for a young boy's father joins strangers Dora (Fernanda Montenegro) and Josue (Vinicius De Oliveira) in the acclaimed Brazilian drama *Central Station*.

Reports of the death of Brazilian cinema, although numerous, are indeed greatly exaggerated. The kind of energy and productivity that marked filmmaking in that country has been greatly reduced over the last decade or two (by 1992 economic collapse had halted feature filmmaking entirely), but there is now a discernible re-birth underway. Filmmaker Walter Salles stands at the forefront of that blossoming, and his new feature *Central Station* has a potential for wide appeal, although it never loses sight of the deeply tragic plight of the country where it takes place. The film is so powerful and yet so watchable that it just might put Brazilian cinema back on the map. Salles makes the most of Brazil's landscape, and by both focusing closely on the squalor of São Paulo and taking us to the very edges of the country he shows just how desolate and poor his homeland really is. The film does, however, have some real heart-jerking moments, some of which threaten to send it careening into the realm of the sentimental. Fortunately, Salles tempers this with a sober ending, making *Central Station* a clearheaded, involving film. It's something of a departure from Salles' earlier film *A Foreign Land* (1995), but what he sacrifices in visual innovation and explicit political comment he makes up for in emotional impact and broader social concern.

The film begins by introducing us to Dora (played by the famous Brazilian actress Fernanda Montenegro), who makes her living by writing letters for illiterate people from a little table she sets up in the train station. It quickly comes out that as a kind of revenge for the fact that she can no longer teach school as she used to, she never mails the letters, taking cruel advantage of those who are among Brazil's most desperate. This is how she comes to meet Josué (Vinicíus de Olivera), whose mother wanted Dora to write a letter encouraging his father, living in Brazil's remote Northeast, to come and see his boy. There's little doubt that because of de Olivera's gentle, intelligent, and painfully realistic performance that he will go down alongside other great child-stars-in-distress such as *The Bicycle Thief*'s Enzo Staiola or *Pixote*'s Ramos de Silva. Josué's real distress begins when his mom is killed by a bus right after having her letter written. Dora takes him in and agrees to give him to men who say they run an orphanage, and who also agree to give her enough money to buy a new TV. When it becomes clear that the men actually mean to kill Josué and sell his organs, Dora is overcome with guilt and flees with him in search of his father. They meet the usual colorful cast of characters, some of which begin to restore the very cynical Dora's faith in humanity. Along the way she, of course, develops a motherly relationship with Josué, although when they locate Josué's brothers, she knows that she has to give it up. This is certainly hard for her, but Salles keenly plays

this as a less than tragic moment—Josué's life has been given new possibility, and Dora has been redeemed. In the midst of unimaginable poverty and depravity, all is well.

Salles is not a fantastically famous filmmaker, although his work has gotten some international exposure, and his trademark visual style can certainly be seen in *Central Station*. His 1995 film, *A Foreign Land*, co-directed by Daniela Thomas, was much more visually adventurous than *Central Station*, although both share a preponderance towards documentary-style realism and huge, gorgeous panoramas and a road-movie-esque motif of wandering. *Land* dealt with immigration from Brazil to Portugal in the wake of Brazil's currency collapse in the early 1990s, and its narrative is much more closely connected to specific political events in Brazil than *Station*, whose focus on urban and rural poverty makes the film seem less connected to a single historical moment. Nevertheless, *A Foreign Land* marked Salles as a filmmaker who was just as concerned with both radical form *and* content as any of the *Cinema Novo* filmmakers who had first brought Brazilian cinema to wide attention in the 1960s.

Whether *Central Station* lives up to its film legacy is another matter, although the ways in which it departs from that cinematic practice do not necessarily make it a weaker film. The plot is much more theatrical than would be expected from some of the more politically fiery work of the 1960s, and in that way it harkens back to an even earlier era of Latin American cinema, the 1940s and 50s, also known as the golden age of the melodrama. Salles is using melodrama in a way that makes the most of its emotional appeal, arousing outrage and sadness at conditions that are very much the product of the economic irresponsibility that has perhaps irreparably scarred Brazil. When Josué's mom is killed by a bus, it seems almost impossibly sudden but also inevitable: from the moment the little scamp comes on to the screen it's obvious something really bad is going to happen to him. Rather than only milk this plot twist for its handkerchief value (which Salles certainly does), he also uses it to call attention to the really awful things that happen to orphans in a country that doesn't have the financial resources to look after them.

The purchase of the television by Dora clearly echoes

> Director Walter Salles discovered Vinicius de Oliveira at the airport where the boy shined shoes.

AWARDS AND NOMINATIONS

Golden Globes 1999:   Foreign Film
Los Angeles Film Critics 1998:   Actress (Fernanda Montenegro)
National Board of Review 1998:   Actress (Fernanda Montenegro); Foreign Film
Academy Awards 1998 Nominations: Actress (Fernanda Montenegro); Foreign Film

the moment in the Douglas Sirk melodrama *All That Heaven Allows* (1955) when Jane Wyman's kids give her a TV and thereby signal her apparent spiritual death. However, Salles is able to invest what was originally a manipulative emotional moment about purely inner turmoil with some very acidic commentary about the price of materialism in a country defined by scarcity. This kind of "enhanced" melodrama is what defines *Central Station*: Salles is unwilling to give his viewer the kind of emotional pleasure that is melodrama's stock in trade without also forcing an understanding of the social realities of Brazil. It's not as politically explicit a strategy as would be favored by more radical filmmakers, but it does eschew the difficulties inherent in watching so many of the films that came out of Latin America in the 1960s, many of which eschewed such bourgeois trappings as coherent narrative or realistic performances. In a way that many of the *Cinema Novo* filmmakers never understood, *Station* is a populist film, and one that invests the popular forms with a call to reform systems that hold people under the boot of poverty.

Salles' decision to set most of the film in the rural hinterlands of Brazil is an especially important aspect of the film, given how utterly different this empty place is from the country's impossibly crowded cities. *Central Station* remains unsparing in its depiction of extreme poverty, although the kinds of dangers and struggles that Salles shows to go on "out there" are quite different from what Dora had become accustomed to dealing with during her comparatively comfortable life in S;atao Paulo. What's impressive about the way that Salles represents rural life is the way that he does away with the expected strategy of making the place look dusty, windswept, and mysterious. It's all of those things, of course, but Salles always counteracts such romanticism with illustrations of nastiness and squalor.

What's most impressive, though, is that despite making his viewer understand this place as harsh and nasty, Salles is able to turn the tables 360° and make the rural setting the place where the film finds its happy ending. This landscape ends up being where Josué is able to find a life for himself, as the film climaxes with the discovery of his brothers, who live in a very eerie, half-unfinished town. While Salles' rural Brazil is a place of harshness, it is also a place of possibility in a way that the city is not. This is a keen insight, rendered with a minimum of sentimentality and a maximum of socio-political impact.

Central Station is, finally, a mixture of Brazil's cinematic traditions. It is just as politically aware and insurgent in spirit as any of the radical films of the 1960s, but Salles also brings a sense of optimism and a common touch to the project. It's important not to underestimate the power of such revisions: the film is likely to do more to bring the plight of average Brazilians to international attention than almost all of the esoteric, often difficult to watch films of the *Cinema Novo* movement. Salles leaves himself open to charges of manipulation and simplification, of course, but such compromises pale in comparison to the sheer breadth of his concerns and insights on what it means to live in the third world at the end of the 20th century. Much more than a simple tearjerker, *Central Station* visualizes in painful detail what happens when a country on the way to economic prosperity goes badly and perhaps permanently bust. Salles' mixture of the popular and the political is something that a great number of filmmakers could learn from.

—Jerry White

CREDITS

Dora: Fernanda Montenegro
Irene: Marilia Pera
Josue: Vinicius de Oliveira
Cesar: Othon Bastos

Origin: Brazil, France
Released: 1998
Production: Arthur Cohn and Martine de Clermont-Tonnerre for MACT Productions, Videofilms, Riofilme, and Canal Plus; released by Sony Pictures Classics
Direction: Walter Salles
Screenplay: Joao Emanuel Carneiro and Marcos Bernstein
Cinematography: Walter Carvalho
Editing: Isabelle Rathery, Felipe Lacerda
Music: Antonio Pinto, Jacques Morelembaum
Production design: Cassio Amarante, Carla Caffe
Costumes: Cristina Camargo
MPAA rating: Unrated
Running Time: 110 minutes

REVIEWS

Daily Variety. November 20, 1998, p. 9.
Entertainment Weekly. November 27, 1998, p. 56.
Los Angeles Times. November 25, 1998, p. F8.
New York Times. November 20, 1998, p. E10.
People. December 7, 1998, p. 31.

Chairman of the Board

Work sucks!—Movie tagline

Box Office: $306, 715

As low as expectations were for Carrot Top's film debut, *Chairman of the Board* still managed to disappoint. Besides being unfunny, the film is unengaging and, after a point, just plain tiresome.

The story stars Carrot Top as Edison, a wacky wannabe inventor who lives in a beach house with his two dim-witted friends, Ty (Mystro Clark) and Freemont (Jock Plotnick). The three spend their time surfing and trying to avoid their landlady (Estelle Harris), who is so crass as to actually want her tenants to pay rent.

One fateful day, Edison helps a man, Armand McMillian (Jack Warden), fix his car. (Surprisingly, Armand doesn't seem to notice that Edison's method of fixing the car involves ripping it apart only to declare the problem a broken fan belt. Hey, thanks.) Later, Edison receives word that Armand is dead and that Armand has declared Edison chairman of the board of his large company. This angers Bradford McMillian (Larry Miller), Armand's evil nephew, who wants the company for himself so he can sell out to the sexy head of a rival company (Raquel Welch).

Much of the "humor" in *Chairman of the Board* revolves around the relationship between Bradford and Edison. Unfortunately for the audience, this relationship never goes any deeper than the one between Sergeant Carter and Gomer Pyle on the old TV show *Gomer Pyle, U.S.M.C.* Edison annoys Bradford, Bradford yells. Edison ruins Bradford's car, Bradford yells.

Although Bradford is an acceptably evil villain, he is too blundering to be an interesting foe. For example, when he attempts to open a lawn chair, he fumbles and hurts himself. Even when he tries a simple maneuver such as applying sunscreen, he squirts it all over himself. Thus, the question of who will finally gain control of the company is never a mystery.

Because the plot lacks any real jeopardy for the characters, the movie is left to follow the antics of Edison and his zany inventions. Most of these inventions are only mildly amusing, at best. One is a special drinking device with a head heater so users can wear it when slurping frozen drinks and avoid "brain freeze." Another is an "anatomically correct fanny pack" shaped like a fanny. Another a catsup bottle with a hand attached so the user doesn't have to hit the bottle themselves. Another is a personal bug zapper—a bug zapper attached to a hat. These inventions are mildly amusing, but certainly not enough to carry a movie.

The editing in the film is quick and jumpy, which seems like it might be a good thing, but is not. Instead of giving the film a brisk pace and a modern MTV sheen, it makes the story seem disjointed. And, unfortunately, no amount of brisk cutting helps make this movie any less tiring.

The only thing that shows any inspiration in *Chairman of the Board* is the set design. Everything, including Edison himself, is brightly colored and fast moving. Edison lives in a Pee Wee Hermanesque world of cartoonish shapes, colorful patterns, and unusual contraptions. When the movie starts, Edison is awakened by a Rube Goldberg-like alarm clock that ejects him from his bed, then plops him in a wacky shower that washes him. It's fairly inventive and a promising start, but is no substitute for an entertaining plot.

Carrot Top's real name is Scott Thompson.

CREDITS

Edison: Carrot Top
Natalie: Courtney Thorne-Smith
Bradford: Larry Miller
Grace Kosik: Raquel Welch
Armand: Jack Warden
Ty: Mystro Clark
Zak: Jack Plotnick
Ms. Krubavitch: Estelle Harris
Freemont: M. Emmet Walsh

Origin: USA
Released: 1998
Production: Peter M. Lenkov and Rupert Harvey for 101st Street Films; released by Trimark Pictures
Direction: Alex Zamm
Screenplay: Al Septien, Turi Meyer, and Alex Zamm
Cinematography: David Lewis
Editing: Jim Hill
Music: Chris Hajian
Production design: Aaron Osborne
Costumes: Seok H. Yoon
Sound: Christopher M. Taylor, Peter V. Meiselmann
Visual effects supervision: John Lindauer
MPAA rating: PG-13
Running Time: 95 minutes

As the main character and the romantic lead, Carrot Top never quite pulls it off. He has a rubbery face and, with his wild shock of red hair, an interesting look, but his character isn't particularly lovable or engaging. Edison, with his slacker ways, doesn't really seem to care what happens to him, so why should the audience?

As Edison's love interest, Natalie Stockwell, Courtney Thorne-Smith proves it is possible to be on a show worse than her former gig, *Melrose Place*. Her part is just as unbelievable a character as anyone on that show. Thorne-Smith has the difficult task of playing a woman who finds it entertaining when Edison takes her on a date and burps really loudly.

Although Carrot Top and his inventions finally save the company in *Chairman of the Board*, they don't do the same for the movie. Simply put, Carrot Top isn't funny enough.

Jokes like "This must be the board room because you all look so bored" might work on Carrot Top's stand-up circuit, but for audiences weaned on edgy comedies like TV's *South Park*, that kind of material is far too tame.

—*Jill Hamilton*

REVIEWS

Entertainment Weekly. March 27, 1998, p. 48.
Los Angeles Times. March 16, 1998, p. F5.
New York Times. March 14, 1998, p. B17.
Variety. March 23, 1998, p. 89.

The Chambermaid on the Titanic; La Femme de Chambre du Titanic; The Chambermaid

There was more than one love story on the Titanic.—Movie tagline

"*Like Water for Chocolate* meets *Titanic*."—Brandon Judell, *America Online*

"A sensuous study of romantic fantasy."—Stephen Farber, *Movieline*

"A lush, crazily romantic movie. Olivier Martinez is frighteningly handsome."—Dennis Dermody, *Paper*

"*The Chambermaid on the Titanic* emphasizes the powers of eroticism and the imagination."—Leslie Camhi, *Village Voice*

"The best foreign film of the year."—Casper Citron, *WOR Radio*

 Box Office: $244,465

French foundry worker Horty (Olivier Martinez) wins a strongman contest and his prize is a trip to Southampton to see the launch of the Titanic. When he's settled in his hotel room, Marie (Aitana Sanchez-Gijon) comes to his door and tells him she is a maid on the ship but has nowhere to stay until the liner's departure because all the hotel rooms are filled. Horty offers to share and, despite Marie's efforts to seduce him, maintains his distance by sleeping in a chair. However, this doesn't stop him from having vivid erotic dreams about the beautiful woman, which will play a significant part in Horty's life.

CREDITS

Horty: Olivier Martinez
Marie: Aitana Sanchez Gijon
Zoe: Romane Bohringer
Simeon: Didier Bezace
Zeppe: Aldo Maccione

Origin: France, Spain
Released: 1997
Production: Yves Marmion and Daniel Toscan du Plantier; released by Samuel Goldwyn Company
Direction: Bigas Luna
Screenplay: Bigas Luna and Cuca Canals; based on the novel by Didier Decoin
Cinematography: Patrick Blossier
Editing: Kenout Peltier
Music: Alberto Iglesias
Production design: Gualtiero Caprara
Sound: Jean Paul Mugel
MPAA rating: Unrated
Running Time: 96 minutes

The next morning, Marie is gone but Horty notices a photograph of her taken by a man recording the big event and buys it as a keepsake. Back home, rumors are rampant that Horty's wife Zoe (Romane Bohringer), who also works at the foundry, has been sleeping with their boss. Horty is given a promotion and an easier job at the foundry and decides that Zoe has been unfaithful, despite her denials. When Horty learns of the Titanic's sinking, he drunkenly shows off Marie's photo to his buddies. They press him for details of his sexual escapade and Horty impulsively recounts his erotic dream of his one-night with a young woman tragically drowned at sea.

Horty's story draws more and more listeners and his retelling grows more and more inventive and elaborate (the story is shown in imaginary flashbacks). When travelling actor Zeppe (Aldo Maccione) hears the saga, he invites Horty to go on the road with him and tell his story to a paying audience. The jealous Zoe even agrees to accompany him and play Marie for the spectators in order to rescue her marriage. By this time, Horty's fantasy has

become so real to him, he doesn't even remember that the story isn't true.

While the cast and the look of the film are both gorgeous, the film is basically stylish fluff with a cold heart. *Chambermaid* follows Luna's Italian-based picture *Bambolla* as the second film in a trilogy dealing with women as objects of desire and obsession. The final film is expected to be a version of *Carmen* to be shot in Spain.

—*Christine Tomassini*

REVIEWS

Boxoffice. August, 1998, p. 45.
Los Angeles Times. September 11, 1998, p. F16.
New York Times. August 14, 1998, p. E6.
People. September 14, 1998, p. 50.
San Francisco Chronicle. September 4, 1998, p. C1.
San Francisco Examiner. September 4, 1998, p. C5.
Variety. October 27, 1997, p. 43.

Character; Karakter

"A spellbinding tale!"—Laurence Chollet, *Bergen Record*

"Superb! A tale of emotion strangled by pride."—Kevin Thomas, *Los Angeles Times*

"A marvelous story! Better than Oscar-worthy! A full-bodied Dickensian delight! The most unforgettable characters you are likely to meet on the screen this year."—Andrew Sarris, *New York Observer*

"Extraordinarily powerful and gripping. First class entertainment, superbly photographed and directed. Four stars, don't miss it."—Paul Wunder, *WBAI Radio*

 Box Office: $713, 413

Character plunges the viewer directly into a fatal struggle between father and son, and the results of their battle with each other pulls us in and wears us out. This Dutch film, winner of the 1997 Academy Award for Best Foreign Film, recreates a world of dark internecine war, but also portrays a mother so reserved she never shares real affection with her only child—or anyone. *Character* is a very well-

known book in the Netherlands; Ferdinand Bordewijk's 1938 novel is read by nearly every high school student. The father, bailiff Dreverhaven, has both stamina and stoicism on his side, and we watch his son, Katadreuffe, flail against his rock-like parent and antagonist with concern and a sense of the inevitable. Does the slender, bookish young man have enough resources to survive his parents? Many reviewers remarked on the Dickensian overtones of the story, but as Janet Maslin of *The New York Times* points out, Kafka comes to mind as well.

The director undertook a difficult task—that of revising a classic: "I changed it a lot. I have always been an original screenplay writer, so that probably gave me the tools to go so freely with it . . . It became a classic because it had these great characters—these monumental, silent, characters . . . What makes it, perhaps, into an interesting film is something that was very much between the lines, but we tried very hard to visualize: the darker side of the father's character, his whole death-defying demeanor, his flirtation with the darkest stuff imaginable."

First-time feature director Mike van Diem is a celebrity in Holland, even before the Oscar. In an interview with *Salon Magazine*, Van Diem said: "Probably the reason why *Character* is so incredibly big is because, . . . the film already had a good reputation at home. Right after the nominations, *Variety* had put the front-runner stamp on it, and the people at home smelled victory—they went all out. Now the media craze in Holland is unimaginable. There are journalists tracking down people I went to film school with, to interview them about me. I am like Monica Lewinsky. At home, I am bigger than Monica Lewinsky."

In adapting this coming-of-age story, Van Diem added a murder mystery, more or less successfully. As the film opens, a violent confrontation between father and son leads to a police interrogation: but if it is patricide, the film says to us, let me show you this monster of a man, and you decide if he deserved to die. The real heart of the story lies in the father-son relationship which is unmarked by tenderness, only by mercantile calculations and psychological one-upsmanship by both of them.

Inspector de Bree (Frans Vorstman): "Dreverhaven. That name sounds like imminent thunder, right?" Katadreuffe (Fedja van Huet): "The name was a legend long before I first heard it."

It is hard to imagine this youth of delicate features and temperament being born of these two people. The fateful event that sets *Character* in motion is an abrupt sexual encounter between the bailiff Dreverhaven (Jan Decleir) and his housekeeper Joba (Betty Schuurman). The stolid Dreverhaven pushes away from the table as if he'd suddenly had a hunger for something else, strides into the room next door where Joba is in her shift, brushing her long red hair. He seizes her and she doesn't struggle or object, merely complies with his desire. Her face registers no emotion, not even surprise. The voice-over informs us that this liaison was a one-time event, never repeated. Joba is anything but clinging—upon finding herself pregnant, she leaves her job and Dreverhaven. She refuses his missives, always bearing the same question: "When will the wedding be?"

She raises her child alone, in poverty, and remains impassive and silent. One shattering scene has the boy set upon by neighborhood bullies; when Joba comes running to pull the boy off one of his tormentors, another woman spits in her face and yells, "Whore!" Joba's response is characteristic—she grimly packs up and moves them to another neighborhood.

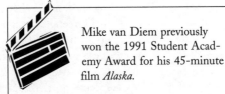

Mike van Diem previously won the 1991 Student Academy Award for his 45-minute film *Alaska*.

Dreverhaven, feared and hated by his tenants and grudgingly respected by the legal establishment who appreciate his zeal in pursuing ne'er-do-wells while deploring his manner and methods, is a towering figure in the community. The boy (who throughout his youth is haplessly caught up in one misadventure after another) is rejected by Dreverhaven when called to rescue him from jail after one such mishap. His illegitimacy is a stigma, but his father's incessant cruelties are what truly mark him. The young Katadreuffe (Fedja van Huet) must contend with his father's efforts to ruin him, first by calling in ruinous loans made to him by a credit com-

pany (the bailiff is a wealthy miser who, it seems, controls the "financial institutions" and housing for the poor of Rotterdam), and in the law firm, a haughty gatekeeper lawyer who dislikes him intensely.

Katadreuffe, a self-educated prodigy, also has two remarkably kind and understanding mentors, his mother's boarder, Jan (Hans Kesting), a young Red who attempts to protect mother and son, and De Gankelaar (Victor Low), a charming and quirky lawyer with a unique and almost comical way of speaking, who helps him overcome class barriers to win admission to the legal profession.

Director Mike van Diem has recreated 1920s Rotterdam with care and remarkable detail— the film's visuals make a more powerful impression since the dialogue is spare and full of significance. The production traveled to Belgium, Poland, and Germany to help recreate the pre-World War II port city. The cinematography of Rogier Stauffers portrays a world of darkness and closed-in interiors; despite that, one set in particular, the wood-paneled beehive of a law office where young Katadreuffe makes his mark as a clerk and then as a lawyer, is exquisite. Van Diem said, "I wanted to keep the camera moving to sort of counterpoint the photography, which is sometimes really breathtaking, but I didn't want to create a perfect picture-book. I wanted a 'motion' picture, in the true meaning of the word." The camera moves with the flow of the office, as Katadreuffe stares upwards in awe, instantly smitten. You readily understand how much he loves this world and will sacrifice to be a part of it. Van Diem also opens up the story into the light— a scene at the beach and in a green, leafy park show the possibilities for a life outside the office that our driven hero turns away from, choosing the ferocious struggle with his father above any happiness.

As for Dreverhaven, his stoic malevolence is matched by his massive presence—Jan Decleir (memorable in *Antonia's Line*, 1995) is superb as the bailiff. Garbed in severe black, unsmiling, with startling eyes that bore into the viewer as he stares down his victims, Decleir gives *Character* its force and validity. Not a shred of scenery chewing mars his rather frightening performance. One dream sequence, wherein the bailiff, naked but for the chain of his office, faces a torch-bearing mob of his angry tenants, is particularly powerful. In his shadow, appropriately enough, is the slighter, but still memorable performance of Fedja van Huet as Katadreuffe. Many reviewers commented on van Huet's likeness to Robert Downey Jr. (while calling the American a far better actor). This is unfair to van Huet, who is required to be wan and easily-led, a person that all his elders seek to toughen or torment (and in the father's case, both—with a vengeance.) His gradual transformation shows van Huet to be a very expressive and subtle performer.

Lorna Te George (Tamar van den Dop), a lovely and perceptive young secretary in the law firm, is as emotionally open and charming as his mother is cold and repressed. Despite his longing for Lorna and a yearning for a family life he's never known, Katadreuffe allows her to slip away. Time passes and the now dying Joba observes their chance meeting in the park where he has taken his mother. Lorna is pushing a stroller, adding to the poignancy of the encounter and the two exchange strained pleasantries. He blurts out to Lorna that he will never marry anyone else. Joba scornfully calls her son a fool for choosing his career over Lorna, now another man's wife. This astringent remark disperses any maudlin feeling in the scene, a characteristic of the screenplay.

Alternately fierce and delicately wrought, *Character* sometimes seems as confused as its hero. As a bildungsroman, it has comic touches and excruciatingly painful moments as Katadreuffe is brought to an understanding of himself, particularly as he reaches his greatest success and finds it less than he imagined. As he says to Dreverhaven in their final confrontation: "Today I have been made a lawyer. You no longer exist for me! You have worked against me all my life," "Or for you," the father answers. As in *Great Expectations,* he is pursued by a Magwitch-like father whose idea of parenting is to exclaim "I'll strangle him for nine tenths and the tenth will make him strong!" Dreverhaven's death hardly sets him free; he inherits his fortune and must now reckon with what his lifelong antagonism has cost him.

—*Mary Hess*

CREDITS

Katadreuffe: Fedja van Juet
Dreverhaven: Jan Decleir
Joba: Betty Schuurman
Lorna Te George: Tamar van den Dop
De Gankelaar: Victor Low
Jan Maan: Hans Kesting
Inspector de Bree: Frans Vorstman

Origin: Netherlands
Released: 1997
Production: Laurens Geels; released by Sony Pictures Classics
Direction: Mike van Diem
Screenplay: Mike van Diem, Laurens Geels, and Ruud van Megen; based on the novel *Karakter* by Ferdinand Bordewijk
Cinematography: Rogier Stoffers
Editing: Jessica de Koning
Music: Paleis van Boem
Production design: Niko Post
Costumes: Jany Temine
MPAA rating: R
Running Time: 114 minutes

REVIEWS

Boxoffice. May, 1998, p. 75.
Entertainment Weekly. April 17, 1998, p. 48.
Los Angeles Times. March 27, 1998, p. F12.
New York Times. March 22, 1998, p. AR1.
New York Times. March 27, 1998, p. E14.
New Yorker. May 11, 1998, p. 107.
People. April 13, 1998, p. 19.
Sight and Sound. September, 1998, p. 40.
Time. April 13, 1998.
Washington Post. April 17, 1998, p. B1.
Washington Post. April 19, 1998, p. G6.
Washington Post Weekend. April 17, 1998, p. 56.

Chile: Obstinate Memory; Chile, la Memoria Obstinada

Patricio Gúzman is one of the most seasoned veterans of third world cinema. His 1974 epic *The Battle of Chile* is a classic of political documentary, and one of his more recent films *The Southern Cross* (made in Spain) tackled head-on the legacy of Spanish exploration just in time for the various 1992 commemorations. His newest work, *Chile: Obstinate Memory*, deals with the memory, or lack thereof, of the coup that toppled Chile's democratically elected Socialist president, Salvador Allende and led to years of brutal repression and military dictatorship by General Augusto Pinochet. It mixes conventional interviews, re-enactments, and group discussions in a very smooth way, making this a powerful, formally varied film. The very fact that he was able to make this film constitutes a kind of moral triumph for Gúzman, but simply as a work of art, it's also a triumph of committed documentary.

Gúzman made his name in the early seventies with *The Battle of Chile*, a film that hangs heavy over *Chile: Obstinate Memory*. He started making that film right before the coup that toppled Allende, and it is compromised largely of newsreel-style footage of demonstrations and clashes with police and soldiers during the weeks when the outcome of the coup was up for grabs. Gúzman was one of the thousands of activists who were rounded up during the coup and detained at the huge soccer stadium in downtown Santiago (Chile's capital city). Unlike many of those detainees, he walked out of the stadium alive, and eventually finished his film in Cuba. *The Battle of Chile* had never actually been shown in Chile, though, so he decided to return to do just that and make a film about the legacy of the coup. The form that *Chile: Obstinate Memory* ends up taking is pretty loose: it moves from one group of people to another without an enormous amount of rhyme or reason for the transitions. What it does do, though, is provide a snapshot of a country defined both by willful amnesia and inescapable memories. Despite the wishes of many Chileans, Gúzman shows, these arguments about Allende and Pinochet are by no means settled.

The interviews that the film draws upon have a decidedly personal aspect to them, which ends up being just fine given both Gúzman's obvious centrality in the nation's struggles and the added sense of melancholia that this intimacy creates. Many of the people who he interviews or gives historical sketches of are filmmakers, and in a way this film is a kind of elegy for the Latin American Cinema of the 1960s and 70s, whose vibrancy and critical sprit won raves all over the world, and which was gradually crushed by the various dictators that came to power throughout the region. As these interviewees each remember the friends and colleagues they lost to military dictatorship, *Chile* begins to feel a little like a wake. This sense of mournfulness is occasionally interrupted in a few different ways. One of them is a fascinating interview with a doctor assigned to treat the wounded and tortured at the soccer stadium. He recalls how Gúzman was brought to him, and Gúzman asks if he looked scared. The doctor, almost fondly, recalls that he didn't.

Another way that Gúzman interrupts the mourning interviews is through the use of lyrical re-enactments. The most powerful of these centers around one of Allende's bodyguards, one of the few who survived the assault on the Presidential palace (one extremely moving sequence comes when he re-visits the palace for the first time since the siege disguised as a member of the film crew). At one point, Gúzman crosscuts newsreel footage of the bodyguards walking along Allende's car during a parade and contemporary footage of them walking alongside an empty black car. It's a sad image, and yet it gives these guys quite a sense of stoicism.

The film concludes with a series of discussions among young people who have just viewed *The Battle of Chile*. As the lights come up they are all silent. One girl manages to say a bit about memory and history, and then the flood gates start to open. Within a few minutes, everyone in the room is in tears, and several people are near-hysterical. These discussions, Gúzman clearly understands, are the only hope for Chile. Old people will mourn their dead friends and bravely accompany empty cars, but the truly difficult, gut-wrenching work of remembering and arguing and making sense, now belongs to the young.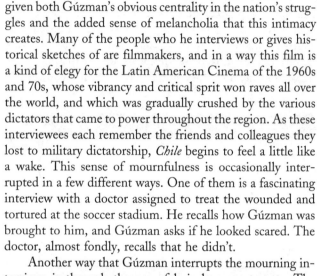

—*Jerry White*

CREDITS

Origin: Canada, France
Released: 1997
Production: Yves Jeanneau and Eric Michel
Direction: Patricio Guzman
Cinematography: Eric Pittard
Editing: Helene Girard
MPAA rating: Unrated
Running Time: 52 minutes

REVIEWS

Village Voice. September 15, 1998, p. 144.

Chinese Box

"Perfection! . . . A brilliant tour de force!"—Hariette Surovell, *Cover Magazine*

"A fragrant love letter to a beautiful, endangered place."—David Hochman, *Entertainment Weekly*

"Drenchingly romantic! Sophisticated, ironic and highly complex."—Kevin Thomas, *Los Angeles Times*

"As sensual as the orient itself! . . . A film of haunting and exotic contrast."—Rex Reed, *New York Observer*

"Ambitious! Haunting! The film's lyrical sweep and refined performances insure that its elegiac echoes linger long after the final credits have rolled!"—Stephen Holden, *New York Times*

"*Chinese Box* is that marvelous rarity . . . vivid, sensual and densely textured . . . Fascinating!"—Joe Morgenstern, *Wall Street Journal*

 Box Office: $2,272,923

Some cities are ripe for love stories, and filmmakers know this well. Place two characters in Paris or Venice, and watch them fall in love. But Hong Kong is different. From the floating restaurants of Aberdeen Harbor to the panoramic view atop Victoria Peak to the neon labyrinths of Kowloon, travelers—including filmmakers—can find themselves distracted and overwhelmed by the city, more apt to fall in love *with* Hong Kong than *in* it.

Anticipation of the July 1997 handover of the (former) British colony to the People's Republic of China only added to Hong Kong's aura. The handover, which seemed to mark the passing of an era, was awaited with hope and fear, nostalgia and anticipation. When the Red Army marched into Hong Kong's rain-soaked streets, filmmaker Wayne Wang was on hand gathering footage for *Chinese Box*. Of all the would-be observers, Hong Kong-born Wang seemed uniquely positioned to capture this moment and work it into a feature-length film. In addition to possessing an insider-outsider perspective on Hong Kong (he has been living abroad since 1967), Wang's proven artistic skill was a match for the city's sensual riches. Yet in lieu of emphasizing the handover itself, Wang enlisted the collective efforts of screenwriters Jean-Claude Carrière (*The Unbearable Lightness of Being* [1988]) and Larry Gross (*48 Hours* [1982]), along with novelist Paul Theroux, to craft a love story set against the backdrop of the handover.

Chinese Box stars Jeremy Irons as John Spencer, an expatriate British economist turned journalist, attempting to record the final days of colonial Hong Kong. Simultaneously fascinated and disgusted with the city, John spends much of his time drifting in and out of homes, brothels, restaurants, and markets, capturing what he can on his video camera. John's restless wandering uncovers aspects of the city not often seen in films—the fabrication of designer copies in private homes or the sadistic training of a race dog by its owners. But like the Hong Kong he has known, John, it turns out, is living on borrowed time. Suffering from a rare form of leukemia, the weakened and befuddled John becomes a parallel for the dying British empire. And this analogy between individuals and nations underlies *Chinese Box*.

Playing opposite to Irons's John is the dazzling Chinese actress Gong Li, best known for her work in the Oscar-nominated *Ju Dou* (1990) and the epic *Farewell My Concubine* (1993). Li plays Vivian, the owner of an upscale bar and John's longtime obsession. To all appearances a successful modern woman, Vivian is actually a kept woman with a dark past. In order to support her boyfriend Chang (Michael Hui), Vivian once worked as a high-class prostitute. As a result, Chang remains indebted to Vivian but cannot, according to Chinese custom, marry her. As Vivian vacillates between Chang and John and contemplates her unsure future, she comes to mirror John's description of Hong Kong as an "honest whore" about to change pimps. Thus, just as John embodies imperialism's last breath, Vivian provides a metaphor for contemporary Hong Kong.

The John-Vivian-Chang love triangle highlights the complicated ways in which cultural politics affect interpersonal relationships. Despite their translocation from mainland China to Hong Kong, Chang and Vivian cannot escape the prejudices and values of their homeland. They even go so far as to pose for "wedding photos" to send to Vivian's mother. Likewise, when Vivian turns to John, she attempts to seduce him by recalling her past and pretending to be a high-class whore named Jenny. The fact that Vivian and John finally consummate their relationship while half-playing these roles in a hotel room illustrates one of the problems inherent in the film's quasi-allegorical narrative. If colonies are like women and imperial powers are like men, the ways of representing their relationship are limited (seduction and rape being the most common). Thus while *Chinese Box* tries hard to transcend

 John (Jeremy Irons) about Hong Kong: "Sometimes you just fall in love with a place without really knowing why, without ever really fully understanding it."

stereotypes associated with East/West interracial relationships—going so far as to dress Gong Li in bluejeans and dark sunglasses—it only succeeds in updating them.

The other problem plaguing *Chinese Box* is its refusal to acknowledge the magnitude of difference separating personal hardship and widescale political change. To date, Wang has set only one other film in Hong Kong, the satirical *Life Is Cheap . . . But Toilet Paper is Expensive*. The tone of that film, coupled with remarks he has made in interviews, suggests an ambivalent attitude towards his birthplace and its future. But while *Chinese Box* does contain one moment of overt political engagement—a young man commits suicide to protest "the loss of personal and cultural freedom"—Britain, Hong Kong, and China are basically reduced to John, Vivian, and Chang. In the end, Gong Li's performance is just so appealing that it is hard not to feel optimistic about Hong Kong's prospects under communist rule when Vivian, a virtual symbol of the city, strides off determinedly remarking, "Like this city, I will have to start over again."

Gong Li puts in a remarkably strong performance in her first English-language feature. Although clearly hampered by the language (while speaking, she is often shot from behind or with her mouth not in full view of the camera), Li manages to communicate a broad range of emotions though expression alone, making Vivian a more complex and poignant character. While Jeremy Irons is utterly believable as the anemic, vaguely cynical but hopelessly besotted Englishman, John Spencer nonetheless comes off as some combination of Irons's last three or four roles. Irons's dyspeptic melancholy is somewhat offset by the jovial, guitar-toting Reubén Blades as photojournalist Jim, but the big surprise in *Chinese Box* is Maggie Cheung. Best known for her work in martial-films, some may recognize Cheung from the quirky arthouse film *Irma Vep,* in which Cheung plays herself playing the vampiric Irma Vep. Here Cheung plays a Janus-faced street hustler named Jean. As Jean, Cheung bristles with nervy and nervous energy, presenting a foil to Li's Vivian and perhaps representing a different side of Hong Kong.

In addition to boasting a strong cast, *Chinese Box* delivers real cinematic fireworks. Exploding with sound and color, the film represents some of Wang's finest work to date. *Slamdance* (1987) and *The Joy Luck Club* (1993) proved that Wang could fill the screen with images of startling beauty: a paintbrush loaded with egg tempera or a string of shattered pearls. In his more improvisational and critically acclaimed works such as *Chan Is Missing* (1982), *Smoke,* and *Blue In the Face* (both 1995), Wang effectively captured the haphazard kinesis of city life. In *Chinese Box,* Wang marries these two cinematic styles. Grainy and jerky hand-held camerawork contributes both immediacy and intimacy as John's video camera peers through subway windows or into backstreet markets. Focused pauses on objects like the stillbeating heart of a gutted fish or a piece of bloodstone jade heighten the sense that Hong Kong is itself a Chinese box, comprising numerous and enigmatic layers. As the first major film to take on the handover of Hong Kong, *Chinese Box* proves disappointingly and typically Hollywood in its tradeoff of politics for romance. Nevertheless, the film comprises such an opulent homage to the textures of Hong Kong that even the armchair traveler might just fall in love.

—*Jacqui Sadashige*

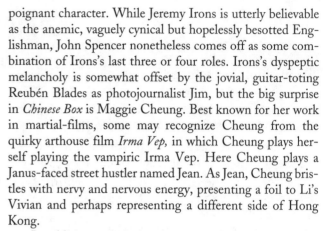

CREDITS

John: Jeremy Irons
Vivian: Gong Li
Jean: Maggie Cheung
Chang: Michael Hui
Jim: Ruben Blades

Origin: USA, France, Japan
Released: 1997
Production: Lydia Dean Pilcher and Jean-Louis Piel for Le Studio Canal Plus, NDF International, Ltd. and Pony Canyon, Inc.; released by Trimark Pictures
Direction: Wayne Wang
Screenplay: Jean-Claude Carriere and Larry Gross
Cinematography: Vilko Filac
Editing: Christopher Tellefsen
Music: Graeme Revell
Production design: Chris Wong
Costumes: Shirley Cgan
Sound: Drew Kunin
MPAA rating: R
Running Time: 99 minutes

REVIEWS

Boxoffice. February, 1998, p. 52.
Entertainment Weekly. April 24, 1998, p. 56.
Hollywood Reporter. April 14, 1998, p. 20.
Los Angeles Times. June 16, 1997, p. F1.
Los Angeles Times. April 17, 1998, p. F8.
New York Times. July 1, 1997, p. C9.
New York Times. April 17, 1998, p. E18.
New Yorker. April 20, 1998, p. 100.
People. April 27, 1998, p. 39.
Variety. September 11, 1997, p. 79.
Washington Post Weekend. May 15, 1998, p. 55.

City of Angels

"A love story with heart and soul."—Mike Cidoni, *ABC-TV*

"A perfect date movie! If you liked *Ghost* you'll love *City of Angels*."—Dan DiNicola, *CBS-TV*

"A heavenly romance if there ever was one! Nicolas Cage and Meg Ryan create one of the screen's most appealing love story duets."—David Sheehan, *KCBS-TV*

"A romantic enchantment that will lift your spirits."—Barbara & Scott Siegel, *Siegel Entertainment Syndicate*

"Cage and Ryan are captivating . . . a must see."—Ann Shatilla, *UPN News*

"Superb entertainment. An imaginative and refreshingly different romantic drama."—Paul Wunder, *WBAI Radio*

Angel Seth (Nicholas Cage) falls in love with heart surgeon Maggie (Meg Ryan) in the romantic drama *City of Angels*.

 Box Office: $78,892,664

Seth (Nicolas Cage) is an angel, literally. Interestingly, he is not a deceased human, but rather is one of God's special beings sent to Earth to escort the newly departed to the afterlife, and to watch over and protect the living. Only those humans near to death can see these ethereal beings, all fashionably clad in black with their long fluid designer overcoats. Although the angels are goodness incarnate, they lack any sense of feeling; they cannot feel such human emotions as joy, sorrow, or pain.

Maggie (Meg Ryan) is a talented and dedicated heart surgeon in Los Angeles, the City of Angels. She is confident and self-assured—until the death of one of her patients sends her into a downward spiral of self-doubt. She is tormented by the possibility that it was a personal failure on her part that caused the man to die.

Seth is the angel sent to help the patient crossover, but he is convinced that Maggie can see him. When Maggie succumbs to her emotions, sitting alone in a stairwell, Seth longs to comfort her, to dry her tears and ease her pain. Finding himself drawn inexplicably in love with her, Seth decides to forgo his eternal existence for a few moments of earthly bliss with Maggie.

Much of the critical writing on the film at the time of its theatrical release centered around the comparison of *City of Angels* to the 1988 Wim Wenders film, *Wings of Desire*,

 Nicolas Cage on his character: "Seth is a kind of rebel angel. He's the Pinocchio angel because he wants to become a human; he wants to be a real boy."

upon which the remake was loosely based. But the concentration of focus on *City of Angels* was not tended to overshadow much of what the film was.

Wings of Desire seems to have been universally applauded by many critics who view it as an exemplary piece of filmmaking, a prototypical example of German New Wave cinema. As such, it was laden with a weighty philosophical bent that, while it might have been "art," was in many ways an alienating viewing experience. Still, *City of Angels* found itself up against the inevitable—yet arguably, undeserved—comparisons to the Wenders film.

There seems to be a tendency in current film criticism to look back on the films that came out of the 1960s and 1970s with the proverbial "rose-colored glasses." It is easy to fall under the spell of nostalgia, and while many of those films were extraordinary pieces of filmmaking, it is important to place them in a broader socio-political framework. Quite simply, the world of 1998 is not the same world of 1967—nor are the viewing audiences the same. It can perhaps be argued that today's filmgoers are not as intellectually demanding of their entertainment—or perhaps, it is simply a case of opting for "Entertainment Lite."

Be that as it may, there remains a certain snobbery when it comes to films, and American critics, in particular, seem to succumb to the notion that anything foreign is by its very nature a more cerebral, more important and therefore, "better" film. It seems necessary at this juncture in time to defend those less weighty films that strive "merely" to entertain. That, of course, demands a dose of "critical distance" and the application of the appropriate set of criteria for judging a film.

Obviously, this should involve looking at a particular film as a singular and distinct entity. If the film in question is a remake of an earlier work, it might be more beneficial to limit comparisons to notation of the differences without a preponderance of critical judgment that attempts to label films as "better or worse."

It seems obvious that the filmmakers of *City of Angels* set out to make a very different film than *Wings of Desire.*

Meg Ryan watched several open-heart surgeries and received technical help from two surgeons in preparation for her role as a cardiac surgeon.

Gone is the philosophical exploration of the dichotomy that existed within the divided city of Berlin. The contemporary tale is set in Los Angeles and it is more of a straightforward romance with a twist, albeit a fatalistic one.

Arguably, one of the elements that *City* handles more adroitly than the Wenders film is the attraction that Seth feels for Maggie. It is a longing so strong that the angel is willing to give up eternity for. By the time Seth makes his decision to hurtle himself from his heavenly stature, the audience is crystal clear on his reasons. In *Wings,* on the other hand, the longing of the Angel (Bruno Ganz) for the mysterious Trapeze Artist (Solveig Dommartin) is far more unclear and unexplained.

Reviews of *City of Angels* were decidedly mixed, but the boxoffice business of this romantic story seemed to prove that the critics had apparently miscalculated its appeal.

—*Patricia Kowal*

CREDITS

Seth: Nicolas Cage
Maggie: Meg Ryan
Cassiel: André Braugher
Messinger: Dennis Franz
Jordan: Colm Feore
Anne: Robin Bartlett
Teresa: Joanna Merlin
Susan: Sarah Dampf

Origin: USA
Released: 1998
Production: Charles Roven and Dawn Steel for Atlas Entertainment and Regency Pictures; released by Warner Bros.
Direction: Brad Silberling
Screenplay: Dana Stevens; based on the film, *Wings of Desire* by Wim Wenders
Cinematography: John Seale
Editing: Lynzee Klingman
Production design: Lilly Kilvert
Art direction: John Warnke
Costumes: Shay Cunliffe
Music: Gabriel Yared
Visual effects supervision: John Nelson
MPAA rating: PG-13
Running Time: 117 minutes

REVIEWS

Boston Globe. April 10, 1998.
Boxoffice. June, 1998, p. 79.
Chicago Sun-Times. April 10, 1998.
Chicago Tribune. April 10, 1998, p. 5.
Entertainment Weekly. April 16, 1998, p. 40.
Los Angeles Daily News. April 10, 1998.
Los Angeles Times. April 10, 1998, p. F1.
NewCity Chicago. April 20, 1998.
New York. April 20, 1998, p. 62.
New York Times. April 10, 1998, p. E12.
People. April 20, 1998, p. 33.
Philadelphia Inquirer. April 10, 1998.
San Francisco Chronicle. April 10, 1998, p. D1.
San Francisco Examiner. April 10, 1998, p. D1.
Sight and Sound. July, 1998, p. 37.
Variety. April 6, 1998, p. 46.
Washington Post. April 10, 1998, p. B1.

A Civil Action

Justice has a price—Movie tagline

"The best film of the year!"—Martin Grove, *CNN*

"I loved *A Civil Action*-A great book has been turned into a great movie!"—Joel Siegel, *Good Morning America*

"A gripping film. A very strong John Travolta is at his best. Robert Duvall is outstanding."—Janet Maslin, *New York Times*

"An engrossing thriller and a riveting drama!"—David Ansen, *Newsweek*

"Two thumbs up!"—*Siskel & Ebert*

"A smart, tough, richly-acted and curiously moving film."—Richard Schickel, *Time*

"A wonderful and important movie that ranks among the best legal thrillers ever!"—Larry King, *USA Today*

 Box Office: $51,632,000

Based on actual events, as the beginning of the film proclaims, *A Civil Action* succeeds in telling a dramatically involving story that could have easily been less interesting or too heavy-handed in its messages about corporate and legal corruption, the victimization of the virtually powerless common citizen, and the consequences and rewards of defending true justice in the face of unbeatable odds. Writer/director Steven Zaillian (director of *Searching for Bobby Fischer* [1993] and screenwriter of *Schindler's List* [1993]), in adapting the book by Jonathan Harr, chooses to focus *A Civil Action* on the often heartless, impersonal realities of the legal world and the emotionally and financially draining "David versus Goliath" battle that ensues when a lawyer commits himself to a cause for reasons of the heart rather than the pocketbook. Featuring fine performances from both John Travolta (as attorney Jan Schlichtmann) and Robert Duvall (as Jerome Facher), the film does a good job of giving the audience a glimpse into the kind of play-to-win mind-set that dominates the legal profession.

Jan Schlichtmann is a very successful personal injury lawyer whose Boston firm boasts an impressive winning track record. The opening scene of the movie demonstrates Schlichtmann's impeccable courtroom strategy. In pleading the case for an injured client, he plays to the sympathy of the jury, and he does it so well that there's hardly a dry eye in the audience. Seeing that the tide's direction has turned strongly in favor of the plaintiff, the defendant offers a substantial settlement. Jan's voice-over narration soon explains that the source of his success lies in never actually going to court. Settling a case outside of court is the goal rather than receiving a favorable verdict. A second tenet of Jan's winning philosophy is to avoid getting personally involved in a case or making the mistake of actually caring about one's clients, which clouds one's judgment. After all, the name of the game is playing to win, not crusading for a cause.

With this understanding of Jan's approach to law, it is no surprise that Schlichtmann turns a deaf ear when one of his associates comes to him with a potential case involving alleged water contamination in a small town. A number of the townspeople claim that two local industries have been dumping waste materials into the river from which the town gets its drinking water, and as a result many children have developed leukemia and died. Convinced that there's little potential profit to be gained by a case like this, Jan travels to the town to explain to the children's families why he cannot take their case. The families, led by Ann Anderson (Kathleen Quinlan), explain that what they're really after is an apology, not money, but that goal of course means nothing to Schlichtmann. However, Jan soon makes a discovery that motivates him to change his mind: the two industries that have polluted the water are owned by two corporate giants, W. R. Grace and Beatrice. Sensing that he has discovered a gold mine ripe for exploitation, Jan decides to represent the families in their lawsuit against W. R. Grace and Beatrice.

A battle of wits follows between Schlichtmann and the lawyers for the two big corporations—Jerome Facher, who represents Beatrice, and William Cheeseman (Bruce Norris), who represents W. R. Grace. Facher is a seasoned, eccentric lawyer who hardly seems concerned about the case, while Cheeseman is almost his opposite—a nervous, uptight man who attempts to enforce the political weight of his client but who does not really seem capable of intimidating or persuading anyone. The former—when he actually talks about the case—argues that there is no demonstrable connection between drinking the water and developing leukemia, while the latter attempts to influence (by keeping under control) the testimony of current and former workers of the leather tanning company owned by W. R. Grace.

Producer Rachel Pfeffer: "This was a tough project. There are no easy heroes. There are many victims. And you can't quite put your finger on the villains. But I always had faith in Steven [Zaillian]."

Facher wisely distances himself and his client from Cheeseman and Grace, for Schlichtmann soon uncovers evidence from employees that the leather tanning company dumped waste products into the water and later attempted to cover up—literally—the truth.

During the process of gathering testimonials from the families involved in the case, Jan finds himself emotionally moved by the story of a father whose cancer-stricken son died while in the car, as well as by the stories of other parents. The more he witnesses the pain suffered by the children and their families, and the more he sees the callous, insensitive, and arrogant attitudes of the defendants, the more Jan wants to see true "justice" served. He makes the "mistake" of actually getting emotionally involved in the cause. When his firm meets with the lawyers of the two corporations to discuss a settlement, Jan names an initial figure that Cheeseman and company are prepared, albeit reluctantly, to accept. But Schlichtmann does not stop there. To the surprise of his colleagues, Jan continues adding to the conditions until he reaches an astounding total. As might be expected, the corporations refuse, and the case is fated to go to trial—the course Jan usually avoids.

Schlichtmann's colleagues, particularly accountant James Gordon (William H. Macy), are mystified by Jan's actions. The firm takes on all the expenses of the cases it handles, costs that are normally covered by huge, profitable settlements, and in order to pursue this case to trial Gordon is forced to take out loan after loan, apply for every credit card he can get his hands on, and mortgage each partner's home. Again and again Gordon and the others try to reason with Jan and encourage him to accept the settlement figure proposed by the opposition, but he insists on going the distance. Ultimately the members of the firm sacrifice almost everything they have. When the case finally goes to trial and the lawyers await a verdict from the jury, Facher offers Schlichtmann a final settlement, but Jan refuses. The verdict is read, and W. R. Grace is found responsible and ordered to compensate the victims' families. Beatrice, on the other hand, escapes judgment, just as Facher had earlier predicted.

The court-ordered compensation amount is barely enough to cover the firm's expenses and reward the families, but ironically the families are not really satisfied, because an acknowledgment of guilt and an apology were all they really sought. Jan's partners, having undergone an experience they never want to repeat and worried that Schlichtmann is not the man he once was, leave the firm.

The last (and rather brief) section of the film shows Jan living in a small apartment with only the bare necessities of life, continuing to research the case and look for evidence

> In light of the film's release, several websites like http://www.civilactive.com have been created to increase the public's awareness of toxic pollution.

of Beatrice's involvement. He is unwilling to simply let go and allow Beatrice to evade responsibility. However, financially unable to do anything more himself, he sends all the research and evidence he and the firm gathered to the Environment Protection Agency (EPA). The federal agency then responds by suing Beatrice, and the final moments of the film explain that ultimately the company was found responsible for contaminating the water and contributing to the deaths of the children.

The drama of *A Civil Action* manages to be quite engaging, helped by an intelligent, fast-moving script and strong performances from Travolta, Duvall, and Macy. What seems a little unusual, though, in light of the story's theme, is that the film tends to focus more on the financial struggles of Schlichtmann's firm—the rapid exhaustion of all their resources as the partners tackle the case—rather than the issue of the water contamination. That is not to say that the tragic consequences of the corporations' irresponsibility is ignored, because the film includes many effective scenes exploring the arrogance of the industries and the concern of several former employees, but much of the middle section of the movie concentrates on the legal firm's descent into debt. That focus is not without its dramatic involvement, but it tends to divert attention from the context of the legal case. Also, since the story seems to be extolling the virtues of steadfastly seeking justice at all costs and paints a rather heroic picture of Jan's struggle and eventual moral victory, one might think the film would spend more time on the events that occurred after the dissolution of his firm and the transfer of his investigation to the EPA. The last minutes of the film move a little too swiftly and lessen the dramatic impact of the final judgment against Beatrice. The weakened conclusion, however, does not overshadow the powerful, intelligent story that has preceded it.

Some critics (who praised the film) suggested that the message in *A Civil Action* is that the best ally in a fight is someone who is an emotionally uninvolved, expert tactician, not a person who's dedicated to you or your cause. Indeed, that is the way Jan Schlichtmann achieved such a winning record, and it is basically the same philosophy followed by the other lawyers in the case, including the experienced, savvy Jerome Facher. In one sense Jan's emotional and eth-

AWARDS AND NOMINATIONS

Screen Actors Guild 1998: Supporting Actor (Robert Duvall)
Academy Awards 1998 Nominations: Supporting Actor (Robert Duvall)

CREDITS

Jan Schlichtmann: John Travolta
Jerome Facher: Robert Duvall
Kevin Conway: Tony Shalhoub
James Gordon: William H. Macy
Bill Crowley: Zeljko Ivanek
William Cheeseman: Bruce Norris
Judge Skinner: John Lithgow
Anne Anderson: Kathleen Quinlan
Neil Jacobs: Peter Jacobson
Al Eustis: Sydney Pollack

Origin: USA
Released: 1998
Production: Scott Rudin, Robert Redford, and Rachel Pfeffer for Touchstone/Paramount Pictures production; released by Buena Vista
Direction: Steven Zaillian
Screenplay: Steven Zaillian; based on the book by Jonathan Harr
Cinematography: Conrad L. Hall
Editing: Wayne Wahrman
Music: Danny Elfman
Production design: David Gropman
Art direction: David J. Bomba
Set decoration: Tracy A. Doyle
Costumes: Shay Cunliffe
MPAA rating: PG-13
Running Time: 112 minutes

ical attachment to the case does lead to his downfall, in that he becomes so single-minded and focused on pursuing true justice that he passes up multiple opportunities to profit through a settlement, and of course he ends up losing everything he has. However, as the conclusion of the film demonstrates, his determination and self-sacrificing efforts eventually lead to victory—perhaps not for him personally, but for the cause he has embraced. The end of the film, which tells us that Schlichtmann continued to take cases like the one against W. R. Grace and Beatrice, suggests that Jan's life was changed and that, even though he lost many of his material possessions, he attained a higher purpose in life. He fought against Goliath and saw the fruits of his efforts lead to the goal he'd sought all along—a judgment of responsibility against the giant. The moral victory is ultimately more important than the material one.

—*David Flanagin*

REVIEWS

Entertainment Weekly. January 1, 1999, p. 47.
Los Angeles Times. December 25, 1998, p. F2.
Los Angeles Times. December 29, 1998, p. F1.
New York Times. December 25, 1998, p. E1.
People. January 11, 1999, p. 35.
Rolling Stone. January 21, 1999, p. 84.
San Francisco Chronicle. January 8, 1999, p. C1.
San Francisco Examiner. January 8, 1999, p. C1.
Variety. December 21, 1998, p. 73.

Clay Pigeons

Lester Long never forgets a friend.—Movie tagline
"A hot-blooded thriller! Vince Vaughn sizzles."—Anne Marie O'Connor, *Mademoiselle*
"One of the choicest sinister comedies in years!"—Stephen Farber, *Movieline*
"A sharp-edged black comedy that has unpredictable plot twists and unexpected laughs coming out of dark corners!"—Bob Graham, *San Francisco Chronicle*
"A riveting whodunit of the first order. One of the best films of the year!"—Jeffrey Lyons, *WNBC-TV*

 Box Office: $1,793,359

The screen has always loved a psychopath. Apparently so does actor Vince Vaughn. Gearing up for his role as Norman Bates in Gus Van Sants' remake of *Psycho* (reviewed in this volume), Vaughn cuts his serial killer teeth as the psychotic, but likable, Lester Long in *Clay Pigeons*. This combination of terrifying and likable would probably make most people label *Clay Pigeons* as a "black comedy." In reality all comedy is black. Falling on banana peels, corrupt politicians, and many other stereotypically comic topics are no laughing matter when you get right down to it. But some topics are just a little too dark, a little too black. Things like child molestation, rape, and murder fall into that forbidden category. However, the unabashed way *Clay Pigeons* uses serial murder for yucks is exactly what makes this so ticklish a film. Being tickled by this type of film, though, poses challenges to its viewers.

Music video director David Dobkin and rookie screenwriter Matthew Healy have concocted the type of film that will forever suffer from the purgatory of mixed reviews. Unlike *Fargo* (1996), another film combining murder with humor, *Clay Pigeons* has more laughs and is more obviously comedic. *Fargo*, however, fits more neatly into the murder-mystery genre, which makes it easier, for those so inclined, to hail it as a masterpiece (which it might be). *Clay Pigeons* (which isn't a masterpiece by the way) will forever be labeled as so-so because of its ambiguities. Clear distinctions between genres make it easier to evaluate a work. Films that merely tease those distinctions, like *Fargo*, are often considered brilliant because they present something new without being threateningly different—the tendency is to believe that they must be great. But then there's poor *Clay Pigeons*. Is it comedy? Is it psychological thriller? Is it noir? The lines are so blurry that the viewer is in the danger zone of being left confused, and thus isolated, and thus cold, and thus we get the dreaded so-so. *Clay Pigeons* is better than that. It may lack the tautness and grand style of *Fargo* but it is certainly a worthwhile effort and on its own terms it's a pretty good show.

Earl (Gregory Sporleder) is the first of many to bite the dust in the shadows of dusty Mercer, Montana. Earl, along with his best friend Clay Birdwell (Joaquin Phoenix), are out in the desert taking pot shots at beer bottles they've emptied and strung to a tree. We learn that Clay has been sleeping with Earl's wife, Amanda (Georgina Cates), and Earl can't stand it one bit. Good writing and good acting credibly build the tension until Earl smashes it by taking a pot shot at himself. Right through the skull. Clay panics because Earl set it up to make it look like murder. He hitches Earl's truck to his own, fastens Earl's body to the steering wheel, and drives off. A bend in the road sends Earl's truck over the side of a cliff. There's nothing left to do but ask Amanda for help.

She'll have none of that, though. Although she's an unashamed nymphomaniac she doesn't want it getting out that she's been cheating on her husband. With a snarl she tells Clay that he's on his own, but she'd still like him to hop into bed with her. He refuses and walks out. Shortly after this Earl's body is found and Sheriff Mooney (Scott Wilson) writes it off as suicide, much to Clay's relief.

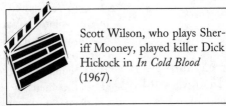

Scott Wilson, who plays Sheriff Mooney, played killer Dick Hickock in *In Cold Blood* (1967).

These opening scenes are just a red herring meant to make Clay look like a suspicious person to the Sheriff. As a red herring this one is kind of confusing. Cinematic red herrings usually come in two varieties: pickled and smoked (real red herrings only come in smoked). With a pickled red herring the hero of the story is in a "pickle." Everybody, including the audience, believes that he or she is guilty of something. A smoked red herring is only a "smoke screen." While the audience knows the hero is innocent, other characters in the film think otherwise. *Clay Pigeons'* red herring doesn't fit either category. We know Clay is innocent of Earl's death, and Sheriff Mooney doesn't really suspect him at this point. What we have in *Clay Pigeons* is a fried red herring. Frying food makes it taste better, and that is the point of this opening. It sets the tone for the film; the mix between comedy, murder, noir, and neatly drawn characters. It's a good mix—and a tasty way to prepare fish.

Lester Long (Vince Vaughn): "Some people just need killin'."

The fish gets tastier when Clay visits a local bar to unwind after his Earl ordeal. As he finishes a game of pool Amanda comes into the bar to confront him. She is raging mad that he has been ignoring all her calls, but most of all she is ragingly horny because he has stopped paying his regular calls. She grabs him by the crotch, telling him that it's been "too long." In an uncharacteristic move Clay slaps her. The slaps succeeds in getting rid of her for the time being but only makes him feel like scum. Someone else, though, thinks otherwise. "You sure handled it right," a stranger says. That stranger is "Lester the molester" as Lester Long introduces himself.

Lester Long is an old-fashioned, larger-than-life, movie character. He is written to the point of becoming unbelievable, but the writer and Vaughn's bubbling performance check him just enough to make sure that he fits snugly into the tone of this film. Lester comes off as being friendly, understanding, and most importantly, extremely likable. Clay and Lester become fast friends. It almost feels destined.

Destiny has a way of walloping one over the head and as the rest of the plot unravels Clay gets walloped pretty hard. The first blow comes when Amanda catches Clay in bed with a local waitress, Gloria (Nikki Arlyn), and puts a bullet through her back. The waitress slumps over dead, smothering Clay. Amanda is ready to push the stiff aside and jump Clay's bones, but he has more urgent needs. Clay ousts Amanda and takes his row boat out to a lake where he drops the body.

Later, while out fishing on the lake with Lester, a body rises to the surface. They drag the body to the shore and on the way to the police station Lester convinces Clay to report the body on his own. At the station Clay reports that he found the body of the missing waitress, shot to death in the lake. This is a funny thing, Sheriff Mooney eventually questions, because this body was stabbed, floating face down, and was not the waitress's. Clay is now a suspicious man for keeps.

Suspicion grows when another person dies. Lester feels that he's doing his buddy a favor when he takes over Clay's Amanda duties. One evening, while Amanda waits for Lester in bed, Lester discovers a stash of very large kitchen knives. Lester selects his weapon as the sound of Elvis singing "It's Now or Never" fills the background. The use of such classic pop-country tunes set against violent crimes is used throughout the film, helping set the silly, but serious, tone. This shtick works surprisingly well. The song continues to play as Lester enters the bedroom and puts the knife into Amanda's back as he does his duty. "Do you like it rough?" he asks. Guess so.

By this time the FBI has been called in to investigate the body Clay found in the lake. Led by Dale Shelby (Janeane Garafalo), the FBI team comes off as intelligent

and organized, a contrast to the local Sheriff and his bumbling deputy, aptly named Barney. This is not to say that Shelby is a straight-laced Jack Webb type. As Garafolo plays her she comes off as having a viewpoint colored by a unique brand of wry cynicism. When Sheriff Mooney and a large entourage show up at the site of Amanda's death, Shelby quips, "Usually I say the more the merrier . . . but a crime scene is not crowd appropriate." During that scene Shelby finds a few joints and pockets the evidence. That evening we see her enjoying that most classic of pleasures: good dope, good movie, and pizza delivery. It's probably no coincidence that the movie she is watching is *Alien* (1979), directed by Ridley Scott who co-produced *Clay Pigeons*.

Later it is discovered that the body Clay found in the lake is of a girl reported missing in another town. This body matches the m.o. of a string of recent murders in the area. Gloria's body is soon found as well, making Clay the number one suspect in all these crimes. The heat turns up and Lester confesses to Clay that he is the serial killer and, if he cooperates, everything will turn out OK. Clay refuses and things start to go even worse, but after a series of tightly written plot twists, the film resolves, albeit ambiguously.

The strangest thing about *Clay Pigeons* is the audience's intended relationship with Lester Long. Even though we know that Lester is a cold-blooded psychopath, we can't help liking the guy. This is part of the fun of this movie. It's a guilty pleasure to commiserate with the heavy. Some people will probably feel uneasy about this and will be inclined to give this film a so-so rating because of it. *Clay Pigeons*, though, really is good fun. However, those so-so reviews are hard to shake, and they will most likely make this one of those films that people will discover on video . . . perhaps while they wait for their pizza to arrive.

—*Rich Silverman*

CREDITS

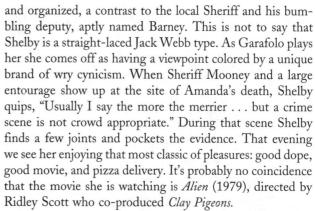

Lester Long: Vince Vaughn
Dale Shelby: Janeane Garofalo
Clay Bidwell: Joaquin Phoenix
Amanda: Georgina Cates
Reynard: Phil Morris
Sheriff Mooney: Scott Wilson
Deputy Barney: Vince Vieluf
Earl: Gregory Sporleder
Gloria: Nikki Arlyn

Origin: USA
Released: 1998
Production: Ridley Scott and Chris Zarpas for Scott Free; released by Gramercy Pictures
Direction: David Dobkin
Screenplay: Matt Healy
Cinematography: Eric Edwards
Editing: Stan Salfas
Music: John Lurie
Production design: Clark Hunter
Art direction: Max Biscoe
Costumes: Laura Goldsmith
Sound: Robert Eber
MPAA rating: R
Running Time: 104 minutes

REVIEWS

Boxoffice. October, 1998, p. 52.
Detroit Free Press. October 2, 1998, p. 9D.
Entertainment Weekly. October 2, 1998, p. 45.
People. October 12, 1998, p. 42.
Variety. September 21, 1998, p. 108.
Village Voice. October 6, 1998, p. 123.
Washington Post. September 25, 1998, p. 63.

Clockwatchers

Four Girls. Four Dreams. One Office.—Movie tagline

Waiting for your life to change . . . can be a full time job.—Movie tagline

"I take hope when I see a movie like this."
—Roger Ebert, *Chicago Sun-Times*

"Delightful to behold!"—Andrew Sarris, *New York Observer*

"A sly fable about women in the workplace."
—Daphne Merkin, *New Yorker*

 Box Office: $444,354

*C*lockwatchers, a film perhaps too subtle for its own good, invades the corporate world and gets into the heads of the people nobody wants to notice—temporary workers. A necessary evil when boring and monotonous work needs to be done and done cheaply, temps, especially women, are everywhere in a downsized corporate America. Director Jill Sprecher collaborated with her sister Karen on the script, which will remind too many people of a day at the office. "There's a lot of drama that takes place in office life," say the writers, both veterans of the temp wars. "This is a story about details and paying attention to minutia. It's about the power that ordinary and mundane events have over people lives." *Clockwatchers* blends that drama with sly comedy, and while the result is uneven, it remains a film to watch.

It helps to have been a one-time denizen of "temp hell" to fully appreciate *Clockwatchers'* surreal atmosphere (described in film publicity as "*Mary Tyler Moore* meets Franz Kafka"), but anyone who has spent long, fruitless hours in a tedious job will recognize the landscape. *Clockwatchers* is explicitly feminist, which may explain why some critics disliked it so much, complaining it offers little "fun," dismissing what are rather thoughtful characterizations of young women at a loss with what to do with themselves, surrounded by a vapid bunch of supercilious permanent workers. *Film Journal's* critic acidly dismissed the quartet: "These girls are, quite simply, losers, of the very type their callous employers would love to believe them to be. Not one of them possesses anything in the way of real attractiveness, wit or style." This completely misses the Sprechers' point in creating 20-somethings who are just struggling to find their way—it would detract from the care-

Margaret (Parker Posey): "Well, the only real challenge with this job is trying to look busy when there's nothing to do."

fully crafted milieu to cast say, Mira Sorvino, or worse, Sandra Bullock as rebellious temps, although that would be the Hollywood way, and they'd be required to torch the office, at very least.

Thankfully, this is an indie, starring Parker Posey (*The House of Yes* [1996]) as Margaret, a live-wire malcontent who desperately wants a permanent position. Then there's Iris (Toni Collette), the newcomer who has no self-esteem, scared of her own shadow. The most fearful day in a temp's life is the "first" day on an "assignment," wandering into a hostile landscape of plastic ferns, disapproving looks and plummeting expectations: when Iris arrives at Global Credit she's told to wait by a snippy receptionist, and wait she does, head hung submissively, for two hours. When somebody finally thinks to notice her, she's shown to a desk that somebody else calls home when they aren't on leave and given forms to stamp. "Try not to make too many mistakes," says Barbara, the draconian office manager (Debra Jo Rupp), "These forms are expensive." Of course poor Iris does mess up, and she throws them away, furtively, in the ladies' room. Into her life blows Margaret, with her rat-a-tat welcome speech: the message is "you're one of us, and here's how they are." Margaret's life as a long-term (read "no future") temp is dedicated to mocking the "haves" while sucking up to a boss important enough to make her "permanent." She taunts the supplies manager Art (Stanley DeSantis), a creepy anal-retentive drone, alternately wheedling and bullying him for more pencils. "Come on, I'm working on a big project!" Art has a prize possession—a ball made of rubber bands which he fondles lovingly. It's one of *Clockwatchers'* best jibes, pointing out the genuinely loony and fetish-driven office workers who feel superior to temps.

Margaret introduces Iris to Paula (Lisa Kudrow) and Jane (Alanna Ubach) when the four share a table at lunch. They bond happily with the new temp, because no one else wants to associate with any of them: they're "corporate orphans" as Margaret says. Paula, the wannabe actress, is just biding her time until she gets a good part, and Jane has her part all planned—she's engaged, and the wedding is when her real life begins. They laugh over how stupid their jobs are, and even go to Happy Hour together after work. Their camaraderie is fun for awhile, and Iris begins to feel a part of their merry band. Her salesman father (Paul Dooley) nags her to apply for a job through his contacts, but she's reluctant. For a brief moment, Global Credit seems like an o.k. place to work, despite the boredom. Then the unthinkable happens: a peculiar, mousy "new girl" is hired, and to their astonishment, she's "permanent," dashing Margaret's dreams of infiltrating the corporate "family" the boss keeps invoking. Cleo (Helen Fitzgerald) seems to want to befriend Iris, but Iris can't quite bring herself to talk with the enemy. Smoking a forbidden cigarette, Margaret raves about Cleo in the bathroom, but slightly embarrassed, her friends put it down to jealousy.

Things go wrong swiftly, as little office knickknacks vanish and a whispering campaign begins. Their invisibility vanishes; suddenly everyone's keeping an eye on the foursome, sequestered into a block of four desks under the watchful eye of a security camera. Suspicion settles on Margaret, and even Iris believes it, suspecting her of stealing from her. The toxic corporate climate scatters the friends, as it must in a world of here today, gone tomorrow: Margaret's fired, Jane marries the man her friends know is two-timing her, and Iris is left to finally depart alone: oddly, Global Credit, or rather her radicalization while temping there, has functioned as a "finishing school" for Iris. A particularly cruel scene where Barbara (always wearing an expensive scarf as a badge of boss-dom) points out that her ripped-out hem violates their "dress code" is resolved when,

by the end of the film, Iris, looking confident and comfortable in a suitably corporate outfit, calmly requests a letter of reference from a glamour-boy boss—for Margaret. He may value her help, but not enough to know who she is. As Jill Sprecher explained, "We wanted to take the least likely person to be triumphant—the most passive person who barely speaks and is so unassertive and allow her to be assertive with dignity at the end."

Parkey Posey's Margaret has energy and anger to burn, and while she may be playing her too-familiar type, she's splendid. Margaret's only superficially a "slacker," but since temp work is all about "looking busy," her fierce intelligence is wasted. She proudly brings a briefcase to work, a present from her parents, only to hear a woman snicker "What does she need that for?" When she's being given the corporate heave-ho, and none too gently, she rages: "How can you fire me? You don't even know my name!" Lisa Kudrow (*The Opposite of Sex,* also reviewed in this edition), always reliable, has some good moments as Paula (particularly during a pregnancy scare), who always pretends to be rehearsing for a play, but her part isn't as strong as Posey's. Alanna Ubach's (*Denise Calls Up* [1995]) Jane similarly has less to do, but her take on the fear leading to her jail-break wedding is dead-on. Collette (*Muriel's Wedding* [1994]) is quietly effective as Iris, who realizes the friends should have stayed together, and stages her own quiet retribution by confronting Cleo, revealed as not only the thief, but a rich woman who hardly needs the job. Debra Jo Rupp's office tyrant Barbara is suitably oppressive as a condescending Queen Bee who lives to inflict petty humiliations in the name of Global Credit. Helen Fitzgerald as Cleo is spooky, but her character is less well-written and pointlessly weird. But in the corporate zoo, those cubicles harbor all kinds of strange creatures: Stanley DeSantis is great as Posey's foil Art.

The slow pace of the film itself proved wearying for a number of critics who failed to grasp what *Clockwatchers* is all about—namely that the boredom of temp work is constant and unrelenting. It's a slice-of-life, so the presence of the thoroughly annoying Muzak which is piped in everywhere is first humorous, then maddening, and finally deadening, as it was surely meant to be. The office itself is perfectly rendered, with ugly, harsh fluorescent light and long, endless hallways where people dodge and duck each other if they are temps and strut and stride if they are permanent. Margaret never understands she's ultimately punished for acting as if she deserved to belong.

As a comedy, *Clockwatchers* only works if you get the joke, and, as a quiet little film with a quirky sense of humor, it succeeds if you see it as a joke on the corporate bosses. Critical reception varied widely, but some appreciated the film. Roger Ebert called it "a wicked, subversive comedy about the hell on earth occupied by temporary office workers." As Sprecher herself revealed in an interview, some au-

CREDITS

Iris: Toni Collette
Margaret: Parker Posey
Paula: Lisa Kudrow
Jane: Alanna Ubach
Cleo: Helen Fitzgerald
Art: Stanley DeSantis
Eddie: Jamie Kennedy
MacNamee: David James Elliott
Barbara: Debra Jo Rupp
Mr. Kilmer: Kevin Cooney
Milton Lasky: Bob Balaban
Bud Chapman: Paul Dooley

Origin: USA
Released: 1998
Production: Gina Resnick; released by Goldcrest Intl.
Direction: Jill Sprecher
Screenplay: Jill Sprecher and Karen Sprecher
Cinematography: Jim Denault
Editing: Stephen Mirrione
Music: Mader
Production design: Pamela Marcotte
Set decoration: Greta Grigorian
Costumes: Edi Giguere
Sound: Christopher M. Taylor
MPAA rating: Unrated
Running Time: 105 minutes

diences are puzzled: "Even though it's the '90s, I think that there are certain attitudes that haven't changed in the last 50 years. After screening the film, certain people have actually asked our producer, 'When are the women going to take off their clothes?' It makes you wonder how far women have really come."

—*Mary Hess*

Cousin Bette

Who knew deception, treachery and revenge could be this much fun . . . —Movie tagline

"A tale of seduction and betrayal reminiscent of *Dangerous Liaisons.*"—*Entertainment Weekly*

"Fabulously sensual, terrifically passionate and wickedly witty. Jessica Lange reminds us once again that she is one of America's finest actors."—*NBC-TV*

"Lots of racy humor."—*New York Times*

"A feast for the eyes."—*Premiere*

 Box Office: $1,295,194

Cousin Bette (Jessica Lange) enlists the help of young courtesan Jenny Cadine (Elisabeth Shue) to help her destroy the lives of the relatives who scorned her.

*C*ousin Bette begins well— the credits appear over an elegant background of old lace, spools, scissors (those scissors will be busy), and you are tempted to think this will be a high-minded costume drama, very Merchant-Ivory. The tools of the dressmaker's trade insinuate the workings of the Fates—spinning, measuring, and finally, cutting—except that one formidable woman, Bette (Jessica Lange) is at once Clotho, Lachesis, and Atropos to a frivolous family to which she is a poor relation. Bette as conceived by Honore de Balzac is malicious, but her intent is concealed in her lifetime costume of a poor but useful country cousin, a lifelong foil to the celebrated beauty of Adeline, the Baroness Hulot.

As portrayed by Jessica Lange, looking stern and drab, Bette is enervated by her hatred of the Hulot family: a powerful scene (one of the best in the film) features a sepulchral-looking Geraldine Chaplin as the Baroness Adeline, Bette's cousin who is on her deathbed. She fondly recalls that her family called Bette "the Countess of Cabbages" (Bette is from Lorraine, and even worked in the fields, which the chic Parisians find amusing). Lange's controlled rage is mani-

fested by a slight flash of her eyes, a trembling quelled instantly. The dying woman rambles on, oblivious to her cousin's reaction. "You will take care of them?" she implores. Bette replies, "I will take care of them all." She is as good as her word.

The reason this adaptation of Balzac's rich feast of a novel fails is simply that the tone is all wrong: many reviewers have classified *Cousin Bette* as a black comedy. There is a comic aspect to the plot, but think scorched-earth, not farce when contemplating the character of Bette herself, whom Balzac described as a "desiccated spinster." Said to have "a long, simian face with warts," a nature "inspired by jealousy," and the manner and appearance of a peasant, Bette is a patient monster of a woman, watching for her chance to devastate her cousin's family. Therein lies another major problem—it strains our credibility to believe that the beautiful Lange could be a realistic Bette. If ever there was a role where looks mattered, this is it—the 1971 BBC adaptation featured Margaret Tyzack as Bette, a perfect bit of casting. Tyzack's appearance and considerable acting gifts have allowed her to play queens and commoners equally well; her stock in trade is the "Plain Jane with a brain."

 Bette (Jessica Lange) to Jenny (Elisabeth Shue): "You shall be the ax that I will wield against them."

Jessica Lange does her best, with her hair and clothes a severe black but her handsome features keep reminding us she is no drab wren, but in fact, an eagle ready to feast on its prey. No one can blame her for choosing a role made to order for the great Bette Davis herself (*The Old Maid* (1939) and *Now, Voyager* (1942) in particular were in this vein), but the movie doesn't support her performance. The vehicles Davis graced as a mature actress were lavishly designed to enhance the effect of a diva daring to play a spinster—this film oversimplifies Bette's malice and distorts the plot—*Newsday*'s Jack Mathews appropriately called it "Balzac for Dummies."

First-time film director Des McAnuff has created a film rooted in the theater; as an accomplished theatrical director with a big reputation for spectacle (*Tommy* and *Big River*), he makes the stage a central focus of the film. The reason for this is ostensibly Bette's work as a costumer, where she meets Jenny Cadine (Elisabeth Shue), mistress to Baron Hulot (Hugh Laurie) and Monsieur Cravel (a mischievous Bob Hoskins, a major scene stealer). Jenny, a pretty but tonedeaf "singer" is the star of a Paris revue. Cheerfully amoral, she tunelessly postures through her showy numbers which are always designed to display her perfect posterior, a running joke that goes on too long. In fact, this one device is what bonds the two in the first place—Bette artfully cuts a strategically placed hole in her leotard to allay Jenny's complaint that the costumer has neglected her "assets." "What about my bosom?" she asks petulantly. "What about my ass?" One snip and the "sisters of the soil" (Jenny is a country girl also) form a partnership that will decimate the Hulots.

The theater setting allows McAnuff to have a great deal of fun in his staging: Jenny first appears as an angel, with subsequent numbers featuring her as a tiger with a hoop of fire, then a devil, a "revolutionary" revue, and finally a nun.

The director also co-wrote the ridiculous songs Jenny sings, and his sly sense of humor allows for a number of bawdy sight gags: notably the scene where the pint-sized Crevel emerges from under Jenny's hoop skirt, explaining her sudden explosive "ardor" to Baron Hulot, who thought they were alone. Such a giddy approach to the film makes it uneven and unconvincing—whatever tension and momentum remained from Balzac's melodrama dissipates quickly.

The film has Bette enraged at not being made the next wife of the Baron—she refuses the offer to become their housekeeper and returns to her own little room in a bad neighborhood. Bette has but one true passion: her love for expatriate Polish sculptor Wenceslas (Aden Young), who lives in a garret room above hers. Starving, he creeps into Bette's room each night to sneak a piece of cheese that baits her mousetrap and sip her wine. In the darkness, Bette listens, her gaze unexpectedly tender. One day she saves Wenceslas from asphyxiation in a suicide attempt. "Foolish boy!" she murmurs. Grateful, he pledges to do whatever she asks in return for sustenance, even to keep to a work schedule which he abhors, since he prefers to work only when the spirit moves him. Perversely, the Hulots' daughter Hortense (Kelly Macdonald) nags Bette about "her sweetheart:" she finds the penniless artist and they begin a covert romance under the nose of his protectress. Their treachery is what moves Bette to action. Through carefully calibrated scheming, she manipulates the weaknesses of all concerned.

The Baron, a notorious libertine, squanders whatever money he has on Jenny, while Hortense and Wenceslas soon discover that their perfect romance sours when he only talks about work, wastes a government commission, and complains that the child they'd had cries constantly. Not satisfied with mere financial ruin and personal misery (Bette suggests a usurious moneylender to "help" the Hulots), she engineers a seduction of Wenceslas by Jenny. However, much to Bette's dismay the two sensualists fall for each other, conducting a messy affair that culminates with a bizarre scene where their naked and writhing bodies are covered with chocolate.

When father and daughter burst into the boudoir, one glimpse is enough to cause them to keel over. He has a stroke, she is driven to try to kill Jenny—of course, she kills him instead and is dragged off to prison. The action shifts to the revolutionary fervor of 1848: a nicely understated (and uncharacteristic) moment has the family maid, long mistreated by the Hulots, contemplating the idea of "freedom" with a smile—the old corrupt aristocracy has been humbled. Cousin Bette remains with the incapacitated Baron, finally lady of the house and "mother" to Wenceslas's son.

The film's missteps are many, but a critical problem is

the helter-skelter rearrangement of the characters and the plot—in the novel, Adeleine and Wenceslas do not die, but Bette does. It is Bette's deathbed, not Adeline's, that figures prominently in the novel. This would be quibbling if it were not such a departure from the plot, which finds Bette dying at the novel's end, chagrined by the Hulots' restored happiness, without even the comfort of their knowing she

had been the agent of their misfortunes. Without the context of history (this film breezily dismisses any attempt to make any real statement on class), *Cousin Bette* lacks bite. The performances are fine (all except Shue, who is miscast) and the production looks handsome enough, but it never quite rises above the irreverent treatment given it by director McAnuff, who clearly enjoyed his first opportunity in this medium.

He uses the stage and Jenny Cadine's performances all out of proportion to the plot—it is as if he could not resist the opportunity to stage a revue within the film. It also seems he felt it necessary not to be reverent in adapting one of Balzac's greatest novels, and while a lack of reverence in interpreting a classic can be a good thing, his *Cousin Bette* veers into farce a bit too often to commend it. Jessica Lange has received mixed reviews from most critics, but her performance is subtle and suitably poisonous—her eyes show her fury while her demeanor remains calm. The production is lavish, the photography striking and the cast generally very able, but this is a disappointment overall. *Cousin Bette* means to be wicked fun, but this film wastes too many opportunities in an effort to be clever.

—*Mary Hess*

CREDITS

Bette Fisher: Jessica Lange
Jenny Cadine: Elisabeth Shue
Cesar Crevel: Bob Hoskins
Baron Hector Hulot: Hugh Laurie
Hortense Hulot: Kelly Macdonald
Count Wenceslas Steinbach: Aden Young
Adeline Hulot: Geraldine Chaplin
Victorin Hulot: Toby Stephens

Origin: USA
Released: 1998
Production: Sarah Radclyffe; produced by Fox Searchlight Pictures
Direction: Des McAnuff
Screenplay: Lynn Siefert and Susan Tarr; based on the novel by Honore de Blazac
Cinematography: Andrzej Sekula
Editing: Tariq Anwar, Barry Alexander Brown
Music: Simon Boswell
Production design: Hugo Luczyc-Wyhowksi
Art direction: Didier Naert
Costumes: Gabriella Pascucci
MPAA rating: R
Running Time: 107 minutes

REVIEWS

Entertainment Weekly. June 12, 1998, p. 50.
New York Times. June 12, 1998, p. E14.
People. July 6, 1998, p. 37.
Time. June 22, 1998.
Variety. June 8, 1998, p. 68.
Village Voice. June 16, 1998, p. 160.
Washington Post Weekend. June 26, 1998, p. 47.

Dance With Me

In the dance of life, love can happen in a heartbeat. *Dance With Me* is a story of hearts in motion.—Movie tagline

"A *Saturday Night Fever* for the 90s with a Latin beat. Vanessa L. Williams and Chayanne are equally hot dancing and romancing."—Jeanne Wolf, *Jeanne Wolf's Hollywood*

"Vanessa L. Williams explodes joyously to life."—Stephen Holden, *New York Times*

"Stuffed to bursting with vivacious, sexy Latin-influenced dance sequences. Adeptly directed by Randa Haines, it's a fun movie."—Leah Rozen, *People*

"Two thumbs up."—*Siskel & Ebert*

Box Office: $15,923,354

The Dance Musical is probably one of the hoariest of Hollywood's tried-and-true formulas, and *Dance With Me* is very much part of the tradition: jaded hoofers, pounding feet, dreams of the big time, and a chorine who makes somebody say, "Hey, the kid's really got something!" On to showbiz glory and true romance: the archetype is *42nd Street* (1933), a cynical confection featuring Ruby Keeler as the ingenue and the worn but suddenly rejuvenated director Warner Baxter. Dick Powell just can't help himself from falling for Ruby and Vanessa L. Williams is similarly wowed by *Dance With Me*'s male "ingenue," Chayanne. The Puerto Rican singer is a Latino sensation, and, in this, his first American film, he shows why. The crusty seen-and-done-it-all role is played by . . . Kris Kristofferson. Not since the Streisand *A Star is Born* debacle (1976) has Kris ventured near musicals-cum-drama, and maybe he should have reconsidered this particular career move. Miscast? Yes, but that's because swallowing the idea of Kris as John Burnett, a ballroom dancing competitor/dance-studio owner is so ludicrous. His current partner Patricia (Jane Krakowski) complains John can't quite manage a "star lift" anymore (a showy move that involves lifting a partner overhead with one hand). We in the audience can't believe he ever would.

Director Randa Haines (*Children of a Lesser God*) has created an entertaining mixed bag of a movie despite such "offbeat" casting. For example, she gives diva Vanessa L. Williams (*Soul Food* [1997]) a chance to show what she can do, as Ruby Sinclair, the older woman in this romance. The *New York Post* observed that the film is a "nostalgic dance movie. Call it 'How Vanessa Got Her Groove Back'." Haines clearly tries to make the story as important as the dance numbers—herself a ballroom dance student, she has filmed the dancing intelligently and with feeling. She is helped considerably by an exciting score featuring Sergio Mendes, Black Machine, Electra, DLG and Thalia, with predictable sweet M.O.R. sounds from Gloria Estefan and Jon Secada, plus Williams' and Chayanne's duet, "You Are My Home."

First-time screenwriter Daryl Matthews also served as choreographer for the film, and predictably, he was more successful staging dances than in creating a script (ominously, the working title was *Shut Up and Dance*). It's not hard to see how Haines got the green light to make *Dance With Me*—since the success of *Selena* (1997), Hollywood has caught on that Latino films can sell tickets, but tapping into the vibrant salsa culture is harder than it looks (witness the Lambada "craze" which died on the vine in the summer of 1990 with two films released in the same week, or *Salsa* (1988), which also fizzled). The possibility that the *Flashdance/Saturday Night Fever* magic might strike again must have been enticing, but the script is too disjointed and slow moving to pull it off. As usual, Hollywood was perplexed by how to market a romance between two gorgeous and talented people of color, and left the film pretty much to its own, hoping no doubt for word-of-mouth to take the place of advertising dollars.

Rafael Infante is leaving Cuba for Houston in search of his late mother's old friend John Burnett, whom the audience has no trouble concluding is his father. Seems his mom and John were performers on a cruise ship, and for old times sake, Burnett offers him a job as a handyman. Sweet-natured Rafael can hardly wait to get to Houston, and he seems to have not a moment's trouble leaving the island, but why mess up a love story with politics? The Cuban scenes are as warm and energetic (he gets a big community send-off, with plenty of dancing) as the ones in Houston are chilly and down-at-the-heels.

Rafael (Chayanne) to Ruby (Vanessa L. Williams): "I'm from Cuba. Of course I know how to dance."

Rafael is delighted when pretty dance instructor Ruby shows up in her little blue VW bug convertible to bring him back to Burnett's Excelsior Dance Studio, which is full of lovable characters like Bea (Joan Plowright), Lovejoy (Beth Grant), and Stefano (William Marquez) who comprise an odd little family. Rafael may have an apartment over the garage, but he can't get anywhere with John or Ruby: John's a loner who just wants to fish and she's down on love since her child's father and erstwhile partner Julian (Rick Valenzuela) left her when she got pregnant. Chayanne's charm carries him a long way in this role—as written, he's Gene Kelly, Cuban-style, right down to a dance he does in a sprinkler a la "Singin' in the Rain."

Randa Haines herself describes the character of Rafael as "magical;" he is a "natural" dancer ("I'm Cuban," he shrugs) while Ruby is a technician. He charms everyone with his dazzling good looks and proves to be just the boost the studio is looking for. When he's asked to put up some decorations for a costume dance "party" he uses all of the decorations—Halloween, Christmas, New Year's—to the delight of the students. Ruby, dressed as a nurse in a strapless white sheath with a zipper that is rapidly headed south with every shimmy, is rescued by Rafael cutting in and surreptitiously zipping her up. He gets John's ancient truck to run—he's Cuban, remember? Patricia needs a new partner and Rafael is only too happy to help. He is, really, too good to be true. How can Ruby resist? She does, for an unreasonably long time.

Dance With Me is remarkably chaste, although there is a sexually charged moment when they kiss in Ruby's apartment with Rafael only wearing a towel. The point is to present a sweet romance with a whole lot of dancing, keeping a young and predominantly female audience very much in mind.

The focus of the plot, such as it is, is that the World Open Dance Championship in Las Vegas is the ultimate destination for the Excelsior hopefuls Ruby and Patricia, each of whom have what it takes but need a good partner to go to the ball. Rafael, encouraged by grudging acceptance from John Burnett, finally risks telling him who he is and is angrily rebuffed. At the same time, Ruby decides she has to choose taking a last chance at the big time over love and leaves to team up again with Julian, who is sleek and villainous. Rick Valenzuela, the assistant choreographer for the film and Latin dance champion, adds some much needed nastiness to this movie.

In Vegas, all conflicts are resolved, but not before some showy and spectacular competition scenes featuring real ballroom and Latin dance champions. Vanessa Williams does overact wildly in the scene where she realizes (in mid-routine!) that she can't live without Rafael. She's being whipped about by Julian and all she can see is Rafael—Julian has to tell her to get with it. Somehow they win but it isn't long before Rafael and Ruby are back together again, dancing happily at the victory party. John has also come to his senses and embraced Rafael, Patricia and Rafael dazzle the crowd, and Chayanne and Joan Plowright even do a cute little turn together. At the film's end, back home in Texas, Rafael and Ruby are happily running the Excelsior.

The dancing scenes themselves really take off, especially when Ruby first agrees to go to a club with Rafael. Vanessa Williams can dance, she looks great in a variety of sparkly spandex frocks, and she and Chayanne work well together. Latin dancing is highly stylized and very exacting, so the cast rehearsed for months to get it right. Said Williams: "What you see in this film is the real thing, every move. No tricks. No doubles. We all did our own dancing—every single step!" After *Shall We Dance* (1997) and *Strictly Ballroom*, (1992) the time was right for this sunny little film, which tries hard to entertain in a traditional way and comment on a cultural phenomenon that is rapidly growing in popularity. Haines explained her fascination with salsa: "My admiration for all things Latin began the instant I entered a salsa club. There is joy there, a feeling of connection, community and culture. Even in the face of adversity, people seem able to put aside the cares of the day and enter the mystery and passion of the night. Many of us could learn from that."

Critics generally found the film flawed but enjoyable: *Entertainment Weekly* said that "the rhythm-equals-soul equation works, not least because Haines makes the dance

CREDITS

Ruby Sinclair: Vanessa L. Williams
Rafael Infante: Chayanne
John Burnett: Kris Kristofferson
Bea Johnson: Joan Plowright
Patricia: Jane Krakowski
Julian: Rick Valenzuela

Origin: USA
Released: 1998
Production: Lauren C. Weissman, Shinya Egawa and Randa Haines for Mandalay Entertainment; released by Columbia Pictures
Direction: Randa Haines
Screenplay: Daryl Matthews
Cinematography: Fred Murphy
Editing: Lisa Fruchtman
Music: Michael Convertino
Production design: Waldemar Kalinowski
Art direction: Barry Kingston
Costumes: Joe I. Tompkins
Sound: David Ronne
Choreography: Daryl Matthews, Liz Curtis
MPAA rating: PG-13
Running Time: 126 minutes

REVIEWS

Entertainment Weekly. September 4, 1998, p. 57.
Los Angeles Times. August 21, 1998, p. F10.
New York Times. August 21, 1998, p. E12.
People. August 31, 1998, p. 31.
Variety. June 8, 1998, p. 67.

floor look like the friendliest of melting pots." Some, less charitably, lambasted the script: Stephen Holden of the *New York Times* called *Dance With Me* "a likable mess" and "Salsa's would-be Sabado Night Fever." As a cross-over vehicle for Chayanne and as an impressive star turn by Vanessa L.

Williams (proving she really can carry a picture), the film works: it is less successful as a drama with something to say beyond "Let's dance!"

—*Mary Hess*

Dancer, Texas Population 81

"Stunning cinematography."—Robert Philpot, *Los Angeles Times*

"A refreshingly uncynical movie."—Kenneth M. Chanko, *Newark Star Ledger*

"*Dancer, Texas* is a town that feels lived in with townsfolk who seem real."—Peter Travers, *Rolling Stone*

"Poignant, believable and funny!"—Jennie Punter, *Toronto Star*

"Immensely charming."—Emanuel Levy, *Variety*

"Enjoyable!"—Joe Morgenstern, *Wall Street Journal*

Small towns have been woven into the tapestry of Americana ever since the beginning of our country and are, in some respect, the roots of our nation. They hold for many people a somewhat mythical quality as well as a longing for simpler times and slower paces. A time when everyone knew each other's name and people were entwined into each other's life. The bonds were strong, as was the desire by the "younguns" to reach beyond the boundaries and explore new horizons—to break free from what they knew and search for the great adventurous unknown. It is a subject that has interested people for years and captured the imaginations of many. Authors have written about it, painters have painted it, singers have sung about it and the cinema has held a fascination for it. Films such as *The Last Picture Show*, *Diner* and *American Graffiti* (to name a few) have focused on particular aspects of the small hamlets of our youth and the sentiment of our memories. Still, yet another film attempts to capture the allure of rural charm and romantic nostalgia of small town life in *Dancer, Texas Population 81*.

Dancer, Texas was written and directed by Tim McCanlies who was a former script doctor for Disney. The setting is not only a small town but also a minuscule one. The popula-

Sue Ann (Shawn Weatherly): "I don't know how the two of you live in this trailer at an angle like this." Squirrel (Ethan Embry): "He was drunk when he parked it. Never got around to leveling it."

tion is a whopping 81 and the inhabitants give new meaning to the word "laid-back." They are bordering on catatonic. It takes place in Texas where not too much happens and the folks are pretty much fine about that—"just fine, thank yeh." The story centers on four close friends who are just graduating from high school and are about to embark on a long awaited trip to bigger and better things. It seems that at age 12, the four lads made a solemn oath that they would all split as soon as they finished high school. The day of reckoning has arrived and now they must decide if they really have the guts to stick to their pact with each other. Keller (Breckin Meyer), who wants to leave Dancer the most, goes about mobilizing the other three friends to make the big leap and go forward with their plans to head for Los Angeles. None of the grads have any concrete plans about what they are going to do when they get there—it just seemed like a good idea when they made their adolescent contract with one another. Keller feels that he cannot do this on his own and desperately tries to convince his friends to pack up and move on out. However, there are complications when push comes to shove. Terrell Lee (Peter Facinelli), the handsome rich kid is the first to back out. His domineering mother (Patricia Wettig from TV's *thirtysomething*) has made it clear that he is to stay and run the family oil business. After all, "he has a responsibility as a Lusk," she reminds him in her inimitable Texas fashion. John (Eddie Mills), the cowboy, is contemplating taking courses at a nearby college and Squirrel (Ethan Embry), the town geek, is really only concerned with meeting girls. Once they are confronted with the reality of getting on the bus, they are forced to face their doubts and fears, much to the anger and frustration of Keller.

Most of the film deals with the events occurring in the lives of the four boys that influence their assessment of the situation and ultimately the direction of their future. None of this is taken lightly by any of them and at this young age, it is certainly understandable—it could influence them for the rest of their lives. "There are no stakes here and trying to figure out which of the gang is going to board the bus at film's end is pretty easy to do, " says Kevin Maynard, critic from the Showbiz web site. It must have been a long time since this reviewer was a teenager. Sometimes deciding what to wear is a big decision when you are an adolescent—coming-of-age and deciding to move could be labeled MONUMENTAL! There are varying degrees of pros and cons in each boy's life that impact their reasons for staying at home. Squirrel's dad is a raging alcoholic and lives in a lopsided, dilapidated trailer that is the quintessential archetype of "trailer trash" living. Not much to keep Squirrel here except, perhaps, a date. Keller's parents are dead and he lives with his gruff grandfather who is surrounded by widows who are baking up a storm to win their way into his bed and possibly his heart. John and Terrell Lee seem to have a lot to keep them in Dancer, as well as a much stronger family support system. So, who decides what to do based on their separate circumstances is engaging and entertaining to watch.

Dancer, Texas was shot completely on location in Fort Davis, Texas and cinematographer Andrew Dintenfass managed to shoot the locations in such a glorious way that they became part of the ensemble of players. The breathtaking landscapes made the city dwellers in the audience want to pack up their bags and get out of Dodge. Another impressive aspect of the film was the success at authentically creating all aspects of a small town atmosphere, as well as the mentality. The cast of townspeople was totally believable in their lazy philosophy of life, which they were all too willing to share with the "fab four." When one of the youths remarked "We don't know what's out there." One of the locals replied, "Yeah, we do—a bunch of nothing." If the smaller roles were well cast by casting directors Laurel Smith and Michael Testa, they surpassed themselves in choosing the main characters. Patricia Wettig is right on the mark playing the rich Texas matriarch with the proper blend of control and sassiness. Breckin Meyer (who played a pothead shaker in *Clueless*) managed to make Keller a deep thinking philosopher without falling into the stereotypical, intense, brooding teenager a la James Dean. His character has warmth and charm and conveys his disappointment and anger without begging the audience for sympathy. Perhaps, the one false note came from Ethan Embry as Squirrel. He was utterly endearing and touching when he was dealing with his father and in the more serious moments in the film. It was when he fell into "goofball—mode" that his physical timing appeared overdone and contrived. It was as if he had watched too many Jerry Lewis and/or Jim Carey films. If it had been toned down a bit, Squirrel would have come across as more sympathetic and authentic.

Certainly, another achievement of this tender film was capturing the essence and difficulty that families have in communicating with their children and openly expressing their feelings. It seems particularly true of the "men folk" in some small, rural communities. The older character actors played the men in the boy's lives with warmth and tenderness. They all managed to convey the deep love that they held for the boys although it was thoroughly encased in a thick Texas machismo. Particularly good were Wayne Tippet as Keller's gruff old granddad and Michael O'Neill as the somewhat submissive Mr. Lusk (Terrell Lee's dad). The amount of love underneath the "manliness" of these men conveyed such a heartfelt compassion for their sons and a desire to see them go after their dreams. It was as if they were passing the torch of manhood to them, encouraging them to take a leap of faith. These actors captured the essence of their characters with strength and intelligence. Their multi-layered performances added subtlety and dimension to the film experience.

In discussing *Dancer, Texas Population 81* the lingering delight of the piece was the richness of imagery and the tenderness of relationships. It had a lyrical quality to it without overindulging in sentimentality and pathos. There was a moment in the film where the four friends came upon a group of four wild Mustangs. They took a moment to look at them in all their wild freedom with longing and admiration. Suddenly, the horses became aware of the boys staring at them and flashed a look back at them. It was as if the horses were challenging them to become the free spirits that they had become—beckoning them to follow their lead. The spell was broken when Terrell Lee said, "I'm not going with

CREDITS

Keller Coleman: Breckin Meyer
Terrell Lee: Peter Facinelli
John: Eddie Mills
Squirrel: Ethan Embry
Josie: Ashley Johnson
Mrs. Lusk: Patricia Wettig
Mr. Lusk: Michael O' Neill
Earl: Eddie Jones
Keller's Grandfather: Wayne Tippet
Squirrel's father: Keith Szarabajka
Sue Ann: Shawn Weatherly

Origin: USA
Released: 1998
Production: Chase Foster, Dana Shaffer, and Peter White for HSX Films and Chase Productions; released by Sony Pictures Entertainment
Direction: Tim McCanlies
Screenplay: Tim McCanlies
Cinematography: Andrew Dintenfass
Editing: Rob Kobrin
Music: Steve Dorff
Production design: Dawn Snyder
Art direction: Jeff Adams
Costumes: Susan Matheson
MPAA rating: PG
Running Time: 97 minutes

you guys. Four of us against 13 million strangers!" Instantly, reality set in and the spell was broken. The ability of this simple moment in the film to evoke such clarity demonstrates the power of film imagery. With minimal dialogue, the filmmaker was able to capture the essence of the piece and expose the heart and soul of his characters. *Dancer, Texas* may not move mountains but it may make a few of the audience members want to try to climb one.

—*Jarred Cooper*

REVIEWS

Entertainment Weekly. May 15, 1998, p. 76.
Los Angeles Times. May 5, 1998, p. F6.
New York Times. May 1, 1998, p. E14.
People. May 18, 1998, p. 36.
Rolling Stone. May 14, 1998, p. 64.
Variety. March 23, 1998, p. 87.
Village Voice. May 5, 1998, p. 119.

Dancing at Lughnasa

Five sisters embrace the spirit of a people.—
Movie tagline

"A really wonderful movie about women! A great celebration!"—Karen Durbin, *Mirabella*

"It's a joy to see *Lughnasa*! If these Mundy sisters had lived in the 90's rather than the 30's they could have conquered the world."—Maeve Binchy, *New York Times*

"Heartbreaking and jubilant!"—Jack Kroll, *Newsweek*

 Box Office: $963,184

The five Mundy sisters, headed by eldest sister Kate (Meryl Streep), are affected by the visit of their older brother in the touching Irish film *Dancing at Lughnasa.*

P at O'Connor may be Ireland's clearest link to Hollywood: he's made some of that country's most financially successful films (*Cal,* [1984] *Circle of Friends* [1994]) and has even made a few films in the United States (*The January Man*). Why that makes him a good candidate to make the film adaptation of Brian Friel's play *Dancing at Lughnasa,* however, is a bit of a puzzle. Certainly the film has much to recommend it, including excellent performances by Meryl Streep, Michael Gambon, and Brid Brennan, and some very nice cinematography by Kenneth MacMillan. Further, the film stays very close to Friel's original material in some ways, resisting the temptation to skirt over the elements specific to Ireland of the 1930s in favor of a simpler, Hollywoodized universalism. The problem with the film overall, though, is less tangible. O'Connor transforms what was originally a very melancholy piece of theater into something that feels very sentimental indeed; this problem stems from some of the very elements that also

Kate (Meryl Streep) to her sisters: "You do not dance!"

recommend it, such as the cinematography. Despite his efforts to remain faithful to Friel's vision, then, O'Connor finally misses some of the most important aspects of it. *Dancing at Lughnasa* is a well-intentioned film, but it is compromised by its need to fit into a Hollywood model.

The story is set near the tiny Irish town of Ballybeg, and centers around the five Mundy sisters who live in a tiny house outside the town itself. The story is guided by a narration from Billy, who in the story is the young son of the unmarried Christina (Catherine McCormack), but who is a sadly sentimental middle-aged man for the purposes of the voice-over. The sisters' lives in Ballybeg begin to radically change when their brother

Jack (Michael Gambon), a priest, returns from missionary work in Africa. He's now a fragile, somewhat dottering old man, and has obviously been transformed by his time abroad. These transformations are of serious concern to the church authorities. These concerns are downplayed by the group's defacto matriarch, Kate (Streep), a serious and very lonely woman, who rules firmly over the clan. The disruptions continue as the flaky, motorcycle-riding lover of Billy's mom, Gerry (Rhys Ifans), returns to the small town, only to get her and his son's hopes up before disappearing on another ill-advised adventure. The opening up of a glove factory hangs heavy over the story, threatening to put the sisters, who do piece-work at home, out of business. When the film ends, sisters Agnes (Brid Brennan) and Rosie (Sophie Thompson) decide to leave for Britain, Kate's job as a schoolteacher is in danger, and Christina takes a job at the glove factory. The voice-over tells how all five of the sisters wound up lost in one way or another, although leaves off with a kind of wistful nostalgia for the days that this dysfunctional family of sisters created such a meaningful little community.

Lugh is the Celtic god of light.

The performances that O'Connor has gotten out of these actors are quite impressive, and simply watching this very skillful and relaxed ensemble at work is one of the film's greatest pleasures. Meryl Streep is her usual magnificent self, and now she has "Irish" to add to her list of foreign accents that she has flawlessly mastered. More importantly, though, she is able to very powerfully convey the strain that defines Kate's everyday life, and so subtly invests her role with such fatigue and unrealized ambition that it almost saves the film from the melodramatic mess that it eventually becomes. Briton Michael Gambon's performance as the brother of the family, Father Jack, is also very nuanced. Although he clearly lost his marbles during his time in Africa, Gambon's Jack is less a crazy person than a haunted and disoriented man. Jack is given to rambling, but Gambon refuses to get cheap laughs out of this little twitch, instead making it clear how far this intelligent and ambitious fella has now fallen. Sophie Thompson plays Rosie, a sister who, like Jack, is not completely there. Thompson, like Gambon, plays this very role in a very understated way, and makes Rosie far more that a mere Gump-esque simpleton. O'Connor could have scarcely assembled a stronger pack of actors.

Dancing is also a gorgeous looking film, with great care paid to both the photography and the replication of Ireland in the 1930s. Ballybeg, where the film is set, is essentially in the middle of nowhere, and the exact time period is often difficult to determine (little changed in this part of Ireland between the end of the famine in the 1850s and the beginning of the 20th century). O'Connor captures this sense of timelessness well, at the same time that he makes

the aspects of the production that *are* time-specific, such as radios and motorcycles, quite central when they do appear in the narrative. The result is a pleasantly disorienting, "gee, what is that doing there" reaction on the part of the viewer that communicates a lot about life in rural Ireland in the 30s. The color scheme of the film—heavy on the greens and browns—creates a soothing atmosphere that is well suited to the quiet melancholia that defines the narrative. The film's costumes aren't all that tall an order, really, but nevertheless they nicely signify the functional, conservative lifestyle that marked rural Ireland, especially in the 1930s. This could also summarize the little house where much of the film's action takes place: there's not much there, but what is there is rendered with great care and expressive possibility by the film's production designer Mark Geraghty. That modest habitation could easily have been played to emphasize the sisters' poverty, but this is one bit of sentimentality that O'Connor avoids. Indeed, an interesting aspect of the original version of *Dancing at Lughnasa* is its potential for a variety of readings and stagings: while there are plenty of places where O'Connor goes overboard and arguably misunderstands some of the most important parts of the play, one part of the film adaptation that works very well is the way that he is able to find a visual equivalent for the sisters' quiet but terminally unquenched determination.

While O'Connor practices restraint in some aspects of the film, he falls into some traps in other parts. *Dancing* is set in the northern part of Ireland (although, importantly, within the Republic of Ireland, or what was in the 1930s called the Free State of Ireland), in a rural locale that offers opportunities aplenty for gorgeous landscape shots. The film is not overly filled with such imagery—there are a few postcard-esque vistas, but certainly not too many. Nevertheless, there are moments when the film veers dangerously close to gooey-eyed romanticizing, and this undercuts a lot of what the narrative seems to be trying to set up. This is especially visible in the sequence where Christina's boyfriend Gerry comes back, and the two enjoy an idyllic afternoon in the back country. It's a nice sequence, lyrical and flirtatious and well acted by both parties. O'Connor uses the very green and bushy landscape in this sequence as an echo of the lush, slightly out of control nature of their relationship. While this isn't done in a *completely* sappy way, O'Connor's use of the landscape makes the moment feel awfully sweet and sentimental, which are emotions that just shouldn't be attached to this relationship given all of the trouble that it's caused for Christina. I understand that this is part of the tension of the story, that she loves him one moment and is furious with him the next. The problem is that O'Connor seems to have a very similar idea of the relationship, and instead of a firm, clear hand on the representation of this really troubled couple, we get a somewhat uneven and often very emotionally manipulative back and forth. It's a sequence that summarizes what is wrong with the film overall. The play *Dancing at Lughnasa* is a clear, quiet tragedy; all too often, the film version lacks that kind of confidence, relying too closely on the emotional impact of melodrama.

Indeed, while there's an awful lot right with *Dancing,* this slip from tragedy into melodrama is a pretty serious compromise. It doesn't destroy the film, but it does seriously undercut its power and also distorts its place in Irish cultural life. Brian Friel was, after all, the founding member of Field Day, a company based in Derry, Northern Ireland, and specifically devoted to creating a politically aware form of theater. His play is about love and family and all that, but it's also very much about the slow, painful extinction of rural Ireland that began in the 1930s. While this is certainly part of the film version, many of the complexities and small tragedies that this entailed seem to have been glossed over. Further, all of Friel's theater work is notable for the way that it so firmly resists emotional manipulation: his plays are nowhere near as clear or understandable or involving as mass-produced narrative demands. O'Connor has, alas, forgotten this so central part of Friel's ethic. Less than a strict adaptation, the film version of *Dancing at Lughnasa* is a transformation, from tragedy into melodrama, from political theater into Hollywood. While not everything has been lost in this shift, the fact that the original has been intangibly, but significantly, watered down, is inescapable.

—Jerry White

CREDITS

Kate Mundy: Meryl Streep
Father Jack Mundy: Michael Gambon
Christina Mundy: Catherine McCormack
Maggie Mundy: Kathie Burke
Rose Mundy: Sophie Thompson
Agnes Mundy: Brid Brennan
Gerry Evans: Rhys Ifans
Michael Mundy: Darrell Johnston
Danny Bradley: Lorcan Cranitch

Origin: USA, Ireland, Great Britain
Released: 1998
Production: Noel Pearson for Capital Films, Channel Four Films, The Irish Film Board; released by Sony Pictures Classics
Direction: Pat O'Connor
Screenplay: Frank McGuinness; based on the play by Brian Friel
Cinematography: Kenneth MacMillan
Editing: Humphrey Dixon
Music: Bill Whelan
Production design: Mark Geraghty
Art direction: Conor Devlin, Clodagh Conroy
Costumes: Joan Bergin
Sound: Kieran Horgan
MPAA rating: PG
Running Time: 92 minutes

REVIEWS

Entertainment Weekly. November 27, 1998, p. 54.
Hollywood Reporter. November 17, 1998, p. 22.
Los Angeles Times. November 20, 1998, p. F14.
People. November 23, 1998, p. 34.
Sight and Sound. December, 1998, p. 42.
Variety. September 14, 1998, p. 38.

Dangerous Beauty

"Unabashedly decadent. A bodice ripper for smart people."—Lisa Henricksson, *GQ*

"An intriguing romance. A strong, spirited performance, played with gusto by Catherine McCormack."—Bruce Williamson, *Playboy*

"Ravishing. A wickedly seductive, remarkable adventure."—Susan Granger, *SSG Syndicate*

"Lavish and erotic! A stunning feast for the eye."—Jeffrey Lyon, *WNBC-TV*

"Sensuous, smart, sexy, fresh and beautiful. Don't miss it!"—Dr. Joy Browne, *WOR-AM Radio*

 Box Office: $4,553,271

*D*angerous Beauty is a luscious, cream-filled Napoleon of a film with a serious, feminist bent beneath its lacy petticoats; that women can and should, at all costs, maintain their sexual freedom. Director Herskovitz has fashioned a film that highlights 16th century Venice in a soft, golden light, clothed men and women alike in handsome finery and lets them lust after one another in between lavish meals and poetry-quoting contests.

Veronica Franco (Catherine McCormack) has loved Marco Venier (Rufus Sewell) since they were children. But now that they are at the marrying age, Marco breaks her heart with the news that he must marry for money to bolster his family's waning fortunes. Devastated, Veronica turns to her mother, the beautiful Paola (Jacqueline Bisset) for comfort and advice. To her shock and surprise, her mother presents her with a scenario that Veronica could never have imagined for herself—the life of a courtesan. Paola explains that despite one's initial feelings about the world's oldest profession, it offers women a life that is wider in scope, intellectual challenges, and power than mere wife-and-

motherhood. For instance, courtesans are widely known to be educated (in order to keep conversation with men of government and politics) and given access to libraries and information unknown to other women. To top off this information, Paola tells her daughter that once she, her own mother, was the best and most popular courtesan in the city! Veteran actress Bisset, still possessed of the most luminous charm and beauty, shines in this role, managing to keep her dignity even when she is taking her daughter through the paces of "Penis 101."

Soon, Veronica is past her freshman jitters and thriving in her new job. She becomes heavily courted in town, and when Marco hears of this news, he confronts his old love. Accusing him of hypocrisy, Veronica tells Marco that she is free to do what she pleases and see whomever she pleases. Despite their bickering, they fall into each other's arms; they find that their love for each other is still strong, despite his wife and her profession.

Indeed, Veronica has become a favorite among men in town—not only for her sexual prowess, but also for her

REVIEWS

Boxoffice. February, 1998, p. 52.
Detroit News. February 27, 1998, p. 6C.
Entertainment Weekly. March 13, 1998, p. 50.
Los Angeles Times. February 20, 1998, p. F10.
New York Times. February 20, 1998, p. E26.
People. March 2, 1998, p. 22.
USA Today. February 27, 1998, p. 9D.
Variety. February 2, 1998, p. 28.
Village Voice. February 24, 1998, p. 61.
Washington Post Weekend. February 27, 1998, p. 44.

CREDITS

Veronica Franco: Catherine McCormack
Marco Venier: Rufus Sewell
Paola Franco: Jacqueline Bisset
Maffio Venier: Oliver Platt
Beatrice Venier: Moira Kelly
King Henry : Jake Weber
Domenico Venier: Fred Ward
Pietro Venier: Jeroen Krabbé
Laura Venier: Joanna Cassidy

Origin: USA
Released: 1998
Production: Arnon Milchan, Marshall Herskovitz, Edward Zwick, and Sarah Caplan for Regency Enterprises and Bedford Falls; released by Warner Bros.
Direction: Marshall Herskovitz
Screenplay: Jeanine Dominy; based on the biography *The Honest Courtesan* by Margaret Rosenthal
Cinematography: Bojan Bazelli
Editing: Arthur Coburn, Steven Rosenblum
Costumes: Gabriella Pescucci
Production design: Norman Garwood
Music: George Fenton
Art direction: Gianni Giovagnoni, Stefania Cella
Sound: David Stephenson
MPAA rating: R
Running Time: 111 minutes

rapier wit and sly poetry. She even bests Marco's cousin Maffio (Oliver Platt) in a poetry duel—much to the bombastic chap's ire. When Venice needs France's fleets to help them stave off the nearby Turks, Veronica is called in to seduce King Henry (Jake Weber), who later is seen limping from her chambers. In fact, new mother Beatrice Venier (Moira Kelly) tells the renowned prostitute that she would almost rather have her baby daughter grow up to follow Veronica's footsteps and be educated and aware of the world, rather than suffer her own stifled and sheltered fate.

It seems that Veronica can do no wrong—until a plague sweeps the city and she is arrested on charges of witchcraft. Veronica faces her toughest foe to date; the new religious zealot Maffio, ready to take revenge on the woman who previously humiliated him. Marco corrals all the men in town who have sampled

Paola (Jacqueline Bisset) to her daughter: "Marriage is a contract, not a perpetual tryst."

The architecture and canals of 16th century Venice were recreated at Italy's Cinecitta Studios in Rome.

Veronica's favors and gathers them together in the courtroom. After Veronica gives a heartfelt speech demanding her right to live and love as she pleases, most of the townsmen rise to cheer her on and give her support. The religious tyrants have no choice but to set her free. A footnote to the film indicates that she and Marco remained lovers until the end of their lives.

McCormack (back from her painful death in *Braveheart* [1995]) shines in this passionate role, as does Rufus Sewell, as her devoted lover. The actors gamely play through the light material, resulting in this romantic fable that sometimes borders on a Harlequin romance. Cinematographer Bojan Bazelli and Costumer Gabriella Pescucci contribute to the film's lush, golden look.

—*G. E. Georges*

Dark City

They built the city to see what makes us tick. Last night one of us went off.—Movie tagline

"A dark and dazzling sci-fi mind-bender in the grand tradition of Serling and Orwell. An eye-popping visual feast!"—Mason Wood, *CBS-TV*

"It does what no other movie has done so far this year. Grip an audience with its sheer visual intensity and deliver a clear, concise humanist message."—Thelma Adams, *New York Post*

"Relentlessly trippy! It could easily inspire a daredevil cult of moviegoers who go back again and again to experience its mind-bending twists and turns. It's a visually arresting ride!"—Stephen Holden, *New York Times*

"Luscious and chilling. *Dark City* is a reminder of how sensuous movie watching can be. It's a wonder to see."—Richard Corliss, *Time*

"An eye-popping convolution of neogothic fantasy and old-school sci-fi paranoia."—Dennis Lim, *Village Voice*

"*Dark City* sets a bold new standard in science fiction. Brilliantly conceived and executed."—Bill Bregoli, *Westwood One*

"A fascinating, bizarre and brilliantly conceived thriller."—Jeffrey Lyons, *WNBC-TV*

Box Office: $14,435,076

*D*ark City is another of the new breed of motion pictures in which special effects and music overwhelm the story. It is not a bad film by any means, but Egyptian-born, Australian-raised director Alex Proyas, whose 1994 film *The Crow* grossed over $50,000,000 at the box-office, did not seem to trust the audience to be sufficiently beguiled by the trials and tribulations of his hero. *Dark City* resembles *Batman and Robin* (1997). Both feature expressionistic cityscapes reminiscent of Lyonel Feininger, state-of-the-art special effects, anti-gravitational ambulation, unrelenting music (evidently inspired by Modest

Dr. Daniel Poe Schreber (Kiefer Sutherland) is responsible for one man's hellish trip in finding the truth in the visionary sci-fi thriller *Dark City*.

Mussorgsky's "Night on the Bald Mountain"), and stygian darkness.

Dark City is well named. The humans never see the sun, and the extraterrestrials who control everything are as photophobic as cockroaches. Like the hero John Murdoch (Rufus Sewell), the viewer tries desperately to understand what is going on. Explanations are parceled out in dialogue which is actually very adroitly handled by the screenwriters—Proyas himself with Lem Dobbs and David S. Goyer. As usual with these alien-invader films, the more they explain, the crazier it gets. The copywriter had the good idea of encapsulating a two-liner in the newspaper ads reading: "They built the city to see what makes us tick. Last night one of us went off."

"They" are a spooky-looking bunch of extraterrestrials, called "Strangers," who all wear black overcoats that come down to their ankles. They conform pretty much to the orthodox conception of flying-saucer invaders—pasty-white, bald, hyper-cerebral, not much good at small talk—except that instead of being little men most Strangers are exceptionally tall, like plants that have grown in air shafts.

Dr. Schreber (Kiefer Sutherland): "First came darkness, then came the strangers."

Along with Murdoch, the viewer comes to realize that this is not Manhattan or any other earthly metropolis but a totally artificial creation where humans are kept like guinea pigs. Dark City is a Manhattan-sized and roughly Manhattan-shaped flying saucer floating among unfamiliar constellations. The Strangers have provided their imitation city with plenty of grime, squalor, dilapidated buildings, and rat-infested alleys to make their human captives feel right at home. As in *The Crow*, the film noir camera work, the mood of big-city anomie, and the glorification of urban ugliness are the best things in *Dark City*. The plot is like one of those little cars at Disneyland, serving only to transport the viewer through a hellish labyrinth which mirrors the reality that human greed has created on Earth.

The Strangers have recruited the hapless Dr. Daniel Poe Schreber (Kiefer Sutherland) to do their hands-on experiments. It is not explained why these supermen can create entire cities by merely willing (or "Tuning") them but need a bumbling human to give injections and extractions. Kiefer Sutherland seems a little young for a "mad doctor" role that would have been perfect for his father Donald. *Los Angeles Times* critic John Anderson observed that Kiefer "speaks in an asthmatic staccato and walks with a limp borrowed from Everett Sloane in *The Lady from Shanghai*" (1948). He drills into each subject's forehead with a futuristic hypodermic-power drill and changes the human's identity by extracting one set of memories and injecting another. Surplus memories are somehow liquefied and stored in vials.

Nobody in Dark City knows who he is. In one amusing sequence, the Strangers do a complete makeover on a working-class couple, "tuning" their humble home into a mansion while they are asleep. When husband and wife are allowed to wake up, they continue dining as if nothing had happened—although their table is now twelve feet long and bedecked with flowers, china and silver, while their conversation has become aristocratic.

What do these Strangers want? Why have they come all this way across space to bedevil us poor humans? Well, you never can tell about aliens. As Carl Jung said, they have become replacements for God among many contemporary agnostics. And people who believe in super-intelligent extraterrestrial visitors have the same trouble explaining their behavior as the theologists have always had in explaining why God does some of the sadistic things He does. Apparently the Strangers are a dying race (as well they should be, since there are no female Strangers among them). They have reached an evolutionary dead-end. They feel the lack of souls more than the lack of feminine companionship and are trying, as the ad says, to figure out what makes us tick. If they could distill the essence of human souls in their vials, they could absorb it themselves and prolong their miserable existence.

Another way in which *Dark City* resembles *Batman and Robin* is that the alien invaders have the power to immobilize the entire city, just as Mr. Freeze could paralyze the population of Gotham City with his freeze-gun. At the stroke of midnight the Strangers put everyone to sleep (except, hopefully, for the members of the audience). These beautifully staged sequences are reminiscent of *The Sleeping Beauty*. Then the vampire-like Strangers come out and select subjects for their next experiments.

There are very few women in Dark City, and most of them are dead. Most, in fact, appear to have been murdered by the hero of this souped-up Cornell Woolrich/Rod Serling-type story. Murdoch wakes up stark naked with a dead prostitute beside the tub where he has been reclining in water that has turned ice-cold. He is the victim of a botched experiment. Instead of having a transplanted memory, he has no memory at all. After dressing in clothes he doesn't recognize, he retrieves a wallet that identifies him as John Murdoch, who is wanted as a serial killer. Naturally he believes he is insane and has really committed these murders. The fact that the half-dozen prostitutes were actually killed by the Strangers shows how cold-blooded they are. They are like vivisectionists seen from the point of view of the laboratory animals in the cages. In his wallet Murdoch finds a photo of himself with a woman who is presumably his wife and a card showing an address where he probably lived. Throughout the film he is driven by push-pull motivations: trying to elude his pursuers while trying to rejoin the woman who may or may not be his wife.

As is often the case in paranoid thrillers, the hero is being chased by both the cops and the bad guys. The cops want him for murder, while the Strangers have to get him back on the table because he has somehow acquired their own psychokinetic powers and can "tune" with the best of them—although it takes him awhile to figure out how to fine-tune his tuning. In the climax Murdoch and the master Stranger who calls himself Mr. Book (Ian Richardson) will fight a duel of the minds in which the sparks will really fly.

The lead detective on the case is world-weary Inspector Frank Bumstead (William Hurt). By shadowing the fugitive's wife, Emma (beautiful Jennifer Connelly), Bumstead eventually catches up with Murdoch himself. But under sufficient emotional stress, Murdoch can make a door materialize in a wall where no door existed before. With infinite patience and innumerable camera and lighting set-ups, the director does an excellent job of creating the illusion of flight through a maze of dark alleys, up and down fire escapes, and over rooftops. The film was created at the new

Fox studios in Sydney, Australia, and the work of production designers George Liddle and Patrick Tatopoulos rivals Hollywood's best.

Whenever Murdoch manages to get away from Bumstead, he is sure to run into a bunch of the Strangers. Rufus Sewell, the young British heartthrob who was appearing concurrently in *Dangerous Beauty*, (reviewed in this edition) does a creditable job in a one-dimensional role. Leaping over banisters and plunging down spiral staircases, he seems as agile as the ill-fated Brandon Lee, whose potentially brilliant career was ended when he was accidentally killed on the set of *The Crow*.

Fifty elaborate studio sets were built at Sydney's Fox Studios for the production.

Movie buffs viewing *Dark City* will catch echoes of many other films. One of the Strangers, for example, twitches and twitters like the nervous Chang (H.B. Warner) in *Lost Horizon* (1937). The many chronological errors the Strangers have made in tuning their replica of an American metropolis will remind some of *2001: A Space Odyssey* (1968), in which the invisible Jupiterian host has sequestered two 21st-century astronauts in an 18th-century apartment. Critics compared *Dark City* to such films as *Metropolis* (1926), *The Trial* (1963), and *Blade Runner* (1982). They might have

CREDITS

John Murdoch: Rufus Sewell
Dr. Daniel Poe Schreber: Kiefer Sutherland
Emma Murdoch/Anna: Jennifer Connelly
Inspector Frank Bumstead: William Hurt
Mr. Hand: Richard O'Brien
Mr. Book: Ian Richardson
Mr. Wall: Bruce Spence
Eddie Walenski: Colin Friels

Origin: USA
Released: 1998
Production: Alex Proyas and Andrew Mason for Mystery Clock; released by New Line Cinema
Direction: Alex Proyas
Screenplay: Alex Proyas, Lem Dobbs, and David S. Goyer
Cinematography: Dariusz Wolski
Editing: Dov Hoenig
Music: Trevor Jones
Production design: George Liddle, Patrick Tatopoulos
Costumes: Liz Keogh
Art direction: Richard Hobbs
Sound: David Lee
MPAA rating: R
Running Time: 103 minutes

named others, including *Escape from New York* (1981), *The Fugitive* (1993), and any number of Hollywood's original noir classics like *D.O.A.* (1949). *New York Times* critic Stephen Holden called Proyas "a walking encyclopedia of weird science-fiction and horror imagery."

Dark City is a step up from *The Crow* for talented director Proyas. It has a bigger budget, a large roster of extras, and bigger names in Kiefer Sutherland, William Hurt, and Ian Richardson. It even tries for more contemporary social significance than *The Crow*, which was little more than a martial arts film following the ancient revenge formula used in *The Count of Monte Cristo* (1934) and countless imitators. Reviews of *Dark City* ran the gamut from negative to enthusiastic. Todd McCarthy, writing for always dollar-conscious *Variety*, predicted that "New Line should rack up decent coin based on strong support from the hard-core sci-fi/fantasy audience." *Time*'s Richard Corliss called the film "a reminder of how sensuous a visual trip movie watching can be."

—*Bill Delaney*

REVIEWS

Chicago Tribune. February 27, 1998, p. 4.
Christian Science Monitor. February 27, 1998, p. B2.
Cinefantastique. April, 1998, p. 35.
Cinescape. September/October, 1997, p. 66.
Detroit News. February 27, 1998, p. 3C.
Entertainment Weekly. March 6, 1998, p. 54.
Los Angeles Times. February 27, 1998, p. F10.
New York Times. February 27, 1998, p. B7.
People. March 9, 1998, p. 24.
San Diego Union-Tribune. February 27, 1998, p. E1.
San Francisco Chronicle. February 27, 1998.
San Francisco Examiner. February 27, 1998.
Sight and Sound. June, 1998, p. 43.
Time. March 2, 1998, p. 85.
USA Today. February 27, 1998, p. 9D.
Variety. February 23, 1998, p. 73.
Village Voice. March 3, 1998, p. 108.
Washington Post. February 27, 1998, p. D1.
Washington Post Weekend. February 27, 1998, p. 43.

Dead Man on Campus

Roommate wanted . . . for a limited time only.—Movie tagline

"A side-splitting, tongue-in-cheek approach to the college freshman experience."—Chad Young, *Blast Magazine*

"The best college movie since *Animal House*."—Dan Deevy, *WNYU*

 Box Office: $15,064,948

College films have been historically silly, and since *Animal House* (1978) they've gotten sillier. It used to be that a few pom-poms and some talk about final exams were enough. But now students in the real world deal with pressures such as drugs, career choices, sexual issues, and parental pressure, so college films can't possibly be as innocent as, say *The Bachelor and the Bobby Soxer* (1947). *Dead Man on Campus* fits right in with these jaded days: it's about the possibility of suicide. And, get this, it's a comedy. Unfortunately, it's not a good comedy. It's not an awful movie, especially if you're a twenty-something college person, it's just an incredibly dumb story, and it would be difficult for most thinking people not to dismiss this film as tripe because of

its questionable premise. All of that having been said, there are some funny moments and some appealing actors which help the film itself transcend its dubious premise. A total waste? No.

A number of first-timers worked on this film, but it certainly doesn't lack in production quality. It is the first live-action feature produced by MTV Productions. The director, Alan Cohn, is a first-time feature director, after having steered MTV's youth-oriented *The Real World*. Cohn allows the story to lag a bit in the middle, and there are moments when the actors seem a bit stiff, but he must be credited with not falling back on MTV-style tricks to tell the story.

The screenplay, written by Michael Traeger and Mike White, has a silly appeal even though the basic premise from a story by Anthony Abrams and Adam Larson Broder is really kind of awful. It's not that black comedy is a bad thing: it's just that it takes a skilled satirist to pull off a comedy about suicide. *Harold and Maude* (1972) dealt successfully with a character obsessed with death, but not many other comedies have been able to pull it off. Another buddy movie about death, *Throw Momma from the Train* (1994), wasn't even helped by Billy Crystal or Danny DeVito. The subject matter is tough, and though Producer Gale Ann Hurd and company are to be commended for trying, it doesn't fully work.

The premise is that shy, academic Josh (Tom Everett Scott), is about to lose his scholarship because his party-minded roommate Cooper (Mark-Paul Gosselaar), has changed Josh from bookworm to party animal in one quick semester. The amoral but lovable Cooper is the scion of a toilet-bowl cleaning fortune, while Josh is a poor young man whose mother expects great things from him ("you've always exceeded my expectations," she says in a phone message, "and I'm expecting straight 'A's.") Once they realize that bad grades will cause Cooper to lose the family fortune and Josh to lose his scholarship, they have to think fast. Somehow (and this is where credibility breaks down) they discover a little-known clause in the school charter claiming that if they have a roommate who commits suicide they can automatically receive straight 'A's.

The problem with the premise is not its outlandishness. An outlandish plot would be fine if the writers had set the film up properly. However, the tone changes radically halfway through. Clearly, the writers are attempting to make a statement about the stress of college and future, etc. on the poor young minds of today, and that's all well and good. The problem is that for the first forty minutes or so, the film is an amiable buddy comedy with two engaging characters played by engaging actors. Josh even finds an engaging young woman named Rachel (Poppy Montgomery) to fall in love with. But once the young men decide to find "Mr. Z," their code name for a likely suicide victim who they can move into their room *tout de suite* the better to collect their straight 'A's when he offs himself, well, it's a little hard to like these guys again. The audience ends up liking the actors more than their characters.

Credit the relationship created by these fine young actors for any enjoyment in the film. The leads and supporting cast are excellent. Gosselaar, who starred in T.V.'s *Saved By The Bell* series for several years, is proving to be a fine young actor. He's truly funny and believable as the lovable bad boy who just wants to party. Gosselaar wisely doesn't overdo it and seems to have a great time. Tom Everett Scott, who starred in Tom Hanks' *That Thing You Do* (1996) is a lanky and charming presence. He is delightful throughout, from his bungling shyness with Montgomery's character, to his hysterical fear that "we're like the Hardy Boys from hell!"

They are a little like the Hardy Boys from hell: Very likable, but you wouldn't want to hang out with them for too long.

—*Kirby Tepper*

Cooper (Mark-Paul Gosselaar): "College is our last chance to go crazy."

CREDITS

Josh Miller: Tom Everett Scott
Cooper: Mark-Paul Gosselaar
Rachel: Poppy Montgomery
Cliff: Lochlyn Munro
Buckley: Randy Pearlstein
Matt: Corey Page
Lucy: Alyson Hannigan
Kristin: Mari Morrow
Zeke: Dave Ruby

Origin: USA
Released: 1998
Production: Gale Ann Hurd for Pacific Western and MTV Films; released by Paramount Pictures
Direction: Alan Cohn
Screenplay: Michael Traeger and Mike White
Cinematography: John Thomas
Editing: Debra Chiate
Music: Mark Mothersbaugh
Production design: Carol Winstread Wood
Set design: Antoinette Judith Gordon
Costumes: Kathleen Detoro
Sound: Walt Martin, Willie Burton
MPAA rating: PG-13
Running Time: 93 minutes

REVIEWS

Entertainment Weekly. April 4, 1998, p. 58.
Los Angeles Times. August 21, 1998, p. F8.
New York Times. August 21, 1998, p. E30.
People. September 7, 1998, p. 40.
Variety. August 24, 1998, p. 27.

Deceiver

There are two sides to every lie.—Movie tagline

Tim Roth as a villain? It wouldn't be the first time to watch the English indie actor in such a role—he has added his brand of menace to films like *Rob Roy* and the underrated *Little Odessa*—but in *Deceiver*, directed and written by the twin brothers Jonas and Joshua Pate, Roth's James Wayland is a more ambiguous specimen. Has he murdered Charleston prostitute Elizabeth Loftus (Renee Zellweger), or is he an innocent man unfairly interrogated by strong-arm police detectives?

In this modest chamber piece of a movie, spanning a Wednesday March 27th to the following Monday, the Pate brothers' focus is on the nature of truth, its verification and its distortion, and the psychology of the criminal mind. As the film opens, two cops, Braxton (Chris Penn) and his senior partner Kennesaw (Michael Rooker), hook Wayland to a lie detector. Each of the trio are introduced by an onscreen description of their age, education, and career background. While Wayland is a Princeton graduate, the IQS and school background of his two adversaries are distinctly inferior. Indeed, Braxton was, we are informed, a guard at Wal-Mart for four years. This narrative device is then dropped, making it, in retrospect, something of an unnecessarily glib device.

While the tough Kennesaw asserts pressure on Wayland by boasting of the detector's spectacular success rate in gleaning confessions from suspects, a subplot is introduced. A worried Braxton is seen paying a visit to a woman called Mook (a heavily-disguised Ellen Burstyn); he owes quite a bit of cash to her, and does not know how he can pay up.

Taking a break from the first round of questions at police HQ, Wayland requests a visit to the bathroom. In the toilet stall, he swallows some pills. Are these drugs, or prescribed medications? A flashback—soon to become a familiar device in this film—reveals Wayland slow-dancing with none other than Elizabeth. Yet to the cops, he claims he only met the dead woman once in the local park.

Wayland proves to be a formidable force in the face of the lie detector and the investigation. He explains that he is an epileptic, for which he requires medication. Blackouts are a symptom of his condition. At the end of the first session, he takes his cool

> Wayland (Tim Roth): "It's ironic . . . that someone who tells the truth about lying is more suspect than someone who actually lies about it."

leave, challenging the competence of the detectives; they have yet to charge him for the murder.

The following day, Wayland is seen drinking absinthe—a potent liquid when mixed with pills, and a combination that might induce blackouts. At a family dinner at his parents' salubrious home, Wayland is bullied by his father, who wants to learn the direction of his son's life and career. A shocking sequence ensues in which a raging Wayland stabs his mother. This is a strange moment, given the father's tyrannical attitude; presumably, it is to introduce the notion that Wayland peruses homicidal ideation.

More information on the main players is supplied. From a shrink (Michael Parks), we discover that epileptics can act out while in a trance, and may not be cognizant of the consequences of their actions. Meanwhile, Braxton is still being pressed for the money he owes to Mook; a brick is thrown through his window at home as a threat. On the domestic front, Kennesaw's wife (Rosanna Arquette) is desperate for him to make love to her, partly to conquer her feelings that he is indifferent to her. He fiercely refuses her; he is tormented by his knowledge of his spouse's infidelity.

Back at work, the police's mind-games continue, but no clear evidence against Wayland is unveiled. What is learned is that the suspect's connection with Elizabeth was more than a passing encounter in the night, especially given that he brought her to his parents' fancy party. Both appear to be stoned as Wayland makes introductions to his horrified family.

Kennesaw supplies $10,000 as a loan to his partner, but 10 more is needed. Wayland, being pushed intently, has a fit and climbs onto the table in the interrogation room. The cops have been warned by the psychiatrist not to touch an epileptic whilst he is in a trance, and this time at least, they refrain from bringing him down.

> The film was shown at the 1997 Venice Film Festival under the title *Liar*.

At the weekend, we discover that Mook is in league with the financially-endowed Wayland, who is weaving a web around the players in this high-stakes game. In another flashback, Elizabeth and Wayland huddle together on a street, and she talks to him of her loneliness. Trying to reach out to Wayland, she kisses him, but he doesn't kiss back.

Monday is April Fool's Day, and Wayland declares that he is ready to confess. The detectives are surprised but expectant. He talks to them of Kennesaw's visit to a shrink and the torment of his wife's unfaithfulness. Kennesaw, he claims, visits prostitutes. Wayland produces a videotape, and the detective is revealed to be with Elizabeth in her room. The physical resemblance between the blonde, lank-haired Mrs. K and Elizabeth is notable. And it is Kennesaw, Wayland charges, who killed Elizabeth in a fit of pique when she ordered him to leave.

It was Wayland, however, who cut Elizabeth's body in half—or so he claims. This is apparently to throw a false trail, to exaggerate the manner of her death, and avert the spotlight from him, even though his fingerprints would be in her room.

In a reversal of fortunes, Kennesaw is connected to his instrument of pleasure, yet he tries to resist telling "the truth." He denies murder, and fights back at Wayland in regards to the severing of the body. Wayland seems to suffer under the duress of his enemy's counter-attack. Seized by his epilepsy, he goes into a trance again, stands up on the table and when touched, thuds to the floor. An ambulance

is summoned to take his body away, but a sly look on the part of one of its personnel suggests a set-up.

One year later, Wayland is back in the park, approaching another lady of the night. So who really did kill Elizabeth?

The film has received few accolades, but it is a competent piece of work. *Variety* sniffed that "this flashy exercise in style and obfuscation represents no threat to the Coens in the sibling auteur stakes." Yet the Pates are not trying to emulate the quirky Coens; their interest seems to be more centered upon psychological truth.

The brothers utilize the cinematography of Bill Butler to vary the angles in the visual telling of their story. Most of the film is set in stuffy rooms, and an attempt is made to lend variety to the shots. Several swooping movements into a close-up, however, serve mainly to draw attention to the camera work rather than fueling our intrigue in the shifting-sands of the mystery.

The acting is solid throughout, although several of the performers are underemployed. Arquette is given little more to do than be a guilt-stricken wife, and Burstyn cannot impress in her vague role. Zellweger plays the vulnerable Elizabeth appealing, yet her role fails to provide insight into her character's soul.

Of the main characters, Rooker sweats bullets as the punitive detective with secrets of his own, while Chris Penn reminds one of his *Short Cuts* character with his slow-thinking earnestness. Roth's American accent, meanwhile, is consistent and not too showy; his expressive eyes and shifty facial expressions certainly prompt one to question whether his character has any veracity within him at all.

This is a tight thriller with suitable claustrophobia and an effective spin on the unveiling of "truth" and "facts." What it isn't, unfortunately—for all its probing into memory—is a film one will readily recall months after its viewing.

—*Paul B. Cohen*

CREDITS

James Wayland: Tim Roth
Braxton: Chris Penn
Kennesaw: Michael Rooker
Elizabeth Loftus: Renee Zellweger
Mrs. Kennesaw: Rosanna Arquette
Mook: Ellen Burstyn

Origin: USA
Released: 1997
Production: Peter Glatzer for MDP Worldwide; released by MGM
Direction: Jonas Pate, Joshua Pate
Screenplay: Jonas Pate, Joshua Pate
Cinematography: Bill Butler
Editing: Dan Lebental
Music: Harry Gregson-Williams
Production design: John Kretschmer
Set decoration: Chuck Potter
Costumes: Dana Allyson Greenberg
Sound: Peter Bentley
MPAA rating: R
Running Time: 102 minutes

REVIEWS

Boxoffice. November, 1997, p. 118.
Entertainment Weekly. February 13, 1998, p. 43.
Los Angeles Times. January 30, 1998, p. F22.
New York Times. January 30, 1998, p. E12.
USA Today. January 30, 1998, p. 7D.
Variety. September 22, 1997, p. 57.

Deep Impact

Oceans rise. Cities fall. Hope survives.—Movie tagline

"Smashing special effects and top-quality actors."—Michael Wilmington, *Chicago Tribune*

"Five hundred billion tons of fun!"—Jami Bernard, *Daily News*

"Exhilarating! The special effects highlight of the year."—Jeffrey Lyons, *NBC-TV*

"Refreshing and inspirational!"—Richard Schickel, *Time*

"A thriller with brains!"—Gene Shalit, *Today Show*

 Box Office: $140,464,664

Onlookers brace themselves for the deadly side effects of a huge asteroid descending to Earth in *Deep Impact*.

If, one day, mankind faces "the end of the world as we know it" (in the words of the popular R.E.M song), most folks would conceive of this terrifying event as the millennium meltdown in the form of the Y2K bug. Hollywood, however, holds a differing notion. In 1988, Tinseltown released two apocalyptic *fin de siecle*, big-budget films. Bruce Willis led the testosterone-inflamed cast in *Armageddon*, but the first, and better, doomsday project was *Deep Impact*.

James Horner's (of *Titanic* and *Legends of the Fall* fame) music sets wind chimes and lyric piano to accompany the peaceful nighttime opening, as young Leo Biederman (Elijah Wood), and girlfriend Sarah Hotchner (Leelee Sobieski) scrutinize the star-rich night sky. With his telescope, Leo spots a celestial object he has never seen before. Intrigued by his discovery, he pops a snapshot and mails it to an astronomer called Wolf (Charles Martin Smith). Chewing pizza, Wolf idly runs the image through the computers, plots the likely trajectory of the object, and is whipped into a panic when his computer model shows it heading right to Earth. Racing off in his jeep with his findings on a floppy disk, he is unfortunately killed by a truck driver not paying attention to the road.

A year has passed—is the world ignorant of the imminent danger from outer space? At MSNBC in Washington D.C., aspiring reporter Jenny Lerner (Téa Leoni) is more concerned with advancing her career, and decides to take up a tip from the news team's anchor Beth (Laura Innes) concerning a senator's rumored infidelity. After playing the politician's wife for information, Jenny believes she has secured the first name of the mistress concerned: Ellie. The senator himself, Alan Rittenhouse (James Cromwell—looking uncannily like Speaker of the

 President Beck (Morgan Freeman) during a speech on television: "Life will go on, we will prevail."

House for a few hours Bob Livingston) gives little help to Jenny. On her way back to the studio, trying to call her story in, she is forced off the road, and taken to meet none other than the President (Morgan Freeman). What Jenny has uncovered is going to be far more significant than she realizes.

Two days later, Jenny is given an unprecedented, prestigious center row seat at a special press conference, at which the President has suggested he will give her first question. Through the Internet, Jenny has learned that "Ellie" is actually "ELE," which stands for "Extermination Level Event," and is so shaken that her meeting with her father Jason (Maximilian Schell) and his new young wife is a debacle. Before she slinks off, Jenny throws at him that he should reunite with her mom, Robin (Vanessa Redgrave). At the press conference, the President tells the world of the onrushing comet, now named Wolf-Biederman. Weighing an estimated 500 billion tons, it represents a grave threat to mankind. But in conjunction with the Russians, a strategy has been developed to divert it from our airspace.

In essence, this strategy has been to build a space ship over the previous year. Somewhat self-consciously named 'The Messiah,' the vehicle is to be manned by a crew that includes Oren Monash (Ron Eldard), Andrea Baker (Mary McCormack), Mark Simon (Blair Underwood), Gus Partenza (Jon Favreau), and moon-lander veteran Spurgeon "Fish" Tanner (Robert Duvall). Full of smiles as it is presented on live television, the team believes it can blow up the comet with a battery of nuclear devices.

As the world prays for 'The Messiah's' success, Jenny has made anchor, and she handles the broadcasts explaining the mission to the viewing public. The ship flies through the tail of the comet, and lands on the surface of its body. Moles implant the nuclear devices, but not before some human intervention by Monash is required. Late to re-board, Gus is lost by the erupting surface of the comet, and Monash is blinded by the surging sun on the horizon as he scrambles to return to the ship.

A second live chat with the President reveals that the mission has been a failure. The devices only split the comet. One piece is six miles wide; the other, one and a half miles in length, and both pieces remain on course to strike this planet. So plan B is unveiled. Titan missiles (which might work) can only be utilized hours before impact, so a computer lottery has randomly chosen 800,000 Americans to join 200,000 pre-selected artists, scientists, teachers (and presumably politicians) to shelter for two years in vast limestone caves in Missouri. For the rest of the American population, apocalypse is now. Martial law is declared, and the future is bleak; predictions are that the bigger comet will bring about the blacking out of the sun. Resigned to imminent destruction, Jenny's mother Robin takes her own life.

Consequently, the time is at hand for reconciliation and decisions. So that her family will be able to accompany the Biedermans into the Missouri caves, Leo persuades Sarah to marry him. Yet when the transports arrive to take the families to safety, the Hotchners are not on the list, and Sarah chooses to stay with her parents when they are refused permission to board the bus. Meanwhile in Washington DC, Jenny's father Jason brings a black and white photo of her as a little girl with him on the beach by their summer house, and says goodbye to his daughter.

Up in space, a tranquil scene between Fish and the blind Oren reveals a touching bond between the pair, and the older man reads *Moby Dick* to his colleague. In Missouri, Leo decides he cannot enter the caves without his new wife, and he says he must return to fetch her. His parents simply allow him to return to the chaos of the cities, and Leo sets off through the thrusting crowd of chosen people and selected animals for this second Noah's ark.

In his final press conference before the comet's double-whammy collision with Earth, a visibly distraught President Beck tells the nation that the missiles have failed, and they must all expect two enormous impacts. With hours remaining, the roads out of the cities are chaotic parking lots, but plucky Leo is somehow able not only to steer his way through the stationary traffic using a motorcycle from his neighbor's home, but to find Sarah and take her with him within the mass of fleeing people. Finally, Jenny gives up her place in the Missouri sanctuary for Beth and Beth's

daughter, racing off to find her father and be with him at the end.

Still in orbit, the crew of the Messiah has a last-gasp plan, knowing they cannot make it back to Earth. They say emotional farewells to their loved ones, and head for the larger piece of the comet to rendezvous with it and employ their remaining nuclear warheads. On our planet, the smaller half of the space object plunges into the Atlantic, and a colossal wave sets its deadly target upon the cities of the eastern seaboard, swiftly obliterating New York. Jenny, reunited with Jason, is at peace in her final moments. Sarah and Leo literally outpace the wave and look to the skies as the second comet is exploded before its impact, provoking a spectacular natural fireworks display. Civilization is saved! After the millions of deaths, President Beck speaks again, vowing to rebuild the country, and the world.

> Picture is dedicated to cinematographer Dietrich Lohmann, who died shortly after lensing was completed.

CREDITS

Spurgeon Tanner: Robert Duvall
Jenny Lerner: Tea Leoni
Leo Biederman: Elijah Wood
President Beck: Morgan Freeman
Robin Lerner: Vanessa Redgrave
Jason Lerner: Maximilian Schell
Alan Rittenhouse: James Cromwell
Oren Monash: Ron Eldard
Gus Partenza: Jon Favreau
Sarah Hotchner: Leelee Sobieski
Eric Venneker: Dougray Scott
Beth Stanley: Laura Innes
Andrea Baker: Mary McCormack
Mark Simon: Blair Underwood
Marcus Wolf: Charles Martin Smith

Origin: USA
Released: 1998
Production: Richard D. Zanuck and David Brown; released by Paramount Pictures and DreamWorks Pictures
Direction: Mimi Leder
Screenplay: Michael Tolkin and Bruce Joel Rubin
Cinematography: Dietrich Lohmann
Editing: David Rosenbloom
Music: James Horner
Production design: Leslie Dilley
Costumes: Ruth Myers
Sound: Mark Hopkins McNabb
Visual effects supervisor: Scott Farrar
MPAA rating: PG-13
Running Time: 120 minutes

While the onset of the massive tidal wave is horrifying (and compelling), I found the spaceship special effects to be less fussy and more evocative. Bruce Joel Rubin and Michael Tolkin's screenplay is competent, it avoids disaster film clichés, and it maintains focus on the tale's human elements by ignoring other aspects of the story. Missing in the script is a contemplation of the broader psychological angst imminent destruction would engender. Even so, the family dramas involving Jenny and Leo are intended to give a human dimension to what might simply have been an overwhelming epic, yet they don't fully succeed as Jenny remains an enigmatic figure, and Leo is hardly more than a standard plucky, if bright, teenager.

Still, Rubin and Tolkin's work is well aware of the intersection of modern culture and media, and this consideration adds an interesting color to the proceedings. Of 'The Messiah' crew, the comment is made, "They're not scared of dying; they're just scared of looking bad on TV." In *Deep Impact*, it's not the revolution that's televised—it's the inexorable path to catastrophe.

Mimi Leder cut her directing teeth on the television show *E.R.* Her debut was the action film *The Peacemaker*, thought to be a strange choice. Here, Leder skillfully handles the space and disaster sequences, as well as the smaller moments of family intimacy, to deliver a surprisingly satisfying—even moving—film. Several steadicam shots recall her television camera choices, but her visual approach is never showy. And under her guidance, the cast gives accomplished performances in roles that, as written, are often more utilitarian than nuanced. Special mention should go to Morgan Freeman, poised and even vulnerable as the stoic President Beck, and Ron Eldard, who turns in an emotional performance as intrepid astronaut Monash blinded and finally extinguished in the race to protect our world. We are left with the recognition that our home in the galaxy is more susceptible to global immolation than most of us are comfortable in acknowledging.

—*Paul B. Cohen*

REVIEWS

Chicago Tribune. May 8, 1998, p. 4.
Cinescape. May, 1998, p. 8.
Entertainment Weekly. May 15, 1998, p. 71.
Los Angeles Times. May 8, 1998, p. F2.
New York Times. May 8, 1998, p. E12.
New Yorker. May 18, 1998, p. 89.
People. May 25, 1998, p. 32.
Sight and Sound. July, 1998, p. 39.
Time. May 11, 1998.
Variety. May 11, 1998, p. 57.
Village Voice. May 19, 1998, p. 134.
Washington Post Weekend. May 8, 1998, p. 61.

Deep Rising

Full scream ahead.—Movie tagline

Women and children first. You're next.—Movie tagline

"Loads of screams and laughs!"—Ron Brewington, *American Urban Radio Network*

"A perfect popcorn movie!"—Barry Krutchik, *Premiere Radio*

 Box Office: $11,203,026

Take *Titanic* (1997), any of the *Alien* films (1979, 1986, 1992, 1997), mix them up with *Ten Little Indians* (1974) and a little bit of the *Die Hard* series (1988, 1990, 1995), add some truly cliché lines ("Wow, man, this is really freaking me out!") and presto, you've got yourself an action-horror-thriller that is unintentionally hilarious called *Deep Rising*.

Led by the stalwart and wry (a good combination) Treat Williams, this film almost gets away with being thought of as entertaining. Williams, who's starred in some fine films, most notably Sidney Lumet's *Prince of the City* (1981), does a fine job here of making us believe that he thinks he is in a movie worthy of his considerable talents. He plays John Finnegan, a man who operates some sort of speedboat service somewhere in the South China Seas. (The lack of specificity should alert audiences to the fact that if they are looking for a sensible story, they are not going to find it here). Finnegan's co-workers include Leila (Una Damon) and Joey (Kevin J. O'Connor, in possibly one of the most irritating performances in memory). At the film's opening, they are ferrying a band of unsavory and ill-tempered thugs, led by Hanover (Wes Studi), to an unknown destination. (There's that pesky lack of specificity again.)

Meanwhile, we also learn that the world's biggest ocean liner, owned by the nasty Simon Canton (Anthony Heald), is cruising the high seas somewhere nearby. Before long, we infer that the atomic missiles and heavy artillery carried by Hanover and his henchmen have something to do with taking over the cruise ship for its loot. Or something. Yet another subplot involves the beautiful Trillian St. James (Famke Janssen) as a clever jewel thief whose life is spared along with a select few passengers. Before you can say "*Twenty Thousand Leagues Under the Sea,*" a giant sea monster takes over the ship and destroys all of its passengers. By the time Finnegan, Hanover, and Hanover's men arrive on board there is an eerie calm all over the ship. They lock and load some heavy artillery, board the ship, and the rest of the film is a proforma journey through the bowels of the ship, with the alien-sea-monster springing up through the pipes and doors, eliminating, one-by-one, all of the characters until the only ones left are the most obvious and the highest paid.

As the characters are killed off, the audience is treated to bits and pieces of back-story. Apparently, shipowner Can-

Joey Pantucci (Kevin J. O'Connor): "I vote we leave. Who votes we leave?"

Director/writer Stephen Sommers created the story after reading a *National Geographic* article on the venomous Bell jellyfish, as well as researching the vampire squid and giant sea anemones.

ton had hired the bad guys to blow up the ship and collect the insurance money. Somebody disarms the ship's computers, then the lifeboats were to take away the passengers, and then the missiles were to sink the ship. "It was my dream," he says, but "I misjudged the market, and discovered that the ship could never make money." Talk about the need for business advice; didn't this guy ever hear of mutual funds?

The tentacled sea monster lustily thrashes through the ship for an hour and a half, and offers no true special effects of interest aside from the occasional good quick scare, which might be credited to the editing of Bob Ducsay and John Wright. Director/writer Stephen Sommers is hard at work on a remake of *The Mummy* as this review is being written, and perhaps that film may bring him more luck as a horror writer/director. As for this film, his style seems to follow the patterns and cliches of others. He tries to blend comedy with horror by inserting inappropriate lines of dialogue simply to get laughs. For instance: when several of the characters are skulking along a hallway, Joey begins to sing "The Girl From Ipanema" and makes some wiseacre comment when everyone gets mad at him for destroying the moment.

Similarly, when Joey and Finnegan are reunited after Joey's leg is wounded, he interrupts Finnegan's entreaties to hurry up by saying, "gee, don't I deserve even a 'hi Joey, how's your leg, Joey?'" Finally, the film's big clever line seems to be "Now what," which are the words Finnegan utters every time another larger monster is discovered. There is nothing wrong in trying to find catchphrases or phrases that a character repeats. Audiences like that sort of thing. But given that the film has already lost credibility with its audience by the time Finnegan says this the first time, most everything he or anyone else says simply becomes irritating and/or laughable.

It's most unpleasant to write a review that doesn't have much nice to say. So we should end by saying that Treat Williams was good and that the monster deserved what he got. Now what?

—*Kirby Tepper*

CREDITS

John Finnegan: Treat Williams
Trillian St. James: Famke Janssen
Simon Canton: Anthony Heald
Joey Pantucci: Kevin J. O'Connor
Leila: Una Damon
Hanover: Wes Studi
Mulligan: Jason Flemying
Vivo: Djimon Hounsou
The Captain: Derrick O'Connor

Origin: USA
Released: 1998
Production: Laurence Mark and John Baldecchi; released by Hollywood Pictures
Direction: Stephen Sommers
Screenplay: Stephen Sommers
Cinematography: Howard Atherton
Editing: Bob Ducsay, John Wright
Music: Jerry Goldsmith
Production design: Holger Gross
Art direction: Kevin Ishioka, Sandy Cochrane
Set decoration: Rose Marie McSherry, Ann Marie Corbett
Costumes: Joseph Porro
Creature design: Rob Bottin
Visual effects supervisor: Mike Shea
Sound: Rob Young, Frank Griffiths
Stunt coordination: Gary Combs
MPAA rating: R
Running Time: 106 minutes

REVIEWS

Entertainment Weekly. February 6, 1998, p. 40.
Los Angeles Times. January 30, 1998, p. F16.
New York Times. January 30, 1998, p. E24.
People. February 9, 1998, p. 19.
USA Today. January 30, 1998, p. 7D.
Variety. February 2, 1998, p. 27.

Deja Vu

A film about love . . . and destiny.—Movie tagline
Your life seems perfect . . . Your future is set . . .
Then you meet the love of your life.—Movie tagline
"A lovely ode to the romantic quest for true love!"—William Wolfe, *Wolfe Entertainment Guide*

Box Office: $1,085,640

*D*eja Vu is the third collaboration between director/writer Henry Jaglom and his wife, actress/writer Victoria Foyt, following *Babyfever* (1994) and *Last Summer in the Hamptons* (1995). Jaglom wrote in his production notes for *Deja Vu* that he has been "obsessed" with the subject for much of his life—the idea that two people, "each of whom is settled in life . . . suddenly meet

Sean (Stephen Dillane) to Dana (Victoria Foyt) on their meeting: "It feels like one of those moments where if you turn the wrong way you regret it forever."

one another and feel that they belong together, feel as if they somehow have *been* together already . . . "

His romantic fable begins with Dana (Victoria Foyt), an American traveling in Jerusalem on business. She shares a cafe table with an older French woman (Aviva Marks), who shares with Dana a story about lost love involving the beautiful ruby and diamond butterfly broach that she's wearing. It's one of a pair, though the woman's lover never had the chance to give her its mate. When the two women part, Dana realizes the woman has left the pin behind.

Dana reschedules her travel plans in order to make a brief stop in Paris to try and (unsuccessfully) return the broach; she then takes the channel crossing to London in order to meet her fiancé, Alex (Michael Brandon), for a pre-honeymoon vacation. At Dover (on the White Cliffs, no less), Dana notices Sean (Stephen Dillane), who's painting a seascape. Their eyes meet and it's love at first sight. As it turns out, Sean is married (seemingly happily) to Claire (Glynis Barber) and Dana does care for Alex. Since this duo happen to be caring adults, neither of them want to hurt their partners, but they're finding it difficult to resist the pull of their very strong attraction for one another.

As fate would have it, Dana and Sean can't seem to avoid one another. Dana visits Sean's art studio and notices an unfinished portrait of a woman. The duo kiss and then part. Then it turns out they have mutual friends in John (Noel Harrison) and Fern (Anna Massey) Stoner and are both guests at their London townhouse. At the Stoner's dinner party is John's exuberant sister, Skelly (Vanessa Redgrave), who notices their mutual desire. Skelly believes in "jumping off the cliff" and advises Sean to live his life as completely as possible.

Dana and Alex return to the U.S. to prepare for their wedding. On her wedding day, Dana's father (Graydon Gould) gives her a ruby and diamond butterfly clip. He tells his daughter he fell in love with a Frenchwoman while he was in Paris during the war and she was the love of his life. Of course, Dana has the matching pin. She decides

CREDITS

Sean: Stephen Dillane
Dana: Victoria Foyt
Skelly: Vanessa Redgrave
Claire: Glynis Barber
Alex: Michael Brandon
Konstantine: Alex Dobtcheff
John Stoner: Noel Harrison
Fern Stoner: Anna Massey
Dana's Father: Graydon Gould
Skelly's Mother: Rachel Kempson
Woman in Jerusalem: Aviva Marks

Origin: USA
Released: 1997
Production: John Goldstone for Jagtoria Film; released by Rainbow Film Co.
Direction: Henry Jaglom
Screenplay: Henry Jaglom and Victoria Foyt
Cinematography: Hanania Baer
Editing: Henry Jaglom
Music: Gaili Schoen
Production design: Helen Scott
Art direction: Helen Scott
Costumes: Rhona Russell
Sound: Tim Fraser
MPAA rating: Unrated
Running Time: 116 minutes

REVIEWS

Boxoffice. June, 1998, p. 77.
Los Angeles Times. April 22, 1998, p. F2.
New York Times. April 24, 1998, p. E12.
San Francisco Chronicle. May 22, 1998, p. C3.
Sight and Sound. October, 1998, p. 40.
Variety. November 3, 1997, p. 100.

this is the sign she's been looking for and calls off the wedding. Dana heads to London and seeks out Sean in his studio. The portrait is now finished and is of the Frenchwoman Dana met in Jerusalem. She's also wearing the butterfly broach. Sean tells Dana that the portrait is of his mother—who has been dead a number of years.

This is the first joint film appearance for Rachel Kempson and her daughter Vanessa Redgrave.

Jaglom's films are an acquired taste. Some critics feel he's narcissistic while others admire his romantic soul-searching. The same is true of Foyt, whose performance was described as of "hysterical self-importance" by *Sight and Sound* critic Melanie McGrath, while Kevin Thomas of the *Los Angeles Times* found her "more radiant than ever." The same dichotomy is also apparent in the reviews for *Deja Vu* itself, which seem to depend on the viewers' tolerance for the romance-with-supernatural-overtones genre that was once so popular.

—*Christine Tomassini*

Desperate Measures

His son needs a DNA donor to live. The clock is ticking. The only match is a vicious killer. Now all Frank Connor has to do is catch him.
—Movie tagline

"*Desperate Measures* is an unrelenting thrill ride that takes it to the limits."—Ron Brewington, *American Radio Networks*

"Suspense you can cut with a knife."—Bonnie Churchill, *National News Syndicate*

"*Desperate Measures* delivers thrills and gore, and a refreshingly ruthless performance from Michael Keaton."—Jeff Craig, *Sixty Second Preview*

 Box Office: $13,806,137

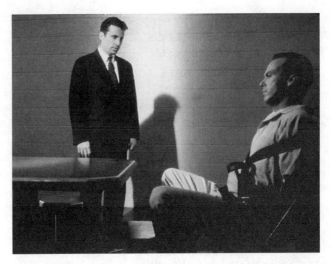

Law enforcer Frank Conner (Andy Garcia) confronts Peter McCabe (Michael Keaton), a sadistic serial killer in the tense thriller *Desperate Measures*.

Die Hard in a hospital? *Desperate Measures* presents the complications involved when a San Francisco cop, Frank Conner (Andy Garcia), learns that the best match for a bone-marrow donor for his leukemia-stricken nine-year-old son Matt (Joseph Cross) is Peter McCabe (Michael Keaton), a four-time murderer and hardened convict who seems to be the most feared inmate in the prison. The long middle portion of the film concentrates on McCabe's escape right before the transplant surgery and his cat-and-mouse game with police in and out of hospital corridors, operating rooms, storage areas, catwalks, and morgues. This film was one of the most negatively reviewed motion pictures of 1998, and part of the critics' sour reactions may owe to the reputation of director Barbet Schroeder and the expectation of more ambitious work from this highly-regarded filmmaker. Though it suffers from many implausibilities, *Desperate Measures* is a polished if superficial action film.

The early scenes stretch plausibility. During the main titles, imaginatively rendered by Robert Danson as shafts of light crawling in ticker-tape fashion along the dark hallways and across the facade of offices at FBI headquarters, Frank breaks into the FBI computers to find the match for his son. Why and how he is able to crack their computers and find the one perfect donor all the while keeping his eye on the door for the night watchman is something the film never clearly explains. This opening sequence sets the tone for some of the later implausibilities.

After McCabe agrees to be the donor, the film shows him planning his escape from the operating room. This sequence requires McCabe to earn back seemingly innocuous privileges such as smoking and access to the prison library, but it is one of the more subtle in the film since McCabe is clearly using these privileges to prepare a larger plan. For example, we see McCabe studying the tunnels and corridors in the old hospital from an interactive encyclopedia in the library while masking the computer screen with a chess game to fool the guard watching him. Later, he practices swallowing an ampule tied to dental floss wrapped around his tooth so that he can store in his mouth a chemical that will counteract some of the effects of the anesthesia before the surgery. The best action scenes are those immediately following his escape from the operating table, as he first takes Matt's doctor (Marcia Gay Harden) as a hostage. Once he is loose in the hospital, the pace quickens.

Cassidy (Brian Cox) to Connor (Andy Garcia): "How many people are gonna have to die here tonight so that kid of yours can live?"

The only interesting dialogue in the film concerns McCabe and his link to Frank and Matt. McCabe finally uses Matt as a hostage in his scramble to escape from the hospital. Their short exchanges of dialogue in a service elevator, in the hospital morgue, and in the basement touch briefly but interestingly on the only ideas the film tries to develop, a notion suggested by the title: the lengths to which someone will go when driven by extreme circumstances. McCabe is driven by desperate measures to obtain his freedom just as Frank is motivated to capture the man who can save his son's life. When Matt sees that McCabe is about to leave the basement carrying a gun, he hits him on the back with a pipe, saying that his father, who is chasing McCabe, doesn't have a gun. McCabe grins at Matt's tenacity and remarks that he and Matt are a perfect match in more ways than one.

The weaknesses in the film multiply quickly. Most of these involve the lengths to which Frank goes as a renegade cop to capture McCabe alive and preserve him for the transplant. As the series of hostages McCabe kidnaps takes him closer and closer to freedom, Frank is similarly driven to block police efforts to shoot McCabe. On a catwalk connecting the hospital with an older structure, Frank shoots ahead of advancing police, forcing them back to safety right before McCabe shoots a propane tank he has planted in the catwalk. The weakest scenes occur in the car chase and on a bridge after McCabe has finally gotten past the police and out of the hospital. The partly humorous tone of the odd final scene suggests that the filmmakers themselves may have finally recognized the cartoon quality that their cop-and-con chase story has acquired.

—Glenn Hopp

CREDITS

Peter McCabe: Michael Keaton
Frank Connor: Andy Garcia
Jeremiah Cassidy: Brian Cox
Samantha Hawkins: Marcia Gay Harden
Matthew Connor: Joseph Cross

Origin: USA
Released: 1998
Production: Barbet Schroeder , Susan Hoffman, Gary Foster, and Lee Rich for Mandalay Entertainment; released by TriStar Pictures
Direction: Barbet Schroeder
Screenplay: David Klass
Cinematography: Luciano Tavioli
Editing: Lee Percy
Music: Trevor Jones
Production design: Geoffrey Kirkland
Art direction: Sandy Getzler
Costumes: Gary Jones
Sound: Steve Nelson
MPAA rating: R
Running Time: 100 minutes

REVIEWS

Entertainment Weekly. January 30, 1998, p. 42.
Los Angeles Times. January 30, 1998, p. F8.
New York Times. January 30, 1998, p. E22.
People. February 9, 1998, p. 20.
USA Today. January 30, 1998, p. 7D.
Variety. January 26, 1998, p. 66.

Digging to China

"... uplifting ... a stirring story."—*Hollywood Reporter*

"There is something to be said about good stories and good acting and *Digging to China* says it ... It is a film that makes you feel."—George Pennacchio, *KABC-TV*

Box Office: $33,556

Digging to China marks the directorial debut of Academy Award-winning (for 1981's *Ordinary People*) actor Timothy Hutton. The story is set in the mid-60s in rural New England and is a predictable, if sweetly told, tale of the friendship between precocious 10-year-old Harriet Frankovitz (Evan Rachel Wood) and 30-year-old retarded Ricky Schroth (Kevin Bacon).

Harriet has a shaky homelife and dreams of getting away. She lives with her vodka-swilling mother (Cathy Moriarty) and her sleep-around sister Gwen (Mary Stuart Masterson) in the run-down, kitschy tourist motel they own and operate called "Mac's Indian Village Cabins." As Harriet narrates: "My mother lived in one world. I was always looking for another. Once I tried to squeeze down a rabbit hole. Then I tried digging all the way to China."

Harriet's definitely the odd-child-out. Her classmates think she's weird and she spends most of her time daydreaming, sitting on the side of the highway watching the cars pass, or running away. She's in her usual vantage point by the side of the road when the Schroth car breaks down. While the car is in for repairs, Leah (Marian Seldes) and her son Ricky settle into the motel for an extended stay. Talkative Harriet immediately tries to befriend Ricky, who's afraid to look her in the eye or speak to her. But since Harriet talks enough for both of them, that's not a problem and she's soon able to persuade Ricky to hang around with her.

Ricky, who's well aware that he's "different," tells Harriet that his mother is taking him to "a home where other people like me live." His mother has cancer and wants him safely settled before she dies. But, it's Harriet's mother, who has a bad tendency to drive on the wrong side of the road, who dies—killed in a car accident. Harriet turns to Ricky for comfort, which soon starts to worry Gwen.

But Gwen has a more immediate problem. After the funeral, she tries to reassure Harriet that she's not an orphan—that Gwen will be her mother. A resentful Harriet tells her sister that her mother's "in a box covered with dirt" and she doesn't need her trying to take her place. But the not-so-big revelation is that Gwen is Harriet's biological mother—"I had you when I was 15." This is not something Harriet wants to believe and only heightens the tension between the two.

Ricky begins to be fearful of going to an institution and leaving his only friend behind. So when his mother's repaired automobile is returned and they're set to leave, he decides to run away. Harriet follows him to one of their familiar hideouts and decides they should both follow the railroad tracks out of town to Canada. They find an abandoned rail car where they set up camp for the night: "Ricky concentrated on food and shelter. My job was to make big pronouncements and worry about the future."

Harriet (Evan Rachel Wood): "My sister Gwen shoulda been a nurse. She was always making some guy feel better."

Their adventure is cut short when Ricky gets sick and wants his mother. Harriet returns home to get help and a worried Gwen tries to make Harriet promise that she'll stay away from Ricky. Instead, Harriet tries to remain Ricky's "secret" friend. The entire situation takes a decidedly melodramatic turn when

---

CREDITS

Harriet Frankovitz: Evan Rachel Wood
Ricky Schroth: Kevin Bacon
Gwen Frankovitz: Mary Stuart Masterson
Leah Schroth: Marian Seldes
Mrs. Frankovitz: Cathy Moriarty

Origin: USA
Released: 1998
Production: Alan Mruvka, Marilyn Vance, John Davis, and J. Todd Harris for Davis Entertainment and the Ministry of Film; released by Moonstone Entertainment
Direction: Timothy Hutton
Screenplay: Karen Janszen
Cinematography: Jorgen Persson
Editing: Dana Congdon, Alain Jakubowicz
Music: Cynthia Miller
Production design: Robert De Vico
Costumes: Mary Zophres
MPAA rating: PG
Running Time: 98 minutes

Harriet tries comforting a crying Ricky, who's told the young girl that their friendship will soon be over anyway because "You're gonna grow up, I'm not."

Gwen sees the two together, misinterprets the situation, and calls the police before a stricken Harriet has a chance to explain. Ricky's soon back and a contrite Gwen tries to make amends by letting the friends say goodbye. Harriet finally decides to give Gwen a chance to act like a mother by having her take over a bedtime ritual about waiting for the Sandman and talking with her about their day.

The film manages not to be mawkish but, besides some attractively woodsy cinematography and an appealing performance by the young Wood, it has little to offer but a sort of wistful nostalgia. Bacon's performance is particularly

unfortunate—a twitchy, hunched-shouldered, ill-dressed, stammering cliché. Masterson deals as well as possible with a character that's all surface and does manage to look attractive in the sixties fashions, while both Moriarty and Seldes make only brief appearances.

—*Christine Tomassini*

REVIEWS

Los Angeles Times. September 11, 1998, p. F8.
New York Times. September 11, 1998, p. E18.
People. September 21, 1998, p. 38.
Variety. February 2, 1998, p. 33.
Village Voice. September 15, 1998, p. 146.

Dirty Work

Nothing tastes sweeter than revenge.—Movie tagline

Revenge Is Sweet (And surprisingly affordable).—Movie tagline

It's sick. It's dirty. It's their job.—Movie tagline

 Box Office: $10,022,221

It's quite easy to have low hopes for *Dirty Work,* the comedy starring Norm Macdonald, the former host of *Saturday Night Live*'s "Weekend Update." For one, the studio didn't allow any advance screenings for reviewers. This is generally a sign that even the studio thinks the film stinks. Another bad sign was that the film was directed by *Full House* alum, the unfunny comedian Bob Saget. For another thing, the trailer for the film featured dead prostitutes in trunks, played for laughs. As a rule, it would be difficult to make comedic fodder out of dead prostitutes in trunks, and *Dirty Work* shows that the rule still stands.

Then there's Norm Macdonald himself. NBC West Coast President Don Ohlmeyer had Macdonald fired from his SNL gig, saying that he just didn't think Macdonald was funny. For once, one of the suits was right. Macdonald really wasn't funny. He was, however, misanthropic and mean-spirited. If his few minutes on "Weekend Update" were painful, the prospect of a long film would not be a happy one. But luckily, that's not a problem. Mostly because, at 81 minutes, the film isn't long at all.

It helps *Dirty Work* tremendously to go in with low expectations. If a viewer expects that Macdonald will behave like a huge jerk, they will be happy to see that he only acts like a semi-huge jerk. If one imagines Saget's directing to be as hideous as his emceeing on *America's Funniest Home Videos,* they will be gladdened to see that it isn't as bad as all that.

The premise of *Dirty Work* is clever. Two loser friends, Mitch (Macdonald) and Sam (Artie Lange), need to raise $50,000 fast to pay for a heart transplant for Sam's father, Pops (Jack Warden). Since their career options are severely limited, they start their own business—a revenge-for-hire business. They graduate from petty revenge like putting popcorn in a bulldozer's motor and hiding smelly fish in someone's house onto more intricate, grandiose plans. Writers Macdonald, Frank Sebastiano and Fred Wolf are generous with their revenge ideas and come up with some fun, subversive ploys.

The rest of the plot is structured straight from a film school diagram. The characters have a goal ($50,000), clearly stated stakes (dear old Pops will die if they don't get the money), and odds stacked against them (a jail term, the wrath of some frat guys, an evil developer who wants revenge, etc . . .) The action marches in a predictable fashion. The odds stack up slowly, one-by-one until they become almost insurmountable and the guys have to fight that final grand battle.

But the plot structure isn't important. Comedy depends on funny ideas and *Dirty Work* has enough of these to make for a mildly entertaining film. After Mitch and Sam get beat up in a big bar brawl, Mitch picks up his ever-present tape recorder. "Note to self," he says, dryly. "Learn to fight."

Otherwise, *Dirty Work* relies on some fairly standard targets. The movie is very big on gay jokes. A typical example: Sam puts his arm around Mitch as a show of friendship. "Keep your distance, Liberace." There are also fat jokes, jokes about women, and a racist line or two. Generally, though, the offensive stuff is focused on gay jokes.

CREDITS

Mitch: Norm Macdonald
Sam: Artie Lange
Pops: Jack Warden
Kathy: Traylor Howard
Hamilton: Don Rickles
Travis Cole: Christopher McDonald
Dr. Farthing: Chevy Chase

Origin: USA
Released: 1998
Production: Robert Simonds; released by Metro-Goldwyn Mayer
Direction: Bob Saget
Screenplay: Frank Sebastiano, Norm Macdonald, and Fred Wolf
Cinematography: Arthur Albert
Editing: George Foley Jr.
Music: Richard Gibbs
Production design: Gregory Keen
Art direction: Gordon Lebredt
Costumes: Beth Pasternak
Sound: Stephen Grubbs
MPAA rating: PG-13
Running Time: 81 minutes

Norm Macdonald plays Mitch in a detached way, like he's sort of mocking the movie while he's acting in it. Although Macdonald can be funny in the film, he's never engaging. There's a certain coldness about him that's kind of chilling. For example, instead of calling anyone by name, he calls them by a label as in, "Settle down, prostitutes."

Lange's Sam is the fat sidekick. He plays it half Belushi (good-natured doofus guy who's good at breaking down doors) and half Ethel Mertz ("Geeeee, Lucy, I don't know if this is such a good idea.") The film is filled with cameos, most notably ex-*Diff'rent Strokes* star Gary Coleman in a hallucination sequence involving weird brownies and Satan. Don Rickles is as cantankerous as usual as a mean theater manager. Also putting in their two minutes are supermodel Rebecca Romaijn-Stamos as a bearded lady, Chevy Chase as a gambling doctor, John Goodman as an emcee, Adam Sandler as Satan and the late Chris Farley as his usual hyped-up down-and-outer.

Although the *Los Angeles Times* reported, "the best way to get revenge on someone who irks you is to force them to sit through this movie," the film isn't nearly as bad as that. As a way to kill 81 minutes on a slow summer day, it's not such a bad bet.

—*Jill Hamilton*

REVIEWS

Entertainment Weekly. June 26, 1998, p. 102.
Los Angeles Times. June 15, 1998, p. F4.
New York Times. June 13, 1998, p. B15.
People. June 29, 1998, p. 35
Variety. June 15, 1998, p. 99.

Disturbing Behavior

It doesn't matter if you're not perfect. You will be.—Movie tagline
Disturbing Behavior. You'll never be the same. —Movie tagline

Box Office: $17,509,368

A couple parked in a car at night kiss. The guy grows anguished, caught in a struggle resisting his sexual urges. He blurts out, "I need my fluids!" sending a laser-like beam from his eyes toward his date. He kills her. From a cliff above, a teenage boy, Gavin Strick (Nick Stahl), watches as the police approach. On discovering the girl's body, one of the officers confronts the murderer—and is slain. But the other cop (Steve Railsback) lets him go free.

Strange things are happening in Cradle Bay, Washington. The local high school misfits are suddenly transforming into ideal students with the help of Dr. Caldicott (Bruce Greenwood), delighting both teachers and parents. This thriller, an adolescent *Stepford Wives* (1975), turns around the theme of the good-kid-gone-bad with an amusing twist.

When teenager Steve Clark (Jimmy Marsden) arrives at his new school, smart-aleck Gavin and his albino buddy U.V. (Chad E. Donella) befriend him with a rundown of the cliqués: Motorheads. Micro-geeks. Skaters . . . and the Athletes or Robots or "Blue Ribbons," a group of clean-cut jocks and cheerleaders that seem to have stepped out of the 50s. In class, stresses between students surface when a rowdy boy gives a teacher a hard time and gets beat up by an apple-polishing Blue Ribbon.

Sneaking a smoke in the basement, Gavin introduces Steve to Mr. Newbury (William Sadler) the janitor, a "Boo Radley/village idiot/Quasimodo" type. The man is tinkering madly with a radio gadget intended to exterminate rats. After school, Steve meets Gavin's friend, Rachel Wagner (Katie Holmes), who wears a nose ring and uses expressions like "razor" for "cool." Driving around, they discover a Blue Ribbon suffering from "toxic jock syndrome" when he becomes unglued and wreaks havoc at a convenience store. Steve decides the violence is due to steroids, unconvinced by Gavin's theories that the group is mysteriously brainwashed.

In an effort to prove his point, they peek in on a rally led by Dr. Caldicott of a group attending the "Enlighten-

Director David Nutter makes his feature debut.

ment Weekend." They overhear the nomination for the next candidate to join the legions of goodniks—Gavin. Steve still thinks the accusations that he'll be changed into a zombie are crazy but the next day, Gavin snubs him saying, "I'll get better results applying myself to this side of the cafeteria." Gavin joins the Blue Ribbons and a fight breaks out when Steve tries to talk with him. The good kids have a habit of exploding into a rage.

Blue Ribbon Lorna Longley (Crystal Carr) shows up at Steve's to supposedly tutor his little sister. Repressing her chaste attitude, she attempts to seduce him but wracked with guilt, she injures herself to stop. Apparently, an implant in the Blue Ribbons' heads has created excessive stimulation to glands causing a rise in dopamine levels. Meanwhile, a Blue Ribboner stalks Rachel to ask her out, freaking out with her "no" answer and flying into a fit as the rat killing device sets off a piercing sound to malfunction his implant.

CREDITS

Steve Clark: James Marsden
Rachel Wagner: Katie Holmes
Gavin Strick: Nick Stahl
Dr. Caldicott: Bruce Greenwood
Officer Cox: Steve Railsback
Dorian Newberry: William Sadler
U.V.: Chad E. Donella
Allen Clark: Ethan Embry
Lindsay Clark: Katherine Isabelle

Origin: USA
Released: 1998
Production: Armyan Bernstein and Jon Shestack for Beacon Communications, Village Roadshow and Hoyts Film Partnership; released by Metro-Goldwyn-Mayer
Direction: David Nutter
Screenplay: Scott Rosenberg
Cinematography: John S. Bartley
Editing: Randy Jon Morgan
Music: Mark Snow
Production design: Nelson Coates
Art direction: Eric Fraser
Costumes: Trish Keating
Sound: Rob Young
MPAA rating: R
Running Time: 83 minutes

Rachel shows Steve a video from Gavin prior to his conversion to mind control. They run off to a psychiatric facility to collect evidence, locating Caldicott's crazy daughter. The suspicious cop tracks them down just as the janitor appears in time to hit the cop over the head. Steve returns home to discover Caldicott convincing his parents to treat him next. The Blue Ribbons capture him and Rachel, taking them off to be programmed with subliminal messages about achieving excellence. Steve manages to escape and save Rachel, and their romance develops further.

With the Blue Ribbons in pursuit, the janitor sets off the rat monitors in the back of a truck lured by the special sound effect. In a *Thelma and Louise* move, he leads them like lemmings over the edge of a cliff. A Pink Floyd song plays on the score, "Hey teacher, leave those kids alone," with a chilling image of Gavin as a teacher, flashing laser-beam eyes at his students.

The irony of troublemakers becoming "A" students only to maim and create mayhem is a welcome theme for teens, as is the clever and snappy dialogue from screenwriter Scott Rosenberg. A youthful audience appreciates U.V.'s humor

when testing Steve to see if he's shifted—"What's the capital of North Dakota?" Steve responds, "How should I know?"

Director David Nutter (*The X-Files* series) displays a stylish approach to this *Scream* wannabe but the acting seem secondary. Katie Holmes (*Dawson's Creek*) gives a sullen and sultry portrayal to a lame role but the standout performances are Stahl and his flip sidekick Donella. Unfortunately, when Stahl joins the Blue Ribbons his quips end and the movie unfolds too predictably.

—Roberta Cruger

REVIEWS

Entertainment Weekly. July 31, 1998, p. 46.
Los Angeles Times. July 24, 1998, p. F13.
New York Times. July 24, 1998, p. E22.
People. August 10, 1998, p. 32.
Variety. July 27, 1998, p. 53.
Village Voice. August 4, 1998, p. 53.

Dr. Dolittle

He doesn't just talk to the animals!—Movie tagline
For thousands of years animals have been trying to tell us something, but their cries have fallen on deaf ears . . . until they found John Dolittle.—Movie tagline

 Box Office: $144,153,418

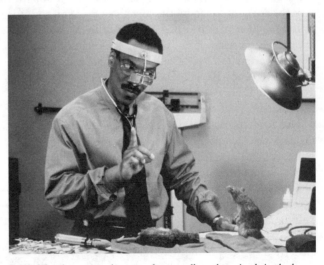

Eddie Murphy stars as the man who can talk to the animals in the box-office hit *Dr. Dolittle*.

Eddie Murphy's *Dr. Dolittle* is a far cry from the 12 whimsical children's books by the English writer Hugh Lofting, which originally appeared between 1920 and 1952 (the last three being published after his death in 1947). About the only element retained in the movie is the idea of a doctor being able to communicate with animals. The new *Dr. Dolittle* might be called a nineties version of Lofting. One of the producers, in fact, was quoted as saying that they were "bringing a contemporary and hip '90s spin to the material." This is a common phenomenon these days, not only in the movies but on television and in other media: the phrase seems to mean "satirical," "irreverent," "sardonic," and "deconstructionist," among other things. Early antecedents can be found in Bugs Bunny and the "Fractured Fairy Tales" portion of television's *The Bullwinkle Show*.

The animals in *Dr. Dolittle* use words that the little readers of the original Lofting stories would never have been permitted to hear. Ironically, Eddie Murphy as Dolittle is forced to act shocked by the same sort of language he has often used himself as a street-smart criminal in films such as *48 Hours* (1982) and its sequel, and as a street-smart detective in the *Beverly Hills Cop* (1984) series. The impressive boxoffice receipts for the opening weeks of *Dr. Dolittle* suggest that Murphy's somewhat shaky career is back on the right track. It is the same track that took him to his 1996 hit, *The Nutty Professor,* and once again it proves that he is more versatile, more durable, and more bankable than many skeptics believed. Given the opportunity, he can play characters other than the jive-talking black hipster who was getting to be a little bit tiresome and redundant. Murphy has come a long way from the prison cell in *48 Hours* to the chemistry professor Sherman Klump and the equally respectable surgeon John Dolittle, who is married, has two cute daughters, and lives in a high-rise apartment building on Union Street with a panoramic view of San Francisco Bay.

Rodney the guinea pig (voice of Chris Rock) to the doctor: "You want gratitude, get a hamster."

Director Betty Thomas and cinematographer Russell Boyd take maximum advantage of San Francisco's famous scenery. At the same time, however, they manage to find new sights and new camera angles, avoiding the old cinematic cliches. Parents who are not captivated by the silly little story can at least enjoy an imaginary visit to the Bay Area during unusually bright and sunny weather.

Dr. Dolittle shares a thriving practice with two partners, Dr. Mark Weller (Oliver Platt) and Dr. Gene Reiss (Richard Schiff). The film is given a gloss of contemporary social significance by the fact that their enterprise is in imminent danger of being swallowed by a giant health maintenance organization (HMO). This soulless corporation is represented by the money-hungry, cost-conscious Calloway (Peter Boyle). Dolittle has misgivings. He is aware that Calloway's proposal would mean downsizing, firing members of their loyal staff, and losing the freedom to give patients the best possible care. He is, however, being pressured by his partners, who can see nothing but the millions being dangled in front of their greedy eyes. The deal would have gone through if Dolittle had not suddenly rediscovered his gift of being able to talk to animals.

A flashback informs the audience that little Johnny Dolittle possessed that gift as a child but lost it as the result of a traumatic event. His father decided it was

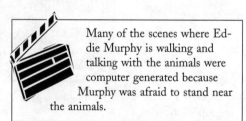

Many of the scenes where Eddie Murphy is walking and talking with the animals were computer generated because Murphy was afraid to stand near the animals.

unhealthy for the little boy to be spending all his time conversing with his dog and sent the beloved pet off to the pound. Suddenly the strange gift comes back to the adult John when he bangs his head on the windshield while swerving to avoid a stray dog. Lucky, the dog (voice of Norm Macdonald), ends up adopting Dolittle and causing him no end of embarrassment.

The doctor naturally thinks he is going crazy when he finds that he can understand not only dogs, but rats, raccoons, owls, his daughter's guinea pig, pigeons, and even an enormous Bengal tiger. With digital imagery, all of these animals seem to be moving their mouths in sync while speaking. These special effects techniques were perfected for *Babe* (1995), the film that received remarkable acclaim for such a lightweight comedy. Dolittle's furry and feathered friends turn out to be a pretty feisty and hip bunch of animals, with voices provided by such actors as Albert Brooks, Chris Rock, Reni Santoni, John Leguizamo, Julie Kavner, Garry Shandling, and Jenna Elfman.

Most of these animals are pursuing Dolittle because he is not only a physician, but the only human who can understand their descriptions of their aches and pains. He tries desperately to keep his gift a secret from his family and his associates. As Leonard Klady wrote in his *Variety* review: "Murphy is largely saddled with a reactive role, and periodically it seems that he's playing to a blue screen where members of the menagerie will be optically inserted later." This sort of computerized hocus-pocus seems, unfortunately, here to stay.

"Reactive" is a good word to describe Murphy's performance in this creature feature. Things keep happening to him and his flexible face reveals his shock, disbelief, bewilderment, distress, panic, or whatever. It is something new for Murphy, and it may be good for him; it takes him away from his shtick as an unflappable, jive-talking egomaniac.

Eventually Dolittle is caught holding long conversations with animals and is whisked off to a sanitarium. By this point he is admitting that he really can communicate with animals, but nobody is buying it. He flunks a sanity test when it turns out that the orangutan who is brought to the psychiatrist's office can only speak Spanish.

The sinister Calloway keeps pressuring the other two doctors to sign on the dotted line, but they cannot consummate the deal without their partner, whose problems have gone from bad to worse. He has gotten involved with a circus tiger who complains of chronic pains so unremitting that he intends to commit suicide. In one scene, having escaped his circus cage, he is preparing to jump off one of San Francisco's famous Landmarks, Coit Memorial Tower. Dolittle, who has now found himself turned into a veterinarian, talks the tiger down by promising to diagnose and cure him.

Now Dolittle is regarded as an escaped lunatic who has stolen a dangerous tiger from the circus and is planning to operate on it without any experience as a veterinarian. All of the principals of the cast have assembled outside the operating room, along with a lot of cops and some burly psychiatric attendants in white coats. But everyone is afraid to enter because the suffering tiger is in a very bad mood. Among those staring horrified through the glass are Dolittle's wife (Kristen Wilson) and his daughters Maya (Kyla Pratt) and Charisse (Raven-Symone). Calloway is aghast at what is going on in the high-tech medical facility he had hoped to add to his HMO empire. Dolittle's partners are still hoping to persuade Calloway that he is only witnessing a temporary aberration caused by the strain of overwork and that his proposed investment is as good as gold. It was possible for them to get around the sight of Dolittle giving mouth-to-nose resuscitation to a rat rescued from a garbage can, but a little hard to ignore a 500-pound tiger on a operating table designed for humans.

Eventually Lisa sees the light. It is her courageous entrance into the operating room to hold the tiger's paw that conveys the film's rather nebulous message. Her husband is not a businessman, not a moneymaker, but a healer. His job is to use his medical expertise to help those in need, regardless of ability to pay. Through his interaction with dumb animals who have no one else to understand them, he has learned that the greatest satisfaction in life is not in getting or spending money but in being of service by exercising one's god-given gifts.

Although Eddie Murphy does not make a schmaltzy speech about family values, as did Jimmy Stewart while embracing wife and kids at the end of *It's a Wonderful Life* (1946), the emotional payoff is similar. Like the Jimmy Stewart film, *Dr. Dolittle* ought to appeal to families with kids still young enough to stay at home at night. As Leonard Klady observed in *Variety*, " . . . the film's big payday [will be] down the line on video."

—*Bill Delaney*

CREDITS

Dr. John Dolittle: Eddie Murphy
Archer Dolittle: Ossie Davis
Charisse Dolittle: Raven-Symone
Lisa Dolittle: Kristen Wilson
Maya Dolittle: Kyla Pratt
Dr. Mark Weller: Oliver Platt
Dr. Gene Reiss: Richard Schiff
Dr. Fish: Jeffrey Tambor
Calloway: Peter Boyle
Rodney the guinea pig: Chris Rock (voice)
Lucky the dog: Norm Macdonald (voice)
Tiger: Albert Brooks (voice)
Rat: Reni Santoni (voice)
Rat: John Leguizamo (voice)
Female pigeon: Julie Kavner (voice)
Male pigeon: Garry Shandling (voice)
Dog: Ellen DeGeneres (voice)
Old Beagle: Brian Doyle-Murray (voice)
Owl: Jenna Elfman (voice)
Raccoon: Paul Reubens (voice)

Origin: USA
Released: 1998
Production: John Davis, David T. Friendly, and Joseph M. Singer; released by 20th Century Fox
Direction: Betty Thomas
Screenplay: Nat Mauldin and Larry Levin; based on the novel by Hugh Lofting
Cinematography: Russell Boyd
Editing: Peter Teschner
Music: Richard Gibbs
Production design: William A. Elliott
Costumes: Sharen Davis
Visual effects: Jon Farhat
Animation special effects : Jonathan R. Banta
MPAA rating: PG-13
Running Time: 85 minutes

REVIEWS

Chicago Tribune. June 26, 1998, p. 5.
Detroit Free Press. June 26, 1998, p. 6D.
Detroit News. June 26, 1998, p. 3C.
Entertainment Weekly. July 10, 1998, p. 48.
Los Angeles Times. June 26, 1998, p. F10.
New York Times. June 26, 1998, p. B16.
People. July 6, 1998, p. 36.
San Diego Union-Tribune. June 25, 1998, p. 23.
San Francisco Chronicle. June 26, 1998, p. C3.
Sight and Sound. August, 1998, p. 37.
Time. July 6, 1998.
Variety. June 29, 1998, p. 38.
Village Voice. July 7, 1998, p. 120.
Washington Post Weekend. June 26, 1998, p. 46.

Down in the Delta

Sometimes the last place you expected to be is the one place you've always belonged.—Movie tagline

Loretta Sinclair is a big city woman with a big city attitude, whose small town cousins are about to show her how to really live!—Movie tagline

"A joyful, entertaining and heartfelt film!"—George Pennacchio, *ABC-TV*

"This year's *Soul Food*! Wesley Snipes shines!"—*Newsweek*

"A remarkable film! Alfre Woodard gives one of her best performances!"—Roger Ebert, *Siskel & Ebert*

"Funny and heartwarming! Maya Angelou's directorial debut is a triumph! Perfect performances from Alfre Woodard and Wesley Snipes!"—Aaron Gell, *Time Out New York*

Box Office: $2,497,557

Not too many poets have succeeded as movie directors. Judging by her initial effort, *Down in the Delta*, Maya Angelou may be one of the first. The acclaimed poet, who has performed at presidential inaugurations, shows a surprising deftness with her handling of this sometimes inspiring, sometimes insipid film about the redemptive power of family heritage.

Angelou's directing of this story about a struggling African-American single mother reborn by a visit to her Southern roots is solid if largely uninspired. Angelou shares none of the writing credits, which go to Myron Goble. But the film shows occasional small touches of her poetic sensibility, helping to salvage what in some ways is a hackneyed saga.

Director Maya Angelou: "A family has the power to heal as well as to damage, to strengthen and build up as well as to tear down. I have always been drawn to stories that affirm life-enhancing relationships."

Unfortunately, *Down in the Delta* also has too many touches of hokey dialogue, unbelievable character transformations and romanticizing of the rural South. Still, it is well acted by a terrific ensemble and qualifies as both a heartfelt and a heartwarming film.

It opens on the mean streets of Chicago's South Side, where a saintly matriarch named Rosa Lynn Sinclair (Mary Alice) tries to cover for her jobless, alcoholic daughter, Loretta (Alfre Woodard). Loretta doesn't have much atten-

tion for mothering her son Thomas (Mpho Koaho) and her autistic daughter Tracy (Kulani Hassen), who spends all her time screaming in a crib. Her mother gets off the couch to feed her only when Rosa Lynn calls to remind her, and even then Loretta mixes soda pop into a bottle of formula.

Alice is splendid at portraying the supremely patient Rosa Lynn, who spends her days working at a church soup kitchen and the rest of the time taking care of Thomas and Tracy while Loretta is out boozing. Thomas, a plucky 12-year-old nicely played by Koaho, secretly earns money by taking pictures of tourists and selling them to his subjects. He hides the money in a stuffed lion to keep it safe from his mother, who is always taking his cash or pawning his other possessions to buy drinks.

Loretta is shiftless and full of excuses. But Angelou intends to redeem her character for us, and in a wonderful scene she lets us glimpse the source of Loretta's pain. At the urging of her son and mother, Loretta applies for a cashier's job at a grocery store. Her son assures her the machines take care of all the math and even fills out her resume for her. But when the manager interviews her, he asks her what change she would give if somebody bought a $3.87 item and handed her $5. Sheepishly, Loretta asks if she could do something else at the store besides cashier.

Loretta leaves the store, dejected. Woodard's face is twisted with humiliation, and you understand what drives her to despair. She goes on a binge and Rosa Lynn tracks her down at a party full of drug users. Inexplicably, however, Loretta has the strength to resist the offer of a crack pipe. Once you go down that road, she says, there's no going back.

Loretta's character is a stereotype of a substance-abusing, irresponsible young woman. It's hard to understand why she has the will to say no to cocaine but can't help binging on alcohol. It's also hard to figure how this terribly disturbed, apparently illiterate young woman is the daughter of the no-nonsense, straight-arrow Rosa Lynn. It's never explained, and it's a major problem for the film's believability.

Desperate for a way out, Rosa Lynn decides to send Loretta and her children to her brother-in-law Earl's home in the Mississippi Delta for the summer. Earl (Al Freeman Jr.) feels compelled to accept them because Loretta is the daughter of his dead brother. But it's not easy for Rosa Lynn to ask this favor. Earl and Rosa Lynn have a feud going over a family heirloom, a silver candelabra they call Nathan. Earl is upset that while he was in the Korean War his brother and Rosa Lynn moved to Chicago and took Nathan with them, and that Rosa Lynn has never returned it.

From the moment Rosa Lynn puts the troubled trio on a Greyhound bus, after pawning Nathan to pay for the trip, there is never a doubt that a summer in the South is going to cleanse Loretta of her evil ways and transform Thomas from a future gunshot victim to a straight-arrow young man. *Down in the Delta* can't be accused of overplaying the grimness of life in a Chicago ghetto. But it does over-sell the beauty of life in the deep South. Angelou portrays the Mississippi Delta as a refuge of rural charm and great beauty, a place for spiritual and racial regeneration. It's picturesque, but doesn't look much like rural Mississippi, just as the street scenes in Chicago didn't look much like that city's South Side. And no wonder. The entire movie was shot in Toronto!

Poverty among rural blacks in Mississippi is the worst in the nation. This story stacks the deck by making Earl the proprietor of the only restaurant in town, a place called "Jus' Chicken" that serves only chicken. Earl lives in a sunny house that used to be the "Big House" on the plantation where his descendants were slaves owned by the "white Sinclairs." Somehow, Earl has become prosperous enough not only to buy the Big House but to hire a woman, Zenia

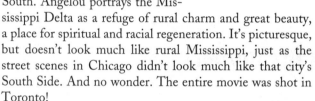

Myron Globe's screenwriting debut was honored with a 1993 Nicholl Fellowship Award.

(Loretta Devine), to help him take care of it and his Alzheimer's-stricken wife, Annie.

Annie is played by the magnificent Esther Rolle, in her last role before her death. It's a remarkable performance, never cloying and never striking a false note. Annie's mind slipping away, and her husband's gentle caring for her, are at the core of the dignity that eventually washes over Loretta. The morning after her arrival, Loretta remarks to her uncle that Annie "should be in a home somewhere." Earl replies simply: "She IS home."

This is the film's traditional moral: Family is the source of pride, dignity, and hope. Caring for your own is essential. Loretta has lost her moral compass in the modern urban world because she has forgotten the importance of family. *Delta* doesn't do a great job of explaining why that happened to Loretta, settling for the simple explanation that alcohol and urban life destroyed her fiber. This isn't a movie that's long on complexity. It does, however, have a big heart.

Freeman is solidly at the film's emotional center. His performance is both simple and enchanting. Earl is a gentle patriarch who is deeply rooted in his family traditions. And after a half-century, he is still smitten with his now-dying wife. Loretta remarks on how unusual that is, how all the men she's ever known don't stay long enough to clean up the messes they have made.

Down in the Delta is essentially one long sermon. It's made bearable by the gentleness of the director's perspective and the heartfelt performances by its characters. Angelou's film has little use for irony or sarcasm. It labors to make its characters real but is content to settle for somewhat farfetched transformations.

The details of Loretta's transformation are glossed over in sunny vignettes. Her guilt over mothering her autistic daughter is never fully explained. And her emergence as an entrepreneur and community leader is sudden and strange. With the aid of Earl's son Will (Wesley Snipes), a buppie Atlanta lawyer, Loretta hatches an idea to save the town and her uncle's business when the local chicken factory announces it's closing. It's a half-baked contrivance which too neatly ties together several disparate threads.

Delta lurches and meanders from subplot to subplot, some involving petty family jealousies involving Will's wife and children. The main events of the film are completely predictable. Finally, Angelou settles on putting the story of the candelabra named Nathan at the center of the film. The complete story of the heirloom—which involves the roots of the family in slavery—unfolds in a herky-jerky fashion. Despite all, the tale is still compelling and powerful.

Angelou's heart is in the right place, and her basic instincts are right. For a first directorial effort, *Down in the*

CREDITS

Loretta: Alfre Woodard
Earl: Al Freeman, Jr.
Rosa Lynn: Mary Alice
Annie: Esther Rolle
Zenia: Loretta Devine
Will: Wesley Snipes
Monica: Anne Marie Johnson
Thomas: Mpho Koaho
Tracy: Julani Hassen
Dr. Rainey: Justin Lord

Origin: USA
Released: 1998
Direction: Maya Angelou
Screenplay: Myron Goble
Cinematography: Williams Wages
Editing: Nancy Richardson
Music: Stanley Clarke
Production design: Lindsey Hermer-Bell
Costumes: Maxyne Baker
Sound: Tom Hidderley
MPAA rating: PG-13
Running Time: 111 minutes

Delta is remarkable. The tapestry of the film is beautiful, if a bit too neatly woven. The spirit of the movie is strong, even if some of the proceedings are a bit too pedestrian. Simply put, it's an old-fashioned story about old-fashioned family values, told in a straightforward, unapologetic way. In an era when too many filmmakers think they need layers of irony or exploitation to sell their ideas, there's nothing wrong with that. Angelou's poetic heart provides this simplistic film with a strong, steady pulse.

—Michael Betzold

REVIEWS

Entertainment Weekly. January 8, 1999, p. 50.
Los Angeles Times. December 25, 1998, p. F16.
New York Times. December 25, 1998, p. E19.
People. January 11, 1999, p. 38.
Variety. September 21, 1998, p. 110.

Dream for an Insomniac

A dreamer who couldn't sleep. An author who couldn't write. A friend who couldn't help but help.—Movie tagline

Writer-director Tiffanie DeBartolo makes her feature film debut with the talky and trite romantic comedy *Dream for an Insomniac*. Set in San Francisco (DeBartolo's father is 49ers owner Eddie), the story revolves around life at the Cafe Blue Eyes coffeehouse, a place where Frank Sinatra is considered king.

Ione Skye stars as Frankie (named for The Chairman), an aspiring actress who works in the coffeeshop and is looking for love. She believes "anything less than mad, extraordinary love is a waste of your time." Frankie longs for a guy "with the soul of a poet and eyes like Frank Sinatra." Aside from the fact that she's a caffeine addict, Frankie claims she hasn't slept a full night since the age of six—that's when her parents died in a car accident.

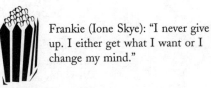

Frankie (Ione Skye): "I never give up. I either get what I want or I change my mind."

Frankie is convinced that once she and her best friend Allison (Jennifer Aniston) leave San Francisco to pursue acting careers in Los Angeles, she'll meet her dream man and then, finally, she'll be able to sleep.

Cafe Blue Eyes is owned by Frankie's Uncle Leo (Seymour Cassel), an Italian immigrant who lives above the store with his son Rob (Michael Landes). A few days before Frankie's departure, Uncle Leo decides to hire a replacement for her (although there's never any customers in the coffeeshop) and in walks David Shrader (MacKenzie Astin). It's love at first sight for Frankie, and at this point, the movie switches from black and white to color. Frankie truly believes that David is her Prince Charming and she has only three days to convince him that she's the love of his life.

New to the area, David is an aspiring writer just in from Michigan. He seems to be attracted to Frankie, yet he doesn't pursue a romantic relationship with her. We later learn that he already, inconveniently, has a nice girlfriend named Molly (Leslie Stevens), whom he keeps a secret from everyone at the coffeeshop. Although David is committed to Molly, he flirts and jokes around with Frankie while working at the Cafe Blue Eyes. They try to stump each other by quoting Kierkegaard, Aristotle, and Nirvana lyrics, among others, all of which is supposed to make us realize that these two are soul mates. Furthering their connection, Frankie reads David's work and praises it. When she learns that he hasn't written a word in ages, they strike a deal—she will try to cure his writer's block and he'll try to cure her insomnia. What happens next is all too predictable.

One of *Dream*'s dull subplots involves Frankie's gay cousin Rob, who's afraid to come out to his gruff, old-world father, even though it's pretty obvious to everyone else what his sexual preference is. Rob, who lives with a boyfriend, enlists Allison to play along as his girlfriend in order to convince Dad that he's straight. After Allison and Frankie leave for L.A., Rob has a change of heart and decides to come out to his father. It turns out the old man wasn't quite so naive all along.

Although *Dream for an Insomniac*'s actors are appealing, the film suffers from an overly talky and tired script. Another serious flaw is that it seems more suited for a play than movie and ends up coming across like a sitcom full of dated

Gen-X cliches. Do we really need another movie about young wannabe actors hanging out in coffee bars, worshipping Sinatra, smoking cigars, and obsessing about pop culture trivia? First-time filmmakers would be better off exploring fresher, more original ideas.

As with the script, all of the characters could have benefitted from more development—and that's especially true of the secondary players. Ms. Aniston, unfortunately, doesn't have much to do except breeze in and out of scenes sporting a variety of annoying accents. Best known for her role as "Rachel" on TV's *Friends*, Aniston has recently enjoyed big screen success with starring roles in *Picture Perfect* (1997) and *The Object of My Affection* (1998).

Writer-director Tiffanie De-Bartolo is the daughter of San Francisco 49ers owner Eddie DeBartolo.

Ione Skye, the star of films such as *Gas Food Lodging* (1992) and *Say Anything* (1989), seems seriously miscast as a depressed intellectual. Skye's airheaded delivery makes it hard to believe her in the role of a brooding and tortured romantic. Nothing really rings true in this film. Besides the subject of romance, Frankie is also supposed to be intense about her career but we never see her pursuing it. In fact, she doesn't even bother to attend any acting auditions. At least we see Allison actually audition and land a gig.

Although there isn't much Astin can do with his largely underwritten role, he is pleasing as David. Besides being extremely good-looking (MacKenzie's the son of Patty Duke and John Astin), David does have his charming moments—especially when he reads Frankie a bedtime story by Dr. Seuss. Overall, though, it's not enough to save this film. Astin can be seen most recently in the third installment of Whit Stillman's preppy trilogy, *The Last Days of Disco* (1998).

While Sinatra is revered at Cafe Blue Eyes, it's actually Frank Sinatra Jr. playing on the soundtrack. That should have been the first clue that things aren't quite up to feature film standards. Overall, *Dream for an Insomniac* tries too hard to be cute and hip. All of its performers have done better work before and since this weak effort was completed three years ago.

Critics were mostly negative in their reviews—with the exception of the San Francisco critics who were kind. Kevin Thomas, writing for the *Los Angeles Times*, calls *Dream* a "snooze" that is "an overly talky yet under-characterized romantic comedy of unstinting artificiality and triteness and no style whatsoever."

—*Beth Fhaner*

CREDITS

Frankie: Ione Skye
Allison: Jennifer Aniston
David Shrader: MacKenzie Astin
Rob: Michael Landes
Uncle Leo: Seymour Cassel
Juice: Sean San Jose Blackman
B.J.:   Michael Streck
Molly: Leslie Stevens
Trent: Robert Kelker Kelly

Origin: USA
Released: 1998
Production: Rita J. Rokisky for Tritone Productions; released by Avalanche Films
Direction: Tiffanie DeBartolo
Screenplay: Tiffanie DeBartolo
Cinematography: Guillermo Navarro
Editing: Tom Fries
Music: John Laraio
Production design: Gary New
Costumes: Charles E. Winston
MPAA rating: R
Running Time: 88 minutes

REVIEWS

Los Angeles Times. June 19, 1998, p. F8.
New York Times. June 19, 1998, p. E24.
San Francisco Chronicle. June 26, 1998, p. C6.
San Francisco Examiner. June 26, 1998, p. C5.

Eden

Let your spirit soar.—Movie tagline

"For everyone who has yearned for the dim recollection of heartfelt filmmaking, for films of passion, sensitivity and bona fide emotional resonance, *Eden* is a must see."—Robert Ellsworth, *Detour*

"Nostalgic and sweetly ethereal."—Janet Maslin, *New York Times*

Eden is a small, heartfelt film that wants very much to recreate a world, and paradoxically, to transcend that world. A young woman retreats from her advancing illness into a spirit existence: this is terra incognita for most filmmakers who prefer their paranormal experience in the shape of sexy specters who visit pining loved ones, a la *Ghost*. One woman's flight from spiritual and physical pain might not seem as if it would have the power to hold an audience, but *Eden* does, though most assuredly it is not a film for everyone.

The *New York Times*' Stephen Holden summed up the film's problems: "*Eden*, which is narrated by Helen, is really two movies in one, and they don't quite fit." *Eden* tries hard to do too many things—it is a family drama, a spiritual odyssey, and an academic tale all at once.

The film takes place in 1965 at a well-heeled prep school, Mt. Eden Academy, the alma mater of Bill Kunen (Dylan Walsh), an economics teacher who is in charge of a group of male students in residence in a rambling, beautiful old house. His sweet-tempered wife, Helen (the lovely Joanna Going) and their two small children coexist with Bill, who seems rather absorbed by his job. Writer/Director Howard Goldberg rather delicately lets us know that Helen has a disability by at first filming her from the waist up, a cheerful, perfect housewife in a skirt and sweater set, then suddenly showing her standing in a doorway. Helen has multiple sclerosis; her leg is encased in a heavy, cumbersome brace—her lithe and slender body seems trapped by this ugly object. Going truly conveys the character's frustration and resiliency; her performance grounds a film which could have easily become a metaphysical mess.

As Helen tells us in a voice-over, "Our lives had been so beautiful, full of grace and joy and promise . . . " as the camera pans over the campus, coming to rest briefly on several coat-and tie-clad students earnestly and tunelessly playing guitars, singing Bob Dylan's "The Times They Are a' Changin'"—stopping abruptly as the bell rings for class. This aspect of *Eden* frequently seems a bit forced, or maybe folk-singing prep students are a hard thing to pull off with a straight face, along with a silly pot smoking sequence late in the film. Goldberg usually manages to preserve some sense of balance in portraying the naiveté of Dave (Sean Patrick Flanery), a smart but underachieving student proto-rebel, contrasting his sometimes goofy idealism with the embittered perspective of Bill, who is 29 but acts as if he were much older. These two lock horns repeatedly, fueled by Dave's barely concealed crush on Helen. Bill resists Helen's entreaties to let Dave be a free spirit by bluntly telling her, "I'm keeping the pressure on until I get results." Helen continues to encourage Dave, tutoring him to help bring up his dismal grades and inventing a motto (she urges him to practice "RIP—Responsibility, Initiative, Progress!" to which he says wryly, "'Rest in Peace' is better!")

The tension over Dave only aggravates what is a slowly deepening rift between Helen and Bill, demonstrated best by a scene where Bill discovers stashed in the kitchen a photo album of their life together, which ends abruptly with a pre-illness smiling photo of them with a newborn. He leans heavily on the refrigerator and sobs, finally displaying some humanity. This comes not a moment too soon for the viewer who would otherwise write him off, as Dave has, as a martinet with no real understanding of his wife, alternately fussing over her and sniping about housework left undone. She also cries in the next room, running the vacuum to conceal the sound of her weeping.

Given her misery, her escape in "flying dreams" makes sense: she tells us "When I was 27, I left my body for the first time. I was so naive and unprepared; I didn't know such things could happen." Once she experiences astral projection, she goes about her daily routine with a new serenity—asleep, she is finally free: "What an incredible sensation! Free to fly, free to roam the world." The scenes of her dream life are soft and buoyant, alluring without being overly specific. The limited budget of this small film no doubt restricted what could be done with special effects, but it's the right approach, far better than indulging in big budget gimmicks.

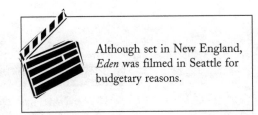

Although set in New England, *Eden* was filmed in Seattle for budgetary reasons.

Goldberg portrays the insular world of Mt. Eden with skill; the quiet, careful touches help the film immensely by reinforcing its WASP-y propriety, which by contrast makes Helen's transformation into a dreamy and mysteriously occupied mystic all the more startling for its suddenness. As a very visible member of the Mt. Eden community, a faculty wife known to all and clearly well-liked, Helen's illness is understood and generates sympathy for Bill. An unexpected discourse on metaphysics in a school assembly dismays and confuses them—the subject of Helen's rather breathless revelation is confused and unintelligible—her illness suddenly supersedes her personality, making her a cause for concern and the once-golden young couple an object of pity.

A remission infuses their lives with hope and possibility—Helen plans a school dance that is a total departure from the norm, a Las Vegas Night which enlivens the entire school and is a personal triumph for her. Unfortunately, the disease reasserts itself, leaving Helen crushed, more dependent than ever on the freedom of astral travel. Goldberg suggests that this pre-feminist culture offers Helen no escape except her illness and her "night life." Unable to share her growing knowledge, Helen withdraws further, this time at a cost to her physical well-being.

Left behind as well is the illusion of Mt. Eden as a paradise—Goldberg deftly explores the prep school as a repressive yet tolerant existence, a duality the fundamentally dishonest and saccharine *Dead Poets Society* was unable to express. Whatever romance clings to the "Mr. Chips" idea of a prep school is given a going-over here, and what remains is more realistic—teachers actually teach without jumping on desks, and while leaning heavily on discipline to make their point, they remain interesting, particularly Dave's acerbic English teacher, Mr. Bainbridge (R. Hamilton Wright). He gives Dave's short story a "D+," praising his idea while deploring his grammar; he says, not unkindly, "Before you can break the rules, young Wordsworth, you must master them." Their scenes together are particularly convincing, providing another view on the headstrong student who only responds to Helen's encouragement.

The final portion of the film is a rather harrowing view into the decline of Helen's physical state—gaunt and hollow-eyed, she spends her days sleeping and dreaming, falling away from her distraught husband and children. The grim, mysterious progress of her withdrawal precipitates outright war between Dave and Bill; a somewhat overwrought scene in Helen's hospital room that began with a serenade by Dave and his friends ends when Bill orders them back to school and Dave, now certain he will be kicked out, impulsively kisses Helen on the lips in front of her smoldering spouse. Dave angrily accuses Bill of not appreciating Helen, and Dave finally sees Bill as an anguished man on the verge of losing the woman he adores.

The transformation that follows their inevitable confrontation affects them both—Helen slips into a coma, as Bill comes to terms, at long last, with his fear and decides to free Helen just as he and his children freed a crow with a broken leg the family nursed back to health. This admission leads to his pulling the plug on Helen's life support—a most uncharacteristic act for Bill, for whom conformity is all-important. As Bill faces arrest, the spirit of Helen returns to her body, a process the viewer watches with decidedly mixed feelings. After all, we've seen her suffer in her body—but as the film ends, there she is at Mt. Eden, blissfully happy in the company of students. "I came back to my family," she says in a voice-over as the film closes.

Critical reaction to *Eden* varied widely, with most reviewers appreciative of the performances (especially Going's) and Goldberg's evocation of time and place, but many found the "New Age" focus on astral travel implausible. The *New York Post* said: "*Eden* gradually evolves from intriguing original to out-of-control nonsense. Granted, the story line deserves credit for going in new directions, but Goldberg's vision is terminally unfocused. It's as brave and unique as it is disjointed and frustrating." A reviewer for *Disability Studies Quarterly* wrote appreciatively of the film's view of the disabled, saying "*Eden* is a film where m.s. is used to help us explore mind, body, spirit, and who we are." The Sundance review (Eden was an Official Selection in the Dramatic Competition) summed up the film's quiet eloquence: "*Eden* is a very unique film, one with an ambitious conception and an admirable reach."

—*Mary Hess*

CREDITS

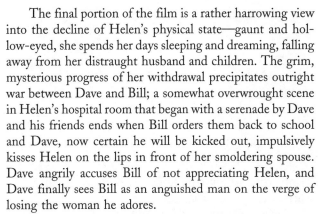

Helen Kunen: Joanna Going
Bill Kunen: Dylan Walsh
Dave Edgerton: Sean Patrick Flanery
Rick: Sean Christensen
Sonny: Edward O'Blenis Jr.
Johnny: Stephen Lennstrom

Origin: USA
Released: 1996, 1998
Production: Harvey Kahn and Chip Duncan for Water Street Pictures; released by BMG Independents
Direction: Howard Goldberg
Screenplay: Howard Goldberg
Cinematography: Hubert Taczanowski
Editing: Steve Nevius
Costumes: Elizabeth Kaye
Art direction: Philip J. Meyer
Music: Brad Fiedel
MPAA rating: R
Running Time: 106 minutes

REVIEWS

Boxoffice. March, 1998, p. 55.
Cinefantastique. April, 1998, p. 12.
Cinescape. May, 1998, p. 59.
Los Angeles Times. August 27, 1998, p. F10.
Variety. February 12, 1996, p. 83.
Village Voice. March 31, 1998, p. 68.

Elizabeth

The world would never be the same.—Movie tagline

Absolute power demands absolute loyalty. —Movie tagline

"An outstanding performance by Cate Blanchett!"—David Sheehan, *CBS-TV*

"The prize entry this fall is *Elizabeth*."—Roger Ebert, *Chicago Sun-Times*

"Magnificently imagined and visualized."—Susan Stark, *Detroit News*

"*Elizabeth* is excellent! Long live this movie!" —George Pennacchio, *KABC-TV*

"Cate Blanchett reigns supreme with one of the best performances of the year!"—Sara Edwards, *NBC Boston*

"One of the year's best!"—Mike Cidoni, *WOKB-TV*

"Cate Blanchett and Geoffrey Rush are phenomenal!"—Dr. Joy Browne, *WWOR Radio*

 Box Office: $15,472,961

This is the most extravagant and spectacular historical epic to treat 16th-century England since Fred Zinnemann's Academy Award-winning *A Man for All Seasons* (1966), which focused upon the reign of King Henry VIII, who severed all ties between England and the Pope of Rome and proclaimed himself head of the Church of England because the Pope refused to grant him permission to divorce Catherine of Aragon, who could not bear him an heir, and marry Anne Boleyn, who gave birth to Elizabeth Tudor in 1533. In 1536 Anne Boleyn was executed after having been charged with adultery and treason, and the infant Princess Elizabeth was taken to Hatfield House in Hartfordshire, where she was raised and very well educated. Henry VIII died in 1547 and was succeeded by his son, King Edward VI, who died young, whereupon Edward's half-sister, a devout Roman Catholic, became Queen Mary I in 1553. Married to King Philip II of Spain, her goal was to reunite the Church of England with Rome, but by then the Protestant Reformation had spread across England and Northern Europe, and the course of history was not easily reversed.

Queen Mary (Kathy Burke) became known as "Bloody Mary" because of severe reprisals taken against English

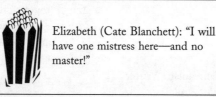

Elizabeth (Cate Blanchett): "I will have one mistress here—and no master!"

Protestants. The film dramatizes the burning at the stake of Bishop Ridley and Master Latimer to demonstrate the oppression and civil unrest caused by the Queen's religious zeal. Master Latimer (Paul Fox) is not identified in the credits, but his lines to Ridley, the Bishop of London (Rod Culbertson), from John Foxe's *Acts and Monuments* (1563), his "Book of Martyrs," are quoted to good effect. The Catholic faction at court is headed by the Duke of Norfolk (Christopher Eccleston), who advises the Queen to sign a death warrant against Princess Elizabeth (Cate Blanchett), who is imprisoned at the Tower of London, because Elizabeth seems to favor the Protestant cause, but the dying Queen Mary refuses to do so, and Elizabeth is finally permitted to return to Hatfield House. After Mary's death in 1558, the Princess assumes the throne as Queen Elizabeth I and is shrewd enough to thread her way through a thickening maze of political intrigue.

At first Elizabeth is guided more by her heart than her head, following an infatuation with the dashing Robert Dudley, Earl of Leicester (Joseph Fiennes), who oversteps his bounds and presumes to control an extraordinarily smart and headstrong woman, then self-destructs by secretly marrying another. Meanwhile, Elizabeth's chief advisor, Sir William Cecil (Richard Attenborough) urges her to take a husband, either her dead half-sister's husband, King Philip II of Spain, or the French Duc d'Anjou (Vincent Cassel), who proves to be a miserable, cross-dressing reprobate, unworthy of her serious attention. Cecil's main concern is that the Queen secure the realm, which is bankrupt, lacking an army and threatened from abroad. The Pope (John Gielgud) dispatches a priest (Daniel Craig) to England to assassinate her, but the assassin is captured just in time and put on the rack. The French have sent troops into Scotland under the "warrior queen" Mary of Guise (Fanny Ardant) to pressure Elizabeth into marrying her nephew, the Duc d'Anjou. The Spanish are equally dangerous and devious, in league with the Duke of Norfolk.

Queen Elizabeth has a strong ally, however, in her Master of Spies, Sir Francis Walsingham (Geoffrey Rush, who, apart from Cate Blanchett, offers the film's most imposing presence, a brutal and ruthless politician, not to be trifled with). During a festival of barges on the Thames River, the Queen survives an assassination attempt, though one of her Beefeaters is killed protecting her. Another assassination attempt fails when one of the Queen's ladies in waiting borrows one of Elizabeth's French silk dresses—only to die because the dress is laced with poison.

Elizabeth sends Walsingham to Scotland, where he first seduces Mary of Guise, then murders her in her bed, nor is the Duke of Norfolk ultimately a match for Walsingham's deviousness.

The film follows Elizabeth's reign to the year 1573, by which time she has consolidated her rule and proclaims that she is married only to England. In preparation for this astonishing transformation, the Queen has her ladies in waiting cut her long hair, then dons white makeup before appearing at Court to make this proclamation, as the camera zooms in to a close-up of her most royal personage and the film ends, not only with a freeze-frame, but with a freeze frieze. She is now every inch a Queen, but also an icon, as the "Virgin Queen" becomes an English symbolic equivalent of the Blessed Virgin Mary. As David Rooney noted in *Variety,* by approximating the iconography of the Virgin Mary, Elizabeth creates "a persona for herself as a holy deity to be adored by her people."

Some reviewers seemed oddly intent upon trivializing this film. *The Baltimore Sun,* for example, dismissed it as "Masterpiece Theatre Lite," which was an insult to television's *Masterpiece Theatre* as well as to Indian director Shekhar Kapur's lavish treatment of this historical spectacle. In his *Rolling Stone* review Peter Travers noted that the film is, at times, "annoyingly enamored with its own campy, post-feminist cleverness," but went on to add, "Stuffy, it's not." Jeff Giles of *Newsweek* claimed that the director could not "decide if he's making an art movie or a melodrama, an opera or a soap opera," but, clearly, the plot is linked to historical facts, despite the ornamentation of character. One might protest that the convoluted screenplay by Michael Hirst is a bit murky and difficult to follow for viewers not acquainted with the historical period and that the debauchery and villainy may seem a bit over-the-top, but the overripe treatment helps to create what *Entertainment Weekly* called "a sensual, psychologically modern costume drama."

At the very least, one doubts that the film will fail to impress the Motion Picture Academy for its art direction

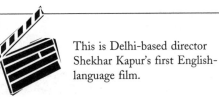

This is Delhi-based director Shekhar Kapur's first English-language film.

(John Myhre gets the credit here) and Alexandra Byrne's excellent costume design, even exceeding the costumes she provided for Kenneth Branagh's *Hamlet* in 1996. In particular, the location shots are stunning. *Elizabeth* was the first feature film to obtain permission to film inside the York Minster in the City of York, the film's setting for Queen Elizabeth's Coronation, and the largest cathedral in Northern Europe. The Nave of Durham Cathedral is used as the setting for the Royal Court, and the Chapter House at Durham doubles for the Whitehall Palace State Room where Elizabeth addresses Parliament. Haddon Hall in Derbyshire, a well preserved Tudor estate, doubles for Hatfield House, where Elizabeth grew up.

The film's outstanding performances by Cate Blanchett, Geoffrey Rush, and Sir Richard Attenborough should also fare well in the acting categories. Joseph Fiennes cuts a dashing figure as Dudley, but his motivation is oddly unexpected and unexplained. *Variety* described Kapur's direction of the

AWARDS AND NOMINATIONS

Academy Awards 1998: Makeup
Broadcast Film Critics Assocation 1998: Actress (Cate Blanchett)
Golden Globes 1999: Drama Actress (Cate Blanchett)
National Board of Review 1998: Director (Shekhar Kapur)
Academy Awards 1998 Nominations: Picture; Actress (Cate Blanchett); Art Direction; Cinematography; Original Dramatic Score; Costume

CREDITS

Elizabeth: Cate Blanchett
Sir Francis Walsingham: Geoffrey Rush
Duke of Norfolk: Christopher Eccleston
Robert Dudley: Joseph Fiennes
Sir William Cecil: Richard Attenborough
Mary of Guise: Fanny Ardant
Queen Mary Tudor: Kathy Burke
Monsieur de Foix: Eric Cantona
Alvaro de la Quadra: James Frain
Duc d'Anjou: Vincent Cassel
John Ballard: Daniel Craig
The Pope: John Gielgud

Origin: Great Britain
Released: 1998
Production: Alison Owen, Eric Fellner, and Tim Bevan for Working Title and Channel Four Films; released by Gramercy Pictures
Direction: Shekhar Kapur
Screenplay: Michael Hirst
Cinematography: Remi Adefarasin
Editing: Jill Bilcock
Music: David Hirschfelder
Production design: John Myhre
Art direction: Lucy Richardson
Sound: David Stephenson
MPAA rating: R
Running Time: 124 minutes

actors as "impeccable" and considered Remi Adefarasin's camerawork "a superb achievement," sure to be considered by the Academy nominations.

A surprising number of reviewers followed the cue planted in the Gramercy Pictures pressbook and compared *Elizabeth* to Francis Ford Coppola's *The Godfather* (1972), a facile and specious comparison that would seem to turn the Virgin Queen into a sort of Renaissance criminal. A far better comparison would be Roberto Rossellini's *The Rise to Power of Louis XIV* (1966), since the film is primarily concerned with Elizabeth's coming to maturity intellectually and consolidating her power politically with the able but devious assistance of Sir Francis Walsingham, for that is the main plot of the film. The quality of the film cannot be denied. The challenge will be to build an audience among people not ordinarily interested in historic events or personages, which might justify the *Godfather* comparisons. Nonetheless, the film tells a story that should be compelling in its own right that carries a strong feminist message, when the Queen declares at the end, "I am no man's Elizabeth," putting Dudley in his place.

The film most certainly has contemporary relevance. It disappoints only in its failure to fully evoke the masterful language and rhetoric of Renaissance England. The closest it comes is in quoting Master Latimer as he is consumed by Catholic fires: "Be of good comfort, Master Ridley, and play the man. We shall this day light such a candle, by God's grace, in England, as I trust shall never be put out." That candle still burns brightly to illuminate the times in this remarkable picture.

—*James M. Welsh*

REVIEWS

Baltimore Sun. November 20, 1998, p. E2.
Boxoffice. August, 1998, p. 16.
Detroit News. November 20, 1998.
Entertainment Weekly. November 13, 1998, p. 53.
New York Times. November 6, 1998, p. B16.
New Yorker. November 16, 1998, p. 114.
Newsweek. November 23, 1998, p. 87.
People. November 16, 1998, p. 34.
Rolling Stone. November 26, 1998, p. 132.
Sight and Sound. November, 1998, p. 47.
USA Today. November 6, 1998, p. E10.
Variety. September 14, 1998, p. 33.
Village Voice. November 10, 1998, p. 115.
Washington Post. November 20, 1998, p. F5.
Washington Post Weekend. November 20, 1998, p. 50.
Washington Times Metropolitan Times. November 20, 1998, p. C16.

Enemy of the State

In God we trust. All others we monitor.—Movie tagline

"A world-class thriller."—Joel Siegel, *Good Morning America*

"Starts with a bang and ends with a boom."—Jeff Strickler, *Minneapolis Star Tribune*

"An action-packed roller-coster ride."—Neil Rosen, *NY1 News*

"Rousing fun . . . A dynamite thriller."—Peter Travers, *Rolling Stone*

"Two thumbs up!"—*Siskel & Ebert*

"The best action film of the year."—Pat Collins, *WWOR-TV*

Box Office: $93,027,903

At first glance, director Tony Scott's espionage thriller *Enemy of the State* seems to be a victim of an ill-timed release date. Autumn is the time for more thoughtful, introspective films; those of a highbrow nature crafted by studios for the sole purpose of nailing down as many Oscar nominations as possible. *Enemy of the State* is purebred action/adventure, chockfull of gadgets, special effects, explosions, and chase scenes. But the British-born Scott has a reputation for delivering brains with his brawn. Like another famous English director, Alfred Hitchcock, many of Scott's films feature a single male protagonist, often left alone to battle forces he has little or no knowledge of. Some might say his new film is merely a modern update of *North By Northwest* (1959); the tale of a white-collar businessman who becomes the target of secret government operatives, who also frame him for murder. These two films have this in common: harrowing, nail-biting action, injected with healthy doses of tongue-in-cheek humor.

Enemy of the State is a picture Scott has been working towards for some time. *Top Gun* (1986), *Beverly Hills Cop2*

Will Smith runs for his life in the action-packed *Enemy of the State*.

provides Dean with an incriminating video tape that collectively raises the hair on the back of a lot of necks and Dean soon becomes an instant target of retribution.

While Dean is contemplating his upcoming confrontation with the underworld, a ruthless, self-serving National Security Agency official named Thomas Reynolds (Jon Voight, rapidly becoming the most sought-after bad guy in the business) and a band of dedicated, carefully-coifed, eerily efficient minions murder a resolute congressman (Jason Robards in an uncredited role), who refuses to back a bill that would give the NSA even more unchecked power to invade citizens' privacy. There's just one small problem: Reynolds and his henchmen have been inadvertently caught in the act on digital tape. With blinding efficiency and an arsenal of high-tech weaponry at their disposal, Reynolds's dogged forces set out to retrieve the incriminating software.

While buying some intimate apparel for his wife, Dean unwittingly comes into possession of the evidence and soon becomes the focal point of Reynolds's wrath. Because of his less-than-cordial relationship with the mob, Dean believes it is they who have quickly turned his life upside down. Various carefully orchestrated set-ups result in Dean losing his job, his credit, the trust of his wife, and his own teetering grasp on reality. On the lam and near his wit's end, Dean

(1987), *The Last Boy Scout* (1991), *True Romance* (1993), and *Crimson Tide* (1995), are all heavy on fireworks and testosterone but never seemed to have lost touch with the human side of storytelling. Starting with *True Romance*, Scott decided to put more emphasis on the heart of the actual plot. The script, written by Quentin Tarantino, was easily the most complex and well-rounded he'd interpreted and certainly gave the director a certain level of validity and dignity that reached beyond the male-based, action/adventure crowd. *Crimson Tide*, with all of its similarities with *The Hunt for Red October* (1990) (and precise script doctoring courtesy of Tarantino), was the first of his projects to use two top-shelf actors (Denzel Washington and Gene Hackman) and marked Scott's first collaboration with producers Don Simpson and Jerry Bruckheimer. Love 'em or hate 'em, the Simpson/Bruckheimer team have upped the ante within the action/adventure genre. Despite Simpson's passing two years ago, Bruckheimer (surely out of respect) still includes his late partners' name in the now familiar, lightning-to-Earth logo.

As the film opens, we see Robert Dean (Will Smith), a Washington, DC attorney who seems to have it all: a Sutton Street townhouse in Georgetown, a beautiful loving wife (Regina King), a precocious son, and a lucrative, promising career as a labor-law specialist. He's currently involved in a case that will send a greasy, corrupt labor leader with mob ties (an uncredited Tom Sizemore) back to jail. Dean is aided in his quest by Rachel Banks (a resurfaced Lisa Bonet), a former college girlfriend who has a "deepthroat" type connection in the intelligence community. Rachel

Brill (Gene Hackman): "Wanna take a poke at me?" Dean (Will Smith): "I don't hit senior citizens."

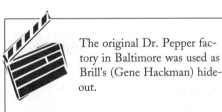

The original Dr. Pepper factory in Baltimore was used as Brill's (Gene Hackman) hideout.

eventually makes contact with Brill (Hackman), a paranoid and jaded former NSA employee who lives alone in an abandoned, nondescript Baltimore warehouse. Much like Smith and Tommy Lee Jones in *Men In Black* (1997), Smith and Hackman quickly form a love/hate, greenhorn/grizzled vet, mismatched-buddy camaraderie that makes for a worthy adversary and allows them to stay (barely) one step ahead of Reynolds. Brill is a Cold War-era geek, with horn-rimmed glasses and receding hairline (Scott even cleverly inserts a still photo of Hackman from the similar 1974 effort, *The Conservation*) who goes toe to toe with a band of technologically advanced, body-pierced punks half his age and truly messes with their minds. Smith was blessed to have had the chance to work alongside Hackman, easily one of the most stalwart and dependable character actors in film history. Whoever shares the screen with Hackman looks better merely by showing up.

Having already snared the lead roles in two of the top ten all-time grossing films ever (*Men In Black, Independence Day* [1995]), the boy or rather man-next-door Smith has an everyman quality that eclipses the threadworn, manufactured allure of Schwarzenegger, Stallone, Willis and a handful of other rapidly-aging monosyllabic action heroes. With his

Clark Gable ears and a baby face that seems to have been frozen in time at age 18, Smith has staying power to burn and a universal appeal that extends far beyond age, race, gender or genre preference. The invariable success of *Enemy* will almost assuredly establish the former rap singer/sitcom star as the most bankable boxoffice draw in the world. With this role, Smith has also established himself as a formidable leading man, taking on the air of a streetwise Cary Grant, able to poke fun at himself without losing a drop of dignity, who can, if needed, still play the young whippersnapper. Talk about versatility. He will be the premier action (and most likely romantic) star of the upcoming millennium.

The script (written by David Marconi, an established espionage novelist) is as intricate as anything ever written by Tom Clancy or John Grisham and is the key ingredient that grabs the audience and pulls them into the action from the start of the first reel. But where Clancy's work is generally loaded down with technical jargon, indecipherable to the common man and Grishman basically recycles the same lightweight legal mumbo-jumbo over and over, Marconi uses these points sparingly—having them compliment Dean's story rather than the other way around.

Scott himself takes advantage of the burgeoning technology at his disposal and delivers the story at breakneck speed. Which is good. If he gave the audience too much time in-between scenes to think about it, they might start poking holes at the many implausible situations regarding Dean's seemingly impeccable timing and immeasurable stamina.

Flawlessly executed, meticulously choreographed chase scenes, coupled with lightning-quick, MTV-style editing, help create the cinematic equivalent of a virtual reality rollercoaster that has no brakes.

It all has to come to a close at some point and, like so many endeavors of this ilk, the ending hasn't got a fighting chance to live-up to its heady build-up. Sizemore and his mob cohorts, silent and unseen since the first half of the first act, suddenly reappear and are confronted by Reynolds and his minions with Dean and Brill caught in the middle. Scott lifts the finale right from his own *True Romance* (which, ironically, also featured Sizemore). A three-way, triangular crossfire, staged indoors, reeks of intellectual pilfering (is it possible for Scott to be sued for stealing from his own film?) Just like the Christian Slater character in *True Romance*, Dean (who has suddenly lost all his energy and bravado) takes himself out of harms way while the bloodletting hits warp speed. Scott's pitifully unoriginal, B-movie conclusion rains on the inferno-level heat, dampening it to mere cinders. But for fans of the getting-there-is-half-the-fun mind-set, the preceding two hours and its addictive adrenaline rush provide the right combination for cinematic fun.

—*J. M. Clark*

CREDITS

Robert Clayton Dean: Will Smith
Brill: Gene Hackman
Reynolds: Jon Voight
Rachel Banks: Lisa Bonet
Carla Dean: Regina King
Congressman Albert: Stuart Wilson
Pintero: Tom Sizemore
Hicks: Loren Dean

Origin: USA
Released: 1998
Production: Jerry Bruckheimer; released by Touchstone Pictures
Direction: Tony Scott
Screenplay: David Marconi
Cinematography: Dan Mindel
Editing: Chris Lebenzon
Music: Trevor Rabin, Harry Gregson-Williams
Production design: Benjamin Fernandez
Art direction: James J. Murkami, Jennifer A. Davis
Set decoration: Peter J. Kelly
Costumes: Narlene Stewart
Sound: Bill Kaplan
Mechanical effects coordination: Mike Meinardus
Surveillance adviser: Martin Kaiser, Steve Uhrig
MPAA rating: R
Running Time: 127 minutes

REVIEWS

Detroit News. November 20, 1998.
Entertainment Weekly. November 27, 1998, p. 51.
Los Angeles Times. November 20, 1998, p. F2.
New York Times. November 20, 1998, p. E1.
People. November 30, 1998, p. 33.
Sight and Sound. January, 1999, p. 45.

Ever After: A Cinderella Story

Desire. Duty. Escape.—Movie tagline

"Magical . . . Enchanting . . . Drew Barrymore steals your heart."—Mike Cidoni, *ABC-TV*

"A great movie. The summer fantasy fun flick."—Patty Spittles, *CBS-TV*

"*Ever After* is something very special indeed."
—Jeffrey Lyons *NBC-TV*

"Enchanting. Moving. It's a must."—Thelma Adams, *New York Post*

"One of the unexpected delights of the summer."—Leah Rozen, *People*

"Drew Barrymore is enchanting. Anjelica Huston is wonderful."—Duane Byrgo, *Rocky Mountain News*

"Funny and touching."—Chris Hewitt, *Saint Paul Pioneer Press*

"Two thumbs up!"—*Siskel & Ebert*

"A dazzling rendering of the Cinderella story."
—Rita Kempley, *Washington Post*

Box Office: $65,667,434

In the film's prologue, the Brothers Grimm are summoned to the home of an elderly French Grande Dame (Jeanne Moreau) who praises their folk tales but informs them that she was "terribly disturbed" by their retelling of the Little Cinder Girl's story. After the brothers admire a portrait of a young woman, the Grande Dame shows them an elaborately beaded shoe and asks if they will allow her to "set the record straight." "What is that phrase you use? Oh yes, once upon a time . . ." And thus begins *Ever After*, a charming retelling of the popular fairy tale, this time set in 16th century France.

High-spirited, eight-year-old Danielle is awaiting the return of her father, Auguste (Jeroen Krabbé), who is bringing back to his small country estate, his new wife, the Baroness Rodmilla (Anjelica Huston), and her two daughters. Tomboyish Danielle has managed to get extremely dirty before her new stepmother arrives—a fact her beloved father doesn't care about but something the elaborately gowned and coiffed Rodmilla notices with disdain. As he tucks her in for the night, Auguste presents his precocious daughter with the

book *Utopia*, Thomas More's vision of the ideal world. Before Auguste can manage to reconcile his daughter with her new family, he dies of a heart attack, leaving Danielle at the mercy of her supercilious stepmother.

Ten years later, 18-year-old Danielle (Drew Barrymore) has been reduced to the place of a servant in her own family home, where she waits on Rodmilla and her two stepsisters, the horribly spoiled Marguerite (Megan Dodds) and the ignored Jacqueline (Melanie Lynskey). Danielle, however, still has her adventurous spirit, and her beloved copy of *Utopia*.

Meanwhile, at the French court, Prince Henry (Dougray Scott) has refused an arranged marriage to the Spanish princess and fled the castle, wishing to be free of his "gilded cage." When Danielle notices a young man stealing one of the manor horses, she beans him with a handy apple, and then discovers he's royalty. Henry asks her to keep silent about his passing by and pays her for the horse. When Danielle discovers Rodmilla has sold one of their servants, separating him from his wife, she dresses as a courtier and heads for town to obtain the man's freedom.

Henry is having his own adventures. Tracked by the royal guard, he stumbles upon a band of gypsies robbing an old traveller. The man begs the Prince to retrieve a painting one of the gypsies has stolen and the Prince is forced to halt his escape and go after the thief. Upon returning the painting, Henry discovers the old man is Leonardo da Vinci (Patrick Godfrey), who has been invited to be artist-in-residence at court by the King of France—only a second-choice however, since first-choice Michelangelo was "busy underneath a ceiling."

Back in town, Henry notices the lovely Danielle demanding the return of her servant and doesn't recognize her from their earlier encounter. He agrees to the servant's release and tries to find out who Danielle is. She secretly thinks

Rodmilla (Anjelica Huston): "Nothing is final until you're dead—and then I'm sure God negotiates."

the Prince is cute but also an arrogant snob and fobs him off with the name of her long-dead mother, Nicole, before she escapes. King Francis (Timothy West) is very displeased with his wayward son and informs him that unless he can find his own bride in five days time, the King will announce Henry's engagement to the Spanish princess at the masked ball he's throwing in da Vinci's honor. His more sympathetic mother, Queen Marie (Judy Parfitt), tells her son: "Choose wisely, Henry. Divorce is only something they do in England." (The fact that the French king and queen are played by plummy-voiced English actors is a little disconcerting, however.)

Leonardo tells Henry he believes that there is one perfect match for everyone but that you can't leave everything to fate—sometimes you have to give her a little help. Danielle has another fateful meeting with Henry and is still managing to pass herself off as a courtier. She likes to scold the privileged young man and tells him "you have everything and still the world has no joy." But the Prince isn't so thick that he doesn't realize Danielle is very intriguing.

Since everyone knows about the King's edict, the Baroness is hard at work promoting Marguerite at court, hoping to marry her off to Henry. She shows Marguerite the elaborately beaded shoes and white dress intended as Danielle's dowry, thinking that Marguerite will wear them to the masque. But when Danielle catches them, Rodmilla covers and instead tells Danielle that she is coming to the ball with them and can wear her late mother's things.

The Prince has discovered Danielle, or Nicole as he believes her to be, is staying with the Baroness and comes calling. Fortunately, they aren't home and Henry is free to take Danielle to a Fransican monastery that has an elaborate library, since reading and knowledge are Danielle's passions. But on their way home, they are waylaid by the band of gypsies, who have a score to settle with the Prince. When Danielle bests the gypsy's leader, he tells her she may take anything she can carry and she manages to pick up Henry, and starts carrying him off. This amuses the gypsies so much that Danielle and Henry are feted at their camp and share their first kiss.

Rodmilla has become suspicious of Danielle's whereabouts and learns at court about a mysterious young woman that the Prince is seeing. When she hears the name Nicole, she and Marguerite realize what Danielle has been doing and vow to get even. After her night at the gypsy camp, Danielle is too tired to do her chores, gets into a furious argument with Marguerite, who has maliciously burned her copy of *Utopia*, and is beaten. Still, she manages to get out of the manor and meet Henry again, trying to tell him who she really is but Henry won't listen. When Danielle gets back home, a furious Rodmilla demands to know what happened to the now missing gown and shoes, and locks Danielle in the cellar.

The servants, who have always been on Danielle's side, manage to get a message to a sympathetic da Vinci, who frees Danielle and tells her she must dress and hurry to the ball. Because of Rodmilla's lies, Henry believes "Nicole" is already engaged and is prepared to do his royal duty. Instead, Danielle shows up at the masked ball, in her mother's dress and shoes, with the addition of a pair of gossamer angel wings, courtesy of da Vinci. (The scene may remind some

of Baz Luhrmann's masked ball in *William Shakespeare's Romeo and Juliet* where Claire Danes' Juliet also appeared in angelic disguise.)

A thrilled Henry rushes to meet her and Danielle once again tries to reveal the truth but she's too late. Rodmilla stops them and informs the Prince that Danielle is merely a servant who has perpetrated an elaborate hoax. Henry is horrified and leaves her and when a crying Danielle runs away, she loses a shoe, which is found by da Vinci. The old man goes to Henry and tries to get him to see reason but Henry doesn't believe he can trust Danielle. Still, da Vinci leaves the shoe behind for Henry.

Henry tries to go through with a wedding ceremony to the Spanish princess but the hysterical young woman refuses to stop crying because she's in love with someone else. Henry understands, calls off the wedding, and finally comes to his

> There are approximately 500 versions of the Cinderella story.

CREDITS

Danielle: Drew Barrymore
Prince Henry: Dougray Scott
Rodmilla: Anjelica Huston
Leonardo da Vinci: Patrick Godfrey
Marguerite: Megan Dodds
Jacqueline: Melanie Lynskey
King Francis: Timothy West
Queen Marie: Judy Parfitt
Gustave: Lee Ingleby
Paulette: Kate Lansbury
Louise: Matyelok Gibbs
Pierre Le Pieu: Richard O'Brien
Auguste: Jeroen Krabbé
Grande Dame: Jeanne Moreau

Origin: USA
Released: 1998
Production: Mireille Soria and Tracey Trench; released by 20th Century Fox
Direction: Andy Tennant
Screenplay: Susannah Grant, Andy Tennant, and Rick Parks; based on the legend "Cinderella."
Cinematography: Andrew Dunn
Editing: Roger Bondelli
Music: George Fenton
Production design: Michael Howells
Art direction: David Allday
Costumes: Jenny Beavan
Sound: Simon Kaye
MPAA rating: PG-13
Running Time: 122 minutes

senses and decides to go after Danielle. Only the evil Rodmilla has sold her despised stepdaughter into servitude to a loathsome neighbor, Monsieur Le Pieu (Richard O'Brien). Henry goes to rescue her but Danielle has already managed to free herself. Still, Henry begs her forgiveness, saying "I kneel before you not as a prince but a man in love," and placing the shoe on her foot.

Back at court, the new Princess confronts her wicked stepmother and stepsister Marguerite and the duo are forced to become servants in the royal laundry for their treatment of Danielle. Da Vinci presents the lovebirds with the portrait he's painted of Danielle, who tells Henry that he is "supposed to be charming." He replies: "And we, Princess, are supposed to live happily ever after." But as the Grande Dame concludes her story to the Brothers Grimm, she informs them that "while Cinderella and her prince did live happily ever after, the point, gentlemen, is that they lived."

The leading roles are well-played by Barrymore as the plucky, opinionated Danielle and Scott as the arrogant prince, who's willing to learn to follow his heart and not his

privileged upbringing. Huston is a hissable villainess who never takes her character too over-the-top, which can't be said for the role of Marguerite, which is played only at the level of spoiled brat. The addition of the genius da Vinci as the voice of reason and Henry's sensible confidante is a nice touch, while the settings, costumes, and scenery all add to the pleasingly picturesque look of the film.

—*Christine Tomassini*

REVIEWS

Chicago Tribune. July 31, 1998, p. 5.
Detroit News. July 31, 1998.
Los Angeles Times. July 31, 1998, p. F1.
New York Times. July 31, 1998, p. E12.
People. August 1, 1998, p. 31.
Sight and Sound. October, 1998, p. 43.
Variety. July 27, 1998, p. 52.
Washington Post Weekend. July 31, 1998, p. 47.

The Faculty

These students are about to discover their teachers really are from another planet.—Movie tagline
"A dazzling sci-fi thriller . . . diabolical fun!"
—*ABC-TV*
"A thrilling ride from beginning to end!"—*CNN*
"Cleverly unpredictable, hip and scary!"—*FOX-TV*
"Consistently funny and clever!"—*Los Angeles Times*
"The perfect blend of thrills, chills and non-stop entertainment!"—*Satellite News Network*

 Box Office: $18,409,135

Herrington High School has no money for the drama club's musical, no funding for new computers, no budget for field trips to New York City, and don't even think about wasting electricity by turning on the air conditioner in the faculty lounge! However, there's no problem finding cash for anything the football team wants. A town full of "football people" and a coach (Robert Patrick) seething with rage see to that. And if you thought Coach Willis was bad about biting people's heads off when his play-

ers don't obey his every command, you should see him after he is taken over by aliens!

How and why this happened is a mystery . . . and so is figuring out how to stop them from taking over other humans once they've started. They get the dowdy old drama teacher Mrs. Olson (Piper Laurie) who shows up the next day looking confident and assured. They get Principal Drake (Bebe Neuwirth) who doesn't change much after being "possessed," probably because she was such a bitch to begin with. Soon the bashful and timid literature teacher Miss Burke (Famke Janssen) is dressed to kill and making lewd propositions to her favorite student, and the science teacher, Mr. Furlong (Jon Stewart) is starting to spread the aliens infestation from the faculty to the students.

Ah, the students. We've seen their likes before. There's the rich, beautiful, and mean-spirited head cheerleader Delilah (Jordana Brewster) who dates the popular but academically-challenged football quarterback Stan (Shawn Hatosy). There's the loner Stokely (Clea DuVall) who immerses herself in science fiction, wears nothing but black and is disparaged as a lesbian by Delilah even though she's not. In fact, she has a crush on Stan. There's the very intelligent underachiever Zeke (Josh Hartnett) who has been left home alone by his parents who, if they returned, would find him selling fake IDs, colorful condoms, and homemade recreational drugs out of the trunk of his car. And there's the poor runt Casey (Elijah Wood) who has smarts and a good heart, but who is also the butt of every bully's mischief. Finally, there's the new girl in town, the sweet and pretty charmer from Atlanta, Marybeth(Laura Harris), eager to make new friends with whoever she can.

If anyone is going to discover the alien takeover, it's going to be Casey. Why? Because as Delilah tells him, "You're that geeky Stephen King kid. There's one in every school." And true to typecasting, Casey finds a seemingly dead "organism" on the football field which he promptly takes to Mr. Furlong for his science class to examine. Imagine their surprise when the inanimate object becomes quite animated after being immersed in water, adroitly swimming about, growing long tentacles, cloning itself, and coming into possession of some very sharp teeth! Casey, who also takes pictures for the school newspaper which Delilah writes for, tries to convince her to run a story about his incredible find in the school paper, but she's more interested in sex and gossip. Consequently the two find themselves snooping in the faculty lounge looking for a steamy scoop. What they end up discovering as they hide in a closet, however, is the body of a dead teacher and the takeover of Nurse Harper (Salma Hayek) by other alien faculty members.

The usual follows: Casey tells his parents what he's seen, they call the police, they all go to the school, the faculty says Casey's imagining things, his parents think he's on drugs and ground him, and the faculty begin to infect the police and parents of the town. So who can the students turn to as their own ranks begin to fall to alien possession? Themselves, of course, that's how these movies are supposed to go.

The schools are always jungles, parents and teachers are figurative if not literal aliens, and the kids have to fend for themselves. Just add some hip dialogue, some fashionable product logos, and it's a calculated attempt to create a teen cult classic. But don't forget the rock and roll! A movie like this has to have a trendy soundtrack CD to increase its marketing appeal and success. There were some obvious music choices: David Bowie's "Changes" done by Shawn Mullins and Alice Cooper's "School's Out" and "I'm 18" (covered by Soul Asylum and Creed, respectively), all have conspicuous plot references. But the best of the oldies revamped for contemporary consumption is "Another Brick In the Wall" performed by Class of '99, an alt-rock, all-star supergroup. This is the first time Pink Floyd has allowed the song to appear in any movie other than their own *The Wall*, and it does work well here, pounding out its background plaint as the Herrington High football team infects their rivals at the big Friday night game. The lyrics "Teacher, leave them kids alone!" is amusingly relevant to the story.

> Casey (Elijah Wood) to Coach Willis (Robert Patrick): "I don't think a person should run unless he's being chased."

A movie this calculated to appeal to teens is the product of one of Hollywood's hottest screenwriters, Kevin Williamson, the wordprocessor behind one of the highest grossing (in terms of money not body counts) horror films ever made, *Scream*. In *Scream*, Williamson tweaked the horror genre with a very self-referential sense of humor that made it an instant hit. "I want to attack every single genre. That is my goal in life," Williamson jokes in *The Faculty*'s press kit. And so he turns his tongue-in-cheek, in-joke style on the sci-fi genre, borrowing a little from *Alien, The Thing, Forbidden Planet,* and *The Puppet Master,* and a lot from *The Invasion of the Body Snatchers.*

However, this time, the borrowing isn't as sharply done, nor as funny, with the possible exception of a scene in which the teens discuss how aliens may have been selling us for years on alien invasion stories like *Men In Black* just so no

CREDITS

Delilah: Jordana Brewster
Stokely: Clea DuVall
Marybeth: Laura Harris
Zeke: Josh Hartnett
Stan: Shawn Hatosy
Casey: Elijah Wood
Nurse Harper: Salma Hayek
Miss Burke: Famke Janssen
Mrs. Olson: Piper Laurie
Casey's Dad: Chris McDonald
Principal Drake: Bebe Neuwirth
Coach Willis: Robert Patrick
Gabe: Usher Raymond
Mr. Furlong: Jon Stewart
Mr. Tate: Daniel Von Bargen

Origin: USA
Released: 1998
Production: Elizabeth Avellan for Los Hooligans; released by Dimension Films
Direction: Robert Rodriguez
Screenplay: Kevin Williamson
Cinematography: Enrique Chediak
Editing: Robert Rodriguez
Production design: Cary White
Art direction: Ed Vega
Set decoration: Jeanette Scott
Costumes: Michael T. Boyd
Music: Alex Steyermark
MPAA rating: R
Running Time: 102 minutes

one would believe it if it actually happened. What most viewers may not believe is the final solution for dealing with the aliens, but then when one is being hip, who has time to finesse plot points or flesh out a story? Besides, it's more fun writing a story with subversive elements such as the positive role recreational drugs play in the film. (And if you really want to think about something unbelievable, some marketing executive at Dimension Films decided to open this horror/sci-fi film on Christmas Day! GO figure!)

If the story and dialogue aren't quite up to par, they are at least given as much help as possible by Enrique Chediak, the director of photography, who truly gives the film the color-saturated look of a '50s sci-fi film. More problematic is the direction of Robert Rodriguez. Best known for his hyperkinetic action films like *El Mariachi* and *From Dusk Til Dawn,* here his usual energy and volatile visual style may work against the brooding, claustrophobic mood that would be more appropriate for the story.

Actually, about the only truly entertaining element of *The Faculty* is the actors. Interestingly enough, virtually all the adults are played by familiar actors, while all the teens—with the exception of Elijah Wood—are played by unknowns. . .at least for now. Wood, a child star with credits ranging from *Flipper* to *The Ice Storm,* is very appealing as the everygeek eventually lifted to responsibility for saving

Robert Rodriguez not only directed *The Faculty* but was also the primary camera operator and the film's editor.

the world. But it's even more entertaining watching the adult professionals have fun with their camp roles. For some, it may be frustrating seeing one of them and thinking, "Where do I know that actor from?" So for those who can't quite place those familiar faces, Salma Hayek here makes her fifth appearance in a Robert Rodriguez film, Famke Janssen was in *Deep Rising* and *Lord of Illusion,* Jon Stewart was an MTV talk show host, Bebe Neuwirth was the acid-tongued ice queen Lilith, married to Frasier on TV's *Cheers,* Piper Laurie has played everything from *Carrie*'s mom to a role in TV's *Twin Peaks,* and Robert Patrick will forever be identified as the unstoppable morphing villain in *Terminator 2.*

In the end, *The Faculty* goes on too long, has no socially redeeming values (mandatory for a teen flick?), has special effects that aren't that great, and fails to be truly innovative in the genre. But all that aside, at least it doesn't take itself all that seriously.

—Beverley Bare Buehrer

REVIEWS

Entertainment Weekly. January 8, 1999, p. 48.
New York Times. December 25, 1998, p. E5.
Variety. December 28, 1998, p. 97.

Fallen

Detective John Hobbes is searching for a criminal he's already met . . . already caught . . . and already killed.—Movie tagline

Don't trust a soul.—Movie tagline

"The most devilish suspense tale since *Seven.*"
—Bob Fenster, *Arizona Republic*

"An excellent supernatural thriller."—Kenneth Turan, *Los Angeles Times*

"Marvelous Twists. The payoff is a gem."—Jack Mathews, *Newsday*

"Intelligent and genuinely creepy."—Mick LaSalle, *San Francisco Chronicle*

"A clever thriller starring one of Hollywood's most charismatic leading men."—Jeffrey Lyons, *WNBC-TV*

"A haunting, sexy thriller that will keep you guessing."—Joy Browne, *WOR Radio*

 Box Office: $25,493,642

Movies that deal with faith (the belief in the unseen or unknown), are a double-edged sword in the hands of filmmakers. Without having a tangible barometer or gauge to make comparisons, any artistic vision or interpretation can be presented without much fear of being off the mark. The majority of films in this category use horror as its messenger, which often demeans or sensationalizes the point. Movies that stay firmly based in reality, without all the unnecessary, overblown histrionics littering up the landscape, generally hit closer to home. Keep the terrain familiar and people will make a deeper connection.

Fallen opens with a confused and manic John Hobbes (Denzel Washington) on all fours, scrambling and flailing in the snow. He starts the tale with a simple line, "I want to tell you about the time I almost died." We're about to see a story told in flashback where the protagonist makes it to the other side intact. Understandably, you might think this tiny sliver of information would remove a large chunk of the mystery surrounding the ending. But things aren't always what they appear to be.

The next scene shows Detective Hobbes at a prison anxiously awaiting a meeting with Edgar Reese (Elias Koteas), a man Hobbes doggedly pursued who was subsequently convicted of murder and is about to be executed. It is clear from their final meeting that the two men have been adversaries for a great while and actually seem to possess some respect for each other. Even as he prepares for death, Reese continues their cat-and-mouse game. While stoic and virtually emotionless, it's clear Hobbes is relishing the moment. He has caught his prey and wants to toy with it just one more time before the death knell is sounded. Suddenly Reese begins speaking in a foreign tongue, Dutch it is presumed, and does so with the intent of rattling Hobbes. He also grabs his hand then teases him with what sounds like a nonsensical riddle. As Reese walks from his cell to the gas chamber, The Rolling Stones' song "Time Is On My Side" begins playing. With his last breaths, Reese too, belts out a few lines from the same song. After being strapped into his seat, Reese makes brief contact with his executioner who releases the poison which soon kills him. Another heinous criminal gone and now little more than a fleeting story on yesterday's news. Although Reese the man is gone, director Gregory Hoblit presents part of the story from the perspective of Reese's spirit—grainy, angular, overexposed stock that will make similar appearances for the rest of the film. This non-human, intangible entity is transferred by touch and can only survive while occupying a flesh and blood host.

While the straight-arrow, beyond reproach Hobbes gets back to the day-to-day of his job, our little spirit, with its very specific agenda, begins leaping from body to body in search of a suitable soul that will allow it to begin a series of baffling, seemingly illogical murders. There are clues left behind but Hobbes and his partner Jonesy (John Goodman) are given little to actually go on. Only after Hobbes is again presented with Reese's riddle at the scene of the crime is he pointed in the right direction. The only key Hobbes has lies with Gretta Milano

John Hobbes (Denzel Washington): "Evil is eternal and knows no bounds."

(Embeth Davidtz), a theology professor who also happens to be the daughter of a slain police officer. The first few moments of their initial meeting indicate that she has little desire to help him. Soon after gently coercing her and under the strict understanding she remain anonymous, Gretta doles out a few more scraps of information. Her father was the primary suspect in a series of murders 30 years ago and rather than face the music, committed suicide.

Hobbes and Jonesy are told that the language used by Reese at the execution is Syrian Aramaic, a 2,000 year old "dead" language. They then are called on to investigate another murder. Ironically, the victim of the second killing turns out to be the perpetrator of the first. A cyclical pattern is developing. Hobbes visits the cabin where Milano's father killed himself and uncovers a floorboard where the name "Azazel" is written. Despite the fact that the crime scene is well over 30 years old, Hobbes visit seems to have been anticipated. He continues to prod Gretta who bluntly tells him to walk away from the case as does Lt. Stanton (Donald Sutherland), Hobbes's boss. Stanton remembers those decades-old events and knows Hobbes is opening a can of worms. He's also starting to lose patience and as the investigations progress, it is starting to look like the killer might be a cop. History begins repeating itself.

Hobbes finally realizes that Azazel is stalking him and (much in the same manner as Morgan Freeman in *Seven* [1995]) immerses himself in literature on anything and everything dealing with possession and the occult. For some viewers, this particular shift in the plot took a little too long to get to and gives us the impression that Hobbes might be oblivious to the obvious. Hoblit is able to overcome this brief misstep with a truly chilling follow-up scene. In the close, cramped quarters of the police station, Azazel passes through well over a dozen people in mere minutes. "Time Is On My Side" is hummed or sung and Hobbes begins receiving cryptic glances from everyone around him. Self-doubt and confusion start eating away at him and he starts showing signs of cracking. His paranoia starts moving at a full-fledged gallop and as a result, he starts looking like someone guilty of a crime. While he just dances around it initially, Stanton eventually comes right out and accuses Hobbes of the killings. Public outcry demands a suspect be named. In short order, the straight-arrow has to start bending the rules and playing a few mind games of his own. One final meeting with Gretta gives him the remainder of the information with which to proceed and he becomes a man possessed.

Although the city in *Fallen* is unnamed, most of the city scenes were shot in Philadelphia.

(Why couldn't she just give him all this information at their first meeting?) Hobbes's way of doing things; living in a world defined solely by hard, indisputable evidence has a head-on collision with theology and he must select certain traits and characteristics of both in order to confront his invisible foe. He does, but not without several immense losses on the both personal and professional front.

The third act drags a bit and screenwriter Kazan throws in an eleventh hour caveat to the transfer process of the spirit that feels too contrived. The ending also seems to cheat the viewer but the overall feel of dread hits home and leaves the viewer with a great deal to contemplate. By the time the film has reached its conclusion, we have grown weary of "Time Is On My Side," which makes way for "Sympathy For The Devil," an even more ham-handed elegy to the man downstairs. Washington turns a solid, understated perfor-

mance that harkens back to Jimmy Stewart or Cary Grant. A well-intended, everyday guy with whom we can all relate. As little screen time as they're given, Davidtz, Sutherland, Goodman and James Gandolfini as a rival cop in Hobbes' precinct go the distance with their sharp support. Accolades also need to be handed out to the virtual dozens of "Azazels," whose looks and pinpoint one-liners contribute so much to the final product.

Hoblit deserves credit here on one very crucial point that separates *Fallen* from any number of like-minded psychological/religious based thrillers. Take a close look at some of the better titles over the years: *Angel Heart, The Exorcist, The Omen, Rosemary's Baby, Seven, The Usual Suspects, The Witches Of Eastwick*. While these films are markably different, they all have an antagonist who can be seen in the flesh and are portrayed by the same performer for the length of the story. Because Azazel travels from person to person, Hobbes never knows who he is looking for; it could be anyone. Hoblit also leads us to believe that once the spirit has come and gone, the previous carrier has no memory of the "occupation." Could it be that Hoblit and writer Nicholas Kazan are trying to tell us that evil has the ability to claim, even if only temporarily, the soul of even the most unsuspecting target? It can come and go in an instant and while it's within you, it can wreak havoc. One of the more underrated writers in the business, Kazan's previous credits (*Frances, At Close Range, Reversal Of Fortune, Dream Lover* and even the children's film *Matilda*) all carry a sinister undercurrent lurking just below the surface that can rear its ugly head at any time. More dangerous is the enemy we can't see.

—*J. M. Clark*

CREDITS

John Hobbes: Denzel Washington
Jonesy: John Goodman
Lt. Stanton: Donald Sutherland
Gretta Milano: Embeth Davidtz
Edgar Reese: Elias Koteas
Lou: James Gandolfini
Art: Gabriel Casseus
Charles: Robert Joy

Origin: USA
Released: 1998
Production: Charles Roven and Dawn Steel for Atlas Entertainment and Turner Pictures; released by Warner Bros.
Direction: Gregory Hoblit
Screenplay: Nicholas Kazan
Cinematography: Newton Thomas Sigel
Editing: Lawrence Jordan
Music: Tan Dun
Production design: Terence Marsh
Art direction: William Cruse
Costumes: Colleen Atwood
Sound: Jay Meagher
Special effects coordination: Jim Fredburg
Visual effects supervision: Kent Houston
MPAA rating: R
Running Time: 124 minutes

REVIEWS

Chicago Tribune. January 16, 1998, p. 5.
Cinefantastique. February, 1998, p. 12.
Detroit News. January 16, 1998, p. 5D.
Entertainment Weekly. January 23, 1998, p. 36.
Los Angeles Times. January 16, 1998, p. F1.
New York Times. January 16, 1998, p. E10.
People. January 26, 1998, p. 21.
Rolling Stone. February 5, 1998, p. 66.
Sight and Sound. March, 1998, p. 46.
USA Today. January 16, 1998, p. 4D.
Variety. January 12, 1998, p. 74.
Village Voice. January 27, 1998, p. 68.

Fallen Angels; Duoluo Tianshi

"Funny and frenetic, hallucinatory & punkishly hip!"—John Anderson, *Newsday*

"Totally irresistible! An orgy of ecstatic style."
—Stephen Talty, *Time Out*

"Extraordinary visual pow! Wong Kar-wai's quintessential work."—J. Hoberman, *Village Voice*

Wong Kar-wai has been acknowledged by many as one of the most important directors in film today. Roger Ebert of the *Chicago Sun-Times* said this of the director, "I felt transported back to the 1960's films of Jean Godard. I was watching a film that was not afraid of its audience. Almost all films, even the best ones, are made with a certain anxiety about what the audience will think: Will it like it? Wong Kar Wai, like Godard, is oblivious to such questions and plunges into his weird, hyper style without a moment's hesitation." This is certainly an extraordinary compliment by the respected critic and illustrates the high regard that many in the film community have for the Chinese director.

Fallen Angels was made after *Chungking Express*, (1994) the film that first drew international attention to Wong, and before*Happy Together*. The bold director refuses to play it safe and watching his work, one is intermittently reminded of many different directors. There is an element of different styles that reflect an eclectic, individual approach that does not fit into one category. There are sections that remind one of Quentin Tarantino and John Woo and then, at times Martin Scorsese with some Woody Allen thrown into the mix. Ultimately, however, it all adds up to Wong Kar-wai's own unique and extraordinary vision. The one prominent aspect that emerges in this film is the director's love for cinema and his ability to incorporate all the different elements of film to create his illusion. The camera is used with such daring and dazzling agility that it becomes like a main character. Lighting becomes a tapestry of mood and emotion, the editing is crisp and at times incisive, underscoring every nuance of the action. Music adds depth and drama and dizzying boldness to the action that is unfolding. It is a complete visual and in some ways sensuous experience that entices and seduces the audience into the stylistic kaleidoscope that is Wong Kar's cinematic world.

Perhaps the one thing that is most neglected in this work is a sense of narrative and linearity. *Fallen Angels* intertwines two separate stories of love, isolation, alienation, and disillusionment. One story is set in the neon-illuminated underworld of Hong Kong and the other is centered in the claustrophobic business district. Wong Chi-Ming (Leon Lai) is a ruthless contract killer who is partners with the gorgeous Michelle Reis (who plays his agent). She hands out the assignments and he blows everyone away without the flinch of an eye. He is detached from his work and shows little emotion or compassion for his victims. The only drawback for him is that he "hates digging bullets out of his body." She cleans up afterwards for him so there is no trace, while also passionately fantasizing about him. While all of this dark and exhilarating action is taking place, there is another story unfolding in the business district.

He Zhiwu (Takeshi Kaneshiro), who stopped speaking after eating a date-expired can of pineapple, lives with his father and takes over other people's shops when they are closed for the night and intimidates customers into buying from him. When not force-feeding people ice cream, he videotapes his father's every action with voyeuristic precision. On the one hand, the action is brutal, filled with carnage and excitement. On the other side, there is silliness and humor mixed with genuine tenderness. This approach, although interesting, tends to make the piece disjointed and at times, somewhat difficult to follow. Although Wong Kar does tie the pieces together at the end, the parallel story lines tends to distract the viewer, diminishing the impact of both stories. At times, it felt that there were two separate movies going on at the same time — albeit both were entertaining. However, it seems that structure was not what Wong Kar wanted to emphasize in this multi-faceted cacophony of visuals. He chose, instead to use the medium to create an almost surrealistic world of sight and sound, colored with texture and dimension. As Kevin Thomas from the *Los Angeles*

CREDITS

Killer: Leon Lai Ming
Agent: Michelle Reis
Ho: Takashi Kaneshiro
Cherry: Charlie Young
Blondie: Karen Mok

Origin: Hong Kong
Released: 1995, 1998
Production: Wong Kar-wai for Jet Tone; released by Kino International
Direction: Wong Kar-wai
Screenplay: Wong Kar-wai
Cinematography: Christopher Doyle
Editing: William Chang, Wong Ming Lam
Music: Frankie Chan, Roel A. Garcia
Production design: William Chang
MPAA rating: Unrated
Running Time: 96 minutes

Times, so aptly put it, "an exhilarating rush of a movie—go for broke visual bravura."

There has been much criticism of films by critics that charge that the film has all style and no substance. In many cases that may very well be true, however, due to the daring and creative talents of the filmmaker, style *became* substance in the case of *Fallen Angels.* Some critics have called this the director's "quintessential work." Whether this is true or not, it does indeed capture the breathtaking immediacy that is captured onscreen by the blending of so many cinematic techniques. Wong Kar succeeded in assembling a visual montage of sight and sound that not only heightens the pleasure of the film experience but also, possibly may have created a new form. It is the bold originality of the work

that makes it so compelling to watch. It may not be for everyone but for the audience who delights in taking risks and challenging set rules, it is a definite must see.

—Jarred Cooper

REVIEWS

Hollywood Reporter. January 27, 1998, p. 20.
Los Angeles Times. May 22, 1998, p. F9.
New York Times. October 7, 1997, p. E5.
Sight and Sound. September, 1996, p. 6.
Variety. October 2, 1995, p. 43.

Fear and Loathing in Las Vegas

Take the ride.—Movie tagline

 Box Office: $10,672,165

Dr. Hunter S. Thompson was (and still is) a counter-culture writer who gained notoriety in the late sixties and early seventies for his own unique, "take no prisoners" brand of reporting that came to be known affectionately as "gonzo journalism." A socio-political writer for *Rolling Stone* magazine, among others, Thompson quickly gained cult status with his 1971 book, *Fear and Loathing in Las Vegas,* an hallucinatory verbal rant on the demise of the American Dream. In many ways, Thompson would be forever regarded as the iconoclastic symbol of the sixties intelligentsia, a man trying desperately to make sense of the cultural transformation of America from Flower Power to the Me Generation of the 1980s.

Audacious filmmaker Terry Gilliam seemed the perfect choice for this second attempt at bringing the drug-addled adventures of Thompson's alter ego, Raoul Duke and his lawyer and partner-in-excess, Dr. Gonzo, to full-tilt visual articulation. A former member of the Monty Python comedy troupe, Gilliam is the visionary director of such visual feasts as *Brazil* (1985) and *The Adventures of Baron Munchausen* (1989), films rich in set design and meticulous detail. *Fear and Loathing* presented its own set of challenges for director Gilliam. Working on a paltry budget of only

 Dr. Gonzo (Benicio Del Toro) to Raoul Duke (Johnny Depp): "Are you ready for that, checking into a Vegas hotel under a phony name with the intent to commit capital fraud on a head full of acid. I sure hope so."

$18.5 million, Gilliam was not afforded the luxury of indulging his characteristic creative perfectionism. Instead, he would find himself too close to "gonzo filmmaking" for comfort. The filmmaker later admitted during press junket interviews that in many ways, the restrictive budget took off the onus of responsibility for translating Thompson's book and "getting it right."

Chameleon actor Johnny Depp plays Raoul Duke, the somewhat demented journalist sent to Las Vegas to cover a motorcross race in the desert for *Sports Illustrated* magazine. The film's plot is minimal, more a series of vignettes as Duke and his corpulent Samoan attorney, Dr. Gonzo (a nearly unrecognizable Benicio Del Toro of *The Usual Suspects* [1996]), navigate their way through one long, acid-fueled trip.

Fear and Loathing in Las Vegas did not garner widespread critical praise. Perhaps the story is a dated one; perhaps American viewers were too far entrenched in the War Against Drugs cultural landscape of the 1990s to see past the method to the message. The film takes neither a pro- nor an anti-drug stance; it is far more concerned with documenting what Thompson saw as the demise of the American Dream and the perversion of "legitimate" excess. For Raoul Duke, the bright lights of the Las Vegas Strip were far more terrifying than any psychedelic acid trip.

If one can suspend judgment over the drug use and view the film as a social document, *Fear and Loathing* can be a humorous look at a time in America when contrasting social values and mores collided in an often cataclysmic way.

One can argue that the true message contained within Thompson's book is not merely a tale of two outlaws flying high on drug cocktails, but rather the struggle of two romantics trying to make sense of an America they no longer recognized. Gilliam concisely articulates this point during a scene in which Duke ventures into a Las Vegas hotel bar populated by true Lounge Lizards. The visual effects, created in part by Special Make-up Effects wizard Rob Bottin, are an impressive and intertextual homage to George Lucas's *Star Wars* (1977).

If the vivid recreation of a microcosm of the American social milieu of *Fear and Loathing in Las Vegas* is shocking, it is nothing compared to the physical transformation of Johnny Depp, arguably the finest actor of his generation. Shaving his head down the middle to

Initial director/writer Alex Cox and his co-writer Tod Davies were given screen credit by the Writers Guild of America even though they dropped out of the project in 1996.

emulate Hunter S. Thompson's balding pate, clenching a cigarette holder firmly between his teeth so as to render most of the dialogue incomprehensible and donning tinted aviator glasses and an array of safari hats, Depp so nailed down the journalist's twitches and quirks that many critics viewed his performance as merely a superficial impersonation. It was a risky venture on Depp's part, to be sure, but no more than his hilarious turn as the schlock filmmaker in Tim Burton's *Ed Wood* (1994). One can even argue that Depp's performance is even more impressive given the fact that the film's voiceover narration is done by another actor (Donald Morrow). In much the same way as Harpo of the famed Marx Brothers communicated a staggering array of emotions without uttering a single word, Depp manages to convey an emotional litany that ranged from shock to bewilderment to disgust.

Actor Benicio Del Toro fared equally successfully with his boorish portrayal of the vile Dr. Gonzo, a character, to be fair, that was far more alienating and threatening than the physically benign, but intellectually aggressive Raoul Duke. Gaining some 45 pounds to obscure his sensuality, Del Toro used his physicality to convey an enraged societal anger that reaches its nadir in perhaps the film's grossest scene in which the flailing Dr. Gonzo wallows in a garbage-filled bathtub, waving a gun and threatening to do in Duke.

Thompson's book was first tackled onscreen in the ill-conceived *Where the Buffalo Roam* (1980), which starred the woefully miscast Bill Murray as the gonzo journalist. Gilliam's *Fear and Loathing in Las Vegas*, in contrast, is a wild ride down one man's warped memory lane, one paved with every pharmaceutical excess imaginable. It might be a flawed journey, but as Hunter S. Thompson once wrote: "Buy the ticket, take the ride."

—*Patricia Kowal*

CREDITS

Raoul Duke: Johnny Depp
Dr. Gonzo: Benicio Del Torro
Hitchhiker: Tobey Maguire
Highway Patrolman: Gary Busey
Lucy: Christina Ricci
North Star Waitress: Ellen Barkin
Blonde TV Reporter: Cameron Diaz
Judge: Harry Dean Stanton
Road Person: Lyle Lovett
Lacerda: Craig Bierko
Musician: Flea
Magazine Reporter: Mark Harmon
L. Ron Bumquist: Michael Jeter

Origin: USA
Released: 1998
Production: Laila Nabulsi, Patrick Cassavetti, and Stephen Nemeth for Rhino Films; released by Universal Pictures
Direction: Terry Gilliam
Screenplay: Terry Gilliam, Tony Grisoni, Tod Davies, and Alex Cox; based on the book by Hunter S. Thompson
Cinematography: Nicola Pecorini
Editing: Lesley Walker
Production design: Alex McDowell
Art direction: Chris Gorak, Steve Arnold
Costumes: Julie Weiss
Sound: Jay Meagher
Visual effects supervision: Kent Houston
Music: Ray Cooper
MPAA rating: R
Running Time: 128 minutes

REVIEWS

Chicago Sun-Times. May 22, 1998.
Chicago Tribune. May 22, 1998, p. 5.
Entertainment Weekly. May 22, 1998, p. 51.
Los Angeles Times. May 22, 1998, p. F1.
New York Times. May 22, 1998, p. E14.
New Yorker. May 25, 1998, p. 74.
Newsday. May 22, 1998.
People. June 1, 1998, p. 32.
Philadelphia Inquirer. May 22, 1998.
USA Today. May 22, 1998, p. 4E.
Variety. May 18, 1998, p. 72.
Village Voice. May 26, 1998, p. 127.
Washington Post Weekend. May 22, 1998, p. 21.

54

"Mike Myers is a phenomenal revelation in a film that is extremely accurate in capturing the bright light of Studio 54."—Dennis Cunningham, *CBS-TV*

"*54* is fun."—Graham Fuller, *Interview*

"Sexy, smart and entertaining!"—Bill Bellamy, *MTV*

"Mike Myers gives a poignant and funny performance."—Michael O'Sullivan, *Washington Post*

 Box Office: $16,757,163

There is always something better on the rainbow's other side. For some it is Oz. For others it is simply where they are not. And for the majority it is as close as the neighbor's yard, where the grass is always greener, so the saying goes. But wherever it is it is almost always illusion, visceral, living for only as long as you can steady your concentration under tightly shut eyes. Open them and it is gone.

During a special time in the late 1970s Oz became real. It sucked in the dirty juices and vibes of the era and spat them out with perfect clarity. Some actually found a sort of home there, but for most this Oz was an idealized gem shining in the distance, a never-reachable place filled with those who had made it, those who soon would, and those who were lucky enough to be touched by some strange kind of magic. That Oz was a disco. It was named Studio 54.

A place, a legend, an idea, *54* is now a film, written and directed by Mark Christopher, that tries to make sense of these various qualities by viewing the club through a number of characters. But in film it is difficult to draw philosophical conclusions without turning into something weighty and dialogue-laden, qualities the American cinema and the American audience have never been easy with. This dilemma is *54*'s downfall. Instead of substance *54* gives us casually drawn story lines and characters that are so one-dimensional that the more interesting story behind Studio 54, both real and philosophical, gets stoned by these chunks of sugar-candy.

 Steve Rubell (Mike Myers) about his profit skimming: "What the IRS don't know won't hurt them."

Shane O'Shea, adequately played by Ryan Phillippe as a likable dimwit, is frustrated by his blue collar, New Jersey life and spends his time gazing at the city across the river. He feels chained by the expectations of his Korean War veteran father, Harlan O'Shea (Skip Sudduth), a man whose happiness in life is Schlitz and frozen dinners. The elder O'Shea comes across as the blue-collar stereotype of the

Disco singing sensation Anita (Salma Hayek) lights up the dance floor in *54*.

overprotective but decent man who just can't understand the way in which the world is running and why his son would want to go to that foolish Studio 54. What his dad doesn't know about is the girl. Julie Black (Neve Campbell) is a soap actress who Shane is infatuated with and who is formerly from his town. When Shane reads that she frequents the club, the allure is too much and Shane makes the journey across the river.

Upon Shane's arrival the great and powerful Oz is presiding over his dominions. No man behind a curtain, this Oz confronts the world with all the subtlety of a Mac truck. He is the man who runs and controls the greatest party every thrown, the owner of Studio 54, Steve Rubell (Mike Myers). Rubell's aversion to labels, his predilection for Quaaludes, and his penchant for philosophical aphorisms make him a perfect disco Midas, and as a Midas he becomes another layer of fantasy added atop the one he himself created.

As that disco Midas, the man who took a former CBS studio and turned it into a Disneyland for the drug, disco, and sexually liberated crowd, Rubell is by far the most interesting character in *54*. Rubell got his start in business with a chain of steak houses opened with business partner Ian Schrager, a person who is left out of the film but represented by the character of the accountant, Viv (Sherry Stringfield). From there they got into the disco game and eventually opened their most infamous club.

Playing Rubell is Mike Meyers in his first dramatic role. Here is a performance that is completely natural—there is no acting, just Steve Rubell. This is truly a remarkable performance, possibly the best in this decade and certainly the finest supporting player this year. It's a shame that Rubell had to be written as a secondary role. Meyers should have been given more space to run. Instead, Rubell winds up as nothing more than the mischievously grinning elf who created all the madness and then stepped back to observe as the stories unfold.

The only really active part Rubell takes in the story is in choosing Shane out of the crowd, which serves as the story's springboard. Outside of Studio 54 hundreds of would be disco-goers clamor for the chance to be invited in. Club regulars like Truman Capote and Andy Warhol, and Studio 54 celebrities like Disco Sally, Dottie (Ellen Albertini Dow) in the film, an 80-year-old lawyer hip to drugs and muscular flesh, never had to go through such elitist indignities. But the majority of the people awaiting permission to enter Oz, like Shane, had to put up with the whims of Rubell. In the film Rubell spots Shane in the crowd and is taken by his cherubic looks. However, Rubell tells Shane that he doesn't like his shirt. Urged on by the cheering of the other peasants-in-waiting, Shane strips off his shirt and gains entry. "Welcome to my party," Rubell intones mystically.

Being chosen, however, often comes with a heavy price and undoubtedly it proved to be too high for many. In an interview a couple of months before Steve Rubell's death in 1989 he recalled that, "I was walking down 5th Avenue, and all of a sudden I see these faces I knew from Studio 54 coming out of a church. Lots of them. I knew them. Then I looked and I saw the bulletin board of the church and they were coming out of an AA meeting." Being chosen to enter the magic realm proved to be the beginning of Shane's undoing, as well as the beginning of a predictable story.

After that first night, Shane is hooked. He continues coming back night after night until he secures a job as a bus boy. He befriends Greg Randazzo (Breckin Meyer), another bus boy who longs to be a bartender, and Greg's wife, Anita (Salma Hayek), a young women aspiring to be the next Donna Summers. Greg and Anita invite Shane to stay with them in their New York apartment and they become an instant family.

Shane quickly grows popular with the club's clientele, especially its female half, and he begins to use and supply drugs. Meanwhile, Greg rejects Rubell's sexual advances and loses his chance at becoming a bartender, only to see Shane obtain that coveted position. Irked by this, Greg begins to embezzle money from the club by skimming money that Rubell is already skimming for himself to avoid the IRS.

While this is happening Anita struggles to get noticed as a singer and in the process grows close to Shane. This causes a strain on Greg and Anita's marriage and also his relationship with Shane. Greg accuses Shane of becoming

Cameos include Lauren Hutton, Michael York, Ron Jeremy, and Thelma Houston.

conceited and arrogant because of his celebrity with the club. This is a strange scene since Shane doesn't come across as being these things at all. This is one of the pitfalls of using characters as tools to explore something else rather than as real flesh and blood with stories of their own.

Eventually Shane meets and dates Julie. The two of them discover that they have strayed far from their blue-collar roots and they determine to whip their lives back into order. In an incredibly sophomoric moment Shane throws his bong out his car window and with it, his party lifestyle. He patches up his relationship with Greg and Greg patches up his relationship with Anita. This all happens around the New Year's Eve party that Rubell is throwing, and it is at this party that Rubell's story comes to an end as well.

A rather weak subplot in the film involves Rubell's skimming operation. It's never really clear exactly what is happening or why, and the episodes involving this seem contrived and forced. In actuality there was more to the skim operation and his tax troubles than is depicted in the film. Fifty IRS agents bursting into your business is no small mat-

CREDITS

Shane O'Shea: Ryan Phillippe
Steve Rubell: Mike Myers
Anita: Salma Hayek
Julie Black: Neve Campbell
Billie Auster: Sela Ward
Greg Randazzo: Brecklin Meyer
Viv: Sherry Stringfield
Grace O'Shea: Heather Matarazzo
Harlan O'Shea: Skipp Sudduth
Disco Dottie: Ellen Albertini Dow

Origin: USA
Released: 1998
Production: Richard N. Gladstein, Dolly Hall, and Ira Deutchman for Redeemable Features, Dollface, and Film Colony; released by Miramax Films
Direction: Mark Christopher
Screenplay: Mark Christopher
Cinematography: Alexander Gruszynski
Editing: Lee Percy
Music: Marco Beltrami
Production design: Kevin Thompson
Art direction: Tamara Deverall
Costumes: Ellen Lutter
Sound: David Lee
MPAA rating: R
Running Time: 92 minutes

ter. Being thrown in jail for three years because of it is even bigger. In the film, however, it becomes a tidy way to wrap everything up.

But when the party ends, the questions begin. This is a film that needs to be pricked and probed for the complex ideas that lie beneath its simple story line. Surprise and meaning lurked in every darkened shadow of Rubell's mind as well as his club. In the film, during a scene where Rubell is being interviewed on a TV talk show, he refers to himself as a philosopher. It was obvious, even at the time, that Studio 54 was more than loud music and drugs and flimflam. In the end, however, it would be the flim-flam that would spell the club's end. Money, drugs, sex, and conceit overwhelmed Steve Rubell, made him careless, made him a target. Midas's touch of gold turned sour as well, and the concentration required to maintain one's dream can not be held steady under such circumstances.

As the IRS descends on Studio 54 during Rubell's New Year's Eve bash, Disco Dottie dies of a drug overdose. House lights flash on, illuminating the club, spotlighting the corpse. The party-goers are thrown into confusion and disarray, for around them is not a land of dreams, but a dingy and dirty old television studio, cavernous and cold. Their eyes had been opened. The dream was done.

—*Rich Silverman*

REVIEWS

Chicago Tribune. August 28, 1998, p. 5.
Entertainment Weekly. September 4, 1998, p. 49.
Hollywood Reporter. August 25, 1998, p. 21.
Los Angeles Times. August 28, 1998, p. F2.
New York Times. August 28, 1998, p. E10.
People. September 14, 1998, p. 50.
Sight and Sound. February, 1999, p. 42.
Variety. August 31, 1998, p. 94.
Washington Post Weekend. August 28, 1998, p. 41.

Firelight

Passion has no limits.—Movie tagline

"A superb and intriguing romance. Don't miss it."—Paul Wunder, *WBAI Radio*

"Sophie Marceau gives a great performance."
—Jeffrey Lyons, *WNBC-TV*

Sophie Marceau (Princess Isabelle in *Braveheart* [1995]) is enough reason to see *Firelight*; this moody drama set in the 1830s has other attractions, such as a keenly-observed sense of place and time, but its primary draw is the erotic tension that Marceau seems to convey merely by breathing. The plot is fairly obvious if you know the canon of Bronte and DuMaurier, but its elements are surefire: a beautiful and impecunious governess with a shadowy past, a tormented, handsome man with a secret, and a just-barely-living and most-inconvenient wife. Add to this a spoiled monster of a little girl and you have a potent (if familiar) brew—but wait, there's more—the early sequences in a seaside hotel strongly echo *The French Lieutenant's Woman* (1981), right down to the heroine's voluminous cape as she walks on the stormy shore. *Firelight* is the kind of film that has fascinated a largely female audience for decades—Bette Davis (*All That Heaven Allows* and,

Charles (Stephen Dillane): "This breeding business can become something of an obsession."

particularly, *The Old Maid*) and Joan Fontaine (*Rebecca* and *Jane Eyre*) captivated audiences in the Forties, and the sexual scenes in *Firelight* are of the fervent, artfully lit variety that show little but imply volcanic passion. Very "art house" in tone, *Firelight* doesn't forget to entertain its audience and it knows just what buttons to push to make them sigh with appreciation.

A young Swiss woman interviews for a position only hinted at—Elisabeth stands to be looked over and appraised as if she were a horse at auction. Mrs. Jago (Maggie McCarthy), an ample, kindly sort of matron, asks the very personal and pointed questions of a buttoned-up Elisabeth while the real purchaser/employer remains hidden. Elisabeth's anger comes to the surface when she asks to see him.

The humiliation implicit in such a situation makes you question how the sphinx-like woman got herself into this; it is revealed she desperately needs money to pay her father's debts. A bargain is struck, and tension builds as she arrives at the hotel where she will meet the mystery man. She eats alone in the dining room, furtively looking at men's faces. When she finally meets him face-to-face in her room, her chilly demeanor is counteracted by his abashed but similarly business-like attitude. The task at hand is to impregnate her—he wants a child desperately but must hire a surrogate for reasons left unexplained. They have a weekend together to accomplish this, and he instructs her not to compromise their bargain by acknowledging him outside their room. She asks if she might keep on an undergarment, signaling her distress and embarrassment, which he agrees to, and it is clear he is intrigued by her. As the camera focuses on her very expressive eyes, her pride and distress clearly visible, the fire crackles and jumps in the background. This may be not be a terribly original device, but this provides the cinematographer with a great opportunity to use the fire's glow to heighten the erotic atmosphere.

Of course, the dutiful coupling leads to passion, with the lovely Ms. Marceau demonstrating Elisabeth's surrender to desire with few words but transparent emotions. She is a terrific choice to play in a costume drama (as was proven in *Braveheart*), because she has tremendous presence and looks perfectly natural in period dress. Even drably clothed, with her hair pulled into a severe bun, she easily commands the attention of all the men in her orbit. The weekend over, the lovers part reluctantly—forever, they think. Elisabeth bears the child, and miserably turns her daughter over to Mrs. Jago.

Seven years pass, and the child Louisa (Dominique Belcourt) has become a willful hoyden no governess can tame. Charles Godwin (Stephen Dillane), her doting father, will let no one discipline the girl. His patient sister-in-law Constance (Lia Williams) hires yet another governess—who else but Elisabeth to the rescue; she's come to the end of her long and unexplained search for her child. All her longing has been expressed in a picture book of watercolors she paints "for my daughter." An aristocrat happier by far to be a sheep breeder, Charles and his family live in a huge, elegant estate in the East of England. Charles is suitably shocked by Elisabeth's appearance, and angrily insists she honor her bargain and leave. Elisabeth refuses to abandon the child, who needs attention and a firm hand. Her efforts to educate Louisa, a wild child who is notorious for defeating governesses, are patient and ingenious. She prevails, even through a stormy confrontation that Charles tries to abort but relents when Elisabeth insists on doing it her way.

When Charles sees that his daughter is actually responding well, he similarly softens towards Elisabeth. It isn't long before their relationship resumes, though now the shadow over their romance is his "Sleeping Beauty" wife, suspended in a coma since a fall from a horse many years ago. This is a nice Gothic turn on the *Jane Eyre* model—absolutely implausible, yes, but in keeping with the fervid romanticism of the story. Unlike Rochester, Charles is genuinely anguished, visiting her and speaking to her. He has even more to worry about with his spendthrift father (Joss Acklund) squandering what's left of their estate (this aspect of the story is familiar to Jane Austen fans, and it creates an atmosphere of anxiety and economic upheaval that strength-

ens the impact of the story). Another semi-comic thread of the story concerns Charles' sheep breeding—the entire movie seems to be obsessed with breeding, so much so his randy father complains that's all he seems to care for (as he leers at Elisabeth).

Firelight, according to Elisabeth, refers to the time when no rules apply and nothing that happens matters. The two revel in their renewed affair, and when one night Louisa discovers their secret, the confused little girl tries to reach her island summerhouse retreat by walking on the ice and falls in. In a stunning scene made more so by Nic Morris' striking photography, Elisabeth leaps into the ice-clogged lagoon to rescue her. Soon after, the precocious child finds her watercolor book, and confronts Elisabeth. But since Elisabeth overcomes every obstacle, even the heavy burden of "selling" her child (as she puts it), it isn't long before the little girl is embracing her fervently.

Her ferocity in protecting the child presages how she will similarly protect Charles as his world crumbles. Charles allows his comatose wife to die of exposure by leaving a window open and extinguishing the fire; he is suspected, but not prosecuted. His sister-in-law professes her love for him, which is obvious to everyone but Charles. A generous soul, she guesses the truth about Elisabeth and Charles at her sister's funeral, and in a melodramatic turn tells Elisabeth to "love him for both of us." The last scenes find Charles, Elisabeth, and Louisa leaving their home, now sold for his father's debts in a long shot that resembles a funeral procession. Elisabeth is satisfied— she, like Jane Eyre, has the man and the child she adores.

CREDITS

Elisabeth: Sophie Marceau
Charles Godwin: Stephen Dillane
John Taylor: Kevin Anderson
Lord Clare: Joss Ackland
Constance: Lia Williams
Louisa: Dominique Belcourt

Origin: USA, Great Britain
Released: 1997
Production: Brian Eastman for Wind Dancer Films and Carnival Films; released by Hollywood Pictures
Direction: William Nicholson
Screenplay: William Nicholson
Cinematography: Nic Morris
Editing: Chris Wimble
Music: Christopher Gunning
Production design: Rob Harris
Costumes: Andrea Galer
Sound: Sandy Macrae
MPAA rating: R
Running Time: 99 minutes

Everything about this scenario—virtually anonymous sex with a handsome and mysterious man who proves to be the love of a lifetime—is a staple of romance novels, and writer and first-time director William Nicholson (who wrote *Shadowlands* [1993] and the less-successful *Nell* [1994]) knows how to extract the maximum mileage from what could have been a conventional script in lesser hands. His skill comes in rendering the familiar and the obvious aspects of the plot while subtly elevating the heroine from the traditional passivity of a romantic heroine to a strong, determined woman who seeks out both her lover and child and claims them. Many critics were dismissive of this device, but Marceau makes it work.

Stephen Holden of *The New York Times* called *Firelight* "a lush, high-toned bodice-ripper" and many critics were quite scathing in their assessment of the film, with a few kind words for the actors, with the inevitable comments about sexy Sophie. Stephen Dillane (*Welcome to Sarajevo* [1997]) more than holds his own with Marceau, and many critics also singled out Joss Acklund and Lia Williams. Williams invests the role of the aptly-named Constance with a sweetness and strength of character that really transforms

a two-dimensional part, as written. Certainly logical inconsistencies plague the script (how does Elisabeth find Charles Godwin when she never knew his name? How does Mrs. Godwin exist so prettily in a vegetative state all those years?) and if you can get past these, *Firelight* will entertain with its old fashioned romantic appeal. The *San Francisco Chronicle* said: "*Firelight* is not a film of great surprises. The biggest surprise is that it's so well done."

—*Mary Hess*

REVIEWS

Boxoffice. October, 1998, p. 53.
Chicago Tribune. September 4, 1998, p. 5.
Los Angeles Times. September 4, 1998, p. F10.
New York Times. September 4, 1998, p. E17.
People. September 14, 1998, p. 48.
Sight and Sound. August, 1998, p. 39.
Variety. September 29, 1997, p. 60.
Washington Post Weekend. September 4, 1998, p. 37.

Firestorm

"Red-hot action!"—Mark S. Allen, *Good Day Sacramento*

"Howie Long scores as a hero . . . The most spectacular fire scenes since *Backdraft*."—Jeanne Wolf, *Jeanne Wolf's Hollywood*

 Box Office: $8,164,661

1998 may just go down in history as the year of the disaster movie. Forget Irwin Allen and his '70s disaster epics, we've got *Armageddon, Deep Impact, Titanic,* and with cinematographer Dean Semler's directorial debut, we've got the majesty that is *Firestorm.* What *Backdraft* did for city firefighters, *Firestorm* attempts to do for smokejumpers, a group of brave souls who parachute into forest fires when no other means is available to help contain them. This seems like a natural topic for an action movie, but rather than giving us any insight into these people's lives and work, *Firestorm* gives us a routine adventure film that clings to that genre's overused conventions including such favorites as the male

weepie-bonding scene and a damsel in distress who really knows how to kick ass.

Our story begins with the never-fail method of putting a petrified child in the middle of a horrific situation, filmed in terrifying detail. Smokejumper Jesse Graves, a wooden character woodenly played by ex-football jock Howie Long, comes rushing to the rescue of a little girl trapped in a flaming cabin. After this daring escapade we are shown a few cursory scenes of Jesse, now the chief, training a crew of rookie smokejumpers. Apparently *Firestorm* doesn't think the audience wants to know anything more about its main subject than those two opening sequences, for from there the film moves to a penitentiary where a sinister plot is about to unfold: the county uses convicts to help put out forest fires, and a volatile prisoner, Earl Shaye (William Forsythe), has arranged through his lawyer to have a fire set to use as cover for escape. Don't ask why he can escape during a fire while other convicts never have, or why he has to have one set in the middle of the dry season—just accept it.

The fire gets set and the convicts are sent in to control it. Shaye kills his guards and herds the remaining convicts and some professional firefighters into the prison van, and escapes into the woods. The trapped convicts and firefighters somehow manage to break down the grate separating them from the driver's seat . . . but there are no keys. In a moment of brilliant hilarity, a firefighter asks the convicts if any of them can hotwire a van. They all raise their hands. Ha Ha.

Meanwhile, Jesse has taken to the skies to investigate this fire, which is getting out of control. He leaps from a helicopter, and wouldn't you know it, out of this whole gigantic forest he lands squarely next to Shaye, who by now has captured an ornithologist named Jennifer, played with 1990s earthy-crunchy, organically grown zest by Suzy Amis. Jesse rescues Jennifer and they flee into the forest, but Shaye, crazier by the minute, goes after them because Jennifer knows of his plans to escape via boat.

> The film is set in Wyoming, but it was shot entirely in Vancouver, Canada.

After some explosions, fisticuffs, motorcycling, and general ass-kicking, Jennifer and Jesse make it to the safety of the river. Shaye arrives shortly after and recaptures Jennifer. Here is where Howie Long . . . Jesse's . . . football skills really come in handy. Picking up his ax, he hurls it majestically in a ridiculous, almost slo-mo shot that painfully records each precise turn of the blade until it lands, a football field's length away, smack dab in the middle of Shaye's chest.

That hardly stops him at all. His rage ignites in sync with a firestorm, a condition where all the oxygen is sucked out of the air causing a fire to rage mercilessly. In a tear-jerking sequence of events, Jesse and Jennifer are reunited, Shaye's head explodes, the firestorm ends, and all is right with the world.

This meatball of a movie has something for everyone. It's got lots of sweaty men running through a blazing forest, screaming with their lips snarled up in the classic tradition of Stallone's Rambo. It has some great effects cinematography, although the last few shots are reminiscent of the forest fire sequence in *Bambi*. It's got loud music, bullets whizzing, male camaraderie, comfortable predictability, and a sexy heroine for female relief. What it doesn't have much of, and what it sorely needs, is more information on the lives and daring of real smokejumpers. While there are a couple of smokejumping terms like "ground pounders" and "backfire" thrown in for good measure, this element is mostly missing. Who knows, with a plot that made sense, rounded characters, and a real examination of an overlooked profession, *Firestorm* could have shaped up into a buffed piece of work, just like Jennifer and her smokejumping friends.

—*Rich Silverman*

CREDITS

Jesse Graves: Howie Long
Wynt Perkins: Scott Glenn
Earl Shaye: William Forsythe
Jennifer: Suzy Amis
Monica: Christianne Hirt
Cowboy: Sebastian Spence

Origin: USA
Released: 1998
Production: Joseph Loeb III, Matthew Weisman, and Thomas M. Hammel; released by 20th Century Fox
Direction: Dean Semler
Screenplay: Chris Soth
Cinematography: Stephen F. Windon
Editing: Jack Hofstra
Music: J. Peter Robinson
Production design: Richard Paris, Linda Del Rosario
Sound: David Husby
MPAA rating: R
Running Time: 89 minutes

REVIEWS

Boxoffice. March, 1998, p. 55.
Entertainment Weekly. January 23, 1998, p. 39.
New York Times. January 9, 1998, p. E20.
Variety. January 12, 1998, p. 63.
Washington Post. January 9, 1998, p. D6.

Fireworks; Hana-Bi

Blood, bullets and redemption.—Movie tagline

"Remarkable! Astonishing! Visually rich and formally paced."—Eleanor Ringel, *Atlanta Journal-Constitution*

"Impressive and haunting!"—Jay Carr, *Boston Globe*

"*Fireworks* is in a class by itself—a cinematic fugue with harsh, funny unforgettable rhythms . . . (it) takes off like a Roman candle. There are scenes of brutal violence and of a tenderness rarely seen on the screen."—Jane Sumner, *Dallas Morning News*

"Bracing and original. Almost every moment pops out in unexpected ways."—Kenneth Turan, *Los Angeles Times*

"A masterpiece in violence! Walks the line between exquisite calm and explosive tragedy. When *Fireworks* explodes, hang on to your seat."—Melanie McFarland, *Seattle Times*

Over a decade has passed since John Woo established Hong Kong's place in the world of action film with *A Better Tomorrow* (1986). Since then, not only have western audiences eagerly welcomed male stars Jackie Chan and Chow Yun-Fat, but Michelle Yeoh earned a privileged place in western cinematic history when she appeared as the most recent Bond girl in *Tomorrow Never Dies* (1997). Despite the steady influx of cinematic offerings from Asia—ranging from arthouse films by Chinese new-wave directors Zhang Yimou and Chiang Kaige to anime serials—the work of Japanese auteur Takeshi Kitano has only now become available in the United States. As if to make up for lost time, *Sonatine* (1992) and *Fireworks* (1997) were released nearly simultaneously in April 1998. Thus, while Kitano may come belatedly to American audiences, this double bill affords a tantalizing glimpse into the development of an eclectic writer-, director-, and actor-virtuoso.

Like Woo, Kitano has been credited with the invention of a now-recognizable genre: the yakuza (Japanese gangster) film. But whereas fast chases, highly choreographed fight scenes, and appropriately frenetic camerawork characterize Hong Kong cinema, yakuza films betray the Japanese love of arthouse film. This is readily apparent in *Fireworks*, where moments of eerie silence and eye-popping violence punctuate extended static shots. In addition to the inclusion of an exquisitely atmospheric score by Joe Hisaishi, Kitano has indulged in skilled yet potentially confusing edits as scenes from the past and present play and replay, flowing seamlessly into one another. Such artistry elevates *Fireworks* well above the standard action flick, but it also provides an appropriate format for the film's thematic concerns.

As the Japanese title suggests, *Hana-Bi* focuses on the interplay of opposites. *Fireworks*, the English translation of the film's title, is usually rendered "hanabi." Kitano, however, has inserted a hyphen into the title, pointing out that the term actually comprises two elements: *hana*, "flower" and *bi*, "heat" or "fire." Both elements find literal representation throughout the film as gunfire alternates with naive-art paintings of floral animals and people. But the opposition between fire and flower recurs repeatedly in numerous variations and forms a structuring principle upon which the film builds.

Perhaps the most obvious dichotomy is manifested through the contrast between protagonists Nishi (played with drop-dead cool by Kitano), a disillusioned cop, and Horibe (Ren Osugi), his former partner. Near the film's outset, Horibe and Nishi are trapped in a bungled stakeout. Horibe suffers doubly when he is paralyzed during the shooting and then abandoned by his family. Not only does Nishi feel partly responsible for Horibe's injury, but he must simultaneously contend with his wife's leukemia. In this way, *Fireworks*, like Atom Egoyan's *The Sweet Hereafter* (1997), traces its characters' reactions to tragedy and, in particular, the concomitant need to confront questions about loss, responsible action, guilt, and blame. But whereas the significance of Egoyan's characters is ultimately located in the way that they are caught in the larger organisms of community and story, Kitano treats action and reaction as means for exploring character. Thus at first Nishi seems to embody the wanton destruction of fire, uncontrollably emptying his gun into a corpse and robbing a bank to pay off loan sharks. In contrast, Horibe finds artistic inspiration and a reason to live while staring into the window of a flower shop. But as with the film's other dichotomies, the marked contrast between these men quickly breaks down. Horibe angrily splashes red paint across one of his works of art, and Nishi reveals a playful tenderness as he ineptly sets off fireworks to entertain his wife Miyuki (played with understated charm by Kayoko Kishimoto).

The characters and actions of *Fireworks*, however, constitute more than a study in opposites. Although it is potentially limiting to view films soley through the lens of a writer's or director's personal life, *Fireworks* all but demands the consideration of some biographical material. In 1994 Kitano was involved in a near-fatal motorcycle accident. As a result, he suffered from partial paralysis (which has been used to explain his stone-faced performance) and took up painting during his recuperation. Kitano's paintings adorn the film's credits and its settings and, more importantly, are featured as Horibe's creations. This use of Kitano's works suggests that Horibe represents something of an alter ego for the director, but it also complicates the relationship between Nishi and Horibe. Viewed against the background of Kitano's recent experiences, Nishi and Horibe appear to be cinematic self-portraits of the director at different moments in his life. Likewise *Fireworks* seems to express the veritable schizophrenia that comes with looking back and forth between one's past and the present, between who one once was and what one might or might have become.

To a certain extent, *Fireworks* ultimately comes across as an artful marriage of two films belonging to two different genres, each with its own subject. At one level it *is* a cop movie or gangster film, following Nishi's actions as he beats up thugs, robs a bank, and dodges (or, more often, kills) yakuza henchmen. At the same time, Nishi's actions are motivated by his disillusionment with the world as well as the desire to do what he can for his dying wife. Thus, although the bank robbery allows him to pay off his debts (which are never explained), his obvious intent is to compensate Horibe and, above all, to finance a road trip through Japan for his wife. Nishi and Miyuki visit temples, camp in view of Mt. Fuji, drive northward to see snow, and fish quietly by a lake. In moments like these, *Fireworks* borders on predictable, sentimental, and whimsical—for instance, while reaching for his lens cap, Nishi falls onto (and thus ruins) a perfectly manicured rock garden. Although the inclusion of such scenes may disappoint long-time fans, Kitano deploys them artfully. More importantly, he plays the film's sentimentality against its violent action to produce two crucial effects.

In the first place, the bulk of the film's action emanates from Nishi. But Nishi rarely speaks, and, aside from the occasional laughter he shares with his wife, remains virtually expressionless. This renders any clear understanding of mo-

tivation and/or psychology nearly impossible. Kitano thus leaves it for his audience to ponder the relationship between tenderness and violence, between performing card tricks for one's ailing wife and poking out someone's eye with a chopstick. Do such acts represent the extreme polarities found within any individual? Can they be rooted in a single impulse or sentiment? *Fireworks* offers no answers regarding the individual psyche. Instead the film's various elements seem deliberately interwoven in order to confuse the boundaries that separate, for instance, committing a crime from doting on one's wife. Kitano seems to have included moments of whimsy and sentimentality specifically to complicate easy judgements and categories like right and wrong. The world of *Fireworks* ultimately emerges as a world of in-betweens, but it is also one made intensely lyrical by that imperfection.

In addition to its contribution to the film's philosophical musings, its sentimentality lends it emotional depth. The interaction between Nishi and his wife Miyuki—which is often wordless—can only be described as achingly precious. Despite the fact that Miyuki is dying, and that she and Nishi both know this, the knowledge makes neither of them desperate or reckless, nor does it produce any life-changing insights. Instead the couple treat everything from divvying up French pastries to touring Japan with a casual matter-of-factness. For instance, they drive a minivan and never leave Honshu, the main island. Nishi even employs a vehicle salvaged from a junkyard to conduct his bank robbery. This attitude is mirrored by the film at large, for *Fireworks* halts its flow of action to consider such things as the price of bean cakes and proper dressing for dates. Not only do such details suggest that nothing is unequivocally expendable, they also underline the fleeting and wondrous potential of everyday life. The film's ending, which may surprise some, renders these sentiments all the more poignant. For while events like first dates or final journeys often find their significance retroactively, Kitano makes it clear that the greatest meaning cannot be found outside of simple human relations. In the end, viewers looking for a slick but simple action adventure may be disappointed by *Fireworks*. The film, however, consistently exhibits the complexity and grace that earned it the Golden Lion at the 1997 Venice Film Festival.

—*Jacqui Sadashige*

CREDITS

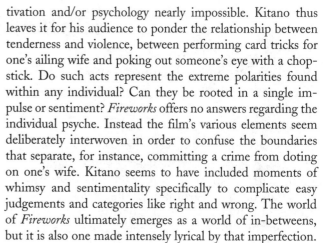

Nishi: Beat Takeshi
Miyuki: Kayoko Kishimoto
Horibe: Ren Osugi
Nakamura: Susumu Terajima
Tesuka: Tetsu Watanabe

Origin: Japan
Released: 1998
Production: Masayuki Mori, Yasushi Tsuge, and Takio Yoshida for Office Kitano; released by Milestone Films
Direction: Takeshi Kitano
Screenplay: Takeshi Kitano
Cinematography: Hideo Yamamoto
Editing: Takeshi Kitano, Yoshinori Oto
Music: Joe Hisaishi
Art direction: Norihiro Isoda
Costumes: Masami Saito
Sound: Senji Horiuchi
MPAA rating: Unrated
Running Time: 103 minutes

REVIEWS

A. Magazine. April/May, 1998.
Daily Yomiuri. January 22, 1998.
Entertainment Weekly. April 10, 1998, p. 46.
Los Angeles Times. March 20, 1998, p. F4.
New York Times. September 27, 1997, p. B12.
New Yorker. March 30, 1998, p. 124.
SPIN. April, 1998.
Variety. September 8, 1997, p. 77.
Village Voice. March 24, 1998, p. 65.
Washington Post. April 17, 1998, p. B5.

First Love, Last Rites

Set in the steamy bayou country of Louisiana, *First Love, Last Rites* lazily hangs there on the screen like the Spanish moss on the area's trees. It is the very thin story of two fairly dim lovers in their late teens who spend the summer having sex, listening to records, having odd conversations, and then starting the cycle over again with more sex. It seeps steadily but ever so casually along. The principal characters, Sissel (Natasha Gregson Wagner) and Joey (Giovanni Ribisi), live in an apartment on stilts which regularly gets to smelling so bad that they finally decide to keep a window open at all times. Joey is haunted by the constant scratching sounds of a rat inside the wall. Sissel, sexually charged and rather loopily vague and detached, comes from a broken home. Her wild-eyed, smooth-talking ne'er-do-well of a father spends much of his time endlessly backing in and out of his ex-wife's driveway while blaring Chinese opera music, which usually results in her calling the police. Sissel's hyper little brother pops in to visit his sister from time to time, often loudly pretending to shoot or blow up people. Joey, the more open and romantic of the two, feels that something wonderful and permanent is gelling with his first love. Looking toward a future together, he accepts an offer from Sissel's smooth-talking loser of a father to trap eels and make a fortune selling them to local markets. Of course, after Joey supplies the venture's money and makes the traps, the ill-conceived venture ends with empty traps and equally empty pockets. Undeterred, Sissel's father simply devises a new scheme for the two of them, this one to haul garbage from homes along the river. Gradually, Sissel begins to feel trapped by Joey's understandable feelings that their apparently serious relationship is actually headed somewhere, and it appears to be her desire to maintain her independence which gives her just enough ambition to get a job at the local sugar factory. She announces that whatever they had is over, and blows off steam by continuing her increasing decimation of the apartment's record collection by tossing them into pots of boiling water. "Promise me you'll always know I'm only yours so much as I want to be yours," she insists. "You don't own me." Soon after the large (as a result of being pregnant) rat is beaten to a bloody pulp, Sissel, also apparently pregnant, makes up with a confused but relieved Joey, and the film ends with the camera drifting away from the couple in their usual spot—on the mattress.

First Love, Last Rites is an adaptation of the Ian McEwan short story of the same name which was set in England. The film was directed and co-written by Jesse Peretz, former bassists for the group the Lemonheads and music video director. This is his feature debut. With attractive cinematography and constant talk of heat, he competently establishes a sense of place and the necessary atmosphere. The film is, however, decidedly inert stuff, and has virtually nothing to make you care about these oddballs or get you emotionally involved in their lives. We feel like we are voyeurs, but unless you are satisfyingly titillated by the film's nudity and sex, there is not enough here to keep your attention from wandering.

Much of the dialogue is simply annoying to listen to. Included in the film are stupefying dream sequences, colored either red or blue, which exhibit Joey's anxiety and confusion, and feature either Sissel, eels, the rat, or all three. The only real spark that the film has is Ribisi (*subUrbia* and *Saving Private Ryan*), who gives an admirable and believable performance as awkward, earnest Joey. Wagner, the daughter of Natalie Wood and producer Richard Gregson and step-daughter of Robert Wagner, often comes off as irritatingly odd.

First Love, Last Rites earned just over $40,000 in extremely limited release, and, while a few critics admired it, the predominant reaction was a collective yawn. There is not much to love in Peretz's first film, but it would be premature to perform the last rites over his feature film career.

—*David L. Boxerbaum*

CREDITS

Sissel: Natasha Gregson Wagner
Joey: Giovanni Ribisi
Henry: Robert John Burke
Sissel's Mom: Jeanetta Arnette

Origin: USA
Released: 1998
Production: Herbert Beigel, Scott Macaulay, and Robin O'Hara for Forensic Films and Toast Films; released by Strand Releasing
Direction: Jesse Peretz
Screenplay: Jesse Peretz and David Ryan; based on a short story by Ian McEwan
Cinematography: Tom Richmond
Editing: James Lyons
Production design: Dan Estabrook
Music: Craig Wedren
Sound: Steve Borne
MPAA rating: R
Running Time: 101 minutes

REVIEWS

Boston Globe. August 14, 1998, p. C4.
Entertainment Weekly. August 4, 1998, p. 50.
Los Angeles Times. August 7, 1998, p. F10.
National Review. September 14, 1998, p. 73.
New Republic. September 7, 1998, p. 24.
Variety. October 20, 1997, p. 72.

Follow the Bitch

It's about the guys, it's about poker, it's about *time* a woman taught them a lesson.—Movie tagline

"Illuminating . . . well worth your time."—Eric Layton, *Entertainment Today*

"Well written and entertaining."—Stuart Halperin, *Hollywood Online*

"Funny, touching, totally entertaining!"—Fred Saxon, *KUSI-TV*

"Considerable humor and passion."—Kevin Thomas, *Los Angeles Times*

"Clever comedy dexterously handled."—Dennis Harvey, *Variety*

Lately, smaller independent films have had increasing power in the marketplace, bringing raw new talent to Hollywood. *The Brothers McMullen* (1995) brought Ed Burns, and *Sling Blade* (1996) brought Billy Bob Thornton. These films were boxoffice successes that showed the public that America could produce more than blockbusters. With the incredible success of the aforementioned are some more modest critical successes which deserve mention. *Follow the Bitch* is one. It's not a perfect film; in fact much of it is very raw. But it is unquestionably a film to be appreciated by anyone who values ideas above noise.

The audience learns that the men—all in their 30's—have been playing poker together for a long time. Like a play, the "event" of this film is that one Friday night someone Cannot make it, and Andy (Dion Luther) invites a friend from work to join them. The catch is that the friend turns out to be a woman, Liz (Melissa Lechner.) Her appearance causes varying degrees of trouble to the men for varying reasons, not the least of which is that she is a tough, canny poker-player. She outmaneuvers the men while retaining her femininity, throwing the entire affair into turmoil, especially for the overbearing, nasty, and cynical Bill (Ray Porter). The evening wears on: secrets are revealed, relationships are questioned and realigned, and warm personal revelation is had by all.

Some of it—okay, most of it—is a bit trite in form. The characters spend a long night together and emerge with a greater wisdom and understanding. Not that this isn't a good film, but it's a little hard at times to think that one night of pizza and beer is going to change a cynic like Bill into a big teddy bear. It's equally as difficult to see how writer/director

Julian Stone justifies keeping one or two of the characters there during some significant crises. For example, Andy has just become engaged, but spends time on the phone from Bill's apartment at one a.m. telling his fiancee he's having second thoughts about the wedding. Why doesn't he go home and work out the problem? Answer: Because if he did, the characters could not leave at 5:00 a.m. having learned something.

Another example is Gordon's (Thomas Napier) constant deal-making (he's apparently a "Jerry Maguire"–style sports agent). Why is he doing deals at 3:00 a.m., sitting on the sofa and watching *Bewitched* in Bill's living room? Why isn't he playing poker? If his business is important enough to be receiving calls at 3:00 a.m., why is he still there? "Because we've done it for a long time" isn't a strong answer: Andy or Gordon were perfectly willing to change the poker night from Friday to Saturday.

Stone has written a film about the relationships between men and women. For it to work, it has to be like *Who's Afraid of Virginia Woolf?* (1966), where the characters pass the night for reasons that are completely justifiable within the universe of the play; where they are forced to stay in that location and confront the issues before them.

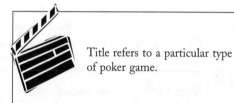

Title refers to a particular type of poker game.

CREDITS

Bill: Ray Porter
Liz: Melissa Lechner
Andy: Dion Luther
Ty: Michael Cudlitz
Blake: Matt Foyer
Gordon: Thomas Napier
Karl: David Teitelbaum

Origin: USA
Released: 1998
Production: Julian Stone and Dion Luther; released by Gurney Releasing
Direction: Julian Stone
Screenplay: Julian Stone
Cinematography: Joe Backes
Editing: Julian Stone
Music: Dane A. Davis
Costumes: Barbara Inglehart
Production design: Rachel Kamerman
MPAA rating: R
Running Time: 87 minutes

Stone has much to say about how men and women interact, about their expectations of themselves and of the opposite sex, and about how sexual attraction and competition are interwoven. The fiercely competitive Bill represents the furthest end of the spectrum and has the most to learn to become a fully actualized nineties type of guy. As played by Ray Porter, he's a mess. Porter has a tricky role; the third act turnaround is a bit hard to take, possibly because Porter has been so incredibly unlikable through the first part of the film.

Melissa Lechner is simply terrific. She plays many levels of her character, rarely appearing obvious and always, therefore, interesting. She delivers her sharp-edged zingers to the dull males around her with understated, sexy glee. The other actors are fine in rather one-note roles. Each role represents a "type:" the "good guy," the "married guy," the "dumb guy," etc. Sometimes Stone's direction and writing are a bit obvious. It is clear that his theme is that men have a great deal to learn from women, if the male competitive instinct would allow them to listen and learn. His is a fine premise, and *Follow the Bitch* is well-done, although—forgive the cliche—at times Stone gets simplistic and shows his hand.

—*Kirby Tepper*

REVIEWS

Daily Variety. April 3, 1998.
Los Angeles Times. April 3, 1998.

Four Days in September

Their goal: Freedom. Their only hope: An international incident. Their target: The American ambassador.—Movie tagline

"Alan Arkin gives a heartfelt and humanizing performance."—Jay Carr, *Boston Globe*

"Engrossing, smart and compassionate."—Michael Wilmington, *Chicago Tribune*

"A powerful and exciting thriller."—Jeff Craig, *Sixty Second Preview*

Four Days in September is a searching, compelling study of modern terrorism, revolutionary zeal, liberalism, and reactionary counter-terror. The film is based on the memoirs of a Brazilian student turned terrorist, who became part of a cohort of idealized youth seeking to bring down a ruthless dictatorship in the mid 1960s. Director Bruno Barreto brings the sensitivity of a novelist to his material, making his audience see the humanity of three very different sets of characters—all of whom are greatly flawed

AWARDS AND NOMINATIONS

Academy Awards 1997 Nominations: Foreign Language Film.

A group of Brazilian terrorists kidnap the American ambassador in the award-winning *Four Days in September.*

and caught up in a cruel history they can barely cope with, let alone change.

Leopoldo Serran's script focuses first on the young terrorists. They are young and amateurish. They don't know how to shoot guns. They don't know how to conceal their identities. They have to be taught everything by professionals—men active in previous revolutions and wars. What these young people do have is a burning idealism and a revulsion toward a government that suppresses free speech and tortures its people. The most eloquent of the young. Fernando (Pedro Cardoso)—his terrorist name is Paulo—is a bespectacled intellectual who never does learn how to shoot straight. But he is a superb writer, and it is his idea to kidnap the American ambassador, Charles Burke Elbrick (Alan Arkin). Paulo persuades his comrades that the Brazilian government can be made to release political prisoners rather than deal with the repercussions of a murdered American ambassador.

Anti-terrorist Artur (Eduardo Moskovis): "Kidnapping an ambassador is like shooting the soldier carrying the white flag."

Paulo believes in the revolution—indeed he thinks America itself is being transformed by the likes of the Black Panthers—but it is clear that he has not really thought out whether or not he is ready to kill for his convictions. His close friend has already been captured by the police during a bank robbery (the terrorists call it an expropriation of funds for the revolution) because he hesitated in shooting back at the police and was wounded and captured. The film succeeds in showing Paulo and his young comrades as both naive and cunning, enthusiastic and also scared to death of torture. They

In 1979, Brazil granted amnesty to all its revolutionaries. After his prison term, Fernando Gabreira became a member of the Brazilian Congress, representing the Green Party.

share the exhilaration of commitment to a dangerous cause and the panic of the untested. They are neither ridiculed nor idealized.

On the other side hunting down the terrorists is Henrique (Marco Ricca). He extracts information about the terrorists by torturing their captured comrades. He cannot sleep at night. He has dreams about bodies hanging upside down. His wife threatens to leave him unless he tells her about his job. He tells her. She flinches, aghast at his brutality. He tells her that he has no choice. It is his job. What is more, if these terrorists come to power, there will not only be torture but executions, many, many executions. Henrique seems to believe this, but he also knows that most of his victims are pathetic, naive, and misguided. He is destroying the pawns of the revolution, not its heads. But there is yet another side to Henrique: he loves the thrill of the hunt. He would rather capture and torture these terrorists than worry about saving the ambassador's life, and he has to be reigned in by his superior.

In the middle is the ambassador. Alan Arkin is the liberal. The script portrays him as a decent man. Arkin endows his role with great dignity and careful understatement. In less competent hands, the ambassador's role might seem somewhat preachy. Arkin calls Paulo "son" several times. They have conversations in which Paulo affirms his revolutionary faith, and Elbrick mildly but firmly suggests Paulo has little sense of how the world actually works.

Elbrick is never condescending. Indeed, he seems to have a good grasp of why these young people have turned to terrorism, although he cannot condone it. The film, however, does not endorse Elbrick any more than it endorses any of the other characters. For all his decency, Elbrick is also complicit in the terror. He makes a point in saying that his personal opinion is that the United States should not support dictatorships—that such tyrannies may in the short term seem stable, but in the long terms they only sow division among the people. Also in Elbrick's "per-

CREDITS

Charles Burke Elbrick: Alan Arkin
Fernando Gabeira/Paulo: Pedro Cardoso
Maria: Fernanda Torres
Henrique: Marco Ricca
Marcao: Luiz Fernand Gulmaraes
Renee: Claudia Arbreu
Toledo: Nelson Dantas
Jonas: Mattheus Nachtegaele
Artur: Eduardo Moskovis
Elvira Elbrick: Caroline Kava
Mowinkel: Fisher Stevens

Origin: Brazil
Released: 1997
Production: Lucy Barreto for Filmes de Equador and Pandora Cinema; released by Miramax Films
Direction: Bruno Barreto
Screenplay: Leopoldo Serran; based on the book *What's Up, Comrade?* by Fernando Gabeira
Cinematography: Felix Monti
Editing: Isabelle Rathery
Music: Stewart Copeland
Production design: Angelo Gastal
Costumes: Emilia Duncan
MPAA rating: R
Running Time: 105 minutes

REVIEWS

Boxoffice. June, 1997, p. 48.
Entertainment Weekly. February 13, 1998, p. 46.
Los Angeles Times. January 30, 1998, p. F24.
New York Times. January 25, 1998, p. 13.
New York Times. January 30, 1998, p. E8.
USA Today. February 27, 1998, p. 9D.
Village Voice. February 3, 1998, p. 49.
Washington Post. February 13, 1998, p. D7.

sonal opinion" the United States should not have become involved in Vietnam. Elbrick is sincere. But can such a man contribute to beneficial change? What good are such personal opinions?

Such questions are not posed by the film, but they naturally arise out of the film's complex presentation of historical, psychological, and political issues. *Four Days in September* seems perfectly poised between the personal and the political. It offers no solutions, but like most works of art it poses the perennial problems of humanity.

—Carl Rollyson

A Friend of the Deceased; Priatiel Pakoinika

"Powerful and engrossing! Krishtofovich's moral tale features cunning twists and witty dialogue on the contradictions facing Russia."—David Poole, *Cover Magazine*

"Elegant and tantalizing! A jewel!"—Kevin Thomas, *Los Angeles Times*

"O'Henry's penchant for deliciously ironic endings lives on, as perfectly showcased in *A Friend of the Deceased*. Resurrects old fashioned drama in new fangled hues."—Larry Worth, *New York Post*

"A quirky deadpan comedy!"—Bruce Williamson, *Playboy*

Acclaimed director Vyacheslav Krishtofovich has a propensity for showing his native country, Russia, as a country evolving. Just as his first film *Adam's Rib* (1990) revealed the crumblings of the old Russia through the eyes of four weary housewives, Krishtofovich's latest, *A Friend of the Deceased*, examines this country's transition from old school Communism to new school capitalism through the malaise of one troubled man.

Anatoli (Alexandre Lazarev) is an old-fashioned man displaced in a modern Russia. He is a highly educated English literature scholar who can't find a job to match his skills in a country rapidly growing due to its capitalist ventures. In order to make ends meet, he takes up a slew of odd jobs. If Anatoli's professional life isn't depressing enough, he soon realizes that his advertising executive wife, whose career is on an upswing, has decided to leave him for a more financially sound man.

With his career non-existent and his marriage crumbling, Anatoli goes on a drinking binge and confesses his woes to his shady friend Dima (Evgueni Pachin). Noticing that his pal has reached rock bottom, Dima mentions his "friends" who can cure Anatoli of some of his problems. He suggests to Anatoli that he should hire a hit man to kill his wife's lover. With little good going for him, the downcast Anatoli agrees with the plan. When Anatoli is told to send a photo of the doomed man, the emotionally vapid Anatoli sends his photo instead. Content with his fate, Anatoli awaits his demise at a café. But before he gets to meet the hit man, the cafe closes early, putting Anatoli out on the seamy streets where he bumps into prostitute Lena (Tatiana Krivitska), a lost soul with a heart of gold. Through Lena's kindness and sexual proclivity, Anatoli breaks out of his hopelessness. With a new outlook on life, Anatoli tries to contact the contract killer, but Dima informs him that it's too late. With only one choice left, Anatoli hires another hit man to kill the one he hired previously. When Anatoli finds the body of the first hit man, guilt overwhelms him and he obtains the man's wallet only to discover that the hit

CREDITS

Anatoli: Alexandre Lazarev
Lena: Tatiana Krivitskaia
Dima: Evgueni Pachin
Marina: Elena Korikova
Katia: Angelika Nevolina
Kostia: Constanit Kostychin
Ivan: Serrguei Romaniouk

Origin: Russia
Released: 1998
Production: Nikola Machenko and Pierre Rival for Compagnie des Films/Compagnie Est-Ouest/National Dovjenko Film Studios/Studios du Kazakhstan production; released by Columbia Tristar
Direction: Vyacheslav Krishtofovitch
Screenplay: Andrei Kourkov
Cinematography: Vilen Kolouta
Editing: Elvira Soumovskaia
Music: Vladimir Gronski
Art direction: Roman Adamovtich
Costumes: Lioudmila Serdinova
Sound: Gueorgui Stremovski
MPAA rating: R
Running Time: 105 minutes

man was a family man. Anatoli visits the newly widowed woman, Marina (Elena Korikova) who, surprisingly, seems less grief-stricken by her loss than expected. She quickly begins to flirt with Anatoli. He rebuffs her affection because of his feelings for Lena, who he finds out is going to marry a very wealthy entrepreneur.

The offbeat adventures of the film's main character has a mixture of brilliance and absurdity. Kourkov's script is witty enough to ignore such temptations to brush off Anatoli's misadventures as nonsensical and contrived. Actors, with Lazarev leading, do add passion to their performances and create finely etched characters that peek interest. Director Krishtofovitch has a firm handle on the heady materials, creating a subtle examination of human despair.

Although *A Friend of the Deceased* centers on Russia's tumultuous shift from Communism to capitalism, its cynicism is universal.

—*Michelle Banks*

REVIEWS

Boxoffice. April, 1998, p. 199.
Entertainment Weekly. May 15, 1998, p. 76.
Los Angeles Times. May 15, 1998, p. F13.
New York Times. May 1, 1998, p. E 28.
People. May 15, 1998, p. 35.
San Francisco Chronicle. May 15, 1998, p. C3.
San Francisco Examiner. May 15, 1998, p. C3.
Variety. May 26, 1997, p. 68.

Dima (Evgueni Pachin): "Friendship went out with the Soviets. Now it's just business."

Gadjo Dilo

In every soul there is a gypsy–Movie tagline

"Exotic, hypnotic and mysterious."—*Details*

"A celebration . . . Infectious!"—Graham Fuller, *Interview Magazine*

"Intoxicating . . . joyous."—Kevin Thomas, *Los Angeles Times*

"Gorgeous . . . heartwarming."—*New York Times*

"4 stars!"—John Anderson, *Newsday*

"Wonderful!"—Edward Guthmann, *San Francisco Chronicle*

Gadjo Dilo is an aimless, clumsy, intermittently fascinating but largely unwatchable look at the life of Romanian gypsies through the eyes of a young French visitor, Stephane. The film's Algerian-born writer-director Tony Gatlif has made other well-received films about the gypsies (*Les Princes,* [1983] *Latcho Drom* [1993]) from his base in Paris. This time, however, Gatlif badly misfires. He seems mesmerized with the gypsy culture but is incapable of making that culture compelling for Western viewers.

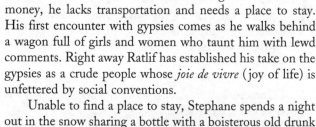

Head gypsy Izidor (Isidor Serban) lamenting after his son is sent to prison: "May I die! May I rot!"

As the film opens, Stephane (Romain Duris) has arrived in Romania fresh from Paris. Though he has a wad of money, he lacks transportation and needs a place to stay. His first encounter with gypsies comes as he walks behind a wagon full of girls and women who taunt him with lewd comments. Right away Ratlif has established his take on the gypsies as a crude people whose *joie de vivre* (joy of life) is unfettered by social conventions.

Unable to find a place to stay, Stephane spends a night out in the snow sharing a bottle with a boisterous old drunk named Izidor (Isidor Serban). Izidor's son, Adriani, has just been hauled off to prison and Izidor complains dramatically: "For us gypsies, there is no justice!" For some reason which is never explained, Izidor believes Stephane is a godsend. "A saint sent him to me," Izidor says to himself. He gets Stephane drunk and takes him to his house for the night.

In the morning, Stephane awakens to a village full of gypsies riled up about the "gadjo dilo"— the "crazy outsider." Children scream that he's huge, though he is of average size. As Stephane walks down the main street of the village, crowds gather on each side, accusing him of being "a chicken thief." They also castigate him as a slovenly "bum" because his boots are worn and torn. Gatlif's joke is that the gypsies' prejudices against the Frenchmen mirror the typical Parisian prejudices against the gypsies who live in France.

But Gatlif overplays his hand. The gypsies he depicts are so outlandishly histrionic, so ridiculously childish, and so loud and overbearing that they cross the line from being charmingly ribald to being childishly stupid and cartoonish. And their innocence defies logic. We are asked to believe that they are familiar with automobiles and modern life and frequently travel to perform music at weddings and parties, yet they gather to cheer when someone rigs up a light bulb or when Stephane concocts a primitive phonograph, as if they've never seen such wonders before.

Izidor calls Stephane "my Frenchman" and appears to adopt him as a temporary substitute for his son, but it's never at all clear why Izidor considers him such a prize. It's gradually revealed that Stephane is searching for a musician named Nora Luca, and late in the film the reason for his search is explained. Her wailing song that he carries about on a cassette tape was the favorite of his father, a wanderer among native cultures who recently died. Stephane says the song is stuck inside his head and he can't get it out. He is apparently repeating the quests of his father as a sort of amateur anthropologist. Other than that, it's hard to understand why he continues to stay with the gypsies.

For most of the film, even this cursory explanation is withheld, and Stephane appears simply to be a gypsy music groupie. Stephane's questions about Nora Luca are met with uncomprehending or misleading half-answers from Izidor. Izidor tells everyone that Stephane is staying so he can learn the Romanes language from Izidor, but in fact they barely can communicate. With subtitles, it's difficult for the English-speaking viewer to understand what's going on, and often nothing much is. Jumping from one meaningless scene to another, Gatlif tries to effect a comedy of miscommunication but instead produces simply a mess of a movie.

Amid scenes of chaotic life in the muddy gypsy village, there are a few prized vignettes. One occurs when Izidor and other villagers are invited to be the musicians at a fancy wedding. First the bride's father ritually fends off the groom's party with epithets and an axe, then he quickly succumbs to a peace offer of a beverage. The bride and groom sit on the floor as the wedding guests dance around them and throw money onto them. Gypsy women writhe on the floor. This is the real deal, Gatlif seems to be saying.

There follows a poignant scene when Izidor takes Stephane to the home of a musician friend who may know Nora Luca and finds him recently dead. Izidor pours vodka on the man's fresh grave, a musician plays an accordion and wails a funeral song, and Izidor dances by the graveside.

> *Gadjo Dilo* is considered writer/director Gatlif's continuing trilogy on gypsies, which began with *Little Princes* in 1982.

Eventually, Stephane becomes entwined with Sabina (Roma Hartner), the former wife of a Belgian man, with whom he can carry on conversations in French. Now the desultory film, which has spent nearly 90 minutes wandering aimlessly from scene to scene, suddenly becomes purposeful. Sabina leads Stephane from village to village, where Stephane records various authentic musicians, compiling a collection of notes and tapes. Gatlif rushes through this part of the film almost perfunctorily, as if he has no faith in the central purpose of Stephane's quest for real gypsy music.

The romance between Stephane and Sabina is decidedly unconventional. One funny scene has the pair of lovers lying outside, breathing heavily, and graphically describing what they want to do to each other. But they are interrupted by the return of Adriani, back from prison. A spontaneous celebration ensues. Not even the prospect of sex, it seems, can stem the gypsy's tribal urge to party. When they finally consummate their affair, Stephane and Sabina run naked through the woods, coarsely underlining Gatlif's view of gypsy life as innocent and connected with nature. Meanwhile, however, Adriani has prompted a fight in a bar which leads to a violent confrontation between local gadjos and the gypsies. Apparently Adriani is a sort of juvenile gangster, or

CREDITS

Stephane: Romain Duris
Sabina: Rona Hartner
Izidor: Isidor Serban
Sami: Ovidiu Balan
Angela: Angela Serban
Aurica: Aurica Ursan
Vasile: Vasile Serban
Joan: Joan Serban

Origin: France, Romania
Released: 1998
Production: Guy Marignane for a Princes Films and Canal+ production; released by Lions Gate
Direction: Tony Gatlif
Screenplay: Tony Gatlif
Cinematography: Eric Guichard
Editing: Monique Dartonne
Art direction: Brigitte Brassart
Music: Tony Gatlif
Costumes: Mihaela Ularu
Make-up: Jeana Mocanu
Sound: Nicolas Naegelen
MPAA rating: Unrated
Running Time: 101 minutes

perhaps merely he is a victim of the prejudices of those who think he is. No matter. Gatlif just wants to set up a painful retribution which leads to a tragic ending. The problem is that the violence comes out of nowhere, without warning. Gatlif never bothered to show the roots of the conflict or to give hints that the gypsies were in constant peril of being rooted out of their village and sent on the run.

Gadjo Dilo is an enormous muddle. Gatlif's Parisian hero, Stephane, learns the hard lessons of gypsy life by living through its meager but earnest joys and its sudden eruptions of great tragedy. But Gatlif never explains the whys and wherefores of the oppression of the gypsies, or exactly how they fit into the larger life of Romania. Neither does he set out a personal story that revolves around a discernible plot with dramatic tension and character development. And *Gadjo Dilo* also falls short of a quasi-documentary, slice-of-life film, because it doesn't pay enough attention to the everyday existence of the gypsies. For all of Gatlif's earnest attempts to show the gypsies, warts and all, he does seem to indulge in his own stereotyping. All the girls have one or more gold or silver teeth and wear scarves, and nearly everyone in the village is loud, crude, simpleminded, and often drunk.

Gatlif lurches from one perfunctory scene to the next. Relying on his boyish good looks, Duris simply grins through the movie, wearing the blank expression of an aimless young man who delights in everything he sees and follows wherever he is led. Serban is terrific but he is inhabiting a caricatured role. Only Hartner seems to strain at the bounds of her limited character, breaking through with genuine understated emotion. For the most part, though, *Gadjo Dilo* is neither illuminating nor entertaining. It seems amateurish and mightily self-indulgent, and it is carelessly put together.

—*Michael Betzold*

REVIEWS

Boxoffice. August, 1998, p. 46.
Los Angeles Times. August 14, 1998, p. F6.
New York Times. August 7, 1998, p. E12.
Sight and Sound. August 8, 1998, p. 40.

Genealogies of a Crime; Genealogies D'Un Crime

Enigmatic director Raoul Ruiz once again tackles some serious metaphysical questions about the nature of identity in the philosophical fantasy/thriller, *Genealogies of a Crime*. The cool beauty of timeless French icon Catherine Deneuve intensifies her detached demeanor as both victim and avenger in this labyrinthine narrative that is as exasperating as it is intriguing.

Solange (Catherine Deneuve) is a defense attorney known for taking on lost causes. Her claim to fame is that she has never won a court case; so it is no surprise when she agrees to represent a young psychopath named Rene (Melvil Poupaud) who has confessed to the murder of his Aunt Jeanne, a well-renowned psychologist (Ms. Deneuve in a red wig). Jeanne was Rene's legal guardian when he was orphaned at the age of five and as he matured, he also became her faithless lover.

When she first interviews her client, Solange is struck by Rene's resemblance to her own son, recently killed in a car crash. She employs the gestalt technique of reverse role-playing, encouraging the young man to take on the questioning while she answers for the murderer. Later, Solange visits Jeanne's office and finds the psychologist's journals documenting Rene's case. Nicknamed "the Monster" by his

aunt, Rene already displayed homicidal tendencies at the age of five and Jeanne, a member of a creepy psychoanalytical organization, believed it would only be a matter of time before Rene's destiny would run its predetermined course.

It is at this point in the story that Ruiz begins to manipulate time and space in a fascinating and complex way straight out of the classic *Through the Looking Glass* and thus further complicating the puzzle with an element of synchronicity. As she stares at a portrait of the deceased woman, Solange appears to lose herself in Jeanne's persona, becoming the avenging ghost of the murder victim. This narrative element is treated in the less-than-subtle way of having a poem about a man who fell in love with the ghost of a woman he killed and then is later killed by the ghost read aloud several times throughout the film.

Solange's life takes a destructive turn as she is drawn deeper into the psychoanalytical maze inhabited by the certifiably mad intellectual rivals, Georges Didier (Michel Piccoli) and Christian (Andrzej Seweryn), analysts enmeshed in a not-always-professional feud and mounting conspiracies that ultimately leads to a sweetly droll mass suicide. *Crime* is a scathing indictment of Freudian psychoanalysis, portraying the profession as a kind of powerless cult. Particularly amusing is a ceremony in which members of the Franco-Belgian Psychoanalytical Society engage in role-playing while taking turns wearing blindfolds and spying through one-way mirrors on the commission of a violent crime.

The Chilean-born, French-based avant-garde film-maker Ruiz and his co-writer Pascal Bonitzer reportedly based their story on actual events involving Hermine van Hug, a Viennese child psychologist who firmly believed that our personalities are developed by the time we are five and no external influences can alter it. She had predicted that her toddler nephew would become a murderer and indeed, he did kill her years later.

CREDITS

Jeanne/Solange: Catherine Deneuve
Georges: Michel Piccoli
Rene: Melvil Poupaud
Christian: Andrzej Seweryn
Esther: Bernadette LaFont
Louise: Monique Melinand

Origin: France
Released: 1997
Production: Paulo Branco for Canal Plus, Gemini Films, and Madragoa Filmes; released by Strand Releasing
Direction: Raul Ruiz
Screenplay: Pascal Bonitzer and Raul Ruiz
Cinematography: Stefan Ivanov
Editing: Valeria Sarmiento
Production design: Luc Chalon, Solange Zeitoun
Costumes: Elisabeth Tavernier
Music: Jorge Arriagada
MPAA rating: Unrated
Running Time: 113 minutes

Ruiz sets out to explore the philosophical arguments of fatalism versus the existential school of free will and determinism. His film asks the ultimate question: if people are destined to follow predetermined patterns demonstrated in early childhood, what should be done? Should sociopaths and psychopaths be incarcerated before they commit the heinous crimes to which that are fated?

As if this metaphysical stew were not thick enough, Ruiz further tantalizes us with the proposition that we humans may be nothing more than players in a few archetypal scenarios that form the foundation of all universal interaction, a limited number of dramas, sculpted by divine intervention yet fueled by human frailty, that comprise all human existence. (Could Ruiz also be commenting on the power of the cinema to shape our lives by further asking us to take on countless personalities as we relate to and through the characters we identify with while staring at that movie screen as we sit in the dark?)

Genealogies of a Crime can be a mindboggling meditation on the role of human existence, but only if the viewer is in the proper philosophical mind-set. On a more mundane level, however, Ruiz's film, no matter how intellectually ambitious, can be tedious, a slowly evolving thriller that is not necessarily much of a mystery.

—*Patricia Kowal*

REVIEWS

Boxoffice. June, 1997, p. 50.
Los Angeles Times. April 10, 1998, p. F14.
New York Times. March 27, 1998, p. E14.
People. April 13, 1998, p. 23.
San Francisco Examiner. August 28, 1998, p. C3.
Variety. February 24, 1997, p. 80.
Village Voice. March 31, 1998, p. 64.

The General

Irish thief Martin Cahill (Brendan Gleeson) finds he has less of a future when listening to police chief Kenney (Jon Voight) in *The General*.

 Box Office: $869,848

I n a 20-year career that ended with his murder by the Irish Republican Army in 1994, Martin Cahill (Brendan Gleeson) and his gang stole money and property with an estimated value over $60,000,000. Writer-director John Boorman's sympathetic portrait of the Irish gangster presents the essence of Cahill's character as a sense of working-class outrage at being relegated to the margins of society. Boorman shows the young Cahill (Eamonn Owens) stealing both to provide for his poor family and as an act of rebellion. A 1960s–style anti-establishment attitude runs through many of Boorman's films and is clearly on display in *The General*, which also resembles British films of the 1960s in its visual style and its mixture of violence and rough-edged sentimentality.

The film's social and political context is best demonstrated near the beginning of *The General* when Cahill is released from prison to discover everyone is being evicted from the rundown apartment complex where he grew up. After all the other tenants have left, Cahill, his wife, Frances (Maria Doyle Kennedy), their children, and his sister-in-law, Tina (Angeline Ball), stay behind even as the building is being demolished around them. When they can stay in the flat no longer, Cahill retreats to a tiny trailer on the complex's grounds. When the trailer is firebombed, he moves into a tent before finally forcing the authorities to give his family an apartment in a middle-class neighborhood.

 Cahill (Brendan Gleeson) to Inspector Kenny (Jon Voight): "You're getting to be like me: trespass, harassment, intimidation, beating people up. You've had to come down to my level."

Cahill's thumbing his nose at authority appears throughout *The General*. When Frances convinces him to buy a house, he goes to a bank to exchange $80,000 pounds in cash for a banker's draft. While he is across the street at a police station chatting with his longtime nemesis, Inspector Ned Kenny (Jon Voight), two of his gang rob the bank, taking back the cash. Followed 24-hours a day by police, he outwits them by driving deep into the countryside until he runs out of gasoline. Cahill, however, has brought along some spare fuel, unlike those trailing him. On trial for robbery, he breaks into a law library to find a legal loophole to get himself off and finds one, though it involves intimidating a witness. When his opponents spread the false rumor that the Cahill gang is dealing in illegal drugs and the neighbors of gang member Noel (Adrian Dunbar) stage a protest, Cahill arranges a counter-demonstration under the heading "Concerned Criminals Against Drugs."

Boorman's point is the stubbornness and audacity at the heart of the Irish character. The gangster revealed by Boorman, an Englishman who has lived in Ireland for 30 years, and Gleeson is also a bit of a contradiction. Kind and generous to his family and friends, Cahill is praised by Frances for being good, for not smoking, drinking, or using drugs. Because Tina can find no man to match Martin, Frances asks her husband to have an affair with her sister. Tearfully, he agrees. A Dublin version of Robin Hood, he shares his loot with his neighbors, cheerfully accepting their lies about their needs. Stealing 11 Old Masters paintings, Cahill becomes enchanted by Vermeer's "Lady Writing a Letter with Her Maid." But he is also a thug. Wrongly suspecting one of his gang, Jimmy (Eanna McLiam), of cheating the group, Cahill nails the young man's hands to a snooker table. Realizing he has made a mistake, Cahill tenderly takes his victim to an emergency room only to dump him unceremoniously. When another member, Gary (Sean McGinley), drunkenly mistakes his 14-year-old daughter for his late wife and sexually assaults her, Cahill shoots his friend in the knee as a ploy to delay prosecution.

Boorman keeps the audience on the side of Cahill, whose nickname gives the film its title, by constantly stressing his strength in the face of persecution. Attempting to sneak back onto his property, he is urinated on by a policeman, but Cahill lies there until dawn because he refuses to let others think they can get the better of him. Similarly, when another officer's ferret is sent to kill Cahill's beloved racing pigeons, he forces his teenaged son to stop crying and laugh so that the police can have no satisfaction. Cahill is assassinated by the IRA when he has difficulty getting rid of the Old Masters and sells one to a Protestant militia group. Hearing of his death, the police celebrate exuberantly and congratulate Kenny, who feels distaste rather than happiness. Boorman's Cahill is not simply a master criminal. He is the ultimate outsider at war with a society that holds him in complete disdain.

Boorman is one of those directors highly regarded by cineastes and other film directors despite a uneven record of accomplishment. He has had only two commercial hits: *Deliverance* (1972) and *Excalibur* (1981). Films such as *Hell In the Pacific* (1968), *Leo the Last* (1970), *The Emerald Forest* (1985), *Where the Heart Is* (1990), and *Beyond Rangoon* (1997) are most notable for their heavy-handed approach to social criticism. Films like *Zardoz* (1974) and *Exorcist II: The Heretic* (1977), despite some visual flourishes, are unrelentingly silly.

Boorman's considerable reputation rests primarily on five films. *Having a Wild Weekend* (1965) attempts to do with the Dave Clark Five what Richard Lester's *A Hard Day's Night* (1964) did for the Beatles and succeeds with surprising style. *Point Blank* (1967), easily the director's greatest film, combines film noir conventions with the cinematic existentialism borrowed from the French New Wave and pushes them to delirious heights. Boorman shows uncharacteristic restraint with the overrated *Deliverance*, from James Dickey's equally overrated survivalist novel, when the film needs some stylistic excess to enliven it. *Excalibur* is his most technically accomplished film with an excellent balance between reverence for the Arthurian legend and playful exaggeration. *Hope and Glory* (1987), an autobiographical look at growing up in World War II London, is unique for a child's-eye look at war that emphasizes joy instead of the conventional senses of deprivation and loss.

These five films convey the exhilaration of filmmaking. This love of cinema is also evident in *The General* to a degree, but despite the overwhelming critical praise the film has received, including Boorman's being named best director at the 1998 Cannes Film Festival and the year's best director by the Boston Film Critics, it is slightly disappointing. Boorman, who also wrote the screenplay, sets up an adversarial relationship between Cahill and Kenny only to have the inspector, the film's moral conscience, disappear for much of the film. The robberies themselves are staged rather indifferently with the director passing up opportunities to entertain his audience and cultivate the legend of his hero's daring. More importantly, the viewer cannot always be certain why Cahill acts as he does or what the filmmaker's point is. Too many events are depicted simply because they actually happened.

Gleeson's much heralded performance is quite good. The range of conflicting emotions he effortlessly displays when Cahill is about to shoot Gary is a highlight of the film. As a lovingly father, Cahill wants to kill Gary but cannot bring himself to do this to his friend. In a few seconds, Gleeson's Cahill moves from pride in coming up with a temporary solution to an unpleasant situation, to indecision about what exactly to do, to almost committing murder, to arriving at a compromise. Leaving Gary bleeding, Gleeson reveals Cahill's satisfaction at finding a way to remain true to his code of conduct and mete out punishment at the same time. Gleeson, best known as Hamish, Mel Gibson's sidekick in *Braveheart* (1995), makes Cahill someone alert to both his mythic proportions and his commonality. Gleeson is prevented, however, from giving the full performance he is capable of by having to hold his hand over his face for much of the film simply because the real Cahill did so when appearing in public. The mannerism is soon quite tiresome.

The final significant aspect of *The General* is Boorman's decision to film it in black and white. The lack of color is appropriate to the life of a character surrounded by a moral grayness. Cinematographer Seamus Deasy shot the film with color stock and printed it as black and white to prevent the usual loss of grayish texture. Boorman may have also intended an homage to an earlier *The General* (1927), Buster Keaton's masterpiece which blends slapstick and violence in telling an outsider's story. Boorman is also clearly making an homage to the black-and-white angry-young-men British films of the early 1960s: Karel Reisz's *Saturday*

Among the burglary victims of the real Martin Cahill was director John Boorman. The items stolen included the gold record Boorman received for "Dueling Banjos" from *Deliverance*.

Night and Sunday Morning (1960), Lindsay Anderson's *This Sporting Life* (1963), and Tony Richardson's *A Taste of Honey* (1961) and *The Loneliness of the Long-Distance Runner* (1962), especially the latter. Black and white best conveys

CREDITS

Martin Cahill: Brendan Gleeson
Inspector Ned Kenny: Jon Voight
Noel Curley: Adrian Dunbar
Frances Cahill: Maria Doyle Kennedy
Tina: Angeline Ball
Gary: Sean McGinley
Jimmy: Eanna McLiam
Willie Byrne: Tom Murphy
Young Martin Cahill: Eamonn Owens
Anthony: Paul Hickey
Paddy: Tommy O'Neill
Shea: John O'Toole
Tommy: Ciaran Fitzgerald

Origin: Ireland
Released: 1998
Production: John Boorman for Merlin Films and J&M Entertainment; released by Sony Pictures Classics
Direction: John Boorman
Screenplay: John Boorman; based on the book *The General, Godfather of Crime* by Paul Williams
Cinematography: Seamus Deasy
Editing: Ron Davis
Production design: Derek Wallace
Costumes: Maeve Paterson
Sound: Brendan Deasy
Music: Richie Buckley
MPAA rating: R
Running Time: 129 minutes

the desperation of the working-class regardless of the decade. Boorman also told *Sight and Sound* that the lack of color gives the film a greater "mythic dimension."

Boorman's film works best in capturing a time, a place, and an attitude, but it is not the best Irish film of 1998. Neil Jordan's magnificent *The Butcher Boy* (reviewed in this edition) shows even better the lengths to which the Irish poor can be driven and celebrates the joy of telling a morally ambiguous story cinematically. *The General* is not the best Irish crime film of the year, nor does it feature Gleeson's best performance. His low-level crook in Paddy Breathnach's *I Went Down,* brilliantly written by Conor McPherson, is grittier and more comic than his Cahill. (Gleeson also appears briefly in *The Butcher Boy*). *The General* is not even the best Boorman film of 1998. *Lee Marvin: A Personal Portrait,* the documentary he made for the BBC and American Movie Classics, captures a contradictory personality more memorably than does his treatment of Cahill. *The General* finally does not engage on either the emotional or the aesthetic level as much as it should have. 🎞

—*Michael Adams*

REVIEWS

Entertainment Weekly. January 15, 1999, p. 42.
Los Angeles Times. December 23, 1998, p. F1.
New Republic. December 28, 1998, p. 32.
New York Times. October 2, 1998, p. B1.
New Yorker. December 21, 1998, p. 114.
The Observer. May 31, 1998, p. 7.
People. January 25, 1999, p. 36.
Sight and Sound. June, 1998, p. 44.
USA Today. December 18, 1998, p. E13.
Variety. May 25, 1998, p. 63.
Village Voice. December 22, 1998, p. 132.

The Gingerbread Man

 Box Office: $1,677,131

Based on an original story by John Grisham (rather than one of his best-selling novels), Robert Altman's *The Gingerbread Man* boasts a talented cast, an appropriately dark and dreary atmosphere, and a suspenseful storyline, but the film fails to capture enough of the dramatic ingenuity that gives most of Grisham's tales their appeal. Previous Grisham–based films, including *The Firm* (1993), *The Pelican Brief* (1993), *The Client* (1994), *A Time to Kill* (1996), *The Chamber* (1996), and *The Rainmaker* (1997), varied in their faithfulness to the original books and varied in quality, but all of them shared a certain "Grisham-esque" atmosphere that includes interesting, likable main characters (usually an idealistic lawyer being one of them), suspenseful and fast-paced plots, and illuminating glimpses into the legal world. *The Gingerbread Man*, however, somehow lacks the inspiration and substantive plotting usually found in Grisham's stories. On its own, *The Gingerbread Man* succeeds in weaving an intense story of intrigue and deception, but when compared to previous Grisham movies, it is a less satisfying film, primarily due to weaker character development and a more simplistic plot (it does have its twists and turns, but at the same time the story seems more formulaic). Considering the overall lackluster appeal of *The Gingerbread Man*, it is really no surprise that the movie experienced only a brief and very limited run in theaters.

Clyde Pell (Robert Downey Jr.) commenting on Mallory's father: "No offense ma'am, but it's always appeared to me your Dad's [been] a few beers shy of a six-pack."

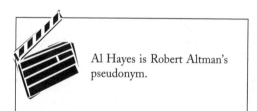
Al Hayes is Robert Altman's pseudonym.

Like all of Grisham's stories, the main character in *The Gingerbread Man* is a lawyer. His name is Rick Magruder (Kenneth Branagh), and he is a savvy southern lawyer (living in Savannah, Georgia) with a successful firm and an unsuccessful marriage. Magruder is soon to be divorced from his estranged wife, Leeanne (Famke Janssen), with whom he has two children, and early in the story it becomes clear that neither party in the marriage felt a strong devotion to faithfulness. The night of a party celebrating a courtroom victory sees the beginning of a whole new set of problems for Magruder when he meets a young woman outside who says her car has been stolen. The quirky, angry woman is named Mallory Doss (Embeth Davidtz), and Magruder offers to take her home. When they arrive, her car is there, and the front door of the house is unlocked. Magruder is puzzled, of course, and Mallory seems upset, but strangely enough she does not appear to be surprised. She indicates that things like this have happened to her before, and she suggests that her "weird" father might have something to do with it.

Magruder follows her into the house, which seems to be empty, and listens to the disturbed Mallory as she angrily and fearfully frets about her father. In a particularly odd moment, demonstrating the eccentricity of the woman, Mallory unabashedly—and seemingly unconsciously—begins undressing in front of Magruder, and quite soon she is standing before him completely nude. Predictably, he takes advantage of the situation and ends up spending the night with her. The next morning when he wakes up, she is still asleep (she actually looks lifeless), so Magruder takes off. Throughout the day he wonders and worries about her, then finally returns to her house to check up on her. To his horror, he finds a dead cat hanging in the doorway. Mallory is unharmed but enraged and heartbroken when she sees her dead feline. Again she casts blame on her father, Dixon Doss (Robert Duvall), telling Magruder that the man is "dangerous." She also suggests that he is mentally ill and says that he belongs to a suspicious, hell-raising organization—"group."

Magruder elects himself and his law firm to help Mallory institutionalize her father. In gathering evidence to prove to the court that the unruly and dirty Dixon is mentally disturbed and should be put away, Magruder solicits the testimony of Mallory's ex-husband, Pete Randle (Tom Berenger), who claims that he was beaten by Mallory's father. The court orders that Dixon be institutionalized, but he eventually escapes the hospital, aided by his backwoods cohorts. In the meantime, Magruder and Mallory continue their affair.

Now it appears Dixon now wants revenge on his daughter. Mallory's car is blown to pieces and she fears for her life. Soon it becomes clear that Magruder is a target as well, for he receives a picture of his children with their faces cut out—an obvious threat. Horrified that his children are in danger, he takes them out of school and decides to take them and Mallory someplace where they will be safe. Unfortunately, one brief moment in which the children are out of his sight is enough for them to disappear. Panic-stricken and enraged, Magruder enlists Mallory to help him look for the compound where Dixon and his group have gathered, located on some old property Dixon has owned for years. When Magruder finds the compound and Dixon's group, he demands the return of his children but initiates a full-scale gunfight, ultimately shooting Dixon Doss to death. But a shocking revelation is made: his children are not there. He discovers that the children are at the police station, having been dropped off there by the stranger who picked them up. Suddenly Magruder finds himself harboring massive legal troubles which could result in either disbarment or imprisonment. What did he do wrong? Magruder pinpoints his misfortune with the arrival of his new friend Mallory.

Magruder's friend and private investigator Clyde Pell (Robert Downey Jr.) uncovers some startling information. Mallory is in fact still married to Pete, and the property where Dixon's compound was located has recently become very valuable. Hence the insidious truth comes to light: Mallory, along with her husband Pete, is the true villain and has set everything up to get rid of her father, take possession of his property, and frame Magruder in the process. Ultimately, of course, Magruder confronts Mallory and Pete and clears his name.

The atmosphere pervading *The Gingerbread Man*, literally and figuratively, is embroiled in a brewing storm (the film was actually shot in the midst of a tropical storm.) The darkness, the wetness, and the noise all provide an appropriate backdrop for this sordid story of betrayal, lust, greed, and murder. For Magruder (and for everyone else, really) a storm truly is brewing, but it is not the storm he thinks he sees. The plot-twist at the end of the film is an effective device, forcing the viewer to go back and carefully evaluate and re-interpret everything that has gone before, but this type of convolution, in which a supposed ally or friend turns out to be an enemy, is not unique—and not really very surprising, either, since Mallory has been a rather enigmatic, cryptic person all along. And that is one of the chief weaknesses of the film: as intense as the story might be at times (such as when the children disappear), and as eccentric as many of the characters are, none of it is very surprising and only brief moments are really suspenseful, which is what the film aspires to be. The revelation that Mallory is the worst villain in the story is interesting inasmuch as it provokes the audience to realize that things are not always what they seem, but the truth is not that much of a revelation at all. Essentially, we've seen this story many times before, and there's not enough freshness in it to distinguish it from the rest.

In most Grisham stories, the protagonist—no matter how much he or she is flawed—is a likeable person who quickly engenders the support of the audience. The character of Rick Magruder may be more difficult to identify with and root for. From the beginning of the film, in which Magruder seems to talk without end, the character often comes

across as annoying and arrogant. Kenneth Branagh's awkward southern drawl does not help matters any (Branagh's a splendid actor, but somehow he doesn't seem quite right in the role of a southern lawyer). Magruder seems as if he could be as untrustworthy as anyone else in the film, and he also projects a certain amount of foolishness—one might think this savvy lawyer would know better than to trust a strange woman like Mallory so quickly. Additionally, his first attachment to Mallory arises more from lust than from a genuine interest in her. Unfortunately, there are no other characters that really make up for Magruder's lack of appeal. Most of the people who inhabit this dark, wet world are equally as questionable. Clyde Pell, for instance, seems to always be drunk or hanging onto several women at once. Sordid characters like these do populate most of Grisham's stories, but they are not usually the main characters. That could either be considered a strength (departure from habit can be good) or a weakness (failing to gain audience sympathy can distance the story from people emotionally).

Surprisingly, this attempt from auteur Altman isn't unique enough to elevate this suspense thriller to any higher ground. The director had all the elements in place to make his debut into the mystery-thriller genre a memorable one,

CREDITS

Rick Magruder: Kenneth Branagh
Mallory Doss: Embeth Davidtz
Clyde Pell: Robert Downey Jr.
Lois Harlan: Daryl Hannah
Pete Randle: Tom Berenger
Leeanne: Famke Janssen
Libby: Mae Whitman
Jeff: Jesse James
Dixon Doss: Robert Duvall

Origin: USA
Released: 1998
Production: Jeremy Tannebaum for Island Pictures and Enchanter Entertainment production; released by Polygram Filmed Entertainment
Direction: Robert Altman
Screenplay: Al Hayes; based on an original story by John Grisham
Cinematography: Changwei Gu
Editing: Geraldine Peroni
Music: Mark Isham
Production design: Stephen Altman
Art direction: Jack Ballance
Set design: Glenn Rivers
Set decoration: Brian Kasch
Sound: John Pritchett
MPAA rating: R
Running Time: 115 minutes

but little of Altman's ingenuity is shown on the screen. Reason for such a lack of display of creativity that also could have attributed to *The Gingerbread Man*'s brief fling in theaters was Altman's public battle with the studio Polygram Filmed Entertainment. Unhappy with test screening results, Polygram ordered Altman to re-edit the film. He refused, causing Polygram to hire another editor to re-cut the film. The final cut became something very different to what Altman envisioned. As a result, Altman disowned the film shortly before its theatrical release.

Perhaps there is good reason Grisham intended *The Gingerbread Man* to be a script rather than a novel. The story is laced with some standard elements common in his best-selling novels—a lawyer who gets caught up in an unpredictably "stormy" case, a plot featuring several twists and turns, and elements of suspense—but at the same time *The*

Gingerbread Man feels like an outline of a tale that could have been richer, more complex, and more surprising.

—*David Flanagin*

REVIEWS

Boxoffice. February, 1998, p. 52.
Entertainment Weekly. January 23, 1998, pp. 38-39.
Entertainment Weekly. January 30, 1998, p. 16.
Los Angeles Times. January 23, 1998, p. F2.
New York Times. (online) June 1, 1997.
New York Times. January 23, 1998, p. E1.
New Yorker. February 2, 1998, p. 81.
People. February 2, 1998, p. 19.
Rolling Stone. February 19, 1998, p. 64.
Variety. January 19, 1998, p. 88.

Go Now

Love now, Live now . . . *Go Now*—Movie tagline

"Robert Carlyle gives the best performance by anyone this year."—Howard Feinstein, *Detour*

"A poignant, affecting and funny movie."—Anne Marie O'Connor, *Mademoiselle*

"A triumphant affirmation of life and love. A great love story."—Andrew Sarris, *New York Observer*

"Distinguished by the performance of a passionately good actor and by lucid, engaging direction."—Janet Maslin, *The New York Times*

"Remarkable! A superb love story. Carlyle is terrific."—Jack Mathews, *Newsday*

He was a psychotic drinker in *Trainspotting* (1996), and a quietly desperate father with a plan to make money in the immensely charming *The Full Monty* (1997). Now American audiences have an opportunity to watch the versatile Robert Carlyle in Michael Winterbottom's modestly affecting *Go Now*, a film receiving a slither more attention than it might ordinarily, given Carlyle's exposure and fame thanks to the worldwide triumphs of *The Full Monty*.

Go Now, however, won't make even half of the impact of the above-mentioned films, despite the quality of Carlyle's work. A co-production with the BBC, one feels that this film would sit comfortably in a television slot. Indeed, it originally aired on British TV, but has enjoyed a theatrical release in this country. The story is set entirely in Bristol, which serves as an urban setting different from London—yet the specific location is all but irrelevant to the

story. A soulful, and sometimes funky soundtrack is continually utilized to promote mood.

The film opens by depicting the boisterousness of Nick Cameron's (Carlyle) football team. Constant banter is the name of the game, ranging from the good-natured (and even bad-natured) comments at Nick's misses at goal, led by the ebullient Tony (James Nesbitt), Nick's pal and workmate. It is with Tony that Nick first encounters Karen (Juliet Aubrey) and her roommate Paula (Sophie Okonedo), following an altercation in a nightclub as Nick tries to show his protectiveness towards Karen. The two lads walk the girls home, hoping to be invited inside, but they are thanked and sent on their way. "Lesbians," grumbles Tony.

Yet Nick's fortuitous encounter with Karen at a local video store leads to a pleasant evening and tender lovemaking. Nick has scored, and a relationship is in the offing. Life is good. But at work, Nick drops a hammer and it smashes a plaster fresco. A trip to the hospital to treat his numb hand makes the incident seem inconsequential.

As his relationship with Karen grows, Nick takes a trip to Gambia with his football team. Upon his return, he asks Karen to move in with him, and she agrees. Still fit and able, Nick swings a hammer and demolishes a wall in his flat in preparation for his girlfriend's arrival. And back on the football ground, he continues to miss goals for his team, provoking the usual comments as to his ability. Seeing double during a jog with Karen, however, prompts him to take an eye test. The optician suggests the problem to be a trapped nerve, and Nick gets glasses.

But things are changing for Nick. In his kitchen at home, he burns his hand but cannot feel a thing. Karen, beginning to be worried, looks for information on the Internet, and believes it might be the start of multiple sclerosis. Her secretive return to the optician doesn't clarify the situation, but still she is told to talk with Nick by the eye-care professional.

Nick is jealous of the attention paid to Karen by her boss Charlie (Sean Rocks)—he gives her a ride home each night—but she brushes off his suspicions. Whilst driving, Nick appears to lose the brakes off his car—or is it the numbness in his legs? In the hospital, he agrees to undergo a spinal tap and an MRI to pinpoint his ailment. A possibility of AIDS is raised, with a question hovering about Nick's possible infidelity during his African trip, but that is dismissed as MS is to become the diagnosis following more tests.

 Film takes its title from the Moody Blues song.

Nick waits four weeks at home for this diagnosis. Using a stick now to walk, and being protected by the taller Karen, his frustration mounts. Wetting himself in bed and impotence with Karen naturally crushes him. And when he gets the phone call with the confirmation of his condition, it is time to talk to his family.

His clan come down from Scotland and receives the news with some stoicism, fortified by a huge drinking session in the pub. Nick no longer drinks, but any liquid he consumes fills up his urine bag, and in the pub's toilets, a mishap leads to his brother and father being sprayed. His father is a lugubrious man when not loosened up by alcohol, and believes his son should throw his sticks away. But Nick knows he cannot do that.

He feels useless and full of rage. He is resistant to Karen's suggestion that he follow a diet that might help, and wants to work again, to contribute to his half of the rent. When Karen proffers the notion that they move up to Glasgow and have his family help out, Nick interprets this as the first move in her casting him off.

We learn that Karen has finally succumbed to gleaning consolation with Charlie; their afternoon trysts take place in hotel rooms. Nick, playing pool with his mates, becomes furious at being patronized; he is all but unbearable at this point. Charlie, meantime, is suggesting to Karen that she leave Nick, and even offers sending a truck to their home for her things.

Karen will not forsake him, and she bullies him through physical therapy sessions that are painful to watch. Tony's banter in the soccer team's dressing room pushes the now wheelchaired Nick too far, and at home, in an attempt to goad her to pack her bags, Nick tells Karen that in Africa he was wildly unfaithful. He wants her to leave; he cannot stand his dependency on her, and the two come to blows as Nick bellows: "Go!" Not averse to blackmail, he screams: "If you don't go, I'll kill myself"—this in the pouring rain when he wheels himself out to her as she shivers in the streets. Yet she stands resolute, and Nick comes back inside once more. A simple "I love you" brings them back together.

Their wedding concludes the film. Even Tony gets a girl of his dreams, and Nick and Karen dance to the soul number "Go Now." Where ever these two people will venture, it will be together.

An intermittent employment of black and white photos complemented by humorous captions is one attempt to lighten the load of this serious-minded film. The workman-like script is written by MS sufferer Paul Powell and Jimmy McGovern, a major television writer in Britain; his work is best known in the U.S. in the film *Priest* (1994), which co-starred Carlyle. A number of contemporary soccer references will mystify American viewers, but this is only a slight loss. The dialogue is never inspired, not least in the emotional climax of the film, but the story has some power to move us.

CREDITS

Nick Cameron: Robert Carlyle
Karen Walker: Juliet Aubrey
Tony: James Nesbitt
Paula: Sophie Okonedo
Charlie: Sean Rocks

Origin: Great Britain
Released: 1995, 1998
Production: Andrew Eaton for BBC Television and Revolution Films; released by Gramercy Pictures
Direction: Michael Winterbottom
Screenplay: Paul Powell and Jimmy McGovern
Cinematography: Daf Hobson
Editing: Trevor Waite
Music: Alastair Gavin
Production design: Hayden Pearce
Art direction: Frazer Pearce
Costumes: Rachel Fleming
Sound: Martin Trevis
MPAA rating: Unrated
Running Time: 88 minutes

REVIEWS

Entertainment Weekly. May 15, 1998, p. 74.
Los Angeles Times. May 27, 1998, p. F5.
New York Times. May 1, 1998, p. E22.
People. May 18, 1998, p. 37.
San Francisco Chronicle. May 15, 1998, p. C6.
Variety. August 28, 1995, p. 65.
Village Voice. May 5, 1998, p. 128.

Where *Go Now* succeeds is in its sure-handed, if never spectacular, direction of Michael Winterbottom (*Jude* [1996], *Welcome to Sarajevo* [1997]), who has the ability to render real situations dramatically. Most of all, however, leading actors Juliet Aubrey and Robert Carlyle are wonderfully grounded and believable in their roles. Aubrey veers close to portraying a saint in her role, but her canonization is prevented by her affair with Charlie, and the understanding of her role as a highly-loyal, yet vulnerable, woman. Carlyle, a subtle actor with a very good range, plots the trajectory of his character's journey with assurance. One feels for Nick, yet he sorely tests the patience, even the commitments, of his lover and his friends, but never quite loses the connection with them or us.

Go Now is a modestly affecting look at a horrific affliction. It manages to raise itself a notch above a "disease of the week" movie by avoiding cliches of the noble struggle of illness, and with the fine work of the principals. Thus, one looks forward to new projects featuring Aubrey, director Winterbottom, and especially Scottish actor Robert Carlyle.

—Paul B. Cohen

Gods and Monsters

He was the father of Frankenstein, but he was only human.—Movie tagline

Gods and Monsters. In Hollywood it's hard to tell them apart.—Movie tagline

"Exceptional! Enormous in its insight, imagination and humanity. Without question this is one of the year's best films, a sure Oscar contender!"—Dennis Cunningham, *CBS-TV*

"Lovely . . . There are so many colors to McKellen's performance . . . better work by an actor will not be seen this year!"—Kenneth Turan, *Los Angeles Times*

"The most beautiful ending of any American film in years."—Dave Kehr, *New York Daily News*

"An unalloyed success! A performance that well deserves to be remembered at year's end . . . beautifully acted, witty and heart-tugging." —Janet Maslin, *New York Times*

"Riveting! One of the best films of the year." —Jack Mathews, *Newsday*

"Transfixing! Elegantly witty and haunting. Ian McKellen gives the performance of his film career. Brendan Fraser excels! Lynn Redgrave is fantastic!"—Peter Travers, *Rolling Stone*

"Two thumbs up!"—*Siskel & Ebert*

 Box Office: $1,677,131

Film director James Whale (Ian McKellen) finds a charming companion in his gardener Clayton Boone (Brendan Fraser) in the indie hit *Gods and Monsters.*

Gods and Monsters, directed by Bill Condon and starring the incomparable Sir Ian McKellen and Brendan Fraser in a most unusual character piece, charms, entertains and moves. Featuring McKellen as the ailing director James Whale—(recovering from a stroke) this film allows the talented actor to create a complex portrait of a complicated man, which will surely be remembered at nomination and award time and introduce him to a new generation of fans.

Although he was mainly known to the public for directing the first two Frankenstein movies ("I directed the first two—the rest were done by hacks"—Whale amusingly relates), Whale was an educated, urbane man with a myriad of sophisticated tastes. He also directed the musical *Showboat* and lived openly as a gay man when others in Hollywood kept their lives tightly closeted. As the film opens, Whale is recovering from a mild stroke in his home, while being clucked over by the almost unrecognizable Lynn Redgrave as his devoted housekeeper, Hanna.

 James Whale (Ian McKellen) goes to a party at closeted George Cukor's home where the guest of honor is to be Princess Margaret: "He's never met a princess before, only old queens."

Whale's eye is caught by the sight of handsome gardener Clayton Boone (Brendan Fraser) removing his sweaty shirt, and subsequently Whale asks the young man to pose for him. Boone is a well-meaning young man, honest and hardworking, but certainly not the sophisticated type who have graced Whale's door in the past. Once Boone is smoothly convinced by the charming director that he is not looking to get into his pants, the two embark on a most unusual friendship. (Of course, even though Whale assures the young man that he has no sexual designs on him, the possibility of seduction with the amusing director somehow always lurks around the corner . . . .).

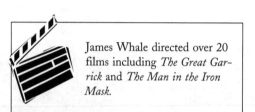 James Whale directed over 20 films including *The Great Garrick* and *The Man in the Iron Mask.*

Boone comes from a broken family, marked by drinking and abuse. He had a failed career with the Marines, and is basically living in a beat-up trailer by the ocean, putting in time on his day job and looking to pick up girls at night. Although he seems to be in his mid-twenties, he has no idea what he wants to do with his life, and lacks a drive and focus that would define his existence—even in his own eyes, much less in others. When someone as successful and educated as Whale takes an interest in him, Boone is dumbfounded. No doubt, lunch at Whale's home is the first time he uses linen napkins, drinks wine instead of beer and is asked his opinion on art, music, and life.

While Whale and his loyal housekeeper watch a late night TV showing of *Frankenstein* Boone and his buddies also watch at the local bar. Boone attempts to get his friends to shush and appreciate this film that his new "friend" had directed, but most of his barmates ridicule the now campy material and stagy overacting. Betty (Lolita Davidovich), a divorced waitress with whom Boone occasionally dallies, snidely remarks that Boone's new friend is probably more interested in him sexually than utilizing him for his gardening abilities. She and Boone angrily square off; they are obviously only physically attracted to one another, a union borne more out of proximity than any real or lasting feelings of affection.

Director Condon is to be commended for instilling so much characterization in one film. The film is loosely based

on the theoretical novel by Christopher Bram, and takes liberties right and left with his subject—but all done with affection and love. Although one could write off the character of Boone as a one-dimensional hulking beefcake, Fraser and the director infuse him with pathos and yearning that is deeply moving. When Boone has a meaningless one-night stand and faces himself with self-loathing the next morning, the director turns this simple sequence into a superlative character epiphany. It is after another empty encounter that Boone hungrily turns to the older man for some human respect and guidance.

McKellen will most certainly be gifted with multiple awards, if not nominations. His character is flooded with feelings and emotions both imagined and real, and watching McKellen's face as he struggles to discern his dreams from reality is painful and moving. Whale's stroke has loosened up his synapses and he is bombarded with memories that director Condon shows in the most revealing and imaginative way. Whale was shown to be a precocious, artistic young boy, born into an impoverished Cockney family that had no use for drawing, painting, acting or stories. He knew of his homosexuality early on and hid it well. In a beautifully realized sequence, Condon shows the young Whale as a soldier in the foxholes of WWI, and his first love—a delicate young man—meeting in a foxhole, surreptitiously courting and falling in love.

As Whale and Boone become better friends, Boone becomes more relaxed around him and even agrees to accompany Whale to a cocktail party given by one of Hollywood's most revered directors, George Cukor. In one of the most bittersweet sequences the film, Whale is crushed to realize that he has been invited to the party by a reporter merely to get an "old Hollywood" reunion picture of him and his *Frankenstein* actors, not merely for the pleasure of his com-

AWARDS AND NOMINATIONS

Academy Awards 1998: Adapted Screenplay
Broadcast Film Critics Association 1998: Actor (Ian McKellen)
Golden Globes 1999: Supporting Actress (Lynn Redgrave)
Independent Spirit Awards 1999: Film; Actor (Ian McKellen); Supporting Actress (Lynn Redgrave)
National Board of Review 1998: Film; Actor (Ian McKellen)
Academy Awards 1998 Nominations: Actor (Ian McKellen); Supporting Actress (Lynn Redgrave)

pany. At the party Whale runs into his former companion David Lewis (David Dukes). David chides him on his open gayness: "You may not care, but the rest of us still care." Whale gleefully tut-tuts him; he has never had time for this kind of hypocrisy, much less at this juncture of his life.

In one of the most amusing metaphors of the film, Condon juxtaposes the broad-shouldered, crew-cutted

CREDITS

James Whale: Ian McKellen
Clayton Boone: Brendan Fraser
Hanna: Lynn Redgrave
Betty: Lolita Davidovich
Harry: Kevin J. O'Connor
David Lewis: David Dukes

Origin: USA
Released: 1998
Production: Paul Colichman, Gregg Fienberg, and Mark Harris for Showtime, Flashpoint, BBC Films, and Regent Entertainment; released by Lion's Gate Films
Direction: Bill Condon
Screenplay: Bill Condon; based on the novel *Father of Frankenstein* by Christopher Bram
Cinematography: Steven M. Katz
Editing: Virginia Katz
Costumes: Bruce Finlayson
Production design: Richard Sherman
Music: Carter Burwell
Sound: Shawn Holden
MPAA rating: Unrated
Running Time: 105 minutes

Boone with the Frankenstein character that Whale has created on film. In the dream sequences that Whale increasingly finds himself drawn into, it becomes obvious that Boone is the new, young Frankenstein to whom Whale wants to surrender his life. One of the film's last sequences finds Whale begging Boone to relieve him of his pain, to send him back to his fond memories.

Unlikely friendships are powerful and moving; they are also the hardest to create and convincingly portray. This film achieves all this and more; Condon has captured a graceful mix of reality and whimsy, comedy and drama, past and present. Rarely have there been two more unlikely people to form a friendship than Whale and Boone; both were enormously enriched by the experience. The final scene of Boone years later, married and explaining to his young son the story of how he knew the creator of *Frankenstein* shows Boone with a character and maturity that could not be imagined years earlier. When Boone lurches around in the rain, imitating the creation of his friend, it is a truly odd and touching testament.

—G. E. Georges

REVIEWS

Cinefantastique. November, 1997, p. 5.
Cinefantastique. December, 1998, p. 50.
Detroit News. December 18, 1998, p. 3D.
Entertainment Weekly. November 13, 1998, p. 53.
Los Angeles Times. November 4, 1998, p. F3.
New York Times. September 26, 1998, p. 87.
People. November 23, 1998, p. 36.
Variety. January 26, 1998, p. 69.
Village Voice. November 10, 1998, p. 120.

Godzilla

Size does matter.—Movie tagline

"A sheer spectacle, this Reptilian spree outdoes *Independence Day.*"—Jay Carr, *Boston Globe*

"The E-ticket ride of the summer!"—Mark McEwen, *CBS This Morning*

"A terrific popcorn movie that will blast you out of your seat! It's big, it's loud and it's fun!"—Joel Siegel, *Good Morning America*

"The spectacle that is *Godzilla* is simply stupendous! It packs nonstop thrills with one jaw-dropping sequence after another!"—Kevin Thomas, *Los Angeles Times*

 Box Office: $136,314,294

Godzilla, the behemoth lizard from Japan, makes a lasting impression in the Big Apple.

There is no doubt that Godzilla is a beloved monster of baby boomers. Like them, he is the product of post World War II Cold War trauma. Like them, he reflects the threat of nuclear annihilation. But unlike them, where they learned the laughable nuclear defense of "duck and cover," he angrily retaliated against the atomic menace by becoming one himself and trashing Tokyo. How boomer kids at matinees everywhere envied his power. Yeah, they knew he was nothing more than some actor in a rubber suit, but he was their monster, camp and all.

When *Godzilla, King of the Monsters* was released in 1954 by Toho studios, his name was really Gojira, a hybrid of "Kujira" (whale) and "Gorira" (gorilla). But two years later, in an attempt to make the film more marketable to US audiences, his name was retooled to reflect a more lizard quality and scenes were spliced in featuring Raymond Burr as an American reporter. Unfortunately, America still hasn't finished tampering with the big guy from the land of the rising sun.

Now boomers are sporting grey hair and bifocals, but even after 22 films, Godzilla always looked about the same. However, in the search for a new generation of kids to entertain, this 1998 version of Godzilla just ain't the same. In fact, he's been so revamped that the only shred of the original remaining is his haunting, high-pitched roar which for some reason an entire team of audio experts couldn't duplicate and finally had to resort to Toho's original sound library.

Boomers loved the one thing the filmmakers of this incarnation of Godzilla worried about . . . "the cheese factor."

 Tatopoulos (Matthew Broderick): "Find out what he eats and he'll come to you."

Camp was fun and boomers embraced it. But in a post *Jurassic Park* (1993) world, film monsters couldn't just be fun, they had to be scary . . . really scary. Unfortunately, this Godzilla is only minimally fun, and it isn't that scary.

Using *Godzilla* as a follow-up to their previous summer blockbuster *Independence Day* (1996), director/producer Roland Emmerich and writer/producer Dean Devlin have kept the monster huge ("Size does matter" the promos promise), but this size may be exactly what works against him. This monster lumbers and seems easily avoidable. He's not menacing like Steven Spielberg's human-sized velociraptors who can open doors we think we're safely hiding behind. He's not threatening like the elusive alien that was small enough to incubate inside a human chest and even when grown could avoid Ripley in heating ducts. No, this monster is like being terrorized by an advancing freight train. All one has to do is step off the tracks to be safe. This monster is too mechanical, too impersonal, to be scary.

However, that hasn't prevented Sony and TriStar from creating a carefully hyped campaign of secrecy around their entry into this summer's boxoffice sweepstakes. They have been extremely coy about showing their Godzilla—a foot here, an eye there—as if they knew there would be a backlash at the more iguana-looking monster. (It also made it difficult for the more than 200 licensees hoping to cash in on *Godzilla*'s success.) And it may be the case that the filmmakers were already worrying about the film lasting long beyond the Memorial Day opening weekend. Sony opened it on a record 7,000 plus screens and, in an unprecedented move, tried to get 80% of the opening weeks' grosses from theaters in an attempt to recoup the film's $100 million-plus budget and $50 million advertising costs.

The basic plot for *Godzilla* is simple. Near Polynesia where the French have tested their nuclear weapons, a mutant lizard has started to make its way from the Pacific Ocean, across Panama, into the Atlantic and up the coast to Manhattan where it terrorizes New York City, lays some eggs in Madison Square Garden and sets us up for a sequel.

And believe it or not, within that simple plot there are a bounty of illogical ideas. For example, why Manhattan? Usually when an animal migrates to procreate, there's a reason for it: better weather, an abundance of food, or just plain old homing instinct. None of these reasons, however, explain why anything would wander out of the tropical and plentiful paradise of Polynesia in order to lay its eggs in New York City. They claim it needs a protected island, well, isn't Japan an island and a lot closer to Polynesia?

And how does a 300-foot-tall creature, one who stands equal to skyscrapers, fit so easily inside a subway tunnel? And how come it fits in subway tunnels but can't get inside the Park Avenue tunnel? And for that matter, if it's that big, how can it totally disappear in a pre-evacuated, teaming city? Wouldn't someone dial 911 to report the latest sighting? Or is this another example of how New Yorkers just don't want to get involved?

But maybe plot coherence is not something the core audience for this film would be interested in. Maybe the filmmakers have sacrificed the boomers and are hoping instead for the pre-pubescent children of boomers. And if that's the case, it's a shame.

There were seeds here for a better film. This Godzilla is more naturalistic. "He's an animal, not an enemy," says the obligatory scientist. This Godzilla adapts and learns—like Spielberg's velociraptors. But this intelligence factor is sacrificed for the thrill of special effects.

And special effects have come quite a distance since 1954. No rubber suit here. Ninety-five percent of the Emmerich-Devlin Godzilla was generated through computer graphics which required developing new software programs in order to put a moving, digital creature into a moving frame. However, this visual advance is offset by the fact that it rains through almost the entire film and scenes are shot at night. This darkness and rain is passed off as adding to the film's grittiness, its mystery and danger, but instead it just adds to the general audience discomfort and disillusionment. (Are they using darkness and rain to obscure poor special effects? How can I get a really good look at Godzilla through all this?)

Sometimes, however, Godzilla's SFX do work. It is fun to watch its tail swish a hole through the New York skyline, but it wears thin after a while. More fun—and more menacing—are the smaller baby-zillas, slipping on gumballs and chasing the main characters at an eyeball-to-eyeball height.

And this brings up another problem with *Godzilla*, the characters. As is usual for this type of film, there is the head butting between politicians protecting the economy of their turf and their reelection chances, army personnel who want to destroy the monster, and scientists who want to preserve and study it. Add a few reporters butting their heads in, and that's about the extent of the character development.

> This is the 23rd installment of the Godzilla franchise. Filmmakers Emmerich and Devlin were approached by TriStar Pictures four times before they decided to commit to the movie.

CREDITS

Dr. Nick Tatopoulos: Matthew Broderick
Philippe Roache: Jean Reno
Audrey Timmonds: Maria Pitillo
Victor "Animal" Palotti: Hank Azaria
Colonel Hicks: Kevin Dunn
Mayor Ebert: Michael Lerner
Charles Caiman: Harry Shearer
Lucy Palotti: Arabella Field
Dr. Elsie Chapman: Vicki Lewis
Sergeant O'Neal: Doug Savant
Dr. Mendel Craven: Malcolm Danare
Gene, the Mayor's assistant: Lorry Goldman

Origin: USA
Released: 1998
Production: Dean Devlin for Centropolis Entertainment Production, Fried Films, and Independent Pictures; released by TriStar Pictures
Direction: Roland Emmerich
Screenplay: Dean Devlin and Roland Emmerich; based on the character Godzilla, owned and created by the Toho Company Ltd.
Cinematography: Ueli Steiger
Editing: Peter Amundson, David J. Siegel
Production design: Oliver Scholl
Art direction: Robert Woodruff
Set decoration: Victor Zolfo
Costumes: Joseph Porro
Godzilla design and supervision: Patrick Tatopoulos
Visual effects supervision: Volker Engel
Music: David Arnold
MPAA rating: PG-13
Running Time: 139 minutes

In the film's lead is Matthew Broderick as Dr. Niko Tatopoulos (a bow to Patrick Tatopoulos, the designer of this Godzilla) humorously called "the worm guy" because he's spent three years studying mutant worms near Chernobyl. He's supposed to be the voice of science and reason, but Broderick spends most of the film wide-eyed and innocent. This is Ferris Bueller's day off at Jurassic Park.

Nick's love interest (as if the film needed one) is his character's ex-sweetheart, Audrey (Maria Pitillo), an aspiring television reporter whose boss (Harry Shearer) is a camera-hogging weasel. But Pitillo's Audrey is tedious verging on whiny. No fit heroine for a modern film. It would have been more fun to dump her character and make the other scientist, Dr. Elsie Chapman (Vicki Lewis) the foil for Broderick. Lewis' edgy characterizations would be much more interesting to watch bounce off the bland Broderick.

The potentially two best characters in the film have their own problems. Hank Azaria who plays video cameraman "Animal" is given very little to do, and considering how he practically walked off with *The Birdcage* (1995) the filmmakers should have invested more in his character. Similarly Jean Reno (so terrific in *The Professional*, 1994) is basically a superfluous character, a French secret service agent posing as an insurance adjuster. His running gag is that he can't find a decent cup of coffee in America, and there's a sub gag involving his four agents who all have names beginning with Jean.

Unfortunately, gags are the only level of humor Godzilla can attain. For example, New York City's rotund mayor is named Ebert (as in Roger) and he has a thinner, balding assistant named Gene (as in Siskel). Needless to say, "thumbs up/down" will show up. But gags are not humor. Humor is appreciated by adults, gags appeal to kids. And in the end, that's probably who will be the main audience for this film. Children won't notice the limited humor, the lack of real style, the unconvincing characters, the illogical plot. Maybe Godzilla will scare the smallest viewers, but older ones will be disappointed by its lack of a sense of wonder or awe. Feelings that even a guy in a rubber suit inspired 44 years ago.

—*Beverley Bare Buehrer*

REVIEWS

Chicago Sun Times. May 25, 1998.
Chicago Tribune. May 26, 1998.
Cinescape. May, 1998, p. 10.
Entertainment Weekly. May 29, 1998, p. 49.
Los Angeles Times. May 19, 1998, p. F1.
New York Times. May 19, 1998, p. E1.
People. June 1, 1998, p. 31.
Rolling Stone. June 25, 1998, p. 100.
Time. May 25, 1998.
Variety. May 25, 1998, p. 55.

Gone With the Wind

See it as you've never seen it before.—Movie tagline

"*Gone With the Wind* looks better than it has in years."—Leonard Maltin, *Good Morning, America*

"The best print you've ever seen of one of the best movies you've ever seen."—Joel Siegel, *Good Morning America*

"Everyone should see *Gone With the Wind* at least once on a big screen."—Leah Rozen, *People*

"Catch *Gone With the Wind* in a dazzling, digitally remastered version."—Peter Travers, *Rolling Stone*

 Box Office: $6,750,112

Witnessing the newly-restored version of *Gone With the Wind* means more than discovering a piece of celluloid that forever changed filmmaking. This film (save

perhaps for the benchmark novel of the same name) is viewed as the most beloved, revered artifact among all sacred cows in the deep South. Seen through the eyes of Scarlett O'Hara (Vivien Leigh), the woman for whom the term "Southern Belle" must have been coined, it represents not only a bygone era of opulence and grandeur, it preserves an attitude and a way of life, the likes of which will never be seen again. Even though it is a fictionalized story, indigenous residents of Dixie place upon it a value commensurate to that of Biblical scripture. The words and actions of Scarlett, delivered in a manner both coy and overt, winsome and bombastic, symbolize the credo of a large portion of Americans whose life and lifestyle was summarily removed from them by other Americans.

Scarlett O'Hara is, quite simply, the most well-rounded, all-encompassing female character in the history of the movies. She was both modern and old-fashioned, demure and demanding, wise and reckless, a woman whose surface vanity and core self-absorption represented narcissism in its purest form, but could also (when it really counted) dispose of any and all lingering pretense and become the embodiment of the indestructible human spirit. She was the original women's-libber, unafraid to take on men and champion her cause at a time when women were regarded as little more than ornamental decorations. While she was fiercely independent, she was never able to fully shake the desire (or need) to be dominated completely by a man. While she unabashedly preyed on the gender as a group, the two most prominent men in her life (who couldn't have been more diametrically opposed) wreaked havoc on her psyche in a manner with which she was completely unaccustomed. She was a control freak who couldn't stave off her own monumental insecurities. Those insurmountable foibles, the ones that prevented her from ever experiencing true love, also proved to be the ammunition that enabled her to overcome staggering odds and become the victor in a war in which she lost practically all the battles. She was the first diva, the original femme fatale, the first screen heroine to use her sexuality as both a weapon and a reward. She was a dichotomy, a walking contradiction who defended a way of life that now seems so impossible to fathom, yet while it was happening, seemed utterly infeasible to relinquish.

The British-born Vivien Leigh won the 1939 Academy Award for Best Lead Actress for her portrayal of Scarlett O'Hara. As the most identifiable and embraced character in the film, Leigh became the *de facto* icon for the movie itself. Leigh achieved, not only cinematic, but a cultural and quasi-historical immortality with her role as well. While her professional life enjoyed varying degrees of success for another 30 years hence, Leigh's career went basically downhill after *GWTW*. Her only major triumph during that time was the Oscar-winning role of Blanche du Bois (which was basically an update on Scarlett) in *A Streetcar Named Desire* (1951). Like so many performers who rode in on her wake, Leigh was destined to be remembered to virtually the entire world as Scarlett which, while lending her enduring fame, hamstringed any chance for her to ever diversify as an artist. Sadly, Leigh's personal life was just as turbulent and scandalous as Scarlett's.

For the entirety of the film, Scarlett carries a torch for Ashley Wilkes (Leslie Howard), a sedate, low-key country squire who is about the only man she knows who doesn't fawn all over her. From the beginning, it is clear that Ashley's affections belong to the heart-of-gold, somewhat oblivious Melanie Hamilton (Olivia de Havilland), who is also his cousin. In the flaxen-haired Ashley, Scarlett sees the one

thing she can't have; a noble, caring gentleman with whom she can build a future. She would give up all the other generic male suitors at her beck and call and retire from the role of Queen Bee if Ashley was to have a change of heart, but she continually hits a brick wall when trying to persuade him to see things her way. While polite and eminently cordial towards her, it's clear that Scarlett's constant overtures and nonstop berating of Melanie rattles Ashley to the core.

Rhett Butler (Clark Cable) is a shrewd, devil-may-care, bon vivant opportunist from Charleston, South Carolina. Refined, aloof, and impeccably dressed, he possesses many of the same traits as Scarlett; most notable—vanity run amuck and an unwavering desire to go against the grain. His past is somewhat shady (he was expelled from West Point and possibly fathered a child out of wedlock) and he marches to the beat of a different drummer. Upon first sight of her (while visiting the Wilkes plantation), Rhett takes an immediate shine to Scarlett, who instantaneously discounts him as a boorish charlatan. The tumultuous, yin and yang relationship that develops between Rhett and Scarlett is the bedrock from which the rest of the story is built upon. These two characters generated more sparks and created more epic tension than any other couple in cinematic history. Just like Leigh, many thought Gable bore an uncanny resemblance to his printed-page character, yet the Oklahoma born actor made no attempt to get cast in the role of Rhett. Although he had been a mainstay in Hollywood for years, with two dozen projects and an Best Actor Oscar (for *It Happened One Night* [1934]) to his credit, he wasn't on the short list of candidates for the job. While executives might have initially discounted him, Gable was a perennial favorite among fans who were responsible, at least in part, for landing him the role. When it was revealed that the book was going to make the transition to the screen, 98% of the letters that inundated Selznick's office making casting recommendations chose Gable. On August 25, 1938, he became the first cast member to sign on to the project.

After spending 10 years laboring over her manuscript, Atlanta native Margaret Mitchell completed her novel in June of 1936. Three weeks later it was optioned by producer David O. Selznick for a (then unheard of) $50,000. Paring down a 719 page book into screenplay form was a daunting, unenviable task. Selznick eventually chose Sidney Howard for the job, a man who had never before (nor after) written a screenplay. Mitchell's book and Howard's script (with heavy input from Selznick) came at a time when mainstream literature and film played their cards very close

Ashley (Leslie Howard) to Scarlett (Vivien Leigh) even as he rejects her: "You've always had my heart —you cut your teeth on it."

The original film was a Technicolor three-strip nitrate negative; this restoration was struck from a later dye-transfer copy and digitally enhanced.

to the vest. Call it what you will— love, romantic relationships, sexual tension—on the Hollywood screen and the printed page, it was treated as taboo and handled with kid gloves. *GWTW* changed that forever. Not only was the nature of romantic entanglements in future films permanently altered, this movie created the blueprint for each and every daytime and nighttime soap opera to ever come down the pike. The television industry owes its very existence to this movie.

The historical aspect of *GWTW*, while in no way the principal plot line, was the thread that held the very fabric of the story together. While the contentious banter between Gable and Leigh is engrossing and engaging, it's not nearly enough to keep our attention for four hours. As one of the first films to give any kind of historical account of the Civil War, *GWTW* was also one of the few pictures to portray the war from the losing perspective. In looking back (as director Ken Burns did so eloquently in his PBS documentary, *The Civil War*), it's clear that the South had no chance to ever win the war. The North had more men, more money, a stronger economy (the entire annual economic output of the South at the time was less than the state of New York alone), and a more sophisticated rail system.

Most importantly, the North had The Cause on their side. Some say it all started to prevent cessation, but that was mere window dressing. Considering the ideological chasm that existed between the two geographic regions concerning the issue of slavery, it's a wonder that the war didn't occur sooner and take place on a greater scale. The one thing the South had going for them, the intangible that seemed to escape the notice of their Northern brethren, was will. They fought harder longer, with less, under worse conditions and waited until it was far past obvious that they would lose, to finally surrender. Once the conflict began, it wasn't so much the preservation of slavery that kept the South going, it was the fact that Yankee strangers were telling them how to run their lives. In their own backyard. If the Confederates had deeper pockets and a few more bodies, they would have won. It's simple as that. They possessed a more fervent passion and passion goes a long way.

GWTW serves as a time capsule for an era that found Americans fighting and dying for a cause (owning other Americans) far less than noble than virtually every other conflict that ever preceded it. But in losing (something Americans had never experienced in war), these same people who had fought for the most abhorrent of causes, showed their tenacity and rose from the ashes as only Americans can. If there is anything wrong with the movie, it is the embarrassingly self-deluded viewpoint regarding the issue of slavery. Treated as happy-go-lucky, largely ignorant minions, the slaves here (referred to as "darkies") were white-washed and depicted in a way that eased the guilt of their owners' progeny. This disturbingly antiquated and rose-colored perspective results in the movie losing a large chunk of credi-

bility, leaving it, at least in some way, painfully inaccurate. While the words, "story of the old south" appear underneath the main title in the opening credits, slavery as a concept and lifestyle was never vanquished completely and is still held in high regard in certain pockets of the South (particularly in Alabama and Georgia).

Winning 10 Academy Awards (including Best Picture) in what experts refer to as the greatest year in film history (1939), *Gone With the Wind* beat out, among others, *Mr. Smith Goes to Washington*, *Goodbye Mr. Chips*, *Love Affair*, *Of Mice & Men*, *Stagecoach*, *Wuthering Heights*, and *The Wizard of Oz* (which, ironically was also directed by *GWTW* helmsman Victor Fleming) for the top prize. For its time, it was a technical marvel. With a final budget of close to $4 million, only *Cleopatra* (1960) cost more (based on inflationary adjustments) to produce. Despite the fact that *Titanic* (1997) has made more money worldwide ($1 billion and counting) at the boxoffice, *GWTW* still holds the record of being seen by more people in theaters than any film in history.

Although it has been rereleased nearly a dozen times since 1939, the 1998 version underwent an extensive, meticulously detailed overhaul. Over $1 million was spent on digital enhancements, color regulation, and dirt clean-up, freeing it of print manufacturing flaws and all variables resulting in differing theatrical exhibition conditions. The film was put back to its original 1.33x1 ratio (previous theatrical re-

CREDITS

Scarlett O'Hara: Vivien Leigh
Rhett Butler: Clark Gable
Ashley Wilkes: Leslie Howard
Melanie Hamilton: Olivia de Havilland
Mammy: Hattie McDaniel
Prissy: Butterfly McQueen
Gerald O'Hara: Thomas Mitchell
Charles Hamilton: Rand Brooks
Aunt Pittypat Hamilton: Laura Hope Crews
Frank Kennedy: Carroll Nye
Bell Watling: Ona Munson

Origin: USA
Released: 1939, 1998
Production: David O. Selznick for Metro-Goldwyn-Mayer; re-released by New Line Cinema
Direction: Victor Fleming
Screenplay: Sidney Howard; based on the novel by Margaret Mitchell
Cinematography: Ernest Haller, Lee Garmes
Editing: Hal C. Kern, James E. Newcom
Music: Max Steiner
Costumes: Walter Plunkett
MPAA rating: G
Running Time: 220 minutes

issues have presented it in a ratio of 1.85x1, a widescreen display that essentially cut off the top third of the frame). All new prints were struck in Technicolor (not used on it since 1961) using a dye transfer printing process. Two scenes in particular benefited immensely from the renovation. One, the burning of Atlanta (which was chronologically the first scene shot) and the scene depicting the fallout of Union General William Sherman's attack on Atlanta. Fleming's long, panoramic crane shot that starts with Scarlett and ends with thousands of dead and wounded soldiers and a tattered Confederate flag are especially impressive. Also included is a digitally remastered, 5.1 multi-stereo soundtrack.

The crowning achievement for *Gone With the Wind* (as would be the case with any well-written film) is the growth and development of its principal character. Scarlett, starting as a pampered socialite and ignorant to the needs of those around her, gets involved with the war effort as a nurse. Because of a promise she made to Ashley, she risks life and limb to transport her pregnant arch-rival Melanie through enemy lines, winding up at the O'Hara plantation, known simply as Tara, and finding it in absolute shambles. She kills an errant Union soldier then, like the proverbial Phoenix rising from the embers, rebuilds Tara. She survives the death of two husbands and slowly hones her strength as a businesswoman. Still pining for the ever elusive Ashley, she succumbs to Rhett's proposal of marriage and becomes (begrudgingly) Mrs. Butler. Never realizing what she's got or learning from her past mistakes, she is eventually left alone with only the land under her feet; the one constant in her turbulent life. Her final epiphany, contained in both the book and film's last words, "Tomorrow is another day." reveals that the lurking spirit and the will to live never dies, whether it be aflame within the impetuous Scarlett, the slowly rejuvenated South or the essence of dormant achievement lying deep within us all.

—*J. M. Clark*

REVIEWS

Entertainment Weekly. July 10, 1998, p. 53.
Variety. June 22, 1998, p. 51.

The Governess

Torn between the love and lust of two men, hiding the secret of her Jewish roots, Mary Blackchurch lives in a world about to change.
—Movie tagline

"Feisty and sensual! Minnie Driver enchants."
—Michele Shapiro, *Glamour*

"Saucy and lusty! An accomplished, touching and original movie."—Ruthe Stein, *San Francisco Chronicle*

"Two thumbs up!"—*Siskel & Ebert*

"Exquisite, erotic! A sexy, sensuous feast for the eye."—Susan Granger, *SSG Syndicate*

"Sink into it! *The Governess* is authentically beautiful and as convincing as a Bronte novel!"
—Stephan Talty, *Time Out New York*

"Mix Judaica with erotica and Scotland sizzles!"—Joe Morgenstern, *Wall Street Journal*

 Box Office: $4,012,658

I wanted it to be quite strange and hard and odd to create . . . two different worlds," is Sandra Goldbacher's comment about the intersection of two realms that are merged in the director's inaugural feature, *The Governess.* Already a noted arts documentarian in Britain, Goldbacher describes these two universes as the "exotic, labyrinthine almost subterranean world of the Sephardic Jewish quarter . . . and the gentile world as Rosina first sees it, which is harsh and cold, bleak and disturbing. Hopefully all the visuals have emotional connections."

The Governess, in fact, is replete with gorgeous visuals, and lyrical passages of music; the "emotional connections" she seeks, however, are less compelling, despite the empathy one develops for her plucky heroine.

An opening sequence, burnished with golden images, takes us from a packed synagogue, with Rosina (Minnie Driver) watching the men at prayer from the customary women's gallery upstairs. Before the service has concluded, Rosina drifts away and out into a teeming London street of her neighborhood; there's an underground, somewhat secretive, and yet colorful quality to the scene.

Rosina's clan is a Sephardi family, meaning that her family hail originally from Spain—until the dispersal of the once affluent and influential community to far-flung havens throughout Europe. There is warmth and celebration in the household, snapped in two upon the sudden murder of Rosina's father (Bruce Myers). Suddenly the font of income that has richly fed the home has been cut off, and Rosina, whom we have learned wishes to become an actress, declares that she will assume an identity to pry open the doors of employment to support her family.

Taking the moniker of Mary Blackchurch, Rosina is engaged to become the governess for a family in Scotland. The coach journey itself is an oppressive and lengthy one, but Rosina eventually finds herself in front of a vast stone mansion, home of the Cavendish family. Her world has indeed changed, and radically.

Rosina (Minnie Driver): "We can be any self we want."

First of the family to greet her is Clementina (Florence Hoath) the predictably precocious young girl who will be her charge. The house, with its slate gray roof, is murky, furnished with dark wood panneling and it possesses a hint of the foreboding. Mrs. Cavendish (Harriet Walter), however, does make Rosina welcome. At dinner, Rosina first meets Charles Cavendish (Tom Wilkinson), a friendly but remote man.

Cavendish is obsessed with the expanding science of photography, and with one issue in particular: How to fix an image on photographic paper? Rosina is ignorant of this fact in the early days of her relocation. She struggles to instill discipline within her pupil, but soon the young woman and the girl bond. Sporting hats and long dresses on the windy beach one day, they encounter Cavendish, and a first connection is made over the search for fossils.

Exteriors for the Cavendish's Scottish mansion were shot on the Isle of Arran.

Rosina is invited to a new part of the house—the photo laboratory. She is enraptured by what she finds there, watched by the thoughtful Cavendish. Yet this discovery is not enough to quell Rosina's loneliness. Alone in her room, she is silent and sad, and she pours out her feelings to her London family, as far from her as the moon.

Still, the challenge of Cavendish's quest has intrigued her mind, yet it is by accident that Rosina uncovers the secret of fixing an image. It comes from her recreation of the Passover ceremony in the privacy of her bedroom. At the traditional seder, an egg in saltwater is eaten, and an accidental spill of the saltwater on a fading photograph is the epiphany Rosina and Cavendish have sought.

She tests her discovery by soaking prints in the sea, and assures herself she is correct. Excited, she takes her work to Cavendish, and he is ecstatic. Hand-in-hand with this breakthrough, their secret relationship begins. She poses one

day as Salome and prevails upon Cavendish to capture her on film.

The return from Oxford of Henry (Jonathan Rhys Meyers), the Cavendish's troubled son, begins innocuously for Rosina, but soon his lugubrious intentions begin to weigh on her. Nonetheless, her passionate tryst with Cavendish continues, and after allowing her lover to photograph her without her clothes, she takes her turn to snap shots of her naked companion; in fact she quietly removes his pants while he is sleeping.

Rosina craves recognition of their love; Cavendish, although drawn to her, is turning his attentions to the visit of a man from Edinburgh. Their visitor will be the first to know of the discovery. Gradually, Rosina sees herself being edged out of Cavendish's life, both as his lover and his colleague. The Edinburgh visitor is told nothing of Rosina's major contribution to the advancement in photography.

Henry's attentions are becoming intolerable. Moreover, he has discovered her Jewish identity, and Rosina fears blackmail. At her lowest point, the young man visits her one night. She rejects his crude advance at first, then demands he strip, relishing the power she holds over him. But there is no consummation.

Given the hopelessness of her affair with Cavendish, Rosina accepts that her tenure in the household is at an end. Hurriedly Rosina packs her few belongings, and gleans a small revenge upon Cavendish by displaying one of her nude photos of him before his shocked family. She returns to a cholera-infested London, and from the pale faces of her sister and brother, learns at once that her mother is dead. Goldbacher doesn't dwell on Rosina's anguish; instead, a new series of photographs reveal Rosina's new path in life.

An unannounced visit by Cavendish puts a ripple in her equilibrium, but there is a sense that he both regrets his actions, and given the fact that she has taken some of his equipment to set up her own studio, there's an unspoken reconciliation. Our heroine faces a future as an independent professional photographer, capturing the myriad faces of her Jewish community in black and white images of beauty.

Despite the unusual, and welcome, charting of Separdic Jewish culture, Rosina and Cavendish's ultimate parting is less one of Christian discarding pariah Jew than the callous act of the nineteenth century man not willing to displace his wife with his lover. Wilkinson has described his character as a "control freak," but he's more than that. Cavendish is the head of the family, and someone whose authority cannot be questioned. While he may dally with a woman who is not his wife, propriety must be retained. Even more, his scientific investigations and discoveries cannot be attributed to a young girl.

Director of Photography Ashley Rowe, and Goldbacher, can take much credit for the beautiful look of the picture. The visuals are often exquisite than not, ranging from the opening sequence of synagogue and bustling street in the Sephardic London microcosm, to the fertile greenery of the British countryside and the wind-swept grandeur of a Scottish island beach. Indeed, the effect of the film can be hypnotic, supplemented by Edward Shearmur's (also re-

sponsible for the excellent score to *The Wings of the Dove* [1997]) wonderfully evocative music, full of lingering notes, tambourine shakes, and the vocabulary of drumbeats.

Of the supporting cast, one can have no complaints, other than to say that the venerable Harriet Walter and emerging actor Jonathan Rhys Meyers are fine within the limitations of their roles. For this is undoubtedly Minnie Driver and Tom Wilkinson's picture. Wilkinson, who is habitually polished, remains a mysterious male presence who intrigues and eventually betrays the central female figure of the story. If his character is never revealed in daylight, one feels that Goldbacher herself doesn't fully fathom his motives. We dislike his treatment of Rosina, and certainly feel pity for her, but we do not weep at her plight.

Rosina, however, is—for all her little deceptions—an open book for the audience to read. High-spirited, inventive, she is ultimately a young woman craving love and a connection to a place, a community to which she can cling. Love eludes after its furtive beginnings with Cavendish; by the film's end, one senses she has found her attachment back in London—yet has lost, possibly forever, the love for which she aches.

—*Paul B. Cohen*

CREDITS

Rosina DaSilva/Mary Blackchurch: Minnie Driver
Cavendish: Tom Wilkinson
Clementina: Florence Hoath
Henry: Jonathan Rhys Meyers
Mrs. Cavendish: Harriet Walter

Origin: Great Britain
Released: 1998
Production: Sarah Curtis for Pandora Cinema and Parallax Pictures; released by Sony Pictures Classics
Direction: Sandra Goldbacher
Screenplay: Sandra Goldbacher
Cinematography: Ashley Rowe
Editing: Isabel Lorente
Music: Edward Shearmur
Production design: Sarah Greenwood
Art direction: Philip Robinson
Costumes: Caroline Harris
Sound: Danny Hambrook
MPAA rating: R
Running Time: 114 minutes

REVIEWS

Entertainment Weekly. August 7, 1998, p. 51.
Los Angeles Times. July 31, 1998, p. F16.
New York Times. July 31, 1998, p. E12.
People. August 10, 1998, p. 34.
Sight and Sound. November, 1998, p. 51.
Variety. June 15, 1998, p. 99.
Village Voice. August 4, 1998, p. 102.
Washington Post. August 14, 1998, p. D5.

Grease

Grease is *still* the word.—Movie tagline

"Electrifying . . . Greased lightning strikes twice!"—Amy Longsdorf, *LA Times Syndicate*

"Hugely entertaining! One of the most enduring musicals of all time."—Gene Siskel, *Siskel & Ebert*

 Box Office: $28,411,018

To celebrate its 20th anniversary, Randal Kleiser's *Grease* has been given a theatrical rerelease, complete with new prints and digitally re-mastered six-track stereo sound. While this frothy musical was not considered a critical favorite or a landmark film of its genre in 1978, it was the highest grossing film of the year and has endured as an audience favorite. *Grease* is not only one of the most beloved of all musicals but also the only blockbuster musical of the last twenty years. Moreover, it represents the apex of John Travolta's superstardom in the late 1970s, and his recent screen comeback, beginning with 1994's *Pulp Fiction* and including his Clintonesque turn in 1998's *Primary Colors,* makes a nostalgic return to Rydell High School all the sweeter.

Grease, even in its initial release, was about a return to the good old days. Set in an idealized world of 1950s high school life—whose sites include the familiar malt shop, big dance, drive-in theater, and climactic drag-race—*Grease* has a very simple plot. Danny (John Travolta) and Sandy (Olivia Newton-John) share a summer romance and unexpectedly meet again when school starts. Danny, however, is the leader of the T-Birds and has a tough-guy persona to maintain, which would be hard to do while dating the virginal Sandy. She is befriended by Frenchy (Didi Conn), a member of the Pink Ladies, the female counterparts to the T-Birds. The plot is a series of boy-losing-girl and boy-winning-girl-back episodes with a lot of musical numbers on which to hang the story. There are some subplots as well—tough girl Rizzo (Stockard Channing) and Danny's pal, Kenickie (Jeff Conaway), have a turbulent romance, and the T-Birds restore an old jalopy for a big race with the Scorpions, a rival gang.

Trying to maintain his aura of cool, Danny is rude to Sandy when he first sees her with his friends around him but later apologizes at the malt shop. Travolta displays a

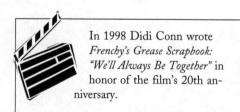

In 1998 Didi Conn wrote *Frenchy's Grease Scrapbook: "We'll Always Be Together"* in honor of the film's 20th anniversary.

pleasing boyishness in this scene—the tough guy letting down his guard to try to win the girl he loves. Even when Danny tries to turn jock to impress Sandy and fails miserably (yet comically) at several sports, Travolta still imbues Danny with enough charm so that he never seems completely foolish. Danny and Sandy have their ups and downs, but the true joys of *Grease,* as in most classic musicals, lie not in the plot but rather in the song and dance numbers.

Choreographed by Patricia Birch, the dance sequences show off the energy of the material's rock and roll origins while possessing their own goofy pleasures. The first musical number, "Summer Nights," takes place on the first day of school during lunch hour and shifts back and forth between Danny and Sandy each telling about their summer romance. The essential joke is that Danny tells a racy story, while Sandy tells of an innocent encounter. Danny struts along the bleachers as the guys form a chorus around him, while Sandy and the girls dance around the tables of an outdoor cafeteria.

"Greased Lightning," a fantasy sequence in which Danny and his buddies pay homage to their dream car, perhaps shows off the young Travolta to his best advantage. Sexy and charismatic as he dances all around and on top of the car, Travolta is all macho swagger with his swiveling hips and lean body. Likewise, the high school dance sequence becomes a showcase for Danny, whether he is dancing with Sandy or Cha Cha (Annette Charles), a bad girl who cuts in and finishes the dance contest with him. Travolta commands the dance floor with a physical grace and assurance, as if he were born to be there. No other actor of his generation could have been a musical star, if only the genre had not died out many years before.

When *Grease* was released in 1978, it had the nostalgic value of the 1950s—a decade fondly remembered for its innocence. Even '50s idol Frankie Avalon pops up for a cameo as the Teen Angel who convinces Frenchy to "go back to high school" in the corny but cute "Beauty School Dropout" number. In 1998, the movie has a second layer of nostalgia—namely, seeing John Travolta in his heyday. Travolta defined superstardom in the late 1970s when he made a smooth transition from TV to movies, from the popular sitcom *Welcome Back, Kotter* to 1977's *Saturday Night Fever* (bringing him his first Oscar nomination) and then to *Grease,* which remains his biggest hit.

While his career slumped in the '80s, his recent comeback and seemingly nonstop work schedule have made him once again a huge star. Indeed, as Janet Maslin pointed out in *The New York Times* (March 27, 1998), "it's a lot easier to watch Mr. Travolta take a date for a milk shake knowing that he always had the *Pulp Fiction* version of this same scene—not to mention the movie Presidency—in his future." However, *Grease* captures him at the exact moment when he reached his peak as a superstar. From his first post-titles appearance as the camera zooms in on him in a leather jacket with his head cocked to the side and a cigarette dangling from his mouth, Travolta is the essence of cool in *Grease*. In the tradition of James Dean, Travolta effortlessly combines self-assurance and toughness with a sweetness and warmth just ready to emerge from below the surface. Indeed, in a *Los Angeles Times/Calendar* (March 15, 1998) article reflecting on the making of *Grease,* Kleiser reveals a brief homage: "Travolta's red windbreaker in the opening scene was based on James Dean's in *Rebel Without a Cause.*"

Travolta's performance may seem better today than it did in 1978. While the role of Danny Zuko may not have

CREDITS

Danny Zuko: John Travolta
Sandy Olsen: Olivia Newton-John
Frenchy: Didi Conn
Rizzo: Stockard Channing
Kenickie: Jeff Conaway
Doody: Barry Pearl
Cha Cha: Annette Charles
Sonny: Michael Tucci
Putzie: Kelly Ward
Marty: Dinah Manoff
Jan: Jamie Donnelly
Principal McGee: Eve Arden
Teen Angel: Frankie Avalon
Vince Fontaine: Edd Byrnes
Coach Calhoun: Sid Caesar
Vi: Joan Blondell
Mrs. Murdock: Alice Ghostley

Origin: USA
Released: 1978, 1998
Production: Robert Stigwood and Allan Carr for Paramount Pictures; released by Paramount Pictures
Direction: Randel Kleiser
Screenplay: Bronte Woodard; adapted by Allan Carr from the musical by Jim Jacobs and Warren Casey
Cinematography: Bill Butler
Editing: John F. Burnett
Choreography: Pat Birch
Costumes: Albert Wolsky
Production design: Philip M. Jeffries
MPAA rating: PG
Running Time: 110 minutes

the depth of his Tony Manero from *Saturday Night Fever,* it has a similar character arc—a young man who is part of a group of friends and who is gradually growing up and away from them. His love for Sandy encourages him to be a better man, and, from the beginning, Danny possesses a maturity that the other T-Birds lack. It simply has to find expression. On more than one occasion, he actually walks away from his buddies and seems conflicted over how to win this sweet girl. Even though *Grease* is a light musical comedy and it would be a mistake to ascribe too much meaning to it, Travolta does capture something of young, insecure manhood in the role. The boy/man tension in Danny is best summed up after Sandy walks out on him at the drive-in when he comes on to her; he sings the heartfelt "Sandy" in a children's swing as a cartoon advertisement featuring dancing ice cream plays on the screen behind him.

Stockard Channing brings humor and passion to Rizzo and demonstrates her musical talent in two very different numbers. The first, "Look at Me, I'm Sandra Dee," is a raucous lampoon of Sandy's goody two-shoes image, and the second, "There Are Worse Things I Could Do," a rather moving self-defense after word gets out she is pregnant. (Things are resolved neatly when it turns out she is not.) After John Travolta, Channing has had the most successful film career and received an Oscar nomination for 1993's *Six Degrees of Separation.*

The T-Birds, Doody (Barry Pearl), Sonny (Michael Tucci), and Putzie (Kelly Ward), provide comic relief and do some Three Stooges-like shtick, but they do not really stand out as individuals. The Pink Ladies, however, have more distinct personalities. Marty (Dinah Manoff) is the pretty, sophisticated one who uses a cigarette holder, Jan (Jamie Donnelly) the funny one always snacking on junk food, and Frenchy the sweet beauty school dropout who becomes Sandy's ally in the end.

Olivia Newton-John's role as Sandy dovetailed nicely with her offscreen wholesome image, and, in the film's last sequence, she actually gets to play against type. To win Danny, Sandy undergoes a complete image makeover with Frenchy's help and triumphantly becomes a siren wearing skintight pants and spiked heels and sporting a wild new hairdo. Ironically, Danny ends up lettering in track as a way of winning her over so they really end up switching roles. She gets to break out of her goody-goody mode and flaunt her sex appeal, and he gets a touch of respectability. Thankfully, though, overt sexuality carries the day as they sing and dance their big number together, "You're the One That I Want," at the school carnival, where the film ends in a boisterous celebration.

Grease is a buoyant, exuberant movie that is a joy to watch on a big screen, from the cute animated main titles to the closing credits on the pages of a high school yearbook. The colors are bright, the songs bubbly, and, if some of it seems rather corny, that is also part of the fun. For those of us who first saw *Grease* during its initial run in 1978, seeing it again in 1998 is like returning to a group of old friends. Other more critically acclaimed films are routinely rereleased, but few elicit the sheer affection of a crowd-pleasing movie like *Grease*. Watching it with an appreciative audience means seeing people mouthing the words to favorite songs (the album remains one of the top-selling soundtracks of all time) and even bouncing along in their seats.

Indeed, some of the newspaper articles celebrating *Grease*'s return to theaters compared the experience to a viewing of *The Rocky Horror Picture Show*. Janet Maslin speculated that "it could be a *Rocky Horror*-style hoot to watch *Grease* with an enthusiastic audience, and anyone else who revisits it will probably feel exactly as you do." After its first weekend back in theaters, Susan Wloszczyna wrote in *USA Today* (April 2, 1998) that "fans young and old were war-

bling 'Greased Lightning' while aping John Travolta's sexy moves and dressing in poodle skirts and leather jackets '50s style." While it is unlikely that *Grease* will become a fixture on the midnight movie circuit, such reactions confirm the personal attachment many people feel for the movie. Next to John Travolta, the loyal fans themselves may be the biggest stars of this revival of *Grease*.

—*Peter N. Chumo II*

REVIEWS

Los Angeles Times/Calendar. March 15, 1998, p. 9.
New York Times. March 27, 1998, p. E14.
USA Today. April 2, 1998.

Great Expectations

Let desire be your destiny.—Movie tagline
"This is the one, the must-see love story!"
—*National News Syndicate*
"Wildly romantic."—David Ansen, *Newsweek*
"Gwyneth Paltrow and Ethan Hawke are dazzling! *Great Expectations* is imbued with genuine romantic spirit."—Peter Travers, *Rolling Stone*
"Two thumbs up!"—*Siskel & Ebert*

 Box Office: $26,420,672

There are several reasons for having great and lesser expectations for the latest film adaptation of Charles Dickens' *Great Expectations* (1861). The first version of Dickens' masterpiece to be set either in the present or in the United States, *Great Expectations* is directed by Alfonso Cuaron and photographed by Emmanuel Lubezki who collaborated previously on *The Little Princess* (1996), one of the most visually striking films of the 1990s. However, *Great Expectations* is written by Mitch Glazer, who also co-wrote *Scrooged* (1988), a generally unsuccessful updated, Americanized version of Dickens' *A Christmas Carol* (1843). *Great Expectations* stars Gwyneth

Paltrow, one of the decade's brightest new stars, but its main character is played by Ethan Hawke who, despite occasional moments in his earlier films, has specialized in grungy sullenness. A major supporting role is filled by Robert De Niro, one of the greatest actors of his time, yet another is played by Anne Bancroft who has often been prone to overacting. Despite all these conflicting qualities, the film works much better than might have been expected but still lacks something.

Glazer's mostly effective updating sets *Great Expectations* in the 1980s and 1990s, beginning with young Finnegan Bell (Jeremy James Kissner) living on the Gulf Coast of Florida with his sister, Maggie (Kim Dickens), and her commercial fisherman boyfriend, Joe (Chris Cooper). Finn, who spends his days at the beach drawing fish and birds, happens upon an escaped convict, Arthur Lustig (De Niro), who threatens to kill him if the boy does not bring him food. After helping Lustig, Finn sees on television that the murderer has been captured and returned to prison to be executed.

Finn is then summoned to the decaying estate of the eccentric Nora Dinsmoor (Bancroft) who orders him to appear each Saturday to dance with her niece, Estella (Raquel Beaudene). Ms. Dinsmoor, as she is called, was abandoned on her wedding day years earlier and is raising Estella to help her wreak revenge on men. (This motivation

> Finn (Ethan Hawke) to Estella (Gwyneth Paltrow): "Everything I've ever done has been for you!"

is considerably underplayed compared to Dickens' novel and earlier adaptations.) Finn, of course, falls in love with the teasing, heartless Estella.

When the teenaged Estella (Paltrow) goes off to Europe, heartbroken Finn (Hawke) gives up art and works full-time with Joe, whom Maggie has left. Years later, a lawyer, Jerry Ragno (Josh Mostel), appears with a bequest to send Finn to New York to be an artist, and he goes, thinking that Ms. Dinsmoor is behind it all. In Soho, Finn becomes caught up, with the help of gallery owner Erica Thrall (Nell Campbell), in the Manhattan art swirl and meets the adult Estella, now engaged to the pompous Walter Plane (Hank Azaria). Through artistic success, an embarrassing visit from Joe, the loss yet again of Estella, Ms. Dinsmoor's remorse, and a surprise visit from the thought-to-be-dead Lustig, Finn is forced into maturity.

Glazer's screenplay sticks to Dickens' basic story, excising a few characters and plot points, adding a few others, but the problem is the emphasis on telling the story without making its moral consequences resonate. Glazer's Finn is too insubstantial to carry the burden of the film's themes. Like the character's naive, almost childlike drawings and paintings, Finn is more an outline than a fully developed character. While Dickens' Pip slowly grows from youthful innocence to adult snobbishness to moral growth, Finn's changes, especially the successful artist's conceit, are rather arbitrary, merely hinted at. Glazer can be commended, however, for the locale changes and making the protagonist an artist. The contrast between rural Florida and sophisticated New York makes up for some of the deficiencies in Finn's development, and his paintings of Estella well convey Finn's romantic obsession. (The screenplay is not entirely Glazer's. The omnipresent David Mamet wrote Finn's voice-over narration.)

Great Expectations, despite its limitations, is a highly watchable film because of Cuaron's skillful direction which proves that *The Little Princess* was no fluke. Cuaron, with the help of editor Steven Weisberg, moves the film fluidly from one scene to the next, giving the audience little time to notice the holes in the story. He frames shots just as expertly, reaching back to the days of classical Hollywood filmmaking with tilted angles to convey confusion and conflict during the final confrontation between Finn and Ms. Dinsmoor.

Stylistic flourishes that lesser directors would go out of their way to call attention to are much more subtle in Cuaron's hands. Young Finn is sketching in shallow water when he (and the viewer) sees something red unexpectedly beneath the surface. The red suddenly surges out of the water to take the human shape of the convict in his prison uni-

form. After Lustig delivers his orders, the camera pulls back to emphasize that the boy is now caught up in the struggles of a much larger world. In the right corner of the frame, Lustig is seen falling back into the water as if disappearing into some magical underwater realm.

Cuaron unifies the young and older Finn and Estella by having them meet on the Dinsmoor estate when the boy drinks from an elaborate fountain and his mouth is joined by that of the girl who merges her open mouth with his, compelling him to experience the chaos of romance. The adult Finn meets the long-lost Estella in the same way at a more mundane Manhattan fountain, their kiss underscoring how he will always be trapped in her snare.

The visual style of *The Little Princess* centers around the contrast between the protagonist's brightly colored vision of an idealized India and the gloomy, even Dickensian, reality of her life in New York after her father goes missing in World War I. With *Great Expectations,* Cuaron and Lubezki avoid the cliché of presenting Finn's Florida as a paradise compared to evil New York. Despite a few bright shots, the Florida scenes are set under overcast skies, at night, or within the dismal Dinsmoor mansion. With Lubezki's suggestive lighting and the production design of Tony Burrough, who transformed the John and Mabel Ringling Museum of Art near Sarasota into a neglected, filthy mess, the audience can almost smell the dank Dinsmoor decay. The contrast in the New York scenes between the wet, noirish nightmare of the city and some dazzlingly beautiful images of Central Park reflects the turmoil within Finn, the raging war between fear of rejection and passionate hope for love.

Artist Francesco Clemente provided Finn's artwork.

Bancroft does overact but in a way true to the character's strangeness. One of Glazer's more effective changes is making the morbidly disillusioned Miss Havisham become the outrageous Ms. Dinsmoor who drowns her sorrow in the tango, ever-changing wigs, and bright green apparel, wonderfully created by Julianna Makovsky. (As Cuaron's favorite color, green dominates both *Great Expectations* and *The Little Princess.*) While providing some needed humor, Bancroft gives the character enough humanity, without self-pity, to keep her from being a cartoon. When Finn forces the old woman to see what she has done to him, Bancroft conveys true horror.

As several reviews have observed, De Niro offers the most Dickensian interpretation of his character. The scene in which the elderly Lustig slowly, teasingly reveals to Finn his real benefactor is masterfully done with the actor displaying the criminal's innocent pride in his accomplishment. Azaria depicts Plane's stuffiness without making him a caricature. Cooper, however, always makes weak or good characters too much like sad sacks.

Hawke, whose least unctuous prior performance is probably *Before Sunrise* (1995), is better than might have been expected, though limited by the script's weaknesses. He does callowness and desperation well but seems a bit smug as the mature Finn at the end of the film. Finn's development is aided considerably by Francesco Clemente's drawings and paintings. Rather than use his own style, more sexual and much darker than Finn's, Clemente creates simple, but not simplistic, art that conveys the character's innocence, confusion, and potential with an economy of strokes.

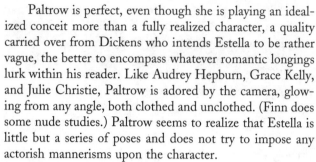

CREDITS

Finnegan Bell: Ethan Hawke
Estella: Gwyneth Paltrow
Nora Dinsmoor: Anne Bancroft
Arthur Lustig: Robert De Niro
Joe: Chris Cooper
Walter Plane: Hank Azaria
Jerry Ragno: Josh Mostel
Maggie Bell: Kim Dickens
Young Finn: Jeremy James Kissner
Young Estella: Raquel Beaudene
Erica Thrall: Nell Campbell
Carter Macleish: Stephen Spinella

Origin: USA
Released: 1998
Production: Art Linson; released by 20th Century Fox
Direction: Alfonso Cuaron
Screenplay: Mitch Glazer; based on the novel by Charles Dickens
Cinematography: Emmanuel Lubezki
Editing: Steven Weisberg
Production design: Tony Burrough
Art direction: John Kasarda
Set decoration: Susan Bode
Costumes: Julianna Makovsky
Sound: Tom Nelson
Music: Patrick Doyle
MPAA rating: R
Running Time: 111 minutes

Paltrow is perfect, even though she is playing an idealized conceit more than a fully realized character, a quality carried over from Dickens who intends Estella to be rather vague, the better to encompass whatever romantic longings lurk within his reader. Like Audrey Hepburn, Grace Kelly, and Julie Christie, Paltrow is adored by the camera, glowing from any angle, both clothed and unclothed. (Finn does some nude studies.) Paltrow seems to realize that Estella is little but a series of poses and does not try to impose any actorish mannerisms upon the character.

This *Great Expectations* pales beside David Lean's wonderful 1946 film, one of the few satisfying adaptations of a literary masterpiece, but the two films have several similarities. Lean's star, John Mills, is as good as he was capable of being but not quite the ideal hero, and Lean's young Estella, Jean Simmons, is as radiant as Paltrow. Cuaron's film improves here by having the same person play both the teenaged and adult Estella. Valerie Hobson is too cold in Lean's version. Lean's *Great Expectations* is also notable for its expert pacing and visual style with brilliant cinematography by Guy Green: The shots of the marshes are among the most beautiful black-and-white images in the history of the medium. Lubezki's work, though excellent, is not quite in that league. This *Great Expectations* is much better than many reviewers have claimed, but it misses greatness by a wide margin. 🎞

—Michael Adams

REVIEWS

Boxoffice. March, 1998, p. 55.
Entertainment Weekly. January 30, 1998, p. 39.
Maclean's. February 2, 1998, p. 78.
New York Times. October 27, 1996.
New York Times. January 30, 1998, p. E10.
Newsweek. February 2, 1998, p. 61.
People. February 2, 1998, p. 19.
Rolling Stone. February 19, 1998, p. 64.
Sight and Sound. May, 1998, p. 44.
USA Today. January 30, 1998, p. D7.
Variety. January 19, 1998, p. 88.
Washington Post Weekend. January 30, 1998, p. 48.

Half-Baked

The feel-good movie of the year.—Movie tagline
A comedy about best buds.—Movie tagline

 Box Office: $17,460,020

At a midday showing of *Half-Baked*, a ticket taker said, "Everyone's seeing that movie today." Of course, who else but stoners would have the free time to check out a movie in the middle of the day? And if nothing else, *Half-Baked* is a stoner's movie.

It's hard to believe in the Just Say No late 1990s, a movie so non-judgmental about drugs could make the screen. The drugs in *Half-Baked* are actually one drug—marijuana, or pot, or Mary Jane or whatever the lingo is in your burg. As much pot is smoked in this movie as any Cheech and Chong movie back in their day. Actually, *Half-Baked* has the same feel as a Cheech and Chong flick—pot as a benevolent force coupled with freewheeling stoner humor. A bong in the movie, for example, is called "Billy Bong Thornton" (as opposed to their pipe, "Wesley Pipes.")

Life is good for main character Thurgood Jenkins (comic Dave Chappelle, the same guy who played the skinny annoying comic in Eddie Murphy's *The Nutty Professor* [1996]). He's a custodian at a pharmaceutical company, Frankincense and Burr, and he and his stoner friends Brian (Jim Breuer of *Saturday Night Live*), Kenny (Harland Williams of *Rocket Man* [1997]) and Scarface (Guillermo Diaz) spend their days in a daze of bong hits and Cheetos. But their utopia is upset when gentle Kenny gets sent to jail for feeding a diabetic police horse junk food and killing the creature. The remaining three friends put their limited brainpower to use and come up with the idea that they should steal the high quality pot from Thurgood's job, and sell it to raise money to bail their friend out of jail. The three print up business cards and hand out the cards plus free samples of the goods (which is a variety so good it causes people to float.) Confounding this plan slightly is Thurgood's love interest named, naturally, Mary Jane (Rachel True).

So there is actually a plot, but it's really not that important. What is important is the comedy between. And like *Wayne's World*, for a "dumb" comedy, *Half-Baked* is actually quite smart. There are clever touches and pop culture references everywhere in the film. One segue between scenes is marked with a spinning marijuana leaf, àla the Batman symbol used in the Batman TV show. And, at one point, when Thurgood goes on a date with Mary Jane and has only $8,

a counter at the bottom of the screen tallies the date's expenditures. If nothing else, the film has the funniest sex scene of the year. Or maybe it's just the weirdest. When Thurgood and Mary Jane get together we see still photographs of the two engaged in goofy sex poses (i.e. Thurgood getting spanked). Over the still photos, loopy carnival music plays while Thurgood chants in a sing-songy voice-over, "I got some booty." It's surreal and wildly creative.

The film has a lot of cameos and instead of having the famous faces onscreen just for a "Hey, there's (blank)" effect, the cameos are used to good effect. Many of them are used to illustrate the different kinds of pot smokers: Janeane Garofalo as an arty chick who thinks pot makes her more artistic; Jon Stewart as an "enhancement smoker," that is, one who thinks everything is enhanced by pot and Snoop Doggy Dogg is the Scavenger Smoker who never seems to have any marijuana of his own. Steven Wright has a role as The Guy on the Couch, that guy who's always hanging out who no one seems to know, and Willie Nelson is an old-timer "You shoulda been there" smoker (sample line: "In the '60s everyone was getting high in the street, and nobody said anything because the cops were smoking too.") The most shocking cameo is wholesome Bob Saget (TV's *Full House* and *America's Funniest Home Videos*) who spouts vulgarities

CREDITS

Thurgood: Dave Chappelle
Scarface: Guillermo Diaz
Brian: Jim Breur
Kenny: Harland Williams
Mary Jane: Rachel True
Samson Simpson: Clarence Williams III
Squirrel Master: Tommy Chong

Origin: USA
Released: 1998
Production: Robert Simonds; released by Universal Pictures
Direction: Tamra Davis
Screenplay: Dave Chappelle and Neal Brennan
Cinematography: Steven Bernstein
Editing: Don Zimmerman
Music: Alf Clausen
Production design: Perry Andelin Blake
Art direction: Paul Austerberry
Costumes: Vicki Graef
Sound: Gary S. Gerlich, Richard Legrand Jr.
MPAA rating: R
Running Time: 84 minutes

at a rehab meeting. And, in perhaps the most fitting cameo, Kenny's jail friend, Squirrel Master, is played by original pothead Tommy Chong.

In this film Dave Chappelle emerges as a comedic force. He co-wrote the script (with Neil Brennan) and his manic energy carries much of the movie. Chappelle is quick with the witticisms and an unpredictable live wire, but also goofily likable.

With its subject matter *Half-Baked* was probably already guaranteed a long life with a certain segment of the population—those stoners who couldn't make it to the matinees. But most likely, the film will be a cult classic to a larger au-

dience because the film is such an anomaly—a smart dope comedy.

—*Jill Hamilton*

REVIEWS

Detroit News. January 17, 1998, p. 5C.
Entertainment Weekly. January 30, 1998, p. 46.
Los Angeles Times. January 19, 1998, p. F8.
New York Times. January 17, 1998, p. B16.
Variety. January 26, 1998, p. 66.

Halloween H20

Blood Is Thicker Than Water—Movie tagline
This summer, terror won't be taking a vacation—Movie tagline
"Terrific fun!"—Joel Siegel, *Good Morning America*
"The scares come at a clip and so do the surprises!"—Peter Travers, *Rolling Stone*
"Non-stop suspense makes this thriller an instant classic!"—Pat Collins, *WWOR-TV*

 Box Office: $55,041,738

After 20 years, Laurie Strode/Keri Tate (Jamie Lee Curtis) still can't escape from her homicidal brother Michael Meyers in *Halloween H20*.

People tend to remember John Carpenter's first *Halloween* (1978) as being a horror masterpiece. They may be right. In any case it launched a whole generation of terrible "slasher" movies. *Halloween*'s first six sequels fall into that dismal category, following the convoluted story of escaped loony Michael Meyers and his dealings with his sister, Laurie Strode, until her death in the fourth movie. The latest offering, *Halloween H20*, is certainly the best since the original movie and, to the joy of *Halloween* fans, the first, since the second entry, to star Jamie Lee Curtis as Laurie Strode. With the uncredited help of Kevin Williamson, the creator of *Scream*, (1996) the writers do as intelligent a job as possible of tying together the messy story line the previous sequels left behind.

It turns out that Laurie Strode faked her death, changed her identity to Keri Tate, and is now the headmistress of a posh, northern California high school. Meanwhile, Meyers,

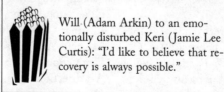

Will (Adam Arkin) to an emotionally disturbed Keri (Jamie Lee Curtis): "I'd like to believe that recovery is always possible."

still on the loose, has discovered his sister's new identity and has set out from Illinois with the sole purpose of killing her. This has been the hallmark of the Meyers character: he is so evil, so heinous, that his only function is to kill. The closing credits of the original *Halloween* don't even list his name, simply calling him "the shape."

How Keri Tate rose to the position of headmistress is anybody's guess. Wracked with the memory of horrors past, she has become addicted to pills and booze, and is a psychological mess—frayed, frazzled, and falling to pieces. Her seventeen-year-old son, John (Josh Hartnett), is fighting for his independence, and by all rights he should have it.

Keri is less successful in alienating her boyfriend, the school guidance counselor, Will (Adam Arkin): "Are you tired of my bullsh**?" she asks him. "I'm a counselor. I'm used to it," he replies.

Every Halloween Keri worries that her brother will show up with his kitchen knives. This Halloween is no exception . . . except that he does. Meyers arrives on campus the day of a school trip to Yosemite and no one is around except for Keri, Will, John and his friends, and a security guard (LL Cool J). The expected havoc ensues until Keri is left to confront her brother alone. Rather then letting him lead the chase, she grabs an ax and goes on the attack in an attempt to not only destroy him, but the psychological and spiritual demons that have been plaguing her for twenty years.

While not a great film, *Halloween H20* isn't a bad piece of horror moviemaking. Rather than serving up the expected

The car that Janet Leigh's character drives in *Halloween H20* is the same model she drove in *Psycho*. (1960).

horror clichés straight, or even with tongue-in-cheek, it gives them to us with a wry smile. One of these clichés is the repeated use of poor electrical wiring. For one reason or another, either nobody ever thinks to flip on a light switch when they enter a dark room, or the power has been cut from that circuit only, which makes one wonder why Michael Meyers didn't pursue a more profitable career as an electrician. Best of all is the ending that spoofs the convention of the bad guy who refuses to die. This time, however, he pops back to life after being "killed" at least half a dozen times. Each time gets more and more ridiculous, with Keri egging him on to get back up and fight. These types of conventions are not filmed seriously, but neither are they played for comedy. Rather, their use seems to be a kitschy homage to the clichés that the first *Halloween* originated, designed to make us chuckle, not laugh, at ourselves for still falling for them.

What this movie lacks is the barren feeling of the first film. Carpenter had to make due with a budget of $300,000, so he filled his frame with chilly autumnal shots of leaves blowing down barren streets. This sequel feels too slick. It attempts to mimic the haunted mood in various shots of the deserted campus, but the high production quality exposes its multi-million dollar budget. Even the music has been slicked up. Carpenter wrote the familiar theme to the first film, a few notes strung together repetitively like a Philip Glass composition. The theme now has additional grace notes and a large orchestra behind it.

Still, *Halloween H20* solidly ends this long and profitable series. Let's just hope that part eight isn't being plotted. "The Ghost of Michael Meyers" would be too bitter a pill to swallow. Even for Keri Tate.

—*Rich Silverman*

CREDITS

Laurie Strode/Keri Tate: Jamie Lee Curtis
Will: Adam Arkin
John: Josh Hartnett
Molly: Michelle Williams
Charlie: Adam Hann-Byrd
Sarah: Jodi Lyn O'Keefe
Norma: Janet Leigh
Ronny: LL Cool J

Origin: USA
Released: 1998
Production: Paul Freeman for a Nightfall production; released by Dimension Films
Direction: Steve Miner
Screenplay: Robert Zappia and Matt Greenberg; based on characters created by Debra Hill and John Carpenter
Cinematography: Daryn Okada
Editing: Patrick Lusser
Music: John Ottman
Production design: John Willet
Art direction: Dawn Snyder
Set design: Thomas Reta, Dawn Swiderski
Costumes: Deborah Everton
Sound: Jim Tanenbaum
MPAA rating: R
Running Time: 85 minutes

REVIEWS

Entertainment Weekly. August 14, 1998, p. 46.
Los Angeles Times. August 5, 1998, p. F1.
New York Times. August 5, 1998, p. E5.
People. August 17, 1998, p. 27.
Sight and Sound. November, 1998, pp. 51-52.
Variety. August 3, 1998, p. 35.
Washington Post Weekend. August 7, 1998, p. 41.

The Hanging Garden

"This film will melt your heart . . . A brave story of love, redemption and rescue."—Lindsay Brown, *Daily News*

"An audacious, imaginative work."—Stephen Farber, *Movieline*

"Sensual . . . A haunting, luminous tale of survival and reconciliation."—Sean M. Smith, *Premiere*

"The performances are exceptional, and writer-director Thom Fitzgerald laces the poignant drama with enough devilish wit to score an impressive feature debut."—Peter Travers, *Rolling Stone*

"Fiercely intelligent and emotionally insightful."—Susan Granger, *SSG Syndicate*

"Funny, terse and offhandedly incisive."—Dennis Lim, *Village Voice*

The east coast of Canada is extremely underrepresented cinematically, and that's a real shame given the region's rugged beauty and quite intact Celtic traditions. Thom Fitzgerald has lived up to much of the promise of "The Maritimes," as Canadians call their easternmost provinces, with his first feature film *The Hanging Garden*. Fitzgerald understands Nova Scotia to be a place where history—including your personal history—never fully moves forward, and a place whose dense, lush landscape inland hides a harsh, rocky shore on the edges. Using a garden as a kind of organizing metaphor, Fitzgerald makes the most of this sense of place, evoking richly contradictory characters that embody the frustrations and possibilities of small town life in the late 20th century. The film won several richly deserved "Genies" (the Canadian version of the Oscar©), including best film of 1997, and these awards only confirmed that *The Hanging Garden* announces a major new Canadian filmmaker.

The film's three acts are named after plants: 'The Lady in the Locket,' 'Lad's Love,' and 'Mums.'

The story begins with a wedding in a small Nova Scotia town. Rosemary (Kerry Fox) and Fletcher (Joel S. Keller) are getting married, and when Rosemary's brother William (Chris Leavins) shows up for the ceremony late, it sets off a cascade of emotional turmoil. William hadn't been back to the town since he ran away as a teenager, and his family expresses a combination of surprise, relief and anxiety when he finally appears. The rest of the film juggles two narratives, the present day as William get to know his family again, and the past, as a teenage William (Troy Veinotte) struggles with his homosexuality and his incredibly repres-

sive family life. His father's garden, which William had to meticulously tend as a boy, is an especially potent catalyst for his memories, and several sequences feature the adult William watching and sometimes talking to the childhood William. As the film progresses, the past narrative gradually becomes more centrally concerned with how his family dealt with young William's sexuality, and the present narrative becomes more and more concerned with the consequences of these ill-conceived correctives. What the narrative finally seems to confirm is that family is a tricky, evolving, and dense structure, resembling in more ways than one the garden where young William had to toil.

One of the ways that Nova Scotia fits this story so well is that the place is arguably somewhere that history is still more intact than much of (increasingly Americanized) Canada. This cultural specificity is made pretty clear at the wedding, which clearly takes place at a house that is remote to say the least, and features a fiddler played by Ashley MacIssac, probably the best known Celtic fiddler in Canada (who hails from Newfoundland, also part of the Maritime provinces). *The Hanging Garden* takes place in a very distinct place, and this would probably be recognized by a Canadian audience in fairly short order. Fitzgerald's project, though, is clearly not to depict the Maritimes as a timeless paradise, but instead as somewhere that time and culture frustratingly seem to stand still and remain quite isolated from the world outside. William ended his time in this little capsule when he escaped to the mysterious and far-away Toronto, a journey that has utterly transformed him: when he returns he's no longer a shy, obese misfit but a confident, good-looking aspiring actor. His family, on the other hand, has remained almost exactly the same, constantly re-hashing the same petty arguments and exhibiting the same closed-off worldview. Their home is a kind of repository of old memories and staid histories, a place that may look beautiful but could never survive outside of this very controlled environment. What William finds when he returns is that the memories that he left behind, then, are still quite intact, and indeed inescapable so long as he stays there.

Like the garden, though, these memories and histories have grown and changed in some important ways. The aforementioned bridegroom, Fletcher, for instance, turns out to be William's first boyfriend. Although he has grown into the figure of an aspiring husband, it's clear that the root of his identity is, of course, unchanged. William's sister, also Fletcher's new wife, seems to know this ("you're not fooling anyone," she sharply tells him), but like the rest of the family, she keeps her resentment and anxiety buried as deep as she can, only occasionally allowing it to bubble to the top. Another subplot focuses on the consequences of William's mother's attempt to make her young, sexually confused son a good heterosexual (she takes him to a local woman who agrees to have sex with him). Although William had thought this whole traumatic little experience to be part of the past, his return to this world shows that while it may have assumed a new form, that little bit of his history has also refused to die.

Fitzgerald's view of small town life eventually emerges as an extremely conflicted one, full both of anger towards the repression that it embodied and a kind of nostalgia for the possibilities that it failed to live up to. While films that biliously damn the (usually suburban) childhood upbringings of their makers have lately been numerous (*The Ice Storm* [1997] is a recent example), *The Hanging Garden*, like its Canadian contemporary *Kitchen Party* (reviewed in this volume), is much more clearheaded and moderate in its critique. The way that Fitzgerald lingers on images of the garden and of the landscape that surrounds the family home makes William's genuine fondness for the place quite clear, a fondness that becomes melancholic and indeed tragic in light of the difficulties that he suffered through when he actually lived here. Indeed, this kind of conflict is what defines the film, an uncertainty as to the difference between happiness and despair, contentment and longing.

The Hanging Garden is also quite clearheaded in the way that it handles the more fantastic aspects of its form. Fitzgerald's two narratives occasionally leak into one another, such as when the present day William speaks to his younger, hallucinated counterpart, and what comes out of these interactions is central to William's movement towards reconciliation. These sequences are rendered in a very matter-of-fact way, though, despite their surrealistic overtones. This straightforward approach is much closer to a spirit of magical realism than most films that aspire to that status, since the core of a magic realist project is the attempt to make the fantastic seem everyday, and therefore more real. Eschewing visual pyrotechnics that might clearly brand these sequences as fantasy, Fitzgerald essentially declines to elaborate on the difference between internal contemplation or remembrance and external reality. Like his conflict between contentment and longing, for the purposes of this film the difference really doesn't matter.

Indeed, what's central to understanding *The Hanging Garden* is realizing that it's not a conventional narrative, and so doesn't obey a lot of the rules that many such films might be expected to. The story does fall together a little too neatly at the end, but minor lapses in credibility don't undermine Fitzgerald's argument that history is essentially circular but still has some variations. Similarly, the details of narrative ends that the film leaves loose—such as the relationship between Fletcher and Rosemary, or the fate of William's dad after his wife leaves him—are ultimately irrelevant. Instead, all of these little lapses in narrative closure or realist credibility help to point to the fact that this is a film about something much larger than the interactions between its characters. That Fitzgerald makes these interactions such a pleasure to watch (his dialogue is very smooth and his actors all play off of each other most gracefully) is what makes this a vibrant meditation on serious, almost existential problems, and not simply a pretentious allegory.

The Hanging Garden, then, is a most satisfying film, one of the best works to come out of Canada in 1998 and certainly the best work about the east coast of that country in recent memory. Thom Fitzgerald's handling of both landscape and actors is confident and ambitious, although his

CREDITS

Sweet William: Chris Leavins
Rosemary: Kerry Fox
Iris: Seana McKenna
Whiskey Mac: Peter MacNeil
Violet: Christine Dunsworth
Teen Sweet Williams: Troy Veinotte
Teen Rosemary: Sarah Polley
Fletcher: Joel S. Keller
Granny Grace: Joan Orenstein

Origin: Canada
Released: 1997
Production: Louise Garfield, Arnie Gelbart, and Thom Fitzagerald for Triptych Media, Galafilm, and Emotion Pictures; released by Goldwyn
Direction: Thom Fitzgerald
Screenplay: Thom Fitzgerald
Cinematography: Daniel Jobin
Editing: Susan Shanks
Music: John Roby
Art direction: Taavo Soodor
Sound: Georges Hannon
Costumes: James A. Worthen
MPAA rating: R
Running Time: 91 minutes

REVIEWS

Boxoffice. April, 1998, p. 202.
Detroit Free Press. July 10, 1998, p. 9D.
Entertainment Weekly. June 12, 1998, p. 52.
Los Angeles Times. May 15, 1998, p. F12.
New York Times. May 15, 1998, p. E19.
Sight and Sound. May, 1998, p. 46.
Variety. September 22, 1997, p. 39.
Village Voice. May 19, 1998, p. 132.

touch is light enough to keep the film from careening into the realms of the melodramatic. Indeed , although it's sometimes promoted as such, this is in no way a family melodrama. Nor, however, is it artsy, navel-gazing indulgence by a rookie filmmaker. Rather, it's a very intense, sometimes surreal, and often comic look at how interior contemplation and struggles are related to the world outside. Perhaps what makes it most remarkable is simply its tone: the way that Fitzgerald handles these situations is to treat them as the stuff of everyday life, sometimes intense, sometimes banal, sometimes magical, but probably familiar to any thoughtful person. This kind of restraint is almost unheard of in recent American independent film, and *The Hanging Garden* (like a lot of recent Canadian independent films) certainly has a thing or two to teach the current generation of aspiring *cineastes*. It's the first major work of someone who could very well become one of Canada's most important filmmakers, and it deserves to be shown as widely as possible.

—*Jerry White*

Happiness

"Subtly savage . . . Evilly funny!"—Janet Maslin, *New York Times*

"Deeply disturbing and shockingly funny."
—David Ansen, *Newsweek*

"Unique and unmissable."—Peter Travers, *Rolling Stone*

"The ultimate black comedy!"—Richard Corliss, *Time*

"Hilarious, shocking and completely unforgettable . . . just might be the year's best movie."
—*Time Out*

"The most electrifying American film to break at Cannes since *Pulp Fiction!*"—John Powers, *Vogue*

 Box Office: $2,756,587

Awkwardness is Todd Solondz's grail. Most filmmakers avoid delicate subjects, tongue-tied characters, and awkward moments. More daring directors employ awkwardness judiciously to make an ironic or jarring statement. But to Solondz, awkwardness is a defining part of being human. His films are peopled by characters who are achingly, sometimes disgustingly, real.

In *Welcome to the Dollhouse* (1997), writer-director Solondz focused on the tribulations of a terribly unhappy 11-year-old girl. Frank discussions of adolescent sexuality and disturbing scenes of emotional torment were part of that film's bleak take on the brutalities of growing up a misfit in postmodern America. Now, with *Happiness,* Solondz has fast-forwarded into postmodern adulthood, where things are just as bad. His characters are desperately un-happy, warped and sometimes pathetic, but undeniably authentic.

Welcome to the Dollhouse lacked just enough polish for some critics to be able to dismiss it as perverse or insignificant. But *Happiness* is a masterful piece of moviemaking. Technically, the film is superb; emotionally, Solondz forces audiences to confront his view of the world. *Happiness* is a powerful, engaging and courageous depiction of the serious voids in the lives of a group of adults. The film is packed with gutsy, understated, memorable performances; unnerving, unforgettable scenes; compelling and groundbreaking dialogue; and a commanding, almost flawless direction. Still, it will disturb and annoy more critics than it will charm, for Solondz refuses to make concessions to marketability.

Solondz is so unflinching that he puts most other avant-garde filmmakers to shame. Who else has the courage to put a pedophile at the center of his emotional canvas? Who else makes sexuality not glamorous or enticing, but sordid and mundane? Who else dares to make human beings tragically flawed and debased, yet still manages to make them sympathetic?

There is nothing coy or tricky about Solondz. But starting with its title, *Happiness* is just droll enough to be entertaining, just ironic enough to appeal to a hip sensibility that Solondz mostly eschews. À la Robert Altman, Solondz introduces an interweaving collection of characters, centering on three sisters living in suburban New Jersey, the same place where *Dollhouse* was set.

The first sister we meet is Joy Jordan (Jane Adams), a self-abnegating latter-day hippie who is desperately lonely yet frightened of intimacy. The film opens with a very awkward moment, as Joy is telling her date Andy (Jon Lovitz) that she doesn't want to become involved with him. "Is it someone else?" Andy asks. "No, it's just you," explains Joy. It's a typical snippet of Solondz dialogue: the people in his films try to speak sympathetically, but come off a little clumsy; they are not good at pretense, though they try hard.

When Andy shows Joy a special gift he has bought for her, she says "I'll always treasure it." But Andy knows she is insincere and snatches it back, saying, "No, you won't." He says he knows he's "pathetic, a nerd, a lard-ass, a fatso," but it's what's inside that counts, and inside he's "champagne." Because Joy doesn't recognize that, he curses her: "You're shit until you die."

Joy is a magnet for such abuse. In a priceless scene, her chirpy sister Trish (Cynthia Stevenson) confides in her that the family always feared Joy wouldn't amount to anything. Now, however, Trish says she is happy to see that Joy is making progress with a career (she's some sort of telemarketer) and her music (she composes maudlin folk songs on her guitar, one of which, "Happiness," serves as the film's theme). As for men, Trish and her successful trendy poet sister Helen (Lara Flynn Boyle) are always trying and failing to make a match for the forlorn Joy.

Joy is *Dollhouse*'s protagonist Dawn Weiner grown up. She has no self-confidence, keeps getting gratuitously abused, lacks judgment, and is a constant loser in love. After she learns Andy has committed suicide, Joy takes a new job where she can indulge her flower-child need to do good for others. She signs up to teach English to newly arrived refugees, but the job is open only because the regular employees are striking. To her dismay, her class of immigrants shouts at her for being a "scab." (A line-crossing colleague tells her to counter proudly with, "I'm not a scab, I'm a strikebreaker!") Only one student befriends her, and too much so. He's a Russian immigrant, Vlad (Jared Harris), who seduces Joy as a Barry Manilow song swamps the soundtrack. Vlad, an incorrigible thief, steals her guitar and CD player, turns out to have a common-law wife whom he abuses, yet still talks Joy into "loaning" him $1,000.

Joy envies Trish, who seems to have it all: the suburban house; the successful husband, psychiatrist Dr. Bill Maplewood (Dylan Baker), and three apparently happy children. Trish, played to annoying perfection by Stephenson, projects an air of smug self-contentment. But it barely masks her envy of Helen, who has a rewarding career and all the sexy studs she can handle. To Helen, however, life is a meaningless round of banal interviews and celebrity couplings. Drop-dead-stunning, Helen believes herself to be a vapid hypocrite and complains that the legions of men who bed her do so for selfish reasons. "Nobody wants me for me," she tells her astonished sister. "I wish I had your life—husband, kids, car pools."

In this trio of perfectly realized sisters—they even look like they could be related—Solondz has constructed a hierarchy of dissatisfaction. At each level of greater self-

 Helen (Lara Flynn Boyle) to sister Joy (Jane Adams): "I'm not laughing at you, I'm laughing with you!" Joy: "I'm not laughing!"

actualization, there is greater misery and deeper irony. Trish believes herself superior to Joy, and Helen feels superior to both her sisters, yet for each something is missing. In fact, Helen is so hungry for authentic attention that she becomes obsessed with obscene phone-caller Allen (Philip Seymour Hoffman), who tells her that she is an overrated nothing. It's the same thing he tells most women, but it's what Helen, in a stupor of disgust at her inauthenticity, thinks she wants to hear. When Helen finds that the caller is her plump, greasy, sweaty, tongue-tied apartment neighbor who is so inept he can't even put a move on her, she recovers her sanity enough to tell him: "This isn't working."

Hoffman's exquisitely played heavy-breather touches the lives of all three sisters. He sits in his room in his underwear and randomly calls woman's names from a phone book, at one time hitting upon Joy, who at first mistakes him for a guy Trish has set her up with. His psychiatrist is Bill Maplewood. In a priceless scene, Maplewood tunes out, mentally running through the day's errands, as his client complains about how boring everybody thinks he is.

The men in *Happiness* are even sicker than the women, yet Solondz manages to make them all understandable. Besides Hoffman's porno-reading, masturbatory, self-loathing caller, there is Vlad the merciless impaler (who zips up and jumps out of Joy's bed as soon as he has completed his conquest); Lenny (Ben Gazzara), the sisters' father, who no longer feels love for his wife (Louise Lasser) or passion of any kind; and, centrally, Bill Maplewood, an apparent paragon of a father who turns out to be a pedophile.

In one of his few missteps, Solondz overplays his hand by making Bill Maplewood look like a Father-Knows-Best caricature in plaid shirts and a 1950s demeanor. The first clue that Bill has a problem comes in the film's only dream sequence, in which Bill enters a pastoral park and randomly shoots everyone. Maplewood tells his own psychiatrist that the dream leaves him feeling happy. Bill is an excellent manipulator; he makes Trish think it's her problem that they don't have a sex life, and at one point convinces her they had sex but she was too tired to remember it. When his son's friend comes for a sleepover, Bill drugs everyone in order to prey on the visitor. And when his son tells him another boy's parents have gone on vacation and left him alone, he seizes the opportunity.

Baker is breathtakingly good at portraying the compartmentalized Maplewood. Solondz is brave for scripting Bill as a decent, confused man with a problem that is overtaking him. In fact, he is kinder to his children than Trish, who punishes one son for pretending to vomit at dinner by making him go straight to bed. That Bill can be a calculating pederast shows how completely in thrall he is to his disorder; yet the film does not make any excuses for his behavior and metes out appropriate punishment.

The movie's most excruciating scenes are those in which Bill's son Billy (Rufus Read) comes to his father for sex advice. As in his first film, Solondz ventures deeply into some of what little taboo territory is left in modern cinema. The fatherly advice is frank, helpful, and salacious all at once. At its most basic, these painful conversations get at the root of the male misidentification of sexual gratification with manhood and self-assurance. After Bill has been apprehended, there is a final, incredible dialogue between father and son in which the son is both repelled by his father's actions and hurt that he cannot share in them.

Original distributor October Films (and its parent company Universal) dropped the controversial film and agreed to its release by production company Good Machine.

Solondz's relentless authenticity gives *Happiness* and its characters an abiding humanity. While some will be repulsed by his refusal to make a pedophile into a monster, Solondz's method is to go deep into forbidden inner life and familial relationships to reveal the essence of what makes us human: our struggle for the acceptance of self and others. "I am trying to be as truthful as I can," Solondz told interviewer Glenn Collins of *Indie* magazine. "Dysfunctionality is an aspect of the world we all live in. But the point is not dysfunction, alienation or misery, but that we are struggling through it to achieve some kind of intimacy. To me, it always comes down to the characters' need for real tenderness. I don't see these as ugly people."

Ugly they're not, but they can be shallow and cruel and terribly misguided. Unfolding like the petals of a noxious flower, *Happiness* includes opportunities for all its characters to obtain satisfaction and redemption of a sort. Solondz flirts with Hollywood happy endings in which his lovesick losers are paired off, only to lampoon them with schmaltzy songs on the soundtrack. For Solondz's characters, there are no neat resolutions. Hoffman's heavy-breather eventually accedes to the supplications of the overweight Kristina (Camryn Mannheim), only to find out that she hates sex so much that she has killed and chopped up a lovesick doorman, Pedro, who has lost his wife and is so lonely that he somehow overcomes her. Kristina is at least double Pedro's weight, but insists that she was raped and that her revenge was a "crime of passion." She tells the whole story while eating ice cream at a diner. It is this mixture of outrageousness and realism that makes *Happiness* so disarming.

Gazzara's Lenny feels no passion, not even when coupling with a oversexed divorcee (Elizabeth Ashley). He's disappointed when his doctor tells him he's healthy as an ox and might live to be 100. With everyone in his Florida retirement community negotiating death or running from it, Lenny needs to connect somehow, so he heavily salts his food. There are many little things like that going on in *Happiness*, which is deviously clever.

In *Welcome to the Dollhouse*, Solondz was often overbearing. In *Happiness* he has found the right touch, mixing his heavy topics with a leavening of humor that pokes gentle fun at his characters without devastating them. This leavening helps you notice how none of his characters, at bottom, is morally superior or inferior to any other. Trish's self-righteous emotional cruelty to her children goes unpunished, but it is part of what will turn her children into dysfunctional adults.

The film is not a whine of victimology. Dr. Maplewood loses his wife and family. Joy's cruelty, though not as intentional nor egregious, nonetheless exacts the price of Andy's life. Whether people mean to hurt or do so unintentionally or simply can't help themselves, their acts have consequences. Solondz doesn't judge, but neither does he let anyone off the hook.

CREDITS

Trish Maplewood: Cynthia Stevenson
Helen Jordan: Lara Flynn Boyle
Joy Jordan: Jane Adams
Bill Maplewood: Dylan Baker
Allen: Philip Seymour Hoffman
Lenny Jordan: Ben Gazzara
Mona Jordan: Louise Lasser
Billy Maplewood: Rufus Read
Vlad: Jared Harris
Kristina: Camryn Manheim
Andy: Jon Lovitz
Diane: Elizabeth Ashley
Ann: Marla Maples

Origin: USA
Released: 1998
Production: Ted Hope and Christine Vachon for Killer Films; released by Good Machine
Direction: Todd Solondz
Screenplay: Todd Solondz
Cinematography: Maryse Alberti
Editing: Alan Oxman
Music: Robbie Kondor
Production design: Therese Deprez
Art direction: John Bruce
Costumes: Kathryn Nixon
Sound: Neil Danziger
MPAA rating: Unrated
Running Time: 135 minutes

Happiness possesses a remarkable ability to be uplifting even as it casts a dour gaze on the human condition. You recognize your own small failings writ large in the canvases of these tortured souls. People who think base instincts and shameful acts are not part of everyone's capacity will be repelled by *Happiness*. Those with a broader perspective may be amused or even exhilarated. More perceptive and more honest films that are this entertaining and clever are rare.

Solondz has taken a giant step into his own quirky and uncharted territory and toward a new definition of what it means to be genuine in filmmaking. Here is a movie that, in the words of *Entertainment Weekly* reviewer Owen Gleiberman, "marks the emergence of a major American filmmaker." Solondz is a force to be reckoned with on his own terms.

Happiness is not everyone's cup of tea. But it is hard to think of a contemporary film with a better ensemble of performances, and a more accurate, if excruciatingly, depiction of the way people talk and behave while desperately pursuing fulfillment. Awkward? Yes. But life's not a Hollywood movie. And real people aren't smooth operators.

—*Michael Betzold*

REVIEWS

Detroit Free Press. October 23, 1998.
Entertainment Weekly. October 16, 1998, p. 57.
New York Times. October 9, 1998, p. E10.
People. October 26, 1998, p. 37.
Premiere. November, 1998, p. 61.
Variety. May 18, 1998, p. 73.
Washington Post. October 23, 1998, p. 54.

Hard Core Logo

A punk rock odyssey.—Movie tagline

"The best rock 'n' roll movie in history! A masterful exercise in edgy virtuoso film craft, subversive propaganda and exhilarating entertainment."—John Griffin, *Montreal Gazette*

"Excellent! You should see this sharp, smart, riveting film."—Ben Greenman, *New Times Los Angeles*

"Zany, powerful and poignant! *Hard Core Logo* is pure punk poetry."—Bruce Kirkland, *Toronto Sun*

There's a magically still moment in Bruce McDonald's congenial but retrogressive *Hard Core Logo* when all the rough and frenetic neurosis of this fictional 'rockumentary' ceases, and what is revealed is a slice of the everyday extracted out of a countercultural expanse of psychosexual liberation. Billy Tallent (Callum Keith Rennie), the likable, wiry lead guitarist of the eponymous rock group, is seated on a porch in the country, in the early light of dawn, desultorily picking his guitar, after a night of psychedelic mindwrecking. It beats anything in the film's illustrious, and now classic, predecessor, Rob Reiner's *This Is Spinal Tap* (1982).

Sadly, McDonald appears so starstruck by Reiner's film, adopting its narrative device of intertitles and chapter headings, that despite all his own innovations, he cannot seem to shake off that structural mold. This has shot the film dead in the water. *Logo* doesn't emerge anything as innovative for 1998 as *Tap* does for 1982.

What made Reiner's film work so well was his willingness to fictionalize the supposedly real, even satirizing himself as the character of the documentary filmmaker *within* the film; McDonald, as a pseudo-serious documentarist, insists on remaining on the outside looking in, thereby offering us a staccato, insular 'punk film;' one that leaves non-punk viewers on the outside as well.

Hard Core Logo can thus best be described as a series of adulatory snippets of confession, interspersed with *cinema verite*—like flashes of life at the edge of sanity, all revolving around a punk rock group's tour across Western Canada. The jaunt is intended to aid a former star, Bucky Haight (Julian Richings), who has been forced into early retirement supposedly by an attempt on his life resulting in the loss of both his legs. By all indications, this reunion tour for Haight looks like the Logo's last. The occasion does, however, provide enough of a license for the band to party like it's 1999.

For all except the abusive lead singer and songwriter, Joe Dick (Hugh Dillon), who, beneath his spit-in-your-face recalcitrance, cannot come to terms with the virtuosic Billy

Lead singer Joe Dick (Hugh Dillon) about the band and guitarist Billy (Callum Keith Rennie): "There's different ways of looking at this: Billy wants the models and limousines; I'm happy with hookers and taxicabs."

leaving to join a far more successful group at the end of the tour. McDonald apparently believes this is all the story line he needs to adopt from the Michael Turner novel on which the screenplay is based. This allows him to indulge in MTV-like cuts of the Logo performing on stage, their ordeal of confinement within their van on the road, and individual members of the group confessing to his camera in sound bites about how they feel about each other.

When the group manages to locate the famous Bucky on his country estate, he turns out to be walking around, fit and healthy, enjoying the life of a recluse. At this point, Joe admits to having lied about Bucky so as to get Billy to tour. Bucky, on his part, proves a gallant host. With a punko-cratic air, he distributes tiny pieces of his sacrament-on-paper, even to the filmmaker, looking into his camera and towards us, while saying, "We're all in this together."

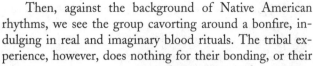

Director Bruce McDonald has described the film as the last in his rock 'n' roll trilogy following *Roadkill* and *Highway 61*.

Then, against the background of Native American rhythms, we see the group cavorting around a bonfire, indulging in real and imaginary blood rituals. The tribal experience, however, does nothing for their bonding, or their musical creativity, and so, proves just another episode in the dissolution of the band, and their youth.

Joe's jealous rage at Billy's plan to cop out comes to a head during the group's final concert in Edmonton. John Oxenberger (John Pyper-Ferguson), the hirsute bass player whose musings on the soundtrack serve as the group's conscience, provides a prelude by reciting barely decipherable poetry about being "dead on a bedrock of evil." He then thrashes his guitar, while the wild-eyed hippie drummer, Pipefitter (Bernie Coulson), destroys his drum set, as Joe spits in Billy's face and lashes out at him, drawing blood. Billy's head remains bloody but unbowed, the mere fact of survival having been established as an indicator of triumph on the punk rock scene.

Outside the stage door, Joe inquires of McDonald, still hiding behind his camera, "Got everything you needed? What about one last shot?" The next moment, a gunshot from the dark strikes Joe dead.

Critics seem to have been receptive to the film's unwavering 'mockumentary' style, calling it an "arresting look at rock's unchecked excesses" (Renee Graham in the *Boston Globe*), and even "a kind of romantic elegy to the punk-rock movement" (Stephen Holden in *The New York Times*), with John Anderson in *Newsday* vouching for it as "the best rock movie of the past several years" and more.

—*Vivek Adarkar*

CREDITS

Joe Dick: Hugh Dillon
Billy Tallent: Callum Keith Rennie
Pipefitter: Bernie Coulson
John Oxenberger: John Pyper-Ferguson
Bucky Haight: Julian Richings

Origin: Canada
Released: 1996, 1998
Production: Christine Haebler and Brian Dennis; released by Rolling Thunder Pictures and Cowboy Booking International
Direction: Bruce McDonald
Screenplay: Noel S. Baker; based on the novel by Michael Turner
Cinematography: Danny Nowak
Editing: Reginald Harkema
Production design: David Willson
Music: Schaun Tozer
MPAA rating: R
Running Time: 92 minutes

REVIEWS

Boston Globe. December 4, 1998.
Entertainment Weekly. November 27, 1998, p. 56.
Los Angeles Times. November 13, 1998, p. F16.
New York Times. November 13, 1998, p. E18.
Newsday. November 13, 1998.
Variety. May 27, 1996, p. 70.

Hard Rain

A simple plan. An instant fortune. Just add water.—Movie tagline

"Top action chemistry between Slater and Freeman! This cast delivers heart-pounding thrills!"—Ron Brewington, *American Urban Radio Networks*

"An impressive spectacle."—Dan DiNicola, *Daily Gazette Albany*

"The efffects are startlingly vivid."—Chris Hewitt, *Knight-Ridder*

"A compelling, fast-paced thriller of the first order."—Jeffrey Lyons, *NBC-TV*

Box Office: $19,870,567

The most daring aspect of the overlooked *Hard Rain* is not its unusual action sequences involving boats and jet skis in a flooded town, nor its disaster-epic scenes of a breaking dam washing away homes. The best part is that it doesn't have any over-the-top villains. The film's criminal mastermind is a quiet, sometimes likeable fellow named Jim (Morgan Freeman), who's ruthless enough in his pursuit of a three-million-dollar haul from an armored car but decent enough not to want to spray people with bullets just for the heck of it. *Hard Rain* is a brave, almost believable story of rather ordinary people in unusual circumstances who all are afflicted, more or less, with the understandable desire to make some easy money.

Originally shot in 1996 and titled *The Flood*, this film was retooled, long delayed and renamed in an effort to move it away from the overloaded disaster-flick category and position it more as an action suspense film, where it belongs. Written by Graham Yost, who penned the hit *Speed* (1996), it also shares three of that film's producers. Released early in 1998, *Hard Rain* ended up, by a quirk of timing, to be a contemporary of *Titanic*, a far more acclaimed film with which it shares several scenes of heroes and heroines trapped by rising water. Though *Titanic* got much greater attention, *Hard Rain* has more suspense and inventiveness in its danger, far more ingenious action, and more realistic characters.

Underneath its often overlong cops-and-robbers chase scenes through the flooded fictional town of Huntingburg, Indiana, *Hard Rain* is a muted story of working-class rage. With a bluesy score by Christopher Young, sophomore director Mikael Salomon (who debuted with *The Abyss*) sets us down in the dark, flooded streets of small-town USA, a place where hardworking people don't feel they've gotten their just desserts. Three cops have stayed behind to protect the town. The Sheriff (Randy Quaid) and his partner Wayne (Mark Rolston) are cynical, beaten-down working stiffs who are glad to see the oily mayor leaving town. The Sheriff is a lame duck, having recently lost a re-election campaign after 20 years on the job, and when the mayor drives away with the rest of the late evacuees, the Sheriff and his partner discuss the idea of torching his house, or putting a dead cow in it. Their young, still-uncorrupted partner Phil (Peter Murnik) wants only to do his job and get to higher ground.

The intriguing thing about Yost's script is that he doesn't feel the need to explain such simmering resentments. His characters' personalities and motivations are revealed through their actions, not a lot of talk. But when their rage and frustration boil over, they connect to a presumed shared experience with an audience, based on unspoken understandings among working people. The characters in *Hard Rain* have struggled, as most Americans do, and in the face of disaster their tensions rise with the water, and their seamier side surfaces. The prospect of stealing money initially appeals to the already criminalized and marginalized, but as social barriers break down and the disaster grows, the idea grows more intriguing to all the characters, and why not? It's not only criminals who are tempted by greed.

As the rains fall and the dam above the town keeps releasing more water, two armored-car drivers pick up loot from banks, which are eager to get their assets out of the disaster area. Charlie (Ed Asner), the older driver, is pricklier than usual, and barks back at the ribbing of his nephew and partner Tom (Christian Slater). It's a lousy job, Charlie finally admits, putting your life on the line protecting other people's money. On their way out of town, the truck breaks down in the rising flood. Stranded, another truck pulls up, and the two uniformed men signal in the glare of a blinding searchlight mounted atop the oncoming truck. We've already met the truck's occupants in a scene at a local bar. The motley gang is headed by Freeman's stoic Jim and includes an ex-high-school science teacher, Mr. Mehlor (Dann Florek), who provides technical knowhow; and two young men, the Bible-quoting Ray (Ricky Harris), and the jittery, loose-cannon Kenny (Michael Goorjian).

Despite Jim's orders not to shoot, Kenny starts a gunfight and Charlie dies. When the gang arrives at the truck, Tom has made his escape with the bag of money. He swims

Except for a week of outdoor shooting in Indiana, the film was shot inside an airplane hangar in Palmdale, California.

to the cemetery and ties it to a partially submerged tombstone, knowing his life depends on being able to lead the criminals to the loot. Then the chases begin. The first is the most inventive. Tom flees to a middle school, and Kenny and Ray pursue him on jet skis down the flooded hallways. It's more than a bit bizarre, as the bad guys hunt down their prey by roaring like overgrown kids through the school.

Eventually, Tom seizes one of the jet skis and finds refuge in a church, where he is bonked with a crucifix by the feisty Karen (Minnie Driver), who figures he's a looter. Karen has just spent eight months restoring the church's stained-glass windows, which of course will be great targets for criminals on speeding boats. Despite warnings from the lawmen to evacuate, she's determined to stay behind to pump water and keep her art dry. When Tom wakes up, he's in a jail cell. He tells the Sheriff about the robbery, but Wayne, who doesn't trust him, keeps him locked up. Phil is told to take Karen to safety, but Karen pushes him out of the boat and returns to church. There's a sudden dam release, the water rises, and Tom is trapped in his cell. It's Karen to the rescue, and Tom finds an emotional reason for living as they flee the criminals, hiding in a partially submerged car and then in the home of a pair of senior citizens. The shrewish Doreen (in a fine turn by the veteran Betty White) and her henpecked husband Henry (Richard Dysart) provide most of the film's comic relief, though it is sometimes lame.

With a few more plot twists and plenty of watery chases, the tension builds. The gang of four continues to terrorize the town while the Sheriff and his partners seem incompetent, always three steps behind the criminals. It finally becomes clear there's a reason for that. In a showdown gunfight in the submerged cemetery, the tables turn as the Sheriff declares he's had enough of protecting the flea-bitten town. "For twenty years I've been eatin' shit for breakfast, lunch and dinner," Quaid declares. "Now I'm changin' the menu. From now on, everything I eat is gonna be shit-free."

In the film's final half-hour, the film's minor characters fall by the wayside, victims of gunshots, drowning and electrocution. Left standing tall are the three principals: Jim, who's seen his plans for easy money fall apart but remains determined; the Sheriff, who's now after the money; and Tom, who's thrown in with Jim. Jim tells Tom that Charlie was part of the robbery plot. Sitting in that truck for years with all that money, a man couldn't keep from thinking about stealing it, Jim argues, and Tom agrees. Tom now must decide between abiding by the law and going for the loot.

The final action is mostly in the church, where Jim and Tom are holed up, and it provides plenty of firepower. As befits the genre, there's blood and gruesome twists and turns, and a flying boat motor is one of the instruments of vengeance. Unfortunately, Karen, who provides most of the film's brains and courage in the first half, ends up playing the damsel-in-distress role, handcuffed to a stairwell. This gives Tom the opportunity to return the favor and rescue her as the dam breaks and a tidal wave ruins the town.

Hard Rain is no masterpiece. The dialogue is sometimes corny and the action contrived. But the suspense is thick, the characters murky and intriguing, and the action relentless enough to make for an entertaining film. The special effects are worth the price of admission—a collapsing dam, uprooted houses, boats roaring through stained-glass windows. And there are a few clever touches—including a scene in which the sword of a submerged Civil War statue ruins the propeller of a boat.

The actors are serviceable. Freeman is characteristically stoic and somewhat bland, but he captures both the depravity and the submerged decency of a complicated man who has chosen the crooked path knowingly, not through some kind of compulsion. Quaid is a believable good old boy whose startling transformation rings as true as it can. Driver is fine in an underwritten part that diminishes as the film progresses. And Slater might revive his uneven career with an understated but finely nuanced performance as the Everyman making moral choices under fire.

It's hard to understand why *Hard Rain* was shelved for so long and then received such poor reviews and middling box-office reception. Evocative of 1997's underrated *Breakdown*, *Hard Rain* is a suspenseful, action-packed thriller which doesn't leave its brains behind. Maybe that's why it failed: it re-

CREDITS

Jim: Morgan Freeman
Tom: Christian Slater
Sheriff: Randy Quaid
Karen: Minnie Driver
Charlie: Ed Asner
Henry: Richard Dysart
Doreen: Betty White

Origin: USA
Released: 1998
Production: Mark Gordon, Gary Levinsohn, and Ian Bryce for Mutual Film Co.; released by Paramount Pictures
Direction: Mikael Solomon
Screenplay: Graham Yost
Cinematography: Peter Menzies Jr.
Editing: Paul Hirsch
Music: Christopher Young
Production design: J. Michael Riva
Art direction: Richard Mays
Sound: Lee Orloff
Visual effects supervision: Ed Jones
Special effects supervision: John Frazier
MPAA rating: R
Running Time: 96 minutes

fuses to make its characters into crowd-pleasing lunatics. It also keeps its disaster in perspective, making it an ever-more-menacing backdrop to the action rather than the centerpiece of the film. It's not the rising water that's chilling in *Hard Rain*, it's the rising malevolence and desperation that overwhelm the decency of its characters. Credibly, *Hard Rain* illustrates that crisis is a test of character that produces sometimes surprising revelations about what's inside of people under stress. And it does so without ever getting preachy or maudlin. For those who like their action and their morality straight up, *Hard Rain* is a stiff little jolt of unexpected potency.

—*Michael Betzold*

REVIEWS

Cinescape. March/April, 1997, p. 40.
Detroit News. January 16, 1998, p. 3D.
Entertainment Weekly. January 23, 1998, p. 39.
Los Angeles Times. January 16, 1998, p. F10.
New York Times. January 16, 1998, p. E10.
People. January 26, 1998, p. 21.
Rolling Stone. February 5, 1998, p. 67.
USA Today. January 16, 1998, p. 4D.
Variety. January 12, 1998, p. 63.
Village Voice. January 27, 1998, p. 68.

Hav Plenty

Lee Plenty has never been lucky in love. This weekend, that's about to change.—Movie tagline

"One of the year's most charming debuts! *Hav Plenty* is a delight!"—Marshall Fine, *Gannett Newspaper*

"Director Chris Cherot has created one of the most original and likeable characters to pop up in a movie in quite a while . . . a hybrid of Woody Allen and Spike Lee!"—Stephen Holden, *New York Times*

"Clever, romantic and sophisticated! *Hav Plenty* has a lot of heart!"—John Anderson, *Newsday*

 Box Office: $2,337,637

Barely 15 years ago, film theorists were questioning the value of young blacks becoming filmmakers within a film industry dominated by whites. Breakthrough works, such as Spike Lee's *She's Gotta Have It* (1986) and Darnell Martin's *I Like It Like That* (1994) put an end to such speculation with full-blown practice, but only partly. Those films, and others like them, seemed pretty sure of themselves of what 'black' and 'white' stood for as cultural indicators. What is so refreshing about Christopher Scott Cherot's debut feature *Hav Plenty* is that it shuffles these very terms of reference, and comes up with, what can oxymoronically be called, a 'white black movie,' or perhaps

 Christopher Scott Cherot on the idea for his film: "I was a heart-broken, lovesick fool and I had to do something to get over it. Writing helped."

a 'black white movie.' Either way, what we end up feeling grateful for is that it isn't a 'black and white movie.'

What makes this ingenuous erotic comedy, supposedly based on "a true story," so disarming is the manner in which its protagonist, Lee Plenty, a struggling graduate student, portrayed by the director himself, appears so removed from the power plays linked to the bed-as-battlefield. His stance allows Cherot, as both actor, writer and director, to tear down some of the basic conventions of a white dominated cinema. Cherot's film storytelling thus allows Lee to address us directly via the camera, taking us into his confidence, as it were, so that we remain on his side while he has fun with the unsuspecting tigresses who seek involvement with him.

As expected, the one young woman who doesn't try to get any closer to him than she already is is the one Lee is serious about, on the days when he can get himself to be serious about anything, that is. Thus, through all the muddling under, over and around the sheets, the film's focus of desire remains the willful, intelligent, strikingly attractive and successful Havilland Savage (Chenoa Maxwell), who is engaged to an immensely popular rap artist, Michael (Hill Harper), who plays the role of fiancé only when he can spare the time.

The film opens with the peculiar intimacy shared by Lee and Hav, as she is called. No doubt feeling guilty about her super-rich family background, Hav extends any kind of help she can to the financially strapped, yet hang loose and fancy free, Lee, convinced she can keep him at the precise distance she wants. Lee is in fact living in her New York apartment when we see him first. Hav, who has gone to her mother's house in Washington, D.C. for the New Year's weekend, rings to shake him out of his introverted stupor, and invite him over.

The film then becomes a revel of sorts, as Lee has to ward off, in turn, the sirens he finds at the house, so that he can maintain the mental equilibrium he needs for the book he is writing on his laptop. First to advance on him is the slinky, haughty Caroline (Tammi Katherine Jones). "What do you do when you're not babysitting Havilland's cat?" is her idea of an opening line. "You have lipstick on your teeth," Lee shoots back, matter-of-factly. Not to be deterred, Caroline gets her way, in the early hours of the New Year, when she climbs over Lee as The Pointer Sisters begin their rendition of "Fire" on the soundtrack. Before the kiss that is sung about can take place, however, Lee turns his face away. This results in the song, like Caroline, stopping abruptly just before its title refrain.

In the morning, Lee is urged by Hav to stay on, so that he can serve as an escort , first to a lunch with relatives, then on a visit to her grandmother's. Michael isn't the only obstacle, or source of tension, preventing Lee and Hav from attaining greater intimacy. Lee's conscience leads him to erupt when he learns of Hav's plans to employ her married

> Director/writer Christopher Scott Cherot wound up playing the role of Lee Plenty when the actor originally cast bowed out two weeks before the start of shooting.

sister, Leigh (Robinne Lee) as her personal assistant. "Who do you think you are that you can talk to me like that?" Hav flares. "Who do you think you are that I can't?" Lee retorts, to which Hav has no answer.

It is at this stage that the film's narrative begins to thin out, as there is no real advancement in the relationship between Lee and Hav. Instead, Cherot, as writer, provides one scene of domestic socializing after another. Even scenes of Lee "curing" the affable Leigh of her married woes, and the misunderstanding this leads to with her husband, Felix (Reginald James), cannot fill this dramatic lacuna. We thus feel the need for a subplot, something tangential to Lee's need for Hav, that could have lent the film some ideological resonance. It is to Cherot's credit that his comedic style always keeps us amused, so we don't really tire of the goings-on.

When Hav feels that Lee is the true thing in her life, she still cannot get him to understand her for "the freak" she feels she is. Lee, on the other hand, perceives her reaching out to him as a "power trip." Much later, of course, he admits his love for her in a letter, after which the film cuts to an epilogue of sorts, where we see some of the events we have been watching in the form of the film that Lee has made, which is being screened at a local festival. This becomes the occasion for the film's upbeat ending. A distribution deal seems to bring Lee, now on the brink of success, and Hav, still single, together again.

Reviewers have been unable to resist the film's infectious charm, Dave Kehr in the *New York Daily News* calling it "highly entertaining." Stephen Holden in *The New York Times* can be taken to represent the thrust of critical opinion when he writes: "*Hav Plenty* may be a featherweight social comedy without a political bone in its body, but its characters are refreshingly buoyant." He then concludes, "Lee is one of the most original and likable characters to pop up in a movie in quite a while."

—*Vivek Adarkar*

CREDITS

Havilland Savage: Chenoa Maxwell
Lee Plenty: Christopher Scott Cherot
Michael Simmons: Hill Harper
Caroline Gooden: Tammi Katherine Jones
Grandma Moore: Betty Vaughn
Leigh Darling: Robinne Lee
Felix Darling: Reginald James

Origin: USA
Released: 1997
Production: Christopher Scott Cherot and Robyn M. Greene for Wanderlust Pictures and Edmonds Entertainment; released by Miramax Films
Direction: Christopher Scott Cherot
Screenplay: Christopher Scott Cherot
Cinematography: Kerwin De Vonish
Editing: Christopher Scott Cherot
Sound: Damian Canelos
Music: Wendy Melvoin, Lisa Coleman
MPAA rating: R
Running Time: 105 minutes

REVIEWS

Entertainment Weekly. June 26, 1998, p. 101.
Los Angeles Times. June 19, 1998, p. F8.
New York Daily News. June 19, 1998.
New York Times. June 19, 1998, p. E26.
People. June 29, 1998, p. 34.
Variety. October 20, 1997, p. 71.
Village Voice. June 23, 1998, p. 140.

He Got Game

The father, the son and the holy game—Movie tagline

"This is a wonderful father-son story."—Gene Siskel, *Chicago Tribune*

"Mr. Lee returns full blast to what he does best . . . Mr. Washington gives a splendid, carefully measured performance."—Janet Maslin, *New York Times*

"Ambitious and absorbing."—David Ansen, *Newsweek*

"*He Got Game* is a triumph! The first great film of 1998!"—Neil Rosen, *NY-1 News*

"Two thumbs up!"—*Siskel & Ebert*

"*He Got Game* is a real movie, and I bet you haven't seen many of those lately."—Amy Taubin, *Village Voice*

"Spike Lee sets his own rules, and comes up a winner."—Joe Morgenstern, *Wall Street Journal*

 Box Office: $21,567,853

The clock is ticking for temporarily released con Jake Shuttlesworth (Denzel Washington) to reconcile with his basketball star son Jesus (Ray Allen) in Spike Lee's *He's Got Game.*

S pike Lee's *He Got Game* is the story of a high school basketball star from Coney Island which succeeds neither as a sports film nor the social parable the filmmaker apparently intends. Coming on the heels of *Hoop Dreams* (1994), *He Got Game* is another story of inner-city kids trying to make the jump to the big time. But it lacks the genuine tension of *Hoop Dreams*. Almost the entire film takes place in the two weeks leading up to number one high school prospect Jesus Shuttlesworth's decision about which college he's going to attend. Into this shallow vessel of the basketball recruitment game Lee attempts to pour a muddled fable about American values—and fails badly.

The plot is ridiculous. Jake Shuttlesworth (Denzel Washington) is a felon at Attica Prison who loves playing basketball. One day the warden (Ned Beatty) makes him an offer he can't refuse. It seems the governor is a big basketball fan, and he wants to see Jesus Shuttlesworth go to his alma mater, Big State University. The warden says that if Jake can sign his son for Big State, the governor will reduce his time. But from the vague words of the warden's promise, it's obvious the authorities are going to renege on their deal.

 Jesus' (Ray Allen) reaction upon seeing his father for the first time in years: "I don't have a father. Why is there a stranger in the house?"

The warden stages a food poisoning incident to get Jake out of prison for two weeks. He's guarded by two parole officers, a mean black man (Jim Brown) and a more forgiving white partner (Joseph Lyle Taylor). They put an electronic tether on Jake, set him up in a fleabag hotel, and give him a deadline to deliver Jesus or return to prison.

Jake surprises his daughter Mary (Zelda Harris) on her way home from school. She invites him up to the highrise apartment she shares with her older brother. But when Jesus (Ray Allen, who plays with the National Basketball Association's Milwaukee Bucks) comes home, he orders Jake to leave, telling him he no longer considers him his father.

Belatedly it becomes clear why Jesus can't forgive his dad. It's not just that Jake has pushed Jesus hard, ever since he was a little kid, to be the basketball star Jake wished he had been. A flashback shows late nights on the neighborhood basketball court, with father and boy playing one-on-one. Tired of his dad's endless taunting, Jesus throws the ball over a fence. That sends Jake into a tantrum which he carries into the house. When Jesus remains defiant, Jake starts to pummel the boy. His mother steps in, and Jake pushes her. She hits her head on a kitchen counter, falls to the floor, and is instantly dead.

It's the kind of death that could occur only in a Spike Lee film, and so is the retribution. Jake is convicted of murder for a situation that surely should not merit more than a manslaughter charge. Apparently, Lee can't be bothered with the credibility of his central plot premises.

Lee's approach to this saga is pretentious—complete with an Aaron Copland score and endless slow-motion shots of arching basketballs against Normal Rockwell-like backgrounds. The stylistic flourish can't mask a story as flimsy as a dime-novel melodrama: A father goes to prison for accidentally killing his wife. He gets one last chance to redeem himself with a phony mission in which his hateful son must do him a favor. In doing so, the son overcomes his own venom and grief. It's pure sop.

Lee, as usual, telegraphs his messages. If he were on a basketball court, all his passes would be intercepted. Not only does he name his central character Jesus, he subjects him to an endless series of temptations. Everyone's coming at Jesus with money and promises. His girlfriend, Lala (Rosario Dawson), is two-timing him with the partner of a sports agent. The agent tries to give him a $35,000 watch and a quarter-million-dollar sports car. His uncle, Bubba (Bill Nunn), tries to lure him with a brand new Lexus bestowed by an unnamed college ("they said it would be O.K. as long as it's in my name," he tells Jesus). Even his high school coach tries to hand off $10,000 in cash. During a recruiting visit to one college, a would-be teammate plies him with co-eds. Even his kid sister Mary feels she deserves a piece of the action.

Lee portrays Jesus as the last hope for virtue in a society despoiled by the crass mercantilism of basketball recruiting. It's an interesting idea for a filmmaker who has his own commercial contract with Nike, one of the leading proponents of the apparel endorsements that have corrupted collegiate athletics. Perhaps it's understandable, then, that for all Jesus's self-righteous piety (he likes to take the city bus to school because "these are my people"), he is not above skimming a little off the top himself, dipping in a few co-eds and taking cash from his coach to pay for a nice apartment.

Constantly cartoonish, *He Got Game* goes way over the top in satirizing the recruitment frenzy. Montages of real basketball coaches sing the praises of Jesus, video tributes pop up everywhere, and one college coach (John Turturro) goes down on his knees to pray that God deliver Jesus to him. Lee relentlessly exploits the parodies involving his character's name before revealing that his dad simply named him after an old NBA star's nickname. Of course, it's hard to miss the point that the never-subtle Lee is making by naming his character for a savior: that basketball is seen as the only salvation for young black men from the ghetto.

Yet Coney Island seems far away from the south-side Chicago of *Hoop Dreams*. Though the old resort is a little seedy, Jesus and his pals don't seem underprivileged at all.

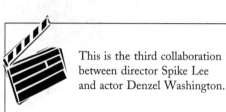

This is the third collaboration between director Spike Lee and actor Denzel Washington.

Though one of the TV bios in the film describes Jesus as being "deprived," none of these young people appear to be deprived. Maybe that explains why Lee inserts a sequence in which a local crime lord outlines all the ways athletes from the 'hood can be waylaid: drugs, alcohol, gambling, and sex.

It's hard to imagine a more misogynist film. *He Got Game* paints females as the dangerous enemy, waiting to leech the precious bodily fluids from their prey or betray them for a pound of flesh. The petty crime boss warns that women can give you HIV. Warning Jesus about his girlfriend, Lala, Jake talks of how craven women can exploit men's weaknesses, as Delilah did to Sampson. In another flashback, we see Lala deceiving Jesus about birth control in order to trap Jesus with a child he doesn't want and the ball and chain of family life. Lee's Madonna/whore complex is in full rut in this film. The murdered mother is almost literally the Madonna, since she is the mother of Jesus, and she seems to have saintly patience. On the other pole, the white co-eds at a college Jesus visits are supercharged sexual vixens; in one of the film's many embarrassingly laughable scenes, Jesus is escorted into a dorm room where two buxom co-eds are waiting half-naked on a bed.

Then there's the nonsensical subplot which pairs up Jake with a prostitute named Dakota (Milla Jovovich), who works out of the room next door to where he is staying. She's the stereotyped whore with a heart of gold. Even more preposterously, Jake, though locked away for more than six years, only wants to have heartfelt talks with her, and when they do have sex, he is impotent. What's going on with these scenes, other than demonstrating Jake's unbelievable mild-manneredness, is anyone's guess. Lee does have to fill up his 136 minutes with something other than Jesus continually announcing he hasn't made his decision yet.

In the end, the climatic scene in which Jake and Jesus go one-on-one to see whether Jesus will agree to sign with Big State is a flop. Allen was recruited to lend authenticity to the basketball scenes, but he so outmatches Washington that the tension of the showdown is missing. And since Allen's on-court moves aren't exploited sufficiently—there is no real game action—it seems that casting him was a big mistake, because his wooden acting destroys many scenes.

For all of Lee's attempts at lyrical shots of pick-up games and efforts to make basketball an icon for the American dream with the Copland score, there is surprisingly little in *He Got Game* about the guts of basketball. Lee himself adores basketball, but he can't seem to convey the reason for that admiration. Longing camera shots don't do it. Gazing adoringly at a sport doesn't make it riveting.

Similarly, Lee's big gamble with the Copland score is a loser. There's at least a little authenticity in the few scenes when the rap group Public Enemy provides the backdrop. But the ubiquitous pastoral Copland orchestral music is jarringly out of place. Again, it's painfully obvious what Lee is trying to do. See, he is saying, isn't basketball really the American pastime of our era? His use of Copland in other scenes, like Jake's big night with Dakota, makes no sense at all.

CREDITS

Jake Shuttlesworth: Denzel Washington
Jesus Shuttlesworth: Ray Allen
Dakota Burns: Milla Jovovich
Lala Bonilla: Rosario Dawson
Coleman (Bogger) Sykes: Hill Harper
Mary Shuttlesworth: Zelda Harris
Spivey: Jim Brown
Warden Wyatt: Ned Beatty
Uncle Bubba: Bill Nunn
Martha Shuttlesworth: Lonette McKee
Coach Billy Sunday: John Turturro

Origin: USA
Released: 1998
Production: Jon Kilik, Spike Lee for 40 Acres and a Mule Filmworks production; released by Buena Vista
Direction: Spike Lee
Screenplay: Spike Lee
Cinematography: Malik Hassan Sayeed
Editing: Barry Alexander Brown
Production design: Wynn Thomas
Art direction: David Stein
Set decoration: Carolyn Cartwright
Costumes: Sandra Hernandez
Sound: Allan Byer, Mathew Price
Music: Aaron Copland
MPAA rating: R
Running Time: 134 minutes

Neither does much of the stunningly insipid dialogue. Lee once had an ear for street talk, but he has been so long in the ranks of the media elite that he seems to have lost it. And all the white people in the film speak stilted lines, especially a rich sports agent who gives such an unconvincing pitch that it's a wonder clients don't run from him.

Under an Afro hairdo, Washington tries to inhabit Jake, but his character is so meek he's almost bland, and his few explosions of temper seem to emerge from nowhere. Washington is great at conveying the pain of his many losses, but we never understand the reason for Jake's smoldering. We are meant to believe he is a hero for pushing his son so hard because that's the only way he thinks Jesus will escape Coney Island. But *He Got Game* never seems to resolve its ambivalence about the role of basketball in dominating the dreams of deprived black youth. What showed early promise as a depiction of sports obsession quickly degenerates into an aimless and vapid paean to sport and a sentimental story of father-son conflict and its resolution. With his usual grandstanding techniques, Lee's canvas seems large, but it is stretched thin over a thoroughly unconvincing plot.

—*Michael Betzold*

REVIEWS

Boxoffice. June, 1998, p. 75.
Chicago Tribune. May 1, 1998, p. 4.
Detroit Free Press. May 1, 1998, p. D1.
Detroit News. May 1, 1998, p. 3D.
Entertainment Weekly. May 8, 1998, p. 46.
Los Angeles Times. May 1, 1998, p. F1.
New York Times. May 1, 1998, p. E16.
People. May 4, 1998, p. 31.
Rolling Stone. May 14, 1998, p. 63.
Sight and Sound. October, 1998, p. 44.
USA Today. May 1, 1998, p. 11E.
Village Voice. May 5, 1998, p. 110.
Washington Post. May 1, 1998, p. 53.

Henry Fool

"A career milestone and a film that could become a landmark in American independent cinema. A hilarious comedy."—Kevin Thomas, *Los Angeles Times*

"Big, audacious! . . . This breakthrough film is the most energetic and far reaching work [Hartley's] done. A hilarious comedy of art, commerce and friendship."—Janet Maslin, *New York Times*

"Astounding!"—John Anderson, *Newsday*

"Spectacular."—Leah Rozen, *People*

"Brutally funny!"—Peter Travers, *Rolling Stone*

"There are levels of truth and observation here that few filmmakers ever reach."—Nick LaSalle, *San Francisco Chronicle*

Box Office: $1,385,002

In Hal Hartley's *Henry Fool,* a common garbage man named Simon Grim (James Urbaniak) becomes a literary sensation under the tutelage of a mysterious stranger who changes his life forever. Hartley has had a certain cult following for years, but many reviews proclaimed *Henry Fool* a breakthrough. *Time*'s Richard Corliss, for example, wrote that, "in Hal Hartley's world the pain blends with humor in a way that gives one a reason to believe in the complexity of life and the future of movies." Unfortunately, this feels like a huge overstatement for a film that may work as a literary conceit but not as a fully realized story. *Henry Fool* wants to be many things—an exploration of friendship and dead-end lives and a meditation on the writing life and the vicissitudes of celebrity, but it bogs down in pointless, highly stylized dialogue and sloppy, unfocused storytelling without offering real insight into the friendship at its core.

Simon is a sadsack, nerdy garbage man who lives a bleak existence with his depressed mother, Mary (Maria Porter), and his promiscuous sister, Fay (Parker Posey in a raunchy, vital performance). Into his life one day walks Henry Fool (Thomas Jay Ryan), an intellectual fellow who constantly speaks in philosophical digressions and quickly takes up residence in the basement of the Grim house. Henry is the archetypal outsider who comes out of nowhere to shake things

Henry (Thomas Jay Ryan) to Simon (James Urbaniak): "I've been bad—repeatedly."

up. He has supposedly lived a colorful life and, we eventually learn, is an ex-con who spent seven years in prison for statutory rape. A man of Joycean ambitions who declares, "I'm sort of what you might call in exile," he is writing an epic work he calls "my confession," an all-encompassing tome that is "a philosophy, a poetics, a politics if you will, a literature of protest, a novel of ideas, a pornographic magazine of truly comic-book proportions."

Henry Fool starts with an intriguing premise—the meeting of two idiosyncratic characters who, at least initially, are amusing in their interchanges and make an oddly complementary pair. Henry typically pontificates on some large, esoteric philosophical or literary issue in elliptical sentences, and Simon speaks in short, halting sentences or fragments befitting a nervous and shy loner with a limited view of the world. As time passes, however, he sometimes sounds more like Henry.

Because Simon has difficulty expressing himself verbally, Henry gives him a notebook and pencil and tells him to write down his thoughts, and very quickly Simon writes an epic poem that has a profound influence on their small Queens community and then the world beyond. Henry immediately recognizes the brilliance of the work—Simon naturally writes in verse without really knowing what he is doing—and gets it read by various locals. The mute daughter of the owner of the donut shop/convenience store inexplicably starts singing when she reads Simon's work, and, as more people read it, a storm of controversy swells. A high school newspaper publishes some of his work, and the parents' association denounces him for his poem's alleged pornographic content. No matter how widely read and praised Simon's poem becomes—Henry eventually puts part of it on the Internet when traditional publishing routes prove futile—we feel distanced from the work's impact. We hear about the public reaction but never understand how it affects Simon.

Indeed, the main problem is the character of Simon, who remains a cipher throughout the film. We can see how Henry's inspiration is offering Simon a way out of a deadening home life, but we never learn what motivates him as a writer. The specific content of his work (as well as that of Henry's) is kept secret from us on purpose so that it will not lose its air of mystery and can stand for general literary ambitions, but, because we never know Simon's passion, nothing is really at stake. We cannot get involved emotionally because we are always distanced from the characters and their motives.

Simon seems to be a perpetual wreck disparaged by just about everyone except the eccentric Henry and later the poem's supporters. Simon initially is brutalized by a bully named Warren (Kevin Corrigan) and his girlfriend after Simon sees them having sex in an alley (the girl later becomes one of Simon's fans), and Fay throws boiling water on her brother when he mentions her sex life. Simon is so downtrodden to begin with that even his mother's eventual suicide has little lasting effect; it feels like an arbitrary plot point emphasizing what we have seen from the beginning—the utter despair of the Grim household.

At the periphery is a community of supporting characters, including the proprietor of the donut shop where Henry and Simon hang out and a clergyman who questions his faith and who advises Simon when he gets a book deal. (Simon's publisher—recommended by Henry—is a fatuous sort who rejects the manuscript until its Internet success convinces him it will make a lot of money.) The most troubling figure is Warren, who undergoes so many changes in character, all of them negative, it is hard to see him as anything but a simplistic character type representing the worst in American culture. He begins as the aimless punk who brutalizes Simon. When an election comes up, he finds direction as the ardent supporter of a right-wing candidate and even begins dressing in a suit and tie. (The candidate's name, incidentally, is Owen Feer, pronounced "Fear," thus compounding the heavy-handedness already inherent in names like "Grim" and "Fool.") When his candidate loses, Warren becomes disillusioned with the system and is worse than ever. By the end, he has married Vicky (Jan Leslie Harding), a local waitress, and abuses her and his stepdaughter, Pearl, who becomes the crux of the film's climax.

Garbage, waste, excrement—scatology is a recurring motif throughout. Simon's very existence is trashy—both literally and metaphorically. Our first glimpse of him is on his garbage truck, and garbage itself proves valuable when Simon finds some old books in his truck, retrieves them, and uses them as the start of his literary education. Later, Henry finds a kind of ring in a garbage truck, and it becomes the wedding ring in his marriage to Fay after he gets her pregnant. When Henry must support his family, he too gets a job as a garbage man (even Henry's connection to the publisher he recommends to Simon was as a janitor in an office building). However, the film takes its fascination with excrement to disgusting levels in two scenes: Simon vomits on one of the bullies who torments him early in the film, and Henry gets a severe, prolonged attack of diarrhea when he learns Fay is pregnant. Perhaps Hartley is making some kind of statement about the conversion of waste into art or emphasizing the ultimate degradation of this world, but such

Thomas Jay Ryan, who plays the title character, makes his feature film debut.

extremes seem gratuitous since we are immersed in squalor from the outset.

Simon reads Henry's work and thinks it is awful but tries to get it published when he finally gets his own book deal because he feels indebted to Henry. He fails his friend, and, in one of the film's strongest scenes, Simon must reveal to Henry that he does not like his writing but tried his best for him. In effect, he destroys Henry's illusions about himself as a writer. It is a moving confrontation because, for once, the characters are really discussing something that matters—the nature of their friendship and Simon's loyalty to Henry—instead of speaking in clever abstractions.

In the end, they have switched places. A few years after the main action of the film, Henry is now the garbage collector living a dead-end life with Fay and their little son, and Simon is living the writer's life—even being awarded the Nobel Prize. Ultimately, we can accept the fact that Simon is a man of genius and Henry really has no talent or ponder the possibility that fate has simply smiled on one and frowned on the other. The film, however, takes a final, arbitrary turn. Pearl, the little girl we have seen from time to time throughout the film, is now a teenager, knows Henry's sexual past, and offers him sexual favors for killing her stepfather, Warren. Henry goes to see if Vicky is all right, gets beat up by Warren, but kills him with a screwdriver in self-defense. Given his criminal background, Henry fears it will look like he killed Warren to have sex with Pearl.

CREDITS

Henry Fool: Thomas Jay Ryan
Simon Grim: James Urbaniak
Fay: Parker Posey
Mary: Maria Porter
Mr. Deng: James Saito
Warren: Kevin Corrigan

Origin: USA
Released: 1998
Production: Hal Hartley for True Fiction Pictures and The Shooting Gallery; released by Sony Pictures Classics
Direction: Hal Hartley
Screenplay: Hal Hartley
Cinematography: Michael Spiller
Editing: Steve Hamilton
Music: Hal Hartley
Production design: Steve Rosenzweig
Costumes: Jocelyn Joson
MPAA rating: R
Running Time: 138 minutes

Henry's little son seeks out the now-reclusive Simon, who comes to see his old friend and makes an extraordinary gift. He gives Henry his passport (after first altering it) so Henry can flee the country for Stockholm, where Simon is supposed to receive his Nobel Prize. Henry in effect becomes Simon—even garnering the praise of the airline clerk on his way to the plane. As its own little vignette, the ending is compelling, but, as the culmination of everything that has gone before, it feels tacked-on—a melodramatic plot twist designed to redeem a friendship whose essential nature was always sketchy at best.

While *Henry Fool* has moments of humor and even poignancy, as a whole it feels shallow and pointless, especially for its long–running time of two hours and eighteen minutes. Hartley seems to want to take us on a trip through the lives of two common men who aspire to the literary life and show the way fate deals them very different destinies, but he offers no real insight into these characters and their

relationships. *Henry Fool* finally does not rise above being a frustrating curiosity—a film whose premise has great potential for exploring grand themes of literature and culture but whose execution finally takes it nowhere.

—*Peter N. Chumo II*

REVIEWS

Boxoffice. April, 1998, p. 198.
Entertainment Weekly. June 26, 1998, p. 102.
Los Angeles Times. June 26, 1998, p. F10.
New York Times. June 19, 1998, p. E13.
People. July 6, 1998, p. 38.
Sight and Sound. November, 1998, p. 53.
Time. July 13, 1998.
Village Voice. June 23, 1998, p. 135.

The Hi-Lo Country

A land without boundaries. A passion without limits.—Movie tagline

"Ideally cast. A fascinating, uncompromising drama set against the wide open New Mexico skies. It captures the unspoiled beauty of the untamed West."—Bob Thomas, *Associated Press*

"Woody Harrelson gives the performance of his career."—Glenn Whipp, *Los Angeles Daily News*

"*The Hi-Lo Country* offers plenty of action and color. Woody Harrelson, in a spectacularly kinetic performance, whirls and dances through his part like a man on fire!"—Stephen Holden, *New York Times*

"A tense, superbly acted drama. One of the best films of the year!"—Jeffrey Lyons, *WNBC-TV*

"A solid winner! Go see it!"—Stewart Klein, *WNYW/FOX-TV*

The Hi-Lo Country sure sounded like a good idea on paper. It was directed by Stephen Frears, the English director of a slew of acclaimed films like *My Beautiful Laundrette* (1985), *Dangerous Liaisons* (1988), and *The Grifters* (1990). The stars are noteworthy and respected actors like Woody Harrelson, Billy Crudup, and Patricia Arquette. The writer, Walon Green, has done fine work on films (*The Border*) and television (*Law & Order, NYPD Blue*)

and he was also the person who wrote *The Wild Bunch* for Sam Peckinpah. The story came from a 1961 book by Max Evans and had plenty of cowboy cred—for years Peckinpah reportedly had wanted to film the story himself. All the elements were in place and *The Hi-Lo Country* seemed to be a sure thing.

But to make a western in 1999, there has to be more of a "why" than just having all of the right elements in place. Westerns have had their heyday and to resurrect the genre, the filmmakers, presumably would have to have something new to say. But, *The Hi-Lo Country* doesn't break any new ground. In fact, it seems content to be a perfectly normal, regular old western. Which is fine in 1950. But in 1999, lines like "Big Boy was like his paw. Ever since he was born, I feared it would come to violence" seem more corny than foreboding.

Maybe Frears's intention was to conquer the genre and make the quintessential American western. Which is exactly what he does. It is an old time western, through and through, without a false move in it. But the film is too true to its roots—it comes across as overly-mannered and lacking any real passion. It is as though Frears is afraid to tamper with the magic western formula.

The story, set in the 1940s, focuses on the friendship between Pete Calder (Billy Crudup) and Big Boy Matson (Woody Harrelson). The two cattle herders meet on the vast wide open spaces of New Mexico when Big Boy buys Pete's misbehaving horse, Old Sorrel. Big Boy is one of the last great cowboys. He's the kind of man who can tame a can-tankerous horse and who finishes up a night drinking at the bar by picking a fight, which, naturally, he always wins. Pete is impressed with Big Boy's manly, bigger-than-life ways.

They do a lot of old West male-bonding activities, like chasing each other on horses or wrestling and perhaps a little hooting here and there. Then World War II happens and they're shipped off to different battlefields. Cut to a few years later, it's the end of the war and Pete and Big Boy are reunited. "Good thing I came back or you'd be squattin' to pee," says Big Boy, typically, when he sees Pete. But it won't all be drinking and fighting. Some things have changed with the old town and the guys will have to deal with them.

Big Boy (Woody Harrelson) on Mona (Patricia Arquette): "Just looking at her makes my teeth itch."

Number one on the list is the West itself. During the war, evil guy Jim Ed Love (Sam Elliott) has been buying up cattle farms and modernizing the business. Instead of holding big cattle drives to get the cattle to the train—the whole fun of being a cowboy, according to Big Boy—Love just takes the cattle by truck. Jim Ed represents the fact that the small-time rancher isn't going to make it in post-War New Mexico. And if it weren't already bad enough that Jim Ed represents all that is killing the good, true cowboy ways, he's also a big jerk too. This is to make sure that we all know that he is indeed, The Bad Guy.

The other thing that's getting to the boys is one Mona Birk (Patricia Arquette), the wife of one of Jim Ed's foremen (John Diehl). When Pete gets back from the war, Mona flirts with him at a dance, saying that she'd only married her husband because he was the only guy left during the war. She seems open to more than a dance, which suits Pete just fine. As he says in a voice-over, "When she came up against me like silver foil, all fragrance and warm pressure, everything else was gone from my mind."

Unfortunately, Pete soon finds out that he's not the only one that Mona's coming up against like silver foil. And his rival for Mona's affections is none other than Big Boy. Since Pete worships Big Boy as a sort of older brother, Alpha Male type, he says nothing and lets Big Boy have Mona. Pete tries to console himself with his ultra-nice girlfriend, Josepha (Penelope Cruz), who waited for him to return from the war, but he wants Mona, not Josepha. This leads to a lot of pouting on Pete's part. In fact, for the last two-thirds of the film, that's pretty much all he does.

Even though it's the womenfolk that are causing the troubles, the real story is about being macho and manly. If they're not drinking, they're fighting or swaggering. Pete is so worshipful of Big Boy that, at times, he seems to be mooning over Big Boy more than Mona.

Besides lots of male bonding, there are three other things that make a western work or not work. They are the settings, characters, and action. On the settings, *The Hi-Lo Country* does the job. It's all vast plains, fiery orange sunsets, and dusty hills. Big Boy's mother (or Ma, that is) and his grandmother live in a tiny, wind-blown house that sits alone in the middle of huge nothingness. The poor house seems like it doesn't stand a chance in the long run, against the vast steady forces of wind, sun, and sands.

Woody Harrelson is the film's other big asset. The character of the wild, lusty Big Boy is a meaty part, and Harrelson's the kind of actor that can handle the challenge. Harrelson has the swagger to make a cowboyism like "The only time to let out a yell is when you're by yourself—or with other people" sound like a reasonable thing to say. With a cocky smile constantly on his face, Harrelson's Big Boy is the kind of crazy, charismatic guy that others flock to, if only to see what happens next.

Actually, the whole film needs Big Boy to provide the excitement because not much else is happening with the other characters. Crudup's Pete doesn't have a lot to do. He's

CREDITS

Big Boy Matson: Woody Harrelson
Peter Calder: Billy Crudup
Mona Birk: Patricia Arquette
Josepha O'Neil: Penelope Cruz
Jim Ed Love: Sam Elliott
Les Birk: John Diehl
Steve Shaw: Lane Smith
Little Boy Matson: Cole Hauser
Hoover Young: James Gammon
Meesa: Katy Jurado

Origin: USA
Released: 1998
Production: Barbara De Fina, Martin Scorsese, Eric Fellner, and Tim Bevan for Working Title and Cappa/De Fina Productions; released by Polygram Filmed Entertainment
Direction: Stephen Frears
Screenplay: Walon Green; based on the novel by Max Evans
Cinematography: Oliver Stapleton
Editing: Masahiro Hirakubo
Music: Carter Burwell
Production design: Patricia Norris
Costumes: Patricia Norris
Art direction: Russell J. Smith
Sound: Drew Kunin
MPAA rating: R
Running Time: 114 minutes

either gazing longingly at Mona, pretending to like Josepha or looking on admiringly as Big Boy pulls off another smooth move. Crudup does have the cowboy look though. His skin and face are tanned to the right leathery sheen, perfect for squinting moodily into the sun.

While Pete tends to squint moodily, Mona leans more toward staring blankly. This seems to be more the fault of Arquette's acting than the character of Mona. Instead of playing Mona like a fiery femme fatale, Arquette seems to be in some sort of daze. She says all of her lines in a slow and dreamy monotone—not slow and dreamy in a sexy way, but more of a slow-witted way. It's hard to believe anyone would be getting all riled up to hang out with her. Elliott's Jim Ed is fine, though the part mainly involves smiling evilly, which Elliott does, indeed, do.

The action is where the film falters. The film is all ominous foreboding, complete with all the old West cliches like the lonesome, mournful guitar sounds on the soundtrack and a fortune teller who predicts trouble. But somehow, the film never pays off. Things happen but not in a final, climactic way as the film is leading you to expect. And the things that do happen are not worth suffering through lines like, "Shootin' been a curse on this family."

Through the entire film, Frears never veers from the old, dusty trail laid by countless cowboy movies that have gone before. He ends his with the perfect cowboy ending, a character riding alone into the sunset. It's too bad it's all been done before.

—*Jill Hamilton*

REVIEWS

Chicago Tribune. January 22, 1999, p. 5.
Entertainment Weekly. January 8, 1999, p. 50.
Los Angeles Times. December 30, 1998, p. F8.
Rolling Stone. February 4, 1999, p. 73.
Variety. January 4, 1999, p. 97.

High Art

A story of ambition, sacrifice, seduction and other career moves.—Movie tagline

"Astonishing."—Peter Keough, *Boston Pheonix*

"Decadent."—Owen Gleiberman, *Entertainment Weekly*

"Passionate."—Jack Mathews, *Los Angeles Times*

"Stunning and seductive."—Thelma Adams, *New York Post*

"Two thumbs up! One of the year's most absorbing films."—*Siskel & Ebert*

 Box Office: $1,936, 997

Art by definition risks pretension. And "high" art, perhaps more than any other art, doubles the risk. First-time director Lisa Cholodenko has played the odds by placing her film in the highly competitive New York City SoHo visual arts scene. Yet not satisfied with this one theme, she increases her wager by giving the film the additional intrigue of lesbian-chic and heroin hell.

Cholodenko's producer, Dolly Hall has previously mined countercultural territory with *All Over Me* (1996) and *The Incredibly True Adventures of Two Girls in Love* (1995). But Cholodenko's take on sexual politics takes a distant second place to the high stakes machinations endemic to New York City's fine arts scene and the sometimes nerve-racking toll the rarefied atmosphere takes on its players.

Youthful Syd (Radha Mitchell) is an ambitious, newly promoted assistant editor of "Frame," a glossy New York City fine arts photography magazine. As the film opens, she busily bundles photo submissions and leaves them at the receptionist's desk on her way out the door. She then travels home by way of the subway in Manhattan to the sparsely furnished SoHo flat she shares with her boyfriend, James (Gabriel Mann). As they drink martinis, she and James discuss her work at "Frame" and his belief that the magazine's senior editors are taking advantage of her hard work.

One night, while taking a leisurely bath, a water leak from the ceiling leads Syd to Lucy Berliner's (Ally Sheedy) apartment directly above her and James's flat. Raw-boned, late-thirtyish Lucy lives with Greta (Patricia Clarkson), a beautiful but faded red-haired German actress. When Syd knocks on the door, Lucy, Greta, and some of their friends are sitting around the apartment's couch snorting rails of heroin off a glass plate.

Syd offers to inspect Lucy's bathtub and the women establish an immediate, yet also unspoken rapport. Syd inquires about the many framed photographic portraits covering the apartment's walls and Lucy—while offhandedly discounting her talent—also admits that the work is hers. Syd, sensing an artist superior to the work she's been studying for "Frame," offers to advance Lucy's career with the magazine's senior editors. Lucy refuses Syd's gambit telling her that she's retired from a career in art photography.

When Syd returns to the magazine the next day, she asks associate editor Harry (David Thornton) if he's heard of Lucy. But since she doesn't know Lucy's last name, Harry shows little interest. At roughly the same time, Lucy has gone to her upper middle-class home to visit her Jewish mother, Vera (Tammy Grimes). Vera expresses her disapproval of Lucy's relationship with Greta—because she's both a woman and German—and the women's chilly conversation reveals that they've settled into a distant relationship where the mother controls her daughter's finances. When Lucy tries to explain herself, she's met with little success or approval.

Syd returns to Lucy's apartment that evening and fixes the leaking bathtub pipe. When she finishes, Lucy introduces Syd to her circle of heroin-addled friends. Lethargic Arnie (Bill Sage) ambles off to the bedroom to shoot some drugs while Syd joins the conversation at the couch. When Syd again expresses an admiration for her work, Lucy informally gives her an art photo book bearing her name.

The next day, Syd passes the book to Harry and "Frame's" senior editor, Dominique (Anh Duong), at an editorial conference. Dominique expresses surprise and interest that Lucy has returned from Germany to live in Manhattan. She explains that Lucy Berliner had once been a major talent but had been difficult to work with. As a result, Berliner had abandoned professional photography. Dominique and Harry then express their willingness to publish Lucy's most recent work. Harry proposes a lunch to offer Lucy a contract.

Syd's continued involvement with Lucy and her drug addict friends soon wears on her relationship with James. But Syd is persistent in persuading Lucy to meet with her superiors and in advancing her career at "Frame." Lucy agrees to lunch with Harry, Dominique, and Syd and accepts their offer on the single condition that Syd be her editor. Despite the older editors' surprise, Syd has scored her first major coup in the world of photo-journalism.

Soon their professional relationship opens the door to a sexual one with the audience wondering if Syd truly is embarking on this lesbian affair out of sincere emotion or out of determination to acquiesce her star photographer, who has her career in the palm of her hand. When Lucy and Syd spend a weekend together in a country cottage, their relationship grows deeper and more passionate when Lucy begins to embrace Syd and the younger woman pauses for a moment and hesitatingly declares her love for Lucy.

Lucy pulls out her camera the morning after in a sun-drenched fade-in and with an inspired reverie, she pho-

tographs the sleeping Syd as she lies drowsily in bed. As Syd halfheartedly protests, Lucy puts her camera on a nearby dresser and sets its automatic shutter. The camera photographs them huddled together. Syd looks thoughtfully at the camera and Lucy looks pointedly at Syd.

Lucy is obviously the most torn as a result of the relationship. Coming from the predictable, yet comforting drug moments of her current, washed-up actress girlfriend, Lucy becomes invigorated with the proximity of Syd and what she represents. A new start. She tries to explain the situation to her mother: She's not sure if she has a "love issue" and a "drug problem" or a "love problem" and a "drug issue." Lucy finds it very difficult to walk away from Greta and her world. The two women agree that their relationship has caused tremendous disorder in their prior relationships. As such, Lucy tells Syd that she's temporarily going to leave New York City to think things through and she hands Syd a folder of photographs taken during their rendezvous. Syd resists the notion that this is the assignment for "Frame" and asks that photos taken earlier of Greta be used instead.

When the magazine's editors see Greta's photos they are disappointed by the lack of structure or meaning to the work. Syd then goes back to her desk and pulls out the photos of her taken by Lucy and she gives the photos to Dominique. After carefully studying the quality of these compositions, Dominique is both impressed and puzzled by the photographs.

Lucy returns from her respite to find the customary hanger-ons are sitting at the couch snorting heroin and Greta is seated with them. Shortly afterward, Lucy and Greta retire to their bedroom and they have a confrontation about their impending break-up. In desperation, Greta asks to spend one final evening with her lover. Lucy reluctantly, reaches in her bag for a vial and finally, snorts the heroin laid on the glass plate after Greta.

The next morning, Syd walks out of her brownstone and finds Arnie sitting disconsolately at the wheel of Lucy's Mercedes. She's disbelieving when he tells her that Lucy and Greta have died from a drug overdose. As the preceding scene subtly implies with Lucy's hesitation that the deaths were not accidental. When Syd returns to work, she's congratulated for the vitality of Lucy's most recent photographs. The magazine's cover is the photo of the two women lying together:

> Lucy (Ally Sheedy) about her career: "I loved the attention but I couldn't handle the impact. I sort of felt pigeonholed."

AWARDS AND NOMINATIONS

Independent Spirit Awards 1999: Actress (Ally Sheedy)
Los Angeles Film Critics: Actress (Ally Sheedy)

Syd looking at the camera and Lucy looking at her. Syd intently studies the magazine cover then gets up from her desk and forlornly walks out of "Frame's" offices.

Director Lisa Cholodenko's direction is so minimalist—and cinematographer Tami Reiker's photography is so formally composed—*High Art* seems contradictorily lifelike yet artificial. Cholodenko's apparent instruction to her actors and actresses to deliver their lines in near-monotones aid in creating the impression that the film is a documentary investigation into these people's lives. What initially seems to be a pretentious actorly tic creates the illusion of complexity because the often non-linear manner in which the actors speak advances the story's narrative in densely episodic fashion. Rather than have the plot's action propel the story, it's the conversation—often seemingly random at the time of delivery—that keeps moving the story forward.

It is also perhaps an irony that Reiker's cinematography is such a polished counterpoint to the contrasting set designs that pass for Syd and Lucy's apartments. The icy blue palette of Syd's place reflects a submerged coolness in her relationship with James, while the warm rose and orange tones of Lucy's apartment reflect an overheated environment and lifestyle. Add to this the harsh neon-lit offices of "Frame"; the darkly luscious mahogany texture of Vera's dining room; and the sun-drenched cottage where Lucy and Syd consummate their relationship, and the high art of the

title is ably reflected by the film's carefully considered production design and camerawork.

If the film has a serious shortcoming, it's probably the condensed time-line in which the story unfolds. Granted plausibility is always a problem with all narrative—after all, there has to be a high degree of coincidence for any story to unfold—but the constricted narrative of *High Art* creates circumstances that sometimes seem contrived. When coupled with the actor and actresses' flat deliveries, the relationships sometimes seem equally labored. In particular, Syd and James' pairing is the least convincing and the passion between Syd and Lucy seems more of an ambitious mating—Lucy using Syd to give her life meaning and Syd using Lucy to advance her career—than heartfelt character transitions.

Yet Cholodenko's handling of her actors is superb. In particular, Lucy and Greta's relationship indicates Cholodenko has a bright future ahead of her. Ally Sheedy and Patricia Clarkson's intimate bickering in their scenes together is the stuff of life. The need these two highly intelligent, but ultimately flawed women have to expose their weaknesses to each other is convincing. Indeed, the high caliber of acting, conviction of delivery, and remarkably relaxed body language Sheedy and Clarkson share in their scenes not only gives the film its greatest tension, but it also gives *High Art* its poignancy. When Lucy must choose between Greta and her drugs, or the tentative counteroffer Syd has provided her, *High Art* moves well beyond the realm of mawkish soap opera to legitimate tragedy.

Mingling ambition with ennui—and countering love with the ever-present specter of hard drugs—in virtually every sequence, Cholodenko's *High Art* is more a cautionary than critical tale. The film's self-satisfied background gives it a cultural panache that seemingly fits the characters' seeming nihilism. It's Lucy's sitting at the odd personal and professional crossroads of success and despair that gives the film its peculiar charm.

In the hands of a less talented filmmaker, *High Art*'s sometimes pretentious forays into art photography, journalism, and other such questionable past-times might have fallen flat. That the film is engrossing is demonstration of the power of art—in both its cinematic and photographic forms—sometimes despite itself.

—*John Carlos Cantu*

CREDITS

Lucy Berliner: Ally Sheedy
Syd: Radha Mitchell
Greta: Patricia Clarkson
James: Gabriel Mann
Arnie: Bill Sage
Dominique: Anh Doung
Vera: Tammy Grimes
Harry: David Thornton

Origin: USA
Released: 1998
Production: Jeff Levy-Hinte, Susan Stover, Dolly Hall; released by October Films
Direction: Lisa Cholodenko
Screenplay: Lisa Cholodenko
Cinematography: Tami Reiker
Editing: Amy E. Duddleston
Music: Shudder to Think
Production design: Bernhard Blythe
Art direction: Caryn Marcus
Costumes: Victoria Farrell
Sound: Noah Timan
MPAA rating: R
Running Time: 102 minutes

REVIEWS

Boxoffice. June, 1998, p. 64.
Chicago Tribune. August 3, 1998, p. 5.
Detroit Free Press. June 26, 1998, p. 5D.
Los Angeles Times. June 12, 1998, p. F8.
New York Times. May 12, 1998, p. E12.
People. June 22, 1998, p. 32.
USA Today. June 12, 1998, p. E12.
Variety. February 2, 1998, p. 29.

Hilary and Jackie

The true story of two sisters who shared a passion, a madness and a man.—Movie tagline

"Emily Watson delivers a stunning performance that commands attention and merits a best actress Oscar nomination. I'm putting *Hilary and Jackie* on my Top Ten List."—Martin Grove, *CNN*

"Bravo! A beautifully crafted performance by Emily Watson gives this wrenching story a haunting power."—Jeanne Wolf, *Jeanne Wolf's Hollywood*

"Superbly acted! Difficult to resist. Watson more than fulfills the promise of her celebrated Oscar-nominated work in *Breaking the Waves*."—Kenneth Turan, *Los Angeles Times*

"One of the best films of the year! Gutsy, moving, provocative and intelligent with two sensational Oscar-caliber performances."—Jonathan Foreman, *New York Post*

"Astounding! As beautifully acted as it is directed, edited and written. A blazing performance by Watson."—Stephen Holden, *New York Times*

"Outstanding! Emily Watson is mesmerizing." —Janet Maslin, *New York Times*

"One of the year's best!"—Paul Wunder, *WBAI-TV*

"Brilliant! A mesmerizing, poignant and powerful story. Two of the best performances of the year."—Jeffery Lyons, *WNBC-TV*

Box Office: $2,532,000

A complex study of two women and the rivalry and love that bonded them together, Anand Tucker's *Hilary and Jackie* is a stunning biography that explores the tumultuous relationship between the renowned English cellist, Jacqueline Du Pre, and her sister, Hilary. A child prodigy, Jackie reached the heights of the classical music world before multiple sclerosis cut short her career at the age of 28 and ended her life in 1987 at the age of 42.

Anchored by two strong performances and Frank Cottrell Boyce's intriguing script, *Hilary and Jackie* is adapted from a memoir entitled *A Genius in the Family* by Jackie's siblings,

Hilary (Rachel Griffiths) to Jackie (Emily Watson): "If you think that being an ordinary person is any easier than being an extraordinary one, you're wrong. If you didn't have that cello to prop you up, you'd be nothing."

Hilary and Piers, and the change in title reflects a certain shift in emphasis. *A Genius in the Family* explores the myriad ways a whole family supports and struggles with the genius of one of its members, while the film adaptation narrows the focus to the often odd and difficult yet, ultimately, loving relationship between the two sisters. (The parents play a small role in the film, and Piers barely registers as a character.)

The film begins with an opening section on Hilary and Jackie from childhood to early adulthood and is followed by sections named after each sister that relay key events from that character's point of view.

The film begins in Hilary's and Jackie's childhood, specifically an idyllic romp on the beach that plays like a beautiful dream. Both girls love music—Hilary plays the flute, and Jackie, the cello—and, while they love to perform together, they are also rivals. When Hilary receives an invitation to perform in a BBC production, Jackie begs to go along, and Hilary refuses to go if Jackie cannot be included. (Jackie gets to play a drum and ends up smashing it.) Jackie practices constantly to be as good as her sister so they can always be together and soon excels at the cello. In one stunning scene, the camera swirls around the young Jackie playing her cello so that we can share the rapture she feels. Both girls win musical competitions, but Jackie clearly becomes the star of the family, and Hilary is forced to live in her sister's shadow. This tension between rivalry and love will influence their relationship as adults, when Jackie and Hilary are played by Emily Watson and Rachel Griffiths, respectively. Jackie makes great strides; she has a defining triumph at Wigmore Hall, and an anonymous benefactor gives her a valuable cello.

The film then enters a new chapter, the "Hilary" section, which begins in Hilary's early adulthood. She struggles in her flute lessons and fails in front of a demanding teacher, but, despite her problems, is pursued ardently by Kiffer Finzi (David Morrissey), who wants her to play in a concert. Kiffer has an energy and boundless enthusiasm that fills a room when he enters it, and he quickly falls in love with Hilary and marries her. Soon Jackie brings home a renowned pianist-conductor named Daniel Barenboim (James Frain), and they too get married.

Time passes, and Hilary takes on a simple life working a farm with Kiffer and raising their children. Then one day Jackie appears unexpectedly and soon makes the extraordinary request of wanting to sleep with Kiffer. Hilary refuses until she finds

Jackie naked in the woods with her clothes strewn about and mutilating herself. Because Jackie apparently has suffered a breakdown, Hilary asks Kiffer to fulfill Jackie's request as "proof that somebody loves her," and he finally acquiesces.

The affair between Kiffer and Jackie was the most controversial aspect of *A Genius in the Family* (some musicians in England felt that such revelations besmirched Jackie's reputation), and the matter-of-fact way it is handled in the movie is shocking. Only because Griffiths is utterly convincing as a woman who feels total empathy for her sister, do we believe Hilary could make such a request of her husband. A section shot in the style of home movies shows Jackie usurping Hilary's role as wife and mother, treating Hilary's children as her own, and taking refuge in a domestic life on the farm. Hilary finally cannot take it any longer, and Jackie is forced to leave. A glaring weakness of the screenplay, however, is that the consequences of the affair are never really addressed.

Director Anand Tucker makes his directorial debut with this film after an extensive career in British television.

The next section, "Jackie," takes us back in time when she first went away performing abroad. Jackie obviously loves playing the cello—she throws her whole body into her performances and seems to lose herself in the music—and yet she hates it at the same time. While she is a musical prodigy, she is not emotionally equipped to deal with being alone, and she feels homesick as she travels across Europe.

When she returns home, we see some scenes that were also part of the "Hilary" section, but now they are filled out to give us Jackie's point of view. It is a cunning strategy that forces us to reconsider events from a different perspective. Most telling is a key conversation between the sisters played with slight variations. In Hilary's section, when Hilary tells Jackie that she plans to marry Kiffer because he makes her feel special, Jackie responds, in the film's cruelest moment, that "you're not special." The scene is replayed in Jackie's section, but this time Hilary fights back with a biting response. It is as if Hilary had recalled her sister's cutting remark but conveniently forgot her own retort that Jackie recalls in her section. The film thus honors the subjectivity of each character and acknowledges the way each woman focuses on the words that strike a nerve and are most hurtful to her.

We then are filled in on Jackie's courtship with Daniel and the passion for music that brings them together. They collaborate musically, but very soon the first signs of Jackie's multiple sclerosis begin. When they listen to one of her recordings, he notices her playing is slow. Soon she says her hands are cold, and, in a heartbreaking moment, she drops her bow in mid-performance. In close-up, it clatters to the floor in slow-motion and lands with several loud thuds. The great tragedy of her disease will be that it will rob her of the ability to play music, and so the visual punctuation of this moment is quite powerful.

Jackie's fear of losing her ability brings her to Hilary's farm as an emotional wreck. Her strange behavior is now understandable as an odd attempt to create a life for herself away from music, where she is slowly losing control but does not know why. When she leaves the farm, the signs of MS begin to appear in full force, from loss of bladder control to loss of finger control on the strings of her cello. She is finally diagnosed with the disease, and her condition deteriorates.

Jackie's gradual decline is a predictable plot trajectory; indeed, her slow descent into helplessness is the most conventional aspect of the film, but it is heartbreaking nonetheless because it cuts her off from the one thing that defines her—making music.

In a complex role, Watson plays the many facets of Jackie—the petulant child-woman, the charismatic musician, the emotionally unstable woman talking to her cello, and the helpless invalid shaking in her wheelchair listening to her old recording of Elgar's *Cello Concerto*, her signature piece. It is a challenging part because we may not always

CREDITS

Jacqueline Du Pre: Emily Watson
Hilary Du Pre: Rachel Griffiths
Daniel Barenboim: James Frain
Kiffer Finzi: David Morrissey
Piers Du Pre: Rupert Penry-Jones
Derek Du Pre: Charles Dance
Iris Du Pre: Celia Imrie
Young Jackie: Auriol Evans
Young Hilary: Keeley Flanders

Origin: Great Britain
Released: 1998
Production: Andy Patterson and Nicolas Kent for Intermedia Films/Film Four, British Screen, the Arts Council of England, and Oxford Films production; released by October Films
Direction: Anand Tucker
Screenplay: Frank Cottrell-Boyce; based on the book *A Genius in the Family* by Hilary and Piers Du Pre
Cinematography: David Johnson
Editing: Martin Walsh
Music: Barrington Pheloung
Production design: Alice Normington
Costumes: Sandy Powell
Sound: David Crozier
Cellist: Caroline Dale
MPAA rating: R
Running Time: 124 minutes

like Jackie, who often seems like a spoiled brat, but, because of Watson's intelligent performance, we understand her burdens—the isolation and loneliness genius can breed and the helplessness it leaves when it is suddenly stripped away.

In their last meeting before Jackie dies, Hilary visits her sister, who shakes violently and seems to have lost all bodily control. Hilary cradles Jackie as she tries to get liquid down her throat. The sisters share an intense bond and, in the end, Hilary is the only person who can calm Jackie's tremors. This is Griffiths's greatest scene because it sums up her character—the stabilizing force who has always gone to great lengths to smooth out the rough edges of her sister's life. Hilary is a reactive character, and Griffiths beautifully complements Watson's volcanic mood swings with a quiet intensity.

With Jackie in her arms, Hilary delivers a very moving speech about the power of memory when you think you have

lost that person. Hilary always remembers the day on the beach from the film's opening when they were little and Jackie told her that "everything's going to be all right"—a message we see young Jackie receive from her adult self on the beach at the film's end. Despite the power of the ending, this final message, a banal piece of optimism, seems incongruent with the struggles we have seen.

Ultimately, *Hilary and Jackie* is not a conventional musical bio-pic. While there are memorable scenes of joyful, musical performance, the film is less about the creation of music and more about the burdens and anguish of genius—both for the artist and the person(s) closest to her.

—*Peter N. Chumo II*

AWARDS AND NOMINATIONS

Academy Awards 1998 Nominations: Actress (Emily Watson); Supporting Actress (Rachel Griffith)

REVIEWS

Boxoffice. December, 1998, p. 40.
Entertainment Weekly. January 15, 1999, p. 43.
Los Angeles Times. December 30, 1998, p. F1.
San Francisco Chronicle. January 15, 1999, p. D1.
San Francisco Examiner. January 15, 1999, p. D3.
Sight and Sound. February, 1999, p. 44.
Variety. September 14, 1998, p. 37.

Holy Man

God's gift to home shopping—Movie tagline

 Box Office: $12,069,719

At one point in the film *Holy Man,* a character simply known as G (Eddie Murphy) takes a chainsaw from a pitchman's hands and rhetorically asks the audience of a home shopping show which they would rather see: should he use the chainsaw to create a Mona Lisa or should he use it to destroy the picnic table in front of him? Everyone knows the answer, destruction sells much better than creation. "We yawn at creation but thrill at destruction," says G. It's a revelation the makers of this film should have recognized in themselves. Which would audiences rather see, they might have asked themselves, a gently funny film that creates messages of love or a biting satire that takes on and destroys an

He's mystical, mysterious, and money for a home shopping network benefitting from G's (Eddie Murphy) popular spiritual selling in the comedy *Holy Man.*

industry? The answer would seem to be the latter. So why did the filmmakers go for the former?

Of course that's just one of the many inexplicable questions that surround *Holy Man,* a movie that is hard to pan because of its positive messages (a rarity nowadays), but not easy to admire because it's just so darned bland.

Ricky Hayman (Jeff Goldblum) is an executive at the Good Buy Shopping Network, a home shopping television station. Unfortunately, he has two problems. First, he seems constantly short of money. He obviously loves living the high life, but his car and house payments are long overdue. Second, the television station is under new management, an apoplectic and devious man named McBainbridge (Robert Loggia) who not only won't give Ricky a raise to help underwrite his lavish tastes, but says that the station's sales have been flat for 27 months and if they don't go up soon, Ricky will be fired.

To help boost sales, McBainbridge has brought in market analyst Kate Newell (Kelly Preston) who is supposed to create a new and dynamic identity for the station and raise sales eight percent over the next few weeks. Needless to say, Kate and Ricky take an instant dislike to each other although they hide it beneath a veneer of professionalism.

Then, as the story finds Ricky and Kate inexplicably driving down an expressway together, Ricky's car gets a flat tire. Of course these two Yuppies immediately pick up their respective cell phones to call the auto club, but they're in a dead zone. As they fumblingly undertake the menial job of changing the tire themselves, they are approached by a strange man, walking down the freeway median strip in caftan pajamas. The stranger offers them assistance, but Ricky is determined to ignore the stranger. For some reason, however, Kate is especially friendly to him. And when he crosses four lanes of highway with no concern for oncoming traffic (and for some reason the cars never swerve—is he invisible?) we begin to suspect he may be a little odd.

The stranger turns out to be G (Eddie Murphy). "Just G with a period, that's it," he says of his name. (Is it supposed to stand for God? Gee, isn't that subtle?) When G faints on the freeway, Ricky and Kate are forced to take him to the hospital where a diagnosis of heat exhaustion and heart problems is followed by a prescription for weeks of rest in a shady place. Needless to say, under Kate's withering humanitarian stare, Ricky is further forced to take G on as a roommate in his bachelor's pad on Miami Beach.

When at a party G cures fashion designer Nino Cerruti of his fear of flying, Ricky has the idea that G might make

Station owner McBainbridge (Robert Loggia): "It's about making people feel they have to have it when they don't really want it."

a great pitchman for his station. And so G is given his first show—selling mixing bowls. But G just can't follow a script and instead wanders around the studio interfering with other shows such as that of Morgan Fairchild who is pitching a face-lift machine called "Insta-tuck." But G is lecturing about true beauty . . . it's an anti-sales pitch for Fairchild's product. And as incredulous as it may seem, it causes sales to increase 30 percent.

And so G gets his own show—*The G Spot*—in which every anti-product message he delivers to the audience is strangely turned into a product endorsement by the public who buys, buys, and buys. As stated by a very enthusiastic announcer at the start of *The G Spot,* it's a show where one can find "philosophy, a higher state of consciousness and nonstop shopping." G's popularity spawns G t-shirts, a G-Whiz cheese product, and G-String wrapping ribbon. There seems to be no end to the crassness to which Ricky can turn G's image.

But you know what's going to happen next, don't you? Ricky and Kate fall in love, then Kate gets angry at how Ricky exploits the gentle G and eventually G will bring them back together again by getting Ricky to redeem himself in her eyes.

And that's part of the problem with *Holy Man.* It's formula. There are no surprises here. And although one may feel guilty for picking on so gentle a film, that still can't excuse the film's slow pace, its limping plot, its routine dialogue, nor its lame characters. How amusing can this movie be when the funniest lines are given to minor characters in the director's booth who act like a Greek chorus for G's actions on the studio floor.

If ever there were a concept in dire need of lampooning it's home shopping shows. The wealth of material here to be mined is phenomenal: Why do we buy? Why do celebrities sell? Why are they so boring? What role do they fill in our lives? What makes them addictive to some people? None of this is addressed in *Holy Man.* And if one tried to excuse the film on the grounds that its message is a different one, then one has to ask exactly what it is? How can we possibly believe that a man with no possessions and only contempt for the products he is talking about could possibly increase sales? An ascetic pitchman is an oxymoron no one ever credibly explains. If his messages do make people feel better about themselves, they shouldn't be buying at all!

Initially Eddie Murphy was offered the part of Ricky, but he must have realized that any actor who played G would probably steal the film. His character, initially, is interesting but being an enigma will only carry audience curiosity so far. Also, unfortunately, the part must never have been

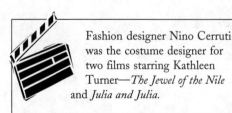

Fashion designer Nino Cerruti was the costume designer for two films starring Kathleen Turner—*The Jewel of the Nile* and *Julia and Julia.*

CREDITS

G: Eddie Murphy
Ricky Hayman: Jeff Goldblum
Kate Newell: Kelly Preston
John McBainbridge: Robert Loggia
Barry: Jon Cryer
Scott Hawkes: Eric McCormack
Director: Sam Kitchin
Assistant Director: Robert Small
Cameraman (Brutus): Marc Macaulay
Morgan Fairchild: Herself
Florence Henderson: Herself
Betty White: Herself
James Brown: Himself
Soupy Sales: Himself
Dan Marino: Himself
Nino Cerruti: Himself

Origin: USA
Released: 1998
Production: Roger Birnbaum and Stephen Herek for a Caravan Pictures; released by Touchstone Pictures
Direction: Stephen Herek
Screenplay: Tom Schulman
Cinematography: Adrian Biddle
Editing: Trudy Ship
Production design: Andrew McAlpine
Art direction: James Tocci
Set decoration: Chris Spellman
Costumes: Aggie Guerard Rodgers
Music: Alan Silvestri
MPAA rating: PG
Running Time: 113 minutes

rewritten for Murphy for his lines aren't that funny and, even worse, he becomes nothing more than a supporting player in the film, disappearing for scenes on end.

Goldblum does a credible job with Ricky, whose slick and shiny suits reflect not only the tropical neon colors of Miami where the movie was filmed, but also his superficial persona. But as to why G takes him on as a pet project is totally unclear. Surely there are other, more worthy candidates for G's redemption. Wouldn't he do more good converting McBainbridge? Also, unfortunately, there's no chemistry between Ricky and Kate. We don't really care if they get together or not. Consequently, whenever G disappears, there's little left to watch. And even when he is on-screen, there's little to laugh at.

And audiences must realize this. *Holy Man* had the lowest opening weekend boxoffice grosses of any Eddie Murphy film. I guess light comedies need to deliver more than trite messages to entertain an audience. When *Holy Man* asks, "Would you rather be a *Baywatch* babe or the Dalai Lama?" Would you rather have beauty or wisdom? They know most people would say beauty, it's just the way our society tends to be. So why did they deliver the Dalai Lama?

—Beverley Bare Buehrer

REVIEWS

Chicago Sun Times. October 9, 1998.
Chicago Tribune. October 9, 1998.
Entertainment Weekly. October 16, 1998, p. 54.
Los Angeles Times. October 9, 1998, p. F1.
New York Times. October 9, 1998. p. E14.
People. October 19, 1998, p. 40.
Variety. October 10, 1998, p. 39.
Washington Post. October 9, 1998, p. 49.

Home Fries

A long shot romance in a short order world.
—Movie tagline

"A super-sized comedy and a spicy romance."
—Maria Salas, *CBS Telenoticias*

"Hilariously zany and fun. Enormously original. Drew Barrymore shines yet again."—Ann Shatilla, *KCOP-TV*

"A rich and quirky comedy with the best performance of Drew Barrymore's career."—Jim Svedja, *KNX/CBS Radio*

"Wickedly funny with superb performances."
—Jeffrey Lyons, *NBC-TV*

"Deliciously demented."—Susan Granger, *SSG Syndicate*

"A cutting-edge romantic comedy."—Bill Bragoli, *Westwood One*

 Box Office: $10,053,369

Dean Parisot's *Home Fries* is a strange hybrid of sweet romance and dark comedy that never really finds its footing or settles into its own rhythm. Some scenes are funny, others fall flat and go on too long, and the resulting hodgepodge is less than satisfying. Set in the middle of rural America, the movie stars Drew Barrymore as Sally, a young woman working the drive-thru window at the local Burger-Matic. She is pregnant by an older man named Henry (Chris Ellis), who, in the bizarre opening scenes, is pursued in his car by a helicopter and is literally scared to death when he suffers a heart attack. We soon learn that the pilots of the helicopter, two International Guardsmen named Angus (Jake Busey) and Dorian (Luke Wilson), are Henry's stepsons. They committed the strange deed at the prodding of their mother, Mrs.

 Dorian (Luke Wilson) to Sally (Drew Barrymore): "This is a gift for your baby. It's an A.H.-1 Cobra. I fly them for the Army National Guard. The Viet Cong called them the 'muttering death.'" Sally: "Thank you." Dorian: "And it's non-toxic, I think."

Beatrice Lever (Catherine O'Hara), who wanted revenge on Henry for cheating on her. It is an odd premise, to be sure, but the darkly comic possibilities of the situation are initially promising.

The brothers heard some interference on their headphones during their attack on Henry and speculate that someone who uses headphones, like the employees at the Burger-Matic, may know what they did. Angus is crazy,

while Dorian is levelheaded, but Angus bullies his brother into getting a job there to check out the situation (there is a cute scene in which Dorian is taught how to assemble a burger but does not quite get the knack of it). Dorian falls for Sally, but neither knows the other's relationship to Henry.

The film seems to be aiming for a manic, screwball sensibility but ends up with individual, wacky scenes that go nowhere. When Dorian has to put on the Burger-Matic robot costume for a children's birthday party, he ends up disarming a crazed gunman named Red (Lanny Flaherty), who turns out to be the father of the birthday boy and apparently goes nuts when he gets drunk. Strange familial relationships run throughout the film and contribute to the sense of small-town craziness but ultimately do not add much to the characters. There are other farcical scenes—Henry's wake, for example, where Angus pulls a jacket off of a corpse for Dorian to wear—but most never reach the level of outrageousness they seem to be shooting for.

Vince Gilligan's script really has two tracks: a sweet, if rather conventional, love story between Dorian and Sally, and Mrs. Lever's machinations to learn the identity of her late husband's mistress and then have her killed. The love story is quite sweet. Dorian gives Sally a toy helicopter for her baby, comes to her defense when he gets rid of a rude customer, and consents to be her Lamaze partner. In Lamaze class, Dorian at first looks uncomfortable but seems to be falling in love with her as he helps her prepare for childbirth. While they share some tender moments, their romance does not gel with the rest of the movie.

Nonetheless, the love story has a certain charm, mainly because of Drew Barrymore. First as the sweet object of Adam Sandler's affection in *The Wedding Singer* and then as the feisty Cinderella in *Ever After* (see both film reviews in this edition), Barrymore gave two winning performances in 1998, and her Sally, pregnant and struggling to do her best in a bad situation, gives *Home Fries* its few sparks. Barrymore embodies the plucky, no-nonsense spirit of her other recent roles along with an appealing mixture of innocence and experience, even if the script gives her a pretty thin characterization. As Mick LaSalle pointed out in the *San Francisco Chronicle*, her face "radiates a worldly-wise, mischievous, very uncorny niceness—not a typical combination."

When Sally appears at Henry's funeral, Dorian seems to figure out who she is and confirms his suspicions when he later asks her about the father of her baby. She tells him that Henry lied to her, that she at first did not know he was married. Dorian is on the verge of telling her about his relationship to Henry, but they kiss instead. When Sally confesses that she wants to explain herself to Henry's wife before she finds certain pictures, Dorian runs off in a panic to retrieve them.

As Dorian is going through his stepfather's photos, Angus appears. Dorian has removed the pictures of Sally to protect her, but Angus sees pictures of another woman with his stepfather and assumes this woman was Henry's mistress. Angus then embarks on an elaborate scheme to gas her with carbon monoxide via a tube running underground and up her toilet, but Dorian foils the scheme and saves the woman just in time, even as he nearly gets gassed himself. This sequence goes on for a long time and ultimately is not very funny or inventive. In fact, it is rather pointless and simply sidetracks the movie from its main story.

The later scenes amount to a series of family squabbles to wrap up the picture. When Sally learns Dorian is Henry's

Producer Mark Johnson first came across the script for *Home Fries* while judging a screenwriting contest in 1988.

stepson, she is angry and hurt that he did not tell her the truth earlier. Angus develops the missing photos from the negatives and learns Sally's identity. Later, when Beatrice is having a violent fit over Dorian dating Sally, Beatrice reveals that Dorian is her favorite child, which unhinges Angus. The Oedipal tension between Angus and his mother is a subtext throughout the film, especially in the subtle ways she coaxes him to do her dirty work, but now he is more crazed than ever and desperate to prove his love to her. Dorian is locked in a closet by Angus, and when he breaks free, he runs to Sally's house, where he is startled to find his mother getting along with Sally. Thinking that Angus has set some kind of booby trap for Sally, Dorian checks the toilet, overturns the gas stove, and destroys the dinner. When Dorian finally confesses to the killing of Henry, Beatrice acts like he is the one who is crazy.

In the film's ludicrous climax, Angus appears overhead in his helicopter and flies after his mom, Sally, and Dorian in his truck. To please his mother, Angus wants to shoot Sally, who, incidentally, is going into labor, but Dorian tries to talk him out of it. After a long standoff, Dorian succeeds, and Angus simply relents and flies away—yet another scene that really goes nowhere. In essence, the big showdown just peters out.

Dorian takes Sally to the hospital, where she delivers her baby. Dorian is with her and the baby at the end, and the implication is that they will be a happy, if somewhat odd, family. When Dorian says that he is the baby's stepbrother (in an offbeat way) but would like to be the father, Sally tells him that he cannot be both because "that's the kind of thing that messes kids up." It is one of the film's few memorable lines and suggests the deadpan wittiness to which the screenplay could have aspired.

Reviews of *Home Fries* were generally negative and the boxoffice grosses poor. Playing on the film's title, *USA Today*'s Mike Clark wrote that the film lacked "any acting or visual condiments to give it a tangy taste." The *Chicago Sun-Times*'s Roger Ebert gave the movie a favorable review but admitted that he had to watch it twice before he could appreciate it and doubted "it's worth seeing two times just to

CREDITS

Sally: Drew Barrymore
Dorian: Luke Wilson
Mrs. Lever: Catherine O'Hara
Angus: Jake Busey
Mrs. Jackson: Shelley Duvall
Billy: Kim Robillard
Roy: Daryl Mitchell
Red: Lanny Flaherty
Henry Lever: Chris Ellis

Origin: USA
Released: 1998
Production: Mark Johnson, Barry Levinson, Lawrence Kasdan, and Charles Newirth for a Baltimore Pictures production; released by Warner Bros.
Direction: Dean Parisot
Screenplay: Vince Gilligan
Cinematography: Jerzy Zielinski
Editing: Nicholas C. Smith
Production design: Barry Robison
Art direction: Phil Dagort
Set design: Andrew Menzies
Costumes: Jill Ohanneson
Sound: Jennifer Murphy
Music: Rachel Portman
MPAA rating: PG-13
Running Time: 93 minutes

REVIEWS

Boxoffice. October, 1998, p. 53.
Entertainment Weekly. December 4, 1998, p. 67.
Los Angeles Times. November 25, 1998, p. F1.
New York Times. November 25, 1998, p. E6.
People. December 7, 1998, p. 34.
Variety. September 21, 1998, p. 109.
Washington Post. November 27, 1998, p. 57.

get into the rhythm. More character and less plot might have been a good idea."

Home Fries has some funny moments, especially in its sweet, albeit routine, romance between Dorian and Sally. Unfortunately, all of the disparate elements do not mesh. The dark comedy is not sharp enough, and Busey's manic performance as a mother-fixated boy who relishes the idea of a creative murder does not provide enough juice to send the movie into truly screwball heights. Shelley Duvall is wasted in the small role of Sally's mother, Mrs. Jackson, and

Catherine O'Hara is sometimes funny but generally underused as the manipulative mother who has Angus in her thrall. The main problem, though, is the plot itself, which lacks a sense of energy and pacing. Also, it is very thin, and, despite the air of craziness at its core and the odd familial situations, pretty lackluster. In the year of the outrageously screwball *There's Something About Mary* (also reviewed in this edition), a few goofy characters colliding with each other is just not enough to sustain a supposedly madcap comedy.

—*Peter N. Chumo II*

Homegrown

Millionaires today. Fugitives tomorrow. Buds forever. The comedy that goes to your head.
—Movie tagline

"A rousing adventure story, with a persuasive sense of bitter irony and a strong comic chemistry among its stars."—William Arnold, *Seattle Post-Intelligencer*

Box Office: $215,553

Homegrown was one of a small spate of films in early 1998 about pot heads. The small trend included the comedy *Half-Baked, Fear and Loathing in Las Vegas,* and Jeff Bridges's generally stoned title character in *The Big Lebowski.* It's hard to imagine why they all came out at once. It was hardly as though there was a public outcry for more films about marijuana. And given the films' generally low boxoffice performances, the public showed no interest in developing reefer madness. It was more like reefer disregard. Or reefer apathy.

But there were still stoners in 1998, and some of these dutifully showed up for *Homegrown.* At one afternoon showing, some audience members were either a bit high themselves or else they just were the type of people who happened to think everything was really, really funny. This audience was dying laughing at the previews before the film. They even laughed at a sadly unfunny promo of a Chris Farley movie. It became apparent that if you're going to screen a comedy, maybe stacking the audience with some giggling stoners wouldn't be such a bad idea.

Jack (Billy Bob Thornton): "Harlan, you don't dare a guy to kill you."

So, the story. Jack (Billy Bob Thornton), Carter (Hank Azaria), and the young Harlan (Ryan Phillippe) are the caretakers of a big pot farm in Northern California. One day as they watch their boss, Malcolm Stockman (John Lithgow), landing in a helicopter to make a routine check-in visit, they notice that Malcolm doesn't stand up to greet them. That's mainly because he's dead—shot by the helicopter pilot who speeds off after doing the deed. The three men panic for a bit, then decide on a plan. They hack off a few big buds and run, taking their loot to their associate, Lucy (Kelly Lynch), for processing. After reaping the benefits of their theft and seeing that nothing bad has happened yet, they decide to go back to the farm to see what condition it's in. Miraculously, it seems that the land is untouched. Malcolm is still lying there dead, no one knows about it, and, well, there are those millions of dollars' worth of marijuana plants just sitting there. So they hatch plan number two. If no one knows that Malcolm is gone, they can pretend that he is still alive and control the business themselves, thus making a huge profit.

Naturally there are complications. For one, they discover a host of other interested parties to whom Malcolm had promised a cut. And then there's the matter of who actually killed Malcolm. This person could still be a very real threat and Malcolm has plenty of enemies to choose from. And finally, there's the matter of the three themselves. As pot farm lackeys, they aren't exactly skilled businessmen. Although Thornton's Jack gives it a good shot, adopting his former boss's mannerisms and style of dress, Carter and Harlan have been dope heads too long. Somehow you sense that there's just no way that they're going to pull off some big financial coup.

Homegrown was billed as part comedy, part mystery/caper film. But it's not really strong in either aspect. The mystery isn't that engaging because of the loose, easygoing style of the story. The laid-back plot style may strike just the right tone for reflecting the '60s throwback weed-smoking characters, but it's not so great for giving a mystery a tight, suspenseful feel.

The comedy part of the equation is barely there. A lot of the humor comes from Jack and Carter teasing young Harlan about his supposed lack of intelligence. It's mainly insult humor such as the line, "Why don't you just wear your underwear on the outside of your f***ing pants?" The humor could depend on one's state of mind, however. The audience stoners found the scene where Harlan gets the uncontrollable giggles to be the height of hilarity.

The film does have its moments. When Jack is discussing an issue with the others, he refuses to listen to their suggestions to think it over. "I have thought about it and I agree with myself," he says grumpily. Also good is the mandatory shoot-out scene. Instead of the usual ho-hum men-with-guns scene, this shoot-out has the added bonus that Jack is wearing boxer shorts and a robe. Seeing Billy Bob Thornton half-naked, with his big old flabby stomach hanging out, was an inspired touch.

Also good is the Northern California town's acceptance of pot as the local business. The townies not only know about it, they support it. When there's trouble up at the ranch, a local gas station attendant alerts Jack. When the guys bribe a local policeman (a less-goofy-than-usual Judge Reinhold), he crows happily about a new auditorium where his nephew is going to perform a play, "We never had a place like that when lumber was the cash crop!"

The cast seems to be in full glory. Billy Bob Thornton is wonderful as the redneck, cranky, semi-leader Jack. Jack has to rise to the occasion, not so much because he's a natural leader, but because, well, who else is going to do it? Watching Thornton is fun, even if it's just to listen to his Southern accent.

Hank Azaria, in a totally different mode here than his sexy, semi-clad houseboy character in *The Birdcage* (1995), is the stoner Everyman. Azaria seems to have a bit of a ham in him and here his inner ham gets a good workout. He's the '60s throwback who hasn't really accepted that times have changed. He sports unfashionably long hair, knows all the best ways to crossbreed marijuana plants, accepts paranoia as part of the pot-smoker's life, and still tries to get in some anachronistic free love with Lucy.

Especially good is Ryan Phillippe, who perfectly captures the energy of youth. With his sticky blond hairstyle and innocent energy, Harlan's the eager puppy of the group, taking everyone else's ribbing with a good-natured attitude. When he spies the older Lucy sweaty and chopping wood (while she's inexplicably wearing lingerie), you can almost hear his hormones rage. Phillippe skillfully brings a touching quality to his role instead of just playing it as a young doofus.

Kelly Lynch works hard to make Lucy come alive as a full character. It's commendable since, as written, Lucy is pretty much only there to serve as a source of conflict between the men. When the lovelorn Harlan gives Lucy a necklace, she seems simultaneously touched and sort of sad that the best she can do is some lovesick kid. She also brings a poignancy to her plight as a woman who is trying to be loose with Carter, but really just wants him to be hers and hers alone.

The film is chock-full of cameos. Jamie Lee Curtis is earthy as an aging flower child/town matriarch who's sympathetic to the cause. Ted Danson is appropriately weird as an off-kilter Mafia boss. And Jon Bon Jovi is good as a drug buyer who may or may not know more than he lets on.

One surprise element of the film is set design. The decor in the scenes is noticeably artistic, with emphasis on old, dark wood furniture pieces. Even the men's tent camp on the pot farm looks like it could have come from a tasteful Pottery Barn catalogue. The design touches aren't exactly in character—if you really think about it, it's pretty implausible that left to their own devices, these three men would be setting out lovely candle holders and candles for themselves—but it looks good on the screen.

The combination of director Stephen Gyllenhaal (*Losing Isaiah* [1994], *A Dangerous Woman* [1993], and *Waterland* [1991]) and co-writer Nicholas Kazan (*Reversal of Fortune* [1990] and *Fallen* [1998]) sounds like it could be promising, but it never really works. It's almost as if the two

CREDITS

Jack Madsen: Billy Bob Thornton
Carter: Hank Azaria
Harlan: Ryan Phillippe
Lucy: Kelly Lynch
Malcolm: John Lithgow
Danny: Jon Bon Jovi
Sierra: Jamie Lee Curtis
Gianni: Ted Danson
Pilot: Jon Tenney
Policeman: Judge Reinhold

Origin: USA
Released: 1998
Production: Jason Clark for Lakeshore Entertainment and Rollercoaster Films; released by TriStar Pictures
Direction: Stephen Gyllenhaal
Screenplay: Stephen Gyllenhaal and Nicholas Kazan
Cinematography: Greg Gardiner
Editing: Michael Jablow
Music: Trevor Rabin
Production design: Richard Sherman
Set decoration: Maurin Scarlata
Costumes: Joseph Porro
Sound: Albee Gordon
MPAA rating: R
Running Time: 101 minutes

were not devoting their full attention to the project, and they end up with something that has the feel of a throwaway. The story isn't clever or clear enough to make for a strong movie and it's hard to tell just what the film is trying to be. In the end, it's as wispy and weightless as a puff of smoke rising from one of Carter's joints.

—Jill Hamilton

REVIEWS

Los Angeles Times. May 8, 1998, p. F8.
New York Times. May 6, 1998, p. E16.
Variety. April 20, 1998, p. 44.
Village Voice. April 28, 1998, p. 124.

Hope Floats

When life fell apart, love fell into place.—Movie tagline

"Sandra Bullock delivers a superlative performance."—David Sheehan, *CBS-TV*

"I laughed, I cried, I spun the emotional wheel."—Geri Richter Campbell, *Jane Magazine*

"Sandra Bullock's finest performance ever. Emotions soar in *Hope Floats*."—Larry Ratliff, *KABB-TV*

"Emotionally on target. *Hope Floats* is distinguished by its acting."—Anne Marie O'Connor, *Mademoiselle*

"Emotionally charged. Strong performances all around."—Sarah Goldsmith, *Seventeen Magazine*

"Sandra Bullock and Harry Connick, Jr. are one of the most romantic couples of the summer. A touching story that will make you laugh and cry."—Maria Salas, *Telenoticias*

"Intimate and heartfelt."—Josh Rosstenberg, *US Magazine*

 Box Office: $60,110,313

Hope Floats is sweet, sentimental, sappy, sniffling, scatterbrained, a little draggy, a little obvious, and the kind of movie you go to with your girlfriend when you need relief from your problems (by watching someone else's) and you're guaranteed a happy ending. Sandra Bullock has to be one of the most likeable actresses onscreen today, so you're willing to forgive her a lot (such as *Speed 2* [1997]) and she's probably the best crier since Demi Moore in *Ghost* (1990). The rest of the cast also prove appealing. Not much more is expected of Harry Con-

Ramona (Gena Rowlands) to daughter Birdee (Sandra Bullock): "Your love life has always been a disaster area. They ought to have those orange cones all around you."

nick Jr. than aw-shucks charm, which he delivers easily, while Gena Rowlands offers generational backbone and young Mae Whitman shows that all child performers don't mug for the camera.

Things start off in the dreadful world of the TV tabloid talk show—Chicago host Toni Post (Kathy Najimy) is about to ambush unassuming Birdee Pruitt (Sandra Bullock) with the knowledge that her husband Bill (Michael Pare) is having an affair with Birdee's "best friend" Connie (an unbilled Rosanna Arquette). Watch Birdee crumple on national TV, with her young daughter Bernice (Mae Whitman) in the audience. The next episode is Birdee and Bernice packing up and heading back to her hometown of Smithville, Texas. Her eccentric mother Ramona (Gena Rowlands) is a fanatical taxidermist who dresses up her stuffed creations in a variety of outfits and then displays them throughout the house, while her sweet father (James N. Harrell) is now in a home suffering the effects of a stroke and "old-timers" disease. Birdee's young nephew Travis (Cameron Finley) is also living with his grandma and is not discouraged from dressing up in various costumes such as a dog, a frog, and a dinosaur. All odd behavior is obviously taken in stride.

Birdee was once the town's Queen of Corn (three years running), a high school cheerleader, and the prom queen who married the quarterback. As she tells her bewildered daughter: "Once upon a time your mama knew what it meant to shine." Now what Birdee does is stay in her pajamas all day, sleeping and moping. When she pulls herself together enough to look for a job, she realizes everyone seems to have seen her TV humiliation and some ex-classmates aren't too sorry to see the prom queen brought low. She manages to land a job at the local quickie photo developing shop, which gets her out of the house and into some kind of routine.

Meanwhile, unsubtle Ramona, who never liked Birdee's husband Bill, has been setting Birdee up with local handyman Justin Matisse (Harry Connick Jr.), a polite charmer who had a crush on Birdee in high school. She's flattered by, if nominally resistant to, his attentions, when they go fishing together and on a drive to the former high school hot spot, the now-closed drive-in. Birdee cuts loose with Justin at a local dance and is impressed when he takes her to the home he's designed and is building for himself. Justin left his post–high school life in California when he realized that his "American Dream" had become so twisted that he didn't recognize it anymore—now Smithville's slower pace suits him fine, as does Birdie. They wind up spending the night together, which Birdee immediately regrets.

What's worse for Birdee is Bernice's resentment. The young girl naturally misses her father and blames her mother

for breaking up their family and leaving their home in Chicago. She's angry at Justin's presence in their lives and is happy to see him leave when Birdee can't give him any encouragement about their relationship. This is small potatoes when Ramona suddenly dies of a heart attack (this is pushing credulity) and Bill turns up at the funeral. Bernice thinks he's come for her but what he wants is a divorce. The distraught child is left to lean on her mother, who's discovered that she does have the strength to cope with whatever life manages to put in her path. Birdee, Justin, Bernice, and Travis are shown together at the town's parade, where Birdee informs her daughter that the best times are before her since "childhood is what you spend your life trying to overcome" and that you just have to "give hope a chance to float up, and it will."

The movie has an excellent soundtrack that is used a little too heavily to punctuate every moment in Birdee's life. It would have been fine if every change weren't accompanied by a tuneful ballad. And it really wants to tug on your heartstrings at every opportunity—although it's a genuinely teary moment when Birdee dances with her father, who probably isn't too sure who the young woman is. Also, the scenes of the bookish Bernice as the new kid in school, who's picked on by class bully "Big Dolores," just slow things down since they don't have any specific consequences and the emotional payoff comes in other mother/daughter scenes. There's also a scene between Justin and Travis, having a man-to-man chat after Ramona's funeral, that's touching but only distracts from Birdee's story. Still, you get a nice fuzzy feeling knowing that you can go home again—Birdee has made a life for herself and Bernice, has a nice guy giving her flowers, and gets a second shot at a self-made happy ending. 🎞

—*Christine Tomassini*

CREDITS

Birdee Pruitt: Sandra Bullock
Ramona Calvert: Gena Rowlands
Justin Matisse: Harry Connick Jr.
Bernice Pruitt: Mae Whitman
Travis: Cameron Finley
Bill Pruitt: Michael Pare
Harry Calvert: James N. Harrell
Mr. Davis: Norman Bennett
Toni Post: Kathy Najimy
Connie: Rosanna Arquette
Nurse: Bill Cobbs

Origin: USA
Released: 1998
Production: Lynda Obst for Fortis Films; released by 20th Century Fox
Direction: Forest Whitaker
Screenplay: Steven Rogers
Cinematography: Caleb Deschanel
Editing: Richard Chew
Music: Dave Grusin
Production design: Larry Fulton
Art direction: Christa Munro
Costumes: Susie DeSanto
Sound: Felipe Borrero
MPAA rating: PG-13
Running Time: 114 minutes

REVIEWS

Chicago Tribune. May 29, 1998, p. 4.
Detroit News. May 29, 1998, p. F1.
Entertainment Weekly. May 29, 1998, p. 52.
Hollywood Reporter. May 26, 1998, p. 18.
People. June 8, 1998, p. 37.
Variety. May 25, 1998, p. 57.
Village Voice. June 2, 1998, p. 155.
Washington Post Weekend. May 29, 1998, p. 49.

The Horse Whisperer

"Moving, involving. A gorgeous film."—Joel Siegel, *Good Morning America*

"Mr. Redford has found his own visually eloquent way to turn the potboiler into a panorama, with a deep-seated love for the Montana landscape against which his rapturously beautiful film unfolds."—Janet Maslin, *New York Times*

"One of the best films of the year! Masterfully directed, marvelously acted, stunningly photographed. It's a winner!"—Neil Rosen, *NY1*

"Visual and intellectually stunning."—Pat Collins, *WWOR-TV*

Box Office: $75,373,563

Robert Redford stars as *The Horse Whisperer,* helping a mother and daughter overcome a tragedy.

Robert Redford's adaptation of Nicholas Evans's *The Horse Whisperer* might just be both the most and the least romantic film of the year. Make no mistake, it oozes with romanticism. Tension mounts as the New York publisher Annie MacLean (Kristin Scott Thomas) and Tom Booker (Robert Redford), the sensitive and earthy horse trainer of the film's title, are steadily drawn to one another. Meanwhile, the distance between Annie and her devoted husband Robert (Sam Neill) becomes painfully visible. Thus on the one hand, *The Horse Whisperer* proffers all the emotional and romantic entanglements that characterize a classic love triangle.

On the other hand, *The Horse Whisperer* constitutes a visually expansive realization of America's romance with its mythic frontier. For nearly three hours, Redford woos his audience with aerial views of patchworked farmlands, breathtaking panoramas of Montana's legendary "big sky," and lulling sequences documenting hay harvests, cattle roundups, and the ebb and flow of seasonal snows. The inclusion of such scenes, coupled with the sheer length of this film, may tire some viewers—especially those looking for a simple love story. At times these two forms of romanticism—the love story and the romance of the land—seem in competition with one another. But it is precisely on account of this tension that the film can offer substantial aesthetic, emotional, and intellectual appeal.

Approximately the first forty-five minutes of *The Horse Whisperer* introduce both the film's central characters and

> Annie (Kristin Scott Thomas): "The more I try and fix things, the more everything falls apart." Tom (Robert Redford): "Maybe you should let them fall."

the catalyst that will bring them all together. During a graphically filmed accident (which accounts for its PG-13 rating), Annie and Robert's daughter Grace (Scarlett Johansson, in a noteworthy performance) and her horse Pilgrim are physically and emotionally shattered. The once beloved horse becomes a black and twisted monster—a childhood nightmare brought to life. Grace, meanwhile, loses a leg and is fitted with a prosthetic. As Grace struggles against the stares of her classmates or asks questions like, "Who's ever going to want me like this?" we see that Grace's plight represents both the aftermath of trauma and a magnification of the pain and self-doubt that always accompanies adolescence. In this way Redford's film is bigger than Evans's novel. The conflicts and anxieties that beset Redford's characters resonate well beyond the specifics of their situations. Thus, when Annie drives both daughter and horse halfway across the country in a desperate attempt to fix everything, her journey becomes one about soothing the American psyche and healing its broken families.

The bulk of *The Horse Whisperer* takes place on and

AWARDS AND NOMINATIONS

Academy Awards 1998 Nominations: Song ("A Soft Place to Fall")

around a cattle farm owned and run by the Booker family. Annie delivers Pilgrim into Tom's hands because she has heard that he possesses a nearly mystical ability to communicate with and heal "horses with people problems." And healing Pilgrim, she believes, will go a long way towards healing Grace. The scenes documenting Pilgrim's training are intriguing in and of themselves, but Redford does not reduce this aspect of the film to documentary. As Booker teaches Pilgrim to accept rope and saddle, close-ups of Grace and Annie betray their fascination. Likewise, the use of shot and reverse-shot close-ups between Tom and Pilgrim give depth to Pilgrim's character while establishing the bond between horse and trainer. Through scenes such as these and those that lyrically record farm life, *The Horse Whisperer* celebrates not merely Tom's relationship to nature but a way of life that seems all but lost to most of us. The simple and organic harmony of the Bookers' lives stands in sharp contrast

Last role for Jeanette Nolan who died on June 5, 1998.

to the disfunctional relationships existing between Grace and Annie, and between Annie and Robert.

Amidst the splendor of the western landscape and under Tom's watchful eye, Pilgrim, Grace, and Annie all confront and conquer their internal demons. Pilgrim learns "how to be a horse again," and Grace and Annie reveal their fears of inadequacy to one another. The idyllic world of Redford's West provides a visually pleasing setting for recuperation, but it is not without its problems. This is a world in which women must devote their lives to childcare and cooking—spaghetti sauce from a jar is a once-in-a-lifetime experiment; homemade is the rule—while the men ride off to herd cattle. By offering the Bookers as a model, *The Horse Whisperer* suggests that what lie at the root of so many family problems are the difficult personalities of its women. Like Pilgrim, all that Annie really needs is a bit of "domestication," and Tom Booker, in short, can teach her "how to be a woman again." The fact that Annie blossoms as she and Tom grow closer only confirms this.

As Pilgrim heals and Grace learns to cope and even ride with her new leg, Annie realizes that she will soon be forced to choose between Robert and Tom. Veteran actors Redford and Scott Thomas artfully instill their characters with a mixture of longing and haunted melancholy that renders their dilemma all the more poignant. In adapting Evans's novel to film, Redford has dramatically rewritten the ending. By closing with Annie's decision, *The Horse Whisperer* brings its two romantic threads together, leaving its audience to ponder difficult questions about being and belonging, about the excitement of new love and places versus the security of a long-established relationship, and, finally, about the self-delusions and fantasies that go hand in hand with wondering "what if" and "how things might have been different."

—*Jacqui Sadashige*

CREDITS

Tom Booker: Robert Redford
Annie MacLean: Kristin Scott Thomas
Robert MacLean: Sam Neill
Grace MacLean: Scarlett Johansson
Diane Booker: Dianne Wiest
Frank Booker: Chris Cooper
Liz Hammond: Cherry Jones
Ellen Booker: Jeanette Nolan
Joe Booker: Ty Hillman

Origin: USA
Released: 1998
Production: Robert Redford and Patrick Markey for Wildwood Enterprises; released by Touchstone Pictures
Direction: Robert Redford
Screenplay: Eric Roth and Richard LaGravenese; based on the novel by Nicholas Evans
Cinematography: Robert Richardson
Editing: Tom Rolf, Freeman Davies, Hank Corwin
Music: Thomas Newman
Production design: Jon Hutman
Art direction: Raymond Kluga
Set design: Clare Scarpulla
Costumes: Judy L. Ruskin
Sound: Tod A. Maitland
Visual effects supervision: Peter Donen, Peter Crosman
Equine technical advice: Buck Brannaman
MPAA rating: PG-13
Running Time: 168 minutes

REVIEWS

Chicago Tribune. May 15, 1998, p. 4.
Entertainment Weekly. May 22, 1998, p. 44.
Los Angeles Times. May 15, 1998, p. F1.
New York Times. May 15, 1998, p. E10.
New Yorker. May 18, 1998, p. 60.
People. May 25, 1998, p. 31.
Sight and Sound. September, 1998, p. 42.
Time. May 18, 1998.
USA Today. May 15, 1998, p. 9E.
Variety. May 4, 1998, p. 83.
Washington Post Weekend. May 15, 1998, p. 55.

How Stella Got Her Groove Back

Sometimes you have to break the rules to free your heart.—Movie tagline

"Whoopi Goldberg delivers a hilarious performance!"—*San Francisco Examiner*

"Angela Bassett smolders and glows!"—*Time*

Box Office: $37,665,439

"Age ain't nothing but a number," is the adage that attractive, affluent, and middle-aged Stella Payne (Angela Bassett) must brainwash herself with as she plummets head-first into a romantic relationship with a man half her age. *How Stella Got Her Groove Back* is a polished if lightweight recounting of one woman's struggle to find Mr. Right and true love in the place and person she least expected.

Based on a semi-autobiographical account of author and screenwriter Terry McMillan's own experiences on a Caribbean vacation, *How Stella Got Her Groove Back* looks at the life of successful financial analyst Stella Payne. Divorced and the mother of a precocious twelve year old, she lives in a swanky pad on the outskirts of San Francisco. Many may think Stella has it all, but all work and no play makes Stella a dull, lovelorn wreck. When her son goes away for a week to visit his father, Stella takes advantage of the moment and suggests to her best friend Delilah (Whoopi Goldberg) that they drop everything and head to Jamaica for a little fun and sun, with the emphasis on the fun.

Shortly after arriving on the lavish and tantalizing resort, Delilah, who is as blasé and carefree as Stella is reserved and responsible, encourages her stiff best friend to cut loose. She soon flirts with the idea when a handsome man piques her interest. Immediately she's physically attracted to the man known as Winston Shakespeare (Taye Diggs) and through casual conversation, he reveals to Stella that he is only twenty years old. To the forty-year-old Stella, the age difference is a glaring stumbling block and she immediately pushes away Winston's compliments and steady advances. Always combating Winston's approving eyes with her age, Stella increasingly becomes drawn to Winston. On advice of her

> Stella (Angela Bassett) to her friend Delilah (Whoopi Goldberg): "Oh, Dee, he's never done anything, he's never been anyplace, he hasn't even had his heart broken."

> Not long after the release of the film, author Terry McMillan married her young suitor, who was the basis of the Winston Shakespeare character from both the book and film.

friend and throwing caution to the wind, Stella decides to act on her strong physical attraction for Winston and their relationship turns heatedly romantic and sexual.

With Stella unsure how serious she's willing to take her relationship with Winston, the film, in brief and choppy sequences, displays the tension and happiness that such a relationship brings the two main characters. Through a convenient plot point (the death of Stella's friend), Stella's and Winston's love affair is brought to Stella's home turf and under the scrutiny of Stella's family. Stella's two sisters: moocher Vanessa (Regina King) is nonchalant about Stella's choice of mate as long as she can always hit big sister up for a loan, while snooty sister Angela (Suzzanne Douglas) considers Stella's choice an indication of desperation. Ironically, one would expect Angela to be more sympathetic toward her sister, since Angela is married to a white man and together they are expecting their first child. If love can be color blind, can it not be age blind, too? There is no subtext to Angela's marriage or a hint of animosity between Stella's ex-husband or son toward Winston, which turns *How Stella Got Her Groove Back* into a demonstration of multi-cultural and multi-generational togetherness that is more fairy tale than reality-based.

Such creative license taken on behalf of screenwriters McMillan and Ron Bass only proves that McMillan's novel, which makes for a relaxing afternoon read, doesn't necessarily make an interesting story on the big screen. One way the writers sought to ignite the film version is by the creation of Whoopi Goldberg's character, Delilah. In the novel, Delilah has died years before Stella even contemplates a vacation in Jamaica, but the film has her playing Stella's hip-talking soul mate/sidekick, a role that the Oscar-winning Goldberg plays to full effect. She is the film's most potent source of comic relief in its first half. And the film suffers a bit when Goldberg is no longer needed.

Wanting to pack both the comical and dramatic punch that propelled the similar *Waiting to Exhale* (1995), *Stella* turns up the melodrama when Delilah dies of cancer, leaving Stella devastated over her loss and seeking comfort in Winston's arms. Through the stoic direction of first-timer Sullivan, the suspense of whether Stella and Winston will make it together not only gets muddled with conventional side plots (Stella being fired from her job and Winston encouraging her to take up her life-long passion of making furniture), it becomes mute by the film's excessive running time and the inkling that these two individuals (one an ambitious youth, the other a creative and resourceful woman) wouldn't be too bad off if they decided to break up or not.

This romantic story may not hold your interest, but the look of it will. The photography makes every grain of beach sand and every pool dip just as enticing as it is. With the postcard scenery of the Jamaican landscape, it's easy to escape into the film's utopian view of romance with blinders on. The beauty of the land is also accentuated with the two beautiful leads. Bassett is nothing short of gorgeous as the physically fit and alluring Stella. She's always mesmerizing to watch even when what's going on around her is flat. Newcomer Diggs, fresh from the Broadway hit *Rent,* is truly a find with a flawless and chiseled body and sensuous smile that would no doubt melt the heart of any woman, regardless of age. With the lush scenery and perfect bodies before you, you'll certainly be inclined to seek out a travel guide or a Stairmaster.

How Stella Got Her Groove Back is definitely not as perfect as its leads. But it remains distinctive for two reasons: it's one of few films geared toward African Americans with all the ingredients to expand into the mainstream; and with the recent flak about Hollywood films teaming older men with much-younger women, it counters that concept with Stella happily setting up house with her younger mate. Audiences have grown accustomed to such pairings (seen most recently with Warren Beatty and Halle Berry in *Bulworth* [1998] or with Michael Douglas and Gwyneth Paltrow in *A Perfect Murder* [1998]—both films reviewed in this edition) and their inherent notion that happy endings come when a nubile young woman finds the solace and love needed in a father-figure type. It's refreshing to see that notion turned on its head by the likes of Bassett's Stella and Diggs's Winston.

—*Michelle Banks*

CREDITS

Stella: Angela Bassett
Winston Shakespeare: Taye Diggs
Delilah: Whoopi Goldberg
Vanessa: Regina King
Angela: Suzzanne Douglas
Quincy: Michael J. Pagan
Chantel: Sicily
Jack: Richard Lawson
Buddy: Barry (Shabaka) Henley

Origin: USA
Released: 1998
Production: Deborah Schindler; released by 20th Century Fox
Direction: Kevin Rodney Sullivan
Screenplay: Terry McMillan and Ron Bass; based on the novel by Terry McMillan
Cinematography: Jeffrey Jur
Editing: George Bowers
Production design: Chester Kaczenski
Art direction: Marc Dabe
Set decoration: Judi Giovanni
Costumes: Ruth E. Carter
Sound: Susumu Tokunow
Music: Michel Colombier
MPAA rating: R
Running Time: 124 minutes

REVIEWS

Chicago Sun-Times. August, 1998.
Chicago Tribune. August 14, 1998, p. 4.
Entertainment Weekly. August 14, 1998. p. 48.
Los Angeles Times. August 14, 1998, p. F1.
New York Times. August 14, 1998, p. E9.
People. August 24, 1998, p. 33.
San Francisco Chronicle. August 14, 1998, p. C1.
San Francisco Examiner. August 14, 1998, p. C1.
Sight and Sound. February, 1999, p. 45.
Variety. August 10, 1998, p. 41.
Washington Post. August 14, 1998, p. 39.

Hurlyburly

"A triumph! The ensemble acting surpasses that of any other film this year!"—Stephen Holden, *New York Times*

"A fireball! Powerhouse filmmaking."—Peter Travers, *Rolling Stone*

"This year's *Leaving Las Vegas*!"—Jennifer Mendalsohn, *USA Weekend*

 Box Office: $1,792,000

Hollywood players Mickey (Kevin Spacey) and Eddie (Sean Penn) are about to show young Donna (Anna Paquin) the ropes in the scathing *Hurlyburly*.

Depending on whom you ask, *Hurlyburly* was either "a misanthropic triumph" or "off-putting in the extreme." The *New York Times*'s Stephen Holden said it had the best ensemble performances of the year, while *USA Today* writer Andy Seiler thought he would have had more fun sitting in L.A. traffic than watching the film.

There are a few points the critics can agree on. 1. *Hurlyburly* is based on a play by David Rabe that was on Broadway about fifteen years ago. 2. It takes place in Los Angeles' Hollywood Hills. 3. It has an ensemble cast. The aforementioned and agreed-upon ensemble cast features Sean Penn, Kevin Spacey, Robin Wright Penn, Chazz Palminteri, Garry Shandling, Anna Paquin, and Meg Ryan taking over the roles that were developed on the stage by William Hurt, Christopher Walken, Sigourney Weaver, Harvey Keitel, Jerry Stiller, Cynthia Nixon, and Judith Ivey.

The film centers on Penn as Eddie, a coked-up casting director. When the film opens, his housemate and business partner, Mickey (Spacey), shakes him awake with, "Are you awake?" Eddie blinks, looks dazedly around the room, and responds, "I don't know." But in his own misguided way, Eddie is getting by—that is, until Mickey rocks his world by dating his ex, the cool blonde Darlene (Wright Penn). True to his character, Eddie starts obsessing—over Darlene, over television, over the pending Gulf War. Eddie questions his own existence and wonders, aloud and often, why things in life happen the way they do.

Mickey, a suave, glib, and cold man, really isn't all that interested. He doesn't care that much about Darlene and is just amusing himself while "taking a break" from the wife and kids. When Mickey tires of Darlene, he manipulates the situation so that it looks like he is giving her back to Eddie out of the kindness of his heart. As with most of Mickey's plans, it's exactingly calculated to make him look good.

 Bonnie (Meg Ryan) to Eddie (Sean Penn): "Oh boy, Eddie, I think I'm going to need a magnifying glass to find what's left of your good points."

Even after Eddie gets Darlene back, he continues to obsess, partly because Darlene doesn't love him as much as he'd like, partly because he's the kind of guy who needs to explore his every feeling and impulse. Somehow, Eddie has found himself a pack of friends who don't seem to mind his ceaseless chatter. Phil (Chazz Palminteri) is a violent ex-con trying to make it as an actor. Eddie's friend Artie (Garry Shandling) rightly suggests that the only reason Eddie hangs out with Phil is so that no matter how low Eddie falls in life, he can always look at Phil and see someone who is lower. These guys live in the kind of moral universe where it's completely acceptable for Artie to bring a runaway girl, Donna (Anna Paquin), to Eddie and Mickey's house so that they can use her however they see fit. "This is a perfectly viable piece of a**," says Artie, crudely, as he tries to convince them to take her in.

The film's roots as a play mixed with Eddie's ceaseless questioning of everything make *Hurlyburly* a long-winded film. To break up the monotony of seeing a bunch of guys sitting around a house talking, director Anthony Drazan occasionally tries to break it up by having Eddie rant to the others in the car, on the phone, or the combo—on a phone while in a car.

Now, there's nothing inherently wrong with talkie films. Practically every Woody Allen film manages to stay entertaining and engaging despite their heavy-on-the-dialogue/light-on-the-action plots. But *Hurlyburly* doesn't work as well as those for the simple reason that the characters aren't very interesting. That's not exactly true—they are interesting, but not as metaphysical seekers of truth. Perhaps if these characters got together and committed the perfect crime or something, then we'd have a film. But hearing these guys expound upon their theories is as absurd as reading a magazine profile on an actor in which the actor tries to explain his deep, philosophical viewpoint on the nature of life.

The first weird thing about *Hurlyburly* is that the characters are sometimes right with their theories. After all, it is reasonable to be upset about a pending war, to wonder whether so much bad TV is hurting us, or to want to find some sort of meaning to life. But by the time any of the characters say anything vaguely insightful, they've already lost credibility as any kind of source of wisdom. After violent Phil says something so dumb as, "This is my karma in life—to whack people in the face when they do such f***ed up things," who cares what other insights he might have? Likewise, when he says, "I have thoughts sometimes that can break my head open," it's hard to work up any desire to hear those thoughts.

The second weird thing about *Hurlyburly* is that the characters often break into long-winded monologues that sound more like they came from a writer's pen than from these character's brains. It's an interesting technique, but one that doesn't particularly work. Hearing a dumb character use big words is kind of amusing, but it's not worth the sacrifice of realism.

The third weird thing about *Hurlyburly* is that, while the characters aren't that interesting, the performances are

quite interesting. Sean Penn is typically intense as the over-the-top Eddie. He's always believable as he plays Eddie through his various phases, whether a clean-living go-getter or the kind of guy who is snorting coke at 8 a.m. At one point, when Darlene spurns him, Eddie becomes like a little angry child. "My girlfriend doesn't love me," he whines, making his mouth into a tiny, childish pout. Penn throws himself into the role and seems to be really enjoying himself.

Kevin Spacey is perfect as the cold, calculating Mickey. After the funeral of a close friend, Eddie complains about Mickey's sarcastic comments. "I'm not being sarcastic, I'm being glib," Mickey says, giving a little sarcastic (or is it glib?) speech about the difference between sarcastic remarks and glib ones. It's the kind of character that Spacey plays best—a guy who is a lot more than he lets on. He is above situations, coolly observing them so that nothing will catch him off guard.

Chazz Palminteri is believable as Phil and does, indeed, come across as an animalistic, violent jerk. When he goes on a blind date with working mother/stripper Bonnie (Meg Ryan) and she says something that he doesn't like, he handles the situation by throwing her out of a moving vehicle. Phil tells Eddie that the reason he doesn't want to have any more children is that "I don't want any kids rolling around in bed with a sick, f***ing hatred for me."

Robin Wright Penn's Darlene is The Blonde, the glamorous Hollywood status symbol rather than a real person. Wright Penn has the thoroughbred looks to pull off the role. Anna Paquin is all grown up as Donna, the runaway who's wiser than the supposed grown-ups around her. And Meg Ryan is serviceable as Bonnie. Although Ryan has the ability to play non-perky roles—like her streetwise chick in *Addicted to Love* (1997)—here, she sometimes lapses back into perkiness. When she smokes some pot with Eddie, she wrinkles her nose prettily at the smoke. At that moment, it's hard to believe that she's a hard-living stripper.

They're all great characters, they're just in the wrong movie. These are characters that should be doing something—a heist, a scam, anything—besides just sitting around talking. Watching the film is like talking to someone who just discovered therapy—you'd just like them to shut up already. Or as the review in the *Los Angeles Times* was headlined, "Yo, *Hurlyburly*, Put a Lid on It."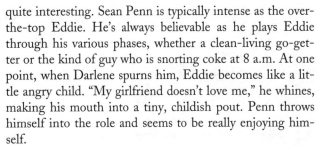

—*Jill Hamilton*

CREDITS

Eddie: Sean Penn
Mickey: Kevin Spacey
Darlene: Robin Wright Penn
Phil: Chazz Palminteri
Artie: Garry Shandling
Donna: Anna Paquin
Bonnie: Meg Ryan

Origin: USA
Released: 1998
Production: Anthony Drazan, Richard Gladstein, and David Hamburger for Storm Entertainment; released by Fine Line Features
Direction: Anthony Drazan
Screenplay: David Rabe; based on his play
Cinematography: Gu Changwei
Editing: Dylan Tichenor
Music: David Baerwald, Steve Lindsay
Production design: Michael Haller
Art direction: Derek Hill
Costumes: Mary Claire Hannan
Sound: Jeffrey S. Wexler
MPAA rating: R
Running Time: 122 minutes

REVIEWS

Boxoffice. January, 1999, p. 52.
Entertainment Weekly. January 8, 1999, p. 49.
New York Times. December 24, 1998, p. E1.
Variety. September 14, 1998, p. 36.

Hurricane Streets

know life. no limits.—Movie tagline

Hurricane Streets had a brilliant debut at the 1997 Sundance Film Festival, winning the Director and Audience awards, as well as Best Cinematography, and yet since has somehow failed to find commercial success. The first feature directorial effort of Morgan J. Freeman, *Hurricane Streets* deserves an audience. Even if the script is a bit formulaic, the overall effect of the film is potent and, at times, electric. Freeman's use of the camera to follow his brigade of five backpack-toting, bike-riding young thieves as they sweep down the streets of New York's Lower East Side is the film's best asset. There's an atmosphere of freedom, but he's pulled the camera back just far enough to show us how very young these boys are, despite their bravado and attitude, peddling away on their children's bikes.

The boys themselves are black, Latino, and white; one, Harold (Antoine McLean), is very young and desperate to please, and the edgy Chip (David Roland Frank) is constantly trying new looks (one of the film's running jokes is how he changes hair color often, and his self-body piercing predictably ends in a nasty infection). To say Chip has attitude is an understatement: he's sullen and constantly looking to one-up the others. He wants to graduate to stealing cars and he's the one to bring drugs into their hideout. Fifteen-year-old Marcus (Brendan Sexton III) is the de facto leader of their group by virtue of his decency and his ability to do business—when the others can only grab one or two CDs when they hit a music store, Marcus has his backpack stuffed full. But he's tired of it, dreaming of escaping the city for New Mexico, where he can find clean air (he sucks on an inhaler constantly) and open spaces. His uncle has promised to send a ticket, which his grandmother Lucy (Lynn Cohen) doubts. Lucy owns a neighborhood bar where Mack (L.M. Kit Carson) is a fixture—he's a shambling, charming character who is the closest thing Marcus has to a father figure. (Carson, a well-known indie figure, is also executive producer.) Like nearly all *Hurricane Streets'* adult principals, they are kind, empathetic souls who worry about the kids. Even the cop who pursues them, Kramer (Jose Zuniga), is decent.

Marcus dutifully visits his mother Joanne (Edie Falco) in prison, who wanly promises they'll go to New Mexico "in a year" when she's released. Marcus is busy at the schoolyard selling stolen CDs to even younger kids (one pays with a bag of quarters) when he meets a roller skating Melena, a shy, pretty Latina (Isidra Vega). When Kramer shows up, a warning hoot from Chip sends Marcus flying away on his bike with the cop running after and Melena holding on as they give him the slip. Melena promises to try to come to Marcus's birthday party at the bar, but she doesn't reckon on her father, Paco (Shawn Elliot), refusing to let her out. When she sneaks out anyway, arriving after the party, their hesitant attraction warms up. Their relationship is sweet and innocent, but Melena's father senses trouble. He rages at the girl—predictably, he knocks her around a bit to make the point. Freeman doesn't break any new ground here ("You're just like your mother, running around all the time!"), but Elliot's portrayal of the confused, angry Paco is scary, relentless in his need to hold on to his young daughter.

As Marcus and Melena's friendship grows (she skips school to hang out by the river with him, and apparently the boys never go), Paco prowls the neighborhood in his tow truck looking for her. Marcus has other problems. He's picked up by the police, and he finds out that his mother is not in jail for helping illegal aliens as he'd been told, but for killing his father, who had abused her. Chip is insistent on moving up to car theft and grand larceny in general, and he issues a challenge to Marcus. Marcus just wants out, and he's thrilled when the promised ticket arrives. Much to Lucy's chagrin, it's really Mack's doing: he wants Marcus to take to the road as he supposedly did. When Mack is in trouble and on the run, Marcus gives him the ticket. After an angry confrontation with Melena's father, Marcus shows up at their apartment, decks the father, and they make plans to escape.

The film was shown at the 1997 Sundance Film Festival under the title *Hurricane*.

Louis (Mtume Gant), the boy who believes his criminal career is a just a phase until he takes over his uncle's grocery store, proposes they rob an apartment. Marcus agrees only because he needs the money to take off with Melena. Harold (whom Chip dismissively calls "Chubbs") finds a wad of bills and a gun; as it turns out, they've broken into a policeman's apartment, reinforcing just how inexperienced and unlucky this crew really is. Back at the hideout, Paco is waiting for them to return. He hides in a closet that has a dart board and a pinup photo on the outside of door. He's enraged, ready to exact his vengeance on the boy who has taken his daughter away. But in a rather heavy-handed climax, it's Harold's show-off shot with his stolen gun at the bulls-eye that goes right through Paco. This turn of events finally breaks up their unity—they dispose of the body in the river, Chip takes off, Harold is a little boy overwhelmed by terror, and Benny (Carlo Alban), the least as-sertive, indignantly tells Marcus he can't just leave them now. The police arrest Chip, after being tipped off by Benny. Marcus, desperate to meet Melena at Penn Station as they'd planned, robs Louis's uncle's store and makes his getaway on the bike. He takes a spill and, dazed, sprints desperately down the street. He arrives just in time to run on to a train with Melena—we don't know where they are going or how they'll live when they get there. Melena, still unaware of what's happened, murmurs, "My father's gonna kill me . . . ," as if she were just late coming home. To his credit, Free-man doesn't make the ending either upbeat or morose: they are getting out of the city, and that's all.

Hurricane Streets shows us people who sound right and look right, and evoking a sense of place, Freeman films the New York of bodegas and backstreets brilliantly. Unfortu-nately, the clubhouse is a set decorator's idea of how a street kids' hangout should look—it has an artificial look, right down to artfully placed signs and comfy furniture. Perhaps the idea here was to give the idea that since they have such

a hangout, like the junior gangsters that they are, they are too far down the road to turn back from a life of crime and violence. Or maybe Freeman intended to pay less attention to the way things are likely to be, and more to how their bond is forged by commerce and convenience: they come to the clubhouse to kick back and divide the spoils of the day's work.

Who is Freeman trying to reach with this film? Is it a liberal's look at street kids, decrying their limited lives? Or did he hope to have comparisons made to *Kids* (1995), or is it an homage to Truffaut's *The 400 Blows* (1959)? The *Boston Phoenix* praised the film's humanity: "All of Free-man's characters are needy humans looking for and capable of giving love. The kids are fighting (and often failing) to find their places in an imperfect world; the adults are just trying to protect what little they've got."

Hurricane Streets manages to straddle the fence: it was praised as a look at street life, yet it was primarily marketed to a young audience, with a web site that imitated the club-house. MGM seemed to be at a loss as to how to promote this film, leaving it to prove itself in a few short engage-ments in major cities and hoping it would get attention from black and Latino teenagers. The soundtrack is a major at-traction, percolating away under Freeman's look at the other New York of weedy back lots and unfashionable neighbor-hoods: the standout track, "Staying Alive" by Supple, is about as far from the insipid Bee Gees original as possible, while a nod to the New York film of another era, *Saturday Night Fever*. Freeman and Sexton's collaboration (begun on *Wel-come to the Dollhouse* [1996] where Freeman was assistant di-rector) has now continued in *Desert Blue* (a little-known film shown at last year's Toronto Film Festival, which also fea-tures Isidra Vega); Sexton's vivid performance is more than enough reason to see this film. Vega and David Roland Frank also impress; both have remarkable presence and seem completely natural and unaffected. With few exceptions, the young cast holds its own and the movie really only works when they are front and center of the action.

—*Mary Hess*

CREDITS

Marcus: Brendan Sexton III
Paco: Shawn Elliot
Melena: Isidra Vega
Chip: David Roland Frank
Mack: L.M. Kit Carson
Kramer: Jose Zuniga
Harold: Antoine McLean
Lucy: Lynn Cohen
Joanne: Edie Falco
Ashley: Heather Matarazzo
Louis: Mtume Gant

Origin: USA
Released: 1997
Production: Galt Neiderhoffer, Gill Holland, and Mor-gan J. Freeman for Posthorn Pictures; released by United Artists
Direction: Morgan J. Freeman
Screenplay: Morgan J. Freeman
Cinematography: Enrique Chediak
Editing: Sabine Hoffman
Production design: Petra Barchi
Art direction: Iliana Sakus
Costumes: Nancy Brous
Sound: Robert Taz Larrea
MPAA rating: R
Running Time: 88 minutes

REVIEWS

Boxoffice. April, 1997, p. 179.
Boxoffice. September, 1997, p. 34.
Entertainment Weekly. February 20, 1998, p. 90.
Los Angeles Times. February 13, 1998, p. F24.
New York Times. February 13, 1998, p. E28.
Sight and Sound. June, 1998, p. 46.
Variety. February 3, 1997, p. 44.
Village Voice. February 17, 1998, p. 116.

Hush

Box Office: $13,587,246

"Of course, there must be subtleties," writer-director Billy Wilder is supposed to have once joked about scriptwriting, "just be sure you make them obvious." *Hush*, a suspense film about the crazed plotting of a mother-in-law trying to hold on to her son's affections, could be taken as an illustration of both implications of Wilder's quip. In the first half of the film, co-writer and director Jonathan Darby makes the subtleties subtle and comes up with a few intriguing touches; in the second half, however, plot and character become far too labored and obvious, as Martha, the mother-in-law played by Jessica Lange, turns into a shrill maniac and robs the film of its interest.

The exposition features some slick and stylish moments. Helen (Gwyneth Paltrow) is the first girl that Jackson (Johnathon Schaech) has ever brought home to his mother Martha. The couple has traveled to the South from New York to spend Christmas at Kilronan, the sprawling horse-breeding farm that has long been in Jackson's family. Though Martha has assigned them different rooms, Helen sneaks into Jackson's bed early the next morning. The filmmakers devise an effective introduction when Martha takes some cut flowers to Jackson's bedroom. Helen has just spotted the breakfast tray and struts naked to the door expecting Jackson ("An angel in the kitchen and a devil in the bedroom—now that's what I like in a man") when Martha enters and gets her first glimpse of her guest. Helen dashes back, crumpling under the covers, but Martha coolly savors her advantage: "Well, I guess I better hurry up and be embarrassed . . . I'll look

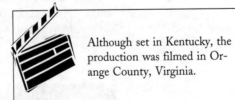
Although set in Kentucky, the production was filmed in Orange County, Virginia.

forward to seeing a lot less of you downstairs."

Initially, Helen responds favorably to Martha, to the farm, to the South. She recognizes the way they connect Jackson with his past and "the architecture of a life," as she calls it. Though Jackson and Helen had planned to return to New York after Christmas, Jackson submits to his mother's pleas and agrees that they will stay until the new year. Helen does not resist.

The next sequence subtly establishes Martha's manipulative nature. Director Darby drops a series of visual hints that Martha is coyly maneuvering herself to be a grandmother. For example, on New Year's Eve Helen returns to her room in the afternoon to find Jackson sitting on the bed ("You cleaned up? I'm shocked!"). He explains that it was his mother who had cleaned the room; in the bathroom Helen sees her diaphragm on the spotless counter under a pink Kleenex. After the party later that night, we see Helen and Jackson celebrating the new year by making love on the sofa as Martha looks down inexpressively from the shadows at the top of the staircase. Shortly after their return to New York, Helen reports to Jackson: "I'm pregnant . . . It seems that my diaphragm is broken." When they call Martha to announce that they are going to marry, Martha says to Jackson, "She's pregnant, isn't she?" At the wedding at Kilronan, Helen meets Jackson's grandmother, Alice Baring (Nina Foch), a blunt-speaking, long-standing nemesis of Martha. Alice tries at once to alert Helen to the dangers of her mother-in-law. What Alice's words to Helen accomplish, however, is the perfect summation of Martha's oblique scheming during the preceding scenes. Alice also correctly guesses that Helen is pregnant: "You can't be stupid and breed horses. It takes a lot of know-how and control. One man to help the stallion. One man to help the mare. One to hold the tail. And one to finesse the situation. Now Martha—she can manage all that by herself." Alice's words deftly confirm the film's clever analogy between horse breeding and possessive mothering.

When the newlyweds relocate from their life in New York to run Kilronan, the audience will also assume Martha's possible involvement. A mugger had threatened Helen and stolen her locket with the picture of her deceased parents. Though she did not suffer a miscarriage, the close call, coupled with Martha's surprise visit to New York, finally convinces them to undertake running the farm and trying to reverse its two years of declining revenues. The mysterious circumstances of the death of Jackson's father years ago have also led Helen to want to return to the farm with Jackson and face the ghosts of his past.

In its later scenes, the film loses most of its appeal as it sheds its subtleties. Helen spots Alice at a garden party and goes to greet her when Martha suddenly shouts, "No, I forbid it." As Martha drops her guard and behaves more overtly malicious, she begins to seem like yet another movie psychopath. The thinness of Jackson's character also proves to be a drawback. The plot requires him to become generally more passive and distant to Helen after their move back to Kilronan. In one scene Jackson arrives at the stables covered in mud from working with the horses, and Martha orders him to strip off his shirt while she hoses him down, laughing and leering at him. Martha's later threatening visit to Alice at her nursing home is also ineffective in its too-overt villainy.

The best moment in the second half of the film involves the drug-laced strawberry shortcake Martha employs as a weapon of sorts on Helen. In a few economical moments of setting the scene, we see Martha pumping the local doctor (Hal Holbrook) for the information that oxytocin, which she uses for her horses, is also the preferred drug for inducing labor in women. Next, Martha slips this drug from the medicine cabinet in the barn. In a slow traveling shot, the camera next moves closer to Martha as she carefully adorns the top of a cake with strawberries, an effective moment that suggests visually rather than states directly that Martha has prepared Helen's dessert with the labor-inducing drug.

The promise of these scenes is fulfilled a bit awkwardly with something of a twist in what follows. Similar to the direction of Alfred Hitchcock, the innocuous dinner-table conversation between Martha and Helen involves cutaways of the spiked shortcake, thereby building suspense by exploiting the knowledge the audience has of Martha's plans. Thanks to this technique, the filmmakers pare the dinner scene down to a minimum. Helen merely decides to take her cake upstairs to bed. Before she eats it, however, Darby creates an edgy, ironic montage of Martha praying at church and asking forgiveness for her sins. While Martha's voice continues on the soundtrack reading from the Old Testament book of Ruth about a daughter-in-law's godly obedience to her mother-in-law, we see Helen packing to leave Kilronan. Later that night in bed she finally eats the cake. The structuring of this scene oddly bypasses a rich opportunity for suspense, but it does succeed at bringing out stylishly Martha's mad self-delusion. The ironic use of scripture to convey Martha's crafty villainy lets the audience both enjoy the film's dark wit and recognize that Martha herself seems blind to her own malice. (For an example of how a similar situation is handled for maximum emotional impact, watch the scenes that depict the poisoning of Ingrid Bergman's character in Hitchcock's 1946 *Notorious*.)

The remainder of the film never rises again to this level. The combination of the oxytocin and Helen's desperate attempt to escape the farm estate brings on her labor. Jackson is away at the important first race for a horse he has nurtured while Helen is stretched out in bed under Martha's evil glare. Martha's plan is to nurse Helen through the childbirth, safeguard her infant grandson, and then kill Helen with an overdose of morphine. Coincidence foils these efforts, however, as Jackson returns unexpectedly just as Martha plunges a needle into Helen's arm. When Martha goes to detain Jackson, Helen flings the syringe onto the carpet. The final scene the next morning exposes the machinations of Martha by tying the events of the recent present with, predictably, those of the distant past and the death of Jackson's father.

A number of effective film elements are wasted thanks to the deteriorating script. The beautiful photography of the farm, especially the horseback riding scenes in the winter,

CREDITS

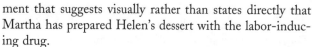

Martha Baring: Jessica Lange
Helen: Gwyneth Paltrow
Jackson Baring: Johnathon Schaech
Alice Baring: Nina Foch
Lisa: Debi Mazar
Sister O'Shaughnessy: Kaiulani Lee
Gavin: David Thornton
Dr. Hill: Hal Holbrook

Origin: USA
Released: 1998
Production: Douglas Wick; released by TriStar Pictures
Direction: Jonathan Darby
Screenplay: Jonathan Darby and Jane Rusconi
Cinematography: Andrew Dunn
Editing: Dan Rae, Lynzee Klingman, Robert Leighton
Music: Christopher Young
Production design: Thomas A. Walsh, Michael Johnston
Art direction: James Truesdale
Set design: Easton Michael Smith
Costumes: Ann Roth
Sound: Jay Meagher
MPAA rating: PG-13
Running Time: 95 minutes

REVIEWS

Entertainment Weekly. March 20, 1998, p. 56.
Los Angeles Times. March 9, 1998, p. F4.
People. March 23, 1998, p. 23.
USA Today. March 6, 1998, p. 4D.
Variety. March 9, 1998, p. 41.
Washington Post. March 6, 1998, p. D7.

and the church scenes will ultimately be overlooked by most viewers since the story becomes so flat and unimaginative. The first-rate cast is also squandered except for the few scenes mentioned above where some subtext gives the performers something to work with. The big climax of the childbirth scene lacks tension, and the resolution of saving Helen through the coincidence of Jackson's timely arrival appears artificial and forced. Finally, Helen's explanations about the events concerning the death of Jackson's father and the resulting behavior by Jackson and Martha settle the family drama too conveniently, making for a resolution that seems hurried and implausible. *Hush* offers a few well-realized sequences, but its lack of subtleties, as Billy Wilder's remark suggests, finally becomes far too obvious.

—Glenn Hopp

I Got the Hook-Up

These three entrepreneurs have the neighborhood wired, but the Feds want them disconnected . . . permanently.—Movie tagline

 Box Office: $10,317,779

One thing about *I Got the Hook-Up*—it uses its R rating to the fullest. In an R movie, you can show some topless women (check), graphically discuss sex (check), and curse like a mother— well, like someone who curses a lot (check, definitely check). Actually, *I Got the Hook-Up* probably earns the R rating in the first 20 seconds of the film when two minor characters unleash a stream of obscenities that includes more curse words than regular words.

The film is the project of Master P, a rapper who became hugely successful with his debut "Ghetto D" and his own indie label. After the surprise success of his straight-to-video autobiographical film *I'm Bout It*, which sold 250,000 copies, Master P ended up with a film deal.

In *I Got the Hook-Up*, Master P wrote, financed, and stars in the film. He plays Black, who runs a junkyard store in a down-and-out South Central L.A. neighborhood with a partner, Blue (A. J. Johnson). One day they con a truck driver into delivering a load of cell phones to their address instead of the proper destination. With the help of Black's sexy girlfriend Sweet Lorraine (Gretchen Palmer), who works at a cell phone company, and his mechanical brother (Anthony Boswell), they get the phones up and running and start to hook up their neighborhood. First they get rich, then they get problems. The phone lines start getting crossed. In the process, Black and Blue manage to anger the F.B.I., the cell phone company, and the local bad guy and his thugs. They also manage to anger most film critics, though that's not part of the story.

Most critics were upset by the film's "low" humor, racist attitude, and profanity. It's understandable. This is a film that plays retarded people, midgets, and fat people for laughs. It is rare for a full ten seconds to go by without a profanity. And, true, women are not respectfully treated. How most reviewers handled the issue was to make a race issue of the thing. Plenty of critics worked the term "blaxploitation" into their reviews and fretted about how the white people were portrayed as incompetent. What most lost sight of was the fact that a comedy can be stupid, vulgar, or even unfunny without race being a factor at all. Did anyone note that Jeff Daniels's graphic toilet scene in *Dumb and Dumber* (1994) was a low moment for Caucasians in film?

Most of the humor is pretty bad, a lot of it offensive. For example, when Black and Blue are trying to get a Latino man to do something for them, they offer him a piñata "with a lot of candy." Similarly, it's supposed to be funny in one scene that an old grandma has a drug dealer of her own. But just because most of the movie is crass and completely non-P.C., that doesn't mean it is completely void of inspired moments. In one scene, Black is making a date with a woman for the next day. Black describes what he'll be wearing. Blue, wanting to go too, chimes in that he'll be there and he'll be the one "buck naked." Right there, in the middle of the scene, the filmmakers stick in several outtakes of Blue describing various equally absurd outfits. It's a clever and fresh moment.

Unfortunately, the few good moments don't save the film. Working against the movie is a too-slow plot and a lack of dramatic tension. And the movie doesn't score any points for originality when, for perhaps the 187th time in a film, a fruit stand is upset during a car chase.

Despite the film's rather obvious flaws, Master P does have a strong onscreen presence. It will be interesting, if he can live down the poison reviews for *I Got the Hook-Up*, to see what he might do in another film—preferably a film not

CREDITS

Black: Master P
Blue: A. J. Johnson
Sweet Lorraine: Gretchen Palmer
T-Lay: Tommy "Tiny" Lister Jr.
Dalton: Frantz Turner
Little Brother: Anthony Boswell
Mr. Mims: John Witherspoon

Origin: USA
Released: 1998
Production: Jonathan Heuer for Shooting Star Pictures, No Limit Films, and Priority Films; released by Dimension Films
Direction: Michael Martin
Screenplay: Master P
Cinematography: Antonio Calvache
Editing: T. Davis Binns
Music: Tommy Coster, Brad Fairman
Production design: Michael Pearce
Costumes: Jhane Isaacs
Sound: David Bach
MPAA rating: R
Running Time: 93 minutes

written by him. A. J. Johnson does a good job in his role as the short, hyper, unlucky-in-love sidekick Blue. Ice Cube and Snoop Doggy Dogg dutifully put in some uneventful cameos, and at first glance it looks as if an overweight Martin Sheen puts in a cameo, too, as a zealous government agent. But it turns out that it's Sheen's portly lookalike brother, Joe Estevez.

I Got the Hook-Up is not a good film by anyone's standards. But it's a bad film because it's slow, pretty offensive, and not funny; not because of color.

—Jill Hamilton

REVIEWS

Entertainment Weekly. June 5, 1998, p. 54.
Los Angeles Times. May 27, 1998, p. F4.
New York Times. May 27, 1998, p. E5.
People. June 8, 1998, p. 40.
USA Today. April 8, 1998, p. 7D.
Variety. June 1, 1998, p. 34.
Village Voice. June 9, 1998, p. 148.

I Love You, Don't Touch Me

Just your typical boy-loves-girl who doesn't love boy till he loves other girl story.—Movie tagline
"Honest, sexy and consistently funny!"—*Los Angeles Times*
"Smart, sweet, audacious, original!"—*New York Post*
"Bright and energetic!"—*New York Times*

Less "Cosmo" and more class would've helped this low-budget romantic comedy that, despite its pretentiously strained attempts, doesn't offer any fresh insight on relationships between the sexes. Cliched dialogue and annoying voiceovers announcing the obvious don't add to the trite story in this freshman effort by Julie Davis. Although this film looks more than its reported $65,000 budget with decent editing and production values, poor lighting and odd camera work make it generally undisciplined and uneven in its quality.

Writer/director/editor Davis, who appropriately went on to do editing and directing for The Playboy Channel,

generously peppers the almost single-mindedly carnal dialogue with an embarrassing amount of vulgarities. Neophyte lead (and Davis's childhood buddy) Marla Schaffel (Katie) is obliged to spew offhanded obscenities that, with her prudish, stilted delivery, seem like a foreign language.

Schaffel's character, Katie, is a virgin songstress in Los Angeles, searching for the mythical Mr. Right after all her early relationships soured due to unfaithful partners. She is self-righteous in these pursuits and looks down at her more liberal friends who date and sleep with people they don't actually love, including co-worker Janet (Meredith Scott Lynn) and her randy neighbor Jones (Darryl Theirse). Constantly at odds with her best friend and hopeful suitor, Ben (Mitchell Whitfield), Katie flicks off his admitted adoration of her in a poem he sheepishly gives her. As heard in a voiceover announcing her inner monologue: "Poor Ben, he loves me for all the right reasons and I feel nothing for him." Although perhaps truthful, this makes her egotistic character rather hard to root for. Ben is in therapy trying to deal with his unrequited love, whereas Katie's idea of an answer is to set Ben up with Janet. Much to Katie's secret dismay, the two hit it off immediately.

A somewhat novel idea of a virgin in the '90s *and* in Los Angeles does start with some potential, until Katie literally runs into her future deflowerer driving a yellow Ferrari. Albeit predictable, the interludes with composer Richard Webber (Michael Harris) also prove unbelievable. He is the picture of pomposity and supposed worldliness sent to usher Katie into a world of culture, freedom, and sexuality. She fights it kicking and screaming all the way but gives in to his irresistible "charm." Harris plays this role without an ounce of likability or genuine feeling, yet we are supposed to believe that this is who Katie has been waiting for. His banter with Katie is also the worst of the film, with unrelenting food analogies such as this little exchange after a first-date dinner when he mentions that, in the love department, he has "sampled many dishes," and Katie asks, "What dishes have you sampled

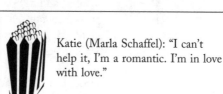

Katie (Marla Schaffel): "I can't help it, I'm a romantic. I'm in love with love."

lately?" Richard: "None. I haven't had much of an appetite, lately." Katie: "Maybe you've overeaten." Richard: "Or maybe I've just eaten the wrong dishes." It does not end here and these delightful metaphors continue until they come full circle when things between the lovers come to a bitter end and Katie berates Richard with, "Women are not like food. You cannot consume us and shit us out when you're done." The fantasy sequences throughout the film designed to show the passion alive within the uptight Katie are similarly trite and uninventive.

Conversely, Whitfield's Ben has some of the film's best exchanges and funniest lines, which he delivers with ease and insight. Ben is earnest in his pursuit of the spunky Janet (played with great ingenuity by Meredith Scott Lynn), whose honesty and practicality seem to suit Ben's style. Janet senses, however, that he is still harboring love for Katie. In one moment, Katie sulks that Richard is not emotionally open enough after sex, while Janet is simultaneously berating Ben for not just being able to be intimate without opening up to her. It is clear these two are destined to eventually get together.

Other than both characters ending up in therapy and the fact that Katie is a total neurotic, comparisons to Woody Allen seem to end there. There are some accurate observations to be heard in the film about love and lust, men and women, sexual liberation, and just plain sluttiness, but it's nothing we haven't all heard before. Schaffel's singing talent does lend some credibility to her role, but carrying the entire film with her performance is a big job that she sometimes cannot handle.

—Hilary Weber

CREDITS

Katie: Marla Schaffel
Ben: Mitchell Whitfield
Janet: Meredith Scott Lynn
Richard: Michael Harris
Elizabeth: Nancy Sorel
Jones: Darryl Theirse

Origin: USA
Released: 1998
Production: Julie Davis and Scott Chosed for Westie Films and Big Hair Productions; released by Goldwyn Entertainment Company
Direction: Julie Davis
Screenplay: Julie Davis
Cinematography: Mark Putnam
Editing: Julie Davis
Music: Jane Ford
Production design: Carol Strober
MPAA rating: R
Running Time: 90 minutes

REVIEWS

Hollywood Reporter. February 17, 1998, p. 18.
Los Angeles Times. February 20, 1998, p. F16.
New York Times. February 20, 1998, p. E14.

I Still Know What You Did Last Summer

The sequel that will hook you . . . again.—Movie tagline

Get Hooked Again.—Movie tagline

"Scarier than the first!"—Teri Hart, *TMN Toronto*

"If you were *hooked* by the original, you'll *die* for this one!"—Sam Hallenbeck, *The Theater Radio Network*

 Box Office: $38,889,884

He still knows and he's still after Julie James (Jennifer Love Hewitt) and her new friend Karla Wilson (Brandy) in *I Still Know What You Did Last Summer*.

Even before 1997's *I Know What You Did Last Summer* went to number one in ticket sales and set a box-office record for an October opening, the filmmakers had already made it clear that a sequel was a big option. The tip-off, as if anyone really needed one, was an ending featuring a not-so-dead villain. Of course, all horror films must feature that now-expected "surprise" ending with the villain who is not . . . really . . . dead!, but the success of *I Know* guaranteed that the remaining living cast members would be back for more slicing n' dicing.

I Still Know What You Did Last Summer takes off where *I Know* left off, borrowing the plot, but leaving the humor behind. In the first movie, Julie James (Jennifer Love Hewitt), boyfriend Ray Bronson (Freddie Prinze Jr.), and two of their friends are driving back from a double date when they accidentally hit a man, Ben Willis (Muse Watson), with their car. The sensible Julie wants to call the police and get help for Willis, but the others convince her that it would be smarter to finish the job by killing him and tossing his body into the ocean. They go with that plan and all is well until someone shows up in their town on the anniversary of the accident and starts killing off the group.

In the second movie, the killer—who, really, should be so dead from the last movie—is back. You see, it's again the anniversary of the accident, July 4, the time when the killer gets riled up about it and goes on a killing spree. The rest of the year, presumably, the killer shops at the grocery store, watches *Oprah,* and otherwise leads a normal, murder-free life. This killing-on-the-anniversary plan gives the movie a title problem. Since the accident was two years ago, shouldn't the film be called *I Know What You Did the Summer Before Last*?

This time out, Julie is off at college with Karla Wilson (Brandy), her new best friend—since her old best friend was killed off and all. Julie is having problems with her sailor

 Tourist: "What do you do around here for fun?" Bartender: "Make fun of tourists."

boyfriend, Ray, because she won't visit him at their old home town, the charming North Carolina coast village, South Port. It's not that Julie doesn't like Ray, it's just that South Port reminds her of the murders. For no apparent reason, except to further the plot, Ray can't seem to accept that perfectly logical explanation. So when Karla answers a question on a radio contest and wins a weekend trip for four to the Bahamas, Julie's back-up boy, Will (Tom Cruise lookalike Matthew Settle), goes in Ray's place.

Once Julie, Will, Karla, and Karla's concupiscent boyfriend Tyrell (Mekhi Phifer of *Soul Food* [1997]) arrive on the tiny island, things start getting bleak. For one thing, they get rooms #201 and #202 (which causes a few versions of this exchange: Hotel Worker, ominously: "You're in 201 and 202!?" Julie: "Yes, why?" Hotel Worker, too casually: "Oh . . . no reason"). It's also the beginning of hurricane season, and not only is the hotel's help unfriendly, they are dying off at an alarming rate.

At first, Julie's friends don't believe that someone on the island is killing people—they think that Julie is just jumpy. Julie has every right to be jumpy because director Danny Cannon makes sure that about every five or ten minutes there's a big scare in the movie. The scares come with such regularity that they become almost tedious. It's as though the filmmakers figured out exactly how frequently the audience should be scared, then had a computer program write the script using the command that a scare occur every x number of minutes. Because the killer can only get around to killing so many people, the movie is littered with fake scares to keep the audience on edge. Fake scare moments include firecrackers going off, a barking dog, and—help!—a clothes dryer making a loud thumping noise.

There's a scene in the movie that's played as a real scare, but seems far more akin to a fake scare. Karla wants Julie to relax and suggests she get a tan in the hotel's tanning bed (because, of course, what better way to relax from being chased by a killer than separating from your friends). Once Julie is in the tanning bed with stereo headphones on, the

Most of the movie's interior shots were done in a once abandoned hotel in Mexico that was reconstructed solely for the film.

killer sneaks in and, with something that looks about as strong as a bread twist-tie, binds the door shut. Julie screams, her friends rush into the room, and the soundtrack roars— all over this little twist-tie.

But not all the scares are so lame. There is plenty of mayhem and some gore, the most memorable being a character who gets hooked in the throat just after saying "This is the worst f***ing vacation of my entire life." Indeed. But for the most part, the deaths in *I Still Know* tend not to be all that inventive, and that probably has something to do with the limitations of the Willis character. Freddie Kruger can kill people in their dreams, Jason has the scary hockey mask, but Willis has . . . a fisherman's rain slicker and hat. As more than one critic put it, Willis looks an awful lot like the Gordon's fisherman. Besides the sensible rain gear, Willis's other distinguishing characteristic is a hook hand. By necessity, then, most of his kills involve . . . hooking someone with the hook. That's fine, but it would add a little variety if he could just shoot somebody once in a while. Even his name lacks ominousness. Is Ben Willis really a name for a killer?

The thing that Willis has going for him is that he's a very industrious killer. To make sure that Julie and her friends stay riled up, he has a habit of planting dead bodies around so that they find them and scream. One can only imagine how much effort it takes to drag all those bodies around to prop them up in various hiding places. In one such scene, he even takes the time to arrange the dead body at a desk, festoon the room with blood, and scrawl out in blood, "I know what you did. . . ." This is a man who spends a lot of time on his work.

Of course, a killer who can remove all traces of blood and a dead body from a closet in the time it takes Julie to run downstairs and back should surely be able to do his real job, that is, killing Julie. Not to tell anyone how to do his job, but it seems like his time could be spent a lot more effectively by just killing Julie instead of wasting all his energy killing innocent bystanders and dreaming up elaborate ways to scare people. In the tanning bed incident, for example, he might have tried killing Julie instead of using the twist-tie closure to try to tan her to death. (Yes, ultraviolet rays are dangerous, but their damaging effects could take years. Why not go for a faster kill?)

The cast of "I Still Know" does a good job considering the script limitations. They are playing characters so two-dimensional that they don't even have a flicker of mourning when a close friend or boyfriend is killed. Brandy is perky and watchable as Julie's energetic friend. Jennifer Love Hewitt is appropriately pretty as she runs from the killer wearing one of her many wet shirts. The wet shirts are there to highlight the real stars of the movie, that is, Hewitt's am-

CREDITS

Julie James: Jennifer Love Hewitt
Ray Bronson: Freddie Prinze Jr.
Karla Wilson: Brandy
Tyrell: Mekhi Phifer
Ben Willis: Muse Watson
Will Benson: Matthew Settle

Origin: USA
Released: 1998
Production: Neil H. Moritz, Erik Feig, Stokely Chaffin, and William S. Beasley for a Mandalay Entertainment and Columbia Pictures production; released by Sony Pictures
Direction: Danny Cannon
Screenplay: Trey Callaway; based on characters written by Kevin Williamson, which were based on the novel by Lois Duncan
Cinematography: Vernon Layton
Editing: Peck Prior
Production design: Doug Kraner
Art direction: Charles Butcher, Scott Ritenour
Set decoration: Jan Bergstrom
Costumes: Dan Lester
Sound: David Ronne
Music: John Frizzell
MPAA rating: R
Running Time: 101 minutes

ple bosom. As a critic at the *L.A. Weekly* wrote, "they are indeed the perkiest, most alert aspects of the film."

Will this be it for the *I Know* franchise? If the filmmakers have their way, future generations will be watching something like, *I Still Know What Your Grandparents Did That One Summer in the '90s.*

—*Jill Hamilton*

REVIEWS

Chicago Tribune. November 13, 1998, p. 5.
Entertainment Weekly. November 20, 1998, p. 94.
Los Angeles Times. November 13, 1998, p. F8.
New York Times. November 13, 1998, p. E14.
People. November 23, 1998, p. 34.
San Francisco Chronicle. November 13, 1998.
Variety. November 9, 1998, p. 31.

I Think I Do

Two couples. One wedding. No funerals.—Movie tagline

Anyone that ever went to see a friend (or a friend's kid, perhaps) in a school play was faced with a terrible dilemma: what do you say when you hated the show but you don't hate the friend? "Very interesting." "You kids must have put a lot of work into that." "I loved that part where (fill in the blank)." But it's pretty hard to truly say you liked it when the show was just, well, not good. That's the case with *I Think I Do*, a low-budget comedy from Brian Sloan. You can say the kids worked pretty hard, and that they must have put a lot of work into it, but alas, it's just not entertaining.

And what's worse is that the buildup was good. Expectations were high. Sloan was one of the filmmakers who contributed to *Boy's Life* (1996), a trio of short films (Sloan's was titled *Pool Days*) that was highly regarded by critics. *I Think I Do* was the feature-length step on the ladder that Sloan needed to secure his place as a filmmaker of talent and originality. Unfortunately, audiences will have to wait for his next film to decide whether Sloan was a one-note wonder, for *I Think* displays no large amount of talent or originality, sad to say.

It is the story of Bob (Alexis Arquette), his college chums, their sexual problems and peccadilloes, and their romantic entanglements. If it has a theme, it is that you can never be sure about anything in the romance department. But to say that this film has a theme, or to go about trying to find one, is not the point (and in all fairness to the filmmakers, it shouldn't have to be). This is a screwball comedy where bed-hopping replaces the kind of identity issues that might have been found in *Some Like It Hot* (1959) or in *Pillow Talk* (1959). *I Think I Do* aspires to the level of *The Big Chill* (1983), with its group of friends who discover that love is never what you expect (or something like that). And it attempts to find a frothy-but-sophisticated wit found in *The*

Philadelphia Story (1940) or any of the Preston Sturges comedies. But it doesn't succeed.

What it does have is the twist that the characters are both gay and straight, and that the storyline does not involve just one or the other. Bob (Arquette) and his college roommate and best buddy Brendan (Christian Maelen) are seen, in the film's opening, wrestling around platonically. But what Brendan doesn't know is that Bob has been in love with him for a long time. Things quickly become heated and Brendan becomes scared, ending their relationship, and causing reverberations with the rest of their friends (Maddie Corman, Marianne Hagan, Lauren Velez, and Jamie Harrold).

Fast forward to years later, when Carol (Velez) and Matt (Harrold) are getting married. Bob attends the wedding with his hunky boyfriend Sterling (Tuc Watkins), the star of the soap opera Bob writes and produces. Sterling wants to make their situation permanent, but Bob still aches for Brendan. Brendan shows up at the wedding too, and announces that he has a secret: he's gay now, and he's decided that Bob is and always has been the guy for him. What about Sterling, who may be dumb but has a great body and is crazy about Bob? What about those poor other straight lady friends of Bob and Brendan's who can't find nice guys? Why are they only hanging out with gay guys? What about the seriously mismatched Matt and Carol? And most importantly, what will Bob do about Brendan's newfound attention?

Suffice it to say that many sexual situations and much soul-searching is required before the denouement. But you can bet Bob's final decision won't be a disappointment. This type of film should usually be incredibly witty because it is clearly going to end the way you want it to. The story isn't what attracts audiences to films like *Four Weddings and a Funeral* (1994). It's the style: the dialogue, the performances, and the direction. But unfortunately, other than Arquette's sweetly cynical Bob and Tuc Watkins' standout as the dumb-as-dirt Sterling, the performances are perfunctory at

CREDITS

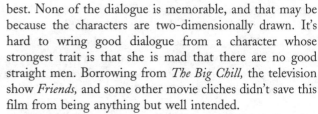

Bob: Alexis Arquette
Brendan: Christian Maelen
Beth: Maddie Corman
Eric: Guillermo Diaz
Sarah: Marianne Hagan
Carol: Lauren Velez
Sterling: Tuc Watkins
Matt: Jamie Harrold

Origin: USA
Released: 1997
Production: Lane Janger for Danger Filmworks and House of Pain; released by Strand Releasing
Direction: Brian Sloan
Screenplay: Brian Sloan
Cinematography: Milton Kam
Editing: Francois Keraudren
Production design: Debbie Devilla
Costumes: Kevin Donaldson, Victoria Farell
Sound: Robert Taz Larrea
MPAA rating: Unrated
Running Time: 92 minutes

best. None of the dialogue is memorable, and that may be because the characters are two-dimensionally drawn. It's hard to wring good dialogue from a character whose strongest trait is that she is mad that there are no good straight men. Borrowing from *The Big Chill*, the television show *Friends*, and some other movie cliches didn't save this film from being anything but well intended.

The best thing that can be said, and this is important, is that the mixture of gay and straight romance is unusual to see on the big screen. Perhaps *I Think I Do* should be remembered and congratulated for that.

—*Kirby Tepper*

REVIEWS

Boxoffice. April, 1998, p. 198.
Los Angeles Times. April 15, 1998, p. F9.
New York Times. April 10, 1998, p. E14.
Variety. June 30, 1997, p. 66.
Village Voice. April 14, 1998, p. 64.

I Went Down

A film about sex, friendship and one incredibly talkative hostage.—Movie tagline
"The cinematic equivalent to a night in an Irish pub."—Ray Greene, *Boxoffice*
"A sharp, droll comedy."—Lisa Schwartzbaum, *Entertainment Weekly*
"A great film! Unfolds with the racy abandon of a pulp thriller, with dialogue that is both deliriously obscene and highly literary."—Richard Rayner, *Harper's Bazaar*
"Colorful, off-color, and packed with impertinent zingers, *I Went Down* delights in sidestepping cliches."—Dennis Lim, *Interview*
"Sharply etched and tartly written."—Janet Maslin, *New York Times*
"The flood of lively new movies from Ireland hits a crest with *I Went Down*! A deft, darkly comic thriller with a coolly inventive plot."—Bruce Williamson, *Playboy*

"If you can't enjoy this one, you may give up on movies altogether."—*Time Out London*
"Hilarious, good hearted and thoroughly unpredictable! It should make stars of its talented director, dazzling writer and flawless cast."—Amy Taubin, *Village Voice*

Paddy Breathnach is one of Irish cinema's mavericks. His 1991 film *Alisa* was an intense, brooding piece of work that could stand alongside some of the dreariest and most thoughtful contemporary European art films. His second and most recent feature, *I Went Down*, is a considerable departure from that mold, although he's still interested in making highly artificial the troubles that define everyday life. *I Went Down* is a gangster film, and it incorporates many of the elements, both narrative and stylistic, common to that genre. Breathnach rides a fine line throughout the film, though, between making this an enjoyable pop film and something else entirely, something more complex and tragic. In so doing, he shows you just how strange and wonderful a genre the gangster flick could be, were it used to its full potential more often. Overall *I Went Down* is a smashing example of what American film critic Manny Farber once called Termite Art: its raw love for generic conventions and its ability to speak to a wide audience make it far more subversive than most "art films." Breathnach is not among Ireland's best known filmmakers, although *I Went Down* certainly shows why he deserves to be. He may, of course, be well on his way to broader acclaim, since this film has enjoyed both a theatrical release in Europe and North America, after winning great acclaim at the 1998 edition of that hippest of American film festivals, Sundance.

The film starts when our hero, Git Haynes (Peter McDonald), is released from jail. His old girlfriend is now with his best friend, and he agrees to tell his guilt-stricken pal that it's OK. Before he can do this, though, Git badly beats up two gangsters who were roughing his mate up. Their boss, gangster kingpin Tom French (Tom Doyle), is upset, especially since one of the guys Git roughed up lost his eye (in a moment of especially harsh Catholic expression, Tom French says that under normal circumstances he'd simply have taken Git's eye in return). To make things right, he demands that Git go down to the countryside around Cork to retrieve an old business associate, Frank Grogan (Peter Caffery), and the $25,000 that he supposedly still has. He's sent along with Bunny Kelly (Brendan Gleeson), who insists that they focus purely on getting the job done and ignore any larger moral concerns that might present themselves. Of course, this cynical strategy doesn't work, and when the job starts to become complicated the two find it difficult to know whom they should be loyal to. As the job slowly disintegrates and their lives become increasingly endangered, Git and Bunny develop a close relationship, a pairing that feels much less contrived and more meaningful than what would be found in a typical buddy movie. The end of the film nicely combines harsh justice with profound redemption (more of Breathnach showing his Catholic background?) and still manages to leave the characters' most interesting ambiguities unresolved.

There's no question that *I Went Down* is in many ways a straightforward gangster film, and certainly contains most of the stylistic and thematic quirks of that genre. All the tough guys are sufficiently surly and badly dressed, and Git is supposed to be playing the role of the nice kid gone just a little bit wrong. The film's also got plenty of moments of violent catharsis that are the gangster flick's stock in trade. One especially impressive example of this is when Frank is taking a bath in a luxurious hotel, believing that he has evaded Git and Bunny. Shot from a ridiculously (Hitchcockian) high angle (which has the benefit of illustrating how comically gaudy the bathroom is), Bunny suddenly breaks down the door and darn near shoots Frank just out of spite. A more conventional example of the film's fondness of gangster conventions comes at the climax, when Git gets over his anxiety about shooting at people, leans out of the car during a high-speed chase, and shoots out the windshield of the pursuing car. For fans of fast-paced crime movies, there's plenty of high-testosterone kicks in *I Went Down*.

Breathnach alters the genre in other ways, though, and one of those ways is to make certain minor aspects of it conform to the reality of rural Ireland, where much of it is set. One example of this comes when Git and Bunny first go to get Frank, who is hiding out deep in the countryside, and Git falls into a bog. It's kind of an odd little narrative kink, and doesn't effect the story all that much, but it does have a way of reminding the viewer where they are. The minor problems they encounter on Ireland's ridiculously narrow roads have a similar effect. At one point Bunny tells Git that they have to be especially careful, since they're driving a stolen car and that on these roads, there'd be no way that they could avoid being trapped by the police if they got into a chase. These may seem like minor points, but Breathnach actually brings up the road issue a few more times, and overall these little pieces of Irish complication give the film a sense of being just a little bit off, not quite what a viewer would expect from a Hollywood-style gangster flick.

This sense is confirmed by other elements of the film, most notably the way that the relationship between the characters develops and then twists all around. Git is early on established as a guy who values loyalty above almost everything else, and Breathnach seems to be playing his idealism off of the more hardened Bunny. What eventually becomes clear, though, is that Git gives away his loyalty too easily, and it is the cynical, seemingly amoral Bunny who ends up having the truly clearheaded sense of loyalty and its role in this harsh life. The narrative settles quickly into the usual confusing gangster twists and turns, but the male bonding subplot, always present in gangster films, is developed in an especially interesting way here. Buddy films seem to always have something of a homoerotic subtext, but *I Went Down* makes this aspect of the experience explicit in a fairly fascinating way. A scene where, after a few beers, Bunny tells Git that he was forced to do this job because Tom French threatened

 Frank (Peter Caffrey) to his captors: "Did you ever make love to a gangster's wife? You can't really enjoy yourself."

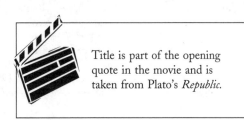 Title is part of the opening quote in the movie and is taken from Plato's *Republic*.

to tell his wife about a homosexual liaison he had in jail, a liaison that seems to have really meant something to him, is a moment of real intimacy and openness between two men. Such ambiguous, painful, and genuine emotion is not within the moral universe of most gangster flicks, and the way that the exchange cements the relationship between the two men is what makes this one of the few films to be worthy of the name "buddy film."

Overall the film rides a very fine line between irony and involvement, although the sheer zestiness of the film is enough to keep it from being an overly arty pastiche. Different segments of the film are separated by title cards that cryptically summarize what's going to follow, and while this might seem just a little bit too clever and film-schoolish, the absurdity of the device makes it effective and comical. Fur-

ther, while Breathnach's tongue is pretty firmly in his cheek, he never condescends to his material. His actors are going more or less all out through the entire film, and the kinetic pace that makes gangster flicks such crowd pleasers never lets up. At the same time, Breathnach's understanding of the genre's mainstays—such as loyalty and male bonding—is far more nuanced and fully considered than the genre usually allows. He has, astonishingly, the best of both worlds: *I Went Down* is a gangster film that is highly aware of its own limitations at the same time that it shamelessly pushes the cheap thrills that are supposed to make the viewer forget about such limitations.

There have been quite a few oh-so-hip gangster imitations over the last few years that have tried to capitalize off the success of *Pulp Fiction* (1994). Most of them are possessed of a smarmy superiority towards a genre that they are supposed to be reveling in: seeming to want to eat their slam-bang cake and have it too. Breathnach's film is different: he is blessed with a sense of lunacy and excitement, but also has a gentle, patient sense of directing, allowing his actors enough space to slowly illustrate the complexity of their characters. He has managed to give a uniquely American genre a sense of Irish geography with a pinch of European slowness and deliberation for good measure: that this cinematic soup doesn't feel overseasoned is remarkable, but it doesn't. Instead, *I Went Down* is an exciting, self-conscious, and enjoyable film, one of the most original works to come out of Ireland, or anywhere, in quite some while.

—*Jerry White*

CREDITS

Bunny Kelly: Brendan Gleeson
Git Hynes: Peter McDonald
Frank Grogan: Peter Caffrey
Tom French: Tony Doyle
Sabrina Bradley: Antoine Byrne
The Friendly Face: Donal O'Kelly
Anto: David Wilmot

Origin: Great Britain, Ireland
Released: 1997
Production: Robert Walpole for Treasure Films, Euskal Media, Radio Telefis Eireann, Irish Film Board, and BBC Films; released by The Shooting Gallery
Direction: Paddy Breathnach
Screenplay: Conor McPherson
Cinematography: Cian de Buitlear
Editing: Emer Reynolds
Cinematography: Music Dario Marianelli
Production design: Zoe MacLeod
Art direction: Tim McCullogh
Sound: Simon J. Willis
MPAA rating: R
Running Time: 108 minutes

REVIEWS

Boxoffice. April, 1998, p. 182.
Detroit Free Press. July 3, 1998, p. 3C.
Entertainment Weekly. July 10, 1998, p. 54.
Los Angeles Times. July 1, 1998, p. F4.
New York Times. June 24, 1998, p. E5.
Sight and Sound. February, 1998, p. 44.
Variety. October 13, 1997, p. 98.
Village Voice. June 30, 1998, p. 138.
Washington Post Weekend. July 3, 1998, p. 46.

I'll Be Home for Christmas

Somewhere between L.A. and N.Y. Jake found the true meaning of Christmas.—Movie tagline

Box Office: $12,025,266

I'll Be Home for Christmas is a dismal attempt to cash in on the teen heartthrob fame of its star, Jonathan Taylor Thomas, and a woeful miscalculation it is. *Christmas,* released by Walt Disney Pictures (sister studio to the Disney Television studio that produces *Home Improvement,* the hit sitcom in which Taylor Thomas stars), fails to deliver the kind of charm or draw that other teen films have done this past year.

Jake Wilkinson (Taylor Thomas) attends college in southern California with his girlfriend, Allie (Jessica Biel), where he majors in being a slick hipster. Jake spends most of his time pulling scams for money, such as procuring concert tickets for himself and his pals, selling goods, and helping his fellow students cheat on tests. When Jake's father (Gary Cole) contacts Jake and asks him to come home to suburban New York for Christmas, Jake tells him that he is taking Allie with him to Cabo San Lucas instead. It seems that Jake's mother died within the last few years and Jake is resentful that his father has remarried (although to a perfectly nice woman who hungers to connect with Jake). To cap off the conversation, Jake's dad offers his prize 1957 Porsche if Jake makes it home by 6 p.m. Christmas Eve. This bribe entices Jake to travel

back home, though not to spend any time with his family.

Allie informs Jake that she wants to go back East and have a white Christmas, not travel to Mexico. And with the vision of the Porsche dancing in his head, Jake decides to go back East as well. But an exam scam of Jake's falls through and his football player buddies fail their tests. They exact revenge on Jake by stranding him in the desert with a Santa Claus suit and beard glued on. When Jake fails to appear to take Allie to the airport, she reluctantly accepts a ride back East with Eddie (Adam Lavorgna), an obnoxious wanna-be stud who has his eye on her.

Alone, broke, and dressed like Santa, Jake starts to hitchhike to New York. Thus begins the road trip wherein Jake encounters a variety of travails trying to get back East in time to get his father's Porsche and to win back his girlfriend's heart. In typical "road-movie" fashion, Jake has a myriad of experiences that are meant to change his way of thinking about life and himself: he gives presents to sick kids in a hospital, he reunites estranged lovers, he shares a ride with some adorable elderly Tom Jones fans.

None of these scenes are presented in any sort of moving or emotional manner; part of this has to do with Taylor Thomas's glib, slick manner. He simply cannot pull off acting like such a charming scamp; he is obnoxious rather than endearing. One thinks of how delicious Matthew Broderick was in *Ferris Bueller,* or the smoothness of Michael J. Fox in numerous roles. Thomas may make hearts race on television, but he cannot bring the same excitement to the big screen. Biel, herself a veteran of television (the show *Seventh Heaven*), has an extremely likable, easygoing presence and shows great promise in her acting. The problems with her character lie in the remote possibility that someone as strong, capable, and directed as Allie would even have a conversation with someone as unpleasant and phony as Jake.

The characters seem to be cutout versions of old Brady Bunch episodes, yet unlike the very funny, sardonic *Brady Bunch* I & II (in which Gary Cole played the unflappable patriarch, Mike Brady [1995 & 1996]), this kind of dull, lifeless comedy doesn't work on any level at all. To say nothing of the odious underlying issues of bribing kids to spend time with their families, and having the hero of a kids' film involved with helping other kids cheat on tests.

—*G. E. Georges*

CREDITS

Jake: Jonathan Taylor Thomas
Allie: Jessica Biel
Eddie: Adam LaVorgna
Jake's Dad: Gary Cole

Origin: USA
Released: 1998
Production: David Hoberman and Tracey Trench for Mandeville Films; released by Walt Disney Pictures
Direction: Arlene Sanford
Screenplay: Tom Nursall and Harris Goldberg
Cinematography: Hiro Narita
Editing: Anita Brandt-Burgoyne
Costumes: Maya Mani
Production design: Cynthia Kay Charette
Art direction: Alexander Cochrane
Sound: Rob Young
Music: John Debney
MPAA rating: PG
Running Time: 86 minutes

REVIEWS

Entertainment Weekly. November 20, 1998, p. 98.
Los Angeles Times. November 13, 1998, p. F10.
New York Times. November 13, 1998, p. E18.
Variety. November 16, 1998, p. 34.

Illtown

The love that never dies.—Movie tagline

"Unique and compelling. Nick Gomez goes through the looking glass minting a bold new style."—Gavin Smith, *Film Comment*

"Riveting. Michael Rapaport is superb. Adam Trese is a born star."—Matt Zoller Seitz, *New York Press*

"Powerful. A cool, dreamy gangster's paradise."—Janet Maslin, *New York Times*

"As original as any American film of the last decade. Nick Gomez creates images that transform the way you see the world. The cast is utterly electric. An amazing film."—Amy Taubin, *Village Voice*

With *Illtown*, writer-director Nick Gomez returns to the gritty urban underworld that won him critical praise for his earlier films, but his latest attempt succumbs to oppressive allegorical symbolism, a paper-thin narrative, and a vapid visual style that one film critic so aptly dubbed "narcotic realism"—a hazy soporific stupor undoubtedly akin to a heroin nod that is likely to overcome the viewer.

In this perverted tale of naughty and nice, Dante (Michael Rapaport) and his girlfriend Micky (independent film favorite Lili Taylor) are a pair of "respectable" petty Florida drug dealers trying to get out of the business and start a family. They play golf with their goofy friend and partner, Francis/Cisco (Kevin Corrigan), espouse family values to their crew of sociopathic teenaged peddlers (played mostly by amateurs recruited from local high schools), and have the moral fortitude to refrain from shooting up themselves.

The trio have a comfortable little operation going, their own slice of the American Dream. But all hell breaks out when the nefarious competition—a group of drug-addicted "bad guys" with no sense of common decency—starts elbowing into their territory. Things unravel even further when former partner and avenging fallen angel, Gabriel (Adam Trese), is released from jail. Convinced that it was Dante who sold him out to the cops years earlier, Gabriel comes seeking revenge. As the story makes its way to the requisite final showdown, Dante is thrust into his own inferno, forced to give up his passivist ways and shooting up in order to forget, as well as remember, the past.

Gomez has insisted in press interviews that his film was an attempt at experimental filmmaking born of necessity. He had planned to tell a linear, neo-noir crime story, an adaptation of Terry Williams's book, *The Cocaine Kids*, but

when he exhausted his funds, Gomez was forced to adopt a more fragmented narrative, replete with dreamy stylization and brooding postmodern religious iconography. The result is an uneasy fusion of Old Testament spiritual allegory with contemporary urban crime drama.

The manipulation of time and space within *Illtown*, achieved through elliptical editing by Tracy Granger, produces a slow build towards the tale's ultimate revelations. The film's hallucinatory style and pretentious metaphysical didacticism tend to alienate, prohibiting the audience from identifying with or having sympathy for any of the film's characters. When the violence erupts onscreen—it is interspersed throughout and may serve as a literal wake-up call for the viewer, a counter to the narcoleptic episodes—the viewer is likely not to care who is murdered or what their motivations might be.

While the visuals are handled artfully by cinematographer Jim Denault (Michael Almereyda's *Nadja* [1995]), it is the dialogue that is most egregious. When Gabriel is first introduced, he is on a staircase, cloaked in an all-white flowing wardrobe. He remarks, "I died and went to heaven . . . they kicked me out." Later, facing the camera in a style rem-

CREDITS

Dante: Michael Rapaport
Micky: Lili Taylor
Gabriel: Adam Trese
Francis (Cisco):   Kevin Corrigan
Lucas: Paul Schulze
Lilly: Angela Featherstone
Gunther: Saul Stein
D'Avalon: Tony Danza
George: Isaac Hayes

Origin: USA
Released: 1996, 1998
Production: David L. Bushell; released by The Shooting Gallery
Direction: Nick Gomez
Screenplay: Nick Gomez; based on the book *The Cocaine Kids* by Terry Williams
Cinematography: Jim Denault
Editing: Tracy Granger
Production design: Susan Bolles
Sound: Jeff Kushner
Costumes: Sarah Jane Slotnick
Music: Brian Keane
MPAA rating: R
Running Time: 97 minutes

iniscent of Jean-Luc Godard, he tells us, "Money is easy . . . Philosophy is hard," while other characters carry the burden of such ponderous lines as: "Everyone has done things they're not proud of, but that's how you transcend weakness" and "You were blind and now you can see."

Director-writer Nick Gomez, twenty-nine at the time, attracted critical attention and spawned relentless comparisons to director Martin Scorsese with his debut film, *Laws of Gravity* (1992). It was a gritty urban tale that employed a cinema verite style to convey the tense and violent milieu, a deliberate attempt to emulate Scorsese's powerful *Mean Streets* (1973). Gomez's other films include the less impressive *New Jersey Drive* (1995).

Lili Taylor is woefully underutilized in the obligatory girlfriend role, but her talent enables her to still make an impact, infusing Micky with far more depth than is scripted. Michael Rapaport is refreshingly and uncharacteristically restrained in the lead role, while former television sitcom star Tony Danza is cast against type as the sinister gay head of the heroin empire. Isaac Hayes, the first African American

to win an Academy Award in music for *Shaft* (1971), as well as the voice of "Chef" in the subversive comedy *South Park,* appears as Dante's mysterious police contact/spiritual advisor.

Illtown was first shown at the 1996 New York Film Festival. Reviews for the film, which appeared in limited theatrical release, were decidedly mixed.

—Patricia Kowal

REVIEWS

Boxoffice. April, 1997, p. 197.
Entertainment Weekly. January 23, 1998, p. 42.
Hollywood Reporter. November 12, 1996, p. 14.
Los Angeles Times. January 30, 1998, p. F6.
New York Times. October 3, 1996, p. C18.
Sacramento Bee. January 30, 1998.
San Francisco Chronicle. January 20, 1998, p. E16.
Variety. September 23, 1996, p. 125.
Village Voice. January 20, 1998, p. 90.

The Impostors

Why be yourself when you can be somebody else?–Movie tagline

Headlines got you down? At last, the perfect comic relief. A musical, magical, cross-dressing, mistaken identity, cream puff-eating, hidden bomb kind of comedy!—Movie tagline

"Fast, funny and fabulous. *The Impostors* is one great cruise."—Anne Marie O'Connor, *Mademoiselle*

"Stanley Tucci struts his comic stuff way out on a limb, and then he invokes the Marx Brothers by setting the increasingly hilarious, slapstick proceedings on a luxury liner."—Karen Durbin, *Mirabella*

"One of the year's funniest, most inventive and brilliantly conceived comedies."—Jeffrey Lyons, *NBC-TV*

"A can't lose cruise. Stanley Tucci's *The Impostors* is refreshing. Oliver Platt is uproarious. Hectic and hilarious."—Thelma Adams, *New York Post*

"More than a dozen of New York's finest actors ham it up with unrestrained glee."—Stephen Holden, *New York Times*

Stanley Tucci and Oliver Platt are two unemployed actors who stow away on a cruise ship to escape the police in the hilarious comedy *The Impostors.*

"Exuberant and scintillating. *The Impostors* is a tour de force. Brilliant."—Desmond Ryan, *The Philadelphia Inquirer*

"Fun and frothy . . . with echoes of Peter Sellers' *Pink Panther* pictures."—Judy Gerstel, *Toronto Star*

Box Office: $2,194,929

Writer-director Stanley Tucci's *The Impostors* is an old-fashioned farce, a broad comedy of slapstick, pratfalls, and disguises. Tucci and Oliver Platt star as unemployed actors who get caught up in shenanigans aboard a luxury ocean liner filled with an assortment of screwball types reminiscent of old Hollywood comedy. Unfortunately, the story itself is fairly thin, and, while the movie has some funny bits, many comic routines simply fall flat, and ultimately there are not enough inspired moments to sustain the length of a feature film.

The movie begins promisingly. Intercut with the opening credits is a cute homage to silent movies. We meet Platt's Maurice and Tucci's Arthur at separate tables at an outdoor café when they get into a fight over a woman. The people around them think the altercation is real (especially when it escalates into a knife fight and concludes with Maurice's "death"), but it is actually a staged confrontation that they perform to practice their acting skills. The piece works as a fun takeoff on silent cinema in the exaggerated poses and movements of the players and is a delightful introduction to Arthur and Maurice as actors and to early comic forms that the film will imitate. In the next scene, Arthur is upset that Maurice stole his death; Arthur, we soon learn, treasures a grand death scene, and it was his turn to die.

It is the early 1930s, and Maurice and Arthur are struggling to get work. They go on an audition for a director played by Woody Allen in an unbilled cameo, and, in the middle of their scene, they see their latest opportunity dashed when the director's wife phones to tell him she is leaving him and pulling out the funding for the play. Next Arthur and Maurice try to run a scam on a small bakery in the hope of getting an assortment of pastries. They fumble their roles, but the baker ends up giving Maurice two tickets to a production of *Hamlet*. Platt and Tucci work well together as a comedy team, but, while these expository scenes are amusing, they point out a problem of the film in general; the actors often strain for laughs in skits that are funny at first but do not deliver the big payoff at the end.

The production of *Hamlet* stars the pretentious Jeremy Burtom (Alfred Molina), a bad actor who comes out drunk after the play's intermission and attacks his fellow actor on stage. Later that night in a bar, Maurice is denouncing Burtom when the puffed-up actor himself enters. Soon Arthur and Maurice are being chased out of the bar and down the street. They run to the edge of a dock, take refuge in a huge crate, and the next morning find themselves aboard an ocean liner as accidental stowaways.

Arthur (Stanley Tucci): "I'm going to die if I don't get work."

Once on board, Arthur and Maurice soon discover that Burtom is also there and that the police think they attacked him. The plot then becomes a cat-and-mouse game in which Arthur and Maurice are basically chased around the ship as slapstick and pratfalls ensue in the Marx Brothers tradition. Arthur and Maurice don steward uniforms and meet Lily (Lili Taylor), the head stewardess. The most normal of the characters they encounter, she is sympathetic to their plight and helps them. Lily is in love with Marco (Matt McGrath), the ship's detective, but is pursued by the head steward, the jealous Meistrich (Campbell Scott doing a German accent). Scott's impersonation of a sexually frustrated, Nazi-like disciplinarian is fun for a while but soon grows tiresome.

Among the film's supporting actors, only a few are allowed to make much of an impression. Steve Buscemi is the best as Happy Franks, an ironically named crooner who is actually suicidal over a recent divorce, and, in a running joke, keeps failing in his attempts to kill himself. He is pursued by Emily (Hope Davis), a brooding young woman on board with her mother, Mrs. Essendine (Dana Ivey). She is eager to marry Emily off to a rich man, but the depressed Happy seems to bring out the romantic in Emily, and the two morose people finally find true love in each other.

Many of the other performances are really extended cameos. Elizabeth Bracco plays Pancetta Leaky, the ship's social director, and Isabella Rossellini has a very thin part as a deposed queen who does not do much but look depressed. Billy Connolly appears as Sparks, a gay tennis champion who flirts with Maurice, and Teagle F. Bougere is a sheik whose big scene centers on an odd but not very funny dance with Arthur and Maurice. Most of these oddballs have a funny moment here and there, but ultimately the film feels overstuffed with minor characters doing various pieces of shtick.

While they are hiding out from Burtom, the heroes discover some bad guys on the ship, people who, like themselves, are "impostors." Maurice, hiding in the room of the first mate (Tony Shalhoub), learns that he is really a foreign spy planning to set off explosives on the ship. The film's funniest and most inventive gag occurs as Maurice hides under the bed and eavesdrops on the first mate revealing his plans on a two-way radio in his native tongue; Maurice actually sees the English subtitles, but they are backwards to him until he looks in a mirror. This is an inspired moment, and indeed the film would have benefited from more loopy and unexpected gags like this one that actually plays with the mechanics of cinema. Meanwhile, Arthur learns of the scheme of a pair of con artists, Johnny (Richard Jenkins) and Maxi (Allison Janney), who are pretending to be French and are planning to woo and kill Mrs. Essendine and the sheik for their money.

From this point on, Arthur and Maurice are not just being chased, they are on a mission to save the day. "The time has come to act," Maurice declares in a line that links the mission to their profession. However, because we really have little emotional investment in the secondary characters, it is hard to care about these plot contrivances, which really do not generate any suspense and become excuses for a gala ball where Maurice dresses in drag and Arthur in full disguise, including wig, glasses, and mustache. As everyone dances, Maurice tries to warn Mrs. Essendine and the sheik that they are targets of a murder plot. Arthur's wig eventually falls off in front of Burtom, who repeatedly screams, "Impostor!" All the impostors, thinking they have been discovered, flee, and everyone eventually meets in a lifeboat, where the heroes and Lily have donned more disguises to fool the various bad guys.

In the film's climax, the first mate threatens to detonate the bombs he has planted all over the ship. He babbles on against pretense and disguise and wants a world in which all have "One single face!" His ideology, it seems, is in direct opposition to the idea of being an impostor that the film celebrates, but, because this conflict has not been developed, the showdown means nothing. The detonator falls into Happy's hands, but, now in love with Emily, he chooses life over suicide. The con artists have been captured, and the conflict with Burtom seems to have been forgotten. Many people have paired off—Emily and Happy, the ship's captain (Allan Corduner) and the queen, Mrs. Essendine and the sheik, Lily and Marco—to give the film a big happy ending.

During the film's end credits, the whole cast dances on the ship's deck and gradually dances its way off the ocean liner, among the film's crew, and finally off the film set itself—in essence breaking the fourth wall. It is a sweet ending and a great capper that makes one wish the movie itself had been more whimsical all along.

A homage to slapstick comedies of the 1930s, to the frenetic humor of the Marx Brothers, and to comedy teams like Laurel and Hardy, *The Impostors* is a nostalgic throwback and a sometimes refreshing change of pace for 1990s humor. Platt and Tucci exhibit some nice teamwork, especially in the early scenes, and there are also some fun moments on the ship, like Arthur getting the death scene he has craved for so long when he pretends to be dead after Marco shoots and misses him. However, the movie too often feels like a patchwork of chase scenes and comic bits, some of which bring a smile to the face but many of which feel hackneyed. Because the story is simple, the gags need to be sharper and more fast-paced to make *The Impostors* the madcap, zany romp it wants to be.

What makes *The Impostors* particularly disappointing is that Stanley Tucci was the co-creator of *Big Night*, one of the best movies of 1996, and *The Impostors* features many of the same actors. *Big Night* was a very heartfelt, funny, and ultimately bittersweet character-driven piece about two immigrant brothers struggling to keep their Italian restaurant in business. Admittedly, *The Impostors* is a different kind of film, and Tucci should be commended for trying to do a farce, which is very difficult to pull off. Nonetheless, it does not come close to capturing the magic of his first feature.

—*Peter N. Chumo II*

CREDITS

Maurice: Oliver Platt
Arthur: Stanley Tucci
Sheik: Teagle F. Bougere
Pancetta Leaky: Elizabeth Bracco
Happy Franks: Steve Buscemi
Sparks: Billy Connolly
Emily: Hope Davis
Mrs. Essendine: Dana Ivey
Captain: Allan Corduner
Maxine: Allison Janney
Johnny: Richard Jenkins
Jeremy Burtom: Alfred Molina
Marco: Matt McGrath
Queen: Isabella Rossellini
Meistrich: Campbell Scott
First Mate: Tony Shalhoub
Lily: Lili Taylor
Theater Director: Woody Allen

Origin: USA
Released: 1998
Production: Beth Alexander and Stanley Tucci for First Cold Press; released by Fox Searchlight
Direction: Stanley Tucci
Screenplay: Stanley Tucci
Cinematography: Ken Kelsch
Editing: Suzy Elmiger
Music: Gary DeMichele
Production design: Andrew Jackness
Art direction: Chris Shriver
Costumes: Juliet Polcsa
Sound: William Sarokin
MPAA rating: R
Running Time: 102 minutes

REVIEWS

Boxoffice. July, 1998, p. 126.
Detroit Free Press. October 2, 1998, p. 9D.
Entertainment Weekly. October 16, 1998, p. 58.
New York Times. October 2, 1998, p. E12.
People. October 12, 1998, p. 42.
San Francisco Chronicle. October 2, 1998, p. C3.
San Francisco Examiner. October 2, 1998, p. C3.
Sight and Sound. January, 1999, p. 47.
Variety. May 25, 1998, p. 58.
Village Voice. October 13, 1998, p. 126.
Washington Post Weekend. October 2, 1998, p. 47.

In God's Hands

Fortune favors the brave.—Movie tagline

"*In God's Hands* is a supremely gorgeous film, all those lush locales, thundering waves and perfect bodies, that unfolds accompanied by a rapturous, rousing score by Paradise."—Kevin Thomas, *Los Angeles Times*

"Contains some wild and clearly dangerous surfing footage that is probably the closest most viewers will ever get to the sport."—Jamie Bernard, *New York Post*

"As pretty as a scenic calendar. The waves are awesome and spectacular, and the members of Mr. King's crew who captured their sight and sound deserve no end of credits."—Lawrence Van Gelder, *New York Times*

"Stunning surf photography . . . a dazzle of daredevils on water mountains."—Peter Stack, *San Francisco Chronicle*

 Box Office: $1,546,414

Surf movies are a unique breed and have always occupied their own special place in the world of film. Countless pictures have explored the lure of the ocean waves over the past three decades but only a few have achieved cult status. Surf aficionados cite Bruce Brown's classic *Endless Summer* (1966) and John Milius's *Big Wednesday* (1978) as two films that have truly captured the surfing life. Brown's sequel, *Endless Summer 2* (1994), also offers an entertaining glimpse into the subculture and traces the evolution of surfing from the '60s to the worldwide phenomenon it is today. *In God's Hands,* the latest entry in the surf genre, is a gorgeously shot film full of stunning surf footage, but it wipes out when it turns away from the spectacular ocean imagery.

Filled with lush locales (Bali, Hawaii, Africa, Mexico), golden sunsets, thundering waves, and a rousing score by Paradise, *In God's Hands* makes for an attractive travelogue. However, the film is seriously lacking in narrative and dramatic development. If one can overlook the

Wyatt (Shaun Tomson): "Technology is taking surfing into another dimension . . . To ride waves this big is to put yourself in God's hands."

Besides the three pro surfers who star in the film, the movie also features Rush Randle, a world-class sailboarder; Brian Keaulana, the world's best ocean rescue lifeguard; big wave legend Derrick Doerner; and world sailboarding champion Pete Cabrinha.

wooden acting, flimsy plot, and cheesy dialogue, and just go with the superior visuals, this can be worthwhile entertainment.

What's most surprising about this latest surf pic is that it's directed by Zalman King, who is best known for erotica like *9 1/2 Weeks* (1986), *Wild Orchid* (1990), and Showtime's *Red Shoe Diaries.* Although King's sultry, music video style is apparent throughout, there is thankfully little sex here. To his credit, King and crew (lenser John Aronson and special water photographer Sonny Miller) do an excellent job with the water imagery. Indeed, shooting surfers curled inside fifty-foot waves is no easy feat. The technical superiority is evident in these scenes and the powerful waves are clearly the highlight of the film.

In God's Hands follows three world-class surfers around the globe in their quest for awesome-sized waves. The guys are in fact real pro surfers, which makes for breathtaking surfing sequences, but whose acting leaves much to be desired. At times their reading of dialogue is so unnatural and stilted that it's downright laughable.

One of the surfers, thirty-five-year-old Matt George, not only co-stars in the film but also co-wrote the script with King. George, a former top professional surfer, plays the extroverted Mickey, an aging ex-champ who's aware that his day is over and that he'll never adapt to new techniques like the use of jet skis to tow surfers into the biggest waves. Seventeen-year-old Matty Liu, a sometime actor who was five-time Hawaiian Surfing Champion, plays Keoni, the wide-eyed novice from Hawaii. And rounding out the trio is twenty-two-year-old Patrick Shane Dorian (currently ranked No. 2 in the world), starring as the gifted wave rider Shane, who despite his enormous talent has no interest in turning pro. These three surfing companions travel from Madagascar to Bali to Hawaii to Mexico as they seek the challenge of riding the world's biggest, deadliest waves.

Tracking them along the way is Wyatt (Shaun Tomson), a Bali-based writer who bails out the guys when they get into trouble by paying for bribes with an endless supply of black pearls. Wyatt always seems to be around when the trio needs him most. Since the surfers have no visible means of support and are always training when not out shredding monster waves, the black

CREDITS

Shane: Patrick Shane Dorian
Mickey: Matt George
Keoni: Matty Liu
Wyatt: Shaun Tomson
Serena: Maylin Pultar
Philips: Bret Michaels
Captain: Brion James

Origin: USA
Released: 1998
Production: Tom Stern for Triumph Films; released by TriStar Pictures
Direction: Zalman King
Screenplay: Zalman King and Matt George
Cinematography: John Aronson
Editing: James Gavin Bedford, Joe Shugart
Production design: Marc Greville-Mason, Paul Holt
Art direction: Jacqueline R. Masson
Costumes: Jolie Anna Andreatta
Sound: Adam Joseph
Special water photography: Sonny Miller
MPAA rating: PG-13
Running Time: 96 minutes

pearls also pay for their support. None of this makes much sense or really matters as it adds no dramatic value to the movie whatsoever.

When not focusing on surfing, the threadbare plot turns to a romance between Shane and Serena (Maylin Pultar), a beautiful girl from Ipanema; Keoni suffers from a bout of malaria; and Mickey engages in a fistfight for money in Bali. These lame plot devices exist only as an excuse to show more luscious scenery and gargantuan waves.

In God's Hands does not make for a compelling drama, but it does offer up lots of big-wave thrills and some of the best surf footage ever filmed. If director King would have focused exclusively on surfing and dropped the jerry-built storyline, it would have been close to nirvana for surf fans and sports-minded audiences alike. *In God's Hands* opened to mixed reviews, though the film was widely praised for its cinematography.

—*Beth Fhaner*

REVIEWS

Boxoffice. June, 1998, p. 77.
Los Angeles Times. April 24, 1998.
New York Times. May 15, 1998, p. E24.
San Francisco Chronicle. May 8, 1998, p. C10.
San Francisco Examiner. May 8, 1998, p. B2.
Variety. April 27, 1998, p. 59.

Incognito

It is often an international event when someone announces the serendipitous discovery of a previously unknown poem by Shakespeare, a newly uncovered Van Gogh canvas, or even Hitler's diaries. This last case from the 1980s ultimately proved to be a notorious fake. The diaries were brilliantly executed, and they fooled a number of experts along the way. Furthermore, plenty of money was at stake in the diaries' authentication. And hence we arrive at the premise of *Incognito*.

The film opens with the flinging of a painting into a bonfire, and the police mug shots of Harry Donovan (Jason Patric); from there, we flash back to the events that led to this sequence. Donovan is an American painter whose talents have been overlooked. He has therefore all but forsaken the creation of original art in favor of a line of work that is proving to be more lucrative: forgeries.

In his dingy New York apartment, Donovan halfheartedly instructs an attractive model to disrobe. Abruptly he dismisses her, along with her advances, and as she stomps off down the stairway, three men, led by Alastair (Thomas Lockyer), come up. They have a proposition: for the master faker to create a "new" Rembrandt. Donovan is initially dismissive of the offer, but in the end he succumbs to the lure of $50,000.

A walk in the park with Dad, Milton (Rod Steiger), reveals that Donovan père was once an artist of note, and he believes his son could reach the heights of excellence if only he dedicates himself to his talents. But the brooding son is now committed to his new task, and what follows is a slightly cheesy montage focusing on Donovan's sight-seeing, detail-collecting visits to Amsterdam—specifically the Rijksmuseum to investigate Rembrandt's seminal "Night Watch"—and thence onto Paris.

In the city of light, he bumps into Professor Marieke van den Broeck (Swiss actress Irène Jacob), or rather, she bumps into him as he sketches at an outdoor cafe. He doesn't show much interest in her genuine apology, but that's our Donovan—he's a surly sort. His interest is revived, however, when he's trying to sneak into the restoration department in the Bouffes du Nord to check out a particular Rembrandt painting. Happily, Marieke is on her way there. She's a member of staff, thus easing Donovan's way to the inner sanctum. Secretly, he scratches a sampling of original paintwork from the work in question, depositing his vandalism into a tiny glass tube.

Thus armed, our hero procures any number of old-fashioned and esoteric paints, emulsions, and ingredients for his project. He sets up his studio in an attic and obsessively gets to work, taking inspiration for his forgery from a photograph of his father's face. The painting he produces is of a work alluded to in textbooks but believed lost, namely, a portrait of the artist's father. The result is astounding.

Paris might be a huge city, yet, at least in this film, it allows Donovan rapidly to encounter Marieke anew at another outdoor cafe. It isn't long before they are tearing each other's clothes off. Waking up in her bed the next morning, Donovan watches her dress and leave for work. Smiles all around.

Our European tour continues as we are whisked from Alastair's Spanish villa to London—but not before a local man sells a framed picture to the Englishmen; it will serve as a cover for the sudden appearance of the Rembrandt masterpiece. The unveiling of the discovery is set up in Alastair's tony Soho gallery. The explanation will be that the painting lay for centuries in the Spaniard's humble home. Cohort Iain (Simon Chandler) and a Japanese gentleman called Agachi (Togo Igawa) are also in attendance.

Downstairs, Donovan waits for his money. But before he can get paid, verification from a quartet of experts must be gained. And leading this verification team is none other than Marieke—no less than the world's foremost authority on Rembrandt—and she isn't convinced. The sale is suddenly in doubt, and Marieke takes off for an opera at Covent Garden. The enraged Donovan, learning that his payment is dependent on "authentication," rolls up the painting. In the ensuing chaos, a pistol is drawn, and it appears, after a struggle, that Donovan shoots the Japanese man to death.

A fleeing Donovan catches Marieke on the street, but she waves him off; their sexual encounter in Paris, she reports, was a mistake. She continues on to the performance of *Aida*, but will leave before its end to take the Channel Tunnel over to Belgium. Disconsolate, Donovan takes to a bar, where British police apprehend him. But this is an American tough guy they are dealing with, and he breaks free of their arrest, despite handcuffs hanging on his wrist. At one of London's train stations, Donovan pickpockets an Englishman's jacket for his passport, catches up with Marieke—she just happens to be there at that moment—cuffs her, and they get on board.

Eluding the attentions of the police, the unlikely couple remain inextricably linked as the train heads toward the coast. But the British police are a dogged lot, forcing Dono-

van to drag Marieke off the train to escape their pursuit; after all, they believe him to be a murderer. The pair ends up in a picturesque village, and Marieke demands to know what he wants of her. He needs her to verify his work's provenance, and then he will sell the "Rembrandt" on the open market.

While the pair enjoys a parade of bucolic adventures, one is reminded of *Two for the Road* (1967) with Albert Finney and Audrey Hepburn. Marieke finds herself being swayed by Donovan's charm (such as it is), and kisses and embraces are resumed. The pair travels the countryside in a stolen classic car, and Donovan's various attempts to fence the painting either come to naught, or endanger them both. A visit to former mentor Old John (Ian Holm)—the man who highlighted Donovan's work for Alastair's group—turns out to be a trap, and it is here that the desperate Donovan flings his work into the flames of a rustic fire.

In London, he is tried for murder. His prospects are dim indeed. Experts other than Marieke testify that the painting is too convincing to be a fake. Worse, Donovan's father dies; the artist only learns of this during Alastair's taunting prison visit. Back in court, prosecuting counsel Turley (Ian Richardson) skewers the defense. One opportunity to convince the jury that the picture is a fake arrives when Donovan recreates his work, but he backs down after a day's work, emotionally shattered by drawing his father's visage anew. The painting, ironically, continues to be thought of as genuine.

All seems lost, until Marieke talks with Iain, and tries to persuade him that Alastair will get rid of him after the trial, just as he did with their Japanese colleague. For Marieke now believes her lover is innocent. Finally, Iain realizes the truth in this observation, and blurts out the truth in court. Alastair is arrested, and Donovan released, but the painting still belongs to the English group.

At a swank party, Iain celebrates the massive sale of the painting on the market, until his lawyer announces that the Spanish government has taken custody of the artwork as its sale wasn't properly documented. Cut to sunny Spain, and a now-rich Spaniard thanking Donovan for his efforts; we recall that Donovan gave Marieke a letter just before his final arrest in England, and this letter alerted the Spanish government. Our artist is now a wealthy man (to the tune of about five million dollars) because the Spaniard insists on cutting him in. A final scene, with the Seine and the Eiffel Tower as background, shows Donovan smooching with Marieke.

Despite the presence of Steiger and the fact that Badham is a well-known Hollywood director, *Incognito* made little impact as a theatrical release. And perhaps deservedly so, despite its modest merits. Certainly, as a travelogue picture, there is some appeal. The sights of Europe are always welcome, and one may include in this the beautiful Irène Jacob, known best for her work with the late Polish director Krystof Kieslowski. Her role has little weight, despite the intellectual kudos that attach to her title as a professor, but she adds some glamour to the cast. A good actress, she never seems uncomfortable speaking in English—even given screenwriter Jordan Katz's unexceptional dialogue.

As for Steiger, he is fine in his small supporting role, and his tough demeanor makes him a persuasive progenitor

CREDITS

Harry Donovan: Jason Patric
Marieke van den Broeck: Irène Jacob
Alastair: Thomas Lockyer
Turley: Ian Richardson
Iain: Simon Chandler
Milton Donovan: Rod Steiger
White: Pip Torrens
John: Ian Holm
Agachi: Togo Igawa

Origin: USA
Released: 1997
Production: James G. Robinson for Morgan Creek; released by Warner Bros.
Direction: John Badham
Screenplay: Jordan Katz
Cinematography: Denis Crossan
Editing: Frank Morriss
Music: John Ottman
Production design: Jaime Leonard
Art direction: Mark Roggett
Costumes: Louise Stjernsward
Sound: Nancy MacLeod
MPAA rating: Unrated
Running Time: 106 minutes

of the misanthropic Donovan. British luminaries Richardson and Holm are similarly competent as nemeses. The biggest problem comes with Patric. To be sure, his character is that of a rogue, but Patric's range is narrow. Most of the time he presents a sour face to everyone with whom he interacts, and it is hard to root for him for much of the picture. There is pathos when he lingers in prison, but one cannot help but wonder how such a luminous woman as Jacob's Marieke would stick with the dark Donovan. Presumably, she is in awe of his talent—however misdirected toward forgeries it might be.

Katz's plotting is more successful than his dialogue, and certainly the subject matter is one of contemporary interest. Irony, when it appears, adds needed spice to the film. As for Badham, one feels that here is an experienced director neither stretching himself nor neglecting his professional duties on the picture. There is little discernible style in the direction, save for the backgrounding of European tourist spots, and perhaps Badham could have lifted Patric from the latter's persistent scowling. Sadly, he fails to do so.

In sum, the film would make an agreeable rainy afternoon rental. Enjoy the scenery, the whispers of romance, and James Gemmill's wonderfully rendered Rembrandts. On the landscape of recent movies, this release is, unfortunately, incognito.

—Paul B. Cohen

REVIEWS

Sight and Sound. January, 1998, p. 46.
Variety. November 17, 1997, p. 64.

Insomnia

"Psychic and emotional darkness are played out against a background of unremitting light."—Jay Carr, *Boston Globe*

"Absolutely brilliant acting . . . my pick for best film at this year's Cannes Film Festival!"
—Michael Kilian, *Chicago Tribune*

"Taut, spare and riveting. Stellan Skarsgard is sensational."—Peter Stack, *San Francisco Chronicle*

"Two enthusiastic thumbs up."—*Siskel & Ebert*

"An eye-opener with the edgy visual panache and off-kilter sensibilities of *Barton Fink* and *Seven*!"—Steven Gaydos, *Variety*

A first-rate performance by Stellan Skarsgard as a troubled police investigator highlights Erik Skjoldbjaerg's first feature. Jonas Engstrom (Skarsgard) is a Swedish homicide detective who has left his native country under a cloud and is working in Oslo with aging veteran Erik Vik (Sverre Anker Ousdal). When the brutal murder of a young woman is discovered in a small northern Nor-

 Crime writer Jon Holt (Bjorn Floberg) to homicide detective Jonas Engstrom (Stellan Skarsgard): "Sometimes one has to alter the truth a bit. An author understands that."

wegian town, the local cops realize their limitations and send for the pros. The case turns out to be a particular challenge because the elusive killer went to great trouble to clean up both the victim and the crime scene, leaving the detectives with few clues.

It's also summer and the region is going through its period of twenty-four-hour daylight, which only heightens the insomnia that Jonas is already suffering. It quickly becomes clear that the normally authoritative Jonas has lost his detachment and is precariously balanced on the brink of a nervous breakdown. With no clear motive or suspect, Jonas tries to trap the killer using a television interview as a ruse to lure the killer to a remote area where a piece of evidence was found. But when the local cops screw up their stakeout, Jonas accidentally shoots and kills his partner in the thick morning fog. Before anyone else can get to the scene, he engineers a cover-up, placing blame on the original killer, and now the corrosion of his psyche begins in earnest.

Suspicious local detective Ane (Maria Bonnevie) isn't sure what to believe, but she still helps Jonas uncover evidence that links the girl's murder to crime writer Jon Holt (Bjorn Floberg). But when Jonas does corner Holt, he discovers his killer witnessed Jonas's own crime and so the fates of both men are inexorably intertwined. It's a film noir set in sunshine (much like the equally unnerving *Purple Noon* [1960]), where the film's "good guy" becomes increasingly paranoid and caught in the trap of his own lies. In the end, Jonas manages to get his killer and get away with his own crime, but at a cost that will haunt him for the rest of his life.

—*Christine Tomassini*

CREDITS

Jonas Engstrom: Stellan Skarsgard
Erik Vik: Sverre Anker Ousdal
Jon Holt: Bjorn Floberg
Hilde Hagen: Gisken Armand
Ane: Maria Bonnevie

Origin: Norway
Released: 1997
Production: Petter J. Borgli, Tomas Backstrom, and Tom Remlov for Norsk Film and Nordic Screen; released by First Run Features
Direction: Erik Skjoldbjaerg
Screenplay: Erik Skjoldbjaerg and Nikolaj Frobenius
Cinematography: Erling Thurmann-Andersen
Editing: Hakon Overas
Music: Geir Jenssen
Production design: Eli Bo
Costumes: Runa Fonne
Sound: Randall Meyers
MPAA rating: Unrated
Running Time: 97 minutes

REVIEWS

Austin Chronicle. December 14, 1998.
Cinefantastique. October, 1998, p. 121.
Entertainment Weekly. June 6, 1998, p. 54.
Hollywood Reporter. May 29, 1997, p. 5.
Los Angeles Times. June 5, 1998, p. F10.
New York Times. May 29, 1998, p. E14.
San Francisco Chronicle. October 1, 1998, p. C6.
Sight and Sound. December, 1998, p. 46.
Variety. May 19, 1997, p. 52.
Village Voice. June 2, 1998, p. 160.
Washington Post. August 14, 1998, p. D5.

Jack Frost

Miracles can happen.—Movie tagline

Jack Frost is getting a second chance to be the world's coolest dad . . . if he doesn't melt first. —Movie tagline

"*Jack Frost* will warm your heart."—Maria Salas, *CBS-Telenoticias*

"Amazing state-of-the-art, computer-generated special effects."—John Monaghan, *Detroit Free Press*

"*Jack Frost* is the perfect holiday film. Wonderful!"—Joel Siegel, *Good Morning America*

"Non-stop magical fun. The best in family entertainment."—Joanna Levenglick, *Kids News Network*

"A wonderful treat for the holidays."—Paul Clinton, *Turner Entertainment Report*

 Box Office: $34,545,000

Before he is reincarnated as a snowman, Jack (Michael Keaton) has a moment of quality time with his son Charlie (Joseph Cross) in the heartwarming *Jack Frost*.

Frosty the Snow Man is a fairy tale, they say/He was made of snow, but the children know how he came to life one day." So goes the 1950 Nelson-Rollins song that inspired the 1969 animated film *Frosty the Snowman* with Jimmy Durante, which makes an appearance on television every year around the holidays. Both of these creations have been dubbed "classics," not because of any unparalleled richness about them, but because they have a certain sweet, innocent, and lovable quality, and because of their ability to capture the imaginations of children and strike a nostalgic chord in adults for a simpler time of life when you could almost believe that a snowman could come to life. The aforementioned lyrics were also the source of inspiration for *Jack Frost*, and while no assertion will be made here that this film is destined to become a classic like the song and film cited above, it, too, succeeds in being gently appealing family fare for the holidays.

As the film begins, life for the Frost family is going along as it apparently always has: Jack (Michael Keaton) is singing in a nightclub with his blues band, his loving and supportive wife, Gabby (the radiant Kelly Preston), is busy fixing the kitchen sink because Jack never got around to doing it, and their bright and spirited eleven-year-old son, Charlie (Joseph Cross), cleverly holds his own in a snowball fight with the local bully. While the Frost's Colorado home is a happy one, filled with warm feelings and cheerful banter, there is a problem: Charlie is sometimes lost in the shuffle due to his well-in-

 A local bully to Charlie (Joseph Cross): "Well, I guess a snowdad is better than no dad."

tentioned father's focus on making it in the music business. To make sure that his son feels connected to him despite his busy schedule, the amusing music man gives his son one of his harmonicas, and jokingly claims that it possesses magical powers. "When you play that," he asserts, "no matter where I am, I can hear it."

The instrument would have come in handy at Charlie's next hockey game, as his father lost track of time in the recording studio and failed to make a promised appearance. Afterward, Gabby tries to impress upon her husband that he's going to regret it if he continues to miss the precious moments in his son's life. Jack apologizes to Charlie, and explains that he wants to follow his dream to be able to provide for his family by doing something he truly loves. He tries to make it up to his disappointed but understanding son by planning a three-day Christmas getaway to their mountain cabin, where nothing can intrude on their togetherness. When the phone starts ringing as they are cheerfully packing the car, we know that there will be a hitch in their plans. Jack announces that he must immediately head to an audition that could lead to a recording contract. Hurt and disappointed, Charlie returns the harmonica and walks away. Later on, when Jack leaves his bandmates to meet his family at the cabin after all, he is faced with driving through a relentless snowstorm, and his perseverance leads to his death on an icy mountain highway.

The film then skips to a year after Jack's death, and it seems that the life has been drained out of his family, as well. Now, his forlorn son cannot be enticed into the fun of snowball fights. Charlie's excellent grades have dropped, and he has quit his beloved hockey team. The family's house has an uncharacteristic lack of Christmas decorations. Jack's best friend Mac (Mark Addy of 1997's *The Full Monty*), who is virtually a member of the family, has lost the joy he got from playing music. Amidst her own pain, Gabby tries her best to comfort her son, but Charlie cannot help crying while building a snowman alone. Afterward, he huddles in his bed and wistfully plays the "magical" harmonica his father had wanted him to have.

Suddenly, as snow swirls around Charlie's icy creation on the front lawn, Jack's soul enters the snowman. Jack, now a self-described "frozen freak of nature," has some unfortunate run-ins with a snowplow and a dog with a decidedly full bladder. Naturally, Charlie is incredulous when it appears that his snowman has come to life, and it is only after it saves him from the bully in a chase across the snowy Colorado countryside that the boy realizes his father has returned. Both are astonished that the harmonica actually did have powers. Charlie apologizes for giving it back, and Jack finally takes the time to practice a tricky hockey shot with his son. Jack advises his son to get back to playing the game he loves, and to re-enter his life in general. He also expresses his love and concern for Gabby. Charlie soon rejoins his team, and Jack finds a slick way of getting in to see Charlie score his first goal.

A bout of unseasonably warm temperatures threatens to terminate this better-late-than-never father-son bonding session, and Charlie desperately tries to prevent losing his father for the second time. He hatches a plan to transport his father to the mountain cabin, where it is much colder. "I was so busy trying to make my mark on the world," Jack says to Charlie with both regret and new understanding. "You are my mark on the world. Thanks for the second chance to be your dad." Gabby finds herself believing her son's assertions that Jack is the snowman when she receives a call from her late husband requesting her presence at the cabin. Having set things right with his family, Jack, expressing his love and unending devotion, departs amidst another swirl of snow shortly after his wife's arrival. As a result of the dead musician's "return engagement," Jack's wife goes back to decorating the house for Christmas, Charlie prospers in school and in the rink, and Mac's love of playing music is reawakened.

While *Jack Frost* did receive a number of positive reviews, many critics gave the fantasy a distinctly cold shoulder. It succeeded in being one of the top ten movies at the

> To play a credible musician, Michael Keaton worked with the film's composer (and former Yes rock band member), Trevor Rabin, and even co-wrote two songs with Rabin for the film.

boxoffice in its first three weeks of release, but did not do as much business as the swarm of other family movies also out at the time, such as *A Bug's Life*, *The Prince of Egypt*, and *The Rugrats Movie*. Like its title character, the film has its shortcomings. The writing does not always sparkle, and sometimes its light touch skates too close to being merely lightweight. Some of the more moving scenes fall perceptively short of eliciting the necessary lumps in the throat. The important moment when Charlie scores his first goal, for instance, does not possess the emotional payoff one would expect. Despite the fact that the bully also lost his father, the boy's reaction to learning the snowman's true identity, his cheerful agreement to help save Jack from melting, and his subsequent friendship with Charlie, ring false. Jack's second departure also comes a little too abruptly. While these problems may have given many viewers pause, how much they like *Jack Frost* seems for the most part to have hinged upon how they responded to the snowman itself.

The snowman was brought to life through the skill of the puppeteers at Jim Henson's Creature Shop and the computerized special effects wizardry of George Lucas's Industrial Light & Magic. It is actually quite convincing, for the most part, although a number of reviewers were apparently looking for something a little more impressive. Admittedly,

CREDITS

Jack Frost: Michael Keaton
Gabby Frost: Kelly Preston
Charlie Frost: Joseph Cross
Mac MacArthur: Mark Addy
Sid Gronic: Henry Rollins

Origin: USA
Released: 1998
Production: Mark Canton and Irving Azoff; released by Warner Bros.
Direction: Troy Miller
Screenplay: Mark Steven Johnson, Steve Bloom, Jonathan Roberts, and Jeff Cesario
Cinematography: Laszlo Kovacs
Editing: Lawrence Jordan
Music: Trevor Rabin
Production design: Mayne Berke
Costumes: Sarah Edwards
Sound: Gregory King
Special effects supervision: Steve Galich
Visual effects supervision: Joe Letteri
MPAA rating: PG
Running Time: 95 minutes

he sometimes looks too obviously like someone dressed in a snowman's costume. If nothing else, he would have benefitted from a little glitter to make him glisten more like the frosty form he is supposed to be. Of all the negative reactions, no one was more indignant than Roger Ebert, who stated that it "gave me the creeps. Never have I disliked a movie character more . . . They say that state-of-the-art special effects can create the illusion of anything on the screen, and now we have proof: It's possible for the Jim Henson folks and Industrial Light & Magic to put their heads together and come up with the most repulsive single creature in the history of special effects, and I am not forgetting the Chucky doll or the desert intestine from *Star Wars*."

Michael Keaton, in his seventh film for producer Mark Canton, does a good job playing Jack in both incarnations, and the tang of his wisecracking snowman helps the film negotiate its second half. Preston and Cross also acquit themselves well, as does Addy, although he has very little to do. Henry Rollins is quite amusing as bombastic Sid Gronic, whose encounter with Jack upon his return to Earth

leaves the hockey coach horribly traumatized by even the word *snowman*. What this talent brought forth is a pleasant-enough bit of undemanding seasonal fluff. While nothing spectacular, it did not deserve the disdain of Ebert and the other critics, who, like the dog in the film, enthusiastically lifted their leg on *Jack Frost*.

—*David L. Boxerbaum*

REVIEWS

Boston Globe. December 12, 1998, p. C4.
Christian Science Monitor. December 11, 1998, p. 12.
Entertainment Weekly. December 18, 1998, p. 54.
Los Angeles Times. December 11, 1998, p. F14.
New York Times. December 11, 1998, p. E28.
People. December 21, 1998, p. 31.
Variety. December 14, 1998, p. 131.
Wall Street Journal. December 11, 1998, p. W11.
Washington Post. December 11, 1998, p. W51.

John Carpenter's Vampires

Prepare for the dawn.—Movie tagline

"John Carpenter's best film since *Halloween*!"
—Tony Timpone, *Fangoria*

"One of the best vampire films of the modern era."—Bruce Westbrook, *Houston Chronicle*

"A bracing blend of fright and fun!"—Peter Travers, *Rolling Stone*

"Rousing entertainment!"—Gene Siskel, *Siskel & Ebert*

"John Carpenter's most entertaining movie in years!"—Andrew Johnston, *Timeout Magazine*

 Box Office: $19,967,510

Vampire hunter Jack Crow (James Woods) is in dogged pursuit of head vampire Valek in *John Carpenter's Vampires*.

With *Vampires*, John Carpenter once again proves that he is almost a great filmmaker. There is something inherently frustrating with a Carpenter production. Many of his films, including the maligned *They Live* (1988), could have been cinematic feasts serving up both gourmet fare and pizza delivery. Granted, this is a difficult menu to balance, but Carpenter comes painfully close at times. Tainting his films are the presence of too many Hollywoodisms that cloud his natural sense of style and technique. John Car-

penter is the Brian DePalma of the horror genre and *Vampires*, written by Don Jakoby and based on the novel by John Steakly, is no exception to this rule.

As *Vampires* begins, Jack Crow (James Woods) is proving his skills as the Catholic Church's "master slayer." Jack, with the help of Tony Montoya (Daniel Baldwin) and a team of recruited men, is "sweeping out a nest" of vampires in New Mexico. In this well-executed sequence, which uses Carpenter's score effectively for the only time in the movie, a horde of vampires is killed, but the "master" they are looking for is not found.

That night, at a prostitute-filled party, the master, named Valek (Thomas Ian Griffith), shows up and kills the team. One of the prostitutes, Katrina (Sheryl Lee), is bitten by Valek and found by Jack, who decides to use her to his advantage. It's not what you think. Forty-eight hours after a person is bitten by a master, a telepathic connection is forged between them; Katrina, therefore, will become a homing device. This plot point is one of many that pose logical goofs. Katrina can see through Valek's eyes but not the other way around. This must be pretty embarrassing for the most powerful vampire on Earth.

Valek, and not Bela Lugosi, was the original vampire. In the middle 1300s, Valek was a priest who denounced his faith and an exorcism was performed on him using a jeweled cross. Something went wrong, the ceremony wasn't finished, and Valek became old toothy. If Valek finds this cross and completes the ceremony, he will be able to walk in daylight. This wouldn't be good so Jack's boss, Cardinal Alba

> Jack Crow (James Woods): "I killed my own father, padre. I got no trouble killing you."

(Maximilian Schell), sends a wimpy priest, Father Adam Guiteau (Tim Guinee), to help Jack hunt for Valek.

Valek finds the cross and a big showdown begins in a condemned prison building that features another logical error. Strangely, cameras all over the building still work perfectly fine, transmitting their images back to guard room monitors. Jack and Father Adam try to use them to their advantage but Valek captures Jack anyway. Cardinal Alba then makes a surprise entrance, explaining that he has lost his faith and made a bargain with Valek to acquire eternal life. Cardinal Alba admits to losing his faith yet he performs Valek's overtly religious ceremony with great conviction . . . but to no avail.

When daylight comes, Jack escapes and skewers Valek. However, he's too late to prevent Katrina and Montoya from both becoming vampires. But that's OK. Somehow they've managed to fall in love even though Katrina spent the majority of this film passed out. With a hug and a warning that he'll hunt them down, Jack sends the couple on their way.

Vampires features some grizzly special effects and certain scenes may not be for the faint of heart. Scarier yet is Daniel Baldwin's performance. Rather than looking tough, he looks stupid and fat. This contrasts with James Woods's machismo, which is more fitting for a film that is a western at heart. What isn't fitting is the music. In *Vampires*, Carpenter recycles the same three-note theme he wrote for *They Live* and pounds it to death. Near the climax, he throws in a western-style theme, but it sounds synthesized and ridiculous. It ruins the mood rather than enhancing it.

Vampires is enhanced, however, by smart pacing and some interesting twists on the vampire legend. The presence of religious overtones adds a richness and sense of history to the movie. But these things aren't enough to save *Vampires*, because its genre-clinging persistence makes it far too predictable. Combining a few elements from a chase movie and a few elements from a western does not produce original art. If Carpenter had spent more time exploring the mythical world of *Vampires*, a world where the church breeds vampire slayers and ancient legends come to life, then he may have had something here. Oh well. Maybe next time.

—*Rich Silverman*

CREDITS

Jack Crow: James Woods
Tony Montoya: Daniel Baldwin
Katrina: Sheryl Lee
Valek: Thomas Ian Griffith
Father Adam Guiteau: Tim Guinee
Cardinal Alba: Maximilian Schell

Origin: USA
Released: 1998
Production: Sandy King for Largo Entertainment; released by Columbia Pictures
Direction: John Carpenter
Screenplay: Don Jakoby; based on the novel *Vampire$* by John Steakley
Cinematography: Gary B. Kibble
Editing: Edward A. Warschilka
Music: John Carpenter
Production design: Thomas A. Walsh
Art direction: Kim Hix
Sound: Hank Garfield
Costumes: Robin Michel Bush
Makeup: Greg Nicotero, Robert Kurtzman, Howard Berger
MPAA rating: R
Running Time: 104 minutes

REVIEWS

Cinefantastique. May, 1998, p. 7.
Detroit News. October 30, 1998, p. 3F.
Entertainment Weekly. November 6, 1998, p. 56.
People. November 9, 1998, p. 34.
Variety. May 4, 1998, p. 83.

Just Write

She's a star in need of a hero . . . he's about to create one.—Movie tagline

A comedy about falling in love . . . the write way.—Movie tagline

"Piven is just perfect . . . Fenn turns on the charm."—*The Hollywood Reporter*

"An incisive romantic comedy . . . *Just Write* is just right!"—*Los Angeles Times*

"A hilarious, romantic Hollywood ride that's absolutely just right!"—*Santa Barbara International Film Festival*

Just Write is a sweet, slight, somewhat silly, and old-fashioned Hollywood love story. Harold McMurphy (Jeremy Pivens) has just turned thirty and works for his father (Alex Rocco) as a Hollywood tour bus driver for their overextended company, Trolleywood Tours (so-called because the tour bus is trolley-shaped). As Harold informs in a voiceover, since he was six years old, he always wanted to be a tour bus driver like his father. But now Harold is vaguely dissatisfied. Passing by a church famous for its Hollywood weddings, Harold has a fantasy that his faceless bride (Nancy McKeon) refuses to marry him when she discovers he has no money and no concrete ambitions. Harold's father tells him: "You're like your mother was, God bless her, a dreamer." His advice to his son is to "get out more—get drunk—get laid—do something."

So Harold goes to hang out at the chichi restaurant where his model/aspiring actor best friend Danny (Jeffrey Sams) works as a bartender. Harold wants to find a woman who will love him for himself, but, of course, things don't exactly start out that way. Danny points out to Harold that rising star Amanda Clark (Sherilyn Fenn) is having lunch with her barracuda of an agent, Sydney Stone (JoBeth Williams). Amanda is complaining about the script for the potential blockbuster (with Brad Pitt, no less) that Sydney has her signed for. Amanda thinks her role is one-dimensional and she wants to take a pass if her part can't be rewritten.

Sydney is called away to take a phone call and Harold takes the opportunity to tell Amanda how much he enjoys her work. He makes some perceptive comments about her

> Agent Arthur Blake (Wallace Shawn) to Harold (Jeremy Piven): "Do me a favor. Go on home and just—write!"

> Jeffrey Sams also co-starred with Jeremy Piven in the brief ABC series *Cupid*.

roles and, impressed, Amanda asks him what he does for a living. Harold hems and haws and finally tells her that he tells stories for a living (referring to his tour bus spiel). Amanda immediately assumes he's a writer and asks him to take a look at her lousy script. Stunned (and mortified), Harold takes the script and agrees to meet Amanda the next day to discuss it.

At a beachside restaurant, Amanda is sitting with macho actor boyfriend Rich Adams (Costas Mandylor). After telling Amanda he's too busy to see her that evening, Rich immediately gets a pinprick of jealousy when Harold shows up for his meeting with Amanda. Finally left alone with Amanda, Harold proceeds to unknowingly echo all Amanda's concerns about the script and, thrilled, she immediately wants him to tell her agent his reservations. Amanda takes Harold to a lavish Hollywood party to find Sydney and introduces him around. No one is willing to admit that they never heard of Harold, so they praise his writing abilities. Sydney's none too happy about Harold's interference and insists on talking to Harold's agent before they make a deal. Harold blurts out the only name he knows, that of well-connected Arthur Blake (Wallace Shawn).

Amanda then runs into Rich at the party with another girl and angrily confronts him. Humiliated, she has Harold drive her home and invites him in. They have a sweet evening together drinking hot cocoa and looking at family photos. Amanda tells Harold she's going to call things off with Rich because of his lies to her: "If I'm going to have a relationship I want it to be with someone that I can trust—someone that will always tell me the truth." Of course, this causes essentially honest, nice guy Harold to squirm with misery. Still, Harold invites Amanda out the next evening (they go to an amusement park) and agrees to attempt an actual rewrite of her script.

Worried that Sydney will check him out, Harold manages to sneak into agent Arthur Blake's office and actually tells the man the truth. Arthur thinks Harold's story is so crazy that it must be true (and even offers to sell the story to the studios), finally agreeing to give the tour bus driver a shot for Amanda's sake. Harold's father is appalled when he realizes how far the deception has gone and tells his frantic son, "We show folks movie stars' homes. We do not date them!" But Harold complains that his well-meaning father has never had any faith in him.

A comedy of errors ensues when Amanda tries to get in touch with Harold to thank him for flowers he's sent her. She reaches the tour bus company and, thanks to a bad connection, Harold's father assumes that Amanda is the woman (Yeardley Smith) that he set Harold up with on what turned out to be a disastrous date. He tells Amanda that Harold never wants to see her again. Amanda talks to Sydney, who tells her that "when you're hot everybody has their own agenda." Harold's problems are compounded when he goes to see Danny at the restaurant, gets drunk and friendly with a couple of actresses, and is spotted by Sydney.

Sydney promptly calls Amanda, who checks out the situation for herself and decides Harold is basically Hollywood slime. Harold does blurt out the truth when trying to apologize to Amanda but she doesn't hear him. In order to redeem himself, Harold decides to actually try rewriting the script he's been given even though Amanda refuses to see him. After pulling some all-nighters, Harold finally finishes

and leaves the script with his father in order to take his usual tour bus run. By this time, Harold's dad has realized his telephone conversation was with the wrong woman and takes the finished script to Amanda's home in order to explain things to her.

A heartbroken Harold is driving his tour trolley through Beverly Hills when he's spotted by Rich (who's in his HumVee). There's a wild chase through the streets before Harold manages to lose Rich, but it prompts Harold to decide he has to face Amanda. So, he drives to her house with his tourist-filled trolley and greets her on the steps. Amanda informs him that his father (who's taking a dip in her pool) has told her the truth and, by the way, she's read the rewritten script. She complains Harold doesn't know how to write the love scene—and proceeds to demonstrate what she would do by kissing Harold in front of his bus full of tourists.

Over the end credits, you find out what's happened: Sydney reassures her client, Harold, about a new script he's writing; Harold's father is driving the tour trolley and points out the home of movie star Amanda Clark and award-winning writer Harold McMurphy; and Danny, who's found his own acting success, guest-stars on Jay Leno, where Jay asks him the scoop about Amanda Clark and a tour bus driver. As Danny replies: "Well, Jay, it's a love story, I have to tell you that."

The beautiful Sherilyn Fenn may still be best known for her sexpot roles, but she's equally believable as the vulnerable Amanda. Amanda is a relatively down-to-earth homebody who wants to find someone who'll love her and not just the star-trappings. Jeremy Piven, who can be annoyingly smirky, sets aside any attempt at hip to play (and well) a guy who wears his heart on his sleeve and dares to dream. The supporting cast also does fine work, particularly JoBeth Williams, who takes her clichéd hard-charging agent and works it for all she can. *Just Write* may not break any new cinematic ground but it is a love story with a happy ending and Hollywood really can't turn out too many of those.

—*Christine Tomassini*

CREDITS

Harold McMurphy: Jeremy Piven
Amanda Clark: Sherilyn Fenn
Sydney Stone: JoBeth Williams
Harold's father: Alex Rocco
Danny: Jeffrey Sams
Arthur Blake: Wallace Shawn
Rich Adams: Costas Mandylor
Lulu: Yeardley Smith
Emma: Holland Taylor
Fantasy Bride: Nancy McKeon
Luncheon Chairman: Ed McMahon

Origin: USA
Released: 1998
Production: Heath McLaughlin for Wind Chill Productions; released by BMG Independents
Direction: Andrew Gallerani
Screenplay: Stan Williamson
Cinematography: Michael Brown
Editing: Laura M. Grody
Music: Leland Bond
Production design: Roger Collins
Costumes: Arlene Toback
MPAA rating: PG-13
Running Time: 106 minutes

REVIEWS

Boxoffice. April, 1998, p. 208.
Chicago Tribune. September 27, 1998, p. 17.
Dallas Morning News. September 25, 1998.
Los Angeles Times. September 25, 1998, p. F10.
Variety. September 28, 1998, p. 38.

Killing Time

Revenge is a dish best served cold.—Movie tagline

For those who ask for nothing more than entertainment and do not mind a little murder, *Killing Time* will do just fine. The film has some fine effects and a little humor. The main attraction is a lanky Italian woman; if any Italian character in recent film might be described as lanky, surely Kendra Torgan's the one. She is so thin that it is amazing how easily her clothes hide her guns. For she is a nameless assassin hired to eliminate a very sophisticated and very perverse villain, Jacob Reilly (Nigel Leach), who can quote James Joyce as he is skewering one of his victims.

The suave Reilly has eluded police pursuit, enraging cop Bryant (Craig Fairbrass) so much that he is the one who has hired the assassin. There is only one problem: Bryant does not have the money to pay for the hit. Instead, he tries for a discount by hiring a band of local thugs to assassinate the assassin. Everything goes wrong, though, because (predictably) the locals are bumblers, thinking they can take this foreign woman while she picks them off one by one.

Whatever tension the film builds is fastened on watching each man go up against this professional. When she shoots, she never misses. She also never ducks when men shoot at her. It is a real fantasy, of course, and just one of many that make this film implausible. It cannot be enjoyed at all unless the doctrine of verisimilitude is forsaken and the viewer simply gets caught up in the action.

One pleasure the film should provide is sorely lacking. As genre film, it ought to have some new wrinkle. Reviewers have suggested that perhaps *Killing Time* is a kind of knock-off of Quentin Tarantino. But the characters are neither freshly offbeat nor particularly menacing. Even the assassin is more a cartoon or fantasy than a character. Especially disappointing is Craig Fairbrass, whose looks inspire the hope that he might be some kind of low-rent Mel Gibson. There is a very slight resemblance, but Fairbrass plays his part pathetically. It might be argued that the character is pathetic—what halfway decent cop would think he could ever get away with such a stupid scheme? Even so, a better actor than Fairbrass might have found a way to make his character at least a little more comic or edgy.

The best scenes in the film do provide some comic relief. There is, for example, the well-meaning bellhop who seems to be constantly at the assassin's door offering all kinds of help. He pays for his solicitousness with his life. When he barges in, saying that there have been some complaints about noise in the assassin's room (she has already shot a couple of her erstwhile assassins), he notices that her toilet is plugged up. She has stuffed one of the men's cell phones in it, and when the bellhop comes up with it, holding it triumphantly, he notices the body of one of the assassin's victims. That is the end of his friendly service. The assassin looks slightly annoyed, perhaps just a little dismayed, that this likeable intruder has to be iced.

One of her (she is never given a name) assassins is actually stupid enough to follow her to her room, thinking that she is going to make love to him. But then, the point about this beautiful assassin is that she is all business and does not let emotion interfere with her job—a discipline that neither the local thugs nor their cop boss can maintain.

Quite aside from the trite plot, the barely competent acting, and the jejune script, *Killing Time* almost seems to revel in its implausibility. No one ever seems to be around except the film's characters, even though it is a large hotel and an urban environment. The film has none of the texture or density of motivation that distinguishes the best works in its particular genre.

Especially inept is the film's ending when Bryant manages to get his sensible partner killed, although the villain also gets his. Capping off the improbability of the action is the final series of shots in which the Italian assassin calmly rides the escalator to the top after a full day of killing. She

CREDITS

Assassin: Kendra Torgan
Bryant: Craig Fairbrass
Jacob Reilly: Nigel Leach
Madison: Peter Harding

Origin: Great Britain
Released: 1998
Production: Richard Johns for Metrodome Films and Pilgrim Film; released by Avalanche Releasing
Direction: Bharat Nalluri
Screenplay: Neil Marshall, Fleur Costello, and Caspar Berry
Cinematography: Sam McCurdy
Editing: Neil Marshall
Music: Christopher Slaski
Production design: Ronald Gow
MPAA rating: Unrated
Running Time: 88 minutes

is not concerned about witnesses. She is not in a hurry. It is as if she is there just to be filmed, making *Killing Time* a rather pointless exercise.

—Carl Rollyson

REVIEWS

Los Angeles Times. January 30, 1998, p. F16.
New York Times. January 30, 1998, p. E16.

The Kingdom, Part 2; Riget 2

"Hilarious, haunting and wildly imaginative!"
—Dave Kehr, *New York Daily News*

"Remarkable! Uproariously entertaining . . . As outrageous as it is inexhaustibly inventive."
—Stephen Holden, *New York Times*

The Kingdom, Part 2 is a continuation of the epic film that director Lars von Trier made for Danish television. Part 1 is now available on video, and Part 2 continues the story of a huge, modern hospital, built on an ancient, swampy site, and dubbed "The Kingdom." Each part of the film is prefaced by foggy shots of people plunging garments into water that was used in a bleaching process. The misty, fluid environs are evocative of the primordial soup out of which all life arises. The portentous voiceover narration suggests that the modern, antiseptic attitudes of the doctors in the film, and their pride in therapeutic institutions, merely mask the upheavals of the primitive life below its foundations. The massive edifice not only of the hospital, but of the contemporary life—the film implies—is actually unstable. Indeed, the voiceover narrator says in so many words that modern medicine and science ignore the religious dimension, the struggle between good and evil, replacing it with the simpler categories of sickness and health.

The Kingdom is epic both in its ambitious theme and in its cast of characters. Yet it is also a grand made-for-television soap opera. And like many soap operas, the plot and the character conflicts are easily grasped, for they are essentially melodramatic. Thus Part 2 can be enjoyed even without knowledge of Part 1. Nevertheless, a reprise of what happens in Part 1 does enhance an appreciation of Part 2, especially in evaluating how Trier manages to keep his narrative not only intact but engrossing.

Stig Helmer (Ernst-Hugo Jaregard) is the Dane-hating Swedish neurosurgeon, one of the film's amusing princi-

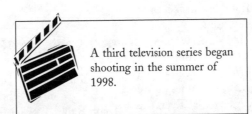

A third television series began shooting in the summer of 1998.

pal villains. He finds the Danes to be idiotic (one of his favorite words). He is a caricature of the arrogant doctor who never admits a mistake. In his case, his pretensions are ludicrous. He has badly botched an operation on a young girl and is being investigated for malpractice. He scorns alternative medicine in Part 1, but in his hysterical quest to cover up his incompetence turns to voodoo in order to put a curse on his rival, junior surgeon Krogen (Soren Pilmark). It takes nothing away from the fun to reveal that in Part 2, Helmer succeeds in both killing Krogen and turning him into a zombie.

Then there is Mrs. Drusse (Kirsten Rolffes), an old woman with psychic talents. She is aware that the hospital is haunted by spirits who cannot rest because of an evil crime committed by a doctor at the turn of the century—a doctor who has now become a demon and impregnated a staff doctor, who has given birth to a half-human, bloated, and rapidly aging baby. Mrs. Drusse roams the hospital's enormous corridors, seeking out the troubling origins of the hospital's evil. Whereas in Part 1 her eccentricity marginalized her, in Part 2, virtually the whole action of the film is marginalized, so to speak, or subordinated to her acute sense of the paranormal and the spiritual. Much of the film, in other words, is viewed through her eyes.

By making Mrs. Drusse the central figure, the organized world of the hospital seems like an highly efficient illusion. Thus the fanatical cancer researcher, Professor Bondo (Baard Owe), seems far more wacky than Mrs. Drusse. He has allowed his own liver to develop a tumor, the largest tumor in the world, he brags. Only when the mass has reached its final life-threatening stage does he allow it to be removed. And even then he hesitates in the classroom, not wanting to dissect the tumor because then it will no longer be the world's largest. As one of his students tells him, he has to make a choice: does he want to continue the program of research or become a collector? It seems like an absurd question, but the surrealism of this scene effectively makes the point that modern medicine and its adjunctive activities in the classroom and laboratory can become a kind of farce removed from reality. Bondo, his finger in the air, abjures his students with the single word "science," which they repeat, like a mantra, "science." They seem serious, but they are also joking.

Indeed, the ultimate absurdity is that the sense of privilege, of being the holder of recondite knowledge, isolates the doctors into a kind of occult, priestly class. Thus it is natural (in this film) for them to meet as a secret society performing absurd ceremonies—like the rite of initiation that compels the initiate to hold onto a lemon with his teeth while another doctor uses a sword to slash off a piece of the fruit. Constant aerial shots of the gargantuan medical complex emphasize that it is a kingdom, a world unto itself that does not recognize its own imbecility.

Such an isolated world not only develops its own rituals, it also seeks ways to divert itself, to make its insularity less tedious, less routinized. This is, after all, a denatured world. It is a set of interiors where people work long hours and seem to have no life outside of their jobs. To amuse themselves, to put some thrill back into their lives, the hospital staff organizes a betting pool, which is keyed to timing how long it takes an ambulance driver to make it to the hospital from a pre-arranged point. The driver is competing against himself, with each ambulance run aimed at besting his previous record run. He wears a ski mask and crash helmet and drives recklessly. Everyone admires this derring-do, and the only one to make the obvious point that this dangerous game is the antithesis of what the hospital is meant to do is constantly called "boring." He is rejected by the woman he loves because he is too predictable. The irony is obvious though no less forceful: the hospital is built on a paradox. On the one hand, modern medicine represents the human quest to regulate life, to save it, to heal it, to make it ordinary in the sense that the drama of illness and disease are conquered. Yet that very therapeutic process takes the adventure out of life for the doctors and the rest of the staff. They want risks; they envy the rash and the wild.

The Kingdom, Part 2 does not end the story. Rather it is suspended at another climax. Whereas Part 1 ended with the birth of the demon-child, Part 2 apparently ends with that child's death, and with Mrs. Drusse's confrontation with evil in an elevator plunging downward during a power outage caused by the zombie Krogen. However the film ends, its style suggests that the human story is about a never-ending conflict between good and evil that science can never master.

Reviewers of *The Kingdom* have been wary of taking it too seriously. After all, it was a television series. The portentous music and narration seem like a parody of horror films. Can a work with so much humor be taken seriously?

Can the techniques of mass entertainment be used to make a profound statement? Such questions reflect reviewers' fears that their legs are being pulled, and that to take *The Kingdom* seriously is to risk being called pretentious and even foolish.

The Kingdom is popular and serious in the same way that Poe or Dickens are popular and profound. Like Dickens, *The Kingdom* is serial art; its episodes are deliberately contrived to amuse, to shock, and even to scare. Exaggeration is its modus operandi, and its black humor has much in common with the theater of absurd—but one that has been domesticated, brought into daily life, so to speak. Like Poe, the film delights in the grotesque and questions the concept of normality—so precious to concepts of modern medicine and the therapeutic.

Stig Helmer laughs scornfully when he is told that doctors can get ill too. Of course they can, he sneers, remarking again at the stupidity of the people he must deal with. But then the phrase keeps recurring to him, and he begins to question his own health. The words penetrate his facade of impregnability, a facade as seemingly rigid as the concrete and steel complex he works in. But like that complex, Helmer has an unstable foundation. When he confides his health concerns to Professor Moesgaard (Holger Juul Hansen)—the fussy, earnest head of neurosurgery who is beginning to doubt his own sanity—Moesgaard recommends that Helmer examine his feces. If Helmer has floaters, he is fine, but if he has sinkers, well . . . There follows throughout the film shots of Helmer peering into

CREDITS

Stig Helmer: Ernst-Hugo Jaregard
Mrs. Drusse: Kirsten Rolffes
Dr. Moesgaard: Holger Juul Hansen
Krogen: Soren Pilmark
Rigmore: Ghita Norby
Bulder: Jens Okking
Miss Svendsen: Birthe Neumann
Bondo: Baard Owe
Judith: Birgitte Raaberg
Mutant baby: Udo Kier

Origin: Denmark
Released: 1997
Production: Vibeke Windelov and Svend Abrahamsen for Zentropa Entertainment and the Danish Broadcasting Corporation; released by October Films
Direction: Lars von Trier
Screenplay: Lars von Trier and Niels Vorsel
Cinematography: Eric Kress
Editing: Molly Malene Stensgaard, Pernille Beach Christensen

a toilet bowl, worrying about his waste products, and cursing the Danish scum. He is ridiculous, but he is also most human and infantile at those moments when he is concerned with his own evacuations and what they mean. Like *The Kingdom,* Helmer is actually staring into an abyss, wondering how to replace his sense of dread with a fulfilling ambition.

—*Carl Rollyson*

REVIEWS

Boxoffice. June, 1998, p. 74.
Detroit Free Press. May 17, 1998, p. 7F.
Los Angeles Times. May 8, 1998, p. F6.
San Francisco Chronicle. May 29, 1998, p. C3.
San Francisco Examiner. May 29, 1998, p. C3.
Variety. September 15, 1997, p. 80.
Village Voice. May 12, 1998, p. 130.

Kissing a Fool

There are three sides to every story.—Movie tagline

"David Schwimmer in a hilarious turn."—Monica Eng, *Chicago Tribune*

"Irresistible."—Michael Medved, *New York Post*

"A lot of fun. Jason Lee is smart and funny."
—Anita Gates, *New York Times*

"A witty romantic comedy."—Jane Horowitz, *Washington Post*

  Box Office: $4,106,388

A few prominent critics were not kind to *Kissing a Fool.* One particularly uncomplimentary review in *Entertainment Weekly* said, "And you thought *Ed* scraped the bottom of the features-by-*Friends*-folks. Wrong-o." Lest anyone miss the point, the review also called it "coarse, tedious, unfunny, utterly disposable" and branded it with a D- grade for good measure.

This was unnecessary. Although *Kissing a Fool* is no *Dr. Zhivago,* it's certainly not as bad as *Ed*—though few things are. *Kissing a Fool* is merely a light, forgettable comedy, no more, no less. As that, it does the job.

As is required of romantic comedies, *Kissing a Fool* has a cockamamie set-up. Max Abbitt (David Schwimmer) is a Chicago sportscaster who is a man's man. He likes the ladies, sports, and the minor celebrity that comes with his job. He's also kind of a jerk. Jay Murphy (Jason Lee), Max's best friend since birth, is a writer who is working on a book detailing the painful breakup with his ex-girlfriend. During a

spare moment not spent moping about his lost love, Jay decides he may have found the woman that can get Max to settle down—his smart, beautiful editor, Samantha Andrews (Mili Avital, the Israeli film star).

Jay is right. Even though Max and Sam have nothing in common (she hates sports, he hates books), they hit it off immediately. They hit it off so well, in fact, that they are engaged within weeks.

For a ladies' man like Max, this is a scary thought. He knows he is having trouble keeping his wandering eyes in check and begins to wonder if his fiancee is also attracted to others. This is where the requisite kooky set-up comes in. Max asks his old buddy Jay to try to seduce Sam to see if she can resist the temptation. "C'mon, you're a fairly good-looking guy," Max says, trying to convince Jay. Jay does not want to go through with Max's convoluted scheme because he is such a sensitive guy (or perhaps he is just offended by the silliness of the movie's plotting).

Even though Jay nixes Max's plan, he and Sam do have to spend a lot of time together working on his book and they do have a lot in common. With all the long days hunched over the computer together, somehow the probable ending of the movie becomes a whole lot clearer.

As if there weren't enough cutesy contrivance going around for at least two light, romantic comedies, screenwriters James Frey and Doug Ellin (who is also the film's director) use an awkward framing device. The movie begins with a wedding involving Sam, Jay, and Max (who is actually marrying is obscured). The wedding is held at the sprawling mansion of Linda (Bonnie Hunt), the rich boss at the publishing house that employs Sam and owns Jay's book. Cornered by some overbearing and uncouth wedding guests, Linda begins to tell

Max (David Schwimmer) to Jay (Jason Lee): "What if Sam isn't The One after all? What if she is the first woman who could actually dump Max Abbitt?"

the tale of how the day's newly married couple got together. Throughout the rest of the film, the action occasionally cuts back to Linda telling the story while the uncouth couple look on, saying things like "Wow!" and "And then what happened?" While the framing device isn't offensive, it adds nothing to the film and could have been left on the cutting room floor.

What takes the film above its too-obviously plotted plot is the general likability of the actors. David Schwimmer (who also was an executive producer on the film) generously lets Jason Lee be the big hero, but also seems to be having fun hamming it up as the selfish, semi-dense Max. Max is no Ross Gellar (Schwimmer's character on *Friends*). He shares the same penchant for shiny hair goo, but you can tell Max is no Ross because his lines actually work on women, plus he cusses a lot more (one memorable un-Ross-like string of epithets: "F– f–ing fair!" What would Monica think!). If nothing else, it's nice to see Schwimmer playing something other than a shy, puppy dog–eyed wimp. He doesn't quite pull it off—the puppy dog eyes betray him—but he gets close.

Mili Avital is fresh-faced and bright in her role as the bookish Sam. Not only is Sam smart and gainfully employed, but she even occasionally wears glasses. Kudos to the writers for creating a non-ditsy female lead in a romantic comedy.

> Jerusalem-born Mili Avital won an Israeli Academy Award for best supporting actress for *Over the Ocean* and received a best actress nomination for *Groupie*.

Bonnie Hunt is wasted in the role of Linda the storyteller. Any of her frequent guest appearances on David Letterman's *Late Show* show much more of a comic flair than her thankless role here. The funny Hunt seems like she should be mocking such a role, not playing it.

The standout member of the cast is Jason Lee. He brings the same sort of easy charisma to the film that he had in *Chasing Amy*. Lee's performance is even better considering how badly the role was written. Jay's character—a sensitive, bookish, lovelorn guy—could have been a big dud if played by someone less edgy (like Schwimmer, perhaps). Lee makes Jay seem like a real guy, a guy from down the hall in the dorm or office. Lee even makes Jay's incessant mourning over his old girlfriend seem semi-charming. A critic in *L.A. Weekly* described Lee as "a decent haircut away from stardom." Stardom could happen for Lee, though smart role choices will help as much as a haircut.

As the romantic portion of the romantic comedy combo is slight, so is the comedy part. The jokes are light and not knee-slappingly funny but they're not bad. And with the exception of one fat joke, they're not offensive either. In a world full of *Beverly Hills Ninja*-style comedies, that's saying a lot. A sample joke: Linda says, "You wouldn't believe how happy Jay was when he heard the news." Jump cut to the past and Jay blandly saying to her, "I'm very happy." It's clever and there are more than a few laugh-out-loud moments.

The dialogue is similarly fine. A sample line from Max on the subject of therapy: "Right, I always wanted to pay someone a hundred bucks an hour to talk myself out of being happy." It would be fair to say that the dialogue is sometimes almost even snappy, though Nick and Nora Charles could talk verbal circles around these characters.

The film makes good use of its Chicago setting, also the setting of *My Best Friend's Wedding*. Apparently Chicago is good for romance, especially romances that take place in the non-snowy summer months. And, fortunately for the theater seat traveler, the film's characters tend to have many of their big conversations out in some of Chicago's most

CREDITS

Max Abbitt: David Schwimmer
Jay Murphy: Jason Lee
Samantha Andrews: Mili Avital
Linda: Bonnie Hunt
Natasha: Vanessa Angel
Dara: Kari Wuhrer

Origin: USA
Released: 1998
Production: Tag Mendillo, Andrew Form, and Rick Lashbrook for Largo Entertainment and R. L. Entertainment; released by Universal Pictures
Direction: Doug Ellin
Screenplay: Doug Ellin and James Frey
Cinematography: Thomas Del Ruth
Editing: David Finfer
Music: Joseph Vitarelli
Production design: Charles Breen
Costumes: Sue Kaufmann
Sound: David Obermeyer
MPAA rating: R
Running Time: 93 minutes

REVIEWS

Entertainment Weekly. March 6, 1998, p. 58.
Hollywood Reporter. February 24, 1998, p. 14.
Los Angeles Times. February 27, 1998, p. F12.
New York Times. February 27, 1998, p. E23.
Sight and Sound. October, 1998, p. 45.
USA Today. February 27, 1998, p. 9D.
Variety. February 23, 1998, p. 73.
Village Voice. March 10, 1998, p. 118.

scenic locations, and there's some beautiful aerial photography of the town over the opening credits.

When all the various *Friends* movies are lined up and analyzed, *Kissing a Fool* won't be one of the shining examples of greatness, but as *Friends* movies go, it's not that bad. And although Schwimmer didn't get the career-making hit he might have been hoping for with *Kissing a Fool*, he also didn't make the kind of movie that will ruin his career. *Kissing a Fool* is the nice, likable movie that exists solely so that dating couples will have something to watch while killing time before the good-night kiss.

—*Jill Hamilton*

Kitchen Party

I don't think you get what's going on here.
—Movie tagline
If they found out, they'd kill me.—Movie tagline

Although it has some of the marks of a run-of-the-mill teen pic, Gary Burns's second feature film *Kitchen Party* is a real breath of fresh air. Drawing on a very impressive ensemble of young actors, Burns manages to sidestep the easy path of sneering at the suburbs, instead carefully, and sometimes painfully, mapping out the contradictions and hypocrisies of middle-class life. Burns even manages to redeem the sterile, spiritually empty setting (some nameless suburb of Vancouver) through a humorous treatment that is both clearheaded and harshly critical. Burns's first feature, *The Suburbanators* (1996), didn't get much play outside of film festivals, but with this second film he shows that he's much more than just a hipster one-shot wonder, and is indeed a skilled storyteller, making intelligent small films.

The film opens with a fairly run-of-the-mill family dispute as the insanely neat Mom and Dad get ready to go to a dinner party, leaving their eighteen-year-old son Scott (Scott Speedman) home for the night. It is the end of summer, and Scott has just finished high school but has been told by Dad that if he gets in any more trouble then Dad won't pay for him to go to university in the fall, meaning that he'll be confined to his personal suburban hell indefinitely. He of course decides to tempt fate by inviting his friends over for a party, but insists that they all stay in the kitchen, since the living room is so immaculately vacuumed that any footprints from his friends would give him away. Various snags in the evening arise, some predictable (one of Scott's friends crashes his dad's car), some quite unexpected (his malcontent brother finally snaps and leads police on an absurd motorcycle chase across a golf course).

What's most immediately notable about the film is the performances that Burns elicits from his very young crew of players. The narrative very much revolves around Scott, and

Speedman shows himself to be a very solid actor indeed. His performance is marked by a sense of restraint that at first seems to be a logical response to the excess that surrounds him, but that eventually proves to be more a product of the repression that seems to have defined his upbringing. This duality seems pretty clear by the end of the film, but it takes a while to come to that realization. Speedman does an admirable job of playing his cards close to his chest, only to reveal at the end that the very qualities that have made him so likable are indeed what make him something of a schmuck. This realization is facilitated by Tammy (Laura Harris), and Harris also gives a solid performance as a young woman who moves from being Scott's object of lust to his Jiminy Cricket–esque conscience. This is also something of a remarkable progression, one that Harris brings about quite gradually and skillfully. Rather than suddenly turning shrill and moralistic, she makes it clear that she was always a strong, moral person and if Scott had just bothered to pay attention, that would've been obvious.

There is also a narrative parallel to the madness in the kitchen: a dinner party that the parents of the "kitchen kids" have gone to. Burns resists the urge to make the parents literal duplicates of their kids, and while it's clear that none of the apples have fallen terribly far from the trees, a lot of these kids have evolved more as a reaction to their parents than as a reflection. A case in point is one of Scott's friends, Lester Jr. (Dave Cox), who ends up wrecking his dad's car. Dad is a boisterous but insecure fella, who nearly gets into a fist fight at the dinner party over whether or not Junior is gay. Junior himself, though, is morose, quiet but extremely impulsive, and indeed self-destructive (one of the film's subplots revolves around the handgun that Junior is carrying around in the car). It's clear that he's gotten his rather nihilistic worldview from dealing with his overbearing dad and his utterly defeated mom. Scott has a similar relationship with his extremely overbearing dad and neat-freak mom, and it's clear that his perpetually mellow nature has evolved as a coping mechanism. Less than an echo of their offspring, then, this menagerie of parents serves as a kind of extended explanation for the young characters with whom we spend most of the film.

Burns's film is also notable for the massive amount of suburban ground that it covers in a fairly short period, and this geographic sweep makes the film feel almost epic. Of course the idea of a suburban epic is a little silly in and of itself, but Burns's narrative wanders pretty far and wide for a film that is, at its core, about what happens in someone's kitchen. While part of Burns's purpose in this getting out of Scott's house and into the world seems to be to mock the epic form, part of what he accomplishes is showing this personality-free suburb to be a fairly unstable and constantly shifting landscape. Although he begins by basing the narrative purely on hemmed-in interior spaces (the kids in the kitchen, the adults in the dining room across town), as the film progresses the action becomes more and more dependent on sprawling, uncontrollable spaces, such as a garden party that the parents eventually adjourn to and the golf course where the surreal motorcycle chase takes place. This duality constitutes one of Burns's keenest insights into suburban life. Even though suburbs are supposed to create a stable, controllable space with easily identifiable borders, the reality is that even these places have large, potentially chaotic quarters where people's most uncontrollable urges tend to get lived out.

This insight, that suburbs are not as stable as they appear to be, could easily be filed under many of the suburban-angst films to have come out of the North American indie scene in the last ten years or so (Richard Linklater's *subUrbia* [1997] may be the best known of this cycle of films). And yet, *Kitchen Party* avoids much of the smarminess that seems to be endemic to films about the suburbs, and in some ways is defined by an almost anthropological coolness instead of a bitter sneer. This coolness is really what makes the film stand out, for not only does Burns resist the urge to demonize his fallen minions of suburbia, but he conveys some very real, unpatronizing sympathy for the condition in which they find themselves. Scott wants to escape the place so badly that the viewer can just taste his wanderlust, but Burns shows this to be equal parts desire to escape repression and a passion for anything new that is a defining part of late adolescence and may or may not have anything to do with the suburbs as such. Burns maintains a very clear head about the root of the middle-class angst that he chronicles then, resisting the ease of blaming it all on the 'burbs and showing instead that a sense of discontent tends to permeate middle-class life, seeping into the psyches of those who are both young and middle-aged. Angst may tend to settle in the suburbs, but it begins in the tormented interior life (and family life) of its inhabitants.

Indeed, Burns's main project here seems to be to chronicle the kinds of power relationships and hierarchies that inevitably emerge among small groups of people, a project that

doesn't necessarily have much to do with suburbia. Our young anti-hero Scott is quite obviously the leader of his group of friends, and while there are occasional attempts (often by the girls) to challenge him, what he says pretty much goes. Inevitably the strains of command catch up with him, though, and perhaps the most touching revelation of the film is when Tammy shows him just how not-in-control he really is. At the end of the film he abandons his psychotic brother, who is riding his motorcycle and being chased across a golf course by the police, and Tammy opts to stand by the one she hopes will become her man. While Tammy has been set up as the conscience of the group, though, the one who's really smarter than most of these other goofy teens, this final situation also proves too much for her, leading her, like Scott, towards a realization that she's not really in control after all. Burns's final insight, then, is that these hierarchies, although undoubtedly a central part of social interaction, are really just elaborate ruses that people perpetuate, ruses that can come unraveled at any moment given an intense enough situation.

Although it's been billed by the online movie review service JAM! as "Canada's answer to the slacker flick," *Kitchen Party* is really much more complex and sensible than most examples of that GenX exploitation genre (maybe that's what makes it "Canada's answer"). Burns has a keen eye for both suburban landscape and social relations, but he never allows himself to get carried away with sneering at the excesses of either teenagers or malcontent yuppies. Instead, he's fashioned a gentle, insightful portrait of middle-class life, one that could do much to cor-

CREDITS

Scott: Scott Speedman
Tammy: Laura Harris
Brent: Kevin McNulty
Barb: Gillian Barber
Cynthia: Sarah Strange
Cal: James McBirney
Steve: Jason Wiles
Lester Jr.: Dave Cox

Origin: Canada
Released: 1997
Production: Christine Haebler and John Hazlett for Sub Urban Film Co.; released by Cineplex Odeon Films
Direction: Gary Burns
Screenplay: Gary Burns
Cinematography: Robert Aschmann
Editing: Mark Lemmon, Reginald Harkema
Music: Schaun Tozer
Art direction: Douglas Hardwick
MPAA rating: Unrated
Running Time: 87 minutes

rect some of the simplifications and distortions of that social group that's appeared in a lot of recent North American independent film.

—Jerry White

REVIEWS

New York Times. April 10, 1998, p. E18.
Variety. October 6, 1997, p. 58.

Knock Off

Capitalism is exploding in the Far East!—Movie tagline

 Box Office: $10,319,915

Jean-Claude Van Damme has done it again. His latest film, *Knock Off*, is a fun and wickedly fast-paced action film with enough wit to satisfy audiences who don't usually enjoy this type of fare. The film's director is Tsui Hark, one of China and Hong Kong's most prolific and successful action filmmakers. It is written by Steven E. De Souza, the prolific screenwriter of *Judge Dredd* (1995), *Beverly Hills Cop III* (1994), *The Flintstones* (1994), and the first two *Die Hard* films (1988, 1990). Together with co-stars Lela Rochon, Paul Sorvino, and Rob Schneider, they have made an amusing and fast-paced film.

The plot revolves around a pair of buddies, Marcus Ray (Van Damme) and Tommy Hendricks (Schneider), who work in Hong Kong's fashion industry. They work in the area of import/export for a large blue jean manufacturer. As in many action films, the specifics of their work remains a bit murky, but they seem to run a large warehouse, and have done so for four years. The plot thickens immediately with the arrival of several Russian thugs who seem to be smugglers and are out to get Ray's adopted brother, Ling Ho (Carmen Lee). Not only are the Russian bad guys on the scene, but a few other characters seem to have an interest in Ray and Hendricks's business: Karen Leigh (Lela Rochon), an executive from the headquarters of the blue-jean company who has come to investigate Ray and Tommy's import/export

operation; and Harry Johannson (Paul Sorvino), a CIA agent who is also looking into their business.

What everyone seems to be looking for is the source of several bombs that turn out to be exported in the jeans. It seems that the jeans are knock-offs (copies of originals) and someone is skimming money, adding the bombs, exporting them, and may just end the world through these blue-jean-button-bombs. Or, at least, that appears to be the plot. It's all a bit hard to follow, but that's the fun of the film. Just when it seems clear who the good guys are, they are exposed as something different. Metaphorically speaking, every character is a "knock-off." No one in the film is what they seem to be, and the twists and turns each new discovery causes are part of what make this film a hoot. De Souza and Tsui keep the audience guessing until the very end, and they don't ever let the action stop long enough for anyone to notice that there isn't much there in the way of a plot in the first place. It's a few bad guys and some smuggling with some quick plot changes, but the action never ceases, and that's where the filmmakers show their craft. The opening sequence grabs attention immediately, with several scuba divers opening boxes of children's dolls. The dolls prove to be "knock-offs" filled with bombs; the bombs go off; a great action sequence ensues; the film is underway.

This kind of fast-paced action is where director Hark excels. There are numerous set action sequences in interesting locales, each sequence piling on top of the last like vanquished losers in one of those crowded wrestling challenges on television. For example, no sooner does the first (aforementioned) underwater sequence end before another sequence begins. In it, the audience finds itself introduced to Van Damme and Schneider's characters via an inexplicable rickshaw race. The characters careen through

> Marcus (Jean-Claude Van Damme) on his clothing business: "I always made a quality piece of crap."

> Tsui Hark and Jean-Claude Van Damme also worked together on 1997's *Double Team.*

the crowded alleys and markets of Hong Kong's busiest districts, overturning food stalls and causing a lot of destruction along the way. Somehow, though, a fair amount of ex-

CREDITS

Marcus Ray: Jean-Claude Van Damme
Tommy Hendricks: Rob Schneider
Karen: Lela Rochon
Johansson: Paul Sorvino
Ling Ho: Carmen Lee
Eddie: Wyman Wong
Lt. Han: Michael Fitzgerald Wong

Origin: USA
Released: 1998
Production: Nansun Shi for Film Workshop Company Ltd.; released by TriStar Pictures
Direction: Tsui Hark
Screenplay: Steven E. De Souza
Cinematography: Arthur Wong
Editing: Mak Chi Sin
Music: Ron Mael, Russell Mael
Production design: James Leung, Bill Lui
Costumes: Ben Luk, William Fung, Mable Kwan
Sound: Gary Wilkins
Stunt coordination: Yuen Bing
MPAA rating: R
Running Time: 91 minutes

position occurs during this sequence: the audience learns about the relationship of Van Damme and Schneider's characters, a bit about their history, about where they work, who their enemies are, who the enemies of the film itself might be, and more. That's quite an accomplishment on the part of Hark and writer De Souza.

With all this praise, it shouldn't be construed that this is any classic film. It's just a very fun film that requires nothing of its audience but to enjoy Van Damme's endearing screen presence (he continues to improve as he becomes more and more the international action veteran) and some lively action. There are holes in the plot, and there are some inadequate performances in a few of the supporting roles (Schneider was better in a similar role in De Souza's *Judge Dredd*). However, Hark's interesting camera angles and use of close-ups and cutaways, combined with great action, make it all worthwhile. And the fact that this was all filmed during the final days of Hong Kong's British rule makes it all the more impressive an accomplishment.

—*Kirby Tepper*

REVIEWS

Entertainment Weekly. September 18, 1998, p. 62.
Hollywood Reporter. September 8, 1998, p. 18.
New York Times. September 5, 1998, p. B17.
People. September 21, 1998, p. 38.
Variety. September 7, 1998, p. 72.

Krippendorf's Tribe

"Wildly hilarious!"—David Sheehan, *CBS-TV*

"The rib-tickling film of the year!"—Bonnie Churchill, *Group W*

"Fresh and funny, a rollicking good time!"—Bill Bregoli, *Westwood One*

 Box Office: $7,571,115

Someday, there may very well be a Trivial Pursuit question that reads as follows: "Name the film from a Walt Disney studio that begins with the line, 'Give this to your mother. She's the one without the penis shield.'" The answer will be *Krippendorf's Tribe*, a frenetic, often low-brow farce from Disney's Touchstone Pictures that tries hard to

be hilarious and heartwarming and falls short of being either. The aforementioned immortal line is uttered by anthropology professor James Krippendorf (Richard Dreyfuss) to the youngest of his three children while on an expedition in the jungles of New Guinea to study primitive man. In these brief introductory scenes, captured on film during the trek, we see the Krippendorf family in happier times, before the death of Krippendorf's wife, Jennifer (Barbara Williams). Also an admired anthropologist, Mrs. Krippendorf was beautiful, fun, intelligent, and had a close, loving family. Indeed, she appears to have had it all (except, of course, the aforementioned shield).

These lighthearted moments from their past are in stark contrast to the present state of affairs in the Krippendorf household. We see the professor lying in the dark on his living room couch, dispirited and disheveled, staring at these flickering images of a person and a time he sorely misses.

To avoid ridicule from his peers, anthropologist James Krippendorf (Richard Dreyfuss) and his children simulate a lost tribe in the family comedy *Krippendorf's Tribe.*

The premature death of his wife has set Krippendorf adrift, both personally and professionally. His unkempt house contains dirty laundry, spoiled food, and a great deal of hostility and resentment. Into these gloomy surroundings breezes Veronica Micelli (Jenna Elfman of TV's *Dharma & Greg*), an effervescent addition to the anthropology department who greatly admires Krippendorf's work and is looking forward to his lecture that night. The much-anticipated talk will announce the results of his quest to locate and study a previously undiscovered tribe. It seems, however, that Krippendorf's funk has prevented him from undertaking any such expedition, and, what is worse, he has been using his grant money to pay his family's bills.

Hearing that a colleague who also misappropriated funds was shown no mercy and sent to prison, a frazzled Krippendorf enters a packed university auditorium and proceeds to make up his findings as he goes along. His family and their circumstances become fodder for his imaginative creation: he names the fictitious tribe Shelmikedmu after the members of his own "tribe," which consists of daughter Shelly (Natasha Lyonne), and sons Mickey (Gregory Smith) and Edmund (Carl Michael Lindner). He also states that the tribal children are raised by the male parent and the boys are all circumcised. The audience is stunned and thrilled by these unusual findings, and a request is made to see Krippendorf's films of the Shelmikedmu. The professor hatches a desperate plan to transform his backyard into a jungle setting, create costumes and makeup for his children, and shoot films that will satisfy everyone and get him out of his predicament. While his daughter is disdainful and his littlest son continues not to speak to him, the

older son warms to the task. Soon all are involved in the production, and the children, lost since their mother's passing, come together—and to their father's rescue—by portraying his lost tribe.

Despite the fact that Krippendorf's creative juices are now coursing through his body, he wants to contain his deception before doubts arise. He is therefore exasperated when Veronica, who smells more grant money, arranges further lectures and gets the media to trumpet the professor's findings. Things get even more out of control when Krippendorf gets Veronica drunk, puts her in a Shelmikedmu costume, and films the two of them having sex, thereby documenting tribal mating rituals. (He also claims that a broken, cylindrical piece of a souvenir from a family vacation is a sexual aid used by the women of the tribe.) Veronica is appalled when she recognizes herself in the film, and realizes that Krippendorf's tribe is a sham. She shows up on a television program where he is pretending to be a Shelmikedmu chieftain, and forces the seething professor to eat bugs.

Meanwhile, Ruth Allen (Lily Tomlin), a colleague who is jealous and suspicious of Krippendorf's findings, has headed to New Guinea to look for the Shelmikedmu. When Krippendorf and Veronica are awarded a Proxmire Grant to continue researching the tribe at a lavish dinner, Ruth sends a fax that exposes the hoax. His children come to his defense with a last-ditch effort to convince the crowd, but touching words from long-mute little Edmund make Krippendorf realize that it is time to end the charade. In the end, a call comes from an astounded Ruth saying that the Shelmikedmu do exist after all, thanks to some creative intervention from Shelly. Veronica and Krippendorf, now a couple, are seen presiding over a cheerful family barbecue. Krippendorf's tribe is, indeed, no longer lost.

Krippendorf's Tribe received mostly negative reviews, and by its second week in release, business was already down fifty percent. The film's basic problem is that it is nowhere near as hilarious as it clearly thinks it is. Its aim is for broad, exuberant, ribald humor, but despite the tremendous energy put into the performances, the film fails to shine. Dreyfuss generates a number of smiles, but nothing more. Tomlin and Elfman add some degree of sparkle to their roles, and the great Elaine Stritch and the always-welcome Tom Poston do what they can in small roles. The children are, for the most part, utterly resistible. Excellent veteran character actor Phil Leeds delivers two of the film's most memorable lines, including the following one to the decidedly decrepit, 100-year-old Mrs. Proxmire: "Nice to see you. Was it you who died, or was it your sister?" (This was apparently Leeds' final feature film role, as he died in August at the age of 82.)

Krippendorf (Richard Dreyfuss) as his children leave for school: "Have a good day, kids. Make me proud. Come home different."

CREDITS

James Krippendorf: Richard Dreyfuss
Veronica Micelli: Jenna Elfman
Mickey: Gregory Smith
Shelly: Natasha Lyonne
Edmund: Carl Michael Linder
Henry Spivey: David Ogden Stiers
Gerald Adams: Stephen Root
Irene Harding: Elaine Stritch
Gordon Harding: Tom Poston
Ruth Allen: Lily Tomlin
Jennifer: Barbara Williams

Origin: USA
Released: 1998
Production: Larry Brezner; released by Touchstone Pictures
Direction: Todd Holland
Screenplay: Charlie Peters; based on the book by Frank Parkin
Cinematography: Dean Cundey
Editing: Jon Poll
Music: Bruce Broughton
Production design: Scott Chambliss
Art direction: Bill Rea
Costumes: Iris Mussenden
Sound: James F. Webb
MPAA rating: PG-13
Running Time: 94 minutes

Another of the film's significant shortcomings is that the script, based on the 1985 book by Frank Parkin, never makes us especially like, or care about what happens to, Krippendorf and his family. The film is directed by Emmy-winner Todd Holland, who has acquitted himself nicely on such television shows as *The Larry Sanders Show, Tales from the Crypt,* and *My So-Called Life. Krippendorf*'s producer, Larry Brezner, burst onto the scene with 1987's *Good Morning Vietnam* and *Throw Momma from the Train* after co-producing *Arthur* (1981), but his subsequent films have failed to live up to this initial show of promise. Add *Krippendorf's Tribe* to that list.

—David L. Boxerbaum

REVIEWS

Chicago Tribune. February 27, 1998, p. 7F.
Entertainment Weekly. March 6, 1998, p. 24.
Hollywood Reporter. February 24, 1998, p. 14.
Los Angeles Times. February 27, 1998, p. F4.
New York. March 9, 1998, p. 48.
New York Times. February 27, 1998, p. E12.
People. March 9, 1998, p. 24.
USA Today. February 27, 1998, p. D9.
Variety. March 2, 1998, p. 84.
Washington Post Weekend. February 27, 1998, p. D7.

Kurt and Courtney

"Electrifying . . . incendiary . . . sensational!"
—Entertainment Weekly

"Absorbing . . . well worth a trip!"*—New York Times*

"A must-see!"*—Rolling Stone*

A cause célèbre at the 1998 Sundance Film Festival, where it was pulled due to legal threats, Nick Broomfield's *Kurt and Courtney* made its premiere at San Francisco's Roxie Cinema and set house records before opening in other cities. *Kurt and Courtney* examines the relationship of the first couple of grunge rock in the early 1990s, Kurt Cobain and Courtney Love, and focuses on the possibility that Cobain's death in 1994 was not, as officially declared, the result of a self-inflicted gunshot wound but rather a murder plot engineered by Love herself.

The documentary opens with the discovery of Cobain's body on April 8, 1994. Broomfield tells us that people could not accept the suicide of Nirvana's lead singer, and murder theories developed. The early part of the film gives us some background on Cobain. Particularly interesting is his Aunt Mary, who plays a very early recording of Kurt at the age of two. Aunt Mary also helped him record his first tracks as a teenager—tracks that Broomfield could not use in the film because of Love's legal threats. This is just the first of several instances where Love's censorial influence is felt. (One of the film's themes, in fact, is Broomfield's struggle to maintain financing in the wake of Love's pressure on the film's backers.)

We get the general sketch of Cobain's childhood—his parents' divorce, his often rootless existence living with a teacher and his family for a while, and later under a bridge.

Broomfield talks to a former girlfriend of Kurt, Tracy Marander, with whom he lived for three years. She shows some of Cobain's artwork, disturbing pieces like a self-portrait of himself as a thin skeleton and a picture of a fetus.

In some interview clips, we see the humble, sweet side of Kurt Cobain. He comes across as a regular guy uncomfortable with fame and fortune and unexpectedly happy about fatherhood. Diehard Nirvana fans will be most interested in this section of the film, which offers these little insights into Kurt's early years and thoughts. However, the bulk of the film is dedicated to investigating the murder theory surrounding his death.

The most notable of the witnesses espousing this theory is Love's estranged father, Hank Harrison, who used pit bulls to discipline his daughter as a little girl and calls this technique "tough love." He claims that Cobain and Love were about to get divorced and Cobain was about to change his will. Courtney would thus get more money if Kurt died before the divorce. Harrison has written two books on Cobain, one of them titled *Who Killed Kurt?* Like many of the people Broomfield interviews, Harrison does not come off very well. He clearly has a vendetta against his daughter, and, in one very disturbing scene, shouts, "I'll keep kicking your ass." He genuinely loves playing to the camera, and his motives seem less about exposing what he sees as the truth and more about hawking his books. In his last meeting with Broomfield, Harrison notes Broomfield's nice car. Broomfield says the BBC provides for him, and Harrison cynically responds, "Well, I didn't get any of it, but that's okay"—a throwaway remark that seems to sum up Harrison's motivations.

Indeed, so many of those interviewed seem to have a grudge against Love that the film soon becomes one long diatribe against her. Rozz Rezabek, an old boyfriend, says that Love was very ambitious and felt her way to the top of the music world was through a man, and her attempt to turn him into a rock star made him quit music. Blaming her for his failure, he bitterly accuses her, "You stole my career and made me run away from it."

While Rezabek seems pathetic as he reminisces over lost dreams, other people are downright freakish. One girl named Amy bears an eerily striking resemblance to Love in her grunge years and claims she has photos of herself shooting up with Kurt and Courtney. However, Amy can never produce these pictures proving she knew them. The extent of her insight is that Kurt was "very nice, very courteous" and Courtney "a harpy"—an idea reiterated in various ways throughout the film. A friend of Kurt, Dylan Carlson, is incoherent in explaining why he does not believe the murder theory. Near the end, when Chelsea, a friend of one of the couple's former nannies, comes forward to speak, it looks

like Broomfield will indulge anyone with anything to say. Chelsea looks like an older, washed-out version of Love. The nanny herself believes Kurt killed himself, or, at worst, Courtney drove him to do it, which is not a farfetched idea given the film's unflattering picture of Love.

The most disturbing figure in the film is a rock singer named El Duce, described as "a debaucherous sort of fellow" and having an S&M stage persona. He claims Love offered him "fifty grand to whack Kurt Cobain" but does not know if she was joking. He is a burly, scary fellow who looks like a wrestler or a killer and loves playing up this persona for Broomfield, who doubts his veracity but seems to enjoy filming him anyway. El Duce even says he regrets not taking the job, and, in a bizarre epilogue to his story, we learn he was killed by a train.

Interviewee El Duce about Courtney Love: "She offered me fifty grand to whack Kurt Cobain." Broomfield: "People might not think you're the most reliable witness."

The most levelheaded, because he actually speaks coherently and not venomously, espouser of the murder theory is Tom Grant, a private investigator whom Courtney hired to find Kurt days before he was found dead. However, Grant's pivotal claim, that the level of heroin in Kurt's system would have made it impossible for him to lift a shotgun, is disputed by a doctor.

As a portrait of a conspiracy theory, the film raises suspicions but no hard evidence and so becomes a hatchet job on Love, who is portrayed, at the very least, as an opportunist and a schemer. What separates her from her accusers, though, is that she has succeeded where they have not, and they are trying to make a name for themselves by trashing her. Ultimately, Broomfield has assembled an assortment of losers and misfits—some of them pathetic, some of them scary—who have come in contact with the famous but will never make it to the top like Kurt and Courtney and are clearly out to get their fifteen minutes of fame in the wake of the Cobain tragedy.

In the world of the wannabes and acquaintances who populate Broomfield's film, Cobain's Aunt Mary comes off

CREDITS

Origin: Great Britain
Released: 1997
Production: Nick Broomfield for Strength Ltd.; released by Roxie Releasing
Direction: Nick Broomfield
Cinematography: Joan Churchill
Editing: Mark Atkins
Sound: Nick Broomfield
MPAA rating: Unrated
Running Time: 95 minutes

the best. She does not have an ax to grind or a desire to make a name for herself by trashing Love. Mary believes her nephew's death was a suicide (she even remembers some suicide-related song lyrics Kurt wrote as a teenager), and she seems the most credible witness.

Love is depicted as a woman who was at the periphery of the music business for a long time, and, once she got to the top of the grunge/punk world, was very eager to abandon it for Hollywood glamour, which calls into question her authenticity. Cobain and Love, while similar in their troubled backgrounds and drug addictions, were clearly very different. Cobain was embarrassed "by the fame and by the trappings of fame" (as an old friend, Alice Wheeler, points out), while Love has embraced fame and wants to make it big in the movies, as demonstrated in her glamorous arrival at the 1997 Academy Awards.

Love is clearly not a saint. The last part of the film is dedicated to her violence towards the press, and, in light of these attacks, it is not surprising that she and her legal team tried so hard to stop the release of *Kurt and Courtney. Vanity Fair*'s Lynn Hirschberg, for example, mentioned Love's heroin habit while pregnant in a story about her, and this led to a threatening letter and Love's attempt to bludgeon her with Quentin Tarantino's Oscar the night of the 1995 Academy Awards. We also hear Love's threatening phone message to Victoria Clarke, who was writing a book on Nirvana, and Clarke's account of Love physically attacking her at a club. (In the film's only instance of showing a dark side of Cobain, he joins in the threats on Clarke's answering machine.)

In the film's coup de grace, Love attends an ACLU gala, where she presents a very prestigious award—a rich

irony given her past and future attacks on freedom of expression. Before the event, Broomfield interviews her briefly, but Love walks away when he brings up her death threats against journalists. Then we see Love make her presentation and hear her trumpet the value of freedom of speech. Broomfield takes the podium to question her and is quickly hustled away. While the scene is clearly self-serving in making Broomfield the martyr of the First Amendment, it is still a great moment demonstrating Love's hypocrisy.

Kurt and Courtney is fairly entertaining and often darkly comic in its tour of the fringes of fame and the depths to which some people will go for a moment in the spotlight. At the same time, because the film stems from a tragedy and finally offers a very biased view of the Cobain-Love marriage and only speculation regarding the murder theory (even Broomfield ends up not believing it), one cannot help feeling the whole enterprise a fairly tawdry affair.

—*Peter N. Chumo II*

REVIEWS

Boston Phoenix. June 15, 1998.
Chicago Tribune. June 5, 1998, p. 5.
Detroit News. June 19, 1998, p. 11D.
Entertainment Weekly. April 10, 1998, p. 40.
Los Angeles Times. April 17, 1998, p. F4.
New York Times. June 5, 1998, p. E12.
People. June 1, 1998, p. 33.
Portland Oregonian. April 10, 1998.
San Francisco Chronicle. February 27, 1998, p. C3.
San Francisco Examiner. February 27, 1998, p. C1.
Variety. January 26, 1998, p. 71.

The Land Girls

The story of three young women and the events that would change their lives . . . The friendships that would stay with them forever . . . and the loves that would change their hearts.—Movie tagline

David Leland's *The Land Girls,* based on the 1994 novel by Angela Huth, is a nostalgic tribute to the Women's Land Army during World War II, when the German U-boat campaign was threatening to starve the British into capitulation. Accustomed to importing so much of its food, Britain was faced with the necessity of growing much bigger crops, while at the same time conscripting thousands of young farmers into its armed forces. The Women's Land Army was founded during World War I. It was revived when war broke out again in 1939 and was not disbanded until 1950. During that time, over 100,000 women had served in the WLA. They wore distinctive uniforms with high boots and jodhpur-like breeches, and they paraded with shovels on their shoulders instead of rifles.

The Land Girls were mostly young women from the cities who had been given a minimum of training for such jobs as milking cows and driving tractors. One of them confesses to her crusty old employer John Lawrence (Tom Georgeson) that her instruction in milking had consisted of squeezing water out of the holes poked in the fingers of a rubber glove. John is more than a little skeptical about the three young women assigned to his Dorset farm. He tells his patient, over-worked wife (Maureen O'Brien) that they are lazy, incompetent, and merely "out for a lark." The story might have been more dramatic if the three heroines—Stella (Catherine McCormack), Prudence (Anna Friel), and Ag (Rachel Weisz)—had shown more of these characteristics at the beginning. They do seem pretty incompetent at first when it comes to milking the family's herd of cows, but otherwise they take to farming with surprising ease. Not only that, but they prove themselves to be hard workers. Each of them is just as valuable as any male farmhand, which, of course, supports the thesis of the film that the Land Girls were gutsy heroines of Great Britain's "finest hour."

The audience is reminded that there is a war on by the fact that from a hilltop the three young women can see the lights of bombs and anti-aircraft fire where a city is under nightly attack by Hermann Goering's *Luftwaffe.* The year is 1941. The Battle of Britain is at its height. In one strik-

ing scene the war is brought directly home to the Lawrence farm when a burning German fighter plane crashes in their field and the mortally wounded pilot jumps out covered in flames.

The Land Girls was given an R rating but hardly seems to deserve it. The only scenes of nudity occur when the three girlfriends are taking much-needed baths together in an old-fashioned tin tub, and the camera seems to respect their natural modesty. There is also a scene involving *coitus* involuntarily *interruptus* in the hayloft, but both lovers keep most of their clothes on and do not get far with their lovemaking before John barges in and forces his son Joe (Steven Mackintosh) to jump out the window.

Although the three girlfriends do a lot of talking about sex, most of their dialogue only reveals their naivety and inexperience. The feeling of being on their own, away from people and places they have known, seems to have liberated their repressed libidos. Their conversations, however, are not much different from those now heard on American family sitcoms during prime time. Viewers will be reminded of such PG-rated American films as *Swing Shift* (1984) and *A League of Their Own* (1992), in which women take over for men during World War II and not only prove themselves competent but discover their true identities. As Kevin Thomas commented in his review in the *Los Angeles Times,* "World War II marked the beginning of a social revolution

Prue (Anna Friel) about Joe (Steven Mackintosh): "I'm going to have him—total fornication."

in which women began to consider alternatives to their traditional roles as housewives and mothers . . . young people of conventional backgrounds were tempted to throw aside strictures against pre-marital sex and to question whether they really loved those whom they were supposed to marry."

With so many young farmers off to fight the war, Joe Lawrence suddenly finds himself very popular with the ladies. All three of the visiting Land Girls eventually have what they call "a go" at him. Prue, a worldly wise working-class girl, only wants sex. Ag, an inhibited academic type decides that at age 26 she is long overdue to lose her virginity. Stella's interest in Joe begins as mere sexual attraction but becomes tragically serious. Stella is engaged to a handsome young upper-class Royal Navy officer, Philip (Paul Bettany). The conflict between her love for both of these men provides the main dramatic interest in the story.

Joe is already engaged himself. He carries on his affair with Stella without the knowledge of his fiancee. In spite of their honorable intentions, Joe and Stella find themselves falling more and more deeply in love. Joe aspires to join the

Royal Air Force and fly Spitfires, but he is rejected for a congenital heart ailment. Stella has just decided to become a Dorset farmer's wife when she receives word that her fiancé has been hospitalized and is asking to see her. Joe drives her to the train station and promises to be waiting there when she returns to Dorset after she has gone through the ordeal of breaking her engagement to the other man she still loves. Every day Joe comes to the picturesque old station and awaits the arrival of the huffing and puffing little two-car passenger train. (What would an English picture be without a train and a train station?) Every day he returns to the farm disappointed. Eventually, he stops coming to the station.

What has happened is that Stella has visited the crowded hospital ward full of suffering men and has discovered that her handsome, devoted fiancé has had both legs amputated at the knees. Philip very nobly tells her that he will understand if, under the circumstances, she should wish to break their engagement—which is exactly what she had come to do. The camera fades out on this touching scene before it is resolved, but the viewer has already realized that

> The Women's Land Army numbered more than 80,000 workers during World War II.

Stella (whom *New York Times* reviewer Stephen Holden described as "attractive, well-mannered, and too highly principled for her own good") will not be able to inflict such an emotional blow upon a man who has already suffered so heroically.

Several years after the war has ended, Prue, Ag, and Stella are reunited for a christening in the Dorset village near the Lawrence farm. In contrast to the uniforms and drab work clothes they wore before, they are now dressed in colorful, feminine summer attire inspired by the New Look of the late 1940s. The camera feasts on sunlight, which had been conspicuously absent during the first hundred minutes of the film. Prue and Ag are both married and have small children. Ironically, Stella tells them that her own marriage has already ended in divorce. The viewer who may be hoping to see a reunion between Stella and Joe is quickly disillusioned when the two former lovers meet again in an orchard. Joe has married his childhood sweetheart and is the father of two children, who appear at his side as if to symbolize his responsibility and commitment. He is now running the family farm and deeply rooted in a way of life it would be impossible for him to change, although it is obvious that Stella is still the only woman he has ever really loved. He is right where he belongs—and Stella realizes that she is intruding where she might have belonged temporarily during wartime, and might have adjusted to if she had married Joe, but clearly does not belong anymore. They dare not even kiss goodbye. They only touch with the tips of their fingers in a farewell scene reminiscent of the classic *Brief Encounter* (1946), another wartime story in which a pair of English lovers place duty above personal happiness.

The film's outstanding feature is its beautiful cinematography directed by Henry Braham. The camera lavishes attention on the rolling hills and ancient trees, the pristine pastures being torn up by the plow to raise more food for the war effort, the country roads by day and night, the venerable village church, the huge, patient draft horses and docile cows, the authentic old English farmhouse and the commodious barn whose hayloft offers such a convenient and aesthetically appealing place for bucolic lovemaking. The viewer could easily forget about the war (which happened so long ago anyway), except for occasional sight of a Spitfire roaring through the peaceful sky or the occasional arrival of an official letter regretfully informing some member of the tightly knit community that a loved one had been killed in action.

This unpretentious film feels patriotic without being propagandistic. With characteristic British understatement, the people's unity and patriotism are taken for granted. Not a word is said about the monster Hitler or the wicked enemy. There

CREDITS

Stella: Catherine McCormack
Ag: Rachel Weisz
Prue: Anna Friel
Joe Lawrence: Steven Mackintosh
Mr. John Lawrence: Tom Georgeson
Mrs. Lawrence: Maureen O'Brien
Janet: Lucy Akhurst
Philip: Paul Bettany

Origin: Great Britain
Released: 1997
Production: Simon Relph for Greenpoint Film, Channel Four Films, Intermedia Films, and West Eleven Films; released by Polygram Filmed Entertainment
Direction: David Leland
Screenplay: David Leland and Keith Dewhurst; based on the novel by Angela Huth
Cinematography: Henry Braham
Editing: Nicholas Moore
Music: Brian Lock
Costumes: Shuna Harwood
Production design: Caroline Amies
Art direction: Frank Walsh
Sound: Stuart Wilson
MPAA rating: R
Running Time: 110 minutes

are a couple of obligatory scenes in which all the armed forces are represented and the speaker acknowledges the contribution of the members of Women's Land Army. Otherwise, *The Land Girls* seems more like a tribute to English country life and the honest, industrious farmers upon whom the rest of a complex modern society will always depend.

—*Bill Delaney*

REVIEWS

Los Angeles Times. June 12, 1998, p. F18.
New York Times. June 12, 1998, p. B12.
San Diego Union-Tribune. June 25, 1998, p. 24.
San Francisco Chronicle. June 12, 1998, p. D3.
Sight and Sound. September, 1998, p. 44.

The Last Days of Disco

History is made at night.—Movie tagline

"Touching and funny—often simultaneously. An oasis of civilized delights."—Jay Carr, *Boston Globe*

"A perfect mood-booster."—Michele Shapiro, *Glamour*

"Wonderfully clever, sharp-eyed and charming with wit and a whimsical sense of humor."—Kenneth Turan, *Los Angeles Times*

"Whit Stillman's best movie yet!"—Karen Durbin, *Mirabella*

"A small miracle of comic social portraiture . . . deeply evocative and enjoyable."—Dave Kehr, *New York Daily News*

"Deft, funny and improbably touching."—Janet Maslin, *New York Times*

"Brilliantly amusing. Stillman's cast, one and all, is perfect."—Steven Rea, *Philadelphia Inquirer*

"Comic bliss."—Peter Travers, *Rolling Stone*

Box Office: $3,024,198

Alice (Chloë Sevigny) and Charlotte (Kate Beckinsale) look for everlasting love at the end of the disco era in *The Last Days of Disco*.

C ritiquing any film by Whit Stillman can put a person in an awkward position. Criticize or dismiss the film outright and Stillman devotees will claim that you just don't get the social satire. Assume that Stillman is only about satire, that his characters exist fundamentally as objects of ridicule, and an insider might assume that you are still bitter about never having gotten into an exclusive New England college. Laugh at all the in-jokes, sympathize with those articulate overeducated preppies, reminisce about debutante balls or armchair Marxism—basically, take the film at its word—and, well, you end up sounding like

> Des McGrath (Chris Eigeman): "Our bodies are not really designed for group social life. We're really designed for pairing off."

you walked (or strutted) straight out of *The Last Days of Disco*, Stillman's last installment in the trilogy that began with *Metropolitan* (1990) and *Barcelona* (1994).

Like other recent films set in the "disco era," such as *Boogie Nights* (1997) and *54* (1998), *The Last Days of Disco* simultaneously is and is not about presenting a faithful recreation of that era. Typically Stillman-esque, the film features an ensemble of young, white, well-educated members of the "urban haute bourgeoisie" (UHBs), who spend more time talking about themselves, their beliefs, and the social politics of popular culture than they do actually dancing, dating, or having sex. For this reason, viewers not familiar with Stillman's previous works may feel that the film's title is more than a bit misleading and find his characters at best amusing and at worst ridiculous, boring, or just plain annoying. To film connoisseurs, or merely the duly warned,

Stillman's trilogy will recall Krzysztof Kieslowski's magnificent *Trois Colours/Three Colors* (*Blue*, 1993; *White* and *Red*, 1994)—although Stillman's work is intentionally smaller and far wryer than Kieslowski's. In *Barcelona*, for instance, moments of cross-cultural conflict lead up to a final resolution in which Spanish women concede that real American hamburgers taste great. Yet both trilogies use individual characters to explore the definitions of national culture alongside abstract questions about chance and fate through artful and provocative series of interlocking narratives.

Writer/director Whit Stillman refers to his three films as his "Doomed Bourgeois in Love" series.

The Last Days of Disco tracks the days and nights of dowdy Alice Kinnon (Chloë Sevigny) and the exquisitely bitchy Charlotte Pingress (Kate Beckinsale), two recent Hampshire College graduates trying to make it in the business of publishing. Their social circle consists of other New England-educated young professionals—mostly Harvard guys—with whom they frequent an exclusive Manhattan dance club. Alice, whose vulnerability is accentuated by Sevigny's awkward physicality, provides the film with its moral and narrative anchor. Throughout *Disco*, we watch painfully as Alice sifts through a motley collection of males, in part at Charlotte's instigation. Included in the line-up are Des (Stillman regular Chris Eigeman)—the college drop-out, dance club floor manager who disposes of girlfriends by "coming out" to them—and Tom the environmental lawyer (Robert Sean Leonard)—a stereotypical enlightened male whose morning-after routine includes lamenting, "What I was craving was a sort of sentient individual who wouldn't abandon her intelligence to hop into bed with every guy she meets in a nightclub." By the film's end, Alice has more or less hooked up with Josh (Matthew Kesslar), a sincere but manic-depressive, out-of-work assistant district attorney.

Despite all this coupling, the film strays about as far from romantic comedy as one could imagine. Romance, or merely its possibility, provides these characters—all played with biting precision—with yet another topic of conversation. Did the disco era, with its pulsating music and hoards of sweaty dancing bodies, really herald "a whole new era of social models," as Charlotte claims? Is group social life more important than "all that ferocious pairing off?" And do guys really like it when women insert the word "sexy" at random into their conversation? It is precisely questions like these that Stillman's characters and his film overall are primarily interested in exploring. Thus, subplots about apartment hunting and I.R.S. investigations aside, the film reaches its highpoint in a hilariously articulate debate between Josh and Des over the meaning of Disney's *Lady and the Tramp* (1955). Josh claims that the dogs actually represent "human types" in a "primer for love and marriage directed at very young people." He bitterly charges, "Films like this program women [like Lady] to adore jerks [like Tramp]" and argues that Lady ought to have cho-

sen the "loyal old Scottie." Des—recognizing that Josh's interpretation contains a thinly veiled objection to women like Alice choosing men like Des over himself (Josh)—suggests that Tramp undergoes a Lady-inspired transformation and deserves credit for changing his ways.

Viewers may or may not agree with either Des's or Josh's final analysis. And a good number of film critics have written off their debate as something of a joke. But the discussion of *Lady and the Tramp* actually lies at the heart of *The Last Days of Disco*. From Tom's claim that "The environmental movement of our times was sparked by the re-release of *Bambi* in the 1950s," to Josh's messianic pronouncement that "Disco was too great and too much fun to be gone forever," the film ultimately offers a simple statement about the powerful and lasting influence that popular culture exerts on our lives. Alice, Charlotte, Josh, and Tom may all boast degrees from the crème de la crème of American higher education, and the quality of their education may enable them to express their opinions in complex sentences, but in the end their behavior and beliefs, like that of everyone else, has been shaped by Disney features, dress codes, and dance styles.

CREDITS

Alice: Chloë Sevigny
Charlotte: Kate Beckinsale
Des: Chris Eigeman
Josh: Matt Kesslar
Jimmy: MacKenzie Astin
Dan: Matthew Ross
Holly: Tara Subkoff
Hap: Michael Westerly
Tom: Robert Sean Leonard
Nina: Jennifer Beals

Origin: USA
Released: 1998
Production: Whit Stillman for Westerly Films and Castle Rock Entertainment; released by Gramercy Pictures
Direction: Whit Stillman
Screenplay: Whit Stillman
Cinematography: John Thomas
Editing: Andrew Hafitz, Jay Pires
Music: Mark Suozzo
Production design: Ginger Tougas
Costumes: Sarah Edwards
Sound: Scott Breindel
Choreography: John Carrafa
MPAA rating: R
Running Time: 113 minutes

Embedding a message about the power of pop in the depths of a quirky highbrow vehicle indicates either true edginess or plain inconsistency. And, to a certain extent all of Stillman's films carry this potential flaw. It is never wholly clear how much of an "insider" Stillman really is. For example, anyone schooled in the 60s-throwback liberal climate of New England colleges during "the very early 80s"—as Josh and Des are supposed to have been—would find *Lady and the Tramp* easy prey, but they would bypass the Tramp vs. Scottie dilemma and go straight for an attack on its "compulsory heterosexuality." But very few viewers care about historical accuracy to this extent. For most viewers, Stillman's message will ring true. And as the film draws to a close, and subway commuters begin dancing to the infectious strains of "Love Train," the unequivocal truths of pop music and disco dancing become hard to deny indeed.

—*Jacqui Sadashige*

REVIEWS

Chicago Tribune. May 29, 1998, p. 5.
Entertainment Weekly. June 5, 1998, p. 46.
Hollywood Reporter. May 26, 1998, p. 20.
Los Angeles Times. May 29, 1998, p. F1.
New York Times. May 29, 1998, p. E12.
New Yorker. June 18, 1998, p. 81.
People. June 8, 1998, p. 38.
Rolling Stone. June 25, 1998, p. 100.
Sight and Sound. September, 1998, p. 44.
USA Today. May 29, 1998, p. 4E.
Variety. May 25, 1998, p. 55.
Village Voice. June 2, 1998, p. 155.
Washington Post Weekend. May 29, 1998, p. 48.

Last Night

It's not the end of the world . . . there's still six hours left.—Movie tagline

Don McKellar has been the subject of a lot of joking about what it means to be famous in Canada. He was one of the real toasts of the 1998 Cannes and Toronto film festivals, having co-written and acted in the award-winning, François-Girard-directed, Samuel Jackson-starring film *The Red Violin*, in addition to writing, directing, and starring in his own film, *Last Night*. Along with *Violin*, McKellar's first foray into directing is a fantastic example of Canadian cinema's increasing comfort with the possibilities of a reasonably commercial, but also reasonably intelligent national cinema. In this way, McKellar is king of the moderates, which may seem a ludicrously Canadian way of classifying him, but I'll stick to it. *Last Night*, in its sensibility and its willingness to thoughtfully innovate, is a film that has the potential to put Canadian film on the map internationally.

That potential is an important part of the film, actually, because it was commissioned as part of a multinational project. It was part of a series for French television, which asked directors from all corners of the globe to contribute a film about what would happen on the last day of the millennium. Several of the other entries have deservedly received some international exposure. The episode from Mali, *Life on Earth* (by Abderrahmane Sissako), where essentially nothing happens on the fateful New Year's Eve, which says

a lot about living in the third world during the age of globalization, is one of the best of the series. A waterlogged, squalid, oppressively urban and brilliant film called *The Hole*, which was made by the Taiwanese filmmaker Tsai Ming-Liang, is also a biting, highly visual film. *Last Night* gains a lot when it's considered as part of this international gathering, since such company makes it clear that McKellar is a fully-fledged member of the new generation of international *cineastes* who are struggling to balance well crafted filmmaking with narrative accessibility and social relevance.

McKellar's basic take on the last day of the millennium is that the world is simply going to end. This may seem like something of a cliché, but the way he handles it is especially original: the exact details of why or how the world is going to end are left unexplained. Everyone in the film has totally accepted that it's just all over at exactly midnight, Toronto time. The typical elements of millennial/apocalyptic narrative are still here, including street riots and infrastructure breakdown and separation from loved ones and all that. Nevertheless, the way that all these characters are so completely resigned to the inevitability of it all is the creepiest part of the story. The kind of tension that would be expected in an apocalypse film is almost totally absent here: the most dramatic moments of the film are much more interior-oriented than related to any sort of end-of-the-world kind of stuff. Indeed, the film's climax, where the camera swirls around McKellar and Sandra Oh as they try to decide whether to complete a suicide pact, is excruciatingly suspenseful, far more powerful than anything in *Deep Impact* or *Armageddon*'s moral universe precisely because the moment is unrelated to the fact of the apocalypse as such. It relies instead on an abstract, rawly emotional impact.

Simply as a piece of narrative, *Last Night* is exceptional. McKellar is quite a skilled narrative artist, juggling an unusually large number of characters, giving each one a sufficient amount of depth so we understand their own individual crises and connecting them all in a way that is apparent and not overly clever. McKellar himself plays Patrick, the character at the center of the film, and his deadpan humor and gently confused expression gives all these sometimes disjointed situations an odd kind of moral center. The great Québécois actress Geneviève Bujold is especially memorable in a minor role as McKellar's former French teacher (who, as a way of going out with a bang, has sex with McKellar's coitus-obsessed friend Craig [Callum Keith Rennie]). She gives the role a very real gravity that miraculously escapes melodrama. When she spontaneously quizzes McKellar on the French that she had taught him a decade earlier she is toughly amused by his pathetic attempts to respond. Her emotions turn gently sad when she begins to realize that it'll be the last time she sees him. "It's nice you remember some of it," she mumbles, as the elevator closes on her. It's a nice moment, played with a thoughtfulness and world-weariness that is all too uncommon these days. Sandra Oh's performance as Sandra, a woman hopelessly trying to re-unite with her husband for the big moment, is also a marvel. The presence and force that she's brought to other roles (most famously *Double Happiness* (1994), although she also has a bit part in *The Red Violin*) seems oddly out of place in this environment of impossibility, but it's just that intensity and seriousness of purpose that gives her part of the film its tragic sense.

Visually, *Last Night* is somewhat less than revolutionary, but I'd argue that this is part of its power. Rather than seeking some equivalent of the apocalypse, like gloomy lighting or oppressive urban spaces or whatever, *Last Night*'s visual scheme emphasizes long takes of open spaces (like the city) or tight compositions of closed spaces (like the characters houses and apartments). The way that the outside world feels so wide open is important because it exists in this film as a place where anything can happen, as McKellar often shows us through occasional, random and oddly flat acts of violence. One of the closing sequences, where McKellar's brother-in-law pummels a rioter with a golf club as McKellar unwittingly tries to get through a traffic jam, is an especially potent example of the unstable, multi-layered bits of reality that the film is based upon. The interiors, though, give a sense of comfort and intimacy that also don't seem quite right for a film about the apocalypse. This ends up working perfectly, though, because all of these characters have to find some sort of solace in the most plain and quotidian of domestic spaces, before it's too late. The intimacy that these spaces take on has a certain sense of urgency to it. This conflict between comfort and haste is perfectly summed up in a hilarious sequence when McKellar agrees to go to a big dinner at his family's suburban nest. This is where (predictably enough) countless long-suppressed arguments and conflicts come bubbling to the surface, but McKellar refuses to play the sequence for easy laughs. Instead, there's real poignancy here, with a pair of well-intentioned parents struggling quietly to regain the world of McKellar's childhood, a world that was difficult but which seemed a whole lot clearer. The film may look plain, but that's precisely the point: the apocalypse, in McKellar's universe, is something that happens unexpectedly, but which must be accepted and dealt with and finally internalized and normalized.

Last Night, much like *The Red Violin* (also reviewed in this edition) and the earlier McKellar-Girard collaboration *32 Short Films About Glenn Gould* (1993), is notable for the way that it mixes a commercial film practice with a more aestheticized, less accessible mode of cinema, thereby resisting a conventional distinction between "art film" and "Hollywood film." *Last Night* is not your grandfather's Canadian cinema: McKellar, along with Girard and filmmakers like Bruce McDonald (*Hard Core Logo* also reviewed in this edition) is trying to form a commercially viable but

CREDITS

Patrick Wheeler: Don McKellar
Sandra: Sandra Oh
Craig Zwiller: Callum Keith Rennie
Jennifer Wheeler: Sarah Polley
Duncan: David Cronenberg
Donna: Tracy Wright
Mrs. Carlton: Geneviève Bujold
Mrs. Wheeler: Roberta Maxwell
Mr. Wheeler: Robin Gammel
Jogger: Jackie Burroughs

Origin: Canada
Released: 1998
Production: Niv Fichman and Daniel Iron for Rhombus Media, Arte, and the Canadian Broadcasting Corporation; released by Cineplex
Direction: Don McKellar
Screenplay: Don McKellar
Cinematography: Douglas Koch
Editing: Reginald Harkema
Music: Alexina Louie, Alex Pauk
Production design: John Dondertman
Costumes: Lea Carlson
Sound: John L. Thompson
MPAA rating: Unrated
Running Time: 94 minutes

still innovative form of filmmaking. It's not an easy task, and these new Canadian films are marked by a real conflict in expectations: they're fun to watch, but they feel much odder than an average Hollywood film. All three of these filmmakers are graduates of the Canadian Film Centre, a school started by Norman Jewison in hopes of building a film industry north of the 49th parallel and ending Hollywood domination on Canadian screens. That hasn't exactly come to pass, but the films coming out of the Centre's grads, especially those by McKellar and Girard, have done a great deal to bolster domestic and international confidence in Canadian film, and to come up with new ways of telling stories that resists both European-influenced esoteric and Hollywood-style simplicity.

Finally, then, *Last Night* is a film about very big ideas, which come to include the end of the world, the need for companionship, the randomness of love, the value of human life, and the impossibility of reconciliation. It's also a film that deals with these ideals in a very straightforward way, Don McKellar's refusal to indulge in this material's possibilities for philosophical pretense or melodrama is especially impressive. The film well deserves its multinational character, and indeed synthesizes the most important elements of Canadian cinema (concern with civic life, a gentle nihilism, visual utilitarianism, and narrative expertise) into a humorous, emotionally satisfying whole. I can think of no better person to be famous in Canada than Don McKellar.

—*Jerry White*

REVIEWS

Boxoffice. July, 1998, p. 131
eye weekly. September 3, 1998.
Variety. June 1, 1998, p. 36.

Lawn Dogs

"Beautiful, brilliant, bold and daring; don't miss it."—*Instinct Magazine*

"Reveals the truth and humor of growing up in a sheltered, unforgiving suburbia . . ."—*Premiere*

"Playful, tragic and, literally, quite magical . . . a truly original contemporary fable . . ."—*Premiere UK*

"Haunting . . . hypnotic."—*Time Out UK*

Lawn Dogs is an uneven drama with fairy-tale elements about the unlikely friendship between a 10-year-old girl and the working class young man who mows lawns in her affluent Kentucky suburb. Based on an original screenplay by award-winning playwright and poet Naomi Wallace, it is an exploration of the growing physical space between the social classes in America, a story of how innocence is no match for the power of prejudice. Directed by Australian John Duigan, *Lawn Dogs* strains under the weight of overextended expectations: a didactic comedy-drama-fable that strives to be both quirky and explosive.

Devon (Mischa Barton) is a strange, intelligent and precocious—is there any other kind in today's films?—outcast, not unlike Christina Ricci's character in *The Addams Family* (1991). She lives in a gated community christened Camelot with her affluent parents, Clare (Kathleen Quin-

lan), a "Mrs. Robinson" who is sexually serviced by one of the local college boys, and Morton (Christopher McDonald), a successful businessman with political aspirations. Trent (Sam Rockwell) is the twenty-one-year-old lowerclass man who is paid as much to keep a low profile as he is to mow lawns.

Sent out by her parents to sell Scout cookies to the neighbors, Devon instead ventures outside the walls of Camelot. As she walks down the road, the girl recounts the Russian fairy tale of a little girl who is saved from the monster Baba Yaga only by her own cunning and a touch of magic. Soon Devon finds herself at the trailer of the Big Bad Sexual Wolf, Trent. He is polite, but perhaps cognizant of the possible ramifications of their friendship, discourages the young girl. But like a moth drawn to a flame, Devon returns to wear down Trent's resistance, ultimately resulting in the community's misunderstandings that Trent had feared all along.

Unlike the touching *Edward Scissorhands* (1990) or the overlooked urban rendering of Little Red Riding Hood, *Freeway* (1995), *Lawn Dogs* is far less successful in combining the elements of contemporary storytelling with timeless fairy tales.

While the sexual elements within the story are buried just below the surface, director Duigan chooses to exploit the emerging sexuality of the young Devon. Quite disturbing is his choice to photograph the prepubescent actress

Mischa Barton in ways that rival Adrian Lynne's controversial film adaptation of Vladimir Nabokov's novel, *Lolita* (reviewed in this edition). During a scene obviously meant to demonstrate Devon's free-spirit nature, the girl climbs out onto her bedroom roof, strips off her nightgown and releases it into the breezy night. It is not the content of this scene that is unnerving but rather the inappropriate way in which it is shot. The young actress is photographed not from the rear (which would have afforded some degree of decency since she wore underpants) but from the front, exposing her budding breasts. Given societal concerns over sexual abuse and the proliferation of child pornography, particularly over the Internet, it seems irresponsible of the filmmakers to venture into such uneasy territory. Other scenes that focus on the latent sexuality of the main characters often seem gratuitous in nature and only muddy the narrative.

The argument can certainly be made that this exploration of the sexuality that lingers beneath the relationship between Devon and Trent is an integral part of the story, and some viewers may find Duigan's film to be a "brave" look at the complex nature of friendship. It can further be argued that because there is no overt sexual activity between the protagonists, there is nothing inappropriate nor libidinous about their behavior. It is true that Devon initiates physical contact, but the manner in which Trent runs his finger down the girl's scar is equally unsettling. It is often difficult to decipher such interactions, perhaps because of the filmmaker's ambiguous treatment of both characters and story. Without access to Ms. Wallace's original screenplay, it is impossible to know whether the relationship between Devon and Trent was more clearly articulated and its boundaries carefully delineated; as a result, the responsibility of cohesive storytelling rests squarely on the director, John Duigan, and to this end, his efforts fall short.

The talented ensemble of actors are for the most part wasted in underdeveloped roles. Academy Award–nominee Kathleen Quinlan (*Apollo 13* [1995]) and veteran character actor Christopher McDonald (*Thelma and Louise* [1991]) are saddled with roles that are more caricature than character. Sam Rockwell's filmography includes *Box of Moonlight* (1997), *The Search for One-Eyed Jimmy* (1996), and interestingly enough, *Lolita.*

—*Patricia Kowal*

CREDITS

Devon: Mischa Barton
Trent: Sam Rockwell
Clare: Kathleen Quinlan
Morton: Christopher McDonald
Nash: Bruce McGill
Sean: Eric Mabius
Brett: David Barry Gray
Billy: Miles Meehan
Beth: Beth Grant
Jake: Tom Aldredge
Pam: Angie Harmon

Origin: Great Britain
Released: 1997
Production: Duncan Kenworthy for Toledo Pictures; released by Strand Releasing
Direction: John Duigan
Screenplay: Naomi Wallace
Cinematography: Elliot Davis
Editing: Humphrey Dixon
Production design: John Myhre
Costumes: John Dunn
Music: Trevor Jones
MPAA rating: Unrated
Running Time: 101 minutes

REVIEWS

Boxoffice. May, 1998, p. 73.
Chicago Sun Times. May 15, 1998.
Entertainment Weekly. May 29, 1998, p. 54.
Los Angeles Times. May 15, 1998, p. F10.
New York Times. May 15, 1998, p. E10.
San Francisco Chronicle. June 12, 1998, p. D5.
San Francisco Examiner. June 12, 1998, p. D5.
Sight and Sound. November, 1997, p. 46.
Variety. September 1, 1997, p. 78.
Washington Post. June 5, 1998.

The Leading Man

His method is seduction.—Movie tagline

He knew just what he wanted . . . and just how to get it.—Movie tagline

"Wickedly witty . . . *The Leading Man* is terrific backstabbing fun."—Philip Wuntch, *Dallas Morning News*

"Jon Bon Jovi ends up seducing everyone in sight, including the audience."—Owen Gleiberman, *Entertainment Weekly*

"Jon Bon Jovi gives an assured, sexy performance . . . sexy and sly as a fox."—Dennis Dermody, *Paper Magazine*

"Immensely enjoyable, intellectually intriguing, well-acted and genuinely sophisticated."—William Arnold, *Seattle Post-Intelligencer*

Rock star Jon Bon Jovi tests the big-screen limelight as a Machievellian manipulator and world-class womanizer in John Duigan's *The Leading Man,* a comedy of manners revolving around adultery and duplicity in the backstage world of London theatre.

Revered London playwright Felix Webb (Lambert Wilson) has built a romantic house of cards that is teetering on the brink of collapse. His wife, and the mother of his three children, Elena (Italian actress Anna Galiena) is beginning to unravel emotionally over her husband's public flaunting of his extramarital affair with his latest leading lady, Hilary Rule (Thandie Newton). Felix has promised the comely actress that he will leave his wife; but when Elena takes to angrily shredding his neckties and shorning off his boyish forelock while he sleeps, Felix fears for his wife's sanity—as well as the welfare of a treasured piece of his anatomy!

With his wife's outrage intensifying and his mistress's impatience growing, Felix cannot find a safe haven anywhere. He is mired in such escalating emotional turmoil that he readily accepts the outlandish proposition offered up by his leading man, the American film star seeking legitimacy on the London stage, Robin Grange (Jon Bon Jovi). In exchange for beefing up his part in the play, the sexy screen idol offers to distract Elena by seducing her in order to bolster her self-esteem

Elena (Anna Galiena) to husband Felix (Lambert Wilson): "You can't even make time to discuss breaking up your family! You can't even make time for that!"

and restore her independence, thereby paving the way to divorce for Felix.

Robin, a self-described "mercenary of the heart," studies his prey carefully, making lists of the music Elena listens to and the books she reads. With Robin's encouragement, Elena blossoms both as a woman and as a playwright—a talent she had secreted away in the shadow of her husband's success.

The conniving and manipulative Robin is so adept at playing games of the heart, as well as in the professional arena, that his intentions are always ambiguous and seldom honorable. Not content to have stolen away Felix's wife, Robin also seduces Hilary. His motivations are somewhat confusing, as is the presence of the handgun that Grange keeps in his briefcase. "I like to play with matches," reveals the womanizer who is rumored to have fled the United States to escape a romantic indiscretion with a producer's wife.

The acting in *The Leading Man* is strongest in the supporting roles, most notably David Warner as the mischievous veteran actor. While Bon Jovi is competent as Robin Grange, bringing a confident swagger befitting a Hollywood heartthrob, he lacks the acting depth to imbue his character with the complexity required if we are to understand Grange's ambiguous and duplicitous nature.

The film lays the seeds for a rich exploration of the precarious nature of love and romance, but disappoints in the execution. The predictable storyline is, as one character remarks in the film, "a classic banal plot." Written by Virginia Duigan, a former theatre critic, wife of Australian director Bruce Beresford and sister of director Duigan, *The Leading Man* is more entertaining in its tart glimpses into the backstage melodramas of the theatre. Not as scathing an indictment as was the witty and cynical *All About Eve* (1950), Duigan's film feels closer to the satiric Warren Beatty vehicle, *Shampoo* (1975).

John Duigan has displayed a fondness for rich character studies rather than projects that rely on fast-paced narrative. Arguably his best film to date, *Flirting* (1990) was a charming coming-of-age tale of adolescent love that was both witty and sensitive. Duigan's other work includes: *The Winter of Our Dreams* (1982), an exploration of love between a heroin-addicted prostitute and an

Actress Nicole Kidman appears in a cameo as an Oscar presenter. She previously worked with Thandie Newton and John Duigan in *Flirting* (1990).

unhappy bookshop owner; *Sirens* (1994), a provocative comedy of manners most notable for its rampant nudity; and *Journey of August King* (1995), a slow, thoughtful period piece about a runaway slave and the lonely farmer who comes

CREDITS

Robin Grange: Jon Bon Jovi
Elena Webb: Anna Galiena
Felix Webb: Lambert Wilson
Hilary Rule: Thandie Newton
Humphrey Beal: Barry Humphries
Delvene: Patricia Hodge
Susan: Diana Quick
Tod: David Warner

Origin: Great Britain
Released: 1996, 1998
Production: Bertil Ohlsson and Paul Raphael for J&M Entertainment; released by BMG Independents
Direction: John Duigan
Screenplay: Virginia Duigan
Cinematography: Jean-Francois Robin
Editing: Humphrey Dixon
Production design: Caroline Hanania
Art direction: Andrew Munro
Costumes: Rachel Fleming
Music: Edward Shearmur
Sound: Colin Nicolson
MPAA rating: R
Running Time: 99 minutes

to her rescue. Also released in 1998 was his Southern fable of friendship and prejudice, *Lawn Dogs* (reviewed in this volume).

Jon Bon Jovi made his film debut in a brief appearance in the "Brat Pack" Western, *Young Guns II* (1990), but had his first major role as the sexy housepainter in *Moonlight and Valentino* (1995). He appeared in two other films released in 1998: *Homegrown* with Billy Bob Thornton and Edward Burns's *No Looking Back* (both reviewed in this edition).

The Leading Man is a pleasant enough diversion; it certainly is not the worst film to be made. But it is disappointing in the familiar road it travels to an unpredictably bittersweet denouement.

—Patricia Kowal

REVIEWS

Boxoffice. April, 1997, p. 197.
Chicago Sun-Times. March 13, 1998.
Cinema Papers. June, 1997, p. 35.
Entertainment Weekly. March 20, 1998, p. 59.
Hollywood Reporter. November 12, 1996, p. 10.
Los Angeles Times. March 6, 1998, p. F27.
New York Times. March 20, 1998, p. E12.
People. March 16, 1998, p. 24.
Rolling Stone. April 2, 1998, p. 80.
Sight and Sound. September, 1997, p. 47.
Variety. September 16, 1996, p. 68.
Village Voice. March 10, 1998, p. 66.

Les Miserables

"This classic saga is new again and it's magnificent. A compelling and powerful human drama with terrific performances by Liam Neeson and Geoffrey Rush."—Bill Diehl, *ABC Radio*

"Geoffrey Rush is a magnetic force. Liam Neeson is a monument of penance, intelligence and charity."—John Anderson, *Los Angeles Times*

"A first-rate cast and a venerable storytelling style with suspenseful momentum. Mr. Neeson plays the role with sure physical authority and profound decency. Mr. Rush does a fine job."
—Janet Maslin, *New York Times*

"Solid and handsomely mounted! Savor the heft the well-cast Liam Neeson brings to the role. Marvel at Geoffrey Rush's reptilian, dead-eyed stillness."—David Ansen, *Newsweek*

"Strikingly photographed and exquisitely acted."—Andy Seiler, *USA Today*

"The movie sustains perfection from shot to shot. Absorbing, evocative and beautifully illuminated."—Gary Arnold, *Washington Times*

 Box Office: $14,096,321

I f ever a classic needed to be saved from the sticky and sentimental clutch of pop culture, it's *Les Miserables*. With his spare, intelligent film, Danish director Bille August (*Pelle the Conqueror* [1988]) has done just that. Liam Neeson (*Michael Collins* [1997]) has the strong physical presence and astute intelligence to inhabit the role of Jean Valjean. His compassion and contrition seem real, not scripted. Similarly, Geoffrey Rush (*Shine* [1995]) is a Javert of calculating menace—a different flavor than the benchmark performance of Charles Laughton in the 1935 classic version, but a very interesting interpretation nonetheless, one that emphasizes Javert's unthinking worship of the law, and examines how corrupt his soul becomes in his pursuit of Valjean. Released in the very thick of the Kenneth Starr-Bill Clinton showdown, this film prompted more than a few observers to draw parallels between Starr and Javert. Even cartoonist Garry Trudeau's *Doonesbury* comic strip featured a character opining that ". . . like the obsessed inspector in *Les Miserables*, he should put on manacles and throw himself into the river."

 Javert (Geoffrey Rush): "I've tried to live my life without breaking a single rule."

August's evocation of the look of early 19th–century France was achieved by shooting the film in the Czech Republic as well as Paris. Calling the film "wonderfully gray and dark," *The Washington Post* observed that "August's cold Scandinavian sensibility comes in handy in creating a dramatically under-lit world of mud, stone and misery." For misery is at the heart of the matter: Victor Hugo's 1862 novel was an indictment of his society, and this film seems to understand that, bypassing the all-too-familiar cliché of the hunter and the hunted. This tale is far more than *The Fugitive* in 19th century dress: by trimming Hugo's sprawling epic novel ("boiling it down" in the words of the screenwriter, novelist Raphael Yglesias), the film earns its place in the ever-expanding *Les Miserables* canon, which includes the wildly popular stage musical (publicity for this film says it has been seen by 40 million people) and even an animated Disney-esque children's film. Said Yglesias, "I realized that the central theme of Hugo's novel is redemption. I couldn't possibly tell the whole story, so I decided to focus on Valjean's struggle toward goodness and the relationship between him and Javert, which drive the plot forward."

The very well-known story is often reduced to a sentence: poor man steals a loaf of bread and serves nineteen years at hard labor; he reforms but is found out by a police inspector who hounds him mercilessly. Too many adaptations have taken this "Cliff Notes" approach with plenty of scenery chewing for the principals, but this one has much of the spirit of the Fredric March/Charles Laughton version, generally conceded to be the best film version by many critics. In keeping with the general discernment and sensitivity that mark this adaptation, writer and director both chose Neeson because of his subtlety and intelligence. Neeson commented: ". . . [Valjean] is no saint, and I did not want to play him as a goody-two-shoes. I have to play him as a human being, as a three-dimensional man in order to make it true to life and because cinema audiences want to see flesh and blood. I have concentrated very hard on showing that, every day, Valjean struggles to be good. It was as hard then as it is now to be good, so I wanted to show that struggle."

As the film opens, Jean Valjean has just been released from prison, and cannot find shelter or food anywhere—his past is inexorably with him. Shivering and famished, he is consumed with bitterness. Neeson looks suitably ferocious (his build and physiognomy are perfect for this part) and when directed by a kind woman to knock on a door, he is taken by a Bishop (Peter Vaughan) who is famously devoted to the poor and unfortunate. When Valjean steals the silver candlesticks from the home and escapes into the night, only to be returned by the police, he fully expects to be returned to the galleys. When the Bishop instead insists he gave them to the former convict, Valjean is astonished and accepts the Bishop's mandate: "You no longer belong to evil, but to good." These scenes are very effectively staged and flow smoothly into the next phase of the story, where we meet the scruffy Valjean transformed into the Mayor of Vigau, a successful and benevolent factory owner.

Fantine (Uma Thurman) is a worker who loses her position when it is discovered she has an illegitimate child in another village. Dismissed for "immorality", the consumptive Fantine is desperate to support her daughter Cosette who lives with a usurious couple, the Thernadiers, who constantly ask for more money and who, unknown to the mother, have virtually enslaved the little girl. When Javert suddenly appears in Vigau and presents his credentials to the Mayor, he does not recognize Valjean. When Fantine is arrested for prostitution, she angrily blames the Mayor for her misfortune, who defends her from Javert, thus setting the fateful events of Valjean's flight in motion. Valjean brings the dying woman home and tenderly cares for her. Javert, who had suspected the Mayor of being Valjean, instead concedes his error and asks the Mayor to dismiss him. He refuses to do so, earning him the eternal enmity of Javert: his pride will not tolerate being forgiven. Another man is accused, and in a powerfully staged

CREDITS

Jean Valjean: Liam Neeson
Javert: Geoffrey Rush
Fantine: Uma Thurman
Cosette: Claire Danes
Marius: Hans Matheson
Captain Beauvais: Reine Brynolfsson
Bishop: Peter Vaughan

Origin: USA
Released: 1998
Production: Sarah Radclyffe and James Gorman for Mandalay Entertainment; released by Columbia Pictures
Direction: Bille August
Screenplay: Rafael Yglesias; based on the novel by Victor Hugo
Cinematography: Jorgen Persson
Editing: Janus Billeskov-Jansen
Music: Basil Poledouris
Production design: Anna Asp
Art direction: Peter Grant
Costumes: Gabriells Pescucci
Sound: David John
MPAA rating: PG-13
Running Time: 131 minutes

courtroom scene, Valjean reveals himself. At Fantine's deathbed, Valjean vows to find Cosette; he rescues her and escapes to Paris in an exciting sequence with Javert hot in pursuit. The two find shelter shut away in a convent for a decade; it is only when the teenage Cosette (Claire Danes) falls in love with Marius (Hans Matheson), a young student revolutionary, that the final chapter of the manhunt is played out against the background of the 1832 Paris Rebellion.

The *New York Times* critic Andre Sennwald wrote in 1935 that "one of the great merits of the screen play [is] that it brings Valjean and Javert down to the end of the story together, eliminating the anticlimax of Valjean's death. Thus the drama fades out powerfully with Valjean free at last, and Javert a suicide in the nearby Seine for the sin of mercy for which he could atone only by forfeiting his own life." Boleslawski's film is almost a textbook example of the power of black and white film to express tragedy; the climax in this newest interpretation loses much of its force by being sunlit and in full color. Of course, there is the hopeful (and rueful) walk that Valjean takes away from his own nightmare that concludes this film: August and Yglesias are careful not to blare the triumph of Valjean, which would go against the austere atmosphere so carefully created.

Newsday said Bille August's adaptation of Hugo's greatest work is "an eager, earnest, broadly constructed pageant of ideas and characters whose greatest asset may be the service it pays to literature." Since fewer people are likely to tackle this enormous, complex book than see a film or play, being faithful to the spirit of the original is significant. Successful adaptations are not necessarily crowd pleasers, so for some, August's verisimilitude might be disturbing—but the life of the poor as Hugo depicted it was shocking and demoralizing. Valjean spends much of his life as a prisoner, brutalized by injustice and by the particular sadism of Javert. Audiences during the Great Depression were riveted by the tale that ensues from the theft of a loaf of bread; August wisely first focused on the psychology that drives both men to engage us, and only secondarily drew on the political themes so present in the novel.

This *Les Miserables* is blunt and relentless in depicting poverty: Fantine's steady descent into prostitution isn't prettified—in the novel, a particularly gruesome passage has her selling her front teeth—but a small complaint is that we never grasp how far she's fallen since we first meet her working in the factory. Fantine was once a great beauty, so casting Thurman made sense, and the actress works hard to achieve an otherworldly quality in the squalor of her life. Haggard and rheumy-eyed, she pulls back the blanket of her sickbed to "entice" a creditor to take out his debt in trade. It's a disturbing moment, and characteristic of August not to allow sentiment to overwhelm the story. Rush's Javert is similarly ascerbic and contained, yet when he realizes his instinct about the Mayor was correct, he roars "I knew it!" with the satisfaction of a man who has no belief whatsoever in redemption. "Reform is a discarded fantasy," says Javert.

His performance and Neeson's save the last quarter of the film, which sags badly due to the miscasting of Claire Danes and the too-pretty Hans Matheson. Other performances worthy of note include Peter Vaughan as the Bishop and Mimi Newman as the child Cosette.

Most critics, while not overly enthusiastic, considered this a worthy (if somewhat dull) interpretation. Said Roger Ebert: "Here we have a dutiful, even respectable, adaptation that lacks the rabble-rousing usually associated with *Les Miserables*." *Rough Cut* disagreed: "Overall, the story sells itself as the epic it is and, yes, audiences will be pleased."

—*Mary Hess*

REVIEWS

Boxoffice. June, 1998, p. 76.
Chicago Tribune. May 1, 1998, p. 5.
Entertainment Weekly. May 8, 1998, p. 48.
Los Angeles Times. May 1, 1998, p. F1.
New York Times. May 1, 1998, p. E22.
People. May 11, 1998, p. 33.
Sight and Sound. December, 1998, p. 49.
USA Today. May 1, 1998, p. 11E.
Variety. April 27, 1998, p. 58.
Washington Post Weekend. May 1, 1998, p. 53.

Lethal Weapon 4

The gang's all here.—Movie tagline
"A flamboyant tongue-in-cheek adventure!"
—Janet Maslin, *New York Times*

Box Office: $130,444,603

Detectives Murtaugh (Danny Glover) and Riggs (Mel Gibson) team up again for more crime fighting mayhem in *Lethal Weapon 4.*

Richard Donner, the action director who launched the *Lethal Weapon* series over ten years ago in 1987, directed this *Lethal* sequel at breakneck pace, working from an inchoate and inane screenplay by Channing Gibson, developed from a story concocted by Jonathan Lemkin, Alfred Gough, and Miles Millar. The film's tag line promises that "The Gang's All Here," and it is: Mel Gibson is back as the once wild and crazy Martin Riggs, of course, and Danny Glover is back as Roger Murtaugh, his older and more sedate sidekick. Joe Pesci is back as Leo Getz, more irritating than ever. Rene Russo is back as Lorna Cole, pregnant this time with Riggs's child, but alive and kickboxing. Perhaps a dog is missing here, but everyone else is back.

Donner pumps up the action immediately. The opening shots show an unexplained psycho with a flame-thrower and an automatic weapon torching stores and cars on the city streets for no apparent reason. This is an obvious prelude to the mass destruction that is sure to follow, but there is no clear link to the main plot, other than to remind viewers how Riggs and Murtaugh work together as oddball partners. After the torcher is torched, Riggs and Murtaugh go fishing with Leo in order to have a comic moment with a shark they have landed, but then the fishing boat, owned by

Murtaugh, is nearly crushed by a passing freighter. When they give chase, they are attacked when the crew commences firing upon them. Our heroes somehow manage to disable the freighter, which is loaded with illegal aliens from China, by running it aground. Never a dull moment, here.

After the illegal aliens are rounded up, Murtaugh discovers the Hong family, hidden under the tarp of a lifeboat. When he learns they were brought to the U.S. as slave laborers, in sympathy he decides to take them home and harbor them. It turns out that the grandfather's brother, an expert engraver, is already in America, under the control of a "triad" of Chinese criminals who have forced him to counterfeit Chinese currency to be paid to a corrupt Communist

General (Dana Lee) as ransom for four members of the triad family, originally imprisoned in China, but now released and flown to America. If the engraver does not cooperate, his own family will be murdered. When they are found and "rescued" from Murtaugh's home, the consequences turn nasty. Riggs and Murtaugh are subdued and tied up with Murtaugh's family, then Murtaugh's home is torched. The crooks depart hastily with their hostages, but a little Chinese boy is missed. He comes out of hiding, finds a pair of scissors, and cuts the duct tape used to bind up Riggs and Murtaugh, who then manage to save Murtaugh's family as the house burns.

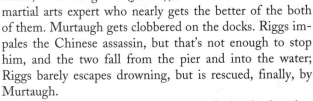

Producer/Director Richard Donner: "Audiences have lived with these guys for a long time. They're characters that audiences have fallen for—people have a relationship with them."

Murtaugh, a grandfather-to-be, has bonded with Mr. Hong and plans to find and rescue the kidnapped family. Murtaugh and Riggs track down the Chinese restaurant owner and godfather, Uncle Benny (Kim Chan), as he is having work done at the dentist's office. Madcap Leo creates a diversion by pretending to need emergency dental work (which he gets, by the way), while Riggs and Murtaugh use laughing gas to get Uncle Benny to tell them where the family has been taken. Apparently nitrous oxide also works, for the purposes of this movie, as a truth serum, though apparently Chinese dentistry is 70 years behind American practices in anesthetic procedures. Anyway, they get Uncle Benny's cheerful assistance in this way. They are also assisted by yet another detective, Lee Butters (Chris Rock, in a hard role), who has secretly married Murtaugh's daughter after getting her pregnant. Murtaugh doesn't know this, but while they are all high on laughing gas, Riggs breaks the news to his partner.

Once the laughter has stopped and this surreal sequence is over, they discover the counterfeiting ring and that Mr. Hong (Eddy Ko), has been murdered. This is enough to motivate them to go after the triad, whom they reach just before the prisoner exchange is about to take place, letting the General know that he is about to be paid in counterfeit bills. A terrible shoot-out follows in which Riggs and Murtaugh fight to the death with a triad enforcer, Wah Sing Ku (Jet Li), a

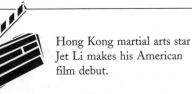

Hong Kong martial arts star Jet Li makes his American film debut.

martial arts expert who nearly gets the better of the both of them. Murtaugh gets clobbered on the docks. Riggs impales the Chinese assassin, but that's not enough to stop him, and the two fall from the pier and into the water; Riggs barely escapes drowning, but is rescued, finally, by Murtaugh.

The film ends in a family way at the hospital, where babies are born. After the exhausting finale, Riggs and Murtaugh race to the hospital and get there in time for Riggs to marry Lorna before their baby is born. Murtaugh's daughter has her baby at the same hospital at the same time in this conveniently contrived conclusion. In a final coda, which is not above shameless sentimentality, Riggs visits the grave of his first wife, who died in 1984. Leo is there to console him and explains that Riggs and Murtaugh are the only family he has.

Although consistently goofy, the film effectively delivers action-adventure as it careens from one chase to another, on foot, in cars, and on boats, to its unlikely conclusion. It is a film designed more to please the fans than to impress the critics. And yet it has a sense of humor, however infantile, and moments that suggest self-parody. The big action moments are too big and too absurd to be taken seriously. They must have been planned tongue-in-cheek, as when, for example, in one car chase Riggs and Murtaugh crash through the plate-glass side of a building. The car sweeps through an architectural office, with workers scrambling to get out of the way (of course, no one seems to get hurt), then crashes through the plate glass at the opposite end of the building, hurtles airborne, and is carried by its momentum to the street below to resume its chase behind the Chinese hood who thought he had eluded them. Later on, Riggs squirms out of the window of a moving car and jumps onto a wide-load mobile home being towed, climbs over it, gets to the enemy car being pursued, and reaches down and pulls the driver out so they can have a slugfest without interrupting the chase. Finally, they break through the plastic shield covering the open side of the mobile home. The bad guy goes bouncing like an India rubber ball into the freeway traffic, but the heroic Riggs ends up astride a table on the plastic strip being pulled behind the mobile home and somehow manages to survive.

Director Richard Donner understands stuntwork and pushes his stunt crew to achieve impossible feats of derring-do, making fun of the excesses of action-adventure filmmaking. Donner, a well-established Hollywood professional, surely knows the action sequences are absurd, but he seems to be issuing a challenge to other action directors: Can you top this? He is also challenging the critics to chill out. He knows more about the kind of movie he is making than they do, and he has been making them longer than Jerry Bruckheimer. No one beats Richard Donner at his own game. After all, he helped design the rules of the game. No moment is too outrageous or too absurd.

At its deepest core, however, this is a family film, a film about families and family values. Murtaugh has always been a family man, and in *Lethal Weapon 4* he becomes a grandfather. He advises Riggs that Riggs should marry pregnant Lorna. Riggs breaks the news that Lee Butters is Murtaugh's new son-in-law, and by the end of the picture, Murtaugh is reconciled to that fact. Murtaugh is willing to break immigration laws by sheltering the Chinese Hong family. The Chinese triad family works their counterfeit scam in order to get family members released from prison in Red China, including Wah Sing Ku's brother, who is killed during the failed prisoner exchange. Wah Sing Ku dies while attempting to avenge his brother's death. At the end, after Leo tells Murtaugh that he considers Murtaugh and Riggs his family and as the credits roll, snapshot family pictures are in the background, including pictures of Richard Donner himself, suggesting that the film production group has become like a family after three sequels over an eleven-year run.

The message, then, clearly is "We are family." The combined family harmony theme might be considered a sort of farewell conclusion to the series. If another sequel follows, one suspects that Murtaugh might be ripe for retirement, in

which case Riggs could become the senior partner to Chris Rock's Lee Butters to keep the black-white partnership intact and to keep Glover in the picture, though moving him into the background. Can an action hero grow old gracefully? In the first *Lethal Weapon* (1987), Mel Gibson's Martin Riggs, a one-time sniper in Vietnam who is burnt out and also grieving the recent death of his wife, was borderline psychotic and fearless because he didn't seem to care if he lived or died. Ten years later he had become domesticated and is about to propose marriage to the woman he loves and who bears his child. He now has a reason for living. He has tamed down and lost much of his manic energy and devil-may-care attitude. The problem with changing the character in this way is that it also changes the very successful formula.

Although reviews were mixed, *Lethal Weapon 4* knocked *Armageddon* out of the number one spot, grossing $34 million during its debut weekend. The film did better than any of the previous openings in the series. Brian McTavish of the *Kansas City Star* found the film silly and too long, though "passably entertaining." Joe Morgenstern of the *Wall Street Journal* described it as a "preposterously overblown hymn to friendship, family, and pyromania." Richard Schickel of *Time* magazine questioned the wisdom of redefining Riggs. If the character is made less manic, he becomes less interesting and more ordinary. In general reviewers seemed to find Chris Rock's "fresh comic improvisation" agreeable, though the actor's motormouthed babble might also be considered irritating. Andy Seller of *USA Today* thought Kim Chan stole the show as Uncle Benny, "an aged Chinese restaurant owner and heroin dealer who is as vicious with an enemy as he is cute on laughing gas," though to some the cuteness may seem utterly unanticipated and contrived. Janet Maslin of the *New York Times* wrote that the film was at least "pro-friends and family" and "anti-slavery."

"The stunts are staggering, the jokes funny, the human stories plausible," in the opinion of *Associated Press* reviewer

CREDITS

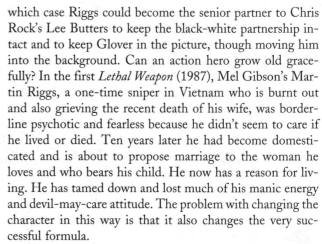

Martin Riggs: Mel Gibson
Roger Murtaugh: Danny Glover
Leo Getz: Joe Pesci
Lorna Cole: Rene Russo
Lee Butters: Chris Rock
Wah Sing Ku: Jet Li
Capt. Ed Murphy: Steve Kahan
Uncle Benny: Kim Chan
Trish Murtaugh: Darlene Love
Rianne: Traci Wolfe
Hong: Eddy Ko

Origin: USA
Released: 1998
Production: Joel Silver and Richard Donner for Silver Pictures and Doshudo Productions; released by Warner Bros.
Direction: Richard Donner
Screenplay: Channing Gibson; based on characters created by Shane Black
Cinematography: Andrzej Bartkowiak
Editing: Frank J. Urioste, Dallas Puett
Music: Michael Kamen, Eric Clapton, David Sanborn
Production design: J. Michael Riva
Art direction: David Klassen
Costumes: Ha Nguyen
Sound: Tim Cooney
Special effects coordination: Jon Belyeu
MPAA rating: R
Running Time: 127 minutes

REVIEWS

Chicago Tribune. July 10, 1998, p. 4.
Entertainment Weekly. July 17, 1998, p. 56.
Kansas City Star Preview. July 10, 1998, p. 7.
New York Times. July 10, 1998, p. B13.
Newsweek. July 20, 1998, p. 66.
People. July 13, 1998, p. 31.
Philadelphia Inquirer Weekend. July 10, 1998, p. 3.
Sight and Sound. September, 1998, p. 45.
Time. July 20, 1998, p. 58.
USA Today. July 10, 1998, p. E9.
Variety. July 13, 1998, p. 53.
Wall Street Journal. July 19, 1998, p. W1.
Washington Post. July 10, 1998, p. D1.
Washington Post Weekend. July 10, 1998, p. 43.

Bob Thomas. "Curiously, the formula works," he concluded. What is really curious here, however, is that after three sequels and considerable tinkering, the formula continues to work, demonstrably, with audiences. Within a month of its release, for example, the film had earned $108 million at the boxoffice. The most interesting point to be made about *Lethal Weapon 4*, then, is the way the filmmakers have man-

aged to violate the prime rule of genre filmmaking, tampering with a very successful formula by taming down Riggs and altering the basic chemistry between the film's characters, while still somehow maintaining the integrity of the product, and the interest of the fans.

— *James M. Welsh*

Life Is Beautiful; La Vita E Bella

"This film will restore your faith in movies."
—*Boston Herald*

"Powerful and extremely emotional. I predict it will be nominated for Best Picture."—Roger Ebert, *Chicago Sun-Times*

"Writer, director and star Roberto Benigni has Chaplin's genius for combining comedy and compassion."—Joel Siegel, *Good Morning America*

"A masterpiece."—*Los Angeles Daily News*

"An extraordinary tale of love and the affirmation of life."—Jack Mathews, *New York Newsday*

"Two thumbs up."—*Siskel & Ebert*

 Box Office: $10,336,425

Life Is Beautiful, a tour de force by Italy's Roberto Benigni, combines laughter and tears in a story of family love amidst the horrors of the Holocaust.

Roberto Benigni, Italy's national treasure, directs, co-authors, and stars in this unlikely comedy about family, catastrophe and sacrifice. Not many would dare to make a comedy set in a concentration camp in 1945 fascist Italy, and herein lies the film's greatest strength and weakness. The film has raised controversy from both the right-wing in Italy and the left-wing critics at Cannes. Unsettling at times for its audacity, the film's passion and daring manages to overcome the difficulty of its subject matter and make a case for human will and caprice.

The film is divided into two parts. The first half traces the courtship of Guido (Roberto Benigni) and Dora (Nicoletta Braschi). In Chaplin style the film opens with Guido barreling into town in a car with no brakes, being mistaken for a visiting dignitary by a crowd of onlookers, appearing to give the SS salute while really trying to signal the onlookers to get out of the way. While

 Roberto Benigni: "I never asked myself if the idea for *Life Is Beautiful* was similar to or different from those tackled in my previous movies. I just felt extremely attracted to it, overwhelmed by it. I could even say that I didn't seek out this idea; it sought me."

stopping to repair the car he meets Dora, or rather she falls out of a barn and lands in his arms just minutes after he has declared himself a prince in search of his princess. The two repeatedly encounter one another in similar, accidental collisions.

As Guido grows increasingly enamored with Dora he begins to carefully stage his coincidences. He arrives disguised as the school inspector at the school where she teaches, improvising and distorting the expected speech on racial superiority. He appears at the opera she is attending and after the performance he arranges for her to mistake his car for her fiancé's. He impresses her with repeated acts of apparent magic that lead her to believe they were fated to come together. When he discovers that she is about to be married he breaks up the engagement party by entering on his uncle's horse, which has been painted green with anti-Jewish sentiments, and steals her away. This ability to transform even what is an act of violence and hatred into a spectacle of enchantment is Guido's signature and the underlying message of the film. That one can take up and transform the same forces which threaten to limit and overcome, is the ultimate act of freedom. Turning evil into beauty is presented as a game, but a game that veils a struggle for life.

The role of fate, destiny, and will is strong in this film. Guido's friend reads the philosopher Schopenhaeur to be saying that the will is supreme and if one wants something they simply need will it. Guido actively pursues this power and freedom by playing with and thus shaping fate. His greatest charm is that he lives as if life were a dream, and he had unlimited freedom to make of it what he will. And what he makes of it is a vast puzzle, in which he is both puppet and puppeteer. He finds a comrade in a German, Dr. Lessing (Horst Buchholz), who frequents the cafe where he waits tables and shares his obsession with riddles. The different ways in which they apply the game in the end will distinguish Guido and justify the difficult relation in this film between comedy and tragedy.

The second half of the film cuts to the life of Dora and Guido five years later. They are now married and have a five-year-old son Giosue (Giorgio Cantarini). They own a small bookstore, ride around on a rusty bike, and live a modest but happy existence. On Giosue's birthday Dora returns home to find her house ransacked and her husband and son missing. She heads for the train station where they are being deported as Jews. She insists the train be stopped and she be permitted to board. The remainder of the film takes place in the concentration camp. The family is split up and Giosue is left in the care of his father. Confused and frightened, he demands to know what is going on. Guido responds by creating a fabulous fiction whereby this is all a game designed for his birthday, and whoever gets 1000 points wins a real tank at the end. To win one must endure countless trials and tribulations, hunger, cold, fatigue, and separation from mother. The antics that Guido goes through to convince his son of the benevolence of a situation which is catastrophic are both desperate and amusing.

Although not Jewish, Roberto Benigni's father was imprisoned in a German labor camp during World War II.

Children and elderly are killed first. Giosue escapes, because he never was one to want to take a shower, and throughout the remainder of his internment must remain hidden in the bunkers. The worried Dora is reassured when Guido and Giosue sneak into headquarters and relay a message in Italian to their "princess." Guido's hopes for escape are inspired by the presence of his friend the German doctor. Dr. Lessing makes arrangements to have Guido serve as a waiter for a German party held at the camps. When the doctor's desperate attempts to speak to Guido in privacy are finally met, Guido learns that the doctor simply wants to know the solution to a silly riddle which is keeping him up nights. While both friends have turned inward to the world of dreams and play to cope, Guido's game is a sacrificial one, about hope, perseverance, and redemption, whereas Dr. Lessing's has become an empty and selfish obsession, a game merely for the sake of a game.

Just when all hope seems lost the war is won and the camp stands on the verge of liberation. The Germans busy themselves trying to dispose of as many prisoners as possible. Guido hides Giosue and convinces him this is the finale of the game and if he can stay hidden until everyone vanishes, he will win. He then desperately tries to find his Dora. During his frantic search he is caught and shot by a

AWARDS AND NOMINATIONS

Academy Awards 1998:   Actor (Roberto Benigni); Foreign Film; Original Dramatic Score
Broadcast Film Critics Association 1998: Foreign Film
Screen Actors Guild 1998:   Actor (Roberto Benigni)
Academy Awards 1998 Nominations: Film; Director (Roberto Benigni); Original Screenplay

CREDITS

Guido: Roberto Benigni
Dora: Nicoletta Braschi
Giosue: Giorgio Cantarini
Ferruccio: Sergio Bustric
Uncle: Giustino Durano
Dora's mother: Marisa Paredes
Dr. Lessing: Horst Buchholz
Guicciardini: Lydia Alfonsi

Origin: Italy
Released: 1997
Production: Elda Ferri and Gianluigi Braschi for Melampo Cinematografica; released by Miramax Films
Direction: Roberto Benigni
Screenplay: Vincenzo Cerami and Roberto Benigni
Cinematography: Tonino Delli Colli
Editing: Simona Paggi
Music: Nicola Piovani
Art direction: Danilo Donati
Costumes: Danilo Donati
Sound: Tullio Morganti
MPAA rating: PG-13
Running Time: 122 minutes

German soldier. When the camp clears out, Giosue steps out of his hiding place just as an enormous American tank approaches the camp. He shrieks with delight, convinced now that the game was for real and that this is his big prize. He rides on the tank out of the camps where he is reunited with his mother. The father has sacrificed himself for the life of his family.

The performances of both Benigni and Braschi are expressive and enchanting, reminiscent of the silent era. *Life Is Beautiful* won many awards including the Grand Jury Prize at the Cannes Film Festival, and the Audience Awards at the Toronto and Vancouver Film Festivals, and eight Donatello awards in Italy. It also made history at the 1999 Academy Awards with a surprise win by Benigni as best actor. The first foreign actor to do so since Sophia Loren won in 1961 for *La Ciociara* (*Two Women*).

The driving message of this film is that life is beautiful, despite its harshness and that love and games overcome even the gravest seriousness. But the vaudeville theatrics of the film do not always lend themselves to the graveness of the content. While it's not a musical, there is an ambiance of otherworldliness and staginess to the concentration camp scenes that can at times seem irreverent and unrealistic. The death camps are softened to accommodate humor, but sometimes this makes it even more difficult to laugh. The film is to be applauded though for challenging limits, taking risks, and making a case for the power of human caprice in the face of disaster.

—Reni Celeste

REVIEWS

Boxoffice. July, 1998, p. 125.
Chicago Tribune. October 3, 1998, p. 5.
Detroit News. October 30, 1998, p. 3F.
Entertainment Weekly. November 6, 1998, p. 54.
New York Times. October 23, 1998, p. E14.
People. November 2, 1998, p. 34.
Sight and Sound. February, 1999, p. 46.
Vanity Fair. October, 1998.
Variety. December 22, 1997, p. 60.
Washington Post Weekend. October 30, 1998, p. 64.

Little Men; Louisa May Alcott's Little Men

"For everybody who loved *Little Women*, *Little Men* is just the ticket. I recommend it."—Bill Hoffman, *New York Post*

"A great adventure for young audiences!" —*Newsday*

"Everything about this movie is first rate." —Moira McCormick, *TV Guide*

Little Men is a careful, faithful rendition of Louisa May Alcott's classic novel, published in 1871. It is a very quiet film punctuated by a few dramatic moments. It is a bucolic, anti-urban work in which the country setting evokes the conventions of the pastoral. In this genre of literature, transformed into film, human nature is put out to pasture, so to speak; that is, what human beings should be and what they are is gently revealed in an unthreatening environment. Here no one has to steal to survive, to compete for a job or a place in life. Rather the personality is lovingly cultivated like a piece of good earth.

Jo March (Mariel Hemingway), the spunky heroine of *Little Women*, is mother/teacher to a group of six boys and two girls. She and her beloved husband, Professor Bhaer (Chris Sarandon) run a boarding school designed to teach proper values—no lying, fighting, swearing, and so on). When a new boy, Nat Blake (Michael Caloz) is caught in a lie, Professor Bhaer has the boy strike him six times with a ruler, telling Nat that he is less likely to lie again if he sees that his bad behavior hurts others as much as it demeans him.

As gentle as Professor Bhaer is, he believes in human depravity, and he is suspicious of Dan (Ben Cook) who shows up from Boston to team up again with Nat. The two boys had cruised the streets, homeless and on the look out for the main chance. Nat has reformed, but Dan fails to believe in the Bhaers' goodness. He confirms Professor Bhaer's misgivings when he introduces card playing and cigar smoking to the boys, who almost burn down the house.

Jo has steadfastly defended Dan. She sees potential in this spirited, if devious boy. He shows real courage in helping her to put out the fire, and it is odd that his heroic act is not even mentioned. Instead, Jo reluctantly consents to her husband's decision to banish Dan to a school for problem boys. When Dan runs away and returns to the Bhaers, he is given a second chance, and the film revolves around this wayward boy: will he succeed in redeeming himself?

The film makes no concessions to contemporary taste. To many reviewers it seems too idyllic, although this is precisely the spirit of the pastoral and of Alcott's work. Evil is not absent from her world, but it bound by a genteel design. Nostalgia for the past was overtaking Alcott even as she wrote her books, so it is not surprising that a film based on her work should be treated as unrealistic.

Like another recent childrens' film, *Madeline* (reviewed in this edition), *Little Men* is unabashed by its sweet and sentimental message about proper values. Both films suggest that adults with a moral vision of the world can raise children to recognize right and wrong and to be good citizens. The children rebel, get into trouble, but they also look to the adults for guidance. The children want to do good, even if it is their nature to do mischief.

What both Professor Bhaer and Jo do so well is establish a tone of authority. Of course, they have no competition. There is no television, no outside world (except for Dan) to tempt the children away from the proper path. The world of Little Men cocoons the children. But then the pastoral has always performed such a safeguarding function. The point is not so much that the country is the seat of virtue and the city the trough of sin but that in the simpler, stripped-down rural scene, the ethical way to live can be seen more clearly. On the farm, trouble can be seen coming; it can be isolated. The consequences of behaving badly are conspicuous. Crime is not a potential lurking down every street.

With films like *Little Men* and *Madeline*, filmmakers have explicitly forsaken the violence and the fancy techniques that stud so many of Hollywood's products. There are no special effects. No explosions. The closest *Little Men* comes to bloodshed is a scene in which Jo cleanses the burn a child has gotten in the fire. The reddened arm is all the more shocking because gore is so absent from the film. The only potential violence is the scene where Dan challenges one of the boys to a drop the switchblade game, in which the two boys point the knife at the space between their feet. Each time the knife hits the ground, the boy has to put his foot to the spot where the blade dropped. It is a game of chicken to see which boy will call it quits before the knife hits a foot. The tension mounts as the camera focuses on the plump young feet of these boys. Finally Dan calls the game off—saying nonchalantly that it is not worth continuing with the risk of a knife wound becoming infected. His intervention comes as a great relief to the boys; it also suggests that he is indeed a redeemable human being.

In the city, Dan could not have backed off. Too much would have been at stake in terms of his reputation and his very survival. The country does not make him good, but it does allow him the possibility of virtue. The pastoral, in other words, is a form of therapy, a clarification of first principles that sometimes get lost in the crowded scene of contemporary life.

The performances of the main characters are done well, but it is the casting that perhaps contributes most to the success of *Little Men*. Mariel Hemingway has the strong fea-

tures of her grandfather, the novelist Ernest Hemingway. She is handsome but without a hint of glamour. She looks like what she is supposed to be: the salt of the earth. She is so kindhearted as to almost seem unbelievable, but Hemingway puts just enough edge and authority in Jo's voice so that she never loses command. Hemingway's Jo is simply solid, there for the children in a way that they can never doubt.

Chris Sarandon presents a surprisingly delicate Bhaer to Jo's robust figure. There is nothing of the wimp about Bhaer, but he is an extremely quiet man, who speaks with subdued authority, a sort of formal, European resignation. He does not speak in a German accent, which is just as well since no point at all is made of his foreignness, which would only stick out if his accent called attention to itself. When Nat lies, Sarandon's Bhaer is rueful, telling the boy about his own youthful lying and punishment. Although the word is never used, Bhaer is very good at making Nat feel guilty. Like a good parent, Bhaer knows how to make the children feel they have let him down without making them feel resentful about it.

Through Nat, played with just the right wide-eyed innocence by Michael Caloz, *Little Men* reflects Alcott's esthetic sense of life. Nat plays the violin, sharing with Professor Bhaer and his nephew a love of music. Caloz's androgynous quality—his delicate features often make him look like a girl dressed in boy's clothing—make him a universal figure, a blend of passive and aggressive traits exquis-

CREDITS

Nat Blake: Michael Caloz
Jo Bhaer: Mariel Hemingway
Dan: Ben Cooks
Tommy Bangs: Ricky Mabe
Fritz Bhaer: Chris Sarandon
Nan Harding: Gabrielle Boni

Origin: Canada
Released: 1998
Production: Pierre David and Franco Battista for Allegro Films, Image Organization, and Brainstorm Media; released by Legacy
Direction: Rodney Gibbons
Screenplay: Mark Evan Schwartz; based on the novel by Louisa May Alcott
Cinematography: Georges Archambault
Editing: Andre Corriveau
Music: Milan Kymlicka
Production design: Donna Noonan
Costumes: Janet Campbell
Sound: Tim Archer
MPAA rating: PG
Running Time: 98 minutes

itely refined by the Bhaers into an ideal form: sensitive and vigorous.

Ben Cook gives Dan an edge without, even at the beginning, overdoing his illicit side. Here clothes and props make a difference. Fresh from the city, Dan sports a modified bowler hat and walking stick. When banished from the Bhaers, he resumes this urban dress. It demarcates the boundaries of his world. In the city, or when he dons his city mentality, he is something of a con man, with part of his nature concealed. The stick could be a weapon; it certainly is part of his armature, the protectiveness he had to learn to survive on mean streets. But at the Bhaers, his city clothes come off, and bareheaded he suddenly seems more like the other boys. He is more vulnerable and more responsive than his city self. Without the hat his face seems more open and accessible. He has nowhere to hide. What is more, he does not need to hide his feelings.

A couple of spunky girls (played by Gabrielle Boni and Julian Garland) round out this picture of the pastoral family. Boni as Nan Harding is a perfect foil for Nat. Her feminine but bold featured face, and her ability to hit a baseball, mark her as another child who is a blend of gender traits and fits well into the Bhaer school and household.

Little Men will probably appeal most to younger children; the older ones may be too jaded to accept Alcott's idyll. Seen not as a realistic picture of family life or of nineteenth-century America, but rather as what critic William Empson would have called a version of pastoral, *Little Men* is a satisfying and very accomplished film.

—Carl Rollyson

REVIEWS

Detroit News. May 8, 1998, p. 7D.
Los Angeles Times. May 8, 1998, p. F14.
New York Times. May 8, 1998, p. E12.
Variety. May 11, 1998, p. 60.

Little Voice

Finding your own voice can be magic.—Movie tagline

"Delightful! Jane Horrocks gives an amazing performance!"—Roger Ebert, *Chicago Sun-Times*

"A brilliant and stunning film!"—Steve Oldfield, *FOX-TV*

"*Little Voice* is a remarkable film. Brilliantly acted and moving. Michael Caine, Brenda Blethyn and Jane Horrocks offer three of the year's most exquisite performances."—Rod Dreher, *New York Post*

 Box Office: $4,595,000

Jane Horrocks shines as the title character of Mark Herman's *Little Voice,* the story of a young woman's brief but stunning moment in the musical spotlight. Laura, better known as Little Voice or LV because she is soft-spoken, is so withdrawn that answering a telephone is a major challenge for her. She stays in her room listening to her late father's record collection, highlighted by the music of Judy Garland, Marilyn Monroe, and Shirley Bassey, and has a special talent for mimicking the voices of her favorite singers. Horrocks's dead-on impersonation of each diva is so amazing that we might think she were lip-synching to the original recordings if a credit at the film's end did not tell us that she performed all of her own songs. Her musical performances were also filmed entirely live without recorded vocal tracks synched to the stage show.

Adapted from Jim Cartwright's stage play, *The Rise and Fall of Little Voice,* the movie introduces us to characters living ordinary, even dead-end lives, and then attempts to find a bit of magic in their mundane world. While the storytelling is uneven and sputters out near the end, the film, more than any other since Woody Allen's *The Purple Rose of Cairo,* (1985) beautifully captures the way popular entertainment can become a vehicle not only of escape but also of transcendence.

LV lives in an English seaside town with her widowed mother, Mari Hoff (Brenda Blethyn), a shrill, strident woman who dominates and abuses her daughter. Past her prime and desperate to be loved, Mari is a lusty woman who seems to be trying to recapture her youth or at least stave off the passing years. She is a bundle of nerves who is always mouthing off, dancing around the house, and wearing sexy clothes that are not very becoming. Slowing down, it seems, would mean facing the emptiness of her life.

Mari is seeing a sleazy talent agent, Ray Say (Michael Caine), and one night comes home drunk with him. LV is upstairs listening to a Judy Garland record, while her mother is downstairs making out with Ray and trying to drown out her daughter's music with her Tom Jones record. The electricity goes out, and yet the voice of Garland can seemingly be heard. It is of course LV, and she is singing "The Man That Got Away" to the picture of her late father hanging on the wall. LV feels a special connection to her father, and his record collection binds them together.

The next day, when the power is restored, Ray questions LV about the voices she can do. When LV asks Ray about the famous people he has met, it turns out they are all small-timers. Ray, it appears, has spent a life on the fringes of showbiz as a failed promoter, and so he immediately sees LV's talent as his ticket to the top.

Although Michael Caine and Brenda Blethyn are playing stock types, they are still able to bring out glimpses of their characters' humanity. While Ray is essentially a loser, the poor fellow tries to act like a winner, whether he is driving his beloved, red convertible or promoting a stripper as if she were a major talent. We feel at least some measure of sympathy for these characters, especially Mari, although Blethyn's over-the-top portrayal becomes grating fairly quickly. She never shuts up, so we can understand why her daughter is so quiet. In one special moment, though, we get to see her vulnerability. When Ray boasts that he has found "one of those once-in-a-lifetime things," she thinks he is talking about her, but he is really talking about the talents of her daughter, and, when the realization hits Mari, it is a quietly stunning moment.

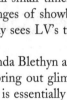

Nightclub owner Mr. Boo (Jim Broadbent) introducing Little Voice (Jane Horrocks) to the audience: "The girl with the greats queuing up in her gullet!"

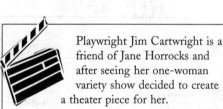

Playwright Jim Cartwright is a friend of Jane Horrocks and after seeing her one-woman variety show decided to create a theater piece for her.

When Ray brings the owner of a local nightclub, Mr. Boo (Jim Broadbent) to see LV, she refuses to come downstairs, but soon they can hear her singing "Over the Rainbow" (she is performing for a vision of her father) and are amazed at her imitation of Garland. When they get her onstage, however, she does fine until the lights are turned on and she becomes frightened and runs away.

A young telephone lineman named Billy (Ewan McGregor), whose hobby is caring for homing pigeons, develops an interest in LV. He is shy and quiet like LV, so we can guess from the outset that they will get together by the end, but their courtship is sweet nonetheless. In a tender, almost fairy tale-like moment, for example, he uses the cherry picker on his phone truck to visit LV through the window of her upstairs bedroom.

The script is often heavy-handed, especially in the recurring bird/flight metaphor. The film's opening song is Frank Sinatra's "Come Fly with Me," LV is often compared to a bird, and Billy's pigeons even become a symbol of LV's spirit. This metaphor for LV's liberation becomes especially obvious when Billy talks about his pigeons flying free and suggests to LV that "you should try it sometime." When Ray visits LV to persuade her to try singing again onstage, he tells a cute story about a bluebird that sang and then flew away to find its freedom.

Ray shrewdly plays upon LV's love for her father and his music to persuade her to do a show revolving around his favorite singers. Caine works a subtle charm in this scene—his Ray is very smooth in winning LV's confidence by taking an interest in her record collection and pretending it is not a big deal to him whether she performs or not. Ray then gets the stage ready, vigorously promotes the event, raises money, loses money at the racetrack, gets LV to try on costumes—all in a montage set to Shirley Bassey's "Goldfinger," which plays as a humorous commentary on Ray and some sly foreshadowing of the villain he will become.

The film's big set piece is LV's live concert at Mr. Boo's, a magical moment for her. As she pictures her father watching her, she does all of her specialties and lets loose in a testament to the power of performance. LV commands the stage, plays to the orchestra, and flirts with the audience. It is an optimistic, liberating view of pop culture—not simply as an escape but as a form of expression; through her favorite entertainers, LV can face the world with confidence and even transcend, albeit momentarily, a dismal life.

The character of LV is the most compelling aspect of the film, and, while her sudden, public blossoming may be predictable, it is nonetheless a thrilling moment. Unfortunately, the plot really has nowhere to go after her triumph and soon falls apart. For her, it was a one-time-only event, but Ray of course wants to get rich. A showbiz big shot agrees to come see LV the next night at Boo's, and Ray almost immediately goes from sleazy to outright nasty. Eager to desert Mr. Boo for the big time, Ray tells him he is nothing and eventually mocks Mari for her age and her delusion that they would ever be a couple. It is a sudden, radical character shift from which the film never quite recovers.

AWARDS AND NOMINATIONS

Golden Globes 1999: Musical/Comedy Actor (Michael Caine)
Academy Awards 1998 Nominations: Supporting Actress (Brenda Blethyn)

When LV is scheduled to appear at Boo's club, she is in bed at home while a series of very bad acts (including Mr. Boo's own pathetic comedy) fills time on stage. Ray tries to get LV out of bed and even turns violent and starts slapping her. She lashes back at him as her voices pour out of her in a mad scramble—almost as if she were possessed and we were now watching a horror film. Her special talent, it seems, is her only defense against the man who wants to exploit her. She knocks Ray down a flight of stairs, and, in a dark, disturbing climax that feels arbitrary, he accidentally triggers an electrical fire (heavily foreshadowed by electrical problems throughout the film). LV ends up trapped in her room with her precious record collection as the fire rages around her until Billy appears outside her window and carries her to safety. Meanwhile, Ray seemingly goes nuts at the club as he takes the stage and madly sings "It's Over" as his creditors wait for him.

The ending is choppy and anti-climactic, as if various loose threads had to be tied up quickly. LV has a showdown with her mother and finally breaks free of her, but the confrontation covers predictable material like Mari mistreating and cheating on LV's father and the record collection being his refuge from Mari before it was LV's. In the film's last scene, LV is with Billy and his pigeons. They begin freeing his birds, and the film concludes with a freeze-frame of LV letting a bird take flight—once again linking a bird's freedom to LV's, as if the connection were not abundantly clear by now.

While the story of an underdog coming into her own is overly familiar to begin with, and the plot falters near the end, *Little Voice* is nonetheless buoyed by its quirky charm. Most importantly, Jane Horrocks's portrayal of LV is an original creation and a touching tribute to the way popular entertainment can sustain and even liberate the most timid of souls.

—*Peter N. Chumo II*

CREDITS

Laura Hoff (LV): Jane Horrocks
Mari Hoff: Brenda Blethyn
Ray Say: Michael Caine
Mr. Boo: Jim Broadbent
Billy: Ewan McGregor
Sadie: Annette Badland
George: Philip Jackson

Origin: Great Britain
Released: 1998
Production: Elizabeth Karlsen for Scala Productions; released by Miramax Films
Direction: Mark Herman
Screenplay: Mark Herman; based on the play *The Rise and Fall of Little Voice* by Jim Cartwright
Cinematography: Andy Collins
Editing: Michael Ellis
Music: John Altman
Production design: Don Taylor
Art direction: Jo Graysmark
Costumes: Lindy Hemming
Sound: Peter Lindsay
MPAA rating: R
Running Time: 96 minutes

REVIEWS

Chicago Tribune. December 4, 1998, p. 4.
Entertainment Weekly. December 11, 1998, p. 48.
New York Times. November 29, 1998, p. A32.
New York Times. December 4, 1998, p. E12.
People. December 14, 1998, p. 34.
Sight and Sound. January, 1999, p. 38.
Variety. September 28, 1998, p. 36.

Live Flesh; Carne Tremula

"Awesome . . . breathtaking."—Kevin Thomas, *Los Angeles Times*

"*Live Flesh* is the best movie from Almodovar since *Women On the Verge of a Nervous Breakdown*. This Spanish bad-boy writer-director does the comedy of sexual passion better than anybody else."—David Denby, *New York Magazine*

"*Live Flesh* is a lover's sigh."—Thelma Adams, *New York Post*

"A stylish, sexy film noir."—Janet Maslin, *New York Times*

"Sensual to the point of succulent."—Tom Gliatto, *People*

"Wildly seductive . . . brimming with lust, betrayal and murder."—Peter Travers, *Rolling Stone*

"Thrillers don't get sexier! Lively, fleshy and just plain terrific."—Andy Seiler, *USA Today*

Spanish director Pedro Almodovar has abandoned most of his sexual burlesque and stylistic excesses in the surprisingly engaging *Live Flesh*. A story of five characters entwined by violent and erotic twists of fate, *Live Flesh* is, despite its titillating title, Almodovar's most down-to-earth and humanistic film yet.

This is a much more mature Almodovar than the raunchy, reckless auteur whose *Women on the Verge of a Nervous Breakdown* (1988) and *Tie Me Up! Tie Me Down!* (1990) confused outrageousness with social satire. In terms of narrative substance and watchability, those and other early Almodovar films are mere trifles compared with *Live Flesh*. *Live Flesh* features solid ensemble performances, some bracing encounters, and fewer of the clumsy, cartoonish sexual encounters that made Almodovar's other films so cheesy and so popular.

Still, erotic obsession continues to be the glue that holds Almodovar's characters together. In *Live Flesh* his five characters all are in the grips of some form of sexual fixation. It's a staple of Almodovar that otherwise strong men and women turn to jelly at the sight of an attractive member of the opposite sex. Sexuality overwhelms judgment, ruins lives and is a desperate relief from tension that can even overcome class and social boundaries. In this, Almodovar is evocative of the great Luis Buñuel, though he is nowhere near Buñuel's excellence as a symbolist and satirist.

It comes as no surprise that the protagonist of *Live Flesh*, a naive young man named Victor (Liberto Rabal), is the bastard child of a prostitute. In a superbly executed and enchanting prologue, the hooker gives birth to Victor, with the help of her landlady, aboard an empty bus with the help of a reluctant driver. The streets are empty because it is Christmas 1970 and Madrid is still gripped by the terror of the Franco regime. The film's final scene shows Madrid celebrating 26 years later in an atmosphere of prosperity and peace. According to the narrator, "in Spain we stopped being scared a long time ago." These bookends serve as a political framework; the rest of the film can be seen as a parable of a society achieving freedom and postwar modernity.

It's easy to interpret Victor as being a modern-day Christ figure. Subtlety has never been Almodovar's long suit, and in his case he endows the twenty-something Victor with a bizarre version of virginal innocence, a love for reading and quoting from the Bible, and a dogged affection for the woman of his dreams. Victor is the persecuted, luckless exile in his own land, a juvenile who has been victimized by being in the wrong place—and the wrong social class—at the wrong time. But his naivete must be placed within the context of Almodovar's relentlessly crude sensibility.

Victor is transfixed by Elena (Francesca Neri), an Italian diplomat's daughter who is a sluttish drug addict. They have had a sexual encounter of a sort in a club, but she is not interested in another because Victor was so clumsy. Victor is entranced because it was his first time. He impulsively enters her apartment on a ruse, a fight ensues, and a pair of plainclothes policemen enter. One is a drunken wife-beater named Sancho (Pepe Sancho) and the other is his seemingly straight-arrow partner, David (Javier Bardem). David is shot and Victor is sent to prison. Only much later in the film is it revealed that Victor was falsely blamed for the crime.

 Sancho (Jose Sancho) to his wife Clara (Angela Molina): "As long as I love you, you're not leaving me."

Flash forward, and Victor is released from jail. His mother has died in the meantime, bequeathing him a trashed apartment. Victor is rehabilitated but has revenge on his mind. David is now a wheelchair basketball champion whose face is on television and billboards. The injury Victor unintentionally inflicted has robbed David of his legs, but brought him fame and a trophy wife, Elena. Elena, mesmerized by the handsome David's heroics that saved her life, has changed from bleached-blonde temptress and druggie to a soft-spoken, generous, brown-haired, doting wife. She bathes and cares for David and contributes her money and time to a shelter for abused children.

Through a series of improbable chance meetings, Victor spirals not only toward a war with David over Elena but toward another war with Sancho over his wife, Clara (Angela Molina). Sancho is a jealous husband who regularly hits Clara and then begs for her forgiveness. Clara provides a reason for that jealousy by seducing Victor. Victor asks the much older Clara to teach him the intricacies of lovemaking, and she willingly does so, in the process falling in love with him.

Victor insinuates himself into a position at the children's shelter. But instead of continuing his plan to exact revenge on Elena, Victor tells David that Sancho made him pull the trigger that handicapped him. Victor has learned from Clara that David was her secret lover at the time of the shooting. David inexplicably confesses the truth to Elena. In this film, characters turn out to be brutally honest at surprising moments.

Victor's plan was to learn how to be the best lover in the world, seduce Elena for one night, and then abandon her. It's a strikingly complex revenge motif which would allow Victor to exact tribute from everyone: using Clara to learn how to hurt Elena and in the processes cuckolding both Sancho and David. But Victor, however, has decided not to pursue the plan, but he tells the plan to Elena. Eventually and somewhat inexplicably, she takes up his implicit invitation for a night of universe-moving sex. Motivations in this script, adapted freely from a difficult Ruth Rendell novel, are more often than not murky. Everything is explained, as is Almodovar's custom, by preoccupation with erotic fulfillment.

But *Live Flesh* is not as awkward as a plot summary suggests. In fact, Almodovar succeeds splendidly in making this round-robin into a tense, intricate thriller. The film is rife with threats of violence and betrayal, secrets kept and secrets told and shifting loyalties. It also is not without its comic moments. When David and Victor grapple in a fight over Elena, they stop in mid-punch to watch a replay of a soccer goal on television. No matter how much enmity there is between men, their bond as sports fans transcends all, Almodovar suggests.

Almodovar can find telling beauty in simple details. When Victor re-enters his dead mother's home, his hand reaches down to find an old plastic toy soldier fallen on the carpet. The extreme close-up evokes an image of Victor's lost childhood, his fall from the grace of innocence to the terrible turmoil of manhood, and his inability to fulfill the promise of his youth—all that in one swift, superb shot. Equally powerful and economical is a shot, near the climax of the film, of Clara and Sancho's two bloodstained hands, clasped so that their wedding rings are nearly touching, gripping a pistol pointing at Victor: an angry symbol of a marriage ruined by mistrust and infidelity. And though much of Victor and Elena's night of love is rendered in typical Hollywood fashion as a set of sweaty calisthenics, there is a remarkable shot of them spooning, their bare legs so close together that they appear to be one flesh.

Though the photography is sometimes lyrical, the dialogue is often clunky. *Live Flesh* falls short of being the stylish film noir to which it aspires, mainly because Almodovar is incapable of noir. He is too attracted to gaudiness, both in the colorful sets and in the splashy, brilliantly stupid words and actions of his characters. Yet the fine acting and the emotional changes the characters go through evoke a fuller, more sympathetic humanism than any of Almodovar's early work. Only Sancho is one-dimensional. Victor is both overly romanticized and, at times, cruelly calculating. David is both macho and weak, cuckold and cuckolded. Elena and Clara both are betrayers and betrayed in love;

CREDITS

David: Javier Bardem
Elena: Francesco Neri
Victor: Liberto Rabal
Clara: Angela Molina
Sancho: Jose Sancho
Isabelle: Penelope Cruz
Dona Centro: Pilar Bardem

Origin: Spain, France
Released: 1997
Production: Augustin Almodovar for Ciby 2000, France 3 Cinema, and El Deseo; released by MGM
Direction: Pedro Almodovar
Screenplay: Pedro Almodovar, Ray Loriga, and Jorge Guerricaechevarria; based on the novel *Live Flesh* by Ruth Rendell
Cinematography: Affonso Beato
Editing: Jose Salcedo
Music: Alberto Iglesias
Art direction: Antxon Gomez
Costumes: Jose Maria de Cossio
Sound: Bernardo Menz, J.A. Bermudez
MPAA rating: R
Running Time: 98 minutes

REVIEWS

Entertainment Weekly. January 23, 1998, p. 41.
Los Angeles Times. January 30, 1998, p. F6.
New York Times. October 10, 1997, p. E1.
New Yorker. January 26, 1998, p. 86.
People. January 26, 1998, p. 22.
Rolling Stone. February 5, 1998, p. 66.
Sight and Sound. May, 1998, p. 50.
Time. February 23, 1998.
USA Today. January 16, 1998, p. 4D.
Variety. October 13, 1997, p. 84.
Village Voice. January 20, 1998, p. 61.
Washington Post. February 13, 1998, p. D1.

Elena as a "strong," modern woman, Clara as a more traditional, long-suffering wife.

Live Flesh suggests that no one is pure and unsullied, that all are both victims of erotic obsession as well as victimizers. Even the film's ending is an unsettling mixture of tragedy and happiness. As "live flesh," born as the result of lust, Almodovar suggests that we all are the products of heat and passion, the pawns of fate and circumstance, and yet, through the force of will, we can sometimes attain our dreams. Those dreams, in Almodovar's crudely romantic world, are not tarnished by being somewhat sordid, for that, too, is part of the curse of being live flesh.

—*Michael Betzold*

Living Out Loud

"*Living Out Loud* is a film of eccentric charm that knows its way around relationships."—Kenneth Turan, *Los Angeles Times*

"At last, a romantic comedy for grown-ups! LaGravenese strikes gold. Holly Hunter is spectacular."—Rod Dreher, *New York Post*

"A delightfully grown-up comedy. The sleeper of the season."—David Ansen, *Newsweek*

"Hunter and DeVito give touchingly nuanced performances, and Latifah proves that her raves for *Set It Off* were no fluke by stealing every scene she's in."—Peter Travers, *Rolling Stone*

Box Office: $12,626,134

A bittersweet comedy about two people trying to pick themselves up and start over in middle age, writer-director Richard LaGravenese's *Living Out Loud* beautifully captures a sense of romantic longing in its two main characters, Judith (Holly Hunter) and Pat (Danny DeVito). However, it also explores big issues like overcoming genuine loss, finding one's place in the world, and dealing with loneliness. Hunter and DeVito give two strong performances, which compensate for a script that, despite its many bright moments, sometimes feels random and disjointed.

In the film's opening scene, Judith faces the dissolution of her marriage. She confronts her cardiologist-husband, Bob (Martin Donovan), with her knowledge of his affair, and, while she is clearly a victim, she is smart and tough and sees through her husband's lame evasions. Judith is the classic woman who married well, gave up her own ambition to be a doctor to support her husband's

Judith (Holly Hunter): "I want to stop agreeing to things I don't really want."

goals, and even agreed not to have children. Now alone in middle age and working as a nurse, Judith is forced to reassess where she is in life and where she wants to go.

From the outset, *Living Out Loud* places us in Judith's subjectivity. We hear the thoughts racing around in her head as she tries to process the disturbing news reports she sees on TV or contemplate the possibility of a future alone. The film also delves into Judith's fantasy life, her own alternate versions of reality. We see her jump out of her high-rise's window, for example, and then see her watch a fantasy news report of her suicide and how her fall also crushed her ex-husband and his new wife. While these digressions feel a little gimmicky at first, after a while they have their own quirky charm and help forge an intimate bond between the audience and Judith.

When we meet Pat, his daughter is dying. Thrown out by his wife after 25 years of marriage and living with his brother, Philly (Richard Schiff), Pat is in debt to local hoods and works as an elevator operator in Judith's Upper East Side co-op. At the age of 52, Pat is still floundering but unwilling to compromise and work for his brother. Pat seems to be a big-idea man with plans for the future, like an Italian import business with a cousin in Sorrento, but he never follows through on them (as his brother is eager to remind him) and so has never really found his niche in life. DeVito lets us see the vulnerable man underneath his usual wise-guy persona, the dreamer who cannot quite make his dreams come true.

Judith and Pat begin talking one day when she sees a picture of his daughter and he tells her that she just died. In a touching moment, she embraces him—one human being reaching out to another in pain. A friendship develops, and the two get to know each other over coffee in Pat's office. He gets her to loan him some money, supposedly to pay the building's gas bill, but he really needs the money for his debts. To pay Judith back, Pat asks Philly for some money in a scene that spells out the way Philly, who owns his own bar, has the upper hand on his brother. When Pat finally admits the truth to Judith, it turns out that she knew he was lying about the gas bill but trusted him anyway to pay back the money. Such plot points do not really matter in the long run (the script is more interested in character), but they serve as markers in the developing friendship.

Judith also makes friends with Liz Bailey (Queen Latifah), a singer at Jasper's, a jazz club she begins visiting. Judith is a fan from the outset (the opening credits feature Judith fantasizing she is singing as Liz), and later Liz becomes her confidant. Judith opens up to her and proceeds to assess her life and the mistakes she made, like dumping old friends when she acquired money and putting up with her husband's infidelities. "I'm not sure where I've been for twenty years," Judith declares as she realizes that she left herself long before her husband did.

Two short stories by Anton Chekhov inspire certain aspects of the film. The protagonist of "Misery" is echoed in Pat's mourning for his daughter, and the central event of "The Kiss" is evoked when Judith opens the wrong door at Jasper's and is kissed by a stranger (Elias Koteas) waiting for someone else. The surprising kiss becomes a defining moment for Judith, the start of her reawakening to the world, to sexual feelings, to the unexpected passion of life itself. In essence, the film traces the progression of a woman who is tired of compromising, and, through a series of epiphanies, slowly comes into her own.

The accidental kiss in fact becomes a catalyst for a flowering of sexual passion, long dormant in Judith. In one funny scene, Judith has a massage from a handsome masseur (sex is implied) and, in another big moment, cuts loose on the dance floor in a lesbian nightclub—two scenes that suggest her willingness to take risks. The story unfolds at a fairly tepid pace, however, and these scenes, while entertaining, feel like set pieces rather than the building blocks of a tight screenplay. These scenes also teeter on the brink of becoming clichés along the way to a kind of feminist awakening, but Hunter's funny, sexy performance keeps us seeing the real person and not a mere type.

Judith also has flashbacks to her teenage self and reconnects with her in a fantasy in the nightclub, but this scene does not pay off since it is not clear what this encounter is supposed to signify, beyond some trite notion of Judith recapturing her youth. Moreover, since Judith is not discovering she is a lesbian, it is not clear why her recovery of lost youth should occur in a lesbian club. This setting is not only a puzzle but something of a distraction as well. The screenplay may be trying too hard to have Judith walk on the wild

Screenwriter Richard LaGravenese makes his directing debut.

side and so in essence is giving her an unnecessarily showy triumph when in fact she already has triumphed in the way she is rebuilding her life and reaching out to other people.

While DeVito is excellent and gives one of his most nuanced performances, the movie belongs to Hunter. She gives a vital performance, whether Judith is standing up to her husband's new wife with a smart retort when she tries to be conciliatory or coming on to Pat and practically jumping on him after Liz gives her a drug that "makes you want to just touch everybody." Judith's transformation from a scared, lonely divorcée to someone taking charge of her life is wholly credible and often hilarious. She has a terrific scene in which she disrupts an important meeting to sell the country house and then lashes out at her husband—both verbally and physically—as if to rid herself of all her rage. The scene itself may be yet another obligatory, grand moment for Judith, but Hunter is funny, angry, and even a little scary all at the same time.

While Judith is slowly coming into her own, Pat is falling in love with her, even though she gently makes it clear that she is not interested in him romantically. Inspired to act on his dream of an import business, one night out at dinner he produces two tickets for a trip to Italy. Well aware

CREDITS

Judith: Holly Hunter
Pat: Danny DeVito
Liz Bailey: Queen Latifah
Bob Nelson: Martin Donovan
Philly: Richard Schiff
The Masseur: Eddie Cibrian
The Kisser: Elias Koteas

Origin: USA
Released: 1998
Production: Danny DeVito, Michael Shamberg, and Stacey Sher for Jersey Films; released by New Line Cinema
Direction: Richard LaGravenese
Screenplay: Richard LaGravenese
Cinematography: John Bailey
Editing: Jon Gregory, Lynzee Klingman
Music: George Fenton
Production design: Nelson Coates
Art direction: Joseph Hodges
Costumes: Jeffrey Kurland
Sound: Petur Hliddal
MPAA rating: R
Running Time: 102 minutes

that she does not return the same feelings, he asks her anyway to accompany him, and, in a very moving declaration, tells her of his need to love another person. She turns him down, though; ultimately, her dreams lie not with him but in a return to medical school to become a pediatrician. Having been rejected, Pat leaves Judith alone at the table, and the camera pulls back, as if to emphasize her isolation. A similar camera move is used in an earlier scene when Judith tries to have a second encounter with the kisser at Jasper's but finds the door locked. Both shots highlight Judith alone; this time, however, Judith has chosen her solitude. Clichéd as it may be, the scene suggests Judith can now face being alone with a certain equanimity.

The film almost ends on this ambiguous note, but a coda that takes place several months later shows that both characters are living out their dreams. Judith is working in a hospital and pursuing her goal of medical school. Pat, who has an Italian girlfriend, delivers a triumphant rendition of "They Can't Take That Away from Me" at Jasper's. The ending may be a little too upbeat for the overall tone of the film, but it leaves one feeling hopeful for Judith and Pat.

Living Out Loud is not perfectly constructed. A few scenes simply go nowhere, and the overall plot lacks suspense since we know from the start that Judith will slowly get her life straightened out. While the general outlines of the story are predictable—middle-aged people overcoming the inertia of their lives and the fear of loneliness to live out their dreams—the true pleasure of the film lies in the details. Indeed, the humor of many of the big scenes and the tender rapport between Judith and Pat ultimately make the film a charming slice-of-life character study.

—*Peter N. Chumo II*

REVIEWS

Entertainment Weekly. November 6, 1998, p. 55.
People. November 9, 1998, p. 33.
Sight and Sound. February, 1999, p. 47.
Variety. September 28, 1998, p. 44.
Village Voice. November 10, 1998, p. 115.
Washington Post Weekend. November 6, 1998, p. 47.

Lolita

"An entrancing, heartbreaking film. As Humbert, Jeremy Irons creates one of the great screen performances."—Caryn James, *New York Times*

 Box Office: $1,475,951

Jeremy Irons and Dominique Swain star in Adrian Lyne's controversial remake *Lolita*.

Lolita made its author, an obscure academic expatriate who had been teaching Russian literature at Cornell, famous, if not notorious, when it appeared in 1955. It told the story of another European expatriate, Humbert Humbert, who had been teaching at Beardsley College in New England and had an affair with an underaged girl before being charged with the murder of his evil twin and rival for the nymphet's affections, Clare Quilty. The novel takes the form of a prison diary written from a psychiatric ward. Adrian Lyne's film begins with the blood-spattered Humbert (Jeremy Irons) driving his station wagon erratically down a country road after the murder but before his being apprehended by the police. In one hand he holds a hairpin, in the other a revolver, as he attempts to keep on the road.

From this disturbed perspective, Humbert begins to tell his story, which is also the story of Lolita, "my sin, my soul, Lolita. But there might have been no Lolita at all had I not first met Annabel." Lyne then provides a flashback to Cannes, 1921, in order to "explain" Humbert's perversion, in a continued voice-over, because, as a 14-year-old boy, he had his first sexual encounter with a young girl who died of typhus four months later: "The child I'd loved was gone, but I kept looking for her long after I'd left my own childhood behind. The poison was in the wound, you see, and the wound wouldn't heal." Therefore, Humbert has spent his life looking for someone like Annabel Leigh.

Unfortunately for him, Humbert finds her years later in the presence of the sluttish Dolores Haze (Dominique Swain), nicknamed Lolita, when he is seeking a room to rent in the New England town of Ramsdale. He not only takes the room but woos and weds Lolita's mother, the vulgar Charlotte Haze (Melanie Griffith), whom he is so repulsed by that he slips her sleeping pills in the evening in order to avoid his "husbandly duties." Charlotte sends Lolita to summer camp and later intends to send her to boarding school. Humbert would like to change those plans, but has no solutions, until fate intervenes. Humbert has kept a journal in which he records his true feelings about Charlotte, whom he describes as a "cow." Charlotte knows about the diary, breaks into the locked drawer where it is kept, and reads it. She informs Humbert that their marriage is over and leaves the house, intending to mail letters that will set her plans in motion, but while crossing the street, she is struck by a car and is killed.

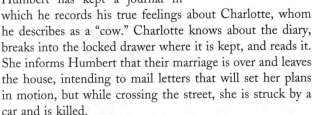

Dominique Swain was fifteen when the movie was filmed and a body double was used for the sexual scenes.

Humbert then drives to the camp to get Lolita and takes her on an extended vacation, a cross-country excursion that lasts for a year in the novel. They then return to Beardsley College, where Humbert is questioned eventually about his daughter's sexual maturity. They decide to leave on another extended vacation, but this time on Lolita's terms. Humbert senses that they are being followed. Lolita feigns illness and Humbert takes her to a hospital for overnight care. The next morning he discovers that she has been "kidnapped" (Humbert prefers to think) by the lecherous Clare Quilty (Frank Langella), who wants to exploit Lolita as a child porn queen, as she tells Humbert three years later, when he finally locates her, after she has written him at Beardsley, asking him for money.

Humbert goes to Lolita and finds her pregnant with another man's child. Humbert then goes to Clare Quilty's mansion and kills his rival, shooting him several times. This brings the action back to the opening shots of Humbert's drive through the countryside, just before he is apprehended by the police. A subtitle at the end informs the viewer that Humbert died in prison in 1950 and that Lolita died in childbirth that same year.

When Stanley Kubrick directed the first film version of *Lolita* in 1962 from a screenplay adapted by Vladimir Nabokov himself, he found, as he explained in 1968, "it was almost impossible to get the film played. Even after it was finished, it laid around for six months. And then, of course,

the audience felt cheated that the erotic weight wasn't in the story." And this was during the so-called sexual revolution of the 1960s.

For nearly half a century Nabokov's *Lolita* has vexed those who would be moral guardians for the country. From the time Nabokov completed the novel in 1953, the publishing trade was afraid to touch it. G.P. Putnam's Sons finally published it in America in 1958, but only after it had already been published in Paris in 1955. Although the novel is shocking in what it suggests about the infatuation of a sophisticated academic pushing forty and a twelve-year-old girl, it "is not about pornography," according to Alfred Appel Jr., editor of *The Annotated Lolita* (Vintage Press, 1991). "It's about a crippling obsession." It was certainly not intended "to gain sympathy for pedophiles."

When the cable network Showtime announced in 1998 that it would broadcast Adrian Lyne's film adaptation, a horrified Jerry Kirk, President of the National Coalition for the Protection of Children and Families, claimed, "This film will increase child molestation and have a harmful effect on pedophiles and healthy men." It took Kubrick nearly a year to get his film adaptation released. Lyne's *Lolita*, started in 1995, was scheduled for release in 1996, the same year the United States Congress passed the Child Pornography Prevention Act, forbidding even the appearance of a minor engaging in a sexual act. By 1997 Lyne had edited the film to qualify for an R rating, but he was still shopping around for a distributor amidst the Woody Allen-Soon-Yi Previn scandal and the later scandal surrounding the murder of young Jon-Benet Ramsey. As Anthony Ramirez wrote in the *New York Times* (August 2), "the latest movie version hews closer to the book" than Stanley Kubrick's film version that featured a fifty-two-year-old James Mason, whose Humbert never kissed the nymphet, "but any depiction of sex with a child, unfiltered by Nabokov's ironic prose, is shocking." As early as 1996 *Newsweek* quoted an anonymous studio executive, who asked: "How do you market a movie about a pedophile?"

The screenplay for Lyne's film was written by Stephen Schiff, a staff writer for *The New Yorker* magazine who had no previous film scripts to his credit, but Schiff followed three other writers, two of whom are among the best playwrights of their generation. According to Christopher C. Hudgins, who has examined all the scripts, the first screenplay, dated October 21, 1991, was by James Dearden, who wrote *Fatal Attraction* for Lyne in 1987; the second, dated September 26, 1994, was written by Harold Pinter; and a third screenplay written by David Mamet was dated March 10, 1995. Though Hudgins would have preferred the Pinter treatment, he concedes that the Stephen Schiff shooting script "clearly displays a critical intelligence at work," but at the same time it reads like a committee effort, since it incorporates elements from the three versions that preceded it.

Reviews were mixed. *Washington Post* television critic Tom Shales, for example, considered Lyne's adaptation "far inferior to the 1962 version," which Pauline Kael had described as a "wild, marvelously enjoyable comedy." Shales described Jeremy Irons as "lugubrious" as Humbert and Dominique Swain's Lolita as "childishly annoying." Melanie Griffith was "flagrantly miscast" as Lolita's mother. For Shales, neither Griffith nor Frank Langella could match the achievements of Shelley Winters and Peter Sellers in Kubrick's film. In Lyne's version, Shales wrote, "we see both more of Quilty [because of the frontal nudity] and less, because he doesn't get nearly as much screen time as in the previous film."

Caryn James of the *New York Times,* on the other hand, found Lyne's film both "entrancing" and "heartbreaking," claiming that "visually and emotionally," the novel survived "its journey to the small screen with its power surprisingly intact." For James, Melanie Griffith was "ideally cast as the annoying, widowed Charlotte," and as Humbert, Jeremy Irons created "one of the great, fearless screen performances," making it clear that "this is Humbert's story, told in his own lyrical voice, from his own passionate, sad, tortured perspective." In fact, the film "is so faithful to the novel that it shares similar flaws." Although Langella is "effectively sinister" as Clare Quilty, "the Grand Guignol scene of his murder belongs in another film (and another novel)." If Humbert is, as he calls himself, an artist and a madman, James contends that Lyne's film succeeds in transforming "Humbert's madness into art."

Adrian Lyne set a kind of record for perseverance in his attempts to get *Lolita* funded (originally with Carolco for $58 million), completed, and finally distributed, even though every major American movie studio refused to touch the film after Carolco's demise. According to *USA Today,* Showtime paid $4 million for rights to the film and helped Lyne get *Lolita* released theatrically through the Samuel Goldwyn Company, a small independent studio, in September after the film's telecast in August, in America, a year after the film had been distributed in Europe without controversy. Had it been released a year earlier, one doubts that it would have held its own against *Titanic* (1997) in the Academy Awards competition, despite claims to the contrary, but the film represents an obviously sincere effort, perhaps more humorless than it needed to be.

— *James M. Welsh* and *John C. Tibbetts*

CREDITS

Humbert Humbert: Jeremy Irons
Lolita: Dominique Swain
Charlotte Haze: Melanie Griffith
Clare Quilty: Frank Langella

Origin: USA, France
Released: 1997
Production: Mario Kassar and Joel B. Michaels for Pathe; released by the Samuel Goldwyn Co.
Direction: Adrian Lyne
Screenplay: Stephen Schiff; based on the novel by Vladimir Nabokov
Cinematography: Howard Atherton
Editing: Julie Monroe, David Bremner, Ennio Morricone
Production design: Jon Hutman
Art direction: W. Steven Graham
Costumes: Jenny Beavan
Sound: Charles Wilborn
MPAA rating: R
Running Time: 137 minutes

REVIEWS

Entertainment Weekly. August 9, 1996, p. 28.
Entertainment Weekly. July 31, 1998, p. 53.
Literature/Film Quarterly. Vol. 25:1 (1997), p. 23.
Los Angeles Times. July 22, 1998, p. F5.
Movieline. September, 1998, p. 48.
New York Times. July 31, 1998, p. B1.
New York Times. August 2, 1998, Sec. 4, pg. 5.
New Yorker. February 23, 1998, p. 79.
Newsweek. December 16, 1996, p. 70.
People. August 3, 1998, p. 21.
Sight and Sound. May, 1998, p. 21.
Time. March 23, 1998.
USA Today. July 31, 1998, p. E1.
Washington Post. August 2, 1998, p. G1.

The Long Way Home

The Long Way Home won an Academy Award for the best documentary in 1997. Sponsored by the Simon Wiesenthal Center, the film begins with extraordinary documentary footage of the Nazi concentration camps, but then it segues into a lesser known story about the fate of camp survivors and the drive to establish the state of Israel.

To assess The Long Way Home's unique power, it is useful to briefly describe other cinematic treatments of the Holocaust and its aftermath. One of the earliest and best films is French director Alan Resnais's Night and Fog (1956). He interspersed scenes (shot in color) of the camps in the 1950s with black-and-white photographs and newsreel footage taken soon after the inmates were liberated from their horror. Resnais's cinematographer probed camp sites relentlessly in tracking shots that seemed to evoke the postwar effort to comprehend the monstrosity of the recent past. Even ten years after World War II, the full dimensions of the Holocaust were not well-known and certainly not confronted in Europe or in America—in spite of the appearance of eyewitness accounts such as Primo Levi's Survival in Auschwitz (1959), Elie Wiesel's Night (1960), and Viktor Frankl's Man's Search for Meaning (1962).

In Exodus (1960), starring Paul Newman and Eva Marie Saint, director Otto Preminger was one of the few Hollywood filmmakers who attempted to dramatize the aftermath of the Holocaust and the founding of the state of Israel. This stirring film concentrates on the heroism of Zionists, who triumph over a seemingly overwhelming number of Arabs. More typical of Hollywood film was The Diary of Anne Frank (1959), based on the Broadway play that emphasized the fate of Anne and her family in universal terms, downplaying their Jewish identities.

Most films, in Europe and in America, did not address the historical context in which the Holocaust was created. Exceptions were the French director, Marcel Ophuls, whose documentary, The Sorrow and the Pity (1971) presented a searing look at French society and those who collaborated with the Nazis in making the world of the camps possible. Similarly, French director Claude Lanzmann employed his documentary Shoah (1985) to probe the complicity of the Poles and others in setting up the camps and in creating an atmosphere in which millions of lives perished.

Two other American films should be mentioned, though, in creating a context for an appraisal of The Long Way Home. The television miniseries Holocaust (1978) tried to make the horrors of the Holocaust comprehensible in terms of individuals and families, just as Roots attempted to make the Middle Passage and slavery an intimate, accessible experience. Neither of these films could escape the sentimentality and simplistic plot structures of the commercial television medium. Similarly, director Steven Spielberg's epic film, Schindler's List (1993), while evoking a good deal of the trauma and human waste of the Holocaust, could not avoid reducing this historical tragedy into the factitious formulas of Hollywood product.

The Long Way Home seems conscious of the strengths and weaknesses of previous efforts to picture the Holocaust and its consequences. Writer and director Mark Jonathan Harris selects for the beginning of his film documentary footage that goes beyond the usual depiction of the concentration camp victims—their emaciated bodies, corpses piled in shallow trenches, and cadaverous figures clinging to wire fences. Such shots are in his film, but so are scenes of camp inmates fighting over food that their rescuers are trying to distribute. American soldiers stare at the inmates in incomprehension, sometimes with sympathetic looks, sometimes with barely concealed disgust. Home makes clear that many Americans did not understand what they were seeing. General George Patton thought of the inmates as animals and did nothing to conceal his anti-Semitism. When General Eisenhower visited the liberated camps under Patton's command, he was so outraged at the poor treatment of the survivors that he had Patton removed from his post.

In its first 30 minutes, The Long Way Home employs professional actors to read from the diaries and letters of concentration camp survivors. Neither the actors nor the actual survivors appear on camera. Instead, as in the Resnais film, the camera roams ceaselessly over concentration camp sites as if trying to match the survivors' words to the hellish places that confined them. By withholding shots of present-day survivors and of the camps as they appear today even as voices of the survivors play over the documentary footage, a tremendous sense of yearning is created, a desire to somehow make contact with the reality that the words and the documentary footage represent. The film makes its audience into searchers of its scenes, so that when the director finally does begin to intercut the documentary footage with scenes of present-day survivors, there is an enormous relief—as if all the previous viewing of the remnants of the past has earned viewers the right to see the survivors. Harris's accomplishment is extraordinary, because he has found a means to honor the past and the sense that it cannot be recaptured while at the same time creating an obsessive need to find out what happened, to see the people who carried on from that seemingly hopeless point, when what they had gone through was understood by almost no one, and when the energy (physical and moral) to retell the story hardly existed.

Out of this despair that the world would never understand, the camp survivors and other Zionists persisted in their drive to create the state of Israel. If Patton was an egregious example of the prejudice and ignorance that the survivors faced, there were nevertheless plenty of others in power who wanted no part in creating a homeland for the Jews. Jews will never be safe, Zionists argued, until they had their own ancestral land.

Much of the remaining part of *The Long Way Home* is taken up with Zionists, their supporters and opponents in the period between 1945 and 1948. Long after the war was over, Jews, like today's Palestinians, were living in camps. They were often referred to as DP's (displaced people), almost as if they were a different race of people. No one seemed to want them. British Foreign Secretary, Ernest Bevan, told Zionist leaders that he thought of the Jews as trouble makers. The British ruled Palestine, and they were much more concerned with offending their Arab neighbors (who controlled such vast amounts of oil) than with doing justice to the Jews.

The film takes an unabashedly pro-Zionist point of view. It spends virtually no time considering the plight of the Arabs (not yet called Palestinians) who occupied land that Zionists wanted for their state. At the same time, it does not blink at the fact that Zionists used terror to create the state of Israel, eventually forcing the British out of Palestine.

But *The Long Way Home* is about the story of a people re-creating themselves, and it has as much right to tell that story as present-day Palestinians would have a right to make a documentary about their camps and displacements. And the fact is that the plight of the Jews, what they continued to suffer in the camps after World War II, would have been ignored if not for Zionist agitation. Gifted with great political leaders such as David Ben Gurion and Abba Eban (interviewed in the film), the Zionists were able to enlist the

United States and, most surprisingly, the Soviet Union as the crucial deciding votes in the United Nations that led to the creation of the state of Israel in 1948.

In some ways, the greatest hero in the film is President Harry Truman. One of his closest advisors, Clark Clifford, is filmed explaining Truman's single-minded support for the idea of Israel. Clearly a dying man, Clifford speaks in a barely audible but firm whisper, recalling Truman's enormous courage and decisiveness. His major advisors, except for Clifford, argued against recognizing Israel. George Marshall, then in Truman's cabinet and the architect of the famous Marshall Plan that did so much to rebuild Western Europe, told his President point-blank that if he did not change his position on Israel, Marshall would not be able to vote for him in the next election. But Truman did not waver.

Of course Truman was lobbied by Zionist leaders (a part of the story the film does not tell). Yet many American Jews also opposed the creation of the state of Israel, some believing that assimilation was inevitable, while certain Orthodox Jews believed Israel would come into existence only upon the arrival of the Messiah. What is more, Truman was hardly responding to a groundswell of support for the idea of Israel. Ernest Bevin, who was restricting Jewish immigration to Palestine and turning away Jews who showed up in boats in their promised land, pointed out that America had its own restrictive policies on immigration.

The Long Way Home does not discount how dispirited many of the Jewish concentration camp survivors were. Some died shortly after liberation, literally eating themselves to death after years of starvation. Others could not bring themselves to share the horror of their experience with their families—if they had any families left. Yet many of those who felt their lives were broken beyond repair continued to have children in the abysmal conditions of refugee camps. Ruth Gruber, an American newspaper correspondent, realized that though "their world was gone, they had to continue for their children." The film's narrator, the distinguished actor Morgan Freeman, speaking for these survivors, concludes: "The world lost, and yet we won. We are going on."

—Carl Rollyson

CREDITS

Origin: USA
Released: 1997
Production: Marvin Hier and Richard Trank for Moriah Films and The Simon Wiesenthal Center; released by Seventh Art Releasing
Direction: Mark Jonathan Harris
Screenplay: Mark Jonathan Harris
Cinematography: Don Lenzer
Editing: Kate Amend
Music: Lee Holdridge
MPAA rating: Unrated
Running Time: 120 minutes

REVIEWS

New York Times. September 19, 1997.
San Francisco Chronicle. May 8, 1998, p. C10.
San Francisco Examiner. May 8, 1998.

Lost in Space

Get lost.—Movie tagline

"Exciting, adventurous, eye-popping fun!"—Bruce Westbrook, *Houston Chronicle*

"Blast into space with a thrill ride you'll never forget."—Bonnie Chruchill, *National News Syndicate*

"A wild, fun ride!"—Bill Zwecker, *NBC-TV*

"A wild ride through nonstop visual effects!" —Peter Stack, *San Francisco Chronicle*

 Box Office: $69,117,629

The Robinson family prep their robot for an exploratory adventure in the big screen version of *Lost In Space*.

Based on the often campy 1960s television series created and produced by Irwin Allen, *Lost in Space* finally arrived on the big screen after years of speculation, unfruitful attempts, and pre-production planning. Hoping to emulate the successful revitalization of *Star Trek* in the form of a lucrative feature film series, various individuals, including some of the stars of the television series, attempted throughout the 1980s to get new *Lost in Space* projects off the ground; however, these ideas never materialized because Irwin Allen, who owned the rights to the series, strongly opposed any such revival. Then, when the rights to *Lost in Space* finally became available, it took still longer to get a film going. As the film went before the cameras at last, featuring a new cast and an updated story, director Stephen Hopkins and screenwriter Akiva Goldsman promised a story that would be a more serious take on the original series, an adventure more in keeping with the original tone of the series when it premiered in 1965 than with the lighthearted, campy direction it took in later episodes. Hoping that *Lost in Space* would be the beginning of a moneymaking franchise, New Line Cinema poured $80 million dollars into the film, making it the most expensive movie ever produced by the small studio.

During the last few years audiences have witnessed an unprecedented number of big screen revivals of old television series, a trend that to some suggests a lack of original creativity in Hollywood and that to others represents the industry's self-protective need to rely on what is tried and true instead of taking new risks. Occasionally these television-inspired films have been commercially and/or critically successful (for example, *The Addams Family*, *The Flintstones*, and *The Brady Bunch Movie*), but just as often they have failed (*The Beverly Hillbillies*, *McHale's Navy*, *Leave It to Beaver*),

 Dr. Zachary Smith (Gary Oldman): "Oh, the pain, the pain!"

giving rise to the question of whether the "TV revival" trend is an artistically and financially wise one. *Lost in Space* doesn't provide any clear answers to that question, because the film has its strengths and its weaknesses, the latter of which derive from the very fact that the movie was designed as both a re-telling of an older story and an intended spawner of sequels. On its own, divorced from the television series which inspired it, *Lost in Space* is a visually exciting and dynamic film, a fast-paced adventure with interesting characters, witty dialogue, and the potential for family drama, but often the potential for drama does not entirely deliver what it promises, partially because it seems that further development has been reserved for future stories.

The year is 2085, and the planet Earth is facing imminent environmental disaster. The effects of global warming and the depletion of the ozone layer will render the planet uninhabitable within two decades, so the scientific community must find a way to relocate Earth's population. As part of this attempt to save humanity, Professor John Robinson (William Hurt) develops the Jupiter project, an extended space flight that will take him and his family to the distant planet of Alpha Prime, a world similar to Earth. There he and the family will begin work on a "hyper-gate" that will allow for faster-than-light transportation to the planet from Earth. As Robinson explains to an audience of news reporters early in the film, without such a hyper-gate, one cannot predict his destination when traveling through hyper-space. Therefore, construction of the gate is crucial to transporting the population of Earth.

Unfortunately for Professor Robinson, his family is not quite as eager to make this journey. While his older daughter Judy (Heather Graham) is a fellow scientist who seems to share his commitment to saving the people of Earth, his wife Maureen (Mimi Rogers) cautions him that he is neglecting the family, his daughter Penny (Lacey Chabert) angrily mourns that she is leaving everything she holds dear, and his brilliant, scientifically-minded son Will (Jack Johnson) believes his father has no interest in anything he does. Finally, their reluctant hotshot young pilot, Major Don West (Matt LeBlanc), would rather be flying a mission with more heroic potential. Shortly after take-off, the family faces a more serious problem than reluctance or unhappy relationships when their flight is sabotaged by the traitorous Dr. Zachary Smith (Gary Oldman), who unintentionally sends their ship, the Jupiter 2, soaring toward the sun. In a last-minute effort to save everyone, Robinson and West take the ship into hyper-space without a hyper-gate. Subsequently, the Robinsons find themselves across the galaxy in unknown areas of space.

Now literally lost in space, the family soon comes across a strange "bubble" in space surrounding a derelict space ship. After boarding the ship, they discover it is evidently an Earth ship from the future, its crew ominously missing. According to onboard logs, the ship was sent out to search for the Jupiter 2 but ran into trouble. The trouble they encountered soon appears in the form of swarms of large, deadly spider-like creatures that can live in space. The Robinsons, West, and Dr. Smith narrowly escape the ship, but in the process Smith is bitten by one of the creatures. To eliminate the pests, West destroys the derelict ship, but the shock wave from the explosion sends the Jupiter 2 into the atmosphere of a nearby planet, where the ship crash lands.

On the planet they find another bubble similar to the one that had surrounded the derelict ship from the future. The strange phenomenon, which Professor Robinson identifies as a temporal bubble, is expanding. Inside it, Robinson encounters a future version of his son, Will (Jared Harris), who has been working on a time traveling device with which he can go back in time to prevent his family from getting lost in space. The only other survivor in this future is Dr. Smith, who has metamorphosized into a huge, half-spider, half-human creature. Will had grown up on the planet believing Smith was his friend and protector, but it turns out that he actually was responsible for the death of the Robinsons and has persuaded Will to build the time device for his own devious plans. Professor Robinson warns his son from the future that if he attempts to travel back in

time, he will actually unravel the fabric of the universe and destroy his family.

After defeating the evil spider Smith and persuading the future Will not to follow through with his plan, the Robinsons escape from the planet and, using incomplete navigational data obtained from the derelict ship they found, head out into space toward what they hope is their original destination. Here the movie ends rather suddenly as Penny says, "Here we go again," and the audience is left to wonder if they will reach Alpha Prime or wind up lost again.

The plot of *Lost in Space* is partially derived from the first few episodes of the television series, but it is also updated and just as much new as it is old. This is in keeping with the tone consistent throughout the movie, which—as intended by the film's writer, director, and producers—is that of paying homage to the television series while simultaneously telling a new story that is more technically sophisticated, more action-packed, more serious, and more hip. What could be disadvantageous—and unavoidable—about this is that much of the film's charm lies in references to the original series that may be missed by many audience members who are herewith introduced to *Lost in Space* for the first time. In fact, what could be described as one of the major weaknesses of the film is that it tends to presume audience familiarity with the show from which the movie takes its inspiration. One example of this problem is the film's conclusion, which reaches a climax rather quickly and then rushes to a cliffhanger-type ending that seems to say "To Be Continued . . ." Such an ending was a staple of the television series but seems awkward in the film, yet it obviously owes to the fact that the producers and the studio hope to tell further big-screen adventures of the Robinson family.

The updated characterizations work well, and in some cases are more developed than they were in the TV show. Judy, for example, is a scientist like her father, with similar motivations, and her strong nature and witty resistance to the sexual advances of Don West make for a more interesting character than her television counterpart. Likewise, Penny has been updated into a more major character (and a stranger one), who obviously was very attached to her life on Earth and who seems to lack a strong relationship with anyone in her family except her brother Will, though her relationship with him is, on the surface, one of sibling rivalry. Will Robinson, who eventually became the focus of the television series along with Dr. Smith, is an interesting character well-acted by young Johnson even though he is less emphasized than in the television show. His attempts to prove himself to his father eventually form the background to the conflict in the latter part of the film, the resolution of which coincides with the underlying thematic is-

> Although many of the original TV series cast have cameos in the film, the only one to recreate his original role is Dick Tufeld as the voice of the robot.

sues *Lost in Space* tries to develop. At the heart of the film lies the story of a dysfunctional family that is actually "lost" before ever traveling into space. Ironically, finding them-selves lost in space forces them to draw closer together and improve their relationships. This problematic family situa-tion is also a '90s update of the TV series, in which the fam-ily could have hardly been more perfect (and sometimes ir-ritatingly so). The added complexity of the imperfect, lacking family relationships provides not only more conflict to the story but more realism and more dramatic dimension.

Despite overall mediocre reviews, in its opening week-end, *Lost in Space* became the first film to knock *Titanic* out of the number one spot at the boxoffice. However, after two weeks the film's large audience numbers began to diminish. Only time will tell whether the movie will eventually turn in a profit or fulfill New Line's plans of starting a franchise se-ries. Should more *Lost in Space* installments be made, it might be wise of the producers to rely less on insider-references and audience familiarity, concentrating more on further charac-ter development and dramatic depth. As a stand-alone prod-uct, *Lost in Space* looks good, boasts some fascinating ef-fects, provides an action-packed ride, and presents some interesting characters that are well-performed by the cast, but there is potential for much more in terms of story and originality.

—*David Flanagin*

CREDITS

John Robinson: William Hurt
Maureen Robinson: Mimi Rogers
Dr. Zachary Smith: Gary Oldman
Judy Robinson: Heather Graham
Will Robinson: Jack Johnson
Don West: Matt LeBlanc
Penny Robinson: Lacey Chabert
Voice of Robot: Dick Tufeld
Older Will: Jared Harris
General: Mark Goddard
Principal: June Lockhart
Reporter No. 1:   Marta Kristen
Reporter No. 2:   Angela Cartwright
Business Man: Edward Fox

Origin: USA
Released: 1998
Production: Mark W. Koch, Stephen Hopkins, Akiva Goldsman, and Carla Fry for Prelude Pictures and Irwin Allen Productions; released by New Line Cinema
Direction: Stephen Hopkins
Screenplay: Akiva Goldsman
Cinematography: Peter Levy
Editing: Ray Lovejoy
Music: Bruce Broughton
Production design: Norman Garwood
Costumes: Vin Burnham, Robert Bell, Gilly Hebden
Art direction: Keith Pain
Sound: Simon Kaye
Visual effects supervision: Angus Bickerton
MPAA rating: PG-13
Running Time: 131 minutes

REVIEWS

Boxoffice. March, 1998, p. 14.
Chicago Tribune. April 3, 1998, p. 4.
Cinefantastique. March, 1998, p. 8.
Cinefantastique. April, 1998, p. 14.
Entertainment Weekly. April 10, 1998, p. 42.
Los Angeles Times. April 3, 1998, p. F8.
People. April 20, 1998, p. 36.
Sight and Sound. August, 1998, p. 48.
USA Today. April 3, 1998, p. 5E.
Variety. April 6, 1998, p. 46.
Village Voice. April 14, 1998, p. 64.
Washington Post Weekend. April 3, 1998, p. 53.

Love and Death on Long Island

"Wonderful!"—Roger Ebert, *Chicago Sun-Times*

"Consistently brilliant! Funny and touching." —Michele Shapiro, *Glamour*

"A wonderfully warm and clever comedy. Perfectly performed."—Jack Mathews, *Los Angeles Times*

"Delightfully droll. John Hurt is simply wonderful!"—Janet Maslin, *New York Times*

"Refreshing! Utterly original!"—Daphne Merkin, *New Yorker*

"A comedy of unusual intelligence and poignancy. A clever beauty of a film."—David Ansen, *Newsweek*

"John Hurt is glorious. Jason Priestley is perfect."—Dennis Dermody, *Paper Magazine*

"Extraordinary! Uniquely funny and touching." —Peter Travers, *Rolling Stone*

"Hilarious! The jokes are sharp and funny. A triumph . . . John Hurt is fabulous."—John Powers, *Vogue*

Box Office: $2,581,014

Love and Death on Long Island *is a surprisingly effective story of romantic longing, an incisive comedy that aches with poignancy and resonants with the agony of unrequited love. Based on the cult novel of the same name by Gilbert Adair, the film marks the feature film debut of writer-director Richard Kwietniowski.

Giles De'Ath (John Hurt) is a reclusive widower, a writer of esoteric British novels who accidentally locks himself out of his London flat one rainy afternoon. To pass the time, Giles makes a rare foray from his cloistered existence to the local cinema, intent on seeing the latest screen adaptation of E. M. Forster. But when he wanders into the wrong theatre, he is appalled to find himself subjected to the idiotic American teen comedy *Hot Pants College II*. Repulsed, Giles is about to storm out when suddenly he is transfixed by the face of the pretty and highly "snoggable" young actor, Ronnie Bostock (Jason Priestley).

Against all logic and reason, the middle-aged Giles soon finds himself deep in the throes of a full-blown adolescent obsession with the sweetly sexy American heartthrob. He surreptitiously rents videos of the rest of Ronnie's oeuvre, films

Giles (John Hurt): "Ronnie, there's nothing more solitary than an artist's life. One yearns for solace without quite knowing where to look for it."

with such complex titles as *Skid Marks* and *Tex Mex*—a feat not easily accomplished since Giles, the "erstwhile fogy," cannot tell the difference between a VCR and a microwave, nor that the videotape player needs a television! Giles locks himself in his study where he scours over teen fan magazines, mooning over color photos and cutting and pasting every journalistic morsel he can find on this elusive love object into a scrapbook he has grandly christened "Bostockiana."

With this obsession showing no signs of waning, Giles spontaneously makes a pilgrimage to New York, determined to track down the object of his affection. Like a fish out of water, Giles, expecting a shine, places his shoes outside his motel door at night; and when he ignores the "Thank You for Not Smoking" sign, Giles flatly informs the astonished cabdriver: "As I am, I don't expect to be thanked."

Arriving in the small Long Island town where Ronnie unfortunately lives with his model girlfriend Audrey (Fiona Loewi), Giles is able to infiltrate his way into the unsuspecting actor's life by flattering Ronnie's "serious" career aspirations. After all, Giles tells him, *Hot Pants College II* and Shakespeare's *Richard III* are both essentially about a quest.

The film's ambiguous denouement is refreshing; there is no easy resolution. Kwietniowski deftly avoids melodrama and farce—albeit at times reaching the fringes of the very same banal universe of light comedy that it parodies—managing instead (with Hurt's artful collaboration) to paint a sympathetic and rich portrait of a character that could have easily lapsed into a pathetic joke.

Love and Death on Long Island *is a rich blend of Thomas Mann's *Death in Venice* and Nabokov's *Lolita*. While both Humbert Humbert and Giles De'Ath find themselves driven down the ladder of social strata by lust, one is tragically destroyed by it, the other miraculously resurrected.

Jason Priestley, best known for his role on the long-running television show *Beverly Hills 90210*, is clearly mocking his own teen heartthrob persona, but he manages to find a glimmer of inner life to his character. It is, however, veteran actor John Hurt's elegant and nuanced performance as the tweedy writer that gives this film, along with the witty writing of Kwietniowski, its emotional resonance. Hurt has twice been nominated for an Academy Award for his powerful work in *Midnight Express* (1978) and *The Elephant Man* (1980), but he is perhaps better known in pop culture as the unfortunate crew member who births the hideous monster aboard the spaceship in Ridley Scott's *Alien* (1979).

As poignant and impressive as the film is, *Love and*

CREDITS

Giles De'Ath: John Hurt
Ronnie Bostock: Jason Priestley
Audrey: Fiona Loewi
Mrs. Barker: Sheila Hancock
Irving: Maury Chaykin
Henry: Gawn Grainger
Mrs. Reed: Elizabeth Quinn

Origin: Canada, Great Britain
Released: 1997
Production: Steve Clark-Hall and Christopher Zimmer for Skyline Films and Imagex; released by Lions Gate Films
Direction: Richard Kwietniowski
Screenplay: Richard Kwietniowski; based on the novel by Gilbert Adair
Cinematography: Oliver Curtis
Editing: Susan Shipton
Production design: David McHenry
Art direction: Emanuel Jannasch
Costumes: Andrea Galer
Music: Richard Grassby-Lewis
Sound: Neil Kingsbury
MPAA rating: PG-13
Running Time: 93 minutes

Death on Long Island can be off-putting. Like the evolution of the relationships it depicts, the story meanders along, sometimes at an agonizingly slow pace, while little is made of the homosexual element of the attraction of the widowed Giles to the virile Ronnie. Perhaps this is indeed part of the point being made: that this attraction is not intended to be sexual, but rather spiritual in nature. Giles is sparked back to life through this "insane" crush, this infatuation with someone that he might otherwise revile. Ultimately, the film is a bittersweet exploration of the power of love, even unrequited love, as well as the power of the cinema to shape our fantasies and our expectations.

—*Patricia Kowal*

REVIEWS

Chicago Sun-Times. March 13, 1998.
Chicago Tribune. March 13, 1998, p. 5.
Entertainment Weekly. March 13, 1998, p. 51.
Los Angeles Times. March 6, 1998, p. F22.
New York Times. March 6, 1998, p. B7.
New Yorker. March 9, 1998, p. 93.
San Francisco Chronicle. March 13, 1998, p. C3.
San Francisco Examiner. March 13, 1998, p. C3.
Time. March 2, 1998, p. 85.
Variety. May 19, 1997, p. 50.

Love is the Devil

"Sensual!"—*The Advocate*

"Jacobi's portrait of Francis Bacon is a masterpiece . . . Outstanding."—*The Guardian*

"Brilliantly realized!"—*Harpers Bazaar*

"Breathtaking visual poetry!"—*Interview*

"Brilliant."—*New York Post*

"Its respect for the viewers intelligence is extraordinary!"—*New York Press*

"Visually striking!"—*Newsweek*

"*Love* is a dark ride, but one that lovers of sumptuous cinema won't want to miss!"—*Time Out, New York*

"One of the finest films made about an artist . . . The performances are terrific."—*Time Out, UK*

"Astonishing."—*Village Voice*

Box Office: $336, 236

The British artist, Francis Bacon, who has been called one of the greatest painters of the twentieth century, created images that depict the isolation, violence, and terror that are hallmarks of our age. *Love is the Devil: Study for a Portrait of Francis Bacon* is the story of a fragment of life, between 1964 and 1971, and explores the relationship between the artist and his model and lover, George Dyer.

Although the substance of the film is about the artist's life, this film is no ordinary biography. Writer/director John Maybury has put together a series of sketches that successfully evoke the ambience of Bacon's work while telling the story of the tragic love affair. The Bacon estate would not allow the filmmaker to use any of the artist's work in the film, and working within those parameters, Maybury has used film sequences to actually recreate some of Bacon's paintings. These cinematic tableaux combined with theatrical sets and special effects create an intentionally dark and often nightmarish backdrop to the story, and the use of distorted images and odd camera angels evoke the same twisted reality found in some of Bacon's paintings. Said Maybury, "We started to look at more subtle ways of interpreting the work on film and looked to the paintings for inspiration; the general claustrophobia of places, the lighting and the color palette throughout ... Basically Bacon was our ultimate production designer."

The film follows similar ground as did the book *The Gilded Gutter Life of Francis Bacon*, written by Bacon's friend and biographer Daniel Farson, who also worked as a consultant on the film. It begins at the opening of Bacon's 1971 retrospective at the Grand Palais in Paris. At the pinnacle of his career, Bacon (Derek Jacobi) accepts international accolades, while back at their hotel room, his lover has just taken a fatal dose of drugs and alcohol. He then slips back into a flashback of the night they met.

One night in 1964, George Dyer (Daniel Craig), an inept East End thief, fell through the skylight of Bacon's flat during a robbery attempt. Dazed by the fall, Dyer looked up to find Bacon staring at him curiously. "Take your clothes off and come to bed and you can have whatever you want," he tells him. Dyer does, and so begins their tumultuous, seven-year affair.

Bacon, in his fifties, showers the young Dyer with gifts, clothes, and money, and then introduces him to his friends at the Colony Room, a drinking club in Soho. Bacon's life centers around gambling, drinking, young men, and painting. His friends include *Vogue* photographer John Deakin (Karl Johnson), whose photos Bacon used in his work, a scathingly facetious Muriel Belcher (Tilda Swinton), and his confidante, Isabel Rawsthorne (Anne Lambton), who all come from upper-class backgrounds. Their brand of camp sophistication excludes the naive, working class Dyer, and he soon becomes the butt of their jokes.

Socially at odds, Bacon and Dyer have only one thing in common: their sadomasochistic relationship. In that one area Dyer is dominant, but in every other way Bacon has the upper hand—financially, socially, and emotionally. Dyer does not fit into Bacon's world and soon no longer fits into his own world. He is adrift and he suffers. First he begins drinking heavily and abusing drugs, while his lover watches on with amused disgust. When he is beset by nightmares,

Bacon tells him that he is even more boring when he is asleep than when he is awake. There follows numerous suicide attempts, and Bacon again reacts with impatient indifference. And yet Bacon's work, using Dyer as his model, portrays his suffering so perfectly that it is almost as if Bacon is a conduit for Dyer's anguish. He expresses Dyer's pain on his canvasses, yet he remains outwardly unmoved.

"I think Dyer had his problems before they met," Maybury said, "but meeting Bacon simply aggravated things. He may have continued a life of petty crime but instead, he became one of the greatest icons of twentieth century art."

Whether Dyer's problems stem from his own life or from his association with Bacon, the viewer is never certain. But what is certain is that Bacon abuses his lover. He starts seeing other men, locking him out of their apartment, insulting him, and—the cruelest abuse of all—he is totally indifferent to Dyer's pain. In fact, he actually feeds on it for the sake of his art. Dyer has become his lover, his model, and his muse, and in his portraits of him, Bacon has crystallized Dyer's agony into art, but as the artist and his art flourishes, the muse begins to die. The irony is that Dyer had come to steal from Bacon, but in the end it is Bacon who takes everything from Dyer.

"What interests me most about Bacon's life are the paintings of Dyer," Maybury said. "The dynamic between an artist and his muse and the choices that an artist has to make between his work and his private life. I find that fascinating."

Maybury carries this to an extreme in a scene where Bacon is working in his studio and the comatose Dyer is passed out in the middle of the floor. Bacon steps back and forth over the body while he is working, oblivious to his lover's dire state. The film underlines Bacon's self-absorption and lack of humanity that sometimes even extends to the way he treats himself. This is no where more evident than in the scene where he is dressing to go out on the town. He brushes his teeth with scouring bleach and touches up his graying hair with brown shoe polish, painting himself in much the same way he paints his canvases. Later we see him literally painting himself in oils, symbolic perhaps of the artist becoming his work.

It is just this sort of symbolism that weakens the emotional impact of the film. The story itself is not strong, and the viewer is given no inkling as to why Bacon is such an emotionally bankrupt individual, although a scene which was removed from the film might have shed some light into his

Francis Bacon (Derek Jacobi): "Champagne for my real friends; real pain for my sham friends."

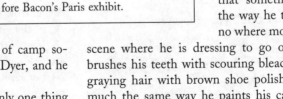

The film has Dyer committing suicide while Bacon is attending his retrospective at the Grand Palais, but Dyer actually ended his life a few days before Bacon's Paris exhibit.

character. The scene shows Bacon as a youth dressing up in his mother's clothes. Bacon's father catches the fifteen-year-old in the act and sends him to the stable to be horsewhipped by the stable hands. This is an allusion to a story in Farson's book about how Bacon lost his innocence among the stable hands. But the scene was deemed irrelevant to the story and was removed to appease the British Film Institute. This obstacle together with the absence of Bacon's paintings from the film keep the viewer from gaining a necessary insight into Bacon's character, and the viewer is left with little sympathy for the painter.

Bacon is played by Sir Derek Jacobi, known to American audiences for his television performances in *I, Claudius*

CREDITS

Francis Bacon: Derek Jacobi
George Dyer: Daniel Craig
Muriel Belcher: Tilda Swinton
Isabel Rawsthorne: Anne Lambton
Daniel Farson: Adrian Scarborough
John Deakin: Karl Johnson
Henrietta Moraes: Annabel Brooks
Blond Billy: Richard Newbold

Origin: Great Britain
Released: 1998
Production: Chiara Menage for British Broadcasting Corporation, British Film Institute, Premiere Heure, Uplink, and Arts Council of England production; released by Strand Releasing
Direction: John Maybury
Screenplay: John Maybury
Cinematography: John Mathieson
Editing: Daniel Goddard
Music: Ryuichi Sakamoto
Production design: Alan Macdonald
Costumes: Annie Symons
Sound: Ken Lee
Casting: Mary Selway
MPAA rating: Unrated
Running Time: 91 minutes

and *Cadfael*. Jacobi brings a believable coldness and indifference to the part, but is not quite convincing as a man who sought out hell in life for the sake of his art. He comes across more as a self-centered sensualist, and because of Jacobi's inherent onscreen charm, he is not altogether unlikable in the part. But the character's indifference infects the viewer, and in the end it is difficult to care for this uncaring man.

Daniel Craig, who plays the doomed Dyer, brings a whole world of pain to the part. He is the emotional centerpiece to this otherwise intellectually and stylistically sterile film, and the only character who seems to have any feelings at all.

Except for fans of Bacon, few will understand the frigid man portrayed in the film, nor will any but the aficionado bring to the film an appreciation of what Bacon has given to the art world. For those unfamiliar with his work, it will be difficult to forgive a man for living only through his art if that art remains unseen. Bacon's rise to prominence and his lover's corresponding sinking into the depths of despair is the only real movement in the film, and it becomes overdone and redundant. The only truly sympathetic character is Dyer, and his inevitable death becomes not only expected but also ultimately anticlimactic.

Although *Love is the Devil* is visually innovative, the film's overriding concern with style and symbolism robs it of its emotional relevance. The viewer is told that Bacon explored the darkest recesses of the soul, but the film never illuminates just what he found there.

—*Diane Hatch-Avis*

REVIEWS

Entertainment Weekly. October 9, 1998, p. 18.
Los Angeles Times. October 9, 1998, p. F12.
New York Times. October 8, 1998, p. E5.
New Yorker. October 12, 1998, p. 82.
People. October 19, 1998, p. 41.
Sight and Sound. September, 1998, p. 47.
Variety. May 25, 1998, p. 58.
Village Voice. October 13, 1998, p. 126.
Washington Post. November 13, 1998, p. D5.

Love Walked In

Nothing is more seductive than temptation.
—Movie tagline

"*Love Walked In* is an involving twisty little sleeper. I advise you to check it out soon."—Jay Carr, *Boston Globe*

"A curiously wonderful old fashioned gem."
—Duane Byrge, *Hollywood Reporter*

"Intelligent and stylish."—Kevin Thomas, *Los Angeles Times*

"Love walked right in and drove the shadows away/Love walked right in and brought my sunniest day ..." These words begin the classic Gershwin song that *Love Walked In* is presumably named after. However, the film doesn't follow the uplifting optimism of the Gershwin brothers, but rather descends into a world where shadows aren't driven away and love walks right on out the door. This ironic mix between title and theme would appear to present all the elements for a pretty good drama, but the filmmakers throw in so many ingredients—a little of *The Fabulous Baker Boys* (1989), a touch of *Indecent Proposal* (1993), a dash of the Sinatra vehicle *Young at Heart* (1954)—that we get alphabet rather than pea soup.

The tone is immediately set through a bitter monologue given by perpetually-broke lounge musician Jack Morrisey (Denis Leary). Addressing a well-heeled audience, Jack expresses his angst over the state of popular music, cursing out such monstrosities as grunge, techno pop, and Michael Bolton. He concludes with the despairing fact that he is "writing second rate Gershwin–esque for an audience that no longer exists." His observations are refreshingly honest and astute, but it's all downhill from there.

After this terrific opening the plot ignores his songwriting and focuses on a simplistic blackmail plot. This scheme is intermixed with scenes from a novel that Jack is writing (of course, he is also a writer and an alcoholic), which explores the two sides of his personality with the help of two cousins: one good, another bad.

An old friend of Jack's, a loser named Eddie (Michael Badalucco), who he hasn't heard from in years, conveniently shows up in town as a private investigator who has been hired to dig up dirt on the town's most prominent citizen, the boring Fred Moore (Terence Stamp). Failing to find anything, Eddie proposes to Jack that they blackmail Fred by photographing him in compromising situations with

The film originally debuted at the Sundance Film Festival under the title *The Bitter End*

Jack's long-suffering lover, Vicky Perez (Aitana Sánchez Gijón). The inevitable happens when Vicki actually falls for Fred and he for her. Eddie discovers this and decides to back out of the plan, which only makes Jack suspicious that Eddie is trying to take all the blackmail money for himself. The friendship falls apart and Jack decides to carry out this clever little espionage on his own.

Unfortunately, Jack finds some un-staged pictures of Vicki and Fred, sending him over the edge. He convinces Vicky to seduce Fred up to his bedroom at Fred's big birthday bash, intending this as a test of Vicky's faithfulness. Jack brings his camera and gun to the party and stakes out a spot in a tree from where he can photograph Fred's bedroom. A maid threatens to squash these plans by closing the curtains on the bedroom window. Jack sneaks up there, opens the curtains, and leaves the party to climb his tree. Vicky gets Fred into the bedroom where she melodramatically closes the curtains and takes him to bed. By this time it is thundering and lightning outside,

CREDITS

Jack Morrisey: Denis Leary
Vicky: Aitana Sánchez Gijón
Fred Moore: Terence Stamp
Eddie: Michael Badalucco
Mrs. Moore: Marj Dusay
Vera: Moira Kelly
Joey: Gene Canfield
Howard: Neal Huff
Matt: Danny Nucci

Origin: USA
Released: 1997
Production: Ricardo Freixa for Apostle Pictures and Jempsa Entertainment; released by TriStar Pictures
Direction: Juan José Campenella
Screenplay: Larry Goldin, Lynn Geller, and Juan José Campenella; based on the novel *Ni el Trio del Final* by José Pablo Feinman
Cinematography: Daniel Shulman
Editing: Darren Kloomok
Music: Wendy Blackstone
Production design: Michael Shaw
Costumes: David Robinson
MPAA rating: R
Running Time: 90 minutes

pouring rain on the drunk and demented Jack. Cut to a violently overwrought scene from his novel where the Good Cousin kills the Bad Cousin. After these images parade through Jack's mind he decides not to kill the two lovers, falls out of the tree, and relinquishes Vicky to Fred, leaving us with these sage words, "You start out by trying to spin a tale and it ends up spinning you."

Love Walked In successfully packs in a walloping number of clichès in its slender 90 minute frame. We get the failed songwriter, the failed writer, and the alcoholic battling pesky inner demons in the character of Jack. In Vicky we get the long-suffering, more talented, stick-by-my-man type. Rounding out this crew is the two-bit private eye who is too honest for his own good, and the wealthy businessman who has it all and has to fight the temptation to do wrong.

Ultimately, this is a disappointing film not because of its stereotyped characters and paper-thin plot, but because it begins so smartly. What starts out as a promising character piece ends up as a thinly plotted noir, a terrible oxymoron. The filmmakers are so caught up in using forced, hard-boiled dialogue and the silly device of Jack's novel that they lose sight of any focus this script, penned by three writers, may have once had. We are left with a film that has flashes of intelligence and honesty, but smothered in an overzealous coating of Parmesan. In other words, cheese.

—*Rich Silverman*

REVIEWS

Los Angeles Times. February 20, 1998, p. F8.
New York Times. February 20, 1998, p. E12.
Variety. January 27, 1997, p. 81.
Village Voice. February 24, 1998, p. 124.

Madeline

You loved her for generations. Now the biggest little girl in Paris is coming to the big screen.
—Movie tagline

In an old house in Paris, that was covered with vines . . . —Movie tagline

"You will fall in love with *Madeline!* It's a treat for the young and old."—Bill Diehl, *ABC Radio Network*

"*Madeline* is divine."—Ron Brewington, *American Urban Radio Networks*

"Enchanting."—Jeffrey Lyons, *NBC-TV*

"*Madeline* will make any child's summer a wonderful world. Funny and filled with adventure."—Gene Shalit, *Today Show*

 Box Office: $29,967,750

The classic children's book series is brought to life with Francis McDormand as Miss Clavel and newcomer Hatty Jones as the mischievous *Madeline*.

L udwig Bemelmans introduced his little heroine, Madeline, in a series of six books he began publishing in 1939. The Madeline of the books, like the Madeline of the recent film adaptation directed by Daisy von Scherler Mayer, is one of a dozen little girls who board at a Parisian school run by a Catholic nun named Miss Clavel. The Madeline of the movie, Hatty Jones—who was nine-years-old when the film was made—does an excellent job of embodying those traits readers treasure about one of their favorite heroines: she is spunky, brave, generous, thoroughly unpretentious, and—above all—red haired.

One of the primary glories of Bemelmans' children's books is their illustrations, which paint Paris in memorable primary colors. Some of these illustrations (or a simulation of them) are revisited during *Madeline*'s opening credits, and when the inanimate paintings begin to melt into color-saturated live action, it does at first seem that the Madeline of childhood memory has been brought to life on the screen. There are, however, more differences than similarities between Bemelmans' creation and Mayer's recreation.

Daisy Mayer's version of *Madeline* combines the plots of four of the Madeline books and adds some Hollywood high jinx for good measure. The result, unsurprisingly, is rather a mishmash. To be fair, though, the filmmaker was presented with a problem that the author did not have to confront: Mayer was working under the constraint of entertaining young girls with MTV-trained short attention spans for nearly an hour and a half, a daunting task.

Some of the film's innovations work: most notably the introduction of Lord Covington, played with admirable stuffiness by Nigel Hawthorne. "Lord Cucuface"—as the movie Madeline calls him behind his back—is presented here as the owner of the boarding school and

Madeline (Hatty Jones): "I can do anything."

The six-book *Madeline* series has sold more than 10 million copies worldwide.

film's primary plot device. The school has been his wife's (Stephane Audran) favorite charity, but after she dies early on in the action, he resolves to sell the lovely old mansion that houses Miss Clavel (Frances McDormand), Madeline, and the eleven other little girls who eat, sleep, and promenade in two straight lines.

Lord Covington's plan will (and here the film plot begins to veer rather wildly away from Bemelmans') have the greatest impact on Madeline, for, as we are repeatedly told, she is an orphan. But Madeline, whose appendicitis brings her in contact in hospital with the dying Lady Covington, is a clever little girl with all manner of inner resources. It is her ability to see past Lord Covington's fearsome persona and touch the deep sadness within him that saves the day. But first, we have to get through the rest of the movie.

Declining to play the role of victim, Madeline decides to take hold of her own fate. After failing to derail Lord Covington's plans by other means, she determines that she will run away with the circus. She does not, however, count on being kidnapped with Pepito (Kristian De La Osa), the pesky son of the Spanish ambassador, who lives next door to the school. The resolution of this plot twist involves a predictable but diverting car chase in which Miss Clavel, piloting a tiny Citroen, saves the day—but not before almost colliding with the kidnappers' truck and providing viewers with one of the more amusing scenes in the movie when she puts her hands across her passenger's eyes to prevent her from witnessing the disaster. Her passenger, of course, is the school's pet dog, Genevieve, who had earlier saved Madeline after she fell into the Seine.

And needless to say, Madeline and Pepito are finally rescued, as is the school. The happy ending—if little else—is certainly in the spirit of Bemelmans' gentle books. And Hatty Jones—with her bright red hair, brighter brown eyes, and convincing way of dismissing problems with a toss of

CREDITS

Madeline: Hatty Jones
Miss Clavel: Frances McDormand
Lord Covington: Nigel Hawthorne
Lady Covington: Stephane Audran
Leopold the Tutor: Ben Daniels
Mr. Spanish Ambassador: Arturo Venegas
Pepito: Kristian de la Osa
Mrs. Spanish Ambassador: Katia Caballero

Origin: USA
Released: 1998
Production: Saul Cooper, Pancho Kohner, and Allyn Stewart; released by TriStar Pictures
Direction: Daisy von Scherler Mayer
Screenplay: Mark Levin and Jennifer Flackett; based on the book by Ludwig Bemelmans
Cinematography: Pierre Aim
Editing: Jeffrey Wolf
Music: Michel Legrand
Production design: Hugo Luczyc-Wyhowski
Costumes: Michael Clancy
Art direction: Betrand Clercq-Roques, Gerard Drolon, Rebecca Holmes
Sound: Michel Kharat
MPAA rating: PG
Running Time: 90 minutes

REVIEWS

Entertainment Weekly. July 17, 1998, p. 61.
Los Angeles Times. July 10, 1998, p. F10.
New York Times. February 18, 1998, p. AR 11.
New York Times. July 10, 1998, p. E18.
People. July 13, 1998, p. 32.
Time. July 13, 1998.
Variety. July 13, 1998, p. 54.
Village Voice. July 28, 1998, p. 115.
Washington Post Weekend. July 10, 1998, p. 42.

her head and a pronounced "Pooh, pooh!"—makes a marvelous Madeline. Her co-stars, too, lend *Madeline* credibility. Frances McDormand is so sweetly satisfying as Miss Clavel that one does not stop to ask how a single nun has come to run a boarding school—let alone why a nun should be called "Miss Clavel." And Nigel Hawthorne performs excellently well as the curmudgeon with a heart of gold. But when the film ends and the credits once again roll against a backdrop of only slightly animated pictures taken from Madeline's more bookish adventures, one cannot help but sigh about what has been lost in translation.

—*Lisa Paddock*

Mafia!; Jane Austen's Mafia!

Murder. Romance. Family. Sheep.—Movie tagline

Box Office: $19,889,299

Audiences have come to expect great comedy from Jim Abrahams. As one third of the ZAZ team that also included Jerry and David Zucker, the trio made their name with such groundbreaking comedies as *Airplane!* (1980), *The Naked Gun* (1988) and the comedy series *Police Squad!* (1982), which spoofed the disaster and detective film genres respectively. Even when Abrahams broke off into a solo act he kept the comedies coming with *Hot Shots!* (1991) and *Hot Shots! Part Deux* (1993), parodies of the Rambo-type war films.

But just as Mel Brooks's quintessential parodies (*Blazing Saddles, Young Frankenstein* (1974), *High Anxiety* (1977) gave way to weaker attempts (who can remember *Robin Hood, Men in Tights?* [1993]), so it now seems that Abrahams, too, is finding his spoofs running out of gas. With *Mafia!* (formerly known as *Jane Austen's Mafia!*) audiences may find a smile or two, but there are few surprises and even fewer outright laughs.

Mafia! is Abrahams's attempt to parody all the many recent films featuring the Italian mob. From Francis Ford Coppola's trio of *Godfather* films through Martin Scorsese's *Goodfellas* (1990) and *Casino* (1995), heaven knows there's a ripe genre for lampooning out there. Unfortunately, like a cross-eyed hit man, *Mafia!* only hits its target occasionally.

Mafia! begins with a take-off on the car bomb explosion from *Casino* with Anthony Cortino (Jay Mohr), whose character is really more of a take on Al Pacino's in the *Godfather,* flying through the explosive air à la Dorothy in the *Wizard of Oz* (1939) as cows and Frisbees make an incongruous appearance. From there we flash back into several different time frames. In one we see Tony as the successful manager of the Peppermill Casino in Las Vegas. In the next it's 1910 Sicily where a young and bumbling Vincenzo Cortino gets himself and his family in such trouble during the Festival of the Day the Olives Turn Black that he has to swim to America having missed his boat, the *Il Pacino.*

We follow this second story for a while as Vincenzo arrives at Ellis Island and an immigration officer almost gives him the name sewn into his clothes, Armani Windbreaker. We see him meet his future wife Rosa and then we flash-forward to the Depression–era New York in which Tony and his brother are raised.

Soon we are back in "the present" at the wedding of the Vincenzo's (Lloyd Bridges) eldest son, the psychotic Joey (Billy Burke). Arriving at the wedding is Anthony, just home from the Korean War, and his WASP girlfriend Diane (Christina Applegate). During the wedding Don Vincenzo is shot and the story now twists into revenge and control of the family.

There are some funny things in this film, many of them part of the stacked jokes the ZAZ team is known for. This refers to the layers of comic items in a scene, many of which are not part of the main action but can be found in the background. For example, while the characters undertake their performances in the casino, we suddenly notice that the games are not the normal ones, but are all from our childhood: Chutes and Ladders, Go Fish, Candyland, and Guess the Number. Even

Diane (Christina Applegate): "I don't belong, Anthony. I'm always just going to be that Protestant chick who never killed anyone!"

The old world of Sicily was filmed at a Tuscan-style villa in Rancho Palos Verde in California.

the ATM machines in the casino are aimed at gambling, and all the slot machines have titles like "Kiss your money goodbye" and "Last red cent." Not a source of belly laughs, but the layered funny business is worth several smiles.

However, there are a lot of unfunny things in *Mafia!* too. Perhaps the worst of these takes place during the parody of the *Godfather*'s famous "baptism by fire" in which the Al Pacino/Jay Mohr characters exact their revenge on their rivals. In this send-up a little child is attacked by *Jurassic Park*–style raptors and a casino boss is beheaded by a flabby and fleet-footed Irish dancer. These are amusing, but when

a fickle girlfriend is torched to death by a farting grandmother played by the esteemed Olympia Dukakis, it's unredeemingly over-the-top.

Most of the actors do a decent job playing their parts with their tongues firmly planted in their cheeks, but of special note is Jay Mohr who is best known for his turns in *Jerry Maguire* (1996) and *Picture Perfect* (1997). He is adept at delivering his dialogue with just the right amount of seriousness amidst the humor. Sadly, *Mafia!* also marks the final screen appearance of veteran actor Lloyd Bridges who died March 10, 1998.

As usual with a ZAZ, and Abrahams' film, the credits are there to be read for the fun of it. Here they not only offer follow-ups on the careers of the main characters but also, as usual, hidden into the normal credits are some "fun facts" and other strange trivia.

In the end, as much as the Mafia genre is perfect for parody, it is a shame that this weak entry can't do more with the overemotional and melodramatic world of murder and family loyalty that is the film genre so beloved by Coppola and Scorsese. And where's the parody of the character Joe Pesci usually plays in these type of films? If ever an actor's onscreen persona was begging for a lampoon, it's that one. But even that probably wouldn't have lifted *Mafia!* out of the realm of the amusing and into the world of the truly hilarious.

—*Beverley Bare Buehrer*

CREDITS

Don Vincenzo Cortino: Lloyd Bridges
Anthony Cortino: Jay Mohr
Sophia Corino: Olympia Dukakis
Diane: Christina Applegate
Joey Cortino: Billy Burke
Pepper: Pamela Gidley
Marzoni: Tony Lo Bianco

Origin: USA
Released: 1998
Production: Bill Badalato for Tapestry Films; released by Touchstone Pictures
Direction: Jim Abrahams
Screenplay: Jim Abrahams, Greg Norberg, Michael McManus
Cinematography: Pierre Letarte
Editing: Terry Stokes
Production design: William Elliott
Art direction: Greg Papalia
Sound: David Ronne
Costumes: Mary Malin
Visual effector supervision: Sam Nicholson
Music: Gianni Frizzelli
MPAA rating: PG-13
Running Time: 86 minutes

REVIEWS

Chicago Sun Times. July 24, 1998.
Chicago Tribune. July 24, 1998, p. 5.
Entertainment Weekly. July 31, 1998, p. 48.
Los Angeles Times. July 24, 1998, p. F8.
New York Times. July 24, 1998, p. E14.
People. August 3, 1998, p. 29.
USA Today. July 23, 1998.
Variety. July 27, 1998, p. 52

Major League: Back to the Minors; Major League III

They're just nine players short of a dream team.—Movie tagline

Major League: Back to the Minors finds Gus Cantrell (Scott Bakula), a veteran minor league ballplayer, on the horns of a dilemma that is all too familiar with fans of this franchise. He is aging, tired, and finds that he is huffing and puffing to keep up with the younger players. He has a loving and supportive girlfriend, Maggie Reynolds (Jensen Daggett), but he plans to retire from baseball at the end of the season and enter into a completely different field.

Enter Roger Dorn (Corbin Bernsen), a smooth-talking baseball tycoon. Not only does Roger own the Minnesota Twins, who are managed by the gratingly obnoxious Leonard Huff (Ted McGinley), he owns a small minor league team in South Carolina called the Buzz. Roger talks Gus into coaching the Buzz for a week or two, to give them the benefit of his knowledge and years on the field. With the vow to leave in a month if he can't take it anymore, Gus is dispatched to Buzz headquarters to meet the team.

Former Los Angeles Dodger catcher Steve Yeager served as baseball consultant.

The team is indeed in desperate need of guidance, populated by a catcher who routinely overthrows into parking lots, an ex-ballet dancer who leaps across the field, an over-the-hill outfielder, and a self-styled therapist outfielder who analyzes everyone's fielding faults and relates it to childhood trauma. The only player that stands out is Downtown Anderson (Walt Goggins), a kid with a killer swing, but a massive ego to go along with it.

Writer/Director John Warren gets warm performances out of these characters—clichés though they may be. The team is bolstered by the addition of previous Major League characters Pedro Cerrano (Dennis Haysbert) and Taka Tanaka (Takaaki Ishibashi). When the team shapes up and actually almost beats the major league Minnesota Twins (losing due to a cheating move by Huff), they form a cohesive unit that is more than its separate parts. The main theme Gus stresses to his men is that they need to work together—it's not a one-man show. Twins' coach Huff steals Downtown Anderson to get back at Gus, whereupon Gus challenges Huff to a year's worth of his (Gus') salary or Huff's coaching job if the Twins can beat the Buzz—fair and square.

The die is cast and the teams assemble at Buzz's home field. Downtown Anderson joins them who, much like Gus predicted, was drummed out of the Twins' organization when he choked under pressure . Gus's guys prevail and they beat Huff's team to the wild cheers of the Buzz fans. When Roger tries to appoint Gus to Huff's position as coach of a Major League team, Gus demurs. He has finally found his home, his true stomping ground. He tells Roger that he has a lot of knowledge to impart to young players; he is of better use and happier in the minors.

Production values are uniformly good (cinematographer Tim Suhrstedt brings a warm glow to the most American of sports—and shows unique vantage points of the baseball itself). This is a pleasant ensemble comedy that makes the case for loving the sport of baseball for the character-building experience that our parents and coaches told us it would be.

—G. E. Georges

CREDITS

Gus Cantrell: Scott Bakula
Pops Morgan: Thom Barry
Roger Dorn: Corbin Bernsen
Leonard Huff: Ted McGinley
Maggie Reynolds: Jensen Daggett
Pedro Cerrano: Dennis Haysbert
Downtown Anderson: Walt Goggins
Hog Ellis: Judson Mills

Origin: USA
Released: 1998
Production: James G. Robinson for Morgan Creek; released by Warner Bros.
Direction: John Warren
Screenplay: John Warren
Cinematography: Tim Suhrstedt
Editing: O. Nicholas Brown, Bryan H. Carroll
Production design: David Crank
Music: Robert Folk
Costumes: Mary MacLeod
Sound: Carl S. Rudisill
MPAA rating: PG-13
Running Time: 102 minutes

REVIEWS

Chicago Tribune. April 23, 1998, p. 4.
Entertainment Weekly. May 1, 1998, p. 42.
New York Times. April 18, 1998, p. B16.
People. May 4, 1998, p. 32.
Variety. April 20, 1998, p. 43.

The Man in the Iron Mask

For the honor of a king. And the destiny of a country.—Movie tagline

"A great action adventure with a once in a life-time cast."—Kyle Osborne, *ABC-TV*

"Leonardo DiCaprio delivers a dazzling duet of performances."—Jeanne Wolf, *Jeanne Wolf's Hollywood*

"So much testosterone, so little time!"—Bonnie Churchill, *National News Syndicate*

" . . . Call it the Heartthrob in the Iron Mask."—David Ansen, *Newsweek*

"All for fun, and fun for all!"—Leah Rozen, *People*

 Box Office: $56,968,169

Leonardo DiCaprio has a dual role as the arrogant King Louis and his imprisoned twin Philippe in the lush retelling of Alexandre Dumas's *The Man in the Iron Mask.*

The *Man in the Iron Mask* offers Leonardo DiCaprio's fans a double helping of the beautiful lad whose role in *Titanic* (1997) helped that film become the biggest moneymaker in cinema history. Writer-director Randall Wallace has reconstituted Alexandre Dumas's classic to give DiCaprio maximum camera exposure as both King Louis and identical twin Philippe. DiCaprio's young fans, who go back again and again just to drool over him, will undoubtedly make *The Man in the Iron Mask* a financial success even though reviews were inauspicious. Siskel and Ebert gave it two thumbs down. Janet Maslin wrote in the *New York Times* that the dialogue is wooden and the movie is "one of [DiCaprio's] most ill-advised film projects," while conceding that he has "a physical beauty that reduces the camera to one more worshipful fan." As Louis XIV, DiCaprio is showcased in golden finery, surrounded by opulence, and deliberately cast with aging male actors who only make the star's youthful beauty more striking by contrast.

At the same time, the seasoned supporting actors buttress DiCaprio's still shaky dramatic talents. When he appears with any of the four musketeers he looks like a kid who has been called to the principal's office. Gerard Depardieu could never have competed with DiCaprio in a beauty contest, but the veteran French actor's presence is more than welcome to viewers who are not as captivated by the hordes of teenyboppers who have never heard of Depardieu. The

King Louis (Leonardo DiCaprio): "He's my twin. A fact which has kept him alive until now."

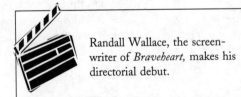

Randall Wallace, the screenwriter of *Braveheart,* makes his directorial debut.

same is true of John Malkovich as the world-weary Athos, Jeremy Irons as the devout Aramis, and Gabriel Byrne as the fourth musketeer D'Artagnan. These professionals give the film a seriousness and dignity it would otherwise have lacked.

Athos and Porthos are living in retirement. Aramis, true to his intellectual nature, has become a Jesuit priest and spends his time in prayer. Porthos spends his time drinking and chasing women. Athos' sole interest is his young son Raoul (Peter Sarsgaard), who wants to become a musketeer. Raoul is engaged to the beautiful Christine (Judith Godreche) but makes the mistake of bringing her to a royal garden party. The lecherous, imperious King Louis starts a train of events that will lead to his downfall by sending Raoul off to the battlefield. When Christine learns Raoul has been killed, she becomes the King's mistress.

Athos, who despises Louis already, is enraged when he receives word of his son's death. He suspects the King's ulterior motives. Aramis and Porthos agree to help him take revenge—and Aramis knows just how to do it. They will free the man in the iron mask and place him on the throne. Their former comrade D'Artagnan represents a serious obstacle as the only person besides Aramis who knows the King's twin is still alive. It was D'Artagnan who took Philippe at birth and placed him in a humble home to be raised in obscurity. The former king, Louis XIII, feared that twin sons competing for the crown would create interminable civil strife. When Louis become King Louis XIV, however, he had Philippe confined to the Bastille, where the poor lad has worn his iron mask for six years with no idea of why he is being punished. Athos, Porthos, and Aramis have a series of adventures and misadventures before they achieve their goal.

There is surprisingly little sword fighting in the film. Depardieu should have known how to fence, since he starred as the super-swordsman/poet in *Cyrano de Bergerac* (1990). And Malkovich engaged in a harrowing fencing duel in *Dangerous Liaisons* (1988). There is a great deal of brandishing of swords in *The Man in the Iron Mask* but not a single sustained duel or one of those swashbuckling scenes in which a musketeer takes on four or five swordsmen and defeats them all. Instead, the musketeers hurl the king's men against walls and into moats, bash them with furniture and assorted bric-a-brac, and knock them out with gloved fists. When one of the musketeers uses a sword, he always seems to pink his opponent in the shoulder (which by cinematic convention symbolizes *hors de combat* but not mortally wounded). D'Artagnan still has his legendary skill with a sword but uses it to slice an apple in half while it is sailing through the air and then to catch another flying apple on the tip of his blade.

Starving Parisians are storming the palace because King Louis has been sending all available food to troops fighting another of his senseless wars. Rioters throw rotten food at D'Artagnan, who has come out to confront them single-handedly. He promises he will persuade Louis to relieve their plight. D'Artagnan, captain of the King's guard and his most trusted advisor, is the only one at court who can do anything with the headstrong, philandering young monarch. On another occasion, D'Artagnan proves his phenomenal loyalty as well as his uncanny skill with his sword by throwing it an incredible distance over end and wounding the king's would-be assassin in the shoulder. (After the King gets through with him off camera, however, the poor fellow might wish D'Artagnan's sword had been better aimed.)

There may have been several reasons why the filmmakers decided to downplay the kind of fencing that was once an indispensable part of Hollywood films of this genre—such as *The Count of Monte Cristo* (1934), *The Prisoner of Zenda* (1937), and the 1939 version of *The Man in the Iron Mask*. Writer-director Wallace may have felt that exciting fencing scenes would distract attention from DiCaprio, who is showcased throughout like a jewel on a velvet cloth. Wallace may have feared that too much impaling and bloodshed would jeopardize the film's innocuous PG-13 rating. He may have been thinking about the all-important videotape receipts in the future. Parents with very young children shy away from overly violent features. Rita Kempley, who reviewed the film for *The Washington Post*, called

it a "less-than-rollicking adaptation" and complained that "derring is long overdue."

The Man in the Iron Mask is one of those new-type non-violent violent films in which there is much combat but nobody gets killed—at least on camera. Another of the many recent examples is *Batman and Robin* (1997), in which Mr. Freeze's victims only get frozen and then presumably thawed out. Is this kind of non-violent film violence better or worse than the old-fashioned kind? Does the more innocuous brand of violence give impressionable young minds the notion that people who get shot and stabbed in real life are not seriously hurt? The recent rash of schoolyard shootings and other shocking murders by children suggests that possibility.

Wallace may have been thinking that he did not want DiCaprio, whose face is his fortune, to run even the slightest risk of having that face injured by a blade. When DiCaprio handles a sword it is only as Philippe, the King's twin. The Dumas story provided the perfect gimmick for the adaptor: Philippe never gets near a sword except when his face is protected by that famous iron mask. DiCaprio's use of a sword is only symbolic. When Philippe is permitted to join the four musketeers in their familiar pledge of "One for all, and all for one," all five men point their crossed blades discreetly at the floor.

CREDITS

King Louis/Philippe: Leonardo DiCaprio
Aramis: Jeremy Irons
Athos: John Malkovich
Porthos: Gerard Depardieu
D'Artagnan: Gabriel Byrne
Queen Anne: Anne Parillaud
Christine: Judith Godreche
Lieutenant Andre: Edward Atterton
Raoul: Peter Sarsgaard

Origin: USA
Released: 1998
Production: Randall Wallace and Russell Smith; released by United Artists
Direction: Randall Wallace
Screenplay: Randall Wallace; based on the novel by Alexandre Dumas
Cinematography: Peter Suschitzky
Editing: William Hoy
Music: Nick Glennie-Smith
Production design: Anthony Pratt
Art direction: Francois de Lamothe, Albert Rajau
Costumes: James Acheson
Sound: David A. Stephenson
MPAA rating: PG-13
Running Time: 132 minutes

Even when the story ends, with Philippe on the throne and Louis screaming his head off in the Bastille and wearing that loathsome mask, there is a disclaimer to soft-pedal the horror of the musketeer's retribution. It is explained that Philippe, now King Louis XIV, eventually pardoned his brother and allowed him to live out his days in peaceful rural seclusion. In the meantime Philippe became France's great Sun King, patron of the arts and protector of the people.

Wallace's version of *The Man in the Iron Mask* represents a "feminization" of the genre. There is a great emphasis on lovemaking, on costumes and dancing, and on women's emotions, including those of the Queen Mother (Anne Parillaud), who grieves over the twin she believes died at birth and is overjoyed when she learns he is alive. If this feminization represents a definite Hollywood trend, acknowledging the boxoffice clout of modern women, it might be a risky one. DiCaprio may be able to carry such a film on the basis of his looks and charisma, but genres are genres because they contain certain essential ingredients. A sword-fighting picture without sword fighting is like a musical comedy without music, or a western without horses—or a Dumas adventure without plenty of bloodshed.

Perhaps the most interesting aspect of the film is its challenge to DiCaprio. As Todd McCarthy of *Variety* put it, "DiCaprio's presence assures a strong opening, and it will be interesting to see how far the film can travel in the wake of *Titanic*." DiCaprio does not have a $200 million budget behind him this time, but *The Man in the Iron Mask* is lavishly produced and bolstered by a brilliant international cast. As the *San Francisco Chronicle* stated, this "separated-at-birth yarn ... is handsome throughout, with gorgeous French settings and lush period costumes. The grandiose architecture, gilded ornamentation and fancy clothes play well—especially in the grand ball scene—against the burning emotions and betrayals at the heart of the story."

—*Bill Delaney*

REVIEWS

Chicago Tribune. March 13, 1998, p. 4.
Entertainment Weekly. March 20, 1998, p. 55.
Los Angeles Times. March 13, 1998, p. F1.
New York Times. March 13, 1998, p. B12.
People. March 23, 1998, p. 23.
San Francisco Chronicle. March 13, 1998, p. C1.
Sight and Sound. April, 1998, p. 43.
USA Today. March 13, 1998, p. 8D.
Variety. March 16, 1998, p. 63.
Village Voice. March 24, 1998, p. 112.
Washington Post. March 13, 1998, p. C1.

Marie Baie des Anges; Marie from the Bay of Angels; Angel Sharks

"A hot ticket!"—*Entertainment Weekly*

"Pulsates with raw intensity!"—Anthony Kauffmann, *Indie Magazine*

"A *Breathless* for 1998!"—*Interview*

"Beautiful and exasperating."—Chuck Wilson, *LA Weekly*

"Gorgeous! A dizzying paganistic ode to Eros. A movie that celebrates the raw sexual energy of adolescence."—Stephen Holden, *New York Times*

Pradal's debut feature of teenage lust gone wrong is a visually stunning nod to Godard and the French New Wave with little heart and less heat as his two neophyte leads, Vahina Giocante (Marie) and Frederic Malgras (Orso), blandly go through the motions of falling passionately in love (or something similar) while unknowingly provoking dire consequences. Pradal discovered his young stars while combing the streets and beaches of France and they do their best, looking good in front of the camera and offering up a certain authentic appeal, but hardly injecting the real spark necessary to match the rest of a fine cinematic package and leaving only the dreamily photographed landscapes to keep the narrative alive.

The French Riviera is the playground for Pradsl's group of Gallic teenage delinquents who drink, smoke, thieve, and Vespa their way through the gorgeous scenery without leaving much of a lasting impression on the audience or, apparently, each other as evidenced by the resident vixen of the tribe, Marie, who flits from her scooter riding boyfriend to any of the various convertible driving American sailors and back again. In the midst of these adventures, Marie then meets Orso. Malgras's Orso is a stoic rebel with a genuine hard-edged glare that hints of a troubled background. This appeals to the precocious, impetuous Marie who strives for maturity, searching for whatever is just beyond her reach. Marie, however, treats Orso casually at first, trying to maintain her status with the U.S. sailors who definitely appreciate her jail-bait efforts at entertaining the troops.

Marie spends much of her time cavorting with the stereotypically drunk and droolingly horny American G.I.s, with the of exception one sympathetic fellow who feels sorry for Marie and when the rest of the boys grow bored and desert her, this lone soldier, in a surreal turn, begins to dance for the lonely girl à la Gene Kelly. Sensing her days with the lads are numbered, Marie turns more of her amorous attentions to her sullen, adolescent paramour Orso. Orso, meanwhile, has been spending his days robbing tourists, getting arrested, becoming incarcerated in a juvenile home, and later making a daring escape back to the beach where Marie and the rest of the juves hang out.

The story plays out in a non-linear style, now jumping to Orso's attempts to obtain a gun from a mysterious seller in some remote woods, then back to Marie swimming in the local Bay of the Angels (named after the Angel Sharks that used to swim there) with her G.I. friends, then back to

Orso in another unknown location, snooping around the elegant home of an older mystery woman (his mother?) who is attending a funeral. The editing and style of this collage is engaging and adds to an unspoken secret that is never revealed. The depth of the film can be found more in the style than the actual events, which take a dramatic turn when Orso and Marie escape the daily ennui of their everyday lives and steal away to a remote island. Here their love is the only thing going and the island becomes their Eden until the restless Orso manages to get his hands on a gun and things take a grim turn in his naive efforts to provide for his new woman. Before this somewhat artificial attempt at reaching a denouement, the film skims along as lightly and dreamily as its story, unforced and engaging. It seems unmotivated that the characters that have been on screen all this time would really want to do anything at all, barring sex, drugs, and rock and roll.

Although teenage rebellion and violence is no longer shocking film fodder, it seems that Pradal found it necessary to find a harder edge in his characters than mere petty crime and illicit sex, although in the era of the brutally realistic *Kids* (1995), *Marie* comes off looking like a quaint throwback to kinder, gentler times. *Marie*'s actual appeal lies in the unspoken mystery of it all. Beauty and mystery is what essentially drive the film and keep it from losing its steam, even with a certain predictability in the turn of events. Worthy, if only for a certain directorial gloss and Christophe Pollock's cinematographic mastery.

—Hilary Weber

CREDITS

Marie: Vahina Giocante
Orso: Frederic Malgras

Origin: France
Released: 1997
Production: Philippe Rousselet; released by Sony Pictures Classics
Direction: Manuel Pradal
Screenplay: Manuel Pradal
Cinematography: Christophe Pollock
Editing: Valerie Deseine
Costumes: Claire Gerard-Hime
Music: Carlo Crivelli
Production design: Javier Po
MPAA rating: R
Running Time: 90 minutes

REVIEWS

Boxoffice. April, 1998, p. 198.
Chicago Tribune. September 4, 1998, p. 5.
Los Angeles Times. July 3, 1998, p. F6.
New York Times. June 19, 1998, p. E13.
Sight and Sound. December, 1998, p. 40.

Marius and Jeannette;
Marius et Jeannette: Un Conte de L'Estaque

"Warm-hearted! Uplifting! It radiates a glow."
—Stephen Holden, *New York Times*

Director/co-writer Guediguian sets his latest of seven films in his favorite venue and hometown, working-class Marseilles, and creates a touching and socially relevant love story about two of its middle-aged residents, Marius and Jeannette. Acting like a "Greek chorus," in Guediguian's words, is the bustling world of the surrounding community, where animated neighbors still gather in the courtyard to argue and discuss politics, marriage, and each other and it also serves as the platform for the director's own opinions. Whether or not one shares these views, Guediguian's frequent explorations of the setting and its people are obvious in the richness of characters and delight in the material.

Jeannette (Ariane Ascaride) is a once widowed and once divorced fortyish cashier at a supermarket trying to raise her two children, Magali (Laetitia Pesenti) and Malek (Milou Nacer). Opinionated and strong from all the hardships she has had to overcome, Jeannette's sudden outburst of temper shouted through the intercom at the check-out counter berating her bosses, costs her her job. Ascaride, the director's wife who has appeared in all his films, injects a vitality and realism in the character, whom she had a hand in creating.

Marius (Gerard Meylan), who created a fake limp to gain employment, works as a security guard at a condemned cement factory. He meets up with a desperate Jeannette, who breaks into the factory to steal a few gallons of paint to redecorate her dismal flat. Marius feels sorry for her and decides to let her off the hook, not calling the police, and amused that afterward she calls him a fascist and tries to convince him to let her take the paint, anyway. He refuses, but later arrives with cans in hand at her apartment, offering to do the job himself. It's clear a love connection has been achieved.

Jeannette's neighbors are as interested in making a match as the couple themselves, and encourage Jeannette as Marius begins his courtship. Jeannette's fear of intimacy after her losses make it difficult for Marius, as she fights her attraction to him. Also keeping them apart is the fact the Jeannette has not had a physical relationship with a man in eight years. Eventually, however, they become close and Marius moves in with Jeannette and her little family. Later, though, Marius inexplicably abandons his new love and his new home due to some secret from his past that causes him to start drinking heavily. The reason for Marius's flight is later revealed in a badly staged barroom brawl that falls flat on its face in this subtle, character-driven film.

Jeannette's neighbors, at this point, intervene and seek to reunite the troubled couple. Among the neighborhood gang another love story emerges, mirroring the main one, when the retired teacher Justin (Jacques Boudet) and the older Caroline (Pascale Roberts), a survivor of a German detention camp, have dinner together in a very touching scene. Another neighbor is a worker (Jean-Pierre Darroussin) who is constantly harassed by his wife for once voting for the National Front. These subplots make for amusing and revealing insight into the main characters' motivations and the character of the city as a whole.

Originally created for television with a relatively low budget ($1 million), the film then became the official selection for the Cannes Film Festival. The deft leads, supporting cast, and clear direction make it obvious why it was chosen Best French Film of the Year by the Foreign Press in Paris and nominated for seven Cesars (the French Oscars), including a win for Best Actress by Ascaride. Her performance is especially a standout, giving life to a real character with who is able to meet life's challenges head-on with a toughness that doesn't completely harden her to the possibilities of romance. Jeannette, throughout the story, loses some of her characteristic grit, possibly under the warming influence of her new relationship, bringing her new hope.

The story in *Marius and Jeannette* are its characters, who all have hardships and struggle daily to make ends

CREDITS

Marius: Gerard Meylan
Caroline: Pascale Roberts
Justin: Jacques Boudet
Monique: Frederique Bonnal
Dede: Jean-Pierre Darroussin

Origin: France
Released: 1997
Production: Gilles Sandoz for Agat Films, Le Sept Cinema, and Canal Plus; released by New Yorker Films
Direction: Robert Guediguian
Screenplay: Robert Guediguian and Jean-Louis Milesi
Cinematography: Bernard Cavalie
Editing: Bernard Sasia
Art direction: Karim Hamzaoui
Sound: Laurent Lafran
Production design: Malek Hamzaoui
MPAA rating: Unrated
Running Time: 102 minutes

meet, yet provide a more fertile ground for pure romance to find them than those with more bourgeois concerns. A more basic way of life, with less of the trappings that keep people apart is portrayed to be a more natural and, perhaps, preferable way of life. Certainly it seems to be a more caring way of life.

—*Hilary Weber*

REVIEWS

Boxoffice. June, 1998, p. 77.
Los Angeles Times. June 19, 1998, p. F13.
New York Times. April 24, 1998, p. E21.
Sight and Sound. December, 1997, p. 46.
Variety. May 26, 1997, p. 69.
Village Voice. April 28, 1998, p. 75.

The Mask of Zorro

"Great fun! I loved it! Anthony Hopkins has got to be one of the best actors ever!"—Joel Siegel, *Good Morning America*

"Antonio Banderas in a role he was born to play! Catherine Zeta-Jones plays her role so show-stoppingly that the film's appeal extends well beyond action adventure."—Janet Maslin, *New York Times*

"This is one crowd-pleaser that actually pleases!"—David Ansen, *Newsweek*

"High romance, pure ideals and dashing heroism!"—Richard Schickel, *Time*

"A gift from the movie gods!"—Joe Morgenstern, *Wall Street Journal*

Box Office: $93,715,262

Antonio Banderas dons the black mask and brandishes the sword to protect a Mexican town from a greedy land developer in *The Mask of Zorro*.

Everyone knows Señor Zorro, but apparently few reviewers knew his background and history. Zorro was born in August of 1919 when journalist-turned-novelist Johnston McCulley first created him in "The Curse of Capistrano," published in five installments in *All-Story Weekly* as a sort of colonial Spanish-American Robin Hood, fighting for justice in California between 1775 and 1800. By day he was the mild-mannered Don Diego Vega, by night the mysterious caped crusader, a masked vigilante who was the scourge of corrupt politicians.

MCulley's friend of the oppressed first slashed his way across the screen in *The Mark of Zorro* (1920), directed by Fred Niblo, but it was Douglas Fairbanks, Sr. in his first costume role who set the comic-acrobatic style for the masked avenger. McCulley's Zorro wore a black mask and a purple

Zorro (Anthony Hopkins) referring to Alejandro's sword: "Do you know how to use that thing?" Alejandro (Antonio Banderas): "Pointy-end goes into other man."

cloak, but Fairbanks would appear to be costumed in all black in black-and-white silent cinema. The slashed "Z" and the foppish mannerisms of Don Diego were invented by Fairbanks, then appropriated by McCulley in his further Zorro stories. Of the later movie Zorros, the best was Tyrone Power, who inherited the role in the remake of *The Mark of Zorro*, directed by Rouben Mamoulian in 1940. Bob Kane admitted to Fairbanks scholar John Tibbetts in 1989 that he had modelled Batman partly on the image of Zorro—Bruce Wayne's double identity, the Batcave, the mask, and cape. Hence the popular image of Zorro throughout the century has been lasting and influential. Writing from a more ignorant perspective, *Philadelphia Inquirer* reviewer Steven Rea accused *The Mask of Zorro* of "borrowing" from the Batman formula ("Zorro's elaborate secret cave set-up"), when, in fact, it was the other way around!

Zorro was a swashbuckler waiting to be ressurrected, and by 1998 the resurrection was long overdue, when Antonio Banderas donned the costume for *The Mask of Zorro.* Although lacking the Fairbanks signature sense of humor, Banderas was impressive in his swordsmanship and feats of derring-do. He is also the paradigm of the Latin lover, making for an appealing characterization. The screenplay borrowed liberally from the Fairbanks features, especially from *Don Q, The Son of Zorro* (1925), in which Fairbanks played both Zorro and his son.

In *The Mask of Zorro,* the older Zorro is played by Anthony Hopkins, whose weapons, like Fairbanks's, are the sword and bullwhip; but in the later sequence the younger Zorro who inherits the cloak (Banderas) is not his biological son, but a peasant boy, Alejandro Murrieta, who has to learn Zorro's aristocratic manners as well as his riding and duelling skills. His motive is to avenge the death of his brother Joaquin (Victor Rivers), killed by an American renegade mercenary, Captain Harrison Love (Matthew Letscher).

The true Zorro (Hopkins) opens the action in the film's prologue when he rescues three randomly chosen peasants from the firing squad of Spanish Governor Don Rafael Montero (Stuart Wilson), the villain of the piece. Montero later tracks Zorro to his home, captures and imprisons him, kidnaps his infant daughter, and burns his hacienda. Montero is secretly in love with Zorro's wife, who is accidently shot and killed when Zorro is apprehended. Montero throws Zorro into prison, while he returns to Spain with Zorro's daughter.

Twenty years later Montero returns to California, intending to turn it into a Republic that he will rule. A grizzled, bearded Zorro escapes from prison and plots his revenge. He finds a younger ally in the Banderas character, whom he trains, so the two of them can work together against Montero and Love. Naturally, the younger man falls in love with Zorro's daughter Elena (Catherine Zeta-Jones), who eventually discovers the identity of her biological father and turns against her adopted father, thanks to her erstwhile nanny, Esperanza (Julieta Rosen), who recognizes Elena in the marketplace because the grown-up Elena resembles her mother.

Thus the film offers two heroes and two villains. The younger Zorro will avenge himself on Montero's American henchman, who wears a United States Cavalry uniform and seems to have been modelled on General George Armstrong Custer, flaxen-haired, ruthless, and dangerous, though his presence in the plot is never satisfactorily explained. He helps Montero exploit the masses through slave labor in a secret gold-mining operation that will provide the resources to fund their political ambitions. The final confrontation

> Swordmaster Robert Anderson has trained and doubled for leading action stars for 45 years, beginning with Errol Flynn, and he trained Anthony Hopkins, Antonio Banderas, and Catherine Zeta-Jones for this film.

takes place at the mine. The senior Zorro kills his adversary but dies himself after the fight, even though it is not immediately clear that he has been seriously wounded.

The film's stuntwork, coordinated by J. Mark Donaldson, is impressive, and the destruction of the gold mine is spectacular, but the action of the final confrontation is filmed awkwardly in a disjointed way. In *Don Q.* Fairbanks had father and son fighting back to back at the same time; but the crosscutting in *The Mask of Zorro* between the two conflicts—between the father and Montero and between the son and Captain Love—is not as seamlessly filmed as it might have been. Moreover, the elder Zorro only achieves his goal with difficulty. He seems far less effective in fighting the older Montero than when he fought the younger Zorro in the earlier training sessions. Of course, Banderas is the featured star, and he is not about to be upstaged by Hopkins.

The reviews were favorable, by and large, and in three weeks' time *The Mask of Zorro* had earned $62 million, covering most of its $70 million production budget. Though certainly nostalgic in its attempt to revive the old-fashioned swashbuckler, the Zorro formula has been effectively redesigned. *Kansas City Star* reviewer Robert W. Butler thought there was too much going on in this "slightly overcooked swashbuckler," including a touch of *My Fair Lady* as the aristocratic Zorro coaches the proletarian Alejandro, part *Rocky* as Alejandro learns how to duel, part family melodrama when Elena comes to realize that the servant "Bernardo" (the escaped Zorro's disguise) is actually her real father, and part *Lethal Weapon* in the film's explosive conclusion when the mine is dynamited. The screenplay steals shamelessly from several tried-and-true formulas in concocting an amusing summer entertainment that was bound to succeed at the boxoffice.

Only Steven Rea of *The Philadelphia Inquirer* attempted, feebly, to criticize the film, claiming that it lacked "an essential element of the swashbuckler: panache." If the swordplay resembles what viewers had already seen in the *Star Wars* trilogy, as Rea complained, it is clearly because consultant swordmaster Robert Anderson stood in for Darth Vader in that space epic. And surely the fact that Indiana Jones used a bullwhip was a gimmick stolen from the orig-

AWARDS AND NOMINATIONS

Academy Awards 1998 Nominations: Sound; Sound Effects Editing

inal Fairbanks Zorro. For *Newsweek*'s David Ansen, on the other hand, Banderas certainly did not lack "panache" but played the younger Zorro "with a delightful combination of dash and self-deprecating humor." Todd McCarthy of *Variety* was impressed by the way the picture "favors dashing adventure, intrigue, well-motivated characters and romance over fashionable cynicism, cheap gags and sensation for sensation's sake."

The often grumpy and sometimes cynical *Time* critic Richard Schickel, who wrote an excellent study of the Zorro character entitled *His Picture in the Papers: A Speculation on Celebrity in America, Based on the Life of Douglas Fairbanks, Sr.* (Charterhouse, 1974), praised *The Mask of Zorro* for its "high romance, pure ideals [and] dashing heroism." Schickel was impressed that this "summer action spectacle" saved "its only explosion until the end, where it has a genuine impact."

The Mask of Zorro effectively exploited a well-known mythic figure and an extraordinarily popular formula. Johnston McCulley went on to write sixty-four Zorro stories for pulp magazines as his own popularity fed off the tremendous popularity of matinee idol Douglas Fairbanks, Sr. during the 1920s. Republic Pictures went on to produce six Zorro pictures between 1936 and 1949. Almost forty Zorro pictures were made between 1952 and 1975, and many actors besides Fairbanks played the role: Tyrone Power, Guy Stockwell, Gordon Scott, Alain Delon, Frank Langella, and George Hamilton.

The studio's marketing strategy was calculatingly effective. Under its first working title *The Mark of Zorro*, the project was originally designed for Sean Connery and Andy Garcia under director Robert Rodriguez on the basis of his film *Desperado* (1996), according to *Entertainment Weekly* (May 15, 1995). In fact, the film was directed by New Zealander Martin Campbell, whose last picture was the James Bond thriller *Goldeneye* (1995), which grossed over $350 million worldwide and rejuvenated the Bond franchise for United Artists. At first the *Zorro* project was seen as a swashbuckler largely for adults, and according to *New York Times*'s James Sterngold this explains why the release was delayed. TriStar Pictures originally planned to release the film in the Christmas market of 1997, but the film was not ready because of production delays. It was to have been released during the spring of 1998, but test screenings indicated that it might have wider audience appeal than first believed. Though *The Mask of Zorro* was originally designed as an adult film, Robert Levin, president for worldwide marketing at Sony Pictures (the parent company of TriStar), concluded "It was a different kind of film than we expected." So the release was delayed until July, when school was out, in order to reach a more youthful audience. The strategy paid off brilliantly, since *The Mask of Zorro* proved to be the most entertaining film of the summer movie market.

—*James M. Welsh*

CREDITS

Alejandro Murrieta/Zorro: Antonio Banderas
Zorro/Don Diego de la Vega: Anthony Hopkins
Elena: Catherine Zeta-Jones
Don Rafael Montero: Stuart Wilson
Capt. Harrison Love: Matt Letscher
Prison Warden: Maury Chaykin
Don Luiz: Tony Amendola
Don Pedro: Pedro Armendariz
Three-Fingered Jack: L.Q. Jones
Espernaza: Julietta Rosen

Origin: USA
Released: 1998
Production: Doug Claybourne and David Foster for Amblin Entertainment; released by TriStar Pictures
Direction: Martin Campbell
Screenplay: John Eskow, Ted Elliott, and Terry Rossio
Cinematography: Phil Meheux
Editing: Thom Noble
Music: James Horner
Production design: Cecilia Montiel
Art direction: Michael Atwell
Set design: Noelle King
Costumes: Graciela Mazon
Sound: Pud Cusack
Swordmaster: Robert Anderson
MPAA rating: PG-13
Running Time: 136 minutes

REVIEWS

Boxoffice. April, 1998, p. 42.
Chicago Tribune. July 17, 1998, p. 4.
Entertainment Weekly. May 15, 1998, p. 49.
Entertainment Weekly. July 24, 1998, p. 50.
Kansas City Star Preview. July 17, 1998, p. 5.
New York Times. July 17, 1998, p. B12.
Newsweek. July 20, 1998, p. 66.
People. July 27, 1998, p. 35.
Philadelphia Inquirer Weekend. July 17, 1998, p. 3.
Sight and Sound. December, 1998, p. 48.
Time. July 20, 1998, p. 62.
Variety. June 29, 1998, p. 37.
Village Voice. July 21, 1998, p. 124.
Washington Post. July 17, 1998, p. B1.
Washington Post Weekend. July 17, 1998, p. 43.

Meet Joe Black

He's expecting you.—Movie tagline

Meet Joe Black: Sooner or later everyone does.
—Movie tagline

"A rich, compelling and extraordinary romance!"—Dennis Cunningham, *CBS*

"One of the year's most romantic and entertaining pictures!"—Gene Siskel, *Chicago Tribune*

"Brad Pitt lights up the screen! Anthony Hopkins has got to be one of the best actors ever. This movie will leave you with a lump in your throat"—Joel Siegel, *Good Morning America*

"Filled with deep emotion and romance!"—David Sheehan, *KCBS*

"Sensational! You'll love it! A moving emotion-filled experience."—Neil Rosen, *NY-1*

"A beautiful love story with a great cast! Brad Pitt is outstanding."—Jim Ferguson, *Prevue Channel*

"Two thumbs up!"—*Siskel & Ebert*

"A splendid . . . other worldly romance!"—Gene Shalit, *Today Show*

"*Meet Joe Black* is what great movies are all about! This movie is incredible."—Larry King, *USA Today*

Box Office: $43,240,705

Willliam Parrish (Anthony Hopkins) is a very, very, very wealthy businessman who has somehow retained his humanity. His opulent lifestyle—which includes a New York City penthouse, a huge waterside mansion, and a private helicopter to carry him between the two—is contrasted by his two doting daughters and the love they obviously feel for him. Parrish has everything . . . . and it appears he hasn't had to sell his soul to get it.

Bill (Anthony Hopkins) to Joe (Brad Pitt): "It's hard to let go, isn't it?" Joe: "Yes, Bill." Bill: "That's life, what more can I tell you?"

But early one morning, just days before his 65th birthday, Bill Parrish runs into a problem even his power and money can't solve. "This is the one situation you knew you never could handle," a disembodied voice softly whispers as Bill's heart pounds, his chest tightens, and his arm numbs. It is a warning of things to come, but Bill has a communications empire to run; mergers are in the offing. Who has time to stop for the inconveniences of a physical problem?

For that matter, who has time to watch a leisurely-paced, three-hour film about Bill's last hours on Earth? That's what director Martin Brest (*Scent of a Woman* [1992]) wants his audience to spend. For some, *Meet Joe Black* won't be a study in life vs. death, it won't be a romantic tale of loves lost and found, it will be an exercise in how long they can sit in a theater seat before fidgeting.

It's not that *Meet Joe Black* is a bad film; it's just that it's a slow film, evenly paced, luxuriant, indulgent. For those only willing to sit three hours for World War II battles or Titanic ship sinkings, this could be an ordeal. But for those who could spend ten times that long just staring at Brad Pitt as he reads a telephone directory, even three hours won't be enough.

Considering the fact that *Meet Joe Black* was inspired by the 1934 film *Death Takes a Holiday* (which itself was inspired by a 1920s stage play), one marvels at how Brest and his team of writers (perhaps too many writers!) transformed the original 78-minute film into a protracted study in reserve and pensiveness. There is no real dramatic arc in *Meet Joe Black*. It moves evenly from scene to scene, carrying the viewer along as if drifting down a lazy river with nary a bend nor a rapid in sight.

We flow along as Bill Parrish worries about his younger daughter Susan (Claire Forlani), a dedicated resident physician engaged to Bill's number two man, Drew (Jake Weber). As much as Bill must trust and like Drew, he fears he is not right for his daughter. "Love is passion, obsession, someone you can't live without," Bill tells his daughter. "There is no sense in living your life without this." And he frets that Drew doesn't do all this for Susan.

And Susan may be starting to believe this herself. Especially after a chance meeting in a coffee shop with a young lawyer (Brad Pitt) who has just moved to the city. He is lively and charming and the two just miss hitting it off right there and then. Perhaps the next time they meet at the coffee shop. But there will be no next time, for the young man is hit by a car as he turns to take one last look at the departing Susan.

Although Susan doesn't know the young man has been in an accident, imagine her surprise when that night at dinner she finds herself face-to-face with the young man again . . . except that he's not quite the same. Now he is stiff, hesitant, almost shy. He seems awkward in his own body, confused by even simple interactions with people. He is innocence and simplicity, and unlike the talkative lawyer she met earlier, he is almost hypnotically silent.

It appears the young man is a friend of her father's, but in reality it is just the young man's body she recognizes, for he no longer inhabits it, death does. In his wisdom, death has chosen Bill as the perfect person to explain life to him: "I chose you for your verve and excellence and ability to teach," he tells Bill. "Show me around, be my guide, and in return you get time." It is a deal Bill can't refuse.

So, death learns about the human love of life and how hard it is to let go of it. He learns this after tasting peanut butter for the first time and after falling in love with Susan. But if Bill wasn't sure of Susan's love of Drew, he's absolutely sure death, even though appealingly packaged as the coffee shop man and now named Joe Black, is not right for her.

The film's birthday party scene took 6 weeks to film, with the fireworks scene alone taking a week.

While all this is going on, Drew has used some offhanded remarks made by Bill's son-in-law, the guileless Quince (Jeffrey Tambor), to sabotage Bill's control of his own company, while Quince's wife, Bill's older daughter, the eager-to-please Allison (Marcia Gay Harden), plans her father's birthday party.

As improbable as Bill Parrish's character sounds (a gentle tycoon sounds like an oxymoron), Anthony Hopkins once again proves he is one of cinema's most gifted actors. Even as he knows he is dying, he is sympathetic without being maudlin and incredibly full of life. We like him despite his wealth, despite his power, and we are more than willing to believe he has no discernible character flaws.

Brad Pitt as death, however, is a bit more problematic. His dialogue is often almost laughable, but there's no denying his romantic appeal. One can almost hear an audible gasp from the women in the theater as Joe sheds tears after the tenderness of his first kiss with Susan.

But as integral as the characters and the plot are to this film, perhaps lending even more to its appeal and ambience is the way it looks. *Meet Joe Black* may be most memorable for its entire atmosphere: the stillness and mystery of death surrounded by the opulence and golden splendor of an almost cold wealth. Credit here belongs to production designer Dante Ferretti, a five-time Oscar nominee for such films as *Interview with the Vampire* (1994) and *Kundun* (1997).

For *Joe,* Ferretti created unprecedented visual affluence. The Parrish country manor was filmed at the Aldrich Mansion, a seventy-five-acre estate on Narragansett Bay in Rhode Island. The Parrish New York City penthouse, complete with swimming pool, however, was created in a National Guard Armory in the Park Slope section of Brooklyn. But whether borrowed or created, there's not a false note in the lavish settings. Each detail, from copies of master paintings on the walls to rare antique furniture, from cascading vases of fresh flowers to the leather-bound books filling cases in the libraries, all add credibility to the wealth and style of its owner.

Similarly, all the golden tones that highlight the gilt of Parrish's life are the handiwork of the director of photography Emmanuel Lubezki who, while receiving an Oscar nomination for *The Little Princess* (1995), is also well-known for creating more than his share of the mood in the steamy *Like Water for Chocolate* (1993). All of Parrish's wealth could have been cold to see, but by filming it in warm hues of grays and blues and tans, the penthouse has a warmth that matches Bill's soul.

What is created on the screen, both the love of life and the love of love, is why we humans are so reluctant to leave it, but eventually we all must. And as the baby boomers get closer to meeting their own Joe Blacks, films too are reflecting that preoccupation. (Witness the fact that this year also saw the release of *What Dreams May Come* and *Jack Frost*.)

So even after three hours of a story that could have greatly benefited by some tighter editing, it's a hard film to dislike. And even as we wonder where the young lawyer's soul has been all this time, or why his body isn't a bit more crumpled

CREDITS

Joe Black/Young Man in Coffee Shop: Brad Pitt
William Parrish: Anthony Hopkins
Susan Parrish: Claire Forlani
Drew: Jake Weber
Allison: Marcia Gay Harden
Quince: Jeffrey Tambor
Eddie Sloane: David S. Howard
Jamaican Woman: Lois Kelly-Miller

Origin: USA
Released: 1998
Production: Martin Brest for City Light Films; released by Universal Pictures
Direction: Martin Brest
Screenplay: Ron Osborn, Jeff Reno, Kevin Wade, Bo Goldman; suggested by the screenplay *Death Takes a Holiday* by Maxwell Anderson and Gladys Lehman; from the play by Alberto Casella, adapted by Walter Ferris
Cinematography: Emmanuel Lubezki
Editing: Michael Tronick, Joe Hutshing
Production design: Dante Ferretti
Art direction: Robert Guerra
Costumes: Aude Bronson-Howard, David C. Robinson
Music: Thomas Newman
MPAA rating: PG-13
Running Time: 154 minutes

after being hit by not one but two cars; and even as we question why Bill doesn't seek medical attention, or communicate more to all his loved ones; or even as we just try to imagine what we would do with just a few days' reprieve from death, one can't help but get caught up with the premise.

And in the end, we very much want to agree with the toast that Bill delivers at his 65th birthday party, with only a few minutes left of his life: "That you would have a life as lucky as mine. That you would wake up one morning not wanting anything more. Sixty-five years, don't they go by in a blink. No regrets, it's a good feeling, isn't it?"

—*Beverley Bare Buehrer*

REVIEWS

Chicago Sun-Times. November 13, 1998.
Chicago Tribune. November 13, 1998, p. 4.
Daily Variety. October 19, 1998, p. A12.
Entertainment Weekly. November 20, 1998, p. 89.
Los Angeles Times. November 13, 1998, p. F1.
New York Times. November 13, 1998, p. E14.
People. November 23, 1998, p. 33.
Sight and Sound. February, 1999, p. 48.
Variety. November 9, 1998, p. 30.

Meet the Deedles

To protect and surf.—Movie tagline
"You'll crave their wave! The most unlikely comic duo since Bill and Ted."—Jeanne Wolf, *Jeanne Wolf's Hollywood*

Box Office: $4,356,126

Every generation looks back on the things it found entertaining in earlier days and wonders, "how could I have ever been so foolish as to like *that*?" Most likely, people who ate goldfish in the Roaring '20s or dressed up in poodle skirts in the '50s laugh at themselves with the (supposed) wisdom of maturity. It is only with this kind of objectivity that one can enjoy the new film, *Meet the Deedles*. This is a solidly made film by director Steve Boyum; it is a notch above the absolute gross stupidity and foolishness of, say, *Dumb and Dumber* (1994) or anything made by Pauly Shore. Of course, it's hardly a Merchant/Ivory film.

That aside, it is innocuous, ingenuous, and actually kind of charming, if you look at it from the perspective of its target audience of teens. You are not likely to enjoy this film if you are over a certain age (somewhere around 15, perhaps, in 1998), but then, this film is not aimed at you if you are older than 15. The lesson here? If you go to *Meet the Deedles* and you don't like it, it's your own darn fault. Go back and watch reruns of *Laverne and Shirley* and you won't feel so smug.

The eponymous Deedles (how many reviews will give you an extravagant word as "eponymous" when referring to a film with the intellectual depth of a Post-it note?) are two brothers, Stew (Steve Van Wormer) and Phil (Paul Walker) Deedle of the Honolulu Deedles. Think of them as the Hardy boys, only they are shiftless, vapid, and have no sense of responsibility. Stew is the smart one, a computer hacker who always gets them out of scrapes with ingenious ideas. Phil is the cute one, who gets the girl in the film's finale.

The initial sequence gets right down to business, as the twin youths celebrate their birthday by breaking the law and damaging property in a drunken party, speaking in some language adults will not easily understand, though you might say their dialect is "fully rad." (One of the film's great lines is, "that idea is so ridiculous it's ri-ridiculous." You get the picture.) Anyway, it turns out that the boys are rich and spoiled by their widower father (Eric Braeden), the fabulously wealthy but busy papa Deedle. He decides to dump the boys for a summer, hoping that by sending them to a camp in Wyoming (Camp Broken Spirit), they will return as responsible adults. Unable to imagine spending time in a world without waves, the Deedle boys react as they react to most anything they don't like: they scream, with their mouths forming two round ovals creating enough sound to cover the landing of a DC-10.

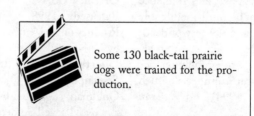

Some 130 black-tail prairie dogs were trained for the production.

In fact, screaming is a major dialogue component of the James Herzfeld and Dale Pollock screenplay. Urbane it ain't, with lines like "I crave your wave," and much yelling of the word "Deedles!" forming some of the more sophisticated of the verbiage. The story that interrupts these bon mots involves the boys' being mistaken for two new ranger recruits at Yellowstone National Park. They are mistakenly charged with ridding the park of a swarm of prairie dogs set upon the park by the villainous Frank Slater (Dennis Hopper), who plays a former ranger gone bad. (And somehow they pull it off.)

CREDITS

Stew Deedle: Steve Van Wormer
Phil Deedle: Paul Walker
Lt. Jesse Ryan: A. J. Langer
Capt. Douglas Pine: John Ashton
Frank Slater: Dennis Hopper
Elton Deedle: Eric Braeden
Nemo: Robert Englund

Origin: USA
Released: 1998
Production: Dale Pollock and Aaron Meyerson for DIC Entertainment and Peak Productions; released by Walt Disney Pictures
Direction: Steve Boyum
Screenplay: Jim Herzfeld and Dale Pollock
Cinematography: David Hennings
Editing: Alan Cody
Music: Steve Bartek
Production design: Stephen Storer
Art direction: Linden Snyder
Costumes: Alexandra Welker, Karyn Wagner
Sound: Kim B. Christenssen
MPAA rating: PG
Running Time: 92 minutes

Dennis Hopper, you ask? Well, that's just what it looks like Hopper is asking himself, appearing to wonder just what turn of events brought him to the first of what might be a Deedles franchise. Turning in a performance that seems as if he came to work, said "where do I stand?", and then asked for a paycheck.

The two boys are completely engaging, however, and they are effortless and believable in their slacker roles. They pull off the dumb moments, like stuffing their faces full of Twinkies, screaming while they are careening down a hill on skateboards, or wearing wet-suits in the Wyoming winter, with a free-spirited energy. Van Wormer carries the love scenes with sexy and winning A. J. Langer (as a young female ranger) with simplicity and charm. And John Ashcroft, known as the beleaguered cop from the *Beverly Hills Cop* series (1983, 1991), is as beleaguered and dependable as always.

Disney may not have made a classic with *Meet the Deedles*, but it's fun for the kids and isn't going to hurt anyone. Unless, of course, someone tries to find a shred of entertainment for the grown-ups. But to do such a thing would be so 'diculous' it would be 'ri-ridiculous.'

—Kirby Tepper

REVIEWS

Entertainment Weekly. April 3, 1998, p. 70.
Hollywood Reporter. March 24, 1998, p. 28.
Los Angeles Times. March 27, 1998, p. F14.
New York Times. March 27, 1998, p. E28.
People. April 13, 1998, p. 20.
Variety. March 30, 1998, p. 42.

Men

So many men. So little time.—Movie tagline

Men, directed by Zoe Clarke-Williams, is a misguided romantic-comedy-drama that attempts to illuminate the ineffable highs and lows of modern day relationships. Instead of offering subtle performances framed by a witty, insightful script, we are treated to a clunky, forced story that portrays no one involved—actors, writers or director—in a good light.

Stella James (Sean Young) is an aspiring chef who lives in New York City in a platonic co-habitation with her best friend Teo (Dylan Walsh). Teo is a mixed up rich kid, on the dole and miserable, who spends most of his time blind drunk. Despite Stella's exhortations to clean up, become useful, and enjoy life, Teo wallows in a most unattractive despair.

Stella decides to move to Los Angeles to both get away from Teo and to broaden her options as a chef. Once in Los Angeles, she quickly finds a home to share and finds a job in Babbington's, a restaurant owned by George (John Heard). Stella relishes her time in a new city; she is a free spirit who engages in many relationships—sexual and otherwise—with many men. In a narrative that's meant to be

Stella (Sean Young): "When—and if—does experience turn into understanding?"

pensive and thought-provoking but is merely cloying and annoying, Stella muses on the nature of love and its foibles. Meanwhile, she starts to sleep with her boss, George and, much to her dismay, he falls for her.

When Stella meets carefree photographer Frank (Richard Hillman), she surprisingly falls head over heels for him. He has long, blond hair and a disarming charm about him. Frank wants to be a professional photographer, and spends his spare time hanging out with gangs in poverty-stricken neighborhoods in order to capture their reality. Stella falls for his direct honesty and they soon embark on a wild, passionate affair, marked by bursts of deep, revelatory confessions. She takes comfort from Frank when she learns that Teo has died in New York.

Trouble erupts one night when Frank brings some of his friends over to dinner with Stella. Although Stella enjoys Alex (Karen Black), she has issues with some other women who flirt mercilessly with Frank. When Frank innocently returns another woman's affections, Stella experiences jealousy for the first time in her life. She runs from the party and spends the rest of the night perched on a hill, thinking.

Stella pledges her love to Frank, telling him that what she has found with him transcends any other relationship that she has had and that she wants to spend the rest of her life with him. All this comes to a tragic end when Frank is killed by a stray bullet from one of his photographic subjects.

Love stories are as old as the Greek myths and Shakespeare—the challenge is to create characters that seem real, true to their selves and show the joy and pain of mere existence. This story fails to rise above the level of the most banal television movie, with glaring clichés abounding, left and right. Sean Young seems to be sleepwalking through this film, with almost no inflection in her voice at any time. John Heard is a terrific actor, but totally wasted here. *Men* fails to exhibit even the slightest quality to amuse, entertain, or move one to muse over their own love life.

—*G. E. Georges*

CREDITS

Stella James: Sean Young
George Babbington: John Heard
Teo Morrison: Dylan Walsh
Frank: Richard Hillman
Alex: Karen Black

Origin: USA
Released: 1997
Production: Paul Williams for Hillman/Williams Productions and Shonderosa Productions; released by Unapix Films
Direction: Zoe Clarke-Williams
Screenplay: James Andronica, Karen Black, and Zoe Clarke-Williams; based on the novel by Margaret Diehl
Cinematography: Susan Emerson
Editing: Stephen Eckelberg, Annamaria Szanto
Music: Mark Mothersbaugh
Production design: Clovis Chamberet
Sound: Neal Spritz
MPAA rating: R
Running Time: 102 minutes

REVIEWS

Los Angeles Times. June 26, 1998, p. F6.
Variety. May 26, 1997, p. 67.

Men With Guns; Hombres Armados

"You wouldn't expect anything less from the relentlessly independent Sayles . . . with grace, humor and a dose of magical realism."—Lisa Henricksson, *GQ*

"This inspiring odyssey takes us where few American movies deign to go!"—Graham Fuller, *Interview*

"A provocative, powerful movie . . . Sayles sails on!"—Leah Rozen, *People* "A compassionate, provocative movie . . . "—Bruce Williamson, *Playboy*

"*Men With Guns* ranks with Sayles' best! This film means to shake us, and it does!"—Peter Travers, *Rolling Stone*

"Two very enthusiastic thumbs up!"—*Siskel & Ebert*

Box Office: $956,145

John Sayles has often ventured far from the beaten path. He has repeatedly gone where few if any filmmakers have trodden. Sayles specializes in projects that have no commercial hooks, from a dramatization of baseball's 1919 Black Sox scandal in *Eight Men Out* (1988) to a West Virginia coal miners' strike in *Matewan* (1987) to a lesbian romance in *Lianna* (1983). Even his more accessible subjects, like the urban corruption in *City of Hope* (1991), come loaded with heavily politicized subtexts.

In *Men With Guns,* Sayles takes us to the outposts of the indigenous peoples of a nameless Latin American country. So remote and forgotten are these villages and so unpublicized are the social upheavals taking place there that even Sayles' learned protagonist, Dr. Humberto Fuentes (Federico Luppi), has no idea what life is like there. In an opening sequence in which the doctor is treating a military commander, Sayles establishes Dr. Fuentes as a political naif. "The world is a savage place," his heavily-decorated patient lectures the doctor.

Fuentes, recently widowed and given to listening to his own heart with a stethoscope (it's obvious what that means), has been working in the country's capital in blithe ignorance. He believes in the march of progress and is proud of a "Doctors for Health" program he once established to train young practitioners to work in clinics among the natives. Now, rather than taking a vacation to the ocean, he decides to journey to the mountains to find his former students and engage in a little self-congratulation. He wants to witness

A local citizen: "Nobody refuses the men with guns."

firsthand the medical benefits his students have bestowed on the poor masses and thereby reassure himself he is leaving behind a worthy legacy.

Fuentes is only partially shaken when he discovers the brightest of his former students has forsaken the outback to become a black-market pharmaceutical dealer in a slum section of the capital. The jolt only strengthens his resolve to find his other students staying the course and making a difference. As he drives far into the interior reaches of his native land, where he has never before visited, he encounters two American tourists (Mandy Patinkin and Kathryn Grody) who ask him about the atrocities that have been reported in the region. Fuentes replies that such stories are folklore, soap opera for "the common people," and insists: "That happens in other countries. Not here."

The doctor's ignorance of the conditions among the lower classes in his own society is an obvious metaphor for an entire privileged culture's avoidance of the ugly truths about the Third World. As in many of his movies, Sayles presents *Men With Guns* as an obvious allegory of relations between social classes. Fuentes stands for a class of rational professionals whose belief in scientific progress exists in a vacuum, not the real world. What *Men With Guns* does is to show Fuentes, and by extension Western audiences, the reality of life among the most exploited peoples of the world.

Arriving in a village where a student was assigned, Fuentes finds the inhabitants skittish and uncooperative. From a gregarious blind woman he learns the young doctor was murdered by the "men with guns." To the indigenous peoples, it matters little whether the "men with guns" are the government troops, the guerillas they are hunting down, or various thieves or rogues. Sayles leaves the politics of the situation completely opaque, as it must be to these villagers. To them, the "men with guns" are to be feared and obeyed, and they are the helpless pawns.

In village after village, the doctor finds the same result: His student has been killed, or kidnapped and then murdered, by the men with guns. His lifelong innocence falls away and he realizes the real plight of the people he thought he was helping and the real forces that are controlling his country. As the radicals in Sayles's debut film *The Return of the Secaucus Seven* (1980) would say, the doctor has his consciousness raised.

As Fuentes's nightmare unfolds, he encounters a starving young boy who takes him to massacre sites and to an abandoned school which was used by the men with guns as a torture chamber. His car is stolen and he is robbed at gunpoint by a military deserter who is wandering aimlessly. Eventually they meet a priest who calls himself "The Ghost" and is filled with guilt. The priest ran away from a village rather than comply with the military's orders that he be among six men who kill themselves to demonstrate their loyalty to the regime. Finally, the motley party hooks up with a young woman who has been raped by the troops and hasn't spoken since. Together they seek a rumored heavenly hideout on the mountaintops.

In this story, which he wrote as well as directed, Sayles obviously is hoping to raise the consciousness of Western audiences who can identify with Fuentes. But the brave Sayles has badly floundered here. Even Sayles's most loyal audiences need a story to hang onto, and *Men With Guns* has only a repetitive and action-starved wail of desperation. Any hope that Sayles had generated of reaching larger audiences with the accessible Irish fairy tale *The Secret of Roan Inish* (1994) and the enigmatic pseudo-thriller *Lone Star* (1995) evaporates in *Men With Guns.* Sayles should have made a documentary, for that would have carried more dramatic weight than the starved narrative he attempts.

Watching *Men With Guns,* whose characters and situations are pregnant with dramatic possibilities, you keep waiting for something to happen. But nothing of interest

Filmed in Spanish and the indigenous Maya, Nahuatl, Tzotzil, and Kuna languages, with English subtitles.

ever does. The doctor's awakening should come with the revelations he finds in the first village he encounters, and up to that point the film has a measure of intrigue. But Sayles spends the last two-thirds of this overlong film giving the same news, over and over, to Fuentes and the film audience.

In a more skillful narrative, Fuentes's initiation into the real world would come with more palpable dangers and threats. But Sayles flubs all chances for such tension. In one scene, the doctor discovers that the deserter's gun is not loaded and smugly assumes he is safe. When the man later puts cartridges into the chambers without Fuentes's knowledge, there should be suspense in wondering how the doctor will get the news the gun he thought was harmless really is lethal. But nothing interesting comes of this. Sayles also doesn't seem to know what to do with the intriguing character of his worldly wise, stoic peasant boy. By the time the priest arrives to tell his tale, Sayles has abandoned dramatic narrative altogether for painfully contrived situations.

About the only relief from these dreary proceedings, spoken in Spanish and native languages and subtitled in English, comes from Patinkin and Grody. The American tourists pop up now and again, in the remotest places, looking for fabulous native ruins. Patinkin and Grody are authentically funny. The joke on Fuentes is that they seem to know more about the history and culture of his country than he does.

Unfortunately, everything else that happens in the last half of this film is an elaboration of points made long before. Sayles has muffed an opportunity to send audiences along with Fuentes on a real nightmare ride that might awaken new understandings of the world. Some movie thrills and chills would not have undermined his points, but would have made them all the more compelling. But instead there is a sanctimonious air about *Men With Guns* that ruins what Sayles is trying to accomplish. It is hard to believe that a director of such reach and achievement has forgotten what makes moviemaking different from—and potentially more powerful than—lecturing.

—*Michael Betzold*

CREDITS

Dr. Fuentes: Federico Luppi
Domingo: Damian Delgado
Conjeo: Dan Rivera Gonzalez
Graciela: Tania Cruz
Padre Portillo: Damian Alcazar
Andrew: Mandy Patinkin
Harriet: Kathryn Grody

Origin: USA
Released: 1997
Production: R. Paul Miller and Maggie Rezzi for Lexington Road and Clear Blue Sky; released by Sony Pictures Classics
Direction: John Sayles
Screenplay: John Sayles
Cinematography: Slawomire Idziak
Editing: John Sayles
Music: Mason Daring
Production design: Felipe Fernandez Del Paso
Art direction: Salvador Parra
Costumes: Mayes C. Rubeco
Sound: Judy Karp
MPAA rating: R
Running Time: 126 minutes

REVIEWS

Boxoffice. February, 1998, p. 51.
Detroit News. April 24, 1998, p. 8C.
Entertainment Weekly. March 20, 1998, p. 60.
GQ. March, 1998, p. 121.
Los Angeles Times. March 13, 1998, p. F14.
New York Times. March 19, 1997, p. H15.
New York Times. March 6, 1998, p. E29.
People. March 30, 1998, p. 20.
Rolling Stone. March 19, 1998, p. 72.
Variety. September 8, 1997, p. 79.
Washington Post. March 27, 1998, p. C7.

Mercury Rising

"Suspense and cliffhanging action. Bruce Willis at his best."—David Sheehan, *KCBS*

"A first rate action-packed thriller."—Paul Wunder, *WBAI*

 Box Office: $32,983,332

Mercury Rising is another of those big-budget action thrillers which Hollywood does so well. The name Bruce Willis is like the Good Housekeeping Seal of Approval for aficionados of this violent genre, guaranteeing that it will be high-quality fluff. The story is derivative, but no expense was spared to make the movie a diverting spectacle. Superstars like Willis can demand fancy packaging. The viewer may be experiencing deja vu all over again but cannot help being impressed by the intricately choreographed chases indoors and outdoors through Chicago's crowded streets and commercial buildings, the multi-vehicle crashes on expressways, the vertiginous helicopter shots of gun fights and fistfights atop skyscrapers, the waves of shattering glass, the multi-stage explosions, and all the other state-of-the-art razzle-dazzle that makes American action films so popular around the world. Willis can also demand a top director. He got one in Harold Becker, whose credits include *The Onion Field* (1979), *Sea of Love* (1989), *Malice* (1993), and *City Hall* (1995).

Willis plays a rogue FBI agent named Art Jeffries who becomes involved in what appears to be a case of murder and suicide with the possible kidnapping of a little boy named Simon (Miko Hughes). It is the possible kidnapping angle that allows the FBI to interfere in what would otherwise be a local police matter. The boy's parents were actually murdered, as the viewers have already seen. They will learn in time that the ruthlessly efficient killer was acting on the orders of Lieutenant Colonel Nicholas Kudrow (Alec Baldwin), a high-ranking official in the National Security Agency (NSA). The principal target was Simon himself, but the terrified boy managed to hide until approaching police sirens forced the hit man to jump into a waiting getaway van and flee down a back alley.

Jeffries, a stereotypical tough guy with a heart of gold, is the only person who suspects that there is something phony about the parents' deaths. His suspicions are confirmed when he goes to visit Simon at the hospital and finds the whole wing eerily deserted in a scene that bears an uncanny resemblance

to the one in *The Godfather* (1972) in which Michael Corleone (Al Pacino) foils the plot to assassinate his father. With the screaming Simon under one arm and a gun in his free hand, Jeffries commandeers an ambulance and flees. From that point on, the movie is mostly hide-and-seek, providing viewers with the visual bonus of a tour of modern-day Chicago. Jeffries' problems are immensely complicated by the fact that Simon has a tendency to disappear and end up in front of an oncoming train or out in the middle of a busy street.

Simon, an autistic child, is also an idiot savant. Although he needs constant supervision because he is lost in his own private world, he has mental powers like those of Raymond Babbitt (Dustin Hoffman) in *Rain Man* (1988). Simon is addicted to the kinds of puzzle magazines that appeal to engineers and scientists with genius or near-genius IQs. One element of the plot is hard to swallow, but the whole story pivots around it: A couple of spaced-out code experts working for the NSA have challenged the readers of a puzzle magazine to supply the answer to a complex question written in "Mercury," the most sophisticated code ever invented, and vital to national defense. Evidently these two nerds believed their new security code was so foolproof that they could safely test it on the eggheads who subscribe to such magazines. Nine-year-old Simon studied the full-page Mercury-encoded cryptogram for a few minutes and then called in the correct answer on their 1-800 number, thereby creating pandemonium at the NSA.

 Kudrow (Alec Baldwin): "A $2 billion code is an open book to people of diminished capacity?!"

The situation is reminiscent of the classic *Three Days of the Condor* (1975). Like Turner (Robert Redford), Simon becomes the quarry of government assassins masterminded by Kudrow. Like Turner, Jeffries manages to find a woman who will believe his crazy story and agree to help him out. Jeffries accosts Stacey (Kim Dickens) in a Starbuck's coffeehouse and asks her to keep an eye on Simon for a few minutes. Jeopardizing her job, she is stuck with the difficult boy for hours before Jeffries comes back all bloody and bruised from one of his encounters with Kudrow's goons. An intimate relationship never develops between Jeffries and Stacey, as it did between Turner and Kathy (Faye Dunaway) in *Three Days of the Condor*. There is so much chasing and killing going on, and Simon proves to be such a handful, that there is really no time for Jeffries and Stacey to get acquainted. Her role is limited to babysitter, thereby freeing Jeffries for some of the rough stuff. Expecting a hero to fight the American government with a struggling kid under one arm is asking too much, even of Bruce Willis.

Willis and Baldwin are stuck with an improbable premise but both do competent professional jobs of making their motivations seem plausible. Baldwin is given long-winded passages of dialogue in which he explains that the Mercury code protects the identities of thousands of secret agents all over the world. This, in his character's opinion, justifies the sacrifice of Simon, Simon's parents, Jeffries, the two bungling computer nerds, and anyone else who threatens to jeopardize Mercury. In contrast to poor Jeffries, who is dirty, unshaven, bleeding, and exhausted, Kudrow is always shown impeccably attired and surrounded by fawning admirers. His Mercury project may be a top secret, but everybody seems to know about it and wants to pat him on the back for conceiving it.

Miko Hughes is a cute kid and an experienced actor with several roles to his credit, but asking him to play an autistic idiot savant was too great a challenge for both the boy and director Harold Becker. As Jack Mathews observed in his *Los Angeles Times* review, the young actor "speaks in a robotic voice, walks as if battery-operated, and he doesn't just avoid eye contact, his eyes float in the sockets, as if there were no muscles attached."

It is inevitable that Jeffries would eventually hit on the

Miko Hughes played the scalpel-wielding toddler Cage in 1989's *Pet Sematary*.

idea of using Simon's unique mental abilities to turn the tables on Kudrow and his small army of rigidly disciplined assassins. The little genius uses a computer to hack into the NSA's most closely guarded files and creates so much trouble that Kudrow has to ask for a parley. He agrees to meet Jeffries in the most cinematically impressive setting available—the rooftop of a Chicago skyscraper. But Kudrow—to nobody's surprise—intends to double-cross Jeffries. And street-smart Jeffries—to nobody's surprise—intends to double-cross the double-crosser. This leads to a spectacular nighttime confrontation between the FBI and the NSA and a hand-to-hand fight between Jeffries and Kudrow with the camera looking straight down at the crawling headlights 51 stories below. In the meantime, Simon amuses himself by walking back and forth on a parapet at the brink of the 500-foot drop. A helicopter whirls just overhead because scenes of this familiar type seem to require at least one such helicopter.

The presence of a cute nine-year-old autistic orphan is the only thing that saves *Mercury Rising* from being a perfect clone of too many previous paranoid thrillers involving some freewheeling government agency. Unfortunately, the camaraderie that develops in *Rain Man* between Charlie Babbitt (Tom Cruise) and his autistic-savant brother Raymond never develops between Jeffries and Simon. The viewer can hardly blame the poor kid for being withdrawn, after having his parents assassinated before his eyes and being chased all over Chicago by the same killers. Even though the film could not avoid an R rating for excessive violence, the casting of a child star will help some home entertainment receipts. Pragmatic *Variety* critic Todd McCarthy predicted: "Pic will be one of Bruce Willis' modest performers in between more muscular outings." The critics were unimpressed by *Mercury Rising*. Siskel and Ebert gave it two thumbs down for being too much of the same old same old. But Bruce Willis can afford to cry all the way to the bank.

—*Bill Delaney*

CREDITS

Art Jeffries: Bruce Willis
Nicholas Kudrow: Alec Baldwin
Simon: Miko Hughes
Tommy B. Jordan: Chi McBride
Stacey: Kim Dickens
Dean Crandell: Robert Stanton
Leo Pedranski: Bodhi Pine Elfman
Emily Lang: Carrie Preston
Shayes: Peter Stormare
Lomax: Kevin Conway

Origin: USA
Released: 1998
Production: Brian Glazer and Karen Kehela for Imagine Entertainment; released by Universal Pictures
Direction: Harold Becker
Screenplay: Lawrence Konner and Mark Rosenthal; based on the book *Simple Simon* by Ryne Douglas Peardon
Cinematography: Michael Seresin
Editing: Peter Honess
Music: John Barry
Production design: Patrizia von Brandenstein
Art direction: Jim Truesdale, Steve Saklad
Costumes: Betsy Heimann
Sound: Kim Ornitz
Visual effects supervision: Michael Owens
MPAA rating: R
Running Time: 112 minutes

REVIEWS

Chicago Tribune. April 3, 1998, p. 4.
Entertainment Weekly. April 10, 1998, p. 44.
Los Angeles Times. April 3, 1998, p. F14.
New York Times. April 3, 1998, p. B9.
People. April 13, 1998, p. 20.
San Diego Union Tribune. April 3, 1998, p. E1.
San Francisco Chronicle. April 3, 1998, p. C3.
Sight and Sound. October, 1998, p. 46.
USA Today. April 3, 1998, p. 5E.
Variety. April 6, 1998, p. 47.
Village Voice. April 14, 1998, p. 64.
Washington Post. April 3, 1998, p. 53.

A Merry War; Keep the Aspidistra Flying

"A wickedly clever piece of satirical fun!"—Ella Taylor, *Atlantic Monthly*

"Heart-tickling!"—Michele Shapiro, *Glamour*

"A first-rate piece of work."—Peter Rainer, *New Times*

"Helena Bonham Carter is splendid."—Richard Corliss, *Time*

Box Office: $373,830

For many years, a musical ran in London's West End entitled 'No Sex Please, We're British!' This might be an unofficial adage for the life of struggling poet Gordon Comstock (Richard E. Grant). Not that it is for want of trying with his girlfriend Rosemary (Helena Bonham Carter). But Gordon is up against that most English of sensibilities: respectability. And as a motif in this film, it is the aspidistra plant, even more than Rosemary, which embodies respectability.

Indeed, *A Merry War* is retitled from *Keep the Aspidistra Flying*, the film's name in England (and the original nomenclature of George Orwell's 1936 novel). The phrase 'a merry war,' can, however, be found in Orwell's text in reference to "the eternal and idiotic question of Man versus Woman."

A wriggling specimen in coat and tie, Gordon bursts to forsake his middle-class life. Although a successful copywriter, he is sick of penning clever slogans. Rosemary, a designer at the advertising firm in which they both find solid employment, sympathizes with her boyfriend's wider ambitions, but she is content to hold down a steady job.

After Gordon's volume of poetry is published, no lesser paper than the August *Times* of London supplies a good review. Ecstatic, he marches to see the boss, Erskine (Jim Carter), to hand in his resignation. Not only is Erskine unwilling to lose one of his best employees, he can't discern Gordon's prospects. "Isn't there enough poetry in the world?"

Gordon's millionaire, champagne socialist publisher Ravelston (Julian Wadham), tries to bring his writer down to earth. There is very little money to be made in poetry, he cautions, so he encourages the unwilling Comstock to take up a job in a bookstore. Soon, Gordon secures a room nearby with the requisite aspidistra (a staple, representing the bour-

geoise). Already manic, our hero is to become unnerved by the challenge of the artistic life—and Rosemary's obdurateness in the face of his romantic ardor.

Gordon tries to bury himself in work, but takes distraction in burning holes in the poor aspidistra plant. A trip to the countryside, however, holds promise. Gordon and Rosemary find themselves inside a high-class hotel restaurant, where, in defiance of the patronizing waiter, they order food from the menu with money Gordon has borrowed from his sister Julia (Harriet Walter), a waitress in a London tea room. The bottle of red wine supplementing the meal blows the rest of their cash.

But the payoff for Gordon appears to be Rosemary's relaxed guard. In a secluded grove, skirts and pants are removed, but since our poet has forgotten to bring precautions, Rosemary's defenses are erected—so to speak.

And then Gordon's luck turns. The grand sum of fifty bucks arrives to laud the acceptance of a poem in a California poetry journal. Gordon wines and dines Rosemary and Ravelston in a posh restaurant, and egged on by his excessive spirits—fueled by alcohol and grandiose hopes for his writing future—he begins to make a fool of himself.

After an altercation in the public house, Gordon lands in jail, and is bailed out by his publisher. Turfed from his book-

Gordon (Richard E. Grant) about a proposed country picnic: "I reject the countryside, it's dark and there are animals."

store job and middle-class lodgings, Gordon embraces misery. He breaks with Rosemary, and takes up a penurious existence in Lambeth, a poor part of London, working for meager wages in a bookshop where the owner no more reads books than paints Picassos.

Rosemary continues to care, and despite her disdain for the squalor of his lodgings, she at last surrenders to him in his attic bedroom. Yet Gordon will not leave this new life—until Rosemary returns and announces her pregnancy. The prospect of a new life, and the attendant responsibilities, steers Gordon back into the middle of the road. He is roundly welcomed back at the advertising firm, and marries Rosemary. The verses he lauds now are his own clever, if trite, ditties. And in his new home, there stands an aspidistra.

Adapting novels into films has been, and will remain, a constant source for the film industry. In many cases, only a flavor of the book's appeal is transferred to the screen, and this is the case in *A Merry War*. Directed by Robert Bierman, and scripted by Alan Plater, a British television writer of caliber, the film is no more than a mild entertainment charting the progression of Gordon's slight rise, precipitous fall, and resurfacing to the middle-class. Production designer Sarah Greenwood's evocative period work stands out, as does

CREDITS

Gordon Comstock: Richard E. Grant
Rosemary: Helena Bonham Carter
Ravelston: Julian Wadham
Erskine: Jim Carter
Julia Comstock: Harriet Walter
Hermione: Lesley Vickerage

Origin: Great Britain
Released: 1997
Production: Peter Shaw for Bonaparte Films and
UBA/Sentinel Films; released by First Look Pictures
Direction: Robert Bierman
Screenplay: Alan Plater; based on the novel by George
Orwell
Cinematography: Giles Nuttgens
Editing: Bill Wright
Music: Mike Batt
Production design: Sarah Greenwood
Art direction: Phillip Robinson
Costumes: James Keast
Sound: Patrick Quirke, Paul Hamblin
MPAA rating: Unrated
Running Time: 101 minutes

Location Manager Colin Plenty's, because the interiors are lovely to observe, and Bierman and Giles Nuttgens's camera relishes the details.

As for the cast, it is Grant as the hero of the film who carries the film. Despite the manic episodes, and his degeneration into self-imposed poverty, in truth our poet is not a compelling character. We sympathize with him, but we are not riveted. Similarly, the accomplished Bonham Carter has to make the best of a prim role; Rosemary is a woman chained to respectability. It's a war between the pair, perhaps, but one might see their conflict as no more than a series of light skirmishes set in an agreeable vision of 1930s England.

—*Paul B. Cohen*

REVIEWS

Boxoffice. April, 1998, p. 199.
Entertainment Weekly. September 11, 1998, p. 106.
New York Times. August 28, 1998, p. E10.
People. September 7, 1998, p. 39.
Sight and Sound. November, 1997, p. 44.
Variety. October 6, 1997, p. 57.

The Mighty

The quest for friendship is the noblest cause of all.—Movie tagline

Courage comes in all sizes.—Movie tagline

"A marvelous film—absolutely terrific. It's Oscar time for everyone involved."—Jan Wahl, *CBS Radio*

"*The Mighty* soars into greatness! A magical fable about friendship, self-esteem and empowerment with superb performances from Sharon Stone, Harry Dean Stanton and Gena Rowlands. This film is something special."—Jack Mathews, *New York Newsday*

"Two thumbs up!"—*Siskel and Ebert*

 Box Office: $2,652,246

If you experienced a nagging sense of déjà vu while viewing *The Mighty* at your local theater, the explanation for that feeling was no further away than that crumpled ticket stub still in your jacket pocket or purse with *Simon Birch* printed on it. Indeed, there are a surprising number of sim-

ilarities between these two worthwhile films, which unfortunately opened just a month apart. Both films were based upon well-received novels by acclaimed authors (*Freak the Mighty* by Rodman Philbrick and *A Prayer for Owen Meany* by John Irving). Both are about two outcast boys who form an unlikely but enriching friendship with each other. In both films, the smaller boy has a smart mouth and a nimble mind despite also having a rare, crippling, and eventually fatal malady known as Morquio's Syndrome. (The actor in *Simon Birch*, Ian Michael Smith, is actually afflicted with this disorder.) In both films, the healthy boy has concerns about his absent father. The films each have a wonderfully warm, loving mother, and the death of a mother figures in both plots. Both utilize a voice-over narration. Finally, both films speak of the enabling power of friendship, the amazing ability of the spirit to triumph over adversity, and the importance of not judging a book by its cover. Because of these similarities, many moviegoers who had just finished drying their eyes after seeing *Simon Birch* were probably less interested than they might otherwise have been in *The Mighty*. While *Simon Birch* apparently had a bigger budget for publicity, this situation undoubtedly also contributed to *The Mighty*'s earning about $1.5 million in its first month of release, compared to *Simon Birch*'s take of almost $14.5 million in its first four weeks out of the gate. *Simon Birch* also benefitted from being a glossy, old-fashioned (and overtly-orchestrated) tearjerker, but the less-showy *Mighty* is also enjoyable and deserving of praise.

The Mighty begins with aerial shots of bridges (shot around Cincinnati, Ohio and Covington, Kentucky), which are symbolic of the sturdy connection which will be established between the film's two main characters, Kevin Dillon (Kieran Culkin) and Max Kane (Elden Henson). Max, in a voice-over, looks back on that unusual and decidedly life-altering bond. He spent most of

Kevin (Kieran Culkin) to Max (Elden Henson): "You need a brain, I need legs—and the Wizard of Oz doesn't live in South Cincinnati."

his childhood with his maternal grandparents because his mother was killed and his father was sent to prison for the crime. He refers to his serious, sober guardians as Gram (Gena Rowlands) and Grim (Harry Dean Stanton), and they remind him of the couple in Grant Wood's painting *American Gothic*. With his full face, husky body, a learning disability, and a murderer for a father, 13-year-old Max is even more self-conscious than most adolescents. He feels as if people view him as some sort of monstrosity, and the especially brutal teasing by town bullies Blade and the Doghouse Boys reinforces that view. They refer to him as the "missing link," and a "freak of nature," and their chants of "Killer Kane! Killer Kane! Had a kid who got no brain!" make him retreat into himself to escape the pain—and the fear that, because he looks just like his father, that he will grow up to be like him in other, more unsettling ways.

Little does Max know that his salvation has arrived when he meets his next-door neighbor Kevin, whose hunched and stunted body are in stark contrast to Max's. Despite Kevin's physical infirmity, he revels in books, words and ideas, prompting his mother (Sharon Stone) to remark proudly that she "gave birth to a healthy, seven-pound dictionary." Kevin is soon chosen to tutor Max in the latter's special reading class, and when he introduces Max to the legend of King Arthur and his noble Knights of the Round Table, the two boys open an unexpected chapter in their lives. During one of their sessions, Kevin asks Max to do him a favor: he needs someone to take him to the Riverfest in exchange for five dollars. Kevin's mother, who hates crowds and fireworks, agrees to let her son go accompanied by his formidably-built new friend. During the fireworks, which diminutive Kevin cannot see in the midst of the dense crowd, Max hoists him up on his shoulders for a better view, and it occurs to both of them that they compliment each other well through this arrangement. Max suddenly feels

that he has a good head on his shoulders, and Kevin feels that he has a healthy, powerful body at his command. Thus begins an empowering merger, and the two refer to their creation as Freak the Mighty. Together, inspired by the bravery, chivalry, and ethics of King Arthur and his men, they are able to save a woman being mistreated in a store, fend off the Doghouse Boys, and return a purse stolen by the menacing hoods from a trashy alcoholic with a good heart named Loretta Lee (Gillian Anderson). Through this quasi metamorphosis, Kevin makes friends and experiences what it is like to slam dunk a basketball, and Max's self-esteem reaches new heights, as well. All of this progress is endangered by the parole of Max's brute of a father (James Gandolfini), who promptly kidnaps his son. In a rather melodramatic and unlikely scene, Kevin drives his mother's van, sleds through the woods, and then rescues his friend with some help from Loretta. Kevin's health soon takes a turn for the worse. The scenes which follow, showing how Max deals with the news of Kevin's death and continues to grow as a result of their friendship, are both heartbreaking and inspiring.

Philbrick's book was published in 1993 by Blue Sky Press, an imprint of Scholastic Inc., which brought the work to the screen through its film production arm. Stone, who does an admirable job in a dressed-down, smaller role, served as co-executive producer for *The Mighty,* the first film made by her recently formed Chaos Productions. She is especially effective in the emotionally-charged scene where she convinces Kevin's school to let him participate in gym class. Culkin, who has previously appeared in a number of minor roles, shows himself to be an actor of greater complexity and range than his older brother Macaulay of *Home Alone* fame. Henson, best known for the *Mighty Ducks* films of the early and mid-'90s, has both the strength and vulnerability necessary for his role, and is particularly good in the scene when Max learns of his pal's death. Anderson of television's *X-Files* is startlingly different here, and highly enjoyable. Veteran actors Rowlands and Stanton are welcome additions, as always.

This is British director Peter Chelsom's first American film, and he builds nicely upon the promise shown in his *Funny Bones* (1995) and *Hear My Song* (1991). The images he gives us of King Arthur's knights, which appear at various times in the movie, could have been intrusive or heavy-handed, but they are effective here. Writer Charles Leavitt brings the story to the screen, complete with some of the book's chapter headings announced as part of Henson's

Rodman Philbrick's book *Freak the Mighty* won the American Library Association's award for "Best Book for Young Adults" in 1993.

CREDITS

Gwen Dillion: Sharon Stone
Maxwell Kane: Elden Henson
Kevin Dillion: Kieran Culkin
Gram: Gena Rowlands
Grim: Harry Dean Stanton
Loretta Lee: Gillian Anderson
Kenny Kane: James Gandolfini
Blade: Joe Perrino
Iggy: Meat Loaf
Mrs. Addison: Jenifer Lewis

Origin: USA
Released: 1998
Production: Jane Startz and Simon Fields for a Scholastic production; released by Miramax Films
Direction: Peter Chelsom
Screenplay: Charles Leavitt; based on the book *Freak the Might* by Rodman Philbrick
Cinematography: John de Borman
Editing: Martin Walsh
Music: Trevor Jones
Production design: Caroline Hanania
Art direction: Dennis Davenport
Set decoration: Cal Loucks
Costumes: Marie Sylvie Deveau
Sound: Bruce Carwadine
MPAA rating: PG-13
Running Time: 100 minutes

narration. His script has more clarity and cohesiveness than in his previous work, *The Sunchaser* (1996). *The Mighty* should appeal to those currently experiencing the growing pains of adolescence, as well as adults who remember their own struggles to negotiate that difficult time of life. A poignant film enlivened by adventure and flashes of humor, *The Mighty* is a modest but worthwhile production. Miramax reportedly held it back for a year, perhaps finally releasing it in an attempt to capitalize on the unexpectedly-positive word of mouth about *Simon Birch*. The idea may have been that there was enough longing for this type of motion picture out there to enable Miramax's film to ride piggyback on *Simon Birch* like Kevin did on Max. If that was the plan, it only served to dilute the strength of *The Mighty.*

—*David L. Boxerbaum*

REVIEWS

Boston Globe. October 16, 1998, p. C5.
Chicago Tribune. October 16, 1998, p. M7.
Entertainment Weekly. October 16, 1998, p. 58.
New York Times. October 9, 1998, p. B14.
Rolling Stone. October 29, 1998, p. 79.
Sight and Sound. January, 1998, p. 50.
USA Today. October 9, 1998, p. E6.
Variety. May 25, 1998, p. 60.
Wall Street Journal. October 13, 1998, p. A20.
Washington Post. October 16, 1998, p. D5.

Mighty Joe Young

"A perfect treat."—Nancy Jay Malosky, *ABC-TV*

"The family movie parents will want to see twice."—Bob Cowan, *Global Television, Toronto*

"*Joe* is a sensation!"—Jack Mathews, *Los Angeles Times*

"The season's must-see adventure!"—Bobbie Wygant, *NBC-TV*

"A suspenseful, humorous, sweet and sentimental film!"—Richard Schickel, *Time*

Box Office: $20,028,356

Jill's (Charlize Theron) circle of friends include boyfriend Gregg (Bill Paxton) and gigantic gorilla *Mighty Joe Young*.

Mighty *Joe Young* strives to be grade "A" family entertainment, the hallmark of the Walt Disney company. Director Ron Underwood (*City Slickers* [1991] and *Speechless* [1994]) has offered up an entertaining, old-fashioned tale of adventure, loyalty, and friendship. Although lacking the sardonic and witty edge of last year's Disney's *George of the Jungle*, the film achieves a by-the-book retelling of a Hollywood classic in a squeaky clean manner. Because of the astounding advancement of special effects, it is pointless to compare this film to the original 1949 film on which it is based; indeed, that film, with its stop-motion action is in itself entertaining and enjoyable.

Eight-year-old Jill Young (Mika Boorman) helps her mother Dr. Ruth Young (Linda Purl) study gorillas in Tanzania. Dr. Ruth has noted the unusual growth of a baby gorilla that they have named Joe; he is indeed, growing larger than his siblings at an alarming rate. Poachers soon invade their pleasant sanctuary, and in an ensuing melee, mercenary hunter Strasser (Rade Sherbedgia) kills Joe's mother and Ruth is fatally wounded trying to protect her charges. Before she dies, Ruth tells Jill to watch over and protect Joe. Uncertain of their future, Jill and Joe cling to one another.

Flash forward twelve years: Jill (Charlize Theron) has matured into a leggy beauty who is the only one who can handle and appease the by now behemoth Joe. Joe has grown so large that he mainly hides in the jungles of a remote mountaintop, and has achieved mythical status among the locals. Enter Gregg O'Hara (Bill Paxton), a scientist from a California conservation preserve. After a terrific action sequence where Gregg and the local natives chase Joe, Jill emerges and tells Gregg to stay away. Even though Gregg is only offering a protective home for Joe, away from

> Terry Moore who played the original Jill and Ray Harryhausen who did the special effects for the first *Mighty Joe Young* have cameos in this remake.

the encroaching poachers, Jill fiercely tells him that Joe must live free in his native environment. Only after a close call with more poachers, does Jill take Gregg up on his offer and agree to send Joe to the animal sanctuary. But on one condition—that she and she alone is completely in charge of Joe.

Joe is greeted at the California Animal Preserve by opportunistic Harry Rueben (David Paymer), the head of the preserve, and Dr. Cicily Banks (Regina King). Thus begins the "fish out of water" sequence in which both Joe and Jill are subjected to the indignities of urban life. The gorilla is amazingly lifelike, thanks to the multi-faceted efforts of Dreamquest images, Industrial Light and Magic, and gorilla impresario Rick Baker (Baker was responsible for the apes in *Gorillas in the Mist* and *Greystoke: The Legend of Tarzan, Lord of the Apes*).

Joe's misfortunes pile one upon the other; Strasser finds his way back to taunt Joe, just as the great ape is being showcased at a huge fund-raiser. Joe goes berserk, smashes his way loose and heads out into open civilization

AWARDS AND NOMINATIONS

Academy Awards 1998 Nominations: Visual Effects

CREDITS

Jill Young: Charlize Theron
Gregg O'Hara: Bill Paxton
Strasser: Rade Sherbedgia
Garth: Peter Firth
Harry Rueben: David Paymer
Cicily Banks: Regina King
Dr. Ruth Young: Linda Purl

Origin: USA
Released: 1998
Production: Ted Hartley and Tom Jacobson for RKO Pictures and Walt Disney Pictures; released by Buena Vista
Direction: Ron Underwood
Screenplay: Mark Rosenthal and Lawrence Konner, based on a screenplay by Ruth Rose and a story by Merian C. Cooper
Cinematography: Don Peterman, Oliver Wood
Editing: Paul Hirsch
Production design: Michael Corenblith
Costumes: Molly Maginnis
Music: James Horner
Visual effects supervision: Hoyt Yeatman
Art direction: Dan Webster
Sound: Richard Bryce Goodman
MPAA rating: PG
Running Time: 114 minutes

to wreck havoc. This sequence seems to be the weakest, and merely exists to have the impressively large and expressive ape climb buildings, hide under freeway passes, and indeed, even jump through the "O" in the Hollywood sign. With Jill and Gregg and the poachers in close pursuit, everyone must save Joe from being killed by the local police. In the largest and most impressive sequence, Joe saves a small boy from a Ferris wheel and nearly perishes himself when the entire wheel topples over. The pathos and emotion that emerge from this great, friendly-yet-misunderstood beast works on the most functional level. The film falls short of impressing its audience with any sense of verve or style, any kind of humor or danger. It is broad and PG-rated, in the most bland sense. There is barely even a kiss between attractive couple Jill and Gregg. Overall, the gorilla and the effects are amazing, but the story itself cannot match their strength.

—G. E. Georges

REVIEWS

Entertainment Weekly. January 8, 1999, p. 49.
New York Times. December 25, 1998, p. E19.
People. January 11, 1999, p. 38.
Variety. December 21, 1998, p. 74.
Village Voice. December 29, 1998, p. 128.

Mrs. Dalloway

"A triumph! It's pure pleasure to watch of one the world's greatest actresses!"—Lorraine Glennon, *More Magazine*

"The elusive, mercurial spirit of Virginia Woolf has been caught, its heart still beating, on the screen."—Daphne Merkin, *New Yorker*

"Extraordinary! Redgrave is astonishing!"—Dennis Dermody, *Paper Magazine*

"Exhilarating!"—Claire Dederer, *Seattle Weekly*

 Box Office: $3,309,421

Vanessa Redgrave dominates *Mrs. Dalloway* the way John Wayne used to dominate his westerns—and like John Wayne she looks taller than everybody else. Both men in her life have to look up to her physically as well as morally.

When lifelong platonic lover Peter Walsh (Michael Kitchen) dances with her, he looks a little like a tugboat guiding the *Queen Elizabeth II*. Redgrave is not only on camera most of the time, but it is understood—eventually, at least—that many of the other characters exist only in her character's consciousness.

There are three main pairs of characters: Mrs. Dalloway in her fifties and as marriageable young maiden Clarissa (Natascha McElhone); Richard Dalloway, the aging husband, a Conservative MP (John Standing) and Clarissa's handsome young suitor in the summer of 1890; Peter Walsh and Young Peter Walsh (Alan Cox), whose hopes of marrying Clarissa were crushed when well-connected, upwardly mobile Young Richard intervened. Whenever something reminds Mrs. Dalloway of the past, the younger characters materialize in flashbacks.

There is a fourth young character, Sally Seton (Lena Headey) who, because of the feminist spin director Marleen Gorris and scriptwriter Eileen Atkins have given Woolf's

Vanessa Redgrave and John Standing star in the British drama of lost love and regrets *Mrs. Dalloway*.

is disorienting. *Citizen Kane* (1941) jumps back and forth in time too. An important difference is that the major characters are played by the same actors—Orson Welles, Joseph Cotton, Everett Sloane, George Coulouris—in youth and old age. Another important difference is that *Citizen Kane* achieves variety by presenting its flashbacks through different characters' points of view.

The story of *Mrs. Dalloway* takes place during one day in June of 1923. The aging heroine is making last-minute preparations for an elaborate soiree at her London home. She has nothing to do but order flowers. It is a beautiful day, but her stream of consciousness takes a bumpy detour when she witnesses a disturbing scene through the flower-shop window. Septimus Smith (Rupert Graves), a shell-shocked World War I veteran, suffers a psychotic episode in which he relives the moment when his best friend was killed in the trenches. (Viewers will see several recurrences of Smith's nightmarish experience in yet more flashbacks.) Smith's devoted Italian wife (Amelia Bullmore), nearing the end of her endurance, is dragging her husband off to a psychiatrist.

The connection between the disheveled working-class veteran and the aristocratic heroine is tenuous. She never speaks to him and sees him only once, yet somehow identifies with him as her alter-ego. At her party when she learns that he has committed suicide by impaling himself on the spikes atop an iron fence, she is tempted to imitate him. (Woolf originally intended to have her novel end with the heroine's suicide. The author herself, who had several nervous breakdowns after WWI, actually did commit suicide in 1941 by filling her pockets with rocks and drowning herself in the Ouse River.)

The other significant event in Mrs. Dalloway's day is a surprise visit from Peter Walsh, who has been living in India for years and has made a complete mess of his life. In his fifties, on the verge of divorce, he is faced with starting out all over again. His reappearance makes her reflect on the turning point in her life: her decision to marry the stable but unexciting Richard rather than the passionate Peter. In telling Peter that "he asked too much of her," she sounded like

novel, seems closer to winning young Clarissa's love than either of the silly, infatuated males. The two maidens hug and kiss with real affection bordering on sexual passion. (Eileen Atkins had starred as Virginia Woolf in her own play, *Vita and Virginia,* dealing with the lesbian relationship between Woolf and Vita Sackville-West. Vanessa Redgrave played Vita.)

Even viewers who have read Woolf's novel have trouble understanding what is going on. The older characters only approximately resemble their young versions. Daphne Merkin wrote in her laudatory review in *The New Yorker:* "The viewer is asked to keep track of so much fleeting material that I found myself wondering whether great novels—especially great flighty novels—should ever leave the printed page. But then somewhere into the first half hour the movie begins to click."

Woolf relied heavily on the stream-of-consciousness technique. Her *Mrs. Dalloway* (1925) resembles James Joyce's *Ulysses* (1922). Both take place in a big city during a single day. In both there is little happening on the outside but a lot going on inside people's heads. In

Peter (Michael Kitchens) on the party: "Oh what snobs the English are. How they love dressing up."

adapting Woolf's complex novel, the filmmakers had to find a cinematic equivalent for stream of consciousness and were forced to use flashbacks and voice-over interior monologues, both of which have long been considered rather clunky contrivances in Hollywood story departments. "Thinking back," wrote Joe Morgenstern in his *Wall Street Journal* review, "that's a literary habit if ever there was one, and a red flag for those who would bring important books to the screen."

Flashbacks are familiar cinematic conventions, but when past and present are shuffled together like a deck of cards it

Daisy, the poor little rich girl in F. Scott Fitzgerald's novel *The Great Gatsby* (1925). Mrs. Dalloway realizes, not only that her own life would have been entirely different if she had opted for Byronic romance and adventure over comfort and security but that she could have made Peter's life different by giving him the spiritual support he needs. Peter and Richard reflect Woolf's negative view of men as selfish, pompous, demanding, parasitical creatures, insensitive to women's emotional needs. Even Septimus Smith, it would appear, is another such man; he is so dependent on his wife that he kills himself when the psychiatrist threatens to tear him away from her mothering arms.

Woolf was a great admirer of Marcel Proust. ("Oh if I could write like that!" she confided to her diary.) She copied the French genius in ending her novel, as Proust ended the last volume of *Remembrance of Things Past*, with a gala party in which the protagonist sees the tragic, comic, ironic changes that age has wrought in people she has known since youth. In her voice-over monologues, she makes cutting observations about the phonies who form England's upper crust, parasites whose way of life was preserved by the deaths of so many young men like Septimus Smith. Sally Seaton, the beautiful young "Sapphist" who believed that "marriage is a catastrophe for women," has become the fat, complacent Lady Rosseter (Sarah Badel), mother of five. Although surrounded by people, including the Prime Minister and the Duke and Duchess of Marlborough, Mrs. Dalloway feels pathologically isolated. According to biographer Lyndall Gordon, Woolf wanted her novel to illuminate one of her chief concerns: "The truth is people scarcely care for each other."

CREDITS

Mrs. Dalloway: Vanessa Redgrave
Clarissa Dalloway: Natascha McElhone
Septimus Warren Smith: Rupert Graves
Peter Walsh: Michael Kitchens
Richard Dalloway: John Standing
Young Peter: Alan Cox
Young Sally: Lena Headey
Lady Bruton: Margaret Tyzack
Lady Rosseter: Sarah Badel
Rezia Smith: Amelia Bullmore

Origin: USA, Great Britain
Released: 1997
Production: Stephen Braly and Lisa Katselas Pare; released by First Look Pictures
Direction: Marleen Gorris
Screenplay: Eileen Atkins; based on the novel by Virginia Woolf
Cinematography: Sue Gibson
Editing: Michiel Reichwein
Music: Ilona Sekacz
Production design: David Richens
Art direction: Alison Wratten, Nik Callan
Costumes: Judy Pepperdine
Sound: Peter Glossop, Brian Simmons
MPAA rating: PG-13
Running Time: 97 minutes

In the end, Mrs. Dalloway comes close to imitating Septimus Smith by jumping out the window. Instead, she goes back for a promised tete-a-tete with the needy Peter Walsh. The viewer understands that the tight-lipped Clarissa has come to the conclusion, familiar to many people facing old age, that being alive is slightly preferable to being dead. She at least has happy memories of a time when the whole world seemed to love her. She can go on giving attention and sympathy to others, fulfilling her supporting role as "Mrs. Dalloway" even though others—and especially those selfish men—can give nothing in return.

Director Marleen Gorris, cinematographer Sue Gibson, screenplay author Eileen Atkins, editor Michiel Reichwein, and others deserve much credit for dedication to a challenging task. Like John Huston's *The Dead* (1987), an adaptation of the short story by James Joyce, *Mrs. Dalloway* is a labor of love and not a product designed to score megabucks at the megaplex. The fact that it is a costume drama will keep it from becoming dated; it can provide enjoyment and edification to people not yet born. It will inspire many to read Virginia Woolf. (Daphne Merkin wrote: "It is high tribute to the movie that after it was over I went home and reread the novel. I kept seeing Vanessa Redgrave standing at Mrs. Dalloway's party, her posture impeccable, her large blue eyes alert with concealed regrets.")

The critics seemed to realize that *Mrs. Dalloway* was not to be treated like standard commercial fodder. (An exception was Joe Morgenstern, who complained about the "flashback epidemic" as well as "laggardly pacing, some atrocious supporting performances and inexplicably flat photography.") *Mrs. Dalloway* is not for everyone, but connoisseurs who enjoy elaborate, full-color adaptations of classics such as Henry James's *The Portrait of a Lady* (1996), *Washington Square*, (1997) and *The Wings of the Dove* (1997) will recognize another of the rare movies that offer food for thought instead of "chewing gum for the eyes."

—*Bill Delaney*

REVIEWS

Boxoffice. February, 1998, p. 52.
Christian Science Monitor. February 27, 1998, p. B3.
Detroit News. March 27, 1998, p. 3C.
Entertainment Weekly. March 6, 1998, p. 55.
Hollywood Reporter. September 23, 1997, p. 10.
Los Angeles Times. February 20, 1998, p. F4.
Movieline. March, 1998, p. 56.
New York Times. February 20, 1998, p. B12.
New Yorker. February 16, 1998, p. 82.
People. March 2, 1998, p. 22.
Sight and Sound. March, 1998, p. 53.
USA Today. February 27, 1998, p. 9D.

Mr. Jealousy

"Mistrust receives a fresh coat of paint . . . Baumbach recalls Truffaut and early Woody Allen!"—Ella Taylor, *Atlantic Monthly*

"Witty . . . romantic in the best sense of the word!"—Patricia Towers, *Elle*

"A witty, wonderfully bittersweet comedy and romance!"—Dennis Dermody, *Paper*

"Diamond-hard and dazzling!"—Peter Travers, *Rolling Stone*

"Sharp and delightful!"—Andrew Johnson, *Time Out New York*

M
r. *Jealousy* is a sweet, small film about relationships; the lack of them, the beginning of them, the delicious, perplexing agony of living through them, and the frustrating and sometimes inexplicable end to them. Noah Baumbach, director of *Kicking and Screaming* (1995), adds to his oeuvre of confused thirtysomethings with this pleasant story of dating confusion, fear of commitment, and urban worries.

Lester (Eric Stoltz) to Dash (Christopher Eigeman): "How can you say at your age that you've never been faithful to anyone? What kind of boyfriend *are* you?"

Lester Grimm (Eric Stoltz) is a seemingly easygoing urban New Yorker; he is an intelligent, aspiring writer, eking out a living as a substitute teacher, dating Ramona Ray (Annabella Sciorra), an attractive, intelligent grad student. By all accounts, they have an enjoyable relationship, jam-packed with dinners with friends, movies, art shows, walks in the park, and passionate sex.

But Lester is tortured by jealousy; indeed, he simmers with resentment and insecurity when Ramona blithely prattles on about her numerous boyfriends—young, old, smart, dumb, burly. Lester is rattled when Ramona's first boyfriend in the city, writer Dashiell Frank (Chris Eigeman), is pronounced the "writer of our generation" with the publication of his latest book. Although Ramona has not spoken to Dash in years, Lester is simply undone by the thought of Ramona being the model for some of the novel's explicit sex scenes.

In an amazing stroke of synchronicity, Lester sees Dash on the street (he recognizes him from his book jacket) and follows him to a psychologist's office. He makes a snap decision to approach the psychologist Dr. Poke (Peter Bogdanovich) and join the group, under the name of his best friend Vince (Carlos Jacott). Coincidentally, Vince is about to marry Lucretia (Marianne Jean-Baptiste) and is himself plagued by doubts and questions about this move. He is thrilled that Lester will be attending the group under his name and gives him a list of questions about his and Lucretia's situation for the group to explore. Thus begins the film's central premise—a gentle comedy of manners and mistaken identities, underscored by a dry narration that reminds one of similar European films, rife with irony, self-deprecation, and awareness.

Lester lambastes Dash for his phoniness and insincerity about women. When he learns that Dash was not faithful to Ramona during their short courtship, he calls Dash on his callousness. Refreshed by Lester's forthrightness, Dash invites him out for a drink and they bond over multiple scotches. Predictably, Lester finds himself in the awkward position of becoming Dash's friend as "Vince" rather than himself, and wants to bail out of group therapy.

Much to his surprise, though, Lester's therapy has become very important to Vince, and when Lester threatens to leave the group, Vince decides to join the group as "Lester" (though for some inexplicable reason he infuses "Lester" with an incredibly lame British accent). As Lester is more and more preoccupied with keeping up his "double life," Ramona feels ignored. Much

CREDITS

Lester Grimm: Eric Stoltz
Ramona Ray: Annabella Sciorra
Dashiell Frank: Christopher Eigeman
Vince: Carlos Scott
Lucretia: Marianne Jean-Baptiste
Dr. Poke: Peter Bogdanovich
Irene: Bridget Fonda
Lint: John Lehr

Origin: USA
Released: 1997
Production: Joel Castleberg; released by Lion's Gate Productions
Direction: Noah Baumbach
Screenplay: Noah Baumbach
Cinematography: Steve Berstein
Editing: J. Kathleen Gibson
Costumes: Katherine Jane Bryant
Production design: Anne Stuhler
Music: Robert Een
Sound: Jeff Pullman, Ken S. Polk
MPAA rating: R
Running Time: 103 minutes

to Lester's chagrin, Ramona breaks a few dates, seems to fib about her whereabouts, and re-establishes contact with a few old flames.

The entire situation blows up in Lester's face when Ramona follows him to group therapy—along with Lucretia—and they see, in succession, Lester, Dash, and Vince file out of the office. Tempers and fists fly and more is revealed to everyone than they can stand. As appalled as Ramona is to learn why Lester joined the group, Lester is even more shocked to learn that Dash and Ramona have recently met for a short tryst.

Baumbach's characters are nothing if not introspective. Couples split, then reconcile. Lester retreats to a teaching position in the Midwest, licking his wounds. Ramona continues with her education, staying in New York. Lucretia and Vince marry and, at the reception, Lester and Ramona circle each other cautiously.

Like his previous film Baumbach favors articulate urbanites, plagued by the large and small issues that single city dwellers focus on: Do people spit into the creamer at the diner? Must I remain friendly with an ex that I see on the street? Am I ever going to meet the right person? Does everyone in my therapy group hate me? Baumbach's ensemble meshes together perfectly, emboldened by some interesting casting choices (Peter Bogdanovich as the psychologist!). Although Stoltz and Sciorra do not have the most arresting screen presence, together they are more than the sum of their parts.

—*G. E. Georges*

REVIEWS

Boxoffice. April, 1998, p. 198.
Entertainment Weekly. June 12, 1998, p. 52.
Los Angeles Times. June 5, 1998, p. F16.
New York Times. June 5, 1998, p. E15.
Rolling Stone. June 25, 1998, p. 100.
Variety. October 6, 1997, p. 57.
Village Voice. June 9, 1998, p. 152.

Mr. Nice Guy; Yatgo Ho Yan

Fight first. Apologize later.—Movie tagline
Nice guys don't get mad. They get even.—Movie tagline
"Awesome and amusing . . . Chan is as appealing as ever."—Kevin Thomas, *Los Angeles Times*
"Thumbs up!"—Roger Ebert, *Siskel & Ebert*

 Box Office: $12,716,953

He's part Charlie Chaplin, part Harold Lloyd, and part Bruce Lee: He's Jackie Chan. And if you haven't seen him do his stuff, sit back and have fun. Jackie Chan is not just an international star. He's an unstoppable force, not to mention a wild mixture of comedy and martial arts. To the uninitiated, Chan is the Chinese (Hong Kong) phenom whose films such as *Supercop* (1996) have made him a hugely popular star throughout the world. He blends truly astonishing physical feats of martial arts with a wry sense of humor. Jackie's films (once you see him, you feel like you know him well enough to call him by his first name) are formulaic, and, shall we say, not overburdened with verbiage. But actions speak louder than words, and in cinema, pictures speak loudest of all. And Jackie delivers both: heart-stopping action and eye-popping pictures, not to mention a charming and thoroughly engaging screen persona. Only recently has he begun to make inroads into the tough U.S. market, and his most recent film, *Mr. Nice Guy* should help. It is filled with the usual Jackie Chan stunts (which he does all by himself), and a healthy dose of humor.

Ever since *The Terminator* (1984) introduced "humor" into the action drama, American audiences have been flooded with would-be Henry Youngmans dodging bullets and plunging knives into the villain's throat. Most often, these guys have been played by Arnold Schwarzenegger, such as in both *Terminator* movies and *True Lies* (1996); these were still action-dramas and the mixture of funny lines and dripping blood has seemed gratuitous. But perhaps reflecting society's numbness to violence, the violent action-comedy has recently become a cinema staple. Many of the famous male stars have tried it: Eddie Murphy did it in *Beverly Hills Cop* (1984, 1987, 1994), Mel Gibson and Danny Glover in the *Lethal Weapon* films (1987, 1989, 1992, 1998). Of course, many others from Stallone to Snipes to Harrison Ford have tried to weave some humor into their action, but let's not get away from the point. The point is this: nobody blends action and comedy together like Jackie Chan, and *Mr. Nice Guy* is funny, charming, and breathtaking even while its story is shallow, its acting marginal, and its violence unnerving.

Here is the wispy plot of *Mr. Nice Guy*. Jackie (Jackie Chan) is the co-host of a popular cooking show in Melbourne, Australia. Coming out of his studio one day, he encounters a damsel-in-distress, a newswoman (Gabrielle Fitzpatrick) who has gotten her hands on a video tape showing damning evidence against Melbourne's most dangerous druglord, Giancarlo (Richard Norton, doing his best Steven Seagal impression). Jackie, being Mr. Nice Guy, helps her to foil the numerous henchmen chasing her all over downtown Melbourne in a chase scene best described as madcap violence. It is destructive and hilarious, appealing to the best and worst in us. But it's fun; and it's the movies.

Anyway, the plot, such as you might call it, thickens, as Jackie's naive Chinese-speaking girlfriend (Miki Lee) arrives in town and is captured by the bad guys. The police bungle her rescue and Jackie takes matters into his own hands. More important than plot, though, is director Samo Hung and Chan's extraordinary mastery and understanding of their genre of film. They are there to entertain like a cartoon entertains, and boy, do they deliver. Several set-piece action sequences are breathtaking in their pace and ingenuity; they build in intensity and each tells a little story of their own. An example is a sequence in a construction site: it is a Feydeau-farce of opened and closed doors with Jackie and Giancarlo's henchmen playing cat-and-mouse. We remember the old silent films in a wonderful sequence where Jackie is in real danger of being cut up by a series of whirling, turning saws. Knowing that Chan put himself in true peril to create the scene is half the fun. The final sequence, with Jackie riding the wheels of the biggest bulldozer you've ever seen, is a satisfying end: just when you think he can't do anymore, there goes Jackie.

Filmgoers should be advised to stay in their seats during the credits: the outtakes of Jackie attempting his death-defying stunts are as much fun as the film itself. This is not a film for the intellectual elite. *Mr. Nice Guy* is an experience where, like seeing a fine magician at work, you will sit like a kid at a Saturday matinee and wonder, "How did he DO that?" What fun.

—*Kirby Tepper*

CREDITS

Jackie: Jackie Chan
Giancarlo: Richard Norton
Miki: Miki Lee
Lakeisha: Karen McLymont
Diana: Gabrielle Fitzpatrick
Romeo: Vince Poletto
Baggio: Barry Otto

Origin: Hong Kong
Released: 1996, 1998
Production: Chua Lam for Golden Harvest; released by New Line Cinema
Direction: Samo Hung
Screenplay: Edward Tang and Fibe Ma
Cinematography: Raymond Lam
Editing: Peter Cheung
Music: J. Peter Robinson
Production design: Horace Ma
Sound: Gretchen Thornburn
MPAA rating: PG-13
Running Time: 90 minutes

REVIEWS

Chicago Tribune. March 20, 1998, p. 5.
Entertainment Weekly. March 27, 1998, p. 47.
Los Angeles Times. March 20, 1998, p. F14.
New York Times. March 20, 1998, p. E12.
Sight and Sound. September, 1998, p. 49.
USA Today. March 20, 1998, p. 8E.
Variety. August 25, 1997, p. 74.

Monument Ave.

Every city has one—Movie tagline

"An Irish *Mean Streets*. Gritty, jolting Leary dominates in the most complex and compelling role of his career."—Jay Carr, *Boston Globe*

"Extraordinarily powerful. An award caliber performance by Denis Leary. Brilliantly directed by Ted Demme."—Paul Wunder, *WBAI*

Based on the memoirs of its star, Denis Leary, *Monument Ave.* is a relentlessly depressing saga about a group of small-time Irish hoods trapped in the insular Charlestown section of Boston. Leary grew up in Charlestown, a peninsula on the north side of Boston that surrounds the Bunker Hill Monument, the site on Breed's Hill of the misnamed battle that opened the American Revolutionary War. The street of the film's title is shown only once, in an early sequence where the drunken young hoods kick the cars that line both sides of the streets just to make their alarms go off. The monument that commemorates the sacrifices which birthed the United States looms in the background at the end of the street, as if watching in silent judgment over this sort of silly vandalism.

This film was shown at the 1998 Sundance Film Festival under the title *Snitch*.

Directed by Ted Demme from a script by Mike Armstrong, *Monument Ave.* is a rude, crude, unforgiving drama that revels in the supercharged authenticity of its working-class dialogue. The film opens with a jolt, a car chase through the Boston streets, with one car bumping another. In between close-ups of one driver, Bobby O'Grady (Leary), there are sudden flashes of homemade slides that show the young man and his gang in happier childhood days. These memories apparently jostle for the attention of O'Grady's addled brain, for they pop up from time to time. It's the film's only concession to sentiment, and even this is an unforgiving one, for it shows the kids playing cowboys and Indians, and sticking toy guns into each other's faces.

For O'Grady and his buddies, those innocent childhood days are long gone, replaced by a confusing, merciless, fuzzy present. The characters in *Monument Ave.* are constantly drinking beer and booze, smoking cigarettes and snorting cocaine. These addictions and their lust for petty trouble leave them easily manipulated by the neighborhood's crime boss, Jackie (Colm Meaney). Jackie commissions them to do various jobs involving car thefts and insurance schemes while he supplies them with coke, pays rent for their mothers and grandmothers, and picks up bar tabs. Apart from Jackie's largesse and his crimes, their lives are aimless.

Just how aimless is detailed in an hilarious and depressing early sequence in which Bobby and his buddies, Mouse and Seamus, spend an evening in Bobby's house doing lines of cocaine. It's true grit time as the boys compile lists of movie actresses they'd like to have sex with and debate the locations of Amsterdam, Holland and the Netherlands, using a bottle and an ashtray. Clearly, these young men are adolescents who have never grown up. They can only make homophobic wisecracks, discuss women as if they were meat, and keep getting more stoned. At the end, in a sudden fit of honesty, Bobby concludes that the actresses they fantasize about wouldn't give them the time of day if they were the last men on earth.

Bobby is just intelligent enough to know that he is wasting his life but he has absolutely no clue as to how to change his circumstances. One thing that's compelling about *Monument Ave.* is how it shows, without being preachy, what drugs can do to lives. These characters are trapped as much by their need for getting high as they are by Jackie's rule. And the drug traffic that is controlled by Jackie has brought a new level of violence into the tightly knit ethnic culture of the neighborhood. After Jackie's hit men rub out one of the buddies who had gotten out of prison by being a stool pigeon, Bobby says to the others: "In the old days we would settle this with our hands. The worst that could happen would be that somebody would come at you with a shovel or a baseball bat." Now that they are adults, though, and participants in the drug trade, punishment is meted out by execution at gunpoint.

After the first member of Bobby's old boyhood chums dies under Jackie's direction, the beat cop arrives at the bar where the shooting occurred. Played by Martin Sheen, the cop is an Irish veteran who knows the score. When these barroom shootings occur, he points out, every potential witness is always in the bathroom. That's because of the "Code of Silence"—nobody wants to rat on Jackie. In fact, there *was* a Code of Silence in Charlestown; for 25 years, not a single murder was solved because nobody talked.

Sheen's savvy cop concentrates his efforts on Seamus, the newest member of Bobby's gang, a cousin who came over from Dublin less than a year before. Seamus lives with Bobby and his mother, and Bobby has set him up working for Jackie. It turns out, however, that Seamus eventually tires of the bizarre life that Bobby and his friends lead. He feels it's a poor substitute for an honest living, a view which Bobby can't understand, since he has never known anything beyond the insular crime culture of the neighborhood.

The director is excellent at atmosphere but poor at exposition. The code of silence is never explained; the origins of the culture or the reason Jackie is in charge are also not clear. Demme's film implies that there is a carry-over from the old ways in Ireland to the newer, even rougher rule of petty mob chieftains in Boston, but it's not clear how Irish culture affects what's happening. Demme gratuitously uses a merry Irish dance as a backdrop for the film's ultimate act of violence, but it's a statement that is too forced: beneath the smiling Irish eyes lurk the meanness of old scores to be settled.

The relationships among the characters are never made clear. They're all just part of one big Irish mob. Fuzziest—and least Irish–looking—of all is Katie (Famke Janssen). Katie is Bobby's girlfriend, but it's not until later in the film that it's also made clear that she's Jackie's concubine and that Bobby is seeing her on the sly. The dramatic tension would have been aided if Demme had made that conflict clearer earlier on. And Bobby's efforts to arouse Katie's jealousy by making a move in a bar on a yuppie girl (the radiant Jeanne Tripplehorn) don't seem to have much rhyme or reason, other than his simmering need to get revenge on Jackie.

Bobby's troubles boil over as his conflict about his relationship with Jackie deepens. As played with oily malign by the apt-named Meany, Jackie is an ingratiating godfather who has the nerve to show up at the funerals of boys he rubs out to comfort their mothers and even give them some money. His word can't be trusted and his justice comes like a bolt from the blue. In fact, all the violence in *Monument Ave.* explodes fast out of nowhere; Demme doesn't believe in buildups or foreshadowing. That makes his film perhaps more true-to-life but also less satisfying as entertainment. The climax, in particular, comes rocketing in with no warning.

Neither is Demme very successful at embroidering the edges of his neighborhood scene or fleshing out his flat, one-dimensional characters. This could be any American urban ethnic enclave, and these could be any group of small-time crooks. In fact, this story has been done time and time again, and the rich texture and background needed to make it unique are lacking. There is too much gritty, inconsequential dialogue and there are long stretches that seem to be there only to pad the film. One embarrassing sequence that involves Bobby's efforts to show up one of the gang's fringe members as a big talker when it comes to racial harassment is both brutal and unhelpful. So is the part where Bobby tries to take out his frustration at Jackie during a street hockey game.

Leary is quietly effective in his central role as an emotionally constipated, developmentally arrested delinquent who realizes too late that he's never managed to grow up, just get older. The actors who play the rest of his buddies are unremarkable, mostly because their characters get little to do other than sit around making stupid remarks and looking for trouble. Janssen is badly off-kilter here, and she and Leary have so little chemistry that when he fends off her drunken sexual attack, it's a relief. Meany and Sheen both overplay their parts, making their characters into near-caricatures.

Still, there are plenty of effective scenes in *Monument Ave.* To the film's credit, no phony happy ending is imposed on the dreary proceedings. Instead, there's just a small sense of relief and a return to the flashback memories of a happier youth. The hero never exactly makes peace with his demons; he just buries them. Demme is to be congratulated for those doses of realism. But overall his effort falls flat.

—*Michael Betzold*

CREDITS

Bobby: Denis Leary
Jackie O'Hara: Colm Meany
Hanlon: Martin Sheen
Katy: Famke Janssen
Teddy: Billy Crudup
Digger: John Diehl
Shang: Greg Dulli
Mouse: Ian Hart

Origin: USA
Released: 1998
Production: Joel Stillerman, Ted Demme, Jim Serpico, Nicolas Clermont, and Elie Samaha for a Filmline International, Phoenician Films, Clinica Estetica, and Tribeca Independent Films production; released by Lions Gate Films
Direction: Ted Demme
Screenplay: Mike Armstrong
Cinematography: Adam Kimmel
Editing: Jeffrey Wolf
Production design: Ruth Ammon
Set decoration: Jacqueline Jacobson
Costumes: Deborah Newhall
Music: Amanda Scheer-Demme
MPAA rating: Unrated
Running Time: 90 minutes

REVIEWS

Entertainment Weekly. October 9, 1998, p. 56.
Hollywood Reporter. September 15-21, p. 20.
Los Angeles Times. September 25, 1998, p. F4.
New York Times. September 25, 1998, p. E15.
Village Voice. September 29, 1998, p. 130.

Moon Over Broadway

For those of us who love film and those of us who love the "theatre", *Moon Over Broadway* offers up a sampling of both mediums. Brought to you by Chris Hegedus and James McCormick, the filmmakers that helmed *The War Room* (1993), *Moon* examines no less a political minefield— the backstage machinations of a Broadway play. From the very first announcement from producer Rocco Landesman that Carol Burnett, star of television, film and theater, will star in *Moon Over Broadway,* the camera follows actors, producers, the writer and director through their exhaustive paces.

One of the producers of the play before the curtain rises: "I'm telling you, I'm telling you, I'm not worried the least!"

Putting on a "show" in the New York Theatre of the 1990s, is very different from the Mickey Rooney-Judy Garland vision of years gone by. Although the mere presence of Burnett guarantees publicity and a certain name-brand familiarity, that's about all it guarantees—the producers still struggle with the script. But as playwright Ken Ludwig blurts out during one particularly testy rehearsal, "having to have

The play *Moon Over Broadway* marks Carol Burnett's return to Broadway after a 30 year hiatus.

a star is like a deal with the devil"! Ludwig, whose previous work includes *Crazy for You,* appears confident at the press conference announcing the play, then waffles between morbid flop sweat and gallows humor for the rest of the process. Director Tom Moore is the very picture of calm and optimism; if he ever had moments of indecision or uncertainty, the directors have left them on the cutting room floor.

Although the filmmakers were obviously striving to assemble a variety of revealing, enlightening, and yes, shocking scenes, nothing is shown that even remotely approaches the turmoil simmering below the surface. In the one scene that almost boils over, actor Phillip Bosco confronts the director and writer over their refusal to allow some improvisation, some "massaging" of the lines, "Don't you want the benefit of our experience? Isn't that why you hired us?" Everyone seems acutely aware that they are being filmed, and in a movement that becomes a pattern, director Moore calms cast, producer, and writer.

When the production travels to Boston for the out of town tryout, the material's kinks become snarls and everyone's stamina and optimism ebbs and flows. The "glamour" of the theatre is revealed to be an endless series of take-out food, late night walks home in the rain, and continuous, insular discussions. Jokes come and go and bits are reworked. The Boston reviews are kind to Burnett, but pine for a more sophisticated turn of phrase. Just as Hollywood writers complain that they have no clout and are dispensable, this playwright is almost replaced by the producers' choice of joke doctor— a Long Island dentist.

The tinkering continues in New York, as the producers, actors, playwright, and director try to put on a good front for their theatre friends and skillfully manage spin control for the press. The filmmakers, either out of deference to Burnett, or perhaps because they were not allowed access to her, have almost no scenes showing the star upset, flustered or uncertain. She comes across as a humble, driven ("Gosh, look at the re-writes!") actor, never hogging the spotlight, unflaggingly generous. (She seems positively down-to-earth compared to a swooning, vain co-star, seen complaining about her poster, "I'm the pretty girl!")

Burnett's overwhelming popularity with audiences comes forth when a production problem causes a winch to break and one performance to come to a screeching halt. Appearing in front of the curtain, Burnett takes questions from the audience, gives her signature Tarzan yell, and generally charms audiences through a rough spot. The reviews

CREDITS

Phillip Bosco: Phillip Bosco
Carol Burnett: Carol Burnett
Ken Ludwig: Ken Ludwig
Tom Moore: Tom Moore
Elizabeth Williams: Elizabeth Williams
Rocco Landesman: Rocco Landesman

Origin: USA
Released: 1998
Production: Wendy Ettinger, Frazer Pennebaker production in association with Bravo Cable; released by Artistic License
Direction: Chris Hegedus. D.A. Pennebaker
Cinematography: James Desmond, Nick Doob, D.A. Pennebaker
Editing: Chris Hegedus, D.A. Pennebaker
Sound: Chris Hegedus, James McCormick
MPAA rating: Unrated
Running Time: 92 minutes

arrive and they are generally kind to Burnett, but range from tepid to snide for the production. As a counterpoint to these reviews, an epilogue to the film indicates that the play ran for a boffo nine months, drawing steady crowds. The film is enjoyable, but presents nothing scandalous, or insightful, and will be most enjoyable to theatre buffs.

—*G. E. Georges*

REVIEWS

Boxoffice. April 4, 1998, p. 202.
Entertainment Weekly. March 20, 1998, p. 62.
Los Angeles Times. March 6, 1998, p. F24.
Los Angeles Times Weekend. March 5, 1998, p.10.
New York Times. February 18, 1998, p. E5.

Mulan

The flower that blooms in adversity is the most rare and beautiful of all.—Movie tagline

"*Mulan* will capture your heart."—Maria Salas, *CBS Telenoticias*

"Magnificent! Destined to become a timeless classic"—Mose Persico, *CFCF-TV*

"An amazing triumph! An Awe-inspiring epic that is fall-off-your-chair funny! *Mulan* will thrill moviegoers of all ages."—Cameron Turner, *Hangin' N Hollywood*

"If you miss *Mulan*, you'll miss magic this summer!"—Diane Kaminsky, *KHOU-TV* .

"Hands down, the best family film of the summer."—Neil Rosen, *NY-1*

"Disney's greatest achievement since *The Lion King*. You've never seen anything like it."—Mike Cidoni, *WOKR-TV*

A brave Chinese maiden joins the army in place of her father and becomes a hero in Disney's 36th animated feature *Mulan*.

Box Office: $120,620,254

Mulan , based on an ancient Chinese legend, represents Disney's first foray into drawing from unfamiliar, non-Western legends, fairy tales, or folktales for the subject of an animated film. The 36th animated feature released by the studio, *Mulan* was met with the best overall critical reviews and highest audience numbers of any animated Disney film since 1994's *The Lion King*. Although Disney's status as the industry's longstanding "king" of top-notch animated movies has been challenged recently by elaborate, high-quality features from other studios (Fox's *Anastasia*, [1997] Warner Brothers' *Quest for Camelot*, and Dream-Works' *The Prince of Egypt* [two films reviewed in this edition]), the charming *Mulan* proves that the Mouse is in no real danger of losing its reputation. This tale of a young

woman who disguises herself as a man to become a soldier, and who ultimately becomes a national hero, provides a successful combination of humor, delightful characters, memorable musical numbers, rich animation, and an interesting story with a number of useful themes. *Mulan* also achieves a nice balance in tone, somewhere in between the solemnity and maturity of *The Hunchback of Notre Dame* (1996) and the lightheartedness and relative simplicity of *Hercules* (1997). The overall spirit of the film is more like that of *Beauty and the Beast* (1991), but even more so than that film, *Mulan* celebrates the ingenuity and courage of its heroine.

The film introduces the girl Mulan (voice of Ming-Na Wen) as she is preparing, along with other young maidens of her village, to meet the Matchmaker (Miriam Margoyles), who will judge her worthiness to be married and, hopefully, find her a mate. Free spirited and unconventional, Mulan is not entirely confident of herself as a "proper" young Chinese woman, and fears that she will disappoint her father and mother. When she meets the Matchmaker, an unfortunate incident with a supposedly lucky cricket results in the Matchmaker telling Mulan that she will not be an honor to her family. Feeling like she cannot please anyone, Mulan returns home, where her father Fa Zhou (Soon-Tek Oh), though somewhat disappointed, reassures her that she is simply a flower that has not bloomed yet.

Meanwhile, China is invaded by the Huns, led by the huge, menacing Shan-Yu (Miguel Ferrer), who takes his army in the direction of the palace of the Emperor (Pat Morita). To fend off this attack, the Chinese army calls on a male from every family to join its ranks. The only male in Mulan's family is her father, who was wounded years before in another war, so he is ordered to report for duty. Fa Zhou considers it an honor to fight for

Mushu (voice of Eddie Murphy) to Mulan: "You're the man—well, sort of."

the protection of his family and country, but Mulan does not want him to go. During the night, she disguises herself as a young man, secretly takes her father's armor and sword, and steals away toward the camp of the army.

When Mulan heads off to join the army, the spirits of her family's ancestors awaken and decide to send a protector to go after her and bring her back. The First Ancestor (George Takei) orders the tiny, clumsy dragon Mushu (Eddie Murphy) to awaken a great stone dragon and send him after Mulan, but Mushu decides to take on the task himself, hoping to impress the ancestors and regain his lost stature as a guardian of the family. However, instead of bringing Mulan back home, Mushu decides to try to help her become a great soldier, but as a primarily comic character, Mushu does not

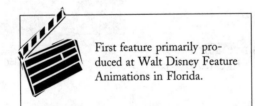

First feature primarily produced at Walt Disney Feature Animations in Florida.

prove to be that much of a help after joining Mulan. Mulan's road to success is one she paves herself.

Initially Mulan has trouble coping with her comrades and the demands of their captain, Shang (B.D. Wong), a stalwart and handsome young man who has been given the task of training the new recruits. However, this changes when she begins relying on her wits and gains confidence in herself. Her progress somehow then motivates the other recruits, who follow her example, and they all become good soldiers—or real "men," as Shang puts it. Mulan's mental and physical prowess proves to be a great asset to the small army of new soldiers when she saves the company from the advancing Huns and literally saves Shang's life. Unfortunately, Mulan's true gender is eventually exposed, and to repay the debt he owes her, Shang spares her life and kicks her out of the company (women, of course, are prohibited from serving in this army). Shang and the rest of the army

then proceed to the Imperial city, believing the Huns to be defeated.

Left behind, Mulan discovers that Shan-Yu and his strongest cohorts have survived and are on their way to the Emperor. She speeds to the Imperial city to warn the people and the army, where she is first ignored. However, her peers in the army still respect her and team up with her to outwit and defeat Shan-Yu once and for all. For her courage and heroism, the Emperor honors Mulan by bowing to her and then bestowing on her an imperial medallion and the sword of Shan-Yu. Shortly after Mulan returns home to the joyous, welcoming arms of her family, Shang shows up to visit her, having developed a strong attraction to this young woman he once believed was a man. Mulan also has feelings for him, and the movie ends with a clear indication that the two will likely become a couple.

Mulan is one of the strongest female characters Disney has ever created for an animated film. In recent years, the women in Disney's features have become increasingly independent, intelligent, unconventional, and heroic. Belle, from *Beauty and the Beast,* was such a character, as were Pocahontas from the same-titled film (1995) and Esmeralda (from 1996's *The Hunchback of Notre Dame*), but Mulan takes such characters several steps further, in that she alone is the true hero of this story (she never has to be rescued by her man) and she successfully blurs the lines between conventional gender roles. The beginning of the story finds Mulan wrestling with her fears that she cannot measure up to what is expected of her as a woman by society or her family. Society expects her to be a proper young woman whose goal is to be matched with the right man and bring honor to her family, but Mulan fears that she "will never pass for the perfect bride or the perfect daughter." She is, in fact, struggling with her identity as an individual, a struggle she describes eloquently in the song "Reflection:" "Why is my reflection someone I don't know? Somehow I cannot hide who I am, though I've tried. When will my reflection show who I am inside?"

Interestingly, and in a move more daring than any Disney heroine before her, Mulan disguises herself and takes on a role that her society reserves only for men. Her experience in the army challenges gender stereotypes and shows that, in many ways, she can be as good a "man" as any male. Amusingly, when Shang first attempts to train his army, the males have as difficult a time as Mulan, and there is sharp irony in Shang's singing to the company that he will "make a man" out of everyone (including, of course, Mulan). The song playfully exposes the relativity of gender roles: according to Shang, his recruits are not "real" men (he sarcastically questions whether he has been sent China's daughters instead of her sons) because they are unskilled and seemingly inept as soldiers, but it is Mulan (truly one of China's daughters) who first demonstrates the traits Shang is looking for from his men.

The complexity in Mulan's character is one of the many highlights of the story. Even though she does join the army to save her father, she eventually realizes that her motives were somewhat selfish as well. As she tells Mushu in a moment of self-revelation, she joined the army for herself as much as for her father. In addition to protecting her father, Mulan hopes to find herself and to prove herself. This moment of enlightenment comes at the lowest point in her adventure, after she has been exposed and left behind, but instead of giving up,

CREDITS

Mulan: Ming-Na Wen (voice)
Mulan: Lea Salonga (singing)
Mushu: Eddie Murphy (voice)
Shang: B.D. Wong (voice)
Shang: Donny Osmond (singing)
Yao: Harvey Fierstein (voice)
Chien-Po: Jerry S. Tondo (voice)
Ling: Gedde Watanabe (voice)
Ling: Matthew Wilder (singing)
Chi-Fu: James Hong (voice)
Shan-Yu: Miguel Ferrer (voice)
Fa Zhou: Soon-Tek Oh (voice)
The Emperor: Pat Morita (voice)
Grandmother Fa: June Foray (voice)
Grandmother Fa: Marni Nixon (singing)
First Ancestor: George Takei (voice)
General Li: James Shigeta (voice)
Matchmaker: Miriam Margoyles (voice)

Origin: USA
Released: 1998
Production: Pam Coate; released by Walt Disney Pictures
Direction: Barry Cook, Tony Bancroft
Screenplay: Rita Hsiao, Christopher Sanders, Philip Lazebnik, Raymond Singer, and Eugenia Bostwick-Singer
Editing: Michael Kelly
Music: Jerry Goldsmith, Matthew Wilder
Lyrics: David Zippel
Production design: Hans Bacher
Art direction: Ric Sluiter
Sound: Lon E. Bender
MPAA rating: G
Running Time: 88 minutes

AWARDS AND NOMINATIONS

Academy Awards 1998 Nominations: Original Musical or Comedy Score

she rises to the occasion once again and valiantly sets out on her own to save her friends and the Emperor.

The puny dragon Mushu, voiced by Eddie Murphy in a hilarious, inspired performance, stands out as one of the other delightful elements of *Mulan*. Mushu is drawn as a comic parallel to Mulan, in that he also embarks on a quest to prove himself and obtain honor that he has lost or failed to achieve. While he genuinely hopes to help Mulan, his underlying goal is also to convince the ancestors to make him a guardian. Mulan's self-revelation prompts his own admittance of selfish aspirations. When Mulan's disguise is removed, and she sees into herself clearly, Mushu has a similar experience. This scene works as a pivotal point in the story and underscores the film's central theme, which is the problem of identity. Both of these characters put on disguises and set out on quests to prove themselves, which ultimately only happens after the disguises are dropped and they embrace the freedom to be themselves.

Mulan should be counted as one of Disney's best animated films, for it shares the qualities of the studio's great classics. There is humor aplenty, exquisite animation, a sophisticated musical score, memorable songs (though the number of songs is small), a scary villain, an entertaining story, and a heroic protagonist whose heroism lies not only in defeating the villain but in challenging and defeating age-old stereotypes and repressive social roles. As long as Disney continues to produce quality, sophisticated features like *Mulan*, the studio should retain its legendary standing at the top of the list.

—*David Flanagin*

REVIEWS

Boxoffice. June, 1998, p. 16.
Chicago Tribune. June 19, 1998, p. 5.
Cinefantastique. June, 1998, p. 7.
Detroit News. June 19, 1998, p. 11D.
Entertainment Weekly. June 19, 1998, p. 47.
Los Angeles Times. June 19, 1998, p. F1.
New York Times. June 19, 1998, p. E13.
People. June 22, 1998, p. 31.
Rolling Stone. July 9, 1998, p. 146.
Time. June 22, 1998.
Variety. June 8, 1998, p. 66.
Washington Post Weekend. June 19, 1998, p. 47.

Music From Another Room

Early on in *Music From Another Room,* Grace Swan (Brenda Blethyn of 1996's *Secrets and Lies*) goes into labor at her kitchen sink, and her baby is in danger of being asphyxiated by the umbilical chord wrapped tightly around its neck. Danny, the five-year-old son of her late best friend who is visiting the Swans along with his father, is able to reach inside Grace with his tiny hands and save little Anna's life. Whether *Music From Another Room* would ever see the light of day seems to have been equally problematic. The romantic comedy was made on a small budget in thirty days at the beginning of 1997. While it was released in Australia and Israel in the Fall of 1998, it was apparently never released in the United States, relegated to being an in-flight movie before finally emerging for the general public's consideration in the form of a video-cassette around the end of 1998.

Anna (Gretchen Mol): "Hi, nice to meet you." Danny (Jude Law): "Last time we met, you were covered in afterbirth."

The bulk of the film deals with the adult Danny's (Jude Law) passionate love for Anna (Gretchen Mol), which began with his vow on the night she was born that he would marry her someday. He meets her for the first time in two decades when he returns to the U.S. after growing up in England. Upon Danny's arrival, his girlfriend breaks up with him, and he swears that he will never fall in love again. He soon breaks that vow, however, when he runs into Anna while making a delivery for the bakery below his new apartment. Is it kismet? An ardent Danny thinks so, but Anna, her feet always planted firmly on the ground, continues to keep herself tightly under control, as she is engaged to marry Eric (Jon Tenney), a rich man who has continued to help her loopy family financially. Anna cares about Eric, but their relationship lacks the spark of exhilarating romance that Danny's love offers.

Danny gets a job working on mosaic tile restoration, his chosen trade, but he spends his free time reading to Anna's blind sister Nina (touchingly portrayed by Jennifer Tilly), appearing in a violently feminist version of *Medea* put on by another sister, Karen (Martha Plimpton), and generally hanging around the Swan clan in the hope of winning an obviously wavering Anna. Before Momma Grace passes away, she states that she hopes to live long enough to see Anna break loose and do one magical, impassioned thing. Thinking over her situation, Anna searches out Danny and spends the night making love to him. After Grace's funeral, however, she returns to Eric, and Danny swears off passion for good. Nina gives her sister the final push she needs towards Danny, who, in a decidedly false note, tells Anna that he is no longer romantic but rational like her, and she should return to Eric. Even though Danny had been hurt, it seems unbelievable that he would need

Anna's dogged pleas to convince him to accept the love of his dream girl. They end up together, of course, in keeping with this genre's conventions. We always figure that the boy and girl will end up together in this type of film, despite all their troubles and bickering, so the audience's enjoyment depends upon how interesting the journey is to get to that point. (Think especially of the screwball comedies of the 1930s and 1940s.)

While *Music From Another Room* often strains in obvious and unsuccessful ways to be funny in a quirky sort of manner, it is comparatively more successful in the romance department. This is due in large part to Law (1997's *Gattaca* and *Midnight in the Garden of Good and Evil*), a fresh and engaging actor who shows the skill which earned him an Olivier Award nomination as "Outstanding Newcomer" followed by a 1995 Tony Award nomination for the play "Indiscretions." He is hobbled in his efforts by a weak script and a pairing with Mol (also seen in this year's *Celebrity*) as Anna, who is certainly pretty but viewers may have a hard time warming up to her Anna even when she finally warms up to Danny. There is something too blank and nondescript about her performance, nothing

CREDITS

Danny: Jude Law
Anna Swan: Gretchen Mol
Nina Swan: Jennifer Tilly
Grace Swan: Brenda Blethyn
Karen Swan: Martha Plimpton
Eric: Jon Tenney
Billy Swan: Jeremy Piven

Origin: USA
Released: 1998
Production: John Bertolli, Brad Krevoy, Steven Stabler, Bradley Thomas; released by MGM-UA
Direction: Charlie Peters
Screenplay: Charlie Peters
Cinematography: Richard Crudo
Editing: Carroll Timothy O'Meara
Music: Richard Gibbs
Production design: Charles Breen
Set decoration: Denise Pizzini
Costumes: Mary Claire Hannan
Sound: David Rawlinson
MPAA rating: PG-13
Running Time: 104 minutes

distinctive, especially when compared to that of her co-star. Law is the one who comes off as affecting in their scenes and gives them what life they have.

Music From Another Room may have an intriguing title and premise, but what follows that title onscreen is uneven and often unsuccessful, with only Law's performance and a few poignant moments that ring true. Most of the family members are rather one-note, sketchy characterizations that are a little too purposefully offbeat. Almost all are peripheral characters we would not especially want to know, and so when they are focused upon we wish that the film would get back to Danny and Anna. The one exception to this is the secondary love story of Nina and Jesus (an effective Vincent Laresca), who have some genuinely tender moments. Their relationship, fleshed out further, might have even been interesting enough for a film of their own, but they are merely here to make a point: that the sister who cannot see but feels deeply can still recognize true love when it stands before her, while her rather icy, sighted sister cannot see it when it is right under her nose.

Many lines in *Music From Another Room* sound too much like they were crafted for effect upon the screenwriter's word processor instead of originating in the minds and hearts of the characters. Still another problem with the film are the times when music is conspicuously used to signal that what we are watching is a stirring moment, as if the director felt the welling-up of music might elicit the welling-up of emotion that the script could not rouse on its own. Despite its troubled path to domestic release, *Music From Another Room* will not make you flee to another room. It should, however, serve to increase your respect for Law.

— *David L. Boxerbaum*

REVIEWS

The Australian. March, 1998.
Boxoffice. February, 1998.

My Giant

"Big laughs, bigger heart!"—Joel Siegel, *Good Morning America*

"A winner! A king-sized charmer."—Alan Silverman, *Voice of America*

"Sharp, funny and very moving."—Paul Wunder, *WBAI Radio*

 Box Office: $8,072,007

By rights, a movie about a friendship between a character played by diminutive comic Billy Crystal and a 7-foot-6 Romanian giant ought to be full of sight gags and other laughs. And, in fact, *My Giant* is billed as a comedy. But it has a gigantic problem: it isn't funny.

There are more good lines in a typical Crystal hosting of an Academy Awards presentation than in this film. Ad-libbing his way through the Oscars, Crystal is wry and original. In *My Giant*, however, Crystal falls victim to a fatal comedian's temptation: the desire to be warmhearted. It's a failing that has plagued many comics since Charlie Chaplin, many of whose films are nearly ruined by treacly sentimentality.

Beware of films where the star is the producer. Judging by its hackneyed plot, *My Giant* would never have been made

if it weren't a Crystal project. Nothing much of interest happens in this film, which feels much longer than its 97 minutes. The story line is forced, flimsy, and full of extraneous detours.

Crystal conceived the idea for the movie while working with Andre the Giant in *The Princess Bride* (1987). After Andre died, Crystal, a pro basketball fan, set his sights on Washington Wizards center Gheorghe Muresan. At 7-foot-6, Muresan is the tallest man in the National Basketball Association. He is also, unlike most of his hoop peers, a true giant, medically speaking. The gigantism accounts not only for his stature, but also his diminished life expectancy, his huge jaw and his slurred speech. The vocal impediments combined with his heavy accent make Muresan extremely problematic as an actor. It's difficult to understand much of what he is saying.

Having found his giant, Crystal seems unable to figure out what to do with him. Concocting a story with screenwriter David Seltzer, Crystal turns himself into Sammy, a talent agent down on his luck. The role is not much of a stretch for Crystal, and allows him basically to play himself: a fast-talking, breezy show-biz type who feels unfulfilled.

Sammy is scripted as a self-centered workaholic who has neglected his teenage son Nick (Zane Carney) and his devoted wife Serena (Kathleen Quinlan). But Sammy doesn't really behave as an egomaniac in the film; he doesn't mistreat anyone. He is more like a little puppy dog who has lost his way. This demeanor allows him to be redeemed, again without much effort, by the purer motives of the giant.

My Giant would have worked better if Crystal had allowed his character to be at least a little mean or venal. But every major role in the film is sickeningly sweet. Muresan, because he is genuinely unactorly, is the only one whose big-heartedness and guilelessness ring true. He is every bit the novice being taken along for a ride.

Crystal and director Michael Lehmann exploit Muresan's dramatic inexperience by making him into a ridiculously untutored innocent. His character is called Maximus, of course, or Max for short. Max is a sweet version of the noble savage, a little boy hidden in an oversized body. The script treats him exactly as many film scripts treat animal pets who show their masters true love, loyalty or courage.

Sammy finds Max living in a Romanian monastery, to which his parents sent him when he was 15, ostensibly because he was growing too fast and eating them out of house and home. The shy Max never leaves the monastery because villagers have heckled him and thrown rocks at him, treating him as a freak.

Sammy is in Romania because his newest young star is playing in a swashbuckling costume epic being shot there. Unfortunately, the conceited star fires Sammy. In despair, Sammy accidentally drives off a road in a rainstorm. His car plunges into a river, but he is lifted out of the water by a pair of giant hands. The hands belong to Max, but Sammy figures it's God. This is Crystal's none-too-subtle way of signaling that Max will be Sammy's salvation from his sins of ambition and greed.

Sammy realizes Max will fit nicely the role of the villain in the epic being shot nearby. Max is such an innocent that he doesn't know what a movie is, and he's afraid to go out in public. Max does desire, however, to go to America, because that's where the girl of his dreams lives. Her name is Lillianna, and he wistfully explains to Sammy that once, when he was 14, they kissed. It was behind the statue of the Virgin Mary,

Basketball player Gheorghe Muresan plays center for the Washington Wizards.

and naturally so, because it was a virginal kiss. Crystal won't let Max be adult enough to be capable of lust, only puppy love. For 23 years, he would have us believe, Max has been writing daily love letters to Lillianna, though she has never answered them.

Though physically Max is overdeveloped, emotionally he is scripted as a case of arrested development. He is impossibly innocent, charmingly loyal, and unsullied by the ways of flesh or gold. The fact that he can't talk clearly and that he is easily frightened makes him even more of a little boy. There's even a scene of Sammy reading a bedtime story to Max. It's actually Shakespeare, an author Max loves. That proves Max is no simpleton, and helps elevate his emotions. But the whole character is an insult to Muresan. He's treated not as a grown person, but as an enlarged eunuch.

While otherwise patronizing him, Lehmann and Crystal resist almost every temptation to exploit Muresan physically. The few times they do so provide some of the film's rare funny bits. When Sammy brings Max to his parents' apartment for dinner, an aunt audaciously asks, "How big is your. . . . " and is quickly hustled away. When Sammy, desperate for money, lets the reluctant Max do a wrestling match in Cleveland against a tag team of seven midgets, the littlest midget taunts the giant, glaring at him and saying: "You're mine." Max is downed, and the tiniest midget sits astride his head and pulls his hair.

Even these scenes are cut short. Max never answers the aunt's question (to do so would ruin his innocence). And Max abruptly quits the wrestling match, offended because the announcer calls him "Diablo Grotesque," the same insult hurled at him by the villagers back in Romania. In these and other scenes, Crystal pulls back every time he starts to use Max's size to make a joke, as if he distrusts his own comic instincts. It's fine not to make a whole film based on height incongruity, but that's the basis of the film's concept, after all.

Contrivance builds on contrivance as the film labors along, a sort of aimless road picture that ends in Hollywood. The last third of the film wallows in unbearable sentimentality, as Sammy learns Max is dying of an enlarged heart. Now, real giants do have real heart problems, and Muresan's life expectancy is therefore shorter than normal, but this plot twist dooms the film to a terribly maudlin finish.

Eventually, Sammy lands Max a dream role in a Steven Seagal movie, and Seagal, playing himself, deadpans: "He's bigger than me. And that's no good." In the film's best scene, a triumphant Sammy puts Seagal on the phone to his son Nick, mistakenly believing Nick worships Seagal. Nick, thinking Seagal is really Sammy doing an imitation of Seagal, blasts the action star: "When you talk, try clearing the phlegm out of your throat. Try taking acting lessons." The mystery is why Seagal signed on for *My Giant*. Maybe he's secure enough in his huge paychecks to take some ribbing.

Curiously, Crystal and the movie lose interest in Max's film stardom, and we never even see Max in Seagal's movie. Instead, Sammy goes off to track down Lillianna (Joanna Pacula), who, in one of the film's few non-fairy-tale moments,

Steven Seagal on giving Max a film role: "The fact of the matter is that he's much bigger than me. And as you know, that's not good."

CREDITS

Sammy Kanin: Billy Crystal
Serena Kanin: Kathleen Quinlan
Max: Gheorghe Muresan
Lillianna: Joanna Pacula
Nick Kanin: Zane Carney
Steven Seagal: Steven Seagal
Justin Allen: Rider Strong
Milt: Harold Gould
Rose: Doris Roberts

Origin: USA
Released: 1998
Production: Billy Crystal for Face; released by Castle Rock Entertainment
Direction: Michael Lehmann
Screenplay: David Seltzer
Cinematography: Michael Coulter
Editing: Stephen Semel
Music: Marc Shaiman
Production design: Jackson DeGovia
Art direction: Tom Reta
Costumes: Rita Ryack
Sound: Jeff Wexler
MPAA rating: PG
Running Time: 103 minutes

expresses no interest in fulfilling Max's dream. The preposterous solution is for Sammy to recruit the dutiful Serena to fake being Lillianna and come to meet with Max. Quinlan, as usual, struggles gamely to give her underwritten part some much-needed believability. But this scene is excruciating.

Throughout, Crystal plays it safe with *My Giant*. It's one of the slowest, tamest, and most meaningless pictures in years. There's nothing wrong with the way Lehmann directs or how the other technical magicians do their work; it's just that Crystal gives them so little to work with. If Crystal really is so infatuated with giants, maybe he should try doing a documentary. To make Muresan into an over-sized stuffed animal betrays the shallowness of Crystal's concept. We didn't need another movie about a show-biz personality who finds his heart. What we really need from a comic are laughs.

—Michael Betzold

REVIEWS

Entertainment Weekly. April 17, 1998, p. 47.
Los Angeles Times. April 10, 1998, p. F4.
New York Times. April 10, 1998, p. E20.
People. April 20, 1998, p. 33.
San Francisco Chronicle. April 10, 1998.
Variety. April 6, 1998, p. 47.
Washington Post. April 10, 1998, p. B7.

The Negotiator

Chicago's two best hostage negotiators are forced to face their worst nightmare . . . each other.—Movie tagline

"The summer's best surprise!"—Joanna Langfield, *Movie Minute*

"Jackson and Spacey are perfect!"—Jeff Craig, *Sixty Second Preview*

"Intense! A high-octane summer sizzler!"—Susan Granger, *SSG Syndicate*

"Positively electrifying!"—Bill Bregoli, *Westwood One Radio Network*

"A winner! A powerful, explosive, action-packed thriller."—Jules Peimer, *WKDM Radio*

Box Office: $44,748,766

This picture demonstrates that a potentially incoherent screenplay can be rescued by competent direction and by superior star acting. It is difficult to say who wins the contest between Samuel L. Jackson and Kevin Spacey, both of whom are at the top of their form here, but it is clear that the two of them are responsible for saving this film. Jackson plays Danny Roman, a tough hostage negotiator with the Chicago police force. The film opens with a tense encounter in which an insanely jealous husband has taken his young daughter hostage. He threatens to kill the child if her mother is not brought to him. This unbalanced and suicidal maniac intends to kill himself in his wife's presence. Danny calms the man down and manages to get into the apartment with him, on the pretext of searching the place before the wife is allowed to enter. He maneuvers the man into a room away from the child and near to a window, where police snipers can get a clear shot. It's a pretty brutal solution.

Danny is a hero, but fame is fleeting, as he is soon to discover. His partner has disturbing information that money

A tense situation develops between hostage negotiators Danny Roman (Samuel L. Jackson) and Chris Sabian (Kevin Spacey) in *The Negotiator*.

is being skimmed from the police pension fund. He arranges a late-night meeting with Roman, but by the time Danny arrives, his partner has been executed in his automobile. Within days it becomes clear that Danny is being framed for the murder, when he is asked to turn in his badge and weapon. Enraged, Danny goes to the 20th floor office of the head of Chicago's Internal Affairs, Inspector Niebaum (played by the late character actor J.T. Walsh, to whom the film is dedicated), his chief accuser. The confrontation quickly escalates, and Roman takes the man hostage, along with his boss, Commander Frost (Ron Rifkin), tough secretary Maggie (Siobahan Fallon), and con man Rudy (Paul Giamatti) who specializes in credit-card fraud.

As a S.W.A.T. team quickly moves into place, as well as the F.B.I., who want to take over the situation, Roman, who fully understands the rules of the deadly game he is playing, takes control, and says that he will only deal with a single "negotiator," Chris Sabian (Kevin Spacey), from the West Side of Chicago rather than downtown, a man he knows by reputation, though the two are not friends. Sabian agrees to cooperate only on one condition—that he be given command of the situation. He doesn't want bloodshed, but when the S.W.A.T. team rappels down from the roof and breaks in through the office windows, risking the lives of the hostages, it soon becomes clear that someone highly placed wants Roman dead.

Roman is able to deal with crisis situations, however,

Sabian (Kevin Spacey) to Roman (Samuel L. Jackson): "You hurt one of them, you burn up any currency you have with me. They're all I care about. Getting you out of here alive . . . a distant second."

Filmed on location in downtown Chicago.

and ends up taking two more police officers hostage. With some help from Maggie and Rudy (who knows how to break computer codes), Danny manages to get incriminating information from Niebaum's hard drive. A second attack results in Niebaum's death. It is clear to Roman that Niebaum was assassinated, since he takes three shots in the chest. Niebaum's death was no accident. Obviously those trying to get Roman were afraid that Niebaum might cave under pressure, and, just as obviously, he knows too much.

Sabian goes to the 20th floor to talk to Roman face-to-face. Concessions are made in return for the release of hostage Frost and the electricity, which has been cut off, is turned back on so that Danny can get to Niebaum's office computer. But meanwhile the situation is getting our of hand, and finally the F.B.I. takes over. By that time, Sabian is convinced that Roman is onto something and possibly innocent. With his help, Roman manages to escape, first through an air vent, then from the building complex, in order to get to Niebaum's home computer, since by that time the office computer has been fried and burnt out during the skirmishes on the 20th floor.

And that is where the final showdown takes place, at Niebaum's home. Clearly Danny has been betrayed by several of his friends and colleagues, but it is not clear until the very end who is dirty and who is not, since even Internal Affairs officers have been on the take. At the end, Danny is exonerated, but not without some strain and pain, as Sabian works a devious deal that apparently involves his shooting Danny. Curiously, the signature tagline featured prominently in the film's trailer, spoken by Kevin Spacey, "Now you have to deal with both of us," is not prominently featured in the film, but that line cuts to the chase in signifying what the film's drama involves.

Reviews were incredibly scrambled and inconsistent. *Time* critic Richard Schickel delayed reviewing the film until ten days after its opening, then gave it what the magazine calls a "short take." Schickel found the framework promising—"two strong actors in a strong situation," and the central mystery puzzling ("if Roman isn't the killer, who is?"), but complained that "Hollywood doesn't trust talk," and in its latter stages, the film exchanges explosions for dialogue, and, "as usual, the main things lost in the hubbub are wit and logic."

Attacking the film from a different direction, *Washington Post* reviewer Stephen Hunter found it "bafflingly constructed" and "about five rewrites shy of intelligibility." Hunter's colleague Michael O'Sullivan of the *Post Weekend* also criticized writers James DeMonaco and Kevin Fox for fabricating a story that "ranges from dumb to average," but he praised the direction of F. Gary Gray, as well as Jackson and Spacey. Chris Kaltenbach of the *Baltimore Sun* was also impressed by the "superlative acting," but believed that Jackson outclassed Spacey, as was not necessarily the case. One could just as easily argue that Spacey's understated style holds its own against Samuel L. Jackson's flamboyance. Both of these reviewers were impressed, however, by David Morse "as a gung-ho SWAT commander with bullets for brains," the actor having "morphed into one scary, hulking ape from his wimpy days as Dr. Morrison" on the network televison show *St. Elsewhere*. "With stars like this," Kaltenbach wrote of Jackson and Spacey, "who thinks about the plot?"

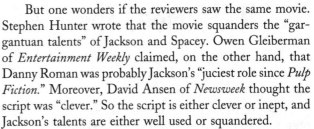

CREDITS

Danny Roman: Samuel L. Jackson
Chris Sabian: Kevin Spacey
Cmdr. Adam Beck: David Morse
Cmdr. Frost: Ron Rifkin
Chief Al Travis: John Spencer
Terence Niebaum: J. T. Walsh
Karen Roman: Regina Taylor
Maggie: Siobahn Fallon
Rudy: Paul Giamatti

Origin: USA
Released: 1998
Production: David Hoberman and Arnon Milchan for Regency Enterprises, Mandeville Films and New Regency; released by Warner Bros.
Direction: F. Gary Gray
Screenplay: James DeMonaco and Kevin Fox
Cinematography: Russell Carpenter
Editing: Christian Wagner
Music: Graeme Revell
Production design: Holger Gross
Art direction: Kevin Ishioka
Costumes: Francine Jamison-Tanchuck
Sound: Russell Williams
Special effects supervision: Dan Suddick
Stunt coordination: Joel Kramer
MPAA rating: R
Running Time: 138 minutes

But one wonders if the reviewers saw the same movie. Stephen Hunter wrote that the movie squanders the "gargantuan talents" of Jackson and Spacey. Owen Gleiberman of *Entertainment Weekly* claimed, on the other hand, that Danny Roman was probably Jackson's "juciest role since *Pulp Fiction*." Moreover, David Ansen of *Newsweek* thought the script was "clever." So the script is either clever or inept, and Jackson's talents are either well used or squandered.

Samuel L. Jackson told Charlie Rose in a PBS television interview (July 30) that the film was originally intended as a Sylvester Stallone project. Perhaps that explains why Gleiberman considered it "a clever B-movie" because "the characters don't have much texture." But a B-movie is ordinarily one that is made quickly on a low budget, and this was a big-budget, high profile movie, the first for director Gray, who manages to escalate the suspense "with an expertise that, most of the time, avoids the meaningless hysteria so many action directors now feel is *de rigueur*," in the opinion of David Ansen. Ansen also praised the film for its sense of humor that managed to turn this "formula film into a frolic."

Is the plot baffling? It's not perfect, but it hangs together well enough, ultimately, and, according to *Variety*, it was "inspired" by an actual case in St. Louis involving police corruption. *Variety* reviewer Emanuel Levy found a comparison to *Face/Off* in the way the film "shrewdly exploits not only its central opposing roles, but the different performance styles of the actors." The bottom line for *Variety* was that *The Negotiator* was an "entertaining suspenser" likely to make money. Regardless of the mixed reviews, *The Negotiator* delivered more entertainment value and smarter acting than most of the noisy, explosive films unleashed on audiences during the summer season.

—*James M. Welsh*

REVIEWS

Baltimore Sun. July 31, 1998, p. E5.
Entertainment Weekly. July 31, 1998, p. 44.
New York Times. July 29, 1998, p. 85.
Newsweek. August 3, 1998, p. 67.
Philadelphia Inquirer. July 29, 1998, p. D4.
Sight and Sound. December, 1998, p. 52.
Time. August 10, 1998, p. 88.
Variety. July 27, 1998, p. 51.
Washington Post. July 29, 1998, p. D1.
Washington Post Weekend. July 31, 1998, p. 47.

Neil Simon's The Odd Couple 2; The Odd Couple 2

Some arguments stand the test of time.—Movie tagline

"The modern world's most deliriously mismatched buddies are at it again."—James Verniere, *Boston Herald*

"Lemmon and Matthau are the champions of comedy. One of Neil Simon's funniest. . . ever!"—Dennis Cunningham, *CBS-TV*

"Lemmon and Matthau make comic gold!"
—Michael Wilmington, *Chicago Tribune*

"Laughs-a-plenty! Neil Simon is the master."
—Jeffrey Lyons, *NBC-TV*

"Our cheeks are sore from laughing! Matthau has the best comic timing in movies and funnyman Simon arms him with zingers to spare."
—Thelma Adams, *New York Post*

"You'll laugh, guffaw, giggle, chuckle and smile. It's absolutely impossible not to enjoy this fun-filled comedy."—Susan Granger, *SSG Syndicate*

 Box Office: $18,912,328

Neil Simon's The Odd Couple 2 received many unfavorable notices, perhaps because critics were comparing it with the original hit film *The Odd Couple* (1968), which was the basis for the long-running television sitcom starring Jack Klugman and Tony Randall. Siskel and Ebert gave the film "two thumbs *way* down" and said the script was the worst Neil Simon had ever written. According to Stephen Holden of the *New York Times*, "Mr. Simon's screenplay is so clunky and devoid of real jokes that the actors are reduced to desperate mugging and shouting to try to pump some energy into their bickering dialogue." Ruth Stein of the *San Francisco Chronicle* compared Lemmon and Matthau to old-time slapstick comedians Laurel and Hardy.

Undeniably, the sequel to *The Odd Couple* falls far short of the brilliant original. On its own merits, however, the new film is at least as funny as Jack Lemmon and Walter Matthau's successful *Grumpy Old Men* (1993) and funnier than its sequel *Grumpier Old Men* (1995). *Variety* critic Joe Leydon wrote: "To their credit, the two veteran actors generate a great deal of goodwill, and do much more for the pic

Oscar (Walter Matthau): "Don't get physical, Felix. I'm too old to hit but I could spit you to death."

than it ever does for them. Director Howard Deutch [who also directed *Grumpier Old Men*] basically keeps out of their way, which, under the circumstances, may have been the wisest possible move." There is also a certain nostalgic pleasure, at least for older viewers, in seeing the neat freak Felix Ungar (Jack Lemmon) and sloppy Oscar Madison (Walter Matthau) brought back together after being separated (in story time) for seventeen years.

The Odd Couple 2 marks the eighth appearance of Lemmon and Matthau as a comedy team. Their first buddy film was *The Fortune Cookie* (1966), a boxoffice success which established their contrasting personas. Their biggest hit was *The Odd Couple*, followed by *The Front Page* (1974), and the disappointing *Buddy Buddy* (1981). *Grumpy Old Men* successfully paired the now aging actors, but *Grumpier Old Men* lacked humor. It looked as if Lemmon and Matthau were getting too old to attract young viewers and had lost the chemistry they had once shared. Then they surprised doomsayers with *Out to Sea* (1997). They looked rejuvenated. They were really funny—and bankable—again.

What brings Oscar and Felix back together is the wedding of Oscar's son Brucey (Jonathan Silverman) to Felix's daughter Hannah (Lisa Waltz) in Southern California. Oscar and Felix will meet again at Los Angeles International Airport and share a rental car to get to the ceremony in a place called San Malina.

Oscar, the former sportswriter, still likes to play poker. The only difference is that he now plays mostly with women because their greater longevity has put them in the vast majority in his retirement community in Sarasota, Florida. In keeping with his feckless character, Oscar has not saved his money and is living on a tight budget like all his friends. They play for nickels and dimes and spend more of their time kvetching and kibitzing than playing cards. Instead of handing out sloppy ham sandwiches and beer as he used to do in New York, Oscar now serves his guests sloppy tofu sandwiches and diet sodas.

When the two old friends meet at LAX, Felix is carrying a suitcase containing $10,000 in cash and a $6,000 silver tray as wedding presents. In keeping with his own obsessive-compulsive character, he has obviously been saving and investing all these years. Inevitably, Oscar leaves the suitcase standing out in front of the car rental office. They only realize what has happened after Oscar has gotten them lost out in the Mojave Desert. After they get out of the car, an infuriated Felix pounds his fists on the car's hood, causing it to start rolling backward and over a cliff, where it explodes. The careless and forgetful Oscar had neglected to shift to park or set the emergency brake.

They walk for miles in the glaring sun without seeing any sign of civilization. Finally they flag down a rattletrap truck piled high with produce. The Mexican driver subsequently asks them to take his truck on to the next town and leave it for him because an emergency forces him to speed off with friends in the opposite direction. When Oscar and Felix run into a police roadblock, they find out that they have been transporting illegal Mexican workers. This leads them to their first encounter with the local sheriff, who finds it hard to believe they are heading for a wedding because they have become so disheveled and have been accidentally sprayed with white insecticide by a crop duster.

The Odd Couple 2 bears a strong resemblance to Neil Simon's *The Out-of-Towners* (1970), in which Lemmon starred as an Ohio rube in New York City to whom everything goes wrong that could go wrong. Simon, however, understands New York much better than he does California. Crop dusters, for example, do not spray sagebrush in the Mojave Desert. Simon's attitude towards California resembles that of Woody Allen, who hated all that horrible sunshine and observed that California's only contribution to culture was passing a law giving motorists the option to turn right on a red light.

Everything goes wrong for Oscar and Felix before they finally make it to the wedding, but the things that go wrong could have gone wrong in Texas or Florida or upstate New York. In a honky-tonk bar in the middle of nowhere, the duo run into a couple of younger women (Christine Baranski and Jean Smart) who seem to have been inspired by the heroines of *Thelma and Louise* (1991). Incurably flirtatious Oscar gets them both into trouble with the women's gun-toting, good-ole-boy husbands, who take them for a wild ride that ends abruptly at another roadblock. They find themselves right back at the sheriff's office trying to explain themselves. Naturally, both keep blaming their problems on each other.

Felix and Oscar believe they are finally on their way to San Malina when they are offered a ride by Beaumont (Barnard Hughes), a kindly old gentleman who owns a vintage Rolls Royce. The boys are a little bit frustrated when they realize that the old man drives so slowly that he is being passed up, not only by cyclists, but by hikers on foot. Then their benefactor drops dead behind the wheel and the sheriff's deputies arrive to find Felix going through Beaumont's wallet. Once again they are back in the sheriff's office. This time he suspects them of murder and attempted robbery. When he finally ascertains that Beaumont died of

natural causes and that Felix was only looking for his identification, he decides to put them on a plane so he will be sure they are out of his territory forever.

Their troubles do not end at this point but take them off on separate tangents. Felix falls in love at first sight with a woman who is attending the wedding but is too shy to talk to her. Oscar throws the two together with characteristic tactlessness. In San Malina, Oscar has to intercede when he finds that his son has developed a serious case of pre-marital cold feet—echoing a similar situation involving a Matthau character in Neil Simon's *Plaza Suite* (1971). As the offspring of divorced parents, Brucey is understandably skeptical about marriage. He has been living happily with Hannah for some time but fears that marriage will spoil their relationship. The gist of what Oscar tells Brucey is that marriage is a gamble but a gamble worth taking. Felix's suitcase shows up and he is able to change into a dark suit in which to give his daughter away.

At the very end of the movie, Oscar is back playing poker with his girlfriends in Sarasota, believing that his life has returned to normal. Then Felix shows up carrying two suitcases and looking as dejected as he did when he came to Oscar's Manhattan apartment 30 years before. Felix's

Jack Klugman and Tony Randall also appeared in a sequel, the 1993 TV movie *The Odd Couple: Together Again.*

CREDITS

Felix Ungar: Jack Lemmon
Oscar Madison: Walter Matthau
Brucey: Jonathan Silverman
Hannah: Lisa Waltz
Beaumont: Barnard Hughes
Thelma: Christine Baranski
Holly: Jean Smart
Leroy: Jay O. Sanders

Origin: USA
Released: 1998
Production: Neil Simon, Robert W. Cort, and David Madden; released by Paramount Pictures
Direction: Howard Deutch
Screenplay: Neil Simon
Cinematography: Jamie Anderson
Editing: Seth Flaum
Music: Alan Silvestri
Production design: Dan Bishop
Costumes: Lisa Jensen
Sound: Lee Orloff
MPAA rating: PG-13
Running Time: 96 minutes

love affair has already fizzled since no woman can put up with his neurotic personality. He wants to move in with Oscar—who is not just reluctant but horrified. He has told Felix, "Nothing has changed. I'm still a pig. You're still a human vacuum cleaner." But Oscar, the kindly grouch, relents and allows his old roommate to share his apartment on a trial basis. Felix immediately begins tidying up the living room and interrupting the poker game by emptying ashtrays and offering to improve on Oscar's lopsided sandwiches.

It would appear that the producers (who include Simon himself) had hopes for another possible sequel, with the same kinds of frictions in Sarasota that existed in New York. Even though the prospects seem remote, an *Odd Couple 3* might be funnier than *The Odd Couple 2*. Simon's story was originally a stage play. The conflict between his two char-

acters, largely territorial, seems to require enforced confinement—something everybody can relate to because it is something everybody has experienced.

—Bill Delaney

REVIEWS

Chicago Tribune. April 10, 1998, p. 5.
Entertainment Weekly. April 17, 1998, p. 47.
Los Angeles Times. April 10, 1998, p. F16.
New York Times. April 10, 1998, p. E25.
People. April 20, 1998, p. 35.
San Francisco Chronicle. April 10, 1998, p. D6.
Sight and Sound. December, 1998, p. 53.
Variety. April 6, 1998, p. 48.
Wall Street Journal. April 10, 1998, p. W4.

The Newton Boys

America's most wanted criminals are about to make history.—Movie tagline

"An action-packed, rip-roaring adventure, with a cast to die for."—Bonnie Churchill, *National News Syndicate*

 Box Office: $10,451,854

"**D**on't kill, don't steal from women and children, and don't rat." That was the gentlemanly motto adhered to by the Newton boys, four young brothers in 1920s Texas who prided themselves on the fact that they became the most prolific bank robbers, and pulled off the largest single heist, in U.S. history by relying on smarts, skillful planning, and an enviable arsenal of Southern charm. According to an excellent 1994 article in *Smithsonian,* the brothers claimed to have stolen more "than Jesse and Frank James, the Dalton Boys, Butch Cassidy and all the other famous outlaw gangs put together." The Newtons did away with numerous bank safes but not a single soul, and they died of natural causes at advanced ages. Newspapers during the boys' heyday reserved their blaring front page headlines for the bloody, dastardly deeds of more ill-mannered outlaws, relegating the New-

tons to relative obscurity despite their legitimate claims to fame.

Billy the Kid and the aforementioned Jesse James are probably the two best known outlaws of the American West because of the unusual ease and frequency with which they dispensed their malevolent behavior. Billy the Kid boasted that he had killed twenty-one men by the time he turned twenty-one, the year he was shot to death. James led a feared gang of murderous ruffians known for their numerous audacious robberies and a decided lack of reverence for human life. He was shot by a member of his gang in 1882, dying at the age of thirty-four. Hollywood recognized the dramatic possibilities inherent in the sensational stories of the violent lives and deaths of such notorious real-life figures. Billy the Kid's story has been told in such films as *The Outlaw* (1943), featuring Jack Beutel and a scandalously-prominent display of cleavage by Jane Russell, and two MGM vehicles, both titled *Billy the Kid,* which starred John Mack Brown in the 1930 version and Robert Taylor eleven years later. There have been at least seven films on James, including 1939's *Jesse James* starring Tyrone Power and 1941's *Jesse James at Bay* with Roy Rogers. None of these films felt particularly constrained by historical fact. In *The Newton Boys,* director Richard Linklater, a Texan, tries to be faithful to the facts which make the brothers noteworthy, but that does not provide exceptionally dramatic, riveting mate-

Willis Newton (Matthew McConaughey): "We was just businessmen like doctors and lawyers and storekeepers. Robbin' banks and trains was our business."

rial for a motion picture. His presentation of the Newtons' story is hampered throughout by this basic problem, relying heavily upon the charisma of its talented group of young performers to keep the audience engaged.

The film starts like a Southern drawl, picking up some momentum when the zealously charming and slick Willis (Matthew McConaughey), the eldest of the Newton brothers, formulates a plan to get his trusted brothers to help him rob banks. Feeling frustration and resentment at their poor, harsh circumstances while the Twenties are roaring for other people, Willis convinces his brothers, Jess (Ethan Hawke), Dock (Vincent D'Onofrio), and Joe (Skeet Ulrich), to join him. Willis rationalizes that the hard-hearted banks are now insured, and so will simply get their money back if it is stolen. The money grubbing insurance companies will undoubtedly have no problem with anything that makes the banks feel insecure. If anything, the boys will merely be "little thieves stealing from big thieves." Robbery will simply be their profession. It is a risky venture, but, as Ma Newton (Gail Cronauer) always said, "God hates a coward." The boys embark upon their well-planned criminal quest aided by nitroglycerin expert Brent Glasscock (country singer Dwight Yoakam, building on his much-deserved critical success in 1996's *Sling Blade*), who blows up the banks' safes.

While pilfering all this money, Willis also steals the heart of Louise (Julianna Margulies, best known for TV's *ER*), who works in a hotel to support herself and her young son and who is unaware of both Willis' real name and occupation. Joe, the youngest and most soulful, contemplative Newton, asks Willis where it will all end, his big brother replies "when we're millionaires" with his usual self-assurance. When they have accumulated a large amount of cash, the Newtons sink their money into an oil well that turns out to be a dry hole. Reasoning that God does not want them to go legit, the boys revert to their criminal ways. As the banks had acquired new and better safes in the meantime, an impatient Willis sets his sights on intercepting a train in Illinois which will be filled with over $3 million in cash, bonds, and jewels. Although Dock is accidentally wounded by one of his comrades during the heist, it is monetarily successful, and the brothers head for Mexico. Soon, the law catches up with them, and the Newtons are brought to trial, along with the other less-than-straight-arrows with whom the brothers have come into contact along the way. At the end of the brief courtroom sequence, Linklater lets us know the jail terms each character had to serve, as well as what happened during the rest of their lives.

The Newton Boys is Linklater's first big budget Hollywood film, having come to some prominence with smaller-

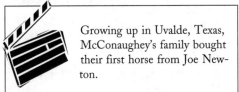

Growing up in Uvalde, Texas, McConaughey's family bought their first horse from Joe Newton.

scale independent films about teen angst such as *Slacker* (1991) and *Dazed and Confused* (1993). Perhaps one can draw a parallel between the characters in those films and the Newtons, although the young people in this film are a little more advanced in their unruly behavior. *The Newton Boys* has many cinematic ancestors, from *The Great Train Robbery* (1903) to *Butch Cassidy and the Sundance Kid* (1969). The subject matter, some directorial choices, and the attention to period and regional detail clearly hark back to Arthur Penn's landmark *Bonnie and Clyde* (1967), a work fueled by the violent exploits of young criminals who met a spectacular, bloody end.

If this comparison is noted, *The Newton Boys* suffers by comparison. None of the robbery scenes in Linklater's film are especially dramatic or suspenseful—they are simply presented as a string of successes, so efficient that they start to seem almost rote, with occasional dashes of humor added for some zest. The all-important train robbery scene is not as taut as it should be, and possesses less potency than expected. The ending of the story is rather anti-climactic. Penn, clearly an expert at his craft, shot his

CREDITS

Willis Newton: Matthew McConaughey
Joe Newton: Skeet Ulrich
Jess Newton: Ethan Hawke
Dock Newton: Vincent D'Onofrio
Louise Brown: Julianna Margulies
Brentwood Glasscock: Dwight Yoakam
Slim: Charles Gunning
Avis Glasscock: Chloe Webb
Slim: Becket Gremmels
Ma Newton: Gail Cronauer

Origin: USA
Released: 1998
Production: Anne Walker-McBay for Detour Films; released by 20th Century Fox
Direction: Richard Linklater
Screenplay: Richard Linklater, Clark Lee Walker, and Claude Stanush; based on the book by Stanush
Cinematography: Peter James
Editing: Sandra Adair
Music: Edward D. Barnes
Production design: Catherine Hardwicke
Art direction: Andrea Dopaso, John Frick
Costumes: Shelley Komarov
Sound: John Pritchett
MPAA rating: PG-13
Running Time: 122 minutes

memorable film armed with interesting, suspenseful and shockingly-dramatic raw materials fashioned into a superb script by David Newman and Robert Benton, in addition to attractive young stars. The main body of *The Newton Boys* also suffers by comparison with the glimpses we get of two real Newtons at the film's conclusion. At that time, we are treated to portions of a 1975 interview with Willis and an appearance by Joe on the *Tonight Show* with Johnny Carson in 1980. Although both brothers were elderly by that time, they still come off as far more fascinating and engaging than the portrayals of the preceding two hours.

All of the lead actors in *The Newton Boys* do competent work in roles filled with exuberance but somehow lacking in sufficient definition and telling detail. McConaughey, who grew up in the Newton's hometown of Uvalde, seems hell-bent on single-handedly thrusting the plot forward with his impassioned portrayal of Willis. He succeeds to an admirable extent, although his often winning performance sometimes seems almost psychotically fervent. Despite the energetic performances of its good-looking young stars, *The Newton Boys* was anemic at the boxoffice, and received mixed reviews. Many critics agreed that the film is like cinematic

cotton candy, a ball of fluff which is passably enjoyable while it lasts, but which lacks anything substantial to stay with you. Despite the laser-like intensity of McConaughey's eyes and regular flashes of his radiant smile, *The Newton Boys* lacks much of an afterglow.

—*David L. Boxerbaum*

REVIEWS

Boston Globe. March 27, 1998, p. D5.
Chicago Tribune. March 27, 1998, p. A7.
Christian Science Monitor. April 3, 1998, p. B3.
Entertainment Weekly. April 3, 1998, p. 64.
Esquire. April, 1998, p. 23.
Houston Chronicle. March 27, 1998, p. G1.
Los Angeles Times. March 27, 1998, p. F6.
New York Times. March 27, 1998, p. E14.
People. April 6, 1998, p. 19.
Rolling Stone. April 16, 1998, p. 88.
Time. April 6, 1998, p. 70.
USA Today. March 27, 1998, p. E4.
Variety. March 16, 1998, p. 67.
Wall Street Journal. March 31, 1998, p. A20.

Next Stop Wonderland

Love is the Destination.—Movie tagline

"Hope Davis gives the sort of breakthrough performance a film critic sees only a handful of times in a career!"—*Boston Herald*

"A winning confection filled with dazzle and spice!"—*Entertainment Weekly*

"A sharply observed film with a fine sense of humor! It's a pleasure to care about these characters!"—*Los Angeles Times*

"Romantic and joyful! As the blockbusters sizzle, it's time for a trip to *Wonderland*! This is a must-see movie!"—Thelma Adams, *New York Post*

"Beautifully acted and filled with smart, savvy dialogue!"—*New York Times*

"A delightful comedy! One of this year's undeniable pleasures!"—David Elliott, *San Diego Union Tribune*

"A refreshingly original and terrifically pleasing romantic comedy!"—Dennis Cunningham, *WCBS-TV*

 Box Office: $3,395,581

*N*ext Stop Wonderland, director Brad Anderson's follow-up to his first feature *The Darien Gap* (1996), is a charming and unconventional romantic comedy that plays on the idea of destiny. Smart and seductive, this indie film examines the concept of fate and the everyday ironies of single life in the late '90s.

Set in contemporary Boston, the title refers to the last train stop on the subway system. Two of the regular passengers on this line are Erin Castleton (Hope Davis) and Alan Montiero (Alan Gelfant), attractive 30-ish singles who have almost given up on romance. *Next Stop Wonderland*'s clever structure lets the audience know right away that the two protagonists are made for each other, but it doesn't know if they'll get together, because they have yet to meet.

Hope Davis (*The Daytrippers* [1996], *The Myth of Fingerprints* [1997]) stars as Erin, a night-shift nurse and medical school dropout who's still mourning the death of her father. She's ready to give up on men after being dumped by her political activist boyfriend Sean (the amusing Philip Seymour Hoffman). Perfectly content to be on her own, Erin doesn't necessarily believe in fate, but admits she'd be delighted if the right man happened to cross her path this way.

Erin's meddling mother (Holland Taylor) doesn't believe her daughter is happy living a life of solitude, so she secretly places a personal ad in a Boston paper on her behalf. She hilariously uses several inaccurate descriptions of her reserved daughter, including the word "frisky" and having a "zest for life." Furious with her mother for doing this, Erin eventually decides to check on her responses and is shocked to discover there are 64. Mostly out of curiosity, Erin decides to meet a few of her suitors and goes on a string of hopeless blind dates. Some of the movie's best comic moments come from Erin's barroom interchanges with this motley group of romantic hopefuls.

"The intent of the movie was to play on the issues of fate and destiny, to explore how people in their private moments create guidance and structure to see themselves through the difficulties of finding love."—writer/director Brad Anderson commenting on his film.

Meanwhile, running on a parallel track to Erin is Alan, an ambitious ex-plumber pursuing his dream of becoming a marine biologist. Plagued by his father's gambling debts and besieged by a seductive classmate, Alan struggles to alter his destiny by working his way through school and volunteering at the Boston Aquarium. There's also an overly complex subplot involving the expansion of the aquarium, a loan shark, and a mob request that Alan "hit" the aquarium's star attraction, a blowfish named Puff. The fishy business with Puff is whimsical and good for a few laughs, however, the rest seems extraneous.

The film's title refers to the last station of the blue line on Boston's subway system.

Although living parallel lives and with their paths nearly crossing several times, Erin and Alan just miss connecting. Anderson's superior editing skills are evident in all of the clever cross-cuts that show the protagonists in a series of near-misses. By keeping the audience on edge as to whether the characters will finally meet or not, Anderson succeeds with a nice balance of solid direction and witty camera work.

Both lead actors are fresh and appealing in their roles. Gelfant gives a subtle performance as the unpretentious and ambitious Alan. Reportedly, Anderson had Gelfant in mind for the role before the script was even written. Anderson had seen him in a film at Sundance (*The Destiny of Michael Fine*) and liked his style. How's that for a twist of fate?

For the role of Erin, Anderson and co-writer Lyn Vaus wanted to create a lead character who embodies the Bossa Nova concept of *saudade*, which encapsulates sadness, happiness, and sexiness all at once. The soulful Ms. Davis fit this role perfectly. In his review for the *Los Angeles Times,* Kenneth Turan states: "In Hope Davis, Anderson has found the classic personification of this notion. It's unusual for a young actress to have the opportunity to carry an entire picture, and rarer still does one succeed with the aplomb Davis displays here."

Wonderland's cool Brazilian soundtrack consists almost entirely of jazzy Bossa Nova and Samba music, which beautifully complements the picture. In the movie's press kit, Anderson explains how Brazilian music helped inspire the film: "I've always loved Brazilian music but I was also interested in the concept of *saudade*. It seemed a good fit for a film that has both humor and a melancholy undertone to it. I also just liked the contrast of setting a film in Boston to Brazilian music. It defies expectation and I like that."

A hit at the 1998 Sundance festival, *Next Stop Wonderland* is an enjoyable and accomplished film. Although it didn't generate much at the boxoffice, critical reaction to *Wonderland* was mostly positive. Stephen Holden, writing for the *New York Times* commented that the film "creates and sustains an intelligent seriocomic mood better than any recent film about the urban single life."

Entertainment Weekly called it an "appealing fairy tale"; and Kenneth Turan of the *Los Angeles Times* wrote: "*Wonderland* succeeds because it shares a sensibility with its heroine: Despite

CREDITS

Erin Castleton: Hope Davis
Alan Monteiro: Alan Gelfant
Frank: Victor Argo
Eric: Jon Benjamin
Julie: Cara Buono
Brett: Larry Gilliard Jr.
Piper Castleton: Holland Taylor
Robert: Robert Stanton
Cricket: Callie Thorne
Daryl: Lyn Vaus

Origin: USA
Released: 1998
Production: Mitchell B. Robbins for Robbins Entertainment production; released by Miramax
Direction: Brad Anderson
Screenplay: Brad Anderson and Lyn Vaus
Cinematography: Uta Briesewitz
Editing: Brad Anderson
Music: Claudio Ragazzi
Production design: Chad Detweiller
MPAA rating: R
Running Time: 111 minutes

REVIEWS

Boxoffice. April, 1998, p. 183.
Detroit Free Press. online. August 27, 1998.
Entertainment Weekly. September 14, 1998, p. 58.
Los Angeles Times. August 21, 1998, p. F1.
New York Times. August 21, 1998, p. E8.
People. September 7, 1998, p. 38.
San Francisco Chronicle. August 28, 1998, p. C3.
Variety. January 26, 1998, p. 68.
Village Voice. August 25, 1998, p. 128.

its clever dialogue, it's an empathetic vehicle at heart, a work whose well-developed characters, even the sillier ones, insist we care even as they're making us laugh." As one of the most delightful and original romantic comedies of the year, filmmaker Anderson has given us a true valentine.

—*Beth Fhaner*

Niagara, Niagara

Love can't be controlled.—Movie tagline

"I can't get it out of my head. A deeply emotional film. Henry Thomas and Robin Tunney shine."—Jordana Brown, *Buzz Weekly*

"Indelibly stamped with soul and integrity. Robin Tunney gives a jolting, powerhouse performance."—Robert Ellsworth, *Detour Magazine*

Niagara, Niagara features two remarkable performances by Robin Tunney (Marcy) and Henry Thomas (Seth), two misfits who fall in love and in the classic American manner hit the road. Seth is a shoplifter. He is also withdrawn and acts like a beaten dog. The film reveals almost nothing about his background, except one domestic scene with his derelict, ex-con father. Seth seems simple almost to the point of retardation. He cannot look at people when he talks, and when he talks his words trail off. To say that he has no confidence in himself is a monumental understatement.

Marcy spots Seth shoplifting and tries to strike up a conversation. She is looking for company, and Seth might be interested—though it is hard to tell because he says so little and is almost expressionless. But he does take some initiative when he offers Marcy a ride in his Plymouth Gran Fury. In his car, he has a little more confidence. He drops Marcy off at the sanitation department, where she works weekends. Clearly, she wants to pursue the

Marcy (Robin Tunney) to Seth (Henry Thomas): "I think that you should give up shoplifting now that we're real criminals. I think we should only do classy crimes."

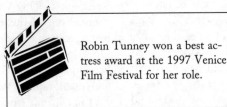

Robin Tunney won a best actress award at the 1997 Venice Film Festival for her role.

relationship, but Seth says nothing. She gets out of the car and slams the door. Then immediately she says "sorry" as Seth drives away. She keeps repeating the word sorry.

Marcy seems angry with herself for expressing anger. But when she encounters Seth a second time at his favorite shoplifting location, she proposes that they drive to Canada to get a certain black doll not available in their town, and en route she explains that she suffers from Tourette's Syndrome and echolalia. The first malady makes her behave aggressively and shout obscenities; the second forces her to repeat a word or phrase incessantly. Sometimes she can will herself to stop this compulsive behavior; sometimes it just bursts out because she has tried to suppress it, and then she is likely to hit someone or some thing. She explains her plight to the passive Seth in a hotel room. He asks her if anything can relieve her symptoms. Yes, she replies matter of factly. Liquor helps (her favorite drink is Jack Daniels), and so does sex. Seth just sits there, not knowing how to react to this plainspoken young woman. But he likes her, and there is obviously nothing he would rather be doing than traveling with her. She is afraid that one of her fits will scare him off. But Seth is incredibly patient.

The trip to Toronto via Niagara Falls is the story of this strange couple's passion. The shots of fountaining Niagara, the wonder of its exploding force, the relentless falling water, is like a cascading destiny that Marcy and Seth are drawn to. While the symbolism is obvious, the sheer sensuousness of the cinematography overwhelms the hackneyed, rather confused story line. But how are Marcy's maladies meant to factor into her criminal behavior? She almost beats a man to death. Is this really supposed to be the product of pent-up rage that she cannot control? She leaves home without her medication (Halidol) and expects a pharmacist to give her the drug without a prescription. Then she tries to forge a prescription. This idiotic behavior, which Seth all too willingly abets, becomes irritating.

Tunney's and Thomas's performances are what make the film interesting and almost unbearable to watch. She

CREDITS

Marcy: Robin Tunney
Seth: Henry Thomas
Walter: Michael Parks
Pharmacist: Stephen Lang
Seth's father: John MacKay

Origin: USA
Released: 1997
Production: David L. Bushnell; released by The Shooting Gallery
Direction: Bob Gosse
Screenplay: Matthew Weiss
Cinematography: Max Spiller
Editing: Rachel Warden
Production design: Clark Hunter
Art direction: Max Biscoe
Costumes: Laura Jean Shannon
Sound: Jeff Pullman
Music: Michael Timmins, Jeff Bird
MPAA rating: R
Running Time: 96 minutes

gives a well-rounded view of Marcy—part demented romantic who wants to get off on a cross-country crime spree à la Bonnie and Clyde, and part social critic who exposes the callous lack of imagination that makes people reject her. It is a wonder, for example, that when she and Seth disrupt a store or demand that a prescription be filled, it is the store manager and the pharmacist who seem like criminals, parroting conventional behaviors that blind them to Marcy's suffering. Thomas plays the perfect foil: he is polite, even diplomatic, which makes his interlocutors look especially intolerant.

But the great performances cannot ultimately mask the film's shopworn romanticism. Ho, hum, another indictment of bourgeois society. The characters deserve attention, yet they are done a disservice by being at the beck and call of a script that is too manipulative. It is just too easy to sneer at the brutalities of society, and to imply that the brutality of criminals is somehow more acceptable because they are victims and reveal in their very brutality a society that does not nurture individuality. There is some truth in that idea, but it is also incredibly sentimental and dangerous—as Walter (a widower who befriends the outlaw couple) learns when Marcy bludgeons him to the ground.

—*Carl Rollyson*

REVIEWS

Boxoffice. March, 1998, p. 54.
Detroit News. April 3, 1998, p. 7D.
Entertainment Weekly. April 10, 1998, p. 46.
Los Angeles Times. March 20, 1998, p. F22.
New York Times. March 20, 1998, p. E12.
Variety. September 22, 1997, p. 52.
Village Voice. March 24, 1998, p. 70.

A Night at the Roxbury

Score!—Movie tagline.

"A Beverly Hills *Beavis and Butthead*."—Elizabeth Burr, *Buffalo News*

"*Dumb & Dumber* on the dance floor."—Nick Carter, *Milwaukee Journal Sentinel*

"This fall's funniest film!"—Chaunce Hayden, *Steppin' Out Magazine*

"Hilarious! Don't miss it."—Joseph Zahn, *TCI Cable*

 Box Office: $30,312,145

Yet another *Saturday Night Live* skit-based movie. What is Lorne Michaels thinking? "Hey, this skit is mediocre at best. Let's make it into a movie!"

Does he have no realization that *SNL*-spawned hits like *Wayne's World* (1992) and *The Blues Brothers* (1980) did well because they were good films, not—repeat, not—because they were skits? If simply slapping together a movie from a *SNL* skit were all it took, then *Coneheads* (1993) would be a hit. Kids everywhere would have *It's Pat: The Movie* (1994) lunch boxes.

A Night at the Roxbury is unique in that, not only is it barely a movie, it was barely a skit to begin with. In the skit, two guys Steve (Will Ferrell) and Doug (Chris Kattan) Butabi are "cool" guys who try to pick up chicks by bobbing their heads incessantly. The movie is similar, but longer.

In the skit or in the movie, the Butabi brothers don't really have personalities so the film has to invent some for them. Writers Kattan and Ferrell, along with Steve Korren take the easy way out and make the brothers dumb, à la *Dumb and Dumber*, (1994) *Cabin Boy*, (1994) nearly all Adam Sandler vehicles, ad nauseum . . . .

Steve and Doug Butabi are two semi-young brothers who still live with their rich parents Barbara (Loni Anderson) and Kamehl (*Clueless'* Dan Hedaya) in L.A. By day, they work in their father's fake flower shop and by night they seek the perfect club experience. They spend nearly all their time perfecting their club banter, including the perfect way to say "What's up?" and their really bad anecdote about seeing Emilio Estevez at a pay phone. Although their club experiences mainly involve being rejected by bouncers, they harbor a dream to one day open a club like the cool Roxbury club. And for a while it looks like it just might happen. The boys meet a successful club owner, inadvertently

score some chicks and have the good fortune to get in a fender bender with the ultra-cool Richard Greico.

But the real plot is the love story between the brothers. Their relationship is set up like any movie romance. They are happy together, they fight, they separate, they moon for each other, they get back together. Near the end of the film, when Doug Butabi finally woos his brother back from the marriage-happy Emily (*SNL*er Molly Shannon), he holds up a radio *Say Anything*-style blaring "their" song, Haddaway's "What Is Love?" Later the two brothers make up on a romantic bridge in a lovely setting. After Doug gives a long, mushy apology to Steve, filled with sentiments like "You complete me," Steve answers tearfully, "You had me at 'hello.'" You almost expect them to start making out right there.

It's a semi-clever moment, but unfortunately, also a rare moment. Most of the jokes in the film range from downright flat to just okay. For example, when Doug mentions something about being ready to "hit his peak," his father says, "If you're going to hit your peak, do it in your room." Still, there exists some clever bits

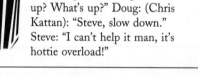

Steve (Will Ferrell): "What's up? What's up? What's up? What's up? What's up? What's up?" Doug: (Chris Kattan): "Steve, slow down." Steve: "I can't help it man, it's hottie overload!"

CREDITS

Steve Bubati: Will Ferrell
Doug Bubati: Chris Kattan
Emily: Molly Shannon
Richard Greico: Richard Greico
Mrs. Bubati: Loni Anderson
Mr. Bubati: Dan Hedaya
Cambi: Elisa Donovan
Viveca: Gigi Rice

Origin: USA
Released: 1998
Production: Lorne Michaels and Amy Heckerling for a SNL Studios production; released by Paramount Pictures
Direction: John Fortenberry
Screenplay: Steve Koren, Will Ferrell, and Chris Kattan
Cinematography: Francis Kenny
Editing: Jay Kramen
Music: David Kitay
Production design: Steven Jordan
Art direction: Carl Stensel
Costumes: Mona May
Sound: Jim Tanenbaum
MPAA rating: PG-13
Running Time: 81 minutes

of slang. At one point, Steve complains, "You're mad-cow-ing on me." Maybe the good slang comes from co-producer Amy Heckerling who directed the similarly slang-filled (but infinitely better) *Clueless*.

There is also some clever use of music. At one point when the boys ride an elevator, an instrumental version of the ubiquitous "What Is Love?" plays in the background. Later, when the brothers are estranged, "He Ain't Heavy, He's My Brother" blares pointedly.

The movie is filled with cameos, and they're fun casting choices. Dwayne Hickman (the guy who played Dobie Gillis), Loni Anderson, ex-Kid in the Hall and fellow *SNL*er Mark McKinney, *SNL* news guy Colin Quinn and Richard Grieco, who plays a washed-up TV star named . . .Richard Grieco, all put in appearances. But the cameos aren't used as well as they could be. The filmmakers could have had a lot of fun with these characters but the best they ever come up with are some scattered references to *21 Jump Street*. And Loni Anderson, in her part as the boys' tacky mom, just

Actor Chazz Palminteri has an unbilled cameo in this film.

looks scary, proving that after a certain point, plastic surgery just no longer works.

A Night at the Roxbury isn't offensive, which for a low level comedy like this one, is something. But the lack of offensiveness is equaled by the lack of humor in the film. It's too bad, because the L.A. club scene is certainly rife with humor possibilities. But *A Night at the Roxbury* doesn't jump on them and in the end, just falls flat.

—*Jill Hamilton*

REVIEWS

Detroit Free Press. October 2, 1998, p. 14D.
Entertainment Weekly. October 16, 1998, p. 60.
Los Angeles Times. October 2, 1998, p. F16.
New York Times. October 2, 1998, p. E20.
People. October 19, 1998, p. 42.
Sight and Sound. February, 1999, p. 49.
Variety. October 5, 1998, p. 68.

Nightwatch

What if someone you trusted was setting you up? What if you were the final piece in a brilliant serial killer's puzzle? The night holds the secret.—Movie tagline

He's the prime suspect in a terrifying mystery. The police are after him and so is the murderer.—Movie tagline

"An edge-of-your-seat thriller! Ewan McGregor and Josh Brolin are brilliant!"—*Entertainment Asylum*

"Prepare to be scared! The entire cast is excellent!"—*Fox-TV*

"An eerie shocker!"—*Playboy*

 Box Office: $1,278,516

Law student Martin Bells (Ewan McGregor) takes a part-time job at the morgue and simultaneously becomes a prime suspect in a series of brutal murders in *Nightwatch*.

With the boxoffice success of the gruesomely violent thriller, *Seven* (1997), Hollywood eagerly sought similar projects to entice the same audience back into the theaters. Films that followed in the same vein of grisly "serial killers on the prowl for young females to sadistically tor-

ture, rape and murder" slasher-thrillers included, among others, *Kiss the Girls* (1998) and Ole Bornedal's *Nightwatch*.

Nightwatch is an American remake of Bornedal's own 1994 Danish film *Nattevagten*. Since the original film was never released in the United States, it is not possible to compare the two films, unfortunate since it might help to dispel the notion that Bornedal's motivation for remaking his own film was merely to gain entry into the lucrative Hollywood market. (Steven Soderbergh, writer/director of 1989's *sex, lies & videotape*, is curiously credited as Bornedal's co-writer.)

Scottish heartthrob Ewan McGregor stars as Martin Bells, a young law student who takes a job as the nightwatchman at the city morgue. While Martin hopes to be able to utilize his time studying, he has the unfortunate timing of starting work just as a homicidal necrophiliac has started murdering young prostitutes.

Before he knows it, Martin finds himself the prime suspect in an investigation headed by the creepy Inspector Cray (Nick Nolte). For reasons known only to the killer, he has chosen to frame Martin for the murders—despite the fact that the young lad is the only character in *Nightwatch* with an ironclad alibi, having to punch several different time clocks as he makes his periodic rounds through the morgue.

The first forty minutes or so of *Nightwatch* is quite effective. The murky lighting, the skewed camera angles and deliberate pacing all work in sync to create an edgy atmosphere of dread and doom. But the plot grows more and more preposterous and the story quickly spirals into a contrived and clumsy climax.

Bornedal invests a great deal of time and energy setting up elaborate diversions and making every character so repulsive that any one of them seem capable of murder, but the structural problems with the plot quickly eliminate the suspects. Martin's brooding and nihilistic best friend James (Josh Brolin) is too obvious a choice, given his overt indulgence in playing sick, and ultimately dangerous, jokes on his friend. Prototypal Hollywood creep Brad Dourif and the character actor John C. Reilly, on the other hand, enjoy far too little screen time to be serious contenders for the villain prize. That leaves the equally unsettling Inspector Cray, the only character with easy access to (a) the morgue, (b) the city's prostitutes, and (c) Martin's semen sample.

Director Bornedal withholds the killer's identity by shooting him within the frame from the waist down, but then reveals him far too early to sustain the suspense. He attempts to build mystery through imbuing the killer with the modus operandi of gouging out his victim's eyeballs and then raping them post-mortem. It is never explained why the homicidal necrophiliac plays the recording of the childhood song, "This Old Man," and perhaps with good reason since it makes little or no sense within the context of the story. It has been postulated that the song is about the infamous Jack the Ripper, which, if true, might explain the connection since the latter murdered British prostitutes. The choice of the song is an intriguing one, but ultimately not exploited to its fullest.

The female characters in *Nightwatch* fall squarely in two camps, both victims. Patricia Arquette and Lauren Graham are the girlfriends involved with men who are afraid to commit to their relationships; both actresses are wasted in their roles. The other women characters are the other Hollywood staple, the prostitute/murder victim. Only young actress Alix Koromzay stands out in the role of the teen hooker.

In the wake of the creative and critical success of Jonathan Demme's *The Silence of the Lambs* (1991)—the film garnered five major Academy Awards, including Best Picture—thrillers seem to have taken on a more exploitive approach to the violence that is portrayed onscreen. Though not explicitly shown, the violence tends to be more insidious; it is alluded to, revealed through gruesome details and insinuated through unsettling flashes, leaving little to the imagination.

What differentiates *Silence* from most, if not all, of its poor imitators is the complexity of the story. While on the surface it was a serial killer-thriller, the screenplay by Ted Tally managed to capture the more novel exploration of the

 Inspector Cray (Nick Nolte) about the killer's motives: "Explanations are just a fiction to make us feel safe."

CREDITS

Martin Bells: Ewan McGregor
Inspector Thomas Cray: Nick Nolte
James Gallman: Josh Brolin
Katherine: Patricia Arquette
Joyce: Alix Koromzay
Marie: Lauren Graham
Inspector Bill Davis: John C. Reilly
The Duty Doc: Brad Dourif

Origin: USA
Released: 1998
Production: Michael Obel; released by Dimension Films
Direction: Ole Bornedal
Screenplay: Ole Bornedal and Steven Soderbergh; based on the film *Nattevagten*
Cinematography: Dan Laustsen
Editing: Sally Menke
Production design: Richard Hoover
Art direction: Kathleen M. McKernin, Adam Scher
Costumes: Louise Mingenbach
Sound: Stephen Halbert
Music: Joachim Holbek
MPAA rating: R
Running Time: 101 minutes

issue of mentor/protégé, thus driving the story to a richer level.

It is this type of complexity that is sorely lacking in *Nightwatch*, a tale that seems to suggest that perversity is the norm, not the aberrance of American society. Serial killers no longer murder because it is sexually or psychologically satisfying, but rather are driven by guilt or shame. And the result is a far from satisfying experience for the viewing audience. Critics were nearly unanimous in their unfavorable reviewing of *Nightwatch*.

—*Patricia Kowal*

REVIEWS

Boxoffice. June, 1998, p. 78.
Chicago Sun-Times. April 17, 1998.
Entertainment Weekly. April 24, 1998, p. 57.
Los Angeles Times. April 17, 1998, p. F18.
New York Times. April 17, 1998, p. E16.
People. April 27, 1998, p. 37.
Rolling Stone. April 30, 1998, p. 74.
San Francisco Examiner. April 17, 1998, p. D3.
USA Today. April 17, 1998, p. 10E.
Variety. April 13, 1998, p. 28.
Washington Post. April 17, 1998, p. B1.

Nil By Mouth

"A remarkable film!"—Roger Ebert, *Bravo TV*
"Brilliantly written . . . a superb cast . . . filmed with real power."—*The Guardian*
"A powerful, neatly executed but harrowing drama."—John Anderson, *Los Angeles Times*
"Powerfully raw!"—Janet Maslin, *New York Times*
"Fierce and compassionate."—*The Times*

Gary Oldman, who has been an acclaimed theater and film actor for twenty years, has recently made his screenwriting and directing debut with the acclaimed *Nil By Mouth*. The title alludes to a medical term applied to those patients who are unable to receive food or medicine orally and forms part of the climactic speech delivered by the film's main character, Ray (Ray Winstone). Ray is a brute of a man, a drug and booze addicted member of the British lower classes, whose unpredictable and ungovernable rage causes him to lash out violently at all those around him. Following years of abuse, his pregnant wife, Valerie (Kathy Burke)—who at thirty looks twice that age—leaves him after an especially vicious and gratuitous beating, and Ray responds by destroying their apartment. Afterward, bereft and full of confused contrition, he delivers a rambling speech to his friend Mark (Jamie Forman). Ray only vaguely intuits that there is some connection between his loutish behavior and his loveless childhood, but he does make an ironic connection between his own father's inability to give him a kind word and the sign that hung over the old man's bed—"Nil by Mouth"—when Ray went to visit his father in the hospital.

Gary Oldman: "Directing is a really rewarding experience and you're finally the boss. It's a bit like being a benevolent dictator."

Much has been made of the autobiographical content of Oldman's film, and the speculation has been fueled by the film's dedication to the director's father. Although in interviews Oldman has repeatedly claimed that Ray is not his father, there seem to be clear similarities between the two, and Oldman has variously denied and confirmed his identification with Ray and Valerie's little girl, Michelle, who witnesses her parents' battles. But, declares Oldman, the father Ray talks about—the withholding old man who could not tell his son he loved him—represents the director's own father. The strict equation of Ray with Oldman's father and of Valerie with Oldman's mother upset his family, which he says is close. And indeed, *Nil By Mouth* is something of a family affair, with the actor's sister—a truck driver billed as "Laila Morse" (an anagram for *mia sorella*, "my sister")—appearing in the key role of Janet, mother to Valerie and her junkie brother, Billy (Charlie Creed-Miles). In addition, Oldman's mother, Kathleen, is responsible for a song sung in the film by Janet's mother, Kath (Edna Dore).

Like the characters in his movie, Oldman had a rough childhood, growing up in a working class section of South London that was scarred by graffiti and violence. Abandoned by his father, a welder, Oldman was employed as a salesman in a sporting goods store when he began training with the Greenwich Young People's Theatre. After working with the Rose Bradford School of Speech and Drama, Oldman emerged as an accomplished stage actor in Britain, then made his breakthrough into film acting starring in *Sid & Nancy* (1986). His portrayal of punk rocker Sid Vicious was devastatingly powerful, and he went on to deliver other highly praised performances in such films as *Prick Up Your Ears* (1987), *Rosencrantz and Guildenstern Are Dead* (1990), and *The Professional* (1994). Lauded as one of the best actors of his generation, he delivered a dead-on portrayal of Lee Harvey Oswald in Oliver Stone's *JFK* (1991), as well as a convincing portrait of Ludwig Van Beethoven in *Immortal Beloved* (1994). In recent years, he has increasingly found himself typecast as a sadistic villain, often appearing in such wholly commercial efforts as *The Scarlet Letter* (1996) and *Air Force One* (1997).

The first-time actress billed as Laila Morse is Gary Oldman's older sister, Maureen Bass.

It was during the filming of the less than classic Demi Moore version of *The Scarlet Letter* that Oldman was finally forced to come to terms with his own longtime alcoholism. Out of his recovery program came *Nil By Mouth*. He continued to accept unchallenging parts, but now he did so for a purpose: he was working to finance his movie, which would help him, at least, to exorcise his demons.

In the end, Oldman financed his film entirely out of his own pocket, getting considerable artistic help from his friends Luc Besson, who produced the film, Francis Ford Coppola, who gave Oldman permission to use footage from *Apocalypse Now* (1979), and Eric Clapton, who composed part of the soundtrack for *Nil By Mouth*. Oldman says that he wrote the first draft of the screenplay in five weeks, driven by the explosive misery that had lingered within him since childhood: "[It] was in me. It was almost like the solution that I'd been looking for to a problem." The rage that had previously fueled his acting was now funneled into writing and directing a fictionalized version of his past. Having made *Nil By Mouth* seems to have resolved a number of lingering problems for Oldman, in the process eradicating his will to act. One of his goals was to break the pattern of drink and emotional violence and poor parenting he had inherited from his father. Having achieved this goal, Oldman now finds he lacks the motivation that drove his acting career.

In *Nil By Mouth*, he does a superior job of conveying the true horror of being caught up in the cycle of addiction. Filmed largely in close up using a hand-held camera, *Nil By Mouth* is at once sharply focused and chaotic. After it opens, the film runs for several minutes before the director introduces an establishing shot. What viewers see initially is a series of talking heads, but they seem to be talking nonsense. For starters, they are speaking in an accent so broad that their working class British dialect seems almost unrelated to English. And their dialogue seems not really to be dialogue, because they appear not to be speaking to one another, instead directing their words to the smoke-filled air. Making sense of it all is rendered more difficult by the repetitive but aimless soundtrack of ambient noise that competes with the characters' voices for viewers' attention. Oldman, in fact, does a wonderful job of letting filmgoers know just how it feels to be inside the disoriented, overwhelmed, and yet deadened consciousness of someone whose life is out of control.

Just whose consciousness viewers are meant to share is also up for grabs. Although the opening scenes focus on a character we come to recognize as Ray, during the early segments of the film the camera follows Billy on his desperate errands, as he begs and steals and cajoles enough money for the next fix. Only when Billy steals some of Ray's stash and Ray retaliates by beating his brother-in-law and biting through the tip of his nose does the focus shift. Gradually it becomes clear that Ray is at the center of this particular maelstrom—although viewers are still treated to several graphic scenes of Billy shooting up, once even in the back of his mother's van while she looks on.

Nil By Mouth is, in a sense, a family saga, but it is hard to imagine a more dysfunctional family. The men, Ray and Billy, are both addicts, and the women, Valerie and Janet, are both co-dependent. Billy is a junkie largely because his mother is willing to support his habit. And after Ray viciously beats Valerie, she at first attempts to shield him from

CREDITS

Raymond: Ray Winstone
Valerie: Kathy Burke
Billy: Charlie Creed-Miles
Janet: Laila Morse
Kath: Edna Dore
Paula: Chrissie Cotterill
Angus: Jon Morrison
Mark: Jamie Forman
Danny: Steve Sweeney

Origin: Great Britain
Released: 1997
Production: Luc Besson, Douglas Urbanski, and Gary Oldman for SE8 Group; released by Sony Pictures Classics
Direction: Gary Oldman
Screenplay: Gary Oldman
Cinematography: Ron Fortunato
Editing: Brad Fuller
Music: Eric Clapton
Production design: Hugo Luczyc-Wyhowski
Art direction: Luana Hanson
Costumes: Barbara Kidd
Sound: Jim Greenhorn
MPAA rating: R
Running Time: 128 minutes

discovery, telling Janet that her gruesome cuts and bruises are the fault of a hit-and-run driver. This is not the first time Ray has beaten his wife, but Janet, although she knows better, is eager to buy into Valerie's lie, swearing she will not rest until the driver is caught. But then friends talk Valerie into leaving Ray, and together the four female generations of the family—Kath, and Janet, and Valerie, and Michelle—attempt to make a go of it.

Oldman has repeatedly asserted his love for the characters in *Nil By Mouth*, but it is difficult to believe that his affection includes the likes of Billy and Ray. Janet, with her spunk and generosity, is admirable in her own way. And when Valerie, stripped of all her defenses and delusions at last, tells Ray that she wants to find someone else—someone kind who will love her—it is a heartbreaking speech. (Kathy Burke won the prize for best actress at Cannes in 1997 for her portrayal of Valerie, and hers is indeed a stunning performance.) Still, these are not strong individuals, and when in the end we see them reunited as a family with Ray in their midst, our awareness that the cycle of dependency and abuse has begun again is devastating.

Nil By Mouth is true to life in every sense of the term. Oldman has given his film the feeling of a documentary, and although he scripted all the dialogue, the actors give their speeches the feeling of improvisation. Oldman has followed in the footsteps of such British directors of cinema verite as Ken Loach and Mike Leigh, and with the help of some very big talents, he has proven that he can hold his own with these predecessors. *Nil By Mouth* makes for an uncomfortable filmgoing experience but an auspicious debut.

—*Lisa Paddock*

REVIEWS

Boxoffice. August, 1997, p. 46.
Entertainment Weekly. February 13, 1998.
The Hollywood Reporter. May 9, 1997, p. 7.
Los Angeles Times. February 6, 1998, p. F12.
New York Times. May 12, 1997, p. B6.
New York Times. February 6, 1998, p. E14.
New Yorker. February 9, 1998, p. 83.
People. February 16, 1998, p. 19.
Rolling Stone. February 19, 1998, p. 64.
Sight and Sound. October, 1997, p. 55.
Variety. May 12, 1997, p. 76.
Washington Post Weekend. February 27, 1998, p. 43.

Nô

Robert Lepage is the leader of a new generation of filmmakers who are rapidly revolutionizing filmmaking in Québec. His newest film, *Nô*, is a typically dense combination of interpersonal confusion, narrative complexity and visual dynamism that somehow ends up feeling modest and self-contained. Overall the film is an attempt to exorcise a number of Québec's cultural demons, and in so doing it offers a highly original interpretation of the recent history of that embattled Francophone province. Lepage is also fairly unique among filmmakers in that his background is in the theater (this is really where he's made his name) and that training is visible throughout, but he also has a very firm grasp on the nature of the cinematic medium, and makes the most of its visual essence. However, even though *Nô* is highly complex politically and innovative visually, it never gets bogged down: its performances are all very affecting and his story is comical and oddly romantic. *Nô* is a witty, biting film, and sheds some much needed light on a culture that is too often ignored or misunderstood in North America.

The story opens at the 1970 World Expo in Osaka, and for much of the duration of the film Lepage follows around the members of the Canadian pavilion. Most prominent among them is Sophie (Anne-Marie Cadieux), who is playing the lead in a French farce being performed by dutiful Québécois anxious to put forward a cultured face. The Canadian ambassador Walter Laponte (Richard Frechette) and his wife Patricia (Marie Gignac) take her out afterwards, and when she gets drunk at dinner things begin to come unraveled. This unraveling is augmented by the occasional presence of her rejected lover François-Xavier (Eric Bernier), who acts in the farce with her, and the painful absence of her much beloved boyfriend Michel (Alexis Martin), who is in Montréal. Indeed, the film sometimes moves from Osaka to Montréal, where Michel has taken up with a group of fairly hapless bombers just as martial law is being declared in order to combat the rise of militant Québec separatism. Various romantic triangles are initiated and go badly awry, and Sophie finds out that she is pregnant. When she hears of the declaration of martial law she fears for Michel's safety, and finally decides that she must get back to Montréal. When she returns to Michel's apartment, which he had accidentally blown to pieces while assembling a bomb, she is arrested in one of the round-ups that marked the period known as "The October Crisis," and miscarries. The closing images are of Sophie and Michel, now married and safely middleclass, watching the returns in the 1980 vote on sovereignty, where the current Prime Minister of Canada (then the federal government's pointman for arguing against separatism) Jean Chrètien is interviewed on why the voters of Québec decided not to separate.

Nô is pretty dense with political and social references, and it's important to know something about the recent history of Québec going in. *Nô* takes place in a most fateful year, 1970, although what happened three years before then is just as important. The 1967 world expo was in Montréal, and that event is credited with opening up a rapidly liberalizing Québec to the wonders of the world abroad. It was a truly epochal moment in what came to be known as Québec's "Quiet Revolution," the period between 1959 and 1970 when a previously provincial and strictly Catholic culture awakened from its long slumber. The fact that Lepage focuses so closely on the Osaka World Expo, which was the first one after the Montréal event, makes it clear that he means to examine the aftermath of Québec's reformation. One of the products of this reformation was the emergence of militant nationalism, which culminated in the bombing campaign of a terrorist group called the Front pour la Liberation du Québec (FLQ).

In the fall of 1970 the FLQ kidnapped Québec's justice minister and a foreign trade representative from Great Britain. When the justice minister turned up dead in a car a few days later, Canadian Prime Minister Pierre Trudeau declared martial law throughout Québec, thus beginning what came to be known as "The October Crisis." Activists of all stripes were rounded up and detained without charge, and tanks patrolled the streets of Montréal. The party of the Quiet Revolution was over. These few weeks remained scarred in the minds of many Québécois, and sharply effected the evolution of the culture in the 1970s, perhaps leading to the rise of a separatist government and a referendum on separation from Canada in 1980. That referendum failed, and the fact that Sophie and Michel (who, recall, was an FLQ–esque bomber ten years earlier) are watching those returns at the end of the film indicates that Lepage sees the vote of "No" as the logical outcome of the troubled Quiet Revolution, a revolution which, in this film, is marked not by triumph or even defeat but confusion.

This interpretation comes at a crucial moment in Québec's political evolution, and has a great deal to contribute to the ongoing arguments about Québec culture and the romanticism of separatism. His revision of the popular perception of the Quiet Revolution is especially important, and his representation of the Canadian pavilion is an especially acidic example of a critical spirit. The promises of a culturally independent and confident Québec are nowhere to be found in this parade of nostalgia—the fact that a *French* play and not a piece of Québec theater (which, in the 1970s, was very vibrant indeed) is used to show to the world how confident Québec now is speaks for itself. Lepage adds to this mix of hypocrisy the boorish diplomat Walter Laponte (who incompetently tries to seduce Sophie, who is young enough to be his daughter) and his icy wife Patricia, who are not exactly the ideals of a new, worldly Québec. All that fuss of the Quiet Revolution, Lepage seems to say, and this is what you wind up with in just a few years: a bad French farce, a slobbish francophone ambassador, and enormous confusion about a personal life that, despite your passionate wishes to be sophisticated and cosmopolitan, remains in Québec, so far away when our protagonist, Sophie, needs its comforts the most. Although Lepage has been one of the keenest chroniclers of contemporary Québec (his other two films, 1993's *Le Confessinale* and 1996's *Le Polygraphe* are minor masterpieces of cultural exposition) he is no propagandist. Instead, he sees Québec as a deeply troubled place, but obviously loves the culture enough to want to point out its collective flaws and self-deceptions.

Lepage's play *The Seven Streams of the River Ota* follows the literal and metaphorical fallout from Hiroshima through several generations of internationally linked characters.

You wouldn't know it from the graceful, cinematic way he makes films, but Lepage is actually better known as a theater director. Indeed, *Nô* is partially based on Lepage's seven-hour play *The Seven Streams of the River Ota*, although this is much more straightforward and narrative than that quite fragmented stage piece. This doesn't mean that *Nô* is conventional: in addition to creating a very engaging narrative, Lepage has allowed his visual sensibilities to run wild. All of the images in Montréal are in black and white: contrasted to the vibrant colors of Osaka this makes it clear, in a purely visual way, just what he thinks of the climate in Québec's supposed cultural capital. Further, he has a pronounced lyrical sensibility: a sequence where a blind Japanese interpreter and her Canadian boyfriend go into a photo booth and start to kiss and giggle is pure bliss, and Lepage has the good sense to sit back and let it unfold. Another sequence in the same photo booth, where Sophie's dejected lover François-Xavier smacks himself over and over, is shot in a similarly simple, and this time upsetting, fashion.

Lepage's theatrical training shows in some ways, of course, and the way that his actors interact with each other is the clearest expression of this part of his background. It's almost impossible to say who the star of this film is, so interdependent are all the performances of this formidable en-

CREDITS

Sophie: Anne-Marie Cadieux
Michel: Alexis Martin
Hanako: Marie Brassard
Walter: Richard Frechette
Patricia: Marie Gignac
Francois-Xavier: Eric Bernier

Origin: Canada
Released: 1998
Production: Bruno Jobin for In Extremis Images; released by Alliance
Direction: Robert Lepage
Screenplay: Robert Lepage and Andre Morency; based on a segment of Lepage's play *The Seven Streams of the River Ota*
Cinematography: Pierre Mignot
Editing: Aube Foglia
Music: Michel F. Cote, Berrnard Falaise
Production design: Fanfan Boudreau
Art direction: Monique Dion
Costumes: Marie-Chantale Vaillancourt
Sound: Veronique Gabillaud
MPAA rating: Unrated
Running Time: 85 minutes

semble. Indeed, Lepage's narrative fits together so tightly that even the smallest detail somehow holds the whole thing together; this sense of integration is achieved in large part by the controlled performances and the care with which the actors develop their characters.

In short, Lepage manages to have the best of both worlds in *Nô*, combining the purely visual artifice of the cinematic artist with a skill working with actors that can come only from years spent on the stage. All this and critical analysis of a marginalized culture, an analysis that is beholden neither to the militants nor those who would cover over Québec's ongoing troubles. Rigorously concerned with both aesthetics and politics, Robert Lepage is the filmmaker laureate for a culture struggling to make sense of a very tumultuous recent history. 🎞

—*Jerry White*

REVIEWS

Sight & Sound. April, 1999, p. 50.
Variety. August 31, 1998, p. 97.

No Looking Back

How can you not fit in . . . in your own hometown?—Movie tagline

"A universal love story. A winner! Edward Burns does it again!"—Jim Ferguson, *KMSB/Fox* (Tucson)

"Deeply satisfying. Holly gives a richly expressive performance. Burns and Bon Jovi handle their roles with zest and style."—Andrew Sarris, *New York Observer*

"Jon Bon Jovi is strikingly good."—Peter Travers, *Rolling Stone*

"Lauren Holly shines."—David Naranjo, *WPLG/ABC*

With his third outing, filmmaker Edward Burns shifts from the romantic comedies of *The Brothers McMullen* (1994) and *She's the One* (1996) to straight drama in *No Looking Back*. Besides playing as a serious, character-driven drama, the multitalented Burns' latest feature is also a

woman's story and the first of his films to be told largely from a woman's point of view.

Writer-director-actor Burns once again focuses on working-class America but this time he ventures outside the Irish-American milieu of his earlier films. *No Looking Back* takes place in an unnamed Eastern seaboard town of very limited opportunities. Cinematographer Frank Prinzi sets the tone with his moody ocean-town photography—giving the film a bleak, desolate feel. Shot in Rockaway, N.Y., in the drizzly off-season, the film evokes the blue-collar melancholy of Bruce Springsteen territory with small-town angst and dead-end futures. Appropriately, The Boss himself lent three songs for the soundtrack.

The film's simple story centers around Claudia (Lauren Holly), a 30ish waitress at the local diner, who is engaged to be married to her sweet, live-in boyfriend Michael (Jon Bon Jovi). She's afraid her future is set in this small town with work, marriage, and a family. Although Michael is attractive, loyal, and hardworking, Claudia knows their future together will be all too predictable and she's afraid of ending up in a rut. Complicating matters further, Charlie (Burns), the love of Claudia's life (and Michael's best friend), blows back into town after abandoning her three years earlier to seek his fortune in California.

Returning home broke, Charlie takes a part-time job pumping gas and immediately starts to reenter his old friends' lives. No one is particularly happy to see the aimless drifter back in town, including his own mother. It turns out Charlie wants Claudia back and he gradually starts breaking down her defenses by promising her that things will be different this time. He tries to convince Claudia that she's selling herself short with Michael and can change her luck if she goes with him the next time he leaves town. Although Charlie is extremely charming and sexy, Claudia is not sure if she can trust him. Will she give the world-class rogue another chance?

That's basically it for the storyline—a working-class love triangle with Claudia caught in the middle. Nothing else really happens here but the ending feels completely appropriate

Claudia (Lauren Holly) to Charlie (Edward Burns): "Do you realize we were in sixth grade the first time we kissed? That's close to twenty years ago. So you've been breaking my heart on and off for twenty years now. I hope you're proud of yourself."

Filmed in Rockaway, N.Y., the movie was shot in muted tones to set the mood of a rain-swept seaside town.

for the film's dynamics. The decision Claudia finally makes is the only one that would work for this movie—no other ending would ring true.

Both Bon Jovi and Burns are solid in their roles and their scenes together are the most honestly depicted in the film. Rocker-turned-actor Bon Jovi gives a good, understated performance as the ultra-nice guy, while Burns is a real scene-stealer as the rakish Charlie. Several critics commented that Burns easily holds the screen with his matinee-idol performance but that he may be too natural a movie star to fit into this scruffy working-class story. (For further proof of his star power, check out his supporting role as Private Reiben in Steven Spielberg's D-day epic, *Saving Private Ryan,* 1998).

Although Holly tries hard with her largely underwritten role, she is too sophisticated and refined to make Claudia's dilemma credible. Many critics cited that Holly, with her model-slim figure and cover girl face, was miscast as a working-class waitress facing a crossroads in her life. No matter how she's dressed, Holly just looks too glamorous for her drab surroundings. As the emotional center of the film, the character of Claudia is too hollow and could have benefitted from more development.

In an interview in the *Los Angeles Times/Calendar,* Burns remarks on the challenges he set for himself with his third feature: "This is a story about dreams, particularly the dreams of people who grow up in small towns, and is the story of a woman who looks at the lives of the people around her and knows she wants something more. I'd never written a story from a woman's point of view, so that was one of the challenges here. And, although I touched on dramatic elements in the previous films, I'd never done a drama."

Although *No Looking Back* only received a brief theatrical release and reviews were mixed, the film succeeds as

CREDITS

Claudia: Lauren Holly
Charlie: Edward Burns
Michael: Jon Bon Jovi
Claudia's Mom: Blythe Danner
Kelly: Connie Britton
Teresa: Jennifer Esposito
Goldie: Nick Sandow

Origin: USA
Released: 1998
Production: Ted Hope, Michael Nozik, and Edward Burns for a Polygram Filmed Entertainment Group, Marlboro Road/Good Machine/South Fork Pictures production; released by Gramercy/20th Century Fox
Direction: Edward Burns
Screenplay: Edward Burns
Cinematography: Frank Prinzi
Editing: Susan Graef
Production design: Therese DePrez
Set decoration: Diane Lederman
Costumes: Sara Jane Slotnick
Sound: Matthew Price
Music: Joe Delia
MPAA rating: R
Running Time: 96 minutes

REVIEWS

Entertainment Weekly. April 3, 1998, p. 64.
Los Angeles Times. March 27, 1998, p. F4.
Los Angeles Times/Calendar. March 29, 1998, p. 3.
New York Times. March 27, 1998, p. E24.
People. April 6, 1998, p. 20.
Rolling Stone. April 16, 1998, p. 87.
USA Today. March 27, 1998, p. 4E.
Variety. March 23, 1998, p. 88.
Village Voice. March 31, 1998.

a minor character and mood piece. Burns is to be commended for taking a risk and trying something different. Fans expecting another *The Brothers McMullen* will be disappointed. However, if given a chance, they'll find this latest feature to be a worthwhile and watchable ensemble piece.

More importantly, this drama proves that Burns is not a one-trick pony, but rather a versatile triple threat (writer-director-actor) who continues to expand his filmmaking boundaries.

—Beth Fhaner

The Object of My Affection

A love story that could only happen between best friends.—Movie tagline

"Jennifer Aniston and Paul Rudd make movie magic. A true delight. *The Object of My Affection* will capture America's heart."—Bill Zwecker, *NBC-TV*

"Absolutely enchanting! One of the happiest, most intelligent American films in years."—Rex Reed, *The New York Observer*

"Jennifer Aniston comes into her own. A strong performance!"—David Ansen, *Newsweek*

"Memorably funny and touching!"—Peter Travers, *Rolling Stone*

 Box Office: $29,187,243

Nina Borowski (Jennifer Aniston) falls in love with her gay roommate George (Paul Rudd) in the unlikely romance *The Object of My Affection*.

Hollywood added a new twist to the romantic comedy this past year with sexual orientation becoming the main obstacle to modern love in the movies. With the success of the 1997 films *My Best Friend's Wedding, In & Out,* and *Chasing Amy, The Object of My Affection* became the fourth romantic comedy in a year to explore a relationship between characters with differing sexual orientations. This contemporary romantic comedy asks whether a gay man and a straight woman can develop a satisfying relationship when there's no hope for passionate sex.

Jennifer Aniston (of TV's *Friends*) stars as Nina Borowski, a social worker who meets nice, grade-school teacher George (Paul Rudd) at a Manhattan dinner party. Upon learning that George has just been dumped by his boyfriend, Robert (Tim Daly), and no longer has a place to live, Nina innocently invites him to share her modest Brooklyn apartment.

 Rodney (Nigel Hawthorne) gives Nina (Jennifer Aniston) some advice: "Don't fix your life so that you're left alone right when you come to the middle of it."

Although Nina's overbearing, lawyer boyfriend Vince (John Pankow) would like to move in, he respects Nina's decision and she assures him that it's only a temporary arrangement.

Once they're living in such close quarters, it doesn't take long for Nina and George to become instant soul mates. They share everything from secrets to late-night ice cream to ballroom dance lessons. The relationship between them grows into a strong bond based on emotional intimacy, trust, and companionship. When Nina learns she's pregnant, she dumps the biological father Vince and suggests raising her child with best friend George instead. After some hesitation, George agrees to the arrangement without giving much thought to the long-term consequences.

Nina envisions a perfect environment where "none of the old rules apply." The problem is that they can't agree on the rules in this unconventional relationship. Things start to get complicated when Nina finds herself sexually drawn to George and starts pushing him for greater intimacy. Although there is a moment when it appears that they're heading for a physical relationship, George backs off—he knows they've went too far. In a somewhat predictable turn of events, George leaves for a weekend trip with his ex, during which time he finds a new romantic interest in Paul (Amo Gulinello), the actor boy-toy of aging drama critic Rodney Fraser (Nigel Hawthorne). When George brings his new beau home, Nina feels rejected and finally grasps the obvious: Their special arrangement won't work on a permanent basis. Although the outcome is hardly surprising, it is a bittersweet and poignant moment as the characters realize the ground has shifted under their friendship.

The film marks the screenwriting debut of playwright Wendy Wasserstein (the Pulitzer Prize-winning *Heidi Chronicles*), who adapted the script based on Stephen McCauley's 1987 novel of the same name.

In her screenwriting debut, playwright Wendy Wasserstein (the Pulitzer Prize-winning *Heidi Chronicles*) adapts Stephen McCauley's 1987 novel with sophisticated new characters, funny dialogue, and contemporary concepts.

CREDITS

Nina Borowski: Jennifer Aniston
George Hanson: Paul Rudd
Sidney Miller: Alan Alda
Rodney Fraser: Nigel Hawthorne
Vince McBride: John Pankow
Dr. Robert Joley: Tim Daly
Constance Miller: Allison Janney
Frank Hanson: Steve Zahn
Paul James: Amo Gulinello

Origin: USA
Released: 1998
Production: Laurence Mark; released by 20th Century Fox
Direction: Nicholas Hytner
Screenplay: Wendy Wasserstein; based on the novel by Stephen McCauley
Cinematography: Oliver Stapleton
Editing: Tariq Anwar
Production design: Jane Musky
Art direction: Patricia Woodbridge
Set decoration: Susan Bode
Costumes: John Dunn
Sound: Michael Barosky
Music: George Fenton
MPAA rating: R
Running Time: 112 minutes

However, the most significant departure from McCauley's charming novel is the point of view. McCauley chose to write his novel from George's perspective, whereas Wasserstein sees the film through Nina. It's such a major departure from the novel that director Nicholas Hytner has called it "a free cinematic adaptation of the novel rather than a slavish retelling of it." The only problem with this concept is that the changes made, which included jettisoning the book's second half and the creation of numerous new characters, have resulted in a less emotionally compelling story.

Hytner, who previously created *The Madness of King George* (1994), directs the script with intelligence and humor, though it occasionally slides into sitcom territory. Under Hytner's direction, both Aniston and Rudd give terrific performances. Despite an adorable turn by Aniston (*Picture Perfect* [1997], *She's the One* [1996]) in her most demanding big-screen role yet, the movie belongs to Rudd, who is best known as Alicia Silverstone's stepbrother turned boyfriend in 1995's *Clueless*.

In his first starring screen role, Rudd makes the character of George so sweet and endearing that the audience can't help but be won over by him. Commenting on Rudd's performance in the *Detroit News*, critic Susan Stark wrote: "Paul Rudd is the movie's major source of charm. He's so appealing that his character will have every heterosexual woman in the audience empathizing with Aniston and all the gay guys in the crowd reveling not only in his good looks and charm, but also in his emotional integrity."

In addition to the attractive and talented leads, *The Object of My Affection* features an equally impressive supporting cast. Alan Alda is gratingly funny as a name-dropping literary agent, and Allison Janney gives a sassy turn as Nina's pushy stepsister. John Pankow as the baby's obnoxious birth father and Tim Daly as Rudd's ex also give solid performances. But the most engaging supporting role is that of the homosexual theatre critic beautifully played by Nigel Hawthorne, who starred for Hytner in the acclaimed stage and screen versions of *The Madness of King George*. He provides one of the film's most poignant moments when he attempts to console Nina and himself with this advice, "One shouldn't be too hard on oneself if the object of one's affection returns the favor with less enthusiasm than one might have hoped."

Although *The Object of My Affection* has an appealing cast and puts a fresh spin on unrequited love, it's tough to buy into this premise in the first place. The audience knows long beforehand that Nina and George's unconventional relationship is never going to work out. It's a heartfelt and well-intentioned tale of modern love, yet a misguided one.

Despite being a crowd-pleaser at the boxoffice, critical reaction to *Object* was mixed. Michael Wilmington in the *Chicago Tribune* summed it up best: "Overall, it's a movie I both liked and disliked, sometimes changing my mind from scene to scene . . . With a bit more universal sympathy, *Object* might have been a shattering romantic comedy instead of a frustrating one. But perhaps, in the end, we shouldn't blame this movie—or Hytner and Wasserstein—for choosing unworthy objects of affection. Isn't that a major flaw in life itself?"

—*Beth Fhaner*

REVIEWS

Chicago Tribune. April 17, 1998, p. 4.
Detroit News. April 17, 1998, p. C1.
Entertainment Weekly. April 24, 1998, p. 55.
Los Angeles Times. April 17, 1998, p. F6.
New York Times. April 17, 1998, p. E22.
People. April 27, 1998, p. 35.
Rolling Stone. April 30, 1998, p. 73.
Sight and Sound. July, 1998, p. 50.
USA Today. April 17, 1998, p. 10E.
Variety. April 13, 1998, p. 27.
Washington Post. April 17, 1998, p. B4.
Washington Post Weekend. April 17, 1998, p. 57.

Off the Menu: The Last Days of Chasen's

The Golden Age of Hollywood is featured in *Off the Menu: The Last Days of Chasen's*, a documentary chronicling the demise of one of Tinseltown's most celebrated restaurants. While staying in an L.A. bed-and-breakfast, the husband-and-wife filmmaking team of Shari Springer Berman and Robert Pulcini learned the landmark restaurant would be closing its doors and decided to document the final two weeks that preceded Chasen's exit on April 1, 1995. For nearly sixty years, Chasen's was the place where the biggest stars came to eat and drink amidst an elegant, exclusive, and expensive atmosphere.

Off the Menu affectionately captures celebrity's most fascinating characters and stories connected to the restaurant's lengthy history. Alfred Hitchcock was a longtime regular, who dined at the same booth every Thursday night. Jimmy Stewart held his bachelor party there. Ronald Reagan proposed to Nancy Davis over a Hobo steak at Chasen's; and Elizabeth Taylor had Chasen's famous chili shipped to her in Rome while filming *Cleopatra* in 1962—these are just a few of the anecdotes recounted by various celebrities, including Angie Dickinson, Don Rickles, Robert Wagner, Rod Steiger, Fay Wray, and Sharon Stone.

Besides reminiscing celebrities, the film also focuses on the restaurant's loyal, longtime staff. Many of these

> "It's like when somebody's sick. Nobody calls, but everybody goes to the funeral."—bartender Pepe Ruiz commenting on Chasen's popularity once it posted its closing notice.

> Elizabeth Taylor was not only a regular but had Chasen's famous chili shipped to her in Rome while she was making *Cleopatra* in 1962.

workers had spent decades at Chasen's entertaining the rich and famous. Among the former employees interviewed is Tommy Gallagher, the legendary headwaiter who hobnobbed with the Rat Pack and had his picture taken with presidents and even Pope John Paul II. The sentimental Gallagher spent so much time at Chasen's that his grown son refers to the restaurant as his father's "other woman." Other employees interviewed include Ronnie Clint, the restaurant's British-born general manager; Val Schwab, who checked coats for years; and Onetta Johnson, the ladies' room attendant who inspired Donna Summer's song "She Works Hard for the Money."

Touching on the value of tradition and the importance of change, the film itself is a testament to the trendiness of Hollywood. Although it continued to host glamorous post-Oscar parties, Chasen's had ceased years ago to be a hotspot for celebrities to be seen. Only when the restaurant posted its closing notice did it become a popular celebrity watering hole again, leaving some people begging to be admitted. As bartender Pepe Ruiz observed, "It's like when somebody's sick. Nobody calls, but everybody goes to the funeral."

The downfall of Chasen's, with its rich menu and formal dress code came when it could not attract Hollywood's younger generations, who went to trendier, more casual places featuring health-conscience menus. Chasen's older clientele began dying off or staying home.

CREDITS

Origin: USA
Released: 1998
Production: Julia Strohm
Direction: Shari Springer Berman, Robert Pulcini
Editing: Robert Pulcini
Cinematography: Ken Kobland, Mark Suozzo
MPAA rating: Unrated
Running Time: 90 minutes

Although a bit long at 90 minutes, *Off the Menu* is a bittersweet tribute to the most enduring restaurant of Hollywood's Golden Era. At the time the documentary was completed, Chasen's had been sold to a strip mall developer. However, three years later, Chasen's was able to relocate to Canon Drive in Beverly Hills and the original location continues to open for special events.

—*Beth Fhaner*

REVIEWS

Los Angeles Times. May 15, 1998.
Washington Post. September 9, 1998, p. D1.

One Tough Cop

There are still real heroes.—Movie tagline

Sometimes the facts get lost in the headlines.
—Movie tagline

"Director Bruno Barreto brings out the best in Stephen Baldwin and Chris Penn, two fine actors. Fresh, solid and diverting from end to end."—F.X. Feeney, *L.A. Weekly*

"A totally absorbing drama. Stephen Baldwin was superb in *The Usual Suspects* and here he's even better."—Jeffrey Lyons, *NBC-TV*

"Strongly acted and pungently written. A hearty two-fisted performance by Stephen Baldwin."
—Stephen Holden, *New York Times*

"For harshly realistic police drama, the film to beat is *One Tough Cop*."—Peter Stack, *San Francisco Chronicle*

 Box Office: $1,313,607

Bo Dietl (Stephen Baldwin) is one tough cop who wanted to be one good cop, a cop who believed that "Becoming a cop was a chance to make a difference." The film, directed by Bruno Barreto, was adapted by Jeremy Iacone from Bo Dietl's autobiographical novel. Considering himself a kind of Dirty Harry operative willing to bend the rules, Dietl was a highly-decorated police detec-

tive in New York City whose controversial methods finally caught up with him. After being reassigned from Manhattan to Brooklyn, he eventually became discouraged enough to retire early at the age of 35. The "true story" framework is destroyed by a disclaimer at the end of the film, however, that states: "Except for the character of Bo Dietl, all characters and situations portrayed in this film are fictional."

The film begins with a demonstration of how frustrating police work can be as Dietl and his short-tempered partner Duke Finnerty (Chris Penn) are thrown into a difficult hostage situation. After killing his wife for infidelity, a father (Luis Guzman) is desperately threatening to kill himself and his daughter. Dietl manages to save the daughter, but the man shoots himself. The primary story, however, involves the brutal rape and murder of a nun at an East Harlem convent school in 1981, so horrendous that a special investigation was mounted.

Dietl acts on a tip he gets from an underworld friend, Richie La Cassa (Mike McGlone) who owns an Italian-American nightclub, a tip that leads to an informant in the rape-murder case, but La Cassa is on the wrong side of the law, being investigated by FBI agents Jean Devlin (Amy Irving) and Bruce Payne (Victor Slezak). Dietl has no business associating with La Cassa, whom he has known since they were schoolmates. Nonetheless, Dietl strikes up an affair with Joey O'Hara (Gina Gershon), La Cassa's ex-mistress, while his partner Duke runs up a hefty gambling debt with La Cassa's mob associates. Joey, who works at the nightclub, has broken up with La Cassa, a family man who is not about to leave his wife for her. The major dilemma comes when the FBI agents give Dietl an ultimatum. They will destroy his career unless he agrees to help them nail his friend La Cassa by rigging a recording device in Richie's car. Dietl also attempts to help Duke, which puts him on the wrong side of Richie's mafia connection. Bo's situation steadily intensifies as the inevitable face-off between cop friend and mob boss friend is brought on when Finnerty's booze and gambling vices place his life in extreme danger.

Police captain to Bo Dietl (Stephen Baldwin): "Bo, you're the best cop I have working for me, but swear to God, you're your own worst enemy!"

The real-life Bo Dietl retired from the force with a 98 percent conviction rate.

Director Barreto, who has been nominated twice for an Academy Award for *Four Days in September* (1998) and *Dora Flor and Her Two Husbands* (1979) captures the grittiness of the tough New York streets, which is amazing since the film was shot mainly in Toronto, but the preachiness and predictability of the script makes it harder to separate film from many of the hard-hitting crime dramas seen on television.

With this tough guy role, Baldwin proves that he has range beyond the usual dimwit, comedic roles he has chosen prior to this film. An intensity comes across, making Baldwin's transition into the nonfiction character of Bo Dietl a convincing one. However, the rest of the cast doesn't come across with much impact. Penn doesn't expand much on a role he's becoming all too familiar with, along with sexy vixen Gershon, who just stands around with her mouth slightly open in bewilderment. Ironically, the one who suffers the most, performance wise, is Barreto's wife, actress Amy Irving. As Dennis Harvey of *Variety* stated, Irving is "badly miscast as a fed."

Bo Dietl's life as a New York City cop was one that truly had the potential to be the next *The French Connection* (1971) or *Serpico,* (1973) or *Bad Lieutenant* (1992). But *One Tough Cop* failed to make that life interesting or entertaining.

—*Jim Welsh* and *Michelle Banks*

CREDITS

Bo Dietl: Stephen Baldwin
Duke Finnerty: Chris Penn
Richie La Cassa: Mike McGlone
Joey O'Hara: Gina Gershon
Frankie (Hot) Salvano: Paul Guilfoyle
FBI Agent Jean Devlin: Amy Irving
FBI Agent Bruce Payne: Victor Slezak
Gunman Popi: Luis Guzman

Origin: USA
Released: 1998
Production: Michael Bregman and Martin Bregman for Patriot Pictures production; released by Stratosphere Entertainment
Direction: Bruno Barreto
Screenplay: Jeremy Iacone; inspired by the novel *One Tough Cop* by Bo Dietl
Cinematography: Ron Fortunato
Editing: Ray Hubley
Production design: Perri Gorrara
Set decoration: Megan Less, Lisa Nilsson
Costumes: Martha Mann, Sue Gandy
Sound: Bryan Day, Fanklin Stetiner
Music: Bruce Broughton
MPAA rating: R
Running Time: 90 minutes

REVIEWS

Detroit Free Press. October 10, 1998, p. 5F.
Entertainment Weekly. October 16, 1998, p. 60.
New York Times. October 9, 1998, p. E14.
People. October 19, 1998, p. 41.
San Francisco Chronicle. October 9, 1998, p. C3.
San Francisco Examiner. October 9, 1998, p. C3.
Variety. October 5, 1998, p. 69.
Village Voice. October 13, 1998, p. 130.

One True Thing

Box Office: $23,523,196

Career-driven journalist Ellen Gulden (Renée Zellweger) re-examines her life and familial relationships when she takes care of her cancer-stricken mother (Meryl Streep) in the tearjerker *One True Thing*.

When you think about it carefully, films about death—more specifically, films surrounding impending death—shouldn't even be made. Based on the promise of escapism and temporary relief from the horrors of the real world, movies were originally designed to entertain us and lift our spirits. Why would we want to pay good money to have someone bring us down? Some might say for the purpose of teaching us more about ourselves. Others find it a semi-therapeutic release to feel the pain of others and react as if it were their own, having a good cry, as it were. Cynics call it "emotional manipulation." By and large, mainstream audiences avoid these types of pictures, yet they are never in short supply. Tragic but far from tragedies, their existence seems based on the need for artistic recognition. Arguably, it allows members of the acting community to test the boundaries, to force themselves into testing the limits of their own emotions and, as a result, to increase their range.

It's no coincidence that these films almost invariably are reserved for fall and winter release. It's not so much that they are the last thing diversionary, action-minded summer audiences would want to pay money to see. Fall and winter equate to prestige time for studios. It's probably the only time of the year when a healthy return isn't the main concern. Some say it's their own self-imposed penance for the wealth they've amassed during the warmer months when the release schedule is practically devoid of anything that can be remotely construed as intellectually stimulating. Others, unafraid to offend or to call something what it is, know it is the time

Ellen (Renée Zellweger) to her mother Kate (Meryl Streep): "How do you do this every day and no one notices?"

when the studios all toss their collective lines into the lake and hope against hope that they can reel in an Oscar nomination or two.

If you're going to make a weepie, you might as well get the best group of actors at your disposal to deliver the material. That's exactly what director Carl Franklin did for *One True Thing*. After a period of inactivity (two years), Meryl Streep decided to mark her return with a role that would test her mettle. Easily the finest, if not the most diverse, actress of her generation, Streep makes her job seem almost effortless. With an arsenal of foreign accents at her disposal, all she need do is don a different hairstyle and she can become anyone she wishes. However, never in her career has she been called on to play a character so ordinary. As Kate Gulden, a New England homemaker whose skills around the house are on a par with Martha Stewart, she is given very little to do. Perfect to a fault, she is what many would label a throwback to the old days when a woman's sole purpose in life was to take care of her family. Perhaps Kate's only fault is her inability to acknowledge that her husband George (William Hurt) is regularly and flagrantly unfaithful.

Pretentious, aloof, and icy, George is a highly respected English professor who has long regarded his family as his second priority. Also of a "traditional" mentality, he sees nothing wrong with maintaining an emotional chasm with his wife and children as long as he dutifully fulfills his role as a provider. He never realizes that "providing" extends far beyond monetary concerns. Content with fleeting affairs with his students and never quite finishing his "great American novel," he appears connected to his family by the thinnest of threads. Hurt was an ideal choice for the part of George. An actor of limited range, his more memorable roles (*The Big Chill, Altered States, The Accidental Tourist, Broadcast News*) are the ones he plays with controlled unemotional detachment. Solemn, taciturn, often brooding, he always seems to do a lot with a little. It's not that it's not in him to go further. Ironically, the role that earned Hurt his sole Oscar was that of a flamboyant, imprisoned transvestite in *Kiss of the Spider Woman*.

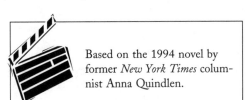

Based on the 1994 novel by former *New York Times* columnist Anna Quindlen.

Early on in the film it is learned that Kate has contracted cancer and, true to form, George shirks the responsibility of caring for his wife by imploring his daughter Ellen (Renée Zellweger) to move back home to play nursemaid. Like her father, Ellen is a writer. It's made clear that she yearns desperately for his approval (which never comes) and she chose her career, in part at least, to win George over. A features writer for *New York* magazine, Ellen leads a life like the city in which she lives: harried, high pressure, get it done yesterday. The demands of her job are many but she seems to thrive and is anxious to prove she's got what it takes. Her life is more or less complete, but all that changes when George calls on her to move back home to look after her mom. Nowhere near as concerned with receiving praise from her mother, Ellen is still nagged by the realization that she can never measure up to Kate. Riddled with guilt, Ellen accommodates George's request and, convinced that she can still do her job, moves back home.

The Guldens do have another child, a son named Brian (Tom Everett Scott). It is presumed that he still lives nearby and has what seems to be (we're never really told) an uneventful life. Why isn't Brian called on to take care of Kate? Or pitch in occasionally? If the screenwriter (Karen Croner) couldn't find a way to develop his character, he should have been written out altogether.

Believing that Ellen can adequately handle the task at hand, George distances himself even further from his familial duties. Had he had a keener eye, he would have seen that, despite her gallant efforts, Ellen is slowly becoming unglued. Her work is suffering, her once rock-steady romantic relationship is unraveling, and, to top it all off, Ellen is getting a much better idea of just how unfaithful her father really is. As Kate's condition worsens, the resentment Ellen has been feeling for George reaches critical mass and the accusations begin flying.

Zellweger, the bright, girl-next-door type who wowed everyone with her performance in *Jerry Maguire*, is to her generation what Streep is to her own. After her debut in *Dazed & Confused* (1993), Zellweger took on a handful of incidental throwaway roles and was still a relative unknown when she took the lead in *Maguire*. Although heralded by critics and audience alike, the Academy ignored her performance of a struggling single mom. Undaunted, she chose to stay away from mainstream fare and instead accepted gutsier parts in other, arthouse-oriented projects including *The Whole Wide World* (1996), *Deceiver,* and the highly underrated *A Price Above Rubies* (two films reviewed in this edition). Despite mixing it up with two screen legends here, Zellweger holds her own and is the de facto lead in the story. She is the true standout in the film and if anyone affiliated with the movie deserves Oscar consideration, it is she. While Streep's character is admittedly the emotional anchor of the story, it is the friction between Zellweger and Hurt that takes center stage.

CREDITS

Kate Gulden: Meryl Streep
Ellen Gulden: Renée Zellweger
George Gulden: William Hurt
Brian Gulden: Tom Everett Scott
Jordan Belzer: Nicky Katt
Jules: Lauren Graham

Origin: USA
Released: 1998
Production: Harry Ulfand and Jesse Beaton for Monarch Pictures; released by Universal Pictures
Direction: Carl Franklin
Screenplay: Karen Croner; based on a novel by Anna Quindlen
Cinematography: Declan Quinn
Editing: Carole Kravetz
Music: Cliff Eidelman
Production design: Paul Peters
Art direction: Jefferson Sage
Costumes: Donna Zakowska
Sound: Allan Byer
MPAA rating: R
Running Time: 127 minutes

AWARDS AND NOMINATIONS

Academy Awards 1998 Nominations: Actress (Meryl Streep)

Director Franklin, with just two feature films to his credit (*One False Move, Devil in a Blue Dress*), is an anomaly among the handful of prominent African American directors working today. With *One True Thing*, he seems to be making a decidedly marked effort of proving to Hollywood that not all black filmmakers are interested in presenting urban-based stories or working on films with predominantly all-black casts. While the first two acts of his film come off with nary a hitch, he eventually slips into the maudlin malaise that invariably overwhelms projects of this ilk; he goes a little overboard with the glares, stares, and awkward silences. Carefully framed, "poignant" moments are accented with a tinkling, new-age score that reeks of emotional manipulation. Told largely in flashback, questions regarding the circumstances surrounding Kate's death are raised but are never given satisfactory closure. We're not sure if she met her end as a result of suicide, mercy killing, murder, or natural causes. An emotional crescendo is never delivered and, in a desperate move to strike a lasting chord with the audience, Franklin instead presents Kate in heavy, over-the-top make-up; a mere shadow of her former self. We wait in vain for the wallop that never posts. This weepie ends with a relative whimper.

—*J. M. Clark*

REVIEWS

Chicago Tribune. September 18, 1998, p. 4.
Entertainment Weekly. September 25, 1998, p. 72.
Hollywood Reporter. September 8, 1998, p. 18.
Los Angeles Times. September 18, 1998, p. F1.
New York Times. September 18, 1998, p. E1.
People. September 28, 1998, p. 39.
Variety. September 7, 1998, p. 72.
Village Voice. September 22, 1998, p. 146.
Washington Post Weekend. September 18, 1998, p. 56.

The Only Thrill

Don't save love for a rainy day . . . —Movie tagline

"Aimed at the same audience that loved *Bridges of Madison County* . . . the movie packs an emotional punch."—Scott Timberg, *Houston Press*

"A heartfelt tale with top drawer acting . . . the charisma and chemistry earn honest tears."
—Michael Begeron, *Public News*

Small town life and romance is invoked in director Peter Masterson's somewhat schmaltzy romantic drama *The Only Thrill*, which does not have a particularly evocative title. (*The Trading Post*, the title of Larry Ketron's stage play, has a good deal more meaning—perhaps someone thought the film would be mistaken for a western if it was used.) The Trading Post in question is the one Reece McHenry (Sam Shepherd) opens up (it's actually a used-clothing store) in a small Texas town in 1966. Reece was a successful land developer who gave up his career after his wife's car accident, which has left her in a permanently comatose state.

Into Reece's life comes widowed seamstress Carol Fitzsimmons (Diane Keaton), who's looking for a job to support herself and her young daughter. She and Reece bond over the stock and are soon engaging in a Wednesday ritual—the afternoon matinee at the local movie house, drinks and a meal at the local watering hole, and then a little love in the afternoon. This situation goes on fairly comfortably for years, although Reece never manages to tell Carol how he truly feels about her.

Meanwhile, echoing their own commitment-shy relationship is the romance that develops between Carol's

CREDITS

Carol Fitzsimmons: Diane Keaton
Reece McHenry: Sam Shepherd
Katherine Fitzsimmons: Diane Lane
Tom McHenry: Robert Patrick

Origin: USA
Released: 1998
Production: Yael Stroh, James Holt, and Gabriel Grunfeld for Prestige Productions and Laureate Films; released by Moonstone Entertainment
Direction: Peter Masterson
Screenplay: Larry Ketron; adapted from his play *The Trading Post*
Cinematography: Don E. Fauntleroy
Editing: Jeff Freeman
Costumes: Jean-Pierre Dorleac
Music: Peter Rodgers Melnick
Production design: John Frick
MPAA rating: R
Running Time: 107 minutes

daughter, Katherine (Diane Lane), and Reece's son, Tom (Robert Patrick). Things come to a crisis in 1978, when Carol's sister contacts her. The sister, who lives in Toronto, Ontario, is terminally ill and needs her sibling. So Carol packs up and heads to Canada, without much hope that the situation with Reece will ever change.

Indeed, the film meanders its way into the present, with Reece and Carol aging and complaining about failing health and memories and regrets about their slipping away from each other. Shepherd and Keaton do well as the lovers who let their second chance at love pass them by, but the story is prosaically told and hardly compelling.

—*Christine Tomassini*

Diane Keaton and Sam Shepherd also starred together in 1986's *Crimes of the Heart* and 1987's *Baby Boom.*

REVIEWS

Austin Chronicle. February 16, 1998.
Los Angeles Times. March 6, 1998, p. F18.

The Opposite of Sex

You'll laugh, you'll cry, you'll be offended.
—Movie tagline

"One of those in your face comedies that has audiences laughing, ducking and not believing their ears!"—Roger Ebert, *Chicago Sun-Times*

"Hilariously nasty!"—Stephen Farber, *Movieline*

"A scathing comedy!"—Janet Maslin, *New York Times*

"Funny and offbeat. Original, quirky and really funny."—*Siskel & Ebert*

Box Office: $6,367,164

W riter-director Don Roos's *The Opposite of Sex* begins in a blast of outrageousness as we meet Dedee Truitt, a smart-mouthed, white-trash sixteen-year-old whose witty and profane voice-over narration immediately grabs our attention. Played with abandon by Christina Ricci, the selfish and scheming Dedee cheerfully wreaks havoc on all the people around her; within the film's first few minutes, she disrupts her stepfather's funeral and runs away from her Louisiana home to take refuge in the Indiana home of her gay half-brother, Bill (Martin Donovan), even as she casually peppers her speech with flip homophobic remarks. *The Opposite of Sex* flirts with nastiness and danger, and, at the outset, there is indeed a certain perverse thrill in watching the manipulative Dedee run roughshod over everyone and even seduce Bill's slow-witted boyfriend, Matt (Ivan

Dedee's (Christina Ricci) narration: "I don't have a heart of gold, and I don't grow one later on. But relax. There are lots of nicer people coming up—we call them losers."

Sergei), who is no match for her wiles. However, whatever energy the film builds up dissipates quickly in a fairly lackluster chase film that feels more like a patchwork of scenes full of attitude than a coherent story.

Bill is a quintessential nice guy—a high school English teacher who, when he discovers a student's homophobic graffiti about him in the boys' bathroom, corrects the student's grammar instead of being outraged. While Bill is passive, Matt is good-looking but fairly dumb and ultimately not a very intriguing character.

The only person who stands up to Dedee's amorality is Lucia (Lisa Kudrow), the sister of Bill's late lover, Tom. Lucia clings to Bill because she feels a connection to Tom through him and probably secretly loves him. She also seems to fear a relationship with a man who could really become her lover. Playing against her usual flighty type, Kudrow is angry, straitlaced, and needy, and she nicely balances Lucia's sarcastic, wisecracking side with an underlying sense of loss and loneliness. She is romanced by the local sheriff, Carl (Lyle Lovett), as he follows her and Bill to help them through their trials with Dedee. Lovett plays Carl in his usual deadpan, laconic style but brings a certain loopy tenderness to his romance with Kudrow's Lucia.

After Dedee announces she is pregnant by Matt and they steal ten thousand dollars of Bill's money and run away, the script loses its footing. Jason (Johnny Galecki) appears and tells Bill that he, too, is Matt's boyfriend. He threatens Bill that, if he does not tell him where Matt went, he will accuse Bill of molesting him in school when he was a student four years ago. A '90s-style media scandal breaks, and Bill is suspended with pay. Then Bill and Lucia take a trip to Los Angeles, where a call from Matt has been traced. When they catch up with Dedee and Matt, Lucia figures out that Matt is not the father of the baby, and Dedee tries to extort money from Bill with Tom's ashes, which she has stolen. Playing with false charges of homosexual molestation in high school and with the memory of a loved one who died of AIDS is meant to be shocking and daring. Ultimately, though, such jabs at political correctness amount to a lot of hip posturing and help create a movie that *USA Today*'s Susan Wloszczyna called "a self-satisfied soap opera from hell."

Soon Dedee's old boyfriend, a punk named Randy (William Lee Scott), the true father of the baby, appears in Los Angeles. Dedee forces Matt to give her what is left of the money they stole and then goes off with Randy, whose main characteristics—a missing testicle and a fanatical Christian streak—are played for laughs but are not very funny. He is killed with Dedee's gun in a fight when he turns violent on her, and soon Dedee flees with Matt, who still cares about her and the fate of the baby.

With its assortment of misfits and oddballs clashing with each other in a series of supposedly goofy situations, the movie is clearly aspiring to a sense of lunacy, but unfortunately the episodic script lacks the narrative drive and fast pace needed for a no-holds-barred comedy. Moreover, none of the male characters are very interesting or pose a challenge to Dedee, and so we seldom feel any sense of urgency. Bill, for example, is independently wealthy from Tom's death, so losing his teaching job is not a real blow to him, and the threat to his reputation never seems to concern him.

Bill eventually returns to Indiana, only to learn Jason has disappeared, and so a hearing cannot be held to determine Bill's fate at school. The plot is so unimportant by this point that we probably would not remember a job was at stake if Dedee did not fill us in with her voiceover narration. Bill resigns from his job anyway, and Jason reappears to extort money for Dedee in exchange for recanting his false accusations. Bill, though, comes to life and forces Jason to take him to Dedee, and they head off to Canada in the last of the film's road trips. Lucia follows, and soon everything is sorted out. Bill must face the fact that he has lost Matt to Jason and has a heart-to-heart talk with Matt about the demise of their relationship, after which Dedee sarcastically undercuts the emotion of the moment. Dedee has her baby, and at the same time Carl declares his love for Lucia, who tells him that they too are having a baby.

One inventive aspect of the film is the self-conscious way it plays with the conventions of moviemaking itself. Dedee's voiceover narration not only tells the story but manipulates the way it is told. When she takes a gun with her at the outset, she tells us to pay attention—she is putting it in her bag "for foreshadowing, which we covered when we did Dickens. If you're smart, you won't forget I've got it."

When she and Matt run away, she tells us that Bill was distraught. When we see Bill alone, Dedee announces, "I can really lay it on," which cues grand, sentimental music to swell up to highlight Bill's sadness as he pines away for Matt. Then she shows Bill doing normal household activities to show that he carried on just fine alone. While this sequence is clever, it is emblematic of one of the film's major problems. Any time we generate genuine concern for a character, Dedee's comments quickly undercut it. We are supposed to think this is funny, but, by the end, we really are supposed to care what happens to all these people, so we are put in the weird position of laughing at stock characters and then being expected to develop a certain empathy for them.

While the self-conscious play can be fun, it also grows tiresome. Twice Dedee tries to make us believe she is dead—first in the scuffle with Randy when the gun is shot off-screen and later during childbirth when she even shows us a fictional scene of Bill and the others feeling sad for her alleged demise. (Both times she chides us for falling for the trick.) If the film were a pure, over-the-top comedy or a commentary on the conventions of narrative filmmaking, these techniques might be effective, but in this context they become gimmicks that keep distancing us from the characters so that the poignant moments seem more jarring than genuine. *The Opposite of Sex* finally tries to have it both ways—to shock and offend us and yet finally have us care about the characters (even giving just about everyone a happy ending).

In the end, in fact, all the supporting characters have paired off. Matt and Jason are together, as are Bill and Dedee's parole officer (Bill gets his job back, and Dedee has to spend six months in jail for not reporting Randy's death and is then paroled to Indiana). Carl and Lucia are together, and Lucia has her baby. Dedee, though, leaves her baby with Bill and runs away again, claiming that sex results in attachments like children, disease, and relationships, and she wants "the opposite of all that." She told us at the outset that she would not grow "a heart of gold," but at the end her future is left open-ended. When we see a montage of life's happy and sad moments for the various characters, we get the impression that Dedee is wrong, that the attachments actually make life worth living (a rather conventional lesson for a film that has tried to be edgy and darkly comic). Dedee looks toward the camera and addresses us directly with the implication that she may return to the group she

AWARDS AND NOMINATIONS

Independent Spirit Awards 1999: First Feature Award; Screenplay
National Board of Review 1998: Supporting Actress (Christina Ricci)
New York Film Critics 1998: Supporting Actress (Lisa Kudrow)

just left behind. She simply does not want us to see her going soft. Except for Lucia's newfound love with Carl, not much has really happened (it is hard to take seriously Dedee's possible transformation), but all the journeys everyone has taken are meant to convince us that everything has changed.

Some critics were impressed with *The Opposite of Sex.* Lavishing praise on the film, *Time*'s Richard Corliss called it "the smartest, edgiest, most human and handsomely acted romantic comedy in elephant years." In the *Los Angeles Times,* Kristine McKenna wrote that the film "verges on screwball comedy," but, aside from the sassiness of Dedee and her quick-witted repartee with Lucia, *The Opposite of Sex* does not crackle with the madcap energy of the best screwballs, especially when Dedee is offscreen and the film loses its major spark.

Finally, *The Opposite of Sex* feels both overstuffed with its group of misfits who frantically run all over the country and yet somehow empty in its listless plot that too often goes nowhere. Roos has created a memorable *femme fatale* in Dedee and a sharp foil in Lucia and has sprinkled patches of wicked dialogue throughout the film. However, the thin plot and unsatisfying mixture of dark humor and poignancy make *The Opposite of Sex* an uneven experience.

—*Peter N. Chumo II*

CREDITS

Dedee Truitt: Christina Ricci
Bill Truitt: Martin Donovan
Lucia: Lisa Kudrow
Matt Mateo: Ivan Sergei
Sheriff Carl Tippett: Lyle Lovett
Jason: Johnny Galecki
Randy: William Lee Scott

Origin: USA
Released: 1998
Production: David Kirkpatrick and Michael Besman for Rysher Entertainment; released by Sony Pictures Classics
Direction: Don Roos
Screenplay: Don Roos
Cinematography: Hubert Taczanowski
Editing: David Codron
Music: Mason Daring
Production design: Michael Clausen
Costumes: Peter Mitchell
Sound: Jon Ailetcher
MPAA rating: R
Running Time: 105 minutes

REVIEWS

Boxoffice. May, 1998, p. 72.
Detroit Free Press. July 3, 1998, p. C1.
Entertainment Weekly. June 5, 1998, p. 54.
Los Angeles Times. May 22, 1998, p. F2.
New York Times. May 29, 1998, p. E18.
People. June 8, 1998, p. 49.
Sight and Sound. January, 1998, p. 51.
Time. June 15, 1998.
USA Today. May 29, 1998, p. 4E.
Variety. February 16, 1998, p. 58.
Village Voice. June 2, 1998, p. 166.

Orgazmo

Making sex safe again!—Movie tagline

"Imagine *Boogie Nights*, but funny!"—David Poole, *Cover*

"Hilarious! Rude and riotously funny!"—Dennis Dermody, *Paper*

Orgazmo is crude, perverted, sacrilegious, sophomoric, lewd, and filthy—among other things. The adjectives could race on but the word that describes *Orgazmo* best is funny. This is not always the case in these types of movies where plot is thin and outlandishness high. Refreshingly, *Orgazmo* is funny and downright bawdy in a locker room, bar stool kind of way.

Ben (Dian Belcher), trying to reassure Joe (Trey Parker): "There are so many pornos made every year, no one will ever see your movie."

Fans of cable's *South Park* will recognize *Orgazmo*'s biting style of humor since it was written and directed by *South Park*'s co-creator, Trey Parker. Matt Stone, *South Park*'s other half, only acts in *Orgazmo*, which was produced before *South Park* hit big. At times the film seems a little less sophisticated than the television show, but overall *Orgazmo* manages to nail the same comic mark. Sure, the premise is stupid and the execution amateurish, but after all, what does one expect from a movie about a Mormon becoming a pornographic superhero named Orgazmo?

Orgazmo begins with a shot of the famous Hollywood sign. Moments later the word "Hollywood" is superimposed on the bottom of the screen. This mocking tone carries throughout the movie, starting immediately with the first scene of Joe Young (Trey Parker), a saccharine and clueless Mormon, soliciting people door to door. After he successfully completes this mission work he can return to Utah and marry his longtime girlfriend, the equally saccharine and clueless Lisa (Robyn Lynne Raab).

In order to get married in the Temple, Joe and Lisa need to come up with a large sum of money. Luckily, Joe rings the doorbell of a mansion where a porno is being filmed, featuring the evil Jizz Master Zero, a.k.a. "Clark" (Ron Jeremy). For those not in the know, Ron Jeremy is an adult film star specializing in being fat, hairy, and disgusting. Upon seeing this sleazy prize in her bedroom, a girl screams for help and the superhero Captain Orgazmo comes to the rescue. However, the actor playing the role is ineffectual and the shooting stops. Enter Joe. The director, Maxxx Orbison (Michael Dean Jacobs), sees that Joe would make the perfect Orgazmo. The lure of the money is too great and Joe reluctantly agrees to take the role of the crime-fighting superhero who uses his "orgazmorator" to disable people by bringing them to orgasm.

Every superhero must have a sidekick. Choda Boy (Dian Belcher), a euphemism for an erection, is a scrawny man with a dildo-topped hat who uses various sex toys as crime-fighting weapons. Named Ben Chapelski off the set, he is actually an inventor who constructed a working orgazmorator. When Joe asks him why he does porn when the "heavenly father has given you a gift for science," Ben replies that because of his diminutive height girls don't take him seriously and doing porn "sure beats jerkin' it."

Filming continues with scenes featuring a woman called T-Rex (too disturbing to recount here) and other assorted characters (also too disturbing to recount here). Orgazmo finishes shooting and becomes a huge crossover hit, spawning an Orgazmo franchise featuring children's toys. Joe wins a number of awards and has to remind people that "I'm not a superhero, I'm a Latter-day Saint!"

Maxxx coerces him into making Orgazmo Two, which prevents him from returning to Lisa. During the sequel's filming, which "doesn't have the spirit of the first one," Lisa

CREDITS

Joe Young: Trey Parker
Ben Chapleski: Dian Belcher
Lisa: Robyn Lynne
Maxxx Orbison: Michael Dean Jacobs
Clark: Ron Jeremy
Rodgers: Andrew W. Kembler
Dave: Matt Stone
G-Fresh: Maseo Maki-san

Origin: USA
Released: 1997
Production: Fran Rubel Kuzui, Jason McHugh, and Matt Stone for Kuzui Enterprises, MDP Worldwide, and Avenging Conscience; released by October Films
Direction: Trey Parker
Screenplay: Trey Parker
Cinematography: Kenny Gioseffi
Editing: Trey Parker, Michael R. Miller
Music: Paul Robb
Production design: Tristan Paris Bourne
Costumes: Kristen Anacker
Sound: Jon Ailetcher
MPAA rating: NC-17
Running Time: 95 minutes

comes to surprise Joe and finds out his secret. She is none too happy. Joe goes to Maxxx and quits the movie, but Maxxx retaliates by kidnapping Lisa. Ben and Joe don their crime-fighting costumes, become real superheroes, and rescue Lisa. When she and Joe prepare to go home, Ben convinces them that L.A. needs Orgazmo and Choda Boy to fight real crime. Jesus materializes before Joe and gives him an approving thumbs up.

This is primarily a funny movie, featuring such gems as a discussion between Ron Jeremy and other porn stars about the exploitative nature of the genre. But the middle of the film bogs down with a subplot involving a character named G-Fresh (Maseo Maki-san), a ghetto-talking Japanese man who owns a sushi bar. Also unnecessary is a silly sequence in which Ben reveals that he knows all sorts of martial arts, including the dreaded "hamster style," which he vowed never

to use again. Inevitably he uses it, making one wish that he had stuck to his word. There's a fine line between funny and stupid, and *Orgazmo* crosses it from time to time with sequences like these. For the most part, though, *Orgazmo* is a trite piece of vulgarity that aims to please. And please it does—orgazmorator not included.

—*Rich Silverman*

REVIEWS

Boxoffice. April, 1998, p. 178.
Entertainment Weekly. October 30, 1998, p. 84.
New York Times. October 23, 1998, p. E26.
People. November 2, 1998, p. 36.
Variety. September 22, 1998, p. 40.

Out of Sight

"Smart writing, brilliantly cast characters and an extra romantic edge."—Michael Wilmington, *Chicago Tribune*

"Smart, juicy and consistently deliciously surprising in details as in point of view!"—Susan Stark, *Detroit News*

"Consummately entertaining. The year's most diverse and exciting supporting cast. Director Soderbergh has let it unfold with dry wit and great skill."—Kenneth Turan, *Los Angeles Times*

"A smart, sardonic, fast-paced crime caper with quirky, unpredictable details."—Stephen Farber, *Movieline*

"Clooney and Lopez give *Out of Sight* steam heat!"—Janet Maslin, *New York Times*

"Packed with juicy, vivid performances! The comic timing of this superb ensemble is a joy to behold. Funny and sexy."—David Ansen, *Newsweek*

"A richly textured crime drama with character, plot and humor to spare!"—Leah Rozen, *People*

"The sexiest movie of the summer!"—Peter Travers, *Rolling Stone*

"The actors are terrific and sexy together! What makes this movie work is the kind of cool that made *Get Shorty* go so nicely."—Richard Schickel, *Time*

"Fresh, smart and enchanting. Hilarious!"—Joe Morgenstern, *Wall Street Journal*

 Box Office: $37,562,568

After years of mediocre or worse adaptations of his western and crime fiction, Elmore Leonard has finally seen three pleasing adaptations of his novels: *Get Shorty* (1996), *Jackie Brown* (1997), and, best of all, *Out of Sight*. This film also represents a significant comeback for director Steven Soderbergh, whose career had been foundering since his brilliant debut with *sex, lies, and videotape* (1989).

When bank robber Jack Foley (George Clooney) escapes from a Florida prison with the help of his longtime partner Buddy Bragg (Ving Rhames), they are surprised by shotgun-wielding United States Marshal Karen Sisco (Jennifer Lopez). In what Leonard may have intended as a send-up of cute meeting scenes, Jack and Karen find themselves crammed into the trunk of her car, discussing Faye Dunaway movies. Karen observes that Dunaway falls for abductor Robert Redford too easily in *Three Days of the Condor* (1975). She eventually shoots at Jack before making her escape but finds herself thinking about him afterward in ways law-enforcement officers usually do not apply to hardened criminals. Karen becomes attached to the task force formed to track down Jack, but does she want

Criminal Jack Foley (George Clooney) ponders his next great heist in the dark comedy *Out of Sight*.

But Leonard's greatest attribute is his ability to create compelling characters in just a few strokes. Better even than *Get Shorty* and *Jackie Brown,* the film version of *Out of Sight* displays the quirks that make his characters so Leonardesque. When the recently escaped Jack spots, from a closing elevator door, Karen waiting in the lobby of his hotel to arrest him, he waves like they are old friends. Buddy is wracked by Catholic guilt and always telephones his sister, a nun, to confess his sins. When he makes the mistake of calling her before committing a crime, she notifies the police, and he is arrested. Jack is amused that Buddy spends two hours talking to his sister from having spent forty-five minutes with a prostitute. Best of all, Chino (Luis Guzman), a vengeful escaped convict, visits Adele (Catherine Keener), Jack's ex-wife, only to be surprised by Karen, who throws him to the floor and handcuffs him. While waiting to be taken to jail, lying uncomfortably in a hallway, Chino asks Adele, formerly a magician's assistant, to explain how she was sawn in half.

Leonard's style is best conveyed in the film by the robbery of Ripley. White Boy Bob forgets the diamonds to steal steaks from Ripley's refrigerator. Kenneth combs through Ripley's collection of compact disks to try to find music appropriate for a "home invasion" but finds only classical music. Miller pauses to select the best suits and ties from Ripley's wardrobe. When the thieves finally make their way into Ripley's safe, instead of diamonds, they find the swindler's collection of hairpieces. Jack, remembering that his old prison mate is a fish fancier, knows of somewhere less obvious than a safe. And White Boy Bob learns the hard way that a large gentleman cannot charge up a hardwood staircase while carrying a gun.

While *Get Shorty* accents the comic more than does Leonard's novel and *Jackie Brown* is a bit more somber than necessary, *Out of Sight* finds the right balance between all the elements of the story. Screenwriter Scott Frank, who also adapted *Get Shorty* and wrote Kenneth Branagh's film noir *Dead Again* (1991), takes an unusual approach to adapting a novel by making the film's structure more complex than that of the novel. Even more than Quentin Tarantino's *Pulp Fiction* (1994), to which *Out of Sight* has been compared, Frank fractures time with frequent flashbacks and, in one notable scene, a flashforward. There are even flashbacks within flashbacks. This structure emphasizes how the characters' actions are interrelated. Frank's screenplay is an excellent model for adapting almost any novel. No scene runs too long or is too short to make its point. Several events, such as Buddy's conversations with his sister, are described rather than shown because showing them would slow down the film. Frank also adds a scene at the end to resolve Karen's dilemma over what to do about being true both to Jack and to her job.

Out of Sight places Clooney in a spot because television stars attempting to make the transition to the big screen get

to capture him or protect him? Even she is not certain of her motives.

A second conflict awaits Jack in Detroit, where he and Buddy go because they were once in prison with Richard Ripley (Albert Brooks), a financial wizard who has bragged of having $5 million in uncut diamonds in his Bloomfield Hills mansion. The robbery is complicated by Maurice "Snoopy" Miller (Don Cheadle), a former boxer who was also in prison with Jack and Ripley. Miller plans to steal the diamonds with his goons, the psychotic Kenneth (Isaiah Washington) and the thickheaded White Boy Bob (Keith Loneker), but agrees to let Jack and Buddy tag along. The good thieves go to Ripley's knowing it is unlikely all will leave alive. Karen follows, uncertain what action she will take.

Leonard's 1996 novel is fairly typical of his work: a bit of violence, a bit more humor, a strong sense of place—most of his crime novels take place in South Florida or his native Detroit—highly distinctive, realistic, profane, funny dialogue, subtle social commentary, and a little romance now and then. *Out of Sight* has a stronger love angle than is usual for Leonard, and the filmmakers emphasize it even further.

 Buddy (Ving Rhames) to Jack (George Clooney): "You want to sit down and have cocktails with a woman who tried to shoot you?"

only so many chances. After flops like *One Fine Day* (1996), *The Peacemaker* (1997), and *Batman and Robin* (1997), the star of *ER* finally has a good role in a good film. Using charm as his primary weapon in crime, Jack Foley is almost a gentleman bank robber, and Clooney, with his boyish grin and bedroom eyes, has plenty of charm. His Jack, much more perhaps than Leonard's, is a little boy playing criminal because he does not want to grow up. The goofy expression on his face when Jack waves at Karen captures this quality perfectly.

Both Michael Keaton and Samuel L. Jackson are uncredited in the film.

Clooney's slow Midwestern drawl resembles that of another star in *Three Days of the Condor*: Cliff Robertson. Like Robertson, Clooney seems at times to be a beat behind the other performers in his pacing. Reviewers are constantly comparing Clooney to other actors to try to get a handle on him. Janet Maslin of the *New York Times* keeps insisting that he is like Cary Grant. No way. Lacking the dangerous edge essential to Jack, Clooney most resembles another television star who never quite had an impact in films. Like James Garner, he is likable but lightweight.

Lopez is a more distinctive talent who benefits from no comparisons. She continues to grow from film to film as she becomes more sure of herself. Perhaps the least self-consciously sexy American female star ever, Lopez is so well used by Soderbergh, who elicited wonderful performances from Laura San Giacomo and Andie MacDowell in *sex, lies, and videotape*, that she almost seems credible, despite her youth and beauty, as a federal officer. Her major advance here is how well she listens to the other performers, one of the most demanding of acting skills. Several scenes call upon her to listen to men who think they understand matters much better than she does, and Soderbergh shows Karen's weighing their comments carefully before deciding she still wants to do things her way.

Out of Sight features a uniformly excellent supporting cast. Rhames and Cheadle, two of the most dependable character actors, are outstanding in roles similar to those they have played before. Brooks's role requires him to disappear into a character part for the first time. Bald, wearing horn-rimmed glasses (closely resembling his director), Brooks is almost unrecognizable. Steve Zahn almost steals the film as Jack's unreliable car-thief colleague Glenn Michaels. One of

Leonard's major motifs is the stupidity of criminals, and Glenn is overconfident out of ignorance. Zahn makes Glenn cocky and nervous at once.

The film's best-acted scene comes when Marshall Sisco (Dennis Farina), a retired cop, meets Ray Nicolette (Michael Keaton), an FBI agent and Karen's married lover. Farina is delightful as Marshall does everything he can to express his disdain for Ray, and Keaton, reprising his *Jackie Brown* role, seems oblivious to what the angry father is saying. Another *Jackie Brown* star, the great Samuel L. Jackson, has a cameo at the end of the film in which he almost blows Clooney off the screen.

The five films Soderbergh directed after *sex, lies, and videotape* are interesting failures that show little of the cine-

CREDITS

Jack Foley: George Clooney
Karen Sisco: Jennifer Lopez
Buddy Bragg: Ving Rhames
Maurice "Snoopy" Miller: Don Cheadle
Glenn Michaels: Steve Zahn
Marshall Sisco: Dennis Farina
Richard Ripley: Albert Brooks
Adele: Catherine Keener
Kenneth: Isaiah Washington
Chino: Luis Guzman
Midge: Nancy Allen
White Boy Bob: Keith Loneker
Jack Burdon: Wendell B. Harris Jr.
Raymond Cruz: Paul Calderon
Ray Nicolette: Michael Keaton
Hejira Henry: Samuel L. Jackson

Origin: USA
Released: 1998
Production: Danny DeVito, Michael Shamberg, and Stacey Sher for Jersey Films; released by Universal Pictures
Direction: Steven Soderbergh
Screenplay: Scott Frank; based on the novel by Elmore Leonard
Cinematography: Elliot Davis
Editing: Anne V. Coates
Production design: Gary Frutkoff
Art direction: Phil Messina
Costumes: Betsy Heiman
Sound: Paul Ledford
Music: David Holmes
MPAA rating: R
Running Time: 129 minutes

AWARDS AND NOMINATIONS

National Society of Film Critics 1998: Adapted Screenplay; Director (Steven Soderbergh)
Writers Guild of America 1998: Adapted Screenplay
Academy Awards 1998 Nominations: Adapted Screenplay

matic skills he displays in his first film and again in *Out of Sight*. In interviews, Soderbergh has explained how he had to get a tendency to take himself too seriously out of his system. In terms of framing shots and pacing, *Out of Sight* is almost perfect. The movie's high point shows how film is truly a collaborative art as Soderbergh, Frank, cinematographer Elliot Davis, veteran editor Anne V. Coates, who won an Oscar for *Lawrence of Arabia* (1962), Lopez, and Clooney combine their talents. The scene cuts back and forth between a scene in a Detroit hotel bar in which Karen and Jack try to seduce each other, and the outcome in Karen's room. The stars, at their most appealing, stare longingly at each other, while snowflakes and the lights of downtown Detroit glitter in the background, recalling the fireworks behind Grace Kelly and Cary Grant in Alfred Hitchcock's *To Catch a Thief* (1955). Soderbergh proves here that he, like Hitchcock, knows a thing or two about combining crime and romance.

—*Michael Adams*

REVIEWS

Chicago Tribune. June 26, 1998, p. 4.
Detroit Free Press. June 26, 1998, p. D1.
Detroit News. June 26, 1998, p. C1.
Entertainment Weekly. June 26, 1998, p. 100.
New York Times. June 26, 1998, p. E14.
New Yorker. July 6, 1998, p. 78.
Newsweek. June 29, 1998, p. 66.
People. July 6, 1998, p. 35.
Rolling Stone. July 9, 1998, p. 145.
Sight and Sound. October, 1998, p. 7.
Sight and Sound. December, 1998, p. 55.
Time. July 6, 1998, p. 88.
USA Today. June 26, 1998, p. E12.
Variety. June 22, 1998, p. 50.
Village Voice. June 30, 1998, p. 138.
Washington Post Weekend. June 26, 1998, p. 46.

Palmetto

In a town this bad it's no use being good.
—Movie tagline

"A succulent film noir—Harrelson's acting grows richer with each film."—Owen Gleiberman, *Entertainment Weekly*

"A juicy film noir—deliriously sensual. Shue cast come-hither looks as scorching as hot coals."
—Stephen Holden, *New York Times*

"A story so crafty that just when you think you got it figured out, it does a sly figure eight. Spins enough twists to confound even those know-it-all fans of whodunits."—Gene Shalit, *Today*

 Box Office: $5,878,911

Based on *Just Another Sucker* by 1930s pulp novelist James Hadley Chase, *Palmetto* is a too-familiar tale told in a far too familiar way. This noirish thriller offers up the standard-issue femme fatale, the sexually manipulated should-have-known-better male, and all the double dealing and triple crossing that can fit into this well-tread genre. What it does not do, however, is find a clever new twist to its telling—unfortunate, since the film starts out as a promising, tongue-in-cheek send-up of the film noir genre.

Chase, whose work is relatively unknown in the United States, is the pseudonym of British author Rene Raymond—the boxoffice bomb *Rough Magic* (1995) came from one of his books—a writer whose work is clearly inspired by American pulp fiction writers Raymond Chandler and James M. Cain.

Acclaimed German director Volker Schlondorff, perhaps best known for his previous literary adaptations of Gunter Grass's *Tin Drum* (1979) and Margaret Atwood's *A Handmaid's Tale* (1990), attempts to blend humor with lusty suspense, with mixed results. For those viewers less familiar with the conventions of the film noir genre, those dark, fatalistic films that grew to prominence in World War II America, the twists and turns of *Palmetto*, designed to keep the viewer guessing, may be engaging. The film's languorous pace may intentionally mirror the humid environment of the story, but it also produces a hypnotic trance in the viewer, a costly effect for a thriller.

A palmetto is a fat and juicy cockroach found in Florida. It is also the name of the sleepy seaside town that Harry Barber (Woody Harrelson) is determined to escape from when he is unexpectedly released from a two-year prison stint. Met outside the prison walls by his long-suffering artist girlfriend Nina (Gina Gershon in the thankless role of the Good Girl), Harry is quickly seduced back to Palmetto. And before long, he's also seduced into a kidnapping scam by a mysterious blonde named Rhea Malroux (Elisabeth Shue).

What starts out as a seemingly simple get-rich-quick scheme turns into a complex web of deception that is one long evolving set-up.

Director Schlondorff seems unsure as to what tone to adopt for *Palmetto*. The acting is so wildly divergent that it sends the film skittering between parody and serious drama. While humor is often a welcome addition to this sort of film, it must come internally, from the absurdity of the situations and circumstances, not from ridiculous portrayals and sheer vamping of the characters.

 Harry (Woody Harrelson) about Rhea (Elisabeth Shue): "She played me like a game of Chinese checkers."

Unfortunately, Schlondorff failed to rein in one of his key players, sending *Palmetto* into a cliched spiral from which it cannot recover.

Woody Harrelson brings an interesting complexity to the role of the moral and criminally incompetent journalist, Harry Barber. His brass cockiness is tempered by an amusing underlying naivete that allows Harrelson to find the inherent humor while wallowing in the steamy and sweaty purgatory between fate and existentialism. Harrelson manages to walk a fine line between passivity and aggressiveness, managing a slow burn of resentment and determination. Director Oliver Stone was perhaps one of the first filmmakers to tap into Harrelson's innate duplicitous nature when he cast the comic actor against type in the violent expose *Natural Born Killers* (1994).

While actor Michael Rapaport covers familiar ground, both within and without the confines of the film world, as the smarmy, corrupt ex-cop, he is woefully out of his streetwise element here as a more sophisticated conniver. Relative newcomer Chloe Sevigny turns in the film's most impressive performance as Odette, the lanky and seductive daughter of Rhea's dying wealthy husband. Tom Wright, a frequent collaborator with director John Sayles, is the district attorney who hires Harry to handle the media covering the kidnapping conspiracy.

Many critics noted that actresses Elisabeth Shue and Gina Gershon were each miscast, respectively as the devious femme fatale and the long-suffering stand-by-your-man girlfriend. With her forced sensuality and girlish manner, Shue gives a performance that is more caricature than character, while Gershon (arguably the best thing in *Showgirls*, 1997) has very little material to work with in a part that is sorely underwritten. While admirably determined to undermine any typecasting, this casting misstep contributed greatly to *Palmetto*'s critical demise.

The past several years have witnessed a resurgence in the film noir genre, with filmmakers such as John Dahl deftly wielding shadows and light, patsies and femme fatales in such a way as to breathe new life into a film style that can easily fall victim to cliche. Unfortunately, Volker Schlondorff proves less adept at sidestepping all the inherent storytelling traps of the film noir. As Harry Barber tells us in the opening scene of *Palmetto*, "Nothing's worse than a writer who doesn't have anything to say."

—*Patricia Kowal*

CREDITS

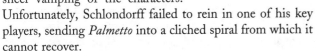

Harry Barber: Woody Harrelson
Rhea Malroux: Elisabeth Shue
Nina: Gina Gershon
Donnelly: Michael Rapaport
Felix Malroux: Rolf Hoppe
Odette: Chloë Sevigny
John Renick: Tom Wright

Origin: USA
Released: 1998
Production: Matthias Wendlandt for Castle Rock Entertainment and Rialto Film; released by Columbia Pictures
Direction: Volker Schlondorff
Screenplay: E. Max Frye; based on the novel *Just Another Sucker* by James Hadley Chase
Cinematography: Thomas Kloss
Editing: Peter Przygodda
Production design: Claire Jenora Brown
Costumes: Terry Dresbach
Music: Klaus Doldinger
Sound: Mark Weingarten
MPAA rating: R
Running Time: 114 minutes

REVIEWS

Boston Phoenix. February 20, 1998.
Chicago Sun-Times. February 20, 1998.
Entertainment Weekly. February 20, 1998, p. 89.
Los Angeles Daily News. February 20, 1998.
Los Angeles Times. February 20, 1998, p. F8.
New York Times. February 20, 1998, p. E14.
People. March 2, 1998, p. 21.
San Francisco Chronicle. February 20, 1998, p. C3.
San Francisco Examiner. February 20, 1998, p. C3.
Variety. February 16, 1998, p. 57.
Washington Post Weekend. February 20, 1998, p. B6.

The Parent Trap

"The best family film in years!"—Diane Kaminsky, *KHOU-TV*

"Irresistible!"—Kenneth Turan, *Los Angeles Times*

"Clever, spirited and unabashedly romantic!" —*People*

"Hugely entertaining!"—Ruthie Stein, *San Francisco Chronicle*

"Two thumbs up!"—*Siskel & Ebert*

"Funny and utterly charming! Don't miss it!" —Paul Wunder, *WBAI Radio*

"It's even better than the original!"—Jeffrey Lyons, *WNBC-TV*

Box Office: $66,308,518

The updated version of *The Parent Trap* has all the trappings of a lively family comedy, though it is basically a load of claptrap. The original *Parent Trap* (1961) was a lighthearted piece of Disney fluff that logged in at a ponderous 129 minutes. It starred the British-born Hayley Mills playing a set of identical twins, separated at birth by their divorced parents. Improbably, when the twins reach age eleven, they meet up at a summer camp. There, they discover their past and conspire to reunite their parents by switching places and going home pretending each to be the other. The original spawned a series of made-for-TV sequels and launched the lackluster career of Mills, which included the likes of *That Darn Cat* (1965) and *The Kingfisher Caper* (1976).

The best news about the remake is that newcomer Lindsay Lohan is more of an adorable pixie than the somewhat stiff Mills. Lohan is effervescent without being cloying; she's precocious without being annoying. Lohan carries the entire film pretty much on her tiny shoulders, and her performance screams "child star." Lohan manages to carry off a quite credible British accent when playing Annie, the twin raised by her British mother Elizabeth (Natasha Richardson). Lohan also pulls off convincing American affectations as Hallie, the twin whose father, Nick (Dennis Quaid), is a northern Cal-

Nick (Dennis Quaid): "It ended so fast." Elizabeth (Natasha Richardson): "It started so fast." Nick: "Well, that part I remember perfectly."

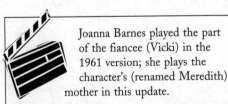

Joanna Barnes played the part of the fiancee (Vicki) in the 1961 version; she plays the character's (renamed Meredith) mother in this update.

ifornia vineyard owner. And after the twins switch places, Lohan carries off a slightly poorer British accent for Holly and a barely convincing American accent for Annie. Lohan is certainly a very accomplished young actress.

That's a good thing, because Lohan's freckled, perky, and thoroughly likeable presence animates the entire picture. The twin roles—and their twists after the switch—are the film's main means of getting attention. The plot and the enjoyment of the film depend almost entirely on sympathizing with and enjoying the twin girls and the actress who carries off the difficult feat of playing the double role. In the original, audiences no doubt marveled at Disney Studio's split-screen and mirror-image techniques that allowed Mills to appear on screen playing both roles simultaneously. These days, of course, with the help of computers, such feats are more seamless but also more commonplace. It is a measure of the sophistication of today's target audience for *The Parent Trap* that my eight-year-old daughter knew Lohan was a single actress playing two parts while my wife wasn't entirely sure that she wasn't two actresses who looked an awful lot alike.

The veteran writer team of Charles Shyer and Nancy Meyers, who have two pre-teen girls of their own, did the necessary script updating, just as they did in the two *Father of the Bride* remakes. They also co-wrote *Baby Boom* (1987) and *Irreconcilable Differences* (1984), so they know this turf well. Meyers makes her directorial debut in *The Parent Trap*. She pushes all the right buttons, but it's basically a paint-by-numbers job, and she seems reluctant to take many risks with the rather cloying and shopworn material. It's all too easy to shrug off the movie. It's so instantly digestible that none of it sticks with you afterwards. Everything happens on the surface and not a moment of opacity is allowed to intrude.

The main problem with the remake is the same as with the original: At 127 minutes, the movie is much too long getting to its foregone conclusion. The other bothersome aspect of this *Parent Trap* is that its settings, dialogue, characters, and even photography appear to be taking place in a time warp. Judging from the language, the clothes, the attitudes, and the relentlessly bright lighting, most of this film seems to be set in an early 1960s that has been transported to the late 1990s wholesale. When Annie's plane lands at northern California's Napa Airport, for instance, everything's so sunny and streamlined it looks like a 1961 *Look* magazine cover. The twins wear outfits no girl would be caught dead in today, and say things in ways that sound awkward and stilted. When, every so often, there's a concession to the late 1990s in words or mood, it seems out of place. Even by the end of the movie, it's unclear what era it's supposed to be taking place in. That's not because the mood created is timeless, it's just inconsistent.

The film's soundtrack can't seem to decide what era it's in or what kind of pop music is appropriate, so it simply samples one of every genre and decade. This is a pop-culture dilettante's movie. When Hallie-pretending-to-be-Annie first follows her mother to work—Elizabeth is an improbably successful fashion designer—they walk across Abbey Road. Meyers freeze-frames them in mid-step, just so audiences don't miss the point that she's sending up the famous Beatles album cover. You can almost hear the parents excitedly whispering to their uncomprehending children in the audience exactly what the director's doing.

The original movie was preposterous enough. The update is thoroughly silly, given that it retains outdated attitudes and mores. Yet despite its thinness, the film works fairly well on its own terms. Thanks go mainly to the cast. Richardson is enchanting, even if her character is slightly farfetched—glamorous, successful, but still secretly pining away for the man she ditched years before. She is an interesting actress, whose good looks get a zaftig quality because she appears to be slightly cross-eyed. Quaid is serviceable as the clueless but warmhearted dad. Elaine Hendrix as the despicable gold-digger Meredith, who is trying to marry Nick, steals her scenes with an over-the-top send-up of Sharon Stone in *Basic Instinct* (1992); hers is a glamor-puss that's easy to hate. And Lisa Ann Walter, who plays Hallie's nanny as a frank Jewish-mother type, and Simon Kunz, who plays Elizabeth's butler as a repressed free spirit, add appreciably to the comedy. Of course, this is the type of film where single parents easily achieve such boundless wealth that they can afford nannies and butlers—another sign that it belongs to that bygone era when every family in film or television was inexplicably well off enough to employ domestic help.

The difficulty with the plot is why the twins—and the audiences who are identifying with them—should go all gooey for two adults who have been cruel enough to separate twins at birth and then have to be forced almost at gunpoint into reuniting them. The twins absolutely adore their parents, pining away for the absent ones, and harboring them no resentment. *The Parent Trap* is a child of divorce's wish-fulfillment orgy: The missing parent not only turns out to be a dreamboat, but Mom and Dad really love one another after all, just like they're supposed to. Just as the twins discover their long-lost best friends in each other, so do their parents.

This material is guaranteed to be sappy, and Meyers certainly lays it on thick. There are so many mandatory sen-timental moments in this plot, however, that there is hardly any excuse for adding so many egregious ones. The film lurches from scene to scene like so many music videos, and the pop-song-theme-for-every-emotional-big-moment approach cements the impression that girls just wanna have fun—rather than construct a serious film. If there was ever a quintessential pajama party movie for nine-year-olds, this is it.

You might not even stay awake until the end. In the last third of the film, there are so many aborted climaxes that you want to scream out for the moviemakers to get it over with. Before the inevitable parental reconciliation, you must endure a pointless reunion in a hotel—a sequence that seems ripe with comic possibilities but falls terribly flat; a camping trip in which the girls get to torture Meredith in predictable ways; and two separate romantic reunions between Nick and Elizabeth that inexplicably go nowhere. How can two people who are in love miss each other's signals this badly? They can't. Why should an 85-minute piece of cinema candy last this long? There's no excuse for it.

Along the way, fortunately, there are some pleasantries, thanks to Lohan and the rest of the crew. But there are also a number of clunkers, as when Meredith tells Annie "Some-

CREDITS

Hallie Parker/Annie James: Lindsay Lohan
Nick Parker: Dennis Quaid
Elizabeth James: Natasha Richardson
Meredith Blake: Elaine Hendrix
Chessy: Lisa Ann Walter
Martin: Simon Kunz
Marva Kulp Sr.: Polly Holliday
Marva Kulp Jr.: Maggie Wheeler
Grandfather: Ronnie Stevens
Vicki Blake: Joanna Barnes

Origin: USA
Released: 1998
Production: Charles Shyer; released by Walt Disney Pictures
Direction: Nancy Meyers
Screenplay: David Swift, Nancy Meyers, and Charles Shyer; based on the book *Das Doppelte Lottchen* by Erich Kastner
Cinematography: Dean A. Cundey
Editing: Stephen A. Rotter
Music: Alan Silvestri
Production design: Dean Tavoularis
Art direction: Alex Tavoularis, John Fenner
Costumes: Penny Rose
Sound: Sean Rush
MPAA rating: PG
Running Time: 127 minutes

day you'll understand what it's like to be in love," and Annie replies: "I don't even have my twelve-year-old molars yet." Gee whiz. This picture is so retro, you almost expect Annette Funicello to pop up in it wearing her Mouseketeer outfit. Lohan is so squeaky-clean and devilishly cherubic, it's jarring when it is revealed her Hallie character has a poster of Leonardo DiCaprio. And it makes absolutely no sense that Annie doesn't know who DiCaprio is.

The Parent Trap circa 1998 is tolerable if you secretly harbor a nostalgic feeling for Disney's version of 1961, which, given how hip Disney is, would be something more like 1956. You almost expect the twins to start gyrating in hula hoops. This film is, in every imaginable way, that outdated. It expresses an almost palpable longing for the joy of being a pre-teen girl in the days just before innocence ended.

Trouble is, it's a thoroughly phony pining and reveals almost nothing about the real feelings of real pre-teen girls of any era. At least it has its fun moments.

—*Michael Betzold*

REVIEWS

Entertainment Weekly. August 7, 1998, p. 50.
Los Angeles Times. July 29, 1998, p. F1.
People. August 3, 1998, p. 26.
Sight and Sound. December, 1998, p. 56.
USA Today. May 5, 1998, p. 4D.
Variety. July 27, 1998, p. 51.

Passion in the Desert; Simoom: A Passion in the Desert

What nature divides, the spirit unites.—Movie tagline

"A beautiful film."—Kenneth Turan, *Los Angeles Times*

"Amazing! Utterly unforgettable entertainment."—Larry Worth, *New York Post*

"Reminiscent of *The English Patient*, *Passion* is an engrossing, visually mesmerizing tale."
—Lawrence Van Gelder, *New York Times*

"*Passion in the Desert* is a fascinating adventure."—Bruce Williamson, *Playboy*

"*Passion* is marvelously suspenseful."—Eve Claxton, *Time Out New York*

"Astonishing! It will mesmerize you!"—Jeffrey Lyons, *WNBC-TV*

A strange bond is formed when soldier Augustin Robert (Ben Daniels) is stranded in the Egyptian desert and befriends a leopard in *Passion in the Desert*.

This feature film debut by Lavinia Currier might have been entitled "Two Men and a Leopard," since it only features two recognizable actors, Ben Daniels and Michel Piccoli, and a trained leopard named Simoom. Or maybe "One Man and a Leopard," since the artist Jean-Michel Venture de Paradis (played by the well-known French New Wave actor Michel Piccoli in a vivid cameo) drops out of the picture about a third of the way into the desert action. The year is 1798 and Napoleon's campaign has entered Egypt, apparently to pillage and deface priceless artifacts of antiquity, one of which, a small sphinx, the French soldiers use for target practice.

A French officer, Augustin Robert (Ben Daniels), has been ordered to locate and retrieve the French painter Ven-

ture and escort him back to Paris. With a small detachment of soldiers, Augustine does indeed protect the bearded, corpulent painter against marauding Arabs; but Venture seems more at home with the elements and the landscape than Augustin is. A crisis arises when the two manage to get themselves lost in a sandstorm, after skirmishes with unfriendly natives, fierce Mamaluke warriors.

Despite Augustin's boast that it is impossible to get lost in Egypt ("where there's the Nile and the Red Sea," discounting what may be betwixt and between), the two parched travelers wander in proverbial circles. Water supplies dwindle. To Augustin's dismay, Venture uses his last few drops of water to mix his paints, out of a desire either to become one with his materials or to commit chemical suicide. Later on, when Augustin leaves the artist, who by that time is unable to continue, in order to scout further ahead, Venture drinks down his paints and then shoots himself dead.

The second half of the film deals with Augustin's struggle to stay alive in the face of starvation and thirst. Pursued by angry Bedouins who dare not follow him, he finds a cave opening that takes him to a palace ruin of some kind (filmed in Petra, Jordan) in a closed canyon with a watering hole. This would seem to be the perfect oasis and his salvation, until he notices the slitted eyes of a huge leopard glowing ominously in the darkness next to him. After a great deal of wary maneuvering, however, each grows accustomed to the other and a strange rapprochement of peaceful co-existence is somehow achieved between them.

Simoom means "breath of the desert."

Before long they are drinking water together and feeding off the freshly slain carcasses of goats and antelope. Eventually, the man is curling up next to the beast and caressing her in either friendship and gratitude or demented "passion." But when the leopard he's named Simoom runs off briefly to mate with a male leopard, Augustin strips himself, plunges into the waterhole, and smears his body with yellow-mud dye and brown spots. This is a startling moment, as, wordlessly, we witness this utter transformation of man into beast. Is he mad or merely jealous? Sure enough, the leopard eventually comes back to Augustin, whom she seems to tolerate as her pet.

Enter the remnants of the French troops, who, unlike the local Arabs, are ignorant that they are entering a leopard's lair. Augustin fashions a rope and ties Simoom to a rock, declaring he must not desert his fellow troops. He dons his uniform and begins to leave, but Simoom wrestles herself free and attacks him. In self defense, he kills her with a knife. Wrenched with grief, Augustin disappears, alone, back into the trackless wastes of the desert. This is an odd conclusion, inasmuch as the film's prologue depicts Augustin's rescue from the desert by a passing camel drover, and the subsequent amputation of his arm. Yet, this ending leaves Augustin utterly alone in a void that fills the screen. Where is his rescuer?

The entire film is virtually wordless. Everything and everyone, including Augustin, is stripped down to its essentials of sound, color, and silence. Special credit must go to the actor Ben Daniels, who is required to endure all manner of all-too-obvious privations, and to cavort with an animal that, no matter how tame it may be, is still very healthy and no doubt somewhat unpredictable. "The leopard was terrifying," the actor recalled to Jean Nathan of the *New York Times*. "I got chewed and scratched and bitten. When the cat would go along with the scene as scripted, I knew she wasn't concentrating on her role. She was thinking, 'So, how can I eat this person I'm playing with?'" This odd film certainly gives animal magnetism a new dimension. Daniels accepted the role because "it was one of the most extraordinary things I had ever read, and I couldn't resist it."

The source for this film was a novella, *Une Passion Dans le Desert*, written in 1830 by Honoré de Balzac (1799–1850), described by playwright-critic Stefan Zweig as "an unexcelled master of the art of the short story." Or, to be more accurate, the film is based on a story within that story. The source seems highly unconventional for Balzac, certainly not the sort of urban society drama for which he is best known. It is hardly surprising that Hollywood would eventually turn to the prodigiously prolific Balzac, who produced over a hundred major works, mainly novels, before he succumbed to caffeine poisoning at the age of fifty-one in 1850.

Over the past decade Hollywood had exploited several nineteenth-century novels, making adaptations of Edith Wharton and Henry James and also Thomas Hardy, Charles Dickens, and Jane Austin. Director Des McAnuff's *Cousin Bette* (reviewed in this edition), perhaps Balzac's best-known novel of manners, written in 1847, was the first recent adaptation of a major Balzac novel, and an excellent vehicle for the actress Jessica Lange. *Passion in the Desert*, on the other hand, was not world famous.

Director Lavinia Currier, a Harvard graduate who majored in comparative literature, worked for ten years to get her film made. *Movieline* critic Stephen Farber praised her "eloquent use of the desert locations while treating the encounters of man and beast with a combination of tenderness and awe." The odd relationship at the center of this "passion," however, was sure to invite ridicule from some reviewers. *Premiere* found this "meditation on the ambiguous distinctions between human civility and animal behavior" to be "sometimes shocking and sometimes moving, but too often merely confusing and disturbing." Rita Kempley of the *Washington Post* dismissed the film as "a loony erotic period drama" and made mirthful comparisons to *The English Patient* (1996), since "Currier's narrative begins with the hero's mutilation and flashes back to the start of his ill-fated journey." Although the tale is not "explicitly sexual," she conceded, "it's clear that there's more than heavy petting" involved here.

Not all reviews were negative, however. Stephen Farber found *Passion* a "strange chronicle" of a French soldier lost in the Sahara "a more thoroughly satisfying adaptation of a Balzac tale" than *Cousin Bette*, which he considered too "streamlined." The film is mainly abstract and non-verbal since one of the principals is not human. It is an allegory concerning man's ability to survive in the wilderness. The challenge recalls Nicolas Roeg's *Walkabout* (1971), adapted from James Vance Marshall's adolescent novel about two children stranded in the Australian Outback. In *Walkabout* the children were befriended by a young Aboriginal boy who comes to their rescue, but since he does not speak English, communication is difficult and nonverbal, as it is also in *Passion in the Desert*.

Like *Walkabout*, David Lean's *Lawrence of Arabia* (1962), and Bernardo Bertolucci's *The Sheltering Sky* (1990), *Passion in the Desert* excels in capturing the abstract beauty and texture of an arid desert landscape, but it is mainly the story of a single man, alone in the desert, co-habitating with a female leopard that not only tolerates him but shares food as though he were her pet. Though some affection is demonstrated between them, the "passion" is not really sexual or beastial (as Rita Kempley mirthfully suggested), but meta-

physical.

The desert is itself a strange and metaphysical setting. During the Middle Ages, anchorites went into the desert wilderness seeking "hesychia" (quietude for prayer) in order to find inner peace and to "see" the "uncreated light." The whole point for these religious mystics was to meditate in order to reach the silence, to shut off the internal dialogue within one's head caused by the distractions of the cultural discourse that surrounds us, and that quietude is enhanced by the nonverbal nature of Lavinia Currie's picture, where silence abounds. "In the desert there is anything and nothing," Balzac wrote: "It is God without mankind."

This film is quite remarkable, a kind of Delacroix Rorshach blot, redolent of Delacroix's Moroccon and Egyptian paintings, drenched in electric blue skies, salmon deserts, and red costume sashes and boots. It has a Rorshach effect because its protracted silences and enigmatic actions allow the mind to fill in the gaps. It meditates on the thin boundaries that ultimately separate man and beast, society and primal waste, soldier and animal. The film's intoxicating images and the superbly mixed palette of color take hold of the imagination. Surely a story about the harmony between man and wild beast is incredible, but the poetry that shimmers off it is authentic in its own way.

— *James M. Welsh and John C. Tibbetts*

CREDITS

Augustin Robert: Ben Daniels
Jean-Michel Venture de Paradis: Michel Piccoli

Origin: USA
Released: 1997
Direction: Lavinia Currier
Screenplay: Lavinia Currier and Martin Edmunds; based on the novella by Honore de Balzac
Cinematography: Alexei Rodionov
Editing: Nicolas Gaster
Music: Jose Nieto
Production design: Amanda McArthur
Costumes: Shuna Harwood
Sound: Michael Stearns
Special effects supervision: Colin Arthur, Randy Pope
MPAA rating: PG-13
Running Time: 93 minutes

REVIEWS

Boxoffice. February, 1998, p. 51.
Entertainment Weekly. June 19, 1998, p. 54.
Los Angeles Times. June 12, 1998, p. F12.
Movieline. July, 1998, p. 43.
New York Times. June 7, 1998, p.14.
New York Times. June 12, 1998, p. E20.
Premiere. July, 1998, p. 19.
Variety. September 22, 1997, p. 39.
Village Voice. June 16, 1998, p. 160.
Washington Post. July 10, 1998, p. D5.

Patch Adams

Laughter is contagious.—Movie tagline

"Robin Williams continues to astonish. Director Tom Shadyac lets the humanity as well as the comedy shine through."—Bob Thomas, *Associated Press*

"Williams is terrific! One of the year's best films."—Steve Oldfield, *FOX*

"The incomparable Robin Williams plays this brilliantly. People will leave the theatre with tears of joy on their cheek."—Gene Shalit, *Today Show*

 Box Office: $46,444,325

There is no doubt that the critics were not overly fond of *Patch Adams*. Some of the words they chose to describe it ranged from "maudlin" and "sappy" to "bullying sentimentality" and "emotionally manipulative." The critical consensus is that none of them appears to want to be treated by a doctor with a sense of humor in his medicine cabinet. And, like a good HMO gatekeeper, these critics tried to keep people away from this example of movie malpractice by giving it pretty bad reviews.

Audiences, on the other hand, did not take the critics' advice, sought a second opinion, and went to the movie in droves. In fact, they made *Patch Adams* one of the highest grossing December releases in history. They loved it, and it may be a bitter pill for the cinematic cognoscenti to swallow.

One of their major complaints is that the story is just too unbelievable, that Dean Walcott (Bob Gunton) was right and anyone who perpetrated all the things depicted in the movie should never have been given access to patients, let alone a medical license. However, truth is stranger than fiction, because *Patch Adams* is based on the true-life story of Hunter Adams. In television interviews following the release of the film, Adams has said more than once that his life is even more outrageous than what was depicted on the film, and if you doubt this, read his 1993 book *Gesundheit: Good Health*

> Carin (Monica Potter): "You're never serious are you?" Patch (Robin Williams): "No, I tried that for years. It never worked for me."

> The real Patch Adams gave up treating patients in 1983 to devote himself to his nonprofit Gesundheit! Institute, which is still under construction.

Is a Laughing Matter, which he co-wrote with Maureen Mylander.

For example, the real Patch actually has filled numerous patients' rooms with balloons as was depicted in the birthday party scene. The same is true of the scene in which Patch arranges for a patient who won't eat to "swim" in a pool of cooked spaghetti. Although he does admit this one was exaggerated for the film.

The film begins Hunter's story as the teenager commits himself to the Fairfax Hospital Psychiatric Ward in 1969 because of his suicidal tendencies. (And although Robin Williams does indeed look a bit old to be playing a teenager, he does play the character throughout the entire film.) While in the hospital Hunter realizes that when he concentrates on other people's troubles and tries to help them, he doesn't feel his own pain as much. And so he sets out to learn and to help those incarcerated in the psychiatric ward with him.

Among those he learns from in the hospital is Arthur Mendelson (Harold Gould), an industrialist millionaire/genius. Hunter has been holding up four fingers and asking people how many they see. Of course everyone sees four, but not Arthur. Eventually Hunter asks him how many he sees. But it's only when Hunter fixes Arthur's leaky paper coffee cup with a piece of paper that Arthur tells him to look beyond the fingers. "If you focus on the problem, you'll never see the solution. See what everyone else refuses to see," he tells Hunter, whom he now calls "Patch" in honor of his paper-cup solution.

Among those he helps is his roommate Rudy (Michael Jeter), who refuses to leave his bed because there are vicious squirrels trying to attack him. So one night Rudy and Patch wage war on the rascally rodents, shooting them with any piece of military equipment their imaginations can concoct from rifles to bazookas. It doesn't take long for all the squirrels to bite the illusory bullet and it's once again safe for Rudy to leave his bed. "Last night with Rudy I connected with another human being. I want to do more of that," Patch tells his therapist.

And with these lessons Patch finally finds a mission for himself: He's going to become a doctor. Patch enrolls in the Virginia Medical University where, as the dean of the school (Bob Gunton) tells the first-year students, the school will "rigorously and ruthlessly train the humanity out of you and turn you into something better." This is not a message Patch wants to hear, and neither is the fact that he won't be seeing patients until his third year.

Consequently Patch begins sneaking into the local teaching hospital, often wearing bedpans on his feet and a bright red enema bulb on his nose. He does the unthinkable for a doctor: he makes friends with the nurses, especially Joletta (Irma P. Hall), and gives patients not medicine from bottles but from his heart. Soon he has friends everywhere, including Truman (Daniel London) and Carin (Monica Potter). At first Carin is icy if not downright hostile to Patch's antics, but eventually he wins her over. In fact, Patch seems to be good at winning just about everyone over, even the surly Bill Davis (Peter Coyote), who is in the hospital dying of pancreatic cancer.

However, the one person Patch seems only to irritate more and more is Dean Walcott, the man who can euthanize all Patch's dreams of becoming a doctor, no matter how terrific his grades (and he's the top of his class), and no matter how sincere his passion to heal. "Passion doesn't make doctors, I make doctors," he warns Patch as he condemns the young student by writing in his personnel file that he is guilty of "excessive happiness."

Needless to say, eventually Patch will so alienate Dean Walcott that he will be expelled, and needless to say, all those who have come to love Patch will come to his rescue. This includes his old friend Arthur Mendelson, who donates 105 acres of land and an old building that Patch will turn into the first fun hospital in the world, the Gesundheit! Institute, where there's no malpractice insurance or fees, and where humor along with medicine is used to heal.

Patch Adams is not a subtle film. It is as over-the-top as Patch is a doctor and Williams is a comedian. To fault it for its excessive silliness and sentimentality would be to condone the mean-spirited Dean Walcott. Yes, Walcott is a one-dimensional character (we never see him helping a patient, only harassing Patch). Yes, the plot is pretty traditional (good-hearted outsider takes on the establishment, which tries to crush him). Yes, the film is sentimentally manipulative (even some of the children in the cancer ward of the hospital were obviously actually ill with the disease—they were in the film because the production company worked closely with the Make-a-Wish Foundation).

Yes, Patch/Williams outrageously clowns around at some very inopportune moments (does someone who is terribly ill really want to be suddenly jolted awake by clowns with balloons for one last safari?). But do audiences care? No. Maybe the critics should take the same leap of faith they might make for a horror or science fiction film. Maybe the good-heartedness of the film is what audiences want, not technically perfect stories, characters, or dialogue. But maybe too many critics have never dealt with a doctor with a hurtful bedside manner or a health insurance company intent on denying patients the care they need. Or maybe too many critics have just had their funny bones surgically removed.

The real Patch is said to have requested, "Please don't make it a goofy doctor film, although I'm a goofy guy."

CREDITS

Patch Adams: Robin Williams
Truman: Daniel London
Carin: Monica Potter
Mitch: Philip Seymour Hoffman
Dean Walcott: Bob Gunton
Dr. Eaton: Josef Sommer
Joletta: Irma P. Hall
Judy: Frances Lee McCain
Dean Anderson: Harve Presnell
Adelane: Daniella Kuhn
Bryan: Jake Bowen
Bill Davis: Peter Coyote
Bile: James Greene
Rudy: Michael Jeter
Arthur Mendelson: Harold Gould
Dr. Titan: Richard Kiley

Origin: USA
Released: 1998
Production: Barry Kemp, Mike Farrell, Marvin Minoff, and Charles Newirth for Blue Wolf, Farrell/Minoff, and Bungalow 78; released by Universal Pictures
Direction: Tom Shadyac
Screenplay: Steve Odekerk; based on the book *Gesundheit: Good Health Is a Laughing Matter* by Hunter Doherty Adams and Maureen Mylander
Cinematography: Phedon Papamichael
Editing: Don Zimmerman
Production design: Linda Descenna
Art direction: Jim Nedza
Set decoration: Ric McElvin
Costumes: Judy Ruskin-Howell
Music: Marc Shaiman
MPAA rating: PG-13
Running Time: 110 minutes

AWARDS AND NOMINATIONS

Academy Awards 1998 Nominations: Original Musical or Comedy Score

Goofy doesn't seem to do him justice if this movie is any indication. I'm just betting that a lot of people who have seen *Patch Adams* wish the producers had sold the rights to film the first meeting between the real Patch and Robin Williams. I'll bet the two of them together must have been something to see. 🎞

—*Beverley Bare Buehrer*

REVIEWS

Chicago Sun Times. December 25, 1998.
Entertainment Weekly. January 8, 1999, p. 47.
Los Angeles Times. December 25, 1998, p. F2.
New York Times. December 24, 1998, p. E6.
People. January 11, 1999, p. 38.
People. February 1, 1999, p. 46.
Variety. December 21, 1998, p. 74.

Paulie

The journey of a thousand miles begins with a single parrot.—Movie tagline

"It's a charmer! Kids will love this enchanting and touching adventure."—Bill Diehl, *ABC Radio Network*

"A heartfelt tale full of the kind of warmth and fun that appeals to all ages."—Glenn Whipp, *LA Daily News*

"*Paulie* is something to behold. A warm and witty film that is fun for adults as well as children."—Lawrence Van Gelder, *New York Times*

"A perfect family movie with intelligence and humor."—Bob Heisler, *Newsday*

"A delightful family movie for kids of all ages."—Jeffrey Lyons, *WNBC-TV*

"A sweet, touching, sassy movie for the whole family."—Joy Browne, *WOR Radio*

Box Office: $27,084,499

A movie about a talking parrot sounds corny. But *Paulie* is a refreshing surprise. Though a bird is not as cuddly as most film animal heroes, *Paulie* has no trouble tugging at the heartstrings without indulging in too much sappy sentimentality. The film is simply a very pleasing piece of entertainment. A smart screenplay by newcomer Laurie Craig, deft direction by John Roberts, and a slew of fine performances topped by Gena Rowlands make *Paulie* a rare bird indeed—a family film that has charm, dignity, wit, and heart.

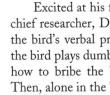

Paulie: "I have a lifelong trait of speaking when I should have kept my beak shut."

Craig's screenplay skates successfully on the thin ice above melodrama and makes an impact simply because it is so honest and understated. Unlike most family films, *Paulie* does not telegraph its moral points, but neither does it descend into the swamp of incivility. It is finely crafted and beautifully made, and director John Roberts obviously did not feel a need to jazz up the proceedings with special effects or crude jokes. It's a movie that's unafraid to be old-fashioned, needing no gimmicks and relying heavily on its simple yet well-realized anthropomorphic yarn.

First we meet Misha (Tony Shalhoub), a shy and conscientious immigrant who has just taken a job as a janitor at an animal research institute. Misha is earnest and caring but awkward with his new country and new work. In his unnamed land of origin, he was a professor of literature; here, he is struggling to start from the bottom of the ladder. He meets a blue-crown conure, a type of parrot, in the building's basement. Soon he discovers that the bird not only can talk, but can hurl insults and carry on conversations like an urbane adult.

Excited at his find, Misha naively corrals the institute's chief researcher, Dr. Reingold (Bruce Davison), to witness the bird's verbal prowess. But in the presence of authority the bird plays dumb. Misha is chastised but soon figures out how to bribe the bird into speech by offering it mango. Then, alone in the basement with Misha, Paulie unfolds his quirky life story, which consumes most of the movie in flashback.

As a baby bird, Paulie was a present to Marie Alweather (Hallie Kate Eisenberg), a young girl with few friends and a speech impediment. When her father (Matt Craven) comes home from Vietnam, he quickly becomes impatient with his daughter's speaking progress despite reassurances from his wife (Laura Harrington). Paulie soon discovers he can talk, and he helps

Marie overcome her stutters. But Paulie has his own problem: a fear of flying that becomes a major worry when the family gets a cat. When Marie tries to help Paulie fly, she falls from her bedroom window. Her father, blaming the bird, takes Paulie away.

This first part of Paulie's life is a bit problematic. Viewers of a young age may have trouble understanding why the bird is taken from Marie. The script fails to give the father sufficient motivation for this cruel act. Marie's minor problems getting a sentence started don't seem to warrant all the fuss. The director should have insisted on a more pronounced stutter in his young actress. It's inconsistent to have her speaking entire phrases without tripping in one scene and then have her struggling to say a single word in another.

Paulie is played by fourteen Blue-Crown Conures and one animatronic bird.

But the plot devices do serve to put Paulie in exile and to begin a lifelong search for Marie. The parrot learns how to hurl toothsome insults while ensconced in a pawn shop run by Artie (Buddy Hackett). Hackett's old-time smart-aleck style seems to have inspired Jay Mohr, who does Paulie's voice in a wisecracking, vaudevillian timbre. This approach saves the bird and the film from being too saccharine.

It's amazing, though, how much the movie is able to make the viewer care about this sometimes abrasive creature. Paulie is "played" by fourteen different conures and one animatronic creation by Stan Winston, which is used for the more difficult sequences. The technical wizardry is near-perfect, allowing for a seamless portrait of a bird who is endowed with many human qualities yet remains essentially a parrot. Shalhoub's endearing performance as Misha helps establish the bond between audience and avian protagonist. Seeing the creature through his tolerant eyes, we become sensitized to his plight.

A widow named Ivy (Gena Rowlands), impressed by Paulie's vocabulary though annoyed at his impertinence, buys him from the pawn shop. At first, her golden locks hidden under a hat, Rowlands is almost unrecognizable as Ivy. But time has not diminished the dignity and range of this actress, who is probably one of our era's most accomplished but largely overlooked performers. Rowlands is always marvelous because she totally inhabits her characters, giving them an almost unbearable authenticity.

Rowlands's Ivy must do some heavy emotional lifting for *Paulie*. First she is won over by the bird's entreaties to help him find Marie. Then, when they discover the Alweathers have moved to Los Angeles, Paulie's love for Marie rouses Ivy from her grief at her husband's absence. She boldly sets out to drive her mobile home across the country. Along the way, Ivy goes blind and Paulie stays on to become her seeing-eye bird. Eventually she dies, before being able to reach the Grand Canyon, a place she had always wanted to

see with her husband. Rowlands infuses this role with zest and courage and saves her character from being pitiable.

Heartened by Ivy's joie de vivre, Paulie plucks up the courage to fly the rest of the way to Los Angeles. There he meets a parrot girlfriend, Lupe, who belongs to a taco-stand owner named Ignacio (Cheech Marin). This half of the comic duo Cheech and Chong makes Ignacio's small role quite charming. Paulie and Lupe become the mainstays in a parrot song-and-dance revue that accompanies a band playing at the taco stand.

Kidnapped by a small-time thief named Benny (also played by Mohr), Paulie next enjoys a brief career as a partner in crime, lifting money from ATM machines. The sudden appearance of the ATMs is a little jarring, because the narrative seems suddenly to have skipped a decade or two. It's a small quibble, because by this point viewers should be totally engrossed in Paulie's quest. When Benny plans a big heist and Paulie goes down a chimney to try to steal some jewels, he is caught and taken to the research institute.

Reingold immediately sees Paulie's potential. There's a great scene when the bird proves his intelligence by riffing

CREDITS

Voice of Paulie/Benny: Jay Mohr
Ivy: Gena Rowlands
Misha: Tony Shalhoub
Ignacio: Cheech Marin
Dr. Reingold: Bruce Davison
Artie: Buddy Hackett
Marie: Hallie Kate Eisenberg

Origin: USA
Released: 1998
Production: Mark Gordon, Gary Levinsohn, and Allison Lyon Segan for Mutual Film Company; released by DreamWorks Pictures
Direction: John Roberts
Screenplay: Laurie Craig
Cinematography: Tony Pierce-Roberts
Editing: Bruce Cannon
Music: John Debney
Production design: Dennis Washington
Art direction: Tom Taylor
Costumes: Mary Zophres
Sound: Joseph Geisinger
Animatronic characters: Stan Winston
Animal stunt coordination: Boone Narr
MPAA rating: PG
Running Time: 91 minutes

verbally on the connotations of the word "pie" after he is shown a flash card by the researchers. Paulie agrees to co-operate with Reingold's work in exchange for a promise to be returned to Marie. But when the scientist reneges on the promise, hoping Paulie will be his meal ticket to success, Paulie is incensed. The bird ruins Reingold's coming-out party by reverting to standard parrot mimicry in front of a room full of chagrined scientists. Enraged, Reingold has Paulie's wings clipped and banishes him to the basement.

Flashbacks completed, it remains for Misha to become a hero by standing up to Reingold, spiriting Paulie away, and tracking down Marie for a predictable yet still satisfying ending. In doing so, Misha overcomes his fears. The movie is about conquering obstacles and learning how to use your voice and your wits in the wisest way. But the message, which is a rather general one, does not carry the movie. The performances and the story do.

In its own quirky way, *Paulie* explores the relationship between animals and human beings. In the course of the film, Paulie performs many roles. To Marie, he is a pet, a teacher, and a friend. To Artie and Benny, he is a material possession. To Ivy, he is a companion who helps ease the loneliness of old age. To Ignacio, he is entertainment. And to Misha, he is a sage of sorts. To all of them, he is a friend.

Paulie is solid entertainment. Its virtues are quiet ones, apt to be lost in the shuffle of bigger special-effects bangs and bigger boxoffice attractions. Never rude or cloying, *Paulie* achieves a timeless quality in its own quiet way. Suitable for all ages, with enough wisecracks to keep adults happy, *Paulie* ranks among the best family films of recent years.

—*Michael Betzold*

REVIEWS

Boxoffice. June, 1998, p. 80.
Detroit News. April 17, 1998, p. 3C.
Entertainment Weekly. April 24, 1998, p. 58.
Hollywood Reporter. April 14, 1998, p. 21.
Los Angeles Times. April 17, 1998, p. F21.
New York Times. April 17, 1998, p. E22.
People. April 27, 1998, p. 37.
USA Today. April 17, 1998, p. 10E.
Variety. April 13, 1998, p. 43.

Pecker

"Uproarious!"—Rob Ellsworth, *Detour*

"John Waters looks as much like a poster boy for good, solid values as a champion of all who live at the margins." —Susan Stark, *Detroit News*

"Nutty and raunchy! *Pecker* is John Waters's funniest movie ever!"—Karen Durbin, *Mirabella*

"We've seen John Waters's *Pecker* and we like it! A merrily subversive satire."—John Elasser, *POV*

"Hilarious! *Pecker* is gleeful, outrageous fun." —Susan Granger, *SSG Syndicate*

"After Monica's dress stain and Mary's hair gel, the godfather of gag seems downright quaint." —*USA Today*

"If scandal, sleaze, and celebrity worship are our national religion, then John Waters is an American prophet." —*Village Voice*

 Box Office: $2,281,761

A feel-good John Waters movie? This is the closest he'll get, and *Pecker* is sweet, in a yucky, ooky white-trash kind of way. *Pecker* is Waters's love letter to Baltimore, a sentimental look at the artist as a young boy. Although less polished than his most recent work, say *Serial Mom* (1994), Waters's latest harkens back to his earlier work in its slap-dash, spontaneous humor and plot development. It smacks of Waters's earlier renegade filmmaking, done commando-style. (In fact, it was done on half the budget of the Kathleen Turner suburban crime epic, and shot in only thirty days.) But what makes *Pecker* still a product of neoWaters is the fact that it is basically harmless. He pokes fun at Baltimore, at Catholics, at gays and straights, white trash, and the upper class; he uses tasteless images such as a little girl with sugared saliva drooling from her mouth in an almost pornographic manner and the invention of a new sex act ("tea bagging"). But Waters's film is really just a coming-of-age story in which the price of fame is demonstrated, and ultimately, the main character finds that there's no place like home.

Edward Furlong plays the title character—so named, it is pointed out in the movie, because he "pecks" at his food. (According to Waters, the MPAA objected to the title until he pointed out that it wasn't really a dirty word—"No one says 'C'mon, baby, suck my pecker.'") Pecker is a budding photographer who is content to snap Baltimorian life (two rats fornicating, homeless people, shoplifting in progress, and so on). Pecker is supported by his loving family, comprising Mary Kay Place as his mother, the proprietor of a second-hand store; his father (Mark Joy), who runs a bar; his grandmother Memama (Jean Schertler), who operates a pit beef stand ("It's just something they eat in Baltimore," explained Waters at the Toronto Film Festival, where the movie premiered) on the front yard; and sisters Tina (Martha Plimpton), emcee at a gay bar, and L'il Chrissy (Lauren Hulsey), a sugar addict. Add in Pecker's best friend, Matt (Brendan Sexton III), a shoplifter, and Pecker's girlfriend, Shelly (Christina Ricci), a workaholic proprietor of a laundromat, who seems

"I always wished statues talked to me, didn't you?" —John Waters regarding the "talking" Virgin Mary.

Director Waters supplies the voice of the pervert on the phone who plagues "stain goddess" Christina Ricci.

to be the kind of girl Waters himself would have hung around with.

Life is happy for Pecker until he is "discovered" by Rorey Wheeler (Lili Taylor), a New York critic who gives Pecker his big break. She unveils his "culturally challenged" world to the public, and Pecker's world begins to fall apart as he and his family and friends are unable to handle the media attention (Shelly, for example, is labeled a "stain goddess"). Here, Waters pokes fun at the upper class as they poke fun at the lower class. In the end, both classes party together in celebration of . . . celebrating. It doesn't need to make sense; Waters is having fun here, and so are his characters. The plot is not involved—it's just a means of binding together a touching and tastelessly humorous video album of Baltimore as Waters see it: Memama's talking statue of the Virgin Mary ("Full of grace," it squawks over and over again, and Memama's lips hardly move at all); a second-hand store where the homeless receive fashion advice and an Easter outfit "for under a quarter"; and bars of all kinds, from "The Pelt Room" (which features nude lesbians) to "The Fudge Palace" (which features nude homosexuals).

Edward Furlong is appealing as the young would-be artist (and bears a comfortable resemblance to the director, as well); Christina Ricci, reigning indie queen, is appropriately sullen and brash, capturing well the Waters brand of Baltimore attitude; and Lauren Hulsey as l'il sis Chrissy is a charmer, even while dripping sugared saliva from her mouth in a most unsettling fashion.

The music is true to earlier Waters works as well; Stewart Copeland's score is appropriately lighthearted, with

CREDITS

Pecker: Edward Furlong
Shelly: Christina Ricci
Matt: Brendan Sexton III
Joyce: Mary Kay Place
Jimmy: Mark Joy
Memama: Jean Schertler
Tina: Martha Plimpton
L'il Chrissy: Lauren Hulsey
Rorey: Lili Taylor
Lynn Wentworth: Patricia Hearst
Precinct captain: Mink Stole
Dr. Klompus: Bess Armstrong

Origin: USA
Released: 1998
Production: John Fiedler and Mark Tarlov for Polar Entertainment; released by Fine Line
Direction: John Waters
Screenplay: John Waters
Cinematography: Robert Stevens
Editing: Janice Hampton
Music: Stewart Copeland
Production design: Vincent Peranio
Costumes: Van Smith
Sound: Rick Angelella
MPAA rating: R
Running Time: 87 minutes

REVIEWS

Boxoffice. September, 1998, p. 61.
Chicago Tribune. September 25, 1998, p. 5.
Detroit Free Press. September 25, 1998, p. 5D.
Detroit News. September 25, 1998, p. 3D.
Entertainment Weekly. October 2, 1998, p. 45.
Los Angeles Times. September 25, 1998, p. F2.
New York Times. September 25, 1998, p. E15.
People. October 5, 1998, p. 38.
Pulse! October, 1998, p. 87-88.
San Francisco Chronicle. September 25, 1998, p. C3.
Time. October 5, 1998.
USA Today. September 25, 1998.
Variety. September 14, 1998, p. 39.
Village Voice. September 22, 1998, p. 139.
Washington Post. September 25, 1998, p. 62.

45-ish cuts reminiscent of Water's beginnings, such as "Happy Go Lucky Me," "In the Mood" as clucked by chickens, and a piece written by Waters and Copeland, "Don't Drop the Soap (For Anyone Else but Me)".

John Waters is a loyal kind of film guy. His regulars Mink Stole, Patty Hearst, and Mary Vivian Pearce appear, and longtime collaborators Pat Moran, Vincent Peranio, and Van Smith are behind the scenes once again. *Pecker* was released by New Line Cinema, continuing the long relationship between studio and auteur that began with *Pink Flamingos* (1972), the first commercially distributed Waters film.

—*Carol Schwartz*

A Perfect Murder

A powerful husband. An unfaithful wife. A jealous lover. All of them have a motive. Each of them has a plan.—Movie tagline

"A terrific, spine-tingling performance by Gwyneth Paltrow."—Bill Diehl, *ABC Radio Network*

"A hold-your-breath thriller."—Joel Siegel, *ABC-TV*

"Drop-dead gorgeous, tense and clever."—Michael Wilmington, *Chicago Tribune*

"*A Perfect Murder* benefits from the gift director Andrew Davis has for adding intelligence to shockers."—Kenneth Turan, *Los Angeles Times*

"Sensuous, engaging, skillfully plotted. Nasty twists and tantalizing clues."—Stephen Holden, *New York Times*

"Diabolical suspense thriller. Intelligent and intriguing."—Susan Granger, *SSG Syndicate*

Box Office: $67,658,331

Steven Taylor (Michael Douglas) devises a clever but fallible plan to murder his wife Emily (Gwyneth Paltrow) in *A Perfect Murder*.

Frederick Knott's classic 1952 play *Dial M for Murder* is best known as the basis of Alfred Hitchcock's 1954 film starring Ray Milland and Grace Kelly. The story of a desperate husband blackmailing someone to murder his younger, wealthy, unfaithful wife is given a few new twists in this adaptation written by Patrick Smith Kelly. Like Hitchcock's film, *A Perfect Murder* is slick and entertaining, but it is not as cohesive as the earlier version and might have been more inventive.

About to go broke, Wall Street bond salesman Steven Taylor (Michael Douglas) decides to convince painter David Shaw (Viggo Mortensen) to murder Emily Bradford Taylor (Gwyneth Paltrow) so that he can inherit her $100 million. In the original, the husband blackmails an old acquaintance who has been conning older women out of their fortunes and may have killed one of them. The major innovation in *A Perfect Murder* is that David Shaw is both Emily's potential killer and her lover. Steven has discovered that David is not only having an affair with his wife but is a former convict and confidence man. He will inform police of the crimes David has committed since his release from prison unless the artist murders Emily. David's dilemma is that he does not want to be exposed and, of course, highly desires the $500,000 Steven will pay him, but he also has feelings for his lover. The film's title is ironic because once her would-be killer enters Emily's apartment, matters develop far from perfectly.

One of the pleasures of the film for those familiar with *Dial M for Murder* should be seeing how it departs from the original. Except for making the lover and the potential killer the same, however, most of the changes are minor. When police detective Mohamed Karaman (David Suchet) enters the picture and stares suspiciously at Steven, it seems that the duplicitous financier has stumbled into someone as smart as or smarter than he is, but Karaman has little to do with the rest of the plot, which could not have developed as it does if the police had simply followed the suspect. The detective is an Arab simply so that Emily, a translator for the United States Delegation to the United Nations, can flash her language skills.

In Hitchcock's film, it is clear that the police inspector (played with comic hauteur by John Williams) will eventually catch the husband, but Steven Taylor is a more inventive and dangerous villain because he keeps making appropriate adjustments as his plan unravels. His finest moments come when he explains away most of Emily's suspicions. In *Dial M for Murder*, the wife is too much a passive victim. Surviving two vicious attacks, Emily is more resourceful, but she is still too passive—the victim, after all, of two men this time.

Kelly provides an extensive background for David but not much about the Taylors. Steven is rich and manipulative, and that's it. He is so clever and controlled in his dealings with Emily and David that it is difficult to understand how he could fail so miserably in his business. Emily is rich, beautiful, and skilled at languages. She is observant enough to recognize when a diplomat is simply repeating a speech he has given previously, but she cannot see the obvious about Steven and David. It is also hard to believe that someone with her background, having family lawyers administering her late father's estate, would marry without a prenuptial agreement.

Kelly also stumbles in updating the story. In the original, the husband's alibi is attending a dinner, ironically with his wife's lover. To make the murder appear to be a case of the wife interrupting a burglary, he arranges to telephone her so that she will be in the right spot for her killer to attack. Steven has two alibis: While attending his weekly poker night, he uses his cellular phone to log in to his home computer to check the foreign markets. With another cell phone that cannot be traced to him, he calls Emily. But why does she, in the age of answering machines, leave her bath to answer the phone?

After the boxoffice success of *The Fugitive* (1993), director Andrew Davis made the critical and commercial flops *Steal Big, Steal Little* (1995) and *Chain Reaction* (1996). He rebounds well with the professionalism of *A Perfect Murder*, directing with enough skill almost to camouflage many of the holes in Kelly's script. Davis seems to take as his model not the Hitchcock of *Dial M for Murder*, which, despite the director's efforts, is somewhat stagy, but the Hitchcock of *Vertigo* (1958). Davis and editors Dennis Virkler and Dov

Steven (Michael Douglas) to Emily (Gwyneth Paltrow), when they meet unexpectedly: "That's not happiness to see me, is it?"

Actor Viggo Mortensen produced the paintings for his artist character.

Hoenig, both of whom worked on *The Fugitive*, give the film a slow, seductive, elegant pace. Most of the scenes are longer than typical for a 1990s American film because there is so much exposition to get out of the way, but Davis makes this deliberateness central to the film's style, giving the film a dreamlike, subdued nightmare quality.

Many reviews and interviews have claimed that Steven Taylor is Douglas's first bad guy since his Oscar-winning megalomaniac in *Wall Street* (1987), but the actor specializes in characters with shaky morals who can become rotten in an instant. See, for example, *Fatal Attraction* (1987), *The War of the Roses* (1989), *Basic Instinct* (1992), *Falling Down* (1993), *Disclosure*, and *The Game* (1997). Douglas makes Steven an attractive villain by downplaying the character's essential sleaziness. Steven is more a comment on American ruthless self-regard than

CREDITS

Steven Taylor: Michael Douglas
Emily Bradford Taylor: Gwyneth Paltrow
David Shaw: Viggo Mortensen
Detective Mohamed Karaman: David Suchet
Detective Bobby Fain: Michael P. Moran
Raquel: Sarita Choudhury
Sandra Bradford: Constance Towers
Ambassador Wills: Novella Nelson
Will Lyman: Jason Gates

Origin: USA
Released: 1998
Production: Arnold Kopelson, Anne Kopelson, Christopher Mankiewicz, and Peter MacGregor-Scott for Kopelson Entertainment; released by Warner Bros.
Direction: Andrew Davis
Screenplay: Patrick Smith Kelly; based on the play *Dial M for Murder* by Frederick Knott
Cinematography: Dariusz Wolski, Dennis Virkler
Editing: Dov Hoenig
Production design: Philip Rosenberg
Art direction: Patricia Woodbridge
Set decoration: Debra Shutt
Costumes: Ellen Mirojnick
Music: James Newton Howard
Sound: Tom Nelson, Lance Brown
MPAA rating: R
Running Time: 105 minutes

an example of true evil. Douglas is a pleasure to watch because the audience can always see him thinking. The fact that Steven's plans keep going awry despite his best efforts almost makes him sympathetic.

Paltrow is, as always, immensely talented, attractive, and likable, but she does not seem quite right as Emily, never gets a handle on the character. Trembling in the dominant shadow of Douglas's Steven, she seems like an awkward teenager pretending to be an adult. Again, she is handicapped by Kelly's failure to develop Emily into anything interesting. Mortensen, glamorously seedy with stubble, scar, and long, slightly unkempt hair, is credible as the kind of outsider a woman such as Emily would go for but who is not to be trusted.

All three actors are aided by the costumes created by Ellen Mirojnick, who gives David an understated downtown look, makes Emily subtly elegant, and dresses Steven in dark clothing that underscores his unscrupulousness. The look of the film, in fact, is its most impressive element. Philip Rosenberg, Patricia Woodbridge, and Debra Shutt create a luxurious apartment that captures perfectly the Taylors' need to display their wealth and live in complete comfort. Including several paintings by fashionable artists such as Fernando Botero, the setting manages to be ostentatious and tasteful at the same time. Davis and his collaborators also

put Manhattan to good use, even though much of the film was shot in Jersey City, setting scenes at the Metropolitan Museum of Art, in Pennsylvania Station, on a Hudson River ferry, in several locations near the United Nations (calling to mind Hitchcock's *North by Northwest* [1959]), and, most spectacularly, the view of Central Park from the Taylors' balcony. Unfortunately, the emotionally unengaging *Perfect Murder* offers mostly surface glamour.

—*Michael Adams*

REVIEWS

Chicago Tribune. June 5, 1998, p. 5.
Detroit Free Press. June 5, 1998, p. 4E.
Detroit News. June 5, 1998, p. 3D.
Entertainment Weekly. June 12, 1998, p. 43.
Los Angeles Times. June 15, 1998, p. F8.
New York Times. June 5, 1998, p. E12.
Newsweek. June 15, 1998, p. 70.
People. June 15, 1998, p. 35.
Rolling Stone. July 9, 1998, p. 146.
Sight and Sound. October, 1998, p. 48.
USA Today. June 5, 1998, p. E8.
Variety. June 1, 1998, p. 33.

Permanent Midnight

"Ben Stiller gives a fierce, fearless performance that is the best of his career."—Stephen Farber, *Movieline Magazine*

"A dramatic tour de force. Stiller's restless, haunting power makes *Permanent Midnight* impossible to shake."—Peter Travers, *Rolling Stone*

"Stiller's performance is a revelation."—*Smug Magazine*

"Extraordinarily funny, powerful, provocative and shocking."—Paul Wunder, *WBAI Radio*

 Box Office: $1,171,001

en Stiller brings his career forward with this dark story of a successful television writer who is addicted to cocaine. Stiller is best known as the creator and star of *Reality Bites* (1994) and as the star of *Something About Mary,* one of 1998's biggest boxoffice hits (reviewed in this edition). He is the son of Jerry Stiller and Anne Meara, best known as comics (Jerry Stiller was Jason Alexander's father

on television's *Seinfeld*), and wrote, produced, and starred in a critically acclaimed, but short-lived television comedy series, *The Ben Stiller Show*, in 1990. With all this comedy in his background, then, Stiller clearly relishes the opportunity to move away from just comic acting and to prove himself a more fully rounded movie star.

Permanent Midnight succeeds in defining Stiller as an actor of wider range than he has shown in his films thus far. Here he plays Jerry Stahl, whose meteoric rise to financial success in television is paralleled by his meteoric fall into the depths of heroin addiction. While he may not be giving Anthony Hopkins a run for his money, Stiller is touching and believable in his depiction of a man whose hubris gets the better of him, and who refuses to see the danger of his behavior until it is nearly too late. By the time his character reaches the nadir of behavior—in a pathetic scene where Jerry shoots heroin in a car while his newborn baby cries for food—Stiller casts aside any concern that he's only a comedian.

The story is a true one: it is the autobiographical story of Jerry Stahl, who wrote television comedy until heroin took over—and nearly destroyed—his life. Stahl wrote the fine script for this film with its thoughtful director, David Veloz.

According to press reports and publicity information, *Permanent Midnight* does not veer far from the truth. The bulk of the story is a flashback, framed by Stahl's release from a rehabilitation center somewhere in California. When we meet Stahl, he is clearly at a crossroads, about to start a new life, and is afraid of what lies ahead. He meets Kitty (Maria Bello), also a former addict, and they share a wild affair in a roadside motel where he tells her his story.

Jerry Stahl's (Ben Stiller) confession to an ex-addict friend before their intimate encounter: "I've never done this straight before. Trust me, on smack I was a real stud."

In flashback we see that Stahl comes to California with no money in his pocket but with a great deal of pretension. His studied, fake–James Dean cool is as ubiquitous as the black leather jacket he wears, and just as out of place in the California sun. He also arrives in L.A. with a chip on his shoulder, intending to be a real writer as opposed to selling out for television. Stahl's artsy pretensions are rather quickly destroyed, however, when the friend of a friend gets him an interview to write for a dreadful television series about an alien named "Mr. Chompers" who moves in with a suburban family. (In real life the show was called "Alf," and ran for several sea-

Jerry Stahl makes a cameo in the film as a doctor in a methadone clinic.

sons on NBC.) Meanwhile, the woman who helps him get the interview, Sandra (Elizabeth Hurley), is in need of a fake marriage to fool the immigration authorities into allowing her to stay in the U.S. Jerry agrees to marry her. The trade is complete, and Jerry finds himself with a job as a television writer on a top-rated show with a beautiful new wife that he has only just met, and more money than he ever dreamed of having.

The film moves quickly into Jerry's heroin-induced decline. It offers little justification for his initial heroin use beyond several interposed scenes with Kitty. In those scenes he continues to tell his story and offer brief but not thorough insights. Though some critics may say that more may be needed to understand the reasons behind his increasingly self-destructive behavior, they may be missing the point. The very vacuity of the addiction as presented here may be Stahl's point: once a person allows himself to try something as lethally addictive as heroin, the psychological reasons why they initially tried it are merely academic. Jerry is hooked. Period. Stahl has lived through an extraordinary tale of loss and redemption and should be applauded for putting it onscreen without "going Hollywood," or without getting overly psychological.

Veloz and cinematographer Robert D. Yeoman have chosen an unusually dark palette of colors and shades to underscore Jerry's ascent. When he is on the road to recovery, the light is all the more welcome, and dramatically highlights his redemption.

It is a gutsy little film, and its performers, from the luminous Elizabeth Hurley to the earthy Liz Torres as a drug pusher to Stiller's pathetic protagonist, contribute to this cautionary tale. It is a fine film, with much promising talent and much to offer those who think they are above falling into the trap of any kind of addiction.

—*Kirby Tepper*

CREDITS

Jerry Stahl: Ben Stiller
Sandra: Elizabeth Hurley
Kitty: Maria Bello
Nicky: Owen Wilson
Vola: Lourdes Benedict
Gus: Peter Greene
Pamela Verlaine: Cheryl Ladd
Craig Ziffer: Fred Willard
Allen from "Mr. Chompers": Charles Fleischer
Jana: Janeane Garofalo

Origin: USA
Released: 1998
Production: Jane Hamsher and Don Murphy for JD Productions; released by Artisan Entertainment
Direction: David Veloz
Screenplay: David Veloz; based on the book by Jerry Stahl
Cinematography: Robert Yeoman
Editing: Steven Weisberg, Cara Silverman
Music: Daniel Licht
Production design: Jerry Fleming
Costumes: Louise Mingenbach, Lori Eskowitz
Sound: Eric Enroth
MPAA rating: R
Running Time: 85 minutes

REVIEWS

Boxoffice. October, 1998, p. 53.
Detroit News. September 18, 1998, p. 3D.
Entertainment Weekly. September 18, 1998, p. 58.
Entertainment Weekly. September 25, 1998, p. 78.
Los Angeles Times. September 18, 1998, p. F12.
New York Times. September 16, 1998, p. E1.
People. September 28, 1998, p. 40.
Variety. September 21, 1998, p. 108
Village Voice. September 22, 1998, p.142.
Washington Post. September 18, 1998, p. 56.

Phantoms

This time, the terror comes from below.—Movie tagline

Nothing is more terrifying than the unknown. —Movie tagline

"Entertaining terror at its best!"—*Academy of Science Fiction and Horror*

"A chillingly original thriller!"—*CBS-TV*

"Slick, scary and intelligent!"—Thelma Adams, *New York Post*

The townspeople of an isolated mountain town in Colorado have disappeared, and "The Ancient Enemy" is responsible. *Phantoms,* written by Dean Koontz, author of the best-selling book, shows that terror lurks under the surface, deep within.

Jennifer Pailey (Joanna Going), the town doctor, has brought her younger sister Lisa (Rose McGowan) to Snowfield, pop. 400, in an attempt to shelter her from the dangerous influences of Los Angeles. From their arrival in the eerily deserted village, the suspense is relentless, though contrived.

On entering Jennifer's home they discover the soup's on but the housekeeper's dead. Her car won't start, so they head for the police—only to find the local cop killed as well. They move through empty streets, past abandoned cars and vacated storefronts, to the bakery, where severed body parts cook in the oven. The frightened sisters flee, unexpectedly running into county sheriff Bryce Hammond (Ben Affleck) and his deputies.

A shrill whistle triggers a cacophony of blaring alarms and flickering lights that stops abruptly—the menace is messing with them. The Candleglow Motel beckons, but no one's at the inn—except a couple of corpses upstairs. A ghostly child whom Sheriff Hammond accidently killed when working for the FBI skulks in a closet, but is just an apparition. A mirror reveals a puzzling clue scribbled in lipstick about "The Ancient Enemy."

Deputy Steve Shanning (Nicky Katt) chases after a shriek, then vanishes. Deputy Stu Wargle (Liev Schreiber) exhibits some strange behavior, including an oddly demonic chuckle. The sheriff radios for help but the signal is unclear. Spooky garbled voices emanate from the phone, lights go out, and a creature pounds at the window. They barrage it with gunfire but a giant moth devours the deputy.

Meanwhile, the Feds visit former paleobiologist Dr. Timothy Flyte (Peter O'Toole) at the offices of the tabloid Wide World News. He's typing an installment in his series "The Ancient Enemy," about his wild theories on a force he believes caused the destruction of the Mayan civilization and an entire Chinese army, and other baffling phenomena. The agents ask him to come with them.

Back in town, awaiting help, Jennifer and Hammond share skeletons in their closets—about the sisters' alcoholic mother and the sheriff's guilt over the little boy he shot. Lisa hears primeval sounds from the drain in the restroom and encounters the creepy dead deputy. She escapes, but so does he.

An armored government vehicle rolls down Main Street with a mobile laboratory, a military team, and Dr. Flyte to record data and fight the foe. They locate a pile of metal, jewelry, and gold teeth—"undigestible remains," explains Flyte, referring to the by-products of the subterranean entity's feeding frenzy.

A soldier is sucked into the sewers as the missing reappear, transforming into a variety of monstrous forms—from humanlike to tentacled—to wipe out the troops. The slain have

Director Joe Chappelle: "It [the antagonist] has an attitude; it has an ego. It's come to believe it's immortal, that it's invincible. It thinks it's God."

CREDITS

Timothy Flyte: Peter O'Toole
Lisa Pailey: Rose McGowan
Jenny Pailey: Joanna Going
Sheriff Bryce Hammond: Ben Affleck
Deputy Stu Wargle: Liev Schreiber
Deputy Steve Shanning: Nicky Katt

Origin: USA
Released: 1998
Production: Joel Soisson, Michael Leahy, Robert Pringle, and Steve Lane for Neo Motion Pictures and Raven House; released by Dimension Films
Direction: Joe Chappelle
Screenplay: Dean Koontz; based on his novel
Cinematography: Richard Clabaugh
Editing: Randolph K. Bricker
Music: David Williams
Production design: Deborah Raymond, Dorian Vernacchio
Art direction: Daniel Bradford, Ken Larson
Set design: Jack Bishop
Costumes: Dana K. Litwak
Sound: Larry Scharf
MPAA rating: R
Running Time: 95 minutes

been resurrected on behalf of the Ancient Enemy, with a message for Flyte, "Tell the world. Preach the gospel." Hiding in the lab, Flyte examines the composition of a piece of the beast, explaining the million-year-old fiend from deep within the earth to the sisters and sheriff.

They determine its point of weakness: When consuming people it absorbs their fear that it can't be destroyed—so it only thinks it's invulnerable. Flyte finds an antidote handily on board in vials—used in oil spills, the bacterial substance feasts on petroleum. They must locate the mother mass to deliver the poison before it annihilates the world.

Flyte tricks the thing up from a manhole. Manifesting into a cyclone of everyone it's guzzled, the horrid energy is blasted by Hammond with the infectious substance. Finishing the job underground, Hammond faces the youngster he shot years back, which shows that only conquering personal demons can stop the force's power.

Squeaky gates, dark alleys, dank tunnels, and cheesy special effects are the sorts of cliches running rampant through this horror film. There's little dramatic suspense, information is spoon-fed, and the flimsy characters with flat lives are merely devices to serve the action, misusing some decent actors. Although the premise could provide a potentially intriguing plot, *Phantoms* isn't developed beyond a scary diversion with an illusory sense of story.

—*Roberta Cruger*

REVIEWS

Entertainment Weekly. February 6, 1998, p. 40.
Los Angeles Times. January 23, 1998, p. F8.
New York Times. January 23, 1998, p. E10.
Variety. January 26, 1998, p. 65.
Washington Post Weekend. January 23, 1998, p. 41.

Pi

Faith in chaos.—Movie tagline

"An artistic and edgy piece of mystification . . . visually stylish."—Kenneth Turan, *Los Angeles Times*

"A bizarre and ingeniously paranoid thriller."
—Janet Maslin, *New York Times*

"*Pi* is a mesmerizing mind bender filled with smarts and kinetic excitement. Aronofsky is a visionary."—Peter Travers, *Rolling Stone*

Box Office: $3,221,152

Encyclopedia Britannica defines *pi* as a symbol denoting the ratio of the circumference of a circle to its diameter. It also calls pi an "irrational" number, meaning it cannot be expressed as a simple fraction or a finite decimal. In freshman director Darren Aronofsky's quirky, compelling first feature, *Pi*, a brilliant but possibly mentally ill mathematician must contend with various forces that seem to want to steal his brain or his soul. There is nothing "simple" about this *Pi* either. In a low-budget landscape littered with an overabundance of raunchy comedies, tired Tarantino rip-offs, and sexual iden-

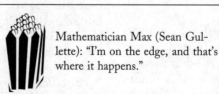

Mathematician Max (Sean Gullette): "I'm on the edge, and that's where it happens."

tity tales, *Pi* offers up a richly cerebral drama of conflict between intellectual obsession and religious desire, and between genuine and artificial knowledge and self-acceptance. Given a wild reception at the 1998 Sundance Film Festival, director Aronofsky and his talented cast have fashioned a truly low-budget story that shows the exploration of the limits of one's mind.

Max Cohen (Sean Gullett) lives in a cramped apartment in Chinatown, dwarfed by banks of homemade computers. He spends his time obsessively playing with numbers on two very different playing fields; trying to gauge a pattern in the stock market and, more close to his heart, trying to find a mathematical order to life through the mystery of the formula of pi. Reclusive, rarely leaving his apartment, Max pores over numbers constantly, searching, probing the universe, looking for patterns in life, finances, and history. When he does leave the apartment he seeks the counsel of his mentor, retired mathematician Sol Robeson (Mark Margolis). Although Sol was once driven and career-minded, he is now content in his retirement and tries to get Max to slow down and enjoy life more. When Max leaves the house he cannot see beyond his intellectual blinders; he can't even respond to the overt advances from his lush and frankly sexual neighbor, Devi (Samia Shoaib), nor enjoy the conversations of an adorable neighborhood child.

Yet one day Max is approached by someone he cannot shake; he gets into a conversation with Orthodox Lenny Meyer (Ben Shenkman) about the relations between numbers and the eternal nature of Judaism. Max is both repelled and intrigued by Lenny's buoyant but passionate love of his religion: "Cohen? You Jewish? So am I." Although he is a passionate non-believer, Max is taken in by Lenny's colorful weavings of the relationship between numbers, families, God, and the universe. The plot thickens when Lenny takes Max to meet the other holy men at his synagogue and they reveal that they want him to use his talents with numbers to unlock an ancient mystery of Judaism.

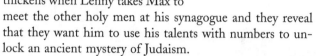

The film was shot for some $60,000.

At the same time Max is hotly pursued by Marcy Dawson (Pamela Hart), an aggressive representative for a major Wall Street Firm that also wants to tap into his affinity for numbers. Despite Max's reclusive nature, she finds his unlisted phone number and calls constantly, trying to lure him into having lunch. Marcy and her cohorts have somehow learned of Max's talents and wish to use them to tap into the unpredictable variables of the stock market. Max runs from her as if she is an apparition.

It seems that Max is only interested in exploring the scope of the formula of pi and how the pattern and reasoning behind this formula could indeed unlock the secrets of all mathematical systems. That this film can so lucidly portray such a heady character is a testament to Aronofsky's wonderfully mature storytelling abilities. Aronofsky excels in creating a world that is nightmarish in its own small scale. Instead of being liberated by the vast scope of his intelligence, Max is constricted and paralyzed. He retreats into his small world, barely leaving his enclave. Aronofsky's choice of shots echos his character's frenetic, disjointed mind. Max suffers from chronic migraines, and the audience is shown over and over quick, jarring cuts of him chugging down pain pills. Low-budget restrictions work to an advantage here (can one imagine what this film could have been with a larger budget?); Aronofsky can wring tension from the simple act of Max hesitating to push "enter" on his computer.

From this simple story emerges a complex, cerebral tale of desire: Max's desire for pure knowledge, the Jewish men's desire to access to their God via Max, and Marcy and the Wall Street gang's desire for unadulterated wealth through Max. Only Sol appears to have a balanced life, despite the fact that—or maybe because—he is sickly.

Aronofsky's style and thematic concerns could be related to David Lynch; his nightmarish view of life, his distorted characters and twisted nomenclature scream out for midnight showings, à la *Eraserhead* (1978). By the time Max is approaching—or so he thinks—a breakthrough to his quest, he is hallucinating heavily and near physical collapse. He fantasizes about his sexy neighbor, imagines that he can hear her making love in the next room. He clashes with his landlady. He finally blows up at Sol, whom he has always venerated. Even a trip in the subway turns into freakish, psychological torture when he visualizes his exposed brain, naked and vulnerable on the platform. A "Frankenstein" allegory—or at the very least, the torturous effect of migraines—comes to mind when Max, in a feverish dream, tries to drill into his own skull. Does he want to let the pain out? Or the embryonic knowledge that is more a curse than a blessing?

The film culminates with a chase that seems somewhat silly, considering the characters involved. Max is being pursued by Marcy and her venal cohorts down a dark alley, when out of nowhere a car full of Hassidic Jews roars up and spirits Max to safety. Not something you see every day.

The films ends as it begins: the camera pans from the cacophony of the city to sweet, soft trees. Max's odyssey has

CREDITS

Maximillian Cohen: Sean Gullette
Sol Robeson: Mark Margolis
Lenny Meyer: Ben Shenkman
Marcy Dawson: Pamela Hart
Rabbi Cohen: Stephen Pearlman
Devi: Samia Shoaib

Origin: USA
Released: 1998
Production: Eric Watson for Harvest Film Works, Truth & Soul, and Plantain Films; released by Artisan Entertainment.
Direction: Darren Aronofsky
Screenplay: Darren Aronofsky
Cinematography: Matthew Libatique
Editing: Oren Sarch
Production design: Matthew Maraffi
Music: Clint Mansell
MPAA rating: R
Running Time: 102 minutes

AWARDS AND NOMINATIONS

Independent Spirit Awards 1999: First Screenplay

brought him full circle; he seems content to commune with nature, not technology. Aronofsky has fashioned a riveting treaty of uncommon intelligence and scope—the limits unfazed by a low budget. His cinematographer, Matthew Libatique, stretched the limitations of the genre with his shaded, eye-popping visualizations, and Clint Mansell's original music propels the action along with pizzazz.

—G. E. Georges

REVIEWS

Boxoffice. April, 1998, p. 80.
Boxoffice. June, 1998, p. 18.
Entertainment Weekly. July 17, 1998, p. 60.
Los Angeles Times. July 24, 1998, p. F6.
People. July 20, 1998, p. 35.
Sight and Sound. January, 1999, p. 52.
Variety. January 26, 1998, p. 67.
Village Voice. July 14, 1998, p. 46.

The Players Club

Sometimes you're the player. Sometimes you're played.—Movie tagline

"Rich with colorful dialogue and characters!" —Roger Ebert, *Chicago Sun-Times*

"Funny, fast-paced, music-backed, power-packed entertainment!"—Sheila Simmons, *Cleveland Plain Dealer*

Box Office: $23,047,939

Rapper–turned–film actor Ice Cube does quadruple duty in this energetic and entertaining film about the underworld of "lap dancing." He is the executive producer, writer, director, and one of the supporting leads in the film, and somehow he manages to wear all of his hats well. The film is no vanity project, as his acting role is relatively small (he plays a small-time hood), and the ratio of action to humor and drama to melodrama is very good indeed. Though lacking the quirky style of Spike Lee or the surefire comedy/drama blend of Woody Allen, Ice Cube is forging his own auteur-ish style with strength and grace.

The film takes an unusually strong overall stand regarding the degradation of women in society, particularly urban society. Though the film is about African-American women, the universality and simplicity of Ice Cube's story clearly indicate that he intends to indict all of society for the misogynistic treatment of women, not just African-American society.

However, some may see *The Players Club* as having its cake and eating it too. And it does. The film is about gorgeous women dancing half-naked, and it is also about how awful and degrading it is. So, while the women are strutting their stuff, audience members can say they are shocked—shocked!—that women should be portrayed that way, even while their eyes are popping out of their sockets. Is that a legitimate quibble? Perhaps so. But welcome to the cinema of the '90s. After all, this is the era where exaggerated violence, such as in *Pulp Fiction,* is supposed to expose it as awful. Rhetorically speaking, then, why shouldn't Ice Cube be able to show some feminine pulchritude in the name of opening discussion on the mistreatment of women?

Be that as it may, it is the story of Diane (LisaRaye), a young single mom trying to make ends meet to get through college, intending to become a television journalist. She quickly discovers that lap-dancing might be a good way for her to earn some real money, and she finds her way to Dollar Bill's (Bernie Mac) Players Club. Afraid at first, she quickly catches on that the big tips come with the private lap dances. She remains a good girl, though, and refuses to become a prostitute, to the displeasure of Ronnie (Chrystale Wilson) and Tricks (Adele Givens), two lesbian strippers who are simply bad, through and through.

Now here is where the film becomes either fun or melodramatic, depending upon the viewer's likes or dislikes. Ronnie and Tricks are so awfully cruel and evil that you wonder if they didn't pop up out of some bad "B" prison movie of the '50s or '60s. Until a climactic scene in which Diane fights with Ronnie, the banter between them teeters on campy fun. The negative part of it all is that the terror that these two bring to the proceedings has to do with their lesbianism, as if poor Diane is powerless against the mean lesbians. The film and the characters are far better served when Ronnie and Tricks

Diana's (LisaRaye) motto: "Make that money, don't let it make you."

are setting Diane's hapless cousin Ebony (Monica Calhoun) up for trouble. The threat of danger in those scenes is far greater and more real than the mere threat that Ronnie and Tricks want to get into a hot tub with Diane. Wilson and Givens, however, are highlights of the movie with their riotous costumes, hairdos, and outlandish characterizations.

CREDITS

Diane Armstrong/Diamond: LisaRaye
Reggie: Ice Cube
Dollar Bill: Bernie Mac
Ebony: Monica Calhoun
Li'l Man: A.J. Johnson
Blue: Jamie Foxx
Ronnie: Chrystale Wilson
Tricks: Adele Givens
Mr. Armstrong: Dick Anthony Williams

Origin: USA
Released: 1998
Production: Patricia Charbonnet; released by New Line Cinema
Direction: Ice Cube
Screenplay: Ice Cube
Cinematography: Malik Sayeed
Editing: Suzanne Hines
Production design: Dina Lipton
Costumes: Dahlia Foroutan
Art direction: Keith Neely
Sound: Russell Williams
MPAA rating: R
Running Time: 104 minutes

Diane (who changes her name to Diamond upon becoming a stripper) is gently and elegantly played by Lisa-Raye as a moral but pragmatic woman caught in seedy circumstances, and knowing when to get out. Bernie Mac is a bit over the top as Dollar Bill, but fun nonetheless. His is one of those roles that Ice Cube doesn't seem to have defined as tragic or comic. Dollar Bill's subplot, involving money and drugs, seems to be played for laughs. His character might have been more effective to the overall story if he contributed to the true darkness of the surroundings in which Diane finds herself.

Speaking of darkness, Cube (Mr. Cube? Mr. Ice?) has created a wonderfully dark and seedy visual look with the help of cinematographer Malik Hassan Sayeed. Sayeed's ability to find different shades of darkness, echoing the sorriness of the Players Club and environs, is an important part of the film's success, as is the work of art director Keith Neely.

In the end, Ice Cube has made a fine film with many laughs even while it becomes a morality play. It all adds up to good entertainment with a message. 🎞️

—*Kirby Tepper*

REVIEWS

Boxoffice. June, 1998, p. 81.
Entertainment Weekly. April 17, 1998, p. 48.
Los Angeles Times. April 8, 1998, p. F5.
Sight and Sound. October, 1998, p. 49.
USA Today. April 8, 1998, p. 7D.
Variety. April 13, 1998, p. 28.
Village Voice. April 21, 1998, p. 72.

Playing by Heart

A romantic comedy with a twist.—Movie tagline

"A hilarious romantic comedy filled with surprising twists!"—*CBS-TV*

"Seductively funny! A superb romantic comedy filled with wonderful performances!"—Marshall Fine, *Gannett Newspapers*

"This all-star cast is beautifully headed by Sean Connery and Gena Rowlands! It takes aim and hits the bull's eye!"—Kevin Thomas, *Los Angeles Times*

"Funny, sexy, wonderful . . . there are more surprises than a first time love affair!"—Bonnie Churchill, *NNS*

"Gillian Anderson and Jon Stewart have comic chemistry and generate sexy sparks! Angelina Jolie gives a star-making performance!"—Andy Seiler, *USA Today*

 Box Office: $3,956,000

*P*laying by Heart is, admittedly, a chick flick. It has all the elements—it's about love, features well-dressed characters in lovely settings, and has the requisite noble dying person (actually, in this case, three noble dying people). But despite having these typical elements, *Playing* rises above its chick flick sisters. This is the kind of film that could give chick flicks a good name.

Witty, smart, and fun, *Playing by Heart* was originally titled *Dancing about Architecture*. The title was taken from something Joan (Angelina Jolie) says at the beginning of the film, quoting a famous adage: "Talking about love is like dancing about architecture." *Playing* takes the challenge and talks about the various love stories of a group of Los Angelinos, with the film alternating between several different stories. In one story, loud, funny actress Joan has a crush on quiet club kid Keenan (Ryan Phillippe), but he keeps blowing her off even though he seems to like her. Meanwhile, funny Trent (Jon Stewart) is trying to start something with Meredith (Gillian Anderson), but she is so burned by her previous relation-

 Writer/director Willard Carroll: "I wanted to make a movie about different ways of looking at love. It's about finding love, it's about holding onto love and it's about losing love."

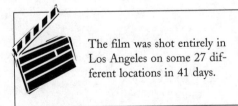 The film was shot entirely in Los Angeles on some 27 different locations in 41 days.

ships—or as she puts it, her "parade of losers"—that she tries to break up with Trent before things even begin.

In some of the other stories, perfect suburban mom Mildred (Ellen Burstyn) sits in a hospital room with her son Mark (Jay Mohr) who is dying from AIDS. Gracie (Madeline Stowe) deals with the boredom of her marriage by having a sex-only affair with Roger (Anthony Edwards). Hugh (Dennis Quaid) spends his time in various bars, telling lies about himself and his life to strangers, including Allison (Patricia Clarkson), Melanie (Nastassja Kinski), and drag queen Lola (Alec Mapa).

The centerpiece story of the film is the love story between television chef Hannah (Gena Rowlands) and her manager/husband Paul (Sean Connery). The two are a perfect pair, lustfully tossing verbal barbs at each other. When Hannah isn't speaking to Paul after a fight, he comes up to her and pleads, "How much longer do I have to wait for my next dose of vitriol?" Their prickly, passionate relationship gets rocked when, on the heels of finding out some bad health news about Paul, Hannah also learns that he might have had an affair twenty-five years earlier. "What are you thinking?" says the guilty Paul as Hannah is cooking. "Hot liquid and facial burns," she replies.

What makes this different from an extended version of *Love Boat* is the writing. The characters are smart and funny and the movie assumes that the audience is, too. When Meredith gets hit by a falling magazine rack at a local store, she signals that she's okay by saying, "I just landed on a stack of *George* so there was plenty of padding." The story between the pessimistic Meredith and her would-be suitor Trent yields some of the best lines. On their first date, Meredith complains about the artificiality of dates and their dress codes by saying to Trent, "I don't imagine you walk about your house wearing an Armani suit." Trent says, "No, in my house, it's black tie."

Earlier in the evening, Meredith notices Trent's wedding ring. "I only wear it to keep the construction workers away," says Trent. "Does it work?" says Meredith. "Depends on what I'm wearing," says Trent. Ba-dum dum.

But it's not the individual lines that make the movie, it's the offhand way in which they populate the movie. The characters say funny things, not to get a big laugh from the audience or because the film is supposed to be a comedy, but simply

CREDITS

Hannah: Gena Rowlands
Paul: Sean Connery
Meredith: Gillian Anderson
Trent: Jon Stewart
Joan: Angelina Jolie
Keenan: Ryan Phillippe
Gracie: Madeleine Stowe
Hugh: Dennis Quaid
Roger: Anthony Edwards
Mildred: Ellen Burstyn
Mark: Jay Mohr
Allison: Patricia Clarkson
Melanie: Nastassja Kinski

Origin: USA
Released: 1998
Production: Willard Carroll, Meg Liberman, and Tom Wilhite for Intermedia Films; released by Miramax Films
Direction: Willard Carroll
Screenplay: Willard Carroll
Cinematography: Vilmos Zsigmond
Editing: Pietro Scalia
Music: John Barry
Production design: Melissa Stewart
Art direction: Charlie Daboub
Costumes: April Ferry
Sound: Arthur Rochester
MPAA rating: R
Running Time: 121 minutes

because they're funny people. The jokes always rise naturally from the circumstances. "You're overwrought," says Paul to Hannah as she reacts strongly to news of his affair. "I'm perfectly wrought," she snaps back, overwrought. "Under the circumstances, I'm probably underwrought."

The film is filled with excellent performances. Especially good are Connery and Rowlands who, according to the *Los Angeles Times*, "are so absolutely right for each other, it's a wonder no one has teamed them before. She is beautiful, he is handsome, and their chemistry is palatable." Jon Stewart tones down his sarcastic talk-show-host persona into a funny, smart, and appealing standout performance. And Angelina Jolie is a wonderfully vulnerable wreck as the insecure, quick-witted Joan.

Playing by Heart is about love, but it goes far beyond the usual boy-meets-girl love stories. There are stories about mature, complicated love, the love between a mother and son, and love between long-married people. In addition to transcending the usual territory, *Playing by Heart* also snaps with bright, lively dialogue and heartfelt, real characters. It's a rare treat.

—*Jill Hamilton*

REVIEWS

Entertaiment Weekly. January 22, 1999, p. 81.
Los Angeles Times. December 30, 1998, p. F8.
New York Times. January 22, 1999, p. E12.
People. February 2, 1999, p. 30.
Time. January 25, 1999, p. 74.
Variety. January 4, 1999, p. 98.
Washington Post Weekend. January 22, 1999, p. 38.

Pleasantville

Nothing is as simple as black and white.—Movie tagline

"Simply brilliant! One of the year's delights. Film itself is being reborn."—Jay Carr, *Boston Globe*

"Brilliant and funny. We will hear from *Pleasantville* come Oscar time."—Joel Siegel, *Good Morning America*

"Priceless scenes and sensational performances."—Rex Reed, *New York Observer*

"An ingenious fantasy."—Janet Maslin, *New York Times*

"A complex and entertaining film that has real ideas."—Jack Kroll, *Newsweek*

"A visionary adventure."—Peter Travers, *Rolling Stone*

"Two big thumbs up."—*Siskel & Ebert*

"An epic-sized entertainment. It's smart fun."—Richard Corliss, *Time*

Modern teenagers David and Jennifer (Toby Maguire and Reese Witherspoon) are transported into an old 1950s sitcom in the fantasy *Pleasantville*.

Box Office: $38,761,264

Pleasantville begins with this pleasant fantasy: a brother and sister from the 1990s are magically transported from the "real" world into the black-and-white world of a 1950s television sitcom called *Pleasantville*, where they enact the roles of children from another era living in a picture-perfect nuclear family. The set-up has David (Tobey Maguire) and Jennifer (Reese Witherspoon) home alone in their dysfunctional household. Their divorced mother (Jane Kaczmarek) has gone off with her "significant other," a man nine years younger than she. As brother and sister, they have nothing in common. David plans to watch a marathon screening of his favorite television sitcom (which happens to be *Pleasantville*) to prepare himself for a forthcoming trivia contest, which he is sure to win, since he seems to have memorized all the episodes and much of the dialogue. Worldly and experienced Jennifer is looking forward to going out on a date.

Bud (Tobey Maguire) about Pleasantville's inhabitants: "These people are happy." His sister Mary Sue (Reese Witherspoon) replies: "Nobody's happy in a poodle skirt and sweater set."

The teenagers fight for control of the TV remote, which gets thrown against the wall and broken, but a TV repairman (Don Knotts, a sitcom icon from *The Andy Griffith Show*) mysteriously appears to remedy the problem. After testing David on his knowledge of *Pleasantville*, the repairman leaves a strange and powerful replacement controller that magically transports David and Jennifer into the sitcom, where they be-

come Bud and Mary Sue, known to her sitcom father (William H. Macy) as "Muffin." In their real world they do not have a father, and David secretly yearns for the perfect nuclear family he now finds himself belonging to. Jennifer, a sexually active rebel, is less satisfied and at first resents being trapped in "nerdville," as she calls it; but she begins to change her mind when she finds herself courted by Skip (Paul Walker), the dreamboat basketball star of Pleasantville High School, whom she soon seduces on Lovers' Lane.

Jennifer's actions on Lovers' Lane serves as a catalyst. When Jennifer's sitcom mother (Joan Allen) asks her what young people do on Lovers' Lane, Jennifer is at first coy, then tells her mom, "Sex." The confused mother wants to know, "What's that?" After Jennifer explains the joys of sex to her mother, her worldly wisdom begins to change not only her mother, but the whole fictive town. As the teenagers begin to realize their human potential, they begin to appear in color against the drab black-and-white setting they inhabit, and the same thing happens to Mom after she does some experimental fiddling in her bathtub.

As the town is transformed, so is the plot, from a simple fantasy to moral allegory, or at least a parable concerning the knowledge of good and evil. If this sounds Edenic, well, it is, and the parallel is stressed through the imagery of a bright red apple. The conservative townspeople, led by Mayor Big Bob (J. T. Walsh in his last movie role), organize a campaign against the "coloreds" (the colorized townsfolk) to protect the status quo, which includes burning books and destroying art. But it's a losing battle. Young David becomes the spokesman for the "coloreds," escaping the nostalgic charm of the status quo and standing up to Big Bob at a public meeting at the courthouse. When he manages to get the mayor really angry, even Big Bob is colorized, as is the whole town after that meeting. In the film's confused conclusion, David decides to return to the "real" world and consoles his real mother after he gets back, since she has split with her younger lover, explaining, "He didn't make me feel younger; he just made me feel older."

But Jennifer, who has discovered the joys of reading in Pleasantville, decides to stay behind in order to continue her mission of education. What will become of this "lost" girl the screenplay by director Gary Ross leaves absurdly open. What will become of Betty, the sitcom mother who has struck up an adulterous relationship with the artistic Mr. Johnson (Jeff Daniels), who owns the malt shop, and what will become of her pathetic husband George, a victim of change who just doesn't get it until it appears to be too late? Such questions are likewise left inconclusive and ambiguous.

"People are nostalgic for something I didn't feel was real," writer-director Gary Ross told the *New York Times* (October 30). "They sanitized this memory. They created a kind of perfection out of the past." But Ross, born in 1956, would have had no clear memory of the period, only a television similitude of the *Father Knows Best* era and the universe of *Ozzie and Harriet*. The film, which was the No. 1 boxoffice draw its opening weekend, deals mainly with television-inspired nostalgia and falters only in its attempt to embrace the uncertainty and ambiguity of the real world, but it does succeed in evoking the Zeitgeist of the era reflected through popular culture. The challenge was to bring an artificial world to life. A "perfect" world is not a real world, of course, and it is entirely appropriate that the one-dimensional characters should first be seen in black and white.

Pleasantville treads near significant issues in what it suggests about the reckless and self-indulgent behavior of parents and their disregard for their offspring, as brilliantly demonstrated in Ang Lee's *The Ice Storm* (1997), but the fabricated characters of *Pleasantville* pale in comparison to the realistic characters of Rick Moody's 1994 novel on which *The Ice Storm* was based. *Pleasantville* opts for easy answers and solutions as

In order for the film to achieve its gradual colorization, the movie was filmed in color, which was removed digitally for the black-and-white sequences.

the children lead the way to human fulfillment and understanding. After his nostalgic mythic quest into a dream world, David brings new-found wisdom back to the "real" world to comfort his mother, who should have known better in the first place. So the children are good, if not entirely innocent, and they shall lead the way. Mature viewers may actively resist such simplistic nonsense as this. Nonetheless, *Pleasantville* won the approval of many reviewers. Peter Travers of *Rolling Stone*, for example, characterized the film as "a visionary adventure" and praised writer-director Gary Ross for his dexterity in exploring "accepted definitions of what's funny and what's scary," as the fantasy starts funny, "then accelerates into a grave parable with the specters of fear and bigotry that arise when so-called normal values are threatened." In fact, the film both valorizes and criticizes the values of the Eisenhower era, and that is to its credit. Those who lived through the 1950s will know that the *Reader's Digest* utopia this film represents is surely exaggerated, but in many respects dead-on in what it suggests about a more naive and innocent small-town America. The film's title is perfect, by the way, since Pleasantville, New York, is the headquarters of *Reader's Digest*.

Yet not all reviews were entirely favorable. Lisa Schwarzbaum of *Entertainment Weekly* described the film as "a vivid yet vacant fantasy" that lacks the "depth, poignance, and brilliance of *The Truman Show*," which it followed three months later, a "lightweight literary sketch" in the old *Reader's Digest* style. Though it may be unfair to question the fable too literally, the details are inconsistent and leave many questions unanswered. David and Jennifer find in Pleasantville a sexless society, a world without bodily functions. When Jennifer goes into the rest room at the malt shop, for example, she discovers that it has stalls but no toilets, which leads one to wonder if the teenagers have genitalia, and, if not, how they could be naughty on Lovers' Lane? Jennifer also discovers that the books in Pleasantville have blank pages, but as David tells the story of Huckleberry Finn, the text of the novel magically appears (corrupted, one wonders, by David's incomplete memory?). After Jennifer educates the young people about sex, one supposes by this logic that form perhaps follows function. So as Jennifer rewrites the script, the world appears to change in really substantial ways. Taking her bath after she has been instructed by daughter Mary Sue, Betty seems to achieve an orgasm, though one knows that her G-spot would never have been originally scripted for the character.

In *The Truman Show*, the viewer saw the creator of the sanitized television utopia struggling to sustain his artificially constructed world, but in *Pleasantville* the focus is entirely on the created rather than the creator. Like Amaurotum, the city of Sir Thomas More's *Utopia*, *Pleasantville* is "dark or dimly seen" in black and white, suggesting through the cinematog-

AWARDS AND NOMINATIONS

Broadcast Film Critics Association 1998:
Supporting Actress (Joan Allen)
Los Angeles Film Critics 1998: Supporting
Actress (Joan Allen)

CREDITS

David/Bud: Tobey Maguire
Mr. Johnson: Jeff Daniels
Betty: Joan Allen
George: William H. Macy
Big Bob: J. T. Walsh
Jennifer/Mary Sue: Reese Witherspoon
TV Repairman: Don Knotts

Origin: USA
Released: 1998
Production: Jon Kilik, Robert J. Degus, Steven Soder-bergh, and Gary Ross for Larger Than Life; released by New Line Cinema
Direction: Gary Ross
Screenplay: Gary Ross
Cinematography: John Lindley
Editing: William Goldenberg
Music: Randy Newman
Production design: Jeannine Oppewall
Art direction: Dianne Wager
Costumes: Judianna Makovsky
Sound: Robert Anderson Jr.
Visual effects supervisor: Chris Watts
Color effects design: Michael Southard
MPAA rating: PG-13
Running Time: 124 minutes

raphy that this world is incompletely realized and more an image of reality than reality itself. But once it takes on color, does it—more to the point, can it?—become "real"? *Pleasantville* works as a fantasized allegory that is decidedly "pleasant" and entirely amusing and entertaining in the way it represents a nostalgic "nowhere," but in comparison to Peter Weir's *The Truman Show*, it appears to be a pretty hollow, though inventive and entertaining, accomplishment. As a purely technical achievement, however, mixing color and black-and-white cinematography to good effect, the film is impressive.

—*James M. Welsh*

REVIEWS

Baltimore Sun. October 23, 1998, p. E13.
Entertainment Weekly. October 30, 1998, p. 77.
New York. November 2, 1998, p. 118.
New York Times. October 23, 1998, p. B23.
New York Times. October 30, 1998, p. B16.
Rolling Stone. November 12, 1998, p. 121.
Time. October 26, 1998, p. 92.
USA Today. October 23, 1998, p. E6.
Variety. September 21, 1998, p. 104.
Village Voice. November 3, 1998, p. 135.
Washington Post. October 23, 1998, p. B1.
Washington Post Weekend. October 23, 1998, p. 54.
Washington Times Metropolitan Times. October 23, 1998, p. C16.

Plump Fiction

From the producers who saw *Pulp Fiction*, *Reservoir Dogs*, and *Twister*.—Movie tagline

Plump Fiction is not, repeat, not a porno. Although the title may imply a film about, shall we say, the physically challenged, this is actually an inventive, and much deserved, spoof of Quentin Tarantino flicks. A grab bag of indie pics are also skewered in this comedy that slides from the hilarious to the simply stupid with a sublimity not seen since the Zucker brothers last worked together. There is a prevailing fallacy that if a film is "independent," then it must be brilliant and sacrosanct. Of course this isn't true and neither is it true that Tarantino is some kind of 1990s wunderkind, although there are legions who would argue otherwise. What Bob Koherr, the writer and director of *Plump Fiction*, understands is that a film is not great just because

it is violent, irreverent, obnoxious, and disjointed. These qualities can make for great art, but often they are gimmicks disguised in wolf's clothing. *Plump Fiction* rips the costume off, fangs and all.

The first half hour of this movie is relentless in its mocking of *Pulp Fiction*. It opens with the familiar sounds of Dick Dale's trippy guitar work, but it's only until you listen closely that you realize that this is not the original *Pulp* music at all, but rather Havah Nagilah. Why is it that whenever a cheap, aural laugh is needed, the strains of Havah Nagilah begin to jam? Why is it that it always works? This instance is funnier yet since Dick Dale actually did the arrangement.

After a brief scene where screenwriter Bunny Roberts (Sandra Bernhard) commands Bumpkin (Dan Castelleta), a *Forrest Gump* rip-off, to bring the last copy of her script to a warehouse where her movie is being shot, the film moves to a spoof of a scene that has become a pivotal sequence in the annals of 1990s cinema. Two black-suited "hit men," Julius (Tommy Davidson) and Jimmy (Paul Dinello), are in a car driving to their latest "extermination." Jimmy has just gotten back from a trip to Europe where he spent most of his time at Paris Disneyland. "Do you know what they call Tomorrowland over there?" he asks. Julius is shocked to find out that it's called "Mañaland." This perfect send-up continues with Jimmy giving other examples of Euroized Disney characters and rides until they arrive at their destination. Mimicking Tarantino's upward shot from the car's trunk, Julius and Jimmy get out their equipment, which turns out to be bug extermination devices. Unfortunately, they have to clean out the apartment of two serial killers, Nicky (Matthew Glave) and Vallory (Pamela Segall), who have been forced into obscurity because of the work of film-maker Gulliver Stone.

These characters' stories, along with those of the "Reservoir Nuns," revolve loosely around the mobster cum exterminator–business owner cum strip club owner, Montello (Robert Costanzo), who has lost a mysterious briefcase. None of these stories make a whole lot of sense, but that is just the point. For some reason Jimmy has to take out Montello's ex-stripper wife, the plump and food-addicted Mimi (Julie Brown). She and Jimmy visit the Independent Café where all your favorite independent film characters, like Priscilla "Queen of the Desserts" (Tim Kazurinsky), come to life.

While this is happening, Bumpkin attempts to get Bunny's script to the warehouse, but along the way he spills the unnumbered script dozens of times. By the time it reaches the director's eager hands it is out of order and completely disjointed. He picks it up, scans it, and declares it brilliant because it is violent, bloody, and incoherent. The title of the script is, of course, "Plump Fiction."

The concept, acting, and much of the writing in *Plump Fiction* is hilarious but uneven. At times the length Koherr goes to mock his subjects slips into banality, but somehow this only heightens the really good parts—and the ending is one of them. The content of the mystery briefcase both is and is probably not what Tarantino had in mind. Inside the briefcase is a *Welcome Back, Kotter* lunch box, but as Julius notes, "It ain't worth a damn thing without the thermos." Inspired touches like these make the duller parts bearable in a film that many will perceive as juvenile and stupid. But juvenile and stupid may very well be the crowning achievement of this movie, because it makes you take a good hard look at the source material, which is just that.

—*Rich Silverman*

CREDITS

Julius: Tommy Davidson
Mimi: Julie Brown
Jimmy: Paul Dinello
Bunny Roberts: Sandra Bernhard
Bumpkin: Dan Castellaneta
Montello: Robert Costanzo
Vallory: Pamela Segall
Nicky: Matthew Glave

Origin: USA
Released: 1998
Production: Gary Binkow for Rhino Films; released by Legacy
Direction: Bob Koherr
Screenplay: Bob Koherr
Cinematography: Rex Nicholson
Editing: Neil Kirk
Production design: Jacques Herbert
Art direction: Robert La Liberte
Costumes: Vincent Lapper
Sound: Eric Enroth
MPAA rating: R
Running Time: 82 minutes

REVIEWS

Los Angeles Times. May 15, 1998, p. F10.
Variety. May 18, 1998, p. 77.

Polish Wedding

Sometimes the further you stray, the closer you are to home.—Movie tagline

"Invite your friends to this wedding."—Michele Shapiro, *Glamour*

"Lena Olin reclaims her title as one of the sexiest women on screen. A colorful, likeable off-kilter slice of life."—Leonard Maltin, *Playboy*

"With piroshkis instead of pizza, *Polish Wedding* strikes a *Moonstruck* note."—*TV Guide*

 Box Office: $563, 143

First-time writer/director Theresa Connelly produces a finely crafted, old-fashioned story of Polish-American immigrants struggling to keep their tight-knit family intact in a suburb of Detroit. Connelly, whose script was plucked by producers from the Sundance Screenwriters' Lab, insisted on keeping the locations as real as her characters and the result is a film that looks as far away from a slick, glossy Hollywood creation as the Hamtramck locales of Connelly's hometown, where it was shot. Considerably enhancing the sites are the international, multi-star cast led by the Swedish Lena Olin and the Irish Gabriel Byrne, who, by virtue of their transcontinental upbringings, also give the film another dimension of reality.

The undoubtedly central and unifying force in the family is Olin's passionate matriarch Jadzia Pzoniak. Passion is the character's resounding trait, as she defends the family and home as fiercely as she attacks the love of her life. Byrne as the breadmaker husband and father, Bolek, is the stoic yet powerful opposite of his stormy wife; he quietly trudges off each night to the bakery in his crisp white uniform. Caught in the middle is Hala, their only daughter among four sons. Although closest to her father, she is the very picture of her lusty mother. Because of this resemblance, Jadzia is probably overly wary with her wayward daughter, thus causing a rift between them. The bond between father and daughter is strengthened, also, by an ever-widening distance between Jadzia and her faithful husband.

Hala is the main focus of the film's action as she runs around with teenage boys and rowdy friends in the back streets of her hometown. Her Lolita-like coquetry and thirst for adventure, not to mention her slight summer dresses, catch the eye of handsome local cop Russell (Adam Trese),

 Jadzia (Lena Olin): "Making love and life, that's my religion."

who is further enticed by her cold treatment of him when he shoos off her intoxicated, underage mates. Following her as she runs down a dark alley, Russell sees Hala disappear headfirst into a basement window, where she sometimes meets up with her nine-year-old brother for a discreet smoke. Just as Jadzia calls for Hala out her window, knowing what her young daughter must be up to, Hala's mother remembers some secret business of her own and slips out of the house to go to her Polish Women's group, whose meetings are becoming more and more frequent. Jadzia, who is a cleaning woman, has also been working increasingly late in the evenings and Bolek starts to suspect what we already know—that Jadzia is having an affair with businessman Roman (Rade Serbedzija).

Notable among the support characters is Mili Avital as Sofie Pzoniak, the put-upon young wife of Hala's oldest brother Ziggi (Daniel Lapaine). Mother to his child and Jadzia's co-worker and daughter-in-law, Sofie doesn't understand Jadzia's unbridled lust to procreate and resents her mother-in-law's frequent urgings to have more children of her own.

Conjuring up images of the excitement and secret pleasures of youth, Connelly also puts as much importance on the yearnings of a middle-aged, happily married woman and a long-suffering but loving husband. Jadzia's and Bolek's drama plays out alongside Hala's, and is just as engaging. The love of the characters for each other is what gives the movie such tremendous heart, as we feel for each one and their dilemmas. When the very young Hala, after a late-night tryst with Russell, suspects she is pregnant and finally tells her father her worst fears, it is just as emotional as when Bolek stands outside the house of his wife's lover and cries. The exquisite drama of such moments are balanced by frequent bursts of comedy, such as when the whole Pzoniak tribe marches over with baseball bats in hand to Russell's to obtain a shotgun wedding for the now pregnant Hala. Some of these comic moments, however, seem to play a little too farcically in such a touching story and at times take away from the action at hand.

Issues of the church, usually vital in immigrant families such as the Pzoniaks, are given consideration as young Hala is chosen by the members of the Catholic Church to head the Festival of the Virgin, underscoring her current, very un-virgin-like situation. The stern young priest seems to represent a community that looks down on behavior such as Hala's. As the family struggles with all these life-altering issues, they fall apart and then come back together again to

CREDITS

Jadzia: Lena Olin
Bolek: Gabriel Byrne
Hala: Claire Danes
Roman: Rade Serbedzija
Russell: Adam Trese
Sofie: Mili Avital
Ziggi: Daniel Lapaine

Origin: USA
Released: 1998
Production: Tom Rosenberg, Julia Chasman, and Geoff Stier for Lakeshore Entertainment; released by Fox Searchlight
Direction: Theresa Connelly
Screenplay: Theresa Connelly
Cinematography: Guy Dufaux
Editing: Curtiss Clayton, Suzanne Fenn
Music: Luis Bacalov
Production design: Kara Lindstrom
Costumes: Donna Zakowska
MPAA rating: PG-13
Running Time: 107 minutes

support each other. It proves a very inspirational message in a time where families are spread out and often lose contact with one another.

Visually, the film takes on an appropriately raw look with expertise provided by cinematographer Guy Dufaux. Production design mirrors this look, with the somewhat shabby sets and costumes that appear to be almost out of the 1940s or '50s yet are still modern and reflective of an aging community. The lively, polka-like soundtrack of Luis Bacalov is infectious and in keeping with the flavor of the well-told, well-acted, and throughly entertaining film.

—*Hilary Weber*

REVIEWS

Boxoffice. September, 1998, p. 63.
Detroit News. July 17, 1998, p. 3D.
Detroit News. August 25, 1996, p. 10A.
Entertainment Weekly. July 24, 1998, p. 51.
Hollywood Reporter. January 20, 1998, p. 20.
Los Angeles Times. July 17, 1998, p. F16.
New York Times. July 17, 1998, p. E18.
People. August 10, 1998, p. 34.
Variety. January 26, 1998, p. 70.
Village Voice. July 21, 1998, p. 124.

Post Coitum; Post Coitum, Animal Triste

Some people fall in love. And some people fall all over it.—Movie tagline
"A brave, witty and very touching film."—Janet Maslin, *New York Times*

Brigitte Rouan co-wrote and directed this vehicle, which does a good job of displaying her acting talent. Starring as Diane Clovier, an editor at a small Parisian publishing house, Rouan portrays a woman who, in her forties, is clearly poised for a mid-life crisis. Seemingly Diane has everything: she is well established in her profession and well liked at work, and she has a stable marriage to a loving husband which has produced two teenaged sons who adore her.

The opening frames of *Post Coitum* intercut scenes of a cat moaning in heat with scenes of Diane wailing as she wallows about in bed. These scenes are starkly filmed, and Rouan presents the aftermath of love

Diane (Brigitte Rouan) to younger Emilio (Boris Terral): "I'm a lifetime ahead of you."

as a less than pretty picture. One of her children (unwittingly) casts a humorous light on the contrast between Diane and the cat by telling the story of a mouse who, wandering along a railroad track one day, loses his tail. The next day, when he goes back in search of his tail, the train comes along and cuts off his head. The moral of the story, the insouciant boy says, is that he who chases tail loses his head. This is a French film, after all, and we are not to take it *too* seriously.

After the opening scenes, *Post Coitum* flashes back to reveal what has brought Diane to such a brutish condition. One of her authors, Francois (Nils Travernier), is suffering from writer's block. One night when Diane visits him in a effort to rouse him from his lethargy, she is the one who experiences an awakening. At Francois's apartment, she meets Emilio (Boris Terral), an Italian engineer half her age who seems the embodiment of animal magnetism. It seems to be a case of lust at first sight, and although it is Emilio who pursues Diane, she quickly capitulates. *Post Coitum* is, for at least half of its running time, both highly erotic and highly romantic. Rouan films several fairly explicit sex scenes between Diane and Emilio, including one urgent consummation in a ladies' room. She also includes a scene of Diane floating on a cloud when she is first caught up in her passion for her young lover.

Not surprisingly, however, things soon go awry. Emilio abruptly announces that he is off to Africa to work on a new engineering project, rather matter of factly breaking off his affair with Diane. It is clear enough to him—and to the audience—that an adulterous affair between a woman in her forties and a young man half her age is not meant to last. Diane, however, is heavily invested in this attempt to recapture her lost youth. In fact, she has been behaving like an irresponsible adolescent, ignoring her family and showing up late for business meetings because she could not leave Emilio's arms. Like the mouse, in her search for "tail," she has lost her head. And when Emilio dumps her, she has a breakdown.

Diane reacts to rejection just like many middle-aged men undergoing a similar crisis: she first restyles her hair, then takes to drink. As passionately as Diane had committed herself to her love affair with Emilio, she now just as passionately mourns its end. She loses her job and (seemingly) her family. The only one who remains true to her is Francois, who has managed to overcome his blockage by turning her tragedy into an award-winning novel. It is indeed a story as old as time, which Rouan manages to keep fresh through the honesty of her acting and the trick of reversing the sexes in a May-December romance.

Rouan and her fellow screenwriters provide an interesting counterpoint to Diane's downfall. While she is pursuing her romance with Emilio, her husband, a criminal lawyer, is defending a neighbor, Madame Lepluche (Francoise Arnoul) who, after forty-three years of marriage to an abusive, unfaithful lout, one day kills him by stabbing him in the neck with a carving fork—seemingly without provocation. While Diane loses her head post coitum, Mme. Lepluche seems to find a kind of equanimity after ending her relationship in a fit of madness. And just as Francois uses Diane's crisis to create his successful novel, so Philippe (Patrick Chesnais) will be able to use his own distress to weave a story that will win the jury over to Mme. Lepluche's side. In the end, Francois and Philippe will save their respective muses. Vita brevis, ars longa.

—Lisa Paddock

The French title *Post Coitum, Animal Triste* translates as "After sex, animal grief."

CREDITS

Diane Clovier: Brigitte Rouan
Philippe Clovier: Patrick Chesnais
Emilio: Boris Terral
Francois Narou: Nils Tavernier
Weyoman-Lebeau: Jean-Louis Richard
Madame Lepluche: Francoise Arnoul

Origin: France
Released: 1997
Production: Humbert Balsan; released by New Yorker Films
Direction: Brigitte Rouan
Screenplay: Brigitte Rouan, Santiago Amigorena, Jean-Louis Richard, and Guy Ziblerstein
Cinematography: Pierre Dupouey
Editing: Laurent Rouan
Music: Michel Musseau, Umberto Tozzi
Production design: Roland Deville
Costumes: Florence Emir, Marika Ingrato
MPAA rating: Unrated
Running Time: 97 minutes

REVIEWS

Boxoffice. September, 1997, p. 111.
Los Angeles Times. March 20, 1998, F14.
New York Times. September 27, 1997, p. B9.
New York Times. March 8, 1998, p. 15.
People. April 13, 1998, p. 22.
San Francisco Examiner. April 3, 1998.
Variety. May 26, 1997, p. 66.
Village Voice. March 17, 1998, p. 64.

Practical Magic

Falling in love is the trickiest spell of all.—Movie tagline

"Spellbinding. A magically romantic comedy." —Maria Salas, *CBS/Telenoticias*

"A fun romantic treat. A must see."—Jim Ferguson, *FOX-TV*

"A terrific brew of fun and fantasy. Bewitching and beguiling. Beautifully acted by Sandra Bullock and Nicole Kidman."—Bonnie Churchill, *National News Syndicate*

"Funny, clever and smart."—Gene Siskel, *Siskel & Ebert*

 Box Office: $46,404,796

One would expect the supernatural film *Practical Magic*, with its first-rate cast of Sandra Bullock, Nicole Kidman, Dianne Wiest, and Stockard Channing, to cast a spell or two on the audience. Unfortunately, there's not much that is magical or practical about this latter-day witch tale.

Based on the popular novel by Alice Hoffman, the plot revolves around Sally (Sandra Bullock) and Gillian (Nicole Kidman) Owens—beautiful, modern-day sister witches descended from a line of New England women dating back to the Puritan era. Besides trying to learn to live with "the Craft," the sisters also share a family curse: Any man truly loved by an Owens woman is destined to die prematurely.

Sally and Gillian have been raised by their eccentric aunts following the death of their parents. Aunt Frances (Stockard Channing) and Aunt Jet (Dianne Wiest) are likable, spinster witches who get blamed for everything that goes wrong in their town. The girls grow up in an atypical household— eating brownies for breakfast, studying spell books, and staying up late to practice the ancient arts.

As the girls mature, they develop contrasting attitudes toward their powers. Sally, whose gift is the strongest, wants nothing more than to live a "normal," magic-free life, while the fiery Gillian embraces her powers and embarks on a hedonistic lifestyle. Ignoring the oath and falling in love, Sally marries and has two daughters, while sexy vamp Gillian is

off chasing men in California.

A short time later, a series of events occurs that leaves Sally a grieving widow and Gillian in trouble with her abusive boyfriend Jimmy (Goran Visnjic), a Bulgarian with a cowboy fetish. When Sally attempts to rescue Gilly, both girls end up abducted by the drunken, obsessive Jimmy. Things turn violent and in an act of self-defense, the two women accidentally kill the bad-news stud with a dose of belladonna. The Owens sisters try to bring him back to life with another spell, only to bury him, at which point he rises from the dead and the movie launches into *Exorcist* mode. (Don't ask.) Gillian and Sally spend the rest of the movie dealing with the evil spirit and dodging police inquiries.

Just when you think this mishmash can't get any worse, Gary Hallet (Aidan Quinn), an Arizona police officer, shows up at the door of the Owens's rambling Victorian house looking for answers. Of course, Sally thinks he's her dream man and falls for the investigator. Will the curse be lifted this time or will Sally suffer another heartbreak?

Directed by actor turned director Griffin Dunne (*Addicted to Love* [1996]), *Practical Magic* suffers from awkward pacing and constantly changing moods. The film shifts so abruptly from a female-bonding comedy to romance to horror that you're not sure what tone Dunne is trying to achieve. Dunne and his trio of

 Gillian Owens (Nicole Kidman): "Did you ever put your arms out and spin and spin and spin? Well, that's what love is like."

screenwriters (Robin Swicord, Akiva Goldsman, and Adam Brooks) downplay the magic and concentrate more on the emotional burdens of being a witch in the '90s. The filmmakers would have been more successful focusing on the witchcraft. After all, what good are special powers if you can't have fun with them?

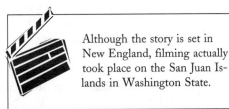 Although the story is set in New England, filming actually took place on the San Juan Islands in Washington State.

While both Bullock (*Speed* [1994], *While You Were Sleeping* [1995], *Hope Floats* [1998]— also reviewed in this edition) and Kidman (*To Die For* [1995], *The Peacemaker* [1997]) have their charming moments, the real highlight of the film is the comic support of Wiest (*Bullets Over Broadway* [1994], *The Birdcage* [1995]) and Channing (*Six Degrees of Separation* [1993], *Twilight* [1998]) as the witchy Aunts. They make a fun pair, hamming it up and bringing some much needed merriment to the muddled storyline.

Critical reaction to *Practical Magic* was mostly negative, although a few reviewers noted that the film worked as amusing, schlocky entertainment. Several critics also com-

CREDITS

Sally Owens: Sandra Bullock
Gillian Owens: Nicole Kidman
Aunt Jet: Dianne Wiest
Aunt Frances: Stockard Channing
Gary Hallet: Aidan Quinn
Jimmy: Goran Visnjic
Kylie: Evan Rachel Wood

Origin: USA
Released: 1998
Production: Deinse Di Novi for Fortis Films and Village Roadshow Pictures; released by Warner Bros.
Direction: Griffin Dunne
Screenplay: Robin Swicord, Akiva Goldsman, and Adam Brooks; based on the novel by Alice Hoffman
Cinematography: Andrew Dunn
Editing: Elizabeth Kling
Music: Alan Silvestri
Production design: Robin Standefer
Set design: Aric Lashee
Costumes: Judianna Makovsky
Sound: Richard B. Goodman
Special effects supervisor: Burt Dalton
MPAA rating: PG-13
Running Time: 105 minutes

mented on Bullock's continual whining and moping around—an act we've seen before. In his review for the *Chicago Tribune*, Mark Caro even suggested the movie be retitled "Hope Floats on a Broomstick."

As far as witch fables go, *Magic* pales in comparison to other pop-culture witch pics like *The Witches of Eastwick* (1987), *Hocus Pocus* (1993), or *The Craft* (1996). However, none of these witchy sagas comes close to capturing the magic of the legendary television sitcom *Bewitched*, which starred Elizabeth Montgomery as the nose-twitching Samantha. Now that was one enchanting spellcaster.

—Beth Fhaner

REVIEWS

Chicago Tribune. October 16, 1998, p. 5.
Cinefantastique. October, 1998, p. 14-16.
Detroit Free Press. October 16, 1998, p. 4E.
Detroit News. October 16, 1998, p. 3D.
Entertainment Weekly. October 23, 1998, p. 47.
Los Angeles Times. October 16, 1998.
New York Times. October 16, 1998, p. E10.
People. October 26, 1998, p. 35.
USA Today online. October 19, 1998.
Variety. October 19, 1998, p. 74.
Washington Post Weekend. October 16, 1998, p. 48.

A Price Above Rubies

In a world defined by its rules, one woman is ruled by her passion.—Movie tagline

"Engrossing and powerfully enveloping! Renee Zellweger gives a lovely performance."—Janet Maslin, *New York Times*

"Two thumbs up! Renee Zellweger's performance is wonderful!"—*Siskel & Ebert*

"Provocative, intelligent and highly entertaining! Writer/director Boaz Yakin has created an extraordinary and powerful story of one woman's quest for individuality."—Paul Wunder, *WBAI Radio*

 Box Office: $1,130,732

R enee Zellweger (*Jerry Maguire* [1997]) stars as a young Hasidic woman who rebels against the confines of her religion and embarks on a personal odyssey of indepen-

dence and sexuality in Boaz Yakim's *A Price Above Rubies.* Though the film elicited protests from New York Hasidic Jews over what they felt was an unfair representation of their close-knit community, Yakim, who is himself Jewish, insisted that his film was not a social indictment, but rather an examination of one woman's struggle for personal emancipation.

The film begins with a fable-like prologue in which the young Sonia (Jackie Ryan), daughter of a jeweler, quickly declares the ruby that her older brother, Yossi (Shelton Dane), has given her fake. To redeem himself, Yossi goes for a midnight swim in the lake and drowns.

In the present, the adult Sonia (Zellweger) gives birth to a baby boy, but is unsuccessful in persuading her devout husband, Mendel (Glenn Fitzgerald), to agree to name the boy after her beloved brother. When the rabbinical scholar Mendel receives an appointment at a prestigious Yashiva in the close-knit Orthodox Jewish community of Borough Park, Sonia finds herself thrust even deeper into a life to which she feels ill suited. One night with her husband, her passion is ignited and when she begins to respond sexually, Mendel is appalled, feeling that lovemaking is a sacred act not to be profaned in God's presence.

Sonia's frustrations, both physical and emotional, mount with no available release until one day when, unsatisfied by her designated role as wife and mother, Sonia allows herself to fall victim to the lecherous advances of her conniving brother-in-law, Sender (Christopher Eccleston). In exchange, Sender, a jeweler, offers Sonia a job appraising gems and the young woman blossoms in her newfound professional independence. However, Sonia's personal fulfillment and ease at mingling with "outsiders" is met with contempt by her relatives, and Sonia soon discovers the emotional costs of being an individual when one's individual needs do not fit into the structure of one's society.

 Writer/director Boaz Yakin on his film: "I wanted to explore the emotional difficulties of being an individual when one's individual needs . . . don't fit into the structure of the society. It's a story that's really adaptable to any time, any place."

A Price Above Rubies is director Boaz Yakim's second film, the follow-up to his feature debut, *Fresh,* winner of the Filmmakers' Trophy at the 1994 Sundance Film Festival. His second film is a less commercial project, more personal and ultimately controversial. Yakim admits to being drawn to stories about "round pegs in square holes."

Yakin mixes a spattering of magical realism into his tale of one woman's rebellion against a restrictive life and her religiously ascribed identity, but unfortunately there is not enough for the viewer to decipher to a satisfying degree. The infusion of such cosmic influences as an old beggar woman (Kathleen Chalfant)—whose true function remains questionable to the end—results in more confusion than complexity and lends little to the narrative. For Yakin, the fable-like love story of the film's prologue represents a perfect romantic love that Sonia would never be able to recapture.

One of the most striking elements of the film is Adam Holender's hauntingly beautiful cinematography. Despite its contemporary setting, the film is photographed in such a way as to visually articulate the sense that this is a culture strongly rooted in the past and in its history.

The actions of the character of Sonia could very easily be regarded as selfish were it not for the strength of actress Renee Zellweger's performance. Yakin alienated some in the Jewish community when he cast the offbeat Texan woman of Swiss and Norwegian ancestry—a "shiksa"—in his film's pivotal role, but Yakin was quick to dismiss the notion of cultural specificity in casting as a specious argument. While promoting the film, Yakin chastised those who felt that only a Jew could portray a Jew onscreen, reminding all that acting was, after all, an imaginative process. "You find the emotional life of the character and emote to express that," Yakin said in a press interview in Los Angeles. "That's what actors do." True to his word, of the lead actors only Julianna Margulies (Emmy Award–winning actress of television's *ER*) is Jewish.

The phrase "a price above rubies" derives from a Biblical proverb that is intended to honor the righteous woman who serves her husband and home: "A woman of fortitude, who can find? For her price is far above rubies . . . " Boaz Yakin's film, however, did not fare quite as well; *A Price Above Rubies* received decidedly mixed critical reviews.

—*Patricia Kowal*

CREDITS

Sonia: Renee Zellweger
Sender: Christopher Eccleston
Rachel: Julianna Margulies
Ramon: Allen Payne
Mendel: Glenn Fitzgerald
Feiga: Edie Falco
Rebbe: John Randolph
Rebbitzn: Kim Hunter

Origin: USA
Released: 1998
Production: Lawrence Bender and John Penotti for Pandora Cinema and Channel Four Films; released by Miramax Films
Direction: Boaz Yakin
Screenplay: Boaz Yakin
Cinematography: Adam Holender
Editing: Arthur Coburn
Production design: Dan Leigh
Sound: William Sarokin
Costumes: Ellen Lutter
Music: Leslie Barber
MPAA rating: R
Running Time: 117 minutes

REVIEWS

Chicago Sun-Times. April 3, 1998.
Chicago Tribune. April 3, 1998, p. 4.
Christian Science Monitor. April 10, 1998.
Entertainment Weekly. March 27, 1998, p. 47.
Houston Chronicle. April 2, 1998.
Los Angeles Times. March 27, 1998, p. F12.
New York Times. March 25, 1998, p. E5.
Oregonian. April 3, 1998.
People. April 6, 1998, p. 19.
Toronto Sun. April 3, 1998.
Variety. February 2, 1998, p. 31.
Village Voice. March 31, 1998, p. 64.

Primary Colors

What went down on the way to the top.—Movie
tagline

How much spin does it take to win?—Movie
tagline

"It's so funny it hurts!"—*Rolling Stone*

"Funny and vibrant!"—*Time*

Box Office: $39,299,835

John Travolta stars as a familiar southern presidential candidate in Mike
Nichols's *Primary Colors*.

If there were an Academy Award for the most misperceived and misunderstood film of the year, *Primary Colors* would be a strong contender for the Oscar. It is dramatic, funny, well written, well acted, and, best of all, intelligent, morally observant, and thought provoking. The mislabeling of this Mike Nichols film resulted in part from the growing White House scandals and the unexpected popularity of *Wag the Dog*, Barry Levinson's witty satire of White House scandal managing. Both the Monica Lewinsky sex scandal and the Levinson film appeared in January 1998, and by the time *Primary Colors* opened in March, moviegoers naturally assumed that the Nichols film, like the Levinson film, would take witty and cynical shots at the Clinton administration. John Travolta's superb evocation of Bill Clinton's complexly compartmentalized personality only furthered these assumptions.

When *Primary Colors* turned out to be much more than savvy political satire, moviegoers were perhaps puzzled or disappointed over not getting what they had wrongly expected. Boxoffice returns quickly fell off, and the film's $39 million gross made it a financial failure in relation to its $65 million budget. Part of this confusion owes no doubt to publicity statements by the filmmakers. Wanting to capitalize on the real-life scandals without misrepresenting his movie, Nichols may have protested too much to reporters. *Entertainment Weekly* magazine, for example, quoted the director as saying, "This movie is *not* about Clinton. It's about the Clinton *thing*. It's about the Kennedys and the Jeffersons and the Lincolns. It's about us—the public—and how we elect these guys. That's a *big* distinction." Writer Benjamin Svetkey's reaction to these words in the magazine apparently paralleled that of the audiences who stayed away: "Uh-huh. And oral sex isn't adultery." The film, however, supports the claims of its director.

Based on the then-anonymous 1996 novel by political journalist Joe Klein, *Primary Colors* benefits from a smart script by Elaine May, who last worked with Nichols on *The Birdcage*. The film follows the primary campaign of presidential candidate Governor Jack Stanton (John Travolta) through the eyes of his new campaign manager, Henry Burton (Adrian Lester). Henry is the film's focal character and also its conscience. The grandson of a civil rights leader, he wonders about the wisdom and the ethics of uniting with a slick operator like Stanton, but he cannot resist Stanton's blandishments and the possibility that Stanton really believes in the ideals he propounds and really wants to make life better for ordinary Americans. In the opening scene, Howard Ferguson (Paul Guilfoyle), one of Stanton's aides, describes with admiration for Henry the governor's variety of handshakes and how each is calculated to affect the recipient in a different way. From the moment Stanton gives Henry his special two-handed, sincere grip, Henry is hopelessly seduced.

The plot is organized around a series of increasingly serious threats to Stanton's campaign and the responses that Henry and others devise to handle them. The first danger comes from the popularity of rival candidate Governor Ozio, an offscreen character, and the lack of attention the Stanton campaign has received. As Stanton's popularity begins to rise, the Stanton circle must next handle the unexpected report of Stanton's long-forgotten anti-war arrest in 1968. This embarrassment begins a mild controversy, but the real bombshell follows when Susan Stanton's (Emma Thompson) former hairdresser, Cashmere McLeod (Gia Carides), publicly accuses Stanton of having had an affair with her. Henry alertly recognizes some of Stanton's comments from the audio tapes Cashmere McLeod plays before the media as the carefully re-edited remarks originally spoken by Stanton in a cell phone conversation with Henry himself. In an ingenious rebuttal of McLeod's accusations, Stanton campaign worker Daisy Green (Maura Tierney) surprises broadcaster Larry King on the air with a tape of some of his own cell phone conversations re-edited into a compromising context. The Stanton campaign scores a big success.

But fresh political concerns soon jeopardize the momentum from this victory. In Florida, candidate Lawrence Harris (Kevin Cooney) leads in the polls through some negative ads against Stanton. Stanton abandons his previous reluctance to respond in kind by making Florida's voters wonder about Harris's commitment to social security and the nation of Israel. Just as the Stanton campaign seems to be taking charge of the primary race, their real disasters commence. Harris is so upset by Stanton's statements that he suffers a heart attack while talking to Stanton live on a radio call-in show. Harris's wife (Bonnie Bartlett) pledges her husband's convention delegates to new candidate Fred Picker (Larry Hagman), whose sincere calm and outsider status bring him a surge of popularity. At the same time, Henry hears from longtime Stanton friend Willie McCollough (Tommy Hollis) that his teenage daughter is pregnant with Stanton's child. The final third of the film shows Henry and the inner ring of the Stanton clique hustling to protect their candidate while wondering exactly what sort of man they are working for. These two concerns, the dramatic and the ethical, converge for a powerful climax.

The consistent focus on Henry and occasionally on Libby Holden (Kathy Bates), the self-styled "dustbuster" for the Stantons, gives the film its moral emphasis. Both suffer from what campaign strategist Richard Jemmons (Billy Bob Thornton) calls "galloping T.B.," true-believerism. Libby ruthlessly shields Stanton from the mud hurled by others—once to get a confession she even pushes a loaded gun into the groin of the lawyer who masterminded the Cashmere McLeod hoax—but she balks at digging into Fred Picker's mysterious past in search of campaign dirt because she doesn't want to defame another candidate. She and Henry keep hoping that Stanton will prove himself to be better than all the other self-serving politicians. Libby remembers young Jack Stanton during the 1972 McGovern campaign

calming her anger over Nixon's dirty tricks: "I said, we got to get the same capability as the CIA . . . We got to be able to do dirt too." And you said, "No. Our job is to end all that. Our job is to make it clean. Because if it's clean, we win. Because our ideas are better. Do you remember, Jack?" Stanton's response is a tired but gentle look of exasperation: "That was a long time ago."

Primary Colors raises intriguing questions about politics and even about America in general. How much do our compromises on important matters really taint us? In all walks of life, do we hunger for promotion, attention, success, and winning so much that we barter our souls to obtain them? Is an effort to remain true to our ideals simply a failure to recognize the reality of a complex world where most decisions involve choices with unwanted alternatives? The film, of course, frames these issues in the context of politics: Do the ends justify the means if a candidate like Stanton, once elected, serves the interests of the people better than other candidates who would merely have basked in the glory of their power? If our motives are good, how much should we be willing to dirty our hands to get elected?

In the final scene, Jack Stanton tries with an odd mixture of realism and idealism to talk a disillusioned Henry out of leaving the campaign: "You don't think Abraham Lincoln was a whore before he was a president? He had to tell his little stories and smile his shit-eating, back-country grin. He did it all just so he'd get the opportunity one day to stand before the nation and appeal to 'the better angels of our nature.' And that's where the bullshit stops." Anyone interested in *Primary Colors* or in films about politics should read Hendrik Hertzberg's stimulating article in *The New Yorker* (March 23, 1998). Hertzberg sees the realism of Nichols's film as an antidote to the impossible idealism of Frank Capra's *Mr. Smith Goes to Washington* (1939) and the long string of political films it inspired, and he claims that *Primary Colors*, "by a considerable margin, [is] the smartest movie ever made about American politics."

In addition to the merits of the script and the richness of the ethical issues, the film features a number of excellent performances. Travolta's work is more than an echo of Clinton's accent and mannerism. He captures the swirl of pas-

Political wife Susan (Emma Thompson) to weary campaign aides: "You'll survive. We all find a way to survive."

AWARDS AND NOMINATIONS

Broadcast Film Critics Association 1998: Supporting Actress (Kathy Bates)
Screen Actors Guild 1998: Supporting Actress (Kathy Bates)
Academy Awards 1998 Nominations: Supporting Actress (Kathy Bates)

sion at the center of the character that reveals itself in both undisciplined sex and the desire to bring political change for the better. The often-cited Krispy Kreme scene illustrates this common touch by Stanton: as the scandals start during the campaign, the camera pans away from a television set to shoot through the hotel-room window at a doughnut shop where Stanton sits talking to a clerk who has only earned the minimum wage all his life. Henry enters to return Stanton to the campaign crisis at the hotel and is so intent on the issues at hand he hardly notices the clerk. It is Stanton who makes Henry stop and consider a nation made up of many people like the doughnut clerk. Travolta's rich performance highlights all the personal contradictions and shows why a majority of Americans can feel both that Bill Clinton has lied about private sexual matters and that he is doing a good job as president.

Other actors do not attempt as close an impersonation of famous figures. Emma Thompson plays Susan Stanton

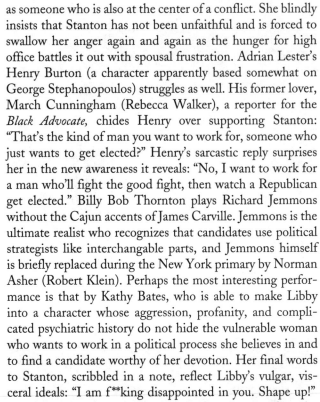

Gov. Jack Stanton: John Travolta
Susan Stanton: Emma Thompson
Richard Jemmons: Billy Bob Thornton
Libby Holden: Kathy Bates
Henry Burton: Adrian Lester
Daisy Green: Maura Tierney
Gov. Fred Picker: Larry Hagman
Mamma Stanton: Diane Ladd
Howard Ferguson: Paul Guilfoyle
Cashmere McLeod: Gia Carides

Origin: USA
Released: 1998
Production: Mike Nichols for Icarus and Mutual Film Company; released by Universal Pictures
Direction: Mike Nichols
Screenplay: Elaine May; based on the novel by Anonymous (Joe Klein)
Cinematography: Michael Ballhaus
Editing: Arthur Schmidt
Music: Ry Cooder
Production design: Bo Welch
Art direction: Tom Duffield
Costumes: Ann Roth
Sound: Chris Newman
MPAA rating: R
Running Time: 143 minutes

as someone who is also at the center of a conflict. She blindly insists that Stanton has not been unfaithful and is forced to swallow her anger again and again as the hunger for high office battles it out with spousal frustration. Adrian Lester's Henry Burton (a character apparently based somewhat on George Stephanopoulos) struggles as well. His former lover, March Cunningham (Rebecca Walker), a reporter for the *Black Advocate*, chides Henry over supporting Stanton: "That's the kind of man you want to work for, someone who just wants to get elected?" Henry's sarcastic reply surprises her in the new awareness it reveals: "No, I want to work for a man who'll fight the good fight, then watch a Republican get elected." Billy Bob Thornton plays Richard Jemmons without the Cajun accents of James Carville. Jemmons is the ultimate realist who recognizes that candidates use political strategists like interchangable parts, and Jemmons himself is briefly replaced during the New York primary by Norman Asher (Robert Klein). Perhaps the most interesting performance is that by Kathy Bates, who is able to make Libby into a character whose aggression, profanity, and complicated psychiatric history do not hide the vulnerable woman who wants to work in a political process she believes in and to find a candidate worthy of her devotion. Her final words to Stanton, scribbled in a note, reflect Libby's vulgar, visceral ideals: "I am f**king disappointed in you. Shape up!"

Primary Colors seems to assume that there are few who have succeeded in life who would not be humbled by a respected voice from their past reminding them of what they once believed in and insisting that they "shape up." Though favorably reviewed by most critics, it is a film whose reputation should only increase in the years ahead.

—*Glenn Hopp*

REVIEWS

Chicago Tribune. March 20, 1998, p. 4.
Detroit News. March 20, 1998, p. D1.
Entertainment Weekly. March 27, 1998, p. 44.
Los Angeles Times. March 20, 1998, p. F1.
New York Times. March 20, 1998, p. E1.
New Yorker. March 23, 1998, p. 86.
People. March 30, 1998, p. 19.
Rolling Stone. April 16, 1998, p. 87.
Sight and Sound. October, 1998, p. 50.
USA Today. March 20, 1998, p. 5E.
Variety. March 16, 1998, p. 63.
Village Voice. March 24, 1998, p. 65.
Washington Post. March 20, 1998, p. B1.

The Prince of Egypt

The power is real. The story is forever. The time is now.—Movie tagline

"Excellent! A family film all ages can enjoy." —Holly McClure, *Orange County Register*

"One of the best movies of the year."—Peter Travers, *Rolling Stone*

"Enchanting! Totally absorbing! Bring the family."—Jeffrey Lyons, *WNBC-TV*

Box Office: $55,106,631

The decision of fledgling studio DreamWorks to develop *The Prince of Egypt* as its first animated feature was an ambitious and bold move. Only recently have other studios made serious, concerted efforts to challenge the preeminence of Walt Disney Pictures' animation division, most notably seen with Fox's release of *Anastasia* in 1997. DreamWorks, of course, had the asset of former Disney mogul Jeffrey Katzenberg behind the reins of the new studio's animation arm (which naturally added another politicized level to the brewing competition between the studios), but choosing a Biblical epic as subject matter for an animated film was not without its risks. For one thing, *The Prince of Egypt*'s cost reportedly rose to $70 million or more, a lot of money to invest in an innovative, untraditional, and unproven kind of animated movie that doesn't quite fit into the same mold as previous Katzenberg-produced hits such as *The Little Mermaid* (1989), *Beauty and the Beast* (1991), or *The Lion King* (1994).

The story of Moses and the liberation of the Israelites from slavery in Egypt is a more somber, more hallowed, and—in many ways—more complex tale than the typical Hollywood animated feature, which tends to be of the "fairy tale" variety. According to Katzenberg, with *The Prince of Egypt*, DreamWorks would be "changing seventy years of perception overnight," creating a film that takes animation in new directions. In this more serious epic-style story, "there are no dancing teapots and no Egyptian statues that suddenly break into song," said Katzenberg. The more mature nature of the film also earned it a PG rating, appropriately and accurately indicating that *The Prince of Egypt* was not primarily intended for an audience of children. Finally, whereas many Disney films benefit from commercial tie-ins (toys and fast-food promotions, for instance), the story of Moses does not

Pharoah Seti (Patrick Stewart): "Sometimes, for the greater good, sacrifices must be made."

quite lend itself to such traditional merchandising. With the impending release of DreamWorks' unconventional animated epic came increased speculation as to what kind of reception the film would have among audiences and critics.

The Prince of Egypt opened to strong boxoffice business, though perhaps not as strong as the studio heads at DreamWorks might have hoped for. Initial reviews were also positive, indicating that the film's producers had a "winner" and a modest hit if not an unqualified blockbuster in the same vein as Disney's biggest successes. As with Fox's *Anastasia* and DreamWorks' own *Antz*, released earlier in 1998 to avoid head-to-head competition with Disney's *A Bug's Life*, the performance of *The Prince of Egypt* suggested that although other studios could produce commercially popular and critically praised animated films of a quality rivaling that of Disney's, there still seems to be something almost "magically" advantageous about having the Disney name attached. Yet, whether the film would have benefited from an association with Walt Disney or from a more traditional approach to animation (which would hardly have seemed appropriate considering the subject matter), *Egypt* as presented by its makers is a dramatically effective, artistically fascinating, and appropriately respectful interpretation of a well-known story.

Like every adaptation of the Biblical story of Moses that has come before, *The Prince of Egypt* takes some liberties with the tale and fills in "gaps" that are not touched upon in the scriptural account. However, in doing so the film maintains a respectful tone and remains faithful to the most crucial elements of the narrative, perhaps even more so than past live-action versions of the story, such as Cecil B. DeMille's classic *The Ten Commandments* (1956). The filmmakers consulted with representatives of every major faith that counts the Exodus tale as an important part of its traditions, and that attitude of respect with which they approached the project shows in the fact that the movie never seems "cartoonish" in a negative sense and carefully avoids the dangers of turning the story into a pretentious melodrama. In fact, one of the primary goals of the film—and one that it fulfills quite nicely—is to portray Moses as a character who is at once likable, genuine, decent, and thoroughly human. This animated Moses is a man with whom the audience can readily identify.

The story begins with the familiar events leading to the baby Moses' adoption into the house of the Pharoah (only in this case his adopted mother appears to be Pharoah's wife rather than his daughter). After Egypt's ruler decrees that all newborn Hebrew males be killed, Moses' mother places her child in a basket, singing to him a lullaby, and sets the basket in the Nile. Her daughter Miriam follows the baby down the river and watches as the Queen (voice of Helen Mirren) takes the child and decides to raise it as her own.

When next we see Moses (voice of Val Kilmer), he is an adventurous, brash, and somewhat mischievous young man who enjoys chariot-racing through the city with his older brother, Rameses (voice of Ralph Fiennes). Seemingly free from worry, he often winds up unintentionally getting his brother into trouble. Rameses usually goes along with his young, impetuous brother, then blames Moses for his trouble when his father, Pharaoh Seti (voice of Patrick Stewart), chastises him. Rameses complains that Moses never receives a harsh word of correction for his wild behavior, but the Pharoah explains to Rameses that, as the heir to the throne, it is he who must learn responsibility and the kind of nobility befitting a king of all Egypt. However, despite the mild rivalry between them, Moses and Rameses develop a close bond, and it is clear they love each other.

Moses first encounters his past when he follows a woman into the streets and inadvertently runs into Miriam (voice of Sandra Bullock), his older sister. She recognizes him and says he has come back to save his people, but Moses thinks she is mad and walks away. As he leaves, Miriam sings the lullaby his mother sang when she gave him up as a baby, which he seems to recognize. Disturbed, he returns to the palace. That night he has a strange, visionary dream that reveals to him his true origins. This dream, which takes the form of "animated" hieroglyphics, is one of the most inventive and interesting sequences in the film, and works as an intriguing and highly creative explanation of the way in which Moses learns that he is actually a Hebrew. When he awakens, Moses finds hieroglyphics on the wall of the palace that verify his dream. Horrified to discover what his father the Pharoah had done to the Hebrews in ordering that their children be killed, Moses faces a painful crisis of discovery. "All I've ever known to be true is a lie," he says. The sorrow and loss of identity that he feels are well portrayed through this sequence of events, and it is easy to feel his horror and empathize with him when he sees an Egyptian beating an old, frail Hebrew slave and rushes to the old man's rescue, accidentally killing the Egyptian in the process.

Realizing that he no longer truly belongs in the house of the Pharaoh, Moses flees, though Rameses tries to stop him and to assure him that the killing of the Egyptian slave-driver can be dismissed since they are royalty. But Moses wants nothing more to do with the Egyptians, for he feels betrayed. He winds up in the land of Midian, where he meets cind becomes a shepherd for Jethro (voice of Danny Glover). He falls in love with Tzipporah (voice of Michelle Pfeiffer), Jethro's daughter, and marries her.

When the voice of God comes to Moses through a burning bush, the moment is a magical one depicted with visual splendor, yet it is also a calm and inspiring one. The voice of God is calm and quiet, yet also confident and authoritative. Though Moses first hears God's bidding with surprise and disbelief, eventually the quest to lead the Hebrews to freedom fills him with purpose, self-confidence, and a self-identity that replaces the one he has lost. Whereas he had lost all faith in the Egyptians to whom he thought he belonged, and although he had lost his sense of the truth, now he has something to believe in. When Tzipporah initially tries to dissuade him from returning to Egypt, Moses tells her, "Look at your life through heaven's eyes." Tzipporah cautions him that, "Moses, you are just one," but he holds on to his confidence and his purpose. Moses' growth from the carefree, impetuous youth to the mature, steadfast man is depicted with an honesty and insight of character that could hardly be rendered better in a live-action film.

The drama at the heart of *The Prince of Egypt* intensifies, of course, when Moses returns to Egypt, where his brother Rameses is now Pharaoh, and demands, "Let my people go!" The conflict between Moses and the Pharaoh achieves a level of tragedy unique to this film in that it is cast in the shadow of rivalry between estranged brothers. Rameses is at first delighted to see his long-lost brother until he discovers his purpose, and then he feels betrayed. This adds an ironic twist to the story, since Moses had justifiably felt betrayed by their "father" Seti—and, in fact, by all Egyptians. Moses still cares for his brother the Pharaoh, and one wonders whether underneath his stubbornness Rameses also retains some love for his Hebrew brother, which at the same time fuels his hateful resentment. To Rameses, the two are still the brothers they were in youth, and the boy who always got him in trouble when they were younger has now returned to challenge his authority.

But the Pharaoh refuses to become "the weak link," determined to be an even stronger ruler than his father was. Thus it is not only a matter of personal betrayal but also of royal pride that feeds his refusal to succumb to Moses' demands, even in the face of the plagues brought upon Egypt.

> Many religious leaders such as Billy Graham and the Reverend Jesse Jackson Sr. were asked for their input while the script was being written.

AWARDS AND NOMINATIONS

Academy Awards 1998: Song ("When You Believe")
Academy Awards 1998 Nominations: Original Musical or Comedy Score

Moses, on the other hand, clearly experiences sorrow that Egypt and his brother must suffer so. "Your stubbornness is bringing this misery on Egypt," he tells Rameses. He even attempts to go to the Pharaoh one last time, before the final plague of death, and warn him, hoping to save him from the loss to come. When the Pharaoh finally relents after the death of his son, Moses returns to his people the Hebrews not only in victory but in pain, dropping to his knees in tears. The compassion and sensitivity displayed here and at other times throughout the movie add to the depth, humanity, and nobility of Moses' character.

While *Egypt* does depart from the style and tone of most animated films, some elements common to animated features survive in this Biblical epic. There are several musical numbers, for instance, all serving to advance the story or to comment on characters, but most of them are more serious than songs in animated films tend to be (with the exception of a number performed by the Pharaoh's magi-

cians). While it is sparse, there is also some comedy in the film, but it tends to be comedy of situation and is never directed at any of the main characters, who are all treated with respect. Rameses' magicians, Hotep (voice of Steve Martin) and Huy (voice of Martin Short), for instance, are played for laughter and are portrayed as foolish tricksters.

To its credit, *The Prince of Egypt* does not shy away from the grim, harsher aspects of the story. The brutal treatment of the Hebrew slaves, for example, is vividly represented, though it is treated less explicitly and more tastefully than it would likely be shown in a live-action version of the film. The complexities of the story and the grim realities of death and suffering set it apart from other animated films. The final plague, in which the firstborn of Egypt are slain, is an effective, moving scene that depicts not only the power of God but also the sad, mournful consequences of Rameses' stubbornness. Yet the dramatic subject matter is not the only area in which the film achieves superb realism. Like the best of Disney, the visual artistry in *The Prince of Egypt* is rich, elaborate, and at times startling. Settings and characters are all given intricate detail. The movement of the characters is fluid and believable, and some of the background settings are breathtakingly realistic. The most spectacular visual effect is the parting of the Red Sea, a fascinating sequence complete with an inspired image of the silhouette of a whale swimming against the wall of water looming over the awestruck Israelites. It is an image one will not soon forget, and it characterizes the film's unique nature: that it achieves the kind of "magic" possible only in wonderful animated movies, yet at the same time it maintains a dramatic depth and realism that is apt to resonate with children and adults alike.

—*David Flanagin*

CREDITS

Moses: Val Kilmer (voice)
Rameses: Ralph Fiennes (voice)
Tzipporah: Michelle Pfeiffer (voice)
Miriam: Sandra Bullock (voice)
Aaron: Jeff Goldblum (voice)
Jethro: Danny Glover (voice)
Pharoah Seti: Patrick Stewart (voice)
The Queen: Helen Mirren (voice)
Hotep: Steve Martin (voice)
Huy: Martin Short (voice)

Origin: USA
Released: 1998
Direction: Brenda Chapman, Steve Hickner, and Simon Wells
Screenplay: Philip LaZebnik
Editing: Nick Fletcher
Music: Hans Simmer
Original songs: Stephen Schwartz
Production design: Darek Gogol
Art direction: Kathy Altieri, Richard Chavez
Visual effects supervision: Don Paul, Dan Philips
Sound: Lon Bender, Wylie Statemen
MPAA rating: PG
Running Time: 97 minutes

REVIEWS

Boxoffice. December, 1998, p. 16.
Detroit Free Press. December 18, 1998, p. D1.
Entertainment Weekly. December 18, 1998, p. 50.
Los Angeles Times. April 6, 1998, p. F1.
New York Times. December 18, 1998, p. E17.
Newsweek. December 14, 1998, p. 80.
People. December 21, 1998, p. 36.
Sight and Sound. January, 1999, p. 54.
Time. April 13, 1998.
Variety. December 14, 1998, p. 130.

The Proposition

One man gave up everything he owned. The other, everything he believed in. *The Proposition*—It would change their lives forever.
—Movie tagline

"It's one of the best movies I have seen in a long time."—Faye Bordy, *Drama-logue*

"Kenneth Branagh is magnificent . . . Madeleine Stowe is luminous."—Alan Silverman, *Hollywood Bytes*

"A real spellbinder."—Bonnie Churchill, *National News Syndicate*

A successful romance is engrossing no matter how preposterous the plot, and to carry us away it needs to convince us, at least for awhile, that we should care about the lovers. *The Proposition*, set in 1930s Boston, while clearly aiming higher than soapy histrionics, is a sorry stew of dynastic drama, intrigue, and formulaic weepie. Flat and unemotional when it needs to be lush and ardent, burdened by a clumsy and impossible plot, the film falters almost immediately and never recovers.

The script is murky and burdened by a rather tortured device—the heroine, Eleanor Barret (Madeleine Stowe), the pampered wife of powerful Boston attorney Arthur (a somber and buttoned-down William Hurt), is a devotee of Virginia Woolf, and herself a "brilliant" and successful writer. In one of the film's more ludicrous scenes (but certainly not the last of such howlers), Eleanor strides down a long hallway in her expensive home, walking through room after exquisite room until at last she arrives, as Father Michael McKinnon's (Kenneth Branagh) respectful voice-over tells us, at a "room of her own." It looks more like a wing of her own, but no matter. It is clear Eleanor is being set up as a tragic heroine, and if you missed that point, there will be plenty of references to "Shakespeare's sister" to come. Feminism is implied, but hardly realized—yet another element thrown in for period color.

Kenneth Branagh, the real center of this film (though he says, without conviction, it is Eleanor's life, her faith, that is his inspiration) is a dashing young Catholic priest who only wants to escape the wealthy and powerful and serve the poor. Of course, his moneyed father intervenes and makes certain his son is "punished" for entering the priesthood by strong-arming the church into assigning McKinnon to a posh Boston parish. He seems determined to avoid contact with the Barrets (think Kennedys) at all costs; but finally pressed into accepting a dinner invitation, he spills his big secret—he's actually a Barret, the son of Arthur's estranged older brother Sam. Michael's mother Julia was Arthur's fiancee, and Sam has always gotten what Arthur wants, including a son. Sam has no scruples about doing business with the Nazis, which has alienated his son, yet another device to give this silly story some substance.

Branagh may look fetching in his Roman collar (as does the lovely Madeleine Stowe in her riding habit), but a handsome couple does not a *Thorn Birds* make. In fact, this film manages to defuse the erotic potential in a love affair between a priest and a lovelorn beauty, usually a thing. Branagh looks absent, as if he were considering his next Shakespearean project, most likely financed by acting jobs like this one (much as Orson Welles and Branagh's model Laurence Olivier did for their productions). Madeleine Stowe has her moments, but she looks distracted too—she's trying hard to make sense of Eleanor's predicament.

She wants a baby, and her husband Arthur can't give her one. His money can buy her the best in surrogate fathers, and scarily, he actually *chooses* Roger (Neal Patrick Harris), a Harvard grad who innocently thinks he's being offered a job with Barret's Beacon Hill firm. While the former Doogie Howser, M.D. feebly attempts a rakish charm, the film has a rather bizarre comedy interlude wherein Eleanor must coax her intimidated surrogate into performing his duty. The sight of the womanly Stowe and the elfin Harris in a bed together is unsettling, but there are even more unlikely plot twists ahead. The always reliable Blythe Danner is on hand as Syril, adopted by the Barret family, once loved by Sam and extravagantly devoted to Arthur, whom she brought up. It is left to Syril to keep directing men to Eleanor's bed, to be Arthur's confidant, and generally to keep the plot afloat.

The film focuses so much on breeding and on Eleanor's cycle (Arthur and Eleanor exchange numerous endearments while discussing the necessity of "trying"—"It's the twelfth day, Arthur!") that the viewer thinks only of procreation, not of any romance. Babymaking is rather a chilly business as contracted by the Barrets, but of course poor Doogie/Roger falls for Eleanor, and becomes a rather hysterical third-wheel in her pregnancy. About the only thing that is realistic about the script is that Eleanor doesn't get pregnant the first time, requiring a return visit of her geeky swain. He threatens to expose the scheme, and Arthur brusquely orders his suave right-hand man Hannibal Thurman (Robert Loggia) to handle it. The next time we see Roger, he's in a plain pine box as Father McKinnon plants him in the parish potter's field. "I never forget *their* faces" he

Eleanor (Madeleine Stowe): "I'd rather starve than sell my soul!"

says piously, pulling back the lid to show Eleanor, who gasps and topples headlong into the newly-dug grave, causing her to miscarry and enraging Arthur. "She had no business being there!" he huffs to the priest, and we are then knee-deep in a murder mystery which will only hold our attention for as long as it takes to plant discord in the idyllic Barret marriage.

As Michael doggedly searches for the truth about Roger's death, he antagonizes Arthur and his superior Father Dryer (Josef Sommer), who warns him repeatedly not to endanger the substantial financial contribution of the Barrets to the parish. In this time of trial, when Eleanor has turned away from her husband in despair, it's Father McKinnon to her emotional rescue. The pair go out riding to try to sort out Eleanor's spiritual crisis, and when the movie finally moves out of the drawing room/bedroom into the great outdoors, you just know something earthshaking is about to happen. A chaste clinch and some guilty murmurings later, nothing has, and any possibility of a grand passion is gone. Not even when Syril manipulates a visit by Father Michael to rescue Eleanor from an occasion of sin on a rainy night with yet another hunky Harvard surrogate does this catch fire. The lovemaking, viewed briefly through a rain-streaked window, with both fully clothed, is a cheat for the very audience it so desperately wants. No bodice-ripping here.

Branagh's self-absorption and scenery-chewing peak when he is told he's being shipped off to Rome and that he is the father of Eleanor's child. He begs to remain, carrying on about his soul—despite what he's saying, you hardly believe he cares for her or the child. He wants to be a priest, you see—all these troublesome Barrets have taken him from his true calling. Branagh finally gets a chance to emote, but the material isn't worth the effort. Eleanor's deathbed provides the other big scene; as she painfully expires, Michael heroically assists the doctor in delivering his twin sons, "breathing life into them" and then claims them both, deciding in a moment to quit the priesthood and be a parent.

A quiet scene by Eleanor's coffin between Syril and Arthur clears up the murder question—Syril poisoned Roger: "I did it for you, Arthur!" Father McKinnon finds he can, after all, leave the boys in Arthur's care and return to his priestly duties. There is one last gothic touch—he insists on burying Eleanor among the poor where she may remain close to him, while Arthur pretends to bury her in the Barret plot. This is the last bargain struck over Eleanor's body, and we see her laid out in another pine box (looking very pre-Raphaelite with flowing curls and flowers) and the audience shrugs or laughs, depending on how this absurd denouement strikes you. Poor stoic Arthur bring his young sons to Father Michael each Sunday for communion; we find out they grow to be "true Barrets—stubborn and proud." He's lost his beloved wife, but he can raise his own great-nephews as his sons. Father McKinnon seems bemused by the workings of fate, and not too unhappy. One of the boys is even named Michael. "Imagine that!" he says with paternal pride.

Despite a good cast and a handsome production, *The Proposition* received scathing reviews, singling out Rick Ramage's screenplay and director Lesli Linka Glatter as largely responsible for the film's excesses. William Hurt's performance alone seemed to garner favorable notices, although all but Branagh make a strong effort to redeem the weak material. As a period melodrama, it may yet find an audience on "The Lifetime Channel" or "Romance Classics"; the director has worked primarily in television and seems to have difficulty finding her way. This story seems best suited to a mini-series, but then again, why bother? *The Thorn Birds* was a success because it was over-the-top and had a tremendous asset in Richard Chamberlain's performance as a tormented priest who chooses ambition before love. Branagh can't fill his cassock, and he shouldn't have tried.

—*Mary Hess*

CREDITS

Father Michael McKinnon: Kenneth Branagh
Eleanor Barret: Madeleine Stowe
Arthur Barret: William Hurt
Roger Martin: Neil Patrick Harris
Hannibal Thurman: Robert Loggia
Father Dryer: Josef Sommer
Syril Danning: Blythe Danner
Dr. Jenkins: David Byrd

Origin: USA
Released: 1998
Production: Ted Field, Diane Nabatoff, and Scott Kroopf for Interscope Communications; released by Polygram Filmed Entertainment
Direction: Lesli Linka Glatter
Screenplay: Rick Ramage
Cinematography: Peter Sova
Editing: Jacqueline Cambas
Music: Stephen Endelman
Production design: David Brisbin
Art direction: Kenneth A. Hardy
Set design: Adam Scher
Costumes: Anna Sheppard
Sound: T. J. O'Mara
MPAA rating: R
Running Time: 114 minutes

REVIEWS

Entertainment Weekly. April 3, 1998, p. 66.
Movieline. May, 1998, p. 46.
New York Times. March 27, 1998, p. F10.
New York Times. March 27, 1998, p. E29.
People. April 6, 1998, p. 20.
Variety. March 16, 1998, p. 69.

Psycho

Check in. Relax. Take a shower.—Movie tagline
The classic story of a boy and his mother.
—Movie tagline
A recreation of the nightmare that started it all
. . .—Movie tagline

"Groundbreaking! Van Sant has assembled a terrific cast."—Ann Hornaday, *Baltimore Sun*

"The ultimate remake! Creepy suspense at its best."—Louis B. Hobson, *Calgary Sun*

"*Psycho* is still crazy after all these years!"—Joanna Connors, *Cleveland Plain Dealer*

"Gripping! Just as gripping a thriller as the classic."—Susan Stark, *Detroit News*

"Scare yourself crazy! It's taut terrifying entertainment."—John Griffin, *Montreal Gazette*

"An artful good-looking remake. It remains the most structurally elegant and sneakily playful of thrillers."—Janet Maslin, *New York Times*

Anne Heche stars as a woman whose stay at the Bates Motel comes to a violent end in the shot-for-shot remake of the 1960 classic *Psycho*.

 Box Office: $20,363,450

One question kept emerging from out of the constant *Psycho*-babble anticipating the release of the 1998 remake of *Psycho* on December 4—"Why?" Why would an obviously gifted director who had made such an original picture as *Good Will Hunting* in 1997 waste his time remaking and slavishly imitating Hitchcock's most famous film? Why had Gus Van Sant suddenly gone psycho? What was he trying to prove? The original left considerable imprint, but that impression would be pulled for anyone who had already seen Hitchcock's classic. The film's shower power would surely be diminished, and there could be no surprises involving Norman's mother for viewers who would know that she is long since dead. The original film was bold in its treatment of utterly psychotic behavior and taboo subjects such as transvestism, and its suggestive violence was certainly revolutionary for the time it was made, but since that time, new thresholds have been crossed in horror films many times over.

To summarize the plot of this film seems as silly and redundant as remaking it. The film opens in Phoenix, Arizona, on December 11, 1998, with the helicopter shot Hitchcock wanted to use but could not because it could not

 "It's a dirty night."—Norman Bates (Vince Vaughn) to Marion Crane (Anne Heche) upon entering his motel on a rainy night.

have been done right back then in 1960. The camera pans the skyline of the city, picks out a building, and zooms into one of the windows, a derivative shot that was used as early as 1928 in King Vidor's *The Crowd*. Inside the window is a cheap hotel room, in which Marion Crane (Anne Heche) has just made love to Sam Loomis (Viggo Mortensen) and is getting ready to go to her job at a real-estate agency. A flamboyant millionaire client, Tom Cassidy (Chad Everett) wants to close a deal with a cash transaction of $400,000 (ten times as much as in the original, to keep up with inflation), and Marion's boss, Mr. Lowery (Rance Howard) asks Marion to take the money to the bank for safekeeping. Marion agrees, but feigns a headache and tells Lowery that after going to the bank, she will be taking the rest of the day off.

Her head filled with thoughts of larceny because a lack of ready cash has somehow impeded her love life, Marion has other plans, however. She goes home, impulsively packs her suitcase, gets in her car and heads for California. Driving through the night, she gets drowsy, pulls off the road, and sleeps in her car, to be awakened the next morning by a highway patrolman (James Remar), who senses that she is behaving suspiciously. He follows her and observes her from a distance as she pulls into a used car lot and trades her car in for a Volvo, paying $4,000 cash from the stolen money. That evening she arrives in the rain at the Bates Motel, conveniently located off the beaten path, and books a room from Norman Bates (Vince

Vaughn), who seems to be having a dispute with his mother in the house on the hill adjacent to the motel, after Norman has offered to make her sandwiches for supper. After supper and a wonderfully disturbed conversation with Norman, Marion decides to return to Phoenix the next day. When she tells Norman her real name, he realizes that she has registered under an assumed name and that perhaps no one knows where she is staying.

The kitchen knife used in the terrifying shower scene is credited as belonging to Hong Kong director John Woo.

After Marion retires to Room No. 1, next to the office, Norman goes to the back room, removes a picture hanging on the wall, and spies on Marion through a hole in the wall while Marion undresses. His voyeurism parallels the original, but in the remake Mister Bates masturbates as he watches Marion. Norman must feel guilty and conflicted, since he knows his mother would not approve of this, and as Marion then takes her shower, a symbolic spiritual cleansing after she has made a moral decision to return the stolen money, she is attacked, apparently by Mrs. Bates, wielding a kitchen knife, and murdered. Norman, apparently, is horrified by what has happened, but cleans up the room and disposes of the body by placing it in the trunk of the Volvo and driving the car into a bog, presumably to protect his mother.

Meanwhile, back in Phoenix, Marion's sister, Lila Crane (Julianne Moore), is alarmed over Marion's strange disappearance and joins forces with a private eye, Milton Arbogast (William H. Macy), hired by the real-estate broker to find her. Abrogast traces her to the Bates Motel, interviews Norman, and asks if he can talk to Mrs. Bates, but Norman will not allow this, for reasons that later become clear. According to Sheriff Chambers (Philip Baker Hall) and his wife (Anne Haney), Mrs. Bates has been dead for several years, but when Abrogast goes into the house to find her, it seems that he is attacked by the knife-wielding Mrs. Bates on the staircase and murdered. Norman disposes of this body in the bog, too.

The mystery is finally solved by Marion's sister and her lover, Sam Loomis, who trace Abrogast to the Bates Motel in search of Marion. Lila Crane discovers the corpse of Mrs. Bates, preserved by her disturbed taxidermist son, who attacks Lila and Loomis but is taken prisoner. At the end, a psychiatrist, Dr. Simon (Robert Forster) explains Norman's disturbance in clinical terms that might have made sense during the 1950s. Mad Norman is seen at the end in custody, speaking in his mother's voice.

This gothic horror story is so bizarre that it strains credulity. Hitchcock's direction made it seem somehow plausible, and Van Sant attempts to work the same magic by careful imitation, claiming that "95% of everything was shot according to the original." Van Sant told David Ansen of *Newsweek* that this was an anti-remake film. "Why do

people take films that are really well done and change the dialogue and change the shots and call it the same movie?" he wanted to know. The changes may be few, but they will be noticeable. The sexual relationship between Marion and Loomis is far more candid in the remake, and Norman's masturbating, despite his name (Master Bates, the pun is as new as Jonathan Swift), could not have been so obviously indicated. Stephen Hunter of the *Washington Post* noted that Van Sant "cranked up the realism about 20 points, but somehow what he achieves for the effort is a larger sense of banality." The point is well taken.

The banality of the remake might have been offset by the novelty of the original. Viewers unfamiliar with the plot would be more likely to be sucked in by it and shocked by its brutal and kinky twists, but without the element of surprise, the plot will be disarmed and disabled. Hitchcock was ingenious enough to get away with a kind of cinematic sleight of hand that would not work for lesser talents. For years Hitchcock was underrated, dismissed as the "master of suspense," a recognized technician capable of making apparently flawless films that were defined by their slickness. Many of his plots are cheesier than they first seem, indulging in psychological fakery, implausible motivations, and unexplained situations. In *Vertigo* (1958), for example, Scottie, the protagonist, is literally left hanging at the end of the film's opening sequence as a result of his phobia. The trick of being Alfred Hitchcock was his skill as the master of manipulation. He was expert at deceiving the audience, which enabled him to carry viewers through all sorts of implausible situations. The closer an imitator comes to making a photocopy of the original, the better the film is likely to be. But, as the *Variety* reviewer noted, the remake seems oddly quaint and old-fashioned.

As a matter of fact, Hitchcock was not above imitating himself. He first made *The Man Who Knew Too Much* in 1934, but that did not stop him from remaking it twenty-two years later in 1956 with Doris Day and Jimmy Stewart. Today, Hitchcock is no longer able to imitate himself, but 1998 offered a bumper crop of Hitchcock imitations. *Dial M For Murder* (1954) was reworked as *A Perfect Murder* (also reviewed in this edition) early in the year, and only a few weeks before the release of Van Sant's *Psycho*, *Rear Window* was remade for television, reshaped for the handicapped actor Christopher Reeve, and in the words of *Washington Post* television critic Tom Shales (November 21), "reconfigured so as to make it a tribute" to the actor's "courage in the face of adversity." Shales protested that remaking Hitchcock has become "perversely fashionable" in Hollywood: the "mere concept" of remaking a classic such as *Rear Window* (1954) Shales considered "cinematic sacrilege." Maybe so, but Van

Sant's remake is still far superior to most of the teen horror vehicles that have clogged the marketplace in 1998. The remake is "new," in that it is shot in color.

Reviews were mixed, though most reviewers registered some level of disappointment over the remake. Ann Hornaday, the eccentric reviewer of the *Baltimore Sun*, claimed that the remake "got all the important stuff right." Stephen Hunter of the *Washington Post* characterized the film as "being drained of genius," however, and Carrie Rickey of the *Philadelphia Inquirer* first quoted the 1960 tag-line, "The picture you must see from the beginning—or not at all," then added this disclaimer about the remake: "The picture

you must see in the original—or not at all." Most reviewers were complimentary about Danny Elfman's reworking of Bernard Herrmann's original score.

At least Van Sant's *Psycho* was more respectful than any remake yet attempted, suggesting that imitation might be the most sincere form of flattery. The film would be sought out by the curious as a sort of novelty feature, but one wonders if that may prove sufficient for Universal Studios to recover its $25 million investment. It is fascinating to watch a ditsy Anne Heche playing Janet Leigh, William H. Macy playing Martin Balsam, Julianne Moore playing Vera Miles, Gus Van Sant playing Alfred Hitchcock (even down to the signature cameo appearance), and to hear Danny Elfman playing Bernard Herrmann's music. But Janet Maslin protested that Vince Vaughn's Norman fell far short of the sensational performance of Anthony Perkins, though Vaughn does manage to bring his own distinctive creepiness to the role. The added masturbation scene did little more than inspire lewd giggles from the audience and arguably violates Hitchcock's sense of taste. The chronology is updated, but not the dialogue. Not all changes were necessarily for the better here, but Van Sant set a very high goal to be imitated. The film is a watchable curiosity.

—*James M. Welsh*

CREDITS

Norman Bates: Vince Vaughn
Marion Crane: Anne Heche
Lila Crane: Julianne Moore
Sam Loomis: Viggo Mortensen
Milton Arbogast: William H. Macy
Dr. Simon: Robert Forster
Sheriff Chambers: Philip Baker Hall

Origin: USA
Released: 1998
Production: Gus Van Sant and Brian Grazer for Imagine Entertainment; released by Universal Pictures
Direction: Gus Van Sant
Screenplay: Joseph Stefano; based on the novel by Robert Bloch
Cinematography: Chris Doyle
Editing: Amy Duddleston
Production design: Tom Foden
Costumes: Beatriz Aruna Pasztor
Art direction: Carlos Barbosa
Music: Danny Elfman; based on the original score by Bernard Herrmann
Sound: Ron Judkins
MPAA rating: R
Running Time: 100 minutes

REVIEWS

Baltimore Sun. December 5, 1998, p. E1.
Detroit News. December 5, 1998, p. C1.
Entertainment Weekly. December 4, 1998, p. 36.
Entertrainment Weekly. December 18, 1998, p. 48.
Movieline. December/January 1999, p. 68.
New York Times. December 5, 1998, p. A15.
New York Times Magazine. November 29, 1998, p. 104.
Newsweek. December 7, 1998 , p. 70.
Newsweek. December 14, 1998, p. 93.
The Philadelphia Inquirer. December 5, 1998, p. D8.
Sight and Sound. February, 1999, p. 36.
Variety. December 7, 1998, p. 53.
Washington Post. December 5, 1998, p. C1.

Quest for Camelot

"An incredible achievement."—Leo Quinones, *The Film Freak*

"Inspiring, hilarious thrill-packed adventure." —Cameron Turner, *Hangin 'n' Hollywood*

"Kids will love it."—Neil Rosen, *NY1 News*

"Comic antics will entertain!"–Leah Rozen, *People*

"Exciting and enchanting. Happily-ever-after entertainment."–Gene Shalit, *Today Show*

Box Office: $22,931,682

Quest for Camelot is Warner Bros.' 1998 effort to create an animated film rivaling those of animation powerhouse Walt Disney. For the past few years almost every major studio has attempted to make significant headway in sharing some of the top-rated glory that has long been enjoyed almost exclusively by Disney. Warner Bros., of course, has been involved in animation for decades, but Bugs Bunny cartoons and features like Snow White and the Seven Dwarfs (1937) or *Beauty and the Beast* (1991) are different breeds of animation. Not until Fox's 1997 release of *Anastasia* did another studio approach Disney's level of aesthetic artistry, technical sophistication, and broad audience appeal (new studio DreamWorks has recently managed to do so again with *Prince of Egypt,* also reviewed in this edition). Disney at its best means colorful, memorable characters, rich, detailed animation, delightful, character-driven musical numbers, and clever storytelling that does not patronize or condescend. The makers of *Quest for Camelot* have strived—perhaps too hard—to include all these elements, in an obvious attempt to create a Warner Bros. "Disney" film. To some extent the effort works, in that *Quest for Camelot* manages to tell a fun, adventurous story that is peopled with some interesting characters, bolstered by regular doses of humor, and touched with some socially positive themes. At the same time, however, the film's desire to duplicate the classic Disney formula ultimately weakens it.

As the title suggests, *Quest for Camelot* is a tale set in the legendary time of King Arthur (voice of Pierce Brosnan).

Two-headed dragon tries to start a fire with two sticks: Cornwall (voice of Don Rickles): "Come on, baby, light my fire . . ." Devon (voice of Eric Idle) : "You know, there's nothing more pathetic than a flame retarded dragon."

Warner Bros. is the first studio to win an Academy Award for an animated short—*Knighty Knight Bugs* in 1958.

The film's opening introduces the main character, a girl named Kayley (adult voice of Jessalyn Gilsig), who is the energetic daughter of Sir Lionel (voice of Gabriel Byrne), an honored knight of the Round Table. Kayley loves hearing about the origins of Camelot and the powerful sword of King Arthur, Excalibur. She is fascinated with her father's life and yearns to be like him. Unfortunately, tragedy strikes when a knight named Sir Ruber (voice of Gary Oldman) betrays Arthur and the Round Table, kills Sir Lionel in an attempt on the king's life, and storms out of Camelot exclaiming that one day Excalibur and the entire realm will be his.

The passage of ten years finds Kayley a young woman longing for a more exciting life. She still identifies with her honored, beloved father, expressing her feelings of connection to him in a song about being "on my father's wings." Seemingly in answer to her yearning for adventure, Camelot is suddenly attacked by an enormous Griffin (voice of Bronson Pinchot) that manages to wrest Excalibur away from King Arthur. The winged creature then soars away from Camelot, meaning to take the sword to the wicked Ruber, but Merlin the magician (voice of John Gielgud) intervenes by sending out a falcon he calls "Silver Wings" to try to stop the Griffin. The bird attacks the Griffin and causes the beast to drop Excalibur. Unfortunately, however, the magical sword drops into the dangerous, living clutches of the Forbidden Forest. The word immediately goes out that the great sword Excalibur has been lost. When Kayley finds out, she wants to set out to find the sword, but her mother, Lady Juliana (voice of Jane Seymour), will not hear of it.

Then, without warning, Sir Ruber himself suddenly appears and takes Juliana hostage, intending to use her in his plan to invade and conquer Camelot. Ruber reveals that he possesses a unique magical potion, which he uses to turn Lady Juliana's workers (and a rooster) into mechanical soldiers. The evil knight threatens to kill Kayley if Juliana does not cooperate with him. The physically adept Kayley, however, escapes her captors and is pursued into the Forbidden Forest, where she encounters a young man who skillfully comes to her rescue and fends off the attackers.

When things calm down a bit, the young man introduces himself as Garrett (voice of Cary Elwes), and shortly thereafter Kayley realizes that he is blind. Garrett, who has clearly learned to cope with his disability quite well, explains to her that he is a hermit, living on his own in the forest. When Kayley tells him that Excalibur has been lost, he declares that he must find it. Kayley asks to go with him, but Garrett insists that he does not need her company. "I stand alone," he sings, and he explains to her that he knows his way around the forest very well. However, despite his protestations (which are actually not that strong) the young woman follows him. Together they set out through the perilous forest to search for Arthur's special sword.

While in the "dragon country" of the forest, the duo comes across a two-headed dragon whose heads are named Devon (voice of Eric Idle) and Cornwall (voice of Don Rickles). Devon and Cornwall do not get along well with each other, and in fact they perform a musical number fantasizing about how wonderful it would be to have only one head. The relatively small dragon (most of the fire-breathing creatures are gargantuan, but Devon and Cornwall are hardly taller than a human) provides most of the comedy in the film. Not only do they frequently throw verbal jabs at each other, they are also very theatrical. As the group travels further into the Forbidden Forest, Kayley learns that Garrett was trained by her father, Sir Lionel. He still holds high regard for the knight, for in many ways he looked at him as his only friend. Lionel describes to Kayley how he lost his sight in an accident. After going blind, he felt he no longer belonged in Camelot, so he disappeared into the forest.

They finally find Excalibur, beating Ruber and his Griffin to the sword, but Garrett refuses to go with Kayley back to Camelot. He tells her that he doesn't "belong in their world," and sadly walks away, thinking about the world he'd left behind many years before. While watching Garrett walk away, Kayley whispers, "But you belong in mine," revealing the love she has developed for him. Saddened that Garrett is not going with her, the young woman heads back toward Camelot, but she is met by Ruber and his mechanical creatures. They take the sword from her, and Ruber uses his magic potion to affix Excalibur to his hand. Kayley is thrown into a wagon with her mother, and the small caravan heads toward the castle.

In the meantime, fortunately for Kayley, Devon and Cornwall hurry back to the Forbidden Forest to tell Garrett what has happened. The young hermit turns around to hurry to Kayley's rescue. Ruber, who has hidden his identity under a black robe, forces Juliana to sit in the front of the wagon so that Arthur will believe the lady is visiting and allow her to enter. Ruber and his soldiers are in fact permitted to enter, but within moments Kayley breaks free and warns everyone that it is a trap. A battle erupts, at which time Garrett returns to add his strength to the defenders of Camelot, and Ruber enters the tower to confront Arthur himself. The evil knight ultimately meets his defeat when Kayley tricks him into driving Excalibur into the great stone from which Arthur first drew the sword many years before as a young man. Excalibur returns to normal and destroys Ruber. At the same

time, the entire realm experiences rejuvenation. Wounds are healed, Ruber's mutant soldiers return to their original forms, and Garrett regains his sight. King Arthur knights Garrett and Kayley out of gratitude for saving Camelot, telling them that they reminded everyone that a "kingdom's strength is based on the strength of the people."

Quest for Camelot has its fun and humorous moments. The plot itself holds quite a bit of potential—the idea of a young woman and a blind man saving King Arthur and the Round Table is original, inventive, and socially inclusive without being preachy—but many elements of the story lack either freshness or originality. Sir Ruber, for instance, is not that memorable as a villain (certainly nothing like the best Disney villains), and one wonders why he should be such a threat to the legendary Arthur. Some scenes, such as the one in which the heroes find the sword with a great stone giant, are simply disappointing because they are not as exciting as they could have been. With more genuine creativity, the story itself could have improved, and that would make the entire film more engaging.

Humor exists throughout the film, as mentioned before, but most of the comedy derives from Devon and Cornwall. The two dragon heads provide some of the best lines in the film. "We're the reasons cousins shouldn't marry," they reply when asked about their size and their two heads. Later, when Garrett tells the dragon to stop singing, Devon responds, "How do you feel about interpretive dance?" Humorous dialogue like this and other dramatic lines throughout the movie (though especially the more sarcastic remarks) are well-written, but the movie tends to fail when it tries to be very sentimental.

Sentimentality tends to be the subject matter for songs in movies like this, and this is one aspect of *Quest for Camelot* that could have been toned down immensely. Obviously, in order to imitate the Disney formula, the makers of the film believed they needed to incorporate musical numbers. In *Quest for Camelot*, the songs themselves are mostly nice, well-written tunes, but the problem is that they appear too often, and frequently they seem completely unnecessary. In fact, *Quest for Camelot* tries so hard to use songs to convey the feelings of the characters that the results often seem sappy or corny. They simply do not seem to fit well into the story, and they are employed to such an extent that character development through regular dialogue sometimes suffers. The film quite possibly would have been much better if the musical numbers were thoroughly excised and replaced

AWARDS AND NOMINATIONS

Academy Awards 1998 Nominations: Song ("The Prayer")

CREDITS

Kayley: Jessalyn Gilsig (voice)
Garrett: Cary Elwes (voice)
Ruber: Gary Oldman (voice)
Devon: Eric Idle (voice)
Cornwall: Don Rickles (voice)
Juliana: Jane Seymour (voice)
King Arthur: Pierce Brosnan (voice)
Griffin: Bronson Pinchot (voice)
Bladebeak: Jaleel White (voice)
Lionel: Gabriel Byrne (voice)
Merlin: John Gielgud (voice)

Origin: USA
Released: 1998
Production: Dalisa Cooper Cohen; released by Warner Bros.
Direction: Frederick Du Chan
Screenplay: Kirk De Micco, William Schifrin, Jacqueline Feather, and David Seidler; based on the novel *The King's Damosel* by Vera Chapman
Editing: Stanford C. Allen
Music: Patrick Doyle
Original Songs: David Foster, Carole Bayer Sager
Production design: Steve Pilcher
Art direction: Carol Kieffer Police, J. Michael Spooner
Animation: Russell Hall
Sound: Alan Robert Murray
MPAA rating: G
Running Time: 85 minutes

with sequences of dialogue. It might not be "Disney-ish" enough, but it would probably benefit this particular story.

Surprisingly (considering the graphic technology available today), the animation in *Quest for Camelot* is not very impressive at all. Clearly the animators attempt to use more detail and color, but movement is not smooth and the objects, landscapes, and characters still do not have the realistic feel that characterizes Disney's animation (even the less-detailed animation). In contrast to the animation, however, the musical score by Patrick Doyle contains some rousing, lively selections and easily qualifies as one of the best aspects of the movie. One might expect to hear a score like this behind a grand-scale, epic, live-action film. Unfortunately, the contrast between the picture on the screen, the musical numbers, and the musical score simply highlights the weaknesses of *Quest for Camelot*. In the future, Warner Bros.—or any other studio—would be wise to try to break new ground in animation than flatter Disney with a rather poor imitation.

—*David Flanagin*

REVIEWS

Chicago Tribune. May 15, 1998, p. 5.
Cinefantastique. June, 1998, pp. 16-17.
Detroit News. May 15, 1998, p. 3D.
Entertainment Weekly. May 22, 1998, p. 48.
New York Times. May 15, 1998, p. E10.
People. May 25, 1998, p. 34.
Sight and Sound. August, 1998, p. 50.
USA Today. May 15, 1998, p. 9E.
Variety. May 5, 1998, p. 58.

A Rat's Tale; Die Story Von Monty Spinneratz

A children's classic in the tradition of
Pinocchio.—Movie tagline

Box Office: $33,768

It can be considered that *A Rat's Tale* is either a throwback to the old-fashioned ways of entertaining children (the use of marionette puppets) or just a cheesy concept (the strings are shown) that can't hold a candle to the new special effects of computer animation. Either way, *A Rat's Tale* has very little entertainment value, for kids or adults.

From an incantation at an altar, where a rat in robes evokes the spirit of life and magic powers, to a Mexican ruin, where a rat on tour is given a couple of shells by a guide with an earnest request to take them to Manhattan, this tale, from the children's book by Tor Seidler, begins. A community of rats, portrayed by the marionette puppets, living under New York City streets, strive to survive an evil exterminator through their own devices and learn that a little magic can help.

The unlikely hero of the story is bashful, and lower-class rodent Monty Mad Rat Jr. who is often harassed by the Pack Rats, a gang of unruly rodents who hang out in the sewers. On one of his walks, Monty encounters rich Isabella Nobel Rat, who lost her ride on the bumper of a taxi. Immediately smitten, he offers to walk her home uptown through a shortcut which gives her a taste of life on the other side of the drains. When they arrive at her fancy home, she's scolded by her mother for spending time in the "gutters with strangers." Monty arrives home to find his visiting aunt from Mexico, Aunt Charlotte, who gives Monty magical shells to paint, since he's an artist.

Meanwhile, Professor Plumpingham (Jerry Stiller) is developing "Rat Away," a potent extermination spray in the Pollution Evolution Labs for nasty boss Lou Dollart (Josef Ostendorf). Mogul Dollart is intent on ridding the city of "those repulsive creatures in the way of progress," despite his wise wife's (Beverly D'Angelo) response, "Rats are very smart. They always find a way."

The creation of the spray has the rats in a panic. A town meeting, organized by Isabella's father and her fiancé, Laurat Ladida, is called to order to discuss the community's options regarding the development of the new lethal spray. Monty is present at the "DemocRATcy" meeting and suggests using his magical shells as a solution to the toxic scourge. Ignoring Monty's input, the rat committee devises a plan to stop Dollart by buying the wharf back from the humans. The rats enlist a marathon fund-raising blitz and stop all other activity to collect the cash. However, stoppage of work flow creates an even bigger problem—by not cleaning the drains, water levels can rise and wash away the rats' homes. Simultaneously, the imminent danger is green "Rat Away" seeping into the sewers as Dollart's crews constantly spray the streets.

With the rat's bad luck situation, Monty places even more faith in his magical shells and goes above the surface to visit his art gallery owner and friend Evelyn Jellybelly (Lauren Hutton) to sell the shells to her. A non-believer at first, she is an instant buyer when the shells break apart and create a beautiful bubble of "post virtual reality." Jellybelly gives Monty a huge sum of money

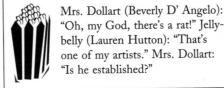

Mrs. Dollart (Beverly D'Angelo): "Oh, my God, there's a rat!" Jellybelly (Lauren Hutton): "That's one of my artists." Mrs. Dollart: "Is he established?"

CREDITS

Evelyn Jellybelly: Lauren Hutton
Mrs. Dollart: Beverly D'Angelo
Prof. Plumpingham: Jerry Stiller
Lou Dollart: Josef Ostendorf
Monty Mad-Rat Jr.: Dee Bradley Baker (voice)
Isabella Noble-Rat: Lynsey Bartilson (voice)
Old Monty: Ray Guth (voice)
Rudi Rake-Rat: Scott MacDonald (voice)
Jean-Paul Canalligator: Donald Arthur (voice)

Origin: Germany
Released: 1998
Production: Hans Peter Clahsen; for Monty Film production; released by Legacy Films
Direction: Michael F. Huse
Screenplay: Werner Morgenrath and Peter Scheerbaum; based on the children's book by Tor Seidler
Cinematography: Piotr Lenar
Editing: Timothy McLeish
Music: Frederic Talgorn
Production design: Austen Spriggs
Set decoration: Chantal Giuliani
Costumes: Eun-Young Kim
Marionette design: Hannelore Marschall-Oehmichen, Jurgen Marschall
Sound: Olav Gross, Josef Porzchen
MPAA rating: G
Running Time: 89 minutes

which will go toward buying the lethal rat poison away from Dollart.

Other antics ensue as Monty, along with Isabella and Cajun pal Jean-Paul Canalligator try to return to their underground dwelling with money in hand. Mean old Dollart is accidentally sprayed with his own rat poison. Through the shells, a port-hole to a mystical place is revealed that houses aloe-vera, the only antidote to the lethal rat spray. Through this lifesaving episode, man and rat soon learn to live together. Truly a fairy tale.

Despite the fifty-year-old tradition of Germany's Augsburger Puppenkiste, marionettes don't work well on the movie screen. Besides the obvious show of strings, the movements are awkward and even two to six-year old kids—who this film is intended for—are accustomed to the sophistication of animation and the Muppets. Director Michael F.

Huse is equally awkward in the movement between the puppets and live action with actors. The script is clumsy, with an odd mixture of a simple plot with complex subplots. This Library of Congress award-winning book might be a preferable choice for the tale. It's worthwhile to see rats in a sympathetic role but their shabby depiction in this film doesn't further their cause.

—*Michelle Banks* and *Roberta Cruger*

REVIEWS

Los Angeles Times. March 20, 1998, p. F12.
New York Times. March 20, 1998, p. E12.
Variety. March 23, 1998, p. 88.

The Real Blonde

"A clever satire! DiCillo's witty observations will make you want to go natural!"—Michael Shapiro, *Glamour*

"Appealing, humorous and heartfelt, this *Blonde* really does have more fun!"—Anne Marie O'Connor, *Mademoiselle*

"DiCillo continues his winning streak in this wickedly observant comedy."—Stephen Farber, *Movieline*

"Edgily funny!"—Janet Maslin, *New York Times*

 Box Office: $247,745

Writer-director Tom DiCillo's *The Real Blonde* is a deliciously wicked farce about sexual illusions and reality. Deftly acted by a splendid ensemble and cannily executed, *The Real Blonde* makes fun of the male preoccupation with artificial standards of beauty. The two men at the center of this film lust for a "real" relationship with an impossibly perfect woman—never quite understanding that you can't package sincerity.

The characters in *The Real Blonde* inhabit a New York City arts subculture where superficiality so dominates relationships that the major activity seems to be superficial conversations

Fashion photographer Blair (Marlo Thomas) checking out some male models: "That's what I want: abs, abs, abs!"

about how superficial life—and other people—are. At the center of this jaded, emotionally bankrupt landscape are Joe Finnigan (Matthew Modine), a chronically unemployed actor who is still holding out for a principled part, and his live-in girlfriend Mary (Catherine Keener), a makeup artist and hairstylist for a fashion photography studio.

Beneath their fashionably smug exteriors, Joe and Mary both are seething with anger at the world they live in. Joe thinks it's unfair that he hasn't landed a plum role just on talent and integrity alone; he resents the success of his friends and stubbornly refuses to compromise his lofty principles to play the success game. He wants his ideal acting job, and he also wants the perfect woman, which in his typically male fantasy is a blonde bombshell who is kinky and aggressive. Those sexual desires serve as a cover for his deep disappointment that Mary doesn't love him enough to let him make love to her without a condom. He criticizes her for not being sufficiently spontaneous sexually.

Mary must put up not only with a deadbeat lover who is always behind on his half of the rent, she also has to tolerate ministering to a self-absorbed airhead fashion model named Sahara (Bridgette Wilson), put up with the whims of the dictatorial photo shoot boss Blair (Marlo Thomas, in her best turn in years), and deal with the crude remarks of a dirty old man who verbally assaults her every day on her way to work. Mary tells her therapist (Buck Henry) that she'd like to punch the guy, but she's afraid to do that. Neither does she want him to "win" by forcing her to take a different route to work. Like Joe, it's a struggle for Mary to retain her self-respect, so when her therapist suggests she take a special self-defense course that deals with everyday verbal abuse, she enrolls.

The first half of the film charges along with a take-no-prisoners satire, making fun of the pretensions of all its characters. While Joe pontificates on how terrible it is that "twenty-five years after women's liberation," magazine fashion ads still portray women as sex objects, Mary buttons a transparent top and asks Joe: "Is this blouse too revealing?" Sahara tells Mary she is "giving up on the whole human race" because "everyone is so superficial" and goes on to discuss the deep spiritual meaning of *The Little Mermaid* and other Disney films. Sahara's real problem is that she is chronically depressed because despite her great looks she can't get a man to stay past the night. The man she met at the bar the previous night tiptoed out the door in the morning without making any promises to return. It turns out the man is Bob (Maxwell Caulfield), Joe's cad of a friend who brags about his sexual conquests but is constantly disappointed when he finds out the blondes he picks up, like Sahara, aren't the "real thing" but bleached imitations.

Joe is confused. On the one hand, he's such a crusader against male exploitation of women that he wants to write a book about the sexual objectification of women in advertising. He even confronts an old man on the street who is bothering a young girl and a man with a gun who is beating his girlfriend. Yet Joe is also envious of Bob's conquests and is influenced by Bob's perception that blonde fashion models are the height of womanhood. Just after Joe rescues the young girl who is being harassed, he passes a stunning blonde sitting in a café and fantasizes that she propositions him on the spot. Joe is a post-feminist man struggling to reconcile competing attitudes about women.

Joe and Bob represent two distinct types of that disappearing species (in New York, anyway) known as the heterosexual male. They work as waiters at museum lunches, and they continuously have to assert that they're not gay like their co-workers. Their boss Ernst (Christopher Lloyd) constantly upbraids Joe for his gauche behavior, but seems to enjoy the instruction a little too much. In DiCillo's world, the struggle to figure out how to be a "real man" is intense. Bob announces to Joe that he's landed a $3,600-a-week job on a soap opera, playing a cad named Dirk Drake—seemingly a perfect fit for him. Joe goes to an audition but tells the casting boss (Kathleen Turner) that he's not interested in doing soaps because "it's fake, it's stupid, it's not even acting." After she berates him, he apologizes and she says she might be able to cast him in a Madonna video.

Joe and Mary have dinner with some old friends. Joe is envious of the man's success as an artist—he's got his work in three galleries now—and Mary is smitten with the couple's baby, hilariously named Cassiopeia. Joe starts an argu-

ment over a popular movie, and in a scene right out of Woody Allen, the whole restaurant begins arguing about the film. Mary is furious about Joe's behavior at the dinner and the audition, and they fight. Many scenes end with the two of them getting undressed, climbing in bed, and fighting. They can't ever seem to get in sync.

The tone of the film remains acerbic as Bob is seduced by his sex-kitten soap co-star, Kelly (Daryl Hannah), who must convince him she's a real blonde by showing him her pubic hair. But the real thing proves too much for Bob to handle. He is impotent with her, and she cuts him down to size both on and off the set. Joe shows up for the Madonna video in a bathing suit that looks like a pair of boxer shorts, gets pushed to the back of the ensemble, and is fired after fighting with a Holocaust-denying assistant director (Steve Buscemi has a small part as the director). But before he is canned, Joe meets Tina (Elizabeth Berkley), the blonde in the café who is Madonna's body double. Joe, who is unbelievably naïve, believes that Madonna herself has called on his answering machine; he later learns that it was a practical joke initiated by Bob.

Mary becomes the star pupil in her self-defense class. The instructor (Denis Leary) tries to tap his students' rage by making degrading remarks to them until they cry, scream, or hit him. Mary's therapist tells Mary she has a problem accepting herself as an attractive woman. She becomes even angrier after the self-defense teacher drives her home and kisses her; when she tells her therapist, he reveals he too is attracted to her.

DiCillo, who succeeded previously with similar material in *Living in Oblivion,* has delicious timing and a sharp ear and eye for the trappings of New York life, but his scenes are too precious by half. By the last half of the film the satire has become tiresome and the plot begins to lurch improbably. What seemed full of promise as a delicately balanced series of illusions tumbles down into a surprisingly pedestrian happy ending in which all the loose ends are neatly knotted up. Joe realizes his dream, discovers who his real love is, and all the characters get their due. The problem is that the resolutions come out of nowhere and seem serendipitous; suddenly things fall into place for no apparent reason.

DiCillo's theme is too obviously that of truth and fakery in relationships and careers, but it is impossible to take anything in this film very seriously. It turns out that when Joe and Bob finally get their real blondes, they don't want them. Besides Blair, Mary is the only woman in the film who is not a blonde or pretending to be one, so she comes to represent authenticity. Joe's favorite lines, which he is constantly practicing, are from the Arthur Miller play, *Death of a Salesman:* "Oh. Everyone around me is so false. I'm constantly lowering my ideals." DiCillo telegraphs all his punches, but until the disappointing ending the spectacle is fairly engrossing.

Modine does his usual bang-up job, bringing just the right mix of sweet-hearted puppy-dog appeal and enor-

CREDITS

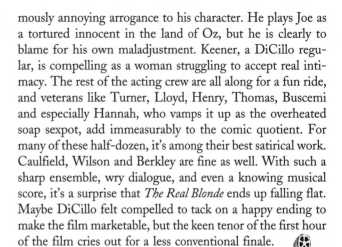

Joe: Matthew Modine
Mary: Catherine Keener
Kelly: Daryl Hannah
Bob: Maxwell Caulfield
Tina: Elizabeth Berkeley
Blair: Marlo Thomas
Sahara: Bridgette Wilson
Dr. Leuter: Buck Henry
Ernst: Christopher Lloyd
Dee Dee Taylor: Kathleen Turner
Doug: Denis Leary

Origin: USA
Released: 1997
Production: Marcus Viscidi and Tom Rosenberg for Lakeshore Entertainment; released by Paramount Pictures
Direction: Tom DiCillo
Screenplay: Tom DiCillo
Cinematography: Frank Prinzi
Editing: Camilla Toniolo
Music: Jim Farmer
Production design: Christopher A. Nowak
Costumes: Jennifer Von Mayrhauser
Sound: Tom Mather, Matthew Price
MPAA rating: R
Running Time: 107 minutes

mously annoying arrogance to his character. He plays Joe as a tortured innocent in the land of Oz, but he is clearly to blame for his own maladjustment. Keener, a DiCillo regular, is compelling as a woman struggling to accept real intimacy. The rest of the acting crew are all along for a fun ride, and veterans like Turner, Lloyd, Henry, Thomas, Buscemi and especially Hannah, who vamps it up as the overheated soap sexpot, add immeasurably to the comic quotient. For many of these half-dozen, it's among their best satirical work. Caulfield, Wilson and Berkley are fine as well. With such a sharp ensemble, wry dialogue, and even a knowing musical score, it's a surprise that *The Real Blonde* ends up falling flat. Maybe DiCillo felt compelled to tack on a happy ending to make the film marketable, but the keen tenor of the first hour of the film cries out for a less conventional finale.

—*Michael Betzold*

REVIEWS

Boxoffice. March, 1998, p. 53.
Entertainment Weekly. March 6, 1998, p. 56.
Los Angeles Times. February 27, 1998, p. F8.
New York Times. February 27, 1998, p. E10.
People. March 9, 1998, p. 21.
Rolling Stone. March 19, 1998, p. 72.
Sight and Sound. June, 1998, p. 52.
Variety. September 29, 1997, p. 61.
Washington Post. March 13, 1998, p. C7.

The Red Violin; Le Violon Rouge

 Box Office: $1,145,646

Although it was one of the most critically acclaimed Canadian films of 1998, *The Red Violin*, in the final analysis, seems to be missing something. Of course, this sense of unease may just be what makes it a completely *Canadian* art film. Indeed, it has all the makings of a American-style, Miramaxy kind of film: a multinational flavor with occasional forays into exoticism, lavishly recreated historical sequences, serious moral purpose, and just a little bit of star power (Samuel L. Jackson has a major role). But it defies these conventions (and it seems fair to say that the "Miramaxy" art film now has a reasonably identifiable set of conventions) in surprising ways: its performances are flat, its narrative is less than straightforward, sometimes diffi-

cult to follow and often very slow, and *The Red Violin*'s climax is distinctively anti-climactic. And yet, these violations are what makes the film a much more interesting work than, say, that paradigmatic Miramax art film, *The English Patient* (itself based on a beloved Canadian novel). It sets you up for a certain kind of easy payoff that it never delivers: it's a pleasant surprise to discover that this isn't as pleasant a film as it at first seems.

The film is directed by François Girard and written by Girard and Don McKellar (who also plays Jackson's assistant). This is also the team who directed and co-wrote the 1995 film *32 Short Films About Glenn Gould,* and these two films are similar in more ways than their common interest in musical subjects. Girard is an intensely visual director, always creating a specifically cinematic equivalent of his musical subjects with visuals that are just as rich and multi-layered as the symphonies that often give his stories their base. Further, he and McKellar have done a great deal to stretch the possibilities of the narrative film: both *The Red Violin* and *Glenn Gould* contain just enough narrative to keep an audience interested at the same time that they freely transgress the limitations that narrative imposes. Girard's films ride a fine line between the conventional and the highly aestheticized, sometimes skillfully avoiding and sometimes intentionally falling into the traps that each one of these cinematic modes can set.

The narrative follows the path of a priceless violin from 17th century Italy, where it is made in the studio of a master, up to the present day, when it is auctioned off at a prestigious Montréal auction house. Several owners of the violin have a representative at that auction (sometimes many generations removed) and it becomes very clear very quickly that it belongs, truly, to nobody. Although the auction suggests that it will find a final owner, there is a plan afoot to keep that from happening, to protect the violin's wandering spirit. At the conclusion of each story about one owner of the violin, the film moves back to the present day, focusing either on the auction itself or the process of discovering and restoring the violin, undertaken by art expert Charles Morritz, played by Jackson. He becomes increasingly obsessed with understanding the instrument, and develops a very deep, spiritual relationship with it, one that stands in contrast to the purely scientific awe experienced by his assistant Evan (McKellar) or the intense financial interest that the auction house has in it (the dignified but slightly slimy auctioneer is played by Colm Feore, who played Glenn Gould in Girard's earlier film).

The Red Violin is marked by a tension between the linear and the elliptical, which is perhaps the first signal that something is awry with the film as a whole. Each story about an individual owner is a very straightforward mini-narrative, very clearly showing how the violin came into someone's possession, what it meant in their lives, and how it came to leave them. They are all told with the precision and visual attention of a high-budget costume drama: this is especially true of the sequences in Italy, where the violin is born, and in Germany, where it a young boy in a orphanage/monastery/school learns to play it. The first segment features noblemen and women galore, each in frilly, painstakingly rendered period dress; the second one features a gorgeous monastery, intense-looking monks, and an angelic boy's choir that every one of the orphans under the monk's care has to belong to. Both sequences also feature some high melodrama: the violin maker's wife has a stillborn child and then dies in childbirth, and the kid in the monastery orphanage/school sees the violin as a means of at last expressing himself. This kind of easy, lush pleasure is much harder to get out of the contemporary sequences, however,

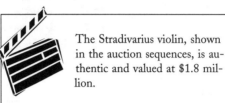

The Stradivarius violin, shown in the auction sequences, is authentic and valued at $1.8 million.

which jump around a great deal (the film's very first shots turn out to be the very last part of the narrative as a whole) and end up advancing a narrative so simple that it hardly seems worth all the confusion.

This split between the straightforward and the impressionistic makes the film hard to follow in places, but it also draws your attention to various important narrative elements that might otherwise go unnoticed, thereby making parts of the film actually *clearer* than would be possible with a completely linear narrative. There are parts of the storyline where Jackson is undertaking the restoration that don't contribute to any narrative momentum, but which emphasize very specific elements of his personality. His interactions with the staff at the hotel where he's staying are rendered in great detail, and so are his ongoing, unsuccessful attempts to speak with his wife. These nonsequiturs, some of which are difficult to place in the film's overall chronology, make the film's conclusion seem entirely logical, indeed the only course of action that this character would logically take. Similarly, the stories of each of the violin's owners are evoked in chronological order, but the jump forward to reveal their modern-day surrogates happens in the auction room, where time is essentially frozen. Girard repeats the same few minutes in the auction over and over again, each time showing us a different person in the room. This makes the film itself seem a little dull and pedantic, but it also shows that the violin could never stay with any of these people. The conclusion, when the violin makes its escape, seems entirely logical given how utterly different this magical instrument is from a space like the auction, which we come to know as so locked into a pre-written history.

Despite the presence of experienced, acclaimed actors, the performances in *The Red Violin* are marked by a understated, often flat quality. This is most noticeable in Jackson's case, since he comes with a reputation as such an intense, forceful actor. There are moments in the film where he lets this side of himself show, such as when he rages at a hotel clerk who doesn't realize how seriously he takes his work. Most of his performance, however, is more brooding and restrained, and there's something about the way that Jackson plays this that makes it feel awkward. The restraint and seriousness that he showed in films like *Eve's Bayou* is present here, but his acting is quieted down so much that it feels a little forced. Much the same could be said for Don McKellar, a Canadian actor well known for his flatness and who is even less expressive here than he's been on other films (like *Highway 61* or *Last Night*).

What's important to understand about this narrative eccentricity and performative flatness is that it's not a problem: indeed, it ends up being the film's salvation. What makes *The Red Violin* more than your run-of-the-mill costume drama is the way that it just doesn't quite work, the way that it resists the easy comforts that the costume drama provides. You could say that this awkwardness is what makes

CREDITS

Charles Morritz: Samuel L. Jackson
Evan Williams: Don McKellar
Nicolo Bussotti: Carlo Cecchi
Anna Bussotti: Irene Grazioli
Frederick Pope: Jason Flemyng
Victoria Byrd: Greta Scacchi
Georges Poussin: Jean-Luc Bideau
Kaspar Weiss: Christoph Koncz
Xiang Pei: Sylvia Chang
Chou Yuan: Liu Zi Feng
Auctioneer: Colm Feore
Production design: Francois Seguin
Costumes: Renee April
Sound: Claude La Haye, Marcel Pothier, Hans Peter Strobl
MPAA rating: Unrated
Running Time: 131 minutes

Origin: Canada, Italy
Released: 1998
Production: Niv Fichman for Rhombus Media, Mikado, Sidecar Films; released by New Line International
Direction: Francois Girard
Screenplay: Don McKellar and Francois Girard
Cinematography: Alain Dostie
Editing: Gaetan Huot
Music: John Corigliano
Solo violin: Joshua Bell

it so very Canadian a film, and while that statement runs the risk of indulging in stereotypes, there's something to it. So much of costume drama is, keep in mind, based on a bleary-eyed nostalgia. The history that these films seem to be longing for is much more present in the everyday life of Canada, with its continued ties to the British monarchy, than it is in the historical United States. As a result, there is a much greater awareness in Canada of the essential falseness of this nostalgia, even though many Canadians are just as drawn to it as Americans. This double bind (we love the stuff but at least we know it's kind of silly) ends up creating some very odd films, and *The Red Violin* is a good example of just such a film. Girard never seems entirely sure of himself and never lets his actors become fully confident either, but he's still drawn to forms that demand such confidence. What emerges is a highly self-conscious mish-mash: *The Red Violin* can't quite deliver the goods, but at least Girard knows that those goods are a little bit damaged anyway. By denying us fluid dialogue, a simple narrative or engaging performances, Girard makes us look elsewhere for pleasure and this film, and its gorgeous visuals and occasional moments of lyricism are there in the wings, waiting for a patient viewer to partake of them. This is a problematic film, but its problems can tell us a lot about what it is we expect from a film and what those expectations too often force us to exclude from our cinemagoing.

—*Jerry White*

REVIEWS

eye weekly. November 12, 1998.
New York Times. May 25, 1997, p. AR9.
Variety. September 7, 1998, p. 74.

Regeneration

Between duty and destiny, loyalty and love, lies the road to *Regeneration*—Movie tagline

"Stunning!"—*The Scotsman*

"Dazzling! A triumph!"—*Toronto Star*

While the war film (as a genre) has endured several peaks and valleys, it has long remained a staple and trump card when original ideas were on the wane. Nary a skirmish or prolonged entanglement during man's history has gone untouched by cinematic storytellers. From the prehistoric era to the Romans, through the Crusades, the many assorted Revolutions and Civil Wars all the way up to the Gulf War of the early 1990s, the man vs. man conflict has provided not only Hollywood but filmmakers the world over with the ideal setting. While the "police actions" that took place in Korea and Vietnam received their fair share of attention, the films that told their tales carried a palpable level of bile, disdain and regret. Perceived largely as defeats, they took place at a time when filmmakers could take more risks than their predecessors.

Films centering on World War II offered propaganda of a different sort. Having won the greatest of all wars, America began to experience unprecedented social, economic and (to a much lesser degree) artistic expansion. Having the blessing of ending smack dab in the middle of its "Golden Era," Hollywood began championing the WWII victory with film after film extolling the seemingly endless stream of feel-good stories (both real and made-up) that was largely one long, non-stop exercise in self-congratulatory back-slapping. There are over nine hundred, that's right, nine hundred different films about World War II now available on home video. How many others that have been lost due to deterioration or neglect is anyone's guess.

One of the reasons 1998's *Saving Private Ryan* (reviewed in this edition) makes such an lasting impact is in the way it is presented. It took the never-say-die heroic grandeur of WWII and tinted it with the this-is-wrong, why-are-we-here, self-doubt of Vietnam. It's unlikely that you'd be able to find anything resembling the carnage and devastation found in *Ryan* contained in any of those other nine hundred efforts. For the first time, the real Hell on Earth of the 1940s was laid out for us in gruesome, unflinching detail. The physical destruction and mental anguish were clear, the psychological fallout, a little less so.

There was another film released in 1998 that talked about war and, like the armed conflict it discusses was for the most part, ignored. World War I, not having the luxury of throngs of motion picture archivists to relive its details upon completion, is a war few living people can recall and one even fewer can relate to. Bridging the collective gap between the Civil War and WWII (for Americans anyway), it is the Forgotten War. Fewer than 100 films about it can be found on video and, by and large, these are non-essential works. However, if there is any justice, Gillies MacKinnon's *Regeneration* will get another chance on video to move people in the same throttling manner *Ryan* does. Without pretense or pomposity, it examines the crippling psychological fallout of war as no other film has ever done.

The movie begins with an aerial shot of dead and dying soldiers whose grayish, soiled uniforms are indistinguishable from the scorched Earth on which they lie. Director of photography Glen MacPherson's opening pan sets the visual tone for the remainder of the film—dark, murky, shivering tones that are a mirror image of the Scottish landscape that is its backdrop. The sun rarely shines at Craiglockhart psychiatric hospital; dread, displacement and helplessness permeate its halls. Just like the war from which it offers temporary shelter. However, the shelter only protects its patients from bullets and bombs. The confrontation soldiers must face inside the hospital walls is with themselves. Craiglockhart treats men suffering from what was labeled as "shell shock," which later evolved into "battle fatigue," then, ultimately, the politically correct "post-traumatic stress disorder."

Siegfried Sassoon (James Wilby): "Now they can explain away my protest—just another loony."

As Wilfred Owen (Stuart Bunce) makes his way through the woods towards the hospital, he notices dead woodland creatures swinging from the limbs of trees. They have all been hanged. As he gets farther up the plank walkway, he encounters a naked man huddled in a clearing with more animal corpses circling him. He is ripping his own flesh with the teeth of a dead rodent. MacKinnon wastes no time in getting to his point—sending men into battle who have neither the talent, need or desire to indiscriminately take the lives of other men—will result in partial or complete mental collapse. Whether it be under the guise of patriotism, the thwarting of imperial aggression or to claim petty amounts of often worthless real estate, the results are the same. From the stone age through the computer age, the single factor that appoints victory or defeat lies in one side's ability to slaughter more people than the other side. We may think we have evolved, become more diplomatic, humane and rational but the bottom line is that man inevitably reverts back to the basic, barbaric law of the jungle—to kill or be killed—in order to get his way.

Shortly after Owen returns the lost man to Craiglockhart, we meet the three principals of the story. William Rivers (Jonathan Price), a soft-spoken psychiatrist, Billy Prior (Jonny Lee Miller), who suffers from mutism, and Siegfried Sassoon (James Wilby), a completely rational man; so proficiently fearless at combat and killing, his underlings call him "Mad Jack." Sassoon has suddenly gone from being a killing machine to complete pacifist, sighting that the objective has changed from the defense of oppression to aggressive conquest. Handsome, well-spoken, a gifted writer and orator, Sassoon has laid down his arms and thrown away his military cross. This highly irregular change in attitude leads his superiors to think that he might have snapped, or worse, changed his mind. They would rather sacrifice the prototypical perfect soldier and chalk it up to fatigue than have scores of civilians catch wind of and perhaps rally around an anti-war protest. MacKinnon wants us to know that not only did anti-war sentiment not start in the Vietnam era, it was often spearheaded by the most sane people of the time. With Sassoon, MacKinnon recalls the Yosarian character from author Joseph Heller's novel (later a Mike Nichols directed film) *Catch-22*. Finding an efficient soldier who can carry out his tasks while remaining neutral from a moral standpoint is a tall order. The last things his superiors want to have happen is letting him develop a conscience or to let his killer instincts slip away. Whether his tenure be complete or not.

Rivers is called on by higher-ups to, not declare whether Sassoon is insane, but rather to convince him that his position is wrong. Rather than having a distinguished soldier question the direction of the war in the House of Commons, the government would rather put him in a position of questioning his own priorities. Idly languish in a hospital full of crazies or do the job for which he is most suited. From the moment they meet, it's clear that Rivers and Sassoon are on the same page. Rivers questions Sassoon, hoping to find a chink in his armor but can find none. He not only likes and respects him but also starts to admire his modest courage and forthright demeanor. The first meeting between Rivers and Prior is more contentious. Nowhere near as balanced or assured as Sassoon, Prior's inability or, as Rivers sees it, refusal to speak, is a result of neurosis. He is a man who is truly in need of psychiatric treatment. Within days, Prior regains his speech and immediately escalates the friction between himself and Rivers. Unlike Sassoon, Prior's leadership abilities do not come so naturally; it takes a marked effort. The war whittles away at his soul. He cannot perform with the same random precision as Sassoon, although he tries with everything that is in him. For Sassoon, soldiering is mere work, for Prior, it is an exhilarating, albeit belabored endeavor.

Author Pat Barker's WWI trilogy consists of : *Regeneration* (1992), *The Eye In the Door* (1994) and *The Ghost Road* (1996).

At various points throughout the film, other methods of treatment by other doctors on other soldiers are shown. One weary conscript is given the charge of marching all-too-eager grade-school students in order to help him get back his confidence. Another group builds model sailboats. In one of the more disturbing vignettes, a ruthless doctor resorts to torture with electrical devices in order to force a man afflicted with mutism to speak. While one extreme of these therapies is sadly elementary and the other sadistically inhumane, MacKinnon shows us that Rivers' methods, simple dialogue and basic conversation between doctor and patient gets more lasting results.

While Rivers notes their progress and considers possible solutions to their problems, Prior and Sassoon establish personal relationships with other newfound friends. Owen, as we discover, is a budding poet and a big fan of Sassoon's. After getting Sassoon's autograph on two of his books, Owen and Sassoon develop a quick spiritual rapport. In Owen, Sassoon sees an impressionable, talented young man who looks to him for guidance. Somewhat selfishly, Sassoon implores his admirer to direct his energies into crafting works devoted exclusively to slamming the war effort. By film's end, Owens' poetry, which he likens to spiritual exorcism, has matured and taken on the characteristics of *Leaves of Grass* by Walt Whitman and *A Farewell to Arms* by Ernest Hemingway— two other immensely gifted writers who took horrific subject matter and managed to lend it a certain winsome, romantic allure.

Prior, growing more impatient and frustrated by the minute with his detainment, decides to visit a local watering hole and falls hard for the beautiful Sarah (Tanya Allen), a local girl who works at a munitions factory near the hospital. Because she calls it "a loony bin," he wishes to keep his stay there a secret. Prior, desperate for relief from Rivers' probing and longing for the warmth of the human touch and Sarah, who recently lost a boyfriend in battle, soon become inseparable.

While *Regeneration*'s parallel stories of Prior and Sassoon are ostensibly the foundation of the first half, it is the combination of their plights that soon begin to take an effect on Rivers, which dominates the second. As he gets further and further into his analysis of the two men, he begins to lose objectivity, starts seeing things with their perspective and actually begins to externalize their symptoms. A man without family or friends—with only his career as his connection with the rest of the world—Rivers sees it all slowly being taken away. It makes quite an impression. What screenwriter Allan Scott (working from the novel by Pat Barker) is driving home, is that even individuals lucky enough to elude actual fighting can still suffer the aftershocks of the battle; that the destructive powers of war can be felt, often in greater degrees, by people who have never experienced it. In curing (some might say "cure" is the wrong word) the young men, Rivers has assumed the position of

CREDITS

Dr. William Rivers: Jonathan Pryce
Siegfried Sassoon: James Wilby
Billy Prior: Jonny Lee Miller
Wilfred Owen: Stuart Bunce
Sarah: Tanya Allen
Robert Graves: Dougray Scott
Dr. Bryce: David Hayman
Dr. Yealland: John Neville

Origin: Canada, Great Britain
Released: 1997
Production: Allan Scott and Peter R. Simpson; released by Alliance Communications
Direction: Gillies MacKinnon
Screenplay: Allan Scott; based on the novel by Pat Barker
Cinematography: Glen MacPherson
Editing: Pia Di Ciaula
Music: Mychael Danna
Production design: Andy Harris
Art direction: John Frankish
Costumes: Kate Carin
Sound: Louis Kramer
MPAA rating: Unrated
Running Time: 113 minutes

conduit, a magnet for their pain, their guilt, their confusion and defiance. He will be the supreme victim in the long run, the one who will suffer the non-physical "slings and arrows" with the greatest pain. Pryce, a veteran of the stage, was the perfect choice for Rivers. His character's austere, seemingly impenetrable, upper-crust demeanor is slowly chipped away, revealing that deep-down, no matter how brave a face or stiff a lip offered, even the most mentally sturdy will crumble and be taken as a prisoner of war.

The efforts of Barker, Scott, MacPherson and MacKinnon and their magnificent casts' bottom line message —dying a horrible death in war might actually be preferable to surviving and tallying the pointless losses. *Regeneration* is not so much an anti-war film as it is a study in what is not seen after the smoke clears. Too many films lead us to believe that to the victors go only the spoils. *Regeneration* digs deeper into our core and blurs the fragile line between victory and defeat. The survivors are the ones who should feel guilty. In war, there are no winners or losers. Only victims.

—*J. M. Clark*

REVIEWS

Los Angeles Times. August 14, 1998, p. F8.
New York Times. August 14, 1998, p. E10.
San Francisco Chronicle. August 21, 1998, p. C3.
San Francisco Examiner. August 21, 1998, p. C7.
Sight and Sound. December, 1997, p. 52.
Variety. August 25, 1997, p. 76.
Village Voice. August 18, 1998, p. 112.

The Replacement Killers

"Chow Yun-Fat ignites the screen!"—*American Urban Radio Network*

"It will blow you away!"—*Detroit News*

"A sleek piece of filmmaking."—*New York Times*

Box Office: $19,204,929

Chow Yun-Fat and Mira Sorvino team up to combat an avenging Chinese mob in the crime thriller *The Replacement Killers.*

Hong Kong action superstar Chow Yun-Fat makes his English-speaking debut in Antoine Fuqua's *The Replacement Killers,* which attempts to bring the Hong Kong action genre to America. Chow Yun-Fat has starred in some of the most notable Hong Kong actioners, like *A Better Tomorrow* (1986) and *Hard-Boiled* (1992), under the direction of John Woo, who is one of the executive producers of *The Replacement Killers.* Chow's good looks and charisma have made him an icon of the genre, but his breakthrough in America may be a challenge. While *The Replacement Killers* is fast-paced and has lots of action, Ken Sanzel's script is thin and the characters very underdeveloped. The film has the very basic plot of a hit man who has turned his back on a job and must flee for his safety.

Chow Yun-Fat plays John Lee. As the film opens, it is night, and John is walking through a nightclub on his way to gunning down a mobster and his henchmen. We first see John from the back; he is the essence of cool as he strides through the crowded dance floor to do his job. The setting is stylish and the action fast and bloody—a precursor to many of the scenes in the movie.

His next assignment is to kill the seven-year-old son of a policeman, Detective Stan Zedkov (Michael Rooker), who killed the son of a big-time mobster, Terence Wei (Kenneth Tsang), in the line of duty and even had the nerve to attend the funeral. John prepares for the job, but once he sees Zedkov playing with his son, he cannot bring himself to complete the assignment and knows he will be a marked man and must flee the country. When John is aiming his rifle, we think the policeman is the target, and only later do we learn that the little boy is Wei's intended victim. The script thus exhibits a bit of cleverness by initially withholding this information from the audience.

John needs a passport to get out and is directed to a forger named Meg Coburn (Mira Sorvino), who can provide the false document. Sorvino's Meg is a tough cookie, tarted up in red lipstick and sexy undergarments, sporting tattoos, and wearing a razor blade for a necklace. As she is

Mira Sorvino majored in Chinese studies at Harvard University.

processing his work, assassins arrive and shoot her place up in an extended gun battle, in which John and Meg are victorious.

There are numerous such shootouts throughout *The Replacement Killers*—in a variety of locations like a car wash, a pinball arcade, and a movie theater. The bullets fly and blood spurts, but, after a while, the action just becomes so much sound and fury. Because there is such a bombardment of violence and the henchmen are fairly anonymous, none of it really matters. We never feel any real sense of danger for John and Meg, and the battles themselves, while often stylish in their use of slow motion, are not cleverly constructed, as in a John Woo film.

Instead of a story in which each event builds on the last, *The Replacement Killers* has a very episodic structure. The bad guys pursue John and Meg, and they move from confrontation to confrontation. The movie also suffers from script implausibilities. The henchmen surprise John and Meg in the car wash, for example, but instead of merely killing them (as the assassins tried to do in Meg's office), they handcuff Meg and punch John, thus giving him time to fight back and engage in a protracted gun battle.

A veteran of commercials and music videos, Fuqua makes his feature film debut with *The Replacement Killers,* and his inexperience in developing narrative drive shows in the way he structures scenes. The rapid-style editing, a carryover from the world of music videos, for example, creates a sense of frenzy but little time for the buildup of suspense within a shootout. Because the plot itself is paper-thin, the action scenes should be more ingenious to hold our interest, but they are fairly routine shoot-'em-up set pieces. Once John and Meg have dispatched the killers, replacements are brought in to kill Zedkov's son. The assassins' entrance is presented in slow motion in a heavy-handed attempt to give them a gravity they have not earned.

The lead characters are fairly thin. The hit man with a conscience and the streetwise chick who ends up having a heart of gold are stereotypes. John and Meg predictably move from hostility and distrust to mutual respect and even a glimmer of love at the end. They share a few tender moments, like the scene in which John explains to Meg his development of conscience. He had to perform three jobs to ensure the safety of his mother and sister in China—the first two assassinations were easy because the targets were criminals, but he could not kill a little boy.

The Replacement Killers is Sorvino's second action movie in a row (after 1997's science-fiction film, *Mimic*), and she acquits herself nicely, although comedy seems to be her true forte. When Zedkov questions Meg after she is taken into custody and runs down her long arrest record dating back to her teens, she tartly replies, "I've always considered myself a feminist pioneer." Later, when she runs into a thug acquaintance and John asks if he is her boyfriend, she wryly answers, "I try to stick to my own species." Such wisecracks give Meg an edge; indeed, the movie could have used more tongue-in-cheek humor to round out the lead characters. Sorvino has proven in *Mighty Aphrodite* (1995) and *Romy and Michele's High School Reunion* (1997) that she is an adept comedian, so it is too bad she was not given the opportunity to develop more fully this aspect of her character.

As a villain, Mr. Wei is fairly one-dimensional and given to making stereotypical pronouncements like "Don't confuse luck with skill" when a henchman tries to explain why John got away. A more complex back story between Mr. Wei and John would have given the film depth and, on a basic level, a greater sense of coherence.

The climactic moral quandary involves John's decision (made with Meg's prodding) to try to save Zedkov's son, even though John is also concerned about getting back to China to look after his own family, who are in hiding from Wei's forces. John learns the location of the proposed killing of the boy, and this leads to the best shootout in the film. The assassins try to ambush the boy in a movie theater where he is watching a Mr. Magoo cartoon with his father, and John saves the boy by leaping over several rows of seats and taking the bullet himself. He is injured but heals himself in the Buddhist temple he regularly visits.

In the film's showdown, an ambush of Wei and his closest henchmen, John comes in with both guns blazing in true Chow Yun-Fat style. Wei and John draw their guns on each other, and John finally kills Wei at point-blank range. While this confrontation should be climactic, by this time in the movie it feels like just one more shootout. The police arrive, and, after a brief Mexican standoff, Zedkov lets John and Meg go because he is grateful John earlier saved his son. More could have been made of this relationship—the assassin and the policeman who finally come to respect each other—but once again weak character development makes this a lost opportunity. In the last scene, Meg bids farewell to John at the airport.

Chow Yun-Fat is a charismatic actor (the camera loves close-ups of his face, which is very expressive), but the pedestrian plot of *The Replacement Killers* does not let him shine. He recently learned English to play this role, and his somewhat stilted delivery betrays his lack of familiarity with the language. However, because he is playing a stoic hit man, his command of the language is not a big problem.

CREDITS

John Lee: Chow Yun-Fat
Meg Coburn: Mira Sorvino
Stan Zedkov: Michael Rooker
Michael Kogan: Jurgen Prochnow
Terence Wei: Kenneth Tsang
Ryker: Til Schweiger
Collins: Danny Trejo
Loco: Clifton Gonzalez Gonzalez
Alan Chan: Randall Duk Kim

Origin: USA
Released: 1998
Production: Bernie Brillstein and Brad Grey for WCG Entertainment; released by Columbia Pictures
Direction: Antoine Fuqua
Screenplay: Ken Sanzel
Cinematography: Peter Lyons Collister
Editing: Jay Cassidy
Music: Harry Gregson-Williams
Production design: Naomi Shohan
Art direction: David Lazan
Costumes: Arianne Philips
Sound: Douglas B. Arnold
MPAA rating: R
Running Time: 86 minutes

REVIEWS

Boxoffice. March, 1998, p. 54.
Entertainment Weekly. February 6, 1998, p. 40.
Los Angeles Times. February 6, 1998, p. F1.
New York Times. February 6, 1998, p. E19.
People. February 23, 1998, p. 21.
Rolling Stone. February 19, 1998, p. 63.
Sight and Sound. June, 1998, p. 54.
Variety. February 2, 1998, p. 27.
Washington Post Weekend. February 6, 1998, p. 41.

The *Replacement Killers* received middling reviews. *Rolling Stone*'s Peter Travers was fairly generous in praising Chow as "a legend in the making" while accurately pointing out that the movie "plays less like a fully realized film than a medley of Chow's greatest hits." *People*'s Leah Rozen was harsher in her assertion that the movie "fails to effectively showcase, much less sell, Chow's brand of guns-in-both-hands, dive-while-you-shoot cool." If Chow Yun-Fat is to make it big in America, he will need a stronger vehicle to show off his talent.

—Peter N. Chumo II

Return to Paradise

Give up three years of their lives or give the life of their friend. They have eight days to decide.—Movie tagline

"*The Midnight Express* of the '90s! Truly Awesome!"—Ron Brewington, *American Urban Radio Networks*

"Vaughn is sensational. This is a leading man."—Lisa Henrickson *GQ*

"See this terrific film."—Bonnie Churchill, *National News Syndicate*

 Box Office: $8,352,677

The dog days of August during the summer of 1998 not only brought heat and humidity to the land but political crisis and scandal as well. Moral responsibility seemed to be the pervasive topic of conversation throughout the country. Of course, everyone has an opinion of its meaning depending on various aspects of their cultural, religious or ethnic backgrounds. Ernest Hemingway, defining morality, once said that "something is good if you feel good after doing it, and evil if you feel bad after doing it". Ultimately, however, the true meaning of this somewhat ambiguous term can only be defined according to individual values.

There haven't been many films released this summer that have concerned themselves with this somewhat personal issue. Perhaps, the reason being that summer audiences usually seem to be attracted to escapist films that distract from the increasingly grim reports of a problematic and chaotic society. The interesting point to note, however is that two of 1998's biggest hits, *The Truman Show* with Jim Carey and Steven Spielberg's *Saving Private Ryan* did not fit into the typical "summer blockbuster genre." *The Truman Show* dealt with the invasion of the media into one's personal life for entertainment purposes and *Private Ryan* dealt with the complete debacle of a world war—both very ruminating and sobering messages. Perhaps, this is indicating a shift in the tastes of an increasingly sophisticated audience.

Polygram's summer release of *Return To Paradise* takes on the weighty topic of individual responsibility and its considerable consequences. The drama starring Vince Vaughn, Anne Heche, and Joaquin Phoenix opened on August 14 as the season's anti-blockbuster "thoughtful summer choice," so said Bob Graham from *The San Francisco Chronicle*. The political thriller, originally titled *Force Majeure* has been called *Midnight Express*—lite by MovieLink's Kevin Maynard. The story centers on three college buddies living it up in Malaysia. They spend their days soaking up the sun and scenery, as well as some real good hash and exotic women. The opening sequence has a laid back, almost home-movie feel to it and serves as an introduction to the three likeable main characters. There's Brooklyn–bred Sheriff (Vince Vaughn), aspiring architect Tony (David Conrad), and animal lover, all around good guy, Lewis (Joaquin Phoenix). All goes well for the three "pals" and at summer's end, Sheriff and Tony decide to return to New York City. Lewis plans to stay and later, go to Borneo for a Greenpeace Project to protect orangutans.

Two years go by and Sheriff is driving a limo through the Big Apple (as far from a Far East paradise as you can get) and Tony is on his way to becoming a successful architect. Their lives are relatively uncomplicated until Sheriff picks up a rider named Beth (Anne Heche), an attractive Manhattan attorney. Suddenly, everything changes and Sheriff is catapulted into what turns out to be, an incredible life changing event. It seems that after Sheriff and Tony left Malaysia, Lewis was arrested for possession of the three friend's left over hash. Since it was over the legal amount for possession charges, he was ar-

Sheriff (Vince Vaughn) recounting his vacation: "It was a paradise of rum, girls, and good cheap hash."

rested for drug trafficking. Lewis was tried and sentenced to die by hanging in one week. All of this comes as a complete shock to the genuinely compassionate Sheriff but Beth hasn't finished her tale. If Sheriff and Tony agree to return to Malaysia to testify that some of the hash belonged to them, Lewis would be spared the death sentence. However, once they confessed—they would have to serve three years in prison. If only one returned, it would be six years. So the no-nonsense, straightforward Beth has laid the cards on the table and now it's Sheriff's move. This certainly is an intriguing conflict to ponder and it puts the audience into the position of asking themselves what they would do if they were put in this situation. It's a great device to keep audiences glued to the screen to watch what decision the central characters are going to make. It is a cerebral experience to ask some penetrating questions while the plot unfolds.

> Even though the script has the three friends vacationing in Malaysia, the tropical scenes were shot in Thailand and the grim prison sequences were shot in a penitentiary in Philadelphia.

Return to Paradise lacks the emotional urgency of a good Costa Garvas political thriller like *Z* or *Missing*—so says Kevin Maynard from MovieLink. Although there is some truth to that statement, it still holds up as an absorbing, well-acted and well-written drama. Director Joseph Ruben (*The Stepfather, Sleeping with the Enemy*) uses a direct, linear approach to the telling of the story leading the viewer through the emotional changes the characters make along the way to their final decision. Ruben has a great ability to create strong visual images that become an integral part of the script. His locations add great illumination to the story and they create a great enhancement to the film's appeal. For instance, the scenes in Malaysia have an almost intoxicating quality to them—Sheriff at one point says: "its like God's own bathtub" and he's right. The almost magical setting makes it easy to see how seductive the surroundings were to these young men. Also, to see that their laid-back attitude could eventually turn deadly. When the action switches to New York, once again, the director manages to use the locale to embellish the plot. With the urban pulse of an electrifying city as the backdrop, the three main characters were plunged back to another time and place and confronted with a monumental decision that would impact the rest of their lives. Ruben's direction was meticulous without being controlled or rigid. The script was intelligent and to the point except for one detour— the romantic involvement between Sheriff and Beth. This aspect of the film, although interesting and thoroughly believable, did distract, somewhat, from the central issue—how far will these men go in order to take responsibility for their actions and thereby save their friend's life? It was inevitable that romance be included to appeal to a wider audience but there was too much time spent on that aspect of the story. Fortunately, Ruben never

allowed it to blur the message of the film but at times it came perilously close.

Anne Heche is a good actress. She brings a quality of intelligence and strength to her roles that are uniquely hers. She is physically a petite woman but it never diminishes the forcefulness of her characters. She has a formidable presence on the screen and yes, she can be sexy when playing opposite a leading man. (See *Six Days, Seven Nights* reviewed in this edition.) In this film, she has all of the above mentioned qualities plus some added new ones. Her portrayal of Beth has a controlled sense of urgency to it that gives it purpose and intensity. At times, it appears that her Beth is about ready to scream but never does. When talking to Sheriff and Lou, she appeals to their sense of decency and humanity but never begs. Beth has a quiet dignity to her that allows the two men to connect with their own sense of morality. Her role is pivotal to the development of the story and Heche manages all of the right elements to bring it together. Alan Silverman from Hollywood Bytes said, "Anne Heche delivers an Oscar–caliber performance." She is certainly an actress of immense possibility and range.

Vince Vaughn caught the attention of famed director,

CREDITS

Sheriff: Vince Vaughn
Beth: Anne Heche
Lewis: Joaquin Phoenix
Tony: David Conrad
M. J. Major: Jada Pinkett Smith
Kerrie: Vera Farmiga

Origin: USA
Released: 1998
Production: Alain Bernheim, Steve Golin for Propaganda Films in association with Tetragram; released by Polygram Films
Direction: Joseph Ruben
Screenplay: Wesley Strick and Bruce Robinson; based on the film *Force Majeure* by Pierre Jolivet and Olivier Schatzky
Cinematography: Reynaldo Villalobos
Editing: Andrew Mondshein, Craig McKay
Music: Mark Mancina
Production design: Bill Groom
Art direction: Dennis Bradford
Set decoration: Betsy Klompus
Sound: William Sarokin
MPAA rating: R
Running Time: 109 minutes

Steven Spielberg in an independent film titled, *Swingers* (1996) and was cast in the summer blockbuster, *Jurassic Park The Lost World*. This mega-hit got the young actor even more attention and he has been working steadily ever since. His subsequent projects include a Texas serial killer in *Clay Pigeons* (reviewed in this edition) and the role of Norman Bates in the much-discussed re-make of *Psycho* directed by Gus Van Sant (also reviewed in this edition). Although Vince Vaughn has leading man good looks, there is a sense of danger lurking underneath the exterior. This smoldering quality is evident in *Return to Paradise* but Sheriff is less dangerous than cynical, more resigned to the world of disappointment and missed opportunities. "Should I beware lawyers bearing gifts," he skeptically asks Beth at one of their meetings. He looks for the con in others because he is so aware of the con in himself. Vaughn does have the quality of dominating a scene when he's in it and has the potential to become one of film's most sought after leading men.

There are so many worthwhile and well-executed moments to this film that it is a thoroughly satisfying experience. The intelligence of the script shines throughout and offers a lot of conscious raising issues to digest and evaluate. It gives the viewer a lot to think about when they are driving home and for some time afterwards. It may not have the shattering impact of a *Midnight Express* (although the ending is quite visceral) but it does offer up a powerful challenge to one's belief system about right and wrong. Whether its message will have any lasting impact on mankind's values toward moral responsibility, it a least raises the issues. Maybe film can play a role in raising the standards and improve the integrity of society while still being entertaining. *Return to Paradise* is certainly heading the medium in the right direction.

—*Jarred Cooper*

REVIEWS

Chicago Tribune. August 14, 1998, p. 5.
Entertainment Weekly. August 21, 1998. p. 94.
Los Angeles Times. August 14, 1998. p. F14.
New York Times. August 14, 1998. p. E9.
People. August 24, 1998. p. 34.
Sight and Sound. January, 1999, p. 55.
Variety. August 3, 1998. p. 36.
Washington Post Weekend. August 14, 1998. p. 39.

Ride

This party makes no stops.—Movie tagline

 Box Office: $5,503,007

A crew of hip-hop musicians take a wild trip from Harlem to Miami in a ramshackle bus to shoot a music video. MTV meets *Speed* meets *House Party* (made by the same producers)—this genre-bender covers all the bases—romantic-comedy musical adventure. An ensemble cast weaves its tales in and out of each other's lives while rapping along for the ride.

At an audition for extras, Leta Evans (Melissa De Sousa), who is smack out of film school, gets thrown into a production mess. She will transport the artists on impresario Freddy B's record label from New York to Florida as fast and cheaply as possible if she can direct the company's next video.

 Writer/director Millicent Shelton: "The main thing was to create a really fun movie that has heart."

Waiting outside the studio for everyone to gather, the World Records performers are introduced and their variety of soap-opera scenarios: Tuesday (Kellie Williams), one half of a female duo, fears she's pregnant by rap artist Brotha (Sticky Fingaz), who fancies himself a star. Casper (Reuben Asher), the white half of a contentious rap act, is searching for the long-lost father he believes is black. Meanwhile, the other half of the duo, Geronimo (Fredro Starr), escapes from a *Bonnie and Clyde* getaway car—grabbing the robber's stash in his backpack and rushing off to meet everyone in time to leave Manhattan.

The bus arrives in a cloud of exhaust. The madcap drivers, Roscoe (John Witherspoon) and Bo (Cedric the Entertainer), break into Wilson Pickett's "In the Midnight Hour" to demonstrate real music. Fending off complaints about the raggedy vehicle, haughty Leta, who's appalled by the state of affairs, realizes there's no choice but to accept the deplorable conditions, including a foul restroom.

At the first rest stop, Leta hands out "per diem" pay—trying to manage the group with the assistance of Geronimo's big brother, Poppa (Malik Yoba). Besides keeping a cautious eye on his out-of-control sibling, he reveals he's headed south to obtain financial support from Freddy B for his inner-city youth program, "Rites of Passage." Tuesday confronts the philandering Brotha, who's now making time with a young female hopeful traveling with them. A spontaneous rap outside the convenience store is interrupted when the robbers arrive in a hijacked big rig in search of their innocent accomplice. Before driving on again, Leta takes roll call, only to find Geronimo hanging off the bumper on a skateboard.

Although the film's advertising tagline claims, "This party makes no stops," they take a lunch break at a South Carolina carnival. Geronimo is accidentally left behind. The dilapidated bus breaks down, and they pull off the road for repairs. While stranded, they join a dance at a nearby club and romance develops between Poppa and Leta. Geronimo catches up, his pursuers right behind—but so is the sheriff. Then Geronimo saves the day, handing over the money for the mechanic with the amount stolen from the hoods who robbed the "hood."

Upon hitting their Miami destination, the dramas are wrapped up, so to speak. Tuesday realizes she's worth more than the treatment she's receiving from Brotha; after ignoring Poppa's pleas on behalf of his cause, Freddy finally commits to the program; and at a poolside shoot, snobby director Bleau Kelly (Downtown Julie Brown) walks off the set when confronted with a strike . . . with Leta at the controls sooner than expected.

Writer/director Millicent Shelton seems to have created an autobiographical tale with an authentic feel to the details of the rap scene, although it's filled with music business clichés. Tuesday and Poppa are particularly believable, but much of the other acting is uneven. A successful rap soundtrack seems more relevant to this film and in true music-video fashion, the contrived and uncohesive storylines move briskly, although not as quickly or rhythmically as a song.

—*Roberta Cruger*

CREDITS

Poppa: Malik Yoba
Leta: Melissa De Sousa
Roscoe: John Witherspoon
Geronimo: Fredro Starr
Tuesday: Kellie Williams
Charity: Idalis de Leon
Bird: Dartanyan Edmonds
Bleau: Downtown Julie Brown

Origin: USA
Released: 1998
Production: Reginald and Warren Hudlin for Hudlin Bros.; released by Dimension Films
Direction: Millicent Shelton
Screenplay: Millicent Shelton
Cinematography: Frank Byers
Editing: Earl Watson
Music: Dunn Pearson Jr.
Production design: Bryan Jones
Art direction: Vera Mills
Costumes: Richard Owings
MPAA rating: R
Running Time: 83 minutes

REVIEWS

Entertainment Weekly. April 10, 1998, p. 46.
New York Times. March 28, 1998, p. B12.
Variety. March 30, 1998, p. 41.

Ringmaster

"Totally outrageous."—Ron Brewington, American Urban Radio

"Guilty pleasure"—Stephen Holden, *The New York Times*

"Poetry in motion"—Michael Rechtshaffen, *The Hollywood Reporter*

"Shrewd and funny"—Kevin Thomas, *Los Angeles Times*

 Box Office: $8,695,301

Game boy. BMW. 444-FILM. Coca Cola. IMAX 3-D. These commercials, plus a slew of mind-numbing previews, weaseled across the screen before the evening's feature amusement: Jerry Springer in *Ringmaster*. This prologue was sickeningly appropriate since *Ringmaster* is a marketer's dream and probably was. The script is dreary. The acting is ludicrous, and the whole package compiles to an experience so painful that it should be thrust upon one's worst enemies only after serious thought and proper contemplation. That this movie will probably turn a profit is evidence that America is doomed forever to be the cultural toilet bowl of the world.

We live in a society that bathes itself in the exhibition of other people's problems in an attempt at self-conviction that somewhere out there exists people who are more screwed up than us. It's all a placebo, a kind of escapism for a society that has become too jaded, too "sophisticated," to accept pleasure from something without the tang of boob jobs and lycra. Springer's show is Disneyland and Jerry is "Uncle Walt"—but you probably wouldn't want to sit on his knee.

The story focuses on two groups of people dying to get on the Jerry Show in order to bloat their egos and air their laundry. The first group revolves around a girl named Angel Zorzak (Jaime Pressly) who works as a motel maid and a prostitute on the side, with an affinity toward performing oral sex. Whether she does this for money or just for the hell of it is unclear, but it doesn't really matter. As in real life, sexual liaisons are ubiquitous in this movie and are accompanied on the soundtrack with slide whistles and whizzing ratchets. Hilarious, isn't it?

The only person not getting a piece of the action is Angel's boyfriend, Willie (Ashley Holbrook). She saves those for Rusty (Michael Dudikoff), her step-father. Conni (Molly Hagan), Angel's mom, catches them and books them all on the Jerry Show. It's dreams come true time for the Zorzak clan as they leave their trailer park to embark on their complimentary "vacation."

The second group focuses on Demond (Michael Jai White), a muscular African American who is sleeping around on his girlfriend, Starletta (Wendy Raquel Robinson). She and her friends are none too happy about it. Just as the Zorzak shtick gives us trailer park clichés, this African-American group gives us all the stereotypes one can stomach and some that takes a healthy dosage of Tums to recover from. A scene where they rap up a storm aboard the plane flying them into L. A. could require a stomach pumping.

Interspersed throughout are glimpses into the backstage, onstage, and offstage life of Jerry Springer, all of which have flashing boobs to spare. One particularly creepy incident puts Jerry at a country-western bar, making a promotional appearance. Dressed as a cowboy he sings a song about talk show hosts. It is truly vomit inducing. We also get to see Jerry having sex with an unnamed woman, schmoozing to his producer Mel (John Capodice), and self-righteously trying to justify his existence.

CREDITS

Jerry Farrelly: Jerry Springer
Angel Zorzak: Jaime Pressly
Connie Zorzak: Molly Hagan
Troy: William McNamara
Rusty: Michael Dudikoff
Desmond: Michael Jai White
Starletta: Wendy Raquel Robinson
Vonda: Tangie Ambrose
Leshawnette: Nicki Micheaux

Origin: USA
Released: 1998
Production: Jerry Springer, Gina Rugolo-Judd, Brad Jenkel, Steve Stabler, and Gary W. Goldstein for a Kushner-Locke Co. production; released by Artisan Entertainment
Direction: Neil Abramson
Screenplay: Jon Bernstein
Cinematography: Russell Lyster
Editing: Suzanne Hines
Production design: Dorian Vernacchio, Deborah Raymond
Set decoration: Jodi Ginnever
Costumes: Gail McMullen
Music: Kennard Ramsey
MPAA rating: R
Running Time: 89 minutes

All this madness ends when the two groups meet for the show. Nasty vibes explode during the taping where they proceed to beat each other silly before a live, studio audience. After a round of verbal attacks ("bitch" seems to be the word of choice), an audience member stands up and begins to lash out at the disgrace on the stage and at the disgrace of the show itself. Springer shuts him up with the convincing argument of, "This is a slice of American life and if you don't like it, bite something else." Thank you, we will.

Another attempt to explain the show, to validate its existence as populist entertainment, involves a female reporter who says to Jerry that his show is "bleak and depressing." Jerry retorts that most of his guests are poor, and poverty is bleak and depressing and the show reminds her of things she doesn't want to see. Jerry's guests represent the poor about as well as the sentiment that the poor are noble. What his guests represent is a frightening rift in our society, a breakdown of norms that veer so far off the beaten path that

> Angel (Jaime Pressly) to her mother Connie (Molly Hagen): "I didn't say you could borrow my jacket." Connie: " I didn't say you could sleep with my husband."

they would have been displayed in a freak show eighty years ago. Today they have television and Jerry Springer is aptly enough, their *Ringmaster*.

But in the end, even the heckler is wrong. The joke is not on the guests. Nor is it on Jerry Springer. After the cash registers have stopped ringing, and a lull of smoky silence fills the air, it becomes clear that the joke is not on them at all. It is on us.

—*Rich Silverman*

REVIEWS

Detroit Free Press. November 25, 1998, p. 7D.
Detroit News. November 25, 1998, p. 6D.
Entertainment Weekly. December 4, 1998, p. 64.
Los Angeles Times. November 25, 1998, p. F7.
People. December 14, 1998, p. 34.
Variety. November 23, 1998, p. 48.
Village Voice. December 1, 1998, p. 128.

Ronin

"A first-rate thriller from the veteran director John Frankenheimer ... The movie has sensational car chases, the stomach-sinking likes of which moviegoers haven't seen since *The French Connection*."—Leah Rozen, *People*

"*Ronin* is the real deal in action fireworks ... "
—Peter Travers, *Rolling Stone*

"A sly masterpiece."—Richard Schickel, *Time*

Box Office: $41,552,061

Robert DeNiro stars as a skillful member of a mercenary team in the espionage thriller *Ronin*.

*R*onin has been widely praised as a low-tech thriller reminiscent of those of the 1960s and 1970s. It is a vastly entertaining, for the most part, action film, the best film director John Frankenheimer has made since the very similar *French Connection II* (1975), but as good as it is, *Ronin* is sloppy around the edges and empty at its core.

Deirdre (Natascha McElhone), a young Irish woman, assembles a group of specialized mercenaries in Paris to carry out a heist planned by a mastermind whose identity is kept secret from all but her. Larry (Skip Sudduth) is a getaway

driver; Vincent (Jean Reno) is in charge of finding whatever the operation needs; Gregor (Stellan Skarsgard), formerly with the KGB, is an expert in computer technology; Spence (Sean Bean), who claims a military background, knows weapons; and Sam (Robert De Niro), reportedly an ex-CIA agent, is a strategist. Their objective is a metallic suitcase whose contents are of utmost importance to the current owner, the Irish, and some Russians.

Sam's crew goes to Nice to steal the suitcase only to have Gregor swipe it, the first in a series of double-crosses. Sam, Dierdre, Vincent, and Larry—Spence has been dismissed for incompetence—follow Gregor's trail first to Arles and then back to Paris. Soon, Sam, Gregor, Seamus (Jonathan Pryce), the mastermind, and the sleazy Russian Mikhi (Feodor Atkine) are fighting each other and their cohorts for possession of the case.

Deirdre (Natascha McElhone): "Are you afraid?" Sam (Robert De Niro): "Of course I'm afraid. You think I'm reluctant because I'm happy?"

Ronin is a generally well-constructed film with just enough time devoted to assembling the gang, planning the heist, arguing among themselves, and dealing with the resulting duplicities, the inevitable romance between Deirdre and Sam fitting smoothly into the narrative. The essence of the film, however, is three complicated, high-speed car chases in Nice, Arles, and Paris. The chases give *Ronin* its main energy, making it more than a caper film or a thriller with political overtones.

The screenplay for *Ronin* is credited to J. D. Zeik and Richard Weisz (a pseudonym for David Mamet), but there has been some controversy over whether the film reflects more the efforts of Zeik or Mamet. *The Los Angeles Times* reported that Mamet has decided not to include his real name in the credits when he works on a screenplay created by another writer, partly because of his experience of failing to receive sole credit for *Wag the Dog* (1997). The newspaper quoted Frankenheimer's contention that the shooting screenplay was the creation of Mamet, but two months later, it published a brief article in which Frankenheimer refuted his previous statements, asserting Zeik's contribution to the film. Regardless of who did what, *Ronin* is notable as a no-nonsense throwback to an earlier era, the kind of film most enjoyed, as a character in Quentin Tarantino's *Reservoir Dogs* (1992) says, by those who like Lee Marvin films.

Given Mamet's participation, however, the characters are surprisingly underdeveloped. This matter would be of less concern had the film striven for some sort of existential overtones like those in Jean-Pierre Melville's *Le Samourai* (1967) or John Boorman's *Point Blank* (1967). *Ronin* begins as if the crew is composed of world-weary men drawn to crime either because they do not fit into the bourgeois world or because they are addicted to danger. Vincent's friend Jean-Pierre (Michael Lonsdale), named in honor of French director Melville, spends all his time painstakingly making miniature samurai figures, villages,

and battlefields from Japan's feudal era. Jean-Pierre explains to Sam about the ronin, the wandering warriors who had lost their masters, much like Sam and Gregor have. The film tries to portray Deirdre's gang, especially Sam, as being disgraced warriors, but the end of *Ronin* reveals Sam to be something else altogether, destroying the film's mythic and existential pretensions and much of its sense of dirty fun. Once Sam and Vincent return to Paris to confront the Russians, in fact, *Ronin* begins to lose its impetus, turning unpleasantly nasty as Mikhi allows the ice skater (Katarina Witt) he manages and seemingly adores to be murdered to protect the suitcase.

Most of the credit for the slickness of *Ronin* has gone to 68-year-old Frankenheimer who, in his prime, made one truly great film, *The Manchurian Candidate* (1962), and several good ones, including *The Birdman of Alcatraz* (1962), *Seven Days in May* (1964), *The Train* (1964), and *French Connection II*. After the big-budget failure of the soulless thriller *Black Sunday* (1977), Frankenheimer's big-screen career went downhill. Then he surprisingly resurrected his career by winning four Emmys for directing cable television films about social, political, and historical issues, as with *George Wallace* (1997). *Ronin* demonstrates the director's affinity for outsiders and his skill at creating an almost-documentary style of realism.

Most of the reviewers of *Ronin* praised Frankenheimer's old-fashioned professionalism, but when examined carefully, that professionalism is a tad ragged. The Paris car chase features one black Audi following another, and in most of the shots, it is impossible to tell which is the pursuer and which the pursued. As the cars charge down one-way lanes against the traffic flow, it is obvious that the oncoming vehicles are being driven slowly and are spaced so that the protagonists' cars can weave in and out of the traffic. Several of the civilian drivers also hang their heads out of their windows and shake their fists angrily as if the wrong-way drivers did not know they are careening against the flow. Likewise, the Nice chase features cars crashing into fruit-and-vegetable carts, the sort of cliché that indicates the filmmakers are either lazy or have not seen many films. In the shootout after the chase, members of the innocent public just stand around waiting to be shot, a tired means of expressing the ruthlessness of the antagonists. Compare how Michael Mann stages similar situations in the magnificent *Heat* (1995), a film with the existential overtones *Ronin* lacks.

Sam discovers Gregor's treachery when he sees that the case he is carrying is a non-metallic one painted silver. Gre-

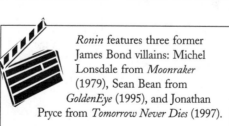

Ronin features three former James Bond villains: Michel Lonsdale from *Moonraker* (1979), Sean Bean from *GoldenEye* (1995), and Jonathan Pryce from *Tomorrow Never Dies* (1997).

gor could not have easily found an exact copy of the case to delay the discovery of his switch? *Ronin* is too good a film to be flawed by such sloppiness.

A few reviewers were annoyed that the contents of the suitcase are never revealed, but the case, as most reviewers recognized, is what Alfred Hitchcock called a McGuffin, a device whose sole purpose is to set the plot in motion: the key in *Dial M for Murder* (1954), the microfilm in *North by*

CREDITS

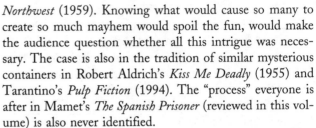

Sam: Robert De Niro
Deirdre: Natascha McElhone
Vincent: Jean Reno
Gregor: Stellan Skarsgard
Seamus: Jonathan Pryce
Spence: Sean Bean
Larry: Skip Sudduth
Jean-Pierre: Michael Lonsdale
Mikhi: Feodor Atkine
Dapper Gent: Jan Triska
Natacha Kirilova: Katarina Witt
Sergi: Bernard Bloch

Origin: USA
Released: 1998
Production: Frank Mancuso, Jr., for FGM Entertainment; released by United Artists
Direction: John Frankenheimer
Screenplay: J.D. Zeik and Richard Weisz
Cinematography: Robert Fraisse
Editing: Tony Gibbs
Production design: Michael Z. Hanan
Art direction: Gerard Viard
Costumes: May Routh
Sound: Bernard Bats
Music: Elia Cmiral
Physical stunt coordination: Joe Dunne
Car stunt coordination: Jean-Claude Lagniez, Patrick Ronchin
MPAA rating: R
Running Time: 121 minutes

Northwest (1959). Knowing what would cause so many to create so much mayhem would spoil the fun, would make the audience question whether all this intrigue was necessary. The case is also in the tradition of similar mysterious containers in Robert Aldrich's *Kiss Me Deadly* (1955) and Tarantino's *Pulp Fiction* (1994). The "process" everyone is after in Mamet's *The Spanish Prisoner* (reviewed in this volume) is also never identified.

This McGuffin is one of several elements that help *Ronin*'s virtues outweigh its defects. Others include the inventive use of the French scenery with the Paris scenes having an ominous, noirish gloom and the bright, sunny streets of Nice in contrast to the chaos raging on them; Tony Gibbs' expert editing of the chases (almost hiding their flaws), making them the best since Popeye Doyle's pursuit of the subway in William Friedkin's *The French Connection* (1971); and the performances, especially that of De Niro. This great actor is an unlikely action hero, but his commanding presence lends authenticity to his Sam. The character has several comic one-liners in the first half of the film, and De Niro makes them seem appropriate to Sam's cynical worldview rather than imposed on the material as in most of the Mel Gibson or Bruce Willis action films. If only the film had even approached the epic scale of *Heat*, in which De Niro gives a truly great performance.

—*Michael Adams*

REVIEWS

Boston Globe. September 25, 1998, p. D6.
Entertainment Weekly. October 2, 1998, p. 43.
Los Angeles Times. September 25, 1998, p. F1.
New York Times. September 25, 1998, p. B12.
New Yorker. October 5, 1998, p. 113.
Rolling Stone. October 15, 1998, p. 133.
San Francisco Chronicle. September 25, 1998, p. C1.
Sight and Sound. December, 1998, p. 58.
Time. September 21, 1998, p. 100.
USA Today. September 25, 1998, p. E3.
Variety. September 14, 1998, p. 34.
Wall Street Journal. September 25, 1998, p. W1.
Washington Post. September 25, 1998, p. N62.

Rounders

"Completely enjoyable and vastly entertaining. The center of the movie is the rapturous dialogue between Matt Damon and Edward Norton."—David Denby, *New York Magazine*

"Magnificent no-holds-barred performances from Matt Damon, Edward Norton, and John Malkovich. You will be mesmerized by all the scene-stealing sparks of electricity."—Andrew Sarris, *New York Observer*

"Stylish and fun entertainment. Matt Damon is a winner."—Peter Travers, *Rolling Stone*

"Two thumbs up."—*Siskel & Ebert*

Box Office: $22,921,898

Mike McDermott (Matt Damon) is a bright young man and a promising law student with a beautiful girl friend and law-school colleague Jo (Gretchen Mol), who loves him, but for his fatal flaw, an addiction to gambling, particularly high-stakes backroom poker. The film begins with a demonstration of Mike's skill at the gaming table, but he miscalculates and loses everything he has to a Russian mafia kingpin known only as Teddy KGB (John Malkovich). To further his law school ambitions and protect his love life, Mike vows not to gamble again and takes a night job as a delivery boy to bankroll his law degree.

But Mike never feels so alive as when he is gambling, and his reformation is shaken when his best friend, Les "Worm" Murphy (Edward Norton), is released from prison, where Worm was honing his own skills as a cardshark, perfecting all the dirty tricks a con-artist hustler needs to succeed at the gaming tables. The day Worm is released, Mike is there to pick him up. He learns that Worm has a long-standing debt and needs $15,000 to cover it. Worm's erstwhile partner in crime, Grama (Michael Rispoli), is now a loan shark, has ties with Teddy KGB, and muscles Worm for the money owed. Out of friendship, Mike agrees to play poker to help bankroll Worm, but Worm cannot stay out of trouble and Mike gets deeper and deeper into debt trying to help his friend, until, finally, his girl leaves him and his studies begin to suffer.

Grama roughs up Worm and takes everything that Mike has staked him as part of his loan payment. So the card sharks go looking for games as far away as Binghamp-

Mike (Matt Damon): "If you play poker for a living, it's like any job—you grind it out."

ton, New York, a five-hour drive from New York City. Worm tells Mike it's a game for municipal workers, but they turn out to be policemen. Mike enters the game by using the password Worm had got from playing poker with prison guards. Mike sends Worm to the bowling alley to get him out of the way, but Worm later turns up at the game and gets caught dealing off the bottom of the deck. Even though Mike has been winning by playing fair, the cops conclude that Mike and Worm are in cahoots and beat them both to a pulp. Meanwhile, Mike has taken the responsibility for Worm's debt and the clock is running, since Grama expects full payment in two days. After getting Mike in this fix, Worm's solution is to skip town.

Desperate for money, Mike goes to one of his mentors, Professor Abe Petrovsky (Martin Landau), who, amazingly, gives him $10,000, not enough to cover the debt, but as much as the Professor can lay hands on. Mike takes the money to Teddy KGB and challenges him to a game of Texas Hold 'Em, pitting his skills against Teddy's and knowing that if he loses, he could lose his life. This makes for an exciting conclusion as the two play into the night. Although he had earlier lost $30,000 to Teddy in a similar all-night game, Mike believes that poker is a game of skill, not luck, as long as the gambler is smart enough to remember the cards and to "read" his opponents' reactions. This is a great opportunity for Mike to realize his calling as a poker champ in the making, but if he loses, he might lose his life.

The film is more about relationships than gambling, and, although there is not much of a plot here in the screenplay by David Levien and Brian Koppelman, it is character-driven. Norton is effectively disturbing as Worm, and, just as Norton brings the same kind of energy he brought to his role as an accused killer in *Primal Fear* (1996), Damon brings the same level of intelligence to his character that he had also done in *Good Will Hunting* (1997), which was a better and more rewarding film. John Turturro is effectively creepy as Joey Knish, another "rounder" who knows the game and has respect for Mike's skills, but cannot or will not help when Mike hits rock bottom because of Worm's stupidity. Martin Landau is quite good as the sympathetic Jewish professor, but his motive for helping Mike is not as strong as it needs to be, though the screenplay labors to establish a paternal link. Petrovsky gives Mike advice at one point, drawing upon his own career. His father wanted him to become a Rabbi, but Petrovsky knew that was not his calling and opted for secular law over Jewish law, at the risk of alienating himself from his family. "We can't run from who we are," he advises. "Our destiny chooses us." In a jucier role, John Malkovich is way over-the-top as the mad Russian who munches Oreo cookies as he faces down his opponents, but his Russian accents are often amusing.

Reviews were mixed. Though most reviewers favored the film, Rita Kempley of the *Washington Post* criticized the screenplay by first-timers David Levien and Brian Koppelman. Though she believed they had done their research on the netherworld atmosphere, the language and psychology of high-stakes gamblers, she complained that there was "no

Title refers to a serious, high-stakes poker player.

passion, no purpose, and not much of an engine." Mike McDermott, the central figure, does not really change: "instead, change happens to him." What we have here, however, is the story of a reformed gambler who is smart enough to succeed in the straight world but who finally chooses to make a career of doing what he does best. He is "changed" by his decision to help his friend and at that point destiny takes over, but he does ultimately take control of his life.

The dilemma faced by the Damon character resembles that of *Good Will Hunting*, as the character seems reluctant to sever ties with his past, and for that reason Kempley suggested that the film might have been called "Good Will Hustling." Of course, *the Hustler* (1961) set the style for all such films as Paul Newman's pool shark waited to challenge the champ, Minnesota Fats (Jackie Gleason) and got roughed up as he attempted to hustle his way to the top. In *Rounders*, Mike McDermott is far different from Newman's drifter because he is not necessarily trapped in the netherworld he chooses to inhabit, but finally he is headed in the same direction by testing his skills. Teddy KGB is his Minnesota Fats. After he proves himself at Teddy's table, he will be on his way to Las Vegas.

The atmosphere is effectively created by director John Dahl, who made his reputation on the basis of two neo-noir features, *Red Rock West* (1993) and *The Last Seduction* (1994), with the help of cinematographer Jean-Yves Escoffier. Though the characters are seen by day, most of the action takes place at night in dark and secret places. In his *Time* review, Richard Schickel praised the film for its atmospherics and the acting talent but missed the "sardonically twisted plots and people of Dahl's best work" in this picture. The low-life characters, according to Janet Maslin of the *New York Times,* were "inspired" by Martin Scorsese's New York films, especially *Mean Streets* (1973), and other reviewers also mentioned the film's debt to Scorsese, who, in the opinion of one, might have done it better. The film's actresses, Gretchen Mol as Jo and Famke Janssen as Petra, her low-life counterpart in Mike's life, are pretty much excluded from the action and function mainly as window dressings in this male-dominant story. At times the film's pacing slows down to a crawl as Mike studies his cards and faces down his opponents, though such pauses do enhance the dramatic content. Most surprising, according to the *USA Today* review, was the film's message "that the real sin isn't

CREDITS

Mike McDermott: Matt Damon
Worm: Edward Norton
Joey Kinish: John Turturro
Jo: Gretchen Mol
Petra: Famke Janssen
Teddy KGB: John Malkovich
Abe Petrovsky: Martin Landau
Grama: Michael Rispoli
Barbara: Melina Kanakaredes
Zagosh: Josh Mostel

Origin: USA
Released: 1998
Production: Joel Stillerman and Ted Demme for Spanky Pictures; released by Miramax Films
Direction: John Dahl
Screenplay: David Levien and Brian Koppelman
Cinematography: Jean Yves Escoffier
Editing: Scott Chestnut
Music: Christopher Young
Production design: Rob Pearson
Art direction: Rick Butler
Costumes: Terry Dresbach
Sound: Mark Weingarten
MPAA rating: R
Running Time: 120 minutes

REVIEWS

Baltimore Sun. September 11, 1998, p. E1.
Entertainment Weekly. September 18, 1998, p. 55.
New York Times. September 11, 1998, p. B16.
Newsweek. September 14, 1998, p. 76.
Premiere. October, 1998, p. 51.
Sight and Sound. December, 1998, p. 59.
Time. September 21, 1998, p. 105.
USA Today. September 11, 1998, p. E11.
Variety. September 7, 1998, p. 71.
Washington Post. September 11, 1998, p. D5.
Washington Post Weekend. September 11, 1998, p. 52.
Washington Times Metropolitan Times. September 11, 1998, p. C16.

giving into vice," as Mike does, "but denying your God-given talents and not risking it all."

The film's reviews were generally favorable. *Newsweek* and *The Washington Post* were both critical of the film's accomplishments, but the usually demanding Gary Arnold of *The Washington Times* praised it guardedly as "a thin but smartly performed melodrama" dealing with the "pitfalls of high-stakes gambling." Reviewers for the *Baltimore Sun* and *USA Today* were more enthusiastic. Overall, the acting is outstanding, even if the story is "thin" and the pacing a bit slow for viewers whose interest in the game of poker may be minimal. Given these handicaps, Matt Damon and Edward Norton hold their own in a gamble that pays off agreeably and entertainingly.

— James M. Welsh

The Rugrats Movie

An adventure for anyone who's ever worn diapers.—Movie tagline

"Just in time for the holidays! Fresh and witty, the film has success written all over it."—Kevin Thomas, *Los Angeles Times*

"*The Rugrats Movie* is a delight!"—Anita Gates, *New York Times*

"*The Rugrats Movie* is a treat for young and old!"—John Anderson, *Newsday*

"A blockbuster adventure! The real charm of *Rugrats* lies in the fact that it looks and sounds a lot like your own life."—*Newsweek*

"The animation is distinctive . . . with a smart sense of design and fun!"—Richard Corliss, *Time*

Box Office: $86,430,992

The gang from the popular Nickelodeon series gets lost and must find their way back home in *The Rugrats Movie.*

There hasn't been a funnier and more entertaining children's television cartoon show than *Rugrats* since the days of *Rocky and Bullwinkle*. For much of the 1990s, the Nickelodeon show about five toddlers and their ditzy parents has stood head and shoulders above the competition. What's great about *Rugrats* is that its creators seem to understand perfectly the thinking processes of a young child—which combine wild flights of fancy, outlandishly exaggerated fears, tortured and out-of-proportion emotions, and a false bravado based on a limited understanding of language and the world.

Many adult depictions of children in television and movies, whether animated or not, make the kids outrageously precocious and often drippily sentimental. The *Rugrats* children are neither. Yes, they can talk in approximations of adult language and their powers of thought and

imagination are beyond what many adults believe children address. And yes, they have over-large feelings. But what's funny about *Rugrats* is the same thing that's funny about real children—they think they know a lot more than they do, they are governed by snap, uninformed judgments, and they are frequently misled by others or by their own misunderstandings of situations.

In the world of *Rugrats*, children aren't precious or goofy or ridiculous—they're just immature and misguided. In short, they are like miniature, less developed versions of the well-intentioned but screwed-up adults around them. *Rugrats* is both an enjoyable satire of adults and an hilarious send-up of children who try to make their way through an unfathomable world. *Rugrats* is irreverent while still sympathetic towards its characters. Its humor is edgy and provocative but not mean-spirited. And the children's predicaments are proportionate to their world—such as being afraid of a playground sandbox because they think it is the same as the Sahara Desert.

When *Rugrats* debuted in 1991, its writers were Arlene Klasky and Gabor Csupo, who had helped create *The Simpsons* in the late 1980s. Its producer was Paul Germain. The show focused on the strange misadventures of one-year-old Tommy Pickles, his best friend Chuckie, twins Phil and Lil, and a domineering three-year-old, Angelica. Angelica, who is a petty, self-obsessed bully, continually tortures the younger foursome, whom she collectively refers to as "You dumb babies!"

Angelica became the show's most popular character. Obsessed with her anorexic, disheveled doll Cynthia, Angelica represents a send-up of the most obnoxious elements in consumer-driven girlhood. She often instructs the babies on the properly cynical and materialistic attitudes towards getting ahead in the world. But Klasky became unhappy with the development of Angelica's character; she wanted a more sympathetic figure, and she and Germain battled about Angelica and other issues, until Germain left after the show's third season. After two years of being sustained by reruns, *Rugrats* went back into production, with the writing overseen by Klasky and Csupo and Angelica softened considerably.

It is this tamer version of *Rugrats,* not the earlier, edgier material, that forms the basis of the disappointing *The Rugrats Movie.* Making an episodic TV show into a movie is always problematic; in this case, the transition from the show's customary 12-minute episodes to a feature-length adventure is fatal. The humor of the *Rugrats* show depends on the babies making a mountain out of a molehill. Chuckie is terrified of a talking clown invented by Tommy's father, for example, and imagines the toy as a real menace, or Chuckie gets lost in the backyard and believes he's in a limitless jungle. The children aren't placed in real dangers; they are so easily frightened that they mistake an ordinary household and ordinary things they encounter as threats. And often it is Angelica, lying about something, who frightens the babies with her bullying tactics.

The makers of *The Rugrats Movie*—producers Klasky and Csupo, their new writing team of David Weiss and J. David Stem, and co-directors Norton Virgien and Igor Kovalyov—decided that more length necessitated a more expansive adventure story. They may have been wiser to concoct a series of interrelated vignettes, because they have ended up with something much closer to a traditional Disney movie than a film which adheres to the Rugrats tradi-

Tommy Pickles (voice of E.G. Daily) as he leads his friends on an adventure: "Hold on to your diapies, babies, we're going in!"

Singing voices for the hospital newborns include Jakob Dylan, Laurie Anderson, Beck, and Patti Smith.

tion. The hook for the story is the birth of a new baby brother for Tommy. The emotional conflict centers around Tommy's jealousy of the attention that the baby Dil gets from his parents. Later, Tommy's pals become jealous of the attention Dil gets from Tommy.

The opening part of the movie is entertaining in typical *Rugrats* fashion. Angelica muscles in when her friend is entertaining adults at a baby shower; she turns a song about cute babies into a wicked ditty about how awful babies are.

The family and friends rush to what the kids call the "hopsickle"— their malapropisms are a rich source of humor—when Tommy's mom is ready to deliver. The hospital lobby is topped by a huge monitor announcing "arrivals" and "departures" and the place is a veritable mall full of separate, trendy birthing rooms, including an underwater tank. The kids are left under the unreliable care of Tommy's grandpa, who can be counted on to get distracted or doze off, and they escape to the nursery, somehow convinced that it's a "baby store" and that's where they must go to buy Tommy a little brother or sister.

In the nursery, there is a boffo musical number sung by the newborns in their cribs. Written by Mark Mothersbaugh, it's their complaints about how bright and unforgiving the new world is and what torments the newborns have to put up with. So far, *The Rugrats Movie* has the typical *Rugrats* nerve and slightly twisted imagination, augmented by the greater possibilities of the big screen and the longer format. The animation—by a team predominantly composed of Koreans—is superb, eschewing the wide-screen penchant for super-realistic animation in favor of even broader and more outrageous caricatures. The soundtrack is engaging, the babies are as confused as ever, and the promise of a roaring good time is intoxicating.

Unfortunately, the nursery song is the film's high point. It's all downhill from there into a morass of big-budget sentimentality. First, we must sniffle for Tommy, whose father Stu has to interrupt his bedtime story to help with the constantly crying Dil. The parents forget about Tommy and he cowers in a corner, feeling abandoned. Then there is a mixup involving Stu's latest invention, a Reptarwagon (Reptar being the dinosaur-TV-star icon of the *Rugrats* world), and another case of the dozing Gramps. The upshot is that Dil and the other children are lost—not in the backyard, but in a real forest. When Angelica finds Cynthia is in the wagon, she takes off in hot pursuit.

Though the filmmakers try mightily to squeeze the customary *Rugrats* brand of humor out of the situation, there's nothing funny about three-and-unders being alone in the forest all night, especially when they encounter a train-wreck full of mischievous monkeys and a howling wolf. There are far too many heart-tugging moments involving Tommy's discovery of his role as caretaker for his little brother—and there's even an adult parallel as Stu tries to redeem himself in the eyes of his big brother. Desperately, the filmmakers resort to introducing new characters—a cowardly park ranger and his brave rookie partner (voiced by the ubiquitous Whoopi Goldberg) and a rude, blow-dried TV newsman parody (Tim Curry)—to try to get some desperately needed laughs.

The scenes seem forced, the situations confused and the multiple rescues unbelievable. For a long time the encounters with the monkeys are not full of grave danger; then suddenly they turn into threats. Stu takes off to save the kids in his homemade flying machine, and doesn't arrive at the woods, which is just out of town, until the next morning.

CREDITS

Tommy Pickles: E.G. Daily (voice)
Chuckie Finster :   Christine Cavanaugh (voice)
Phil and Lik DeVille :   Kath Soucie (voice)
Angelica Pickles :   Cheryl Case (voice)
Dil Pickles: Tara Charendoff (voice)
Didi Pickles: Melanie Chartoff (voice)
Stu Pickles :   Jack Riley (voice)
Grandpa Pickles: Joe Alaskey (voice)

Origin: USA
Released: 1998
Production: Arlene Klasky and Gabor Csupo for Nickelodeon Movies; released by Paramount Pictures
Direction: Norton Virgien, Igor Kovalyov
Screenplay: David N. Weiss and J. David Stem
Editing: John Bryant
Music: Mark Mothersbaugh
Art direction: Dima Malanitchev
Sound: Kurt Vanzo
MPAA rating: G
Running Time: 79 minutes

Neither Angelica nor the perpetually congested, lily-livered Chuckie are given enough to do. Their roles are truncated and their actions entirely too predictable. If *Rugrats* is an updated version of *Peanuts,* as some have suggested, Angelica is the Lucy character and Chuckie is the beleaguered Charlie Brown. Angelica is the bully and Chuckie the neurotic. Tommy, Phil and Lil, who hog most of the screen time, are not nearly as interesting characters. But Disney-like films always focus on bland young protagonists, not bullies and neurotics.

With *The Rugrats Movie,* the creators of *Rugrats* have broken an unspoken pact with both sets of target audiences —the young children who have grown up with the cartoon and their parents. Putting the children into real-world peril betrays the premise that the young heroes' problems are mostly in their own heads, and that they are always safe even as they imagine being in trouble. Even very young viewers of *Rugrats* understand that the children are just "dumb babies" who are at no risk of being actually harmed. It's shameful that this movie violates that bond to such an extent that it might be genuinely frightening for the under-six crowd. And parents should feel violated, too, because the movie takes so much of the neurotic edge off the *Rugrats* saga and sanitizes the humor with a huge gooey dollop of morality.

The final insult is that *The Rugrats Movie* comes complete with merchandising and marketing tie-ins. Fast-food joints are giving away Angelica toys, even though Angelica's ruthless affection for Cynthia long ago punctured the commercial crudeness of such dolls. Shamelessly, the creators of *Rugrats* are now just cashing in. They're exploiting the children whose world they once so engagingly championed.

—*Michael Betzold*

REVIEWS

Boxoffice. November, 1998, p. 34.
Entertainment Weekly. November 27, 1998, p. 56.
Los Angeles Times. April 20, 1998, p. F9.
New York Times. November 20, 1998, p. E30.
People. November 30, 1998, p. 33.
Variety. November 16, 1998, p. 34.

Rush Hour

The fastest hands in the East versus the biggest mouth in the West.—Movie tagline

"Two thumbs up!"—*Siskel & Ebert*

"*Rush Hour* is a nice surprise, like a fortune cookie with good news inside."—Richard Corliss, *Time*

"Chan and Tucker are terrific together!"—Jeffrey Lyons, *WNBC*

 Box Office: $136,065,335

New Line Cinema advertised *Rush Hour* as offering "the fastest hands in the East versus the biggest mouth in the West," and that would be accuracy in advertising if Hong Kong superstar Jackie Chan and his new-found American partner Chris Tucker were adversaries, but they are working together here, even though they may sometimes be at odds. *Rush Hour* presents a new departure for Chan by giving him an ethnic partner, the fast-talking Chris Tucker, last seen—and heard—in *Money Talks* (1997). This newly formed police buddy team scours Los Angeles to locate the daughter of a Chinese diplomat after the ten-year-old has been kidnapped. The question is whether or not Chan can hold his own against the antics of his manic partner. He does hold his own, but it's nearly a draw.

The story begins in Hong Kong at the transition point for the transfer of British rule to the People's Republic of China. Detective Lee (Jackie Chan) thwarts a criminal scheme to ship priceless Chinese art treasures out of the city in an action sequence that establishes his character as an heroic supercop, but his martial arts villain escapes to fight another day, later to resurface in Los Angeles, where most of the film's action is set. Lee reports his success to his chief, Han (Tzi Ma), who is soon to be sent to Los Angeles as a diplomat to the Chinese consulate there, with his daughter Soo Yung (a perky Julia Hsu), who has studied martial arts under her bodyguard and master, Lee, who encourages her to practice her "kicks and eye gouges" while in America.

A parallel sequence at the opening of the film establishes the character of renegade L.A.P.D. detective James Carter (Chris Tucker), intercepting a thug who has a load of C-4 plastique explosives in the trunk of his car, a sequence that ends with the car exploding (of course) and the crimi-

 Carter (Chris Tucker): "Fifty million dollars?! Who do you think you just kidnapped? Chelsea Clinton?!"

nal being captured. He is linked to the Chinese conspiracy that involves terrorism and kidnapping, and later is useful to Carter and Lee. Teamwork is not Carter's strong point. He is a loner who neglects his partner (Elizabeth Peña), an explosive expert whose talents are not needed until near the film's conclusion.

After Consul Han and his daughter move to Los Angeles, the girl is sent to school in a limousine with two bodyguards. Caught in rush hour traffic (and that is the only justification for the film's title), the limousine is diverted off the freeway by an Asian police officer. The bodyguards are killed and the girl is kidnapped in a well-paced action sequence. Upon learning about the kidnapping, Consul Han requests the aid of his trusted friend, Detective Lee, who immediately boards a flight for Los Angeles. The FBI wants to keep Lee at arm's length, however, and requests the LAPD to assign an officer to keep Lee out of their way. Carter, who is seen as a renegade and a nuisance, gets this assignment and is sent to the airport to meet Lee's flight. There is a huge cultural gap between them that needs to be closed and this makes for much comic banter, Chris Tucker's speciality. Lee keeps trying to escape from Carter, at one point removing the steering wheel from Carter's convertible to which he has been handcuffed.

The kidnap-ransom conspiracy is masterminded by the mysterious Juntao, who first demands $50 million dollars in exchange for the girl's life, and then ups the ante to $70 million after Carter and Lee unwittingly get in the way of the ransom delivery. The final act of the ransom conspiracy is played out at a Chinese art exposition. The ultimate villain proves to be a British diplomat named Griffin (played by Tom Wilkinson, memorable as the stripping plant manager from *The Full Monty* [1997]), who had planned to smuggle the art treasures out of China, while pretending to be Han's friend. Jackie pursues him to the top of the exposition hall as he attempts to escape with a satchel of millions from the roof via helicopter. This leaves Chris Tucker to deal with Griffin's martial arts henchman, a job that would better have been left for Jackie Chan, and one that ends in a Mexican stand-off and shoot-out. The viewer almost expects Tucker to talk his opponent to death. After the money is recovered and the little girl is saved, Carter returns with Lee to Hong Kong for a well-deserved vacation. The film ends in typical Jackie Chan fashion with a series of comic outtakes as the final credits roll.

Most reviewers found *Rush Hour* amusing and entertaining. The screenplay by Jim Kouf and Ross LaManna is far-fetched but functional. Michael O'Sullivan of the *Washington Post* described the script as "perfunctory and sloppy," tending to rely "on explosions over sense." The *Washington Post* also criticized the direction as being "limp" and "lethargic," though in fact the action moves at a fairly brisk pace. At age 28 director Brett Ratner belongs to the new millennium generation of young directors trained in television commercials and music videos, who, according to Michele Willens of the *New York Times,* have developed technical skills but are short on vision, as evidenced by the work of F. Gary Gray, who directed *The Negotiator* (reviewed in this edition) and David Fincher, who directed *Seven* (1996) and *The Game* (1997). Ratner told the *New York Times* his videos "were more like mini-movies, telling a story," but, he added, "I do have a short attention span." This is not too much of a handicap for a director working on such a project as *Rush Hour.*

Although Jackie Chan's Hong Kong-made movies have been re-edited and released in the U.S., this is his first big budget Hollywood studio movie.

In his *Entertainment Weekly* review, Owen Gleiberman was most favorably impressed by Chris Tucker, whom he compared first to Eddie Murphy, then to Groucho Marx, concluding that Tucker was "the only performer worth watching in *Rush Hour.*" If that be true, then Jackie Chan, a world-class talent, has made a serious career error in his first major American feature by allowing himself to be upstaged by his motormouthed sidekick. On the other hand, the *Baltimore Sun* review objected that Tucker's character "has nothing going for him save an ability to crack wise," and complained that the constant wise-cracking can get tedious. Tucker has an astonishing talent for the flamboyant articulation of character as he demonstrated in *The Fifth Element* (1997) with Ruby Rhod, a freakish and repulsive entertainment queen, celebrity parasite, and interstellar talk-show host of the future. His performance was fascinating, but painfully over-the-top. By comparison, his portrayal of Carter is low-keyed and even likable.

Other reviewers were not so quick to lose sight of Chan, however. "This smartly mounted thriller stirs a good rapport between the stars and proves that, at 44, Asia's top action hero can still kick up a story," Richard Corliss wrote in his *Time* review, concluding that *Rush Hour* was "a nice little surprise, like a fortune cookie with some good news inside." One might question how well matched the talents are, if Jackie Chan, who has been compared to Buster Keaton for his comic stunts is paired with the pathologically verbal Chris Tucker. If he has become a latter-day Groucho Marx, can he work effectively with a latter-day Buster Keaton? The original Groucho played well enough against the mute comedy of Harpo, however, and the inventively mismatched buddy formula works well enough here. For Carrie Rickey of the *Philadelphia Inquirer,* it was like Buster Keaton playing against Jerry Lewis.

In his *Washington Times* review Gary Arnold never questioned that Chan was the star, though mismatched "enjoyably" with Chris Tucker in an "improbable, serendipitous example of teamwork." Each star is placed out of his element for comedic effect—Chan in a black bar, innocently causing a brawl by repeating a racial epithet that Chris Tucker could use with impunity, and Tucker in Chinatown, being equally obnoxious without meaning to be. As one reviewer noted, "it's a given in these films that the partners always act like they don't get along, but they do." The formula goes back to *48 HRS* (1982) and *Lethal Weapon* (1987), though the occasionally crude screenplay of *Rush Hour,* with its comic ethnic jokes, lacks that level of "narrative polish," as Carrie Rickey noted. The film's verbal overdrive comes from Tucker's rapid delivery that in itself is enough to pace the film, while Jackie Chan's Kung Foolishness creates a smashing ballet of bone-crunching mayhem, especially when he takes out the villains while also carefully trying to protect a 500-year-old vase, that is tipped this way and that, but never toppled or broken.

CREDITS

Detective Inspector Lee: Jackie Chan
Detective James Carter: Chris Tucker
Thomas Griffin: Tom Wilkinson
Tania Johnson: Elizabeth Peña
Capt. Diel: Philip Baker Hall
Agent Russ: Mark Rolston
Sang: Ken Leung
Clive: Chris Penn
Consul Han: Tzi Ma
Soo Yung: Julia Hsu

Origin: USA
Released: 1998
Production: Roger Birnbaum, Arthur Sarkissian, and Jonathan Glickman; released by New Line Cinema
Direction: Bret Ratner
Screenplay: Jim Kour and Ross Lamanna
Cinematography: Adam Greenberg
Editing: Mark Helfrich
Music: Lalo Schifrin
Production design: Robb Wilson King
Art direction: Thomas Fichter
Costumes: Sharen Davis
Stunt coordinator: Terry Leonard, Jackie Chan
MPAA rating: PG-13
Running Time: 98 minutes

Jackie Chan's Hong Kong features have always enjoyed a cult following but have seemed a little too exotic for the American mainstream. During its opening weekend, however, *Rush Hour* grossed $33 million, setting a record for September, and it retained its number-one position the following weekend, when it earned over $20 million more. Thanks to Chris Tucker and the crossover audience he no doubt brought with him, *Rush Hour*, Chan's first American movie in 17 years, could also be Chan's breakthrough American feature. A sequel is sure to follow.

—*James M. Welsh*

REVIEWS

Baltimore Sun. September 18, 1998, p. E3.
Boxoffice. July, 1998, p. 20.
Entertainment Weekly. September 25, 1998, p. 74.
New York Times. September 6, 1998, p. 7.
New York Times. September 18, 1998, p. B12.
Philadelphia Inquirer Weekend. September 18, 1998, p. 4.
Sight and Sound. December, 1998, p. 60.
Time. September 21, 1998, p. 105.
USA Today. September 18, 1998, p. E3.
USA Today. September 25, 1998, p. E1.
Variety. September 21, 1998, p. 105.
Washington Post. September 18, 1998, p. C7.
Washington Post Weekend. September 18, 1998, p. 58.
Washington Times Metropolitan Times. September 18, 1998, p. C16.

Rushmore

Love. Expulsion. Revolution.—Movie tagline

"A masterpiece of originality."—Lisa Schwarzbaum, *Entertainment Weekly*

"Smart and spiky. A particular treat for its skewed, hilarious memories of a cut-throat boyhood in a private school named *Rushmore*." —Janet Maslin, *New York Times*

"A marvelous comedy from deep in left field. Immaculately written and unexpectedly touching."—Jeff Giles, *Newsweek*

"Don't miss *Rushmore*, one of the year's 10 best! It deserves a place on every 1998 ten best list— it's the year's most winning surprise. Order an Oscar for Bill Murray."—Peter Travers, *Rolling Stone*

 Box Office: $9,758,000

Offering extra credit to any student who can solve an impossible math equation written on the board, the geometry teacher at Rushmore Academy stumps a classroom of teenage boys until Max Fischer (Jason Schwartzman) is summoned to prove his mathematical genius. This king of extra-curricular activities—from president of the beekeeping society to founder of the stamp collecting club—is actually daydreaming during a surprisingly frank speech by benefactor Herman Blume (Bill Murray). Max is somewhat of a doer than dreamer, even though his life and world consists of surreal acts that levitate this comedy to new heights of originality. Inspired by the industrialist, the precocious underachiever recognizes their kindred spirit and the two befriend each other, Blume actually finding his younger self in the bright boy.

Fischer actually suffers academically at the cost of his endless pursuits and the scholarship student is put on "Sudden Death Probation," by the principal for flunking all of his classes. Undaunted, Fischer heads off to the library and while reading *Diving for Sunken Treasure*, he discovers a meaningful Jacques Cousteau quote hand-written in the margin. While exploring who else checked out the book, the fifteen-year-old locates the pretty and sweet first grade teacher, Mrs. Cross (Olivia Williams), who he immediately falls madly in love with. He hangs out in her classroom and onto her every word, respecting her reverence for Latin by getting it reinstated onto the school schedule, a class he previously worked on replacing with Japanese.

At a wrestling event Fischer endears himself to his hero Blume, claiming his father is a neurosurgeon, instead of a barber. If Max is embarrassed of his father's profession, Blume is equally mortified with his twin son's coarse behavior. The boy brings his friends together to enjoy his plays—a theatrical version of *Serpico* and

> Blume (Bill Murray): "Never in my wildest dreams did I imagine having sons like this."

other pursuits—while Blume and Cross begin to develop a relationship. The widowed Cross sees similarities between her late husband and the eccentric boy, as well as the bewildered and bemusing Blume. Fearing Fischer's infatuation, she says, "You're too young for me. I'm a teacher and you're a student." But he's undaunted and his crush turns delusional, clear to her when he's rude to her date.

The stagnant magnate Blume dives into his swimming pool at a family gathering, floating at the bottom like the classic scene of Benjamin Braddock in *The Graduate*. The allusions to Fischer as a new Benjamin are also obvious, including his interest in the older woman. The odd twists, quirky behavior and humorous events surrounding the love triangle thicken and turn a darker tone as his obsession deepens. He fixates on building her a fish aquarium and convinces Blume International to fund it, unaware that the disgruntled Blume has also fallen for the teacher.

Only one month later, he's kicked out of Rushmore over an extravagant fund-raiser for the project. Fischer goes off to public school, still wearing his navy blazer and blue shirt uniform. He gives a speech to introduce himself to his new class, catching the attention of Margaret Yang (Sara Tanaka) whom he ignores. Adjusting to the school isn't easy but he tries the same flurry of diversions from fencing to backflips on the cheerleading squad.

During one of his regular after school visits to Rushmore, a nasty Scottish kid confronts him with "I know about you and the teacher," but Fischer's response is as immature as the bully's taunts. His defense puts him in jeopardy with a younger schoolmate, Dirk Calloway (Mason Gamble), that Fischer mentored by claiming a sexual relationship with his mother. Through a gossipy chain of comments, Dirk is hurt and strikes back, spilling the beans to Fischer about Cross and Blume's attraction. Max challenges his older friend Blume—"I saved Latin, what did you do?"

War ensues. Max messes with Blume's brake linings. Blume rides over Max's bicycle. But the problem escalates and turns meaner. Blume is attacked in a bee-infested hotel room after his wife kicks him out of the house. Although Blume smiles slightly, amused by the tactics of his rival, the duel continues to heat up with further foolish mischief. Fischer is not just a nerd with few social skills, he borders on sociopathic and as endearing as Blume appears, partly due to Murray's charming performance, the grown man seems deranged and the laughs turn sour. It's not even clear that what they are battling over is Mrs. Cross's dubious affections.

Dirk confronts Fischer on his assertion to a relationship with his mother and unsatisfied with the results, sends snapshots of Cross with Blume to the principle, compro-

mising her position with the school. In her classroom while packing to leave, she apologizes to Fischer, "I'm sorry I hurt your feelings and that I loved your friend instead." He tries to kiss her, stating "Rushmore was my life—now you are." But surrendering to defeat, the young man meets Blume to end all of the shenanigans with an admittance, "She loves you."

Time passes and a despondent Fischer drops out of school, joins his father in the barber shop, and ignores his fellow student Margaret's visits. But it takes a series of events to shake him out of his stupor—his former friend Dirk apologizes for his part in the dilemma, the Rushmore principal has a stroke. While visiting the principal in the hospital, Max bumps into Blume where they both come to the realization that Cross simply can't get over the death of her husband.

> Screenwriter and director Wes Anderson befriended Owen Wilson while a student at the University of Texas.

To make amends with Blume and Cross, Fischer orchestrates another event to expand Rushmore's aquarium. This gala gets Max back into school where he directs another winning play—a Vietnam War drama, equipped with explosives. He maneuvers to have Cross and Blume seated next to each other for the performance which includes lines such as "When the fighting stops, no one gets hurt." Triumphant due to the success of his play, Max is now dressed in a velvet suit with bow tie. His transformation seems to have him appearing more like Austin Powers than a private school boy.

The obscure '60s pop tunes throughout the soundtrack underline many of the film's messages effectively, including "Here Comes My Baby" by Cat Stevens and The Who's "You Are Forgiven." The ending refrain over the credits sums it up quite well—"I wish that I knew what I know now when I was younger."

Director and co-writer Wes Anderson has taken the "revenge of the nerds" theme to a personal level rather than a student retaliating on an entire school population. Supposedly a tale of "all's fair when love is war," the premise would seem to be about romance and revenge. However, *Rushmore* maintains its focus on the strange Max Fischer, played by Schwartzman (actress Talia Shire's son), in a compelling portrayal of an unusual, perhaps bored yet brilliant

AWARDS AND NOMINATIONS

Independent Spirit Awards 1999: Director (Wes Anderson); Supporting Actor (Bill Murray)
Los Angeles Film Critics 1998: Supporting Actor (Bill Murray)
New York Film Critics 1998: Supporting Actor (Bill Murray)

teenager, in a long tradition of this angst-driven character, from Holden Caulfield to Benjamin Braddock. In its terminal uniqueness, the preposterousness becomes part of the atmosphere.

CREDITS

Max Fischer: Jason Schwartzman
Herman Blume: Bill Murray
Rosemary Cross: Olivia Williams
Bert Fischer: Seymour Cassel
Dr. Guggenheim: Brian Cox
Dirk Calloway: Mason Gamble
Margaret Yang: Sara Tanaka
Ronny Blume: Ronnie McCawley
Donny Blume: Keith McCawley

Origin: USA
Released: 1998
Production: Barry Mendel and Paul Schiff for American Empirical production; released by Buena Vista
Direction: Wes Anderson
Screenplay: Wes Anderson and Owen Wilson
Cinematography: Robert Yeoman
Editing: David Moritz
Music: Mark Mothersbaugh
Production design: David Wasco
Art direction: Andrew Laws
Set design: Daniel Bradford
Set decoration: Alexandra Reynolds-Wasco
Costumes: Karen Patch
Sound: Pawel Wdowczak
MPAA rating: R
Running Time: 89 minutes

There are lots of plays-for-laughs and interesting highlights in Anderson's second film (*Bottle Rocket* [1996]) was his debut, also co-written with Owen Wilson). Roger Ebert in the *Chicago Sun-Times* considers the director "a good off-beat filmmaker." G. Allen Johnson from the *San Francisco Examiner* calls *Rushmore,* "Tom Sawyer as done by the Coen brothers. A weird, wonderful and funny work." He adds it's "a comedy with charming naivete and gives Bill Murray his best role in years." The consensus agrees on Murray stealing the show with a dry and deadpan depiction of the goofy Blume, a performance that won him several Film Critics Association awards.

Although critics like Richard Schickel in *Time* magazine believe it's "a delightfully droll comedy that delights in itself a little too much," audiences find it endearing and original. They don't seem to see Fischer as a menacing stalker with an inflated sense of himself but appreciate the actor's lively film debut and the character's individuality. Overall, the entertainment value runs high with plenty of chuckles and clever surprises.

—*Roberta Cruger*

REVIEWS

Chicago Tribune. February 5, 1999, p. 5.
Entertainment Weekly. December 18, 1998, p. 53.
The Hollywood Reporter. October 13, 1998, p. 60.
Los Angeles Times. December 11, 1998, p. F9.
New York Times. October 9, 1999, p. E10.
People. December 21, 1998, p. 38.
Rolling Stone. February 18, 1999, p. 69.
San Francisco Chronicle. February 5, 1999, p. C1.
San Francisco Examiner. February 5, 1999, p. C1.
Variety. September 14, 1998, p. 33.

Saving Private Ryan

The mission is a man.—Movie tagline

In the last great invasion of the last great war, the greatest danger for eight men . . . was saving one.—Movie tagline

"A watershed picture, for both Spielberg and war movies in general. The most exciting movie Steven has ever made."—Michael Wilmington, *Chicago Tribune*

"A movie of staggering virtuosity and raw lyric power; a masterpiece."—Owen Gleiberman, *Entertainment Weekly*

"A magnificent and stunning picture . . . riveting and fascinating. Hanks is perfect."—Louis Parks, *Houston Chronicle*

"A powerful and impressive milestone. Tom Hanks gives an indelible performance. Spielberg is a master storyteller whose gift for narrative film is unsurpassed."—Kenneth Turan, *Los Angeles Times*

"Viscerally enthralling. It holds the audience spellbound. Spielberg's soberly magnificent film is the second pinnacle in a career of magical versatility."—Janet Maslin, *New York Times*

"Two thumbs way up, one of the most powerful war movies we've seen."—*Siskel & Ebert*

"An emotionally electrifying drama. A film to witness, a film to remember, a film never to forget."—Gene Shalit, *Today*

"A staggering new screen chapter in virtuoso period immediacy . . . the rawest, most sustained screen portrayal of 20th century combat."—Mike Clark, *USA Today*

"Searing, heartbreaking . . .this is simply the greatest war movie ever made, and one of the great American movies."—Stephen Hunter, *Washington Post*

"A major achievement in American film. An extraordinary film of astonishing power, intelligence, heart and soul. The finest WWII movie ever, the finest Spielberg movie ever, featuring the finest Hanks performance ever."—Dennis Cunningham, *WCBS-TV*

Box Office: $190,805,259

Tom Hanks stars in Steven Spielberg's war masterpiece *Saving Private Ryan*.

The most riveting aspect of Steven Spielberg's World War II drama *Saving Private Ryan* is the battle scenes themselves. Praised by many critics as the most realistic combat sequences in a narrative film, the battles are graphic and intense depictions of sheer chaos and bloodshed. On a thematic level, the film is a meditation on fulfilling one's duty while trying to live a decent life in the midst of horror. It is also clearly Spielberg's tribute to the Americans who fought World War II. (Veterans praised him for the film's authenticity, and the American Legion honored him.) While *Saving Private Ryan* is not a perfect film—its narrative is fairly thin—it grabs the audience through the sheer force of unforgettable imagery and action and the presence of Tom Hanks in yet another quintessentially American role.

The film's most stunning set piece is the Allied D-Day invasion of Omaha Beach. An orgy of carnage that lasts about 24 minutes, the invasion begins with many men being shot dead before they can even make it out of their landing crafts. Others are killed underwater or mowed down as they attempt to get to shore. A man carries his own severed arm. Another futilely attempts to put back the guts falling out of his body. Captain John Miller (Tom Hanks) drags a man a few yards only to look down and discover, after an explosion, that he is dragging half of a body. Blood gushes from wounds as medics try in vain to repair the damage.

Spielberg uses the filmic medium brilliantly in these scenes. When Miller is disoriented and momentarily loses his hearing, we see the chaos from his point of view. The film seems to speed up and yet slow down at the same time—giving it an almost dream-like quality. The sequence communicates the utter confusion of war (hand-held camera work gives us the visceral experience of being right in the action) while making the progress of the battle totally comprehensible. The Americans make slow, costly strides but finally take control of the beachhead and ultimately the German bunker.

Once the slaughter is over, we move to Washington, D.C., where a woman in the War Department notices that three brothers named Ryan have been killed in action and that their mother will soon be receiving the news. To prevent a repeat of the real-life story of the Sullivans, five brothers killed together on a Navy ship, General George C. Marshall (Harve Presnell) gives the order that the last brother, James, who parachuted into Normandy the night before the invasion, be found and brought home. This becomes Captain Miller's new mission.

While the film's depiction of war is innovative, the composition of Miller's platoon is not. As in many traditional combat films, men from different backgrounds band together to form a relatively cohesive unit. In addition to Miller and his right-hand man, Sergeant Mike Horvath (Tom Sizemore), there is Private Mellish (Adam Goldberg), a Jew who taunts captive German soldiers with his Star of David; Corporal Upham (Jeremy Davies), a bookish writer and translator who quotes Emerson but who has not fired a gun since basic training and predictably ends up a coward; Private Jackson (Barry Pepper), a Christian marksman who prays before taking each shot; and the cynical Brooklynite Private Reiben (Edward Burns), who constantly questions why eight lives should be risked to save one. Two other soldiers, Private Caparzo (Vin Diesel) and T/4 Medic Wade (Giovanni Ribisi), are killed before the film's final battle.

Saving Private Ryan's most mundane aspect is the construction of the story itself. It is a rather episodic affair in which Miller's platoon marches from place to place, faces the enemy in a series of skirmishes on its way to finding Ryan, and bonds as a unit between battles. The men come upon a devastated village and a panicked family in a bombed-out house. The family wants to give its little girl to the soldiers for protection, and Caparzo takes her and ends up exposing himself to a sniper. His is a slow, agonizing death—just one of several scenes that underscore the suffering men endure when they are dying and the way a kind gesture can backfire during war.

After much marching and frustration, Miller finally ascertains Ryan's position from a soldier who knows him, but, on the way to their destination of Ramelle, the men come across a German fortified machine gun nest. Instead of simply going around it, they attack it so that future Allied troops do not face an ambush. In the assault, Wade is killed. Earlier he spoke movingly and regretfully about sometimes pretending to be asleep when his mother came home from work. As he is dying, he calls out to her.

While these scenes are intense and often harrowing—as almost every critic noted, Spielberg has succeeded in deglamorizing war—they do not always feel like a coherent whole but rather a way of passing time until the unit finds Ryan. (Even the opening invasion, after all, a remarkable sequence that ranks with Spielberg's best filmmaking, is a kind of prologue largely divorced from the main story.)

At the same time, certain details in Robert Rodat's screenplay help to unify the film's episodes. When Caparzo dies, Wade retrieves a letter to Caparzo's father from his pocket and copies it over because the original is soaked with blood. When Wade dies, Miller takes it from his corpse, and, when Miller dies at film's end, Reiben retrieves it from Miller's pocket. This is a subtle motif (no one delivers a grandiose speech about it) that emphasizes the notion of a brotherhood slowly bonding in duty to each other.

After the assault on the machine gun nest, the platoon captures a German soldier. Many of the men want to execute their prisoner, but Miller takes the legal, moral action and frees him blindfolded in the hope that he later will be picked up by the Allies. However, the German soldier re-appears in the final battle and fires the shot that kills Miller—thus showing the cost of integrity during war.

The film's most complex character is Miller, who personifies the decent Everyman tested in the maelstrom of war. To his men, Miller is an enigma. They speculate on what he did in civilian life, and there is a running joke about an ever-increasing pool among the men to guess his background. Tensions run high after the captured German is freed, and Reiben grows more frustrated over the mission. When he threatens to leave and Horvath pulls a gun on him, Miller defuses the tense situation by demystifying himself

Capt. John Miller (Tom Hanks): "He [Private Ryan] better be worth it. He better go home and cure a disease, or invent a longer-lasting lightbulb."

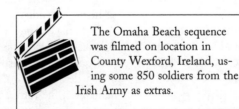

The Omaha Beach sequence was filmed on location in County Wexford, Ireland, using some 850 soldiers from the Irish Army as extras.

and revealing his background, which turns out to be rather ordinary; he was in fact a high school English teacher. Miller is the American ideal—a moral man who acts honorably and bravely in war, a leader who does not shirk from duty (even if he may have personal doubts about his mission), and an educated man who does not show off his knowledge. He even displays a wry sense of humor; when German propaganda announces, "The Statue of Liberty is kaput," Miller deadpans, "That's disconcerting." At the same time, we see the cost of war for such a man. His hand periodically shakes (it is our first glimpse of him), thus suggesting the war is breaking him down, and he even wonders if he has "changed so much my wife is even gonna recognize me whenever it is I get back to her." In one scene, when he questions a line of marching soldiers and refugees to see if they know Ryan's location, Miller seems touched by madness. He even cries alone after the death of Wade. Hanks delivers a complex, subtle portrayal that anchors the film amongst the bloodshed and confusion of war.

The platoon finally finds Ryan (Matt Damon), who, believing it is his duty to fight, refuses to go home and abandon his company, which has the assignment to hold a strategic bridge against German attack. The very rationale for Miller's mission is coming undone, but he and Horvath ultimately decide to have their group stay and join in the upcoming battle. Horvath even speculates that saving Private Ryan could end up being "the one decent thing" they do, which seems like an odd sentiment given the fact that the war itself is being fought for much larger reasons.

While the climactic battle is small in scope compared to the opening invasion, in some ways it is more compelling. The major players are in different locations in the small village, but Michael Kahn's skillful editing enables us to follow the movements of all the soldiers we have come to know. Aside from Hanks's familiar face, most of the men in the film's opening are anonymous, but, by the end, we now identify with specific characters, so the deaths have an extra dimension. Jackson is stationed in a bell tower, and, while he

kills some Germans, a tank ultimately blows him away. Mellish is killed in hand-to-hand combat, while Upham, frozen on a staircase, is too cowardly to climb up and save him. Horvath and finally Miller die in battle. While Upham is useless during the fighting and runs around aimlessly, he does avenge Miller's death by killing the German they once freed, but at this point it feels like a hollow gesture. Air reinforcements arrive, and the bridge is held.

The film opens and closes in the present day with an old man visiting the cemetery in Normandy as his family follows behind him. Only at the end is the man revealed to be Ryan when the face of young Ryan morphs into the old. Throughout the film, the men debated the worthiness of the mission—what is the value of the life of one man, and why should they risk their lives to find him? While the issue can never be definitively resolved, Miller's dying words instructing Ryan to "earn this, earn it" and the image of the older Ryan saluting Miller's grave are meant to assure us that Ryan really was worth all the sacrifice. However, this feels like a pat ending, and the framing device is rendered

AWARDS AND NOMINATIONS

Academy Awards 1998: Director (Steven Spielberg); Cinematography; Sound; Sound Effects Editing; Film Editing
Broadcast Film Critics Association 1998: Film; Director (Steven Spielberg)
Directors Guild of America 1998: Steven Spielberg
Golden Globes 1999: Drama; Director (Steven Spielberg)
Los Angeles Film Critics 1998: Film; Director (Steven Spielberg); Cinematography
New York Film Critics 1998: Film
Academy Awards 1998 Nominations: Picture; Actor (Tom Hanks); Original Screenplay; Art Direction; Original Dramatic Score; Makeup

CREDITS

Capt. John Miller: Tom Hanks
Pvt. Reiben: Edward Burns
Sgt. Horvath: Tom Sizemore
Cpl. Upham: Jeremy Davies
Pvt. Caparzo: Vin Diesel
Pvt. Mellish: Adam Goldberg
Pvt. Jackson: Barry Pepper
T/4 Medic Wade: Giovanni Ribisi
Pvt. James Ryan: Matt Damon
Capt. Hamill: Ted Danson
Gen. George C. Marshall: Harve Presnell

Origin: USA
Released: 1998
Production: Steven Spielberg, Ian Bryce, Mark Gordon, and Gary Levinsohn for Mutual Film Company and Amblin Entertainment; released by DreamWorks Pictures and Paramount Pictures
Direction: Steven Spielberg
Screenplay: Robert Rodat
Cinematography: Janusz Kaminski
Editing: Michael Kahn
Music: John Williams
Production design: Tom Sanders
Costumes: Joanna Johnston
Sound: Ronald Judkins
Special effects supervision: Neil Corbould
Stunt coordination: Simon Crane
Senior military advise: Capt. Dale Dye
MPAA rating: R
Running Time: 169 minutes

superfluous on a dramatic level—a sentimental flourish in an otherwise tough-minded film.

In the summer of 1998, *Saving Private Ryan* was the only Hollywood release that received nearly unanimous critical praise along with blockbuster boxoffice. The film takes us to a place most people will never see and moves audiences through its unforgettable images of combat. It may be going too far to declare *Saving Private Ryan* the greatest war film ever made or even Spielberg's finest achievement, as some critics did. In addition to its unforgettable images, *Schindler's List* (1993) has a more compelling story and complex, ambiguous characters. At the same time, Spielberg's World War II epics complement each other quite nicely. While *Schindler's List* examines the almost accidental heroics of an opportunist and war profiteer, *Saving Private Ryan* is a tribute to American heroism and courage under the most horrifying conditions.

—*Peter N. Chumo II*

REVIEWS

Boxoffice. September, 1998, p. 63.
Chicago Tribune. July 24, 1998, p. 4.
Detroit Free Press. July 24, 1998, p. D1.
Detroit News. July 24, 1998, p. D1.
Entertainment Weekly. July 24, 1998, p. 46.
Los Angeles Times. May 10, 1998.
Los Angeles Times. July 24, 1998, p. F1.
New York Times. July 19, 1998, p. A11.
New York Times. July 24, 1998, p. E1.
Newsweek. July 13, 1998, p. 48.
People. August 3, 1998, p. 25.
San Francisco Chronicle. July 24, 1998, p. C1.
San Francisco Examiner. July 24, 1998. C1.
Sight and Sound. September, 1998, p. 34.
Time. July 27, 1998.
Variety. July 20, 1998, p. 45.

Savior

He's fighting a war he doesn't believe in, hoping to find something he does. Hope is worth fighting for.—Movie tagline

"A portrayal that ranks among the year's finest!"—Kevin Thomas, *Los Angeles Times*

"Dennis Quaid's best performance in years!" —Stephen Farber, *Movieline*

"Dennis Quaid has the role of his career!" —Stephen Holden, *New York Times*

"Two thumbs up!"—*Siskel & Ebert*

Dennis Quaid trades in his usual charming persona to show off his dramatic chops in the compelling war drama, *Savior,* from Serbian director Peter Antonijevic. Screenwriter Robert Orr was a photographer's assistant and relief worker during the war in Bosnia and based his script on the true story of an American mercenary (among other incidents). Quaid stars as the mercenary, a former U.S. military officer named Joshua Rose.

When Rose's wife (Nastassja Kinski) and child are killed by Islamic terrorists in a Paris bombing, he takes revenge by opening fire in the nearest mosque. Rose then disappears

The picture was shot on location in Montenegro.

into the Foreign Legion, changing his name to Guy, and six years later (it's 1993), he's in Bosnia fighting for the Serbs, alongside his best friend Peter (Stellan Skarsgard). Guy has channelled all his rage into becoming a numb, efficient killing machine.

But things change when Guy accompanies Muslim-hating Serb, Goran (Sergej Trifunovic), to a prisoner exchange where they are told to take a very pregnant young Serbian woman, Vera (Natasa Ninkovic), back to her village, which is also Goran's home. Vera's pregnancy is the result of rape by her Muslim captors but Goran accuses her of willingly sleeping with the enemy. When he begins to beat her in order to force a miscarriage, Guy kills him, and then delivers Vera's premature baby girl.

Vera doesn't want the child and is herself rejected by her ashamed father when they reach her village. So Guy decides to drive them to a refugee center. However, Goran's body has been discovered by the local Serbian militia who order Vera's father and brother to pay the blood debt owed to Goran's family by avenging the killing. They catch up and manage to shoot Guy but cannot bring themselves to kill Vera.

Guy decides to try to smuggle Vera and the baby out of the country but their car breaks down on the way. As the wounded Guy hides with the baby, Vera walks to the nearest town to seek help and winds up running into a Croatian patrol, who kill her. Guy again manages to escape with the baby and makes his way to Split, where he finally abandons the child. But a woman brings the baby back to him and asks if he is the father. When Guy says he is, she persuades him to keep the baby.

The film gets off to a shaky start with its prologue establishing Joshua/Guy's motivations for turning mercenary but once that contrivance is out of the way, the rest of the film is bleakly compelling. The violence is brutal and survival is all that matters. Quaid's character is a(n emotionally) dead man walking and even after he accepts responsibility for the child, only the promise of hope is shown—it's not a given.

—*Christine Tomassini*

CREDITS

Joshua Rose/Guy: Dennis Quaid
Maria: Nastassja Kinski
Peter: Stellan Skarsgard
Vera: Natasa Ninkovic
Goran: Sergej Trifunovic

Origin: USA
Released: 1998
Production: Oliver Stone and Janet Yang for Initial Entertainment Group; released by Lions Gate Films
Direction: Peter Antonijevic
Screenplay: Robert Orr
Cinematography: Ian Wilson
Editing: Ian Crafford, Gabriella Cristiani
Music: David Robbins
Production design: Vladislav Lasic
Costumes: Boris Caksiran
Sound: Bill Fiege
MPAA rating: R
Running Time: 103 minutes

REVIEWS

Entertainment Weekly. December 4, 1998, p. 68.
The Hollywood Reporter. November 17, 1998, p. 24.
Los Angeles Times. November 20, 1998, p. F12.
New York Times. November 25, 1998, p. E5.
People. December 7, 1998, p. 34.
Sight and Sound. July, 1998, p. 51.
Variety. June 29, 1998, p. 39.

Senseless

A comedy about the world's most sensitive man.—Movie tagline

"Genuinely hysterical!"—*ABC-TV*

"Marlon Wayans is an outrageous combination of Eddie Murphy and Jim Carrey!"—*Baltimore Times*

"A smart, inspired laugh riot!"—*Los Angeles Times*

"David Spade has never been funnier!"
—*WWBR-FM*

 Box Office: $13,109,234

Following in the footsteps of a show-biz family member can be the sharpest of all double-edged swords. On one hand, getting in the door takes little or no effort. The "it's not what you know, it's who you know" adage doesn't apply; if you've got the genes, getting in the door is your birthright. Sticking around for the long haul is another matter entirely. The expectations for those who coast in on the family plan are (naturally) higher. While being the child of famous parents presents the highest hurdles, riding on the coattails of a high-profile brother or sister can also be daunting. Just ask Janet or Reebie Jackson. Never heard of Reebie Jackson? Point made.

When it was clear that Fox Television's sketch-comedy show *In Living Color* was a bona fide hit, it seemed that each and every one of producer/writer/premier talent Keenan Ivory Wayans's nearly one dozen siblings came out of the woodwork. While brother Damon and sister Kim performed admirably on the show, neither has done much since to distinguish themselves. In 1995, the eldest Wayans produced *Don't Be a Menace to South Central While Drinking Your Juice in the Hood*, a parody of violent urban dramas, written by and starring his brothers Shawn and Marlon. Patently offensive yet absent of any malice, it was gobbled up by the *In Living Color* crowd and quickly forgotten. Before it faded into obscurity, it was able to flag the attention of director Penelope Spheeris who was responsible for some gems (*Wayne's World, Black Sheep*) and some out-and-out clunkers (*The Beverly Hillbillies, The Little Rascals*). Spheeris, no stranger to testing the boundaries of good taste herself, saw in Marlon a handsome good-natured physical comedian who would a perfect fit as the over-achieving everyman in her new *Animal House* meets *Trading Places* meets *Boomerang* project, *Senseless*. Far more than just a vehicle for a string of sight and sound set-up/payoff scenes, *Senseless* is a surprisingly effective, slightly cloaked morality play about setting one's sight on a goal and overcoming often staggering odds in order to achieve it. While it is often sophomoric and base in its delivery, it has moments of downright tenderness and for the most part, keeps us entertained.

Darryl Witherspoon (Wayans) is an economics major at Stratford University who is looking to land a job with Smythe-Bates, a prestigious Wall Street accounting firm. His plethora of odd jobs include selling assorted bodily fluids for cash, working in the school cafeteria and giving quickie tours of the campus. He doesn't work himself into a frazzle for walking around money, it's all done in an effort to keep his financially-strapped family above water. Near exhaustion, Darryl volunteers to be the guinea pig for an experimental drug which heightens the five senses. Despite being read a laundry list of adverse side effects, Darryl begins taking the drug not only for the $3000 in cash that will tide his family over, but also for the added bonus of helping him qualify for the posh job as a numbers cruncher.

After enduring a short period of side effects, Darryl hones his knowledge of finance while trying to fit the mold of the ideal grant candidate. He also starts a relationship with the beautiful Janice (Tamara Taylor) and proceeds to charm the socks off of Randall Tyson (Rip Torn), the man who will choose the lucky finalist for the job. Protocol requires Darryl to play a sport (he picks hockey) and join a fraternity which he endures with a grain of salt, but his biggest battle is staving off Scott Thorpe (David Spade, in peak condescending form), a snotty rich kid who seems pre-ordained to get the coveted job. Initially, Scott considers Darryl a minor distraction whom he deflects with throwaway snide comments but soon realizes that Darryl is a legitimate threat.

With the sense-enhancing formula now giving him the edge he needs to pass Scott, Darryl begins to get a little cocky. Thinking that a double-dose of the drug will double his newfound abilities, Darryl instead becomes confused and disoriented which results in a series of mishaps that basically destroys all of his groundwork. This is where Spheeris's film starts getting a little too formulaic (and some might say racially insensitive). *Senseless* didn't set any boxoffice records when it was released but was able to do what many other lightweight, incidental comedies like it were unable to do: make you think. To be sure, this is a formula film designed for a slapstick-appreciative crowd, but there's more beneath the surface. The Wayans clan should be proud of young Marlon.

—*J. M. Clark*

CREDITS

Darryl Witherspoon: Marlon Wayans
Scott Thorpe: David Spade
Tim LaFlour: Matthew Lillard
Dr. Wheedon: Brad Dourif
Janice: Tamara Taylor
Randall Tyson: Rip Torn

Origin: USA
Released: 1998
Production: David Hoberman for Mandeville Films and Gold/Miller; released by Dimension Films
Direction: Penelope Spheeris
Screenplay: Greg Erb and Craig Mazin
Cinematography: Daryn Okada
Editing: Ross Albert
Production design: Peter Jamison
Art direction: Ann Harris
Costumes: Betsy Cox
Sound: Susumu Tokunow
MPAA rating: R
Running Time: 93 minutes

REVIEWS

Entertainment Weekly. February 20, 1998, p. 92.
Hollywood Reporter. February 17, 1998, p. 18.
Los Angeles Times. February 20, 1998, p. F6.
New York Times. February 20, 1998, p. E26.
People. March 2, 1998, p. 21.
Variety. February 16, 1998, p. 57.
Village Voice. March 3, 1998, p. 108.
Washington Post. February 20, 1998, p. 37.

Shadrach

One man's journey touched another man's heart.—Movie tagline

The last time Pulitzer Prize–winner William Styron's work was adapted for the big screen was in 1982, when his powerful novel *Sophie's Choice* was made into an equally powerful film. Now, Styron's "Shadrach," a short story which first appeared in *Esquire* magazine in 1978, has been made into another worthwhile production. *Shadrach,* a small gem with a warm, pleasing glow, was directed and co-written by Styron's daughter, Susanna, in her promising cinematic debut. It is quiet, meaningful, and deeply human in a way reminiscent of the television classic *The Waltons*. Like that series, *Shadrach* also features a grown-up narrator (Martin Sheen) looking back on events involving a large, deeply-rooted Virginia family struggling through the Great Depression. While the characters in *Sophie's Choice* (1982) were dealing with the reverberations of the Holocaust, the people in *Shadrach* are contending with the echoes of slavery in 1935.

The film is told through the eyes of Paul Whitehurst, who looks back from adulthood on his contact with Shadrach, a 99-year-old former slave who has made a 600-mile trek from Alabama to Virginia in the hope of being buried on the old Dabney plantation, the place where he was born and where the innocence of his youth had allowed him the most carefree days of his life. Young Paul (Scott Terra), the only child of a well-off middle-class family, enjoys spending a great deal of his time with the good-hearted and economically-strapped Dabney family, which includes Vernon (Harvey Keitel), his wife Trixie (Andie MacDowell), and their seven children. Proud Vernon rails against "Franklin D. for Disaster Roosevelt" as he tries to get by on the income his moonshine generates. Trixie is warm and compassionate, and loves her beer. All three of the Dabney boys, nicknamed Little Mole, Middle Mole, and Big Mole, rarely bathe and smell accordingly. The girls, on the other hand, are always "fragrant" in the best sense of the word. It was on one of the many hot summer days Paul spent shooting marbles with Little Mole that Shadrach appears, utterly exhausted, but relieved and full of gratitude to learn that he is once again in the presence of the Dabneys.

After Shadrach (83-year-old newcomer John Franklin Sawyer) collapses and is revived by some of Vernon's alcohol, he tells his life story and expresses his fervent wish to the flabbergasted throng that, upon his imminent death, he be buried among the other slaves on the land where he was born. Everyone, especially the children, takes to Shadrach immediately, and they all set off in the beat-up family car

to what was once the plantation, now the family's "country retreat." They put Shadrach to bed, making him as comfortable as possible, and then transport him in a wheelbarrow to the millpond, which apparently holds many cherished memories for him. Now content, he dies quietly, at which time Vernon is astonished and angered to learn that he can't bury Shadrach on the property; to do so would mean breaking a law prohibiting the burial of someone on private property. Vernon feels that he should be able to do what he wants on his own property, especially when it means keeping his promise to grant the last, harmless wish of a decent old man. Also, he can ill-afford the expense of a funeral for the stranger. Nevertheless, Vernon builds a coffin and makes arrangements for burial in a black churchyard through a black undertaker. It is only after the family returns to the property from the funeral that night that the children learn that Shadrach's body is out by the still and waiting for Vernon, who, smiling triumphantly, honors the old man's request. (Interestingly, the original short story lacks the film's happier ending, concluding with Vernon and Trixie resigning themselves to Shadrach's burial in the churchyard.) The whole experience helps Paul deal with the death of his mother two years later, apparently from tuberculosis.

It is a shame that *Shadrach,* a fine, gently lyrical effort, could not find an audience, especially since it received nu-

CREDITS

Vernon Dabney: Harvey Keitel
Trixie Dabney: Andie MacDowell
Paul Whitehurst: Scott Terra
Edmonia Dabney: Monica Bugajski
Shadrach: John Franklin Sawyer

Origin: USA
Released: 1998
Production: Bridget Terry; released by Columbia Pictures
Direction: Susanna Styron
Screenplay: Susanna Styron and Bridget Terry; based on the short story by William Styron
Cinematography: Hiro Narita
Editing: Colleen Sharp
Production design: Burton Rencher
Set decoration: Valerie Fann
Costumes: Dona Granata
Sound: Larry Long, Carl Rudisill
MPAA rating: PG-13
Running Time: 88 minutes

merous positive reviews. Although its title is certainly appropriate, perhaps too many people did not know what to make of it. Whatever the reason, *Shadrach* was barely released

REVIEWS

Boston Globe. October 16, 1998, p. C6.
Chicago Tribune. October 16, 1998, p. J7.
Entertainment Weekly. October 9, 1998, p. 58.
Los Angeles Times. September 25, 1998, p. F12.
New York Times. September 23, 1998, p. E5.
Playboy. November 1, 1998, p. 21.
Variety. April 20, 1998, p. 45.
Wall Street Journal. September 25, 1998, p. W1.
Washington Post. October 16, 1998, p. WW49.

into theaters before being earmarked for release on videocassette and pay-per-view. *Shadrach* had six executive producers, including Oscar-winning director Jonathan Demme (1991's *Silence of the Lambs*). Fine work by cinematographer Hiro Narit, along with that of production designer Burton Rencher, set decorator Valerie Fann, and costume designer Dona Granata, give us a convincing sense of time and place. The chosen music helps set an appropriate mood.

"Death ain't nothin' to be afraid about. It's life that's fearsome," Vernon states upon Shadrach's passing. "Death," he continues, "ain't much." The same can not be said of *Shadrach.*

—*David L. Boxerbaum*

Shakespeare in Love

Love is the only inspiration.—Movie tagline

A comedy about the greatest love story *almost* never told.—Movie tagline

"An irresistible romantic comedy!"—Bill Diehl, *ABC Radio*

"The richest and most satisfying romantic movie of the year!"—Owen Gleiberman, *Entertainment Weekly*

"*Shakespeare in Love* is a lusty, lavish, freshly captivating epic."—Rex Reed, *New York Observer*

"The year's best and most original comedy!" —Jack Mathews, *Newsday*

"A glorious film that makes moviegoing fun again!"—David Ansen, *Newsweek*

"Two enthusiastic thumbs up!"—*Siskel & Ebert*

"I was swept off my seat. As *Shakespeare in Love* unfolds, we see how ambitious the whole undertaking really is, and how marvelously well director John Madden has pulled it off."—Joe Morgenstern, *Wall Street Journal*

"Absolutely enchanting! One of the must-see movies of the year."—Jeffrey Lyons, *WNBC*

Once costume films as sumptuous and thoughtful as Fred Zinnemann's *A Man for All Seasons* (1966) were less rare, and a spectacularly beautiful, well-crafted film (more or less historically accurate) came along often enough to keep the filmgoers who love them happy. The lusty Tudors were always film worthy, especially Henry the VIII

Young Shakespeare (Joseph Fiennes) shakes off his writer's block by falling in love with wealthy Viola De Lesseps (Gwyneth Paltrow) in the delightful comedy *Shakespeare in Love.*

(Charles Laughton, Richard Burton) and his daughter Elizabeth (Bette Davis, Glenda Jackson). After too long a wait, the winter of 1998 was a feast indeed: first *Elizabeth* (reviewed in this edition), a powerful and popular film based on the life of a young Queen, and, after all that drama, came *Shakespeare in Love*, a playful fancy about the Bard as a very young man, a frustrated writer and sometime actor. From its earliest moments, when the camera explores the empty Rose Theater from the roof right down to the dirt floor, we also realize this is a love song to theater itself.

Marc Norman (*Cutthroat Island* [1995]) and playwright Tom Stoppard (*Rosencrantz and Guildenstern are Dead* [1990]) imagine a Will Shakespeare (Joseph Fiennes) out of funds and without words, anguishing over writer's block as he scratches his name on paper time and again with ink-stained fingers. Meanwhile, his "patron," Philip Henslowe (Geoffrey Rush) quite literally has his feet held to the fire by his angry creditors, particularly the smoldering and disapproving Hugh Fennyman (Tom Wilkinson). He spins a tale of a new play sure to pack the house, with the unlikely name of "Romeo and Ethel, the Pirate's Daughter." Henslowe pursues Shakespeare through the streets, begging for the play (he's off to his weekly visit to pour out his woes to a "therapist"). To distract him, Will tosses off the hated name of Richard Burbage (Martin Clunes), London's most successful actor, who also hopes for a Shakespeare play and who, unlike Henslowe, will pay. While young Shakespeare searches for the lady of his heart to cure both his maladies ("It's as if my quill were broken," he confesses), Henslowe holds off his moneymen and hopes only to keep his doors open. Everyone has their own ideas about the script, especially the beleaguered Henslowe, who says exasperatedly, "A bit of love and a dog, that's what they want." It's a offhand, kindly suggestion from Shakespeare's gentlemanly rival playwright Christopher Marlowe (Rupert Everett, uncredited, memorable and fleetingly present) that finally gets Shakespeare a plot of sorts, and casting, absurdly, begins immediately.

Henslowe (Geoffrey Rush): "It will all work out." Shakespeare (Joseph Fiennes): "How?" Henslowe: "I don't know. It's a mystery."

After a hilarious audition scene of unlikely actors that every director will recognize, Will is riveted by a reading of his "Who is Silvia?"— he demands the actor take off his hat. "He" takes off, with Shakespeare racing after, through the streets and on the Thames with the chase ending at the home of the wealthy young beauty Viola de Lesseps (Gwyneth Paltrow), who Will somehow fails to grasp is his actor, now sans a comical peach-fuzz mustache that appears and disappears along with a short-cropped wig that impossibly covers her spill of blonde curls. Viola is promised to the pompous, cash-poor Lord Wessex (Colin Firth) who plans to wed and pack her off to Virginia, where he thinks "the tobacco crop shows some future." She finds him repulsive, but will do her duty, but not before cuckolding him at every opportunity (with the aid of her Nurse, the delightful Imelda Staunton, who adds immeasurably to the bedroom farce when she guards the door against discovery of the lovers, frantically fanning and rocking to mask the sounds of their ardor).

Judi Dench was so taken with the Rose theatre recreation that Miramax gave the entire set to the actress.

Against all odds, the play does go on, and the presence of the disguised Viola as Romeo transforms the crass atmosphere and the bumptious players into an artistic endeavor, as the lovers implausibly tryst in the wings in gender-bending moments. But as the Queen remarks, the time comes to "settle accounts"— inevitably, the lovers must part, but not before the Lady Viola steps back on the stage, this time as a luminous Juliet to Will's Romeo. There are swordfights that become pillow fights, and the heavy hand of the Elizabethan cultural police threatens to close them down, but finally, the long-anticipated play premieres to a rapt audience. Director John Madden stages this beautifully; every face in the "penny public" is worth watching, and we are swept away as they are.

Shakespeare in Love's nimble and delightful script is its primary attraction, outshining even the radiant Gwyneth Paltrow (*Sliding Doors*) and dark-eyed and passionate Joseph Fiennes (*Elizabeth*). Widely acclaimed as a *literate crowd pleaser* and honored with numerous awards, this handsome, rollicking romp showcases uniformly excellent supporting performances. According to director John Madden (*Mrs. Brown* [1997]), each character has an arc; the talents of all its stellar cast are deftly showcased. *Shakespeare in Love* is a vibrant example of a film completely realized, with a very few and rather minor faults: a sweet and sorrowful love story ("a stolen season" as the Lady Viola says) wrapped up in a farcical contest of rival theaters. As they say, you don't have to know Shakespeare to enjoy the film, but it certainly is pleasant to hear *Romeo and Juliet* read so beautifully in an innovative way that is so sensual and fastmoving that you might lose track of where the familiar lines begin and end, so cleverly have Stoppard and Norman woven them into the script. The intersections of play and love affair seem effortlessly fluid and right, particularly as staged by Madden and as performed by this ensemble.

Joseph Fiennes' Will Shakespeare has the right intensity and quicksilver quality to persuade us: as Romeo and Shakespeare he is perfectly cast, a hot-blooded, gallant lover and endlessly frustrated author. Paltrow's Viola is most worthy of his adoration: declaring "I will have poetry in my life!" Viola's determination to act despite a ban on women actors lifts her character to true muse status. It would be enough if she merely looked like a golden goddess who speaks her lines exceedingly well, but her vivacity and impulsiveness makes her irresistible. Said Janet Maslin: "*Shakespeare in Love* itself seems as smitten with her as the poet is, and as alight with the same love of language and beauty." When

Viola and Will first make love, he unwraps her bound breasts as if he were opening a gift: she twirls around impishly in his arms. Fiennes and Paltrow are almost absurdly good looking; when they dance together it is one of those grand movie moments you remember, like Scarlett and Rhett's scandalous waltz.

The incomparable Judi Dench as Queen Elizabeth is indeed Gloriana: audiences have burst into applause in theaters when she makes a surprise appearance that saves the day. With her chalky-white face and shrewd, snappish mien, when she casts her gimlet eye on the lovely and youthful Viola the film shifts into a higher gear. It's a fact that the Queen loved the theater, but this script uses Elizabeth brilliantly to emphasize just how much plays meant to the English, high and low (it's fun to see frizzy-haired tavern whores approvingly greet Shakespeare the playwright, and then to spot them again in the front row at the performance).

The protean Geoffrey Rush (*Elizabeth, Les Miserables*) is wonderful as the worried Henslowe, ever hoping for the pirates to make their appearance in the play. With his seedy, harried looks, he's a constant joke whenever he appears. As another famous actor of the day, Ned Allyn, (Ben Affleck, *Good Will Hunting* [1997]) is entertaining as a hammy player who Will cozens into participating, promising the play will be titled "Mercutio" after his character. A number of the supporting players are also standouts, including Wilkinson as a businessman suddenly in love with acting and willing to forego Henslowe's debts for a chance to perform on stage.

The *New York Times* observed, "As with *Rosencrantz*, the movie is both Stoppardian and Shakespearean, which is to say it is an antic original but also respectful of its source . . . In each case Stoppard plays fair with Shakespeare, although in the movie he takes literary license with his life. With so little information available, he could be freely inventive." Stoppard has peppered the story with in-jokes and quick asides: even minor characters such as the malicious urchin who haunts the theater turn out to be more than they seem—the John Webster (Joe Roberts) who adores gory

moments is the future author of the blood-soaked Jacobean drama "The Duchess of Malfi." The originality of the script, which won the Writer's Guild of America award, has been questioned by the British press, citing the resemblance to an obscure 1941 novel, *No Bed for Bacon*, by Caryl Brahms and S.J. Simon. Miramax airily dismissed the charge with the oft-repeated reference to Shakespeare himself as the ultimate borrower, and the controversy itself seemed swamped by the praise heaped on the film from critics everywhere and was ignored by the public, which has made *Shakespeare in Love* a popular favorite.

Doubtless legions of English teachers are dispatching students to see the film, hoping to inspire in them a love of the Bard (as Zeffirelli's 1968 *Romeo and Juliet* did), although some might be stopped by its "R" rating, which mystified playwright Stoppard (the MPAA did rate it for sexuality). Both the cinematography and the art direction are splendid, with the scenes at Court and on the Thames

CREDITS

Will Shakespeare: Joseph Fiennes
Viola de Lesseps: Gwyneth Paltrow
Philip Henslowe: Geoffrey Rush
Queen Elizabeth: Judi Dench
Lord Wessex: Colin Firth
Nurse: Imelda Staunton
Ned Alleyn: Ben Affleck
Hugh Fennyman: Tom Wilkinson
Tilney, Master of Revels: Simon Callow
Christopher Marlowe: Rupert Everett
Ralph Bashford: Jim Carter
Richard Burbage: Martin Clunes
Dr. Moth: Antony Sher
Rosaline: Sandra Reinton
John Webster: Joe Roberts

Origin: USA
Released: 1998
Production: David Parfitt, Donna Gigliotti, Harvey Weinstein, Edward Zwick, and Marc Norman for Bedford Falls; released by Miramax Films
Direction: John Madden
Screenplay: Marc Norman and Tom Stoppard
Cinematography: Richard Greatrex
Editing: David Gamble
Music: Stephen Warbeck
Production design: Martin Childs
Art direction: Mark Raggett
Set decoration: Jill Quertier
Costumes: Sandy Powell
Sound: Peter Glossop
MPAA rating: R
Running Time: 122 minutes

AWARDS AND NOMINATIONS

Academy Awards 1998: Picture; Actress (Gwyneth Paltrow); Supporting Actress (Judi Dench); Original Screenplay; Art Direction; Original Musical or Comedy Score; Costume
Broadcast Film Critics Association 1998: Original Screenplay
Golden Globes 1999: Musical/Comedy; Original Screenplay; Musical/Comedy Actress (Gwyneth Paltrow)
New York Film Critics 1998: Original Screenplay
Screen Actors Guild 1998: Actress (Gwyneth Paltrow); Cast
Writers Guild of America 1998: Original Screenplay
Academy Awards 1998 Nominations: Supporting Actor (Geoffrey Rush); Director (John Madden); Cinematography; Sound; Film Editing; Makeup

especially stunning. The score by Stephen Warbeck is lush and merry when need be, while never intrusive as so many seem to be of late. The costumes are *Shakespeare*'s glory: from the Queen's fanciful peacock-feather and pearl-framed face to her tiny slipper-shod feet, designer Sandy Powell outfits Elizabeth perfectly; a riot of rich color and texture makes the Queen's Court dazzle us, but none so thoroughly as Viola, always clad in some golden confection for the camera to revel in, and bathed in a romantic glow. The last moments of the film in which Will envisions his Viola transformed, in a new play and a new land, are particularly stunning. Called "the richest and most satisfying romantic movie of the year" by *Entertainment Weekly*, *Shakespeare in Love* is a decided triumph.

—*Mary Hess*

REVIEWS

Boxoffice. January, 1999, p. 52.
Entertainment Weekly. December 11, 1998, p. 43.
Los Angeles Times. December 11, 1998, p. F1.
New York Times. December 11, 1998, p. E16.
Newsweek. December 14, 1998, p. 78.
People. December 21, 1998, p. 31.
Rolling Stone. January 21, 1999, p. 84.
San Francisco Chronicle. December 25, 1998, p. C1.
San Francisco Examiner. December 25, 1998, p. B1.
Sight and Sound. February, 1999, p. 53.
Time. December 14, 1998.
Variety. December 7, 1998, p. 53.
Village Voice. December 15, 1998, p. 146.
Washington Post. November 20, 1998, p. F5.

Shooting Fish

As con artists they were hard to beat. But they were easy targets for LOVE.—Movie tagline
"*Fish* is definitely worth catching!"—*Mademoiselle*
"Captivating. Kate Beckinsdale has the no nonsense impudence of the young Audrey Hepburn."—*Movieline*
"A thoroughly delightful film right up there with British imports *Four Weddings and a Funeral* and *The Full Monty* . . . You'll leave the theater with a huge grin on your face!"—*People*
"Combines the absurdity of Monty Python with the nonstop intrigue of James Bond!"—*Swing*

Intermittently deligfhtful and dreadful, *Shooting Fish* is a fuzzy-brained British Generation-X romantic comedy about a couple of con men who fall for Kate Beckinsale's character. Falling for the luminous Beckinsale is perfectly understandable, and so is director Stefan Schwartz's penchant for putting her close-up and at the center of as many scenes as possible. She lights up the screen and helps make this lightweight caper film tolerable. But her character is nonsensical, and so is the script by Schwartz and his partner Richard Holmes, the film's producer.

Beckinsale's Georgie first appears in the film as a temp, an office secretary working for con artists Dylan (Dan Futterman) and Jez (Stuart Townsend). Both men are orphans whose dream is to live in a splendid mansion—don't ask why, because no answer is provided. Dylan is the smooth-talking,

jive-spewing American, a super salesman whose eyes glint at the prospect of fleecing rich businessmen and women. Jez is his nerdy British partner, a shy, awkward technical genius.

Together, they concoct both big-time and small-time cons. One big-time con is selling business magnates the latest in voice-operated computers—a model that doesn't even need a keyboard. While Dylan weaves his web of lies about a machine that recognizes millions of words, Jez is hidden in another room, typing in responses and speaking into a microphone to make it appear the computer is talking back.

These guys need a secretary like the James Gang needed an accountant, but Georgie soon proves her worth by saving a deal that was going badly awry. But when she asks what they are using the money for, they tell her it's to send to an orphanage. Georgie finds that a little hard to believe, but accepts the explanation. And she continues to cling to that belief even as she gets to know the con men a lot better. That's preposterous.

As the film unfolds, it's revealed that Georgie is not merely a temp but a medical student, that she's engaged to be married to a rich racehorse owner, and finally that she's an upper-class lady with a mansion and an inheritance of her own. She's smart and sophisticated and a master of verbal repartee. Yet she would have to be as dumb as wood to believe that Dylan and Jez are the "modern day Robin Hoods" they pose as being.

The script for *Shooting Fish* is fine at verbal swordplay but insultingly careless at constructing a believable plot. Why is Georgie temping? Why does she show up just when Dylan and Jez are leaving to have breakfast? Don't ask; no answers are provided. To ask audiences to believe Beckinsale's Georgie is so stupid as to believe Dylan and Jez are altruists is ridiculous. So is the film's happy ending that not only gets the heroes neatly married off but saves a bunch of children with Down's syndrome. That bit of sentiment comes out of left field. But many things come out of nowhere in *Shooting Fish*. Because the script bothers not a whit with plausibility, it ends up being a very silly film in spite of its great good humor.

That's too bad, because Schwartz and his crew obviously have a zest for zany comedy and an ear for a snappy line. It might come from Schwartz's background. He and Holmes were once a comedy act called the Gruber Brothers, and *Shooting Fish* is billed as a "Gruber Brothers film." But despite its considerable charms, *Shooting Fish* has the air of a film that's trying too hard to be cute, hip, cynical and heartwarming all at the same time.

Cute is guaranteed with Beckinsale, best known as the fiery heroine of *Cold Comfort Farm* (1994) and as Hero in Kenneth Branagh's *Much Ado About Nothing* (1993). As Georgie, Beckinsale adopts a short haircut and a slyly seductive combination of sass and sweetness. She carries off the film's most difficult role, making a character that's barely believable into the focal point of the film, and stealing scene after scene from her two increasingly infatuated suitors. Georgie is the only character in the film whose motives are opaque. Apparently, she helped shape the character into one of substance. "When I first saw the script Georgie was a bit 'girl in a miniskirt'—a character in search of a character," Beckinsale wrote in an article in the *London Evening Standard*.

Futterman, who is best known for his role as Robin Williams's son in *The Birdcage* (1995), gives his suave, self-assured Dylan a slightly on-the-edge fervor. Though Dylan always seems to be in control, he's just a slip-up away from being utterly terrified. Futterman is handsome like a fox, but when Dylan blows his chances with Georgie by coming on too strong, the blunder seems totally in character.

While Dylan is the cruder of the two rivals for Georgie's affections, Townsend's mop-top, badly dressed Jez is the old-fashioned romantic one. When Schwartz depicts the guys' fantasies as old movie clips, Dylan pictures Georgie as a femme fatale, but Jez imagines her as a courageous doctor. The Irish-born Townsend is a natural in his role, but he's so low-key he seems almost not to exist in his big romantic scenes with Beckinsale.

The first part of the film is terrific, with the boys' computer caper shot as a suspenseful game. When Georgie's car is burglarized, the two guys embark on an elaborate revenge scheme. Along the way, they prove themselves to be opportunists in crime by using insulation material found in a stolen van to engage in a scam. They tell housewives their husbands have ordered insulation installed, then drag the same pieces from attic to attic along a block of row houses. When the husbands come home, they catch on to the ruse

and pursue. The film's oddball sense of humor is illustrated by a quick shot in which the husbands all pull out computer power books to note down the number of the culprits' fleeing van. Later, the boys return the van to its rightful owners and the owners get blamed for the insulation scam.

Shooting Fish has the breezy air of a '60s British comedy, sharing that era's love for strange domestic sets. Jez and Dylan live in an abandoned water tower, and their lodgings are filled with Rube Goldberg inventions. In a bow to the old TV series, *Get Smart*, they even have a shoe phone. Dylan pulls off minor phone scams to get free calls and free tickets to the theater, where he tries to woo Georgie.

Unfortunately, almost everything goes awry in the film's final half, when Jez and Dylan are finally caught and sent to prison. Georgie's march to the altar is interrupted by last-minute news whose meaning doesn't become clear until later. The plot, so light and feathery at first, becomes ponderous with half-revealed twists and turns. A long caper that involves department-store mannequins posing as funeral home mourners is ridiculous, contrived and unsatisfying. Georgie's attempts to abscond with the loot that Jez and Dylan have accumulated seem out of character, and the film's last several scenes are burdened with ponderous explanations that are needed to clarify what's happened earlier. This is belabored material. And things get even sillier at the end with the Down's orphans and with the sudden appearance of Georgie's sister as a love match for Jez, tying things up much too neatly and sweetly.

CREDITS

Dylan: Dan Futterman
Jez: Stuart Townsend
Georgie: Kate Beckinsale
Mr. Stratton-Luce: Nickolas Grace
Floss: Claire Cox
Mr. Ray: Ralph Ineson

Origin: Great Britain
Released: 1997
Production: Richard Holmes and Glynnis Murray for Winchester Films, Gruber Brothers, Tomboy Films and the Arts Council of England; released by Fox Searchlight Pictures
Direction: Stefan Schwartz
Screenplay: Stefan Schwartz and Richard Holmes
Cinematography: Henry Braham
Editing: Alan Strachan
Production design: Max Gottlieb
Art direction: Sue Ferguson
Costumes: Stewart Meachem
Music: Stanislas Syrewicz
MPAA rating: PG
Running Time: 113 minutes

Shooting Fish is best when it retains its daring, mocking, dangerous air. But while the "Gruber Brothers" know how to do comedy scenes, they don't seem to be able to sustain a consistent clever tone throughout an entire film. While this is a mishmash of a movie, at least it's a reasonably entertaining one. The always mesmerizing Beckinsale and the sporadically amusing Futterman see to that.

—*Michael Betzold*

REVIEWS

Entertainment Weekly. May 8, 1998, p. 52.
Los Angeles Times. May 1, 1998, p. F18.
New York Times. May 1, 1998, p. E30.
People. May 11, 1998, p. 36.
Sight and Sound. October, 1997, p. 56.

The Siege

On November 6th, our freedom is history.
—Movie tagline

"Riveting!"—Bill Diehl, *ABC Radio Network*

"Smart and sophisticated."—Mike Cidoni, *ABC-TV*

"A hold-your-breath thriller."—Joel Siegel, *Good Morning America*

"Exciting and compelling."—Gene Siskel, *Siskel and Ebert*

"Filled with tension and suspense."—Gene Shalit, *The Today Show*

 Box Office: $39,908,508

The *Siege*, directed by Edward Zwick, is a political film that proved to be controversial in the way it fabricates a situation in which New York City is threatened by an Islamic guerrilla organization posing the threat of terrorist bombings. Zwick's earlier films had also broached politically sensitive topics, particularly *Courage Under Fire* (1996), the only Hollywood feature set during the Persian Gulf War, and *Glory* (1989), which concerned African-American soldiers fighting during the American Civil War, earning Denzel Washington an Academy Award for best supporting actor. *The Siege* marked the third collaboration between Zwick and Denzel Washington.

 Elise (Annette Bening): "My first boyfriend was Palestinian. You know, my father used to say they seduce you with their suffering."

Zwick told the *Washington Times* that as a young man he had been influenced by the political films of Constantin Costa-Gavras, who made *State of Siege* (1973), which concerned political terrorism and assassination in Uruguay and was quite controversial in its day. Zwick admires Costa-Gavras, as well he should, but Costa-Gavras was smart enough to focus on political events based in reality. *Z* (1969), his best-known film, for example, was based upon the right-wing takeover of the Generals in Greece, and *Missing* (1982), told the story of Ed Horman's desperate attempt to locate his son, who is "missing" because he has been arrested, tortured, and killed in Latin America.

The Siege, by contrast, is fictive, speculative, and blatantly manipulative. The 1993 bombing of New York's World Trade Center no doubt was the starting point for Lawrence Wright's screenplay, but the political consequences go far beyond the actual events of that disaster. Even before the release of the film, Zwick was criticized by the American-Arab Anti-Discrimination Committee, which claimed, according to the *New York Times*, that the film "perpetuated anti-Arab stereotypes" and protested that it was "insidious, dangerous, and incendiary." Todd McCarthy of *Variety* suggested that the U.S. Army might also have reason to protest the way General Devereaux (Bruce Willis) overreacts by rounding up and detaining Arab suspects. Clips of President Clinton articulating anti-terrorist sentiments seem to suggest his approval of what the film dramatizes.

The film begins with shots of a Mercedes driving through the desert. The path is blocked by goatherders, who are armed and disable the car, killing the driver. The passenger, Iranian Sheik Ahmed Bin Talal (Ahmed Ben Larby) is taken prisoner and later questioned by General William Devereaux (Bruce Willis) and as a consequence, terrorists begin to take action in New York City, operating out of Brooklyn, intending to gain the Sheik's release. Their first target is the #99 bus incident, in which no one is killed but sprayed by exploding blue paint, merely a demonstration of what the terrorists can achieve. The next incident, involving the bombing of bus #87 is for real, however. The terrorists are persuaded by FBI special agent Anthony Hubbard (Denzel Washington) to release children captured on the bus. It looks as though elderly hostages will also be released, but just as the bus door opens, the bus explodes.

Hubbard and his partner Frank Haddad (Tony Shalhoub), a Lebanese American, are advised by CIA operative Elise Kraft (Annette Bening), whose motives seem to be ambiguous and compromised, since she is apparently sleeping with the enemy, a radical named Samir Nazhde (Sami Bouajila), a professor who has sponsored the visa for the terrorist who sacrificed his life in the Brooklyn bus bombing. The first two-thirds of the film involve FBI police work as Hubbard and Haddad attempt to track down the terrorists. Elize Kraft, whose real name is later disclosed to be Sharon Bridger, explains how the terrorists are organized into suicidal cadres that operate independently from one another. After one group is destroyed in achieving its mission, another prepares itself for action. Elise Kraft believes that the terrorists can be traced through her informant, Samir Nazhde, and for that reason she does not want him incarcerated. But it is not entirely clear that she can be trusted.

The official response to there terrorists attacks is at first muted, but when FBI headquarters at One Federal Plaza is bombed and 600 workers are killed, the American President proclaims martial law, and the military takes over, under the command of General Devereaux, who immediately moves in troops from the 82nd Airborne, sealing off Brooklyn in order to contain the threat. Arab-Americans are rounded up and put into concentration camps. The cost of security is freedom that Americans have taken for granted. Though at first he warns against the consequences of martial law, General Devereaux effectively claims command and appears to be out of control as a military dictator, willing to torture prisoners in order to gain information. As he explains in the film, "We will hunt the enemy; we will find the enemy; we will kill the enemy." His extreme measures lead to an ultimate showdown with Hubbard's FBI task force, which is, of course, seriously outnumbered by the military. The dramatic conclusion therefore seems more dramatic than realistic. Todd McCarthy of *Variety* neatly described the film's narrative flaw: the major problem, he noted, is that "the specific focus of the first section, which limits its attention to a few characters and incidents, quickly widens far too much, thus diffusing emotional engagement for the sake of spectacle and the would-be sociopolitical significance of the issues brought into play."

Writing for *The New Yorker*, David Denby was most critical of the film for the way it "offers a far-fetched set of circumstances and then gets all hot under the collar as it criticizes the improbable situation that the movie itself has set up." The Denzel Washington character lectures the fascist

The film was originally titled *Against All Enemies*.

general about his disregard of civil liberties and Constitutional rights, but Denby regarded this as "outright hypocrisy." The film is dominated by its high-powered talent and powerful effects that result in "hysterical opportunism presenting itself, nauseatingly, as a stern cautionary tale." Ultimately, the film "is peddling fear—and perhaps wish-fulfillment." In Denby's well-considered opinion, Zwick is a "Hollywood fool" who loses control "of what he wanted to say."

Reviews were generally mixed. Michael O'Sullivan of the *Washington Post Weekend* was impressed by the way Zwick questions racist assumptions "that all Islamic people are criminals" and claimed that the film was redeemed by its "thoughtful examination of where this country's all-too-prevalent hatred of The Other might one day lead," but he objected to its "puritanical treatment of the only strong female character," misled by her Moslim lover, who turns out to be an activist as well as an intellectual. As Janet Maslin pointed out in the *New York Times*, "Well-intentioned words don't change either the film's visual demonizing of Arab characters or its way of titillating the audience with terrorist stunts."

CREDITS

Anthony Hubbard: Denzel Washington
Elise Kraft/Sharon Bridger: Annette Bening
Gen. William Devereaux: Bruce Willis
Frank Haddad: Tony Shalhoub
Samir Nazhde: Sami Bouajila
Danny Sussman: David Proval
Floyd Rose: Lance Reddick
Mike Johanssen: Mark Valley

Origin: USA
Released: 1998
Direction: Edward Zwick
Production: Lynda Obst and Edward Zwick; released by 20th Century Fox
Screenplay: Lawrence Wright, Menno Meyjes, and Edward Zwick
Cinematography: Roger Deakins
Editing: Steven Rosenblum
Music: Graeme Revell
Production design: Lilly Kilvert
Art direction: Chris Shriver
Costumes: Ann Roth
Sound: Allan Byer
Special effects coordination: Paul Lombardi
Stunt coordination: Joel J. Kramer
MPAA rating: R
Running Time: 116 minutes

Chris Kaltenbach of the *Baltimore Sun* praised the film as being "suspenseful, wonderfully acted, and unsettling" in the way it posed a significant question: "Can a free society exist when it's under attack by a group pledged to destroy it?" Stephen Hunter of the *Washington Post* agreed with other reviewers that Washington and Benning were "terrific," or, in the words of Todd McCarthy, "as good as the limited range of the film will allow." But while the Denzel Washington character poses the overriding Constitutional issues, Bruce Willis turns into a sort of cartoon fascist, a refugee from a rather more predictable and ordinary action-adventure film about terrorists and well filmed explosions, in the words of Janet Maslin, "the loosest military cannon this side of Dr. Strangelove." His actions speak much louder than Denzel Washington's words and Constitutional platitudes. This is more than a mere action-adventure vehicle about mad bombers, but it seems to pander to the action audience to hedge its bet.

—*James M. Welsh*

REVIEWS

Baltimore Sun. November 6, 1998, p. E4.
Entertainment Weekly. November 13, 1998, p. 47.
New York Times. October 30, 1998, p. B16.
New York Times. November 1, 1998, Sec.2, p.17.
New York Times. November 6, 1998, p. B15.
New Yorker. November 15, 1998, p. 114.
Newsweek. November 9, 1998, p. 76.
Rolling Stone. November 26, 1998, p. 132.
Sight and Sound. February, 1999, p. 54.
Time. November 9, 1998, p. 116.
USA Today. November 6, 1998, p. E10.
Variety. November 2, 1998, p. 49.
Washington Post. November 6, 1998, p. D1.
Washington Post. November 8, 1998, p. G1.
Washington Post Weekend. November 6, 1998, p. 46.
Washington Times Metropolitan Times. November 6, 1998, p. C12.

Simon Birch

Destiny has big plans for little Simon Birch.
—Movie tagline

"A surprise delight. A movie with a big heart and a whole new sense of heroism."—David Sheehan, *CBS-TV*

"Unforgettable! An experience you can't miss. One of the most unique and touching films you'll ever see."—Jeanne Wolf, *Jeanne Wolf's Hollywood*

"A curiously entrancing, quite unexpected treat."—Richard Schickel, *Time*

"A very special film. It will touch you for a long time."—Jeffrey Lyons, *WNBC*

 Box Office: $18,253,415

*S*imon Birch is the story of a dwarf-sized boy who believes God has destined him to be a hero. The title character is played by Ian Michael Smith, whose dwarfism is caused by a bone disease, Morquito's syndrome. He was found in a casting call, and he is a find. Although the film is very sentimental—a real tearjerker—Smith is clear-eyed, even stoic. There is nothing self-pitying about his character or his performance. It is fascinating just to watch him re-

late to children and adults. Older boys mock him, but the girls are fascinated not only by his size but by his wit and intelligence, and younger boys admire his bravery and style. A master of self-deprecating humor—naturally it centers on his shortness—Birch/Smith has a big heart and a bold tongue. He denounces the pastor in church for trivializing religion, turning it into social events that demand conformism and inane behavior from children and adults.

Best of all, Smith's character is allowed to have a full range of feelings—particularly about sex. Birch and his best friend, Joe Wenteworth (Joseph Mazzello), are at the edge of puberty and fascinated with girl's body's, especially their breasts. They are too young and innocent (the year is 1964) to do anything about it—until, that is, Simon is cast as the infant Jesus and finds himself staring up at the beckoning breasts of the girl picked to play the Virgin Mary. The resulting chaos when Simon decides to "go for it" during the performance of the church's Christmas play is too much fun to spoil with a description here.

Of course, *Simon Birch* is full of clichés about the stodginess of adults and the unique perceptions of children. But the performances of the children are wonderful and redeem the cliché. David Strathairn plays Reverend Russell as a stuffy disciplinarian who cannot appreciate Simon—or it might be more accurate to say that the man of God cannot afford to admire Simon. For there is just a hint of something troubling the Reverend, some aspect of his own experience that has led him to doubt himself and his religion. When Simon confesses his sense of destiny—his certainty that he was made for heroic action—Russell refuses to confirm Simon's belief that God has a plan for everyone. Even if Russell dislikes Simon, even if he distrusts Simon's convictions, it is surprising that he leaves the child with a troubled look. The film, in fact, is building toward a denouement that shows how Russell has failed himself and his religion even as Simon proves his courage and his belief in his destiny.

> Simon (Ian Michael Smith): "I'm going to be a hero." Ben (Oliver Platt): "Pretty vague job description, isn't it?"

What is most fascinating about *Simon Birch* is to see a child portrayed as having a sense of destiny. Simon knows that he does not have long to live. Indeed, the doctor who delivered Simon told his parents that he would not survive infancy. Living on borrowed time, Simon makes each moment count, and the alert performance of Smith is surely based on his coming to terms with his own disease. Smith lives his role. He is a miracle, a wonder to watch.

Equally good as Smith is Ashley Judd, who sparkles in the role as Rebecca, Joe's mother. As Simon says, Rebecca is the sexiest thing in Gravestown, Maine, the fictional community where the film is set. Judd is sexy but motherly. She loves Simon as much as she loves Joe. Indeed, Joe is a love child, and one of the mysteries to be solved in the film is who fathered Joe. Rebecca won't say. She is a fiercely independent woman who has raised her son by herself, and like Simon she cannot abide the stultifying piety and hypocrisy of church authorities. Any child who has had a crush on a friend's mother or on a babysitter will instantly recognize Rebecca. Her joy, her insouciance, her energy and lack of pretension are just what appeals to children, and Judd seems to perform this role as effortlessly and as genuinely as Smith plays his.

There is an excellent supporting role in the film. Oliver Platt plays Ben, a school drama teacher, who like Rebecca, understands children and knows how to guide them without a heavy hand. Children fortunate enough to have had such teachers know that Ben is not idealized, for he is something of a kid himself who knows how to negotiate the adult world. Of course, this is a didactic film, but the message about how adults should treat children and how children can grow into sensitive adults, is re-presented with great flourish and freshness.

—*Carl Rollyson*

CREDITS

Simon Birch: Ian Michael Smith
Joe Wenteworth: Joseph Mazzello
Rebecca Wenteworth: Ashley Judd
Ben Goodrich: Oliver Platt
Reverend Russell: David Strathairn
Grandmother Wenteworth: Dana Ivey
Adult Joe Wenteworth: Jim Carrey

Origin: USA
Released: 1998
Production: Laurence Mark and Roger Birnbaum for Caravan Pictures; released by Hollywood Pictures
Direction: Mark Steven Johnson
Screenplay: Mark Steven Johnson; suggested by the novel *A Prayer for Owen Meany* by John Irving
Cinematography: Aaron E. Schneider
Editing: Betsy Heimann
Music: Marc Shaiman
Production design: David Chapman
Art direction: Dennis Davenport
Costumes: Betsy Heiman, Abram Waterhouse
Sound: Glen Gauthier
MPAA rating: PG
Running Time: 110 minutes

REVIEWS

Chicago Tribune. September 11, 1998, p. 4.
Detroit News. September 11, 1998, p. 3F.
Entertainment Weekly. September 18, 1998, p. 59.
New York Times. September 11, 1998, p. E18.
People. September 14, 1998, p. 47.
Variety. August 31, 1998, p. 94.
Washington Post Weekend. September 11, 1998, p. 52.

A Simple Plan

Sometimes good people do evil things.—Movie tagline

"One of the tightest, most profound thrillers in this decade."—Rod Lurie, *KABC Radio*

"The picture to beat for the best and rest of 1998 . . . .separates from all the other movies of the holiday season."—Andrew Sarris, *New York Observer*

"Raimi turns the screws of the relentless plot with quiet precision, aiming for queasily escalating suspense."—David Ansen, *Newsweek*

"A shrewdly engrossing, well-cast, and acted thriller . . . Bottom line: Impressive find."—Leah Rozen, *People*

"A stunner!"—Peter Travers, *Rolling Stone*

"Two thumbs up! A razor-sharp thriller."—*Siskel & Ebert*

 Box Office: $10,069,000

A large sum of money creates more havoc than happiness for the Mitchell brothers in Sam Raimi's taut drama *A Simple Plan.*

A Simple Plan bears a strong resemblance to the Coen brothers' *Fargo* (1996), which won a long list of awards and nominations. Both are knee-deep in snow and involve naive Midwestern characters who bite off more than they can chew.

Hank Mitchell (Bill Paxton), his dim-witted brother Jacob (Billy Bob Thornton), and Jacob's buddy Lou (Brent Briscoe) see a fox running off with a neighbor's hen. Naturally they have a couple of rifles in the pickup truck, and they decide to track the marauder. Paw prints lead into a thicket where they find a wrecked private plane half-buried under snow. Crows perch everywhere, drawn by the smell of rotting human flesh. (The dead pilot has had half his face pecked away.) The men regard the crows only as pests, but the viewer senses that the birds symbolize evil and approaching doom.

Hank finds a canvas bag containing $4,400,000 inside the wreckage. Almost immediately the money starts to transform these good old boys into bad old boys. It also begins to turn friends against one another, just as the eight bushels of gold florins did in Chaucer's "The Pardoner's Tale." In *The Canterbury Tales*, the Pardoner keeps repeating "The love of money is the root of all evil," and this is the thesis of *A Simple Plan.* The story of friends corrupted by greed is much older than Chaucer; it has been traced back to ancient India and has served as the basis of countless variations over the centuries, including John Huston's classic film *The Treasure of the Sierra Madre* (1948).

Hank wants to report the crash and turn the money over to the authorities. Lou, however, wants to divide it up and let the plane be discovered when the snow melts. Jacob has mixed loyalties. Hank is his brother but Lou is his best friend. He casts the swing vote in favor of keeping the money. They rationalize that the loot is probably drug money and that keeping it would not really be "stealing."

Hank, the natural leader of the trio, only agrees to keep the money on his own conditions: They all keep their mouths shut and sit tight on the money until the plane is discovered and the money is reported missing. Hank's plan also stipulates that they all move away to avoid suspicion. Such humble men as themselves could never start spending even a fraction of those millions in a community where everybody knows everybody else's business. Hank has a college degree but works for a modest pay in the feed store. Lou is the town drunk and is facing bankruptcy. Jacob lives on welfare.

Billy Bob Thornton plays a character similar to the role that won him an Academy Award nomination for *Sling Blade* (1996). It is hard to tell just how smart or dumb he really is. While the three conspirators are piling the money into the back of Hank's pickup, along comes the local sheriff. Hank is awkwardly improvising a story to explain their presence in this desolate spot when Jacob blurts out, "Did you tell him about the plane?" Hank is forced to lie by saying they thought they heard a sputtering airplane engine but it might have been a snowmobile. The tension in that scene is very intense and from then on, you know in your gut that things are not going to work out for Hank.

When Hank comes home dragging the bag of money, he cannot resist breaking the covenant of secrecy. He is a weak man—which explains why he is working at such a menial, dead-end job. He needs someone to lean on, someone to tell him what to do. The natural candidate is his pregnant wife. He dumps the millions out on the kitchen table to share his secret, and his guilt, with Sarah (Bridget Fonda).

Sarah is the kind of conventional, small-town woman who might be expected to say, "Oh, Hank, we can't keep it. That would be wrong." Instead, she is overcome with more greed than any of the men. She sees the money as her chance-in-a-lifetime to escape the boredom and drudgery of her existence. Although Hank is glad to have Sarah on his side, his new insight into her character adds a drop of poison to their relationship. He keeps his back to her in bed and lies with eyes wide open trying to see into their future. He is the only one of the four with enough intelligence and awareness to realize that there is nothing simple about their simple plan. The money has a life of its own and will dictate their fates.

The wrecked plane and carnivorous crows make the most effective scene in the movie. The screenplay, adapted by Scott B. Smith from his own novel, provides an excuse to bring Hank and his brother back there again. Sarah tells her husband he must return a portion of the loot—say $500,000—to the plane. Anyone who knows about the money will think the dead pilot divided it with henchmen and that this half-million was the only money to be salvaged at this location. If there had been more, why wouldn't the finders have taken it all?

Hank crawls back inside the reeking plane, leaving Jacob back at the truck as a lookout. Jacob is to be changing a tire as a pretext for stopping. When a nosy elderly neighbor comes along on his snowmobile and decides to follow Hank's tracks into the woods, Jacob panics and crowns him with a lug wrench. Hank feels obligated to protect his brother. He also realizes that his possession of the money makes him an accessory to murder. He puts the victim back on the snowmobile, intending to fake an accident at some distant spot. But the old man is not dead. He topples off the snowmobile and tells Hank to call the sheriff and have Jacob arrested. Hank impulsively finishes the job by cutting off the victim's air supply with his heavy glove. The simple plan is getting very complicated indeed.

Lou, the loose cannon, is not fooled by the fake accident. He gets the truth out of Jacob and threatens to report the murder unless Hank immediately forks over his third of the money. Lou is a loud-mouthed moron with an insatiable appetite for liquor; it is obvious that he will expose the trio if he ever gets his hands on over a million in cash. This con-

> Jacob (Billy Bob Thornton): "I wish someone else had found that money."

Mike Nichols was the first to option Scott B. Smith's novel; Ben Stiller and John Boorman also worked on versions before Sam Raimi came in as the film's director.

frontation inevitably leads to a shootout in which Lou is killed by Jacob and Lou's wife Nancy (Becky Ann Baker) is shot by Hank when she goes after Jacob with a revolver. Hank is able to stage the scene to make it appear that Lou and Nancy killed each other in one of their notorious drunken brawls.

Hank and Sarah finally learn the truth about the money. A newspaper article reports that a wealthy man paid $4,400,000 as ransom for his abducted daughter, and the two kidnappers are still at large. Hank and Jacob are called into the sheriff's office and introduced to an FBI agent named Baxter (Gary Cole). Hank is pressured into leading the sheriff and the FBI agent the next morning to the spot where he said he heard the airplane engine. But Sarah, who works in the town's library, has examined the photos of the two kidnappers that appeared in various out-of-town newspapers and tells her husband that the stranger is no FBI agent but the other kidnapper, searching for the ransom money. If he finds it, he will certainly kill both Hank and the sheriff.

Back once more at the crow-infested site of the wrecked plane, there is another shootout in which the sheriff, the kidnapper, and Jacob all die. Miraculously, Hank not only manages to escape with his life but ends up as the person who has sole possession of all the money. But while he is being debriefed by the authorities, he learns that the money is tainted with more than the blood of his brother. Five thousand of the serial numbers were recorded and distributed across the country. Anyone who tries to spend any of that money will certainly get caught.

Much to his wife's distress (and to the distress of the viewer who has been sharing vicariously in the ill-gotten loot), Hank burns the money in the fireplace. The camera lingers on the stacks of banknotes with engraved portraits of Benjamin Franklin being consumed by hungry flames. Director Sam Raimi, who previously specialized in features such as *The Evil Dead* (1983) and *Darkman* (1990), could not resist the temptation to incorporate horror-film sym-

AWARDS AND NOMINATIONS

Broadcast Film Critics Association 1998: Adapted Screenplay; Supporting Actor (Billy Bob Thornton)
Los Angeles Film Critics 1998: Supporting Actor (Billy Bob Thornton)
Academy Awards 1998 Nominations: Supporting Actor (Billy Bob Thornton); Adapted Screenplay

bolism such as crows and hellfire into this otherwise realistic film.

A Simple Plan is a finely tuned film backed by excellent acting from its lead characters. Even though the movie centers on the evils of greed, it touches on the strength of brotherly love. Hank reluctantly kills the nosy neighbor not only to preserve his dreams of wealth, but to keep his brother from going to jail. Hank does become Jacob's keeper. Bill Paxton and Billy Bob Thornton (who previously co-starred together in the critically acclaimed *One False Move* [1991]) are perfectly cast as these two brothers who, despite a sense of rivalry on Jacob's part, still have a sense of loyalty and devotion to one another. Paxton's unwavering performance as the "Average Joe" Hank evokes sympathy even though his judgement quickly becomes impaired. With his all-American good looks and good ole boy charm, it's all the more saddening to watch all his best laid plans go awry.

Thornton gives his Jacob a rough edge. He's unpredictable and "dangerous." He sometimes resents his brother's middle-class status and it would be comforting for Jacob to side with his drinking partner and socio-economic equal Lou. It's in this combination of recklessness and vulnerability that Thornton gives depth to a character that could merely be labelled a "dim bulb." In the end, it's Jacob's demise that jettisons this contemporary melodrama into a richly textured Greek tragedy.

Director Raimi's last film, *The Quick and the Dead* (1994), slightly severed him from the material that made him a household name among fans of cult horror, but he completely makes a seamless transition to layered narrative with *A Simple Plan*. Besides a high gore quotient in his films, Raimi uses a substantial amount of humor and *A Simple Plan* is no exception. Much of the film's humor comes from Jacob's lack of smarts, but it merely demonstrates how someone with Jacob's intelligence would *not* see the danger that lurks when faced with such choices. Raimi's direction is subtle, yet powerful in transforming the serene Midwestern town in which *A Simple Plan* takes place into a chilling location where ghastly acts take place. The story unfolds quietly, which immediately begs viewers to empathize and fantasize along with Hank. The greedy viewer can't help thinking that he wouldn't have made such a hopeless mess of things if given the once-in-the-lifetime opportunity to find all that beautiful cash.

—Bill Delaney and *Michelle Banks*

CREDITS

Hank Mitchell: Bill Paxton
Jacob Mitchell: Billy Bob Thornton
Lou: Brent Briscoe
Sarah: Bridget Fonda
Tom Butler: Jack Walsh
Carl: Chelcie Ross
Nancy: Becky Ann Baker
Baxter: Gary Cole

Origin: USA
Released: 1998
Production: James Jacks and Adam Schroeder for Savoy Pictures and Mutual Film Co.; released by Paramount Pictures
Direction: Sam Raimi
Screenplay: Scott B. Smith; based on his novel
Cinematography: Alar Kivilo
Editing: Arthur Coburn, Eric L. Beason
Music: Danny Elfman
Production design: Patrizia von Brandenstein
Art direction: James F. Truesdale
Set design: Rando Schmook
Costumes: Julie Weiss
Sound: Ed Novick
Special effects supervision: John D. Milinac
MPAA rating: R
Running Time: 121 minutes

REVIEWS

Chicago Sun-Times. December 11, 1998, p. 33.
Detroit Free Press. January 17, 1999, p. 7E.
Entertainment Weekly. December 11, 1998, p. 46.
Los Angeles Times. December 11, 1998, p. F2.
New York Times. December 11, 1998, p. B25.
Newsweek. December 14, 1998, p. 79.
People. December 14, 1998, p. 33.
San Francisco Chronicle. December 11, 1998, p. C3.
USA Today. December 11, 1998, p. E15.
Variety. September 21, 1998, p. 106.
Village Voice. December 8, 1998, p. 129.
Washington Post Weekend. January 22, 1999, p. 38.

Six Days, Seven Nights

After this week in paradise, they're going to need a vacation.—Movie tagline

"Harrison Ford delivers the perfect summer movie!"—Jimmy Carter, *The Nashville Network*

"Fun! Funny! Fabulous!"—Neil Rosen, *NY-1*

"The best romantic comedy since *Pretty Woman*!"—Ann Shatilla, *UPN 13*

 Box Office: $74,339,294

Frank Martin (David Schwimmer) is such a romantic. Three years ago he met Robin Monroe (Anne Heche). It was a cute meet: they argued over possession of a New York City taxi cab and they've been dating ever since. Robin is the high-powered assistant editor of a woman's magazine named *Dazzle* but, in honor of the anniversary of their meeting, Frank wants to whisk Robin away on a six day, seven night vacation on a lush tropical paradise. And once they get there, Frank plans on proposing to her.

Unfortunately, their resort is on an out-of-the-way island that can only be reached by charter airplane, and it looks as if the airplane they've hired won't even make it off the ground, let alone to an island in the middle of the Pacific. However, Quinn Harris (Harrison Ford), the airplane's owner, promises them that he will get them there with no problem. And, with the help of his so-called flight service director and obvious girlfriend Angelica (Jacqueline Obradors) he does exactly that.

Things go just as Frank had planned. The romantic atmosphere melts Robin's workaholic heart and she happily accepts his engagement ring. But before they can truly celebrate, Robin gets a call from her magazine's editor wanting her to fly to Tahiti to supervise a photo shoot. Buying into one of her magazine's own fabricated statistics—that 38% of all women are pressured into giving up their jobs in the first year of marriage—she interrupts her vacation to take on the assignment.

But how to get to Tahiti? Enter Quinn Harris again. Robin offers him $700 to interrupt his own layover to fly her there, and the money is more than the laid-back Quinn

Actor Harrison Ford is a licensed pilot and actually flew the antique De Havilland Beaver airplane in many of the scenes.

Robin (Anne Heche): "I've had just about as much vacation as I can stand."

can pass up. So, as Robin kisses her new fiancé good-bye and Quinn revs up the engines on his old De Havilland Beaver, the two fly off over the Pacific . . . and into some very nasty storm clouds. The turbulence blows the plane off course and when it is struck by lightning, it fries the radio and the emergency locator beacon. This means that when the plane is forced down on a deserted island, no one hears their mayday call and there's no way search teams can locate them.

As the morning breaks, Robin and Quinn assess their situation. They need food, water and shelter, but it would seem that their most immediate problem is that they have such opposite personalities that they'll kill each other before they can scout the island let alone be rescued. You can guess the rest. As they combat the elements, and some pirates, they stop combatting each other and—what a surprise—they first come to respect and then love each other, although they both have trouble admitting it. But everyone knows they will before the final credits role.

Six Days, Seven Nights is not a great picture. In fact, it's only barely a good picture. But two things give it what watchability it does have. One is the tropically inviting and lush scenery very temptingly photographed by cinematographer Michael Chapman (*The Fugitive* [1993], *Raging Bull* [1980]). Filmed not in Tahiti but on Hawaii, the film captures the wild and luxuriant nature of the archipelago's oldest island, Kauai (also the location of movies from *South Pacific* [1958] to *Jurassic Park* [1993].) However, since Hawaii is a rain forest, the filmmakers had to bring in nearly 400 palm trees to simulate Tahiti's tropics. Even the airplane scenes are well-filmed and add believability. This is undoubtedly helped by the fact that Ford is a pilot and insisted on flying the De Havilland himself during the shoot to lend credence to the character.

However, the most interesting aspect of the film are its two very likable lead actors. It is very hard to dislike Harrison Ford no matter what character he plays. He brings a sexy, funny roguishness to his characters that's non-threatening and engaging. Anne Heche (1997's *Donnie Brasco, Wag the Dog*, and *Volcano*) is blooming into a very intelligent actress whose spunk lends energy to her parts. Together they create an appealing, smart, and wisecracking duo. It is a testament to their acting ability that they can carry off the May-December (or at least September) romance between the fifty-five-year-old Ford and the twenty-nine-year-old Heche. And an even better testament of their acting ability is that they can make an audience forget that Heche came out of the proverbial closet and proclaimed her love for TV comedienne Ellen DeGeneres just as the film began shooting. (It is also a testament to Ford and director Ivan Reitman's open-mindedness that this proclamation didn't cause a flurry to recast the female lead.)

CREDITS

Quinn Harris: Harrison Ford
Robin Monroe: Anne Heche
Frank Martin: David Schwimmer
Angelica: Jacqueline Obradors
Jager: Temuera Morrison
Marjorie: Allison Janney
Phillippe: Douglas Weston
Kip: Cliff Curtis
Pierce: Danny Trejo

Origin: USA
Released: 1998
Production: Ivan Reitman, Wallis Nicita, and Roger Birnbaum for Northern Lights Entertainment and Caravan Pictures; released by Touchstone Pictures
Direction: Ivan Reitman
Screenplay: Michael Browning
Cinematography: Michael Chapman
Editing: Sheldon Kahn, Wendy Greene Bricmont
Production design: J. Michael Riva
Art direction: Richard F. Mays
Set design: Pamela Klamer, Patricia Klawonn
Costumes: Gloria Gresham
Music: Randy Edelman
Sound: Gene Cantamessa
Visual effects supervision: David Goldberg
MPAA rating: PG-13
Running Time: 101 minutes

What keeps *Six Days, Seven Nights* from being a better film is its utter lack of originality. First-time screenwriter Michael Browning doesn't seem to have strained his muse coming up with the story for this film. In fact, it rather seems to have been typed together from pages from other scripts. There's a bit from *Heaven Knows Mr. Allison* (1957), and parts of *Romancing the Stone* (1984). Isn't that *Father Goose* (1964) over there, and some of *The African Queen* (1951)? And surely that's the beach kiss from *From Here to Eternity* (1953). The result is lightweight, mainstream fluff. There are no twists or turns, no guessing how things will turn out, no edge-of-your-seat suspense. The only thing that makes this formulaic tale of opposites attracting interesting is wanting to know how the engaging and intelligent actors will pull it off. But maybe in the heat of summer blockbusters this is a nice way to cool off, and if it doesn't do well at the boxoffice, Ford and Heche are sure to appeal on videotape.

—Beverley Bare Buehrer

REVIEWS

Battle Creek Enquirer. June 11, 1998, p. 9.
Boxoffice. June, 1998, p. 22.
Chicago Sun Times. June 12, 1998.
Chicago Tribune. June 12, 1998, p. 4.
Detroit News. June 12, 1998, p. 3D.
Entertainment Weekly. June 19, 1998, p. 45.
Los Angeles Times. June 12, 1998, p. F1.
New York Times. June 12, 1998, p. E1.
People. June 22, 1998, p. 32.
Time. June 15, 1998.
USA Today. March 9, 1998, p. 7D.
USA Today. June 12, 1998, p. 13E.
Variety. June 8, 1998, p. 66.
Village Voice. June 23, 1998, p. 140.
Washington Post. June 12, 1998, p. B1.
Washington Post Weekend. June 12, 1998, p. 44.

Six-String Samurai

Vegas needs a new king.—Movie tagline
"Wildly original and highly entertaining . . . "
—Len Klady, *Variety*

A forced and rather crude attempt to create a grade-B cult film, *Six-String Samurai* is the bizarre story of a post-apocalyptic America whose capital is the fantasy city of Lost Vegas. An opening scroll explains that the Russians dropped the atomic bomb in 1957 and took over the United States, setting up Elvis as king, ruling from Lost Vegas, apparently the only city remaining unleveled. Now, as the film opens, Elvis has died and "every guitar-picking, sword-swinging opportunist" is converging on Lost Vegas to claim Elvis's mantle. Well, at least it's an original premise.

What writer-director Lance Mungia intends by setting up this non-sensical plot—other than some good-hearted fun—is inexplicable. The story line actually sounds better than what the film delivers. The expectation going in might be that *Six-String Samurai* is a gonzo exploration of politics, rock and roll and celebrity. Instead, it's a rather tame, lame road movie in which little of interest happens and everything is filmed in stilted, grandstanding fashion.

We immediately meet the "buddies" who are at the heart of any road picture. They are Buddy (Jeffrey Falcon, who also co-wrote the script), a frozen-in-time Buddy Holly icon with taped-together big-rim glasses, a guitar, a samurai sword, and a ripped-up umbrella, whose function isn't clear. In an undecipherable opening sequence, he saves The Kid (Justin McGuire), a scruffy, apparently speechless orphan who wears a coonskin hat and tags along on the road to Lost Vegas despite Buddy's initial objections.

They travel a wasteland desert landscape pockmarked by occasional outposts of strange survivors. First stop is a gas station oasis where the film's house band, the Red Elvises, are playing Ukrainian rock 'n' roll amid the ruins of a café. There is also a group of baldheaded karate-kicking thugs in bowling shirts. They have a rumble with Buddy, who demonstrates he can swing a mean samurai sword and execute some gravity-defying leaps, at least with the aid of judicious camera angles. Falcon, who studied martial arts under Jet Li's teacher, gets plenty of opportunities in this film to demonstrate what he's learned.

In Mungia's fight sequences—and in other places in the film—he overindulges in slow-motion, stop-action, exaggerated close-ups, and other overused, pedestrian camera tricks. One can't be positive, but Mungia appears to be lampooning these techniques and the type of low-budget action films that use them. That's the generous explanation. Another possibility is that Mungia thinks this is the most entertaining way to make movies. A third interpretation is that Mungia is consciously striving for a high-camp, cult-film feel.

But there are two problems with setting out to do a cult film that succeeds because it makes fun of really bad movies. The first is that everything feels forced and contrived, and the second is that you walk such a thin line between satire and the thing being satirized that you risk simply making a very bad movie yourself. *Six-String Samurai* has both these problems. It is so overdone in terms of reaching for knowing cynical cineastes that it seems overcooked, like one of those absurdly blackened dishes that passes for nouveau cuisine. And it is so thin on plot and action and acting and authentic technique that it is practically tasteless. Mungia's always-posing satire is so dull that if a filmmaker wanted a road map to satirize stilted B-movies, he would lampoon *Six-String Samurai*.

Throughout the film, Buddy and the Kid grab or steal a variety of conveyances, including an old car, a bike and a motorcycle. But they make most of the journey on foot. They are pursued at one point by a group that looks like overstuffed Australian aborigines who have gone way overboard at the local Halloween costume shop. Throughout the film, they are pursued by Death (Stephen Gauger), a top-hat wearing guitarist, and his two accomplices, who are a couple of stupid archers who speak in synthesized voices. Death, of course, is always a few hours behind the heroes, though he is constantly gaining on them. He is supposed to be a riff on Ingmar Bergman's *The Seventh Seal* specter, but he looks more like Tom Petty in a bad costume.

Along the way, Buddy saves the Kid on several occasions and they begrudgingly develop an affection for each other. But this does not happen until Buddy tries several times to get rid of the Kid. At one point, he drops him off at a post-nuclear-winter nuclear family, which is still acting the role of an exaggerated suburban '50s household. The Kid is about to be roasted and eaten for supper by his hosts until he is saved by the approach of the Windmill People, who scare away the family. The Windmill People turn out to be two guys in space suits. Buddy shows up in the nick of time to dispatch the Windmill People in his characteristic—and by now, excruciatingly boring—fashion. The audience limit for samurai slow-motion is definitely tested in this flick.

Inexplicably, the Kid, who until now has only screeched in animal cries to communicate, starts talking in English. The pair now are officially friends. Their next stop is an outpost with a bar where women with dirt-covered faces hover around Buddy, and one even beds him down. There is a fight in the bar, of course, and Death threatens the Kid, and Buddy confesses his frustration: "I've got to get a new gig. Let somebody else be king!" The Kid talks him down.

Besides the overheated and underbudgeted technique, the real trouble with *Six-String Samurai* is that Buddy is supposed to be the rockingest swordfighter in the land, but Buddy never plays a single lick on his guitar. Apart from the Red Elvises and other coy soundtrack tunes, there isn't a bit of music in a film that is apparently centered around rock iconography. Or maybe it isn't. Mungia seems disinterested in his own topic, and more interested in setting up scenes and snippets of dialogue which refer to dozens of classic films.

Six-String Samurai is a sophomoric attempt at filmmaking, a show-off kind of project which might score points in a student film festival but does not belong in any wider kind of distribution. The ultimate showdown with Death doesn't make much sense. "You here for me?" Buddy tells

CREDITS

Buddy: Jeffrey Falcon
The Kid: Justin McGuire
Death: Stephane Gauger
Russian general: John Sakisian

Origin: USA
Released: 1998
Production: Michael Burns and Leanna Creel for HSX Films; released by Palm Pictures
Direction: Lance Mungia
Screenplay: Lance Mungia and Jeffrey Falcon
Cinematography: Kristian Bernier
Editing: James Frisa
Production design: Jeffrey Falcon
Costumes: Jeffrey Falcon
Art direction: Casey Lurie, Scooter Schamus
MPAA rating: PG-13
Running Time: 89 minutes

Death. "You and every rock 'n' roller is out to claim my throne. I hope you guys can play." But the climax is no battle of the bands, merely another opportunity for Falcon to show what he learned from Jet Li's mentor. Then, when the Kid spits at Death and discovers he can melt him, the veiled references to *The Wizard of Oz* comes to the fore, much too obviously.

To enter Vegas, Buddy must get past the remnants of the Red Army, who are guarding the city. This requires grueling hand-to-hand combat in which Buddy mows down hundreds of men. There is also a long and totally obscure sequence in which the Kid descends into a maze of underground steam tunnels to confront something called the Spinach Monster, which never really materializes. *Six-String Samurai* is not merely indecipherable, it is indigestible.

As a midnight show on college campuses, *Six-String Samurai* at least has the virtue of appealing to a jaded sort of rock and cinematic cultural sensibility. As a video or mass-audience release, it would seem to have absolutely no future. And it seems much too self-important and pretentious to make it into the realm of a cult hit, to which it obviously aspires. Mungia had better go back to scriptwriting school and work up a little plot and character development. The movie doesn't even make sense on its own non-sensical terms. It is more like a series of poorly realized music-video set pieces than a feature film.

—*Michael Betzold*

REVIEWS

Boxoffice. October, 1998, p. 53.
Cinefantastique. October, 1998, p. 52.
Los Angeles Times. September 18, 1998, p. F14.
New York Times. January 22, 1999, p. E20.

Slam

"Triumphant!"—Beth Pinsker, *Dallas Morning News*

"It's the kind of movie that makes you believe in movies!"—Owen Gleiberman, *Entertainment Weekly*

"Brace yourself for a slam dunk of a movie! Independent filmmaking could find no higher ground than a film with an innovative style and social conscience that delivers the message: Art redeems life!"—Kimberly Newman, *Hollywood Reporter*

"Breathtaking!"—James McCarthy, *The Observer*

 Box Office: $1,009,819

Slam, directed by Marc Levin, is a wonderfully realized fiction film that won the Grand Jury Prize at Sundance and both the Audience Award and the Camera d'Or at Cannes. Another recent film, the documentary *Slamnation* highlights this phenomenon, a sort of spoken-word poetry performance. Levin, a veteran of other documentaries, has assembled an inspired cast of actors that evoke intensity and natural flair that belies the structured drama behind the story.

Marion Barry, the former mayor of Washington, DC, has a cameo as an anti-drug judge.

CREDITS

Ray Joshua: Saul Williams
Lauren Bell: Sonja Sohn
Hopha: Bonz Malone
Big Mike: Lawrence Wilson
Jimmy Huang: Beau Sia
China: Andre Taylor

Origin: USA
Released: 1998
Production: Henri M. Kessler, Marc Levin, and Richard Stratton for Offline Entertainment; released by Trimark Films
Direction: Marc Levin
Screenplay: Marc Levin, Bonz Malone, Saul Williams, and Sonja Sohn, and Richard Stratton
Cinematography: Mark Benjamin
Editing: Emir Lewis
Music: DJ Spooky
MPAA rating: R
Running Time: 102 minutes

Ray (Saul Williams) is a petty thief with the rich soul of a poet. One need only see him interact with the young kids of his inner-city Washington D.C. ghetto to see the kindness and optimism seep out of his smile. Unfortunately, Ray is caught with a quarter pound of pot when the police arrive to investigate a nearby shooting.

He is now placed into the system, which does nothing more than virtually assign him a number and project a grim future for him; either plead guilty and face up to ten years, or two years at the very least with a good defense. Ray can barely absorb this; he has no place in this living hell, with its careful hierarchy of caste and unavoidable violence. One day he saves himself from certain maiming—or worse—by spontaneous slamming; the other inmates are astounded and amazed and treat him with respect thereafter. Lauren (Sonja Sohn) also hears him and recognizes his enormous, untapped talent. Lauren teaches writing to the prisoners and is herself a gifted slammer. There are a number of scenes that illustrate the class's burgeoning writing talents, scenes that reveal the vast amount of creativity and brainpower that is wasted, particularly among black men. Lauren also sees Ray's insecurities and longs to help him discover his strong self, and escape from the path of crime and prison that seems to be laid out in front of him.

Levin keeps the story from straying from the main focus—that people can be and have to be in charge of their own destiny. This is definitely "politically correct" territory, but is borne out by the characters' true and valid existence. Ray is unexpectedly bailed out, but he faces an enormous obstacle in front of him; face up to his own personal roadblocks, or take an enormous risk and change his life forever.

Lauren and Ray become intimate. It is more than mere physicality; they have a burning passion for their poetry and words fuel their passion. Lauren wants Ray to look honestly at his choices. She does not have her head in the sand; as a black woman she knows the hard reality of obstacles and prejudices that her students face. But she challenges Ray to break free of his previous pattern. Ray endures some serious self-examination, and visits Lauren at a crowded "slam" session.

One of the final, and most powerful scenes in the film, show Lauren and Ray in their full performance glory. Indeed, it is the slamming scenes that elevate this film above the norm. The theme of rising above one's history and circumstances is strongly supported by the desire of this couple. This film was heavily lauded by both the Sundance and Cannes audiences, which traditionally reward material of a more liberal manner. The general audience will probably re-act well to this film, but perhaps not with such overwhelm-ing enthusiasm as the rarefied film festival crowds.

—G. E. Georges

REVIEWS

Boxoffice. September, 1998, p. 20.
Entertainment Weekly. October 23, 1998, p. 49.
Los Angeles Times. October 21, 1998, p. F5.
New York Times. October 3, 1998, p. B16.
New York Times. October 4, 1998, p. AR28.
Village Voice. October 13, 1998, p. 130.
Washington Post Weekend. October 23, 1998, p. 55.

Sliding Doors

A romantic comedy that lets you experience the two different ways one life could go.—Movie tagline

What if catching a train means one future, and missing it means another?—Movie tagline

There are two sides to every story. Helen is about to live both of them . . . at the same time. Romance was never this much fun.—Movie tagline

"Perfect and very charming! A pleasure for everyone to see!"—Lisa Schwarzbaum, *Entertainment Weekly*

"A lively romance! Cleverly conceived and su-perbly executed!"—Jack Mathews, *Los Angeles Times*

"*Sliding Doors* asks the same questions we all ask in life. *What if* and *If only.* The answers are de-lightful either way!"—Rex Reed, *New York Observer*

"A lively romance! Cleverly conceived and su-perbly executed."—Jack Mathews, *Newsday*

"The date-night movie of choice! Funny and touching!"—Peter Travers, *Rolling Stone*

"In a world of ordinary movies, *Sliding Doors* stands far above the crowd! I loved its daring, its sizzling wit and its aura of urgent romance! Gwyneth Paltrow gives a terrific performance!"—Joe Morgenstern, *Wall Street Journal*

 Box Office: $11,911,200

Writer-director Peter Howitt's first film takes an un-usual approach to the vagaries of love by showing how much a part chance plays in the lives of four young residents of London. Howitt's gimmick of telling parallel stories with the same characters works well though the pro-tagonists could have used more depth and the story more humor.

After Helen (Gwyneth Paltrow) is fired from her pub-lic-relations job, she heads for the nearest tube station and just misses her train. Or does she? Howitt stops the action, rewinds it, and shows what would have happened if she had caught the train and sat next to the charming James (John Hannah). The remainder of the film switches between what would have happened if she had caught the train and ar-rived home in time to catch her lover, Gerry (John Lynch) in bed with Lydia (Jeanne Tripplehorn) and events that transpire when she arrives just after Lydia leaves. (The shifts are easy to follow since the two Helens have different styles and colors of hair.)

The impetus of the latter story is how she will support herself and Gerry—he is writing a novel and does not have a paying job—how long it will take her to discover Gerry is unfaithful, how much longer Lydia will put up with his re-fusal to leave Helen, and how Helen and James will find each other. In the parallel story, she leaves Gerry immedi-ately, moving in with Anna (Zara Turner), her best friend, and broods considerably. The questions here are how long it will take James to make Helen forget Gerry and whether James is as perfect as he seems to be.

Such parallel or alternating stories are nothing new in films with the best-known perhaps being the account of life in Bedford Falls had the James Stewart character not been born in *It's A Wonderful Life* (1946). The ironic structure of *Sliding Doors,* however, owes more to Frederic Raphael's brilliant screenplay for Stanley Donen's *Two for the Road* (1967), in which a couple's relationship is depicted as dete-riorating over several years with jumps back and forth in time. Both *Sliding Doors* and *Two for the Road* are also time capsules of the fashions and attitudes of their times. In many ways, *Sliding Doors* seems a 1990s updating of 1960s styles, a less zany version of, say, *Georgy Girl* (1966). Julie Christie or Vanessa Redgrave can easily be imagined playing uncertain Helen.

Howitt's efforts concentrate primarily on the film's structure and pay too little attention to character development and motivation. James is little more than his constant references to Monty Python and the Beatles. Much more surprising than the secret he is keeping from Helen is the revelation that he, the cuddly, boy-next-door type, is a business executive, head of a firm carrying his name. Lydia is also an executive, though of the shrewish variety. She clearly eats her underlings for lunch. Lydia's mystery is what she sees in the indecisive, wimpy Gerry.

Gwyneth Paltrow: "It's a story about destiny, about wondering if you've made the right decisions, about knowing that things happen for a reason."

Come to think of it, what does Helen see in him? All the audience knows about Gerry is that he is writing something about something, has to do research in a library and occasionally out of town (the better to sneak off with Lydia), lives off Helen, and does not like Elton John. (Real Londoners of this generation would have more current pop culture references than Howitt provides. Is he simply condescending to his American audience?) Because Gerry is such weak competition for James, the outcome is never in doubt. And Helen is too much the victim of insensitive, untrustworthy men. Her only winning quality is that she is portrayed by the always appealing Paltrow.

Finally, these characters are mere pawns in a pair of tales aimed at nothing less than getting them from one crucial point to the next. In the stays-with-Gerry arc, Helen must work two jobs to support herself and her boyfriend. In the leaves-Gerry version, how is he buying groceries? Howitt, formerly an actor best known in the United Kingdom for playing a lout in the 1980s situation comedy *Bread,* also brings matters to a climax by having both women become pregnant. Both? Sophisticated businesswomen? In the late 1990s? Even worse is the overly melodramatic resolution of the leaves-Gerry story which puts a considerable damper on the cute, optimistic ending of the other.

Lynch can be quite effective in small roles as tortured souls in such films as *The Secret Garden* (1993) and *The Secret of Roan Inish* (1995), but he has no clue about a boor like Gerry. At least cinematographer Remi Adefarasin lights Lynch to flatter his dark, angular looks and bushy eyebrows. Tripplehorn is not so fortunate. Just because Lydia is the villain does not justify lighting Tripplehorn in varying degrees of horridness, making her look pasty and bloated in almost every shot. She is appropriately shrill in this thankless role.

Hannah, best known as the surviving half of the homosexual couple in *Four Weddings and a Funeral* (1994), displays considerable charm. Because James is the only one of the four protagonists with much of an active sense of humor, Hannah's appearances are welcome, and he and Paltrow play off each other effectively. Paltrow has said in interviews that *Sliding Doors* is one of the few films she is proud of, but Helen is still an underwritten role. Paltrow coasts along on her looks and charisma, but her naturally nasal whine is more pronounced when she does a British accent and becomes irritating at times.

The most appealing characters are Turner's commonsense Anna and McFerran's Russell, the best friend Gerry pours his heart out to in their pub. McFerran gives the film's best performance because of the delight he takes in Russell's joy over his friend's anguish. Russell feels that Gerry deserves all he gets for thinking he can have two affairs at once and roars in

Former actor Peter Howitt was inspired to write *Sliding Doors* after almost being struck by a car while crossing London's Charing Cross Road.

CREDITS

Helen:	Gwyneth Paltrow
James:	John Hannah
Gerry:	John Lynch
Lydia:	Jeanne Tripplehorn
Anna:	Zara Turner
Russell:	Douglas McFerran
Clive:	Paul Brightwell
Claudia:	Nina Young
Paul:	Kevin McNally
James' mother:	Virginia McKenna

Origin: USA, Great Britain
Released: 1997
Production: Sydney Pollack, Philippa Braithwaite, and William Horberg for Mirage and Intermedia Films; released by Miramax Films and Paramount Pictures
Direction: Peter Howitt
Screenplay: Peter Howitt
Cinematography: Remi Adefarasin
Editing: John Smith
Production design: Maria Djurkovic
Art direction: Martyn John
Costumes: Jill Taylor
Music: David Hirschfelder
Sound: John Midgley
MPAA rating: R
Running Time: 108 minutes

laughter at revelations he considers better than an episode of *Seinfeld*.

The ultimate irony of *Sliding Doors* is that Russell sees the ridiculousness of the situation much better than his creator. The film is watchable and occasionally entertaining. It moves along quite smoothly and looks good, with the notable exception of Tripplehorn. But it is not thought out carefully enough, falling back on what is simply convenient and easy rather than finding anything original beyond its premise.

—*Michael Adams*

REVIEWS

Boxoffice. March, 1998, p. 53.
Chicago Tribune. April 24, 1998, p. 4.
Detroit Free Press. April 24, 1998, p. D1.
Detroit News. April 24, 1998, p. C1.
Entertainment Weekly. May 1, 1998, p. 36.
Los Angeles Times. April 24, 1998, p. F1.
New York Times. April 24, 1998, p. B14.
The Observer. May 3, 1998, p. 9.
People. May 1, 1998, p. 33.
Rolling Stone. March 5, 1998, p. 74.
Sight and Sound. June, 1998, p. 55.
Time. April 27, 1998, p. 68.
USA Today. April 24, 1998, p. E6.
Variety. January 19, 1998, p. 89.
Village Voice. April 28, 1998, p. 75.
Vogue. March, 1998, p. 292.
Washington Post. April 24, 1998, p. B5.
Washington Post Weekend. April 24, 1998, p. 56.

Slums of Beverly Hills

"*Slums of Beverly Hills* has a big heart, strong voice, vivid look, and original sense of humor. Natasha Lyonne is a comic discovery."—Lisa Schwarzbaum, *Entertainment Weekly*

"Tamara Jenkins, who makes her writing and directing debut with wit and confidence, keeps the small surprises frequent."—Janet Maslin, *New York Times*

"Startlingly funny."—Joe Morgenstern, *Wall Street Journal*

 Box Office: $5,480,868

In director Tamara Jenkins's wry, appealing coming-of-age story *Slums of Beverly Hills*, Vivian Abramowitz (Natasha Lyonne), like most other teen-agers, is constantly embarrassed by her family. Although this is a common feeling of most adolescents, in this case Vivian may very well be justified by her mortification. In the very first scene, overbearing Murray Abramowitz (Alan Arkin) takes his newly blossomed daughter to the local lingerie shop to suit her up for her first (and very badly needed) bra. As

Vivian (Natasha Lyonne) to her father (Alan Arkin): "I hate us. We're *freaks*."

Murray delicately puts it to the adoring saleslady, "I don't know what happened—overnight—she got stacked, just like her mother!"

The mother in question is absent, living on the east coast, while Murray, Vivian, and her two brothers Rickey (Eli Marienthal) and Ben (David Krumholtz) trundle from one down-scale Beverly Hills apartment complex to another. Murray maintains that he wants the kids to have the excellent education obtained by the Beverly Hills zip code. So what if he routinely wakes them up in the middle of the night, abruptly packs up and races from the livid landlady? "We're Jewish Joads" complains Vivian as they settle into another marginal complex—"The Capri."

Murray's self-confidence and bravado wanes in proportion to his finances; he is constantly reminded by his older, successful brother Mickey (Carl Reiner) that he can't manage his life or his money. Instead of merely begging for more money from Mickey, Murray hits upon the idea of taking care of Mickey's wayward, drug addict daughter, Rita (Marisa Tomei). She's a recent escapee from a sanitarium and needs direction in life. Murray promises to take care of her, enroll her in nursing school, and generally keep her out of trouble. Murray finds himself with a lusty, (pregnant—though she tells no one but Vivian) out-of-control woman who's almost thirty years old.

(Murray and Rita actually have a special relationship founded on them being the family "fuck-ups").

Jenkins's semi-autobiographical screenplay (developed at the Sundance lab, Robert Redford is the film's executive producer) sketches a wide array of characters that are truly original, with a wonderfully charming premise. However, her downfall lays in her weak editing, her tendency to let scenes run on too long and letting her actors flail helplessly in scenes that have worn out their welcome. Jenkins contrasts Vivian's sexual awakening, with slovenly but likeable boy-next-door Eliot (Kevin Corrigan—a staple of independent films), and Rita's vibrator, with the very real and poignant story of her father, a man who is lost in life but needs to pull it together for the sake of his children.

Women have always been denied a witty and compelling coming-of-age story along the lines of *Summer of '42* (1971) or *Stand by Me* (1986). Somewhere between *The Trouble with Angels* (1966) and *Julia* (1977) there lies a film that would address the delicious agony of adolescence, families, and sexuality from the girl/woman's point of view but this film isn't it. The film doesn't always achieve its lofty goals, but Jenkins shows an assured eye for character and detail that will undoubtedly emerge again in other work. Arkin does well in a role that could be somewhat compared to Jason Robards in *A Thousand Clowns* (1965) in terms of balancing pathos and charm. But the real find is Lyonne, who so aptly captures the angst of teenage life, coupled with an unusually trying home life, with the wry wit of Dorothy Parker and the fierce optimism of Mary Richards.

—G. E. Georges

CREDITS

Vivian Abramowitz: Natasha Lyonne
Murray Abramowitz: Alan Arkin
Rita Abramowitz: Marisa Tomei
Ben Abramowitz: David Krumholtz
Rickey Abramowitz: Eli Marienthal
Eliot: Kevin Corrigan
Doris: Jessica Walter
Mickey Abramowitz: Carl Reiner
Belle Abramowitz: Rita Moreno

Origin: USA
Released: 1998
Production: Michael Nozik and Stan Wlodkowski for South Fork Pictures; released by Fox Searchlight Pictures
Direction: Tamara Jenkins
Screenplay: Tamara Jenkins
Cinematography: Tom Richmond
Editing: Pamela Martin
Production design: Dena Roth
Music: Rolfe Kent
Costumes: Kirsten Everberg
MPAA rating: R
Running Time: 91 minutes

REVIEWS

Detroit News. August 28, 1998, p. 3D.
Entertainment Weekly. August 21, 1998, p. 96.
Los Angeles Times. August 14, 1998, p. F16.
People. August 31, 1998, p. 33.
Sight and Sound. December, 1998, p. 61.
Village Voice. August 18, 1998, p. 112.
Washington Post Weekend. August 28, 1998, p. 41.

Small Soldiers

The few, the proud, the small.—Movie tagline
Big Movie!—Movie tagline

 Box Office: $55,143,823

Joe Dante's *Small Soldiers* is such a smart, witty, all-purpose spoof that you hardly mind that it seems coldly calculated to hook in every age group from toddler to aging Baby Boomer. There is something for just about everyone in this grab bag of brain candy. Adults dragged into watching this film about lethal talking toys will be pleasantly surprised at its sharp satirical punches. Teenage girls have Kirsten Dunst to identify with, and pubescent boys can pine for Dunst along with Gregory Smith's 14-year-old Alan Abernathy character. Kids can marvel at the special effects, and even the youngest can appreciate the imaginative squads of commandos and aliens.

The animatronic wizardry of Stan Winston is at the center of the film's appeal. Going *Toy Story* one better, Winston's crew has created two opposing armies of hilarious toy stereotypes—a squadron of gung-ho GI-Joe mercenaries called the Commando Elite and a ragtag group of monstrous but likeable lost creatures, the Gorgonites. The toys' powers are formidable because an eager-to-succeed toy company employee (Jay Mohr) has installed "smart" computer chips in them, obtained from a batch of rejected Pentagon weapons.

The film labors a bit at the beginning to set up its far-fetched plot and introduce all its characters. Mohr's Larry Benson is carelessly intent on obeying his cut-throat boss of toy manufacturer Globotech, Gil Mars (Denis Leary). Mars suggests that Benson and his nerdish partner Irwin (David Cross) try to create action toys that can actually play with children. As Mars puts it, he wants toys that fight back. With such explicit instructions, Benson uses a computer code to crack into a cache of super-smart Defense Department microprocessors and installs the chips in toys. Triumphantly, Globotech introduces its new product line with the slogan: "Everything else is just a toy."

Abernathy is a smart but troublesome son trying vainly to prove to his father that he is responsible enough to run the family toy store while Dad's away. His father, Stuart (Kevin Dunn), is an aging hippie whose store, called The Inner Child, is filled with non-mechanical treasures that Alan thinks are lame. Dad absolutely forbids war toys. But when truck driver Joe (Dick Miller) comes by with a ship-

Archer (voice of Frank Langella): "What's your name?" Alan (Gregory Smith): "Alan. Now shut up!" Archer: "Greetings, Alan now shut up."

Young Alan Abernathy (Gregory Smith) has his life turned upside down by a band of interactive dolls in *Small Soldiers*.

ment of the impressive Commando Elite and the Gorgonites on a Friday afternoon, Alan becomes convinced that the toys will sell like hotcakes and make a profit for his dad's fledgling toy store. He persuades the driver to let him have a set.

The toys are not supposed to be sold until Monday, but they attract the attention of Dunst's Christy Fimple, who has the full attention of Alan. Christy wants to buy one of the toys for her little brother. Alan just wants to impress Christy. You can almost hear Smith's hormones firing up when Dunst comes on scene, but the dialogue between them is weak. "You're not like other girls," Alan tells Christy after they both agree they dislike a popular TV show. "I know," replies Dunst, who looks much older than Smith.

It doesn't take long for the situation to get out of hand. Alan takes home the Gorgonites' leader, Archer (voiced by Frank Langella), who soon exhibits his startling powers of comprehension and becomes Alan's friend. Meanwhile, back at the deserted store, Commando leader Chip Hazard (voiced by Tommy Lee Jones) bursts out of his box and rallies his troops for an assault on the enemy Gorgonites. The troops include demolitions expert Nick Nitro, artillery specialist Brick Bazooka, communications man Link Static, and mercenaries Butch Meathook and Kip Killigan. Standing in front of an American flag on a toy store shelf—in homage to the movie *Patton*—Chip Hazard delivers a hilarious speech that is a collage of famous war-movie and political clichés. Then the toys attack the Gorgonites.

Dante's prior experience with the film *Gremlins* comes in handy as the second half of the movie pits the relentless toy soldiers with the inventive families who are providing safe harbor for the Gorgonites. *Small Soldiers* not only makes fun of war-movie clichés, it also shoots bullets at warring neighbors and warring families. The simple-is better Abernathys have a running feud with the techno-crazed Fimples, Phil (Phil Hartman, in his last role) and Marion (Wendy Schaal). Alan is in a running battle with his father, with mother Irene (Ann Magnuson) trying to cool everyone down with deep breathing and head massages. Christy and her parents are also engaging in a cold war of sorts.

The voices of the Gorgonites are provided by the actors who portray the aging rockers in *This Is Spinal Tap*—Christopher Guest, Michael McKean, and Harry Shearer.

Fortunately, *Small Soldiers* is equally adept at poking fun at peaceniks like the Abernathys, at the obsession of adolescent girls with dolls, at megacorporate greed, and at puppy love. It's an equal opportunity lambaster. The film shifts into high gear as the Commando troops commandeer lawn and garden equipment and power tools and come at Alan and Archer tooth and nail. Clichés fly as fast as the action. "We have ways of making you talk," a commando says to a captured Gorgonite. Some survivors of the original *Dirty Dozen* film do the voices for the commandos.

The Gorgonites eventually win sympathy as the good guys, even though they are deformed and alien. Thanks to the powerful microchips, the Commandos are under direct orders to defend their country. It's just one of the ways Dante turns everything askew. The Gorgonites include a reptilian creature with one prominent eye named Ocula, a stand-up comic named Insaniac, a shy critter named Slamfist, and a gentle monster named Freakenstein. When they bounce around Alan's room, the Gorgonites provide plenty of energy and laughs. The Gorgonites are programmed to hide and lose to the Commando Elite, but with Alan's help they find a new meaning to their existence.

The film goes over the top when the commandos take Christy hostage to flush out Alan and the Gorgonites. In need of recruits, Chip Hazard creates a new army of crazed toys from Christy's Barbie-like dolls named "Wendy." Hazard gives them new "brains" in a Frankenstein fashion, observing: "A mind is a terrible thing to waste." The Wendys first tie up and torture Christy, then her boyfriend, and finally Alan, all the while mouthing Valley Girl clichés about makeovers and malls. These are riot girls par excellence.

As the film careens toward an apocalyptic ending, Dante pulls out all the stops. Chip Hazard gets a helicopter and, as the score from *Apocalypse Now* soars, intones: "I love the smell of polyurethane in the morning." The parents—and the toy inventors who have belatedly arrived to contain the situation—all become war recruits, trapped in the Abernathys' house as the commandos attack by launching flam-

ing tennis balls. The resourceful Marion Fimple volleys them back. In the end, Alan must go on a daring mission to fry the commandos with a high-voltage jolt from a utility transformer. And Mars arrives to pay off everyone's potential litigations with massive amounts of money.

Dante keeps the movie on the right edge between horrifying and hilarious. War is hell, to be sure, but Dante seems to be implying that the toy business is too, even as the movie's marketers concoct product tie-ins for the film. Prospects for merchandising of the film would seem to run into a few snags. Impressionable youngsters who see the film might be afraid that the toys may come to life. As Christy's little brother confesses to his parents after the holocaust is finished: "I just want clothes for my birthday."

Small Soldiers makes great use of Winston's animatronics and thirty years' worth of popular music. The soundtrack is as coy as the script, screeching into Pat Benatar's "Love is a Battlefield" when Alan sees Christy's jock

CREDITS

Christy Fimple: Kirsten Dunst
Alan Abernathy: Gregory Smith
Larry Benson: Jay Mohr
Phil Fimple: Phil Hartman
Stuart Abernathy: Kevin Dunn
Gil Mars: Denis Leary
Irene Abernathy: Ann Magnuson
Marion Fimple: Wendy Schaal
Irwin: David Cross

Origin: USA
Released: 1998
Production: Mike Finnell and Colin Wilson for DreamWorks/Universal; released by DreamWorks
Direction: Joe Dante
Screenplay: Gavin Scott, Adam Rifkin, Ted Elliott, and Terry Rossio
Cinematography: Jamie Anderson
Editing: Marshall Harvey
Music: Jerry Goldsmith
Production design: William Sandell
Art direction: Mark Mansbridge
Set decoration: Rosemary Brandenburg
Costume design: Carole Brown-James
Animatronic design: Stan Winston
Visual effects supervision: Stefen Fangmeier
Sound: Ken King
MPAA rating: PG-13

boyfriend roll up on a motor scooter. Dante's film is full of energy and terrific in-jokes for adults, especially film buffs. It almost succeeds in being all things to all people but manages nonetheless to maintain a winning zaniness. It's a festival of lunatic fun concealed beneath the ridiculous menace of war toys that actually make war. The ultimate message (if you want it) is that our consumer culture is killing us, but Dante delivers this bombshell with such pizazz that you won't feel wounded. In the best traditions of satire, *Small Soldiers* is disarmingly subversive. It's also a whole lot of fun.

—*Michael Betzold*

REVIEWS

Chicago Tribune. July 10, 1998, p. 5.
Detroit Free Press. July 10, 1998, p. D1.
Entertainment Weekly. July 17, 1998, p. 58.
Los Angeles Times. July 10, 1998, F1.
New York Times. July 10, 1998, E18.
People. July 27, 1998, p. 36.
Sight and Sound. October, 1998, p. 55-56.
Variety. July 13, 1998, p. 54.
Village Voice. July 21, 1998, p. 124.
Washington Post. July 10, 1998, p. D5.

Smoke Signals

A new film from the heart of native America.
—Movie tagline

"Warmly comic with charming performances and a splendid screenplay!"—Janet Maslin, *New York Times*

"One of the best films of the year! A heartfelt and wryly hilarious tale. Writer Sherman Alexie and director Chris Eyre have a keen eye for humor and nuance."—Peter Travers, *Rolling Stone*

"Two thumbs up!"—*Siskel & Ebert*

"Funny, charming and entertaining! Don't miss *Smoke Signals*!"—Dennis Cunningham, *WCBS-TV*

Smoke Signals, winner of the Filmmaker's Trophy and the Audience Award at the 1998 Sundance Festival, covers a road trip between two friends, Victor Joseph (Adam Beach) and Thomas Builds-the-Fire (Evan Adams), from their childhood home of the Idaho Coer d'Alene reservation to Phoenix. Although the twenty-ish young Indian men are not close friends, they are linked by early tragedy.

Based on award-winning Indian writer Sherman Alexie's collection of stories entitled *The Lone Ranger and Tonto Fistfight in Heaven*, director Chris Eyre explores the roadblocks to manhood in the young Indian man's life: alcohol, parental abandonment, and the odd prejudices from the "white world off the rez" with style and grace.

Victor's father, Arnold Joseph (Gary Farmer), saved baby Thomas from a fire in Thomas' parents' home after a

Victor (Adam Beach) to the goofy Thomas (Evan Adams): "Indians aren't supposed to smile like that. Get stoic."

party gets out of hand. Thomas's parents perish in the fire, and the sweetly nerdy Thomas shyly looks up to Arnold as a sort of surrogate father figure, as he grows up with his equally nerdy Grandma Builds-the-Fire (Monique Mojica). When Arlene (Tantoo Cardinal), Victor's mother, tells her husband Arnold that they must stop drinking so much, Arnold abandons his family in a heart-shattering scene.

Years later Arlene receives a call from Suzy Song (Irene Bedard), Arnold's neighbor in Phoenix. She has found Arnold dead in his home and wants his family to know. Victor decides to drive to Phoenix to pick up his father's ashes. Upon learning of this journey, Thomas tells Victor that he wants to join him. Thomas is deceivingly annoying; he is the type of low-key charmer that usually gets his way, and, after much bickering, the two men hit the road.

Victor is the strong, silent type; he needs stillness on this trip to process all that is running through his head about his father. Through flashbacks we see happy memories between Arnold and Victor, then unsettling, violent ones. It soon becomes apparent, through a story that Thomas tells over and over about Arnold taking Thomas to a Denny's for a "Grand Slam Breakfast," that Thomas also holds Arnold to be a father figure.

Writer Alexie and director Eyre play with Indian stereotypes and yet somehow manage to show the true individuality behind the facades. Even though Victor chides Thomas for his "grinning Indian" act, they later gleefully stun their fellow bus passengers by singing a ditty entitled "John Wayne's Teeth," which pokes fun at the Indians' historic nemesis. *Smoke Signals* is a simple, mature, and quietly confident coming-of-age story about a group dealing with problems both specific and general to their age and gender.

When Victor and Thomas reach Arnold's home, Victor must come to terms with the remains of his father's—figuratively and literally. Looking through his father's belongings, he finds many pictures and memories of himself and his mother. His neighbor Suzy tells Victor that his fa-

CREDITS

Victor Joseph: Adam Beach
Thomas Builds-the-Fire: Evan Adams
Suzy Song: Irene Bedard
Arnold Joseph: Gary Farmer
Arlene Joseph: Tantoo Cardinal
Police Chief: Tom Skerrit
Grandma Builds-the-Fire: Monique Mojica
Lucy: Elaine Miles
Penny: Molly Cheek
Young Victor: Cody Lightning
Young Thomas: Simon Baker
Randy Peone: John Trudell
Junior Polatkin: Michael Greyeyes

Origin: USA
Released: 1998
Production: Larry Estes and Scott M. Rosenfelt for Shadow Catcher Entertainment; released by Miramax Entertainment
Direction: Chris Eyre
Screenplay: Sherman Alexie; based on stories from his novel *Tonto and the Lone Ranger Fistfight in Heaven*
Cinematography: Brian Capener
Editing: Brian Berdan
Costumes: Ron Leamon
Production design: Charles Armstrong
Music: B. C. Smith
Art direction: Jonathon Saturen
Sound: Douglas Tburtelot
MPAA rating: PG-13
Running Time: 88 minutes

AWARDS AND NOMINATIONS

Independent Spirit Awards 1999:   Debut Performance (Evan Adams)

ther thought of them and that fire every day; sober, pensive and trying to forgive himself, Arnold was a changed man by the time of his death.

Letting go of anger is never easy, and Victor must face the anger and selfishness inside himself. When Thomas tells Victor that he has punished his mother every day for years by not growing to be a man, Victor faces the reality that he is at the precipice of a turning point in his own life.

Like other coming-of-age stories (*Boyz N the Hood* [1991] comes to mind) the obstacles and problems are not particularly new (besides the Indian specifics), but the writing, direction, and wonderful performances make this film memorable. Near the end, Thomas narrates movingly, "After we forgive our fathers . . . then what?," a question that applies to not only American Indians, but rings especially evocative here.

—G. E. Georges

REVIEWS

Chicago Tribune. July 3, 1998, p. 5.
Detroit Free Press. July 10, 1998, p. 9D.
Detroit News. July 10, 1998, p. 4D.
Entertainment Weekly. July 10, 1998, p. 50.
Los Angeles Times. June 26, 1998, p. F8.
People. July 13, 1998, p. 33.
Rolling Stone. July 9, 1998, p. 146.
Time. July 29, 1998.
Variety. February 2, 1998, p. 29.
Washington Post Weekend. July 3, 1998, p. 47.

Snake Eyes

Believe everything except your eyes.—Movie tagline

"Stylish and entertainingly feverish!"—Jay Carr, *Boston Globe*

"A nerve-jangling thriller!"—Michael Wilmington, *Chicago Tribune*

"*Snake Eyes* is a hot new thriller with adrenaline-pumping excitement!"—Stephen Holden, *New York Times*

"*Snake Eyes* is a high energy thriller! The opening is worth the price of admission!"—Jack Mathews, *Newsday*

"A breath-taking mystery thriller."—Andy Seiler, *USA Today*

"Brian De Palma rolls a winning *Snake Eyes* with Cage and Sinise! Cage is super-heated and Sinise is deadly cool."—Joe Morgenstern, *Wall Street Journal*

Box Office: $55,591,409

B rian De Palma is a film director who is obsessed with technique, which may help to explain why so many of his earlier films made him appear to be an artist intent on imitating Alfred Hitchcock, the "master of suspense." The downside of De Palma the technician is that style always overwhelms substance, creating a moral vacuum at the center of his films as art imitates art rather than nature. After seeing *Snake Eyes*, one reviewer dismissed De Palma as "the masturbator of suspense." But it would not be accurate to say that there is more than meets the eye here. In *Snake Eyes* everything meets the eye in a sensory overload.

The opening shot of the film was praised by National Public Radio critic Bob Mandala and others as an impressive demonstration of bravura filmmaking. De Palma begins his film with an apparently uninterrupted take that lasts for anywhere from twelve to twenty minutes (but if the latter estimate is correct, one suspects cinema trickery and "invisible" editing to fake an impossibly long take). The opening shot(s) involve 14,000 actors and introduce all of the major players and some minor ones, such as a television reporter covering a coming story outside the casino which is the film's main setting. She keeps

Kevin Dunne (Gary Sinise) to corrupt cop Rick Santoro (Nicolas Cage): "Do what you always do! Take the money!"

blowing her lines. Why? Because, Mandala speculated, De Palma is telling his audience that in an opening long take as complicated as this one, no actor will have the luxury of missing a cue or of fluffing the lines, for this would force the director to begin the shot anew, an expensive consequence.

Nicolas Cage plays Atlantic City police detective Rick Santoro, sporting a gold cell phone and a flamboyant Hawaiian shirt that matches his overstated personality. As the German proverb goes, "Kleider machen Leute" ("Clothes make the man"). The camera picks him up inside the arena, after the camera has moved from the reporter outside to video monitors inside. Rick is really pumped up for the coming prizefight, which the camera almost completely ignores at first, when it begins. De Palma will later show the fight action in replay, as Rick attempts to reconstruct the crime, an assassination timed to coincide with the knockout punch. Rick eventually realizes that the fight is fixed. The champ has been instructed to take a fall when he hears a planted "fan" scream, "I feel your pain!" What the champ does not know is that at the very minute the champ falls, the Secretary of Defense, Charles Kirkland (Joel Fabiani) sitting at ringside, will be assassinated. And that is why at first De Palma's camera remains on the fans, not on the ring.

The Secretary of Defense arrives at the championship event with a military bodyguard, Naval Commander Kevin Dunne (Gary Sinise), who is an old friend of Rick Santoro and has helped Rick get a ringside seat, and defense contractor Gilbert Powell (John Heard). The political plot, rather vaguely sketched, reveals that the Secretary plans to cut back military spending and research on sophisticated weaponry. To prevent that from happening, Dunne, who is a right-wing super-patriot, has hatched a conspiracy to murder the Secretary at the boxing arena, and the champ, Lincoln Tyler (Stan Shaw), has been bribed to take his fall in order to create a diversion amongst 14,000 screaming fans while the assassin does his dirty work. It's all carefully planned so as to bamboozle Rick and the spectators, and De Palma is an expert at this kind of audience manipulation.

A redhead in a red dress plants herself in a seat near the Secretary. Dunne is careful to tell Rick that it's odd for a woman to be seen at a prizefight unescorted. When Dunne asks her to show her ticket, she runs off and Dunne follows her, but this has all been prearranged, for Dunne's motive is to position himself so that he can murder the assassin immediately after the man has done his work to get him out of the way. In fact, he methodically plans to murder all the conspirators, except, perhaps, for Powell, the industrialist. And Rick stupidly thinks that Dunne is his friend. Dunne has purposefully planted him at ringside because he believes that Rick is irresponsible and incompetent, as at first he seems to be.

At ringside, however, Rick is watching the fallen champ when the shots are fired and sees the champ look up, surprised, when he is supposed to be floored. He therefore senses that something is amiss. Rick may be brash, vulgar, and tainted, but he is not stupid. Just before the shots are fired, the Secretary is approached by a whistleblower, Julia Costello (Carla Gugino), who works for the defense contractor and has an en-velope filled with incriminating evidence. Wearing an obviously fake blond wig, she takes Dunne's seat next to Rick when Dunne goes after the redhead. The Secretary takes a bullet to the throat and the whistleblower takes one in the arm as Rick shoves her to the floor.

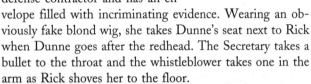

Director De Palma recon-structed a Montreal skating arena to simulate a boxing arena.

In the confusion that follows, she escapes, pursued by Rick and by Dunne, who wants her dead. She ditches the wig and manages to disguise herself, but she is unable to get out of the casino, since Rick has ordered the doors sealed. She pretends to be a hooker in order to find refuge in a nerdy low-roller's hotel room, stalked by both Rick and Dunne. Fortunately, Rick is smart enough to reach her first and gets her to a safer hiding place, near the outer wall of the building, on ground floor. He knows she was also an in-tended target.

The plot is unraveled for Rick when Dunne apprehends him and demands to know where she is hiding. When Rick refuses to tell him, Dunne has the prizefighter attempt to beat the information out of him, but Rick still refuses to co-operate. So Dunne releases the badly beaten Rick, intend-ing to track him to where the woman is. At this point, Rick is not thinking too clearly and can barely walk. So far, the film has been all too carefully plotted by De Palma and screenwriter David Koepp, who also scripted *Jurassic Park* (1993), but the finale is carelessly contrived and disap-pointing. Outside the casino a hurricane has been raging and the wind blows debris against the outer wall of the room in which Rick has locked Julie, tearing a hole in the wall. A squad car arrives at just the right moment, as Dunne breaks into the room. Rather than being captured when told by the police to drop his weapon, he shoots himself and dies the death of a warrior. Rick becomes the hero of the day, but his tainted past catches up with him eventually, and before the film ends, he seems to be facing a jail term. Presumably, grateful Julie, whose life he saved, will be waiting for him.

So what is one to make of Rick Santoro, a sleazy cop on the take who is willing to do the right thing in a crisis situation and behave bravely when push comes to shove? This is "a man of many vices," Rita Kempley wrote in her *Washington Post* review, who "must redeem his virtues while investigating the shooting." The story is as sleazy as the set-ting, the Trump Taj Mahal casino in Atlantic City, but it does not necessarily follow that the film is sleazy. De Palma is an easy target for critics who object to his alleged misogy-ny and his voyeur trickery, but, Kempley conceded, in a left-handed way, that Sinise, Shaw, and Gugino are surprisingly good, considering that all are obliged to play "characters who do not exist in nature."

The Sinise character is as far over the top as his counterpart, Rick Santoro, but Gugino as the whistleblower and Stan Shaw as the crooked prizefighter are more nearly within normal boundaries. Nicolas Cage is unbelievably manic as Rick San-toro, but the performance is still fun to watch as the char-acter is put through his paces on the way to moral rejuve-nation—and survival, for that matter. In his *New York Times* review, Stephen Hunter noted that the film had "deeper is-sues on its mind than cheap thrills, conspiracy theories, and the titillating joys of surveillance," as it moves to question "the limits of friendship and loyalty and what constitutes character." But Holden did not find Rick's moral transfor-mation especially convincing, and, in fact, the manipulation of his character is pretty transparent.

Viewers are not likely to expect too much by way of moral allegory from Brian De Palma. Gary Arnold of the *Washington Times* criticized a glaring tactical error in the plot-ting because the "chief villain is unmasked" about forty min-utes into the story, but if the film is really about menace rather than Rick's moral redemption, it is not a tactical er-ror to establish the Sinise character as a dangerous, ruthless, cold-blooded killer. When he is stalking Julie in the casino hotel corridors, it is clear that he intends to murder her and that knowledge is more than adequate to sustain suspense.

Gary Arnold also complained that the picture "ex-hausted its powers of invention with the opening shot," which he estimated as lasting about twenty minutes, "a vir-tuoso stunt for the Steadicam," which, he points out, "needs to be reloaded about every six minutes." Hence the "open-ing shot" is really a montage of shots involving long takes and cleverly disguised as a single continuous take. The vi-sual follow-up and follow-through are equally impressive. The prizefight was videotaped by several cameras that also recorded events in the arena that Santoro plays back for analysis, and the casino's surveillance cameras provide a larger context for following the action from multiple per-spectives. Visually, the film is splendid.

Although these multiple perspectives are sophisticated and clever, there is little justification here to draw comparisons with Akira Kurosawa's masterpiece *Rashomon* (1950), however, where the framework was supernatural and psychological rather than merely technological, even though rather too many reviewers made this absurd leap of logic. Better comparisons, perhaps, were made to De Palma's own *Blow Out* (1981), which really owed more to Antonioni's *Blow-Up* (1966) than to Francis Ford Coppola's *The Conversation* (1979). But all of this allusive critical woolgathering is merely misleading and has little or nothing to do with *Snake Eyes,* other than the mechanical replication of evidence of a seriously wrongdoing, painstakingly pieced together.

In an interview published in *USA Today,* De Palma made it clear that *Snake Eyes* involved more than self-imitation, advancing the technique of "most glance-back movies" that simply show "the same scenes" over and over again: "This time I tried to go back through this stuff and make it seem like you've never seen it before, [to] show stuff that the audience has a taste of, something maybe they heard, but they weren't exactly sure so that they're really intrigued in going back. That's the trick of this movie."

CREDITS

Rick Santoro: Nicolas Cage
Kevin Dunne: Gary Sinise
Gilbert Powell: John Heard
Julia Costello: Carla Gugino
Lincoln Tyler: Stan Shaw
Lou Logan: Kevin Dunn
Jimmy George: Michael Rispoli
Charles Kirkland: Joel Fabiani

Origin: USA
Released: 1998
Production: Brian De Palma for DeBart; released by Paramount Pictures
Direction: Brian De Palma
Screenplay: David Koepp
Cinematography: Stephen H. Burum
Editing: Bill Pankow
Music: Ryuichi Sakamoto
Production design: Anne Pritchard
Costumes: Odette Gadoury
Sound: Patrick Rouseau, James Sabat Sr.
Visual effects supervisor: Eric Brevig
MPAA rating: R
Running Time: 99 minutes

Reviews were mixed, as might be expected for a De Palma picture. *Variety*'s Todd McCarthy dismissed the plot of this "hyperactive thriller" as "contrived and almost laughably superficial." The *Washington Post*'s Michael O'Sullivan called it a "dunderheaded murder mystery." Daphne Merkin of the *New Yorker* attempted to put *Snake Eyes* in the context of De Palma's career, but she apparently despises De Palma for his cynicism and alleged misogyny and consequently overstated her case. Jeff Giles of *Newsweek* was rather more generous: "De Palma didn't hit the jackpot here, but he certainly didn't roll snake eyes."

The problem is that De Palma, a gifted filmmaker though not a perfect one, is on the outs with the critical establishment, but his work has clicked with audiences, and this film is worth seeing for Cage's over-the-top performance. Ronald S. Librach offers a thoughtful assessment of De Palma's technique in *Literature/Film Quarterly,* claiming that after De Palma sets up a framework, he manipulates his audience into chasing thematic and narrative leads through all manner of heuristic smokescreens, creating a cinema of interacting absurdities. "When you make a film that plays with form," De Palma has stated, "it throws a lot of people off." It's too bad more reviewers are not willing to take his work seriously, but, then, that was the fate of Hitchcock, too, for most of his career.

—*James M. Welsh*

REVIEWS

Boxoffice. July, 1998, p. 18.
Chicago Tribune. August 7, 1998, p. 4.
Entertainment Weekly. August 14, 1998, p. 46.
Literature/Film Quarterly. Vol. 26, no. 3, 1998, p. 166.
New York Times. August 7, 1998, p. B12.
New Yorker. August 17, 1998. p. 82.
Newsweek. August 17, 1998, p. 61.
Philadelphia Inquirer Weekend. August 7, 1998, p.3.
Sight and Sound. November, 1998, p. 61.
USA Today. August 7, 1998, p. E6.
Variety. August 10, 1998, p. 41.
Village Voice. August 18, 1998, p. 107.
Washington Post. August 7, 1998, p. D1.
Washington Post Weekend. August 7, 1998, p. 40.
Washington Times Metropolitan Times. August 7, 1998, p. C16.

Soldier

Left for dead on a remote planet for obsolete machines and people, a fallen hero has one last battle to fight.—Movie tagline

"This dark and edgy sci-fi thriller is a real gripper!"—Jeanne Wolf, *Jeanne Wolf's Hollywood*

"A great action film!"—Tim Reid, *MTV Radio*

"Kurt Russell is a one-man intergalactic army!"—Bill Bregoli, *Westwood One*

"A rousing, supercharged, futuristic thriller!" —Jules Peimer, *WKDM Radio*

 Box Office: $14,623,082

Science fiction has come a long way in Hollywood since the days of Flash Gordon and Ming the Merciless. It used to be the ugly stepchild of the industry. Early sci-fi films featured unknown actors, costumes that resembled long underwear, toy rocket ships suspended on not entirely invisible threads, and ray guns that worked on flashlight batteries.

The big breakthrough for science fiction was Stanley Kubrick's mind-expanding masterpiece *2001: A Space Odyssey* (1968), which happened to come out a year before man first landed on the moon. The Kubrick film was not only a critical and financial success but showed filmmakers that the cinematic potential for science fiction was as vast as space itself. Science fiction was made to order for the big screen, and the big screen was made to order for science fiction. It was something that relied heavily on visual effects. It needed and merited big budgets. Young science fiction addicts had always known this. They put up with the weak characterization and often improbable stories because they recognized space as the last frontier and the hope of the future.

Soldier, competently directed by Paul Anderson and impressively photographed by David Tattersall, is not a great motion picture, but it is an example of the kind of thing that Hollywood and only Hollywood does well. It features a superstar in Kurt Russell and obviously has a big budget behind it. The special effects are so overwhelming that they make the actors look like mice. And if the special visual effects fail to wow the audience sufficiently, the ominous musical score by Joel McNeely deals the other half of a one-two punch.

In *Soldier* we are in the world of the future (where else?) at a time when our galaxy has been colonized and our "civilization" is expanding to the rest of the cosmos. Humans are living on planets that revolve around other stars and on moons that revolve around other planets. Traffic in space is about as heavy as the Santa Monica Freeway at rush hour. One unnamed planet apparently used to be covered with spaceports and other high-tech installations. But because its exploitable resources have been exhausted, it has been abandoned and turned into a gigantic junkyard. Man's ecological destruction has led to vast, unpredictable dust storms with hurricane velocity. Enormous unmanned spaceships fly over regularly and add to the mountains of debris that desecrate the landscape. In one place we see an obsolete aircraft carrier tilted on its side. The spaceship that brought it was so big that this once mighty warship was only a fraction of its cargo.

After three soldiers are dropped onto a pile of rubbish, it becomes apparent that one is still alive. His name, rank and serial number are tattooed on his cheek. All his battles are tattooed on his arm, including the War of the Six Cities, the Moscow Incident, and the Battle of the Argentine Moons. Sergeant Todd (Kurt Russell) was thought to have been killed along with the other two soldiers in a deadly exhibition match with Caine 607 (Jason Scott Lee), a representative of a new breed genetically engineered to be superior warriors. Todd, like a lot of men in their dangerous forties, suddenly found himself obsolete and too highly specialized to adapt to another vocation. (Kevin Thomas observed in his *Los Angeles Times* review: "*Soldier* is the kind of picture described as being aimed at young urban males but may have an unexpected resonance for older viewers, who know only too well that obsolescence is something that nowadays extends to human beings and not just to machines.")

Todd's life story is summarized in a series of vignettes. He never had a mother or father but was conceived in a laboratory. While still in his cradle and not yet able to open his eyes, he is classified 1A and drafted into the army. By kindergarten age he has been conditioned to obey without question and kill without mercy. In one scene a young cadet who is unable to keep up with the others in a cross-country marathon is shot dead by one of the adult officers. The film does not specify that Todd is in the American army. More likely he serves in a futuristic amalgamation of the military forces of industrialized nations imposing their new order on the rest of the universe with dollar diplomacy and,

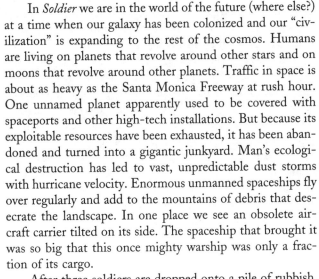 Director Paul Anderson: "The story is basically a western set in space . . . It has the classic narrative structure of a western like *Shane* set in a science-fiction backdrop."

if necessary, with high-tech blitzkriegs reminiscent of the Gulf War in Kuwait and Iraq.

Todd discovers that this supposedly uninhabited planet actually supports a colony of space pioneers whose ship crash landed many years before. They have been unable to make contact with the outside world. The only spaceships that ever come are completely robotized. They are struggling to survive on a planet where dust hurricanes are a common occurrence and spaceships continue dumping more debris on their homes and gardens.

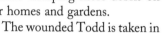

The four-story main set was built on Stage 16 of the Warner Bros. Studio's lot and covered 38,000 square feet.

The wounded Todd is taken in by these peace-loving, vegetarian colonists and placed in the care of beautiful Sandra (Connie Nielsen) and her husband Mace (Sean Pertwee), who have a little boy. It doesn't take long for Todd and Sandra to fall in love—although Todd hasn't the slightest idea what love means. (He keeps calling Sandra "Sir.") The poor husband is conveniently eliminated when a visiting patrol ship (piloted by none other than Caine 607) discovers the planet is inhabited by "hostiles" and is ordered to wipe them out.

It is never logically explained why they are not rescued and brought back to civilization. The commander of the patrol ship, Colonel Mekum (Jason Isaacs) is a sadistic martinet who just doesn't want to be bothered with such unauthorized and unbudgeted diversions. In fact, he might blow up the whole planet with one of the special little planet-atomizers he carries in his arsenal rather than get thrown off schedule. His crew, except for Captain Church (Gary Busey) and a few obsolete veterans, consists of the new breed of DNA-engineered soldiers who care nothing about unarmed civilians. Church, who belongs to the same old school as Sergeant Todd, has quaint ideas about military honor that only infuriate the Colonel.

Todd takes charge of the situation. He finds plenty of arms and ammunition in the junk piles and single-handedly confronts the 17 new-breed commandos wreaking havoc with flame throwers, machine guns, and futuristic bazookas. The battle ends in a long anticipated showdown with Caine 607. Todd commandeers the patrol ship and rescues the surviving colonists, who are now mostly widows and orphans. Russell plays his role with only one facial expression, very much like Sylvester Stallone, who played the obsolete Vietnam veteran Rambo in *First Blood* (1982) and its two sequels, or Arnold Schwarzenegger as the homicidal cyborg in *Terminator* (1984).

Soldier is about obsolescence. The obsolete Todd is dumped on an obsolete planet, which is being buried under obsolete materials. The marooned homesteaders are not exactly obsolete but superfluous. The script was written by the gifted David Webb Peoples, whose credits include two film classics: the futuristic *Blade Runner* (1982), starring Harri-

son Ford, and the acclaimed western *Unforgiven* (1992), starring Clint Eastwood. Peoples, now in his late fifties, may have consciously or unconsciously allowed his own apprehension to creep into his story. James Bates reported in the *Los Angeles Times* (October 26, 1998) that "Writing jobs in today's youth-obsessed Hollywood are increasingly going to young, usually white, males as writers fifty years and older are virtually shut out from many of the top film and television assignments ... While older, experienced writers were once the most highly paid in the industry, changing market dynamics since the early 1980s have made writers in their thirties the ones most highly valued by the industry, the study, commissioned by the West Coast branch of the Writers Guild of America, concludes."

While those older writers tended to draw their inspiration from real world experience, younger screenwriters tend to draw theirs from the films they grew up with. This may explain all the recycling coming out of Hollywood today. There is something ominous about this cinematic inbreeding. Young viewers may be getting more and more distanced from reality, like the two nerds in *Beavis and Butt-head Do America* (1996).

Paradoxically, although *Soldier* was given a well-deserved R rating for violence (at least fifty people killed and a planet obliterated), the film is full of little kids. The opening scenes

CREDITS

Sergeant Todd: Kurt Russell
Caine 607: Jason Scott Lee
Sandra: Connie Nielsen
Mace: Sean Pertwee
Colonel Mekum: Jason Isaacs
Captain Church: Gary Busey
Jimmy Pig: Michael Chiklis

Origin: USA
Released: 1998
Production: Jerry Weintraub for Morgan Creek and Impact Pictures; released by Warner Bros.
Direction: Paul Anderson
Screenplay: David Webb Peoples
Cinematography: David Tattersall
Editing: Martin Hunter
Music: Joel McNeely
Production design: David L. Snyder
Visual effects supervision: Ed Jones
Costumes: Erica Phillips
MPAA rating: R
Running Time: 99 minutes

show a whole roomful of infants and then dozens of little boys training to be soldiers. The marooned colonists appear to have been spending most of their time producing children. Todd develops a loving relationship with Sandra's little son and is holding him in his arms at the end, a shot that was used in newspaper and television ads for this heavily promoted release. When Todd takes over the patrol ship, most of those he saves are children. There are more kids in this picture than adults. The producers were obviously thinking of the home video market (which Glenn Lovell in his *Variety* review calls "ancillary afterlife"), where the children have a dominant voice in deciding what the family will

view. Kids may be interpreting R ratings, not as "You can't see this," but as "You can't *miss* this!"

—*Bill Delaney*

REVIEWS

Entertainment Weekly. October 30, 1998, p. 82.
Los Angeles Times. October 23, 1998, p. F18.
New York Times. October 23, 1998, p. B25.
People. November 2, 1998, p. 38.
Variety. October 26, 1998, p. 41.

A Soldier's Daughter Never Cries

The city of lights. A famous American author and the decade that changed a generation . . . forever.—Movie tagline

"One of the most beautifully acted and unabashedly loving films you'll see this year!"—Jay Carr, *Boston Globe*

"A sure candidate for Best Picture! As touching and entertaining as anything Merchant Ivory has given us."—David Sterritt, *Christian Science Monitor*

"Belongs in the top rank of Merchant Ivory films."—Karen Durbin, *Mirabella*

"A great movie! It makes you laugh and cry at the same time."—Rex Reed, *New York Observer*

"Kris Kristofferson is magnetic."—Peter Travers, *Rolling Stone*

"One of the year's best films! Two thumbs way up! Original and powerful!"—Roger Ebert, *Siskel & Ebert*

"A beautiful film."—Jeff Craig, *Sixty Second Preview*

 Box Office: $1,799,537

A *Soldier's Daughter Never Cries* details the close and loving relationships between a most unusual family; a bicultural writer, his wife and two children who move from Paris to New England. Based on Kaylie Jones's autobiographical novel, this story traces the life of a tough yet sensitive writer in post WWII Paris, his glamorous wife and their two children—one their own, and one an adopted

The life of a celebrated American author living in Paris is seen through the eyes of his daughter Kaylie (Leelee Sobieski) in *A Soldier's Daughter Never Cries.*

French boy. Skillfully directed with a steady hand by James Ivory (known for his other rich character dramas such as *Howard's End* [1992] and *A Room with a View* [1986]) from a screenplay from his distinguished collaborator, screenwriter Ruth Prawer Jhabvla, this story perfectly captures a unique blend of familial love and sophistication.

Divided into three sections, "Billy," "Francis," and "Daddy," one for each of the males that profoundly affected Channe, Ivory gracefully lets the enormity and scope of all his characters' lives emerge through the most simplistic and everyday actions. This is the kind of writing and directing that one rarely sees in current film and television; long, involved scenes that develop a beautiful rhythm and reveal reams of information and emotion.

Charlotte Ann (Leelee Sobieski), "Channe," as her parents Bill Willis (Kris Kristofferson) and Marcella (Barbara Hershey) call her, is well-adjusted and loved by them and her doting nanny/housekeeper, Candida (Dominique Blanc). They live an exciting expatriate life in Paris in the 1960s, where her father is known for his tough, best-selling book portraying men and wartime.

Eight-year-old Channe is surprised when her parents decide to adopt a little six-year-old boy from a young unmarried Parisian woman (Virginie Ledoyen) who cannot keep him. "Billy" (Jesse Bradford) is at first shy, but warms to the intense and genuine love that Bill and Marcella give him. Channe and Candida are a little jealous at the outset. Candida gives Channe the intense, smothering love that befits an older, unmarried woman who has dedicated her life to serving another family, and she views Billy as an outsider. Although Channe is far from spoiled, she enjoys all the attention that her parents give, and she is not sure that she wants to share it.

Channe (Leelee Sobieski): "I'm a *writer's* daughter."

Bill and Marcella enjoy a sophisticated life in Paris, marked by rowdy parties with their group of intellectual compatriots, and always punctuated by heavy drinking. They are both lenient and disciplined with their children, encouraging an intellectual atmosphere of reading, writing, and thoughtful discourse. Where one might expect such a tough character to be bearish and overbearing with his children, Bill is, in fact, a big softy, exhibiting tenderness and unabashed love.

Anthony Roth Costanzo, who plays Francis, is a trained countertenor and does his own singing on camera.

Channe relents in her dislike of Billy and they bond together in the eternal battle of kids against their teachers. When their teacher takes a dislike to Billy and makes him spend long hours in the classroom closet, Channe tells Marcella—who flips and slaps the offending martinet. This is a family given to flamboyant gestures, rich in the enjoyment of life and all that it can offer. But despite a hearty revelry in their everyday life, the family takes their responsibilities seriously. When Channe forges her father's signature on a school note, Bill sits her down and gives her a very adult talk about the serious ramifications of such an act.

By the time Ivory moves on to the teenage years of Channe and Billy, the focus lands on Francis Fortescue (Anthony Roth Costanzo), a new friend of Channe's from school. An odd, effeminate boy, who lives with his indulgent single mother (Jane Birkin), Francis will nevertheless have a strong impact on Channe. When Channe hears Francis movingly sing an aria in class, she is touched in a way that illustrates the awe of discovering something so exquisite and beautiful heretofore unknown. Francis and his

mother routinely take in avant-garde theater such as a wacky, modern version of *Salome,* complete with wild Afros and hip-hugger bell-bottoms (this is the late '60s, after all). Channe and Francis become close, and indulge in a variety of sophisticated games, such as flouncing around her family's apartment acting out scenes from operas.

Conflict arises when Channe experiences a growing interest in boys and parties, which does not set well with the iconoclastic Francis. Francis exhibits an almost eerie understanding of how odd he is, and how no matter how close he and Channe are, that she will break off from him to pursue a "normal" social life. To make matters more complicated, Bill takes Channe aside and tells her that he is moving the entire family back to America. Bill, it seems, has suffered from a long-standing heart condition and he now feels that it is necessary to move to facilitate better treatment for him. For the first time, Channe experiences a strong sense of loss relating to two people quite dear to her—Candida and Francis.

Both Channe and Billy are devastated. Their entire life is centered on school, their friends, their parents and the sophistication of life in an enormously cultured city. Suddenly the family has left their charming apartment in Paris and find themselves in a rambling house in a remote New England suburb. Billy is so traumatized that he can only manage to make it to school and back, content to sit on the couch and watch enormous quantities of banal American television. Instead of conversing with Francis about art, music, and opera, Channe finds herself trying to make conversation with ordinary American high school kids about football, clothes, and rock music. No one really talks about Bill's increasingly bad heart condition.

Ivory details this enormous cultural change with love and subtlety. Although everyone feels displaced, only Channe seems to respond by turning outward, not inward. She begins to experiment with sex, sleeping with two or three boys in rapid succession. This leads to one of the film's more amazing exchanges as Bill explains to his daughter that boys are not as mature as girls in accepting sex as a tender exchange between two willing partners; boys at her age consider it a game that they have "won," if they sleep with girls. The characters interact in such a realistic, warm way that defines the entire emotional range of this picture.

The fact that there are so many wonderfully realized, small subplots that fit together so perfectly and do not weigh down the story beautifully illustrates the skill and mastery of Ivory and Jhablvala. There are many smaller story points—the small romance of Candida with an ardent black suitor, the mystery of Billy's real mother and the journal she left behind, the quirkiness of Francis and the life of cultured enlightenment that he opens up for Channe—that are only briefly touched upon. The writer and director merely sprinkle their canvas with these issues to highlight how rich and varied peoples' lives really are.

The third chapter of this film deals with Bill's worsening illness and its effect on him and the family. Kris Kristofferson and Barbara Hershey have never been so moving or restrained in their performances. Much has been made of lead actress Leelee Sobieski's resemblance to the actress Helen Hunt, and it is indeed true. Beyond her looks, she appears to have an incredible future ahead of her; she shines in this role, unlike her small part in the 1998 summer blockbuster *Deep Impact*, playing a teenage bride. All of the actors, including Jesse Bradford as Billy and Anthony Roth Costanzo as Francis, make the most of their wonderfully written parts. *A Soldier's Daughter* is one of the finest films so far this year, beautifully realized in every aspect.

—*G. E. Georges*

CREDITS

Bill Willis: Kris Kristofferson
Marcella Willis: Barbara Hershey
Channe Willis: Leelee Sobieski
Billy Willis: Jesse Bardford
Francis Fortescue: Anthony Roth Costanzo
Candida: Dominique Blanc
Mrs. Fortesque: Jane Birkin
Billy's Mother: Virginie Ledoyen

Origin: USA
Released: 1998
Production: Ismail Merchant for Merchant Ivory Productions; released by October Films
Direction: James Ivory
Screenplay: James Ivory and Ruth Prawer Jhabvala; based on the novel by Kaylie Jones
Cinematography: Jean-Marc Fabre
Editing: Noelle Boisson
Costumes: Carol Ramsey
Production design: Jacques Bufnoir, Pat Garner
Music: Richard Robbins
Sound: Ludovic Henault
MPAA rating: R
Running Time: 127 minutes

REVIEWS

Boxoffice. September, 1998, p. 54.
Detroit Free Press. September 25, 1998, p. 9D.
Detroit News. September 25, 1998, p. 3D.
Entertainment Weekly. September 25, 1998, p. 76.
New York Times. September 18, 1998, p. E12.
People. September 28, 1998, p. 41.
Sight and Sound. October, 1998, p. 56.
Variety. September 7, 1998, p. 71.
Village Voice. September 22, 1998, p. 142.
Washington Post Weekend. September 25, 1998, p. 63.

Sonatine

The mob put the finger on him . . . so he gave them the finger back—curled tight around a trigger!—Movie tagline

"A splendid film with a driving visual style!" —Kevin Thomas, *Los Angeles Times*

Sonatine is the second film to be released by actor-director Takeshi Kitano, although it was made before *Fireworks* (1997), the American debut work that earned significant critical praise. *Sonatine* is built around its director, who plays a jaded gangster considering retirement. At first, *Sonatine* seems just like a routine crime drama. Gangsters stoically kill each other and battle over turf. In a sense, this is what bothers Murakawa (Kitano). What is one more murder, one more shakedown, one more gang war to him?

The film does not fully shed cliches until Murakawa and his buddies have to ship out of Okinawa, where the gang war becomes so fierce that Murakawa and company have to regroup and wait for word from higher-ups in the crime syndicates. Will there be a truce or an all-out war? Murakawa suspects he is being set up for the kill, since his territory has become especially profitable. But he keeps his own counsel. Only his face, which seems to get stonier and stonier, reflects how bored he is.

In part, Murakawa's stoicism seems to grow because his young companions are so edgy and impatient. They play at

CREDITS

Murakama: Beat Takeshi
Uechi: Tetsu Watanabe
Mituki: Aya Kokumai
Ryoki: Masanobu Katsumura
Takahashi: Kenichi Yajima

Origin: Japan
Released: 1993, 1998
Production: Masayuki Mori, Hisao Nabeshima, and Takeo Yoshida for Shochiku; released by Rolling Thunder Pictures and Miramax Films
Direction: Takeshi Kitano
Screenplay: Takeshi Kitano
Cinematography: Katsumi Yanagishima
Editing: Takeshi Kitano
Music: Jo Hosaishi
Costumes: Hirohide Shibata
Art direction: Osamu Saseki
MPAA rating: R
Running Time: 94 minutes

shooting tin cans off their heads and with other forms of simulated violence. Murakawa occasionally takes part. He even laughs and seems to enjoy himself, but his face soon resumes its hardened cast.

The Murakawa hideout is a beach house. The scenes by the sea are beautifully photographed. The gangster idyll is enhanced by the presence of a beautiful young woman, Miyuki (Aya Kokumai). Murakawa happens to witness her rape on the beach and then shoots the rapist when he tries to assault Murakawa. Miyuki tells Murakawa that she loves tough guys. Soon Murakawa is taking Miyuki out on "dates"—as one of his henchmen scornfully puts it. The girl has fallen in love with him, dazzled by his offhand violence. He is charmed with her. If they become lovers, the films does not show it, for sex is hardly the issue. She is fascinated with this older man's experience, and he is taken with her innocent wonder. Murakawa does not brag about his exploits. Nor does his interest in Miyuki soften him in the least. He remains what he is—a cold-blooded killer. Earlier in the film he has watched a man hoisted by a crane and then dunked into the sea. Can the man survive two minutes or three under water? The man drowns as Murakawa and his associates discuss other matters and forget that the three-minute time limit has been exceeded. "Cover it up," Murakawa says as the dead is brought to the surface.

Miyuki begins to reflect on what it means to be able to murder at will. She observes that if Murakawa can kill others so easily, it would be just as simple to off himself. He does not disagree. Her speculations are prophetic. She wants him to return to her—after he has dealt with his gang war. Murakawa is noncommittal.

The climatic scene—when Murakawa goes in single-handed to machine gun the gang lords who have conspired to cut him out of his territory is nothing like an American gangster film. Indeed, the shoot-out is hardly seen, for it occurs in a darkened room (Murakawa has had the electrical power shut off). Just glimpses of him shooting and of gunmen falling give off the flickering images of fireworks. Shots of Miyuki playing with fireworks on the beach are juxtaposed against this gruesome, yet understated scene.

Both the play-acted violence on the beach and the real-life gore seem childish—like the pranks Murakawa plays on his young subordinates. Murakawa triumphs in the blood bath, but he never makes it back to Miyuki. He is a terrible driver (he concedes in an earlier scene), and though his death is not a car accident, it takes place in a car and by his own hand. Murakawa is a man who has lost his direction and the will to live, the will that he has (Miyuki realizes) all too easily killed in so many other men.

Sonatine is a triumph of form over content, of style over substance. It yields no profound thoughts about violence. It has nothing new to say about the genre of the gangster film. Yet *Sonatine* is absorbing as pure cinema, satisfying the desire to just watch someone like Murakawa, so self-contained and impregnable. Seldom has cinematography (the wide open beach shots) seem so poignant set against the contours of a closed face. It is no wonder at the end of the film that Miyuki watches the road, hoping for his return but looking forlorn, having seen so often the look of death in Murakawa's frozen eyes.

—*Carl Rollyson*

REVIEWS

Entertainment Weekly. May 1, 1998, p. 42.
Los Angeles Times. April 10, 1998, p. F10.
New York Times. April 10, 1998, p. E14.
Village Voice. April 14, 1998, p. 59.

Sour Grapes

If nothing else, *Sour Grapes* had timing going for it. The film came out a few weeks before the final episode of *Seinfeld,* that is, right in the middle of the Seinfeld-mania that swept the country in spring of 1998. What's the connection? *Sour Grapes* was written and directed by Larry David, the co-creator of *Seinfeld,* who left before the last season and came back only for the famous final episode. (David is often credited by *Seinfeld* fans as being the true creative force behind the series.) The film studio, apparently hoping that a lot of Seinfeld's viewers would be interested in such TV staffing minutia as what David's role was with the show, went so far as to make David the selling point of the ads for *Sour Grapes.* David doesn't have the same cache as Leonardo DiCaprio, perhaps, but it was an interesting tactic nonetheless. In reality, the studio didn't have much choice on who they would focus the ads, since there are no well-known stars in the film.

Those wondering whether *Sour Grapes* contains any similarities to *Seinfeld* will be mollified immediately. There, in the opening credits, a lovely still life of a bowl of grapes sits by a window sill. As the credits keep rolling, the grapes start drying up, turning into raisins, then finally collapse into a big pile of rotten goo. That pretty much sums up David's skewed, look-on-the-cloudy-side-of-life outlook. It's the same grouchy outlook that lurks behind the idea of basing a sitcom on four people who are selfish, greedy, and petty.

The plot of *Sour Grapes* revolves around a high concept premise. It's the kind of concept that would make for a good . . . sitcom. Brain surgeon Evan (Steven Weber) and his cousin, tennis shoe sole designer Richie (Craig Bierko) take their girlfriends Joan (Karen Sillas) and Roberta (Robyn Pe-

Richie (Craig Bierko): "I can't be in an enclosed space with fruit. It nauseates me."

terman) to Atlantic City for a weekend trip. After losing about a thousand dollars apiece, the two guys get rid of their excess quarters by dropping them in slot machines. Evan tells Richie to play three quarters so he'll be eligible for a bigger jackpot. Richie only has one quarter. Evan gives him two quarters. "Go crazy," he advises absently. And what do you know, Richie hits the jackpot. Lights flash, bells ring and Richie is over $400,000 richer. This presents a little problem. Evan thinks he deserves a cut—after all, they were his quarters—and Richie thinks he doesn't. Or as he puts it, often and loudly, "He gets nothing!"

Here the film gets into two big *Seinfeld* territories—the escalating of minor incidents into major traumas and the obsession over minor points to absurdity. Everything that happens from this point on in the movie has to do with Richie and Evan obsessing over the division of the money. And the consequences of their ceaseless obsession are wide-ranging and numerous. Girlfriends leave, mothers get hurt, the police get involved, and the cousins' friendship is ruined. It's the kind of concept that could have just as easily worked in a half-hour, but David milks it for all it's worth. What he ends up with never approaches the genius of his TV work, but it's a serviceable comedy nonetheless.

In its sensibilities, the movie is almost like an episode of *Seinfeld,* but with characters no one knows. For fans of the show, half the fun of watching is trying to pick all the Seinfeld-esque touches. For example, David's obsession with tiny slights and moments of selfishness comes into play in a scene when Richie is running to catch an elevator. As the doors close before Richie can get to them, the doctor inside the elevator mimes a "Whoops. I'm sorry" shrug. Later

Richie, still obsessing about it (of course) complains that the doctor just pretended to hit the "open door" button, instead of actually pushing it. "He just leaned!" gripes Richie, sounding just like George Costansza.

Another David touch is Richie's stereotypical overbearing mother (Viola Harris) who is fond of suffocating hugs, worrying and feeding her beloved son. At one point, when Richie is raving about the money again, screaming, "He gets nothing!" the mother nods sympathetically then asks cloyingly, "Did you eat?" When Richie decides he doesn't want a bowl of soup, his mother is shocked. "You changed your mind about the soup? That's crazy talk!"

David also has a knack for pointing out ways of human behavior (especially human dating behavior) and giving them a name. In Sour Grapes, he comes up with "hotel sex." When Richie is trying to convince his cousin Evan to go on the trip to Atlantic City with Joan, Richie reminds him that the trip will mean "hotel sex." In another scene, after Richie's girlfriend Roberta leaves him, he yells after her, "I've seen you naked. That was my only goal!"

In David's universe, big problems and trivial concerns are granted equal weight. When Evan is sitting glumly in an empty bar, complaining of messing up a big operation, he immediately forgets his woes when another customer takes the seat right next to him. "What's wrong with you?" he yells, completely incensed that someone would sit too close to him when there are plenty of other places to sit.

David's interest in language and absurdity is very much in full force. When one character has another at gunpoint, he mentions that he wants everything to be "Hanky dory." "It's not 'hanky dory,' it's 'hunky dory,'" corrects the victim. At another point, Evan and Richie are making up. "I'm sorry," says Evan. "I'm sorrier," says Richie. "Why do you have to be sorrier?! Can't we be equally sorry?" says Evan, miffed again.

One of the better scenes in the movie plays on white people's uncertainty about how to discuss African Americans. When an older white couple is questioned about seeing an African-American suspect fleeing their neighborhood, they refuse to mention his race. Finally, the exasperated African-American policeman asks if the suspect was black. "He happened to be black," the woman says too casually. "But he could have been any color," says her husband, afraid of offending. When the couple is trying to describe the man's hair style, the woman stammers, unsure of whether saying the word "Afro" is racist or not. "You can say Afro," the policeman advises. Also good is a TV show called Guys and Dolls that skewers Friends. It's dead-on, even down to a perky "I'll Be There For You" type of theme song that says, "I'll catch you if you fall."

Not all the comedy comes from dry observations of human behavior, some of it gets pretty sophomoric. One of the recurring jokes involves Richie's ability to, er, pleasure himself orally. Another crotch-oriented subplot involves a botched groin operation on a star of Guys and Dolls (Matt Keeslar) that leaves him with a falsetto voice.

The lack of famous faces isn't a drawback for the movie, but it probably didn't help boxoffice-wise. Besides the minor cache of being in Wings, Steven Weber has the added edge of looking a lot like Jerry Seinfeld. It's appropriate, since in Sour Grapes, he plays the Jerry role. He is the calmer one, but not without selfish quirks of his own. As the Jerry, Weber's a better actor than Seinfeld, but then, almost anyone would be. Weber is able to engage in his silly, immature battle with his cousin while still seeming believable as a respected brain surgeon.

Craig Bierko's Richie is almost a spawn of George and Kramer. He's definitely George with the overbearing mother, the pettiness and the penchant for screaming anything that could just as well be spoken. But he's also like Kramer in his ability to use his body as a comedic device. One reviewer called him a "human R. Crumb cartoon." Some might call Bierko's hamminess overacting, but it is fun to watch his bulging eyes and overdone movements. The one way in which Bierko is unlike George or Kramer is that he's handsome and charming. Seeing a handsome man with George's personality is a little strange. It's almost like he's from the Bizarro episode of Seinfeld where everything was opposite.

The rest of the cast, including Karen Sillas as Evan's feminist girlfriend Joan, are perfectly serviceable. In one interesting casting twist, Robyn Peterman, who plays Richie's girlfriend Roberta, is the real-life daughter of the catalog Peterman who is caricatured on Seinfeld.

CREDITS

Evan Maxwell: Steven Weber
Richie Maxwell: Craig Bierko
Danny Pepper: Matt Keeslar
Joan: Karen Sillas
Roberta: Robyn Peterman
Selma Maxwell: Viola Harris

Origin: USA
Released: 1998
Production: Laurie Lennard for Castle Rock Entertainment; released by Columbia Pictures
Direction: Larry David
Screenplay: Larry David
Cinematography: Victor Hammer
Editing: Priscilla Nedd-Friendly
Production design: Charles Rosen
Art direction: Chas. Butcher
Costumes: Debra McGuire
Sound: Robert Janiger
MPAA rating: R
Running Time: 91 minutes

Despite some moments of cleverness and an ideal release date, *Sour Grapes* didn't become the big comedy of 1998. Reviewers tended not to like it (*Entertainment Weekly* gave it a grumpy C-) and viewers decided that they'd rather just stay home and watch *Seinfeld* reruns.

—*Jill Hamilton*

REVIEWS

Boxoffice. June, 1998, p. 79.
Entertainment Weekly. May 1, 1998, p. 39.
Los Angeles Times. April 17, 1998, p. F6.
New York Times. April 17, 1998, p. E18.
Variety. April 13, 1998, p. 27.
Washington Post Weekend. May 1, 1998, p. 54.

The Spanish Prisoner

"David Mamet has finally made the ingenious, seductive puzzle movie he's been aiming for."
—Karen Durben, *Mirabella*

"The most unequivocal hit of the Sundance Film Festival. The most satisfying feat of gamesmanship Mr. Mamet has yet brought to the screen. Diabolically tricky!"—Janet Maslin, *New York Times*

"A classic scam! Mamet keeps his audience guessing as to who's doing whom right up to the wry, cinematic finish."—Bruce Williamson, *Playboy*

Box Office: $10,272,230

Joe Ross (Campbell Scott) finds himself the target of an elaborate con game in David Mamet's intricate yarn *The Spanish Prisoner*.

David Mamet's *The Spanish Prisoner* is a suspense tale of an Everyman named Joe Ross (Campbell Scott), who has invented something called "The Process," which will make his company a fortune. The Process is, in Hitchcockian terms, the MacGuffin—the device that motivates the plot but does not have any importance in itself. Indeed, we never learn what The Process does but merely see a notebook containing pages of complex mathematical formulae. Even the huge amount of money it is expected to bring the company is kept out of camera sight when Joe writes the figure on a blackboard. A superbly executed thriller, *The Spanish Prisoner* finally is not concerned with the specific details of Joe's work but rather with the elaborate con game to which he falls prey.

The Spanish Prisoner is built around a Hitchcockian plot—the quintessential decent man caught in a web of deception—filtered through Mamet's sensibility. The characters speak in his typically clipped, staccato dialogue filled with repetitions, and, while the situations are often tense and turn on reversals and betrayals, everyone maintains a cool exterior.

The film opens with Joe's arrival on a Caribbean island, where he makes a presentation to his boss, Mr. Klein (Ben Gazzara), and the company's top executives. Along for the trip is his colleague and friend, George Lang (Ricky Jay), who is constantly spouting aphorisms, and a new secretary at the firm, Susan Ricci (Rebecca Pidgeon), who flirts with Joe and acts like she has a big crush on him.

Pidgeon, Mamet's real-life wife, appeared in his recent Broadway production, *The Old Neighborhood* (1997), and effectively delivers Mamet's elliptical dialogue. Susan often seems very artificial—she is very perky and chirpy and given to making big pronouncements to Joe like "You're a real gent" and "I'm loyal and true, and I'm not too hard to look at"—but her wide-eyed openness is ultimately a cover for something sinister.

Joe and Susan have been taking pictures on the beach when a mysterious stranger named Jimmy Dell (Steve Martin) offers Joe a thousand dollars for his camera. Obviously offended at the way a wealthy man can throw money around to try to get his way, Joe simply gives Jimmy the cheap camera. Joe later runs into Jimmy, who explains that he wanted the camera because he and a woman married to one of his friends were in the background when Joe took a picture. Before Joe leaves the island, he agrees to deliver a package to Jimmy's sister back in New York, and it appears Joe has made a new friend.

Meanwhile, Joe treats Susan to a first-class ticket home with the casino winnings George has shared with him. On the plane, Susan speculates on the essential mystery of identity. "Who in this world is what they seem?" she muses in a line emblematic of the plot as a whole, and, as she poses the question in a variety of ways, Joe becomes nervous about the package he accepted from Jimmy. Joe opens it and discovers a book on tennis (Jimmy's sister is a tennis player) with a note inside recommending Joe as a potential date, which of course flatters him. Ever the gentleman, upon his return home, Joe buys a copy of the book in better condition and delivers that one instead.

Joe soon has a falling-out with Jimmy after Joe drops off the book with a doorman instead of delivering it directly to the sister. The rift is patched up when Jimmy apologizes and takes Joe under his wing. Jimmy opens a Swiss bank account for Joe, gains him membership in an exclusive club, and offers legal help when Joe expresses his misgivings about his company's intentions. While The Process will enable the company to corner the market, Mr. Klein is always evasive about Joe's compensation when he raises the issue.

Susan (Rebecca Pidgeon): "How do we know who people are?"

Jimmy is playing just one part in a complex scheme against Joe and is very smooth in the way he gets Joe into his confidence. Steve Martin delivers a finely calibrated performance as a man who does not come on too strong or lavish the good life on his new friend to the point that Joe might become suspicious but rather makes small gestures of friendship that gradually draw him in. Jimmy makes Joe feel special and appreciated for his goodness and manners, while the company seems to take him for granted.

Moreover, Jimmy is able to get inside Joe's mind and articulate what Joe believes—"Good people, bad people, they generally look like what they are"—and also what he fears—"Always do business as if the person you're doing business with is trying to screw you. Because most likely they are, and if they're not, you can be pleasantly surprised." Joe initially favors the former view but must finally develop a more realistic view of human nature.

Jimmy predicts the company will try to cheat Joe and then act cruelly to cover its guilt. Sure enough, Klein tries to coerce Joe into signing some new documents, whereupon Joe accepts Jimmy's offer of legal help. Soon, though, Joe's trust is shaken when he learns that Jimmy's sister does not exist and the woman with Jimmy on the beach is not a

princess, as he had claimed. At this point, Joe recalls Susan's encounter with an FBI agent in the Caribbean, gets the agent's business card out of Susan's scrapbook commemorating their trip, and calls the agent, Pat McCune (Felicity Huffman). The FBI tells Joe that Jimmy is a con man performing a variation on an old scam called the Spanish Prisoner, and they arrange a sting operation.

Campbell Scott anchors the film as the brilliant but naïve hero, whose genius at work does not equip him for the duplicity around him. When Jimmy mentions "The Process" in one of their conversations, for example, Joe should be suspicious since he never used this term with Jimmy. Joe's most glaring mistake, though, is taking his only copy of The Process out of the safe and bringing it to the proposed meeting with Jimmy just because the FBI told him to follow Jimmy's instructions.

All of this preparation leads to the major plot twist of the film. Joe waits at the designated spot, a carousel (perhaps an homage to Hitchcock's *Strangers on a Train* [1951], Jimmy never arrives, and Joe soon discovers that he has a notebook filled with blank pages. This incident highlights Joe's goodness in contrast to the chicanery all around him—when he switched tennis books, he did it out of kindness, but here the FBI agents, who, of course, are not real agents, pulled a switch to ruin him. Like Jimmy, they are part of the elaborate trap that, we learn at film's end, was set up by Klein so he could frame Joe for stealing The Process and reap the huge rewards by selling it to a rival. Because Joe is constantly dealing with the attentions of Jimmy and Susan, Klein's role as the head villain working behind the scenes is an effective surprise.

The film carefully builds its themes of paranoia and betrayal—not just in the complex plot machinations but also in small details like a poster declaring "SOMEONE TALKED!" hanging in the company's lobby and the song "I Wonder Who's Kissing Her Now" playing on the carousel. The Swiss bank account was created so it would look like Joe has a place to hide the money after selling The Process. The club where he and Jimmy ate does not exist, and the membership paper Joe signed was really a request for asylum to Venezuela, which does not have an extradition treaty with the United States.

Klein bails Joe out of jail, only to have him framed for the murder of George, the one person who could have helped clear him. George has been killed with Joe's Boy Scout knife, a fitting device since Susan has joked about him being a Boy Scout and earlier admired the knife. The motto "BE PREPARED" on the knife handle even becomes a kind of mockery of Joe, who is the essential *noir* hero on the run in the big city. He finally goes to Susan for help and gets the idea to fly back to the Caribbean island to retrieve the hotel's security videotape, which will prove Jimmy's existence to the police. However, the police are looking for Joe, so he and Susan drive to the Boston airport, where she gives him the return ticket she received when Joe treated her to the first-class ticket home.

However, at the airport, a mother scolding her little boy for smudging the cover of his book makes Joe recall he has Jimmy's fingerprints on the original tennis book, and Joe leaves. (In a nice detail, the boy's book is the children's classic *The Giving Tree*, about a tree that, like Joe, constantly gives of itself.) We soon learn what many audience members will already suspect, that Susan too is part of the plot against Joe. She substituted the Caribbean ticket for a ticket to Venezuela and put a gun in a bag she gave him so that he would be stopped by airport security. Joe learns of Susan's duplicity, and they board a ferryboat, where Jimmy is waiting. However, United States marshals are also present, and Jimmy is shot with a tranquilizer gun before he can shoot Joe. When Susan is arrested, she asks Joe if he will help her, if he will be a good Boy Scout and let her be his

good deed. She smiles wryly when he has the backbone to refuse.

Throughout the film, Joe's company fears that the Japanese will steal The Process. In one encounter between Jimmy and Joe, Jimmy sees Japanese tourists taking pictures and sarcastically comments, "Someone should do a book—Japanese all over the world in front of the world's greatest monuments taking pictures of each other." It is fitting, then, that the undercover marshals who save Joe are Japanese-Americans posing as tourists. It not only reverses the stereotype of the Japanese as potential villains or objects of fun but also highlights the theme of being fooled by surfaces. As a policeman points out, "Nobody looks at a Japanese tourist." Joe looked at the surface and was tricked by just about everyone, and here the best way to hide something, to fool the bad guys, is to have them see nothing. Indeed, from the film's opening scene of an airport X-ray machine revealing the interiors of packages, the film constantly encourages us to look under the surface of things.

In his short book *On Directing Film*, Mamet advocates a method based in simplicity: tell your story through uninflected shots, and have your actors perform simple physical actions instead of emoting. *The Spanish Prisoner* is a textbook example of this economical method. There are no fancy camera moves, the action is never heavy-handed, and the film is not cluttered with extraneous material. Mamet cuts to the heart of the con and delivers an intelligent and witty thriller whose seemingly disparate pieces snap beautifully into place.

—*Peter N. Chumo II*

CREDITS

Joe Ross: Campbell Scott
Susan Ricci: Rebecca Pidgeon
Jimmy Dell: Steve Martin
George Lang: Ricky Jay
Klein: Ben Gazzara
Pat McCune: Felicity Huffman
FBI Team Leader: Ed O'Neill

Origin: USA
Released: 1998
Production: Jean Doumanian for Sweetland Films; released by Sony Pictures Classics
Direction: David Mamet
Screenplay: David Mamet
Cinematography: Gabriel Beristain
Editing: Barbara Tulliver
Music: Carter Burwell
Production design: Tim Galvin
Costumes: Susan Lyall
Art direction: Kathleen Rosen
Sound: John Patrick Pritchett
MPAA rating: PG
Running Time: 112 minutes

REVIEWS

Boxoffice. April, 1998, p. 40.
Chicago Tribune. April 24, 1998, p. 5.
Detroit Free Press. April 24, 1998, p. 6D.
Detroit News. April 24, 1998, p. 5C.
Entertainment Weekly. April 10, 1998, p. 44.
Los Angeles Times. April 3, 1998, p. F10.
New Yorker. April 13, 1998, p. 81.
People. April 13, 1998, p. 19.
Rolling Stone. April 30, 1998, p. 74.
Time. April 6, 1998.
USA Today. April 3, 1998, p. 5E.
Variety. September 15, 1997, p. 70.
Village Voice. April 7, 1998, p. 68.
Washington Post. April 24, 1998, p. B5.

Species II

Species II

There is life on Mars . . . and now it's here.
—Movie tagline

It's mating season . . . again.—Movie tagline

 Box Office: $19,221,174

From *Star Trek* (1979) to *Nightmare on Elm Street* (1984), to the *Alien* series, sci-fi and horror films are a staple of contemporary moviegoing. And so have the sequels: *Star Trek II: The Wrath of Khan* (1982), *Nightmare on Elm Street II, III, IV,* etc. (1985, 1987, 1988) and more represent only a part of the film franchises on the video shelves today. *Species II* attempts to cash in on the apparent success of *Species* (1996), a sci-fi picture which never seemed to cry out for a sequel in the first place. (If truth be told, the first film wasn't so great, but that is part of another review).

In the initial *Species,* a blonde bombshell (Natasha Henstridge) named Sil comes to earth (to America, specifically) in order to find a husband. Like many frustrated singles, she becomes enraged at the lack of good men, and (unlike most people) unleashes superhuman, alien powers to kill, maim, and destroy anything in her quest to mate. The first film starred Michael Madsen as a sort of mercenary who destroys Sil, and also starred Marg Helgenberger as a scientist who tries to understand her.

Well, they're back. All of them. This time out, Henstridge plays Eve, a clone of Sil who is trapped in a glass bubble (literally) and being studied by Dr. Laura Baker (Helgenberger), presumably to understand who and where she originated. Dr. Baker's research is funded by some typically oily bureaucrats and military types, from Col. Carter Burgess Jr. (George Dzundza, another holdover from the first film), and Senator Ross (James Cromwell). Where Sil once was trying to mate with anything she could find in order to continue her race of nefarious, disgusting pod-type-dinosauresque creatures, now the propagating is being done by the Senator's astronaut son, Patrick (Justin Lazard), who has been taken over by the aliens. He stores the embryos in his father's farmhouse, and generally makes himself a nuisance until he meets Eve.

And as soon as these two quasi-aliens-in-heat meet, all heck breaks loose. Eve throws herself against the glass bubble until it breaks, dying to get to the man/alien she's meant to mate with. The action kicks into high gear. Nothing can stop either of them. That is, of course, nothing except the team thrown together by expert alien-destroyer Press Lennox (Michael Madsen) and sidekick Dennis Gamble (Mykelti Williamson.) Eventually all parties end up in a doomsday battle in a country house near Washington and the world is saved once again.

In between the introduction of Eve and the climactic battle, it would be nice to report that director Peter Medak was able to make something out of this dreadful material, but he hasn't. The formula is simply stale: an alien comes to take over the world and is destroyed by the help of a mixed-gender and ethnically appropriate group who overcome their differences to do battle with evil. The bad guys are in the government, and the good guys are rebels who once worked for the government. Nothing new here. But then, this is a sequel, and perhaps Medak and company needed to keep things the same, just in case the folks at Metro-Goldwyn-Mayer got afraid that *Species II* may not sell like

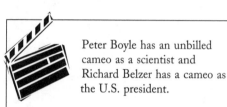

Peter Boyle has an unbilled cameo as a scientist and Richard Belzer has a cameo as the U.S. president.

CREDITS

Press Lennox: Michael Madsen
Eve: Natasha Henstridge
Patrick Ross: Justin Lazard
Dr. Laura Baker: Marg Helgenberger
Dennis Gamble: Mykelti Williamson
Col. Carter Burgess Jr.: George Dzundza
Sen. Ross: James Cromwell

Origin: USA
Released: 1998
Production: Frank Mancuso Jr. for FGM Entertainment; released by Metro-Goldwyn-Mayer
Direction: Peter Medak
Screenplay: Chris Brancato; based on characters created by Dennis Feldman
Cinematography: Matthew F. Leonetti
Editing: Richard Nord
Music: Edward Shearmur
Production design: Miljen Kreka Kljakovic
Art direction: Mark Zuelzke
Costumes: Richard Bruno
Sound: Steve Nelson
MPAA rating: R
Running Time: 93 minutes

Species I. But let's be realistic . . . how well did the original film do at the boxoffice? Maybe a little originality in the script (by Chris Brancato) and in Medak's direction might have helped *Species II* be more than the boxoffice fizzler that it was.

It is difficult to say much good about the film, which does not bring pleasure. Many people put countless hours into these endeavors, and it's no fun to say that it doesn't work. The makers of the creatures have created aliens that seem too similar to those found in the *Alien* series. The music by Ed Shearmur serves its purpose but is uninspired. The actors in particular seem to walk through their paces, and it is difficult to know whether to blame them, director Medak, editor Richard Nord, writer Brancato, or to suggest that the blame lay everywhere. Wherever it lay, there is a sort of torpor over much of the film that renders it dull. It is not a scary film, just a violent one. It is not a fun film, just a color-by-numbers sequel.

It's worth repeating that writing a negative review is no fun. It is a good idea to make a sequel to a film that everyone loved. Perhaps it isn't such a good idea to make a sequel to a film that most people found rather dull the first time around.

—*Kirby Tepper*

REVIEWS

Boxoffice. June, 1998, p. 81.
Chicago Tribune. April 15, 1998, p. 2.
Cinefantastique. March, 1998, p. 7.
Entertainment Weekly. April 24, 1998, p. 58.
Los Angeles Times. April 13, 1998, p. F5.
New York Times. April 11, 1998, p. B13.
People. April 27, 1998, p. 39.
Variety. April 20, 1998, p. 44.

Sphere

Terror can fill any space.—Movie tagline
Scientists have discovered an alien intelligence under the sea waiting to kill us all.—Movie tagline

 Box Office: $37,297,851

Writer Michael Crichton and director Barry Levinson are known for their intelligent mastery of their respective crafts, but when one computes the math for their latest combined effort, *Sphere,* something just doesn't add up. An "A-list" director, an "A-list" writer, and a host of "A-list" actors, here only seem to add up to a "B" movie. How can this be?

There is no denying that *Sphere* is initially an intriguing film. Psychologist Norman Goodman (Dustin Hoffman) thinks he has been called on to counsel the survivors of a plane crash in the middle of the Pacific ocean, but when he is met by a mysterious—and one imagines military—official named Barnes (Peter Coyote), he suspects there's more to the story than what he has been told.

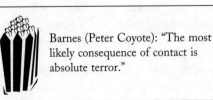

Barnes (Peter Coyote): "The most likely consequence of contact is absolute terror."

To Norman's surprise, also on the ship at the staging site in the Pacific are mathematician Harry Adams (Samuel Jackson), astrophysicist Ted Fielding (Liev Schreiber), and biochemist Beth Halperin (Sharon Stone). Except for Barnes, Norman shares a history with all the members of this disparate group, and he's puzzled as to what they have to do with plane crashes. As it turns out, what all these people have in common is that during the Bush administration, Norman had written a report on what kind of team should be put together for Earth's first contact with an alien life-form. However, Norman only researched half his report and "borrowed" the other half from writers like Isaac Asimov and Rod Serling. To add authenticity, he added the names of the experts he knew, namely Beth, Harry, and Ted, but basically he just made it all up in order to collect the $35,000 paycheck.

And that's why they're all there, to investigate a spaceship that has been found 1,000 feet down on the Pacific floor. To do this, they must take a mini-sub to an underwater habitat from which they will do their research on the ship. Once there, they make the first of several startling discoveries. For one thing, the ship is covered with coral. As Beth notes, coral grows at a rate of one inch per year, and this causes Harry to compute that the ship must have crashed 288 years ago! They are further astonished to find that the aircraft is in perfect shape (which they at first attributed to an ultra hard hull), but when they attempt to break through the door, the paint easily chips. The spaceship didn't crash, it landed.

And then the door opens . . . by itself. But there are more surprises awaiting the crew inside. First they find a bin marked "trash-basura." Could this be a spacecraft from Earth? It's a suspicion confirmed when they find a desiccated human corpse clutching a bag of Smokehouse Blue Diamond Almonds. But if the craft is from Earth, how could it have landed in the Pacific in 1709? The answer? It's from our future. But the question still remains as to how it came to be on the bottom of the Pacific.

Just when the crew believes they've figured out the basics of the spacecraft, they stumble upon an even stranger mystery—a huge sphere that looks as if it were made of undulating, mirror-like golden liquid. It has no entryway, and seems to have no purpose, but what's really odd is that it only reflects what it wants to reflect. Does this mean it is a conscious entity?

The underwater scenes for *Sphere* were filmed at the 142-year-old Mare Island Naval Shipyard near the city of Vallejo, California.

The only clue the crew can find as to what happened to the ship is a holographic log that indicates that around the year 2043 the ship experienced an "unknown event" that Ted indicates looks as if it went through a black hole. Elsewhere on the ship, while staring at the sphere, Harry disappears, and when he reappears, he's not quite the same. He sleeps a lot, snoozes right through some very noisy emergencies, awakens with a huge appetite, and can't stop reading *Twenty-thousand Leagues Under the Sea.*

Then, suddenly, the sphere makes contact using a mathematical code and the habitat's computer. The crew stares at the habitat's computer screen in astonishment as they read, "Hello, How are you? I am fine. What's your name? My name is Jerry." But when it says, "I am happy." Norman worries and asks, "What happens if Jerry gets mad?" It's a good question, because it doesn't take long for Jerry to lose his temper and send the message "I will kill you all."

Sphere is quite a collection of typical science-fiction standbys. The chatty computer from *2001,* the psychological drama of Andrei Tarkovsky's *Solaris* or 1956's *Forbidden Planet* (or even the more recent *Event Horizon*), the stalwart unisex crew of *Alien,* and the claustrophobic underwater setting of James Cameron's *Abyss,* all can be seen here. And at first, the derivativeness of the story is disregarded out of curiosity as to what this "A-list" team will do with it.

Crichton is a master of creating science fiction that is rich in character and thought, where science is discussed and not just seen in the background. *The Andromeda Strain, Jurassic Park, Rising Sun,* and *Congo* were all best-sellers turned into films precisely because of their intelligence as well as their rousing plots. But *Sphere,* at least as it is translated to the screen, has a plot with more holes in it than Swiss cheese. So many events, ideas, and devices are left unexplained that all the intrigue of the first half of the film is diffused by the end because we feel cheated. Did the filmmakers think we wouldn't notice or think about all the unanswered questions? If we're that dumb, why would we want to see an intelligent film? And considering how many writers they had working on the screenplay, one could legitimately expect one of them to have noticed all the dangling threads.

Director Barry Levinson (who worked with Crichton once before on *Disclosure*) is known for his realistic, thoughtful, and very human films like *Rain Man* and *Diner,* and with *Sphere,* he makes his first foray into science fiction. He supposedly tried to shoot the scenes in this story in sequence in an attempt to keep building on the dramatic integrity of the plot, but as it starts to unravel, even this trick won't keep the viewer interested. Maybe he should stick to comedies and dramas. A much better film of Levinson's which was in theaters at the same time as *Sphere* is his wickedly funny political satire *Wag the Dog (1997).*

Also a bit of a letdown are the film's special effects. The holographic ship's log was inventive, but our first glimpse of the ship itself was sheer disappointment. Hidden beneath mountains of coral and obscured by murky water, we can barely make it out. Hardly awe inspiring.

On the other hand, the diving suits used in *Sphere* (designed by costume designer Gloria Gresham and Bev Morgan, the celebrated designer of underwater suits and equipment), actually revolutionized diving technology, creating a new type of underwater suit and helmet. In fact, the helmet, with its enlarged front and side windows and its advanced breathing and communications system created such a huge jump in technology that several international navies expressed interest in the new inventions. But while this may be an interesting bit of background information, it's hardly enough to carry our interest in the film.

Only the actors can say they did justice to the material they were given. Hoffman is always good, imbuing his character not only with strength but also with that droll Hoffman humor. Samuel L. Jackson does a solid job of making his character eccentrically brainy and scornful while keeping us guessing as to whether we should like or fear him after he comes out of the sphere. Sharon Stone does her best with a character that is unfortunately cool and strong one minute and popping pills and being hysterical the next. Peter Coyote lends Barnes an icy and impenetrable exterior that never allows us to fathom his motives, which for a mysterious and presumably military character

CREDITS

Dr. Norman Goodman: Dustin Hoffman
Beth Halperin: Sharon Stone
Harry Adams: Samuel L. Jackson
Barnes: Peter Coyote
Ted Fielding: Liev Schreiber
Fletcher: Queen Latifah
Jane Edmunds: Marga Gomez
Helicopter Pilot: Huey Lewis
Seaman: Bernard Hocke
OSSA Instructor: James Pickens Jr.

Origin: USA
Released: 1998
Production: Barry Levinson, Michael Crichton, and Andrew Wald for Baltimore Pictures/Constant c Production in association with Punch Productions, Inc.; released by Warner Bros.
Direction: Barry Levinson
Screenplay: Stephen Hauser and Paul Attanasio; based on the novel by Michael Crichton
Cinematography: Adam Greenberg
Editing: Stu Linder
Production design: Norman Reynolds
Art direction: Mark Mansbridge, Jonathan McKinstry
Set decoration: Anne Kuljian
Set design: Geoff Hubbard
Costumes: Gloria Gresham
Music: Elliot Goldenthal
Visual effects supervision: Jeffrey A. Okun
MPAA rating: PG-13
Running Time: 132 minutes

is probably most appropriate. And Liev Schreiber, most well known for his work in such indie films as *Denise Calls Up* and *Walking and Talking* (and the not-so-indie *Scream 2*), imparts Ted with a degree of innocence and competitiveness that is endearing.

In the end, however, even all this talent can't save a film that starts to fizzle halfway through. Perhaps the fact that the first half offers such promise, raises such interesting possibilities and our hopes, only to have them ignored and dashed by the end that compounds the disappointment. Even science fiction needs to offer an audience a sense of completion and final understanding, of rising to its potential. And a film that prides itself on its intelligence must especially obey all the laws of logic. It's OK for this kind of film to start with a mystery—in fact those are some of the best in the genre—but when the film's over, the mystery should pretty much be resolved. To leave it hanging is just plain creatively lazy, and asking too much of an audience.

—*Beverley Bare Buehrer*

REVIEWS

Chicago Sun-Times. February 13, 1998.
Chicago Tribune. February 13, 1998, p. 4.
Cinefantastique. March, 1998, p. 10.
Entertainment Weekly. February 20, 1997, p. 86.
Los Angeles Times. February 13, 1998, p. F1.
New York Times. February 13, 1998, p. E18.
People. February 23, 1998, p. 21.
Time. February 23, 1998.
USA Today. February 13, 1998, p. 3D.
Variety. February 16, 1998, p. 56.
Village Voice. February 24, 1998, p. 122.

Spice World

"*Spice World* is a bubble-gum movie—snappy, colorful . . ."—*Atlanta Journal-Constitution*

"Sure-fire delight for Spice Girl fans everywhere!"—David Sheehan, *CBS-TV*

"Sunny . . . The whole group radiates energy, color and good cheer!"—Janet Maslin, *New York Times*

"Lively . . . Fans will find exactly what they want, what they really, really want."—*St. Petersburg Times*

Box Office: $29,342,592

I t's not really surprising that *Spice World* is not a good movie, but in a way, it sort of is. The surprising part is that even if a viewer goes in with very low expectations, the movie somehow still disappoints.

Surely the filmmakers went into the project knowing the movie was going to get a critical drubbing, but it would have been nice if they would have defied expectations by making something good, or maybe campy and kitschy, or, at least, something that sort of made sense.

The movie is loosely based on the Beatles *A Hard Day's Night* (1964), but where that movie had the wit of John Lennon going for it, *Spice World* is stuck with jokes like a character saying, "Or if they find a cure for déjà vu," twice.

But then, the movie isn't supposed to be a comedy, it's more like a product advertising for the band. Basically, the movie provides a chance to see the Spice Girls perform a few songs and to check out some of their outfits. In that sense, it doesn't disappoint. The quintet do, indeed, perform several songs and they do wear some wild clothes. If nothing else, *Spice World* certainly features the most examples of absurdly tall platform shoes.

We learn the stereotypes behind each member. Mel B. (Melanie Brown) is often leopard-clad Scary Spice. Emma (Emma Burton) is the blonde Baby Spice. Mel C. (Melanie Chisholm) is the athletic Sporty Spice. Geri (Geri Halliwell) is the smart one, Ginger Spice. And Victoria (Victoria Adams) is the designer-clad Posh Spice. In one of the better sequences in the film, the group pokes fun at their stereotypes by dressing in the style of another one. But this just makes all the more clear that their various "personalities" don't really go beyond their choices in clothing.

Musical arranger about a rehearsal: "That was absolutely perfect without actually being any good."

The plot, though surely that isn't the right word, is that the five women ride around in their big double-decker bus and get ready for the big concert. It's by no means a documentary and gives no sense of what a typical "Spice Day" is really like. It's too bad because that would have made for an interesting movie. Instead it just pretends to be about their typical days—unless, of course, their days really do consist of getting involved in high-speed chases through town, helping pregnant friends have a baby, and meeting an alien space ship (really). When they're not busy doing things like saving drowning fans, they

CREDITS

Baby Spice: Emma Burton
Ginger Spice: Geri Halliwell
Posh Spice: Victoria Adams
Sporty Spice: Melanie Chisholm
Scary Spice: Melanie Brown
Clifford: Richard E. Grant
Piers: Alan Cumming
Graydon: Mark McKinney
Film Producer: George Wendt
Deborah: Claire Rushbrook
Chief: Roger Moore
Kevin McMaxford: Barry Humphries
Brad: Jason Flemyng
Dennis: Meatloaf

Origin: Great Britain
Released: 1997
Production: Uri Fruchtman and Barnaby Thompson for Icon Entertainment and Fragile Films; released by Columbia Pictures
Direction: Bob Spiers
Screenplay: Kim Fuller
Cinematography: Clive Tickner
Editing: Andrea MacArthur
Production design: Grenville Horner
Art direction: David Walley, Colin Blaymires
Costumes: Kate Carin
Makeup: Graham Johnston
Music: Paul Newcastle
Sound: Colin Nicolson
MPAA rating: PG
Running Time: 92 minutes

also aggravate their nervous manager Clifford (Richard E. Grant). It's a shame to see Grant, who was great in the cult film *Withnail & I* (1987) stuck in such a silly role.

Actually it's painful to see a lot of the cast members in their various bad roles. The most crushing example is seeing ex-*Kids in the Hall* member Mark McKinney as a bland potential screenwriter of a Spice Girls movie. *Cheers'* George Wendt's talent is completely wasted in an unnoticeable film producer role. Little is done with the cameos, too. Elton John's appearance consists entirely of the girls meeting him in the hall and hugging him. And other cameos are just pointless including Elvis Costello, Jools Holland, *Absolutely Fabulous'* Jennifer Saunders, and Bob Geldof (Bob, from Live Aid to this?). Some attempts at "in" jokes are made with some of the cameos. In Meatloaf's role as the girls' bus driver, he says at one point, "I would do anything for them but I won't do that," paraphrasing one of his songs. Roger Moore's appearance as Chief, a Dr. No-ish boss, contains a few less-than-clever Bond references, like having his character caressing and stroking a pig instead of a white pussycat.

The Spice Girls were the first all-girl band to hit #1 on the U.K. charts with their 1996 debut single, "Wannabe."

Spice World could have been a good movie. All the elements were there—a good cast, a fun, energetic and photogenic band with the promising subject matter of pop stardom madness—but the filmmakers don't exploit what they have going for them. However, the filmmakers did exploit the band's popularity at just the right time, making *Spice World* the number two movie the week it came out.

—*Jill Hamilton*

REVIEWS

Chicago Tribune. January 23, 1998, p. 5.
Entertainment Weekly. January 30, 1998, p. 41.
Los Angeles Times. January 23, 1998, p. F18.
New York Times. January 23, 1998, p. E18.
New Yorker. January 26, 1998, p. 85.
People. February 2, 1998, p. 20.
Sight and Sound. February, 1998, p. 49.
Variety. December 22, 1997, p. 58.
Washington Post Weekend. January 23, 1998, p. 41.

Star Kid

"*Star Kid* pushes the right buttons . . . it has heart and a lot of sly wit."—Roger Ebert, *Chicago Sun-Times*

"Heartfelt in the tradition of *E.T.*"—John Walsh, *TV Guide Entertainment Network*

"Ideal for the whole family! The kind of movie we need more of."—Doug Moore, *WDAF-TV*

 Box Office: $6,966,021

"If you run away from things you're scared of, it doesn't get any easier." That's the advice 12-year-old Spencer Griffith (Joseph Mazzello) gets from his sympathetic science teacher Janet Holloway (Corinne Bohrer) near the beginning of *Star Kid*. Miss Holloway has just witnessed the lily-livered Spencer getting shoved around on the playground by the school bully, Turbo Bruntley (Joey Simmrin), then getting tongue-tied when approached by Michelle (Lauren Eckstrom), a girl he has a crush on. Holloway tells

Spencer that she once feared spiders but then her father got a pet tarantula and made her change the water in the spider's cage and she overcame her fears, learned to love arachnids, and became a science teacher. Spencer takes Miss Holloway's advice to heart because she is so cool—in class, she compares a bat's emitting of a protective odor as "like a really gnarly fart."

Growing up is just that easy, in the world of dumb movies. For a girl, it's learning to love creepy crawlers. For a boy, the trick is to witness the landing of an alien war machine, climb inside it, fight off other aliens, and save mankind. Along the way, of course, you reconcile with your snotty big sister, make friends with the bully, and teach your dad not to be late picking you up for school. After that, it's a relatively simple matter to be cool at school. You can even muster the gumption to sit down next to Michelle and start a conversation.

In terms of its object lesson and plot, *Star Kid* treads a well-worn path for kids' films. "Face your fears" is the message of hundreds of movie fairy tales for kids. And for boys, the usual device for facing fears is to become a lean and mean fighting machine, like Spencer's Marvel Comics super hero, Knight Warrior. For Spencer, opportunity knocks when he notices the good-guy alien Trelkins' experimental robot-warrior landing in the junkyard across from his bedroom window. He's had a real bad day—not only because of Turbo and Michelle, but because his dad (Richard Gilliland) is neglecting him for his job and his sister Stacey (Ashlee Levitch) is furious because she had to give up a date to babysit him. (Mom, of course, is dead; there's always a dead or divorced parent in these films.)

The Trelkins are the good aliens—you know that because they've got big goo-goo eyes and they're smart enough to program the robot-warriors to understand English. The Trelkins have been attacked by the Broodwarriors, the bad aliens who are out to conquer the universe. You know they're bad because they look like reptiles combined with insects. They are slimy and oozy and they can tear off pieces of their bodies and make them into weapons or ropes.

The only hope for the Trelkins was to launch their experimental war machine into space and hope it landed on a friendly planet where an unhappy 12-year-old male was trying to figure out how to jump-start his testosterone. Luckily for the Trelkins, their trajectory is perfect, and Spencer meets Cyborsuit, who looks like C3P0 but needs a "biotic host" to activate his powers. With little prodding, Spencer is convinced to take the job. "My life couldn't get much worse," he reasons. The Cyborsuit unzips itself from the back, folding out like the petals of a flower, and Spencer climbs aboard. Pretty brave move for a kid who can't even muster a word when Michelle visits his desk.

Little about the Cyborsuit—or the movie, for that matter—makes sense. It's basically a supercomputer in the form of a bodysuit, and it can move by jet propulsion. But, surprisingly, ordinary walking seems to be beyond its powers. Most of the time it moves clumsily, in response to Spencer's movements. Of course, the alien creation understands English but not English slang, which makes for some low humor.

The Cyborsuit (played by Alex Daniels) has its own voice (spoken by Arthur Burghardt), which sounds like a tape being played at slow speed. But it can also speak with Spencer's voice, though it seems to do so arbitrarily. Behind the face, Spencer can look through the robot's eyes and see a picture with various computer readouts. But when Cyborsuit wants to say something meaningful, the screen melts into a wrinkly, expressive face that looks inward and talks to Spencer. Cy, as Spencer calls him, explains he is only a prototype and that's why things don't always go as planned. That provides grist for some pratfalls.

Spencer, played broadly by Mazzello, loves his new-found powers, but fails to use them wisely. First he seeks revenge against Turbo. He pays a call at the Bruntley family business, an auto shop, where Turbo is inside a car atop a hoist playing loud rock music. The empowered Spencer takes him for a real spin. Next Spencer decides to go to the

town fair to see what Michelle's up to. That proves to be a bad idea when Cy mistakes a man in a Barney suit for a Broodwarrior and starts shooting up the carnival. Michelle and Spencer's friends are atop a ride when Cy blasts it, but the Cy-enclosed Spencer makes a diving catch of their ride car just before it hits the ground. Score it an error and a save. The police come, so Cy escapes by rocketing at top speed right across the ground—another semi-malfunction.

There's a crude pleasure in these ridiculous scenes, like watching the original *Godzilla* movies. So many kids' films these days are such technical marvels that it's almost refreshing to see such cheesy special effects. The animatronics and the computer wizardry in *Star Kid* are decidedly second-rate. As Cy stalks around the carnival and nobody notices him (?), you can almost hear the snarky comments from the *Mystery Science Theater* reviewers. This has the makings of a cult hit—it's so bad that it's funny.

After frying the fair, Spencer takes Cy home, but the Suit gets his head stuck in the refrigerator and wrecks the place, using the fridge as a battering ram. Still seeking food, Spencer has Cy order a burger at a drive-thru. Spencer no longer finds the burger appetizing after Cy processes it into a "cyborsuit turd" and then force-feeds it to the boy. When Spencer wants out of the suit to relieve himself, he gets the bad news that Cy won't let him go until he has accomplished his mission of testing the suit's powers in combat. After many false tries, Spencer finally remembers the non-slang word for what he wants to do (urination), but a design flaw has the urination aperture coming out of Cy's neck. Desperate, Spencer goes to Miss Holloway's house to get help, and, after fainting, she loosens a few screws so Spencer can use the bathroom. Boy, who could have thought being a biotic host was this much trouble?

The rest of the film can't measure up to these sequences for sheer absurdity. The movie makes the mistake of taking itself a little too seriously. Once a Broodwarrior finally tracks Cy down and the battle begins, Spencer must decide between saving his own skin and saving the human race. After one skirmish, Spencer exercises his exit option and returns home, his fears overcoming his affection for Cy.

At home Spencer finds his nonentity of a dad and his spoiled sister are refusing to believe Miss Holloway's story, which is no wonder since Bohrer is such a bad actress. Dad welcomes his son home, though you wonder why he wasn't out looking for him. A few minutes later, Spencer gets another piece of advice from his sister, who tells him to do whatever the person he admires most would do—which, of course, is his comic-book hero, the Knight Warrior. So Spencer decides to go back into the warrior biz, and enlists Turbo, who steals his father's car and drives out to the spot where Spencer left Cy. But the Broodwarrior dude has already taken him away.

I was betting at this point that Michelle would be held hostage by the bad aliens, that Spencer and the good aliens would rescue her, and that Mrs. Holloway and dear old dad would hit it off. It's not quite so formulaic, but it also isn't quite so ambitious. Instead, Spencer and Turbo bond in the junkyard, teaming up with an off-again, on-again Cy to

CREDITS

Spencer Griffith: Joseph Mazzello
Turbo Bruntley: Joey Simmrin
Cyborsuit: Alex Daniels
Cyborsuit voice: Arthur Burghardt
Janet Holloway: Corinne Bohrer
Rolan Griffith: Richard Gilliland
Michelle: Lauren Eckstrom
Stacey: Ashlee Levitch

Origin: USA
Released: 1998
Production: Jennie Lew Tugend; released by Trimark Pictures
Direction: Manny Coto
Screenplay: Manny Coto
Cinematography: Ronn Schmidt
Editing: Bob Ducsay
Production design: C. J. Strawn
Art direction: Michael D. Welch
Costumes: Ileane Meltzer
Music: Nicholas Pike
MPAA rating: PG
Running Time: 101 minutes

crush the Broodwarrior, literally. The prolonged battle is even cheesier and dumber than the rest of the movie—the bad alien disappears inexplicably for long stretches and ends up making like Ed Scissorshands before Turbo comes to the rescue with the help of a car compactor. Cy "ceases to function," but his cute Trelkin creators suddenly land, fix him up with some new powers, and blast off after sharing a few jokes and giving the tearful Spencer a medal for bravery. And, needless to say, Spencer has acquired a lifelong friend, who would no doubt be available to return for sequels.

Even on its own terms, writer/director Manny Coto's film makes no sense. Why have the powerful Broodwarriors sent only one alien to Earth? How is the Cyborsuit going to save the Trelkins from the enemy when it wasn't even capable of beating one Broodwarrior without the help of a schoolyard bully? No matter. This is one weird, wacky, terribly stupid movie that is a lot of fun to watch. Go ahead, face your fears about second-rate kids' movies. If you run away, it doesn't get any easier.

—*Michael Betzold*

REVIEWS

Boxoffice. January, 1998, p. 44.
Cinefantastique. February, 1998, p. 53.
Hollywood Reporter. January 13, 1998, p. 23.
Los Angeles Times. January 16, 1998, p. F10.
New York Times. January 16, 1998, p. E14.
Variety. January 12, 1998, p. 74.

Star Trek: Insurrection

The battle for paradise has begun.—Movie tagline

"Exciting conflict and cutting-edge effects that truly entertain. One of the best in the series with a good story."—Gene Siskel, *Chicago Tribune*

"Even if you've never seen a *Star Trek* movie or TV episode, you'll love this film."—Steve Oldfield, *FOX-TV*

"It's the best *Star Trek* voyage yet. There's plenty of pulse-pounding action and unexpected humor."—Amy Longsdorf, *Gannett News Service*

"Definitely the best *Next Generation* movie so far!"—Jonathan Foreman, *New York Post*

"Seductively apealing. All the ingredients that have made it a perennial."—Stephen Holden, *New York Times*

"The jokes, action sequences and special effects come faster than photon torpedoes."—Colin Covert, *Star Tribune*

"It's old-fashioned sci-fi in the best sense of the word."—Michael O'Sullivan, *Washington Post Weekend*

 Box Office: $67,191,000

Since the mid–1980s there has been talk among *Star Trek* fans and film critics—some of it tongue-in-cheek and some of it quite serious—of an "odd-numbered curse" supposedly plaguing Paramount's twenty-year-old film franchise. According to this theory, all the even-numbered *Star Trek* films have been superior to the odd-numbered ones.

While many people would disagree that all the odd-numbered films have been weaker than the even-numbered ones (some critics, for instance, rated 1994's *Star Trek Generations*, technically number seven in the series, as strong as 1986's *Star Trek IV: The Voyage Home*), the latter tend to show up more often at the top of fans' and critics' lists. When the original *Trek* cast headed by William Shatner's Captain James T. Kirk was replaced on the big screen by the crew of *Star Trek: The Next Generation* the "curse" still seemed alive: 1996's *Star Trek: First Contact*, number eight in the series, was a much more successful film both critically and financially than *Generations*. As production began in 1998 on the ninth installment, eventually titled *Star Trek: Insurrection*, speculation arose as to whether the new film would fall prey to the same pattern or be the movie that would finally break the curse (though some fans argued that the curse had already been broken with *Generations*).

Initial expectations were high when producer Rick Berman selected Michael Piller, writer of some of *The Next Generation*'s most highly esteemed episodes and co-creator of both *Deep Space Nine* and *Voyager,* to write the script for the film that would become *Insurrection*. (The previous two films had been scripted by the writing team of Ronald D. Moore and Brannon Braga, both veterans of the television series.) Berman and Piller intended a slightly different approach with the latest adventure of the *U.S.S. Enterprise,* focusing more on the comradery of the crew and the portrayal of Captain Jean-Luc Picard (Patrick Stewart) as the "thinking man's hero." According to Piller, in *Generations* and *First Contact,* Captain Picard "as a hero had not been truly defined to the big screen audience . . . I felt we had never seen the Picard who was a man of principle, who had the moral and ethical drive that I thought was so important to the character as a television hero." While *First Contact* in particular had pictured the captain as an action hero, Piller wanted to bring out the "intellect and verbal skills" of Picard, as well as the way in which the captain serves as "the center of a family of characters who look up to him, who follow him into danger." As fans eagerly (and nervously) awaited the release of a film whose creators promised adventure, humor, interesting character development, and a plot initially inspired by Joseph Conrad's *Heart of Darkness,* leaking of early drafts of the script on the Internet sparked a maelstrom of rumors and premature mixed reactions, many of which proclaimed that the odd-numbered curse was still alive. However, when *Insurrection* finally appeared on the big screen, the film delivered most, if not all, that was promised by its makers, suggesting that the only "curse" on the series may be a sort of self-fulfilling prophecy in the minds of pessimistic fans. The film opened to respectable business (it took the number one spot at the box

office its opening weekend) and somewhat mixed reviews, but overall audience reaction tended to judge it as weaker than *First Contact* but stronger than *Generations*.

The story of *Insurrection* concerns a moral dilemma for Captain Picard involving his loyalty to the United Federation of Planets which he serves. Picard first realizes that something is amiss when he gets a report from *Starfleet* Admiral Dougherty (Anthony Zerbe) that the android Lieutenant Commander Data (Brent Spiner), who had been assigned to a Federation team on a distant planet covertly observing a small race of people called the Ba'ku, has seemingly run amok, exposing the observation team to the Ba'ku and taking the *Starfleet* officers hostage. Although Dougherty tells Picard his assistance in the situation is unnecessary, Picard's loyalty to his officer and friend Data moves him to take the *Enterprise* into the mysterious area of space known as the Briar Patch, where the Ba'ku planet is located. After arriving at the Ba'ku home world, Captain Picard and Commander Worf (Michael Dorn) apprehend Data and discover that his "hostages" are actually being treated as guests by the Ba'ku, a peaceful group of people who have chosen to reject all the modern advances of technology in favor of embracing a simple, agrarian way of life. Back on the *Enterprise,* Chief Engineer Geordi LaForge (LeVar Burton) examines Data and learns that the android malfunctioned after having been hit by phaser fire from a weapon belonging to the Son'a, a race of aging aliens participating with *Starfleet* in the observation of the Ba'ku. Suspicions raised, Picard takes the repaired Data back with him to the planet's surface to investigate.

The search for answers on the Ba'ku planet uncovers a hidden "holodeck" ship, constructed by the Federation, that contains a holographic recreation of the Ba'ku village. The captain deduces that the ship was prepared for the purpose of secretly relocating the Ba'ku villagers, and he soon discovers the motivation behind this plot. The rings around the Ba'ku planet are permeated with a type of "metaphasic" radiation that constantly regenerates living cells. As a result, the inhabitants on the planet, who originally came from another world over 300 years before, have not aged—and, in fact, many of them regained their youth. Led by the aging Ru'afo (F. Murray Abraham), the Son'a race, who have secured the alliance of Admiral Dougherty and the Federation Council, intend to relocate the Ba'ku to another planet so that they may collect all the radiation in the planet's rings and harness it to restore youth to themselves—a procedure that will destroy the Ba'ku home world in the process. Captain Picard confronts Admiral Dougherty with his discovery of the plot and argues that it goes against the principles of non-interference for which the Federation stands, but Dougherty is unpersuaded, insisting that *Starfleet* needs the

Jean-Luc Picard (Patrick Stewart): "We are participating in the outright theft of a world."

alliance with the Son'a. "We are only moving 600 people," the admiral rationalizes. "How many people does it take before it becomes wrong?" Picard counters, pointing out that the history of humanity before the Federation was replete with immoral relocations of people for reasons of personal gain. Dougherty dismisses the captain's argument and orders Picard to take the *Enterprise* out of the Briar Patch.

Torn between his loyalty to *Starfleet* and his moral principles, Picard chooses to stand up for what he knows is right. Accompanied by Worf, Data, Counselor Deanna Troi (Marina Sirtis), and Dr. Beverly Crusher (Gates McFadden), the captain heads to the Ba'ku planet to lead the villagers to safety in mountains where the Son'a will not be able to abduct them easily. In the meantime, Commander Will Riker (Jonathan Frakes) and LaForge take the *Enterprise* back toward the Federation to try to convince the Council of the immorality of the Son'a plot. Unwilling to tolerate this defiance and the trouble the *Enterprise* crew has caused him, Ru'afo orders his men to track down the Ba'ku and forcibly remove them from the planet, and he convinces Dougherty to allow him to send Son'a battleships after the *Enterprise* to prevent Riker's message from getting through to the Federation Council.

As the conflict heightens, a space battle ensues between the *Enterprise* and the Son'a ships, but with ingenuity Riker leads the *Enterprise* to victory. Meanwhile, Picard and his crew uncover another part of the story that has chilling implications: the Son'a are actually the same race as the Ba'ku. They are in fact children of the Ba'ku who left the home world a century before in defiance of the Ba'ku philosophy of life. Faced with this unsettling information, Dougherty tells Ru'afo to put an end to his plans, but Ru'afo kills him and orders the initiation of the procedure that will collect the radiation from the planet's rings and destroy all life on the world, including his own people, the Ba'ku. The tide turns, however, when Picard convinces Ru'afo's second-in-command, Gallatin (Gregg Henry)—who opposes the idea of killing his own family—to help him outwit the murderous, vengeful Son'a leader. Picard eventually manages to barely stop Ru'afo before the deadly procedure can be carried out.

Ever since the inception of Gene Roddenberry's *Star Trek* in 1966, some of the best installments in the series have tackled difficult social and political questions, and through this vision of the future, Roddenberry and his progeny have portrayed a humanity that has escaped many of the perils of the past and that adheres to firm moral and ethical principles. The philosophy of non-interference with the natural development of a society, the basis of the "Prime Directive" at the core of the Federation's laws, has long been a theme addressed in *Star Trek*. Often the adventures of the *Enterprise,* whether led by Captain Kirk or Captain Picard, put the crew into situations in which they encountered necessary exceptions to that fundamental law, but one of the interesting things about *Insurrection* is that the story illustrates

the ethical rationale for adhering to such a principle. In that vein, the film is very much in the traditional spirit of Roddenberry's creation. The dramatic conflict that propels the story celebrates the virtues of fighting for one's beliefs without compromise, of adhering to what is right in the face of overwhelming pressure to overlook injustice.

Some critics took issue with the principle underlying the *Enterprise* crew's rebellion and felt the conflict lacked real conviction, thus weakening the film's plot. Roger Ebert, for example, questioned in his review what was wrong about sacrificing the happiness and the home of 600 people if it meant extending the lives of others. He also wondered why the Son'a could not simply live on the planet along with the Ba'ku. The first question is one which Picard addresses directly in the film when he asks how many lives it would take to make the action wrong. In principle, Picard insists, the idea of moving people from their homeland in order to benefit others is a dangerous one—and a morally wrong one. The Son'a are an unprincipled, often savage people (both Picard and Dougherty refer to them as "thugs"), and the Federation alliance with them is not one of principle but one of selfish pragmatism. Picard's unwavering adherence to his principles is a laudable, heroic decision that invites the viewer to consider how often, in our own world, alliances have been made with "thugs" based on political or economic pragmatism even though the "partnership" caused some people to suffer. Secondly, the Son'a were unwilling to return to the planet to live (for several reasons) and intended to destroy it. The revelation that the Son'a are actually Ba'ku adds another sinister level to the conflict, for Ru'afo and many of his cohorts are as motivated by revenge as they are driven by self-preservation.

While the ethical issues underlying *Star Trek: Insurrection* provide an interesting dramatic element, the film also has its share of enjoyable romance, humor, and action. Picard's developing relationship with the Ba'ku woman Anij (Donna Murphy) is rendered effectively and realistically, bolstered by strong performances from both Stewart and Murphy. The peaceful, reflective, philosophical Anij seems the ideal woman to attract the intellectual and stalwart captain, and she serves as an alluring, convincing representative of her gentle people. The bond that develops between her and Picard occurs so naturally and smoothly that it seems a shame they never share a kiss. There are other emotionally moving scenes in the film as well, such as when Geordi LaForge, who has been blind from birth, regains his eyesight as a result of the regenerative radiation. The final scene also includes a touching moment when Gallatin reunites with his mother in the Ba'ku village and she gives him a welcoming hug. Much of the character-driven humor in the film arises from the regenerative, youth-giving effects of the planet's rings, such as Worf's experiencing a phase of Klingon puberty (complete with a huge pimple on his nose) and the rekindling of an old romance between Troi and Riker. The humor of the film gives the story a more lighthearted

CREDITS

Captain Jean-Luc Picard: Patrick Stewart
Commander William Riker: Jonathan Frakes
Lieutenant Commander Data: Brent Spiner
Lieutenant Commander Geordi La Forge: LeVar Burton
Lieutenant Commander Worf: Michael Dorn
Dr. Beverly Crusher: Gates McFadden
Lieutenant Commander Deana Troi: Martina Sirtis
Ru'afo: F. Murray Abraham
Anij: Donna Murphy
Admiral Dougherty: Anthony Zerbe
Gallatin: Gregg Henry
Sojef: Daniel Hugh Kelly
Artim: Michael Welch

Origin: USA
Released: 1998
Production: Rick Berman; released by Paramount Pictures
Direction: Jonathan Frakes
Screenplay: Michael Piller
Cinematography: Matthew F. Leonetti
Editing: Peter E. Berger
Production design: Herman Zimmerman
Art direction: Ron Wilkinson
Set design: John M. Dwyer
Costumes: Sanja Milkovic Hays
Music: Jerry Goldsmith
Sound: Thomas Causey
MPAA rating: PG
Running Time: 100 minutes

tone that hearkens back more to the fun of *The Voyage Home* than to the darker, more somber *First Contact*.

One criticism aimed at *Insurrection* is that in some ways it seems more like a big-budget, extended television episode than a feature film, namely due to its plot. Several episodes of *The Next Generation*, in fact, involved storylines vaguely similar (in theme at least) to that of this movie. One tends to expect bigger villains and perhaps a more epic, grand-scale adventure in a feature film, but the comparison of the film to the plots of television episodes does not say much about its value as a dramatic story worthy of standing on its own merits. What can be said about *Insurrection*, however, and has been pointed out by some viewers, is that the film seems rather short. This impression highlights one weakness of the story, which is that it could have been extended a little more. The characters in the film are interesting enough, the performances are strong enough, the conflict is thought-provoking enough, and the overall story is enjoyable enough that additional development may have enhanced the movie's effectiveness. Perhaps the filmmakers rushed the story in order to make it move more quickly and have more of an "action-oriented" feel, but in the process the full dramatic potential of the film has been shortchanged somewhat.

—*David Flanagin*

REVIEWS

Boxoffice. November, 1998, p. 36.
Entertainment Weekly. December 18, 1998, p. 52.
New York Times. December 11, 1998, p. E14.
Sight and Sound. February, 1999, p. 55.
Variety. December 14, 1998, p. 131.
Village Voice. December 22, 1998, p. 138.

Stephen King's The Night Flier

Fly the deadly skies.—Movie tagline

"Never believe what you publish and never publish what you believe." These are the words of wisdom offered to cub reporter, Katherine Blair (Julie Entwisle) by the chronically cynical, yet persistent Richard Dees (Miguel Ferrer) in Stephen King's latest blood fest *Night Flier*. Perhaps these words are an insightful and revealing look into the author's own complex mind and words that he lives by himself. It's reassuring that he does not believe what he publishes or he might be in serious psychological jeopardy.

Dees is the star reporter for a newspaper/rag called "The Inside View." As he himself describes it: "it is an illustration of the insane, a diary of the deranged and dangerously sick." Its headlines cover such appetizing subjects as serial killers, UFO abductions, and tales of molestation, mayhem, and murder. It is not for the faint of heart (nor is the film, for that matter). Merton Morrison, the paper's editor, played with appropriate deviousness by Dan Monahan (of *Porky's* fame) has a hot new item that he wants Dees to investigate. It seems that there is a modern-day Dracula on the loose who calls himself Dwight Renfield (Michael H. Moss). He flies around in a black Cessna jet and lands on isolated airfields across America where he proceeds to create as much carnage as inhumanly possible. This sinister, shadowy figure is devoid of all human emotion in his demonic desire to inflict pain and his insatiable lust for blood. In short, he is the perfect subject for the cover of the ghoulish "Inside View."

Dees (played remarkably well by Ferrer) is the central character in this nightmarish environment. Dees smells journalistic gold and mutters such innocuous dialogue as, "You're gonna be my one way ticket back to the front page." (referring to Count Renfield). Dees also happens to fly around the country in search of his storylines in a Cessna jet of his own, except his is white. Is this some sort of a macabre coincidence or a symbolic parallel? More will be revealed! To complicate matters even more, Morrison (the editor) tries to pit Dees against fledgling reporter, Katherine Blair. At first, she tries to get Dees to warm up to her by exchanging office niceties to which Dees replies, "If you want a friend, go buy a dog." What a charmer! Undaunted by his overt hostility, Blair continues to search for clues on her own only to find that she's taken off the case (or so she thinks) and is forced to turn everything over to Dees.

The Stephen King short story was first published in the 1988 anthology *Prime Evil*.

In the meantime, the bodies are piling up and Dees takes off hot on the trail of his next cover story. The more persistent he becomes, the more gore Renfield creates and the body count mounts. As a calling card, this caped crusader leaves a pile of maggot infested dumpsites, not to mention human heads and dire warnings to Dees to "cease and desist—or else." The feud between the reporters becomes increasingly complicated and they both end up working on the same blood-stained story. Much of the film from this point on deals with the chase to get the scoop first and to take the story to the final scene. When the film reaches the climatic ending, it pulls out all the stops and the special effects department has a field day. There's actually not much that doesn't happen and as stated earlier, it is not for the faint of heart. Stephen King fans should appreciate the bedlam that takes place—a bird's eye view of hell.

"Startling, non-stop horror," so says the *Star Telegram* (Fort Worth). This should be welcome news to the many King followers who have been disappointed in the past. Since *Night Flier* was made to go directly to video (it opened

CREDITS

Richard Dees: Miguel Ferrer
Katherine Blair: Julie Entwisle
Merton Morrison: Dan Monahan
Dwight Renfield: Michael H. Moss

Origin: USA
Released: 1998
Production: Richard P. Rubenstein and Mitchell Galin for New Amsterdam Entertainment, Stardust International Ltd., and Medusa Film; released by New Line Cinema
Direction: Mark Pavia
Screenplay: Mark Pavia and Jack O'Donnell; based on a story by Stephen King
Cinematography: David Connell
Editing: Elizabeth Schwartz
Production design: Burton Rencher
Set design: Andrew Menzies
Costumes: Pauline White
Music: Brian Keane
Sound: Jay Meagher
MPAA rating: R
Running Time: 97 minutes

only on about 100 theatrical screens), it does not have the professional veneer of King's other successful screen adaptations. This one, however, does succeed on many levels and manages to create the appropriate atmosphere of evil and suspense. It utilizes pacing to its advantage and builds slowly (murder by murder) to the final showdown between Dees and Renfield. At this point it becomes the "clash of the Titans," only the Titans actually appear to be on the same side in a metaphorical way. Another interesting aspect to this film is the parallel that it makes to tabloid journalists and the focus on the sick and depraved. This topic was certainly highlighted with the recent death of Princess Diana and the role that the press may have played in causing the accident. The image of a group of news reporters flashing their cameras at the scene of the accident certainly made everyone, who had any kind of a moral conscience, shudder. Death and violence does seem to have gained a solid foothold in the media of late and this point is hard to miss in *Night Flier,* although some may argue that these types of films are part of the problem.

The film succeeds when it relies on the telling of a chilling story—building suspense and expectation. Its weakest moments are when it gets into the close-ups of the dis-

membered bodies and the eyes popping out of the faces frying on a griddle. At these points, it starts to look very much like Halloween in Los Angeles. The indication of unrealistic-looking special effects breaks the illusion and the spell is gone. Suddenly, as an audience member, you are transported into the studio prop room and taken on a tour. The experience is similar to visiting the haunted house exhibit at Disneyland. Perhaps, Stephen King is at his most scary when he lives in the imagination of his readers and not in close-ups. The evil that lurks in man's mind is by far more terrifying than any that can be conjured by the special affects department.

—*Jarred Cooper*

REVIEWS

Cinefantastique. April, 1998, p. 54.
Entertainment Weekly. February 20, 1998, p. 90.
Los Angeles Times. February 6, 1998, p. F10.
New York Times. February 6, 1998, p. E10.
Variety. February 9, 1998, p. 71.

Stepmom

Be there for the joy. Be there for the tears. Be there for each other.—Movie tagline

"The best performance by an actress this year, Susan Sarandon in *Stepmom.*"—Joel Siegel, *Good Morning America*

"One of the best films of the year! Wonderful, funny, emotional, and uplifting. Julia Roberts delivers the best performance of her career!" —Sara Edwards, *NBC-TV*

"Two extraordinary actresses ignite the screen!"—Susan Granger, *SSG Syndicate*

 Box Office: $83,619,000

Isabel (Julia Roberts) learns some parenting tips from rival Jackie (Susan Sarandon) in the family drama *Stepmom.*

There is no doubt that *Stepmom* is a "chick flick" weepie. It seems to be written with the obvious intent of playing just right so that the female members of the audience will whip out their handkerchiefs in unison.

Jackie (Susan Sarandon) and Luke (Ed Harris) must have been *the* ideal couple at one time. He's a lawyer and she gave up her career in publishing to stay at home and take care of their two children, twelve-year-old Anna (Jena Malone) and seven-year-old Ben (Liam Aiken). They have a postcard perfect home in the country, tastefully decorated and brimming with homemade foods and crafts. At least they used to have all this. Now, however, they are divorced. The kids still primarily live with Jackie, but Luke now lives with his younger girlfriend Isabel (Julia Roberts) in a trendy New York City loft, and has his children just on the weekends.

While Luke is very happy to be living with Isabel, he still tries to be friends with Jackie for the kids' sake, but Jackie is very embittered about their breakup, and she's determined to demean Isabel in her children's eyes as often as possible. She is too much of a lady, though, to come right out and call Isabel names, so she resorts to snide comments (as when she responds to Ben's question on whether Isabel is rich: "self-centered people often do make a lot of money") and mean little gestures (throwing the brown-bag lunches Isabel has made for the children into the trash) to further drive home to the kids what a terrible person Isabel is.

In reality, Isabel is the consummate professional, a top-of-the-line fashion photographer, but Jackie tries to make Isabel out as a woman so obsessed with her career that she has no maternal instincts, when in actuality, Isabel is doing the best she can to keep doing her job professionally while also dealing with the emotionally-charged situation that exists between Luke and Jackie.

And then there's those kids. Oh sure, divorce scars kids, but in all honesty, Ben is a brat and Anna is a bitch. Ben is into magic and even goes so far as to try and concoct a magic potion (cocoa) to make Isabel fall asleep for 100 years. And when she dozes off while reading to him in bed, he's ecstatic to think he's actually "killed" her. Anna is a spoiled brat whose impertinent mouth would win her a slap from most parents. These kids are self-absorbed, inconsiderate, and obnoxious, and if Jackie is supposed to be such a great mother, where did these spawn of hell come from?

All of Jackie's contempt for Isabel is confirmed one weekend when Isabel has to take both Anna and Ben with her on a photo shoot in Central Park. When Ben wanders away and gets lost, Isabel is frantic, and Jackie is incensed. Now she threatens to get a court order so Isabel is never left alone with her precious children again.

But on one afternoon, Jackie, the perfect mother, the woman who has all the children's activities color coded on post-it notes attached to the refrigerator, forgets to pick the children up after school. Isabel is called and selflessly tells the kids it was her fault—that she, not Jackie, had forgotten to pick them up. It is a friendly gesture Jackie ignores when she finally does show up at school. Later, when Isabel suggests that she and Anna might bond better if they went to a Pearl Jam concert, Jackie indignantly squashes the idea . . . only to buy the tickets for herself and Anna.

At this point the scriptwriters have to come up with something to make Jackie's character a little more sympa-

> Jackie (Susan Sarandon) to Isabel (Julia Roberts): "I have the children's past and you have their future."

thetic and to set the viewer up for the requisite emotionally satisfying reconciliation between the two women. Hey, let's give Jackie cancer. And let's make it terminal so Isabel will have a clear future with the kids. Jackie tries to hide her illness from her family, but you know they'll figure it out sooner or later, and this will lead to the kinder and gentler part of the film after all the anger and frustration during the first half. Now Isabel and Jackie will become friends instead of combatants.

Stepmom is a glossy formula film from director Chris Columbus (*Home Alone, Mrs. Doubtfire*) whose movies specialize in sentiment. In this production, he unabashedly opens the floodgates, and may the gods help anyone who can't swim. There is no doubt that his intention is to emotionally manipulate the viewer, and his skills as a director allow him to do it in a style that is very popular with audiences.

The writers of this story (and there were five of them—a sure sign of trouble) have resorted to virtually every cliché for this type of film, and they didn't even bother to look for new twists to carry them through. The characters are standard issue and painted in an ugly black or white. Maybe that's

CREDITS

Isabel Kelly: Julia Roberts
Jackie Harrison: Susan Sarandon
Luke Harrison: Ed Harris
Ben Harrison: Liam Aiken
Anna Harrison: Jena Malone
Dr. Sweikert: Lynn Whitfield
Duncan Samuels: Darrell Larson
School Counselor: Mary Louise Wilson

Origin: USA
Released: 1998
Production: Wendy Finerman, Chris Columbus, Mark Radcliffe, and Michael Barnathan for 1492 Productions; released by Columbia Pictures
Direction: Chris Columbus
Screenplay: Gigi Levangie, Jessie Nelson, Steven Rogers, Karen Leigh Hopkins, and Ron Bass
Cinematography: Donald M. McAlpine
Editing: Neil Travis
Production design: Stuart Wurtzel
Art direction: Raymond Kluga
Set decoration: George De Titta Jr.
Costumes: Joseph G. Aulisi
Music: John Williams
Sound: Tod Maitland
MPAA rating: PG-13
Running Time: 127 minutes

because it's easier for those being manipulated to see when the villains become heroes at the half-way point of the movie. It's easier than actually thinking. The fact that one of the writers, Gigi Levangie, supposedly became a stepmother in a way similar to the Julia Roberts's character doesn't even help to give the story the ring of truth. The reason is that the story is just too preachy, too easy to figure out, too superficial and trite a treatment of problems that all too many families can probably identify with.

What eventually saves *Stepmom* are the performances. Ed Harris is always a strong performer, it's just too bad his character is little more than a background prop for the two women and the kids. He's not given much to do. Julia Roberts once again shows that she is an amiable and popular actress and the performance she turns in here is solid—although her performance in *My Best Friend's Wedding* was a much better one. In reality, though, it is Susan Sarandon's film. She has played this Earth Mother type of role before (*Lorenzo's Oil, Little Women*) so it's not much of a stretch for her, but the problem for her character is that it is poorly written; it lacks the nuance and true believability that she is capable of bringing to more fully-created characters. So, considering the shallowness of the character, she still brings a high degree of acceptance to it because of her superior acting ability.

Stepmom is, by turns, overwrought and underdeveloped. It is shamelessly manipulative, calculatedly shifting between comedy and drama, between laughs and tears, as the writers deem fit, without so much as a thought for the audience. For those who prefer to be taught something in their movie-going experiences, *Stepmom* will be a disappointment. For those who just want to sit back and let someone else push their emotional buttons, *Stepmom* will work just fine. They should be warned to take along a big box of tissues. 🎞️

—*Beverley Bare Buehrer*

REVIEWS

Chicago Tribune. January 5, 1999.
Entertainment Weekly. January 8, 1999, p. 46.
Los Angeles Times. December 25, 1998.
New York Times. December 24, 1998.
People. January 11, 1999, p. 35.
San Francisco Chronicle. December 25, 1998.
San Francisco Examiner. December 25, 1998.
Sight and Sound. February, 1999, p. 56.
Variety. December 14, 1998, p. 131.
Village Voice. December 29, 1998, p. 122.

Still Crazy

They were called "Strange Fruit." Some called them the greatest rock band of the '70s. They haven't played together in 20 years. No wonder they're worried about their performance.—Movie tagline

A coming-of-middle-age comedy.—Movie tagline

". . . with the warmth, humor, and wisdom of *The Full Monty.*"–Kevin Thomas, *Los Angeles Times*

"The best British comedy of the year."—*Smash Hits/UK*

"The sleeper hit of the year!"—Paul Clinton, *Turner Entertainment Report*

The print ads for *Still Crazy* were a little misleading. The ads showed a guitar neck, drooping suggestively toward the ground, and lest the point be lost, there was the tagline "No wonder they're worried about their performance." It's too bad about jokey, wink-wink-nudge-nudge ads, because although they do convey the themes of the film—rock and roll and aging—they don't convey the right tone.

Still Crazy is a British film. These Brits wouldn't forsake the trademark, dry Brit humor to stoop to easy impotence jokes. Instead, *Still Crazy* is a wise, wry, tender look at aging rockers. There are jokes, of course, but they go beyond the obvious Viagra gags and are always tempered with affection for the characters.

Back in the 1970s, Tony Costello (Stephen Rea) was a keyboardist for the progressive rock and roll band, Strange Fruit. Now a guy who restocks condom vending machines in restrooms, Tony is only too happy to oblige when a young concert promoter invites the band to reunite for a big music festival. The only problem is that the band is no longer speaking to each other. What's left of them, that is. Original singer, Keith, is dead and his fragile brother, guitarist Brian (Bruce Robinson) has disappeared. And the rest of them are practically as big a challenge. Guitarist Les Wickes (Jimmy Nail) says he's happy to stay on at his job as a roofer and, besides, he's never really gotten over Keith's death. The replacement for Keith, the pompous, mystical lead singer Ray Simms (Bill Nighy) is busy on a solo record, or so his domineering wife

Astrid (Helena Bergstrom) insists. Fat, sloppy drummer "Beano" Baggot (Timothy Spall) is now working in a nursery and dodging the taxman.

But the guys quickly realize that they want to—need to—get back together again. Did they peak in their lives too early? Do they have what it takes to make it again? Along with old-time roadie, Hughie (Billy Connolly, from TV's *Head of the Class*) and their biggest fan-turned-manager, Karen Knowles (Juliet Aubrey), they set off to find out. Here the movie veers into *This Is Spinal Tap* territory, as the band suffers the many small and large indignities that confound low-level bands. Strange Fruit suffers the embarrassingly tiny gigs, getting ditched by an MTV-type reporter when a "cooler" band walks by, and having to pay for a broken ceiling pipe when Ray flails about too eagerly at a show.

It's the little touches in the movie that make this film ring true. When the guys get a touring bus, they are assured by Hughie that it's tops. "It has a first class collection of pornog-

Band manager Karen Knowles (Juliet Aubrey): "I still love their music, and I want to stand in the dark and see an audience feel the same way that I do."

Brian Gibson also directed the Tina Turner biopic *What's Love Got To Do With It?*

raphy, courtesy of the Psychedelic Furs," he says. When one band member is trying to remember something, another prods him with, "Remember we dropped some acid in the Druid's circle?" There are several quick flashbacks to the band's past that remind us that once upon a time in the '70s, it wouldn't have seemed at all corny to drop acid in a Druid's circle.

Another part of the realism is Strange Fruit's music. It's all original and was written by Chris Difford (Squeeze), Jeff Lynne (ELO, Traveling Wilburys), and Mick Jones (Foreigner). Their music sounds like it really did come from the 1970s—it's grandiose, mystical, and overdone.

Overall, the performances are outstanding. Juliet Aubrey's Karen fairly aches for the past and the thrill of being in love with music and Brian. The band members themselves all look so right, exactly like a once young and handsome band would look 20 years later. Stephen Rea's usual hang-dog expression works well for him here, giving him the look of an older Bob Geldof. Timothy Spall plays drummer "Beano" as a big, sloppy goof. "The Hollywood Bowl—that was a great gig," he reminisces. When a bandmate reminds him that they never played there, Beano pouts and says, "But that's one of my most favorites memories."

Best of all is Bill Nighy's amazing performance as aging lead singer Ray Simms. At first, it seems he has kept his rock star looks, but on closer inspection, it's more doubtful. Are those chiseled features or a drawn, hollowed face? Is that a lean frame or maybe frailty? Ray is at once a great performer and out-of-touch and pitiful. It is a rich performance, showing both Ray's extreme vanity and his admirable dignity in the face of the indignity of aging.

Like *This is Spinal Tap, Still Crazy* makes fun of the band, but in this film it's always tempered with a great affection and respect. *Still Crazy* is both a fun romp and send-up of rock and roll, and a fine, almost wistful, thought-provoking movie.

—*Jill Hamilton*

CREDITS

Tony Costello: Stephen Rea
Hughie: Billy Connolly
Les Wickes: Jimmy Nail
David "Beano" Baggot: Timothy Spall
Ray Simms: Bill Nighy
Karen Knowles: Juliet Aubrey
Astrid Simms: Helena Bergstrom
Brian Lovell: Bruce Robinson
Luke Shand: Hans Matheson

Origin: USA
Released: 1998
Production: Amanda Marmot for Greenlight Fund; released by Columbia TriStar Films
Direction: Brian Gibson
Screenplay: Dick Clement and Ian La Frenais
Cinematography: Ashley Rowe
Editing: Peter Boyle
Production design: Max Gottlieb
Art direction: Sarah-Jane Cornish
Costumes: Caroline Harris
Music: Clive Langer
Sound: Colin Nicolson
Casting: Gail Stevens
MPAA rating: R
Running Time: 95 minutes

REVIEWS

Daily Variety. November 4, 1998, p. 9.
Entertainment Weekly. February 5, 1999, p. 47.
Los Angeles Times. December 11, 1998, p. F20.
New York Times. January 22, 1999, p. E14.
People. February 1, 1999, p. 29.
Rolling Stone. February 4, 1998, p. 72.
Sight and Sound. November, 1998, p. 62.
Village Voice. January 26, 1999, p. 106.

Suicide Kings

It's all or nothing.—Movie tagline

Their plan was perfect . . . they weren't.—Movie tagline

"Slick and quirky entertainment."—*Harper's Bazaar*

"A brilliant, twisting plot that'll keep you on the edge of your seat."—*Mademoiselle*

"Walken gives a silky, hypnotic performance."
—*Movieline*

"A grabber, laced with sardonic humor."—*Playboy*

"A jagged, captivating first feature by director Peter O'Fallon"—*Village Voice*

Box Office: $1,740,156

A group of amateur criminals ponder their options in the quirky crime drama *Suicide Kings*.

*S*uicide Kings is a fast-paced comedic thriller that falls into the realm of pictures that pay homage to the oeuvre of Quentin Tarantino; yet *Kings* stands up to scrutiny as a witty, well-directed piece of filmmaking on its own merits. Although the plot treads on familiar territory—a botched kidnapping—*Kings* allows its impressive ensemble to flex their muscles with razor-sharp dialogue and succinct characterizations.

Director Peter O'Fallon's first feature foray (he has worked in television) exhibits dark humor, glib hit men, buckets of booze, and truckloads of attitude. Swinging into action immediately, the picture opens with suave, confident Charles Barrett (Christopher Walken) striding into a downtown bistro for his regular nightcap. Finding a group of college-age kids at his regular table he joins them for a drink (instead of giving them the boot) and the martinis and conversation flow freely. At the table are four old friends; Avery Casten (Henry Thomas), Brett Campbell (Jay Mohr), Max Minot (Sean Patrick Flannery), and T.K. (Jeremy Sisto). Avery is the spoiled son of wealthy parents, T.K. is a handsome pre-med student, Max is madly in love with Avery's sister, Lisa (Laura Harris), and Brett is the very picture of an obnoxious young yuppie. When Avery rises to leave to meet his father for dinner, he offers to give all of the guys and Charlie a ride crosstown. Although Charlie has other plans, he is charmed by these young toughs—they remind him of his own youthful arrogance.

However, once Charlie is in the car, the boys spring into a carefully rehearsed plan. T.K. injects Charlie with a sedative, rendering him unconscious—but not before the doped-up mobster manages to kick out windows and send the Mercedes spinning in traffic. Charlie awakens in a deserted mansion, taped to a chair, with one of his fingers cut off. It seems that Avery's sister, Lisa, has been kidnapped and the boys need a $2 million windfall to get her back. Avery explains that he can't go to his father for the money, so they are appealing to Charlie's underworld connections (the finger is in exchange for a finger of Lisa's that they have supposedly received). While Charlie is trying to process all of this information, the proceedings are interrupted by Ira (Johnny Galecki), whose home they are using. Predictably, nerdy Ira is incensed by the actions going on—and by the fact that the guys are drinking his dad's liquor and putting their feet on the furniture.

Charlie phones his trusty lawyer Marty (Cliff De Young) who goes about raising the money and trying to find out who both sets of kidnappers are. Marty calls one of Charlie's henchmen, Lono (Denis Leary), who applies his formidable detective powers—and his short temper—to the case. In the meantime, Charlie, strapped to the chair, has nothing to do but pick at his tormentors and try to undermine them at their own game.

Marty (Cliff De Young): "Don't go dying on me. Remember, I'm a lawyer. I've got friends in hell."

When the boys' plan starts to unravel (they have neglected to think certain things through—such as how Charlie's men are supposed to contact them when they have gathered the money), Charlie roars with derisive laughter "You didn't think this thing through too good, did you?" Or as he snidely tells Marty, "Listen to me—don't send your kids to boarding school." This is a plum role for Walken, who excels in playing these maniacal, over-the-top characters; he shines in almost every scene, and is very generous with all the younger actors. It is a pleasure to watch him operate.

Brett emerges as the hothead leader of the group, despite the fact that the kidnap victim is Avery's sister and Max's lover. Charlie receives information from Marty that indicates that this kidnapping may be engineered by an "inside" party. Charlie takes this information and runs with it, planting this tidbit in T.K.'s mind. One by one, Charlie plays all the guys for suckers, pulling information out of them, pitting one against the other. A self-aware mobster is at times a psychologist, and he correctly hones in on everyone's weaknesses. Cocky as they seem, they are no match for someone as snake-like and tenacious as Charlie; when it's pointed out that they have the upper hand, and Charlie seems to be tied down to a chair, the experienced mobster even has the confidence to laugh along with them. He knows, as does the audience, that it's only a matter of time until he regains control.

Meanwhile, Lono is piecing together the puzzle on the streets, using a wonderful array of actors performing cameos.These scenarios range from the frightening (Lono saves a good girl [Nina Siemaszko] from her abusive stepfather) to the hilarious (prostitute-turned-madam Lydia [Laura San Giacomo] recalls how Charlie saved her from her brutal pimp and helped her go out on her own). It's worth the price of admission to see Walken in badass "Superfly" clothing and platform shoes, mugging and dancing.

Director O'Fallon keeps the action moving, despite the fact that the great majority of the film takes place in one location, the mansion. Credit goes to his cinematographer Christopher Baffa, whose fluid, stylish images heighten the sharpness of the action and give form to the many flashbacks.

As T.K. predictably lets the "insider" information loose among the guys, nerves shatter and fray. All of the younger actors get a chance to shine, particularly Mohr and Thomas (Thomas is quickly shaping up to be the most versatile young actor of his generation, stretching his range from the ubiquitous *E.T.* as a child to high caliber TV fare such as *The McMartin Trial* and *Moby Dick* to offbeat independent material such as last year's *Niagara, Niagara*). Avery reveals to Charlie that he has kidnapped his sister himself to offset a horrific college gambling debt. Charlie watches the boys scramble and freak—all except Max, who calmly directs the ransom money to the correct venue. Charlie astutely gathers that boyfriend Max has dirty hands as well.

At the break of dawn Lono breaks into the mansion to rescue Charlie (quite in the nick of time, as Charlie's advanced alcoholism is wrecking havoc with the drugs he has been given) and fires off a round of shots to scare the guys. Avery rushes to the hospital where his sister will supposedly be dropped off. When Lisa is nowhere to be found, a quick series of cuts show Lisa and someone else—a man—boarding a boat and taking flight by sea.

Once recovered (with his severed finger successfully reattached) Charlie and Lono put the pieces of the puzzle together to get the money back. It isn't long before they land on Avery's father's yacht and find Max and Lisa sunning in the warm California sun. Under pressure, Lisa admits that the entire scenario was her idea. Just as Lono is about to kill both Lisa and Max, Charlie compliments Max on his choice of women; Charlie has to admire anyone as ruthless and greedy as himself.

Despite a few holes in the screenplay—and a few diversions into subplots that exist for no other reason except to get a laugh or two—the action moves at a taut pace. Walken and Leary emerge as extremely fair and likeable gangsters, as one always hopes gangsters would be. Johnny Galecki's wimpy Ira benefits from his encounter with Walken; Walken compliments him on his sense of decency and fair play—something that he has obviously never gotten from his family or his friends. One character has at least come through intact and better for the experience.

—G. E. Georges

CREDITS

Charles Barrett: Christopher Walken
Lono Vecchio: Denis Leary
Avery Chasten: Henry Thomas
Max Minot: Sean Patrick Flanery
Brett Campbell: Jay Mohr
T.K.:   Jeremy Sisto
Ira Reder: Johnny Galecki
Lydia: Laura San Giacomo
Marty: Cliff De Young

Origin: USA
Released: 1997
Production: Wayne Rice and Morrie Eisenman for Eyes 'n' Rice; released by Live Entertainment
Direction: Peter O'Fallon
Screenplay: Wayne Rice and Gina Goldman
Cinematography: Christopher Baffa
Editing: Chris Peppe
Production design: Clark Hunter
Art direction: Max Briscoe
Music: Graeme Revell
Sound: Eric Enroth
MPAA rating: R
Running Time: 106 minutes

REVIEWS

Boxoffice. October, 1997, p. 38.
Entertainment Weekly. May 1, 1998, p. 39.
Los Angeles Times. April 17, 1998, p. F10.
New York Times. April 17, 1998, p. E26.
Variety. September 22, 1997, p. 39.

Swept From the Sea

In the heart of an outcast, he found his destiny. In the passion of an outsider, she found her home.—Movie tagline

"Beautiful! Hypnotic!"—Jim Svejda, *CBS Radio*

"Passionate . . . A tale of pure love."—David Sheehan, *CBS-TV*

"An inspired romance that sweeps you away. Rachel Weisz is captivating and Vincent Perez wins your heart."—Alan Silverman, *Hollywood Bytes*

"A superb, epic and moving romance."—Paul Wunder, *WBAI Radio*

"A gorgeous film that's everything you want a film to be. Romantic, touching, and just plain wonderful."—Dr. Joy Browne, *WOR Radio*

Creating a successful historical drama is a chancy thing. Beautiful, atmospheric scenery helps. Superb character actors in support help even more. But too much depends on the plausibility of the leads, which is where *Swept From the Sea* falters. What might have been an intriguing reading of a minor Joseph Conrad novella ("Amy Foster") becomes a pretty-looking excuse for a love story. It's too bad, because a superb performance by Ian McKellen is swamped by the silliness surrounding him.

Swept From the Sea has a lyrical, promising beginning—the camera moves over the waves and up a sheer cliff to fix on a young woman and a boy looking out to sea. Mother and son are hypnotized by the sight: "You come from the sea," she says fondly. They are called back to earth by an old man in a buggy, Mr. Swaffer (Joss Ackland), who comes to fetch Amy Foster (Rachel Weisz) to attend to the bedside of his gravely ill daughter. Amy dutifully returns to the bedside of Miss Swaffer (Kathy Bates), but as she prepares to nurse her patient, Dr. Kennedy (Ian McKellen) arrives and abruptly dismisses her. The patient objects to the gruff behavior of the doctor, and insists he reveal the source of his animus against the girl. Reluctantly, Kennedy begins the tale of Amy Foster.

Kennedy's musings reveal that Amy barely interests him, which is in keeping with Conrad's story—the doctor describes the "inertness of her mind." Rachel Weisz, predictably, hardly resembles Conrad's Amy as described: "her dull face, red, not with a mantling blush, but as if her flat cheeks had been vigorously slapped, and to take in the squat figure, the scanty, dusty brown hair drawn into a tight knot at the back of the head." Her very beauty takes away one of the most interesting aspects of the plot, for her lover is certainly intended to be handsome by Conrad and in the person of Vincent Perez he is suitably so, though his long hair and peasant shirts make him look suspiciously like the cover of a bodice-ripping romance novel.

Kennedy actually tells the story of Yanko Gooral, the lone survivor of an immigrant ship bound for America that is shipwrecked off the Cornish coast. He begins with a rather clichéd scene of zesty bearded men and babushka-wearing women chanting and dancing—this noisy vignette of his Ukrainian family and friends the night before Yanko sets out for America is nonetheless the liveliest this solemn film will get. Arriving by train in Hamburg, Yanko is bewildered by the dark nastiness of the immigrant trafficking—he hails a friend from his village "To America!," and it takes little imagination to sense this is their last meeting. As Kennedy's voice describes Yanko's plight, the camera peers into the hold of the ship, full of retching, sobbing people, and when he falls overboard, it is a relief from the claustrophobic misery of the doomed ship.

One of the film's strongest scenes reveals a grim assembly of the dead washed ashore; as Conrad put it, "by the afternoon you could see along three miles of beach dark figures with bare legs dashing in and out of the tumbling foam, and rough-looking men, women with hard faces, children, most fair-haired, were being carried, stiff and dripping, on stretchers, on wattles, on ladders, in a long procession past the door of the 'Ship Inn,' to be laid out in a row under the north wall of the Brenzett Church." Dr. Kennedy stands among the bodies, silently assessing the nameless dead, hoping for a sign of life. McKellen's refinement and perfect pitch make Kennedy most affecting in his scenes and if Conrad's intent survives this glossy makeover, it is largely his doing.

When a battered and disoriented Yanko stumbles off the beach and finds his way to the Smith farm, he is taken for an escaped lunatic. He first spies Amy standing at a window, and they gaze into each others' eyes in a brief moment punctuated by Mrs. Smith's hysterical screams. Amy, thought slow and odd by all, has one signal quality—a tender heart. She defends the man and is rebuked as the farmer locks the pleading "madman" in a barn. Later, she sneaks out to feed him and dress his wounds. They communicate largely by actions and by long, searching looks, which are well-played. At the end of the film, after too much exposure to Perez's attempts at an Eastern European accent, these seem refreshing in retrospect. Yanko, desperately grateful for her kindness, is instantly smitten. If Amy were the plain woman Conrad created whose only grace was her kind heart, *Swept* would have more force. As it is, it's "Wuthering Heights Lite" with a beautiful pair of star-crossed lovers who need an "English in 7 Days" Berlitz class in the worst way.

Dr. Kennedy accidentally discovers that the so-called madman is in fact a foreigner and a castaway, and he befriends Yanko. Their chess games and conversations allow both to express their frustration with the thick-witted and intolerant townspeople, and of course, the lonely older man feels jealous when Yanko courts Amy, whom he considers beneath him. Amy has another life, a secret "home" in a cave by the sea where she takes her lover. She even vamps him a bit with a shawl, suddenly more animated. Here she keeps her treasures washed up by the sea, of which Yanko is the most recent. Oddly, she calls him "my pretty" as Yanko is supposed to be the attractive one.

Despite a savage beating precipitated by Amy's poisonous father (Tom Bell), Yanko is determined to marry her, and the Swaffers help by giving them a cottage. When their son is born, Yanko is jubilant; however, tragedy is about to reclaim the pair. During a violent storm, Yanko, weakened by pneumonia, becomes delirious and threatens Amy and the baby. Terrified, unable to understand as he raves in Ukrainian, Amy runs out into the storm with the child. By the time she has fought her way to the Swaffers miles away (after having sought help in vain from her mother and a neighbor), she returns to find Kennedy trying to revive the dying Yanko. More lucid now, he asks why Amy left him: "I only asked for a little water!" He expires and the sorrowing Kennedy turns away as Amy presses her lips to his in a grim last kiss. "Why did you leave him?" Kennedy demands. Amy seems not to be able to say.

Concluding his narrative, he remarks bitterly, "She did not take care for him." Miss Swaffer demurs, asking him gently, "Did your own love blind you to hers?" Absurdly, the contrivance of the screenplay forces the doctor to go to Amy and seek her forgiveness. Conrad's own ending finds Yanko's son the only trace left of him—there is no such neat and wistful ending, and the doctor is left with his resentment and sorrow.

Weisz's emotional range is severely restricted by the screenplay, which as the film would have it, is a girl completely misunderstood by her family and the entire village. Amy's remote mien and few words cause some to call her a witch, and her moody staring at the sea only adds to the impression that something is "wrong" with her. This is a real misstep by writer Tim Willocks, and only muddles what might have been affecting if left alone. By far, the most ruinous element of the plot is the family drama of the Fosters: Amy is rejected but used by her parents, a haggard pair who seem intent on keeping her from marriage with Yanko. Even strong performances by Zoe Wanamaker and Tom Bell don't help explain why the Fosters treat Amy so shamefully—that's left to Wanamaker to reveal in a concocted moment meant to be devastating ("He's your brother, not your father!") but is oddly irrelevant, just as the "witch" storyline is. Wanamaker does get a nice chance to hiss, "Bad you were conceived and bad you have remained!" making the best of the often embarrassing dialogue.

Many reviewers took the screenplay to task for leaving it to McKellen to insinuate the doctor's love for Yanko, and once again, what is primarily used as a plot device might have given the script some energy and tension. The elegant and expressive scenes that McKellen has with Perez give a hint of what might have been possible in a script less insistent to being a conventional romance. There is very little heat generated by their love, only angst. Critics were not kind to *Swept From the Sea*, and it sank quickly.

UK critic Patrick Humphries offered this assessment: "Still, those addicted to the fulminating fusion of corset and countryside should find just about enough to sate their appetites." Director Beeban Kidron (*To Wong Foo, Thanks for Everything, Julie Newmar* [1995]) fails to pull this off because she lacks the courage to make *Swept* less pretty and more challenging. Had she and Willocks stuck closer to "Amy Foster," the film might have had a chance to honestly speak to its audience.

—*Mary Hess*

CREDITS

Yanko Goorall: Vincent Perez
Amy Foster: Rachel Weisz
Dr. James Kennedy: Ian McKellen
Mr. Swaffer: Joss Ackland
Miss Swaffer: Kathy Bates
Isaac Foster: Tom Bell
Mary Foster: Zoe Wanamaker
William Smith: Tony Haygarth

Origin: Great Britain
Released: 1998
Production: Polly Tapson, Charles Steel, and Beeban Kidron for Phoenix Pictures, Greenlight Fund, and Tapson Steel Films; released by TriStar Pictures
Direction: Beeban Kidron
Screenplay: Tim Willocks; inspired by the short story "Amy Foster" by Joseph Conrad
Cinematography: Dick Pope
Editing: Alex Mackie, Andrew Monshein
Production design: Simon Holland
Art direction: Gordon Toms
Costumes: Caroline Harris
Music: John Barry
Sound: George Richards
MPAA rating: PG-13
Running Time: 115 minutes

REVIEWS

Boxoffice. November, 1997, p. 123.
Chicago Tribune. January 23, 1998, p. 5.
Entertainment Weekly. February 6, 1998, p. 42.
Los Angeles Times. January 23, 1998, p. F12.
New York Times. January 23, 1998, p. E10.
People. February 16, 1998, p. 20.
Sight and Sound. May, 1998, p. 40.
USA Today. January 30, 1998, p. 7D.
Variety. September 15, 1997, p. 78.

Talk of Angels

Some passions cross all boundaries—Movie tagline

"A stirring, romantic film filled with rich humor and vivid performances!"—David Noh, *Film Journal International*

"A lush and dazzling romance! Polly Walker is ravishing!"—Stephen Farber, *Movieline*

Box Office: $22,422

A forbidden love between Spanish aristocrat Francisco Areavaga (Vincent Perez) and Irish governess Mary Lavelle (Polly Walker) is the centerpiece for the sweeping *Talk of Angels*.

Talk of Angels is Gothic romance at its most bland. Replete with a beautiful and spirited young governess, an aristocratic family living on an isolated estate, a few adoring children, and a troubled, though dashing, love interest, burdened by his ambitious but frigid wife. The plot reads like a Harlequin romance novel and is just as predictable. The story line is so formulaic that even the few modern twists in the story can not redeem the film's hackneyed theme. Yet viewers often forgive cliche'-driven films, so the romance genre is rife with them. But what is unforgivable is the total absence of sexual tension between the lovers.

Based on the novel *Mary Lavelle* by Kate O' Brien, *Talk of Angels* tells the story of Mary (Polly Walker), an Irish governess who has been sent to northern Spain to teach English to the daughters of the wealthy Dr. Areavaga (Franco Nero). It is 1936 and Spain is on the brink of civil war, and Mary enters a home that is as politically divided as the country itself. Dr. Areavaga and his son Francisco's (Vincent Perez) sympathies are with the Popular Front, while both their wives are pro-fascist. The men keep their allegiance a secret until the new governess finds a wounded protester hiding in the stable. The protester finds a willing conspirator in Mary, and when Francisco returns home to the family estate, the doctor lets him know that she is on their side.

Francisco has left his government post in Madrid to work against Franco and the military, clandestinely meeting with others to plan a demonstration in Madrid. This alienates him from his wife, Beatriz (Ariadna Gil), who leaves him, but Francisco soon finds political and emotional support in Mary's open arms.

When the novel, *Mary Lavelle,* was first published in the '30s, it stirred up a firestorm of controversy in two countries. It was banned in Ireland for its portrayal of adultery, and the Franco regime prevented O'Brien from ever re-

Kate O'Brien's novel *Mary Lavelle* was banned in Ireland upon its publication.

turning to Spain because of her anti-fascist stance in the novel. Unlike the novel, *Talk of Angels* is bereft of anything that could be even misconstrued as controversy.

Although we are to believe that the story takes place in the 1930s, the characters seem absolutely Victorian in their behavior. Francisco gazes at Mary from afar, sometimes even needing binoculars, and except for one dance in the town square, there is so little contact between the two, that when they finally do get together for a tryst, it feels like somebody lost a reel of film.

Perhaps the greatest problem is in the casting. Polly Walker as Mary is expected to play a demure, convent-bred girl, when she actually is a stunning woman. All the downcast eyes and thumb biting in the world can not disguise that fact. The story is about a girl blossoming into a woman, but Walker begins the film in full bloom.

Her love interest is played by Vincent Perez, who is a lithe, handsome young man who doesn't even look like a suitable dance partner for Walker, much less her lover. There is no chemistry between the two, and this becomes even more apparent when she has scenes with Franco Nero, who plays the father. When these two play a scene there is more sexual energy on the screen than in any of the love scenes with Perez.

This is not to say that they are not a handsome couple. All of the characters in the film, save the lecherous priest,

Don Jorge (Francisco Rabal), are beautiful. The children are beautiful, the people in the street are beautiful, the sets are beautiful, the costumes are beautiful, even the corpses in the morgue are beautiful. It is a beautifully vapid film, full of lovely vignettes that leave the viewer unaffected.

This is especially distressing in a film so full of talent. Cinematographer Alexei Rodionov has captured the excitement of a bullfight, the magnificence of Spanish scenery, and the confusion of political upheaval with a masterly use of light and color.

CREDITS

Mary Lavelle: Polly Walker
Francisco Areavaga: Vincent Perez
Dr. Vicente Areavaga: France Nero
Dona Consuelo: Marisa Paredes
Milagros: Leire Berrocal
Pilar: Penelope Cruz
Conlon: Frances McDormand
O'Toole: Ruth McCabe
Don Jorge: Francisco Rabal

Origin: Great Britain
Released: 1998
Production: Patrick Cassavetti for Polaris Pictures Ltd.; released by Miramax Films
Direction: Nick Hamm
Screenplay: Ann Guedes and Frank McGuinness; based on the novel *Mary Lavelle* by Kate O'Brien
Cinematography: Alexei Rodionov
Editing: Gerry Hambling
Production design: Michael Howells
Art direction: Eduardo Hidalgo
Costumes: Liz Waller, Lala Huete
Music: Trevor Jones
Sound: Peter Glossop
Casting: Mary Selway
MPAA rating: PG-13
Running Time: 96 minutes

Frances McDormand brings an intensity to her small role as the free-spirited nanny Conlon, who develops a crush on Mary. But her talent is sadly underutilized, and her role serves no other purpose in the film than to modernize this Gothic tale. Another wasted performance is that of O'Toole (Ruth McCabe), the aging romantic who is treated like a simpering fool until the end of the film, when, ennobled by marriage, she shares her new-found wisdom with Mary. Both these performances seem to be simple backdrop and lead nowhere. If they could have been better integrated into the film's story line they might have added the needed depth that the film lacks. Instead there is no depth, no building of tension between the lovers, and even the long-delayed first kiss has on impact.

This feature debut of West End theater director Nick Hamm seems more a tribute to other films, than an original work. In a scene where Mary is looking for Francisco among the wounded or dying in a square, *Gone With the Wind* (1939) comes to mind. As she reads to the young girls as they cling to her in her bed, one half expects her to belt out "My Favorite Things." Discovering the wounded man in the stable, and sharing in the doctor's secret was like Jane Eyre promising not to tell about Emma Poole's nocturnal walks.

By the end of *Talk of Angels*, the viewer is left with only a loose string of beautiful scenes, as forgettable as a sunset.

—*Diane Hatch-Avis*

REVIEWS

Boxoffice. September, 1998, p. 118.
Hollywood Reporter. October 26, 1998, p. 6.
Los Angeles Times. October 20, 1998, p. F12.
People. November 9, 1998, p. 35.
Variety. October 26, 1998, p. 42.

Tarzan and the Lost City

A new Tarzan for a new generation.—Movie tagline

Box Office: $2,172,941

John Clayton/Tarzan: Casper Van Dien
Jane Porter: Jane March
Nigel Ravens: Steven Waddington
Mugambi: Winston Ntshona
Kaya: Rapulana Seiphemo
Capt. Dooley: Ian Roberts

Origin: USA
Released: 1998
Production: Stanley Canter, Dieter Geissler, and Michael Lake for Village Roadshow and Clipsal Film Partnership; released by Warner Bros.
Direction: Carl Schenkel
Screenplay: Bayard Johnson and J. Anderson Black; based on the stories by Edgar Rice Burroughs
Cinematography: Paul Gilpin
Editing: Harry Hitner
Production design: Herbert Pinter
Art direction: Emilia Roux, Anna Lennox
Visual effects supervision: Julian Parry
Costumes: Jo Katsaras-Barklem
Music: Christopher Franke
Sound: Colin McFarlane
MPAA rating: PG
Running Time: 105 minutes

If you view *Tarzan and the Lost City* in the spirit of an old-fashioned Saturday adventure matinee, this jungle movie will provide a pleasant passage of time. A crawl briefly explains that John Clayton was raised in the African jungle and given the name "Tarzan" by the natives. He is, however, English aristocracy (Lord Greystoke) and eventually returns to England for his education. In 1913, Clayton (Casper Van Dien) is at his bachelor party when he sees a vision—the spiritual leader of the native tribe that befriended him, Mugambi (Winston Ntshona), calls Tarzan back to defend his home from a marauding band of poachers and thieves. They are led by Nigel Ravens (Steven Waddington), who has stolen a sacred amulet and is mounting an expedition to the mystical lost city of Opar and its legendary treasure.

John's fiancee, Jane Porter (Jane March), doesn't take his leaving her a week before their wedding with very good grace but she soon follows him to Africa. Unfortunately, Jane first meets Ravens who attempts to charm her. Tarzan's already had a run-in with Ravens, who tried to persuade the "Ape Man" to join forces with him. When Ravens learns Tarzan is Jane's betrothed, he plans to kidnap her, but Tarzan gets to her first and, with a lot of vine-swinging and some sappy romantic music, introduces her to the beauties of the jungle and his treehouse abode. (He even has a pet chimpanzee who is, mercifully, only a brief part of the story and is not called Cheetah.) Jane is also introduced to Mugambi and Kaya (Rapulana Seiphemo), a rather impatient chieftain's son who believes Tarzan has gone soft and that the tribe doesn't need his help.

Meanwhile, Ravens and his motley crew have begun their expedition to Opar, with Tarzan and Jane trailing them. When Tarzan is bitten by a cobra, Jane leads Ravens and his men away from her beloved but is captured. Until now the story and adventures have been pretty straightforward—there's your usual elephant-riding, vine-swinging, and hand-to-

Ravens (Steven Waddington) to Tarzan (Casper Van Dien) on reaching legendary Opar: "The cradle of civilization and nobody, not one person, believed in me."

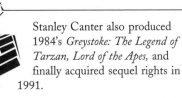

Stanley Canter also produced 1984's *Greystoke: The Legend of Tarzan, Lord of the Apes*, and finally acquired sequel rights in 1991.

hand combat—but some supernatural elements make their appearance. A swarm of bees cover the fallen Tarzan, preventing Ravens's men from seeing him, but when the coast is clear, the "bees" turn into Mugambi who magically heals our hero. When Tarzan wakes up, he's dressed in his de rigueur loincloth and has his trusty bow and quiver of arrows.

Ravens and his men (and the captured Jane) find the gateway to Opar and manage to dynamite it open before they're attacked by Kaya and his tribe. Tarzan follows Ravens into the entrance, as, eventually, does Kaya himself. Tarzan frees Jane and then the magically-appearing Magumbi conjures up some spirit warriors to help the good guys fight back. However, Ravens escapes to a temple anteroom with Tarzan in pursuit and, though wounded in the ensuing fight with Tarzan, crawls into

Opar's ancient throne room and drags himself to sit on the throne. This is a mistake, since the unseen guardians of Opar do not take kindly to this interloper and some sacred lightning basically turns Ravens into dust and sucks him up out of the city. It seems kind of a letdown that Tarzan doesn't get to finish the job himself and bring Ravens to justice. Instead, he has to settle for a jungle wedding to Jane and your basic happy ever after.

March's Jane is a spirited character (although the actress is a frail-looking thing), who takes to life in the jungle (except for the snakes) and does her best to help her man out rather than just getting in his way. Van Dien's got the proper physique (no flab on this Tarzan) and the requisite acrobatic action skills, as well as a not half-bad Lord of the Apes yell (and he talks in complete sentences), but this role can't be considered a big intellectual challenge. Filmed in South Africa, the beautiful locations are a definite plus.

—*Christine Tomassini*

REVIEWS

Boxoffice. June, 1998, p. 77.
Cinescape. May, 1998, p. 36.
Detroit Free Press. April 25, 1998, p. 2A.
Entertainment Weekly. May 8, 1998, p. 52.
Los Angeles Times. April 27, 1998, p. F4.
New York Times. April 25, 1998.
Variety. April 27, 1998, p. 59.

The Theory of Flight

"A beguiling romantic comedy that becomes another personal triumph for its stars, Helena Bonham Carter and Kenneth Branagh."—Kevin Thomas, *Los Angeles Times*

"A sweet, charming love story."—Anne Marie O'Connor, *Mademoiselle*

"Funny, intelligent and deeply poignant. Helena Bonham Carter gives a tour de force performance. Kenneth Branagh is outstanding." —Stephen Farber, *Movieline*

"An original and funny film!"—Jeannie Williams, *USA Today*

A flimsy exercise in sentimental uplift, Paul Greengrass's *The Theory of Flight* stars real-life couple Helena Bonham Carter and Kenneth Branagh in the story of a friendship between a physically disabled woman and a psychologically scarred painter. While Richard Hawkins's script introduces potentially compelling issues of disability and sexual desire, the narrative is underwritten and the characters reduced to clichés.

At the beginning of the film, Richard (Kenneth Branagh) is perched on the roof of a building in full flying gear, including a wing-like apparatus made from his old artwork. In a brief flashback, we see that Richard is a frustrated artist destroying his studio and making life miserable for his girlfriend, Julie (Holly Aird). She tries to get him to come down from the roof, but instead he attempts flight, crashes down, and is sentenced to 120 hours of community service. The first and perhaps biggest problem with *The Theory of Flight* is the character of Richard. He has obviously experi-

enced a breakdown of sorts and suffers from some malaise, but we never learn his exact problem or feel his sense of desperation. True to formula, though, we can rest assured that his community service will heal whatever is ailing him.

His community service project is Jane (Helena Bonham Carter), a plucky young woman confined to a wheelchair and suffering from Motor Neuron Disease. She is in the final stages, and, while she is alert mentally, her voice is deteriorating. Indeed, it is sometimes difficult to make out all of her words, and, when she needs to give big speeches, she communicates through messages she records on her speech machine. Bonham Carter is denied the chance to deliver her most impassioned pleas in her own voice, but, if she did, it is unlikely we would be able to understand all of her words.

Richard rents a dilapidated barn and begins putting together a primitive flying machine. In an attempt to transform his old failures into something new, he uses his old canvases for the plane's wings. When he finally explains his obsession to Jane, he tells her that flight was just something he knew nothing about but thought he should try since it seemed important. This feels like a very weak, arbitrary rationale for one of the major plot lines of the film, especially since flight is supposed to be the protagonist's obsession. Moreover, because we never sense that he has passion for what he is doing, we never feel invested in his plan.

There are of course metaphoric implications regarding flight and the notion of soaring above the earth, and the film hammers away at them. Indeed, one of the most glaring weaknesses of the screenplay is that, instead of allowing such themes to develop organically out of the situations, the characters make grand pronouncements. When Richard tries to fly at the beginning, he tells us in voice-over that he hoped to take what was "keeping me down and to try to reinvent it into something that would get me up." He also says that he wanted to "get my life off the ground." At the end, just in case we did not get the message, Jane spells out the metaphor when she declares, "Taking flight has more than one meaning."

The plot follows the general outline we would expect. Richard and Jane go from uneasiness and distrust to a kind of tenderness and respect, and finally, friendship and the hint of love. Richard is uncomfortable at first and does not know what to do with Jane. They go to a museum, a carnival, and a restaurant, but their relationship only gains a kind of focus when she asks him to help her lose her virginity. Before she was struck with her disease, as a teenager she passed on an opportunity to have sex with her boyfriend. She has regretted it ever since and now wants to do it before she dies.

Jane's Motor Neuron Disease is better known in the U.S. as Lou Gehrig's Disease or ALS (Amyotrophic Lateral Sclerosis).

Richard at first refuses to help Jane and even does community service for other people, but these assignments involve unpleasant tasks like cleaning a blocked toilet. The man Richard is renting the barn from wants him to leave soon, and he is having trouble with the airplane, so he decides to help Jane in her mission. Agencies for the disabled will not help, and a seedy nightclub for the disabled does not appeal to Jane, who wants her experience to be special, so they finally go to a fancy hotel where Richard propositions a gigolo. Because the price is too high, Richard decides to rob a bank for Jane. While we are supposed to believe Richard is a little off-balance, this plan reveals him to be plain nuts. When he declares that he "can't reinvent something by adapting what's gone before," but rather must be bold and radical, Richard is talking as if he were a philosopher making a profound statement, but it is really just one more meaningless platitude.

The pacing becomes very sluggish as we wait for the big day. Richard practices his robbery technique, and, in anticipation of her sexual encounter, Jane wears a beautiful red dress, which is somehow sad and unsettling. She makes a final plea via her speech machine for Richard to have sex with her, but he cannot bring himself to do it and so proceeds with the robbery plan.

While he heads to the bank, the gigolo is with Jane, and the two events are crosscut to form a bizarre sequence. Richard, wearing a stocking over his face, runs into Julie and points his firearm at her until he panics and flees; meanwhile, Jane is screaming in pain with the gigolo on top of her. Richard returns and throws out the gigolo, who says nothing has happened. The juxtaposition of Jane's pain and Richard's silly escapade is not provocative but just distasteful. The script should either have followed through the serious implications of a disabled young woman searching for

sexual fulfillment or simply made the whole enterprise a farce, but playing it both ways makes one feel queasy. Richard finally calms Jane down, and, when he asks her how she feels, she answers, "Like a virgin."

In the aftermath of Richard's botched robbery, Julie confronts Richard, and he gets rid of her by pretending Jane is his girlfriend. Probably meant as a moment of screwball comedy, the scene simply falls flat. Since Julie is actually a sympathetic character, we never understand what prompts Richard's constant rejection and cruelty to her.

The film does have a few moments of humor, like Jane suggesting she and Richard go bungee jumping together and later recommending that he steal ladies' handbags before trying bank robbery, but overall the script is very thin. The filmmakers try to cover up the lack of a decent plot with several musical interludes—songs set to activities like Richard working on his plane and Richard and Jane racing around a supermarket and later living it up in a fancy hotel room when they go to the big city for sex.

In the film's climax, Richard flies his plane, and Jane insists on flying with him, although she is not sure why she must do this (obviously the script demands that they share a big moment of triumph). They remain airborne for a while and then crash, which prompts Jane to beg him to put his life together so she can die in peace. Richard seems moved by her words, but Branagh's acting is not convincing since

CREDITS

Jane: Helena Bonham Carter
Richard: Kenneth Branagh
Anne: Gemma Jones
Julie: Holly Aird
Gigolo: Ray Stevenson

Origin: Great Britain
Released: 1998
Production: Helena Spring, Ruth Caleb, David M. Thompson, and Anant Singh for Distant Horizon and BBC Films; released by Fine Line Features
Direction: Paul Greengrass
Screenplay: Richard Hawkins
Cinematography: Ivan Strasburg
Editing: Mark Day
Production design: Melanie Allen
Costumes: Dinah Collin
Music: Rolfe Kent
Sound: John Taylor, Robert Farr
MPAA rating: R
Running Time: 99 minutes

we do not feel that a genuine bond has developed between them. Why this short flight should spark a transcendent moment is not clear since the idea of flight throughout the film has remained a vague metaphor at best—not something that bears a concrete connection to Richard's life, let alone to Jane's. The ending is full of aerial shots as we fly over the countryside (similar shots open the film), but they feel like a lazy way to fill time. It is also implied that Richard and Jane have sex before she dies. In the end, Richard uses the crashed plane to build a memorial to her. We are supposed to assume Richard's life has been transformed, but, since we never really understand his problem to begin with, the conclusion feels hollow.

While Bonham Carter does a fine job of conveying Jane's disability (her slurred speech and facial and bodily contortions seem right), the character itself is a cliché. She is the spunky, disabled girl who tries her best to enjoy life to the fullest (she watches pornography on her computer, shoplifts, and swears). Most importantly, the physically disabled person helps the supposedly normal yet emotionally crippled protagonist to heal. This formula, with certain variations, has worked in other films like *Rain Man,* but here it fails completely. The main reason is that the character of Richard is so sketchy that we do not understand what he needs, and so his dream of flight never has resonance. Jane's quest for sex is a provocative premise, but the execution fluctuates between the poignant and the comic without ever settling on a consistent tone. Given a very limited release, *The Theory of Flight* died a deservedly quick death at the boxoffice.

—*Peter N. Chumo II*

REVIEWS

Chicago Tribune. January 22, 1999, p. 4.
Entertainment Weekly. January 15, 1999, p. 49.
New York Times. December 23, 1998, p. E5.
Variety. September 28, 1998, p. 42.
Washington Post Weekend. January 22, 1999, p. 39.

There's Something About Mary

"Take your chiropractor if you can because you're going to hurt yourself laughing."—Joel Siegel, *Good Morning America*

"Cheerfully crude and way over the line."
—Kenneth Turan, *Los Angeles Times*

"Destined for instant notoriety is a sequence that ends up with hair gel."—Janet Maslin, *New York Times*

"Outrageous, sweet, raunchy and funny."—Leah Rozen, *People*

"The biggest and boldest laughs around this summer. You won't believe your eyes."—Peter Travers, *Rolling Stone*

"Two thumbs up!"—*Siskel & Ebert*

 Box Office: $174,422,745

I f the fact that *There's Something About Mary* was created by the guys (Peter and Bobby Farrelly) who brought us *Dumb & Dumber* (1994) and *Kingpin* (1996) wasn't warning enough that this film may not fit the "normal" comic mode, then the fact that the opening credit song is being crooned by a guitarist sitting on a tree branch complete with drummer, should be. That singer, Jonathan Richman, once of The Modern Lovers, pops up throughout the film. His music comments on the action like an annoying Greek Chorus (just as the mice did in *Babe* (1995) and Stubby Kaye and Nat King Cole did in *Cat Ballou* (1965), one of the Farrellys' favorite films). Richman sings on the street below Ted's room, croons while running a hot dog stand, serenades as a part of a rumba band, and vocalizes outside Mary's apartment—where the characters finally interact with him to the applause of many audience members. But that's just the first of many jokes that won't be spoiled for you here by being described in detail.

What Richman is initially singing about is the luckless high school geek Ted (Ben Stiller) and his love for the Everydweeb dreamgirl, Mary (Cameron Diaz). The story starts in 1985 Rhode Island. There the long-haired, gawky Ted, complete with braces on his teeth, finds himself suddenly the object of Mary's attention because he has intervened to try and prevent a bully from beating up her retarded brother Warren (W. Earl Brown). Mary is beautiful and popular and obviously kind, so out of a sense of gratitude—and maybe even a bit of attraction—she asks Ted to be her date for the prom. Dumbfounded at his incredible good fortune, Ted accepts.

Oh, that life should be so fortuitous for the nerds of the world, but one knows Ted's date can't possibly go smoothly, otherwise what would the normally crude and gross Farrelly brother's use as fodder for their moviemaking skills? In fact, Ted never even makes it to the dance. While picking Mary up at her home, the most humiliating—and painful—thing that could happen to our hapless hero comes to pass: while in the bathroom he catches himself in his own zipper. So, instead of spending the night dancing in the school gym, Ted ends up bleeding in the hospital. Not long afterward, Mary's stepfather (Keith David) moves the family to Florida and Ted never sees her again. Her memory, however, lingers. Why? Because there's just something about Mary.

Flash forward 13 years and Ted, now a magazine writer, still pines over and wonders about Mary. He's tried to find her, but her number is unlisted. So, one day, Ted's friend Dom (Chris Elliott) suggests he hire Pat Healy (Matt Dillon), an insurance examiner in his office, to go to Miami and find Mary for him. What Ted could never have foreseen is that Healy would not only find Mary but would also fall in love with her himself. Consequently, Healy accurately reports back to Ted that Mary is indeed, still unmarried, but falsely embellishes that she now weighs about 250 pounds, has four kids by three different men, is wheelchair-bound, has a gambling problem, and is on her way to Japan as a mail-order bride. As a result Ted once again retreats into his memories . . . and Healy quits his job and moves to Miami to be near Mary. Why? Because there's just something about Mary.

By listening in on Mary's conversations, Healy soon discovers what the lovely orthopedic surgeon really wants in a man and he sets out to pose as exactly that person. Of course, Mary is at first bowled over by Healy's persona of an architect who has a condo in Nepal and who describes his hobby as "I like to work with retards." But gaffes like that make Mary begin to suspect Healy, especially after another suitor, Tucker (Lee Evans), starts exposing his lies. Why does he do this? Because Tucker, too, has been smitten by the fact that there's just something about Mary. So, Mary becomes disillusioned with Healy. . .and at just that moment, Ted arrives on her doorstep.

One could fill pages recounting the funny "bits" that move this plot along. Mary's overly-tanned and leather-hided neighbor, Magda (Lin Shaye), whose dog Puffy is a pathological man-hater, her brother's obsession with his ears, Ted's run-in with a fish hook, Ted's run-in with a

Ted (Ben Stiller): "I couldn't believe she [Mary] knew my name. Some of my best friends don't know my name."

hitchhiker, the police bust at a roadside rest area, Tucker's problems with his crutches, Dom's obsession with shoes and propensity to skin hives, Puffy's encounters with drugs, and something about hair gel you have to see to believe.

Some of these bits are funnier than others, very few of them would pass a politically correct censor, and most of them make you laugh in spite of yourself. Nothing is sacred to the Farrelly brothers—not handicapped people nor animal rights. Nothing is taboo to them, and one wonders if there is any edge to their envelope to push against! When this duo of indecency was asked if their movies crossed the line, Peter Farrelly replied, "We live on the other side of the line. Do you mean cross it back to normal?" Anything is fair game for their tasteless sense of humor and just about anything can be shown on camera. But, one has to admit, there are some darned funny parts to this movie despite what our conscience tells us is OK to laugh at.

Bobby Farrelly's son and daughter and Peter Farrelly's dog play Chris Elliott's kids and pet in the film.

While the plot itself is not a masterpiece of comedy, the actors are perfectly cast to play the broad characters they are given. Ben Stiller, a consummate comedian (it must be genetic, he's the son of the comedy team of Anne Meara and Jerry Stiller), brings a vulnerability to Ted that never passes over into the realm of the needy. We root for him, wince for him, fear for him, and Stiller allows us to laugh at him. All our worst fears happen to Ted, and Stiller is the perfect everyman who permits us to identify through him as he rises to every preposterous occasion.

Matt Dillon, not usually cast in comedies, brings a real smarminess to his character, including growing a pencil-thin mustache that just screams "don't trust me." While Dillon's Healy is certainly distasteful, there's a sort of innocence to his misdeeds that prevents him from being truly threatening, just strangely obtuse.

But if anyone really saves *There's Something About Mary* from being nothing more than a movie for pre-adolescents, its Mary herself, Cameron Diaz. She is, indeed, cute and perky and sexy—all those things that might make the women in the audience hate her, but darn it, she's incredi-

AWARDS AND NOMINATIONS

New York Film Critics 1998: Actress (Cameron Diaz)

CREDITS

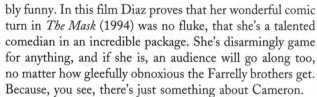

Ted Stroehmann: Ben Stiller
Mary Jenson: Cameron Diaz
Pat Healy: Matt Dillon
Dom: Chris Elliott
Magda: Lin Shaye
Tucker: Lee Evans
Sully: Jeffrey Tambor
Warren: W. Earl Brown
Mary's Mom: Markie Post
Mary's Stepfather: Keith David
Jonathan: Jonathan Richman

Origin: USA
Released: 1998
Production: Frank Beddor, Michael Steinberg, Charles B. Wessler, and Bradley Thomas; released by 20th Century Fox
Direction: Peter Farrelly, Bobby Farrelly
Screenplay: Peter Farrelly, Bobby Farrelly, Ed Decter, and John J. Strauss
Cinematography: Mark Irwin
Editing: Christopher Greenbury
Visual consultant: Sidney J. Bartholomew Jr.
Costumes: Mary Zophres
Music: Jonathan Richman
Sound: Earl Stein
MPAA rating: R
Running Time: 119 minutes

bly funny. In this film Diaz proves that her wonderful comic turn in *The Mask* (1994) was no fluke, that she's a talented comedian in an incredible package. She's disarmingly game for anything, and if she is, an audience will go along too, no matter how gleefully obnoxious the Farrelly brothers get. Because, you see, there's just something about Cameron.

Even though the movie and most of the film seems aimed at a demographic of men in their early twenties, whose sense of humor is stunted around the age of 13, even the most "correct" of us can't help but laugh, too. So, just relax, turn your internal good judgement off, and have fun. But don't say you haven't been warned. This isn't Masterpiece Theater, it's the Farrelly brothers.

—*Beverley Bare Buehrer*

REVIEWS

Chicago Sun-Times. July 15, 1998.
Chicago Tribune. July 15, 1998, p. 1.
Entertainment Weekly. July 15, 1998, p. 59.
New York Times. July 15, 1998, p. E1.
People. July 20, 1998, p. 33.
Sight and Sound. October, 1998, p. 57.
Time. July 20, 1998.
USA Today. July 15, 1998.
Variety. July 13, 1998, p. 53.
Village Voice. July 28, 1998, p. 115.
Washington Post Weekend. July 17, 1998, p. 43.

The Thief; Vor

He'll steal your heart!—Movie tagline

"From Russia, with love! *The Thief* is truly a gem."—Amy Longsdorf, *Courier-Post*

"Superb! Intimate and epic, possessed of lyrical beauty."—Kevin Thomas, *Los Angeles Times*

"Dramatically compelling."—Janet Maslin, *New York Times*

"Magical! A suspenseful, elegant, Oscar-nominated romance . . . Rednikova is stunning!"—John Anderson, *Newsday*

"Two thumbs up!"—*Siskel & Ebert*

   Box Office: $1,124,700

T he Oscar-nominated Russian film *The Thief* is a melancholy, bizarre story of a young boy, whose father has been killed in World War II, his vulnerable mother, and a sinister but seductive man who steals their hearts and their lives. The joint French-Russian production is overpowered by the somber mood it evokes of 1950s Stalinist Russia, and it equates Stalinism with a sort of spiritual deprivation and cultural dishonesty that allows thievery as a form of thwarted capitalism.

The film, written and directed by Pavel Chukhrai, opens with a woman stumbling down an isolated country lane. As the woman falls down in the snow and mud, the voice of a narrator explains that this was how his mother gave birth to him, in 1946. A ghostly image of the boy's father, who died before the birth, fades into the landscape. The next scene has the boy, Sanya (Misha Philipchuk), and his mother, Katya (Yekaterina Rednikova), traveling on a train. Sanya is six. When a rakish soldier, Tolyan (Vladimir Mashkov), joins their compartment, Sanya is immediately intrigued. When Tolyan calls him "squirt" and lets him play with his hat on his bunk, he is mesmerized.

While there is a commotion on the train over a theft, Tolyan uses the opportunity to woo the dewy Katya. Director Chukhrai films their assignation without letting audiences hear their conversation. Their coupling is desperate, secretive, and tawdry. And as young Sanya again sees the ghost of his unknown father disappearing down a corridor, he finds a gun and a woman's purse in Tolyan's kit bag.

Tolyan pretends to be Katya's husband and uses his presumed status as a war veteran to convince a landlord to let the three of them rent a room in a boarding house without paying anything up front. With his mother now absorbed in her new lover, Sanya is treated rudely. Awakening in the night, he sees his mother and the soldier "wrestling" under the covers. Sanya falls off his "bed" of three chairs and runs to his mother. "He was choking you!" he tells his mother, but she replies: "You were dreaming." Tolyan's brutality is unmasked when Sanya tries to climb into bed with his mother. "I sleep here," he commands, "and if you say another word, I'll throw you out that window!"

Katya's complicity in shutting out Sanya is also merciless even if physically more gentle. She is under the spell of the rough soldier, and they spend days having sex in bed, pushing Sanya outside and locking the door. He wanders outside. A group of boys taunts and attacks him because he is a newcomer.

When Sanya returns to his room, Tolyan is upset. "Go and defend yourself," he tells him, "Show you're a real man!" And he orders Sanya to take a stick and return to the fray, while Tolyan returns to bed with Katya. When a man complains that "your son has been hitting kids with a stick," Tolyan comes out, sucker punches the man, holds several of the children, and orders Sanya to pummel them.

As Tolyan sits in his shirt-sleeves on his bed, rolling a razor blade around his mouth with his tongue, he instructs Sanya in his ruthless code of conduct. He tells Sanya that to get along in life, you must scare people. If you scare them, they will respect you, and if they respect you, they will listen to you. And if they don't listen to you, you pummel them. Tolyan shows Sanya his tattoo of Stalin and lies that he's a secret son of the ruler. On the wall above them is a propaganda photo of Stalin with a group of smiling children in a meadow.

The symbolism is inescapable. Chukhrai is suggesting, none too subtly, that behind the image of the loving, paternalistic Stalin lurked the reality of a man who ruled by fear and intimidation. Tolyan's code of conduct is not only

ruthless, it turns out, but dishonest. It gradually becomes clear that Tolyan is not really a soldier, but a con artist. As Tolyan's schemes are revealed in all their insidious immorality, Katya must choose between the man she loves and her own integrity.

Tolyan throws an elaborate dinner party for all the guests at the rooming house. Grateful, they toast Stalin and Tolyan's largesse. He then invites them all to the circus. When Tolyan leaves in the middle of the performance, Katya is suspicious that he has returned to the rooming house for a romp with a flirtatious young woman. She confronts him, only to discover that his purposes are nefarious in a different way—he is robbing the entire house of silverware, jewelry and other valuables. He puts all the stolen goods in a large duffel bag and says he is leaving on the train. Katya balks at going with him, and he tells her he will leave without her. Tolyan is indifferent to her appeals, but asks her tellingly: "Where will you go without me?"

At this juncture, *The Thief* is both a soap opera about doomed love and a metaphor for a nation in thrall to Stalin. Katya has no other prospects except a continued bleak existence in poverty, trying to raise a child by herself and scraping by without skills or steady employment. Katya also has become ridiculously attached to this madman who offers her a chance for a better life. Metaphorically, Katya is like Russia in the postwar era: a nation of widows dependent on a dictatorial patriarch for their salvation. Sanya represents the post-war children who find themselves mesmerized by a powerful but corrupt father figure while longing for the integrity of the brave soldiers who died defending the homeland.

Chukhrai paints Sanya's youthful dilemma as an internal struggle between loyalty to a dead but righteous father he has never known and a terrifying but tempting father substitute who offers a rugged system of survival techniques. Gradually, Tolyan brings Sanya under his sway, teaching him to be a thief and a scoundrel.

The story plays out against a bleak backdrop of crumbling buildings, crowded apartments, trains, and the colossal ruins of a wounded civilization. Cinematographer Vladimir Klimov sketches an unappealing, morose canvas of scruffy open spaces and stultifying interiors. In every aspect of life, there are details which show the hypocrisy of the Stalinist picture of a bright, prosperous, powerful nation marching forward proudly into modern times. *The Thief* is populated by defeated, bludgeoned people stumbling along in a post-war daze.

None are more lost and bewildered than Sanya and his mother. As Tolyan keeps repeating his various scams, Katya becomes more and more impatient to move to another life.

The film won five of the 10 awards it was nominated for at the Nikes, the Russian Oscars, including Best Film.

But Tolyan is obsessed with his self-destructive adventurism. Metaphorically, the idea being advanced is that Stalinism was so corrupted at its center that it had to degenerate into nothing more than political thievery. Culturally and economically, *The Thief* suggests, Stalinism is a dead-end, just as Tolyan's kleptomania is destructive. It brings down everyone who is touched by it.

The Thief is less successful as a story of the miserable early experiences of an abused and confused child than it is as a metaphor for post-war Russia. Sanya has a harrowing life, but it is difficult to believe he has become enthralled with this terrifying father substitute. He feels he has betrayed the memory of his "good" father and is left with no one to follow except Tolyan. Eventually, Tolyan is taken away and imprisoned and Sanya must cope with the tragedy of his mother dying from a botched abortion. The final blow comes when Sanya's carefully cherished memories of his onetime father are exploded by a confrontation with a man who barely remembers the woman and child he once used and abused. The reality is that Tolyan has grown into a

ne'er-do-well, a bum who is constantly on the run, and far from the heroic or saving figure Sanya has concocted from the threads of his memories. Sanya's ultimate revenge doesn't make much sense except as a triumphal shot of societal rebellion.

Chukhrai has let his metaphorical story overwhelm his saga. The very desperation of *The Thief* overwhelms it. It is relentlessly somber but it is low tragedy, not grand. It's a story of ruined lives and shattered, irreparable morals, and its protagonist is simply left alone at the end to try to piece together a life. As such, it may be a brutally honest representation of post-war Russia, mesmerized and finally abandoned by a terrible father who turns out not to have been what he portrayed himself to be. It is a film about vast disillusionment and debilitating corruption.

Essentially a three-actor film, *The Thief* features memorable performances. Rednikova is hauntingly beautiful and wistful, a hollow and tragic picture of womanhood debased and desperate. Mashkov plays Tolyan as a totally unsympathetic macho man and manages to infuse his malevolence with just the slightest hint of a neurotic figure trapped in his own obsessions. And the young Philipchuk, with his wide, deep pools of eyes and his moon face, makes Sanya into a hopelessly lost, confused, and buffeted child.

The Thief may be a sort of exorcism for a generation of post-war Russians. It is a difficult, odd film, especially for non-Russian audiences, who must endure a portrait of a suffocating, luckless land. It's uncomfortable to watch but professionally made and convincingly acted—a sort of bleak, black, paltry treasure.

—*Michael Betzold*

CREDITS

Tolyan: Vladimir Mashkov
Katya: Yekaterina Rednikova
Sanya: Misha Philipchuk

Origin: Russia, France
Released: 1997
Production: Igor Tolstunov; released by Stratosphere Entertainment
Direction: Pavel Chukhrai
Screenplay: Pavel Chukhrai
Cinematography: Vladimir Klimov
Editing: Marina Dobryanskaya, Natalia Kucherenko
Production design: Victor Petrov
Music: Vladimir Dashkevich
MPAA rating: R
Running Time: 87 minutes

REVIEWS

Los Angeles Times. July 17, 1998, p. F12.
New York Times. July 17, 1998, p. E12.
People. July 27, 1998, p. 36.
Sight and Sound. August, 1998, p. 54.

The Thin Red Line

Every man fights his own war.—Movie tagline

"A masterpiece. An instant war film classic."
—Mike Cidoni, *ABC-TV*

"Outstanding and astounding. A masterwork of stunning and haunting imagery."—Dennis Cunningham, *CBS-TV*

"Terrence Malick conjures up visions you'll never be able to shake."—David Ansen, *Newsweek*

"Stunning. Full of power and poetic grandeur. Sean Penn and Nick Nolte are superb."—Peter Travers, *Rolling Stone*

"Two thumbs up!"—*Siskel & Ebert*

"Magnificent!"—Richard Corliss, *Time*

"A film of rare substance and power."—Andrew Johnston, *Time Out New York*

"A powerful film."—Gene Shalit, *The Today Show*

Director Terrence Malick's symbolic and visually stunning look at the madness of war in *The Thin Red Line.*

T*he Thin Red Line* was one of the most anticipated films of 1998 because it is the first film written and directed by Terrence Malick in 20 years. While Malick's name may mean little to the filmgoing public, he is a legendary figure among critics, film historians, and Hollywood insiders because his reclusiveness rivals that of novelists Thomas Pynchon and J.D. Salinger. After making two critics' favorites in the 1970s, Malick turned his back on the industry and retreated into myth. Rumors circulated periodically that he was working on this or that project, that he never intended to direct again. To see what would finally lure the filmmaker out of exile had some film buffs, as well as viewers caught up in the considerable publicity the film generated, panting. The elliptical, often poetic, occasionally violent, slightly awkward result is what fans of *Badlands* (1973) and *Days of Heaven* (1978) would expect. Audiences more attuned to the comparatively visceral impact of Steven Spielberg's *Saving Private Ryan* (1998) are certainly puzzled by all the fuss.

Adapted from James Jones's 1962 novel, *The Thin Red Line* is centered around one of the pivotal battles of World War II. Japanese forces were firmly entrenched on a hilltop on Guadalcanal in the Solomon Islands, but American soldiers, from both the Marines and the Army, eventually prevailed, suffering massive losses in the process.

Like Malick's earlier films, *The Thin Red Line* builds slowly toward this crisis. Much of the first third of the film focuses on two reflective privates. Witt (Jim Caviezel) is a discipline problem who has gone absent without leave several times. Unlike Jones's novel, from which Malick makes radical departures, the film opens with Witt and another de-serter enjoying an idyll on a remote, paradisal island. Captured and returned to his company, Witt suffers the antagonism of the cynical Sergeant Welsh (Sean Penn).

The other private is Bell (Ben Chaplin), a former lieutenant in the Army Corps of Engineers who resigned his commission because his wife (Miranda Otto) objected to his being away from her so much. Bell spends most of his waking moments recalling loving moments with her. These chaste remembrances are so numerous that, unfortunately, they become annoying. Because they are the most sensitive soldiers, Bell and Witt, of course, are also the bravest. Even the most obtuse viewer knows that one or both will die.

In charge of the assault is Lieutenant Colonel Tall (Nick Nolte) who refuses to allow the casualties to affect his determination to win the battle. At the other extreme is Captain Staros (Elias Koteas) who objects to Tall's order to send more of his men to their certain death. Eventually, a patrol led by Captain Gaff (John Cusack) and including Bell and Witt succeeds in knocking out a machine-gun nest, paving the way for a larger assault. The final third of the film presents the soldiers dealing with the consequences of their costly victory.

The Thin Red Line closely resembles the style of Malick's earlier films, particularly Days of Heaven. There are brief conversations, mostly between Witt and Welsh, long shots of soldiers thinking, images of nature, especially waving blades of tall grass and exotic birds. (Part of Malick's personal mystique are his lengthy bird-watching walks.) All this is punctuated by a voice-over narration. While Badlands and Days of Heaven are each narrated by single naïve characters, there are eight voices, principally Witt's and Bell's, in The Thin Red Line.

The frequent shots of flora and fauna are fitting because Malick is saying, some might claim too obviously, that war is a violation of the natural order of things, an order Witt recaptures during his intervals in native villages. The narration, however, is another matter. The voices, except for Nolte's distinctive croak, are often indistinguishable, and the arguments they are presenting about the wastefulness of war would be more effectively made by visual means. Linda Manz's wonderful narration of Days of Heaven works as ironic counterpoint to the understated action, but the inner turmoil conveyed by the narration of The Thin Red Line would be better dramatized. (Cornel Wilde's 1967 cult favorite Beach Red, also about a 1943 assault on a Japanese-held island, features similar interior-monologue narration.)

Welsh (Sean Penn) to Witt (Jim Caviezel): "What difference do you think you could make, one single man in all this madness? You die, it's gonna be for nothing."

The film's breathtaking scenery is mostly the Braintree Rainforest in Queensland, Australia, near the Great Barrier Reef, with some scenes actually shot in the Solomons. Beautifully photographed by John Toll, who won Academy Awards for his first two films, Legends of the Fall (1994) and Braveheart (1995), The Thin Red Line is striking to look at, but too much of it consists of simply watching the soldiers think, placing considerable pressure on the mostly young actors. Both Caviezel and Chaplin have some presence, but Malick's approach reduces them to visual objects. Penn's role is much smaller than many reviews have indicated, but he stands out by uncharacteristically underplaying his role. Koteas, equally understated, has an everyman quality similar to that conveyed by actors such as Dane Clark, Richard Conte, and Frank Lovejoy in World War II films made in the 1940s and 1950s. (Conte's roles include 1943's Guadalcanal Diary.) Koteas' soft-spoken voice is very similar, in fact, to Lovejoy's. Koteas's quiet style is perfect for his confrontations with the volatile Nolte, the veins of whose neck stand out in almost every scene. Some of the newspaper and magazine articles about the making of the film imply that Nolte's intense anger may not simply be acting but a result of his impatience with Malick's lack of specific guidance for his actors and insistence upon repeated takes.

The Thin Red Line was previously filmed in 1964 by Andrew Marton and starred Keir Dullea and Jack Warden.

Malick's screenplay is notable for reducing Jones's complex story and dozens of characters into a mostly cohesive narrative. In addition to eliminating characters, scenes, and a homoerotic subtext, Malick's major change is converting Koteas's character into a Greek American. As Captain Stein in the novel, the character is central to Jones's commentary about anti-Semitism in the army and society at large, a topic the filmmaker was apparently not interested in.

Malick's first edit of the film reportedly lasted six hours. In cutting the film, which was reportedly finished only days before its release, Malick greatly reduced the size of some roles, particularly Corporal Fife (Adrien Brody) and Sergeant Storm (John C. Reilly). Advance publicity for the film heralded Brody's role as central to the film, but he has only two lines of dialogue. Penn's part has also obviously been cut significantly. George Clooney, Woody Harrelson, and John Travolta (as the least convincing general in Hollywood history) essentially have cameos, and Cusack's role is only slightly larger. Roles played by Lukas Haas, Gary Oldman, Bill Pullman, and Mickey Rourke were eliminated and Billy Bob Thornton's narration replaced.

Reducing the size of the actors' roles is strangely appropriate because the message of The Thin Red Line is the dehumanizing effect of war. It is not essential for more than a handful of characters to stand out. By the time the battle is raging, Malick has established the protagonists well enough for their anguish to have an impact. The assault on the hilltop is brilliantly staged, one of the most intense battle sequences ever. This sequence is most notable, however, for its initial aftermath with numerous shots of the humiliation of the captured Japanese soldiers. They become more human for their defeat while the victors question the necessity of what their side has sacrificed. Once the Japanese have been vanquished, the film seems to wander and ends abruptly. Malick, who spent almost two years editing Days of Heaven, may not have had enough time to complete the film as he wished.

Because The Thin Red Line appeared six months after

AWARDS AND NOMINATIONS

New York Film Critics 1998: Director (Terrence Malick)
Academy Awards 1998 Nominations: Picture; Director (Terrence Malick); Adapted Screenplay; Cinematography; Sound; Original Dramatic Score; Film Editing

the hugely successful *Saving Private Ryan,* comparisons between the two films are inevitable but ultimately pointless. Spielberg is an entertainer adept at manipulating audiences, but his intentions are not always clear. His take on World War II apparently intends to make an anti-war statement as intense as Malick's, but *Ryan* seems to suggest that a man is not a real man unless his courage has been tested. The structure of Spielberg's film is superior to Malick's with the contemplative section bookended by two battles, but Spielberg is all about exterior action while Malick is concerned with the inner man, even if he fumbles what he has to say a bit. Spielberg's models are giants of Hollywood's golden age like Frank Capra, John Ford, Howard Hawks, and William Wyler. (*Saving Private Ryan* is one of dozens of films heavily influenced by Ford's 1956 seminal masterpiece *The Searchers.*) Malick's more personal style recalls the austere poetry of Carl Theodor Dreyer and Yasujiro Ozu. Spielberg's Germans are faceless or cartoon villains; Malick's Japanese are painfully human. Spielberg's film is easier to take, even with the Sam Peckinpah-ish violence of its opening; Malick's more demanding.

The Thin Red Line is a heavily flawed masterpiece, resembling Francis Ford Coppola's *Apocalypse Now.* Just as *Hearts of Darkness: A Filmmaker's Apocalypse* (1991), the documentary by Fax Bahr, George Hickenlooper, and Eleanor Coppola about the making of Coppola's Vietnam War epic, is in many ways more satisfying than the film itself, a similar documentary about Malick's tortured attempt to achieve his vision would be fascinating.

—*Michael Adams*

CREDITS

Private Witt: Jim Caviezel
Private Bell: Ben Chaplin
Lieutenant Colonel Tall: Nick Nolte
Captain Staros: Elias Koteas
Sergeant Welsh: Sean Penn
Sergeant Keck: Woody Harrelson
Captain Gaff: John Cusack
Sergeant Storm: John C. Reilly
Sergeant McCron: John Savage
Brigadier General Quintard: John Travolta
Captain Bosche: George Clooney
Corporal Fife: Adrien Brody
Private Doll: Dash Mihok
Corporal Queen: David Harrod
Lieutenant Whyte: Jared Leto
Marty Bell: Miranda Otto

Origin: USA
Released: 1998
Production: Robert Michael Geisler, John Roberdeau, and Grant Hill for Phoenix Pictures and Geisler-Roberdeau Productions; released by Fox 2000 Pictures
Direction: Terrence Malick
Screenplay: Terrence Malick; based on the novel by James Jones
Cinematography: John Toll
Editing: Billy Weber, Leslie Jones
Production design: Jack Fisk
Art direction: Ian Gracie
Costumes: Margot Wilson
Music: Hans Zimmer
Sound: J. Paul Huntsman
MPAA rating: R
Running Time: 166 minutes

REVIEWS

Christian Science Monitor. December 31, 1998, p. 13.
Entertainment Weekly. January 8, 1999, p. 44.
Los Angeles Times. December 23, 1998, p. F1.
New York Times. December 23, 1998, p. E1.
New York Times. January 17, 1999, p. AR11.
New Yorker. December 28, 1998.
New Yorker. January 4, 1999, p. 138.
Newsweek. December 21, 1998, p. 66.
People. January 11, 1999, p. 36.
Rolling Stone. January 21, 1999, p. 83.
San Francisco Chronicle. December 25, 1998, p. C1.
Time. December 28, 1998, p. 173.
USA Today. December 23, 1998, p. D1.
Variety. December 21, 1998, p. 73.
Village Voice. December 29, 1998, p. 117.

Touch of Evil

"One of the greatest movies ever made in America! A wondrous gift no movie lover should miss."—Michael Wilmington, *Chicago Tribune*

"A touch of genius! A great baroque cathedral of film noir!"—David Kehr, *New York Daily News*

"A great thriller! Take a deep breath and enjoy it!"—David Denby, *New York Magazine*

"A real genius at work!"—Jack Kroll, *Newsweek*

"Two thumbs up! Celebrates Welles's great visual sense."—Roger Ebert, *Siskel & Ebert*

 Box Office: $2, 213,147

Among the great directors who worked in the Hollywood studio system, Orson Welles had clearly the worst experience. While John Ford, Howard Hawks, and Alfred Hitchcock flourished within—and perhaps even because of—the system, Welles was one of its victims. After beginning his film-directing career by having complete control over *Citizen Kane* (1941), Welles never enjoyed such autonomy again. His second film, *The Magnificent Ambersons* (1942), was trimmed by RKO from 148 to 88 minutes and had a new ending added. After several similar experiences, he landed at low-budget Republic for his *Macbeth* (1948) and then disappeared into independent productions in Europe until he was given another, unexpected studio assignment. The result, *Touch of Evil*, is one of Welles's greatest films and one of the finest examples of film noir, but it is not all it could have been. After the film was poorly received by a preview audience, Universal International reedited Welles's version of *Touch of Evil* and added a few scenes directed by Harry Keller. Welles then wrote an impassioned 58-page memo describing how the film could be edited yet again to address the studio's wrongheaded changes. Forty years later, acclaimed film editor Walter Murch has created this definitive version from Welles's notes.

Mexico City police detective Mike Vargas (Charlton Heston) and his Philadelphia-born wife, Susan (Janet Leigh), are walking across the border between their countries when an automobile suddenly explodes, killing the wealthy Rudy Linnekar and a woman companion. Because the bomb came from the Mexican side of the border, Vargas interrupts his honeymoon out of a sense of duty. From the beginning, Vargas seems suspicious of jowly, sweaty Hank Quinlan (Orson Welles), a legendary lawman in the border town of Los Robles, who clearly harbors a prejudice against Mexicans. When Quinlan's lackey, Pete Menzies (Joseph Calleia), finds dynamite in the apartment of Manolo Sanchez (Victor Millan), who has been dating Linnekar's daughter, Marcia (Joanna Moore), Vargas knows a frame is in the works.

Complicating matters is the vendetta against Vargas by the criminal Grandi family, one of whose leaders he has sent to prison. Separated from her husband, Susan is confronted by Uncle Joe Grandi (Akim Tamiroff) but refuses to be frightened by his threats. For safety, Susan goes to a remote motel under the supervision of an unusually eccentric "night man" (Dennis Weaver), not knowing Uncle Joe owns the establishment. Grandi sends some hoodlums there to inject narcotics into Susan and take her to a hotel where Quinlan will find and arrest her. More sinister developments, with accompanying deaths, ensue.

Quinlan (Orson Welles): "Come on. Read my future for me." Tana (Marlene Dietrich): "You haven't got any." Quinlan: "What do you mean?" Tana: "Your future's all used up."

Welles was originally hired only to play the villain in *Touch of Evil*, but when star Charlton Heston heard of his involvement, he insisted Welles direct the film as well. Universal International, as the studio was then known, apparently did not mind because this was only a low-budget project for which it did not have great expectations. Welles had just worked for Universal, playing the villain in *Man in the Shadow* (1957), a vehicle for studio star Jeff Chandler. *Man* is a set-bound, predictable melodrama, also set in a small western town, and Universal clearly expected *Touch of Evil* to be more of the same. It is not.

Most sources call Dietrich's character "Tanya" but, according to editor Walter Murch, that is a mistake.

While the studio did make a few minor changes in accordance with Welles's memo, another unsuccessful preview resulted in 15 minutes being trimmed before the film was released. Like most of the classic films noir from the 1940s and 1950s, *Touch of Evil* was not sufficiently appreciated by the critical establishment of its time, many of whom complained, justifiably given Universal's interference, that the film is choppy and incomprehensible. From the very beginning, however, Welles enthusiasts saw in the film's dark lighting, tilted camera angles, and exploration of ambition, excess, and corruption yet another masterpiece. When *Touch of Evil* was shown at the 1958 Brussels World's Fair Film Festival, it was voted best film. Two of the judges included little-known French critics named Jean-Luc Godard and Francois Truffaut.

The film's reputation has grown over the years as later generations of film scholars have recognized Welles's genius and, with the guidance of auteur critics like Truffaut and Godard, acknowledged the efforts of strong directors to impose their styles and visions even on routine genre efforts. Evaluation of Welles's achievement with *Touch of Evil* improved somewhat in the mid-1970s when the 108-minute preview version was rediscovered. The video edition available for several years has been a combination of the 93- and 108-minute versions.

The ultimate *Touch of Evil* is, of course, the one Welles created before Universal began tampering with it, but the studio destroyed everything that had been removed from Welles's cut of the film. The present restoration, the closest possible version to Welles's original intentions, began when film critic and historian Jonathan Rosenbaum was editing Peter Bogdanovich's *This Is Orson Welles* (1992), which was to include a truncated version of Welles's Universal memo, given to Bogdanovich by Heston. (The publisher, ironically, cut the memo from the book because of lack of space.) Rosenbaum published a 1992 article about the memo in *Film Quarterly*. Producer Rick Schmidlin read the article, and after attending a lecture by Walter Murch about the editing of Francis Ford Coppola's *The Conversation* (1974), he tracked down the original memo, enlisted Rosenbaum as consultant, and hired Murch, with sound rerecordists Bill Varney and Peter Reale and picture restorer Bob O'Neil, to reedit the film and its soundtrack according to Welles's instructions.

For the new version of *Touch of Evil*, Murch, who won two Academy Awards as film editor and sound editor of *The English Patient* (1996), deleted the four scenes added by Universal to clarify (that is, make obvious) some of the plot points. Murch also restored Welles's order of the scenes. After Vargas and Susan are separated early in the film, the Universal version stays with Vargas while he meets Quinlan and becomes involved in the bombing investigation and cuts to Susan's encounter with Uncle Joe abruptly after most viewers have concluded that Vargas' story is the essence of the narrative. Welles intended to alternate between the two constantly, emphasizing the equal importance of the two characters.

Perhaps the most significant change comes during the famous three-minute-and-twenty-second crane shot that opens the film, showing the bomb being placed and the Linnekar convertible slowly making its way across the border, encountering the strolling Vargases several times. The shot masterfully establishes the exotic, dangerous milieu in which Susan seems out of her depth. In the Universal version, all

this appears partially hidden beneath the opening credits and with Henry Mancini's jazzy score thundering in the background. Murch and his collaborators have removed the distracting credits and Mancini's music, making the events much easier to follow and restoring Welles's elaborate sound effects, which include a variety of street noises dominated by the mixture of jazz, rock, and Latin rhythms blaring from the nightclubs, bars, and cafes Vargas and Susan pass. Robert Altman pays homage to this scene with the opening of *The Player* (1992), and Altman's famous use of sound effects dominated by overlapping dialogue is clearly inspired by what Welles does with sound in all his films.

Mancini's original title music helps considerably in setting the film's mood, but Welles's more naturalistic approach is even better. Numerous reviewers justifiably chided Murch for eliminating this music, suggesting it could have been

CREDITS

Mike Vargas: Charlton Heston
Hank Quinlan: Orson Welles
Susan Vargas: Janet Leigh
Peter Menzies: Joseph Calleia
Uncle Joe Grandi: Akim Tamiroff
Tana: Marlene Dietrich
Adair: Ray Collins
Schwartz: Mort Mills
Gould: Harry Shannon
Marcia Linnekar: Joanna Moore
Manolo Sanchez: Victor Millan
Pancho: Valentin de Vargas
Motel night man: Dennis Weaver
Hoodlum: Mercedes McCambridge
Blaine: Phil Harvey
Zita: Joi Lansing
Owner of nightclub: Zsa Zsa Gabor
Coroner: Joseph Cotton

Origin: USA
Released: 1958, 1998
Production: Albert Zugsmith; released by Universal Pictures
Direction: Orson Welles
Screenplay: Orson Welles; based on the novel *Badge of Evil* by Whit Masterson
Cinematography: Russell Metty
Editing: Virgil Vogel, Aaron Stell
Art direction: Alexander Golitzen, Robert Clatworthy
Costumes: Bill Thomas
Sound: Leslie I. Carey, Frank Wilkinson
Music: Henry Mancini
MPAA rating: Unrated
Running Time: 108 minutes

used during the closing credits. Mancini's title music is one of the best pieces of film scoring from the 1950s and one of the most memorable in any film noir. Murch's explaination in a *New York Times* article that the music is disposable because it too closely resembles the popular theme Mancini composed for the *Peter Gunn* television series is illogical. If it is good, it should be used somewhere in the film.

Mancini's music in a variety of styles throughout the film adds considerably to the effectiveness of *Touch of Evil*. In slighting it, Murch may be guilty of adhering too mindlessly to the cult of Orson that refuses to recognize the importance of Welles's collaborators. A perfect example is giving the director all the credit for the brilliance of the opening shot. Cinematographer Russell Metty, who worked with Welles previously on *The Stranger* (1946), is famous for complicated crane shots. In fact, he employs a similar, but shorter, one in an earlier low-budget Universal International film, *Naked Alibi* (1954), also set on a border crossing between Mexico and the United States.

Another significant change is the elimination of a closeup of Menzies after Vargas has confronted him with proof that Quinlan has concocted evidence in other cases. Menzies's agonized expression suggests that he has revealed his awareness of his boss' guilt to Vargas and must cooperate as a result. By deleting the shot, Murch makes clear that Menzies is acting as he does in helping Vargas entrap Quinlan of out conscience rather than fear. Instead of betraying Quinlan out of weakness, he is motivated by Quinlan's betrayal of the values Menzies has thought they shared. The subsequent shootout between Quinlan and Menzies takes on more tragic overtones as a result when a good man dies because of his best friend's sins. This change also under-

scores the excellence of Calleia's performance, the best in the film and the best the veteran character actor gave during his almost forty years on the screen. A lesser performer would not have made Menzies's transformation from toady to avenging angel so convincing.

While Murch's changes make the plot and the characters' motivations clearer, a case can be made that they do not enhance the film's greatness. The choppiness of the Universal version is actually fitting for this world of evil and corruption where actions and consequences, as in the best films noir, do not adhere to logic. Though *Touch of Evil* has something to say about friendship and betrayal, about how power corrupts, any thematic content is overshadowed by its visual flourishes, by Welles's obvious delight with the process of filmmaking. It makes the new films of 1998 woefully inadequate in comparison. As Truffaut wrote in 1958, *Touch of Evil* makes "us ashamed to have been so indulgent with cliché-ridden movies made by small talents."

—*Michael Adams*

REVIEWS

Atlanta Constitution. September 18, 1998, p. P11.
Entertainment Weekly. September 18, 1998, p. 60.
Los Angeles Times. September 6, 1998, p. 22.
New York Times. September 6, 1998, p. AR1.
New Yorker. September 21, 1998, p. 146.
Newsweek. September 14, 1998, p. 76.
San Francisco Chronicle. September 18, 1998, p. C10.
USA Today. September 11, 1998, p. E11.
Variety. September 7, 1998, p. 73.

The Truce; La Tregua

At the end of the war, a group of Italian prisoners got lost on their way home. Their journey back transformed everyone they met along the way.—Movie tagline

"A classic memoir stirringly brought to the screen."—Bob Strauss, *Los Angeles Daily News*

"Passionate and involving! John Turturro gives the performance of his life!"—Thelma Adams, *New York Post*

"Turturro gives what may be the performance of his career."—Stephen Holden, *New York Times*

"An absorbing epic."—Andrew Johnston, *Time Out New York*

What war films seem to leave out, more by necessity than intent, is the durational aspect of the hell endured by those caught up in it. The narrative thrust integral to this film genre forces a preoccupation with military maneuvers geared toward achieving set goals. *The Truce*, the first film in English by the Italian film master Francesco Rosi, emerges in its unique way as a kind of extended war film: war is present in the form of its immediate aftermath; for the stragglers and survivors, normalcy is still a distant mirage. It is this limbo, as experienced by the renowned Italian Jewish writer Primo Levi, and accessed through his autobiography, that Rosi boldly adopts as the narrative backbone for his film.

Unfortunately, Rosi's seriousness cripples the impact of his material far more than serving it, resulting in a work overburdened by the humanist conscience of both its real-life subject and that of the filmmaker. We long for an absurdist touch that would have lightened things up a bit. As it is, the film is commanding in its stance: we are expected to absorb it in awe, as the work of a great director.

After a singular Main Title, historical events are condensed through introductory titles, as a background to Primo's odyssey. It is January 1945. As Russian soldiers advance toward the extermination camp of Auschwitz, the Nazis retreat, after frantically setting fire to all records. The film spells out the nature of their misdeeds: "After taking the lives of millions of victims, they now try to cancel their very names."

Then, in complete contrast, against a silent, bleak snowscape, four horsemen appear as silhouettes. An extreme close-up of the Communist insignia tells us that they are Russians. To Primo (John Turturro), however, who is at that moment stumbling toward the camera after having carried a corpse to a mass grave, they could be oppressors or liberators, or both. This ambivalence provides the backdrop for the harrowing images of dehumanization meant to assault our conscience. The prisoners, like semi-human specters, remain transfixed, watching incredulously. Then, as they rush out like cattle, the stirring musical theme by Luis Bacalov stakes out the film's emotional terrain. Primo, however, remains singularly apart from the herd. His bespectacled, sharp gaze looks beyond the momentary release, as his pensive voice-over establishes the film's narrative viewpoint: "Face to face with freedom, we found ourselves lost, emptied, atrophied, unfit for our newfound liberty."

Primo's confusion is justified by the events that follow. A bonfire of camp uniforms is followed by a meal of hot soup, during which Primo sees on the face of his ailing fellow countryman, Daniele (Stefano Dionisi), the despair of the survivor. Daniele offers Primo his half-loaf, as if himself having no use for its nourishment. Primo looks a bit puzzled, then quickly pockets the humble gift. Soon, the two are separated as Primo is herded onto a truck bound for no one knows where. "See you in Italy!" Primo shouts, jubilantly. Daniele, whom we know is headed for a hospital, can only wave back half-heartedly, a trace of envy in his grin.

We then see Primo in a makeshift encampment, strolling idly beside a railroad track. In the bitter cold, he stops near the vacant faces of bereft children huddling around a small fire. As they stare up at him in silence, Primo is moved to part with the half-loaf he had got from Daniele. An approaching train spells hope, as everyone rushes towards it. Again, Primo seems to know better.

Primo Levi's memoir was published in the U.S. as *The Reawakening* in 1965.

Inside the freight car, as the train chugs slowly across the wintry landscape, Primo's plight is made clear to him by the domineering figure holding court, a rambunctious perennial optimist known only as the Greek (Rade Serbedzija). He informs Primo that the train is headed north, toward Italy. When the locomotive breaks down, the Greek takes Primo in hand and suggests they proceed on foot. Without knowing whereto, Primo agrees to the Greek's terms: "I organize. You carry. Then we share what is inside."

As the Greek strides forward majestically, and Primo follows like an overburdened mule, their contrasting sensibilities are thrown into relief along the way. "The war is almost over," Primo says, "and perhaps everything will be easier." The Greek turns round and retorts: "War is always!"

True enough, as Primo is unable to return home from a war without end, his narrative, along with the viewer's experience of the film, takes on an existentialist aspect, but one that Primo, the noble humanist that he is, does not seem to acknowledge. For Primo, the interaction with war-torn social and political institutions that his odyssey will now involve is nothing more than a series of challenges to his belief in the triumph of the universal spirit of man.

In Cracow, when he and the Greek are refused entry into a military shelter for Italians on the grounds that there isn't enough food for the soldiers themselves, it is Primo's reasoning that wins, along with a small bribe from the Greek. "Soldiers, civilians," Primo pleads, "what's the difference? We are all hungry."

While serving to evoke a sense of nostalgia for his homeland as well as the burden of his Jewish identity, Primo's time in Cracow holds little drama. And so, along with most of the sequences that follow, the film emerges as a series of interludes, slices-of-(war)life, as it were, through which Primo moves with the humility of a powerless but observant pawn.

Though an audience accustomed to dramatic cause-and-effect is bound to find the film arduous viewing, the more thoughtful viewer is no doubt meant to ponder the political and metaphysical insights offered. For example, the Greek's view of Hitler and Stalin as mere transitory figures in the sweep of history. Or his musings on the afterlife, when he questions, "When I die, where goes my soul? To heaven or to the worms?" Without requiring a moment's thought, Primo answers, "To the worms."

Soon abandoned by the Greek, Primo is once again herded onto a truck by the Russians. This time, he finds himself in what is described to him as "a transit camp for the rehabilitation of displaced persons liberated from the Nazis." It is also a site of repressed sexuality, as Primo discovers through the loose-living, matronly Russian doctor who supervises the infirmary, and the attractive young nurse, Galina (Agnieszka Wagner), who is assigned to help Primo catalog medicines for sexually transmitted diseases. Just as Primo is about to admit his feelings for Galina, he sees her bestowing her favors on a Russian officer. His stirrings of romantic love crushed, Primo's reentry into the world of familiar human emotions coincides with news of the German surrender, thereby ushering in the next section of his odyssey.

On the train to Odessa, Primo is reunited with Daniele, who is still as melancholic as when last seen. "Why was I the only one spared?" he wonders. "Why did God want this?" To which Primo answers, with the sure air of his hard-won enlightenment, "God cannot exist if Auschwitz exists."

What now becomes clear is the repetitive nature of Primo's fate. As before, he is forced off the train, this time owing to broken tracks. With a ragged group of his countrymen, he then has to trudge north toward Minsk, which he is told is the only undamaged railroad line. He even meets up with the Greek, who is happily running a rustic brothel. In the nearby town, Primo finds a female survivor from Auschwitz with whom he shares a few tender moments.

At last, the train Primo had been waiting for all along does arrive. From Poland, it takes him through Hungary to Vienna, then to Munich, from where he boards another that finally brings him home to Turin. Awaiting him is the sunlit stillness of his study, lined with shelves of knowledge his experience may well have overturned, but in all other respects, just as he had left it, a microcosm untouched by war.

As expected, most critics have found the film an inspiring, accomplished work, but one lacking a cohesive dramatic backbone. John Simon, writing in the *National Review,* justifies this by asking, "But how else to convey desperate errings by foot and rail through a topsy-turvy Eastern Europe?" David Denby, writing in *New York* magazine, also leaps to Rosi's defense, describing the filmmaker as "the last remaining genius of the Italian neorealist movement" who, in *The Truce,* was "working under tremendous constraints to create a peculiar moment of disorder, a moment when civilization exists only through its half-remembered echoes, its scattered fragments." And so, the film emerges as "a series of strange, anomalous moments . . . an epic of gestures and uncompleted acts." Writing from a literary standpoint, Stanley Kaufmann, in *The New Republic,* feels the film does not do justice to its real-life subject's vision of war: "Levi had come to believe that the rooted threat against

CREDITS

Primo: John Turturro
Cesare: Massimo Ghini
The Greek: Rade Serbedzija
Daniele: Stefano Dinisi
Col. Rovi: Teco Celio

Origin: Italy
Released: 1997
Production: Leo Pescarolo and Guido De Laurentiis for Capitol Films, Channel Four Films; released by Miramax Films
Direction: Francesco Rosi
Screenplay: Francesco Rosi, Stefano Rulli, and Sandro Petraglia; based on the book by Primo Levi
Cinematography: Pasqualino de Santis, Marco Pontecorvo
Editing: Ruggero Mastroianni, Bruno Sarandrea
Music: Luis Bacalov
Costumes: Alberto Verso
Production design: Andrea Crisanti
Sound: Alain Curvelier
MPAA rating: R
Running Time: 116 minutes

peace was the inner state of man, that thus peace would always be a mere truce." Kaufmann points out that this could explain Levi's suicide in 1987.

—*Vivek Adarkar*

REVIEWS

Boxoffice. July, 1997, p. 81.
Entertainment Weekly. May 8, 1998, p. 52.
Hollywood Reporter. May 14, 1997, p. 7.
Los Angeles Times. April 24, 1998, p. F4.
National Review. June 1, 1998.
New Republic. May 11, 1998.
New York. May 4, 1998.
New York Post. April 24, 1998.
New York Times. April 19, 1998, p. AR15.
New York Times. April 24, 1998, p. E16.
People. May 4, 1998, p. 34.
Variety. February 24, 1997, p. 78.
Village Voice. September 10, 1996, p. 78.

The Truman Show

On the air. Unaware.—Movie tagline

"You've never seen anything quite like *The Truman Show*! Adventurous, provocative, even daring—who would have thought that Jim Carrey might simultaneously break your heart as easily as he makes you laugh? It's the role of his career."—Kenneth Turan, *Los Angeles Times*

"Peter Weir's *The Truman Show* is a must-see and guaranteed Oscar bait. By comparison Hollywood's usual notion of summer fare, *The Truman Show* is definitely a dazzler. Jim Carrey gives an instantly iconic performance."—Janet Maslin, *New York Times*

"*The Truman Show* is bright as hell and more smoothly provocative than the rest of the summer movies strung together."—Anthony Lane, *New Yorker*

"*The Truman Show* is a miraculous movie! It will rattle both your head and heart, and Jim Carrey's raw, life-size performance will surprise you. Ingenious!"—Jeff Giles, *Newsweek*

"*The Truman Show* may be nothing less than a watershed movie. Jim Carrey is marvelous!"—Gene Siskel, *Siskel & Ebert*

"It's time to celebrate! *The Truman Show* is breathtakingly fresh, a refreshing breeze of originality."—Gene Shalit, *The Today Show*

 Box Office: $125,618,201

Truman Burbank (Jim Carrey) thinks he's just smiling to his neighbors, but his whole life is being telecast to the whole world in *The Truman Show.*

As a rule, Hollywood doesn't like taking many chances. With the average film now costing over $50 million to produce, gambling on an unproven formula or on a vehicle devoid of stars is risky business. When it comes to original thought, the motion picture industry is also notoriously shallow and bereft. They love cloning. There have been two movies focusing on the life and career of Steve Prefontaine, an arrogant 1970s long-distance runner from Oregon. Neither film faired very well at the boxoffice. This year saw two movies about meteors and two animated features dealing with cute, huggable insects. Why roll the dice when the public taste is so easy to figure out?

When *Ace Ventura: Pet Detective* was released in 1993, it didn't have much to lose. It had a small budget and needed one good weekend to break even and if it didn't, who would care? Jim Carrey, that's who. Having just left the sketch comedy show *In Living Color* where he was lovingly referred to as 'the white guy,' Carrey had a lot riding on *Ventura*. Although he'd been on the stand-up circuit since the late 70s (which eventually led to a cable special, *Jim Carrey's Unnatural Act*) and had parts in eight previous films dating back to 1981, he wasn't exactly setting the world on fire.

While *Ventura* only yielded him a six-figure paycheck, it gave Carrey his first real chance to present his talents in front of a mass audience without the constraints of censored network television at his heals. A tightly wound, non-stop ball of perpetual motion, Carrey contorted his face and body in a manner unseen since the likes of Chaplin and Keaton. Physical comedy had found a new star. That's all well and good but those guys come and go with numbing regularity. If he could act with conviction, he might actually be the real deal. Whatever acting skills he had were buried beneath an onslaught of hyperactivity that included Carrey pretending to talk through his backside.

Ventura led to *The Mask* then *Dumb & Dumber* (both with mid-seven figure paychecks), *Ace Ventura: When Nature Calls*, *Batman Forever*, and and finally *The Cable Guy*, where he became the first actor in history to receive $20 million to act in a film. Carrey had finally made it. Well, not really. *The Cable Guy* tanked—big time. Though billed as a dark comedy, it came off as just plain dark. While Carrey toned down the physicality and showed something resembling a newfound vulnerability, it left audiences befuddled and despondent. Carrey was no longer cute. He became a stalker with a lisp and a bad haircut. One dud doesn't end a career, but *The Cable Guy* did force Carrey to realize that he couldn't subject his audience to such a radical about face. Collecting $20 million didn't improve his standing among the acting community either. He was still regarded as a one-trick pony. Wanting respect, Carrey began an unlikely collaboration with highly regarded director Peter Weir.

Known as an actors' director, the Australian born Weir possessed a sterling reputation within Hollywood circles. He made serious pictures that featured top talent that, while not blockbusters with extravagant budgets, still made serious money. He also had an eye for casting talented actors who were in a rut or needed a change of genre. *The Year Of Living Dangerously* took Mel Gibson from action/adventure star to romantic leading man. The same for Harrison Ford in *Witness*. *Dead Poets Society* transformed Robin Williams from earnest jokester to just plain earnest. Weir obviously saw some of Williams in Carrey. A brilliant, physical comedian whose frenetic, often scattershot energy needed some tempering and fine tuning that only Weir could perform. The role Weir had in mind for Carrey was going to be almost exclusively dramatic. Carrey was going to make a mature film, take a pay cut, and stretch as an actor.

Truman Burbank's (Jim Carrey) usual greeting: "Good morning, and in case I don't see you, good afternoon, good evening, and good night!"

When we first see Truman Burbank (Carrey), he's an unassuming man who has been a lifelong resident of Seahaven, a quaint community nestled no where particular on the California coast. He lives in a row house among many other ornately decorated row houses, distinguished only by varying shades of pastel trim. Before he leaves each morning, he has a chipper, wide-toothed greeting to offer his congenial, photogenic neighbors. One day, as he prepares to back out of his driveway, he is momentarily distracted by a whistling sound which is shortly followed by a loud crash. Landing in the street behind him is an overhead spotlight. He searches the heavens vainly for the source and not finding any, tosses it aside. It is his and our first indicator that all is not right in Seahaven. Within the confines of the surrealistic urban sprawl, everyone but Truman is in on the labyrinthian scheme. He is the lone subject of a continuous, 24-hour, thirty-year-long television show. Every move of his existence as been chronicled for all the world to see. His wife, friends, and family have been expertly arranged and choreographed for the sole purpose of providing fodder for a rabid, glassy-eyed, worldwide audience. From birth to adulthood, five thousand carefully hidden cameras captured Truman's mostly uneventful life with wife Meryl (Laura Linney).

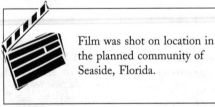

Film was shot on location in the planned community of Seaside, Florida.

Eccentric artist Christof (Ed Harris), a cool but eerily efficient man, oversees, or directs the massive production. Literally and figuratively, Truman is his baby. (It is later revealed that Truman was actually adopted by the show, making Christof his de facto legal guardian). Christof goes to great lengths to insure that the show continues, even if it means temporarily putting Truman in harm's way. As a child, Truman and his "father" decided to take a boat ride and venture beyond the placid shores of Seahaven. Christof orders tsunami-strength winds, which cause the tragic, accidental drowning 'death' of the father and permanently instills a fear of water in Truman.

In order to cover the costs of such a behemoth production (it is a 'round-the-clock pageant and there are no

AWARDS AND NOMINATIONS

Golden Globes 1999: Drama Actor (Jim Carrey); Supporting Actor (Ed Harris); Score
National Board of Review 1998: Supporting Actor (Ed Harris)
Academy Awards 1998 Nominations: Supporting Actor (Ed Harris); Director (Peter Weir); Original Screenplay

commercials), Christof resorts to what Hollywood has been doing for decades: strategic product placement. Christof waves many of these commercial red flags in Truman's face with the help by Donna Reed-clone Meryl. She regularly plugs these products with all the grace and subtly of an airbrushed model from QVC.

For the most part, the actors selected to surround Truman are as diligent as Christof in keeping Truman in the dark. While Truman's mom (Holland Taylor) only makes a cameo appearance or two, Meryl and Truman's best friend Marlon (Noah Emmerich) must remain steadfast. Noah is the most unfliching. In one of the film's most poignant moments, Truman implores and begs Noah to tell him the truth. Noah never gives him a remote indication that their friendship has been fabricated. He looks Truman straight in the eye and lies. It is a truly unsettling scene.

At the heart of *The Truman Show* is a touching love story between Truman and bit player Lauren (Natasha McElhone) from Truman's high school days. A distant flirt who was meant only as a momentary diversion, Truman carries a torch for this girl from the moment he sees her. Waffling between doing her job and following her heart, Lauren tells Truman it is all a ruse and he should get out as quickly as he can. With the efficiency of the Secret Service, Christof has her whisked away and out of Truman's life to Fiji, or so he's told by some supporting actor. A similar fate takes place when Truman's father (Brian Delate) returns "from the dead" to confront his "son." At this point, Truman is convinced that all is not right and starts to uncover the truth. His efforts of escape are thwarted by firm-standing secondary players who do their level best to keep appearances up. In the end, Truman's victory comes as a direct result of him overcoming seemingly insurmountable fears and phobias while outwitting his puppeteer. Even as their inseparable bond whithers away before their very eyes, Truman's worldwide audience cheers his independence.

Weir's scathing commentary on television carries the unabashed social wallop of *Network,* the sarcastic droll of *To Die For* and is presented with a vibrant, yet decidedly surreal tone that recalls the dread-lurking-just-below-the-placid-surface of *Edward Scissorhands.* Sure, our lives would be a lot easier if we had a 24-hour-a-day guardian angel lurking over our shoulders, but like the bird in the gilded cage, we'll never now life completely until we break free of the soft-petaled restraints that jail us. As Weir has proven before, there is much to learn from our failures and shortcomings.

Weir was smart in not trying to completely restrain Carrey (like director-actor Ben Stiller did in *The Cable Guy*). Carrey's crisp, rubbery contortionism serves a distinct purpose; dolling out that trademark, wide-toothed grin in heavy doses keeps him accessible to his original (most loyal) fan base while opening the eyes of a more discerning, high-brow audience. For the first time in his career (save slightly for *The Mask*), Carrey has played the underdog. Here he possesses the same everyman persona as his lifelong hero Jimmy Stewart. People who loathed his previous works have sung his praises for his turn as Truman. The turnaround role here has led to future projects (*Man On The Moon, Incredible Mr. Limpet*) that will allow him to distance himself further from his strictly buffoon image. With *The Truman Show,* Carrey has earned the one thing that has eluded him for the majority of his professional life: outright respect from his merciless critics, audience, and peers. That has to be the most satisfying victory of all.

—*J. M. Clark*

CREDITS

Truman Burbank: Jim Carrey
Christof: Ed Harris
Meryl: Laura Linney
Marlon: Noah Emmerich
Lauren/Sylvia: Natascha McElhone
Truman's mother: Holland Taylor
Truman's father: Brian Delate
Control room director: Paul Giamatti
Network executive: Philip Baker Hall
Network exexutive: John Pleshette

Origin: USA
Released: 1998
Production: Scott Rudin, Andrew Niccol, Edward S. Feldman, and Adam Schroeder; released by Paramount Pictures
Direction: Peter Weir
Screenplay: Andrew Niccol
Cinematography: Peter Biziou
Editing: William Anderson, Lee Smith
Music: Burkhard Dallwitz, Phillip Glass
Production design: Dennis Glassner
Art direction: Richard L. Johnson
Costumes: Marilyn Matthews
Sound: Art Rochester
MPAA rating: PG
Running Time: 102 minutes

REVIEWS

Chicago Tribune. June 5, 1998, p. 4.
Entertainment Weekly. June 5, 1998, p. 43.
Los Angeles Times. June 5, 1998, p. F1.
New York Times. June 5, 1998, p. E1.
People. June 15, 1998, p. 35.
Rolling Stone. June 25, 1998, p. 99.
Sight and Sound. October, 1998, p. 58.
Time. June 1, 1998.
USA Today. June 5, 1998, p. 8E.
Variety. April 27, 1998, p. 57.
Village Voice. June 9, 1998, p. 43.

TwentyFourSeven

Try Love. Try Hate. Try Anything. Just Try.
—Movie tagline

"Shane Meadows has made the best British film of the year."—*Esquire*

"Striking and daring!"—Janet Maslin, *New York Times*

TwentyFourSeven is the debut feature film of Shane Meadows, a young director who first caught the critics' attention in 1996 with the short *Where's the Money, Ronnie?* Meadows co-wrote *TwentyFourSeven,* starring Bob Hoskins as a sensitive but sturdy guy who wants to stop the gangland rivalry in his Midlands town by establishing a boxing club. The role is tailor-made for the feisty Hoskins, who has given many bravura performances without losing his air of vulnerability. His character, Darcy, empathizes with young lads in a community where opportunities are nil. They have no horizon, no sense of the future, and all too easily get involved in drugs and in fights. Darcy fondly remembers his youth, when a boxing club gave him and his chums a sense of discipline and pride. Defending one of his boys he tells a panel at a hearing that the boxing club will keep the crime rate down. He vows to take personal responsibility for shaping up the local misfits.

On the *David Letterman Show,* Hoskins joked about how he was lured into doing this low-budget example of cinema verite. He was told that Meadows was a young, promising filmmaker, and Hoskins liked what he saw of Meadows's work. But then the two met, and Hoskins saw that the filmmaker looked just like him. That cinched the deal, of course. For Hoskins has often had that almost naive, youthful, striving sense of self that has made him such an appealing character. To see himself recreated, so to speak, in a new generation must have been exhilarating indeed.

Without Hoskins, without documentary-style black-and-white, and the authentic regional accents, *TwentyFour-Seven* would be just another trite, sentimental story of moral uplift and tragedy. The elegant direction, acting, and cinematography make this film absorbing even when it does verge on hackneyed. Meadows is exceptionally good at just following his characters about with medium closeups and lots of group shots, which complement the voice-over narrator (Darcy), whose words come straight out of his diary, which tracks his dream of forming his boys into a team that the community will respect.

If Hoskins were not so physical himself, it might seem unlikely that these young roughs would follow his lead. He plays their game (soccer) to get them to play his. He can be harshly critical of a boy when he loses his temper in the ring (stomping an opponent, for example), but he always follows up with a fatherly cajoling, making the lad feel that the success of the boxing club depends upon him.

Darcy is playing a dangerous game, though. He is promising the boys a kind of redemption, not just an activity that will put their time to good use. He manages to get their club funded by a local gangster (though the level of criminality in this community seems quite mild by Anglo-American big city standards), and to get press coverage. He gives the boys short deadlines—in a week, a month, they will be able to box, to compete, to put on a show for the community. He works up a heady atmosphere and a sense of camaraderie even among boys who have been rivals.

Darcy appears to succeed because he is so much like his boys. He is unemployed, and he apparently has no family.

> Darcy: (Bob Hoskins) "The lads and the people in this town have been living the same day their whole life."

CREDITS

Alan Darcy: Bob Hoskins
Tim: Danny Nussbaum
Geoff: Bruce Jones
Pat: Annette Badland
Gadget: Justin Brady
Knighty: James Hooton
Daz: Darren Campbell
Fagash: Mat Hand

Origin: Great Britain
Released: 1997
Production: Imogen West for BBC Films and Scala; released by October Films
Direction: Shane Meadows
Screenplay: Shane Meadows and Paul Fraser
Cinematography: Ashley Rowe
Editing: Bill Diver
Music: Boo Hewerdine, Neil MacColl
Production design: John-Paul Kelly
Art direction: Niall Moroney
Costumes: Philip Crichton
Sound: Rosie Straker
MPAA rating: R
Running Time: 96 minutes

He shyly courts a local woman and goes dancing with an elderly relative. His own horizon has been severely restricted. Yet in his diary he is able to envision a better, more ambitious life. This is really all he wants to impart to his team: the idea that there might be a way out of their narrow lives.

Title is slang for 24 hours a day, seven days a week.

The climax of the fight training and of the film is the match-up with another local boxing team. Darcy's club, judging by the early bouts, is not yet quite up to speed. Faced with well-trained opponents they stumble and gasp, lose their tempers, and turn to street fighting. Yet Darcy and others intervene and the match seems to be just barely under control. What tears it, though, is one of Darcy's boy's parents, a terrible has-been who cannot bear to see his son succeed. He threatens to take his boy home before his bout, and when Darcy takes the aggravating man outside, they get into a fight, and Darcy (just like one of his lads) loses it, pummeling the man into a bloody mass in a heap of garbage. The father's boy goes outside and sees how his coach has hurt and humiliated his father, and in that mo-ment Darcy's dream dissolves. He has done exactly what he has told the boys they must never do: lose control.

To tell the story's ending is to give nothing away. The film begins with a derelict Darcy coming home to die. This is not a film built on suspense; it is, rather, a very contemporary tragedy, designed from the beginning to make one man's story emblematic of a community and of the human condition.

—*Carl Rollyson*

REVIEWS

Boxoffice. April, 1998, p. 200.
Detroit Free Press. May 1, 1998, p. 3D.
Detroit News. May 1, 1998, p. 4D.
Entertainment Weekly. April 24, 1998, p. 57.
New York Times. April 10, 1998, p. E18.
Sight and Sound. April, 1998, p. 55.
Variety. September 15, 1997, p. 78.

Twilight

Some people can buy their way out of anything. Except the past.—Movie tagline

"*Twilight* is a movie with glamour and class. Sarandon is stunningly impressive, Hackman is strong and fascinating, and Newman is a triumph."—Dennis Cunningham, *CBS-TV*

"*Twilight* is a class act in a classic genre. Newman has the ease and panache that only lifelong movie stardom can bring. Sarandon doesn't have to fake glamour, she does it here with sinuous allure."—Janet Maslin, *New York Times*

"Few movies reward us with strong stories and brilliant acting. Newman, Sarandon, and Hackman are gathered in a mystery that's an intrigue of murder, blackmail, devious romance and smoldering sexuality. They show us what fine acting is all about."—Gene Shalit, *The Today Show*

Box Office: $15,055,091

In 1994, Paul Newman teamed up with writer-director Robert Benton for a film adaptation of Richard Russo's novel, *Nobody's Fool.* It was a slice-of-life drama about a man in his later years coming to terms with his family and community. In 1998, the same trio has released *Twilight,* a detective yarn written by Benton and Russo that, as its title suggests, also focuses on characters in their later years. This time around, however, Benton and company have collaborated on a pure genre piece—a film *noir* set among the has-beens and hangers-on of the Hollywood community.

What sets *Twilight* apart from other contemporary *noirs* is its utter sincerity. It is genuinely trying to re-create a genre of the past without the hipness or narrative invention of a Coen brothers or Tarantino film. In a way, this is a refreshing change of pace for the irony-laden 90s. We are given a chance to see great actors like Newman, Gene Hackman, and Susan Sarandon play opposite each other against an old-fashioned background of deception and buried secrets. At the same time, its lack of innovation, its strict adherence to formula without much divergence, prevents it from becoming a classic film, despite its stellar cast.

Newman plays Harry Ross, who, in the opening of the film, is on a mission to retrieve a seventeen-year-old girl, who is in Mexico with her boyfriend. In Harry's attempt to bring her home, the girl, Mel (Reese Witherspoon), the daughter of Jack and Catherine Ames (Hackman and Sarandon), fires Harry's gun, and he is wounded in the leg. Two years later, we see Harry in the process of giving a statement to the police while we hear his laconic voice-over: "My name is Harry Ross, and here's the way my life has gone. First I was a cop, then a private detective, then a drunk. Also in there somewhere a husband and a father. You'd think with all that that the world would lose its power to seduce, but you'd be wrong." From that point the film places itself squarely in the *noir* tradition with the world-weary, cynical hero who has made a mess of his life and is about to share the details.

Ever since the incident with Mel, Harry has lived on the Ameses' property and done odd jobs for Jack. The Ameses are a wealthy couple who were once movie stars, and there is a sexual tension between Harry and Catherine—little flirtations that hint at the attraction Harry feels. Newman and Sarandon play very well off of each other. When we first see them together, Catherine has just gotten out of the swimming pool, and Harry, ever the gentleman, looks away, even though, as Catherine teasingly points out, he has "seen everything there is of me to see" in her movies.

The plot is set in motion when Jack gives Harry a package to deliver to a woman named Gloria Lamar (Margo Martindale), but, when Harry takes the package to its destination, he discovers a man bleeding to death and shooting his gun at him. Harry narrowly escapes getting shot, the man dies, and, from his identification, Harry discovers the man is Lester Ivar (M. Emmet Walsh). Harry goes to Lester's house, breaks in, and discovers Lester had newspaper clippings from twenty years ago covering the disappearance (thought to be a suicide) of Billy Sullivan, Catherine's husband at the time, and her subsequent marriage to Jack. After Harry burns the clippings, the police appear; the officer in charge is Verna (Stockard Channing), an old colleague and flame of Harry. She gives him a hug, notes how long it has been since they have seen each other, then gives the order to "cuff him" in an exchange indicative of the film's often gentle yet sly humor.

After answering a few questions, Harry is soon released and meets his old friend, Raymond Hope (James Garner), who once worked in the police department and then in security at a studio where he looked after Jack. Harry and Raymond share the easygoing camaraderie of two old friends reminiscing about the past. Indeed, running throughout the

Harry (Paul Newman): "I'm tired of people getting killed. I'm tired of being lied to." Catherine (Susan Sarandon): "When have I lied to you?" Harry: "When you acted as though you loved me."

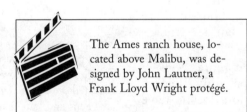

The Ames ranch house, located above Malibu, was designed by John Lautner, a Frank Lloyd Wright protégé.

film is a sense of old age and loss, but, aside from Jack's battle with cancer, these heavy themes are handled with a light touch. Raymond playfully asks Harry about his prostate, the old pals remember how tough they used to be, and Harry clears up a false rumor that he had been emasculated in Mexico in the incident with the gun.

It turns out that Jack is being blackmailed by Jeff (Liev Schreiber), Mel's boyfriend in the film's opening scenes, and his parole officer, Gloria, who learned about the Billy Sullivan incident from Ivar, the investigating officer on the case. He believed Sullivan was murdered and his body buried on the Ameses' ranch, and Gloria thinks she can convince Jack that she knows where the body is buried. Mel has given Jeff the key to the Ameses' ranch house (a rather unbelievable plot point), and Jeff is digging around to find the corpse. Harry gets beat up in his first encounter with the blackmailers but gives them a decoy package and thus forces a second meeting, where Jeff and Gloria are killed when a stranger appears out of nowhere. Harry looks like the murderer and begs Verna for twenty-four hours to solve the case. This is a fairly clichéd request for a detective film, but it is redeemed by a cute moment in which Verna flushes a toilet to illustrate what will happen to her career if he should fail.

Harry ultimately finds Billy's body on the Ameses' property, discovers a bullet hole in the skull, and confronts Jack with what he has found. According to Jack, Billy ended up at the bottom of an empty swimming pool when he learned of Catherine's infidelity and came after Jack in a drunken state. Of course the bullet hole makes this an incomplete story, and soon we learn from Raymond that Billy survived the crash into the pool and Raymond finished him off—Raymond in fact is the one who cleans up the messes for the Ameses and lives quite comfortably as a result. He smoothly tries to persuade Harry to put it all behind them. Harry, however, plans to turn him in, and the result is a climactic shootout in which Harry kills Raymond, and, as far as Harry's statement to the police is concerned, this is the end of the story. However, in a scene not revealed to the police, we see Harry learned that Catherine, in classic *femme fatale* style, was behind the recent killings—even if she did not directly order Raymond to do them, she spoke to him and knew he would kill for her.

There is a subplot concerning one night of adultery between Catherine and Harry, but Jack discovers it almost immediately, and, aside from it being a culmination of Catherine's and Harry's flirtation, it does not have much of an impact on the main blackmail plot. Despite her tryst with Harry, Catherine loves her husband, and Harry must come to terms with this reality. Even Mel occasionally reminds Harry he is an outsider in their home.

In a commentary in the *Los Angeles Times/Calendar* (March 8, 1998), Bill Desowitz declared *Twilight* is "what we used to call a 'movie-movie': well-crafted and executed with such precision and self-reflexiveness that there's a communion between the filmmakers, actors, and filmgoers." He also points out that the film "dispenses with the complicated machinations of plot to concentrate on the complicated machinations of character," and indeed this is where the film succeeds wonderfully, although a few more twists and turns of the plot would have elevated the film. (Think of 1997's *L.A. Confidential,* for example, a neo-*noir* that successfully blends complex characters with an intricate plot.)

Nonetheless, the smooth interaction among the principals and the gentle sense of world-weariness give *Twilight*

CREDITS

Harry Ross: Paul Newman
Catherine Ames: Susan Sarandon
Jack Ames: Gene Hackman
Mel Ames: Reese Witherspoon
Raymond Hope: James Garner
Verna: Stockard Channing
Reuben: Giancarlo Esposito
Jeff Willis: Liev Schreiber
Gloria Lamar: Margo Martindale
Captain Phil Egan: John Spencer
Lester Ivar: M. Emmet Walsh

Origin: USA
Released: 1998
Production: Arlene Donovan and Scott Rudin for Cinehaus; released by Paramount Pictures
Direction: Robert Benton
Screenplay: Robert Benton and Richard Russo
Cinematography: Piotr Sobocinski
Editing: Carol Littleton
Music: Elmer Bernstein
Production design: David Gropman
Art direction: David Bomba
Costumes: Joseph G. Aulisi
Sound: David R. B. Macmillan
MPAA rating: R
Running Time: 94 minutes

its own special charm. Newman has the grace of a man who realizes his shortcomings but is trying to get to the bottom of the puzzle, and Sarandon exudes her usual sex appeal but in a darker role than we have come to expect from her. In the little moments, like Harry and Jack reminiscing over a friendly game of cards, Raymond and Harry confronting the past, or Harry and Verna evoking old times in the way they look at each other as they go off together at the end, the actors communicate the subtle bonds between people whose best years are probably behind them.

One element that does not work is a supporting character named Reuben (Giancarlo Esposito), who used to be a colleague of Harry and is now a chauffeur. He appears out of nowhere to help Harry and becomes the stereotypical sidekick who keeps botching up the job.

The dark secret, the murder of Billy Sullivan, finally does not have the resonance of a pervasive corruption or evil, crucial in so many great *noirs*. In the *New York Times,* Janet Maslin called Jack and Catherine "the Tom and Daisy Buchanan" of the film, and this is perhaps the depth of their evil—two reckless people who make a mess and have other people clean up after them. The reference to *The Great Gatsby* is fitting since *Twilight* is finally a meditation on the insiders like Catherine and Jack who live the glamorous life and the outsiders like Harry and Raymond who do their bidding.

Twilight did not do very well at the boxoffice. Perhaps its rhythm is too slow for audiences accustomed to more fast-paced thrillers. Nonetheless, for fans of these actors and the genre, *Twilight* is a rewarding character study.

—*Peter N. Chumo II*

REVIEWS

Battle Creek Enquirer. March 5, 1998, p. 9.
Detroit News. March 6, 1998, p. 1D.
Entertainment Weekly. March 13, 1998, p. 50.
Los Angeles Times. March 6, 1998, p. F1.
Los Angeles Times. March 8, 1998, p. 27.
New York Times. March 6, 1998, p. E22.
New Yorker. March 16, 1998, p. 83.
People. March 16, 1998, p. 20.
Rolling Stone. March 5, 1998, p. 74.
Sight and Sound. December, 1998, p. 63.
USA Today. March 6, 1998, p. 4D.
Variety. March 2, 1998, p. 83.
Washington Post. March 6, 1998, p. D7.

Twilight of the Ice Nymphs

Guy Maddin has got to be one of the most visually distinctive filmmakers working today. Just look at one single frame of any one of his little anti-masterpieces and you'll know instantly that what you've got in front of you is a Guy Maddin film. And yet, his pictures (he insists on calling them that, as opposed to films or movies) stand out not so much because they are fully realized works of cinematic expression, but simply because they're just so very *peculiar*. His 1991 film *Archangel* is one of the most arresting pieces of cinema of the 1990s, simply because it so expertly duplicated the look of silent films, and yet did so in a way that made the viewer wonder if perhaps some silent films had actually been made by Martians. Alas, that film had very little at its center beyond a kind of visual game-playing, and for that reason didn't really mark Maddin as a major filmmaker. His newest film, *Twilight of the Ice Nymphs*, illustrates a similar lack. It's quite original visually, but Maddin fails to capitalize on his keen eye for eccentricity, remaining content with evoking a world where everyone lives between the sly and the flat, but never using that ambiguous state to express anything of interest.

Like Maddin's other work, *Twilight* is notable first and foremost for its visuals, and the title of the film really says it all. The world that Maddin creates seems to be in a state of perpetual twilight, with the odd, rich light that characterizes that part of the day being on display all the time. It's his first film in color, and there's no doubt that Maddin has made the most of the visual choice. His cinematographer, Michael Marshall, is to be commended, as he has created quite a unified and unique visual feel for the film. Indeed, the look of the film, while not as relentlessly weird as *Archangel* or *Tales from the Gimli Hospital*, is odd at its very root, without any imagery that fails to display the film's trademark look of "twilight." To be able to transpose the feel of Maddin's truly whacked-out visual sense from black and white into color would seem an impossible task, but the washed out images, the preponderance of long shots, and the odd camera movements that define the visuals of *Twilight* manage to convey that sense of artificiality that has made him such a cult favorite.

The setting seems to be an island, known as Mandragora, and really a film like this could only be set on an island. It is utterly detached from the mainland of reality, surrounded on all sides by uncertainty and becoming, as a result, an extremely closed and eccentric community. This sense of isolation is what has driven Maddin from the very beginning of his career, leading him to investigate commu-

nities that, even when based on somewhere real (like the Gimli, Manitoba of *Tales of the Gimli Hospital*) take on a quality of utter otherworldliness. Rather than in fully realized worlds, though, Maddin' films are set in places that we come to understand through implication, suggestion, and confusion. *Twilight* is, in some ways, the peak of this sketchy approach to setting, since historical period is utterly unclear (everyone dresses in costumes that are vaguely 19th century, but since it's so rural a locale maybe they're just supposed to be poor) and understanding a sense of nationality or culture is impossible (everyone speaks with different, and somewhat unidentifiable, accents).

The narrative itself, also as usual for Maddin, is pretty minimal. We follow a young man named Peter (Nigel Whitmey), who is coming back home (to Mandragora) after a stint in jail as a "political prisoner." He finds that his sister Amelia (Shelley Duvall) is entangled in various affairs involving the family ostrich farm, her farm hand (played by Frank Gorshin) and the mysterious Dr. Solti (R.H. Thompson). Although Amelia is madly in love with Solti, the doctor seems to be attached (although the nature of their attachment is not very clear) to Juliana (Pascale Bussières), after whom Peter is also longing. This tension creates the usual assortment of bickering, misunderstanding, and heartbreak.

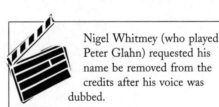

Nigel Whitmey (who played Peter Glahn) requested his name be removed from the credits after his voice was dubbed.

While this may sound like a somewhat dismissive assessment of any other film, that's not necessarily the case with Maddin, who seems to revel in the constant tension between minimalism and excess that defines his films. The plot may be predictable enough, but it has a few quirks that go well beyond the realm of the surreal (the romantic tension between Ameila and the farm hand is resolved when she drives a nail through his head). These sudden emotional explosions hint at a deeper problem with the way that Maddin's narratives work. How seriously, we are left wondering, are we supposed to take all of this? And what parts *exactly* are meant to be taken seriously? These are basic narrative questions that in a Guy Maddin film become unanswerable.

Maddin's earlier films were easier to get your mind around, if for no other reason because they were so utterly strange that it became quite clear they were to be understood as works of visual innovation, and little beyond that. That's not so clear in *Twilight of the Ice Nymphs*, which, while strange, is far more conventional than *Archangel*. *Twilight*'s world, while rendered in unconventional ways (rich in color, stiff in mannerism), is recognizable: he achieves here a sense of veracity that he's gotten nowhere near in his other work. These earlier films, despite their unique visuals, seemed to have precious little behind them. Once the utterly consuming sense of giddiness that defined them is gone, as it more or less is in *Twilight*, there's really not very much left. Maddin has made himself known as the master of distortion, which is something of a dubious distinction, but this film doesn't really manage to live up to that.

In contrast to his earlier work, however, *Twilight* draws upon the talent of some really fantastic actors, although this turns out to be a distinction that doesn't exactly work in Maddin's favor. U.S. audiences are likely to immediately recognize the name of Shelley Duvall, but, alas, she is utterly wasted in this film, delivering flat lines, well, flatly. No doubt that this flatness is supposed to be the point of the entire film, but to employ someone with as much presence as Duvall, who seems to be just bursting at the seams with ec-

centricity and goofiness that Maddin refuses to allow to the surface, seems a real waste. A less familiar but no less distinguished member of the cast is Bussières, who is certainly the most talented French-Canadian actress of her generation. While in other films Bussières has radiated a quiet but powerful presence, she's used here in a way that allows none of her grace or sensuality to become a central part of the film. She's just there to look slender and lovely and to glibly coo some meaningless lines, but never really gets to act. It's clear that Maddin's gifts are visual as opposed to theatrical, so it should come as no surprise that he doesn't deal especially well with his actors. What is striking, though, is that actors of this quality would agree to be in a film that requires so little of them, a film whose very essence precludes the serious attention to their craft that their previous work has exhibited.

Twilight of the Ice Nymphs is a deeply eccentric but in the end a rather vapid exercise in cinematic tomfoolery. Guy Maddin is clearly one of the modern cinema's most adventurous visual stylists, but it's yet to be made clear just what it is he's trying to achieve with his little disorientations. At the 1995 Telluride Film Festival, he was part of a "Tribute to the Surrealists" that included Jan Svankmajer and the Quay Brothers, and this accolade is often used to argue for a shared project with the traditions of surrealism. *Twilight* won't do much to advance that argument, given its lack of a foreboding, dystopic vision that characterizes the best of surrealism (including the work of Svankmajer and the Quays). The early surrealists, goofy and playful though they sometimes were, made it clear that their work was meant to be deadly serious indictments of bourgeois culture. Guy Maddin wastes the potential of his keen visual sensibility by making it equally clear that his work isn't about too much of anything. Really, he's just kidding.

—Jerry White

CREDITS

Juliana Kossel: Pascale Bussières
Amelia Glahn: Shelley Duvall
Cain Ball: Frank Gorshin
Zephyr Eccles: Alice Krige
Dr. Isaac Solti: R.H. Thomson
Matthew Eccles: Ross McMillan
Peter Glahn: Nigel Whitmey

Origin: Canada
Released: 1997
Production: Richard Findlay for Marble Island Pictures; released by Alliance
Direction: Guy Maddin
Screenplay: Georges Toles
Cinematography: Michael Marshall
Editing: Reginald Harkema
Music: John McCulloch
Production design: Rejean Labrie
Art direction: Ian Handford
Costumes: Donna Szoke
MPAA rating: Unrated
Running Time: 91 minutes

REVIEWS

Boxoffice. April, 1998, p. 207.
Sight and Sound. May, 1998, p. 58.
Variety. September 8, 1997, p. 81.

Two Girls and a Guy

Thanks to his two girlfriends, Blake is about to learn a new sexual position. Honesty.—Movie tagline

"An *A*. Brilliant! The movie is ingeniously structured, with an intuitive balance of passion, jokiness and surprise."—Owen Gleiberman, *Entertainment Weekly*

"Robert Downey Jr. is, as always, nothing short of superb!"—Andrew Sarris, *New York Observer*

"This guy, these girls, this movie, are one of a kind. Scorching, smart and painfully hilarious!"—David Ansen, *Newsweek*

"Robert Downey Jr.'s tour de force! Few movies offer a performer the opportunity to let his talents cascade forth in the breathless rush that *Two Girls and a Guy* provides Robert Downey Jr."—Richard Schickel, *Time*

"A very funny and sophisticated look at relationships in the '90s!"—*Time Out New York*

 Box Office: $2,057,193

A romantic triangle begins when the two women in Blake's (Robert Downey Jr.) life confront him in the romantic comedy *Two Girls and a Guy*.

Whoever said that drugs are always bad was probably not a publicist. One of the top reasons that the movie *Two Girls and a Guy* drummed up press coverage was the fact that its star, Robert Downey Jr., the "Guy" of the title, was right in the middle of a jail sentence for drugs during the making of the film. Whenever an article mentioned Downey (or more often, the "troubled Downey"), there would also be a little plug for *Two Girls and a Guy*. And when the movie finally did arrive in theaters, there were probably more than a few filmgoers who went to the movie to see whether Downey could pull it off or to search for signs of trouble in his face.

Was this planned? Actually, yes in a way. According to the *Los Angeles Times*, director James Toback (who directed Downey in 1987's *The Pick-Up Artist*) got the idea for the film after seeing "the disheveled actor making a handcuffed court appearance on TV and wrote the script in a four-day creative frenzy." The filming itself was similarly fast and loose. It was shot in only eleven days and Downey was allowed a lot of improvisation.

No one should be surprised at this sort of move from Toback, making his first film in eight years. He's become known as a provocative film director who follows his passions. His work, from his debut *Fingers* to the documentary *The Big Bang*, has never been bland.

Despite all of Downey's severe and unfortunate drug problems, they—amazingly—have never seemed to interfere with his film work. In fact, with fine work in films like *Chaplin* (1992) and *Natural Born Killers* (1995), he has become one of the more respected actors of his generation. It's a testament to just how talented he is that despite the personal hell he was going through during *Two Girl*'s filming, again, his troubles weren't apparent onscreen.

Which is not to say that *Two Girls and a Guy* doesn't borrow heavily from Downey's predicament. Not Downey's predicament with drugs, exactly, but the situation of being the kind of person who has to lie to others to protect a way of life. One scene in particular is especially raw. In it, Downey's character, Blake, looks in the mirror and watches himself going through an array of emotions. He rages. He cries. He pleads with himself: "Is this what you want to do? Hurt people?" After awhile, something clicks in his head and he becomes more interested in looking at his reflection—how he is reacting rather than the simple fact that he is reacting. Are the emotions real or fake? Can an actor like Blake have emotions without being aware of how they are coming across? The viewer gets the feeling of peering into Downey's real life—perhaps after lying for so long, Downey himself is no longer aware which things he says are true and which are lies. The camera lingers on the scene for a long time and it is almost embarrassing to be a voyeur to such a private display.

This time working with To-back, Downey plays a pick-up artist of a different sort. In this case, he's a man with two girlfriends. It's not surprising that Toback would choose sexual politics as a subject. Toback's own sexual exploits have in the past been the stuff of mag-azine articles. But in the film, Toback's—oops! Blake's—problems start when his two girlfriends decide to wait for him outside his apartment complex. Lou (Natasha Gregson Wagner, the daughter of Natalie Wood), Blake's brunette, talkative, street-wise girlfriend, starts bragging to the cool, blonde Carla (Heather Graham) about her great boyfriend. The two begin comparing notes and realize they're waiting for the same great boyfriend. But instead of stomping off in anger, the two decide to break into Blake's apartment and wait for him to come home.

As they wait, they continue to compare notes. They find out that Blake has charmed them with nearly identical en-dearments. For example, he has told them both that he can't even look at other women because he is so utterly in love with them.

Blake finally arrives in high spirits, not knowing that the women are lurking and watching him. He comes in with a flourish, plops down at the piano and belts out a tune from a Vivaldi opera. He picks up the phone and calls his mother and yells at his agent for not getting him good enough roles. He leaves leering messages for both Carla and Lou. Even-tually Carla decides to make a move and she comes out of hiding. When Blake is confronted with this situation, you can almost see his mind clicking over the possibilities of what he can do. Why is Carla here? Is this good? How should I be reacting?

Then Lou steps into the room and Blake is cornered. How will a smooth-talking, charming man like Blake han-dle this situation? Will he be able to talk his way out of it? Will one girl "win?" Is a ménage à tois in their future? These are the questions that *Two Girls and a Guy* is fascinated with.

The rest of *Two Girls and a Guy* takes place in Blake's apartment over the course of the afternoon. All three of the characters seem fascinated by this new interesting drama in their lives and want to hang around to see what happens. After all, they are all manipulators and now they all have something over on each other.

The plot has the kind of loose, talky, freeform feel of a Henry Jaglom film. Tobacks creates a "what if" situation, then explores all its implications. Even though the action is

Blake (Robert Downey Jr.) to both his girlfriends: "The truth is, I meant everything I said to each of you at the time I said it."

confined to one apartment, it doesn't feel that way, because there's always some new drama to contend with. The action shifts and changes as the afternoon wears on. Without giv-ing the action away between the trio, things keep happen-ing. Two characters decide to get drunk together, a charac-ter fakes a dramatic suicide and two characters have a steamy sexual interlude in the upstairs bedroom. Each character tries to deal with the new developments in their own way. Blake lies, he de-nies, he tells the women he loves them both. Carla is distant and tries to hurt Blake by saying that she hasn't been faithful either. Lou reveals that she is bisexual and suggests a threesome.

Toback's gamble to let Downey loose on his character pays off. Downey puts in one of his best performances ever. His Blake is both charming and repellent. Blake is the kind of person who is "on" all the time. He is full of passion and full of himself. He is always sizing up situations and figur-ing out what he should say. He figures out what makes peo-ple tick and uses it to know how to behave with them. This is what makes him such a desirable lover because he knows exactly the right things to say. It's also what makes him an undesirable lover because he says the right endearments specifically because they're right, not because he means them.

What won particular critical acclaim for the film is Downey's acting. He lets us see Blake's charm in action, but also, skillfully lets us in on the thoughts and planning be-hind the charm. Downey lets us see Blake's mind whirling to figure out the next action to take.

CREDITS

Blake Allen: Robert Downey Jr.
Carla: Heather Graham
Lou: Natasha Gregson Wagner
Tommy: Angel David
Carol: Frederique Van Der Wal

Origin: USA
Released: 1998
Production: Edward R. Pressman and Chris Hanley for Muse Productions; released by Fox Searchlight
Direction: James Toback
Screenplay: James Toback
Cinematography: Barry Markowitz
Editing: Alan Oxman
Production design: Kevin Thompson
Set decoration: Alis Grifo
Sound: Brian Miksis, Itamar Ben Jacob
MPAA rating: R
Running Time: 84 minutes

Hot off the fame of playing Rollergirl in *Boogie Nights* (1997), Heather Graham is serviceable as Carla. Her performance doesn't stand out, but it doesn't need to. Her Carla, a cool blonde who may or may not have a wild side, exists primarily as someone for Blake to react to and to spar with.

Natasha Gregson Wagner's performance is more daring. Her acting veers noticeably, but she captures the sense of Lou being a wild card in the whole situation. Her street-smart character has the daring to call Blake on some of his more generic lines. "I'm not beautiful, I'm cute," she says, correcting him on his choice of compliments.

But while the idea is interesting and Downey's performance fascinating, the movie isn't all it could be. At times, the characters are tiresomely whiny and a little too involved with their whole drama. And Toback adds some unnecessarily heavy-handed moments. When Blake is pacing around his apartment, the song "You Don't Know Me" plays pointedly. Later, the camera lingers on a poster for *Jules and Jim*, the classic Truffaut film that's also about a love triangle. It seems just a bit egoistic to obviously invite comparisons between the two films.

In the end, it isn't the intriguing premise or the sexual politics that make this film, it's Downey's performance. Downey is the guy who makes or breaks the film and, to his credit—especially given the circumstances—he makes it.

—*Jill Hamilton*

REVIEWS

Boxoffice. March, 1998, p. 55.
Entertainment Weekly. April 24, 1998, p. 50.
Hollywood Reporter. April 21, 1998, p. 17.
Los Angeles Times. April 24, 1998, p. F16.
New York Times. April 24, 1998, p. E12.
People. May 4, 1998, p. 31.
Sight and Sound. February, 1999, p. 57.
USA Today. April 24, 1998, p. 6E.
Variety. September 1, 1997, p. 77.
Village Voice. May 5, 1998, p. 128.
Washington Post Weekend. April 24, 1998, p. 56.

The Ugly

"A brilliantly bold psychological tale of dementia!"—Karen Tom, *Coven Magazine*

"A chilling and frightening mind game!"—Tony Timpone, *Fangoria*

There is something unique about *The Ugly*. No, it's not the low, low budget of this psychological, horror yarn from New Zealand, but rather how the money was used. Taking its cue from the dry, laconic style of television's *The X-Files*, *The Ugly* manages to do a lot with very little. The story focuses on a hospitalized serial killer who is being interviewed by a psychiatrist to see if he is fit to stand trial. It's all been done before, but somehow the cheap theatrics, the watery look of the film, it's slow pace, disjointed editing, and dead-pan acting all add up to something more than expected, leaving a dry and perplexed taste in your mouth.

In part this quality comes from the confusion this film creates over what is real and what is being imagined, which is what a good haunting story should do. Confusion is jar-

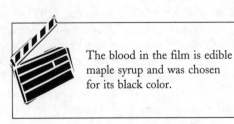

The blood in the film is edible maple syrup and was chosen for its black color.

ring, gets under your toe nails, and makes you scratch where there is no itch. Simon Cartwright (Paolo Rotondo), the killer, is haunted by his childhood, and Dr. Karen Schumaker (Rebecca Hobbs) is haunted by her ambitions and what they have cost her. Riding the crest of a highly publicized case that wrecked her marriage, Dr. Schumaker agrees to interview the hospitalized Simon to see if he is fit to stand trial.

The coldly ambiguous Dr. Marlowe (Roy Ward) oversees the hospital and isn't too anxious about the possibility of his release. He has good reason to feel that way. Simon's story is largely told in flashback and we learn that his parents divorced when he was an infant. His mom, Evelyn (Jennifer Ward-Lealand), poisoned the young Simon's mind against his father, calling him a murderous devil. But Evelyn is no prize herself and spends much of the movie alternately smothering her child with love and beating him ferociously.

School is no better, where Simon is regularly beaten up and mocked by a group of bullies. When the bullies catch him reading a copy of *The Ugly Ducking*, the name sticks and Simon becomes, "the ugly." As a virginal adult "the ugly" becomes something within him that commands him to kill. And he does. *The Ugly* has some of the most effective scenes of murder put on film because they look real. This is not Hollywood blood and guts, but realistic, stomach wrenching, shocking gore. That is the only effective kind of violence on the screen for it doesn't glamorize, but rather exposes it in all its horror.

Supernatural elements come into play when Simon tells Dr. Schumaker that "the visitors" talk to him, tell him to kill. "The visitors" are Simon's victims and they are shown surrounding and taunting him. They command him to kill Dr. Schumaker and Simon lashes out. The hospital guards rescue her in time, but not before she has seen "the visitors" herself. Dr. Marlowe, coldly watching from a one way mirror, isn't surprised by the attack and asks Dr. Schumaker if she saw "them."

CREDITS

Simon Cartwright: Paolo Rotondo
Dr. Karen Shumaker: Rebecca Hobbs
Dr. Marlowe: Roy Ward
Simon's Mother: Jennifer Ward-Lealand

Origin: New Zealand
Released: 1998
Production: Jonathan Dowling for Essential Films and the New Zealand Film Commission; released by Trimark Pictures
Direction: Scott Reynolds
Screenplay: Scott Reynolds
Cinematography: Simon Raby
Editing: Wayne Cook
Music: Victoria Kelly
Production design: Grant Major
Sound: Dick Reade
Special makeup effects: Richard Taylor
MPAA rating: Unrated
Running Time: 92 minutes

Dr. Schumaker goes home, having made the decision that Simon is where he belongs, but Simon somehow manages to escape. Later that night, she dreams that Simon murders her. She wakes with a start to find Simon standing over her bed, with "the visitors" taunting him on to kill. He obeys.

Even though both Dr. Marlowe and Dr. Schumaker seem to see "the visitors," it is never quite clear that they really do. It could just be a cinematic device, meant to clue the audience into the torment inside the mind of the killer. Whatever it is, it doesn't matter, because it works effectively. There are other jarring techniques used as well. The film is non-linear in the extreme, jumping around from the present, to the distant past, the recent past, back to the even more distant past, the present, and so forth. This form of editing creates a sense of imbalance and is handled competently. In other hands this technique just seems silly and confusing. Also effective are the cheap theatrics, like scenes with dropped keys in crisis moments and a metaphorical mask that covers Simon's "ugly" face.

The Ugly, for the most part, is enjoyable and disturbing entertainment, although it's not without flaws. The whole idea of "the ugly" and "the visitors" seems like juvenile pop-psychology. Simon's escape is silly, and the feel of the psychiatric hospital is a cross between *Spellbound* and Mel Brooks's *High Anxiety*. The pluses, though, outweigh the minuses, and this slickly done, "B" movie from New Zealand deserves an American audience.

—*Rich Silverman*

REVIEWS

Boxoffice. June, 1998, p. 76.
Cinema Papers. December, 1997, p. 61.
Cinescape. May, 1998, p. 14.
Los Angeles Times. May 15, 1998, p. F11.
New York Times. May 1, 1998, p. E28.
Sight and Sound. March, 1998, p. 56.
Variety. September 29, 1997, p. 64.

Un Air de Famille; Family Resemblances

"One of the year's most powerful and sincerely affecting films!"—Andrew Johnson, *Time Out NY*

"Flawless! Spellbindingly funny!"—Joe Morgenstern, *Wall Street Journal*

Un Air de Famille is a French family drama that director Cedric Klapisch (*While the Cat's Away* [1996]) injects with a delicious dark humor delivered by unique characters that separates this film from ordinary genre fare. Wholly dialogue-driven, we watch the six main characters of a divided family gradually bare their souls and drop their contrived masks through increasingly bitter and malevolent conversations over dinner. This tête-à-tête fête was deftly adapted from a play by Klapisch and authors Agnes Jaoui and Jean Pierre Bacri.

Taking place almost entirely in a bistro, the family gathers for a birthday party for Yolande (Catherine Frot), who is the wife of one of the three very different siblings, the successful and well-liked software executive Philippe Menaud (Wladimir Yordanoff), who is the golden boy of the family. Philippe's brother, Henri Menaud (Jean-Pierre Bacri), manages the cafe, Au Pere Tranquille (appropriately left to him by his father), where they all gather and is a bitter and gruff person whose wife has just left him. The black sheep of the family is youngest sibling Betty (Agnes Jaoui), an aging rebel who is unhappy with her life and has just broken up with her secret boyfriend and an employee of Henri's, bartender Denis (Jean-Pierre Darroussin). Caustic matriarch of the Menauds (Claire Maurier) is the final addition to the small but very dysfunctional gathering.

Fueled by their mother's barbs, the siblings stew in their own private miseries: Philippe's recent television broadcast proved he made an unfortunate tie choice; Henri is disturbed that his estranged wife Arlette won't be coming to join them and that he may never see her again; and Betty is still distraught over her break-up with Denis, concerned about her still-single status and about the fact that she had some choice words for her boss, who is also a peer of Philippe's. Denis, of course, is also upset about being dumped and the slightly dim Yolande is all but ignored by husband Philippe. Even Henri's dog, the poor old, decrepit Caruso, is fair game for the ill-humored barbs of the clan, as Denis quips, he's "like a rug, but alive." Throughout the dig-fest, however, the director uses contrasting flashbacks to a happier time, when the three children would romp and play with their youthful and energetic parents, signaling that there is hope for even the worst of the lot.

All the actors portraying the characters spent nine months perfecting them in the staged version of *Famille* and

bring them fully realized to the film. They are universally sympathetic portrayals, with standouts by Frot and Darroussin, who each won a Cesar (the French Oscar) for the film, along with Jaoui and Bacri's Cesars for best screenplay. As Yolande, or Yoyo as she is affectionately referred to, gets more tipsy, her honesty and genuine sweetness show through and set her apart from the vitriolic gang. About as close to action as the film comes is when Denis, feeling sorry for the birthday girl, takes her for a celebratory spin on the dance floor while the jukebox plays. Denis, it seems, is the outsider voice of reason for the feuding family and quietly becomes the linchpin for its change.

As the evening and the film concurrently unfold, it becomes clear to everyone that Philippe is not the hero everyone made him out to be, and that underachiever Henri is actually more sensitive and sweet than originally thought. Betty begins to see the reality of her brothers characters, and through them, herself. She begins to rethink her break-up with Denis as she also sees what a genuine human being he is.

Cinematically, the film also satisfies. Although difficult to adapt this one-room theatrical setting to the big screen, Klapisch's use of clever camera work and lighting make it extremely watchable. Artistic use of design was also employed, mainly using primary colors, to bring a specific look to the small film.

CREDITS

Henri: Jean-Pierre Bacri
Betty: Agnes Jaoui
Denis: Jean-Pierre Darroussin
Yolande: Catherine Frot
Mother: Claire Maurier
Philippe: Wladimir Yordanoff

Origin: France
Released: 1998
Production: Telema, Le Studio Canal Plus, France 2 Cinema, and Cofimage 7; released by Leisure Time Features and Cinema Village
Direction: Cedric Klapisch
Screenplay: Cedric Klapisch, Jean-Pierre Bacri, and Agnes Jaoui; based on the play by Bacri and Jaoui
Cinematography: Benoit Delhomme
Editing: Francine Sandberg
Music: Philippe Eidel
Production design: Patrick Lancelot
MPAA rating: Unrated
Running Time: 107 minutes

Dramatic without being a drag and humorous without being simplistic, *Famille* doesn't provide a simple solution to the characters myriad of problems, but merely allows them to slowly discover things about themselves and each other. The film shows the complex relationships families often have and the minor power struggles and hierarchies that naturally occur within them. Lastly, the film also sheds a ray of hope onto the lives of all of these characters, whom have become almost like family to the audience.

—*Hilary Weber*

REVIEWS

Entertainment Weekly. July 10, 1998, p. 54.
Los Angeles Times. June 19, 1998, p. F4.
New York Times. May 12, 1998, p. E12.
People. July 27, 1998, p. 38.
Village Voice. June 16, 1998, p. 160.

Under the Skin

[*Under the Skin*] her passion was undeniable . . .
—Movie tagline

"Samantha Morton is extraordinary!"—Lisa Schwarzbaum, *Entertainment Weekly*

"Outstanding!"—Graham Fuller, *Interview*

"Samantha Morton embodies the central role with incredible abandon, furious intensity and raw presence . . . she is a wild and heartbreaking actress!"—Janet Maslin, *New York Times*

"Hugely exciting . . . eclectic and moody . . . a masterpiece!"—Steven Talty, *Time Out New York*

Carine Adler's *Under the Skin* is forthright and raw in penetrating a young woman's grief; it almost hurts to watch Iris (Samantha Morton) as she immerses herself in a frightening erotic catharsis that threatens to swallow her. The assurance with which Adler pursues death and Eros is astonishing, as is Morton's performance, best known as *Jane Eyre* in a 1997 BBC adaptation. When we first meet Iris, she's drawing on her body with a marker, musing on her love for her mother, a woman who loved flowers: "My mother was everything to me." Then we see Iris sprawled nude on a couch and gazing into the camera: a spiky-haired odalisque in a startling moment that reveals her body and troubled spirit. Cut to a family chat—Iris is a gamine with vivid, energetic features untroubled by anything worse than a bad case of sibling rivalry. This small British film, written and directed by Adler, intelligently and unsparingly examines a woman's soul. Carine Adler, a first-time director, takes tremendous risks, making Iris alternately vulnerable and selfish (so much so that some critics recoiled from the character, protesting that in a "woman's film" she should be more "likable"), but the film is stronger for her daring.

Rose (Claire Rushbrook, from *Secrets and Lies* [1995]), Iris's matronly older sister, is obsessed by her pregnancy ("Look at my fingers! They're swollen like sausages!"). Their mother (Rita Tushingham) sits quietly between them as they chatter to her, vying for her attention. Iris feels no one is listening to her—not her boyfriend Gary (Matthew Delamere), not Rose, or her mother, wrapped up in their familiar intimate confidences. When their Mum is diagnosed with a brain tumor, Rose is terrified and self-pitying, while Iris bravely presents her mother with a healing crystal, and leads her in a cha-cha to cheer her up. Under her too-youthful wig, her mother's expression seems distant, as if some of her spirit had already left; as she twirls in Iris's arms, she smiles and it cuts right to the heart. Their dance slows, and then we see two men solemnly bearing a coffin out of the house. The swiftness of her death is shocking; their loss feels staggering. The awful business of dividing their mother's things is settled, with one exception—a ring which seems to be missing.

It seems as if Rose is having the worst of it, but Iris, trying to control her pain, finds it too much as she returns to her everyday life. A sequence in a dressing room of a women's shop, helping a customer try on brassieres, is a tense, claustrophobic moment—Adler will recreate this feeling numerous times, using her handheld camera to trap us into a space. The customer's full breasts fill the frame as she peels off one bra after another. Iris, feeling overwhelmed by what she feels is a hostile supervisor, angrily chucks the job and lands at the movies. Waking up in an empty theater, she encounters Tom (Stuart Townsend), whom she suddenly turns to in a moment of abandon—her soft voiceover describes their sexual encounter as we see them entwine hungrily, pressed against an alley wall. Director Adler accompanies their embrace with images of Iris's mother's coffin consumed by flames.

Later, Iris can't tolerate her comfortable life with Gary; in their bed she insists she can't breathe; she needs space. Bearing the dying flowers from the funeral, she moves into a strange little apartment (which looks like a hospital room) and assumes a new persona. She shows up at sister Rose's travel agency wearing the mother's wig, pink glasses, a tatty, rabbit fur coat and teetering in stiletto sandals. Rose, astonished, tells her bluntly, "You look like a slut!" Iris shoots back, "Thank you!" As she lays on the black eyeliner and orange lipstick, you want to wipe it away and restore her sweetness: her new appearance and bold demeanor cry out her need to everyone. Gary begs her to come back; her chunky blonde chum Vron (Christine Tremarco) suddenly sneers at her behind her back.

Samantha Morton is a fearless actress; her Iris is driven to seek both comfort and thrills from any man she decides to pick up. Looking like a womanly child dressed up in her dead mother's clothes (the coat in particular is creepy), drinking straight from the bottle, Iris plunges headlong into her sad odyssey into the streets and clubs of Liverpool. "Kiss me!" she says to her pickup, her hungry eyes lined in garish black, lit harshly as the camera comes too close.

Iris decides she wants to sing and is fascinated by a choir of older people. Listening to them, her face softens. Eager to join, she auditions for a kindly woman who registers growing dismay as Iris's voice cracks and strains for the notes. She drifts in and out of her sister's life, mooching money and liquor, using her resentment and jealousy as justification for her erratic behavior. Declaring her intent not to get another "crap job," Iris drifts to a haunted, surreal "Office of Lost Property" where forgotten keys and other articles left on public transportation wait to be claimed. In a charlady's face she thinks she sees her mother coming out of a shadow. The place is hushed and dark as a morgue: a bin of cell phones buzz and ring; she picks it up and hears her mother's voice. It's a dream sequence, but her unsettled dream-life is serene compared to her waking existence.

By day, Iris (who is in nearly every scene) restlessly seeks satisfaction and oblivion. The score is mainly jumpy, pounding electronic music by The Aloof and it works well. A sad touch is the theme "One Love," which accompanies Tom's appearances: he just wants casual sex, he says. Iris says plaintively, "I thought we could talk." Tom keeps her at the end of a phone, waiting for him to call. When her phone is disconnected, she even waits alone by a public phone under the light of a full moon, and grapples with a tough-looking woman who grabs the phone away.

Her desperation leads her to Max (Daniel O'Meara) with whom she has rough sex (the camera focuses tightly on her fear and arousal) and whose graphic humiliation (he blindfolds her, croons "Just trust me!" and then urinates on her) breaks through her pain and begins her return to a saner and safer life. She tries to reach out to Vron, who agrees to meet her and then doesn't show. Iris, mugged by a posse of street-tough, pre-teen girls who snatch her purse (a rude little touch of irony) goes back to Rose, catching up to her at the train and badgers her for money. Iris sees her mother's ring on Rose's hand and grabs her by the hair, screaming and cursing. Rose, insisting their mother gave it to her, boards the train. Iris next lands on Gary's doorstep, begging to talk. He tries, kindly, to defer until morning, but out comes Vron, her hair undone, who defiantly insists Gary set Iris straight—they're a couple now. Typically, Iris flinches in pain, whimpers an apology, then whirls about to attack Gary. He throws her out; she next finds her way to her sister's house and forlornly tries to seduce her brother-in-law Frank (Mark Womack).

The sisters finally reconcile as Rose admits she lied about the ring and Iris shamefacedly produces her mother's ashes. "I want my mum back!" says Rose, and they embrace tearfully. The scene is restrained, poignant, and a tremendous relief—you want these women to heal and help each other. Iris's voiceover, confident again, proudly relates how she filmed Rose's delivery of her son for the out-of-town father. Claire Rushbrook plays Rose as a proper but wounded woman who wants to mother her sister but can't get past her own feelings of abandonment. The cast is uniformly strong, with Delamere and Womack particularly worthy as decent men who struggle to comprehend Iris, and O'Meara as the cold-eyed, predatory Max. Critical reception of the film was generally very favorable: *Salon* called it "an amaz-

CREDITS

Iris: Samantha Morton
Rose: Claire Rushbrook
Their mother: Rita Tushingham
Frank: Mark Womack
Gary: Matthew Delamere
Vron: Christine Tremarco
Tom: Stuart Townsend

Origin: Great Britain
Released: 1998
Production: Kate Ogborn for Strange Dog, Rouge Films, BFI Films, and Merseyside Film production; released by Arrow Release
Direction: Carine Adler
Screenplay: Carine Adler
Cinematography: Barry Ackroyd
Editing: Ewa Lind
Music: Ilona Sekacz
Production design: John-Paul Kelly
Art direction: Niall Mulroney
Costumes: Frances Tempest
Sound: Gary Desmond
MPAA rating: Unrated
Running Time: 81 minutes

ing debut" for director Adler and Samantha Morton, and both have been honored for *Under the Skin*, notably Adler, who received the International Critic's Award at the 1997 Toronto Film Festival.

Rita Tushingham (*A Taste of Honey* [1961]), a legendary actress of rare presence, might have played Iris in her youth. It's a delicate, knowing portrayal: with Rushbrook and Morton, she is the center of an ensemble that feels like family. Her death sets the squabbling sisters' own self-exploration in motion, and unleashes their hostilities as well as their deep love for each other. "Rose and me, we're not that different," says Iris, who finds a new job in a flower shop and finally buries the precious ashes. She sings (not well, but confidently) the surprisingly affecting pop tune "Alone

Again Naturally" in a talent night, looking fresh and young again. Iris strolls on the beach in the sunlight, a fortunate choice for the film's closing scene.

—*Mary Hess*

REVIEWS

Entertainment Weekly. June 5, 1998, p. 54.
Los Angeles Times. June 5, 1998, p. F14.
Movieline. May, 1998, p. 46.
New York Times. March 28, 1998, p. B7.
People. June 8, 1998, p. 41.
Sight and Sound. December, 1997, p. 56.
Variety. September 22, 1997, p. 40.

Underground

"A raging, funny . . . sprawling, mordant, zany epic of a scale and energy you see maybe a few times a decade."—Jay Carr, *Boston Globe*

"Entirely too enjoyable. You leave the film feeling as if you've been in a great bar fight: beat up, exhausted and exhilarated."—Terry Lawson, *Detroit Free Press*

"Impassioned and surreal."—Kenneth Turan, *Los Angeles Times*

"Wild! Rip-roaring! Impassioned! As if the circus had come to town!"—Janet Maslin, *New York Times*

"Magical! Bursting with music, jokes, outrageous behavior, drinking and sex!"—Ray Pride, *Newcity*

"Stunning! Amazing! A raucous mix of politics, sex fantasy, black comedy, brutality, folk culture and historical allegory. A triumph!"—Shawn Levy, *The Oregonian*

"An ambitious epic. Impassioned. Surrealistic. At once brash and touching."—Peter Stack, *San Francisco Chronicle*

"An adrenalin rush of true horror and slapstick humor!"—Paul Goetz, *Washington Free Press*

Winner of the Palme d'Or at Cannes in 1995 and an attraction at the 1996 New York Film Festival, Emir Kusturica's *Underground*, a boisterous, often outra-

geous requiem for the land once called Yugoslavia, has gradually made its way to more American cities in 1997 and 1998. This exceedingly ambitious film traces the story of two buddies through the trauma of Yugoslavian history from 1941 to 1992 and encompasses a wide range of emotions—from sheer delirium to a profound sense of loss when Yugoslavia itself finally crumbles. *Underground* also employs a variety of forms—from buddy comedy to political satire to a climactic moment of transcendence.

The film is divided into three parts—World War II, the Cold War, and the recent war in Bosnia—and begins with a fairy-tale-like opening, "Once upon a time, there was a country." Ultimately, it is a raucous fairy tale and a national epic built on lunacy, tragedy, and finally hope. For Yugoslavia, a land that has endured so much, this mixture of moods and styles may be the truest way to tell the story.

When we first meet Marko (Miki Manojlovic) and Blacky (Lazar Ristovski), it is 1941; they are members of the Communist Party and dedicated to fighting Fascism and making money in the black market. Carousing through the streets, they establish a celebratory mood that will be a hallmark of the film's style. We soon witness the Nazi bombing of Belgrade and the destruction it brings to a zoo where Marko's simple brother, Ivan (Slavko Stimac), works. As some animals are killed and others are freed to roam the streets of the city, we get the sense of a whole social order being turned upside down.

Marko and Blacky are scoundrels, but lovable nonetheless, and their scheming is somehow endearing, even when the married Blacky is trying to romance a beautiful actress named Natalija (Mirjana Jokovic). Soon Marko and Blacky learn they are wanted by the Nazis, and they go into hiding in a cellar along with their comrades. Blacky's wife, Vera (Mirjana Karanovic), dies giving birth to their child, and three years later Blacky sets out to kidnap Natalija in one of the film's most hilarious scenes. Blacky goes on-stage during one of her performances, acts as if he were part of the play, has himself tied to her, and simply walks off-stage after shooting the German officer, Franz (Ernst Stötzner), who is also in love with her. This farcical scene obviously has political overtones—a Yugoslavian claiming a woman away from a German—but it is also outlandishly funny. We get caught up in Blacky's daring invasion of the play, his command of the stage, and the amazement of the actors. Blacky plans to marry Natalija, but the Nazis find the wedding banquet and capture him. Natalija, as much of an opportunist as Blacky and Marko, goes off with Franz, who, it turns out, is not dead.

Film was originally titled *Once Upon a Time There Was a Country.*

All of this leads to a sequence both horrifying and hilarious. The Germans torture Blacky with electric shock to learn information about his arms dealing, but Blacky resists no matter how high they turn up the current. When he keeps resisting, one of the interrogators tries the equipment on himself and is killed. Marko stages a rescue by disguising himself as a doctor, infiltrating the hospital through underground passages, strangling Franz with a stethoscope, and, in a clever flourish, checking his heartbeat with it. In such elaborate sequences, Kusturica brilliantly blends the painful with the absurd. Marko smuggles Blacky and Natalija out of the hospital and into the hideout, where Marko quickly starts seducing Natalija away from his friend; this is just a hint of the major betrayal Marko will perpetrate in the film's second part.

The first part of the film, then, is darkly comic. Marko and Blacky act like a comedy team thumbing their noses at society and engaging in various slapstick antics, and yet the action is often violent and shocking, and the stakes are high—the future of their country. The characters themselves are not terribly deep. Everyone is fairly self-centered and trying to do the best he or she can during wartime but because the comedy is so broad and the plot itself an allegory for Yugoslavian history, the characterizations are fitting.

A character's rise to power provides the transition to the next section, the Cold War years, and, in *Forrest Gump*-like re-creations of history, Marko appears in historical footage alongside this powerful man. In 1961, Marko is married to Natalija and dedicating a statue to Blacky, a national hero who supposedly died fighting the Fascists. However, Blacky is not dead but rather still living underground. Marko has led Blacky and the rest of the cellar dwellers to believe World

War II is still raging and even plays air raid sirens to keep the charade alive. Marko has made himself a confidant and a hero of the Communist Party and is also making money off of the munitions he has his underground people manufacturing. His duplicity represents in a microcosm the way Communism repressed its people for so many years and in essence kept them "underground."

The set piece of this section is an extended wedding banquet for Blacky's son, Jovan (Srdan Todorovic), and his bride, Jelena (Milena Pavlovic). In one of the film's most beautiful images, Jelena floats (with the aid of machinery) through the air to take her seat by the groom. There is great revelry and celebration in this sequence, which best exemplifies Kusturica's exuberant and lively style. The vibrant Blacky offers a lavish toast, and a brass band, present throughout the film, constantly plays in the background. However, tensions are bubbling underneath the surface. We see Natalija's bitterness for the acting career she lost and Blacky's jealousy when he sees Marko with her. A huge tank, the centerpiece of the munitions plant, is an ominous threat in the background, and the celebration, ironically, ends when Ivan's chimpanzee, Soni, gets in the tank and fires it, thus bringing chaos to the underground community.

Underground is epic in its ambitions, and yet it is not a traditional epic. Instead of detailing the triumphs of a hero through grand historical events, it explores the exploits of a sham hero and his creation of another false hero and fictionalized national myths to further his own goals. The film in fact becomes a kind of anti-epic, a satire of heroism—best illustrated in the sequence when Blacky and Jovan, thinking World War II is still being fought, leave the underground and launch an offensive. They run into a film crew shooting a propaganda movie, *Spring Comes on a White Horse,* based on Marko's memoirs. Thinking the actor playing Franz is the real Franz, Blacky shoots him, and then, with Jovan, routs the film crew. It is a surreal moment, to be sure, the real Blacky seeing himself in the actor playing him and commenting, "All brave people look like me." However, the scene also deals with the serious issue of how national myths are constructed out of lies and how one man unwittingly destroys his own myth while it is being created. When Blacky stole Natalija away, he knew he was entering the fictional realm of a play. This time he mistakes a fictional world for the real one. Confusing a Communist propaganda film for real Nazi invaders suggests that it is impossible to separate the various forms of oppression the Yugoslavian people have endured—one is easily substituted for the other.

Underground grows progressively darker. The high jinks of the first part and the raucous festiveness and surreal satire of the second give way to the discovery of betrayal and bitterness in the third part, which is ushered in with a montage covering the death of once powerful political figure in 1980. Then it is 1992 and we find Ivan an emotional wreck in Berlin. He is devastated when he learns of the big lie his brother perpetrated and of the disappearance of Yugoslavia. He makes his way back to his homeland via underground tunnels only to find it is in a state of civil war. Blacky is a commander in the war and looking for his son, who, unbeknownst to him, drowned years earlier. When Ivan finds Marko, Ivan beats him with his cane and then hangs him-self. Soon thereafter, Marko and Natalija are identified as war profiteers. From far away, Blacky—not knowing the names of the criminals—gives the order that they be executed. They are shot and set on fire. Blacky arrives, learns their identities, and watches helplessly as the burned motorized wheelchair (carrying the remains of Marko and Natalija) travels in circles around him. It is the most harrowing image in the film and a final commentary on the tragic fate of Yugoslavia—a summation of the betrayal and slaughter perpetrated by fellow countrymen on each other.

And yet the film ends in a very moving, otherworldly vision of hope. All the principal characters, living and dead, emerge from the sea and gather on the shore for a great banquet and joyous celebration. The ubiquitous band plays in the background, while the whole family celebrates in the foreground. One of the characters turns to the camera and announces, "This story has no end." While the film starts as a fairy tale, the ending is not "happily ever after" but rather somewhat ambiguous. The sense of hope is tempered by a feeling of loss in the way the site of the reunion breaks off from the mainland. Indeed, *Underground* is essentially about disintegration—both the disintegration of a country and the disintegration of relationships in times of war—but there is also great vitality throughout the film and a profound sense of renewal at the end. What begins as farce and culminates in tragedy is magically transformed into a transcendent reconciliation.

—*Peter N. Chumo II*

CREDITS

Marko: Miki Manojlovic
Peter "Blacky" Popara: Lazar Ristovski
Natalija: Mirjana Jokovic
Ivan: Slavko Stimac
Franz: Ernst Stotzner
Jovan: Srdan Todorovic
Jelena: Milena Pavlovic
Vera: Mirjana Karanovic

Origin: France, Germany, Hungary
Released: 1995, 1998
Production: Pierre Spengler for Ciby 2000, Pandora Film, and Novo Film; released by New Yorker Films
Direction: Emir Kusturica
Screenplay: Dusan Kovacevic and Emir Kusturica
Cinematography: Vilko Filac
Editing: Branka Ceperac
Music: Goran Bregovic
Production design: Miljen Kljakovic
Costumes: Nebojsa Lipanovic
Sound: Marko Rodic
MPAA rating: Unrated
Running Time: 192 minutes

REVIEWS

New York Times. October 12, 1996.
Portland Oregonian. January 23, 1998.
San Francisco Examiner. March 13, 1998.
Sight and Sound. March, 1996, p. 53.

Urban Legend

It happened to someone who knows someone you know . . . you're next.—Movie tagline

What you don't believe can kill you.—Movie tagline

"A heart-pounding, edge of your seat treat!—Linda Stotter, *Entertainment Time-Out*

 Box Office: $37,506,463

A college campus becomes the playground for a sadistic killer in *Urban Legend*.

L et's suppose you're on your way to college. You need to get gas, and the attendant is a stuttering Brad Dourif, the voice of Chucky, the demonic doll in the *Child's Play* movies. Then let's suppose the dean of your college turned out to be John Neville, the well-manicured man from the *X-Files* television series and movie. And, let's further suppose that when you get to class, your professor is none other than Robert Englund, Freddy Krueger of *Nightmare on Elm Street* fame. Now, you've got to be asking yourself, "is this normal?" Of course not.

And as if these weren't warnings enough, you discover that every year there are "massacre bash parties" to celebrate the murder of every student but one on a dorm floor by an abnormal psych professor on a rampage. Hey, where was that described in the school catalogue? In fact, not only was that incident not included in Pendleton University's publicity, it has actually been expunged from all archival material. And if you ask that dean with the nicely buffed fingernails, he'll strongly deny that it ever happened. In fact, *U.S. News and World Report* has just named Pendleton the safest campus in the nation. Obviously that Stanley Hall massacre that supposedly happened 25 years ago is nothing more than an urban legend.

You do know what urban legends are, don't you? They're those funny, but often times, frightening stories that someone tells you actually happened to a friend of a friend of a friend of theirs. You know, like The Death of Little Mikey— that cute little Life cereal kid who "eats everything" and ate the candy Pop Rocks while drinking Pepsi causing his stomach and intestines to explode. (Don't worry, Mikey's just fine; he's an ad executive in New York City.) Of course, whether or not urban legends are true is almost irrelevant. They are meant to be cautionary tales.

And that's the kind of urban legend Professor Wexler (Robert England) discusses and tries to debunk in his class

Killer taunts Natalie (Alicia Witt): "Don't you want to be an urban legend? All your friends are now."

at Pendleton. So you can imagine how disconcerting—but not necessarily unexpected—it would be to have a serial killer on campus whose modus operandi is that of fulfilling urban legends and taking those cautionary tales out of the land of folklore and into the realm of reality.

What's really odd, however, is that all the victims of this urban legend murderer are known to Natalie (Alicia Witt). The first victim, Michelle Mancini (Natasha Gregson Wagner) who went to high school with Natalie, falls victim to the old "Killer in the Back Seat" legend. Then when Natalie goes for a ride with her friend Damon (Joshua Jackson) he becomes "The Murdered Boyfriend," his corpse dangling from a tree branch, his toes just barely scraping the top of the car in which she awaits him. Natalie's obnoxious roommate takes the old "Babysitter and the Upstairs Killer" on a slight sideroad when she finds out via a computer chatline instead of a phone that the killer is right behind her instead of upstairs.

And there are more legends lurking in this movie: "The Stuck Couple," "The Microwaved Pet," "The Corpse in the Car," "The Kidney Heist," and "The High Beams Car Chase/Gang Initiation" being most prominently featured.

Luckily for Natalie she has a good friend in Brenda (Rebecca Gayheart) whom she can lean on during these killing times and a journalism student, Paul (Jared Leto), to help her solve the riddle of the urban legends murders. Or maybe one of them is the killer? Or is it the stuttering gas station attendant who is the voice of Chucky, or Professor Wexler who's obviously hiding something besides the fact that in other movies his fingers are tipped by razors? Or maybe it's that all-too-slick Dean who seems to have hidden the X-files on the Stanley Hall massacre? And what about that creepy janitor (Julian Richings) who seems to like lurking around semi-deserted buildings? For that matter, has anyone checked out the campus mascot? Maybe it's one of those crocodiles from the sewers of New York City?

Urban Legends is the latest in modern horror films and has all the usual accoutrements: a cast of up-and-coming actors from TV shows popular with teens, a self-referential humor that winks at the audience indicating that we all know what's going to happen, more than its share of red herrings and possible killers, and music that screeches at just the right moment to make you jump out of your seat . . . even if it's not the killer but a friend about to suddenly appear. These are the formulas for today's horror films.

So it should come as no surprise that this latest entry in the genre is the feature film debut of Jamie Blanks, the 26-year-old director, or that the screenplay is the first one written by Silvio Horta who only graduated from NYU film school in 1996. This young duo may more easily tap into the psyches of the teen audience to whom this film appeals, but they may not have the cinematic maturity to pull of anything but a mere imitation of that which has come before.

> One can check out the urban legends in this film at the Urban Legends Reference Pages at http://www.snopes.com.

While using urban legends as the motif for the killer is a nice hook, and while the film does look good, on the whole it's not much different than either *Scream* (1996) or *I Know What You Did Last Summer* (1997) and in some respects, not as good. For one thing, most of the characters are so annoying or unlikable that one is genuinely pleased not to saddened when they're removed from the film. And with no sympathy for the victims, the scare quotient is limited.

Also limiting the impact of the shocks is the fact that they seem to happen at equal intervals and with equal intensity. There's no build up to the tension. It just seems to follow a pattern of two false scares to one real scare with those shrieking violins acting as a signpost telling us we're supposed to be scared at exactly this moment, even if there's nothing really scary going on. Even the film's climax—when the heroine herself is finally threatened—follows this same pattern.

And patterns, not originality, are what best describes *Urban Legends*. And maybe that's a cautionary tale for today's filmmakers. An urban legend for Hollywood about what happens when young filmmakers are given big budgets. But then again, there's always Matt Damon and Ben Affleck to prove that, as usual, urban legends aren't necessarily true.

—*Beverley Bare Buehrer*

CREDITS

Paul: Jared Leto
Natalie: Alicia Witt
Brenda: Rebecca Gayheart
Parker: Michael Rosenbaum
Reese: Loretta Devine
Damon: Joshua Jackson
Sasha: Tara Reid
Dean Adams: John Neville
Janitor: Julian Richings
Professor Wexler: Robert Englund
Tosh: Danielle Harris
Michelle Mancini: Natasha Gregson Wagner
Gas Station Attendant: Brad Dourif

Origin: USA
Released: 1998
Production: Neal H. Moritz, Gina Matthews, and Michael McDonnell for Phoenix Pictures; released by TriStar Pictures
Direction: Jamie Blanks
Screenplay: Silvio Horta
Cinematography: James Chressanthis
Editing: Jay Cassidy
Production design: Charles Breen
Art direction: Benno Tutter
Set decoration: Cal Loucks
Costumes: Mary Claire Hannan
Sound: Per Hallberg
Music: Christopher Young
MPAA rating: R
Running Time: 100 minutes

REVIEWS

Chicago Sun Times. September 25, 1998.
Chicago Tribune. September 25, 1998.
Detroit Free Press. September 25, 1998, p. 6D.
Entertainment Weekly. October 12, 1998, p. 38.
Hollywood Reporter. September 22-28, 1998, p. 18.
Los Angeles Times. September 25, 1998, p. F8.
New York Times. September 25, 1998, p. E15.
People. October 5, 1998, p. 38.
Variety. September 21, 1998, p. 105.

U.S. Marshals

"If you liked *The Fugitive*, you will love *U.S. Marshals!*"—Ron Brewington, *American Urban Radio Networks*

"*U.S. Marshals* duplicates *The Fugitive*'s breathless moves, hyper-drive acting and ferocious energy from Tommy Lee Jones."—Owen Gleiberman, *Entertainment Weekly*

"You've gotta see *U.S. Marshals*. Make sure you can hold your breath for two hours or the suspense will kill you."—Cary Berglund, *KCAL-TV*

"Solid escapist thrills. Crackling, crisp, gritty action."—Leah Rozen, *People*

"Action city! It moves at Mach III speed!"—Pat Collins, *WWOR-TV*

 Box Office: $57,833,603

After the success of the 1993 blockbuster *The Fugitive*, based on the 1960s television series, the unsurprising response of the studio and the film's producers was to make a sequel. The film, starring Harrison Ford as Dr. Richard Kimble and co-starring Tommy Lee Jones in an Oscar-winning performance as Marshal Samuel Gerard, drew critical praise and lured huge audiences to the theaters. It featured outstanding performances by its top stars, a suspenseful and well-paced story, a convincing plot, and a number of intense action sequences. In making a sequel, the producers chose to capitalize on the commanding, memorable performance of Tommy Lee Jones (who had more lines in *The Fugitive* than Harrison Ford) and center the new story around Chief Deputy Marshal Gerard and his talkative, wisecracking band of marshals. Gone is Harrison Ford's character, but once again Sam Gerard finds himself on the trail of a fugitive (who may or may not have been wrongly convicted of murder), this time in the person of Mark Sheridan (Wesley Snipes). Taking a plot premise very similar to that of its predecessor, *U.S. Marshals* earnestly attempts to duplicate the success of *The Fugitive* and perhaps go a step further in developing the character of Gerard, but unfortunately the film, like many sequels, does not measure up to the original or to its own potential. Despite another strong performance by Tommy Lee Jones, *U.S. Marshals* lacks the originality, the

 U.S. Marshal Sam Gerard: "We have a fugitive."

pacing, the intriguing plotting, the credibility, and the tension of *The Fugitive*.

The first twenty minutes or so of the film function to set up the chase that is to be the focus of the rest of the story, and several coincidences are necessary to put every plot detail into place. The story opens with Mark Sheridan (calling himself Mark Roberts) getting into an automobile accident and then being arrested for the murder of two government agents. The next scene introduces Marshal Sam Gerard, who is staking out a band of criminals while wearing a chicken costume from a fast-food restaurant (this is one of the most humorous moments of the film). After hitting one of the violently resistant thugs while the man is in handcuffs, Gerard is reprimanded by Marshal Walsh (Kate Nelligan), his superior, who puts him on a plane taking the man he arrested and other convicts (including Mark Sheridan) to prison. One of the prisoners on the plane, an Asian man, attempts for some as-yet-unknown reason to kill Sheridan, but the attempt is botched and results in a hole being blasted in the side of the plane, which of course leads to the plane crashing. The plane crash sequence is an intense ride that succeeds in equaling the suspense and excitement of the train wreck in *The Fugitive*, and at the end of the harrowing experience, Sheridan escapes. Joined shortly thereafter by his team of marshals, Gerard prepares to track down the fugitive.

Soon the State Department shows up, explaining that it was two of the agency's men who were murdered by Sheridan. An agent named Royce (Robert Downey Jr.) is assigned to join Gerard's team. Gerard and friends are not too happy with this intrusion into their group, which is not made any easier by the fact that Royce is arrogant and not entirely cooperative. At one point, Gerard finds Royce calling in a cell phone to report to the State Department on their progress, and Gerard grabs his phone and throws it away. Later, when tracking Sheridan down in a swamp, Royce spots the fugitive and goes after him on his own, against Sam's orders. Sheridan winds up surprising Royce and taking his gun, but Sam arrives to intervene. Trapped, Sheridan shoots Sam in the side and escapes. After this episode, Royce seems more cooperative and shows more admiration for Gerard.

Meanwhile, Sheridan contacts his girlfriend, Marie (Irene Jacob), and tells her that he has been set up. He reveals to her that he had worked for the government, and that he was ambushed during an assignment in which he was supposed to deliver a package; he was forced, he says,

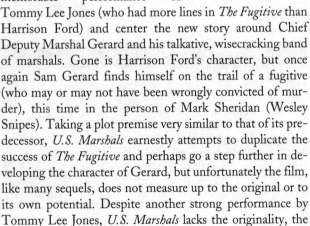

to kill two men in self-defense. Believing that there is "someone on the inside" responsible for setting him up, Sheridan tells Marie that he is going to learn the identity of the guilty party.

While Sheridan initiates his own search for the truth, Sam Gerard is beginning to entertain doubts as to the story he's been told by the State Department, wondering why a 'ruthless assassin' [Sheridan] keeps going out of his way to "make sure people live." After viewing surveillance tapes of the supposed assassination, Gerard realizes that the two men were killed out of self-defense. When confronted with Sam's questions, the State Department claims that Sheridan "went bad" and was selling information to the Korean mafia.

The film was shot in and around Chicago, in New York City, and in the swamps of Tennessee.

The hunt for Sheridan continues, as does an investigation into the Korean mafia. Eventually Gerard's team comes face-to-face with Sheridan again, and Royce pursues the fugitive into a hospital. There he apprehends Sheridan and prepares to shoot him in the head, but suddenly deputy

Newman (Tom Wood) shows up to witness the assasination and Royce shoots him. In the chaos, Sheridan escapes, and when Gerard arrives, Royce claims that Sheridan was responsible for shooting Newman. Enraged that one of his men was killed, Gerard sets out a final time to hunt down Sheridan, accompanied by Royce, but ultimately he discovers that Sheridan has indeed been set up and that Royce is the traitor.

As in *The Fugitive,* Tommy Lee Jones tends to steal the show in the many scenes featuring Gerard. The tough-talking, wisecracking marshal is a role well-suited to the actor, who delivers his lines with a strangely endearing sharpness and vitality that makes the character dominate every scene he's in. Gerard's disguising himself in a chicken suit early in the film is a hilarious image not merely because of the silly disguise but because of its contrast with his character. The rough, cynical, often arrogant Sam Gerard—who can't quite hide the fact that he has a heart of gold—is a character for whom the audience can quickly develop a fondness for. One scene in particular illustrates the manner in which his character elicits audience sympathy even when he's made a mistake. When Sam goes after Sheridan to avenge Newman's death, Deputy Marshal Cosmo Renfro (Joe Pantoliano) tries to dissuade him, saying that Gerard is going against what he has taught his deputies. Cosmo points out that pride is getting in the marshal's way, for he is the "great Sam Gerard." "Yes, I am," replies Sam. "And you always have to win," continues Cosmo, to which Gerard responds, "Yes, I do." To a certain extent, this exchange does illustrate Gerard's pride, but it also gives a sympathetic glimpse into a man who truly cared about his deputy and wants to see justice served, even though he may be going about it in the wrong way.

There is one thing about Gerard's character that does not make much sense, however. Although his instincts lead him early on to question the ruthlessness of Sheridan, and although he later realizes that the man has been framed, Sam's instincts do not seem to serve him so well when Newman is shot and killed. He seems to readily accept Royce's claim that Sheridan did the deed, but one questions why the "great Sam Gerard" has not by this time at least suspected Royce.

While most of the time *U.S. Marshals* is fun to watch, and does tell an interesting story, the plot is not as well executed, organized, or sophisticated as that of *The Fugitive.* At times the film seems to drag on too long, due to uneven plotting and unnecessary elements that are supposed to advance the story but actually do nothing to help the coherence of the plot. Almost half an hour passes before Sheridan actually becomes a fugitive, for example, yet much of the early exposition leading to the plane crash and escape is

CREDITS

Chief Deputy Marshal Sam Gerard: Tommy Lee Jones
Mark Sheridan: Wesley Snipes
John Royce: Robert Downey Jr.
U.S. Marshal Walsh: Kate Nelligan
Deputy Marshal Cosmo Renfro: Joe Pantoliano
Marie: Irene Jacob
Biggs: Daniel Roebuck
Newman: Tom Wood
Cooper: LaTanya Richardson
Chen: Michael Paul Chan

Origin: USA
Released: 1998
Production: Arnold and Anne Kopelson for Kopelson Entertainment; released by Warner Bros.
Direction: Stuart Baird
Screenplay: John Pogue; based on characters created by Roy Huggins
Cinematography: Andrzej Bartkowiak
Editing: Terry Rawlings
Music: Jerry Goldsmith
Production design: Maher Ahmad
Art direction: Bruce Alan Miller, Mark Worthington
Costumes: Louise Frogley
Sound: Scott Smith
Visual effect supervision: Peter Donen
MPAA rating: PG-13
Running Time: 133 minutes

not essential. Similarly, Sheridan's girlfriend Marie really serves little purpose as far as plotting, drama, or character development. Her only usefulness comes into play when Sheridan tells her that he in fact did kill two men, but in self-defense. Some elements of the plot, such as a story point involving Royce's gun, are somewhat muddled and can be easily missed, yet as a whole, the film seems to prolong the obvious. There is less of a puzzle to be unraveled in *U.S. Marshals* than in *The Fugitive,* and the mystery involved is more predictable and solved earlier than that of the first film.

Another aspect of *U.S. Marshals* that can be seen as a weakness is the ambiguity of Sheridan's character. While *The Fugitive's* Richard Kimble was clearly innocent from the beginning of the film, one does not know whether Mark Sheridan can be trusted until late in the story. His background is unknown and his character dubious when he is arrested and when he escapes. Although, as Gerard says, he puts an effort into making sure that people live, Sheridan turns to questionable methods to make his escapes (he hijacks a truck, rams a police car, and shoots Gerard). As a result, he elicits less sympathy. It is difficult to identify with him when his true nature is uncertain. Part of what made *The Fugitive* an

intriguing, suspenseful story was the conflict between two characters who are both honorable and both committed to seeking justice. This element is noticeably absent in *Marshals.* Though the film is suspenseful, intense, at times exciting, and frequently fun to watch due to Gerard's character, a comparison to its predecessor can best be described with the term "absence": there is simply something missing, and that something is not just Harrison Ford.

—*David Flanigan*

REVIEWS

Entertainment Weekly. March 13, 1998, p. 48.
Los Angeles Times. March 6, 1998, p. F10.
New York Times. March 6, 1998, p. E27.
People. March 16, 1998, p. 19.
Sight and Sound. June, 1998, p. 58.
USA Today. March 6, 1998, p. 4D.
Variety. March 2, 1998, p. 83.
Village Voice. March 17, 1998, p. 59.
Washington Post. March 6, 1998, p. D7.

Velvet Goldmine

Leave your expectations at the door.—Movie tagline

"A ravishing rock dream . . . narcotic poetry."
—Owen Gleiberman, *Entertainment Weekly*

"Director Todd Haynes brilliantly reimagines the glam-rock 70s as a brave new world of electrifying theatricality and sexual possibility!"
—Janet Maslin, *New York Times*

"A dazzling triumph and conclusive proof that Todd Haynes is a genuine discovery."—Andrew Johnston, *Time Out, NY*

 Box Office: $1,053,788

Movies that attempt to bring alive countercultural 'scenes' always seem to know just where to draw the blinds, no doubt to suit their own discursive ends. The most spectacular example of such filmmaking remains Robert Altman's *Nashville* (1975), which channelized the ostentatious

professionalism of country-and-western music into a flag-waving affirmation of the inner strength of the American nation. Todd Haynes's glittering *Velvet Goldmine* uses the British glam-rock era of the early 70s to serve the filmmaker's fascination with the politics of sexual identity. One would thus be justified in holding it up to the high standard set by its noteworthy predecessor.

Actually, one should cut it some slack. From the podium of the New York Film Festival, the director made clear that he was laboring under a curse. The original script for the film had six songs by David Bowie, who subsequently decided to withhold all rights. For a filmmaker, this would be like trying to recreate the time of Liverpool in the early 60s without a reference to the Beatles or their music.

That said, we needn't excuse any of the film's other major failings, foremost among them being Haynes's attempt to make up for the lack of authorized support by adopting a perspective that dismisses the veracity of the 'scene' he is trying to portray. Instead, he goes for musicalizing its essence in the form of the 'glam film' he would like to make. The narrative structure that he shamelessly lifts from *Citizen Kane* (1941) allows him to keep us at a distance from the 'scene,' while he is able to visually exploit its sensationalism.

In the process, we are also shortchanged of any kind of drama. Before the emotions of his leads can even start to simmer, the narrative event is either fragmented by a musical number, or brashly underscored by one. Thus, for all of Haynes's artistic intentions, what emerges is the kind of mainstream feature that Haynes is trying so hard to avoid making: the fad musical, or a film hurriedly made to exploit a musical fad. Unlike the classic of this subgenre, Richard Lester's *A Hard Day's Night* (1964), Haynes's effort comes across as an exploitation flick that cannot make up its mind to be one.

A reason for this could be what Haynes has admitted as his primary, if not primal, concern: the sexual ambiguity inherent in the lifestyles portrayed in *Velvet Goldmine.* Conventional films resolve issues of identity, according to Haynes, but resolution, for him, is not as interesting as crisis. While the crisis that Haynes speaks about does surface on the ideological level of his film, his own preoccupation with it as a filmmaker takes its toll on the film as a narrative of dramatic events, thereby resulting in a mess for which only Haynes must take the blame.

To the somber strains of a melodically grand musical score by Carter Burwell, the camera pans down from a starry sky to the Dublin of 1854, as a voiceover intones: "Histories, like ancient ruins, are the fictions of empires, while everything forgotten hangs in dark dreams of the past, ever threatening to return." The film begins with the granddaddy of British nonconformists, Oscar Wilde, as an eight-year-old (Luke Morgan Oliver). A pin he wears on his lapel allows the film to cut to the same pin being worn by seven-year-old Jack Fairy (Osheen Jones), whom we will come to know as a subsidiary character embodying the sexual freedom of the glam-rock scene. The schoolboy Jack, when required to state his ambition, says he wants to be a rock star. The narration then points out how "one mysterious day . . . Jack would discover that somewhere there were others quite like him, singled out for a great gift. And one day, the whole stinking world would be theirs."

The opening credits burst forth, introducing us to the Swinging London of the early 70s with the hysterical young females of the time. Bits from street interviews fill the background, before we are led into, what proves to be, the final concert given by the film's protagonist, pop idol Brian Slade (Jonathan Rhys Meyers). Rock aficionados should be able to recognize the real-life Bowie in the fictional Slade. For the finale, the feathers worn by Slade, as a trademark of his unisexual look, are matched by a shower of feathers raining down upon the audience. Suddenly, an executioner's hand, wielding a revolver, appears to shoot him dead. In the audience is journalist-to-be Arthur Stuart (Christian Bale) who witnesses the event, which is to serve as a linchpin for the film's narrative.

The Velvet Goldmine chronicles Britain's glam-rock music scene during the 1970s.

Manager Jerry Divine (Eddie Izzard) to client Brian Slade (Jonathan Rhys Meyers): "The secret to being a star is to behave like one."

After a quick montage of visual hijinks intended to dislocate our viewing (including an extreme close-up of Slade in flames), the film flashbacks, itself adopting the viewpoint of the media circus on the beginnings of the glam-rock craze. Against the background of "Hot One," a true show-stopper of a musical number, written for the film by Nathan Larson and Shudder to Think, a BBC reporter (Damian Suchet) explains how the long hair and love beads of 60s flower power have given way to glitter make-up and "a whole new taste for glamour, nostalgia, and just plain outrageousness."

Not content with the ability of the film medium to make us experience slices of historical time, Haynes tries to go one better by shifting his narrative to the New York City of 1984.

AWARDS AND NOMINATIONS

Independent Spirit Awards 1999: Cinematography
Academy Awards 1998 Nominations: Costume

Stuart, who is now "the resident Brit" at a tabloid newspaper, is sent forth to uncover the whereabouts of Slade, on the 10th anniversary of what everyone suspects was a fake shooting. Stuart's assignment can be seen to correlate with that of the reporter in *Citizen Kane* who is told to unearth the secret of Rosebud, the last word to be uttered by the dying Kane, but one that no one can make any sense out of.

Stuart, however, has his own memories of his life in England to draw upon, as his voiceover makes clear. Among them, a lecture on Wilde's hero, Dorian Gray, allows him a viewpoint on how the lives he is researching "had in some mysterious way, been his own."

From Slade's manager, Jerry Divine (Eddie Izzard), we and Stuart, learn of Slade's childhood in music hall vaudeville. We see a seven-year-old Slade (Callum Hamilton) performing the rock'n'roll hit "Tutti Fruitti" to an appreciative audience. That trans-culturalism was to take an increasing hold on Slade's life. First, in the form of his American wife, the perennial party girl Mandy (Toni Collette), who bares her chest while introducing Slade at his first gig in a small London club. Then, more significantly, when Slade comes under the influence of the virulent Curt Wild (Ewan Mc-Gregor), who rock fans are bound to perceive as an avatar

Title is taken from a David Bowie B-side recording.

of the real-life Iggy Pop, with shades of The Doors' Jim Morrison. When Wild strips on stage, exposing his penis, Slade is left gasping at the earthy energy, as if realizing the lacuna in his own persona.

Mandy's memories, as related to Stuart, then fill us in on Slade's rising popularity in England, which in turn, seems to spur his sexual experimentation. Diffusely shot lovemaking between Slade and Mandy gives way to scenes of Slade kissing the effeminate Jack Fairy (Micko Westmoreland). It is, however, only when Slade meets Wild in America that his life slides into the abyss of consuming passion.

The relationship between Slade and Wild, which now becomes the film's center of gravity, also allows Haynes to pull off quite a few ideological sleights of hand. Homosexual attraction, as that between Wild and Slade, is made to serve as a paradigm for nonconformity; Wild's heroin habit is made to appear the cause for his slow self-destruction; most troubling, however, remains the indiscriminate sex, as practiced by both Slade and Mandy, being made to represent the ideal of sexual liberation.

Even so, had the above concerns been handled in depth, they could have resulted in engrossing viewing. Instead, we are treated to choppy scenes of extreme close-ups interspersed with postmodernist indulgence, so that even describing the film's storyline in the form of those scenes would bestow on them a dramatic importance absent in the film.

As could have been foretold, Slade and Wild remain at loggerheads when they attempt a musical symbiosis. When Mandy finds them in bed, naked, she becomes convinced that she has lost Slade to a lie that he is now living. As Slade's career takes a downward turn, seemingly owing to

CREDITS

Curt Wild: Ewan McGregor
Brian Slade: Jonathan Rhys Meyers
Arthur Stuart: Christian Bale
Mandy Slade: Toni Collette
Jerry Divine: Eddie Izzard
Shannon: Emily Woof
Cecil: Michael Feast

Origin: USA, Great Britain
Released: 1998
Production: Christine Vachon for Zenith Productions, Killer Films, and Single Cell Pictures; released by Miramax Films
Direction: Todd Haynes
Screenplay: Todd Haynes
Cinematography: Maryse Alberti
Editing: James Lyons
Music: Carter Burwell
Production design: Christopher Hobbs
Art direction: Andrew Munro
Costumes: Sandy Powell
Sound: Peter Lindsay
MPAA rating: R
Running Time: 120 minutes

REVIEWS

Boxoffice. July, 1998, p. 125.
Entertainment Weekly. November 13, 1998, p. 52.
Los Angeles Times. November 6, 1998, p. F8.
New York Post. November 6, 1998.
New York Times. October 1, 1998, p. E5.
New York Times. November 8, 1998, p. AR13.
Newsday. November 6, 1998.
People. November 16, 1998, p. 36.
Rolling Stone. November 26, 1998, p. 64.
Sight and Sound. November, 1998, p. 63.
Variety. May 25, 1998, p. 56.
Village Voice. November 3, 1998, p. 44.
Village Voice. November 10, 1998, p. 115.
Village Voice. November 18, 1998, p. 64.
Washington Post Weekend. November 6, 1998, p. 47.

his "sad affair" with Wild, a fake shooting appears the only way for him to bow out.

The story then returns to 1984, as Stuart begins to suspect that Slade has reinvented himself as the popular evangelist, Tommy Stone (Alastair Cumming), but by that time, his boss at the paper has decided to drop the story. As Stuart continues his probe on his own, it leads to him being sodomized by Wild. Then, as a consummate gesture, Wild presents him with the pin we first saw on the young Oscar Wilde, an heirloom symbolizing sexual freedom.

Understandably, even critics sympathetic to Haynes's previous work (1995's *Safe*) have called *Velvet Goldmine*: "too

arty" and "structurally soft" (Thelma Adams in the *New York Post*); "[with] no center . . . extraneous and diffuse" (Xan Brooks in *Sight and Sound*). Despite its flaws, the film has been showered with more than its share of praise. Janet Maslin in the *New York Times* calls it "dazzlingly surreal," evoking "a brave new world of electrifying theatricality and sexual possibility" with its "explosion(s) of visual sensuality." Even John Anderson in *Newsday*, while describing the film as "an exercise in flamboyance and excess," admits to finding its view of sex spawned by the androgyny of glam-rock "profound and ultimately ingenious."

—*Vivek Adarkar*

Very Bad Things

They've been bad. Very bad.—Movie tagline
"Brazenly shocks you into laughter."—Owen Gleiberman, *Entertainment Weekly*
"Hilarious!"—Stephen Farber, *Movieline*
"Savagely funny!"—Dennis Dermody, *Paper*

Box Office: $9,735,745

If a woman were ever truly interested in becoming a fly on the wall and witnessing the positively abhorrent depths men can reach when assembled in a wolf-like pack, all she need do is sneak a peak at Peter Berg's *Very Bad Things*. While "men only" movies of the past have adequately scratched the surface of what happens when male primeval instincts take over, nothing ever consigned to film has ever done so much with such cutting precision. It is at once vicious, misogynist, mean-spirited, and darkly enriching, and deftly tells a tale of what happens when fear and paranoia overwhelms all other human emotions.

In the '80s, before he became the biggest star on the planet, Tom Hanks starred in *Bachelor Party*, an enjoyable farce loaded to the gills with drugs, drink, hookers, and widespread debauchery. Hanks played a man who recently became engaged and had been talked into the celebrated ritual of the bachelor party by his friends. If it were up to him, he'd just forgo the whole ordeal. Much like funerals, bachelor parties

aren't as much for the honoree as they are for the people who organize and attend them; and Hanks goes through the motions with feigned enthusiasm, and keeping his head while all around him are losing theirs. The hotel room they rent gets completely destroyed, virtually all of the attendees achieve some degree of physical and/or mental gratification and, by and large, no one gets hurt (save for the very large horse that overdoses). It is the scene with a horse in the hotel room that reminds the audience that they were indeed watching a movie; and with everyone coming out on the other side unscathed, the story was wrapped up with a bland, vanilla-flavored flair.

Compared to actor-turned-writer/director Berg's debut, Hanks's outing looks like an afternoon tea with Martha Stewart. Easy-going groom-to-be Kyle Fisher (Jon Favreau) is basically a photocopy of the Hanks character. Affable, amiable, and just a little dim, Kyle is window dressing for both the impending party and his own upcoming wedding.

Robert (Christian Slater): "What we have here was not a good thing, but it was, under the circumstances, the smart play."

He doesn't like to rock the boat too much, so when he and his four cohorts load up the minivan and head from their safe confines of the California suburbs to the glittering lights of Las Vegas, Kyle gets with the program and forges ahead.

As soon as the quintet arrives in Sin City, the festivities get underway in earnest. Berg's first impressive moment comes as the camera perspective changes from idyllically placid to harrowing, disjointed, and violently out of control. The big screen TV in their hotel suite tuned to a sports channel and the song "Dirt" by a band called (ironically) Death in Vegas is blaring on the stereo. On top of the large glass table in the center of the room is a water bong, a pile of marijuana, several lines of cocaine, and assorted liquor bottles. It's crystal clear that the soiree is definitely on it's way. These assorted ingredients—booze, mind-altering chemicals, visual and aural stimuli, all set in the friendly confines of a town that never sleeps, are all staples of the successful bachelor party, yet none is truly complete without the . . . ahem, exotic live "entertainment."

Enter Tina (Carla Scott), the eagerly awaited entertainer. A true professional, she immediately sets her gaze on Kyle, who exhibits the expected nervousness. Seeing that his friend could use a hand, Michael (Jeremy Piven) scoops up Tina and wisks her away to the over-sized bathroom for some stress-relieving sex. Michael's overeagerness and an ill-placed wall-mounted hanger cause Tina's death. Needless to say, this minor "ninety-eight-pound inconvenience," as Robert (Christian Slater) so delicately phrases it, puts a noticeable damper on the proceedings. What to do . . . what to do? Call the police? With some expeditious cleaning and a creative defense attorney, Michael might be able to get off with involuntary manslaughter.

Robert, clearly the group's *de facto* leader (and the only one not freaking out) says absolutely no. Without hesitation, Adam (Daniel Stern), the emotional polar opposite of Robert—wired and scared of his own shadow, emphatically votes yes. This is strange, considering Michael and Adam are brothers. Kyle is on the fence, as is Charles (Leland Orser), his childhood friend, who only moments earlier did a cannonball into the coffee table, which is why someone else is knockin' at the door again. What to do? Smooth talkin' Robert knows: let the burly security guard in, agree to whatever he says, let him leave, and then get the hell out of Dodge. To reveal what happens next in this forum would be patently unfair.

What Berg has said thus far, is that many crimes occur in the blink of an eye and are absent of forethought or malice. It's only when we're given time to contemplate our actions, their repercussions, and the almost certain punishments that follow, do people set in motion the deviant sins of the soul. Denying or covering up the crimes as if they never happened is what eats away at us and wears us down. This is made abundantly clear with Adam: the one who wanted to do the right thing is the one who suffers the greatest mental anguish in the aftermath. Is Berg saying that there is no such thing as an innocent bystander or are some people just victims of bad timing?

Second-billed Cameron Diaz is Kyle's betrothed, Laura. While her fiance is hip-deep in a desert conspiracy, she is busy planning her wedding day. The live-wire, anal-retentive Laura is one of those women who views her nuptials as a quasi-coronation. The idea of being "queen for a day" and the center of attention is what drives her. She is leaving nothing to chance; much of the time Berg devotes to her is spent on locating the right chairs for the ceremony. No detail is too small, and come hell or high water, her day is going to come off without a hitch. Kyle is basically along for the ride and she makes this abundantly clear from the get-go.

Quickly becoming the premiere romantic comedy leading lady of her generation, Diaz takes an all-American outward sheen and injects it with sly, out-there, wild-woman undertones. As a result of her work here and in *There's Something About Mary* (a similarly bad-taste blockbuster that managed to garner almost universal critical acclaim), Diaz's dance card filled up rapidly; she'll be seen in no less than five features in 1999.

Stern and Piven have perhaps the toughest roles in the film; although they look nothing alike, the behavioral traits Berg lends them makes their kinship believable. An interesting actor, Stern only seems to have two speeds: full boar (the *Home Alone* series, *Celtic Pride*) and just mere moments from becoming utterly unglued. Conversely, the voiceover work he performs on television (*The Wonder Years, Dilbert*) finds him taking on the serene demeanor of a terminally mellow, late-night FM disc jockey. Piven's stand-out work can also be found on the small screen, whether it be in his memorable supporting role on *Ellen* or the recently cancelled *Cupid*. As the icy, assertive, ominous Robert, the highly un-

CREDITS

Kyle Fisher: Jon Favreau
Robert Boyd: Christian Slater
Laura Garrety: Cameron Diaz
Adam Berkow: Daniel Stern
Michael Berkow: Jeremy Piven
Lois Berkow: Jeanne Tripplehorn
Charles Moore: Leland Orser
Tina: Carla Scott

Origin: USA
Released: 1998
Production: Michael Schiffer, Diane Nabatoff, and Cindy Cowan for Initial Entertainment Group, Interscope Communications, and BallPark Productions; released by Polygram Filmed Entertainment
Direction: Peter Berg
Screenplay: Peter Berg
Cinematography: David Hennings
Editing: Dan Lebental
Music: Stewart Copeland
Production design: Dina Lipton
Art direction: Michael Atwell
Costumes: Terry Dresbach
Sound: Mark Weingarten, Matthew Iadarola, Gary Gegan
Stunt coordination: Chris Howell
MPAA rating: R
Running Time: 100 minutes

predictable, uneven Slater does his best Nicholson impression since *Heathers,* which (understandably) annoys many viewers. As one of the film's executive producers, Slater seems to be "on" here (as opposed to *Hard Rain,* from earlier in the year). He is the emotional core of the film and shows that with the right material, he can be damn-near perfect.

Having made his mark with 1997's *Swingers* (which he also wrote), Favreau struck a cord with audiences as a "lovable loser." A nice guy you could rally around. That certainly didn't happen here; his role was underwritten and he was called on to play a disposable straight man. Orser, too, is a character that adds little to the proceedings and could have just as easily been omitted.

Receiving little fanfare but proving to be an important facet of the story, Jeanne Tripplehorn, in the role of Adam's equally paranoid and distrusting wife Lois, is awarded little screen time yet does the most with what she's given. A beautiful, statuesque woman, Tripplehorn's strong suit is in offering support. When taking on small roles (*The Firm, Basic Instinct, Sliding Doors*), she exhibits significant range. Sadly, when asked to take the lead (*Waterworld, Til There Was You*), her talents get spread too thin and she flounders.

Many have faulted Berg's movie for being too violent and over the top, and it's not hard to understand that viewpoint. However, it's no mean feat to take a tale this gory and seedy and make it funny, but Berg does it with robust assurance. He crams a lot of material into ninety minutes—nearly too much. The last few scenes slip into pretty silly territory and border on overkill, but his loosey-goosey, dizzying, mile-a-minute pace is a welcomed jolt and never fails to keep our attention. It is as dark as any mainstream-minded effort in memory. A seasoned player of unflinching, often macabre pictures (*Late for Dinner, Fire in the Sky, The Last Seduction, Cop Land*) as well as a regular cast member of the often harrowing television drama *Chicago Hope,* Berg has obviously paid close attention to those directing him. This effort shows a great amount of forethought. Not acting in the film was a wise move; taking on a third job in his behind-the-camera debut could have unnecessarily distracted him. It's rare for anyone to hit a home run on their first at-bat. Berg didn't hit the ball out of the park, but he did manage to electrify the crowd with an exciting, round-the-bases triple.

—*J. M. Clark*

REVIEWS

Entertainment Weekly. December 4, 1998, p. 64.
Hollywood Reporter. September 15, 1998, p. 20.
New York Times. November 25, 1998, p. E10.
People. December 7, 1998, p. 36.
Sight and Sound. January, 1999, p. 59.
Variety. September 21, 1998, p. 107.

Waking Ned Devine

"If you're thinking about buying a lottery ticket, buy a ticket to *Waking Ned Devine* instead. Your chances of winning are much better."—Elliott Forrest, *A&E*

"The perfect antidote to a lousy day."—Lisa Henricksson, *GQ*

"This *Devine* comedy is worth taking a chance on."—Anne Marie O'Connor, *Mademoiselle*

"A dream come true. An absolute delight . . . one of the year's best films."—Jeffrey Lyons, *NBC-TV*

"Adorable. A surprisingly sweet, funny and picturesque movie. Beautiful."—Jeff Giles, *Newsweek*

"A real rarity. You ought to be first in line to see this."—Glenn Kenny, *Premiere*

 Box Office: $5,335,460

Weeks before *Waking Ned Devine* even hit theatres, the hype was already spreading. Most of it involved the words "sleeper" and "the next *Full Monty*." Director Kirk Jones said in a *Los Angeles Times* article that before the film came out, he was wary of Fox promoting the film with an ad campaign like "From the company that brought you *The Full Monty*," but it's hard not to make the comparison. In both movies, there are nude scenes—nude scenes involving men who are not especially young or conventionally attractive. But more on that later.

The two films share more than naked men; both films are low-budget British comedies, and both share a tone.

Waking Ned Devine has the same sort of good-natured gentle comedy of *The Full Monty*, an almost cuteness without being cloying. Both also focus on regular kinds of folks instead of glamorous movie star types.

Waking Ned Devine takes place in the charming Irish village Tully More, population 52. (In reality, it was filmed on the breathtaking British Isle of Man.) *Entertainment Weekly* reports that director Jones got the idea for the film after reading a newspaper story about a small-town postmistress who won a big lottery. *Waking Ned Devine* takes off from there, but instead of it being the postmistress, it's a mystery as to which resident has won.

Upon hearing the news that the lottery winner is from their little town, longtime best friends Jackie O'Shea (Ian Bannen) and Michael O'Sullivan (David Kelly) decide they will figure out who the winner is and befriend them to see what benefits they can reap for themselves. "I'll be their best friend by the time they cash the check," says Jackie.

Jones draws out this first part of the film and has fun with the idea of Jackie and Michael scheming to uncover who their new rich friend is. The two find out who the regular lottery players are in their town and host a chicken dinner for them, plying all with questions like "So will you be buying a bigger house?" They try to get in good with any local residents who seem to be a bit happier than usual. They buy pints and even some "fruity soaps" for a surprised local pig farmer Pig Finn (James Nesbitt). But their efforts lead nowhere until they realize they haven't questioned one resident, Ned Devine.

Jackie walks over to Ned Devine's house carrying his chicken dinner and discovers that poor Ned is dead, still clutching the winning ticket in his hand. After an evening of mourning with his wife Annie (Fionnula Flanagan), Jackie has a dream in which Ned offers to share some of his chicken. Using a very liberal dream interpretation, Jackie decides that Ned is trying to tell him to take the lottery ticket for himself.

The problem is that someone will have to impersonate Ned so that the lottery commission will award the money. At first Jackie, a gifted liar (or as he puts it: "I'm not a great man for telling things the way they are") is going to do it. But somehow poor Michael, a man who has never told a lie in his life, gets more involved with the scheme and ends up having to impersonate Ned himself. He gets so wrapped up with it all that when the lottery agent comes to town, Michael has to rush from his regular nude swim to Ned's house. Without a second thought, Michael hops on a motorcycle, naked but for a helmet, and speeds across town.

Eventually the whole town gets involved and everyone must work together to fool the lottery representative into thinking that Michael is Ned. In the process we meet the locals. There's the cheap, grouchy old lady Lizzie Quinn (Eileen Dromey). There's Pig Finn, the pig farmer who wants to marry the lovely Maggie (Susan Lynch), a greet-

ing card writer and her son, the wise-beyond-his-years Maurice (Robert Hickey).

What makes the movie work are the characters of Jackie and Michael. Ian Bannen (from *Braveheart* and Oscar nominated for 1966's *Flight of the Phoenix*) plays Jackie as a brash Irishman, full of charm and smiles. He seems to radiate joy and good humor. During one scene where he and Michael are trying to fix the expression on the dead Ned's face, he makes what could have been a tasteless scene into one of the most charming ones in the movie. Ned's dental work falls on the floor and Bannen plays it surprised, then giggly. It's amazing acting, the kind that rings completely true.

As the skinny, hawk-nosed Michael, David Kelly (best known for TV's *Fawlty Towers*) is the Ethel to Jackie's Lucy, a semi-willing cohort drawn in the crazy schemes. During his nude motorcycle ride, he manages to upstage his naked, skin-and-bones physique with a priceless facial expression that's simultaneously anxious and determined. In a scene showing Ned Devine's funeral, Jackie is giving the eulogy when the lottery commissioner comes in. Jackie has to quickly change his speech and switches Ned's name to Michael's. Says Jackie, mischievously, "Wouldn't it be wonderful to see one's own funeral? To perhaps sit in the front row and hear what your friends say about you?" Michael, who is indeed sitting in the front row, at first registers shock, then as he hears the warm words being spoken about him, begins to look rather pleased, then finally looks deeply touched. For a scene in which he speaks no words, Kelly conveys quite a bit.

What's nice about the parts of Jackie and Michael, besides the skill of the actors who play them, is that they're the focus of the film, and because older actors tend to be stuck with minor, stereotypical roles—a crazy person, an out-of-touch parent, a weird neighbor, a wise old sage. Jackie and Michael, both hovering around the age of seventy, get to be real, vital people, who are mischievous, daring, funny, and scheming.

The acting by everyone in the film is universally excellent. In a side story, Susan Lynch's Maggie won't marry her true love Pig Finn because he smells like the pigs he tends. "We'd be settled already if it weren't for the pigs," she tells him repeatedly. Nesbitt plays Finn as a lovelorn suitor who, despite the use of his "fruity soaps," can never quite wash the pig scent away. ("Try the raspberry," suggests Jackie helpfully.) When Maggie reads him a greeting card verse she has written, he almost swoons. "That's poetry," he says dreamily.

There are also some good scenes between Maggie's fatherless son Maurice and Father Patrick, who is filling in for the regular priest. After questioning the priest about his line of work and his "boss," God, the precocious Maurice looks doubtful and says, "I don't think I could work for someone I never met and not get paid for it."

One of the most charming characters in the film is the town itself. With its lovely, eccentric occupants and crumbling, ancient stone buildings, it's the old, mythical Ireland come to life. Even if the story in *Waking Ned Devine* weren't as strong, the film would still make for a fine travelogue. The scenery is stunning; there is the vast ocean, winding roads, endlessly wide green fields, and absurdly steep cliffs.

The combination of the wonderful scenery, the engaging characters, and the sly, gentle humor in the film create an atmosphere where subject matter that would ordinarily be tasteless—stealing from a dead man—somehow doesn't seem so at all. And, in the course of the one and a half-hour running time, characters mess around with a dead body, a funeral is made into a joke, and a woman is run over and killed by a van bearing a "Honk if you love Jesus" bumper sticker. But the mood of the film is so carefully laid out that the jokes seem good-natured instead of cruel.

The nudity is handled with the same gentle grace. When Jackie and Michael walk to the ocean for their naked swim, the audience gets a long look at the men's aging backsides—one skinny, one plump. At first there are a few titters, but then there is a certain sweetness that comes from seeing the old friends, as naked and happy as babies, slowly plodding towards the sea.

Waking Ned Devine pulls off quite a trick, being sweet, life-affirming, and very funny all at once. Without a false note in it, it's a lovely film.

—*Jill Hamilton*

CREDITS

Jackie O'Shea: Ian Bannen
Michael O'Sullivan: David Kelly
Annie O'Shea: Fionnula Flanagan
Maggie: Susan Lynch
Pig Finn: James Nesbitt
Dennis Fitzgerald: James Ryland
Brendy: Paddy Ward
Lizzie Quinn: Eileen Dromey
Maurice: Robert Hickey
Father Patrick: Dermot Kerrigan
Lotto man: Brendan F. Dempsey

Origin: Great Britain
Released: 1998
Production: Glynnis Murray and Richard Holmes for Tomboy Films, Gruber Brothers, Mainstream SA, Bonaparte Films, Isle of Man Film Commission, and Overseas Film Group; released by Fox Searchlight Pictures
Direction: Kirk Jones
Screenplay: Kirk Jones
Cinematography: Henry Braham
Editing: Alan Strachan
Music: Shaun Davey
Production design: John Ebden
Art direction: Mark Tanner
Costumes: Rosie Hackett
Sound: David Crozier
MPAA rating: PG
Running Time: 91 minutes

REVIEWS

Entertainment Weekly. November 27, 1998, p. 54.
Los Angeles Times. November 20, 1998, p. F14.
New York Times. November 20, 1998, p. E14.
People. November 30, 1998, p. 34.
Variety. September 2, 1998, p. 106.

The Waterboy

You can mess with him, but don't mess with his water.—Movie tagline

A hero for America.—Movie tagline

 Box Office: $147,895,431

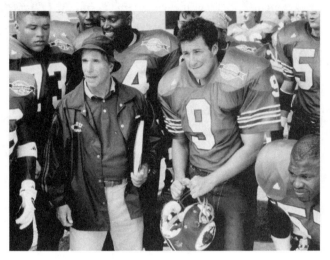

Dimwitted water boy Bobby Boucher (Adam Sandler) becomes a college football superstar in the hit comedy *The Waterboy*.

Bobby Boucher (Adam Sandler) has been the waterboy for the University of Louisiana football team since he was thirteen years old. Now thirty-one, he is still the team's waterboy, but on a level that would make Perrier proud. He's no ordinary waterboy; he's a water distribution engineer. He doesn't offer his team just plain old water, oh no, they have their choice of rain water, spring water, distilled water, or, if they'd like, they can just spit in the water barrel and harass the waterboy.

Well, it seems that harassment is the option the football team likes the most and it's beginning to distract them from their gridiron duties. As a result, Coach Red Beaulieu (Jerry Reed), a bully in his own right, fires Bobby.

Now Bobby has no purpose in life and he returns home to his only friend, his Mama (Kathy Bates). Ever since her husband ran away in 1966 to join the Peace Corps, Mama Boucher has been terrified that her son will abandon her too. Consequently she is very possessive and more than a bit eccentric. She keeps a pet mule in the house who drinks from the toilet, and she is inclined to make gourmet meals out of anything that crawls, hops, or slithers past her shack in the bayou. In order to keep Bobby under her thumb, Mama has home-schooled him which has left him with no social skills and so naïve to the point where he believes that everything from girls to football is the devil's work. And one girl in particular, prison parolee Vicki Vallencourt (Fairuza Balk), who has stolen Bobby's heart, may have more of the devil in her than even Mama expects.

Trying to find another job as a waterboy, Bobby chances into the office of Coach Klein (Henry Winkler) at South Central Louisiana University. Klein's career as a coach

Bobby (Adam Sandler): "Stop making fun of me!"

hit the skids after he suffered a nervous breakdown in the past which has left him only on nodding terms with reality. His mental state isn't helped any by the fact that his team hasn't won a game since 1994 and has an unsullied 40-game losing streak. So besides talking to footballs, he spends a lot of time reading "The Complete Idiot's Guide to Coaching College Football."

But even a losing football team has its share of bullies.

While suffering through his usual abuse at the hands of his new team, Bobby is advised by Coach Klein to fight back. This is a totally new concept to Bobby. He has always been told by his previous coach that the players could get away with anything, including tormenting innocent people, because they are more valuable than anyone else. But when Bobby's years of pent up anger are finally unleashed on his latest hecklers, its explosive nature is immediately identified by Coach Klein as the raw talent needed to be a great linebacker. And so, under the coach's tutelage, Bobby transforms every opposing quarterback into the images of his enemies, releases years of rage on them, and, as a result, breaks the team's losing streak.

In fact, Bobby is so good at furiously tackling his opponents that the team ends its season going to the Bourbon Bowl to face Bobby—and Klein's—old enemy, Red Beaulieu. There's just one problem. Bobby's Mama has refused to let him play "foosball" as she calls it. He has been doing so all these weeks behind her back . . . explaining away his football injuries by blaming an escaped gorilla from the zoo. How can the loyal Bobby continue to be the most valuable player on his team without being disloyal to his beloved mother? Will he ever free himself from her clutches? Does he want to?

Well, if you can't figure out the ending of this movie ten minutes into it, then you're probably still in grade school . . . and that's the audience to which this film was meant to appeal. And appeal it did. *The Waterboy*'s opening weekend scored a touchdown at the boxoffice with $39 million, more than any other November opening in history. It is obvious the creative force behind the film, Adam Sandler, is hitting a responsive chord in younger, primarily male audiences.

However, by relying more on sight gags and physical humor than on intelligently funny dialogue, *The Waterboy* never strives to be anything more than a formulaic sports film in which dopey losers eventually win. Interestingly enough, another film this year, *There's Something About Mary*, took stupidity to the level that Sandler should have strived for but didn't. But where *Mary* was creatively humorous, taking the audience down paths they'd never expect, *The Waterboy* remains formulaic, going for the easy laugh and never being imaginative or inventive enough to lift it out of the cinematicly prosaic.

> Playing themselves in the movie are Lee Corso, Bill Cowher, Dan Fouts, Chris Fowler, Jimmy Johnson, Brent Musburger, Dan Patrick, Lynn Swann and Lawrence Taylor.

Adam Sandler's Bobby Boucher attempts to win favor with audiences through his sweetness and vulnerability, and when combined with the fact that he finally gets his revenge on the bullies in his life, Sandler becomes a kind of everyman for most teenage boys. But even pity won't help most audience members overcome his character's annoying speech impediment or facial mugging.

After a string of movies in which his characters are all too similar, Sandler has no one to blame (or credit) but himself. And since *The Waterboy* caught virtually everyone off guard with its boxoffice receipts, Sandler is now the hot Hollywood property de jour as Jim Carrey was after *Ace Ventura* and *Dumb and Dumber*—the attraction and boxoffice grosses attached to movies about naively dumb heroes could be setting a disquieting prediction for future movie production.

The type and quality of humor in most of Sandler's films makes one imagine that they were written during a drunken night in a college dorm room. So it should come as no surprise that *The Waterboy*, like *The Wedding Singer*, *Happy Gilmore*, and *Billy Madison* before it were all co-written by Sandler with Tim Herlihy, his college pal from his New York University days. Also undergraduate associates are director Frank Coraci (who also directed *The Wedding Singer*) and producer Jack Giarraputo (who also worked on *Singer*, *Billy Madison*, and *Happy Gilmore*). It would be interesting to see what kind of product Sandler's comic talents might generate if he left his college humor and his college pals behind and let someone else do the writing. Until then his films will continue to appeal to a relatively narrow audience who admittedly at least are willing to shell out the price of admission to Sandler's movies, all of which, so far, carry the distinctive stamp of a dumbed-down comedy with a star who relies too heavily on witless, facially mugging heroes. The similarities to Jerry Lewis have been amply delineated by critics. The French should be very excited.

—*Beverley Bare Buehrer*

CREDITS

Bobby Boucher: Adam Sandler
Mama Boucher: Kathy Bates
Coach Klein: Henry Winkler
Vicki Vallencourt: Fairuza Balk
Red Beaulieu: Jerry Reed
Derek Wallace: Larry Gilliard Jr.
Farmer Fran: Blake Clark
Gee Grenouille: Peter Dante
Kyle Robideaux: Jonathan Loughran
Casey Bugge: Al Whiting
Paco: Clint Howard
Walter: Allen Covert
Townie: Rob Schneider
Professor: Robert Kokol

Origin: USA
Released: 1998
Production: Robert Simonds and Jack Giarraputo for Touchstone Pictures; released by Buena Vista Pictures
Direction: Frank Coraci
Screenplay: Tim Herlihy and Adam Sandler
Cinematography: Steven Bernstein
Editing: Tom Lewis
Production design: Perry Andelin Blake
Art direction: Alan Au
Set decoration: Barbara Peterson
Costumes: Tom Bronson
Music: Alan Pasqua
MPAA rating: PG-13
Running Time: 86 minutes

REVIEWS

Chicago Sun Times. November 6, 1998.
Chicago Tribune. November 6, 1998, p. 5.
Entertainment Weekly. November 13, 1998, p. 50.
New York Times. November 6, 1998, p. E18.
People. November 16, 1998, p. 32.
Variety. November 9, 1998, p. 32.

The Wedding Singer

Before the Internet, before cell phones, before roller-blades, there was a time . . . 1985. Don't pretend you don't remember.—Movie tagline

"The Wedding Singer is a sparkling romantic comedy!"—Kevin Thomas, *Los Angeles Times*

"Don't wait! A fresh, screamingly funny '80s flashback. R.S.V.P. *Yes* to *The Wedding Singer*."—Anne Marie O'Connor, *Mademoiselle*

"Sandler and Barrymore make a winning team!"—Peter Travers, *Rolling Stone*

 Box Office: $80,245,725

By the time 1998 rolled around, it seemed like everyone had pretty much figured out Adam Sandler's schtick. His stints on *Saturday Night Live* and movies like *Happy Gilmore* (1996) and *Billy Madison* (1995) showed him to be fond of general obnoxiousness, jokes about flatulence and bad singing (in his semi-famous "Chanukah Song," he sings the couplet "Paul Newman's half-Jewish; Goldie Hawn is too/Put them together, what a fine-lookin' Jew"). Suffice it to say, despite some passing moments of humor here and there, Sandler had never been known as the thinking-man's comic.

But with *The Wedding Singer*, Sandler takes an unexpected direction. He plays it sentimental. And, perhaps even more surprising, it works. Of course, saying that it works is not the same as saying it's a masterpiece. But for what it is—a mere wisp of a movie, the kind of light, romantic comedy that should come out in the summer—it does the job.

Sandler plays nice guy wedding singer Robbie Hart. Robbie is a twentysomething guy who used to be the cool lead singer of rock band Final Warning, but somehow ends up doing wedding gigs instead. He's a small-town guy who's impossibly nice; the kind of guy that gives a dotty old woman weekly singing lessons, even though she only pays him in meatballs. Life is good for Robbie. He's the most popular wedding singer in town and he's about to marry Linda (Angela Featherstone), a heavy metal groupie type he knows from the old Final Warning days.

Robbie's life takes a big downturn when Linda decides to ditch him on the day of the wedding. It seems she loved the old Robbie, the cool Final Warning singer, not the wed-

ding singer Robbie. Robbie, the romantic, doesn't take this news well and freaks out—in a nice guy way, of course. He doesn't shave and gets disheveled and gives one really bad wedding performance where he sings "Love Stinks" and points out undesirable wedding guests who will never find love.

Lucky for Robbie, he has his friend Julia (Drew Barrymore), a sweet waitress to help him through it. With their impossible sweetness and big puppy dog eyes, Julia and Robbie are made for each other, but they don't seem to realize it. And there's another complication. Julia is engaged to jerky Wall Street banker, Glenn (Matthew Glave). If being a Wall Street banker weren't bad enough to show that Glenn's lout, he's also a ladies' man who has no intention of being faithful to Julia.

Since he is a nice guy, Robbie volunteers to help Julia plan her wedding. The two spend a lot of time together and no movie suspense would be ruined to say that Julia and Robbie become fast friends. Will they fall in love? Will Julia realize her fiance is not the man for her?

The love story is so simple and innocent, it could have been set in the 1950s and starred Sandra Dee. Perhaps that's why the movie is set in 1985. The nostalgically remembered 1985 that's in this movie is as sweet and innocent as 1955. Maybe setting the film in the presumably more innocent past allowed writer Tim Herlihy to present such an simple, unironic storyline. Of course it doesn't hurt that the film is one of the first (along with *Grosse Pointe Blank* [1997]) to capitalize on the burgeoning trend of 1980s nostalgia.

 Robbie (Adam Sandler): "Well, we're living in a material world, and I'm a material girl. Or boy."

Besides providing the naïve times to serve as backdrop for the story, the 1980s are also conveniently hilarious, especially from a late–1990s view. The clothes alone are worth some hearty laughs. Robbie's best friend, Sammy (Allen Covert) is big on extreme fashions of the time. In one scene, he shows up in a red leather jacket with a bunch of zippers and the crowning touch, the one sequined glove. Julia's best friend Holly (Christine Taylor, who also played Marcia in the *Brady Bunch* movies) goes for more of a Madonna look. She wears the piles of crucifix necklaces, rubber bracelets and layers of lacy tank tops. But the funniest dresser is George (Alexis Arquette), a member of Robbie's band who tries to dress just like his hero, Boy George. (George's big moment in wedding performances is his heartfelt rendition of Culture Club's "Do You Really Want To Hurt Me?")

And then there's the hair. Big, tall, and puffy. Julia's friend Holly's towering cascade of Madonna curls (circa the

"Like A Virgin" tour), a minor character's Flock of Seagulls look and Robbie's ex's heavy metal chick do are worth a few laughs of recognition. But maybe Sandler himself was the bravest of all, sporting the painfully true to its time long-in-the-back, short-on-the-sides "mullet."

Julia's simple short and straight hairstyle has more of a modern feel to it, as do her outfits of vintage dresses and combat boots. But then the movie, isn't going for strict 1985 verisimilitude. At one point, a character yells "I'm watching *Dallas*! I think J.R. may be dead or something—they shot him!" Either it's a really old *Dallas* rerun, or the movie has a few anachronisms in it.

But even if it's not 100% historically accurate, the references are fun, even if just for the "remember that?" recognition factor. A kid runs around wearing a Freddy Krueger mask, Holly struggles over a Rubik's cube ("No one will ever solve this"), and Julia's fiance sports Don Johnson stubble and makes a point of never missing *Miami Vice*. In a fight with his ex, Linda, Robbie says, "Hey psycho, get out of my Van Halen t-shirt before you jinx the band and they break up."

The movie's music, full of mainly forgotten pop and new wave hits of yesteryear, goes a long way in capturing the feel of the mid-80s. When the novelty hit "Der Kommissar" comes on the radio, a character says "Yeah!" Other blast-from-the-past songs are Nena's "99 Luftballoons," "Pass the Dutchie," the Thompson Twins' "Hold Me Now," and Spandau Ballet's "True."

Another 80's relic in the film is Billy Idol, who shows up at the film's climax, dressed in his old black leather "White Wedding" garb. The Idol appearance is a nice touch, as are the rest of the cameos. Sandler's *Saturday Night Live* alum Kevin Nealon pops up in a brief role as does Jon Lovitz in fine ACT-ING mode as a terrible wedding singer who tries to take Robbie's business away. Best of all, is the always good Steve Buscemi who shows up as a groom's drunken brother and family black sheep.

As Julia, Barrymore is cheery and very sweet. She doesn't have much more to do than act nice and smile, but she does it in a way that seems charming. It helps the movie that Barrymore and Sandler do have some chemistry. For those who have never been big Sandler fans, it may come as a surprise that he's one of the strong points in the film. His willingness to show such vulnerability was a brave move. He sings songs without joking, in his real singing voice and even drops his tired *SNL* technique of laughing at his own jokes. Actually, the Robbie character doesn't even really tell any jokes or have any funny lines. The humor is a more gentle kind, coming from the situations, how the characters react to them and, of course, the bountiful 80's references.

In general, critics liked the film. *Rolling Stone* said, "For those who've written Sandler off as a taste not worth acquiring, *The Wedding Singer* offers a strong case for reconsideration." The *Los Angeles Times* said it is "the kind of picture that glides by so gracefully and unpretentiously that's it's only upon reflection that you realize how much skill, caring and good judgment have gone into its making."

The Wedding Singer is slight, sentimental, and has far too many fat jokes for that. But as a slight, sentimental romantic comedy, it's just fine.

—*Jill Hamilton*

CREDITS

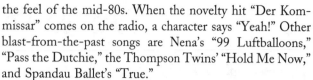

Robbie Hart: Adam Sandler
Julia Sullivan: Drew Barrymore
Holly: Christine Taylor
Sammy: Allen Covert
Glen: Matthew Glave
Linda: Angela Featherstone
George: Alexis Arquette
Rosie: Ellen Albertini Dow
Angie Sullivan: Christina Pickles
Jimmie Moore: Jon Lovitz
David: Steve Buscemi

Origin: USA
Released: 1998
Production: Robert Simonds and Jack Giarraputo; released by New Line Cinema
Direction: Frank Coraci
Screenplay: Tim Herlihy
Cinematography: Tim Suhrstedt
Editing: Tom Lewis
Music: Teddy Castellucci
Production design: Perry Andelin Blake
Art direction: Alan Au
Costumes: Mona May
Sound: Kim Ornitz
MPAA rating: PG-13
Running Time: 96 minutes

REVIEWS

Boxoffice. March, 1998, p. 53.
Chicago Tribune. February 13, 1998, p. 5.
Entertainment Weekly. February 13, 1998, p. 40.
Los Angeles Times. February 13, 1998, p. F10.
New York Times. February 13, 1998, p. E18.
People. February 16, 1998, p. 19.
Rolling Stone. March 5, 1998, p. 73.
Sight and Sound. July, 1998, p. 56.
USA Today. January 13, 1998, p. 3D.
Variety. February 16, 1998, p. 56.
Village Voice. February 17, 1998, p. 111.

Welcome to Woop Woop

There's no place like Hell . . . —Movie tagline

"Hilarious . . . far-out and could become a cult favorite."—Bruce Williamson, *Playboy*

Adapted from the novel *The Dead Heart* by Douglas Kennedy, *Welcome to Woop Woop* is arguably intended as social commentary on the "Unenlightened Age" of early Australian culture, that primitive time before Political Correctness found its way Down Under. Director Stephan Elliott may have intended his film as "a hearty wave goodbye to an old Australia," but the end result is more a painful exercise in grotesque kitsch.

The raucous and relentlessly gross comedy *Welcome to Woop Woop* is Elliott's follow-up to the successful cult favorite, *The Adventures of Priscilla, Queen of the Desert* (1997), a film of surprising warmth and charm. Unlike its predecessor, which conveyed enormous sensitivity in its tale of three drag queens travelling through the Australian desert in a bus, the wildly uneven *Woop Woop* feels devoid of any affection and ripe with ridicule and derision.

Teddy (Johnathon Schaech) is a handsome smuggler who specializes in selling exotic Australian birds to New York's social elite. When his exotic dancer girlfriend kills a couple of mobsters, Teddy flees to the middle of nowhere, the Australian Outback. Driving down a dusty two-lane road, Teddy picks up a pretty, young hitchhiker named Angie (Susie Porter), who soon offers Teddy the best sex of his life. This must be heaven on earth, Teddy thinks, right before everything goes dark.

When he finally comes out of a week-long, drug-induced stupor, Teddy finds himself in a scene straight out of *L'il Abner*: in a pig slough, surrounded by a group of former miners who now earn a living making dog food from kangaroo road kill. Welcome to the town of Woop Woop, an Australian Dogpatch lorded over with an iron fist by Angie's father, the cruel Daddy-O (Rod Taylor).

Teddy's hellish nightmare intensifies when the glowing Angie announces that while he was out, they were married—and that from this day forward his only entertainment will be Rodgers and Hammerstein musicals. Songs emanate from the loudspeaker of the large radio tower in the center of the town and at night, its bizarre citizens sing along to screenings of *South Pacific* and *The Sound of Music*.

The ring of steep red cliffs that surround the asbestos mining pit makes it easy to enforce Daddy-O's number one rule: No one leaves Woop Woop alive. This "Lord of the

Daddy-O (Rod Taylor):"Nobody leaves this town without my permission—which I never give."

Flies" set-up gives free rein to the creative minds of art designer Colin Gibson and costume designer Lizzy Gardner (who last year accepted her Oscar for *Priscilla* outfitted in a dress made of old American Express credit cards). Shacks in this shantytown are cobbled together from beer bottles and Angie's abode takes kitsch to a frighteningly new level.

But beyond the comic sight gags, *Welcome to Woop Woop* is little more than a live-action cartoon. There is little meaning behind the mayhem, although if hard pressed, one could argue that all this escalating eccentricity is in some perverted way a social commentary on the state of the displaced worker in an evolving economy — but that would be pushing it indeed! What it really becomes is a meandering mess of a movie, part John Waters toilet humor and part raunchy Russ Meyers sex farce, all coated with a delusional dose of "Lord of the Flies" import. *There's Something About Mary* (reviewed in this edition) may have changed the face of romantic comedy with its gross-out brand of humor, but it managed to infuse some charm into its tale; *Welcome To Woop Woop* is merely alienating, due in large part to its tonal dischord.

CREDITS

Teddy: Johnathon Schaech
Daddy-O: Rod Taylor
Angie: Susie Porter
Krystal: Dee Smart
Blind Wally: Barry Humphries
Sylvia: Rachel Griffiths
Reggie: Richard Moir

Origin: Australia
Released: 1998
Production: Finola Dwyer for Goldwyn Entertainment Co., Scala/Unthank Films production; released by Metromedia Entertainment Group/MGM
Direction: Stephan Elliott
Screenplay: Michael Thomas
Cinematography: Mike Molloy
Editing: Martin Walsh
Production design: Owen Paterson
Art direction: Colin Gibson
Costume design: Lizzy Gardiner
Music: Guy Gross
MPAA rating: R
Running Time: 103 minutes

Johnathon Schaech (*That Thing You Do!* [1997]) plays Teddy with the appropriate sense of disbelief, but his part is comprised mostly of external motivation, a "to-do list": he tries to escape with Angie's shy sister, Krystal (Dee Smart), while still sexually satiating his new bride, who is prone to squealing with giddy delight, "Sock it to me!" Former Hollywood leading man and Australian native, Rod Taylor (*The Birds* [1963]) is now nearly unrecognizable as the dictatorial Daddy-O, as is Tina Louise, perhaps best known for her role as Ginger on TV's *Gilligan's Island.* Talented young actors, Paul Mercurio (*Strictly Ballroom*, 1992) and Rachel Griffiths (*Muriel's Wedding* [1994]) are sadly wasted in cameo roles.

After a screening at the Cannes Film Festival, director Elliott cut some twenty minutes from his film in an effort to tone down the darker elements that loomed large in the original Michael Thomas novel. It was a questionable choice which most certainly even disappoint those viewers fond of *Dumb and Dumber* (1994).

—*Patricia Kowal*

REVIEWS

Boxoffice. April, 1998, p. 211.
Entertainment Weekly. November 20, 1998, p. 98.
Los Angeles Times. November 13, 1998, p. F14.
New York Times. November 13, 1998, p. E 10.
San Francisco Chronicle. November 13, 1998, p. C3.
Toronto Sun. November 13, 1998.
Variety. May 5, 1997, p. 66.

Western

"A winning entry in the pantheon of buddy road movies."—Elizabeth Weitzman, *Interview*
"Warmly comic, sly and delightful."—Janet Maslin, *New York Times*

Manuel Poirer's breezy fifth feature opens with a freeze frame of a trendily-dressed female hitchhiker facing the camera, caught in the pose of trying to thumb a ride on a road leading out of a French city. It is as if the film is holding its breath, both its form and content held in abeyance, awaiting the play of chance, evoking its own "Wild West."

As the present is set into motion, the first one to stop is the trustful, smiling Paco (Sergi Lopez), a thirtysomething shoe salesman of Spanish decent on a business trip. The hitchhiker, it turns out, doesn't need a ride at all. She is merely helping her friend, the scruffy Nino (Sacha Bourdo), a short, hardened young Russian immigrant. The norms of civilized behavior force Paco into acquiescing to this scam, not suspecting that it is to foreshadow a series of betrayals to come his way, no matter which road, geographical or emotional, he chooses to follow.

As if resigned to the exploitation of his good-natured trust, Paco drives on in silence. Until Nino suggests he check for a "rubbing sound." Paco hasn't heard anything, so he dismisses Nino's fears. Then, no doubt feeling disempowered in relation to the quirks of modern technology, Paco pulls over and gets down to look at each of his tires. This allows Nino to drive off with his car. From Paco's viewpoint, we watch the car neatly merge with the highway traffic. Paco can only curse to the trees.

We later learn that if Paco reports the matter to the police, he will lose his job, since he's not supposed to pick up hitchhikers while on business. Presumably, this is what leaves him slouching by the wayside, pondering his next move. But the film sees things differently. On the highway of chance, the film seems to say, no man is an island, which is to say, a friend unknown could be right round the bend.

A few feet away, a car comes to a halt, and out steps young Marinette (Elisabeth Vitali), who has stopped to adjust her front license plate. Plain-looking but jovial, she appears as trustful of the world as Paco has been. She offers him the temporary refuge of her place, after Paco is fired from his job.

Chance becomes compounded when, the next morning, Paco sees Nino ambling down a sidewalk in town, overloaded with possessions. We later learn the car was stolen from Nino as well. After beating him up mercilessly, Paco makes sure he receives proper medical attention. Paco's conscience, however, eventually leads him to forgive Nino, in gratitude, as he says, for having led him to Marinette.

Over dinner in an elegant restaurant, Paco relates to his newfound love of how he has had to put his emotional life on hold, that he is at present on a month-long leave of separation from his wife, intended to test their feelings for each other.

While strolling with Marinette beside the quiet canal that night, Paco musters up the courage to kiss her briefly.

While playing shy at first, she responds, as expected with passion. Her favors, sexual and otherwise, serve to draw Paco into the comforts of smalltown life, and back towards his original trusting self.

His good nature even leads him to confess lying to Marinette about being married. "Sometimes, one can tell the truth more easily with lies," he reasons. Unconvinced, Marinette has a surprise of her own to spring on him the next morning. She sits beside him at the kitchen table, making him read the thoughts she has put down. We hear her voiceover, as we see the pain her decision is causing her. She admits to having fallen in love with Paco, but would like him to prove his feelings by not seeing her for three weeks, which will also give her time to assure herself of her feelings for him.

His own lie having rebounded on him, Paco is thus set free to roam the "Wild West" of his desires, with the now recovered and repentant Nino as his Tonto.

The film at this stage could have degenerated into a series of picaresque episodic adventures. Instead, what becomes far more important is not what happens to Paco, or who he meets, but the relentless self-questioning he is put through before Marinette's three weeks are up.

Paco and Nino thus hit the road as stray hitchhikers, willing to follow wherever the thumb takes them. While succeeding in getting lifts, from trucks as well as cars, it is a lifestyle that Paco finds alien to his sensibility. He is not use to going without a bath. He therefore agrees to pay for Nino, as they check into a cheap hotel on the outskirts of a small town.

Again, it is eating that brings them closer. While Nino gobbles down everything on his plate, Paco is too lovesick to feel hungry. In the deserted dining room, Nino pursues the beautiful Guenaelle (Melanie Leray), a bartender-cum-waitress, while Paco retires early, obsessed with thoughts of Marinette.

The next morning, the two are back on the road, this time on foot. At a resting spot, overlooking a breathtaking vista of countryside, captured through the anamorphic lens of Nara Keo Kosal, Paco squeezes out of Nino his reason for becoming a full-time hitchhiker. Surprisingly, beneath his gritty exterior, Nino, too, has been harboring a love wound. Having come all the way from Russia to marry a French girl, he found she disappeared, "like smoke," one week before the wedding, taking with her his desire for any kind of stability. What emerges from such a quiet scene is how the two travelers to nowhere have found a common bond in shame, Paco at having lost his job and Nino at not fulfilling the hopes his friends in the old country had for him.

True enough, in keeping with the theme of the film, the two decide to backtrack for the sake of a dinner with Guenaelle and her vivacious friend. Poirer's camera frames the entire event at table level, without needing to change angle or distance. The drunken small talk and innuendos soon

give way to outright erotic advances, as Paco's romantic attachment to Marinette is drowned in wine and momentary sexual release. We remain at the table with a frustrated Nino, listening to the laughter of the two women in bed with Paco.

Nino's pent-up rage at women preferring Paco to him explodes at the end of the lovingly captured festivities of a wedding feast. This segues into the next sequence with the two back on the road again and Paco hatching a plan to find a woman for Nino in the nearby town. The two decide on a poll focused on what women look for in the ideal man.

Their amusing search allows the film to stretch its narrative fabric to include a host of congenial characters: the worldly Baptiste (Basile Siekoua), an Afro-French paraplegic, his French girlfriend (Helene Foubert), and most significantly, the attractive Fougere (Vanina Delannoy), who suddenly develops a suicidal urge while in bed with Nino.

Abandoning their plan, the two are once again walking down a country road. Their goal now becomes to acquire money for survival. Paco can get his company to wire the pay owed to him. Meanwhile, an odd job with a chainsaw almost costs Paco his leg, and results in the two losing their bags and possessions.

Paco's emasculation, however, functions as a cleansing for the twist his life and the film is about to take. When he clumsily hits his bandaged leg against a car parked in town, it turns out to be owned by the attractive but circumspect Nathalie (Marie Matheron). She is the kind of independent, self-assured female who could have stepped out of the films of Poirer's countryman, the great Eric Rohmer. For Paco, however, the chance encounter proves a blow to his emotional stability. While still in love with Marinette, he finds himself captivated by, what he can only describe as, Nathalie's 'personality.'

Even Nino exhibits a submerged, selfless side to his character, as he gets Paco to help draft a letter for a young rebel living in a homeless shelter. Then, delivering the letter to an indignant father, Nino pleads on the youth's behalf, "If you don't have love, it can be very hard."

The site for what proves to be a fresh start for both Paco and Nino is Nathalie's country cottage, swarming with a fatherless breed. As before, a meal provides a sense of direction, but the preparation involved puts Nino on top. Not only does he get to play the master chef in Nathalie's kitchen, but now the film allows him his chance to make Paco jealous of him. When the two set out to replace the container of gas that suddenly runs out, Paco erupts in a rage, accusing Nino of coming on to Nathalie. Again, Poirer shoots the all-important meal at table level, allowing us to see how Nathalie is drawn towards Nino, virtually excluding Paco.

The next night, in a moment of post-coital frankness, Nathalie tells Nino of how the urge to have children has animated her life, so that each of her five children have different biological fathers. Not only can Nino provide a sixth child, she adds, but unlike her other men, she would like him to stay.

Paco's rejection by Nathalie prefigures Marinette's decision to turn him down as well. Nino serves as the go-between for the bad news. Beside a country road, Paco has a showdown with himself, during which he breaks down in tears.

CREDITS

Paco: Sergi Lopez
Nino: Sacha Bourdo
Marinette: Elisabeth Vitali
Nathalie: Marie Matheron
Guenaelle: Melanie Leray

Origin: France
Released: 1997
Production: Maurice Bernart and Michel Saint-Jean for Salome-Diaphana; released by New Yorker Films
Direction: Manuel Poirier
Screenplay: Manuel Poirier and Jean-Francois Goyet
Cinematography: Nara Keo Kosal
Editing: Yann Dedet
Music: Bernardo Sandoval
Art direction: Roland Mabille
Costumes: Sophie Dwernicki
MPAA rating: Unrated
Running Time: 123 minutes

Then, like an epilogue, we see a smiling Paco, with Nino and Nathalie by his side, at the head of a long dining table, presiding over a party for kids of various national origins, presumably Poirer's vision of the France of tomorrow. Amidst the clatter, the film suddenly ends on a freeze frame. Unlike the opening, however, it is a moment evoking stability, as if chance had at last played itself out.

Critics have been unable to resist the film's disarming simplicity. Janet Maslin in the *New York Times* finds the film is really about "travelers who feel like foreigners wherever they go." She points out that Poirer himself, having been born in Peru, must know "all about Paco and Nino's longings." Chris Darke in *Sight and Sound* has a more universal take on the film's two male leads: "Infantilized by their lack of female companionship, these are men shown to be desperate for family and security." For Darke, none of this detracts from the film's charm.

—*Vivek Adarkar*

REVIEWS

Entertainment Weekly. August 7, 1998, p. 54.
New York Times. August 7, 1998, p. F8.
People. August 10, 1998, p. 36.
Sight and Sound. May, 1998, p. 59.

What Dreams May Come

After life there is more.—Movie tagline

"Stunning and totally original."—David Sheehan, *CBS-TV*

"So breathtaking, so beautiful, so bold . . . like nothing you have seen before."—Roger Ebert, *Chicago Sun-Times*

"Awe-inspiring. A visual blast."—Paul Tatara, *CNN*

"One of the best films of the year."—Steve Oldfield, *FOX-TV*

"Two thumbs up!"—*Siskel & Ebert*

"Deeply moving and superbly crafted."—Paul Wunder, *WBAI Radio*

 Box Office: $55,382,891

Based on a novel by Richard Matheson, *What Dreams May Come* is the kind of film that is apt to leave one with a feeling of disappointment that it wasn't far better than it is. The story's basic premise might sound interesting on paper, and in fact the film's trailer looked promising, but the final product unfortunately seems to waste several good performances on a plot that offers little in terms of worthwhile substance. Robin Williams has delivered several strong dramatic performances in his career (most recent his Oscar-winning turn in 1997's *Good Will Hunting*), but even the most powerful performance by an actor cannot carry a film alone. Williams does his best to infuse a spark of dramatic life in his portrayal of Chris Nielsen, a man whose family seems doomed to tragedy and strangely discontent with their true identities.

What Dreams May Come could have been a fascinating film about the afterlife, either as a thoughtful, speculative treatise on the philosophical and theological questions re-

Chris Nielsen (Robin Williams) finds out through guide Albert (Cuba Gooding Jr.) that he can control the beauty of his heaven in *What Dreams May Come*.

Ian (Josh Paddock). Tragedy strikes the happily married couple when Marie and Ian are killed in a car accident. Four years pass, and when we see Chris and Annie again, he is a kind and gentle doctor while she is a nervous and stress-ridden art gallery curator who leans on her husband for emotional support. On the night when the two are supposed to celebrate their "double D" anniversary, Chris is killed by an out-of-control, airborne car while trying to help a victim of a horrible car wreck in a tunnel.

Chris finds himself in heaven, which is a wonderful place where his thoughts create his own reality. The only problem with it is he misses his dear wife. Annie, meanwhile, who is emotionally very unstable and who once before became severely depressed after the death of her children, sinks into despondency, blaming herself for the death of her husband. Finally she commits suicide and goes to hell, the doom awaiting all who take their own lives—not because suicide is an unpardonable sin, but because such people are trapped in denial of what they have done and do not realize they are dead. Although he is told that no one has ever escaped from hell, Chris embarks on a quest to find Annie and save her. He finds her at last, trapped in the illusion that she is still alive and initially unable to recognize her husband. After Chris feels convinced that there is no chance of saving her, he decides to stay with her—at which point (and rather inexplicably) Annie awakens to "reality" and makes the journey with Chris back to heaven. There they are reunited with their children, but instead of staying in heaven with Marie and Ian, Chris and Annie decide to be reincarnated so that they experience meeting one another, falling in love, and living with one another again.

What Dreams May Come is not without its merits. In terms of performances, both Robin Williams and Annabella Sciorra play their roles with dedication and intensity, capitalizing on their abilities as fine dramatic actors to develop the characters of Chris and Annie. Williams' performance makes Chris a very likable, decent human being who has a strong grip on reality and is eternally devoted to his beloved wife. Sciorra convincingly portrays Annie as a sweet but extremely frail and emotionally unstable woman who literally cannot live without her husband. The relationship Chris has to Annie is not only one of a lover but also of a caretaker and a stable rock to which Annie must cling to when she becomes unstable. Although Chris declares that he does not want to spend eternity without Annie, his character is strong and independent enough to live and to cope without her, as

garding the hereafter or as a fantastical and imaginative adventure with no real intentions of seriously tackling the complex spiritual issues involved. Instead of taking either of those two routes, the story attempts to take the middle ground and winds up fumbling through a hodgepodge of inconsistent, half-interesting ideas. The film presents a "Hollywood" portrait of life after death, in that it seems to be attempting to please almost everyone (except atheists, presumably) with its simplistically eclectic vision. Unfortunately, it is actually apt to please very few, dramatically or theologically. In a similar vein, the film tries to deal with so many ideas, character-wise and plot-wise, that it ends up being about very little. Finally, what is arguably the most dissatisfying weakness of *Dreams* is that it tries so hard to end on an uplifting, hopeful note but, once again, stretches too far and loses the very credibility it strives to achieve.

Though *Dreams* is not a short film, and though the film attempts to maintain suspense and interest through several convoluted twists and turns, its plot can be summarized fairly quickly—not necessarily a bad sign, but perhaps indicative of why the storytellers felt the apparent need to "fill in" the storyline. The beginning of the movie depicts the meeting of Chris Nielsen and his future wife Annie (Annabella Sciorra). The two meet and instantly fall in love, and then the story jumps forward several years, at which time Chris and Annie are married and have two children, Marie (Jessica Brooks Grant) and

Chris (Robin Williams): "It's about *not* giving up!"

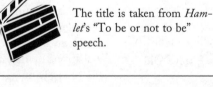

The title is taken from *Hamlet*'s "To be or not to be" speech.

evidenced by his quick assimilation into heaven. Annie, on the other hand, is unable to live without Chris. For her it is not a matter of choice, as it truly is with Chris.

While the filmmakers clearly intend to address the theme of eternal love and the almost supernatural power that love can have between two people, there is also a disturbing subtext underlying the relationship between Chris and Annie—one the filmmakers may not have intended, but one that casts a very different light on their supposedly wonderful, timeless union. The story goes to great lengths to develop the idea that Chris and Annie are soulmates linked by an almost mystical bond that joins them across the worlds of the mortal and the immortal. When Chris first arrives in heaven, he finds himself in a world that is a recreation of one of Annie's paintings. An angel named Albert (Cuba Gooding Jr.) appears and becomes a guide for Chris, explaining to him the nature of the afterlife. Albert tells Chris that one can create any reality one desires in heaven, for in actuality "thought is real" and the "physical is illusion."

Chris creates a reality based on Annie's painting, and he is amazed to discover that when Annie adds something to the painting, it appears in his heaven's reality as well. Story elements such as this work to develop the idea that the two lovers are connected across eternity, but ironically their relationship may not be as wonderful as it appears. When their children died four years before, Annie suffered a horrible bout with depression and even attempted suicide. The situation was so difficult that Chris considered divorcing Annie, but instead he was finally able to rescue her from despair. The night Chris dies provides a perfect example of Annie's extreme dependence on her husband. When she encounters a problem at the art gallery, she nervously calls Chris, frantic because she does not know how to handle the situation. Chris encourages her, assures her everything will be all right, and gives her advice.

Perhaps it is significant that Chris was a physician on earth, a man who spent his life coming to the rescue of others and healing the sick. In a very real sense he functions as a doctor for Annie, saving her life not once but twice and providing the cures for her emotional ills. When examined from this perspective, the relationship suddenly becomes an unhealthy one trapped in antiquated stereotypes that would perturb many viewers. Essentially, when analyzed carefully, *Dreams* is the story of a strong, independent, rational man and a weak, dependent, woman who requires her husband's stability, guidance, and deliverance. Considering Chris's role

as a healer and caretaker, one might even wonder whether his bond to Annie arises at least partially out of her need for him. He, in fact, does not need her in order to survive, but perhaps one reason he feels bound to her is because she cannot live without him.

The film boasts some striking visuals, including the vaguely psychedelic sequence in which Chris finds himself wandering through the "painted" landscape of his heaven, as well as parts of the journey toward hell. Other visual effects, while interesting, offer nothing really new or especially unusual. Similarly, the story occasionally offers interesting speculative ideas about heaven, such as the ability to create one's own reality and the power of thought as contrasted with the limitations of a physical world. Yet again, however, these ideas are not unique and definitely not new. Other elements of the film's vision of heaven seem randomly and eclectically conceived. This "heaven lite," courtesy of Hollywood, combines bits and pieces of different faiths. Heaven exists, as does hell (though in a slightly different form than the traditional "lake of fire"), and the angel Albert assures Chris that God exists "up there," but at no other time does the film refer to God. Yet these familiar images borrowed from Judeo-Christian traditions exist side-by-side with uniquely Eastern concepts such as reincarnation. According to *Dreams,* people go to heaven (unless they kill themselves), but they may also choose to return to earth in another life. It is this hodgepodge and rather shallow treatment of age-

CREDITS

Chris Nielsen: Robin Williams
Albert: Cuba Gooding Jr.
Annie Nielsen: Annabella Sciorra
The Tracker: Max von Sydow
Leona: Rosalind Chao

Origin: USA
Released: 1998
Production: Stephen Simon and Barnet Bain for Interscope Communications and Metafilmics; released by Polygram Films
Direction: Vincent Ward
Screenplay: Ron Bass; based on the novel by Richard Matheson
Cinematography: Eduardo Serra
Editing: David Brenner, Maysie Hoy
Music: Michael Kamen
Production design: Eugenio Zanetti
Art direction: Tomas Voth, Christian Wintter
Costumes: Yvonne Blake
Sound: Nelson Stoll
Visual effects supervision: Ellen M. Somers
MPAA rating: PG-13
Running Time: 113 minutes

AWARDS AND NOMINATIONS

Academy Awards 1998: Visual Effects
Academy Awards 1998 Nominations: Art Direction

old theological questions that makes the metaphysical component of the film (the major component of the film) difficult to accept, even though it is all just a fantasy.

Finally, some aspects of the plot simply don't make much sense. Albert, for instance, turns out to be Ian, Chris's son, who took the appearance of his father's old mentor because he was a man Chris respected. Similarly, Marie first appears as an Oriental woman, Leona (Rosalind Chao). Finally, the Tracker (Max Von Sydow) who guides Chris to hell turns out to be the real Albert. Reasons are provided for each "disguise," but none of them seem very credible. A more likely (and more believable) explanation is that the false facades are used for their surprise value, but they actually come across as gimmicky.

Also, the movie would have ended on a more satisfying note if Chris and Annie had chosen to live in eternity with their children, but their decision to return to earth seems like an undesirable path to take, especially considering all the tragedy they experienced the first time around. Why wouldn't they seize the opportunity to finally be together forever? As a conclusion that evidently attempts to leave the viewer with a good feeling, the last scene depicting the reincarnated versions of Chris and Annie as children falls flat. This final section also illustrates what is wrong throughout the movie: the film rarely achieves what it sets out to do. *What Dreams May Come* initially offers high expectations and attempts to be a dramatically powerful film about love, life, and death, but in the process of trying to involve too many different issues and ideas, the film tells a sad, unappealing, and inexplicable story that its makers probably never intended.

—*David Flanagin*

REVIEWS

Chicago Tribune. October 2, 1998, p. 5.
Entertainment Weekly. October 9, 1998, p. 51.
Hollywood Reporter. September 29, 1998, p. 18.
Los Angeles Times. October 2, 1998, p. F2.
New York Times. October 2, 1998, p. E10.
People. October 12, 1998, p. 38.
Sight and Sound. January, 1999, p. 59.
Variety. October 5, 1998, p. 67.
Washington Post Weekend. October 2, 1998, p. 48.

Whatever

1981. In an era of just say no, they said yes.
—Movie tagline

"One of the more compelling realistic films about teenage angst."—Stephen Holden, *New York Times*

"Remarkably sensitive and knowledgeable depiction of the painful transition from adolescence to maturity."—Bruce Williamson, *Playboy*

"I saw one movie I absolutely adored! Days later, it's still in my veins and buzzing through my head. It's Susan Skoog's *Whatever*."—Nick La Salle, *San Francisco Chronicle*

"Two thumbs way up! Terrific!"—*Siskel & Ebert*

 Box Office: $307,037

"High school is the most formative experience of our lives," asserts Susan Skoog, director, screenwriter, and co-producer of *Whatever*, a brutally frank, unromanticized look at that time of life. "High school is where we become who we are going to be." If this is true for the film's cast of uniformly troubled young characters, then they and the people around them are in for a lot of trouble. *Whatever* takes place in the early 1980's, before AIDS entered our society's vocabulary and when Nancy Reagan was urging young people to simply say no to drugs. The film focuses on Anna Stockard (Liza Weil), a seventeen-year-old New Jersey high school senior who dreams of going to study at the Cooper Union Art School in Manhattan. She anxiously rifles through the mailbox every day hoping to find a letter of acceptance, which will be her ticket out of her family's decidedly unkempt home and uneasy existence. It will also help allay her fear of "being ordinary." While she waits for her means of escape, she spends a great deal of time mouthing off at her over-burdened mother and also trades barbs with her younger brother. Anna appears to feel that she is immensely clever while she pilfers money and liquor, which belong to her mother, and tricks her mom into believing that she is too sick to go to school by scooping fake vomit into the toilet. Her grades are dropping while the number of parties she attends is on the rise. However, despite the fact that Anna spends a lot of her time at gatherings where drugs are everywhere and alcohol and hormones are flowing freely, she is actually the most together teen we get to know in the film. Her wilder best friend, Brenda Talbot (Chad Morgan), begins the film lying in the woods in an alcohol-induced haze, oblivious to the latest guy on top of her who finishes with a satisfied grunt. The guys walk away guffawing and thanking God for the availability of such a "pig." Like Anna's house, Brenda's is also filled with tension, cigarette smoke, and booze, but we also learn that her stepfather has been molesting her. On the day Anna pretends to be sick, she goes with Brenda on an adventurous day trip to New York City. Besides visiting Cooper Union, the two generally enjoy the excitingly different opportunities the city has to offer. They also end up having sex with two guys they meet in a bar, this being the only sex she has had since she lost her virginity earlier in the film to an older artist/ loser she'd had a crush on. (Despite the fact that he clearly wanted her badly, he fails to call or ask her out afterward, as she naively expected.) After Anna is turned down by the art school, and Brenda's stepdad beats her up, the two head down to Florida in a fast car with two equally fast guys. Anna experiences the frightening affects of some serious drugs, and comes to the realization that she, at least, can still go home to better possibilities. Returning home, she finishes her term paper, reconciles with her mother, and talks to her art teacher/mentor about other art schools. She has come out the other side of a rough period with her sassy spark and passion still intact, but just a little bit wiser than before.

Susan Skoog on comparing her film with those of John Hughes's: "They're fine. They are what they are—they're pop—and they're good movies. But I was more interested in realism, in social realism, in what's really going on, and in recreating the world that I saw."

How one reacts to *Whatever* depends, to some degree, upon the viewer's age. Those currently struggling to navigate the turbulent and uncharted waters of adolescence may relate to all the rebellion and general anxiety, while most adults will most likely cringe at much of what goes on in the film, and find the extreme and even dangerous irresponsibility to be a bit repellent. The title of the film reflects the blasé attitude of many teenagers which masks their true, deep, and powerful emotions that are constantly churning just below the surface.

Weil is adequate in the leading role, most effective (but, unfortunately, never especially affecting), when, in silence, her plain, soulful looks come closest to fully revealing her character. She sometimes seems too conscious of performing instead of being the girl she is portraying. Talbot is quite good as Brenda, consistently hitting the proper notes. Not nearly as successful is Frederic Forrest (the veteran actor whose performance in 1979's *The Rose* earned him an Oscar nomination) as Anna's art teacher Mr. Chaminsky, who gives an annoying, mannered performance.

Whatever took in just over $300,000 during the latter half of 1998 in very limited release. Reviews were mixed. The producers of the film drew a comparison between it and *Rebel Without a Cause,* but whatever the merits of Skoog's blunt, straightforward first feature, *Whatever* is nowhere near that classic's depth of feeling and general high quality.

—*David L. Boxerbaum*

CREDITS

Anna Stockard: Liza Weil
Brenda Talbot: Chad Morgan
Carol Stockard: Kathryn Rossetter
Mr. Chaminsky: Frederic Forrest
Eddie: Gary Wolf
Zak: Dan Montano
Woods: John G. Connolly

Origin: USA
Released: 1998
Production: Ellin Baumel, Michelle Yahn, Kevin Seglla, and Susan Skoog for Circle/Du Art Films and Anyway productions; released by Sony Pictures Classics
Direction: Susan Skoog
Screenplay: Susan Skoog
Cinematography: Michael Barrow and Michael Mayers
Editing: Sandi Guthrie
Production design: Dina Goldman
Music: Barklie K. Griggs
MPAA rating: R
Running Time: 112 minutes

REVIEWS

Chicago Tribune. July 17, 1998, p. C7.
Entertainment Weekly. July 17, 1998, p. 62.
Los Angeles Times. July 17, 1998, p. F8.
New York Times. July 10, 1998, p. E14.
Variety. February 16, 1998, p. 60.
Washington Post. July 31, 1998, p. B5.

Why Do Fools Fall in Love

Based on a true story of love, music and money.—Movie tagline

"Great music! Great acting! Great fun!"—George Pennacchio, *KABC-TV*

"A solid gold hit. The entire cast shines."—Neil Rosen, *NY1*

"You will fall in love with this film."—Paul Wunder, *WBAI Radio*

"A rock'n'rollercoaster of love and music."—Bill Bregoli, *Westwood One Radio*

"Enormously entertaining. Poignant, touching, wonderfully done."—Jeffrey Lyons, *WNBC-TV*

 Box Office: $12,506,676

Why Do Fools Fall in Love examines the short and tumultuous life of 50s pop singing sensation Frankie Lymon (Larenz Tate).

If 1950's doo-wop singer Frankie Lymon was as handsome and charismatic as he is portrayed by Larenz Tate in *Why Do Fools Fall in Love*, you can hardly call women fools for falling in love with him. The only problem was that he was also, as two of those women put it in the film, a "lyin', no good, no-bill-payin', home-losin' trigamist." A vibrant, eager, and undeniably talented 13-year-old, he and the neighborhood friends who made up The Teenagers were plucked from a New York street corner by Morris Levy (Paul Mazursky) of Roulette Records, and with Lymon's youthful, high-pitched lead vocals, their "Why Do Fools Fall in Love?" went to No. 1 in 1956. Lymon was the one that the adolescent girls who bought the record swooned over, and The Teenagers, including the group's founder, Herman Santiago, were quickly thought of by Levy as replaceable back-up singers and unceremoniously jettisoned.

Lymon's solo work never equaled his initial burst of success, and as his career continued to falter, his life started a steady downhill skid that was accelerated by his increasing indulgence in drugs and alcohol. In 1968, Lymon, a twenty-five year-old has-been, died while trying yet again to spark a comeback, the love of performing still in his blood, along with a lethal dose of narcotics. Lymon and The Teenagers would be credited with influencing the Motown sound, and paving the way for future black teenage pop stars like the Jackson 5. When Diana Ross's cover of "Why Do Fools Fall In Love?" climbed toward the top of the Billboard charts in 1981, three very different women arrived on the scene with

> Frankie Lymon and The Teenagers were inducted into the Rock and Roll Hall of Fame in 1993.

lawyers in tow to collect a fat royalty check, each calling themselves Mrs. Frankie Lymon.

The singer had married Elizabeth Waters (Vivica A. Fox), a streetwise, shoplifting single mother on welfare who was still married to another man, in 1964. He then left to hook up with the radiantly beautiful and stylish Zola Taylor (Halle Berry), a singer with The Platters who Lymon had previously attracted and gotten to know (in the biblical sense) at the height of his career. They were supposedly married in Mexico in 1965, although Taylor could provide no papers attesting to that fact in court. After he totaled her house while she was out of town, Lymon was drafted into the service, where he met the sister of an army buddy while she was stepping out of the bathtub. (Lymon claimed he was looking for the kitchen at the time.) He married Emira Eagle (Lela Rochon), a sweet, straight-laced Georgian in 1967. Needless to say, when the three women met in Levy's office, each of them was shocked and none too pleased to see the others.

With that farcical encounter, the acid-tongued sniping and go-for-broke legal maneuvering began. A judge would decide who was actually entitled to the money, and, during the court proceedings, each woman told of her time with Lymon. (The case went all the way to the New York State Supreme Court, which finally put a close to the matter by ruling in Emira's favor in 1990.) Because much of the film is comprised of numerous flashbacks to different points in time and from various (and often contradictory) points of view, it makes *Fools* a complex presentation, but its fragmented approach sometimes sacrifices clarity. Still, maybe it is all part of the film's point: that Lymon had many different facets, and no one seems to have gotten a whole, clear picture to fully understand. The marital mess he left behind is certainly an intriguing curiosity, but there is an even more fascinating story to be told if the spotlight is truly on Lymon, with his trigamy an important part, but not the heart, of the story. The film's focus ends up being more on the women, their predicament, and how they fought, bonded, and then fought again while finding themselves in the same unusually-crowded boat.

As for learning about Lymon, by far the most intriguing character here, how does the audience know that each woman's portrait of Lymon is accurate or truthful? There are other stumbling blocks, as well. If one is aware of the specifics of the true story being told, it is hard to accept Tate as a thirteen-year-old in the film's early scenes. It is jarring to see film of the real Frankie Lymon, who looks so exceedingly boyish that he reminds one of actor Gary Coleman, at this film's end. Director Gregory Nava, who previously brought us the story of another young singer who died tragically in *Selena* (1997), has stated that he chose Tate because the actor, who was twenty-two at the time this film was shot, would be believable as Lymon from ages thirteen through twenty-five but a younger actor should have been used in the beginning scenes.

Also, there is a clear difference between Tate's speaking voice and the much-higher pitched voice that comes out of his mouth when he is lip-synching to Lymon's records. Berry's lip-synching is sometimes also too conspicuous. Tate, as mentioned previously, capably flashes a grin that exudes the necessary dynamic charm. Fox shows an undeniable comedic flair, and Rochon and Berry also provide clear-cut characterizations. One wonders if the real women actually acted in the colorful way they are portrayed, or did Hollywood add the sometimes over-the-top comedy, perhaps to balance the film's darker tones? (Emira Lymon has noted that some liberties were taken in the film.) Little Richard, playing himself in the 80's courtroom scenes, is a hoot, as usual. *Why Do Fools Fall in Love* received mixed reviews. Despite its problems, the film is still entertaining and intriguing, if not entirely illuminating.

—*David L. Boxerbaum*

CREDITS

Zola Taylor: Halle Berry
Elizabeth Waters: Vivica A. Fox
Emira Eagle: Lela Rochon
Frankie Lymon: Larenz Tate
Morris Levy: Paul Mazursky
Judge Lambrey: Pamela Reed
Herman Santiago: Alexis Cruz

Origin: USA
Released: 1998
Production: Paul Hall and Stephen Nemeth for Rhino Films; released by Warner Bros.
Direction: Gregory Nava
Screenplay: Tina Andrews
Cinematography: Ed Lachman
Editing: Nancy Richardson
Music: Stephen James Taylor
Production design: Cary White
Art direction: John Chichester
Costumes: Elisabetta Beraldo
Sound: Veda Campbell
MPAA rating: R
Running Time: 115 minutes

REVIEWS

Boston Globe. August 28, 1998, p. E4.
Entertainment Weekly. September 4, 1998, p. 52.
Los Angeles Times. August 28, 1998, p. F8.
New York Times. August 28, 1998, p. E10.
People. September 7, 1998, p. 37.
USA Today. August 28, 1998, p. E5.
Variety. August 10, 1998, p. 42.
Wall Street Journal. September 4, 1998, p. W1.
Washington Post. August 28, 1998, p. WW42.

Wide Awake

A comedy that will raise your spirits and keep you laughing.—Movie tagline

"A wonderful family film! Filled with humor and affection . . . Rosie O'Donnell is terrific! Joseph Cross is a marvel!"—*New York Newsday*

"*Wide Awake* is destined to become a classic coming-of-age film!"—*Sixty-Second Preview*

Wide Awake is a coming-of-age story about a ten-year-old's search for God after the loss of his beloved grandfather. Joshua Beal (Joseph Cross) is on a quest, shown in three parts—the Question, the Signs, and the Answers—that mark his journey through fifth grade as he learns about life beyond Batman and Robin. An elementary school version of *Dead Poet's Society*, this drama is inspirational, as well as filled with humor and mischief.

On the first day of classes at Waldron Academy, Joshua's parents (Dana Delany and Denis Leary) have to literally drag Joshua out of bed and practically brush his teeth to get him moving in the morning. He's inconsolate after his grandfather's (Robert Loggia) death, and spends time reminiscing about their important moments together while sitting in his rocker or wearing Grandpa's shirt. Dressed in his school uniform tie and jacket, at a Catholic school for boys, Joshua begins his inquiry with a discussion on whether non-baptized people go to hell. His teacher, baseball-loving nun Sister Terry (Rosie O'Donnell), manages the students and topic.

Joshua's friend Dave O'Hara (Timothy Reifsnyder) cleverly arranges a prank to skip out of class and watch Brickman, the class nut, imitate a monkey in front of visitors in the hall. At recess the class bully gives Joshua a tough time and the class nerd, persistently tries to befriend Joshua. The new kid, Joshua notes, is even smaller than himself. Crawling into his parents' bed, Joshua asks to join the football team. They're physicians and forbid him to play until he gives them one reason . . . "Grandpa played." However, his helmet won't stay on and he ends up assisting the coach.

While playing games with Dave, Joshua announces he's out to find God to make sure his grandpa is okay. His wisecracking sister reveals that the cardinal, who talks with God, is coming to visit her school. This changes Joshua's previous lack of interest in the girls' school on the other side of

Joshua (Joseph Cross): "My grandpa and me, we always watched out for each other."

the fence. As he tries to escape to check out the cardinal, Joshua is warned by the new kid about the door alarm. Lost in the hallways, Joshua encounters a pretty young girl who befriends him and guides him to meet the clergyman. He has a "biological reaction" to her—his first encounter. Joshua innocently admits, "This mission could take days."

Dumping bad cafeteria food behind nuns' backs and making up stuff in confession are the typical shenanigans that add levity to Joshua's serious pursuit. He asks the priest, "Give it to me straight—is God made up?" The priest explains that doubt is a natural part of faith. Undaunted, Joshua suggests Rome for the family vacation since the Pope is God's best friend. His parents become increasingly concerned about their son's obsession and seek the sisters' counsel. Although Joshua realizes his parents are stressed about him, he stays on his path. "You're wigging," claims best friend Dave.

Narration of Joshua's journal entries provide an insight into his dilemma, but he may have difficulty interpreting the signs. In a flashback, Joshua remembers his grandfather's belief that the proof of God was everywhere—even in the snow. When Joshua opens his eyes from the reverie, snow is falling out the window. By springtime, the answers begin to unfold in unexpected ways. The bully has to leave school and Joshua finds it within himself to reach out and shake his hand goodbye.

Wide Awake was filmed in the Merion area of Philadelphia, where director/writer M. Night Shyamalan grew up.

At a ceremony for the girls' school, his "girlfriend" turns from the altar to give Joshua a rose instead, asking, "Have you found what you're looking for? . . . you will." He also reaches out to the nerd.

When Dave is out sick from school, Joshua stops by his friend's after classes to find him in the playroom closet—laying on the floor after an epileptic fit. Joshua's faith begins to slip. In the hospital, Dave tells him, "Don't give up, dork. You walked in on me—that's a miracle." On the last day of school, Joshua gets dressed up and ready for school without any parental prodding. He reads his report about his year searching . . . "Before, there was Batman and Robin, and now there is family, friends and girls. Before there were weirdos, bullies and daredevils . . . I was asleep before and I woke up." For the fifth grade graduation photo, Joshua tries to catch the small new boy down the hall. But instead of joining them, the youngster simply gives Joshua a cryptic and unexpected, but reassuring message about his grandfather, "He's happy now."

CREDITS

Joshua Beal: Joseph Cross
Dave O'Hara: Timothy Reifsnyder
Mrs. Beal: Dana Delaney
Mr. Beal: Denis Leary
Grandpa Beal: Robert Loggia
Sister Terry: Rosie O'Donnell
Sister Sophia: Camryn Manheim
Sister Beatrice: Vicki Giunta

Origin: USA
Released: 1998
Production: Cary Woods and Cathy Konrad for Wood Entertainment; released by Miramax Films
Direction: M. Night Shyamalan
Screenplay: M. Night Shyamalan
Cinematography: Adam Holender
Editing: Andrew Mondshein
Music: Edmund Choi
Production design: Michael Johnston
Costumes: Bridget Kelly
Sound: Brian Miksis
MPAA rating: PG
Running Time: 88 minutes

A sweet, charming family story, well-written and directed by M. Night Shyamalan, who clearly understands the boy's experience and conveys it meaningfully. The casting of comedic actors like Leary and O'Donnell lends an interesting edge to the performances, taking what could have been a contrived tale and makes it engaging and entertaining. The film deals delicately with the challenging subjects of spirituality and mourning through the eyes of a precocious child without being cloying, but instead, providing insight.

—Roberta Cruger

REVIEWS

Cinefantastique. April, 1998, p. 60.
Entertainment Weekly. March 27, 1998, p. 48.
Los Angeles Times. March 20, 1998, p. F10.
New York Times. March 20, 1998, p. E18.
People. April 6, 1998, p. 20.
USA Today. March 20, 1998, p. 8E.
Variety. March 16, 1998, p. 64.
Village Voice. March 24, 1998, p. 112.

Wild Man Blues

"Sharply insightful and very, very funny!"—Elizabeth Weitzman, *Interview*

"Extraordinary!"—John Anderson, *Newsday*

"Fascinating!"—Jack Kroll, *Newsweek*

Most documentaries about creative artists focus on their work, their lives, or the interrelationship between the two. Barbara Kopple's *Wild Man Blues* is a highly unusual treatment of writer-director-actor-comedian Woody Allen because it deals essentially with his hobby: playing the clarinet in a jazz band. Because Allen takes his music as seriously as he does making his films, what emerges is a compelling, though incomplete, portrait of the artist as well as an amusing, often hilarious, glimpse of the private man. How much of the latter view is spontaneous and how much is calculated to rectify Allen's personal-relations problems resulting from his controversial personal life is impossible to determine.

Allen has for years relaxed by performing with the New Orleans Jazz Band on Monday nights at Michael's Pub in Manhattan, moving to the Cafe Carlyle when Michael's closed. Such a practice by a man known for being intensely shy and private seems contradictory since he is exposing not only himself to public scrutiny but also an art form many in his Monday audiences—those attracted only by the chance to gawk at a celebrity—may be indifferent to. This dichotomy of unease with his public and need to be adored are at the heart of Kopple's portrait of Allen.

The eighteen-city, twenty-three-day 1996 European tour depicted in *Wild Man Blues* came about at the suggestion of Eddy Davis, Allen's longtime banjoist and leader of the ensemble, who thought there would be a European audience for their style of jazz. As Kopple shows, Allen is much more popular in Europe than in the United States because his small-scale, keenly observed films about the details of complicated romantic entanglements and contemporary neuroses appeal to a continental sensibility. Allen's bittersweet films resemble those of Eric Rohmer, Francois Truffaut, the Federico Fellini *Lo Sceicco Bianco* (*The White Sheik*, 1952), and, of course, Ingmar Bergman, his favorite director. (Music Nino Rota composed for Fellini appears on the soundtrack during the Venice visit.)

The audiences captured by *Wild Man Blues*, whose slightly ironic title comes from a Louis Armstrong-Jelly Roll Morton tune performed by Allen's band, in Italy, Spain, Austria, Germany, Switzerland, France, and England come hoping to enjoy the music but are primarily there to bask in the presence of a comic genius. Allen does not let this fact or his playing before hundreds rather than dozens of people for the first time deter him. Peering at the crowd waiting outside his Bologna hotel for a glimpse of the star, he is amused, baffled, and frightened. A man who wants to control all facets of his daily life, Allen is uneasy on unfamiliar turf and moves among his adoring public (and ever-present paparazzi) with forced graciousness.

About half of *Wild Man Blues* is concerned with Allen's music and fans and the rest with his commentaries about not trusting dogs, the plumbing in his extravagant hotel rooms, the danger of gondolas, the claustrophobia of European city streets, and his relations with his entourage, which include his sister, Letty Aronson, who works on the production side of his films, and the woman he refers to as "the notorious Soon-Yi Previn," the adopted daughter of former Allen flame Mia Farrow and the center of the tabloid-press side of his life. (Allen and Previn married in December of 1997.)

Many of Allen's fans may have been uncomfortable with his romantic involvement with a college student over thirty years his junior. Many may have also concluded, having seen only photographs of the couple, that the affair was a case of an older, famous man dominating a naive, inexperienced woman. The big surprise about *Wild Man Blues* has been how self-assured, even domineering, Previn is in their relationship, making fun of him because of their age difference, forcing him to swim (in the pool in their Milan hotel room) longer than he wants, nagging him about speaking only to Davis and not to the other musicians, taking his omelet because hers is too hard. Allen reprimands her only for having seen so few of his films, explaining how she would love *Annie Hall* (1977). After badgering him about how tedious *Interiors* (1978) is, Previn, with a Gioconda smile, admits she likes *Manhattan* (1979), which features the middle-aged Allen character's affair with a high-school student and his friends' disapproval of the relationship.

Wild Man Blues ends with Allen, Previn, and Aronson back in New York visiting Allen's parents, both in their nineties. As his mother recalls how young Woody spent

> Woody Allen about a London audience: "If I'm not good, these people will hate me in my own language."

hours in his room practicing his clarinet, both parents seem unimpressed by the awards he has brought back from Europe (with his father admiring the engraving on one), both lament that he went into show business instead of a more respectable field, such as pharmacy, and Allen's mother wishes he could settle down with "a nice Jewish girl." Previn laughs at this, but the real joke is that in her refusal to baby Allen, to cave in to his many quirks, she resembles his sister and, especially, his mother. She is a nice Jewish girl after all.

Much of the enormous literature about Allen has claimed that in real life he little resembles his screen persona, that he rarely makes jokes and is a model of confidence and control on his film sets. Is the nervous, insecure, whining quipster seen here, who talks just like a Woody Allen character, the real Woody or a clever facade to keep his true self under wraps? According to Farrow's account of their relationship, Allen could be mean-spirited and condescending. This side of Allen appears in *Wild Man Blues* only when he displays profane anger in telling Previn what he is going to do to a bothersome photographer, though he is able to get rid of the man quite civilly.

One of the best scenes occurs when Allen takes his new clarinet to a music store for a minor alteration and asks to play one of the ancient clarinets on display. Finding it much to his liking, he asks the owner if he can buy it. The man declines, saying the instrument is part of the firm's history. He is clearly uncomfortable with these rich Americans who think they can buy anything, and Allen comes off as a cross between a pampered celebrity used to having his way and a child hoping against hope that his wish will be granted.

Best known for socially conscious documentaries like the Academy Award winners *Harlan County, U.S.A.* (1976), about striking Kentucky coal miners, and *American Dream* (1990), about striking meat-plant workers, Kopple seems an unusual choice for what can easily be interpreted as a vanity project, but she delivers an insightful, entertaining film. (The film is produced by Jean Doumanian, producer of all of Allen's recent films.) Kopple and editor Lawrence Silk have skillfully edited fifty hours of film into a concise portrait that expertly balances the musical performances with explorations into Allen's passion for jazz, the European fas-

AWARDS AND NOMINATIONS

Broadcast Film Critics Association 1998:
Documentary
National Board of Review 1998:
Documentary

CREDITS

Woody Allen: Woody Allen
Soon-Yi Previn: Soon-Yi Previn
Letty Aronson: Letty Aronson
Banjoist/band leader: Eddy Davis
Trombonist: Dan Barrett
Bassist: Greg Cohen
Drummer/vocalist: John Gill
Pianist: Cynthia Sayer
Trumpeter: Simon Wettenhall
Nettie Konigsberg: Nettie Konigsberg
Martin Konigsberg: Martin Konigsberg

Origin: USA
Released: 1997
Production: Jean Doumanian for Cabin Creek Films; released by Fine Line Features
Direction: Barbara Kopple
Cinematography: Tom Hurwitz
Editing: Lawrence Silk
Sound: Peter Miller
MPAA rating: PG
Running Time: 105 minutes

cination with this artist, and the New Yorker out of his element. Because the Allen who practices his clarinet every day is the same disciplined writer-director who turns out a film a year—an understanding of the artist develops. Whether the man Kopple shows is the real thing does not really matter. *Wild Man Blues* is the best Woody Allen film not made by Woody Allen.

—*Michael Adams*

REVIEWS

Billboard. April 18, 1998, p. 66.
Boxoffice. April, 1998, p. 179.
Entertainment Weekly. May 1, 1998, p. 38.
New Republic. May 11, 1998, p. 28.
New York. April 27, 1998, p. 57.
New York Times. April 17, 1998, p. B18.
Newsweek. April 13, 1998, p. 73.
People. April 27, 1998, p. 35.
Rolling Stone. April 30, 1998, p. 74.
Sight and Sound. May, 1998, p. 60.
USA Today. April 17, 1998, p. E10.
Variety. September 1, 1996, p. 76.
Washington Post Weekend. May 8, 1998, p. 61.

Wild Things

They're dying to play with you.—Movie tagline

"Fun. Director John McNaughton achieves a sweat-and-champagne atmosphere that sucks you right in."—Owen Glieberman, *Entertainment Weekly*

"Two thumbs up!"—*Siskel & Ebert*

"It has many guilty pleasures. Terrifically cast . . . titillating."—Mike Clark, *USA Today*

"*Wild Things* is wildly entertaining, with more twists than a box of pretzels."—Paul Wunder, *WBAI Radio*

 Box Office: $30,147,739

D irector John McNaughton's films are populated with more than a few characters who are in serious need of counseling. He first became known for the shoestring-budgeted, stunningly brutal *Henry: Portrait of a Serial Killer* (1989), and later he did another study of dysfunctional law-

breakers, *Normal Life*, in 1996. *Mad Dog and Glory* (1993) also had its share of the confused and criminal. McNaughton's latest offering, an erotic mystery aptly titled *Wild Things,* is teeming with stealthy, cunning predators, only a few of which slither in the nearby Everglades. We do not know the exact nature of any of the main characters until the film is over, but by that point, having endured so many twists and turns in the road that Dramamine may have been necessary, viewers may no longer care one way or the other.

In the film's first scene, McNaughton introduces most of his crafty characters. Sam Lombardo (Matt Dillon) is a red-blooded high school guidance counselor in the blue-blooded community of Blue Bay. Kelly Van Ryan (played by the striking Denise Richards of *Starship Troopers* [1997]), a member of the enclave's most prominent family, is squirming with lust in the audience of Sam's senior seminar. Serious police detective Ray Duquette (Kevin Bacon) arrives with his partner to speak on sex crimes. Rebellious Suzie Toller (Neve Campbell of Wes Craven's recent *Scream* films and TV's *Party of Five*) bolts from the auditorium with a sneer and a burst of profanity.

Suzie (Neve Campbell) and Kelly (Denise Richards) strike a pose in the guilty pleasure *Wild Things*.

Soon after the lecture, Kelly volunteers to wash Sam's jeep, although her shining eyes and double entendres offer him much more. She is apparently following in the footsteps, so to speak, of her mother, voluptuous Sandra Van Ryan (Theresa Russell), one of Sam's previous conquests, who places him atop her own extensive list of former lovers. Kelly and a friend caress the car with soapy sponges, and McNaughton gives us many reverential shots from various angles of the girls' sculpted bodies, clearly evident through their drenched, matted clothes. Kelly tells her friend to leave so she can be alone with Sam, and we see her enter his home. The scene fades out, after which we see Kelly, disheveled and upset, running from the residence. She tearfully asserts to her mother that Sam raped her.

Outraged, Sandra hires an attorney Tom Baxter (a scenery-chewing Robert Wagner), and declares that she wants to nail Sam (legally, that is). Sam denies the charges, and retains the slightly unscrupulous and off-kilter Ken Bowen (expertly played by Bill Murray). Sam soon loses his girlfriend (Baxter's daughter), and then nearly his life when he is run off the road and beaten, courtesy of the Van Ryans. Soon after, Suzie claims to have been raped by Sam the year before, and it is deemed that there is enough evidence against him to go to trial. During tough questioning, Suzie admits that both she and Kelly are lying about Sam. She states that Kelly was in love with him and became enraged upon finding out that he was sleeping with Sandra. Vindicated, Sam sues the Van Ryans, and Kelly is livid when her family breaks her trust fund to pay him $8.5 million.

It is at this point that the film reveals its first surprise: Kelly, Suzie, and Sam were in cahoots, and will now divide the money he received. This scheme gives Kelly access to

money that she otherwise could not have touched until she was older. Before the three go their separate ways, they celebrate in the film's second sex scene, the first of which featured a decidedly vigorous Mrs. Van Ryan. Detective Ray suspects that the three were in it together (the scheme, that is). When he questions Kelly by the pool we get another rather heavy-handed pan up her glistening body. Ray tries to destabilize the treacherous trio by playing with their minds and pitting them against each other. (Sam deflects talk of a conspiracy with a crack referring to Bacon's role in Oliver Stone's 1991 film *JFK*.) A brutal fight between Suzie and Kelly in the pool leads, as one would expect, to a lesbian love scene, which Ray videotapes from nearby shrubbery.

The girls meet with Sam a short while later, at which time Suzie is beaten to death and dumped in the Everglades. Ray expresses fear that Kelly will be Sam's next victim, and so he investigates with his partner, Gloria (Daphne Rubin-Vega), who ends up coming uncomfortably close to kissing Sam. When Ray goes into Kelly's house, shots ring out, and he staggers towards the pool. Kelly lies dead, and at a police inquest, Ray states that it was self-defense. As this is the second suspicious shooting incident he has been involved in, the first being a boyfriend of Suzie, Ray loses his job and all of his benefits. At this point comes the next shocking revelation: Ray has been in on the whole thing as well. What is also (briefly) revealed in this scene are Kevin Bacon's genitals, a topic of titillating conversation during the publicity tour for this R-rated movie.

Before Sam gives Ray his cut of the money, he first tries to drown him. When this is not successful, yet another bombshell is dropped when a newly-blond Suzie suddenly reappears and shoots Ray. She then turns on Sam, poisons him, and sails blithely away to split the money with—surprise!—Ken Bowden. A talky scene follows to tie up loose ends, revealing that Ray had had an abusive romance with Suzie, and had killed her boyfriend when the young man interrupted a beating. Suzie had seen Ray do it, so he had her arrested and sent away. During the credits, McNaughton offers us snippets of some key scenes from a different perspective, letting us in on some illuminating information which his camera had not previously revealed.

For the most part, critical reaction to *Wild Things* was lukewarm. It was mainly known to many people as the film in which you get to "see the Bacon." During its first week in release, it was the No. 4 movie in the country, and went on to earn approximately $30 million nationwide over sixteen weeks on *Variety*'s list of the Top 60 moneymakers. Director McNaughton, along with director of photography Jeffrey Kimball (known for such films as 1984's *Beverly Hills Cop* and 1986's *Top Gun*), production designer Edward

Detective Ray Duquette (Kevin Bacon): "People aren't always what they appear to be. Don't forget that!"

McAvoy and the music of George S. Clinton, successfully create the necessary steamy, edgy atmosphere in *Wild Things*. Stephen Peters's script is clearly designed to keep the viewer guessing, but the piling on of drastic revelations and double-crosses calls far too much attention to itself, pulling the audience out of the story. By the last surprise, and with no one left worth rooting for, we no longer care what has happened to this group of good-looking but unpalatable characters.

The film comes off as more of a conscious exercise in screenwriting, with the plot serving the technique instead of the other way around. The attractive cast does a good job negotiating what the studio's production notes call the film's "serpentine script," but viewers will most likely be disappointed—and feel overly-manipulated—when *Wild Things* reaches its conclusion.

—*David L. Boxerbaum*

CREDITS

Ray Duquette: Kevin Bacon
Sam Lombardo: Matt Dillon
Suzie Toller: Neve Campbell
Kelly Van Ryan: Denise Richards
Sandra Van Ryan: Theresa Russell
Gloria Perez: Daphne Rubin-Vega
Tom Baxter: Robert Wagner
Ken Bowden: Bill Murray
Ruby: Carrie Snodgress

Origin: USA
Released: 1998
Production: Rodney Liber and Steven A. Jones for Mandalay Entertainment; released by Columbia Pictures
Direction: John McNaughton
Screenplay: Stephen Peters
Cinematography: Jeffrey L. Kimball
Editing: Elena Maganini
Music: George S. Clinton
Production design: Edward T. McAvoy
Art direction: Bill Hiney
Costumes: Kimberly A. Tilman
Sound: Peter J. Devlin
MPAA rating: R
Running Time: 108 minutes

REVIEWS

Boston Globe. March 20, 1998, p. C4.
Chicago Tribune. March 20, 1998, p. 7D.
Entertainment Weekly. March 27, 1998, p. 46.
Los Angeles Times. March 20, 1998, p. F20.
New York. April 6, 1998, p. 236.
People. March 30, 1998, p. 19.
Rolling Stone. April 2, 1998, p. 80.
Time. March 23, 1998, p. 79.
USA Today. March 20, 1998, p. E8.
Variety. March 23, 1998, p. 87.
Washington Post. March 20, 1998, p. WW47.

Wilde

An ultimate biography of a creative genius.
—Movie tagline

"A fine film!"—Richard Rayner, *Harper's Bazaar*

"Deeply moving! Lustrous! *Wilde* is likely to remain the definitive screen treatment of Oscar Wilde. Fry and Law are triumphant!"—Kevin Thomas, *Los Angeles Times*

"Literate, profound and deeply moving! A titanic performance by Stephen Fry!"—Rex Reed, *New York Observer*

"Remarkably moving!"—Dennis Dermody, *Paper Magazine*

"Elegant!"—Christine Spines, *Premiere*

"Two thumbs up!"—*Siskel & Ebert*

Box Office: $2,412,601

Wilde is a lavish production that brings to life the era when England held dominion over palm and pine and London was the capital of the world. Along with an entertaining and presumably edifying story, the viewer enjoys the visual treat of elaborate costumes, elegant furnishings, ornate architecture, soignee social gatherings, liveried servants, comfort, security, privilege—all the enviable appurtenances of upper-class Victorian life. Stephen Fry bears an uncanny resemblance to the famous playwright-novelist-poet-wit he portrays; however, there are many in the audience who will find it hard to stop seeing him as Jeeves the valet, the role he played so effectively on the PBS *Masterpiece Theatre* series with the equally clever Hugh Laurie as Bertie Wooster.

Fry plays Wilde very much as he played Jeeves. He is poised, smug, prim, proper, wry, unctuous. Like Jeeves, his Wilde is much smarter than everybody else but wise enough not to make it too apparent. Fry was a good choice to play Wilde because—perhaps capitalizing on his experience with Jeeves—he manages to be superior without being insufferable. The real Oscar Wilde could not have done as good a job playing himself. The filmmakers wanted to create sympathy for their anti-hero and could only do so by downplaying his egotism and brilliance. Even when he conducts his notorious affair with the beautiful Lord Alfred Douglas, he does not seem to be flouting convention but really rather modestly going along with the wishes of his headstrong, aristocratic young lover.

The biopic does not cover an entire lifetime. It begins with Wilde's marriage and ends shortly after his release from Reading Gaol. Wilde is very much like a character in one of his plays. He is a fop and a Bunburyist, like his Algernon Moncrief and Jack Worthing characters in *The Importance of Being Earnest* (1895). Wilde is surrounded by the kind of domineering matrons who often appear in his plays. He agrees to get married only because the older women who control the purse strings have decided that it is high time he did so. He chooses Constance Lloyd (Jennifer Ehle) because she is socially acceptable, demure, undemanding, and quiet. He wants a wife who will not interfere with his outside interests and social activities.

At this point Wilde apparently has no idea that he is gay—or at least bisexual. His "coming out of the closet" is the most important event of the film. ("What is there to say about being gay?" asks author Andrew Holleran in his 1996 novel *The Beauty of Men*. "Coming out is the central story told over and over again, like people describing how they found Christ.") For several years Wilde is content to lead a conventional home life with his wife and two sons. He begins to develop a successful career as an author. Then he meets Robbie Ross (Michael Sheen), the handsome young Canadian who serves as a catalyst to bring out Wilde's latent homosexuality.

Wilde seems much more passive and innocent than he probably was in real life. The filmmakers, following the critically acclaimed biography *Oscar Wilde* by Richard Ellman, try hard to deconstruct the flamboyant, supercilious, outrageous image that most people have formed of the eccentric Victorian genius. It is the young men who drag Wilde away from his domestic hearth to a world of illicit pleasures. As an aesthete, he is captivated by the beauty of youth; he seems more in love with youth than with any specific individual.

Wilde (Stephen Fry): "The world is at my command, yet I can't command myself."

The film carefully avoids showing how young some of Wilde's love objects actually were. All the naked young men who appear in the refined orgies are old enough to be men about town. The sex scenes are discreetly handled. The men do more kissing than anything else—at least while on camera. Beauty is like a religion to Wilde—the only religion that many intellectuals of his time believed in. Beauty for Wilde, as for so many aging queens, turns out to be a very false god indeed. It may have been sufficient for the ancient Greeks, but seems lamentably simplistic in the complex modern world. Nobody likes to see him neglecting his wife and adoring sons, neglecting his work, throwing his money away on hedonistic young wastrels who are a constant torment to their own parents.

Wilde manages to walk a thin line between his domestic and gay lives until he meets his young nemesis, Lord Alfred Douglas, played by Jude Law, who had a similar role as the handsome, spoiled elitist Eugene in the futuristic film *Gattaca* (1997). Such spoiled, aristocratic, narcissistic, amoral characters as Lord Alfred scarcely exist anymore—except perhaps in Hollywood. Wilde is of a distinctly lower class, a fact of which Lord Alfred (whom his intimates call Bosie) often reminds him when he is manipulating his older lover to waste time, waste money, or outrage society in a new way. Wilde loves the young man as much for his go-to-hell aristocratic attitude as for his grace and beauty. It is a lethal relationship, resembling the homosexual relationship between poets Arthur Rimbaud and Paul Verlaine portrayed in *Total Eclipse* (1995). There can only be one loser. It is still an age where social rank gives the younger man an invisible cloak of protection and puts his father a few tiers above the law.

Tom Wilkinson, who played the boss of the laid-off workers in *The Full Monty* (1997), does a spectacular job as Bosie's father, the Marquess of Queensbury, a nobleman of the old school who might still horsewhip a commoner who got out of line. It isn't until his fiery lordship bursts upon the scene that the movie becomes really dramatic. Oscar Wilde has had things all his own way and is brimming with self-confidence. The Marquess is the antagonist who has been missing. As is often the case with headstrong young people, it appears that Bosie's exaggerated affection for Wilde is at least partly motivated by a desire to defy and scandalize his father. The outcome is one of the most famous events in literary history. It has already been memorialized on film with Peter Finch in *The Trials of Oscar Wilde* (1960) and Robert Morley in *Oscar Wilde* (1960).

Queensbury accuses Wilde of being a "posing Somdomite" [sic] and Bosie pressures Oscar to sue the Marquess for libel. The tables are turned and Wilde ends up being sentenced to two years of hard labor for "gross indecency." No one who has read Wilde's *The Ballad of Reading Gaol* (1898) can have formed an accurate impression of how truly horrible the place really was, and how excruciating the hard labor could be. Everything is uniformly gray. When the prisoners in their gray uniforms tramp around and around in a circle in the exercise yard, they all wear hideous gray hoods which prevent them from seeing anything but their own feet. In a voiceover narration, Fry very effectively quotes the most famous lines of Wilde's ballad: "And all men kill the thing they love,/By all let this heard,/Some do it with a bitter look,/Some with a flattering word,/The coward does it with a kiss,/The brave man with a sword!"

When Wilde is finally released from Reading Gaol, in 1897, he is bankrupt and disgraced. He is not even permitted to visit his own children. (Constance is living in Italy [she dies in 1898]; the children are in foreign boarding schools.) The viewer cannot help but get the impression that Wilde was a masochist and not only enjoyed at least some aspects of prison life but is even enjoying his disgrace. He had previously allowed Bosie to humiliate him by forcing him to play the voyeur while the young man had sex with multiple lovers at Alfred Taylor's infamous male brothel on Cleveland Street. This masochism may explain Wilde's fatal attraction to that one cruel young man.

Wilde's conceit and arrogance may have been nothing more than an elaborate mask. Only Bosie understood Wilde's need for pain and humiliation. (Most of their ugly scenes are derived from Wilde's accounts in his own *De Profundis*.) This kind of relationship between a sadist and a

Merlin Holland, the son of Vyvyan Holland [Wilde], has written a memoir about his grandfather, Oscar, called *The Wilde Album.*

CREDITS

Oscar Wilde: Stephen Fry
Lord Alfred (Bosie) Douglas: Jude Law
Lady Speranza Wilde: Vanessa Redgrave
Constance Lloyd Wilde: Jennifer Ehle
Lady Queensbury: Gemma Jones
Marquess of Queensbury: Tom Wilkinson
Lady Mount-Temple: Judy Parfitt
Robbie Ross: Michael Sheen
Ada Leverson: Zoe Wanamaker
Judge: Philip Locke

Origin: Great Britain
Released: 1997
Production: Marc Samuelson and Peter Samuelson for Samuelson Production; released by Sony Pictures Classics
Direction: Brian Gilbert
Screenplay: Julian Mitchell; based on the biography *Oscar Wilde* by Richard Ellman
Cinematography: Martin Fuhrer
Editing: Michael Bradsell
Music: Debbie Wiseman
Production design: Maria Djurkovic
Art direction: Martyn John
Costumes: Nic Ede
Sound: Jim Greenhorn
MPAA rating: R
Running Time: 115 minutes

masochist is not uncommon, and it often develops when an older man makes the mistake of falling in love with a young person of either sex. There are many examples in literature and the movies, including *The Blue Angel* (1930), *Baby Doll* (1956), and *Lolita* (1962).

Wilde travels to France with Ross, where he lives on the charity of friends, but eventually meets Bosie in Italy and they resume their relationship. A closing caption appearing just before the credits explains that Wilde broke up with Bosie for good three months later and died in 1900 at the age of only 46. The psychological trauma he had endured, along with the harsh penal servitude, had taken their toll. Bosie himself died in 1945. Robbie Ross, Wilde's truly faithful friend, died in 1918 and his ashes were reinterred with Wilde's in 1950.

Wilde received favorable reviews throughout Great Britain and America. Kevin Thomas writes in his *Los Angeles Times* review: "Coupled with Julian Mitchell's superb script, drawn from Richard Ellman's landmark biography, and director Brian Gilbert's total commitment to it and to

his sterling cast, *Wilde* is likely to remain the definitive screen treatment of Oscar Wilde for years to come."

—*Bill Delaney*

REVIEWS

Boxoffice. June, 1998, p. 76.
Detroit News. May 29, 1998, p. 8F.
Entertainment Weekly. May 8, 1998, p. 50.
Los Angeles Times. May 1, 1998, p. F10.
New York Times. May 1, 1998, p. B22.
New York Times. May 28, 1998, p. F1.
People. May 11, 1998, p. 36.
Rolling Stone. May 14, 1998, p. 64.
Sight and Sound. October, 1997, p. 65.
Spectator. October 25, 1997, p. 65.
Times Literary Supplement. October 24, 1997, p. 20.
USA Today. May 1, 1998, p. E11.
Variety. August 25, 1997, p. 73.
Washington Post Weekend. May 29, 1998, p. 48.

Without Limits

"Donald Sutherland gives a commanding, almost hypnotic performance that is among the actor's best."—Kenneth Turan, *Los Angeles Times*

"Stirring . . . Proudly unconventional."—Janet Maslin, *New York Times*

"*Without Limits* showcases two of the year's best performances, Billy Crudup and Donald Sutherland."—Jack Mathews, *Newsday*

"*Without Limits* scores!"—Bruce Williamson, *Playboy*

"*Without Limits* is worth cheering! Billy Crudup is dynamite."—Peter Travers, *Rolling Stone*

"Breaks free and scores an upset."—Richard Schickel, *Time*

 Box Office: $777, 423

In spite of boxoffice failure and generally lukewarm reviews for *Pre,* the first film made about the brief life of the charismatic champion distance runner Steve Prefontaine, Robert Towne's oft-delayed project about Prefontaine's life and races was anticipated with considerable enthusiasm. Towne's success with *Chinatown* (1974) and his reputation for creating films with an individual style,

such as *Personal Best* (1982), which dealt with athletic competition and social controversy, plus his intense commitment to the Prefontaine film, aroused hopes that *Without Limits* might enjoy the kind of critical acclaim and commercial success of *Chariots of Fire* (1981). But even as road races like the New York or Boston Marathons have had to restrict entries, track and field competition has essentially vanished from public view in the United States, and since the Atlanta Olympics, no single runner has captured attention the way Frank Shorter or Carl Lewis did in past decades. To overcome this kind of indifference, a film about a runner would have to transcend its subject and reach an audience beyond the small coterie of running enthusiasts sure to attend. *Without Limits* tries to make Steve Prefontaine's life representative of crucial and compelling aspects of American individualism and character, an effort that was rewarded by wide-ranging critical enthusiasm, including *Time*'s Top Ten List of 1998, but its focus on running, although handled with imagination and very careful attention to authentic detail, resulted in another total boxoffice disaster.

Aside from a subject that seems to have little visual interest despite the number of people participating in road races, the way in which Warner Bros. handled distribution certainly affected its chances for success in theaters. Both *Pre* and *Without Limits* were postponed beyond their original release dates as distribution tried to maneuver around the scheduled openings of other more heralded films, but even with whatever clout Tom Cruise (co-producer) might have, Warner Bros. still, according to Mark Burger "let this terrific biographical drama of runner Steve Prefontaine slip between the cracks." Films with similarly ineffective promotion, however, have found an audience, especially those that drew comments from respected critics like David Denby who called it "beautifully made and features a marvelous performance by Donald Sutherland," or from Richard Schickel who said it is "a very good movie" but also noted that it "will require a stroke of marketing genius." To overcome advertising neglect and a timid release in only a few places, followed by its immediate withdrawal when it did poorly on its make-or-break first weekend, a kind of undercurrent word-of-mouth momentum might have led to *Without Limits* finding its audience, but such gradual nurturing rarely happens now. As Burger reflected, its remaining hope is to have "a second life on video." While there are certainly enough effective elements in the film to make this a possibility, especially two terrific performances (by Billy Crudup as Prefontaine and Sutherland as his legendary coach Bill Bowerman), some of the same things which made boxoffice success problematic may limit its second release as well.

The project had a long period of gestation, going back to Kenny Moore's idea for a story about his younger Oregon teammate after Prefontaine died when his MG overturned the night after his last race. The accuracy of the details of Prefontaine's life were undoubtedly a major concern for Moore, who wanted to honor the spirit and legacy of an athletic maverick and extraordinary fellow runner, and Moore's skill as a writer at *Sports Illustrated* and as the fourth place finisher in the Marathon at the 1972 Munich Olympics made him a natural choice as a screenwriter. Towne was drawn to the project by Prefontaine's rebel image, recalling that Pre was a "short, barrel-chested, good-looking guy . . . He fooled around with ladies and in general had the volatile persona of a rock star hitting the track." Towne was able to convince (with Cruise's assistance) Warner Bros. to budget the film at $25 million and was determined to make the 5000 meter finals at Munich an experience that would convey something of the competitive zeal, explosive power, tactical tension, and ultimate effort of the field of great runners Prefontaine challenged there. The care and attention to authenticity—filming at the University of Oregon and in Bowerman's home, intermixing footage and commentary from the

Steve Prefontaine (Billy Crudup): "Running is not about winning, it's about guts . . . To give anything less than your best is to sacrifice the gift . . . "

BBC's actual broadcast, and choosing world class runners to recreate the racing scenes—is a testament to the passion that Towne brought to the film, and although he was unable to work out arrangements for his initial choices for the two main figures (Paul Newman and Gene Hackman were considered for Bowerman; Leonardo DiCaprio and Brad Pitt for Prefontaine), Sutherland and Crudup are superb, especially Sutherland whose steely force is nothing like the tentative, tortured (as Towne put it) characters he played in films like *Klute* (1971) or *Ordinary People* (1980). The fascination of these elements led critics like Owen Gleiberman to call *Without Limits* "a richly intimate sports fable."

But as Peter Biskind pointed out in an interview with Towne, "*Without Limits* flies in the face of everything made in Hollywood today. Prefontaine doesn't get the girl, loses the big race, then dies." Towne thought that each of these limitations had the potential of reverse attraction since Prefontaine is an outsider challenging established thinking and the athletic establishment, and a dramatic, wasteful early death has the capacity to carry a hero into legend. His magnificent "failure" at Munich—crossing the line in fourth place after holding nothing back for two all-out-laps against Olympic medalists and world record holders— has a poignancy that is inspiring, and his relationship with a lovely girl (Monica Potter), whose commitments to her own values match his integrity is sweetly appealing. Paradoxically, some of the same things that make the film worth watching may prevent it from finding an audience much beyond the relatively small number of people who have the capacity to appreciate what it accomplishes.

Although *Without Limits* has a fairly large cast, it has only two principal characters. Everyone else—Prefontaine's mother, his teammates, his competitors, his girlfriend—appears briefly and without any development. Then, both Prefontaine and Bowerman are fascinating but not immediately likeable. Crudup projects the outward confidence, idealism, physical presence and inward turmoil of Prefontatine exception-

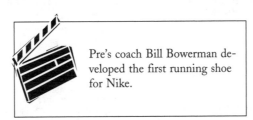

Pre's coach Bill Bowerman developed the first running shoe for Nike.

ally well, running with the distinctive style and evident delight that was Prefontaine's signature, thriving on the attention his success generated, and flaring with justifiable anger at the exploitation of self-serving athletic officials. However, Prefontaine also seems arrogant, self-centered, patronizing, and blindly egotistical at times—a complicated and sometimes irritating person. This makes it more difficult to always root for him and, in his confrontations with Bowerman, two very strong wills come together in combat that may leave a sour residue after each clash.

Sutherland has the demanding task of making Bowerman—already a legend at Oregon where he was regarded as a running guru—into a man whose forbidding manner (Towne told Sutherland, "This man is not tortured. He tortures *other* people and he enjoys it. He does it with a light heart and heavy hand.") conceals how much he cares about the men he coaches, the sport he loves, and the values he believes in. Towne obviously put a great deal of thought into Bowerman's philosophy because it corresponds in some ways to his own and whenever Bowerman tries to get through to Prefontaine, he uses a wry, sardonic, salty kind of humor to throw Prefontaine off stride, and then tries to begin a real conversation. Gradually, Prefontaine (and the audience) begins to realize how much real warmth this forceful and very intelligent man possess. Sutherland makes him so intriguing that his entrances become the most eagerly awaited episodes in the film, as if Prefontaine's problems are actually occasions for Bowerman's intervention and involvement.

The act of running and racing is at the center of the film and here, unfortunately, for all of Towne's efforts to make the races completely gripping and for all of Moore's achievements as a world class runner and writer, there is still something familiar about these sequences. There may be only so many ways to photograph a race, but *Chariots of Fire* set a standard that neither *Without Limits* nor any film since has equaled. Even for a track aficionado, the races seem rather routine, the climactic Munich final not that exceptional. The coach/athlete relationship works very well, though some might find it a bit too grounded in dialogue. However, when Bowerman talks to the team about the reasons for continuing to compete after the murder of Israeli athletes, or when he and Prefontaine get to the heart to their reasons for running and being, *Without Limits* reaches a rare moment of insight that overcomes the film's weaker sections. Prefontaine tells Bowerman that it isn't enough to win; each race for him is a validation of a person's life, or a performance that might be likened to a work of art. This attitude gives the film character, and it may have resulted in a $25 million production that has more in common with independent "art films" than with most commercial ones, and which, so far, has had the same kind of exposure and economic return.

—Leon Lewis

CREDITS

Steve Prefontaine: Billy Crudup
Bill Bowerman: Donald Sutherland
Mary Marckx: Monica Potter
Frank Shorter: Jeremy Sisto
Rosco Devine: Matthew Lillard
Bill Dellinger: Dean Norris
Kenny Moore: Billy Burke
Don Kardong: Gabriel Olds
Mac Wilkins: Adam Setliffe
Lasses Viren: Pat Porter
Barbara Bowerman: Judith Ivey

Origin: USA
Released: 1998
Production: Tom Cruise and Paula Wagner; released by Warner Bros.
Direction: Robert Towne
Screenplay: Robert Towne and Kenny Moore
Cinematography: Conrad L. Hall
Editing: Claire Simpson, Robert K. Lambert
Production design: William Creber
Art direction: William Durrell
Set decoration: Cloudia
Sound: Bruce Bisenz
Costumes: Grania Preston
Track and field technical adviser: Patrice Donnelly
Music: Carlton Kaller
Original score: Randy Miller
MPAA: PG-13
Running Time: 118 minutes

REVIEWS

Boxoffice. February, 1998, p. 21.
Boxoffice. April, 1998, p. 176.
Entertainment Weekly. September 11, 1998, p. 105.
Los Angeles Times. September 11, 1998, p. F1.
Movieline. March, 1998, p. 58.
New York Times. September 11, 1998, p. E16.
New Yorker. September, 1998, p. 99.
People. September 21, 1998, p. 36.
Time. September 7, 1998, p. 75.
Variety. March 16, 1998, p. 68.
Village Voice. September 15, 1998, p. 146.
Winston-Salem Journal. October 31, 1998, p. B3.

The Wizard of Oz

"You owe it to yourself to see it on the big screen—and you definitely owe it to your kids."—Marshall Fine, *Gannett News Service*

"The best children's movie ever made."—Jack Mathews, *Newsday*

"A pure pleasure! Go off to see the Wizard."—Leah Rozen, *People*

"Glorious!"—Gene Siskel, *Siskel & Ebert*

"All dressed up and splashed in splendor. A dazzle of color on a silver screen."—Gene Shalit, *The Today Show*

"A version that looks better than anything you grew up with."—Mike Clark, *USA Today*

"A fabulous movie! The vividness of the restoration is mind-boggling."—Stephen Hunter, *Washington Post*

A scene from the classic film *The Wizard of Oz.*

 Box Office: $14,690,446

Having already taken three generations of Americans (if not the world) from infancy through puberty and beyond, *The Wizard of Oz* is perhaps the most identifiable, enduring children's film of all-time. While everyone who has ever seen it associates it with their carefree, formative years, the majority of those people make it a point to watch *Oz* as often as possible. Before the advent of video tape, laser discs, DVDs, and DI-VXs, the only chance to see *Oz* was by re-arranging one's schedule around the whims of network television. Usually scheduled during a major fall holiday, the annual broadcasts of *Oz* regularly garnered throngs of viewers. Surprisingly, the film failed to make much of a dent at the boxoffice upon its initial release and didn't actually turn a profit until exhibition revenues began pouring in during the late 1950s. This annual marriage of convenience between *Oz* and the small screen also dispelled the assumption that the two mediums could never peacefully co-exist.

Based on a series of early twentieth-century books by L. Frank Baum (himself the subject of a made-for-TV-film starring John Ritter), *Oz* was also one of the first children's adaptations to be melded with the musical and to be produced in color. Like *Gone With the Wind* (which enjoyed its own successful re-release in the spring of 1998), *Oz* was

> The Wizard (Frank Morgan) to the Tinman (Jack Haley): "A heart is not judged by how much you love, but by how much you are loved by others."

originally released in 1939. Unlike *GWTW* however, *Oz* was largely ignored by audiences, panned by critics, and virtually dismissed by the Academy Awards (a fate similar to that of another perennial favorite, *It's a Wonderful Life*). In fact, the only Oscars the film received were for best original song ("Somewhere Over the Rainbow") and best original score.

Many historians believe, rightly so, that the reason *Oz* faired so poorly at the following year's Academy Awards was due to the fact that it was released in what is generally considered to be the greatest year in the history of American film. At that time, nods for Best Picture were double that of the current five. The list of nominees for 1939 read like an historical time capsule. In addition to *Oz*, eight of the remaining features: *Dark Victory, Goodbye Mr. Chips, Love Affair, Mr. Smith Goes to Washington, Ninotchka, Of Mice & Men, Stagecoach,* and *Wuthering Heights* could have all easily won the most coveted Oscar had their timing been better. Even in this greatest of years, *GWTW* seemed pre-ordained to walk away with the top prize (when the dust settled, it walked away with eight awards). One of those went to director Victor Fleming who strangely enough, was the director "of record" for *Oz*. Actually, no less than four of the most notable directors of all-time worked at various points on the production.

Richard Thorpe (*Ivanhoe, The Student Prince*) got everything off the ground and ran with the ball for two weeks until he was fired. Not given a specific reason, this allegedly occurred because producer Mervyn LeRoy didn't like the way the Tin Woodsman chopped down the door in the Wicked Witch's castle. George Cukor (*Gaslight, My Fair Lady*), who considered *Oz* "a minor book full of fourth-rate imagery" and was also an entrenched figure at MGM, was asked to fill Thorpe's shoes and, company man that he was, agreed. His tenure lasted a mere three days but it was time well spent. Cukor took one look at what Thorpe had in the can and was appalled. While obviously not enamored with the story, he knew what kind of parable his higher-ups were aiming for: an unaffected, innocent, plain-Jane, farm girl having to navigate her way home from a foreign place.

Often referred to as "a woman's director," Cukor had a keen eye for small detail and found the Dorothy character Thorpe had filmed to be "too cute and artificial." Replete with a blond wig and an overdose of make-up, she blended in too well with the inhabitants of fairyland Oz. He toned her down, de-glamorized her, ditched the wig, and gave the character a sense of realism and approachability. Along with the shifting of black and white stock to color during the beginning of the dream sequence, this minor alteration changed the texture of the entire production. Having won over the studio, Cukor graciously removed himself. Despite the fact that he had improved the situation, Cukor's departure had again left LeRoy holding the bag and directorless.

While Cukor was "a woman's director," Fleming, the choice, was the polar opposite. Decidedly rough and tumble, Fleming was the definitive "man's man" in a world cluttered with man's men. Hunter, adventurer, pilot, well-dressed rogue, and masculine to the core, he was known for helming action-based productions (*Test Pilot, Captains Courageous, Treasure Island*). While outwardly adventuresome, he was at heart a practical, stable family man who was all business. A doting father of two girls, he was just what LeRoy needed: a take-no-prisoners leader who had the ability to be soft when the situation deemed so. Still not feeling he was the right man for the job, Fleming was wooed incessantly, not only by LeRoy but by the Big Man himself, Louis B. Mayer, to save the film from disaster. Tossing everything Thorpe had already filmed, Fleming gathered the original cast, plus newcomer Jack Haley and started *The Wizard of Oz* over from scratch.

Haley, a vaudeville veteran and an actor of medium-grade ability was not the first choice for the Tin Woodsman. Shortly before the ousting of Thorpe, Buddy Ebsen, a lanky, affable, Jimmy Stewart-type had been hospitalized because the silver makeup he wore (a concoction of chemicals that included aluminum dust) had caused an allergic reaction. How Ebsen's and Haley's career paths would have developed without that infamous chemical reaction is anyone's guess. However, the adage, "one man's poison is another man's cure" never seemed more applicable (at least in the context of Hollywood lore).

Two of Haley's co-stars, the other men sentenced to months of heavy, claustrophobic costumes, also came to the production with vaudeville credentials. The connections contained within this infamous threesome stretched even further than the stages of New York. Haley and Ray Bolger (the Scarecrow) had grown up within a few miles of each other in the Irish Catholic ghettos of Boston. Bert Lahr (the Cowardly Lion) and Bolger had starred together before in *Life Begins at 8:40*, an Ira Gershwin revue. Three "old school" warriors, sharing the bond of dual roles, stifling accouterments, and a penchant for tom-foolery got them through months of tight quarters in a production they all (at one time or another, in hushed, guarded tones) regarded as artistically demoralizing. While all of their careers continued to (in varying degrees) flourish, neither Bolger, Lahr, or Haley were able to get close to the level of notoriety they achieved with *Oz*. It was perhaps the first occurrence of the thespian doubled-edged sword; you can gain immortality now but must give up the hope of every shaking the typecast albatross from your neck.

Judy Garland was awarded a special Oscar for Outstanding Performance by a Screen Juvenile for her role.

The two premiere female roles in *Oz*, The Wicked Witch and Dorothy, also permanently changed the lives of the women who inhabited them. Margaret Hamilton, whose Elvira Gulch alter-ego was just as (if not more) evil than the Witch, couldn't get arrested after *Oz*. A divorced former school teacher with a small child, Hamilton was the one major cast member who had the hardest hurdle to overcome once the cameras stopped rolling. She made approximately one dozen post-*Oz* films (in a thirty-year span), all of them forgettable, and in her autumn years played the role of the lovable Cora in a series of instant coffee commercials. Like Ebsen, Hamilton was required to spend countless hours coated in questionably safe body paint, considered primitive by today's standards.

Judy Garland is the one performer most closely associated with the film and is easily its most calamitous victim. Thrown into a situation that required a maturity far beyond her grasp, the life of the former Francis Gumm was all downhill after Dorothy. Railroaded into studio-conceived "romances" (which included one to then mercurial heartthrob Mickey Rooney), Garland was sucked into the chew-'em-up-and-spit-'em-out assembly line of Hollywood and never made it through to the other side in one piece. Like Shirley Temple before her, she was regarded as a 'juvenile' performer who couldn't make the transformation to adult roles, although that didn't stop a slew of producers and directors from trying.

Shortly after making *Meet Me in St. Louis* in 1944, the still 'innocent' Garland married Vincente Minnelli, the film's director, and tried to assume some level of normalcy. A daughter, Liza, was born and after a decade or so of ever-increasing unsatisfying roles, Garland settled into a semi-lucrative career as a high-profile Vegas lounge singer and host of television specials. In 1969, almost thirty years to the day since the release of the movie that cemented her immortality, Judy Garland, not even fifty-years-old, died of a drug overdose. With the possible exception of Marilyn Monroe, the short rise and long fall of Garland is the textbook example of a Tinseltown tragedy that is unlikely to ever be matched.

As the pre-production phase of *Oz* was drawing to a close, rival producer David O. Selznick was waving the job of director of *Gone With the Wind* under the nose of Fleming. Ultra high-profile even before Margaret Mitchell was done writing the novel, Fleming found the offer too much to resist and departed before principal photography on *Oz* was completed. Once again, LeRoy was left in the lurch. Unlike today, when directors are often more significant than the studios or even the stars, helmsman of years past were considered just part of a stable that could be called on to stop the flood and complete the necessary, mostly uncredited, grunt work of mopping up after their predecessor. LeRoy, whose lucky streak was bordering on the divinely blessed, was able to summon yet another legend to complete the production.

CREDITS

Dorothy: Judy Garland
Hank/The Scarecrow: Ray Bolger
Zeke/The Cowardly Lion: Bert Lahr
Hickory/The Tin Woodsman: Jack Haley
Glinda: Billie Burke
Miss Gulch/The Wicked Witch: Margaret Hamilton
The Wizard: Frank Morgan
Uncle Henry: Charles Grapewin
Auntie Em: Clara Blandick

Origin: USA
Released: 1939, 1998
Production: Mervyn LeRoy; released by Metro-Goldwyn-Mayer
Direction: Victor Fleming
Screenplay: Noel Langley, Florence Ryserson, and Edgar Allen Woolf; based on the book by L. Frank Baum
Cinematography: Harold Rosson
Editing: Blanche Sewell
Music: Herbert Stothart
Art direction: Cedric Gibbons
Costumes: Adrian
MPAA rating: G
Running Time: 101 minutes

King Vidor (*The Fountainhead, War & Peace*), who had about as much clout and power as any director of that era, came in to do the deed. With Vidor, LeRoy's vision found closure and was summarily unleashed on a public that couldn't have cared less. It tanked. But it went far in proving the efficiency of the old studio system. Talent was kept on a short leash, but it was talent of the highest caliber; people who were dedicated completely to the craft. Long before the promise of instant, fleeting exposure courtesy of petri-dish shallow *Entertainment Tonight, People* magazines, and zillion-dollar paychecks, the studios of long ago cranked out film after film with a level of streamline efficiency that dwarfs and embarrasses current standards and benchmarks.

The ripple effects of *Oz* have reached far and wide. It has enjoyed countless reincarnations and reinterpretations and, despite its initially modest performance at the boxoffice, has probably been seen by more people, more often than any other film in history. While seen by more people in theaters, *Gone With the Wind* has only been seen on TV a handful of times. Four hours long, mostly downbeat, and with a decidedly adult appeal, it's not a film that lends itself to family viewing. If *Oz* can make any claim against its once and current 1939 rival, it is in its monopoly on the small screen.

Reissues of films are nothing new but there has been an inordinate amount in the last two years. *The Godfather, American Graffiti, Taxi Driver, The Big Chill,* and *Dirty Dancing* have all been given the royal treatment. Despite a fair amount of hoopla, none of them (including this edition of *Oz*), made much of a dent at the boxoffice. But this is one reissue that makes complete sense; unlike the other above titles, a large chunk of the population has never seen this on a big screen. Even if you were among the millions who queued up in front of the tube year after year to watch Dorothy, Toto, and their three companions battle the Wicked Witch, one look at the restored color will make it feel like the first time (the fact that you don't have to endure countless commercial breaks is an added bonus). The importance of *Oz*, as it relates to the history of the movies, current-day culture, and its artistic influence, even apart from the film industry, cannot be overstated.

If you've come across this essay looking for a review of the film or a detailed explanation of the characters and the plot because you hadn't seen it before, I apologize for not revealing the particulars. I'm also very sorry to inform you, you're on the wrong planet.

REVIEWS

Entertainment Weekly. November 20, 1998, p. 96.
People. November 16, 1998, p. 32.
Variety. November 9, 1998, p. 31.

Woo

It's her world, we're just living in it.—Movie tagline

Box Office: $8,064,972

Woo is the disappointing follow-up to director Daisy von Scherler Mayer's winsome and charming *Party Girl*. As truly appealing as actress Jada Pinkett Smith is, the part of *Woo* will surely not function as the star vehicle the former movie did for Parker Posey.

The story is obviously meant to portray Woo as a carefree modern woman determined to do her own thing and, in the process of having fun, find the man of her dreams. Her good friend transvestite/psychic Celestrial (Girlina) has seen a terrific mate for Woo in her Tarot cards— a studly, financially sound Virgo. When Woo's cousin Claudette (Paula Jai Parker) fixes her up with Tim (Tommy Davidson), her boyfriend's pal, Woo declines—until she learns that Tim's birthday is September 18—solid Virgo territory.

A decent, caring law clerk, Tim is understandably blown away by Woo's sexiness and curves. But then the date pro-

> Tim (Tommy Davidson) to Woo (Jada Pinkett Smith): "Maybe we could be having a good time, if you could control your psychotic mood swings!"

gresses from one mishap to another, mainly because of Woo's self-centeredness and rudeness to others. First, Woo causes a commotion and ultimately a fire at a fancy restaurant. Then, she insists on going to a dive club in a terrible part of town, whereupon Tim's lovely new car gets stolen. There is never any reason for Woo's activity; she merely buzzes annoyingly from one location to another, never slowing down for a minute. And despite the fact that she already knows that Tim is the Virgo that she probably should be with, she persists in treating him shabbily. By the time Tim is accidentally arrested, he has vowed to stay away from this schizophrenic young woman. As he succinctly phrases it, "You got a bad case of fine-itis! You think you are too fine for anyone else!"

When Woo runs to see Celestrial at a drag club, her friend listens to Woo's selfish complaints about her lousy night. The psychic scolds Woo for pushing away a man who seems kind and responsible and tells her to think over her foolish ways. Woo then sets out to find Tim and apologize for her petty, silly ways. Believe it or not, they reconcile.

Almost every aspect of this script is jumbled, senseless, and annoying. As Woo runs from one locale to another, we are forced to tag along and watch forced revelry that makes one long to stay at home and watch television. To make matters worse, David C. Johnson's script blunders from one stereotype to another, providing the talented Pinkett Smith with nothing more to do than rotate her thrusted jaw out and shove her finger at Davidson. One unbelievable sequence has her cousin Claudette dressing up as a chicken and pecking popcorn off her boyfriend's chest to simulate foreplay. There are two amusing sequences that brighten the otherwise dreary surroundings: LL Cool J appears as Tim's suave neighbor, ready to offer advice to help him with the ladies, and Billy Dee Williams appears to Tim as a ghostly specter, ready to dispense the same kind of advice.

—G. E. Georges

CREDITS

Woo: Jada Pinkett Smith
Tim: Tommy Davidson
Lenny: David Chappelle
Claudette: Paula Jai Parker
Celestrial: Girlina
Darryl: LL Cool J

Origin: USA
Released: 1998
Production: Beth Hubbard and Michael Hubbard for New Deal Productions and Gotham Entertainment; released by New Line Cinema
Direction: Daisy von Scherler Mayer
Screenplay: David C. Johnson
Cinematography: Jean Lapine
Editing: Nicholas Eliopoulos, Janice Hampton
Costumes: Michael Clancy
Production design: Ina Mayhew
Music: Michel Colombier
Art direction: Vlasta Svoboda
MPAA rating: R
Running Time: 85 minutes

REVIEWS

Entertainment Weekly. May 22, 1998, p. 45.
Los Angeles Times. May 8, 1998, p. F12.
New York Times. May 8, 1998, p. E12.
People. May 25, 1998, p. 33.
Sight and Sound. October, 1998, p. 60.
USA Today. May 8, 1998, p. 11E.
Variety. May 11, 1998, p. 60.
Village Voice. May 19, 1998, p. 134.
Washington Post Weekend. May 8, 1998, p. 62.

Wrongfully Accused

Somewhere in the naked city lurks a one-armed, one-legged, one-eyed man responsible for the murder for which he's been wrongfully accused. To find him, all Ryan Harrison needs is a clue.—Movie tagline

"Laugh-out-loud funny!"—Paul Wunder, *WBAI Radio*

"Wonderfully wacky!"—Bill Bregoli, *Westwood One Radio*

"A hilariously clever summer laugh!"—Jules Peimer, *WKDM Radio*

"One of Leslie Nielsen's funniest!"—Jeffrey Lyons, *WNBC-TV*

Box Office: $9,717,322

At the very beginning of *Wrongfully Accused*, the latest entry in the *Airplane*-clone parodies, we are told that it is a true story based on real events . . . that have taken place in other movies. It may be the sharpest joke in the entire film.

Writer/director Pat Proft, who was a writer on the earlier clones, *Naked Gun* (1988) and *Hot Shots: Part Deux* (1993) that were directed by either Jim Abrahams or David Zucker of the original *Airplane!* (1980) crew's trio of directors, which also included Jerry Zucker, here not only writes the material but also directs it. Considering that Jim Abrahams's latest solo effort, this year's *Mafia!* (reviewed in this edition), also seems nothing more than a weak imitation of the original comedy, maybe the Zuckers, Abrahams, and Proft should stay a team and not strike out on their own so often.

Ryan (Leslie Nielsen) to Cass (Melinda McGraw): "When you shot me at point-blank range, I knew you loved me."

The problem with *Wrongfully Accused* is not that there are very few jokes, it's that what jokes there are don't inspire a lot of laughter. While primarily being a send-up of *The Fugitive* (1993) (as well as other Harrison Ford roles—i.e. *Star Wars* [1977] and *A Clear and Present Danger* [1994]), there's barely a recent film that escapes lampooning at some point in the film. A cornfield (*Field of Dreams* [1989]) into which a few baseball players disappear quickly becomes the country crossroads dive-bombing scene in *North By Northwerst* (1959). An attempt

to uncover a computer list invokes *Mission: Impossible* (1996), a scene by the shore uncovers *Baywatch* babes and guys, a murder plot set for a Scottish days festival creates a blue-faced *Braveheart* (1995), while a difficult escape is made easier with Mentos. Add a few background jokes such as a PA message requesting that Drs. Ross, Green, Benton, et al. report to the emergency room to pick up their checks, and some terribly mangled *Casablanca* dialogue and it may be hard to keep pace with them all. (But as usual with any Zucker, Abrahams, or Proft effort, some of the best gags may be in the closing credits.)

The story in which all these jokes are set involves Ryan Harrison (Leslie Nielsen), the "Lord of the Violin," whose concert series has been underwritten by the wealthy Hibbing Goodhue (Michael York). Goodhue's wife, Lauren (Kelly Le Brock), however, seduces Ryan when Hibbing isn't looking, but there's also a possibility that Hibbing doesn't notice his wife's antics because he's been a little busy himself with an artist, Cass Lake (Melinda McGraw).

Then one night when Ryan shows up for a tryst with Lauren, he instead finds himself attacked by a man (Aaron Pearl) who turns out to have one artificial leg, one artificial arm, and an artificial eye. Ryan is knocked unconscious during the fight and awakens to find himself framed for the murder of Hibbing Goodhue. Investigating the case is Fergus Falls (Richard Crenna), who arrests Ryan. However, on the way to his execution, Ryan's prison bus slips on a banana peel and is hit by a train. Ryan escapes and sets off to find the one-armed, one-legged, one-eyed killer himself. Falls follows closely behind.

As Ryan pursues and is pursued, he runs into several familiar faces, especially at the fishing supply store where John Walsh from TV's *America's Most Wanted* and the narrator of tales from the Highway Patrol are dazzled by Ryan's tales as he takes on the identity of Buzzin Frog. Only later does Walsh realize he has fabricated the entire story from the products on the wall behind him à la *The Usual Suspects* (1995). Add a few terrorists and some quests for family ties that rival *Chinatown* (1974) and you've got the basic story of *Wrongfully Accused*.

Over the years Leslie Nielsen has developed a distinctive style of delivering his ludicrous lines as if they were serious dialogue, and as Ryan Harrison, he is basically the same

The setting of the film is supposed to be the Minnesota suburb of Columbia Heights, where writer/director Pat Proft was born and raised.

character he has played in every other parody lately—with maybe a little more mugging than usual.

Supporting actors fare no better. Melinda McGraw as Ryan's new love interest is bland while Kelly Le Brock's vil-

CREDITS

Ryan Harrison: Leslie Nielsen
Fergus Falls: Richard Crenna
Lauren Goodhue: Kelly Le Brock
Doctor Fridley: Sandra Bernhard
Hibbing Goodhue: Michael York
Cass Lake: Melinda McGraw
Sgt. Tina Bagley: Leslie Jones
Sgt. Orono: Ben Rather
Sean Laughrea: Aaron Pearl

Origin: USA
Released: 1998
Production: Pat Proft, James G. Robinson, and Bernd Eichinger for Morgan Creek; released by Warner Bros.
Direction: Pat Proft
Screenplay: Pat Proft
Cinematography: Glen MacPherson
Editing: James R. Symons
Production design: Michael S. Bolton
Art direction: Sandy Cochrane
Sound: Rob Young
Music: Bill Conti
MPAA rating: PG-13
Running Time: 85 minutes

lainess is stiffly overdone. Only Richard Crenna manages to add some new sparks to this now aging genre. Crenna's overly-thorough police officer would have every leaf in a forest taken in for evidence while totally overlooking Ryan's unconscious body at the murder scene. Crenna (and often Nielsen's) dialogue is nothing more than inflated purple prose with metaphors that go nowhere. However, in their rapid-fire delivery, maybe there are some hidden jokes that are worth reviewing.

On the whole, however, *Wrongfully Accused* is a parody that only occasionally hits it's comedic bull's-eye . . . even though, heaven knows, there are plenty of targets to aim at. Most of the jokes may be obvious—Proft reached for the easy punchline instead of the unexpected one—but at least he keeps them coming. There is little downtime from the gags in *Wrongfully Accused,* it's just a shame they weren't funnier.

—Beverley Bare Buehrer

REVIEWS

Chicago Tribune. August 28, 1998.
Detroit Free Press. August 22, 1998, p. 2A.
Entertainment Weekly. August 28, 1998, p. 56.
Los Angeles Times. August 22, 1998, p. F8.
New York Times. August 22, 1998.
Variety. August 24, 1998, p. 28.

The X-Files

Fight the Future.—Movie tagline

"Smart, sexy and sensational."—Mike Cidoni, *ABC-TV*

"Intriguing. Full of stunning effects, clever characters and offbeat set-pieces."—Michael Wilmington, *Chicago Tribune*

"Sharp, mysterious and wonderful. A great thriller."—Bill Zwecker, *NBC-TV*

"Imaginative. A corkscrew flume ride. A smart, satisfying summer rip."—Rod Dreher, *New York Post*

"You don't need to have seen the program to appreciate that this is one smart scary movie."—*Newsweek*

"Two thumbs up."—*Siskel & Ebert*

"Offers everything a great action-thriller should: intelligence, excitement and awesome special effects."—Jeff Craig, *Sixty Second Preview*

"A crackling adventure. Enjoy the ride."—Gene Shalit, *The Today Show*

 Box Office: $83,898,313

You don't have to be an X-phile to watch *The X-Files* movie—but it helps. After five TV seasons, creator Chris Carter opted to take his baby to the big screen, using the show's "mythology" episodes as his jumping-off point. The helpful basics for the uninitiated are as follows: FBI agent Fox Mulder (the deadpan David Duchovny), nicknamed "Spooky" by his associates, is relegated to the basement of FBI headquarters where his assignments involve anything "unnatural." This includes a variety of paranormal phenomena, especially anything involving so-called aliens and government conspiracies and cover-ups. Mulder is a UFO believer after having, he believes, witnessed the abduction of his younger sister by aliens when he was a boy.

Mulder's partner is Agent Dana Scully (an intense-but-vulnerable Gillian Anderson), a medical doctor assigned to Mulder specifically because she's a pragmatic skeptic, whose job was to scientifically debunk Mulder's crackpot notions. But after five years and many life-threatening situations together, Scully believes more and Mulder less. What they most believe in and trust is each other.

Agents Mulder (David Duchovny) and Scully (Gillian Anderson) try to escape peril in the big screen adaptation of *The X-Files*.

> Mulder (David Duchovny) to Scully (Gillian Anderson): "It's a global conspiracy that reaches into the lives of every man, woman, and child on the planet."

Much hype was made about the TV series' fifth-season cliff-hanger, which would lead directly into the film, but the most significant carryover is the fact that—once again—the X-Files have been shut down (thanks to their being physically destroyed in a suspicious fire) and Mulder and Scully have been reassigned—this time to an anti-terrorism unit.

However, the movie doesn't start there. In a strange prologue that will only become significant much later, the setting is North Texas in 35,000 B.C. and the viewer follows a couple of prehistoric men into a cave where they are viciously attacked by a creature whose "blood" is a viscous black substance. Cut to the same scene in the present day where young Stevie (Lucas Black) has just fallen into a tunnel while exploring with his friends. He finds a human skull and then the black ooze finds him. Four members of a fire-rescue squad who went after Stevie also disappear and suddenly officious Dr. Ben Bronschweig (Jeffrey DeMunn) turns up and takes over the operation. He makes a phone call and tells his listener "the impossible scenario that we never planned for? Well, we better come up with a plan."

Now, we get to our two heroes. Mulder and Scully are in Dallas, working an alleged bomb threat at a federal building. But Mulder has defied orders and is investigating the building across the street instead. Naturally, he and Scully discover the bomb and the agent in charge, Darius Michaud (Terry O'Quinn), says he'll be able to defuse it. Instead,

Michaud deliberately does nothing—there is a big boom (and some very uncomfortably similar shots to the destroyed Oklahoma City federal building), and Michaud is killed.

Mulder and Scully are back in Washington, up before the Office of Professional Review, whose head, Jana Cassidy (Blythe Danner), seemingly wants to pin the blame on the duo. They also learn that a young boy and three firemen were killed by the explosion. A disgusted Scully tells Mulder she's thinking of quitting the FBI and returning to medicine full time.

Mulder decides to get drunk at his local bar and notices an older man staring at him. An alley chat has Dr. Alvin Kurtzweil (Martin Landau) claiming to be a friend and scientific colleague of Mulder's late father. Kurtzweil tells Mulder that the bodies found in the Dallas wreckage were dead prior to the explosion. And the reason for the bomb was that the building contained offices of a special FEMA (Federal Emergency Management Agency) unit involved with quarantines. Mulder persuades Scully to accompany him to the morgue and autopsy the bodies. Scully discovers the bodies are covered in some kind of goo and that there's evidence of massive infection.

Meanwhile, Mulder's nemesis, the Cigarette-Smoking Man (William B. Davis), known hereafter as CSM, is in North Texas watching Bronschweig's scientific team investigate the caves. The last missing fireman is there and he's been infected by the black goo, which turns out to be an alien virus. In fact, the alien is now gestating inside its human host. Unfortunately, Bronschweig is alone when the alien bursts out of the body (which the viewer doesn't see) and attacks him with razor-sharp claws, lightening speed, and a truly god-awful screaming sound. The doctor is abandoned by his colleagues and the North Texas operation shut down.

In London, the Well-Manicured Man (John Neville) meets with his fellow syndicate members and their leader, Conrad Strughold (Armin Mueller-Stahl). Turns out our cave-dwelling aliens are the original inhabitants of earth and that the syndicate has been working with them since the days of WWII on a project known as "Purity Control." The aliens have always intended to re-colonize earth with their own species and it seems they intend to use humans as "digestives for the creation of a new alien life form." They are creating an alien-human hybrid that is immune to the black oil virus. WMM argues that "this isn't colonization, it's spontaneous re-population."

A follow-up investigation in Texas leads our FBI duo to a corn field growing in the middle of nowhere and two large geodesic domes that turn out to contain millions of

genetically-tinkered with honeybees. They escape the bees only to be chased through the cornfields by a pair of black helicopters. Scully has to return to D.C. for another review board meeting and later tells Mulder that she has resigned. He asks her to reconsider: "I don't know if I want to do this alone. I don't even know if I can." Their moment of closeness, which ALMOST leads to an ACTUAL kiss, is stopped when Scully is stung by a bee that's hidden in her clothes. She immediately goes into shock and collapses.

The ambulance that picks her up is driven by a man Mulder recognizes as working for the syndicate. He shoots Mulder, who wakes up in the hospital peering into the three faces of fellow conspiracy theorists The Lone Gunmen.

With their help, Mulder escapes the hospital and tries to find Kurtzweil to get more information. But Kurtzweil has apparently been killed by the Well-Manicured Man (you never do see the body), who informs Mulder that the alien virus is intended to be spread by the bees (I was never too clear where the corn fit in—something to do with pollen, I think) and it will make human beings into a "slave race." WMM gives Mulder a potential vaccine and co-ordinates to Scully's location and then dies in a car-bomb explosion.

> There are two albums associated with the film: an orchestral score by Mark Snow, who composed the TV series opening theme, and a song album that includes such artists as Sting, Filter, and the Foo Fighters.

The directions lead Mulder to a scientific station in Antarctica, run by old CSM. (Exactly how Mulder gets to such a remote location and just happens to find a Sno-Cat waiting for him is never mentioned.) In an enormous underground labyrinth, Mulder finds both humans and aliens encased in blocks of ice. Discovering Scully, he manages to break through and administer the vaccine but system sensors detect a contaminate and begin an automatic self-destruct of the station. CSM evacuates his people, leaving Scully and Mulder to their fates. After reaching the surface, Mulder looks up and an enormous alien spacecraft rises out of the tundra, hovers a moment, and then vanishes. Scully is unconscious and misses the whole thing.

We don't know how our intrepid agents get rescued but back in Washington, a recovered Scully is trying to give a coherent account of the events to the review board but points out the office that investigates anomalies has been shut down. Mulder complains to Scully that the government has just dug a new hole and covered up everything they've discovered. He says they're "right back at the beginning with nothing" and urges Scully to resume her medical career. She replies: "If I quit now, they win."

An epilogue shows a desert in Tunisia with more domes and another corn crop. CSM finds Strughold and tells him that Mulder is more determined than ever. Strughold thinks that "one man alone cannot fight the future" but CSM hand him a telegram saying that the X-Files have been re-opened.

The details of the plot turn out to be amazingly complicated, much like the mythology episodes of the TV series. And explanations for the aliens, and the virus, and the syndicate pass by very quickly. (This is a movie that will benefit from video release so you can go 'What did he say?' and rewind—a lot.) Assistant FBI Director Walter Skinner (Mitch Pileggi), Mulder and Scully's boss and sometime protector, has little to do in the film but look worried and exasperated. Martin Landau's briefly seen Dr. Kurtzweil serves as a familiar "Deep Throat" but even after Mulder finds a photo showing a younger Kurtzweil posing at a Mulder family gathering, there's no follow-up. Of course, both Duchovny and Anderson have little "acting" to do, but they react very well and have a believable partnership.

As is usual from the TV show, paranoia reigns supreme and government conspiracies abound. Poor FEMA gets the brunt of the mistreatment, since apparently if the President declared a national emergency, FEMA would go into action, in this case being used to spread the alien virus throughout the American population. One good trick is you never fully see the aliens—they're not the green-blooded, shapeshifting humanoids of the TV series but definitely something, well, alien. The film's $63 million budget is certainly on the screen, with some elaborate set pieces, including the Dallas bombing, the helicopter chase, and the Antarctic scenes. What the sixth-season of the TV show will do with the film's many unanswered questions will be interesting to see, although Carter, who is hoping for a film franchise, may leave us all guessing until *The X-Files* has its next big screen appearance.

—*Christine Tomassini*

CREDITS

Agent Fox Mulder: David Duchovny
Agent Dana Scully: Gillian Anderson
The Cigarette-Smoking Man: William B. Davis
Dr. Alvin Kurtzweil: Martin Landau
Conrad Strughold: Armin Mueller-Stahl
The Well-Manicured Man: John Neville
Walter Skinner: Mitch Pileggi
Jana Cassidy: Blythe Danner
Dr. Ben Bronschweig: Jeffrey DeMunn
Darius Michaud: Terry O'Quinn
Langly: Dean Haglund
Byers: Bruce Harwood
Frohike: Tom Braidwood
Stevie: Lucas Black
Barmaid: Glenne Headly

Origin: USA
Released: 1998
Production: Chris Carter and Daniel Sackheim for Ten Thirteen; released by 20th Century Fox
Direction: Rob Bowman
Screenplay: Chris Carter
Cinematography: Ward Russell
Editing: Stephen Mark
Music: Mark Snow
Production design: Christopher Nowak
Art direction: Gregory Bolton, Hugo Santiago
Costumes: Marlene Stewart
Sound: Geoffrey Patterson
Special makeup effects: Alec Gillis, Tom Woodruff Jr.
Visual effects supervision: Mat Beck
MPAA rating: PG-13
Running Time: 120 minutes

REVIEWS

Battle Creek Enquirer. June 18, 1998, p. 9.
Chicago Sun-Times. June 19, 1998.
Chicago Tribune. June 19, 1998.
Cinescape. May, 1998, p. 12.
Detroit Free Press. June 19, 1998.
Detroit News. June 19, 1998, p. 1D.
Entertainment Weekly. June 12, 1998, p. 22.
Entertainment Weekly. June 26, 1998, p. 97.
Film Score Monthly. June, 1998, p. 30.
Los Angeles Times. June 19, 1998, p. F1.
New York Times. June 19, 1998, p. E1.
New York Times Magazine. June 14, 1998, p. 56.
Newsweek. June 22, 1998, p. 70.
People. June 29, 1998, p. 33.
Sight and Sound. September, 1998, p. 55.
Time. June 22, 1998.
Time. June 29, 1998.
USA Today. June 19, 1998.
Variety. June 22, 1998, p. 50.
Washington Post. June 19, 1998, p. B1.
Washington Post Weekend. June 19, 1998, p. 47.

Your Friends & Neighbors

A modern immorality tale.—Movie tagline

"Hilariously savage."—Stephen Farber, *Movieline*

"A cool, sharply funny new film."—Dave Kehr, *New York Daily News*

"A masterly piece of work with as accomplished an acting ensemble as you are likely to find in this year's releases."—Andrew Sarris, *New York Observer*

"The work of an original filmmaker who takes no prisoners."—Janet Maslin, *New York Times*

"Hilariously profane! A virtual symphony of anger, loathing, betrayal, confusion and manipulation."—Jack Mathews, *Newsday*

"Fascinating! Shamefully irresistible."—Jill Bernstein, *Premiere*

"A brutally funny sex comedy that will keep you talking right on through winter."—Peter Travers, *Rolling Stone*

"A spiky new farce!"—Richard Corliss, *Time*

Box Office: $4,714,658

In 1997, writer-director Neil LaBute's debut feature *In the Company of Men* stirred up critical debate for its cold-hearted look at misogyny and betrayal in the corporate world. It was a fairly simplistic, one-dimensional tale, but it at least had a certain narrative drive, even if the payoff could be seen a mile away. With his follow-up feature, *Your Friends & Neighbors,* LaBute has fairly abandoned the notion of a clear narrative in favor of a series of repetitive vignettes in which six yuppies meet in various combinations, have sex, discuss their sex lives ad nauseam, and betray each other in the process. The characters are urban and upscale but relentlessly miserable and self-involved. Indeed, our first glimpse of one of the characters, played by Jason Patric, is of him masturbating while practicing his bedroom talk on a tape recorder. LaBute seems to think he is saying something important about the sterility of modern relationships, but the film ends up a seemingly endless parade of sexual dysfunction and selfishness without offering any significant insight into human motivations.

LaBute's approach is clinical and detached. His characters are never called by their names—indeed, we do not

Terri (Catherine Keener) to husband Jerry (Ben Stiller) on his talking during sex: "I don't need the narration. This is not a travelogue."

know they have names until the end credits reveal them—so that we can feel we are watching supposedly universal types. His filmic style, like his characters, is static to say the least. The camera is usually stationary, and there is little visual variety. (LaBute's background is in theater, and his films could just as easily be performed as plays.)

Mary (Amy Brenneman), a freelance writer, and Barry (Aaron Eckhart), an office worker, are a married couple with an unsatisfying sex life. At least part of the problem is Barry's self-centeredness. Early in the film, Barry tells a co-worker that the best sex he has had is with himself, and the rest of the movie only confirms this. Mary is the most sympathetic of the characters; she at least is not as hard-edged as the others and actually seems quite vulnerable. All she really wants is someone to hold her. Because the characters are thinly drawn, the actors basically play variations on a few emotions, but Brenneman is allowed to flesh out a character, even if she is hemmed in by a script that ultimately goes nowhere. Terri (Catherine Keener), an ad writer, and Jerry (Ben Stiller), a college drama professor, seem even more miserable. Jerry is a "talker," even during sex, and this annoys the shrill, strident Terri to no end. She believes sex is "not a time for sharing."

Two others round out the cast. Cary (Jason Patric), who has an unspecified job in the medical profession, is a classic egotist and user of women—the most disturbed and disturbing of the characters. He is proud of the sexual power he wields over others, boasts of the revenge he takes on the women who supposedly wrong him, and even berates one for staining his sheets with menstrual blood. The other guys seem to admire him. Cheri (Nastassja Kinski) is an artist's assistant who, by seeming coincidence, meets most of the others individually when they visit the gallery where she works. They act out a version of the same scene with her, even repeating patches of the same dialogue as each looks at the same painting. The men reveal their essential natures to her. Cary makes blunt advances, and she walks away. When Barry looks at the painting and asks if it is out of whack or if he is, she points in his direction.

During a visit of the two couples, Jerry comes on to Mary, and she writes her phone number in a book and gives it to him. Meanwhile, Terri meets Cheri at the gallery, and they begin an affair. The nature of their attraction is never made clear. Cheri is the least developed of the characters and seems to function only to have an affair with Terri. Is Terri cheating on Jerry because he is interested in Mary?

Does Terri become a lesbian because she cannot stand Jerry's talking? While this notion may seem silly, the film gives us nothing else to go on.

Mary and Jerry finally get a hotel room, and, while we do not see their attempt at sex, it is obvious from the aftermath that things did not go well. He could not keep his erection. When Barry and Mary go to the same hotel and stay in the same room Mary shared with Jerry, Mary is naturally uncomfortable (we later learn that Jerry actually recommended the room to Barry). Such a scene is typical of the movie as a whole, in which the same locations are used repeatedly—the art gallery, a trendy restaurant, a gym, a book store, the characters' homes—to highlight the insularity of these characters' world. However, instead of enlightening us about their limited milieu, the repetition only makes us feel that we are running in circles, that we are stuck watching the same thing happen over and over.

In the film's most disturbing scene, the three men are in a sauna discussing the best sex they have ever had (a favorite topic for these characters). Cary's response revolves around a homosexual gang rape in high school gym class. In an extended monologue, he goes into excruciating detail and even boasts that he thinks the victim enjoyed it. While shocking and gross in its content, the scene feels like a calculated move to provoke the audience. It just confirms how despicable Cary is but does not really advance the plot or character. Perhaps Cary is a repressed homosexual, but this is never explored. When it is Jerry's turn to reveal his best sex, he answers that it was with Barry's wife—a response purely meant to provoke Barry since we know the attempt at an affair was not successful.

The various entanglements resolve themselves rather matter-of-factly. Terri finds the book in which Mary wrote her phone number for Jerry. Terri calls the number, learns it is Mary, then tears up the book, and continues her affair with Cheri, at least partly to get even with Jerry. One day Jerry is on a field trip with his students when he runs into Mary, who is upset that he suggested the same hotel room to her husband. Jerry claims he was jealous and wanted to pretend he had been there first. Barry prods Mary into admitting her time with Jerry (even though we know nothing has really happened between them), and she moves out. Jerry and Barry meet, and it turns out Mary has not called either one. Jerry also meets with Terri, but she says it is too late for a reconciliation. He needs a number for getting his mail, and she sarcastically writes it in a book. There is no sense that anything is really at stake since no one really cares about anyone else, no sense that anyone has learned anything or even that we have learned anything interesting about these people.

Your Friends & Neighbors is simplistic in that everything revolves around sex; it is the only topic these characters discuss. In a lecture to his students near the film's beginning, Jerry announces that "every story" is about men and women,

and "It's always about fucking." This is clearly meant to be a description of the film, but, even in this limited area, the screenplay has nothing new to say. In the film's coda, Jerry is sleeping with one of his students (a possible affair has been hinted at throughout the film), but the professor having an affair with his student is a cliché. Terri and Cheri are still together, but it is still not clear why, beyond the fact that Cheri is not a talker in bed. Barry, having undergone the least change, is having phone sex.

The only inexplicable outcome is the final pairing of Mary and Cary. Since we have not seen them together before, there is no buildup to the film's last scene, in which they are in bed together and she is pregnant. Why would the relatively nice Mary (at least "nice" by this group's standards) fall for a sleaze like Cary, and how could he seem so accepting of her pregnancy? Perhaps we are simply supposed to see how ironic life is and admit that such improbable, even shocking, matches happen all the time, but this does not make it any more satisfying. *In the Company of Men* also had a surprise ending, but, given the progress of that narrative, it really was not much of a surprise. This ending, though, is genuinely surprising but also completely nonsensical.

Perhaps all of this would be interesting if there were a unique point of view or at least a compelling narrative to give shape to all the nasty proceedings. The notion, however, that people can be mean, selfish, and pathetic in the extreme is not terribly original or profound, and so one is left wondering what is the point? As Kenneth Turan wrote in the *Los Angeles Times*, "Despite what the

CREDITS

Barry: Aaron Eckhart
Cary: Jason Patric
Jerry: Ben Stiller
Mary: Amy Brenneman
Terri: Catherine Keener
Cheri: Nastassja Kinski

Origin: USA
Released: 1998
Production: Steve Godin and Jason Patric for Propaganda Films and Fleece; released by Gramercy Pictures
Direction: Neil LaBute
Screenplay: Neil LaBute
Cinematography: Nancy Schreiber
Editing: Joel Plotch
Production design: Charles Breen
Costumes: April Napier
Sound: Felipe Borrero
MPAA rating: R
Running Time: 99 minutes

modern sensibility dictates, being completely and unalterably bleak about human motivations and relationships is not any wiser, smarter or more realistic than being totally Pollyannish." Ultimately, *Your Friends & Neighbors* is monotonous and smug—a pointless and mannered exercise in pseudo-sophistication that ends up telling us nothing new about the upwardly mobile set or human nature in general.

—*Peter N. Chumo II*

REVIEWS

Boxoffice. August, 1998, p. 44.
Entertainment Weekly. August 21, 1998, p. 92.
Los Angeles Times. August 19, 1998, p. F1.
New York Times. August 19, 1998, p. E1.
People. August 24, 1998, p. 35.
Sight and Sound. October, 1998, p. 61.
Variety. August 10, 1998, p. 43.
Washington Post Weekend. August 21, 1998, p. 39.

You've Got Mail

Someone you pass on the street may already be the love of your life.—Movie tagline

"Romantic comedy at its best!"—Bob Thomas, *Associated Press*

"A great romantic comedy! Tom Hanks and Meg Ryan are magic!"—Joel Siegel, *Good Morning America*

"You'll love it!"—Neil Rosen, *NY1 News*

"A picture-perfect romantic comedy."—Leah Rozen, *People*

"Two thumbs up!"—*Siskel & Ebert*

"A sure-fire hit!"—Gene Shalit, *The Today Show*

Box Office: $63,762,374

Rival bookstore owners Joe Fox (Tom Hanks) and Kathleen Kelly (Meg Ryan) unknowingly are lovers in the anonymous world of Internet chat rooms in the romantic comedy *You've Got Mail.*

In *You've Got Mail*, the cyberized remake of the 1940's romantic comedy *The Shop Around the Corner*, Tom Hanks and Meg Ryan star as two booksellers who are fierce competitors in real life but unwittingly romance each other via the Internet. Hanks plays Joe Fox, a third-generation chain bookstore mogul, who is driving children's bookshop owner Kathleen Kelly (Meg Ryan) out of business.

As the inspiration for *Mail*, Ernst Lubitsch's charming *The Shop Around the Corner* cast Jimmy Stewart and Margaret Sullavan as bickering co-workers who don't realize they're secretly pen pals. Its plot was reworked for the musical *In the Good Old Summertime* (1949) and it was originally scripted as a play, *Parfumerie*, by Miklos Laszlo. With *Mail*, director Nora Ephron

Birdie (Jean Stapleton): "I tried having cyber-sex once, but I kept getting a busy signal."

puts a contemporary spin on this familiar premise by having love blossom in an Internet chat room.

In their third outing together, the dream team of Hanks and Ryan once again exudes the chemistry that endeared them to fans of Ephron's *Sleepless in Seattle* (1993). Like *Sleepless*, where the audience had to wait until the end for the lovers to meet, writer-director Ephron wisely makes us wait again. Although Hanks's and Ryan's characters meet and interact, they don't actually meet as their e-mail alter egos until the very end of the movie.

Corresponding anonymously online as "Shopgirl" (Kathleen's name) and "NY152" (Joe's moniker), Joe and Kathleen have no idea that they're professional rivals. Kathleen owns The Shop Around the Corner, a tiny, one-of-a-kind children's bookstore on Manhattan's Upper West Side, whose existence is threatened by the arrival of a Fox Books superstore on the same block. Kathleen fears her family-owned bookshop, with its personal service and children's storytime, can't compete with the bookstore chain's discounts, huge inventory, and cappuccino bar.

Although both characters are already involved in relationships, she with the narcissistic columnist Frank (Greg Kinnear) and he with hyper, self-obsessed book editor Patricia (Parker Posey), both Kathleen and Joe realize that they're cyber soulmates. Without indulging any personal information, they share musings on New York, and Joe even offers Kathleen advice when she admits she's having a professional crisis. As their e-mail romance grows, they decide to meet. Little do they know, they've already met and don't care much for each other.

Both Hanks and Ryan are as irresistible as ever in the lead roles. In her *New York Times* review, Janet Maslin com-

The two bookstores featured in the film were actually created on the streets of Manhattan. In fact, The Fox Books facade appeared so authentic during its construction that passers-by regularly asked the production crew when the new bookstore would be opening.

ments on their star power: "Ms. Ryan plays her role blithely and credibly this time, with an air of freshness, a minimum of cute fidgeting and a lot of fond chemistry with Hanks. And he continues to amaze. Once again, he fully inhabits a new role without any obvious actorly behavior, to the point where comparisons to James Stewart (who starred with Margaret Sullavan in the Lubitsch film) really cannot be avoided."

Unfortunately, the film's supporting cast doesn't fare as well. Jean Stapleton, Steve Zahn, and Dabney Coleman are all largely wasted in their underwritten parts. Their characters are flashy yet insubstantial. The same can be said for the film's subplots. While the central romance is strongly developed, there are a few subplots that remain undeveloped. Ephron and her co-writer (and sister Delia Ephron) should have fleshed out these scenes a bit more. To their credit, they've managed to successfully capture the lifestyles and trends of the '90s with their comments on the culture of laptops, bookstore economics, online dating, Starbucks, AOL, and our ever increasing dependence on credit cards.

Making the most of its Upper West Side locales, *You've Got Mail* features several restaurants, coffee shops, and stores of this middle-class neighborhood. Both Nora and Delia Ephron live on the Upper West Side and their love of the neighborhood is evident on screen. With its mix of reading and romance, book-lined settings, and characters out of New York literati, *Mail* is a bookworm's cinematic dream.

Focusing on the superstar vs. indie conflict, many independent booksellers across the country received some unexpected publicity with the movie's mid-December release. The superstore, Fox & Sons Books, is a hybrid of Borders and Barnes & Noble, while the independent, The Shop

CREDITS

Joe Fox: Tom Hanks
Kathleen Kelly: Meg Ryan
Patricia Eden: Parker Posey
Frank Navasky: Greg Kinnear
Birdie: Jean Stapleton
George Pappas: Steve Zahn
Kevin Scanlon: David Chappelle
Nelson Fox: Dabney Coleman
Schuyler Fox: John Randolph
Christina: Heather Burns

Origin: USA
Released: 1998
Production: Nora Ephron and Lauren Shuler Donner; released by Warner Bros.
Direction: Nora Ephron
Screenplay: Nora Ephron, Delia Ephron; based on the screenplay "The Shop Around the Corner" by Samson Raphaelson from the play *Parfumerie* by Miklos Laszlo
Cinematography: John Lindley
Editing: Richard Marks
Music: George Fenton
Production design: Dan Davis
Art direction: Ray Kluga
Costumes: Albert Wolsky
Sound: Ron Bochar
MPAA rating: PG-13
Running Time: 119 minutes

REVIEWS

Ann Arbor News. December 18, 1998, p. D1.
Battle Creek Enquirer. December 18, 1998, p. 14.
Detroit Free Press. December 18, 1998, p. D1.
Detroit News. December 18, 1998, p. 3D.
Entertainment Weekly. December 18, 1998, p. 45.
Gannett News Service. December 18, 1998.
Los Angeles Times. December 18, 1998.
New York Times. December 18, 1998, p. E1.
Newhouse News Service. December 18, 1998.
People. December 21, 1998, p. 34.
Publishers Weekly. May 18, 1998, p. 26.
Salon online. December 18, 1998.
San Francisco Chronicle. December 18, 1998, p. C1.
San Francisco Examiner. December 18, 1998, p. B1.
Variety. December 14, 1998, p. 130.

Around the Corner, was modeled after Books of Wonder, an eighteen-year-old children's bookstore in New York City. In *Publishers Weekly*, Ephron explains why she chose the bookstore setting: "You have an actual story that comes right along with this setting, which is the endangered species. It's something I'm very interested in. I'm a writer and a reader, so I care about bookstores far more than I care about any other store."

The chain vs. indie controversy aside, any movie that treasures books and the written word as much as *Mail* does deserves to be honored. And fans of Ephron's earlier work know this isn't the first time she's used a New York City bookstore setting—her protagonists in *When Harry Met Sally* (1989) shop at the now-defunct Upper West Side branch of Shakespeare & Co.

Critical reaction to *Mail* was mixed, although everyone praised the winning Hanks-Ryan chemistry. A few detractors cited the film's length and suggested it could have used further editing. No matter, *Mail* delivered not only at the boxoffice but with holiday moviegoers as well.

—*Beth Fhaner*

Zero Effect

The world's most private detective.—Movie tagline

"Ingenious and delightful. This is one of those movies that creeps up on you, gathering power."—Roger Ebert, *Chicago Sun-Times*

"Smartly hip . . . The freshest detective yarn to come along in a while."—Jack Mathews, *Los Angeles Times*

"Two thumbs up! Way up!"—*Siskel & Ebert*

Box Office: $2,087,471

How to describe Daryl Zero (Bill Pullman)? Well, he's undoubtedly the world's greatest detective: a master of disguise, a genius when it comes to human psychology, an expert at observation, and an artist of logical deduction. He's also elusive and reclusive. Daryl Zero never meets or speaks to his clients. If one has business with Daryl, one deals only with his right-hand man, Steve Arlo (Ben Stiller). Zero is the Sherlock Holmes to Arlo's Dr. Watson. But Steve, who is one of the few people to actually know Daryl, has mixed feelings about his employer. Yes, he can solve a case without ever leaving his desk and computer, but there's something not quite right about Daryl.

Daryl Zero (Bill Pullman): "Help solve a problem first by observation and then by careful intervention. In other words, the zero effect."

As Steve tells a friend, "he never even leaves the house. He's a complete recluse. No social life; no social skills. When he's working, he's the smoothest operator you've ever seen. Brave, slick, cunning, do anything. As soon as he gets off work, it's all gone. He's afraid to go to the dry cleaners, literally. Too uncomfortable in his own skin to go out and eat. Tactless, inept, rude, too, just an asshole." In other words, Zero is a god and a geek.

In the film *Zero Effect*, this disparaging dialogue about Daryl is effectively interspersed with Steve telling a potential customer about Daryl's amazing feats of crime solving. Right from the start, we're curious to meet this Howard Hughes of the Sam Spade set. Interest builds as Steve takes the private elevator to Zero's apartment, obtains initial entrance with a pass card, punches in a combination, uses keys to unlock at least six locks, and then enters a security code. What's behind that contradictory introduction and tight security? We're eager to see what the filmmakers have in store for us, and when we do, we're not disappointed. Daryl Zero is as quirky as we hoped he would be from the buildup.

Yes, he's reclusive, yes, he has all the latest computer equipment, yes, we can easily imagine that whoever lives here is the world's greatest detective, but is that him jumping up and down on the bed playing the guitar and singing one of the world's worst folk songs? This guy is more than reclusive, he's goofy! Is his refrigerator really filled only with TAB? Are those huge bags of Cheerios and cases of tuna fish in his cupboards? And did he really write that awful song he was singing? Yes, yes, yes.

OK, now we're really curious. This guy doesn't even look as if he could get out of his own apartment, let alone claim the title of the world's greatest detective. How in the world is this fool going to solve anything? Well, since his current client Gregory Stark (Ryan O'Neal) has never met Daryl, he's not as concerned as the audience is about the evasive detective. We can't wait to see him at work. Stark's case seems pretty cut and dried: someone has stolen the keys to Stark's safe deposit box and now he is being blackmailed.

The detective can assume a false identity and travel to Portland, Oregon to use his powers of observation to solve the case. He manages to spy on Stark while running right next to him on health club treadmills. He also observes Stark as he delivers the blackmail money. To Zero's surprise, the money is picked up by Gloria Sullivan (Kim Dickens), a paramedic he had met the day before in Stark's health club.

Daryl may have Stark pretty well figured out, but Gloria puzzles him. He is attracted to her (an awkward situation for a recluse) but she is also a bit of an enigma to him. "I have mastered the fine art of detachment," says Daryl, "and while it comes at some cost, this supreme objectivity is what makes me, I dare say, the greatest observer the world has ever known." But while he enjoys observing Gloria, he can't quite see through her veils. Are his emotions clouding his logical ability? Is she the villain or a pawn? Will Daryl really solve the case or go back to writing bad folk songs?

Zero Effect begins seductively. It's well-written, visually enticing, and mentally challenging. We're interested in the characters and attracted to the story. The film sneaks up and involves the audience—involves them not only in the story of the blackmail but also in seeing what in the world Zero will do next and how he will look and act. We're interested not only in the plot's many twists and turns (which will not be revealed here), but also in seeing how Zero's mind works. This last revelation comes not only by watching his antics, but also from some very witty voiceovers in which Zero tells us what he's thinking.

These are high kudos for first-time writer and director, Jake Kasdan. Kasdan, the twenty-two-year-old son of Lawrence Kasdan (*The Big Chill* [1983]), makes an impressive start as he follows in his father's footsteps. However, there is a problem in paradise. *Zero Effect* may begin with all the potential of being a great film, but somewhere at half-time, it begins to run out of touchdowns. Some time after Daryl takes up with Gloria, quirkiness gives way to romance, which humanizes Daryl and undermines the humor. Gloria takes our lovably dysfunctional detective and turns him into just another lovestruck guy. It's not as much fun after that.

In fact, this film that started out so idiosyncratic and engaging, turns quite melancholy by the end. It's at its best when Zero is plying his trade as detective or interacting almost abusively (but nonetheless comically) with Steve, it's at its weakest when he's with Gloria. However, there is no denying that Kasdan has talent and shows great promise. And there's no disputing the fact that Daryl Zero is a great character who deserves a second chance.

There is also no doubt that one of the reasons Daryl Zero is so effective is because he is played by Bill Pullman (*Sleepless in Seattle* [1993], *Independence Day* [1996]). Kasdan evidently wrote this film with Pullman in mind. They had met when Jake was thirteen and his father was making *The Accidental Tourist* (1988). It must have been some impression! Pullman is adroit at playing drama and comedy and here he effortlessly walks a tightrope over insanity. He's likeable, watchable, and does interesting things with his character.

Also helping make *Zero Effect* strong is Ben Stiller. Once again the talent gene pool is working in the film's favor. The son of comedians Jerry Stiller and Anne Meara, Ben has the family comic timing and can play a solid second banana as he does here, but can also carry a film as he did in this year's *There's Something About Mary*. As much fun as it is watching Pullman's Zero take some strange turns in solving his case, it's also fun watching the buddy film develop between Zero and Arlo. Now if we could just get Kasdan to dump the obligatory woman of mystery who softens the story and sends it down the wrong cinematic path.

Supporting players are also in fine form. Ryan O'Neal here returns to his comic roots (*What's Up Doc?* [1972], *Paper Moon* [1973]), while relative newcomer Kim Dickens (1997's *Great Expectations* and *Mercury Rising*) gamely works at a part that in the end torpedoes the film's humor. But that's not necessarily her fault.

If Kasdan had kept the quirky quotient up all the way to the end of the film, this might have been a hit. But even

CREDITS

Daryl Zero: Bill Pullman
Steve Arlo: Ben Stiller
Gregory Stark: Ryan O'Neal
Gloria Sullivan: Kim Dickens
Jess: Angela Featherstone
Bill: Hugh Ross
Daisy: Sara Devincentis
Kragen Vincent: Matt O'Toole
Maid: Michele Mariana

Origin: USA
Released: 1998
Production: Lisa Henson, Janet Yang, and Jake Kasdan for Castle Rock Entertainment; released by Columbia Pictures
Direction: Jake Kasdan
Screenplay: Jake Kasdan
Cinematography: Bill Pope
Editing: Tara Timpone
Production design: Gary Frutkoff
Art direction: Philip J. Messina
Set decoration: Maggie Martin
Costumes: Kym Barrett
Music: Happy Walters, Manish Raval
MPAA rating: R
Running Time: 115 minutes

as it is, the first half of this film is still better than entire other films and deserves a viewing. And as it starts to weaken, we can just sigh and wonder at what might have been. As for why Kasdan allowed the film to venture from its original whimsical premise, well, maybe that's a mystery only Daryl Zero can solve. Although as even he admits, "some questions are for answering, others are better left to torture and torment for all eternity." And so we can only wonder . . . and eagerly await Kasdan's next offering.

—*Beverley Bare Buehrer*

REVIEWS

Boxoffice. February, 1998, p. 50.
Chicago Sun Times. January 30, 1998.
Chicago Tribune. January 30, 1998.
Entertainment Weekly. February 13, 1998, p. 44.
Los Angeles Times. January 30, 1998, p. F12.
New York Times. January 30, 1998, p. E10.
People. February 16, 1998, p. 20.
USA Today. January 30, 1998, p. 7D.
Variety. January 26, 1998, p. 66.
Village Voice. February 3, 1998, p. 54.
Washington Post Weekend. January 30, 1998, p. 49.

List of Awards

Academy Awards

Best Picture: *Shakespeare in Love*

Direction: Steven Spielberg (*Saving Private Ryan*)

Actor: Roberto Benigni (*Life Is Beautiful*)

Actress: Gwyneth Paltrow (*Shakespeare in Love*)

Supporting Actor: James Coburn (*Affliction*)

Supporting Actress: Judi Dench (*Shakespeare in Love*)

Original Screenplay: Marc Norman and Tom Stoppard (*Shakespeare in Love*)

Adapted Screenplay: Bill Condon (*Gods and Monsters*)

Cinematography: Janusz Kaminski (*Saving Private Ryan*)

Editing: Michael Kahn (*Saving Private Ryan*)

Art Direction: Martin Childs and Jill Quertier (*Shakespeare in Love*)

Visual Effects: Joel Hynek, Nicholas Brooks, Stuart Robertson, and Kevin Mack (*What Dreams May Come*)

Sound Effects Editing: Gary Rydstrom and Richard Hymns (*Saving Private Ryan*)

Sound: Gary Rydstrom, Gary Summers, Andy Nelson, and Ronald Judkins (*Saving Private Ryan*)

Makeup: Jenny Shircore (*Elizabeth*)

Costume Design: Sandy Powell (*Shakespeare in Love*)

Original Music or Comedy Score: Stephen Warbeck (*Shakespeare in Love*)

Original Dramatic Score: Nicola Piovani (*Life Is Beautiful*)

Original Song: "When You Believe" (*The Prince of Egypt*: Stephen Schwartz)

Foreign-language Film: *Life Is Beautiful* (Italy)

Short Film, Animated: Chris Wedge (*Bunny*)

Short Film, Live Action: Kim Magnusson and Anders Thomas Jensen (*Election Night*)

Documentary, Feature: James Moll and Ken Lipper (*The Last Days*)

Documentary, Short Subject: Keiko Ibi (*The Personals: Improvisations on Romance in the Golden Years*)

Directors Guild of America Award

Director: Steven Spielberg (*Saving Private Ryan*)

Writers Guild of America Awards

Original Screenplay: Marc Norman and Tom Stoppard (*Shakespeare in Love*)

Adapted Screenplay: Scott Frank (*Out of Sight*)

New York Film Critics Awards

Best Picture: *Saving Private Ryan*

Direction: Terrence Malick (*The Thin Red Line*)

Actor: Nick Nolte (*Affliction*)

Actress: Cameron Diaz (*There's Something About Mary*)

Supporting Actor: Bill Murray (*Rushmore*)

Supporting Actress: Lisa Kudrow (*The Opposite of Sex*)

Screenplay: Marc Norman and Tom Stoppard (*Shakespeare in Love*)

Foreign Film: *Celebration* (The Netherlands)

First Film: Richard Kwietniowski (*Love and Death on Long Island*)

Nonfiction Film: Jonathan Stack, Liz Garbus, and Wilbert Rideau (*The Farm: Angola USA*)

Los Angeles Film Critics Awards

Best Picture: *Saving Private Ryan*

Direction: Steven Spielberg (*Saving Private Ryan*)

Actor: Ian McKellen (*Gods and Monsters*)

Actress: Fernanda Montenegro (*Central Station*) and Ally Sheedy (*High Art*)

Supporting Actor: Bill Murray (*Rushmore*) and Billy Bob Thornton (*A Simple Plan*)

Supporting Actress: Joan Allen (*Pleasantville*)

Screenplay: Warren Beatty and Jeremy Pisker (*Bulworth*)

Cinematography: Janusz Kaminski (*Saving Private Ryan*)

Foreign Film: Elliot Goldenthal (*The Butcher Boy*)

Outstanding Documentary: Jonathan Stack, Liz Garbus, and Wilbert Rideau (*The Farm: Angola USA*)

National Society of Film Critics Awards

Best Picture: *Out of Sight*

Direction: Steven Soderbergh (*Out of Sight*)

Actor: Nick Nolte (*Affliction*)

Actress: Ally Sheedy (*High Art*)

Supporting Actor: Bill Murray (*Rushmore*)

Supporting Actress: Judi Dench (*Shakespeare in Love*)

Screenplay: Scott Frank (*Out of Sight*)

Cinematography: John Toll (*The Thin Red Line*)

Foreign Film: *Taste of Cherry* (Iran)

Nonfiction Film: Jonathan Stack, Liz Garbus, and Wilbert Rideau (*The Farm: Angola USA*)

National Board of Review Awards

Best Picture: *Gods and Monsters*

Direction: Shekhar Kapur (*Elizabeth*)

Actor: Ian McKellen (*Gods and Monsters*)

Actress: Fernanda Montenegro (*Central Station*)

Supporting Actor: Ed Harris (*The Truman Show, Stepmom*)

Supporting Actress: Christina Ricci (*The Opposite of Sex, Buffalo 66, Pecker*)

Foreign Film: *Central Station* (Brazil)

Documentary: Barbara Kopple (*Wild Man Blues*)

Golden Globes

Best Picture, Drama: *Saving Private Ryan*

Best Picture, Comedy: *Shakespeare in Love*

Direction: Steven Spielberg (*Saving Private Ryan*)

Actor, Drama: Jim Carrey (*The Truman Show*)

Actress, Drama: Cate Blanchett (*Elizabeth*)

Actor, Comedy or Musical: Michael Caine (*Little Voice*)

Actress, Comedy or Musical: Gwyneth Paltrow (*Shakespeare in Love*)

Supporting Actor: Ed Harris (*The Truman Show*)

Supporting Actress: Lynn Redgrave (*Gods and Monsters*)

Screenplay: Marc Norman and Tom Stoppard (*Shakespeare in Love*)

Original Score: Burkhard Dallwitz and Philip Glass (*The Truman Show*)

Original Song: "The Prayer" (*Quest for Camelot*: music and lyrics: David Foster and Carole Bayer Sager)

Foreign Film: *Central Station* (Brazil)

Life Achievement Award
Dustin Hoffman

Dustin Hoffman joins an illustrious group of actors and filmmakers, which includes James Cagney, Alfred Hitchcock, Bette Davis, and Jack Nicholson, as recipient of the American Film Institute Life Achievement Award. The Institute voted to award Hoffman its highest honor, and it's a well-deserved tribute for a man whose remarkable career includes films that have become both cultural monuments and deeply personal reflections of our lives. Hoffman is the organization's twenty-seventh distinguished honoree. Along with his predecessors, Hoffman has created a wide range of characters that reveal a craftsman always reinventing himself. The road to his success was neither long nor arduous, for it took just one lead role, over thirty years ago, and the face of cinema never looked the same.

Dustin Hoffman was born in Los Angeles on August 8, 1937, to Lillian and Harry Hoffman, showbiz veterans in their own right. Harry became a prop man at Columbia Pictures, but because of the Depression, he lost his job at the studio and eventually gained employment as a furniture salesman. Lillian was an amateur theater actress who left the big lights to raise her two sons.

Perhaps because of his parents' previous occupations, showing off came easy to young Hoffman but he never really regarded himself as a performer or future actor. Hoffman initially harbored ambitions to become a concert pianist. A college acting class changed his mind and he moved to New York in the late 1950s, eventually getting accepted into Lee Strasberg's Actor Studio. Along with his two roommates, actors Robert Duvall and Gene Hackman, Hoffman beat the pavement looking for work. In between work in plays, Hoffman helped make ends meet with small guest appearances on such shows as *The Naked City* and *The Defenders*. Eventually Hoffman got his break with an off-Broadway role in the play *The Exhaustion of Our Son's Love*. His work in *Exhaustion* won him an Obie Award during the 1965–66 season, a role in the British comedy *Eh!*, and a lead role in the romantic comedy *Tiger Makes Out* (1967). Film director Mike Nichols was familiar with Hoffman's off-Broadway work, but the producers of *The Graduate* wanted to cast Robert Redford in the lead role. Hoffman's audition for *The Graduate* went terribly, but Nichols saw something unique in Hoffman and offered him the role of Benjamin Braddock, the lead character in his adaptation of Charles Webb's novel.

In *The Graduate* (1967), Hoffman's portrayal of Benjamin Braddock as a confused, alienated youth trying to find his place in society resonated with young filmgoers of the day. With uncanny realism Hoffman embodies this character, showing a level of craft and precision unreal for a screen newcomer. The role earned him an Academy Award nomination, and his skills would sharpen further in future roles, solidifying his reputation as one of the screen's top character actors.

With *The Graduate* as a firm launching pad, Hoffman embarked on an incredible cinematic journey over the next fifteen years. During the first phase of his film career, he played a wide range of characters, all with a controlled, technical know-how that fused Hoffman with his roles. This is clearly evident in Hoffman's second major feature, *Midnight Cowboy* (1969). Instead of capitalizing on his success in *The*

Graduate to obtain another leading-man role, Hoffman took a gamble by accepting the co-star role of the tubercular, low-life Ratso Rizzo opposite Jon Voight's naïve hustler, Joe Buck. It's no exaggeration to say that his unforgettable performance, in an equally powerful film, stands up as one of the best character studies in screen history. Hoffman's complex Ratso comes across as pathetic, aggravating, and completely unsympathetic. For his efforts, Hoffman earned his second Oscar nomination.

A string of films of wavering quality followed in quick succession, with notable highlights including *Little Big Man* (1970) and *Straw Dogs* (1971). As Jack Crabb in *Little Big Man*, Hoffman played a 120-year-old survivor of Custer's Last Stand. The scenes where he portrays the old man are inspired pieces of acting, but the rest of the film is not as stimulating. For all its sweep and grandeur, *Little Big Man* doesn't offer much of a script and Hoffman does the best he can with a character that is loosely defined. Hoffman is given much more to work with in Sam Peckinpah's *Straw Dogs*. He is magnificent as the reticent mathematician, David Sumner, in this exquisitely disturbing film of how a once-peaceful man is brought to the brink of unspeakable violence.

After *Straw Dogs*, three years passed before Hoffman appeared in another first-rate film. In 1974's *Lenny*, directed by Bob Fosse, Hoffman plays tortured comedian Lenny Bruce, and it's one of his most deeply honed performances. To prepare for this role, Hoffman spent time interviewing friends and family of the late comic, studying vocal mannerisms from his recorded albums, and repeatedly viewing films of the comedian's stage performances. The results are clearly projected onscreen where Hoffman seems to vanish into his character. Critics acclaimed the film and it won Hoffman his third Oscar nomination.

For the next eight years Hoffman could do no wrong. His subsequent six films are a lexicon of the best American cinema in the second half of the 1970s and early 1980s, beginning with the chilling suspense yarn *Marathon Man* (1976), where Hoffman plays an innocent man inadvertently placed in the path of a sadistic ex-Nazi war criminal played brilliantly by Sir Laurence Oliver. It was in this film that Oliver's character spoke the line, "Is it safe?" and dramatically decreased the number of visits to dentists around the country with his form of torture. Next came the excellent *All the President's Men* (1976) with Robert Redford as Bob Woodward and Hoffman as Carl Bernstein. *All the President's Men* was a daring film that followed closely on the heels of the Watergate scandal and has since become a classic with its realistic and documentary style of filmmaking. *Straight Time* was Hoffman's first foray into film producing. *Straight Time* (1978) was a small film of an ex-convict trying to turn his life around and stay on the right side of the law. It was a restrained, detailed, and brilliant performance that gained notice as a cult favorite in passing years.

With several films and great performances behind him, 1979 proved to be the year Hoffman would win the elusive Oscar. His performance as Ted Kramer, an ambitious advertising executive whose wife leaves him to raise their son by himself in *Kramer vs. Kramer* (1979), was one that he needed to do little preparation for. At the time the movie was shot, Hoffman's marriage to dancer Anne Byrne was slowly deteriorating, and it ended in divorce shortly after he won the Academy Award. Hoffman connected not only with his character but with a legion of men and women who were facing similar traumas. Not since *The Graduate* had a film created such a personal impact with audiences.

Hoffman's next major film would earn him his fifth Oscar nomination. In *Tootsie* (1982), Hoffman gives one of the all-time greatest screen performances as struggling actor Michael Dorsey, who disguises himself as a woman named Dorothy Michaels in order to win a role in a popular soap opera. Hoffman said that he based Dorothy on his own mother, injecting the character with wit, intelligence, and a pugnacious individuality. Equally pugnacious was Hoffman's relationship with the film's director, Sydney Pollack. On and off the set clashes between the two became legendary stories, with the perfectionist Hoffman trying Pollack's patience and perseverance to the extreme. Some of the stories have been exaggerated, but Hoffman is still considered a "difficult" star.

With *Tootsie*, Hoffman ended the first phase of his career and entered the uneven second, which began with a television version of the play *Death of a Salesman*, where he reprised his Broadway role of Willy Loman. A string of top-notch films and downright flops followed throughout the '80s and '90s. During this era, *Rain Man* stands out as his best work, and his portrayal of autistic savant Raymond Babbit earned him his second Oscar and originated a fruitful collaboration with *Rain Man*'s director Barry Levinson. Following *Rain Man*, Hoffman made the much maligned *Ishtar*, a modern-day "road" comedy whose huge budget and terrible script infuriated critics and alienated audiences. Other flops followed, including *Family Business* (1989), *Billy Bathgate* (1991), *Hook* (1991), and *Hero* (1992). At age fifty-five, it seemed that his best work was behind him and that age was eliminating him from better roles.

The last few years, however, have seen a bit of a resurgence in Hoffman's career. The forgettable but profitable disease drama *Outbreak* (1995) was followed by an inspiring performance in David Mamet's *American Buffalo* (1996). His collaboration with Barry Levinson resulted in two strong screen performances from Hoffman. As alcoholic and drug-addicted Danny Snyder in *Sleepers* (1996), Hoffman is believable as a hopeless attorney, even hearkening back to his role as Ratso Rizzo in this underrated drama. With *Wag the Dog* (1997), Hoffman earned his seventh Oscar nomination for his role as Hollywood producer Stanley Motts. The latest Levinson union churned out the sci-fi thriller *Sphere*

(1998). While not a bad performance, Hoffman isn't given much to do in this mediocre film that is overwhelmed with underwater special effects.

Mediocrity, however, is something not typically linked with Hoffman's name or acting. His work has helped define the shape of modern cinema over the past thirty years. Some may claim that his best work is behind him, but a number of his recent and underappreciated efforts prove otherwise. Films such as *American Buffalo, Sleepers,* and *Wag the Dog* reveal an actor at his peak. A roster of future projects promises to bring new and interesting performances from Hoffman to the screen, and the cinema world will be richer for it.Dustin Hoffman is not a star. Dustin Hoffman is an actor, a professional craftsman. Unlike most other actors of his stature, he comes off as self-conscious and humorous in interviews, revealing little of himself, giving nothing to feed the gossip columnists' insatiable appetite. These are the fleeting things of celebrity that he has shunned. His one claim to celebrity infamy is the constant barrage of accusations that he is a perfectionist, obsessing over every detail of a film he's working on. This doesn't detract, but only adds to his luster as one of the most gifted character actors ever to grace the screen.

Rich Silverman

Obituaries

Bob (Tex) Allen   (March 28, 1906–October 9, 1998). Born Irving Theodore Baehr, Allen was an actor who was best known for his starring roles in six "B" Westerns from Columbia Pictures, known as the "Texas Ranger" series. He spent most of his later career acting in stage productions. Allen's film credits include *The Unknown Ranger* (1936), *Rio Grande Ranger* (1936), *Ranger Courage* (1937), *Law of the Ranger* (1937), *Reckless Ranger* (1937), and *The Rangers Step In* (1937).

Eric Ambler   (June 28, 1909–October 22, 1998). Ambler was a British novelist known for introducing antiheroes into the field of espionage literature. His best known novels were *The Mask of Dimitrios* (1939) and *Journey into Fear* (1940). He became involved with cinema as a script consultant for Alexander Korda, worked with a film unit in the British Army in World War II, and ultimately wrote scripts for over a dozen films. He was nominated for an Academy Award for his work on *The Cruel Sea* (1953). His additional film credits include *The Way Ahead* (1944), *The October Man* (1947, which he also produced), *Encore* (1951), *Lease of Life* (1954), and *A Night to Remember* (1958).

Gene Autry   (September 29, 1907–October 2, 1998). Autry was an actor-singer who, along with Roy Rogers, popularized the screen subgenre of the singing cowboy. After being encouraged by fellow Oklahoman Will Rogers to enter show business, Autry began singing on the radio in 1928, and began making records shortly thereafter. His musical talents brought him to Hollywood's attention, and his first lead role was in the science fiction serial *Phantom Empire* (1935). Later that year, he made *Tumbling Tumbleweeds* (1935) and *The Singing Vagabond* (1935), and was on his way to stardom. Autry developed an ensemble that included a sidekick, Smiley Burnette, for comic relief, and his

Gene Autry

faithful horse Champion. He was among Hollywood's most profitable stars every year from 1938–1942. He entered the military in World War II, and in his absence, Republic, his studio, began promoting Roy Rogers as "King of the Cowboys." When Autry mustered out of the service, he went to Columbia Pictures and resumed his film and recording career. He earned his only Academy Award nomination for a song, "Be Honest With Me," which he co-authored and sang in *Ridin' on a Rainbow* (1941). In the late 1940s and early 1950s, he was particularly successful on the record charts, with holiday-themed hits such as "Rudolph the Red-Nosed Reindeer," "Here Comes Santa Claus," and "Peter Cottontail." Autry was an astute businessman, accumulating significant real estate holdings, radio and television stations, and even a major league baseball team. He also recognized the impact of television early, shifting his efforts from film to the new medium in 1950. Autry's screen credits include *Boots and Saddles* (1937), *Springtime in the Rockies* (1937), *South of the Border* (1939), *Melody Ranch* (1940), *Down Mexico Way* (1941), *Robin Hood of Texas* (1947), *Mule Train* (1950), *Texans Never Cry* (1951), and *Winning of the West* (1953).

Binnie Barnes   (March 25, 1905–July 27, 1998). Born Gitelle Gertrude Maude Barnes, Barnes was a British actress who specialized in comic roles. She appeared first in comedy shorts before landing the role of Catherine Howard opposite Charles Laughton in *The Private Life of Henry VIII* (1933). She alternated between leads and second leads in films such as *The Private Life of Don Juan* (1934), *Diamond Jim* (1935), *Broadway Melody of 1938* (1937), *The Three Musketeers* (1939), and *Barbary Coast Gent* (1944). After marriage and retirement in the late 1940s, Barnes resurfaced as an eccentric nun in *The Trouble with Angels* (1966) and its sequel, *Where Angels Go Trouble Follows* (1968). Her additional screen credits include *Murder at Convent Garden* (1932), *The Last of the Mohicans* (1936), *The Adventures of Marco Polo* (1938), *Skylark* (1941), *I Married an Angel* (1942), *The Time of Their Lives* (1946), and *40 Carats* (1973).

Eva Bartok   (June 18, 1926–August 1, 1998). Born Eva Martha Szoeke in Hungary, Bartok was an actress who fled her native country during the postwar Communist takeover and landed in London. She made numerous films between 1951 and 1967, but was better known for her tempestuous romantic life than for her acting. She was married for a time to actor Curt Juergens. Her film credits include *A Tale of Five Cities* (1951), *The Crimson Pirate* (1952), *The Last Waltz* (1953), *Orient Express* (1954), *Ten Thousand Bedrooms* (1957), *Operation Amsterdam* (1959), and *Savina* (1966).

Sonny Bono   (February 16, 1935–January 5, 1998). Born Salvatore Bono, Bono was a musician, politician, and actor. He was also a songwriter and studio musician, working with famous producer Phil Spector in the early 1960s. In 1965, he teamed with his wife, Cher, to record "I Got You Babe," which reached number one on the charts and was followed by a number of other hits, including "Laugh at Me," a solo effort by Bono. Sonny and Cher made two films together, *Wild on the Beach* (1965) and *Good Times* (1967). Bono wrote, produced, and composed songs for *Chastity* (1969), which featured Cher. From 1971–1974, the couple had a successful television variety series, in which Bono served as a foil for his wife's jokes, resulting in the misleading image of Bono as nothing more than an affable buffoon. When the series ended with the couple's divorce, Bono acted in a few films, opened a restaurant in Palm Springs, entered politics, and was elected mayor of that California city in 1988. In 1994, he was elected to the House of Representatives of the United States Congress, one of many freshmen House Republicans that year. He died in a skiing accident. Bono's additional screen credits include *Escape to Athena* (1979), *Balboa* (1982), *Airplane 2 — The Sequel* (1982), *Troll* (1985), and *Hairspray* (1988).

Lloyd Bridges   (January 15, 1913–March 10, 1998).

Lloyd Bridges

Bridges was an actor who specialized in action roles in film and television. He had a stage background, and was signed by Columbia, for whom he appeared in over two dozen low budget pictures from 1941–1945. The quality of his roles improved thereafter, and he had major roles in such Westerns as *High Noon* (1952) and *Wichita* (1955). During this period, he appeared before the House Un-American Activities Committee and acknowledged that he had been a member of the Communist Party. His past politics didn't affect his ability to get roles, and his greatest success came in 1957, when he was cast as Mike Nelson in the syndicated television series *Sea Hunt*. He resumed making films again in the mid–1960s, with *Around the World Under the Sea*

(1966), but his biggest post–*Sea Hunt* role came with *Airplane!* (1980), in which he displayed a hitherto unknown flair for comedy. Most of his memorable later roles were in the same vein, in films such as *Hot Shots!* (1991) and *Mafia!* (1998). He was the father of actors Jeff Bridges and Beau Bridges. His additional film credits include *Here Comes Mr. Jordan* (1941), *Alias Boston Blackie* (1942), *Louisiana Hayride* (1944), *A Walk in the Sun* (1945), *Colt 45* (1950), *The Kid From Left Field* (1953), *The Rainmaker* (1956), *Daring Game* (1968), *Running Wild* (1973), *The Fifth Musketeer* (1977), *Airplane II: The Sequel* (1982), *Joe Versus the Volcano* (1990), *Honey I Blew Up the Kid!* (1992), *Hot Shots! Part Deux* (1993), and *The War at Home* (1996).

Clara Calamai   (September 7, 1915–September 21, 1998). Calamai was an Italian actress who was a top star in Italy during World War II, known for her sensual roles in films such as *Bocaccio* (1940), *Regina di Navarra* (1941), and *La Cena Delle Beffe* (1942). She is best remembered for her work in two films by Luchino Visconti: *Ossessione* (1942) and *White Nights* (1957). Her additional film credits include *Pietro Micca* (1938), *Ettore Fieramosca* (1939), *Adultera* (1944), *Ultimo Amore* (1946), *Aphrodite* (1958), and *The Witches* (1967).

Dane Clark   (February 18, 1913–September 11, 1998). Born Bernard Zanville, Clark was an actor who specialized in tough guy roles in the 1940s and 1950s. He worked under his original name in films such as *Sunday Punch* (1942) and *The Pride of the Yankees* (1942). He took the name of Dane Clark at the suggestion of Humphrey Bogart, his costar in *Action in the North Atlantic* (1943), shortly after the completion of that film. His additional film credits include *Destination Tokyo* (1944), *Hollywood Canteen* (1944), *Pride of the Marines* (1945), *Whiplash* (1948), *Fort Defiance* (1951), *Go Man Go!* (1954), *Massacre* (1956), and *Outlaw's Son* (1957).

Ruth Clifford   (1900–November 30, 1998). Clifford was an actress whose career spanned nearly a half century. She got her start during the Silent Era, in such films as *The Cabaret Girl* (1918) and *The Face on the Barroom Floor* (1923), and appeared in a number of John Ford films, including *Wagonmaster* (1950) and *The Searchers* (1956). Her additional screen credits include *Midnight Madness* (1918), *Tropical Love* (1921), *Thrill Seekers* (1928), *Only Yesterday* (1933), *Hold 'Em Yale!* (1935), *Luck of the Irish* (1948), *A Man Called Peter* (1955), *The Man in the Gray Flannel Suit* (1956), and *Two Rode Together* (1961).

Vittorio Cottafavi   (January 30, 1914–December 13, 1998). Cottafavi was an Italian director best known for his work from 1958–1964, when he brought a number of historical fantasies to the screen, including *Messalina* (1959), *Goliath* *and the Dragon* (1960), *Amazons of Rome* (1961), *Hercules and the Captive Women* (1961), and *The Hundred Horsemen* (1964). His additional screen credits include *I Nostri Sogni* (1942), *La Grande Strada* (1948), *Fiesta Brava* (1956), *The Warrior and the Slave* (1958), and *Legions of the Nile* (1959).

Richard Denning (March 27, 1914–October 11, 1998). Born Ludwig Denninger, Denning was an actor who won leading roles in numerous action-adventure films. He was blond and athletic, and may be better known for his television roles, as he was featured in series from *Mr. and Mrs. North* in the early 1950s to *Hawaii Five-O,* which ran from 1968–1980. He also starred opposite Lucille Ball in the radio series *My Favorite Husband,* which was retitled *I Love Lucy* for television, with Ball's husband Desi Arnaz taking over Denning's role. Denning was married to actress Evelyn Ankers. His film credits include *Hold 'Em Navy* (1937), *Million Dollar Legs* (1939), *Seventeen* (1940), *Beyond the Blue Horizon* (1942), *Black Beauty* (1946), *Creature from the Black Lagoon* (1954), *Target Earth* (1954), *Creature with the Atom Brain* (1955), *An Affair to Remember* (1957), and *The Lady Takes a Flier* (1958).

John Derek (August 12, 1926–May 22, 1998). Born

John Derek

Derek Harris, Derek was an actor and director whose good looks led to roles designed to appeal to teenage girls. His most distinguished acting role was that of Joshua in the biblical epic *The Ten Commandments* (1956). He left acting to take up photography, and ultimately became a director. He is perhaps best known for his succession of blonde actress wives, including Ursula Andress, Linda Evans, and Bo Derek, whose career he guided. He cast his wife Bo in four films that he directed and photographed: *Fantasies* (1981), *Tarzan the Ape Man* (1981), *Bolero* (1984), and *Ghosts Can't Do It* (1990). As an actor, Derek's screen credits include *Rogues of Sherwood Forest* (1950), *Thunderbirds* (1952), *Prince of Pirates* (1954), *The Adventures of Hajii Baba* (1954), and *An Annapolis Story* (1955). As a director and cinematographer, his credits include *A Boy . . . A Girl* (1969) and *Childish Things* (1969).

Richard Dior (1947–October 26, 1998). Dior was a sound engineer best known for his work on *Apollo 13* (1995), which earned him an Academy Award, which he shared with three colleagues. His additional film credits include *Parenthood* (1989), *The Paper* (1994), *Dead Man Walking* (1995), *Ransom* (1996), and *Slam* (1999).

Billie Dove (May 14, 1900–December 31, 1997). Born Lillian Bohney, Dove was an actress who was a leading lady of the Silent Era. She got her start as a model and a Ziegfield Girl in vaudeville while still in her teens, and her stunning looks (she was promoted as "The American Beauty") led to a career in film. She co-starred with Douglas Fairbanks in the early color production *The Black Pirate* (1926). Dove made the transition to sound successfully, but retired in 1932 to marry a wealthy rancher. Her only subsequent role was a bit part in *Diamond Head* (1963). Dove's screen credits include *Get-Rich-Quick Wallingford* (1921), *Polly of the Follies* (1922), *Youth to Youth* (1922), *Yankee Madness* (1924), *Kid Boots* (1926), *Sensation Seekers* (1927), *American Beauty* (1927), *The Heart of a Follies Girl* (1928), *Painted Angel* (1929), *A Notorious Affair* (1930), *The Age of Love* (1931), and *Blondie of the Follies* (1932).

Edward Eliscu (April 2, 1902–June 18, 1998). Eliscu was a songwriter and screenwriter. He wrote the lyrics for such standards as "More Than You Know" and "Without a Song" and worked extensively on Broadway and in television. His film career ended in the early 1950s, when his political views caused him to be blacklisted. As a songwriter, his best known film project was the first Fred Astaire–Ginger Rogers film, *Flying Down to Rio* (1933). His additional screen credits include the songs for *Diplomaniacs* (1933) and screenplays for *Paddy O'Day* (1936) and *Something to Shout About* (1943).

Gene Fowler (May 27, 1917–May 11, 1998). Fowler was an editor and director. Best known as a director for *I Was a Teenage Werewolf* (1957), Fowler was nominated for an Academy Award for his work (with three colleagues) in editing *It's a Mad, Mad, Mad, Mad World* (1963). He also won Emmys for his television editing work. His additional film credits include *The Ox-Bow Incident* (1943).

Linwood Gale Dunn (December 27, 1904–May 15, 1998). Dunn was a cinematographer and an award-winning designer of photographic equipment. With partner Cecil Love, he invented the Acme-Dunn Optical Printer in 1942. It was the first mass produced special effects printer, and Dunn earned four Academy Award citations for his technical achievements, including the Medal of Commendation in 1974 and the Gorden E. Sawyer Award in 1984. His screen credits include *King Kong* (1933), *Bringing Up Baby* (1938), *Citizen Kane* (1941), *West Side Story* (1961), *It's a Mad, Mad, Mad, Mad World* (1963), *My Fair Lady* (1964), and *Hawaii* (1966).

Penny Edwards (August 24, 1928–August 26, 1998). Born Millicent Edwards, Edwards was an actress who played the female lead in numerous "B" Westerns for Republic, occasionally costarring with Roy Rogers. Her screen credits include *Two Guys from Texas* (1948), *Tucson* (1949), *Sunset* *in the West* (1950), *Spoilers of the Plains* (1951), *In Old Amarillo* (1951), *Captive of Billy the Kid* (1952), *Pony Soldier* (1952), *Powder River* (1953), and *Ride a Valiant Mile* (1957).

Gene Evans (July 11, 1922–April 1, 1998). Evans was an actor, most often cast in character parts, in the role of a heavy. He was also featured in the television series *My Friend Flicka* in the 1950s and *Matt Helm* in the 1970s. His screen credits include *Under Colorado Skies* (1947), *It Happens Every Spring* (1949), *The Steel Helmet* (1951), *Park Row* (1952), *Donovan's Brain* (1953), *The Sad Sack* (1957), *Operation Petticoat* (1959), *The War Wagon* (1967), *Support Your Local Sheriff* (1969), *The Ballad of Cable Hogue* (1970), *Pat Garrett and Billy the Kid* (1973), and *The Magic of Lassie* (1978).

Alice Faye (May 5, 1912–May 9, 1998). Born Alice Jeanne Leppert, Faye was an actress-

Alice Faye

singer who was 20th Century-Fox's leading lady for a time in the 1930s. She was discovered as a chorus girl by Rudy Vallee, and through his influence was cast in *George White's Scandals* (1934); when the film's female star, Lillian Harvey, left the film, Vallee insisted that Faye take her role, and she began working her way towards stardom as a spunky, girl-next-door type. After *King of Burlesque* (1936) and *Poor Little Rich Girl* (1936), she was featured in *In Old Chicago* (1938) and *Alexander's Ragtime Band* (1938). She feuded often with Fox studio chief Darryl F. Zanuck, who ultimately replaced her with Betty Grable as the studio's primary female star. Her 1940s films were less than memorable, and she retired after *Fallen Angel* (1945), briefly returning to the screen in *State Fair* (1962) and later films. Faye's additional screen credits include *Every Night at Eight* (1935), *Sing Baby Sing* (1936), *On the Avenue* (1937), *Rose of Washington Square* (1939), *Lillian Russell* (1940), *That Night in Rio* (1941), *Hello Frisco Hello* (1943), *Won Ton Ton—The Dog Who Saved Hollywood* (1976), and *The Magic of Lassie* (1978).

Norman Fell (March 24, 1924–December 14, 1998). Fell was a character actor whose screen career spanned over three decades. He is best remembered as Mr. Roper, a character in the popular 1970s television series *Three's Company* and its spinoff, *The Ropers*. His screen credits include *Pork Chop Hill* (1959), *Ocean's Eleven* (1960), *PT 109* (1963), *The Graduate* (1967), *Bullitt* (1968), *Catch-22* (1970), *Airport 1975* (1974), *Paternity* (1981), and *For the Boys* (1991).

Douglas V. Fowley (May 30, 1911–May 21, 1998). Fowley was a character actor who was featured in numerous films, most often in the role of the heavy. His best remembered roles were as The Director in *Singin' in the Rain* (1952) and as Doc Holliday in the 1950s television series *The Life and Legend of Wyatt Earp*. Fowley's screen credits include *The Mad Game* (1933), *On the Avenue* (1937), *Alexander's Ragtime Band* (1938), *Dodge City* (1939), *See Here Private Hargrove* (1944), *Don't Fence Me In* (1945), *Mighty Joe Young* (1949), *The Naked Jungle* (1954), *Desire in the Dust* (1960), *Walking Tall* (1973), and *The White Buffalo* (1977).

Massimo Franciosa (July 23, 1924–March 30, 1998). Franciosa was an Italian screenwriter who worked most often in collaboration with Pasquale Festa Campanile. The pair first gained recognition for their comedy scripts in such films as *Poor but Beautiful* (1956), but they earned an Academy Award nomination for *The Four Days of Naples* (1963), a realistic evocation of World War II. They also worked extensively with Luchino Visconti on films such as *Rocco and His Brothers* (1960) and *The Leopard* (1963). Franciosa's additional screen credits include *The Lady Killer of Rome* (1961) and *White Voices* (1964), which he also co-directed with Festa Campanile.

James Goldman (June 30, 1927–October 28, 1998). Goldman was a screenwriter, playwright, and novelist who earned an Academy Award for his work on *The Lion in Winter* (1968), which he adapted from his own play. His additional screen credits include *They Might Be Giants* (1971), *Nicholas and Alexandra* (1971), *Robin and Marian* (1976), and *White Nights* (1985).

Phil Hartman (September 28, 1948–May 28, 1998). Hartman was a comedian and actor who was best known for his work in television, where he appeared on *Saturday Night Live* and starred in *News Radio*. Hartman was murdered by his wife, who then committed suicide. His screen credits include *Pee-wee's Big Adventure* (1985), which he also co-wrote, *Jumpin' Jack Flash*

Phil Hartman

(1986), *Three Amigos* (1986), *Coneheads* (1993), *Jingle All the Way* (1996), *Sgt. Bilko* (1996), and *Small Soldiers* (1998).

Hurd Hatfield (December 7, 1918–December 25, 1998). Hatfield was an actor who is best remembered in the title role in *The Picture of Dorian Grey* (1945). He was a handsome leading man who also worked extensively on stage. His additional screen credits include *Dragon Seed* (1944), *Diary* *of a Chambermaid* (1946), *Joan of Arc* (1948), *The Left-Handed Gun* (1958), *King of Kings* (1961), *Mickey One* (1965), *Harlow* (1965), *The Boston Strangler* (1968), and *Crimes of the Heart* (1986).

Irene Hervey (July 11, 1910–December 20, 1998). Born Irene Herwick, Hervey was an actress who played lead roles in many second features of the 1930s and 1940s, and character roles thereafter. Her son is singer Jack Jones. Hervey's screen credits include *The Count of Monte Cristo* (1934), *Charlie Chan in Shanghai* (1935), *Say It in French* (1938), *Destry Rides Again* (1939), *The Boys from Syracuse* (1940), *Frisco Lil* (1942), *Teenage Rebel* (1956), *Going Steady* (1958), *Cactus Flower* (1969), and *Play Misty for Me* (1971).

Josephine Hutchinson (October 12, 1904–June 4, 1998). Hutchinson was an actress whose first role was as a child in Mary Pickford's *The Little Princess* (1917). As an adult, she was a leading lady in her younger years and appeared in character roles as she grew older, usually portraying sympathetic figures. Her screen credits include *Happiness Ahead* (1934), *Oil for the Lamps of China* (1935), *The Story of Louis Pasteur* (1936), *The Son of Frankenstein* (1939), *Tom Brown's School Days* (1940), *Somewhere in the Night* (1946), *Cass Timberlane* (1947), *Many Rivers to Cross* (1955), *North by Northwest* (1959), *The Adventures of Huckleberry Finn* (1960), *Baby the Rain Must Fall* (1965), and *Rabbit Run* (1970).

Persis Khambatta (October 2, 1950–August 18, 1998). Born in Bombay, India, Khambatta is best known for her role as Lieutenant Ilia, the bald, female crewmember of the *Starship Enterprise* in *Star Trek: The Motion Picture* (1979). This former Miss India (1960) remained in supporting roles in such films as *Nighthawks* (1981), *Megaforce* (1982), and *Warriors of the Lost World* (1984).

Keisuke Kinoshita (December 5, 1912–December 30, 1998). Kinoshita was a Japanese director who was greatly respected in his native country. Little known outside of Japan, Kinoshita directed his country's first color film, *Carmen Comes Home* (1951). He worked in a number of different genres, often writing his own screenplays. Kinoshita's screen credits include *The Blossoming Port* (1943), *Marriage* (1947), *Sea of Fireworks* (1951), *She Was Like a Wild Chrysanthemum* (1955), *Ballad of Narayama* (1958), *New Year's Love* (1962), *The Scent of Incense* (1964), *Love and Separation in Sri Lanka* (1975), *Children of Nagasaki* (1983), and *Big Joys, Small Sorrows* (1986).

Leonid Kinskey (April 18, 1903–September 9, 1998). Kinskey was a Russian-born character actor who moved to the United States in the early 1930s. He specialized in playing foreigners, most notably Sascha the bartender in *Casablanca* (1942). His additional screen credits include

Duck Soup (1933), *Les Miserables* (1935), *Rhythm on the Range* (1936), *Cafe Metropole* (1937), *The Story of Vernon and Irene Castle* (1939), *That Night in Rio* (1941), *The Talk of the Town* (1942), *Monsieur Beaucaire* (1946), *The Man with the Golden Arm* (1955), and *Glory* (1956).

Charles Korvin (November 21, 1907–June 18, 1998). Born Geza Korvin Karpathi in Czechoslovakia, Korvin was an actor who was featured in romantic leads and supporting roles in the 1940s and 1950s. He played the title role in *Enter Arsene Lupin* (1944), his film debut. After making *Sangaree* (1953), he ran afoul of the House Un-American Activities Committee, and was unable to work in Hollywood for over a decade, until Stanley Kramer cast him in *Ship of Fools* (1965). Korvin also worked extensively on stage and in television. His additional film credits include *This Love of Ours* (1945), *Temptation* (1946), *Berlin Express* (1948), *The Killer That Stalked New York* (1950), *Lydia Bailey* (1952), *The Man Who Had Power Over Women* (1970), and *Inside Out* (1975).

Akira Kurosawa (March 23, 1910–September 6, 1998). Kurosawa was a Japanese director who was one of the major figures of cinema in the second half of the twentieth century. Educated as a commercial artist, he began working in film in 1936, as an assistant to director Kajiro Yamamoto. By 1943, he was making his own films. The content of his early films, including *Judo Saga* (1943) and *The Most Beautiful* (1944), were dictated by the Japanese government, restricting his artistic freedom in one respect but also leaving him free to focus on developing the craftsmanship for which he became known. At the height of his career, Kurosawa usually produced, directed, wrote, and often edited his own films. After World War II, no longer forced to generate propaganda pieces, Kurosawa came into his own. In 1948, he began a long collaboration with actor Toshiro Mifune in *Drunken Angel* (1948); principally through his work with Kurosawa, Mifune achieved the stature of a cultural icon, representing Japanese values in much the same way that John Wayne came to embody certain American ideals. Kurosawa first became known in the West with *Rashomon* (1950), a story of murder and rape told from four different viewpoints, which won acclaim in Europe and North America, and earned an honorary Academy Award in 1951 as "the most outstanding foreign language film" of the year. Kurosawa's international influence was confirmed when his *Seven Samurai* (1954) inspired the Western *The Magnificent Seven* (1960),

Akira Kurosawa

and *Yojimbo* (1960) was remade as *A Fistful of Dollars* (1964). Following an unproductive period in the late 1960s and the early 1970s, when he was able to complete only one unsuccessful film and even attempted to commit suicide, Kurosawa returned to form with *Dersu Uzala* (1975), which won the Academy Award for Best Foreign Language Film. As he aged, Kurosawa became less prolific, but continued to produce masterpieces such as *Kagemush* (1980) and *Ran* (1985), an adaptation of Shakespeare's *King Lear,* for which he was nominated for an Academy Award as Best Director. In 1989, Kurosawa was given an Honorary Academy Award "for accomplishments that have inspired, delighted, enriched, and entertained audiences and influenced filmmakers throughout the world." His additional film credits include *The Quiet Duel* (1949), *Stray Dog* (1949), *I Live in Fear* (1955), *Throne of Blood* (1957), *Sanjuro* (1962), *Heaven and Hell* (1963), *Red Beard* (1965), *Dodeska-Den* (1970), *Akira Kurosawa's Dreams* (1990), *Rhapsody in August* (1991), and *Madadayo* (1993).

Charles B. Lang   (March 27, 1902–April 3, 1998). Lang was a cinematographer who began working in film during the Silent Era. He worked for Paramount during the 1930s and 1940s and later freelanced. Over his long career, he earned eighteen Academy Award nominations (the most by any artist in a single category), winning the award for *A Farewell to Arms* (1933). His screen credits include *The Right to Love* (1930), *Arise My Love* (1940), *Sundown* (1941), *So Proudly We Hail* (1943), *The Uninvited* (1944), *The Ghost and Mrs. Muir* (1947), *A Foreign Affair* (1948), *Sudden Fear* (1952), *Sabrina* (1954), *Queen Bee* (1955), *Some Like It Hot* (1959), *The Facts of Life* (1960), *How the West Was Won* (1963), *Bob & Carol & Ted & Alice* (1969), and *Butterflies Are Free* (1972) —all of which earned Lang Academy Award nominations.

Jack Lord   (December 30, 1928–January 21, 1998). Born John Joseph Ryan, Lord was an actor best known for his work as detective Steve McGarrett on the long running television series *Hawaii Five-0.*" He also starred as *Stoney Burke* in 1962–63. He was an artist and a screenwriter as well as an actor. Lord's screen credits include *Project X* (1949), *The Court-Martial of Billy Mitchell* (1955), *Tip on a Dead Jockey* (1957), *God's Little Acre* (1958), *Dr. No* (1962), and *The Counterfeit Killer* (1968).

Jack Lord

Roddy McDowall   (September 17, 1928–October 3, 1998). Born in England, McDowall was an actor who made

Roddy McDowall

several popular films as a teenager and sustained a lengthy career as a character actor thereafter. A child actor, McDowall's family moved to the United States in 1940, and he was signed by Darryl F. Zanuck to appear in John Ford's *How Green Was My Valley* (1941). That success led to lead roles in *My Friend Flicka* (1943) as well as *Lassie Come Home* (1943), in which co-starred with Elizabeth Taylor, who became a lifelong friend. McDowall's first adult role was that of Malcom in Orson Welles's production of *Macbeth* (1948). He alternated between stage and film work throughout the 1950s, and in the 1960s appeared with Taylor again in *Cleopatra* (1963). He also had a recurring role as the simian scientist Cornelius in *Planet of the Apes* (1968) and its sequels. He directed one film, *Tam Lin* (1971), also known as *The Devil's Widow*. McDowall was a respected photographer, and also maintained a personal archive of film memorabilia from Hollywood's golden age. His additional film credits include *Son of Fury* (1942), *The White Cliffs of Dover* (1944), *Thunderhead—Son of Flicka* (1945), *Kidnapped* (1948), *The Subterraneans* (1960), *The Longest Day* (1962), *The Greatest Story Ever Told* (1964), *The Loved One* (1965), *Lord Love a Duck* (1966), *Pretty Maids All in a Row* (1971), *Escape from the Planet of the Apes* (1971), *Bedknobs and Broomsticks* (1971), *Conquest of the Planet of the Apes* (1972), *The Poseidon Adventure* (1972), *Battle for the Planet of the Apes* (1973), *Funny Lady* (1975), *Fright Night* (1985), *The Grass Harp* (1996), and *A Bug's Life* (1998).

Wolf Mankowitz   (November 7, 1924–May 20, 1998). Mankowitz was a British novelist, playwright, and screenwriter who wrote or co-authored numerous scripts for English films, including *Expresso Bongo* (1959), a scathing satire on teen culture which he adapted from his own play. His screen credits include *A Kid for Two Farthings* (1955), *The Two Faces of Dr. Jekyll* (1960), *Waltz of the Toreadors* (1962), *Where the Spies Are* (1966), *Casino Royale* (1967), *Black Beauty* (1971), and *Treasure Island* (1972), which he co-authored with Orson Welles.

David Manners   (April 30, 1901–December 23, 1998). Born Rauff de Ryther Duan Acklom, Manners was a Canadian–born actor who is best remembered as Jonathan Harker, one of Bela Lugosi's foils in *Dracula* (1931), and in the title role in *The Mystery of Edwin Drood* (1935). He also appeared in other horror films, notably *The Mummy* (1932) and *The Black Cat* (1934). He retired from films after *A Woman Rebels* (1936). His additional screen credits include

Kismet (1930), *The Truth About Youth* (1930), *The Death Kiss* (1932), *The Moonstone* (1934), *Jalna* (1935), and *Hearts in Bondage* (1936).

Jean Marais (December 11, 1913–November 8, 1998). Marais was a French actor who was the protégé of director Jean Cocteau; together they made such films as *La Belle et la Bete* (1947), *Les Parents Terribles* (1948), *Orpheus* (1950), and *The Testament of Orpheus* (1960). His work with Cocteau established his popularity, and he became one of France's most prominent leading men, making a series of adventure films in the 1960s. Marais's additional film credits include *Le Bonheur* (1934), *Carmen* (1945), *The Secret of Mayerling* (1949), *Le Comte de Monte-Cristo* (1955), *White Nights* (1957), *Le Masque de Fer* (1962), *Fantomas* (1964), *Le Saint prend l'affut* (1966), *Fantomas contre Scotland Yard* (1967), *La Provocation* (1970), *Ombre et Secrets* (1983), and *Le Lien de Parente* (1986).

E.G. Marshall (June 18, 1910–August 24, 1998). Marshall was an actor best known for his forceful role as an attorney in the television series *The Defenders*, which ran from 1961–1965. He also appeared in *The New Doctors* segment of *The Bold Ones* from 1969–1973. His screen credits include *The House on 92nd Street* (1945), *Call Northside 777* (1948), *The Caine Mutiny* (1954), *Twelve Angry Men* (1957), *The Bachelor Party* (1957), *Town Without Pity*

E.G. Marshall

(1961), *The Chase* (1966), *Tora! Tora! Tora!* (1970), *Interiors* (1978), *Superman II* (1980), *Consenting Adults* (1992), and *Nixon* (1995).

Bob Merrill (May 17, 1921–February 17, 1998). Merrill was a composer and screenwriter. He wrote the lyrics to several hit songs of the 1950s and 1960s, including "(How Much Is That) Doggie in the Window" and "My Truly Fair," and wrote extensively for stage. Along with Jule Styne, Merrill was nominated for an Academy Award for the title song in the film *Funny Girl* (1968). As a screenwriter, his screen credits include *Mahogany* (1975) and *W.C. Fields and Me* (1976).

Theresa Merritt (September 24, 1924–June 12, 1998). Merritt was a stage, film, and television actress. The height of her fame came with a starring role in the television series *That's My Mama* in 1974. A decade later, she was nominated for a Tony for her role in *Ma Rainey's Black Bottom*. Her film credits include *The Wiz* (1978), *The Great Santini*

(1980), *The Serpent and the Rainbow* (1988), *Billy Madison* (1995), and *Home Fries* (1998).

Jeanette Nolan (December 30, 1911–June 5, 1998). Nolan was an actress who specialized in character roles. She is best known for her portrayal of Lady Macbeth in Orson Welles's *Macbeth* (1948). She also worked extensively on stage and in radio and television. She was married to actor John McIntire. Nolan's screen credits include *Words and Music* (1948), *Saddle Tramp* (1950), *The Big Heat* (1953), *April Love* (1957), *The Great Impostor* (1961), *The Man Who Shot Liberty Valance* (1962), *The Rescuers* (1977), *True Confessions* (1981), and *The Horse Whisperer* (1998).

Assia Noris (February 26, 1912–January 27, 1998). Born Anastasia von Gerzfeld in Russia, Noris was an actress who starred in numerous Italian films of the 1930s and 1940s. She was married for a time to director Mario Camerini, who cast her in his films. Her talents were unsuited to Italian neo-realism, and she seldom worked after the end of World War II. Noris's screen credits include *Tre Uomini in Frak* (1932), *Giallo* (1933), *Il Signor Max* (1937), *Dora Nelson* (1939), *Una Romantica Avventura* (1940), *Una Storia d'Amore* (1942), *I Dieci Comandamenti* (1945), *Amina* (1949), and *La Celestina* (1964).

Maureen O'Sullivan (May 17, 1911–June 22, 1998). Born in Ireland and educated in London and Paris, O'Sullivan was an actress who was best known for her portrayals of Jane, opposite Johnny Weismuller's Tarzan, in MGM's popular adventure series of the 1930s and 1940s. Her work in other MGM films usually involved lead roles in "B" films and secondary roles in the stu-

Maureen O'Sullivan

dio's more prestigious productions. She married director John Farrow in 1936, and retired from film in 1942 to raise her family, including actress Mia Farrow. O'Sullivan continued to appear in occasional films into the 1980s. Her screen credits include *So This Is London* (1930), *A Connecticut Yankee* (1931), *Tarzan the Ape Man* (1932), *Strange Interlude* (1932), *Tarzan and His Mate* (1934), *The Thin Man* (1934), *The Barretts of Wimpole Street* (1934), *David Copperfield* (1935), *Anna Karenina* (1935), *Tarzan Escapes* (1936), *A Day at the Races* (1937), *Tarzan Finds a Son* (1939), *Pride and Prejudice* (1940), *Tarzan's Secret Treasure* (1941), *Tarzan's New York Adventure* (1942), *Bonzo Goes to College* (1952), *Duffy of San Quentin* (1954), *Hannah and Her Sisters* (1986), *Peggy Sue Got Married* (1986), and *Stranded* (1987).

Alan J. Pakula (April 7, 1928–November 19, 1998). Pakula was a producer and director whose films were both critical and popular successes. After an apprenticeship which included stints at Warner Bros., MGM, and Paramount, he produced his first film, the study of mentally ill baseball player Jimmy Piersall, *Fear Strikes Out* (1957). He soon partnered with director Robert Mulligan to produce *To Kill a Mockingbird* (1962), which earned an Academy Award

Alan J. Pakula

nomination as Best Picture. Working on his own, he directed *The Sterile Cuckoo* (1969), but achieved greater success with the Jane Fonda vehicle *Klute* (1971), which earned Fonda an Academy Award. He became known as an actor's director, and his most acclaimed film of the 1970s was the Watergate-based political thriller *All the President's Men* (1976), which earned four Academy Awards out of eight nominations, including Best Picture and Best Directing for Pakula. *Sophie's Choice* (1982) solidified his reputation, earning the Best Actress Academy Award (Meryl Streep) and nominations in four other categories, including for Pakula's screenplay. In the 1990s, his biggest hits were *Presumed Innocent* (1990) and *The Pelican Brief* (1994). His output slowed over the last decade of his life, but he was still involved with filmmaking when he was killed in an automobile accident. He was married to actress Hope Lange from 1963–1969. Pakula's credits as a producer include *Love With the Proper Stranger* (1963), *Inside Daisy Clover* (1965), and *Up the Down Staircase* (1967). He directed *The Parallax View* (1974), *Comes a Horseman* (1978), *Starting Over* (1979), *Rollover* (1981), *Dream Lover* (1986), *Consenting Adults* (1992), and *The Devil's Own* (1997).

Gene Raymond (August 13, 1908–May 3, 1998). Born Raymond Guion, Raymond was an actor who was a leading man in "B" films of the 1930s. Handsome and blond, he was usually cast in romantic roles. He produced and directed *Million Dollar Weekend* (1948), in which he also acted. After his heyday, he continued to appear in films sporadically into the 1960s. He was married to actress Jeanette MacDonald, and appeared with her in one film, *Smilin' Through* (1941). Raymond's screen credits include *Personal Maid* (1931), *Red Dust* (1932), *Flying Down to Rio* (1933), *The Woman in Red* (1935), *Love on a Bet* (1936), *The Life of the Party* (1937), *Stolen Heaven* (1938), *Assigned to Danger* (1948), *Hit the Deck* (1955), *I'd Rather Be Rich* (1964), and *Five Bloody Graves* (1969).

Jerome Robbins (October 11, 1918–July 29, 1998). Born Jerome Rabinowitz, Robbins was a choreographer much honored in the dance community. His work included elements of both ballet and popular dance, and was highly influential on both stage and screen. His ballet "Fancy Free" (1944) inspired the film *On the Town* (1949). Similarly, his choreography for the Broadway stage plays was the basis for the dance scenes in *Gypsy* (1963) and *Fiddler on the Roof* (1971). He choreographed and co-directed (with Robert Wise) *West Side Story* (1961), earning an Academy Award for his directing efforts.

Roy Rogers (November 5, 1911–July 6, 1998). Born Leonard Slye, Rogers was a singer and actor who starred in "B" Westerns of the "singing cowboy" genre, sharing with Gene Autry the appellation "The King of the Cowboys." Rogers broke into show business as a musician, as one of the founding members of the successful country and western group Sons of the Pioneers. By

Roy Rogers

1935, he was appearing in films, including Gene Autry vehicles such as *Tumbling Tumbleweeds* (1935). When Autry entered the service in World War II, Republic tapped Rogers to fill the role of singing cowboy hero. His stock company included his wife, Dale Evans, sidekick Gabby Hayes, his horse Trigger, and his dog Bullet. Between 1942 and 1951, he made such films as *Sons of the Pioneers* (1942), *King of the Cowboys* (1943), *Don't Fence Me In* (1945), *My Pal Trigger* (1946), *Grand Canyon Trail* (1949), and *Heart of the Rockies* (1951). Like Autry, Rogers quickly realized that his appeal would translate well to the then-new medium of television, and *The Roy Rogers Show* was televised from 1951–1957. Also like Autry, Rogers was a shrewd businessman, and had significant real estate holdings as well as a chain of restaurants named after himself. His additional screen credits include *Under Western Stars* (1938), *The Arizona Kid* (1939), *Romance on the Range* (1942), *The Yellow Rose of Texas* (1944), *Eyes of Texas* (1948), *Son of Paleface* (1952), *Alias Jesse James* (1959), and *Mackintosh and T.J.* (1975).

Esther Rolle (November 8, 1920–November 17, 1998). Rolle became a familiar face to households due to her matriarchal role in the popular television series *Good Times* (1974–1979). But before and after the series, Rolle consistently made television and film appearances. Her credits include *Cleopatra Jones* (1973), *Driving Miss Daisy* (1989), *How to Make an American Quilt* (1995), *Rosewood* (1997), and *Down in the Delta* (1998).

Enrico Sabbatini (January 7, 1922–November 25, 1998). Sabbatini was an Italian costume designer who worked extensively in Europe and Hollywood for over three decades. He earned an Academy Award nomination for his work on *The Mission* (1986). Sabbatini's additional film credits include *The Tenth Victim* (1965), *Casanova '70* (1965), *More Than a Miracle* (1967), *Christ Stopped at Eboli* (1979), *Bloodline* (1979), *The Old Gringo* (1989), *Cutthroat Island* (1995), and *Seven Years in Tibet* (1997).

Frank Sinatra (December 12, 1915–May 14, 1998). Sina-

Frank Sinatra

tra was a singer and actor who became one of the towering figures of twentieth century American popular culture. He got his start as a singer in the big band era, and earned notoriety for inducing fainting and hysteria in his younger female fans, known as bobby-soxers. It was during this period that he made his film debut, with the Tommy Dorsey band in *Las Vegas Nights* (1941) and *Ship Ahoy* (1942). He left the Dorsey band for a career as a solo singer, which was considered something of a risky move at the time, but Sinatra made the transition successfully. His first acting role was in *Higher and Higher* (1943), and he was featured with Gene Kelly in the musicals *Anchors Aweigh* (1945) and *On the Town* (1949). In the early 1950s, problems with his vocal cords combined with the country's changing musical tastes led to a low ebb in Sinatra's career, which was revived when he persuaded Columbia to cast him as Angelo Maggio in *From Here to Eternity* (1953); he earned an Academy Award as Best Supporting Actor, which led to more serious acting roles, as well as feature roles in musicals. At about the same time, his musical career was resuscitated when he signed with Capitol Records and was teamed with arrangers such as Nelson Riddle and Billy May, with whom he made a series of classic "concept" albums in the 1950s. Sinatra made a wide variety of films over the next two decades. He made musicals such as *Guys and Dolls* (1955) and *High Society* (1956). He made serious films such as *The Man with the Golden Arm* (1955), for which he was nominated for an Academy Award, and *The Manchurian Candidate* (1962). He also made a series of action-adventure films with his Rat Pack buddies Dean Martin, Sammy Davis Jr., et al, including *Ocean's Eleven* (1960), *Sergeants 3* (1962), and *Robin and the 7 Hoods* (1964). Finally, he made several hard-boiled detective films, including *Tony Rome* (1967), *The Detective* (1968), *Lady in Cement* (1968), and *The First Deadly Sin* (1980). At the 1971 Academy Awards ceremony, Sinatra was given the Jean Hersholt Humanitarian Award. It is a measure of Sinatra's seminal contributions to popular music that his film career is usually considered an afterthought. Sinatra was always controversial, from his quick temper that led to public fisticuffs, to his occasional association with organized crime figures, to his stormy romantic relationships (he was married for a time to actresses Ava Gardner and Mia Farrow). In politics he was an active Kennedy Democrat until he was snubbed by JFK, at which point he became an outspoken backer of conservatives such as Spiro Agnew and Ronald Reagan, who awarded him the Medal of Freedom in 1985. His children, Frank Sinatra Jr. and Nancy Sinatra, are both singers. Sinatra's additional film credits include *The House I Live In* (1945), *It Happened in Brooklyn* (1947), *Take Me Out to the Ball Game* (1949), *Young at Heart* (1955), *The Tender Trap* (1955), *The Joker Is Wild* (1957), *Pal Joey* (1957), *Kings Go Forth* (1958), *A Hole in the Head* (1959), *Can-Can* (1960), *Come Blow Your Horn* (1963), *None but the Brave* (1965), *Von Ryan's Express* (1965), and *Dirty Dingus Magee* (1970).

Leslie Stevens (February 3, 1924–April 24, 1998). Stevens was a screenwriter, director, and producer who worked extensively in film and television. He created the science-fiction television series *Outer Limits*, which ran from 1963–1965, and also wrote and directed for such series as *McCloud* and *Men From Shiloh* in the 1970s. His first film screenplay was the Paul Newman vehicle *The Left-Handed Gun* (1958), and he also wrote *Marriage-Go-Round* (1961, adapted from his Broadway play), *Hero's Island* (1962), *Incubus* (1965), and *Battlestar Gallactica* (1978).

Catherine Turney (December 26, 1906–September 9, 1998). Turney was a screenwriter who specialized in writing films with strong female roles for actresses such as Bette Davis and Joan Crawford. Her film credits include *Mildred Pierce* (1945), *The Man I Love* (1946), *My Reputation* (1946), *One More Tomorrow* (1946), *Cry Wolf* (1947), and *Winter Meeting* (1948).

J. T. Walsh (April 28, 1943–February 27, 1998). Walsh was a character actor who is best known for his portrayal of a mental patient whose scenes frame Billy Bob Thornton's *Sling Blade* (1996). After beginning his career on stage, he entered film with *Eddie Macon's Run* (1983) and worked extensively in Hollywood thereafter. His additional screen credits include

J. T. Walsh

Good Morning Vietnam (1987), *Tin Men* (1987), *The Grifters* (1990), *A Few Good Men* (1992), *Hoffa* (1992), *Red Rock*

West (1993), *The Client* (1994), *Executive Decision* (1995), *Pleasantville* (1998), and *The Negotiator* (1998).

Robert Wells (October 15, 1922–September 23, 1998). Wells was a songwriter who was best known for writing the lyrics to Mel Torme's perennial hit, "The Christmas Song." He occasionally wrote for film, earning an Academy Award nomination for "It's Easy to Say" in Blake Edwards's *10* (1979). His additional film credits include *So Dear to My Heart* (1948) and *From Here to Eternity* (1953).

Helen Westcott (January 1, 1928–March 17, 1998). Born Myrthas Helen Hickman, Westcott was an actress who began working on stage as a child. At the age of seven, she appeared in *A Midsummer Night's Dream* (1935), and she made her adult film debut in *Adventures of Don Juan* (1948). In her twenties, she earned lead and second lead roles; thereafter, she played character parts. Her additional film credits include *Homicide* (1949), *The Gunfighter* (1950), *With a Song in My Heart* (1952), *Abbott and Costello Meet Dr. Jekyll and Mr. Hyde* (1953), *God's Little Acre* (1958), *The Last Hurrah* (1958), *Studs Lonigan* (1960), *Bourbon Street Shadows* (1962), and *I Love My Wife* (1970).

Freddie Young (October 9, 1902–December 1, 1998). Young was a British cinematographer known for his collaborations with director David Lean. Working with Lean, Young earned Academy Awards for his contributions to *Lawrence of Arabia* (1962), *Doctor Zhivago* (1965), and *Ryan's Daughter* (1970). His additional screen credits include *The Blue Danube* (1932), *When Knights Were Bold* (1936), *Goodbye Mr. Chips* (1939), *The Young Mr. Pitt* (1942), *Treasure Island* (1950), *Mogambo* (1953), *Lust for Life* (1956), *Island in the Sun* (1957), *The Inn of the Sixth Happiness* (1958), *Solomon and Sheba* (1959), *You Only Live Twice* (1967), *Nicholas and Alexandra* (1971), *Rough Cut* (1980), and *Invitation to the Wedding* (1984).

Robert Young (February 22, 1907–July 21, 1998). Young was an actor who achieved success in both film and television. His film career began with *The Black Camel* (1931), and he quickly specialized in affable leading man roles in films such as *The Sin of Madelon Claudet* (1931), *Strange Interlude* (1932), *The Vagabond Lady* (1935), and *Three Comrades* (1938). As he grew older,

Robert Young

he made the transition from romantic lead to the more fatherly type; and indeed, it was his facility in portraying wholesome family men that led to a second career in television. Contemporary audiences probably know Young best for his roles in two long running television series—that of Jim Anderson in *Father Knows Best*, which ran from 1954–1963, and the title role in *Marcus Welby, M.D.*, which ran from 1969–1976. Young acknowledge that, in his private life, he suffered from depression and alcoholism, but he survived both problems. Young's additional screen credits include *Tugboat Annie* (1933), *Death on the Diamond* (1934), *The Bride Wore Red* (1937), *Maisie* (1939), *Northwest Passage* (1940), *The Mortal Storm* (1940), *Western Union* (1941), *Sweet Rosie O'Grady* (1943), *Lady Luck* (1946), *They Won't Believe Me* (1947), *That Forsyte Woman* (1951), and *Secret of the Incas* (1954).

Henny Youngman (January 12, 1906–February 23, 1998). Youngman was a comedian best known for his one liners, including the famous "Take my wife—please!" Born in England, he moved to the United States as a child, and was a musician before becoming a comedian. During the course of his long career, he appeared in several films, including *A WAVE, a WAC and a Marine* (1944), *Nashville Rebel* (1966), *Won Ton Ton—The Dog Who Saved Hollywood* (1976), and *Silent Movie* (1976).

Robert Mitchell

Selected Film Books of 1998

Alpi, Deborah Lazaroff. *Robert Siodmak.*
Jefferson, North Carolina: McFarland, 1998.

Alpi offers a biography of the German-born American director, along with a complete filmography and a detailed analysis of his trademark film noir in the years after World War II.

Ankerich, Michael G. *The Sound of Silence.*
Jefferson, North Carolina: McFarland, 1998.

Ankerich presents interviews with sixteen actors who were active during the transition from the Silent Era to sound pictures.

Aulier, Dan. *Vertigo: The Making of a Hitchcock Classic.*
New York: St. Martin's Press, 1998.

Aulier traces the Hitchcock film from its origins as a French novel, through various screenplays, to the finished product that has fascinated critics for decades.

Bacon, Henry. *Visconti: Explorations of Beauty and Decay.*
New York: Cambridge University Press, 1998.

Bacon suggests that Visconti is the inheritor and renovator of nineteenth century narrative traditions in this scholarly study of the Italian director's film, stage, and operatic work.

Barta, Tony, editor. *Screening the Past: Film and the Representation of History.*
Westport, Connecticut: Praeger, 1998.

Barta offers this collection of sixteen scholarly essays on the relationships between the way historians look at the past and the way filmmakers represent the past on the screen.

Bernheimer, Kathryn. *The 50 Greatest Jewish Movies: A Critic's Ranking of the Very Best.*
Secaucus, New Jersey: Birch Lane, 1998.

Bernheimer discusses the films, famous and obscure, that, in her estimation, best illuminate various aspects of the Jewish experience.

Billingsley, Kenneth Lloyd. *Hollywood Party.*
Rocklin, California: Forum, 1998.

Billingsley is a political conservative who chronicles the Communist Party's attempts to infiltrate the American film industry in the 1930s and 1940s.

Biskind, Peter. *Easy Riders, Raging Bulls: How the Sex-Drugs-and-Rock 'n' Roll Generation Saved Hollywood.*
New York: Simon & Schuster, 1998.

Biskind chronicles the history of the generation of directors, including Lucas, Spielberg, Coppola, Penn, Altman, and Scorsese, who rose to prominence between 1967 and 1980, noting both their excesses and their achievements.

Black, Gregory D. *The Catholic Crusade Against the Movies, 1940–1975.*
New York: Cambridge University Press, 1998.

Black documents the rise and fall of the power of the Legion of Decency that sanctioned Hollywood films and influenced their content for over three decades.

Browne, Nick, editor. *Refiguring American Film Genres: History and Theory.*
Berkeley, California: University of California Press, 1998.

Brown presents nine essays on the evolution of a variety of American film genres in this scholarly volume.

Brunette, Peter. *The Films of Michelangelo Antonioni.*
New York: Cambridge University Press, 1998.

Brunette offers an overview of the Italian filmmaker's career, with special emphasis on his six most important films, including *L'avventura, Blow Up,* and *The Passenger.*

Cardullo, Bert, Harry Geduld, Ronald Gottesman, and Leigh Woods, editors. *Playing to the Camera: Film Actors Discuss Their Craft.*
New Haven, Connecticut: Yale University Press, 1998.

The editors collect forty-two essays and interviews with actors ranging from Louise Brooks and Bette Davis to Meryl Streep and Jack Nicholson, on various aspects of the art of acting for film.

Carroll, Noel. *Interpreting the Moving Image.*
New York: Cambridge University Press, 1998.

This volume collects twenty-four essays on topics ranging from Buster Keaton to contemporary art film, written by film theorist Carroll.

Chan, Jackie, and Jeff Yang. *I Am Jackie Chan: My Life in Action.*
New York: Ballantine Books, 1998.

Hong Kong action superstar Chan reveals the desperate poverty and brutal training regimen of his youth that enable him to do the stunts and other action sequences that have made him famous.

Chaplin, Lita Grey, and Jeffrey Vance. *Wife of the Life of the Party.*
Lanham, Maryland: Scarecrow Press, 1998.

Charlie Chaplin's first wife talks about their scandal-ridden marriage in this autobiography, which includes the first published transcripts of the oft-gossiped about depositions in their divorce proceedings.

Curran, Daniel. *Guide to American Cinema, 1965–1995.*
Westport, Connecticut: Greenwood Press, 1998.

Curran offers brief essays on the significant films and filmmakers during the long transition that began with the demise of the studio system and concludes with the beginning of the technological revolution which continues today.

Daniels, Bill, David Leedy, and Steven D. Stills. *Movie Money.*
Los Angeles: Silman-James Press, 1998.

The authors bring their legal, accounting, and technical expertise to bear on Hollywood's "creative" accounting practices in this volume on the business of filmmaking.

Durham, Carolyn A. *Double Takes: Culture and Gender in French Films and Their American Remakes.*
Hanover, New Hampshire: University Press of New England, 1998.

Hollywood remakes of French films, particularly comedies, have been popular in recent years. Durham analyzes this phenomenon, paying particular attention to issues of gender and culture.

Ehrenstein, David. *Open Secret: Gay Hollywood, 1928–1998.*
York: William Morrow, 1998.

Ehrenstein notes that gay men and women have always been a part of Hollywood and traces their history, from the closeted days to the more open contemporary atmosphere, in this discursive volume.

Erb, Cynthia. *Tracking King Kong: A Hollywood Icon in World Culture.*
Detroit, Michigan: Wayne State University Press, 1998.

Erb analyzes the film *King Kong*, from its production and immediate reception to its influences, in Hollywood and throughout popular culture.

Evans, Joyce A. *Celluloid Mushroom Clouds: Hollywood and the Atomic Bomb.*
Boulder, Colorado: Westview Press, 1998.

Evans studies the impact on American culture of Hollywood's treatment of the threat of atomic warfare, particularly in films made from 1946 to 1964.

Fleming, Charles. *High Concept: Don Simpson and the Hollywood Culture of Excess.*
New York: Doubleday, 1998.

Fleming writes about the career of bad boy producer Simpson, whose fast-lane life eventually led to his untimely death.

Fonda, Peter. *Don't Tell Dad: A Memoir.*
New York: Hyperion, 1998.

Fonda's autobiography chronicles his bumpy road to success in Hollywood and acknowledges his problematic relationship with his famous father.

Freese, Gene Scott. *Hollywood Stunt Performers.*
Jefferson, North Carolina: McFarland, 1998.

Freese has compiled a biographical dictionary of American stuntmen; entries include brief filmographies.

Fujiwara, Chris. *Jacques Tourneur: The Cinema of Nightfall.*
Jefferson, North Carolina: McFarland, 1998.

Fujiwara offers a detailed film-by-film analysis of the career of the filmmaker noted for atmospheric films including *Cat People* in the 1940s.

Fultz, Jay. *In Search of Donna Reed.*
Iowa City, Iowa: University of Iowa Press, 1998.

Fultz offers a biography of the actress who, through her eponymous television series, came to symbolize Eisenhower–era American motherhood.

Gaydos, Steven. *The Variety Guide to Film Festivals.*
New York: Perigee, 1998.

Gaydos provides a list of international film festivals, with annotations by staffers from *Variety* who offer inside information on what makes each event unique.

Gelbart, Larry. *Laughing Matters.*
New York: Random House, 1998.

Gelbart is a screenwriter and portions of this book are written like a screenplay that chronicle his adventures in writing for television's *M*A*S*H* and numerous film comedies.

Gianos, Phillip L. *Politics and Politicians in American Film.*
Westport, Connecticut: Praeger, 1998.

Gianos writes about the interaction between American politics and film, with chapters on film during the Great Depression, World War II, and Vietnam.

Gilmore, Michael T. *Differences in the Dark: American Movies and English Theater.*
New York: Columbia University Press, 1998.

Gilmore examines the difference in American and British culture, using film and theater as his lenses.

Girgus, Sam B. *Hollywood Renaissance.*
New York: Cambridge University Press, 1998.

Girgus examines the work of John Ford, Frank Capra, Howard Hawks, Fred Zinneman, and Elia Kazan, focusing on how these directors worked out their visions of America from the late 1930s into the early 1960s.

Good, Howard. *Girl Reporter: Gender, Journalism, and the Movies.*
Lanham, Maryland: Scarecrow Press, 1998.

Good offers a discursive analysis of the Torchy Blane films, a series of nine Warner Bros. films, released between 1937 and 1939, devoted to the exploits of a female reporter.

Grant, Barry Keith, and Jeannette Sloniowski, editors. *Documenting the Documentary.*
Detroit, Michigan: Wayne State University Press, 1998.

Grant and Sloniowski collect twenty-seven scholarly essays on documentary film classics from *Nanook of the North* to *Roger & Me.*

Green, Philip. *Cracks in the Pedestal: Ideology and Gender in Hollywood.*
Amherst, Massachusetts: University of Massachusetts Press, 1998.

Green offers a scholarly examination of how male-dominated Hollywood has responded to the feminist revolution of the 1970s, arguing that it has been characterized by ambivalence and outright resistance.

Gregg, Robert W. *International Relations on Film.*
Boulder, Colorado: Lynne Reinner, 1998.

Gregg provides a scholarly analysis of the ways in which cinema both reflects and influences American perceptions of foreign policy.

Hammontree, Patsy Guy. *Shirley Temple Black: A Bio-Bibliography.*
Westport, Connecticut: Greenwood Press, 1998.

Hammontree offers a biography of child star Shirley Temple, as well as a filmography of her work and a bibliographical essay on books and articles about the actress.

Harris, Warren G. *Sophia Loren.*
New York: Simon & Schuster, 1998.

Harris chronicles the life of the Italian actress who was a major international star in the 1950s and 1960s, in this biography.

Heston, Charlton, and Jean-Pierre Isbouts. *Charlton Heston's Hollywood.*
New York: GT Publishing, 1998.

Heston offers an anecdotal memoir of his life and career, copiously illustrated with production stills and sketches by the actor himself.

Horton, Andrew, and Stuart Y. McDougal, editors. *Play It Again Sam: Retakes on Remakes.*
Berkeley, California: University of California Press, 1998.

The editors collect nineteen scholarly essays that explore the boundaries of the concept of film remakes, including common characters in multiple films, international remakes, and transitions from one medium to another.

Iaccino, James F. *Jungian Reflections Within the Cinema.*
Westport, Connecticut: Praeger, 1998.

Iaccino analyzes contemporary science fiction and fantasy films from a Jungian psychological perspective, finding primordial archetypes in *Star Wars, Star Trek,* and other films.

Langer, Adam. *The Film Festival Guide.*
Chicago, Illinois: Chicago Review Press, 1998.

This reference work describes the major film festivals of the world, including information for filmmakers on how to enter their films in the competition and for fans on how to get tickets.

Langman, Larry. *American Film Cycles: The Silent Era.*
Westport, Connecticut: Greenwood Press, 1998.

Langman studies American films of the Silent Era in terms of thirty-six common themes, such as biography, divorce, gangsters, and vampires.

Langman, Larry. *Return to Paradise: A Guide to South Sea Island Films.*
Lanham, Maryland: Scarecrow Press, 1998.

Langman provides brief entries on approximately six hundred American films set in the South Sea Islands; annotations emphasize the impact of the Western and native cultures on each other.

Lewis, Jon, editor. *The New American Cinema.*
Durham, North Carolina: Duke University Press, 1998.

Lewis collects thirteen scholarly essays on contemporary American cinema, from Hollywood productions to those of independent filmmakers.

Liebman, Roy. *From Silents to Sound.*
Jefferson, North Carolina: McFarland, 1998.

Liebman offers a compendium of biographical sketches of the actors who made the transition from the silent to sound films; each entry contains a bibliography of critical reviews of the performers' early ventures into sound.

Lopate, Phillip. *Totally Tenderly Tragically.*
New York: Doubleday, 1998.

Lopate uses the three words in his title to describe his infatuation with the movies. His book is a collection of essays chronicling his engagement with films, filmmakers, and critics over the past thirty years.

Lovell, John P. *Insights from Film into Violence and Oppression.*
Westport, Connecticut: Praeger, 1998.

Lovell presents nine essays (including a filmography) on cinematic studies of violence, both personal and political.

McCall, Douglas L. *Film Cartoons.*
Jefferson, North Carolina: McFarland, 1998.

McCall provides a list, with brief annotations, of over 1,600 animated features and shorts produced in the United States in the twentieth century, along with short descriptions of the major American animation studios.

McDougal, Dennis. *The Last Mogul.*
New York: Crown, 1998.

McDougal offers a detailed biography of Lew Wasserman, cofounder of the MCA music and media giant. The coverage, which focuses on the business and politics of Hollywood, also includes extensive information about Wasserman's partner, Jules Stein.

Marlow-Trump, Nancy. *Ruby Keeler: A Photographic Biography.*
Jefferson, North Carolina: McFarland, 1998.

Marlow-Trump was a friend of actress-dancer Ruby Keeler. This biographical appreciation is illustrated with copious production stills and other photographs.

Martin, Len D. *The Republic Pictures Checklist.*
Jefferson, North Carolina: McFarland, 1998.

Martin provides a filmography, with brief plot summaries, of the features, serials, cartoons, shorts, and training films produced by the Republic studio from 1935–1959.

Maturi, Richard J., and Mary Buckingham Maturi. *Francis X. Bushman.*
Jefferson, North Carolina: McFarland, 1998.

Bushman was a prominent leading man in the early days of the Silent Era; the Maturis offer this survey of his life and career, complete with filmography.

Meyer, Janet L. *Sydney Pollack: A Critical Filmography.*
Jefferson, North Carolina: McFarland, 1998.

Meyer offers extended analyses of director Pollack's films, as well as a detailed filmography on all his projects.

Meyers, Jeffrey. *Gary Cooper: American Hero.*
New York: William Morrow, 1998.

Meyer presents an extensive biography of the actor who was an American icon, chronicling both his public career and his private life, and finding Cooper a contradictory figure.

Michaels, Lloyd. *The Phantom of the Cinema: Character in Modern Film.*
Albany, New York: State University of New York Press, 1998.

Michaels refers to feature films, art films, and documentaries in this scholarly examination of "the presence of absence"—the cinematic treatment of ambiguous characters.

Monsell, Thomas. *Nixon on Stage and Screen.*
Jefferson, North Carolina: McFarland, 1998.

Richard Nixon's achievements and mistakes have inspired an entire generation of playwrights and filmmakers; Monsell's work analyzes Nixon's depiction in films, plays, and television.

Morris, Willie. *The Ghosts of Medgar Evers: A Tale of Race, Mississippi, and Hollywood.*
New York: Random House, 1998.

Southern man of letters Morris offers a regional perspective on the making of *Ghosts of Mississippi,* about the murder of civil rights leader Medgar Evers.

Muir, John Kenneth. *Wes Craven: The Art of Horror.*
Jefferson, North Carolina: McFarland, 1998.

Muir offers a detailed analysis of the work of the American director whose films have been seminal to the development of the horror genre over the past quarter of a century.

Naremore, James. *More Than Night: Film Noir in Its Contexts.*
Berkeley, California: University of California Press, 1998.

Naremore examines the literary, political, economic, and cultural contexts of American film noir productions of the classic era of the 1940s and 1950s.

Natoli, Joseph. *Speeding to the Millenium: Film and Culture, 1993–1995.*
Albany, New York: State University of New York Press, 1998.

Natoli analyzes three years' worth of films in the context of life in the United States at the approach of the millenium.

Nevins, Francis M. *Joseph H. Lewis.*
Lanham, Maryland: Scarecrow Press, 1998.

Lewis was a filmmaker best known for his Westerns and film noir work in the 1940s and 1950s; Nevins provides a survey of his career, complete with an interview and filmography.

Nichols, Mary P. *Reconstructing Woody.*
Lanham, Maryland: Bowman & Littlefield, 1998.

Nichols examines a dozen Woody Allen films, released between 1972 and 1995, arguing that Allen constructs a moral world in which truth and virtue are possibilities.

Nourmand, Tony, and Graham Marsh, editors. *Film Posters of the 70s: The Essential Movies of the Decade.*
Woodstock, New York: Overlook Press, 1998.

The authors present a history of American cinema in the 1970s through a succession of posters for the most important films of that decade.

O'Sickey, Ingeborg Majer, and Ingeborg von Zadow, editors. *Triangulated Visions: Women in Recent German Cinema.*
Albany, New York: State University of New York Press, 1998.

The editors collect twenty-one scholarly essays on gender, sexuality, race, and class in German films of the past quarter century.

Parisi, Paula. *Titanic and the Making of James Cameron.*
New York: Newmarket Press, 1998.

Parisi follows the story of the world's most successful film to date, from director Cameron's first attempts to research the film to his Academy Award-winning triumph.

Phillips, Gene D. *Exiles in Hollywood.*
Bethlehem, Pennsylvania: Lehigh University Press, 1998.

Phillips chronicles the careers of the European filmmakers who fled to the United States after Hitler's rise to power in Germany in 1933.

Prince, Stephen. *Savage Cinema: Sam Peckinpah and the Rise of Ultraviolent Movies.*
Austin, Texas: University of Texas Press, 1998.

Prince argues that the violence in Peckinpah films such as *The Wild Bunch* and *Straw Dogs* is grounded in a more humanistic moral sensibility than the work of his contemporary imitators.

Rabkin, Leslie Y. *The Celluloid Couch.*
Lanham, Maryland: Scarecrow Press, 1998.

Rabkin has compiled an annotated filmography of films and television shows which relate to, or contain characters relating to, the mental health profession. The coverage is from the Silent Era to 1990.

Rainey, Buck. *Western Gunslingers in Fact and on Film.*
Jefferson, North Carolina: McFarland, 1998.

Rainey examines the cinematic portrayal of Billy the Kid, Wyatt Earp, and seven other famous Western heroes and villains, separating fact from fiction.

Rasmussen, Randy Loren. *Children of the Night.*
Jefferson, North Carolina: McFarland, 1998.

Rasmussen identifies six archetypal characters in classic horror films, and devotes a chapter each to the discussion of the significance of heroines, heroes, wise elders, mad scientists, servants, and monsters.

Reeve, Christopher. *Still Me.*
New York: Random House, 1998.

Reeve, the actor who was paralyzed in a riding accident, reviews his life and career, and does not avoid the unpleasant details of his life as a quadriplegic, in this autobiography.

Rich, B. Ruby. *Chick Flicks.*
Durham, North Carolina: Duke University Press, 1998.

Rich, a feminist film theorist, offers a collection of her essays, framed by her recollections of the times in which they were written.

Richards, Jeffrey, editor. *The Unknown 1930s: An Alternative History of the British Cinema 1929–1939.*
London: I.B. Tauris, 1998.

Richards's collection of eleven essays on the first decade of British sound film examines the lesser known aspects of English cinema in the 1930s.

Richards, Larry. *African American Films Through 1959.*
Jefferson, North Carolina: McFarland, 1998.

Richards provides a filmography of over 1,300 feature and documentary films with African American casts and/or plots, released between 1895 and 1959.

Ross, Steven J. *Working-Class Hollywood: Silent Film and the Shaping of Class in America.*
Princeton, New Jersey: Princeton University Press, 1998.

Ross argues that, prior to World War I, films for and about the working class dominated American screens, and that these films helped shape class identities in the first quarter of the twentieth century.

Russell, Sharon A. *Guide to African Cinema.*
Westport, Connecticut: Greenwood Press, 1998.

Russell provides a scholarly survey of African film history, with entries on the continent's important films and filmmakers.

Sainer, Arthur. *Zero Dances.*
New York: Limelight Editions, 1998.

Sainer's book is a biography of the popular stage and screen actor Zero Mostel, with a filmography of his feature films.

Samuels, Robert. *Hitchcock's Bi-Textuality: Lacan, Feminisms, and Queer Theory.*
Albany, New York: State University of New York Press, 1998.

Samuels combines a variety of scholarly theoretical approaches to argue that Hitchcock's films can be interpreted from a gay or bisexual perspective.

Sandler, Kevin S., editor. *Reading the Rabbit: Explorations in Warner Bros. Animation.*
New Brunswick, New Jersey: Rutgers University Press, 1998.

Sandler offers this collection of thirteen essays on various aspects of the history of animation at the Warner Bros. studio in this scholarly volume.

Sarris, Andrew, editor. *The St. James Film Directors Encyclopedia.*
Farmington Hills, Michigan: Visible Ink Press, 1998.

This useful reference work contains biographical and critical essays on approximately five hundred directors, from the Silent Era to the present day.

Sarris, Andrew. *"You Ain't Heard Nothin' Yet."*
New York: Oxford University Press, 1998.

Distinguished critic Sarris has produced a history of the first two decades (1927–1949) of American sound film, with chapters covering the important studios, genres, directors, and actors of the period.

Schweizer, Peter, and Rochelle Schweizer. *Disney: The Mouse Betrayed.*
Washington, D.C.: Regnery, 1998.

The Schweizers voice alarm over the transformation of the Disney studio from its axiomatically family friendly films of yesteryear to what they consider to be a profit-driven entertainment conglomerate, with some products unsuitable for children.

Scovell, Jane. *Oona: Living in the Shadows.*
New York: Warner Books, 1998.

Scovell's biography of Oona O'Neill Chaplin, daughter of Eugene O'Neill and wife of Charlie Chaplin, portrays her marriage as a happy one, and a haven from the disdain of her father.

Sherk, Warren M. *The Films of Mack Sennett.*
Lanham, Maryland: Scarecrow Press, 1998.

Sennett was the Silent Era producer responsible for the Keystone Kops and other classic comedies of the time. Sherk has compiled a comprehensive list of his work, complete with cast and credits information for 855 films released between 1912 and 1933.

Sikov, Ed. *On Sunset Boulevard: The Life and Times of Billy Wilder.*
New York: Hyperion, 1998.

Filmmaker Wilder is famous for embellishing the details of his life. Sikov attempts to separate the fact from the fiction in this detailed and well-researched biography.

Silverman, Kaja, and Harun Farocki. *Speaking About Godard.*
New York: New York University Press, 1998. This book records an extended conversation between filmmaker Farocki and professor Silverman about eight films by French director Jean-Luc Godard.

Skal, David J. *Screams of Reason: Mad Science and Modern Culture.*
New York: W.W. Norton, 1998.

Skal investigates the figure of the mad scientist as cinematic villain, and notes the popularity of the "science run amok" theme from the earliest days of the Silent Era to contemporary works such as *Jurassic Park.*

Skarlew, Bruce H., Bonnie S. Kaufman, Ellen Handler Spitz, and Diane Borden, editors. *Bertolucci's The Last Emperor: Multiple Takes.*
Detroit, Michigan: Wayne State University Press, 1998.

The editors present fourteen essays on various aspects of Bernardo Bertolucci's *The Last Emperor* in this scholarly volume, which also includes a foreword by the director himself.

Sklar, Robert, and Vito Sagarrio, editors. *Frank Capra: Authorship and the Studio System.*
Philadelphia, Pennsylvania: Temple University Press, 1998.

This is a collection of nine scholarly essays focusing on the great American filmmaker's achievement of a distinct personal vision in the midst of a corporate studio system at Columbia.

Slide, Anthony. *The New Historical Dictionary of the American Film Industry.*
Lanham, Maryland: Scarecrow Press, 1998.

This is a major revision of Slide's 1986 work, with over eight hundred entries on American film companies, organizations, and studios, as well as definitions of film terminology.

Smith, Scott. *The Film 100.*
Secaucus, New Jersey: Citadel, 1998.

Smith provides essays on the individuals—actors, directors, studio executives, and technicians—whom he considers most important in the history of cinema.

Soila, Tytti, Astrid Soderbergh Widding, and Gunnar Iversen. *Nordic National Cinemas.*
New York: Routledge, 1998.

This volume devotes a chapter each to the history of film in Denmark, Finland, Iceland, Norway, and Sweden, noting the distinctions between the five national cinemas.

Sopocy, Martin. *James Williamson: Studies and Documents of a Pioneer of the Film Narrative.*
Madison, New Jersey: Fairleigh Dickinson University Press, 1998.

Williamson was a pioneer in the art of motion photography. Sopocy presents a study of his work plus a collection of his papers in this scholarly volume.

Stephens, Michael L. *Art Directors in Cinema.*
Jefferson, North Carolina: McFarland, 1998.

Stephens presents a biographical directory, international in scope, of individuals involved in production design; each entry is accompanied by a brief filmmography.

Tashiro, C.S. *Pretty Pictures: Production Design and the History of Film.*
Austin, Texas: University of Texas Press, 1998.

Tashiro offers a scholarly analysis of the role of production design in the evolution of cinema.

Tibbetts, John C., and James M. Welsh. *The Encyclopedia of Novels into Film.*
New York: Facts on File, 1998.

This reference work is arranged alphabetically by the title of each novel; entries include an analysis of the book and film(s) which were derived from it, plus a brief bibliography.

Van Heerden, Bill. *Film and Television In-Jokes.*
Jefferson, North Carolina: McFarland, 1998.

This reference work, arranged by film and television series title, lists nearly two thousand allusions, parodies, cameos, and similar references from one production to another.

Wagg, Stephen, editor. *Because I Tell a Joke Or Two: Comedy, Politics and Social Difference.*
London: Routledge, 1998.

Wagg presents a collection of fifteen scholarly essays which analyze the relationship between comedy and such social issues as ethnicity, gender, class, age, and politics.

Waldman, Harry. *Paramount in Paris.*
Lanham, Maryland: Scarecrow Press, 1998.

Waldman offers a filmography of three hundred films produced at Paramount's Joinville Studios in Paris, from 1930 to 1933.

Watkins, S. Craig. *Representing: Hip Hop Culture and the Production of Black Cinema.*
Chicago, Illinois: University of Chicago Press, 1998.

Watkins analyzes American black youth culture and its representation in contemporary American film.

Weaver, Tom. *Science Fiction and Fantasy Film Flashbacks.*
Jefferson, North Carolina: McFarland, 1998.

Weaver interviews twenty-four actors, writers, producers, and directors who reminisce about their work in "B" science fiction and fantasy films from the 1940s through the 1960s.

Weld, John. *September Song: An Intimate Biography of Walter Huston.*
Lanham, Maryland: Scarecrow Press, 1998.

Weld was a friend of actor Walter Huston, father of director John Huston and grandfather of actress Anjelica Huston; he draws upon his first hand knowledge to produce this biography.

Whissen, Thomas. *Guide to American Cinema, 1930–1965.*
Westport, Connecticut: Greenwood Press, 1998.

Whissen offers brief essays and bibliographies on the films and filmmakers he considers to be of the greatest significance during the first thirty-five years of the sound era.

Winfrey, Oprah. *Journey to Beloved.*
New York: Hyperion, 1998.

This is Winfrey's diary of the production of *Beloved,* which she produced and starred in, illustrated with photographs by Ken Regan.

Wood, Robin. *Sexual Politics and Narrative Film: Hollywood and Beyond.* New York: Columbia University Press, 1998.

Wood offers sixteen scholarly essays on various film and gender issues, including marriage, family, romantic love, and sexism.

Xing, Jun. *Asian America Through the Lens.*
Walnut Creek, California: Alta Mira Press, 1998.

Xing examines the work of Asian American filmmakers, comparing their work to that of other ethnic minorities.

Yaquinto, Marilyn. *Pump 'Em Full of Lead: A Look at Gangsters on Film.*
New York: Twayne, 1998.

Yaquinto surveys the changing image of the gangster on screen from the Silent Era films of D.W. Griffith through the post-modern work of Quentin Tarantino.

Robert Mitchell

Magill's Cinema Annual 1999
Indexes

Directors

Screenwriters

HENSLEIGH, JONATHAN
Armageddon 22

HERLIHY, TIM
The Waterboy 586
The Wedding Singer 588

HERMAN, MARK
Little Voice 298

HERZFELD, JIM
Meet the Deedles 332

HIRST, MICHAEL
Elizabeth 140

HOLMES, RICHARD
Shooting Fish 481

HOPKINS, KAREN LEIGH
Stepmom 529

HORTA, SILVIO
Urban Legend 574

HOWARD, SIDNEY
Gone With the Wind 185

HOWITT, PETER
Sliding Doors 495

HSIAO, RITA
Mulan 354

IACONE, JEREMY
One Tough Cop 382

IVORY, JAMES
A Soldier's Daughter Never
Cries 509

JAGLOM, HENRY
Deja Vu 123

JAKOBY, DON
John Carpenter's Vampires
261

JANSZEN, KAREN
Digging to China 126

JAOUI, AGNES
Un Air de Famille 567

JENKINS, TAMARA
Slums of Beverly Hills 497

**JHABVALA, RUTH
PRAWER**
A Soldier's Daughter Never
Cries 509

JOHNSON, BAYARD
Tarzan and the Lost City
538

JOHNSON, DAVID C.
Woo 613

JOHNSON, MARK STEVEN
Jack Frost 259
Simon Birch 485

JONES, KIRK
Waking Ned Devine 584

KAPLAN, DEBORAH
Can't Hardly Wait 77

KAR-WAI, WONG
Fallen Angels 151

KASDAN, JAKE
Zero Effect 625

KATTAN, CHRIS
A Night at the Roxbury 369

KATZ, JORDAN
Incognito 256

KAZAN, NICHOLAS
Fallen 150
Homegrown 226

KELLY, PATRICK SMITH
A Perfect Murder 407

KETRON, LARRY
The Only Thrill 385

KING, ZALMAN
In God's Hands 253

KITANO, TAKESHI
Fireworks 161
Sonatine 510

KLAPISCH, CEDRIC
Un Air de Famille 567

KLASS, DAVID
Desperate Measures 125

KOEPP, DAVID
Snake Eyes 504

KOHERR, BOB
Plump Fiction 420

KONNER, LAWRENCE
Mercury Rising 337
Mighty Joe Young 342

KOONTZ, DEAN
Phantoms 410

KOPPELMAN, BRIAN
Rounders 461

KOREN, STEVE
A Night at the Roxbury
369

KOUF, JIM
Rush Hour 466

KOURKOV, ANDREI
A Friend of the Deceased
166

KOVACEVIC, DUSAN
Underground 572

KUSTURICA, EMIR
Underground 572

**KWIETNIOWSKI,
RICHARD**
Love and Death on Long Is-
land 311

LA FRENAIS, IAN
Still Crazy 531

LABUTE, NEIL
Your Friends & Neighbors
620

LAGRAVENESE, RICHARD
Beloved 37
Living Out Loud 302
The Horse Whisperer 230

LAMANNA, ROSS
Rush Hour 466

LAMPRELL, MARK
Babe: Pig in the City 31

LANDIS, JOHN
Blues Brothers 2000 56

LANGLEY, NOEL
The Wizard of Oz 612

LAZEBNIK, PHILIP
Mulan 354
The Prince of Egypt 432

LEAVITT, CHARLES
The Mighty 341

LEE, SPIKE
He Got Game 210

LELAND, DAVID
The Land Girls 278

LEPAGE, ROBERT
Nô 375

LEVANGIE, GIGI
Stepmom 529

LEVIEN, DAVID
Rounders 461

LEVIN, LARRY
Dr. Dolittle 132

LEVIN, MARC
Slam 493

LEVIN, MARK
Madeline 317

LINK, CAROLINE
Beyond Silence 40

LINKLATER, RICHARD
The Newton Boys 364

LOCASH, ROBERT
BASEketball 34

LORIGA, RAY
Live Flesh 300

LUNA, BIGAS
The Chambermaid on the
Titanic 85

MA, FIBE
Mr. Nice Guy 348

MACCOBY, NORA
Bongwater 57

MACDONALD, NORM
Dirty Work 128

MACPHERSON, DON
The Avengers 27

MALICK, TERRENCE
The Thin Red Line 548

MALONE, BONZ
Slam 493

MAMET, DAVID
The Spanish Prisoner 515

MANCINI, DON
Bride of Chucky 61

MARCONI, DAVID
Enemy of the State 143

MARSHALL, NEIL
Killing Time 264

MASTER P
I Got the Hook-Up 239

MATTHEWS, DARYL
Dance With Me 105

MAULDIN, NAT
Dr. Dolittle 132

MAY, ELAINE
Primary Colors 429

MAYBURY, JOHN
Love is the Devil 314

MAZIN, CRAIG
Senseless 475

MCCANLIES, TIM
Dancer, Texas Population 81
107

MCENERY, DONALD
A Bug's Life 70

MCGOVERN, JIMMY
Go Now 177

MCGUINNESS, FRANK
Dancing at Lughnasa 110
Talk of Angels 537

Cinematographers

Cinematographers

Editors

Art Directors

Art Directors

Music Directors

Music Directors

Performers

BLEETH, YASMINE
BASEketball 33

BLETHYN, BRENDA
Little Voice 295
Music From Another Room
354

BLOCH, BERNARD
Ronin 456

BLONDELL, JOAN
Grease 188

BODROV JR., SERGEI
Brother 64

BOGDANOVICH, PETER
Mr. Jealousy 345

BOHRER, CORINNE
Star Kid 520

BOHRINGER, ROMANE
The Chambermaid on the
Titanic 84

BOLGER, RAY
The Wizard of Oz 609

BONET, LISA
Enemy of the State 140

BONI, GABRIELLE
Little Men 293

BONIFANT, J. EVAN
Blues Brothers 2000 54

BONNAL, FREDERIQUE
Marius and Jeannette 324

BONNEVIE, MARIA
Insomnia 256

BORGNINE, ERNEST
BASEketball 33

BOSCO, PHILLIP
Moon Over Broadway 350

BOSWELL, ANTHONY
I Got the Hook-Up 238

BOUAJILA, SAMI
The Siege 481

BOUDET, JACQUES
Marius and Jeannette 324

BOUGERE, TEAGLE F.
The Impostors 250

BOURDO, SACHA
Western 589

**BOUTOUSSOV,
VIATCHESLAV**
Brother 64

BOWEN, JAKE
Patch Adams 399

BOYLE, ALAN
The Butcher Boy 73

BOYLE, LARA FLYNN
Happiness 198

BOYLE, PETER
Dr. Dolittle 129

BRACCO, ELIZABETH
The Impostors 250

BRADY, JUSTIN
TwentyFourSeven 556

BRAEDEN, ERIC
Meet the Deedles 330

BRAIDWOOD, TOM
The X-Files 615

BRANAGH, KENNETH
Celebrity 78
The Gingerbread Man 173
The Proposition 432
The Theory of Flight 538

BRANDON, MICHAEL
Déjà Vu 122

BRANDY
I Still Know What You Did
Last Summer 241

BRASCHI, NICOLETTA
Life Is Beautiful 291

BRASSARD, MARIE
Nô 373

BRAUGHER, ANDRÉ
City of Angels 91

BRAZEAU, JAY
Air Bud: Golden Receiver 4

BRENNAN, BRID
Dancing at Lughnasa 107

BRENNEMAN, AMY
Your Friends & Neighbors
618

BREUR, JIM
Half-Baked 193

BREWSTER, JORDANA
The Faculty 145

BRIDGES, JEFF
The Big Lebowski 43

BRIDGES, LLOYD
Mafia! 317

BRIGHTWELL, PAUL
Sliding Doors 493

BRISCOE, BRENT
A Simple Plan 485

BRITTON, CONNIE
No Looking Back 375

BROADBENT, JIM
The Avengers 24
The Borrowers 57
Little Voice 295

BRODERICK, ERIN
Black Dog 49

BRODERICK, MATTHEW
Godzilla 180

BRODY, ADRIEN
The Thin Red Line 545

BROLIN, JOSH
Nightwatch 369

**BROOKHURST,
MICHELLE**
Can't Hardly Wait 75

BROOKS, ALBERT
Dr. Dolittle 129
Out of Sight 389

BROOKS, ANNABEL
Love is the Devil 311

BROOKS, AVERY
American History X 11
The Big Hit 40

BROOKS, RAND
Gone With the Wind 182

BROSNAN, PIERCE
Quest for Camelot 437

**BROWN, DOWNTOWN
JULIE**
Ride 453

BROWN, JAMES
Blues Brothers 2000 54
Holy Man 219

BROWN, JIM
He Got Game 207

BROWN, JULIE
Plump Fiction 418

BROWN, MELANIE
Spice World 519

BROWN, W. EARL
There's Something About
Mary 540

BROWNE, ROSCOE LEE
Babe: Pig in the City 28

BRYNOLFSSON, REINE
Les Miserables 286

BUCHHOLZ, HORST
Life Is Beautiful 291

BUGAJSKI, MONICA
Shadrach 475

BUJOLD, GENEVIÈVE
Last Night 280

BULLMORE, AMELIA
Mrs. Dalloway 342

BULLOCK, SANDRA
Hope Floats 226
Practical Magic 423
The Prince of Egypt 429

BUNCE, STUART
Regeneration 446

BUONO, CARA
Next Stop Wonderland 364

BURGHARDT, ARTHUR
Star Kid 520

BURKE, BILLY
Mafia! 317
Without Limits 606
The Wizard of Oz 609

BURKE, KATHY
Dancing at Lughnasa 107
Elizabeth 138
Nil By Mouth 371

BURKE, ROBERT JOHN
First Love, Last Rites 161

BURNETT, CAROL
Moon Over Broadway 350

BURNS, EDWARD
No Looking Back 375
Saving Private Ryan 469

BURNS, HEATHER
You've Got Mail 620

BURROUGHS, JACKIE
Last Night 280

BURSTYN, ELLEN
Deceiver 116
Playing by Heart 414

BURTON, EMMA
Spice World 519

BURTON, KATE
Celebrity 78

BURTON, LEVAR
Star Trek: Insurrection 522

BUSCEMI, STEVE
Armageddon 18
The Big Lebowski 43
The Impostors 250
The Wedding Singer 586

BUSEY, GARY
Fear and Loathing in Las
Vegas 151
Soldier 504

BUSEY, JAKE
Home Fries 222

BUSSIERES, PASCALE
August 32nd on Earth 23
Twilight of the Ice Nymphs
560

Performers

COBURN, JAMES
Affliction *1*

COHEN, GREG
Wild Man Blues *599*

COHEN, LYNN
Hurricane Streets *234*

COLE, GARY
I'll Be Home for Christmas *247*
A Simple Plan *485*

COLEMAN, DABNEY
You've Got Mail *620*

COLLETTE, TONI
Clockwatchers *98*
Velvet Goldmine *576*

COLLINS, RAY
Touch of Evil *548*

CONAWAY, JEFF
Grease *188*

CONN, DIDI
Grease *188*

CONNELLY, JENNIFER
Dark City *111*

CONNERY, SEAN
The Avengers *24*
Playing by Heart *414*

CONNICK JR., HARRY
Hope Floats *226*

CONNOLLY, BILLY
The Impostors *250*
Still Crazy *529*

CONNOLLY, JOHN G.
Whatever *594*

CONRAD, DAVID
Return to Paradise *451*

CONWAY, KEVIN
Mercury Rising *335*

CONWAY, TIM
Air Bud: Golden Receiver *4*

COOKS, BEN
Little Men *293*

COOLIO
An Alan Smithee Film: Burn Hollywood Burn *6*

COONEY, KEVIN
Clockwatchers *98*

COOPER, CHRIS
Great Expectations *190*
The Horse Whisperer *228*

CORDUNER, ALLAN
The Impostors *250*

CORMAN, MADDIE
I Think I Do *243*

CORRIGAN, KEVIN
Buffalo 66 *65*
Henry Fool *210*
Illtown *248*
Slums of Beverly Hills *495*

COSMO, JAMES
Babe: Pig in the City *28*

COSTANZO, ANTHONY ROTH
A Soldier's Daughter Never Cries *506*

COSTANZO, ROBERT
Air Bud: Golden Receiver *4*
Plump Fiction *418*

COTTERILL, CHRISSIE
Nil By Mouth *371*

COTTON, JOSEPH
Touch of Evil *548*

COULSON, BERNIE
Hard Core Logo *201*

COVERT, ALLEN
The Waterboy *584*
The Wedding Singer *586*

COX, ALAN
Mrs. Dalloway *342*

COX, BRIAN
Desperate Measures *123*
Rushmore *466*

COX, CLAIRE
Shooting Fish *479*

COX, DAVE
Kitchen Party *268*

COYOTE, PETER
Patch Adams *399*
Sphere *516*

CRAIG, DANIEL
Elizabeth *138*
Love is the Devil *311*

CRANITCH, LORCAN
Dancing at Lughnasa *107*

CRANSHAW, PATRICK
Almost Heroes *9*
Broken Vessels *62*

CREED-MILES, CHARLIE
Nil By Mouth *371*

CRENNA, RICHARD
Wrongfully Accused *613*

CREWS, LAURA HOPE
Gone With the Wind *182*

CROMWELL, JAMES
Babe: Pig in the City *28*

Deep Impact *118*
Species II *515*

CRONAUER, GAIL
The Newton Boys *362*

CRONENBERG, DAVID
Last Night *280*

CROSS, DAVID
Small Soldiers *497*

CROSS, JOSEPH
Desperate Measures *123*
Jack Frost *257*
Wide Awake *598*

CRUDUP, BILLY
The Hi-Lo Country *212*
Monument Ave. *348*
Without Limits *606*

CRUZ, ALEXIS
Why Do Fools Fall in Love *596*

CRUZ, PENELOPE
The Hi-Lo Country *212*
Live Flesh *298*
Talk of Angels *535*

CRUZ, TANIA
Men With Guns *333*

CRYER, JON
Holy Man *219*

CRYSTAL, BILLY
My Giant *355*

CUDLITZ, MICHAEL
Follow the Bitch *162*

CULKIN, KIERAN
The Mighty *338*

CUMMING, ALAN
Spice World *519*

CURTIN, JANE
Antz *13*

CURTIS, CLIFF
Six Days, Seven Nights *488*

CURTIS, JAMIE LEE
Halloween H20 *194*
Homegrown *224*

CUSACK, JOHN
The Thin Red Line *545*

CZYPIONKA, HANSA
Beyond Silence *38*

DAGGETT, JENSEN
Major League: Back to the Minors *319*

DAILY, E. G.
Babe: Pig in the City *28*
The Rugrats Movie *461*

DALY, TIM
The Object of My Affection *377*

DAMON, MATT
Rounders *459*
Saving Private Ryan *469*

DAMON, UNA
Deep Rising *120*

DAMPF, SARAH
City of Angels *91*

DANARE, MALCOLM
Godzilla *180*

DANCE, CHARLES
Hilary and Jackie *217*

DANES, CLAIRE
Les Miserables *286*
Polish Wedding *420*

D'ANGELO, BEVERLY
American History X *11*
A Rat's Tale *440*

DANIELS, ALEX
Star Kid *520*

DANIELS, BEN
Madeline *315*
Passion in the Desert *396*

DANIELS, JEFF
Pleasantville *416*

DANNER, BLYTHE
No Looking Back *375*
The Proposition *432*
The X-Files *615*

DANSON, TED
Homegrown *224*
Saving Private Ryan *469*

DANTAS, NELSON
Four Days in September *163*

DANTE, PETER
The Waterboy *584*

DANZA, TONY
Illtown *248*

D'ARBANVILLE, PATTI
Celebrity *78*

DARROUSSIN, JEAN-PIERRE
Marius and Jeannette *324*
Un Air de Famille *566*

DAVID, ANGEL
Two Girls and a Guy *562*

DAVID, KEITH
Armageddon *18*
There's Something About Mary *540*

Performers

Performers

Performers

MAC, BERNIE
The Players Club *412*

MACAULAY, MARC
Holy Man *219*

MACCIONE, ALDO
The Chambermaid on the
Titanic *84*

MACDONALD, KELLY
Cousin Bette *100*

MACDONALD, NORM
Dirty Work *126*
Dr. Dolittle *129*

MACDONALD, SCOTT
A Rat's Tale *440*

MACDOWELL, ANDIE
Shadrach *475*

MACKAY, JOHN
Niagara, Niagara *366*

MACKICHAN, DOON
The Borrowers *57*

MACKINTOSH, STEVEN
The Land Girls *276*

MACNEE, PATRICK
The Avengers *24*

MACNEIL, PETER
The Hanging Garden *196*

MACY, WILLIAM H.
A Civil Action *93*
Pleasantville *416*
Psycho *434*

MADSEN, MICHAEL
Species II *515*

MAELEN, CHRISTIAN
I Think I Do *243*

MAGNUSON, ANN
Small Soldiers *497*

MAGUIRE, TOBEY
Fear and Loathing in Las
Vegas *151*
Pleasantville *416*

MAHONEY, JOHN
Antz *13*

MAKI-SAN, MASEO
Orgazmo *388*

MALGRAS, FREDERIC
Marie Baie des Anges *322*

MALKOVICH, JOHN
The Man in the Iron Mask
320
Rounders *459*

MALONE, BONZ
Slam *492*

MALONE, JENA
Stepmom *527*

MANDYLOR, COSTAS
Just Write *261*

MANHEIM, CAMRYN
Happiness *198*
Wide Awake *598*

MANN, DANNY
Babe: Pig in the City *28*

MANN, GABRIEL
High Art *214*

MANOFF, DINAH
Grease *188*

MANOJLOVIC, MIKI
Artemisia *22*
Underground *569*

MANTEGNA, JOE
Celebrity *78*

MAPLES, MARLA
Happiness *198*

MARCEAU, SOPHIE
Firelight *155*

MARCH, JANE
Tarzan and the Lost City
537

MARGOLIS, MARK
Pi *410*

MARGOYLES, MIRIAM
Mulan *351*

MARGULIES, JULIANNA
The Newton Boys *362*
A Price Above Rubies *424*

MARIANA, MICHELE
Zero Effect *622*

MARIENTHAL, ELI
Slums of Beverly Hills *495*

MARIN, CHEECH
Paulie *401*

MARINO, DAN
Holy Man *219*

MARKS, AVIVA
Déjà Vu *122*

MARSDEN, JAMES
Disturbing Behavior *128*

MARTIN, ALEXIS
August 32nd on Earth *23*
Nô *373*

MARTIN, DICK
Air Bud: Golden Receiver *4*

MARTIN, STEVE
The Prince of Egypt *429*
The Spanish Prisoner *512*

MARTINDALE, MARGO
Twilight *557*

MARTINEZ, OLIVIER
The Chambermaid on the
Titanic *84*

MASHKOV, VLADIMIR
The Thief *542*

MASSEY, ANNA
Déjà... Vu *122*

MASTER P
I Got the Hook-Up *238*

**MASTERSON, MARY
STUART**
Digging to China *125*

MATARAZZO, HEATHER
Hurricane Streets *234*

MATHERON, MARIE
Western *589*

MATHESON, HANS
Les Miserables *286*
Still Crazy *529*

MATTHAU, WALTER
Neil Simon's The Odd Cou-
ple 2 *360*

MAURIER, CLAIRE
Un Air de Famille *566*

MAXWELL, CHENOA
Hav Plenty *205*

MAXWELL, ROBERTA
Last Night *280*

MAZAR, DEBI
Hush *236*

MAZURSKY, PAUL
Antz *13*
Why Do Fools Fall in Love
596

MAZZELLO, JOSEPH
Simon Birch *483*
Star Kid *520*

MCBIRNEY, JAMES
Kitchen Party *268*

MCBRIDE, CHI
Mercury Rising *335*

MCCABE, RUTH
Talk of Angels *535*

MCCAIN, FRANCES LEE
Patch Adams *399*

**MCCAMBRIDGE,
MERCEDES**
Touch of Evil *548*

MCCANN, SEAN
Affliction *1*

MCCARTHY, JENNY
BASEketball *33*

MCCAWLEY, KEITH
Rushmore *466*

MCCAWLEY, RONNIE
Rushmore *466*

MCCOMB, HEATHER
Apt Pupil *16*

**MCCONAUGHEY,
MATTHEW**
The Newton Boys *362*

**MCCORMACK,
CATHERINE**
Dancing at Lughnasa *107*
Dangerous Beauty *110*
The Land Girls *276*

MCCORMACK, ERIC
Holy Man *219*

MCCORMACK, MARY
The Alarmist *8*
Deep Impact *118*

MCCOUCH, GRAYSON
Armageddon *18*

MCDANIEL, HATTIE
Gone With the Wind *182*

**MCDONALD,
CHRISTOPHER**
Dirty Work *126*
The Faculty *145*
Lawn Dogs *282*

MCDONALD, PETER
I Went Down *244*

MCDORMAND, FRANCES
Madeline *315*
Talk of Angels *535*

MCDOWALL, RODDY
A Bug's Life *67*

MCELHONE, NATASCHA
Mrs. Dalloway *342*
Ronin *456*
The Truman Show *553*

MCFADDEN, GATES
Star Trek: Insurrection *522*

MCFERRAN, DOUGLAS
Sliding Doors *493*

MCGILL, BRUCE
Lawn Dogs *282*

MCGINLEY, SEAN
The General *170*

MCGINLEY, TED
Major League: Back to the
Minors *319*

MCGLONE, MIKE
One Tough Cop *380*

Performers

SCOTT, TOM EVERETT
Dead Man on Campus *114*
One True Thing *382*

SCOTT, WILLIAM LEE
The Opposite of Sex *385*

SEAGAL, STEVEN
My Giant *355*

SEAGO, HOWARD
Beyond Silence *38*

SEGALL, PAMELA
Plump Fiction *418*

SEIPHEMO, RAPULANA
Tarzan and the Lost City *537*

SELDES, MARIAN
Affliction *1*
Digging to China *125*

SERBAN, ANGELA
Gadjo Dilo *166*

SERBAN, ISIDOR
Gadjo Dilo *166*

SERBAN, JOAN
Gadjo Dilo *166*

SERBAN, VASILE
Gadjo Dilo *166*

SERBEDZIJA, RADE
Polish Wedding *420*
The Truce *551*

SERGEI, IVAN
The Opposite of Sex *385*

SERRAULT, MICHEL
Artemisia *22*

SETLIFFE, ADAM
Without Limits *606*

SETTLE, MATTHEW
I Still Know What You Did Last Summer *241*

SEVIGNY, CHLOË
The Last Days of Disco *278*
Palmetto *392*

SEWELL, RUFUS
Dangerous Beauty *110*
Dark City *111*

SEWERYN, ANDRZEJ
Genealogies of a Crime *168*

SEXTON III, BRENDAN
Hurricane Streets *234*
Pecker *403*

SEYMOUR, JANE
Quest for Camelot *437*

SHAFFER, PAUL
Blues Brothers 2000 *54*

SHALHOUB, TONY
A Civil Action *93*
The Impostors *250*
Paulie *401*
The Siege *481*

SHANDLING, GARRY
Dr. Dolittle *129*
Hurlyburly *232*

SHANNON, HARRY
Touch of Evil *548*

SHANNON, MOLLY
A Night at the Roxbury *368*

SHAW, FIONA
The Avengers *24*
The Butcher Boy *73*

SHAW, STAN
Snake Eyes *501*

SHAWN, WALLACE
Just Write *261*

SHAYE, LIN
There's Something About Mary *540*

SHEARER, HARRY
Almost Heroes *9*
Godzilla *180*

SHEEDY, ALLY
High Art *214*

SHEEN, MARTIN
Monument Ave. *348*

SHEEN, MICHAEL
Wilde *604*

SHENKMAN, BEN
Pi *410*

SHEPHERD, SAM
The Only Thrill *384*

SHER, ANTONY
Shakespeare in Love *476*

SHERBEDGIA, RADE
Mighty Joe Young *341*

SHIGETA, JAMES
Mulan *351*

SHOAIB, SAMIA
Pi *410*

SHORT, MARTIN
The Prince of Egypt *429*

SHUE, ELISABETH
Cousin Bette *100*
Palmetto *392*

SIA, BEAU
Slam *492*

SICILY
How Stella Got Her Groove Back *230*

SILLAS, KAREN
Sour Grapes *510*

SILVERMAN, JONATHAN
Neil Simon's The Odd Couple 2 *360*

SIMMRIN, JOEY
Star Kid *520*

SINISE, GARY
Snake Eyes *501*

SIRTIS, MARTINA
Star Trek: Insurrection *522*

SISTO, JEREMY
Bongwater *56*
Suicide Kings *531*
Without Limits *606*

SIZEMORE, TOM
Enemy of the State *140*
Saving Private Ryan *469*

SKARSGARD, STELLAN
Insomnia *256*
Ronin *456*
Savior *472*

SKERRIT, TOM
Smoke Signals *499*

SKYE, IONE
Dream for an Insomniac *134*

SLATER, CHRISTIAN
Hard Rain *203*
Very Bad Things *579*

SLEZAK, VICTOR
One Tough Cop *380*

SMALL, ROBERT
Holy Man *219*

SMART, DEE
Welcome to Woop Woop *588*

SMART, JEAN
Neil Simon's The Odd Couple 2 *360*

SMITH, CHARLES MARTIN
Deep Impact *118*

SMITH, GREGORY
Krippendorf's Tribe *271*
Small Soldiers *497*

SMITH, IAN MICHAEL
Simon Birch *483*

SMITH, JADA PINKETT
Return to Paradise *451*
Woo *612*

SMITH, LANE
The Hi-Lo Country *212*

SMITH, WILL
Enemy of the State *140*

SMITH, YEARDLEY
Just Write *261*

SNIPES, WESLEY
Blade *51*
Down in the Delta *132*
U.S. Marshals *574*

SNODGRESS, CARRIE
Wild Things *601*

SNOOP DOGGY DOG
Caught Up *77*

SOBIESKI, LEELEE
Deep Impact *118*
A Soldier's Daughter Never Cries *506*

SOHN, SONJA
Slam *492*

SOMMER, JOSEF
Patch Adams *399*
The Proposition *432*

SOREL, NANCY
I Love You, Don't Touch Me *239*

SORVINO, MIRA
The Replacement Killers *449*

SORVINO, PAUL
Bulworth *70*
Knock Off *270*

SOUCIE, KATH
The Rugrats Movie *461*

SPACEK, SISSY
Affliction *1*

SPACEY, KEVIN
A Bug's Life *67*
Hurlyburly *232*
The Negotiator *357*

SPADE, DAVID
Senseless *473*

SPALL, TIMOTHY
Still Crazy *529*

SPEEDMAN, SCOTT
Kitchen Party *268*

SPENCE, BRUCE
Dark City *111*

SPENCE, SEBASTIAN
Firestorm *157*

SPENCER, JOHN
The Negotiator *357*
Twilight *557*

Performers

VOIGHT, JON
Enemy of the State *140*
The General *170*

VON BARGEN, DANIEL
The Faculty *145*

VON SYDOW, MAX
What Dreams May Come *591*

VORSTMAN, FRANS
Character *85*

WADDINGTON, STEVEN
Tarzan and the Lost City *537*

WADHAM, JULIAN
A Merry War *337*

WAGNER, NATASHA GREGSON
First Love, Last Rites *161*
Two Girls and a Guy *562*
Urban Legend *572*

WAGNER, ROBERT
Wild Things *601*

WAHLBERG, MARK
The Big Hit *40*

WALKEN, CHRISTOPHER
Antz *13*
Suicide Kings *531*

WALKER, PAUL
Meet the Deedles *330*

WALKER, POLLY
Talk of Angels *535*

WALLACE, BASIL
Caught Up *77*

WALSH, DYLAN
Eden *136*
Men *332*

WALSH, J. T.
The Negotiator *357*
Pleasantville *416*

WALSH, JACK
A Simple Plan *485*

WALSH, M. EMMET
Chairman of the Board *83*
Twilight *557*

WALTER, HARRIET
The Governess *185*
A Merry War *337*

WALTER, JESSICA
Slums of Beverly Hills *495*

WALTER, LISA ANN
The Parent Trap *394*

WALTZ, LISA
Neil Simon's The Odd Couple 2 *360*

WANAMAKER, ZOE
Swept From the Sea *533*
Wilde *604*

WARD, FRED
Dangerous Beauty *110*

WARD, KELLY
Grease *188*

WARD, PADDY
Waking Ned Devine *581*

WARD, ROY
The Ugly *564*

WARDEN, JACK
Bulworth *70*
Chairman of the Board *83*
Dirty Work *126*

WARD-LEALAND, JENNIFER
The Ugly *564*

WARNER, DAVID
The Leading Man *284*

WASHINGTON, DENZEL
Fallen *147*
He Got Game *207*
The Siege *481*

WASHINGTON, ISAIAH
Bulworth *70*
Out of Sight *389*

WATANABE, GEDDE
Mulan *351*

WATANABE, TETSU
Fireworks *159*
Sonatine *509*

WATKINS, TUC
I Think I Do *243*

WATSON, EMILY
Hilary and Jackie *217*

WATSON, MUSE
I Still Know What You Did Last Summer *241*

WAYANS, MARLON
Senseless *473*

WEATHERLY, SHAWN
Dancer, Texas Population 81 *105*

WEAVER, DENNIS
Touch of Evil *548*

WEBB, CHLOE
The Newton Boys *362*

WEBER, JAKE
Dangerous Beauty *110*
Meet Joe Black *328*

WEBER, STEVEN
Sour Grapes *510*

WEIL, LIZA
Whatever *594*

WEINSTEIN, HARVEY
An Alan Smithee Film: Burn Hollywood Burn *6*

WEISZ, RACHEL
The Land Girls *276*
Swept From the Sea *533*

WELCH, MICHAEL
Star Trek: Insurrection *522*

WELCH, RAQUEL
Chairman of the Board *83*

WELLES, ORSON
Touch of Evil *548*

WEN, MING-NA
Mulan *351*

WENDT, GEORGE
Spice World *519*

WEST, BOB
Barney's Great Adventure *31*

WEST, TIMOTHY
Ever After: A Cinderella Story *143*

WESTERLY, MICHAEL
The Last Days of Disco *278*

WESTON, DOUGLAS
Six Days, Seven Nights *488*

WETTENHALL, SIMON
Wild Man Blues *599*

WETTIG, PATRICIA
Dancer, Texas Population 81 *105*

WHEELER, MAGGIE
The Parent Trap *394*

WHITE, BETTY
Hard Rain *203*
Holy Man *219*

WHITE, JALEEL
Quest for Camelot *437*

WHITE, MICHAEL JAI
Ringmaster *455*

WHITFIELD, LYNN
Stepmom *527*

WHITFIELD, MITCHELL
I Love You, Don't Touch Me *239*

WHITING, AL
The Waterboy *584*

WHITMAN, MAE
The Gingerbread Man *173*
Hope Floats *226*

WHITMEY, NIGEL
Twilight of the Ice Nymphs *560*

WIEST, DIANNE
The Horse Whisperer *228*
Practical Magic *423*

WILBY, JAMES
Regeneration *446*

WILDER, MATTHEW
Mulan *351*

WILES, JASON
Kitchen Party *268*

WILKINSON, TOM
The Governess *185*
Rush Hour *464*
Shakespeare in Love *476*
Wilde *604*

WILLARD, FRED
Permanent Midnight *407*

WILLIAMS, AARON
Broadway Damage *61*

WILLIAMS, BARBARA
Krippendorf's Tribe *271*

WILLIAMS III, CLARENCE
Half-Baked *193*

WILLIAMS, CYNDA
Caught Up *77*

WILLIAMS, DICK ANTHONY
The Players Club *412*

WILLIAMS, ELIZABETH
Moon Over Broadway *350*

WILLIAMS, HARLAND
Half-Baked *193*

WILLIAMS, JOBETH
Just Write *261*

WILLIAMS, KELLIE
Ride *453*

WILLIAMS, LIA
Firelight *155*

WILLIAMS, MARK
The Borrowers *57*

WILLIAMS, MICHELLE
Halloween H20 *194*

WILLIAMS, OLIVIA
Rushmore *466*

WILLIAMS, ROBIN
Patch Adams *399*

Performers

Subjects

Subjects

Subjects

Subjects

Title Index

This cumulative index is an alphabetical list of all films covered in the seventeen volumes of the *Magill's Cinema Annual.* Film titles are indexed on a word-by-word basis, including articles and prepositions. English and foreign leading articles are ignored. Films reviewed in this volume are cited in bold with an arabic number indicating the page number on which the review begins; films reviewed in past volumes are cited with the year in which the film was originally released. Film sequels are indicated with a roman numeral following the film title. Original and alternate titles are cross-referenced to the American release title. Titles of retrospective films are followed by the year, in brackets, of their original release.

A corps perdu. *See* Straight for
   the Heart.
A la Mode (Fausto) (In Fash-
   ion) 1994
A nos amours 1984
Abgeschminkt! *See* Making Up!.
About Last Night... 1986
Above the Law 1988
Above the Rim 1994
Absence of Malice 1981
Absolute Beginners 1986
Absolute Power 1997
Absolution 1988
Abyss, The 1989
Accidental Tourist, The 1988
Accompanist, The 1993
Accused, The 1988
Ace in the Hole [1951] 1991,
   1986
Ace Ventura: Pet Detective
   1994
Ace Ventura: When Nature
   Calls 1995
Aces: Iron Eagle III 1992
Acqua e sapone. *See* Water and
   Soap.
Across the Tracks 1991
Acting on Impulse 1994
Action Jackson 1988
Actress 1988
Adam's Rib [1950] 1992
Addams Family, The 1991
Addams Family Values 1993
Addicted to Love 1997
Addiction, The 1995
Addition, L'. *See* Patsy, The.
Adjo, Solidaritet. *See* Farewell
   Illusion.
Adjuster, The 1992
Adolescente, L' 1982
Adventure of Huck Finn, The
   1993
Adventures in Babysitting 1987
Adventures of Baron Mun-
   chausen, The 1989
Adventures of Buckaroo Banzai,
   The 1984
Adventures of Ford Fairlane,
   The 1990
Adventures of Mark Twain, The
   1986
Adventures of Milo and Otis,
   The 1989
Adventures of Pinocchio, The
   1996
Adventures of Priscilla, Queen
   of the Desert, The 1994

Adventures of the American
   Rabbit, The 1986
Advocate 1994
Aelita 1994
Affaire de Femmes, Une. *See*
   Story of Women.
Affengeil 1992
Affliction, 1
Afraid of the Dark 1992
Africa the Serengeti 1994
After Dark, My Sweet 1990
After Hours 1985
After Midnight 1989
After the Rehearsal 1984
Afterglow 1997
Against All Odds 1983
Age Isn't Everything (Life in
   the Food Chain) 1994
Age of Innocence, The 1993
Agent on Ice 1986
Agnes of God 1985
Aid 1988
Aileen Wuornos: The Selling of
   a Serial Killer 1994
Air America 1990
Air Bud 1997
Air Bud: Golden Receiver, 4
Air Force One 1997
Air Up There, The 1994
Airborne 1993
Airheads 1994
Airplane II: The Sequel 1982
Akira Kurosawa's Dreams 1990
Aladdin (Corbucci) 1987
Aladdin (Musker & Clements)
   1992
Alamo Bay 1985
Alan and Naomi 1992
Alan Smithee Film, An, 6
Alarmist, The, 8
Alaska 1996
Alberto Express 1992
Albino Alligator 1997
Alchemist, The 1986
Alfred Hitchcock's Bon Voyage
   & Aventure Malgache. *See*
   Aventure Malgache.
Alice (Allen) 1990
Alice (Svankmajer) 1988
Alien Nation 1988
Alien Predator 1987
Alien Resurrection 1997
Alien3 1992
Aliens 1986
Alive 1993
Alive and Kicking 1997
All Dogs Go to Heaven 1989

All Dogs Go to Heaven II,
   1996
All I Desire [1953] 1987
All I Want for Christmas 1991
All of Me 1984
All Over Me 1997
All Quiet on the Western Front
   [1930] 1985
All the Right Moves 1983
All the Vermeers in New York
   1992
All's Fair 1989
All-American High 1987
Allan Quatermain and the Lost
   City of Gold 1987
Alley Cat 1984
Alligator Eyes 1990
Allnighter, The 1987
Almost an Angel 1990
Almost Heroes, 9
Almost You 1985
Aloha Summer 1988
Alphabet City 1983
Alpine Fire 1987
Altars of the World [1976]
   1985
Always (Jaglom) 1985
Always (Spielberg) 1989
Amadeus 1984, 1985
Amanda 1989
Amantes. *See* Lovers.
Amants du Pont Neuf, Les 1994
Amateur 1995
Amateur, The 1982
Amazing Grace and Chuck
   1987
Amazing Panda Adventure, The
   1995
Amazon Women on the Moon
   1987
Ambition 1991
America 1986
American Anthem 1986
American Blue Note 1991
American Buffalo 1996
American Cyborg: Steel Warrior
   1994
American Dream 1992
American Dreamer 1984
American Fabulous 1992
American Flyers 1985
American Friends 1993
American Gothic 1988
American Heart 1993
American History X, 11
American in Paris, An [1951]
   1985

American Justice 1986
American Me 1992
American Ninja 1985
American Ninja II 1987
American Ninja III 1989
American Ninja 1984, 1991
American Pop 1981
American President, The 1995
American Stories 1989
American Summer, An 1991
American Taboo 1984, 1991
American Tail, An 1986
American Tail: Fievel Goes
   West, An 1991
American Werewolf in London,
   An 1981
American Werewolf in Paris,
   An 1997
Ami de mon amie, L'. *See*
   Boyfriends and Girlfriends.
Amin-The Rise and Fall 1983
Amistad 1997
Amityville II: The Possession
   1981
Amityville 3-D 1983
Among People 1988
Amongst Friends 1993
Amor brujo, El 1986
Amos and Andrew 1993
Amour de Swann, Un. *See*
   Swann in Love.
Anaconda 1997
Anastasia 1997
Anchors Aweigh [1945] 1985
And God Created Woman
   1988
...And God Spoke 1994
And Life Goes On (Zebdegi
   Edame Darad) 1994
And Nothing but the Truth
   1984
And the Ship Sails On 1984
And You Thought Your Parents
   Were Weird 1991
Andre 1994
Android 1984
Ane qui a bu la lune, L'. *See*
   Donkey Who Drank the
   Moon, The.
Angel at My Table, An 1991
Angel Baby 1997
Angel Dust 1997
Angel Dust 1987
Angel Heart 1987
Angel 1984
Angel III 1988
Angel Town 1990

Title

Buddy 1997
Buddy Buddy 1981
Buddy System, The 1984
Buffalo 66, 65
Buffy the Vampire Slayer 1992
Bug's Life, A, 67
Bugsy 1991
Building Bombs 1994
Bull Durham 1988
Bulldog Drummond [1929]
    1982
Bulletproof 1988
Bulletproof 1996
Bulletproof Heart 1995
Bullets Over Broadway 1994
Bullies 1986
Bullshot 1985
Bulworth, 70
Bum Rap 1988
'Burbs, The 1989
Burglar 1987
Burglar, The 1988
Buried on Sunday 1994
Burke and Wills 1987
Burnin' Love 1987
Burning Secret 1988
Burnt by the Sun 1994
Bushwhacked 1995
Busted Up 1987
Buster 1988
Butcher Boy, The, 73
Butcher's Wife, The 1991
Butterfield 8 [1960] 1993
Butterflies 1988
Buy and Cell 1988
Buying Time 1989
By Design 1982
By the Sword 1993
Bye Bye Blues 1990
Bye Bye, Love 1995

Cabeza de Vaca 1992
Cabin Boy 88
Cabinet of Dr. Ramirez, The
    1994
Cable Guy, The 1996
Cactus 1986
Caddie [1976] 1982
Caddyshack II 1988
Cadence 1991
Cadillac Man 1990
Cafe Society 1997
Cage 1989
Cage aux folles III, La 1986
Cage/Cunningham 1994
Caged Fury 1984
Cal 1984
Calendar 1994
Calendar Girl 1993
Calhoun. *See* Nightstick.
Call Me 1988
Caller, The 1987
Calling the Shots 1988
Came a Hot Friday 1985
Cameron's Closet 1989
Camilla 1994
Camille Claudel 1988, 1989
Camorra 1986
Camp at Thiaroye, The 1990
Camp Nowhere 1994
Campanadas a medianoche. *See*
    Falstaff.

Campus Man 1987
Can She Bake a Cherry Pie?
    1983
Canadian Bacon 1995
Can't Buy Me Love 1987
Can't Hardly Wait, 75
Candy Mountain 1988
Candyman 1992
Candyman II: Farewell to the
    Flesh 1995
Cannery Row 1982
Cannonball Run II 1984
Cape Fear 1991
Capitano, Il 1994
Captain Ron 1992
Captive Hearts 1987
Captive in the Land, A 1994
Captives 1996
Car 54, Where Are You? 1994
Caravaggio 1986
Cardinal, The [1963] 1986
Care Bears Adventure in Won-
    derland, The 1987
Care Bears Movie, The 1985
Care Bears Movie II 1986
Career Girls 1997
Career Opportunities 1991
Careful He Might Hear You
    1984
Carlito's Way 1993
Carmen 1983
Carnal Knowledge [1971], 680
Carne, La (The Flesh) 1994
Caro Diario (Dear Diary) 1994
Carpenter, The 1988
Carpool 1996
Carried Away 1996
Carrington 1995
Casa in bilico, Una. *See* Totter-
    ing Lives.
Casino 1995
Casper 1995
Casual Sex? 1988
Casualties of War 1989
Cat on a Hot Tin Roof [1958]
    1993
Cat People [1942] 1981, 1982
Catacombs 1988
Catch Me If You Can 1989
Cats Don't Dance 1997
Cattle Annie and Little Britches
    1981
Caught 1996
Caught Up, 77
Cave Girl 1985
CB4 1993
Cease Fire 1985
Celebrity, 78
Céleste 1982
Celestial Clockwork 1996
Celluloid Closet, The 1996
Celtic Pride 1996
Cement Garden , The 1994
Cemetery Club, The 1993
Cemetery Man 1996
Center of the Web 1992
Central do Brasil.*See* Central
    Station.
Central Station, 80
Century 1994
Ceravani tanto Amati. *See* We
    All Loved Each Other So
    Much.

Ceremonie, La 1996
Certain Fury 1985
Certain Regard, Un. *See* Hotel
    Terminus.
C'est la vie 1990
Chain of Desire 1993
Chain Reaction 1996
Chaindance. *See* Common
    Bonds.
Chained Heat 1983
Chairman of the Board, 83
Challenge, The 1982
Chamber, The 1996
**Chambermaid of the Titanic,
    The, 84**
Chameleon Street 1991
Champion [1949] 1991
Champions 1984
Chan Is Missing 1982
Chances Are 1989
Chantilly Lace 1994
Chaos. *See* Ran.
Chaplin 1992
Character, 85
Chariots of Fire 1981
Chase, The 1994
Chasers 1994
Chasing Amy 1988
Château de ma mère, Le. *See*
    My Mother's Castle.
Chattahoochee 1990
Chattanooga Choo Choo 1984
Cheap Shots 1991
Cheatin' Hearts 1993
Check Is in the Mail, The 1986
Checking Out 1989
Cheech & Chong Still Smokin'
    1983
Cheech & Chong's The Corsi-
    can Brothers 1984
Cheetah 1989
Chef in Love, A 1997
Chère Inconnue. *See* I Sent a
    Letter to My Love.
Chèvre, La. *See* Goat, The.
Chicago Joe and the Showgirl
    1990
Chicken Hawk: Men Who Love
    Boys 1994
Chief Zabu 1988
Child's Play 1988
Child's Play II 1990
Child's Play III 1991
Children of a Lesser God 1986
Children of Nature 1994
Children of the Corn II 1993
Children of the Revolution 1997
Chile, la Memoria Obstinada.
    See Chile, Obstinate Memory.
Chile, Obstinate Memory, 88
Chimes at Midnight. *See* Fal-
    staff.
China Cry 1990
China Girl 1987
China Moon 1994
China, My Sorrow 1994
China Syndrome, The [1979]
    1988
Chinatown [1974] 680
Chinese Box, 89
Chinese Ghost Story II, A 1990
Chinese Ghost Story III, A
    1991

Chipmunk Adventure, The
    1987
Chocolat 1989
Chocolate War, The 1988
Choke Canyon 1986
Choose Me 1984, 1985
Chopper Chicks in Zombie
    Town 1991
Chopping Mall 1986
Chorus Line, A 1985
Chorus of Disapproval, A 1989
Chosen, The 1982
Christine 1983
Christine F. 1982
Christmas Story, A 1983
Christopher Columbus: The
    Discovery 1992
Chronos 1985
Chuck Berry: Hail! Hail! Rock
    'n' Roll 1987
C.H.U.D. 1984
Chungking Express 1996
Ciao, Professore! 1994
Cinema Paradiso 1989
Circle of Deceit 1982
Circle of Friends 1995
Circuitry Man 1990
Citizen Ruth 1996
Città della donne, La. *See* City
    of Women.
City Girl, The 1984
City Hall 1996
City Heat 1984
City Limits 1985
City of Angels, 91
City of Hope 1991
City of Industry 1997
City of Joy 1992
City of Lost Children 1996
City of Women 1981
City Slickers 1991
City Slickers II: The Legend of
    Curly's Gold 1994
City Zero 1994
Civil Action, A, 93
Claire of the Moon 1993
Clan of the Cave Bear, The
    1986
Clara's Heart 1988
Clash of the Titans 1981
Class 1982
Class Act 1992
Class Action 1991
Class of 1984 1982
Class of 1999 1990
Class of Nuke 'em High 1986
Class of Nuke 'em High Part II
    1991
Clay Pigeons, 95
Clean and Sober 1988
Clean Slate 1994
Clean Slate. *See* Coup de tor-
    chon.
Clear and Present Danger 1994
Clearcut 1992
Cleopatra [1963] 1993
Clerks 1994
Client, The 1994
Cliffhanger 1993
Clifford 1994
Climate for Killing, A (A Row
    of Crows) 1994
Cloak and Dagger 1984

Title

Title

Final Season 1988
Finders Keepers 1984
Fine Mess, A 1986
Fine Romance, A 1992
Finzan 1994
Fiorile 1994
Fire and Ice (Bakshi) 1983
Fire and Ice (Bogner) 1987
Fire Birds 1990
Fire Down Below 1997
Fire from the Mountain 1987
Fire in Sky 1993
Fire This Time, The 1994
Fire Walk with Me. *See* Twin
    Peaks: Fire Walk with Me.
Fire with Fire 1986
Firefox 1982
Firehead 1991
Firelight, 155
Firemen's Bell, The [1967] 1985
Firestorm, 157
Firewalker 1986
Fireworks, 159
Fires of Kuwait 1994
Firm, The 1993
First Blood 1982
First Kid 1996
First Knight 1995
First Love, Last Rites, 161
First Monday in October 1981
First Name, Carmen 1984
First Power, The 1990
First Wives Club, The 1996
Firstborn 1984
Fish Called Wanda, A 1988
Fisher King, The 1991
Fistfighter 1989
Fitzcarraldo 1982
Five Corners 1987
Five Days One Summer 1982
Five Easy Pieces [1970] 680
Five Graves to Cairo [1943]
    1986
Five Heartbeats, The 1991
Flame in My Heart, A 1987
Flaming Star [1960] 1982
Flamingo Kid, The 1984
Flamme dans mon coeur, Une.
    See Flame in My Heart, A.
Flanagan 1985
Flash of Green, A 1985
Flashback 1990
Flashdance 1983
Flashpoint 1984
Flatliners 1990
Flaxfield, The 1985
Fled 1996
Flesh and Blood 1985
Flesh and Bone 1993
Flesh Gordon Meets the Cos-
    mic Cheerleaders 1994
Fleshburn 1984
Fletch 1985
Fletch Lives 1989
Flight of the Innocent 1993
Flight of the Intruder 1991
Flight of the Navigator 1986
Flight of the Phoenix, The
    [1966] 1984
Flight to Fury [1966] 679
Flintstones, The 1994
Flipper 1996
Flipping 1997

Flirt 1996
Flirting 1992
Flirting with Disaster 1996
Floundering 1994
Flower of My Secret, The 1996
Flowers in the Attic 1987
Flowing 1985
Flubber 1997
Fluke 1995
Fly, The 1986
Fly II, The 1989
Fly Away Home 1996
Fly by Night 1994
Flying Duchman, The (De
    Viegende Hollander) 1995
Folks 1992
Follow the Bitch, 162
Food of the Gods II 1989
Fool for Love 1985
Fools of Fortune 1990
Fools Rush In 1997
Footloose 1984
For a Lost Soldier 1993
For Ever Mozart 1997
For Keeps 1988
For Love or Money 1993
For Me and My Gal [1942]
    1985
For Queen and Country 1988,
    1989
For Richer or Poorer 1997
For Roseanna 1997
For Sasha 1992
For the Boys 1991
For the Moment 1996
For Your Eyes Only 1981
Forbidden Choices. *See* Beans of
    Egypt, Maine, The.
Forbidden Dance, The 1990
Forbidden Quest 1994
Forbidden World 1982
Forced Vengeance 1982
Foreign Affair, A [1948] 1986
Foreign Body 1986
Foreign Student 211
Forever 1994
Forever, Lulu 1987
Forever Mary 1991
Forever Young 1992
Forget Paris 1995
Forrest Gump 1994
Fort Apache [1948] 1983
Fort Apache, the Bronx 1981
Fortress 1993
Fortune Cookie, The [1966]
    1986
48 Hrs. 1982
Foster Daddy, Tora! 1981
Four Adventures of Reinette
    and Mirabelle 1989
Four Days in September, 163
Four Friends 1981
4 Little Girls 1997
Four Rooms 1995
Four Seasons, The 1981
Four Weddings and a Funeral
    1994
1492: Conquest of Paradise
    1992
4th Man, The 1984
Fourth Protocol, The 1987
Fourth War, The 1990
Fox and the Hound, The 1981

Foxfire 1996
Foxtrap 1986
Frances 1982
Frank and Ollie 1995
Frankenhooker 1990
Frankenstein Unbound. *See*
    Roger Corman's Frankenstein
    Unbound.
Frankenstein. *See* Mary Shelley's
    Frankenstein.
Frankie and Johnny 1991
Frankie Starlight 1995
Frantic 1988
Fraternity Vacation 1985
Frauds 1994
Freaked 1993
Freddie as F.R.O.7 1992
Freddy's Dead 1991
Free and Easy 1989
Free Ride 1986
Free Willy 1993
Free Willy II: The Adventure
    Home 1995
Free Willy III: The Rescue 1997
Freedom On My Mind 1994
Freejack 1992
Freeway 1988
Freeway 1996
Freeze-Die-Come to Life 1994
French Connection, The [1971]
    1982
French Kiss 1995
French Lesson 1986
French Lieutenant's Woman,
    The 1981
French Twist 1996
Fresh 1994
Fresh Horses 1988
Freshman, The 1990
Freud [1962] 1983
Friday 1995
Friday the 13th, Part III 1982
Friday the 13th, Part IV 1984
Friday the 13th, Part VI 1986
Friday the 13th Part VII 1988
Friday the 13th Part VIII 1989
Fried Green Tomatoes 1991
Friend of the Deceased, A, 165
Fright Night 1985
Frighteners, The 1996
Fringe Dwellers, The 1987
From Beyond 1986
From Dusk Till Dawn 1996
From Hollywood to Deadwood
    1988
From the Hip 1987
Front, The [1976] 1985
Frosh: Nine Months in a Fresh-
    man Dorm 1994
Frozen Assets 1992
Frühlingssinfonie. *See* Spring
    Symphony.
Fruit Machine, The 1988
Fu-zung cen. *See* Hibiscus
    Town.
Fugitive, The 1993
Full Metal Jacket 1987
Full Monty, The 1997
Full Moon in Paris 1984
Full Moon in the Blue Water
    1988
Fun Down There 1989
Funeral, The 1987

Funeral, The 1996
Funny About Love 1990
Funny Bones 1995
Funny Farm (Clark) 1983
Funny Farm (Hill) 1988
Further Adventures of Ten-
    nessee Buck, The 1988

Gabbeh 1997
Gabriela 1984
Gaby-A True Story 1987
Gadjo Dilo, 166
Galactic Gigolo 1988
Gallipoli 1981
Game, The 1997
Game, The 1989
Gandhi 1982
Gang-Related 1997
Garbage Pail Kids Movie, The
    1987
Garbo Talks 1984
Garde à vue 1982
Garden, The 1994
Gardens of Stone 1987
Gas Food Lodging 1992
Gate, The 1987
Gate II 1992
Gattaca 1997
Gay Divorcée, The [1934] 1981
Genealogies D' Un Crime. *See*
    Genealogies of a Crime.
Genealogies of a Crime, 168
General, The, 170
Gentilezza del tocco, La. *See*
    Gentle Touch, The.
Gentle Touch, The 1988
Gentlemen Don't Eat Poets
    1997
Gentlemen's Agreement [1947]
    1989
Genuine Risk 1990
George Balanchine's The Nut-
    cracker 1993
George of the Jungle 1997
George's Island 1991
Georgia 1988
Georgia 1995
Germinal 1993
Geronimo 1993
Get Back 1991
Get Crazy 1983
Get on the Bus 1996
Get Shorty 1995
Getaway, The 1994
Geteilte Liebe. *See* Maneuvers.
Getting Away with Murder
    1996
Getting Even 1986
Getting Even With Dad 1994
Getting It Right 1989
Gettysburg 1993
Ghare Bhaire. *See* Home and
    the World, The.
Ghost 1990
Ghost and the Darkness, The
    1996
Ghost Dad 1990
Ghost Story 1981
Ghost Town 1988
Ghostbusters 1984
Ghostbusters II 1989
Ghosts Can't Do It 1990

Title

Title

Title

Title

Title

Title